The Arrogance of Power

VIKING
75 years

THE
ARROGANCE
OF POWER

The Secret World of Richard Nixon

A N T H O N Y
S U M M E R S

with Robbyn Swan

Viking

VIKING
Published by the Penguin Group
Penguin Putnam Inc., 375 Hudson Street,
New York, New York 10014, U.S.A.
Penguin Books Ltd, 27 Wrights Lane,
London W8 5TZ, England
Penguin Books Australia Ltd, Ringwood,
Victoria, Australia
Penguin Books Canada Ltd, 10 Alcorn Avenue,
Toronto, Ontario, Canada M4V 3B2
Penguin Books (N.Z.) Ltd, 182–190 Wairau Road,
Auckland 10, New Zealand

Penguin Books Ltd, Registered Offices:
Harmondsworth, Middlesex, England

First published in 2000 by Viking Penguin,
a member of Penguin Putnam Inc.

5   7   9   10   8   6   4

ISBN: 0-670-87151-6

CIP data available.

This book is printed on acid-free paper. ∞

Printed in the United States of America
Set in Sabon
Designed by Jaye Zimet

For Colm, Fionn, and Lara

Ten years ago, during a late-night conversation about investigative writing, Norman Mailer suggested I take on the story of Richard Nixon and Watergate. I barely gave it a thought until Nixon died in 1994. It struck me then that, even allowing for respect for the dead, most public commentary seemed excessively deferential to the memory of the first American president to have resigned in disgrace. Something did not connect. Who was this man in whom so many millions of Americans had placed their trust, who had broken that trust, yet who had achieved political resurrection time and again? One who knew him better than most, John Ehrlichman, said in an interview—with Mailer as it happened—that a Nixon biography was the toughest writing assignment he could imagine. Later, Ehrlichman told me he hoped for "a more solid history of that time, a history that would help our children to comprehend and move forward." The president's former aide was right about the difficulties of the assignment, for the main protagonist was elusive, the evidence scattered—sometimes buried deep. In this book I have reached for the reality of Nixon, from birth in obscurity in California to the fall from the ultimate power of the presidency—for something approaching that "more solid history."

A.S.

Prologue

When Nixon died I thought of the Shakespeare quote about the evil that men do living after them, and the good being interred with their bones. With Nixon the reverse was happening: They wanted the good to live on and the evil to be buried.

—*John Rothmann, longtime supporter, 1996*

April 1994. On a hillside in Southern California two men, one much older than the other, checked their watches and stepped out of shelter into the rain. They had been waiting for nearly an hour. Then, as a convoy of limousines slid funereally slowly into view, a thunderclap split the clouds.

"That's the Lord, welcoming the President to His house of many mansions," said the elderly man.

"You know what it sounds like to me?" responded his companion. "I think it's the Old Man saying, 'Lord, I'm here now if you need any help.'"

This was a rare moment of levity on a day of intense emotions and searing memories. Billy Graham, evangelist and friend to a string of presidents, and veteran Republican advance man Ron Walker had come to California to bury the thirty-seventh president of the United States, Richard Milhous Nixon.

The dominant American politician of the second half of the twentieth century had been felled the previous week by a massive stroke, at the age of eighty-one. He had spent his last active day working on a political speech at his home near New York City. Nixon had left instructions that should catastrophic illness leave him totally incapacitated, he did not wish to be kept alive by artificial means. At the hospital the chief of neurology said Nixon had not wanted to go on living if he could not contribute, could not lead. He had taken his last chance to "exercise moral leadership."

As president, two decades earlier, Nixon had specified that upon his death he wished to lie in state beneath the dome of the Capitol, as had national leaders since Abraham Lincoln. The man he had served as vice president, Dwight D. Eisenhower, his predecessor Lyndon B. Johnson, and his old rival John F. Kennedy, had all lain in state there. In old age, though, Nixon preemptively ensured that no one would be able to deny him the honor. He had ordered that his remains were instead to be flown directly to Yorba Linda, near Los Angeles, and "planted"—his wry word—beside his wife, Pat, in the shadow of the frame house where he had spent his childhood.

The air force brought Richard Nixon home in a simple mahogany coffin draped with American flags, aboard the same blue and white Boeing 707—once designated Air Force One—that had carried him to California in 1974, when he became the first U.S. president ever to resign in disgrace.

America's response to Nixon's dying would probably have surprised him. President Clinton, a Democrat, who as a young man had opposed Nixon and demanded that he resign over Watergate, declared a day of national mourning, closing Congress, the Supreme Court, and the New York Stock Exchange and suspending mail deliveries. Flags were to fly at half-mast at home, and at U.S. installations around the world, for a month. The funeral party left the East Coast to a twenty-one-gun salute and was met at the dead man's birthplace by thousands of people lining the streets. Citizens huddled under umbrellas, clutching wilted bouquets and American flags, in a freak storm that for the *New York Times* reporter covering the ceremony evoked the tempest scene in *King Lear.*

That afternoon and into the night an honor guard stood sentry as citizens filed into the lobby of the Nixon Library, past photographs of the president in his glory moments. They saluted, doffed hats, or stood hand on heart before the closed coffin. The line was three miles long at one point, and by the time the doors were closed forty-two thousand people were estimated to have paid homage.

President Clinton, flanked by all four surviving U.S. presidents—Ford, Carter, Reagan, and Bush—bade farewell at the funeral "on behalf of a grateful nation." "May the day of judging President Nixon on anything less than his entire life and career," he urged, "come to a close." Gerald Ford, who had replaced him after the resignation, that week declared himself more convinced than ever that he had been right to grant Nixon a blanket pardon for crimes he may have committed during the presidency.

Amid the mourners that day stood a phalanx of former secretaries of state, secretaries of defense, an attorney general, members of Congress, and representatives from eighty-five foreign countries. The governor of California, Pete Wilson, and Senate Minority Leader Bob Dole wept during their eulogies. The guttural voice of Henry Kissinger, former secretary of state and national security adviser, cracked when he praised Nixon as "our gallant friend . . . one of the seminal presidents" in the conduct of foreign policy, whose "greatest accomplishment was as much moral as it was political."

The funeral closed with full military honors. Air force fighters flew overhead in the missing man formation, howitzers boomed and rifles cracked, and a lone bugler sounded taps.

The president's surviving brother, Edward, who bore an almost eerie resemblance to his dead sibling, watched—awkward and lonely to one side—as the two American flags on the coffin were handed to Richard's daughters, Tricia and Julie. Then the coffin was lowered into the wet ground.

The Nixon faithful judged this final farewell a resounding success. Ronald Walker, who had organized it with the same efficiency and sense of drama he had once applied to Republican conventions, expressed himself "euphoric." Ron Ziegler, the former press secretary who once had had to admit that previous statements made in Nixon's name were "inoperative," walked away feeling "deep gratitude, in spite of all the shortcomings of Watergate." Peter Flanigan, the former senior assistant who had striven at Nixon's behest to hobble public broadcasting, felt "uplifted. . . . What a story! To come from this depth, to being a senior statesman in the eyes of his countrymen, based solely on guts and intellect." Len Garment, one of Nixon's Watergate attorneys, commented that Nixon had "won the battle . . . he had made his way back." "The Old Man," thought General Vernon Walters, Nixon's translator on foreign trips and his deputy director of the CIA, "must be looking down and taking a delicious revenge."

A poll taken earlier that week, however, indicated that while 27 percent of those questioned thought Nixon would be remembered as a great president, more than 44 percent said he would be remembered as a dishonored leader. An accounting of some of the individuals who attended the funeral, and of some who chose not to, evokes doubts and dark mysteries that Nixonians would prefer forgotten.

On the night that Nixon suffered his fatal stroke, an old enemy had been celebrating his ninetieth birthday at a party in New York. Alger Hiss, the onetime senior State Department official whom Nixon pursued as a Communist and traitor—winning national prominence in the process—had outlived his nemesis. "I am not going to gloat," said Hiss, acknowledging the irony. "There are a lot of things in that man's life that were left unatoned for. . . ."

The adviser who first guided Nixon in the use of the "Red smear" as a means to electoral victory, Murray Chotiner, was long since dead. He had been custodian of many of the man's secrets, including the truth about early support given to Nixon by mobsters.

Robert Maheu, once aide to the billionaire Howard Hughes, had never been thanked by Nixon for having helped extract him from political difficulty and to counter corruption allegations. "I've never believed that death gives a man instant absolution of his sins," Maheu had remarked to dinner companions the night Nixon died. He did not attend the funeral.

Nixon had once spoken casually to Maheu of the possible need to kill a troublesome foreign businessman. In retirement the former president denied having ever been involved in plots to murder foreign leaders. Yet violence and allegations of violence—from the beating of hecklers and demonstrators to assassination rumors—permeated Nixon's career. His first vice president, Spiro Agnew, claimed he resigned—rather than stay on to fight corruption charges—because of pressure by Nixon and what he interpreted as physical threats. "I feared for my life," Agnew recalled, and, although he did attend the funeral, had never spoken to Nixon again.

Also present, and described as looking "more menacing than ever," was G. Gordon Liddy, who had led the botched break-in of the Democratic party headquarters at the Watergate. At the time, according to the chief counsel of the Senate probe, Liddy said he regarded himself as a "prisoner of war" and refused to give more than the metaphorical equivalent of his name, rank, and serial number. Liddy served three years in jail for burglary and wiretapping. Now a maverick talk-show host, he saluted the coffin at the funeral.

Absent was E. Howard Hunt, Liddy's chief cohort, who remained convinced the president had ordered the break-in. He too had served time in prison and regarded Nixon as "despicable" for having saved himself at the expense of others. Not present, too, was James McCord, the security chief for Nixon's reelection committee, who had also gone to prison for his part in the raid. He too continued to believe that Nixon ordered the operation.

Of three senior aides most likely to have known the truth about Watergate and much else about Nixon, only one survived at the time of his death. Both John Mitchell, former attorney general and intimate friend, and H. R. Haldeman, chief of staff, predeceased him. Each had served time for obstruction of justice, as had domestic policy adviser John Ehrlichman. Ehrlichman felt the president had "completely duped" him during Watergate, and the two never spoke again after the resignation. He did not attend the funeral.

For all their differences with Nixon, both his closest aides had retained vast respect for his abilities. "His strengths lay in his intellect," Ehrlichman had said. "He had a brilliant mind." "I doubt if I would ever have served any other man in the office of the president," said Haldeman. "I gained a tremendous appreciation and respect for the greatness in him. . . ."

Another senior White House aide, Charles Colson, was present at the funeral. This was the self-styled "kick-'em-in-the-nuts, anti-press, anti-liberal Nixon fanatic" and dirty tricks man whom Nixon used as liaison with the corrupt leaders of the Teamsters Union. Colson, who had been jailed for obstruction of justice, was moved to tears by Nixon's death.

Haldeman's assistant Gordon Strachan, also at the funeral, has been close-mouthed since 1974, when charges against him were dropped. Then, he admitted having shredded potentially compromising documents and having delivered cash destined to be used as hush money.

The man Nixon denounced as "evil" because he blabbed to investigators, presidential counsel John Dean—yet another aide who went to jail—was not present to see Nixon buried. He was at the time embroiled in a lawsuit arising from a book that suggested he masterminded Watergate and that an alleged sexual element to the affair was somehow connected to the woman who was now his wife.

Nixon's personal attorney, Herb Kalmbach, who did time for campaign violations, stood among the mourners. He had controlled vast sums in secret cash deposits, was accused of selling ambassadorships, was present when the president signed a fraudulent tax return, and traveled around the country under false names while helping Nixon cover up the offenses exposed by Watergate.

Rose Woods, that most faithful of secretaries, had also come to witness the burial of the man she served for twenty-three years. Within months, as the darkness of Alzheimer's disease began to close around her, papers would surface revealing that Nixon's own attorneys had believed that she "intentionally, not accidentally," erased the infamous eighteen and one-half minutes missing from one of Nixon's key Watergate conversations.

Nixon's closest friend, eighty-one-year-old Bebe Rebozo, was at the graveside. He had reportedly been at the hospital when the former president had taken his last breath. Rebozo, who had once covertly received bundles of cash from Howard Hughes on Nixon's behalf, was suspected of having used the bank he owned in Florida as a conduit for cash smuggled in from a Bahamanian casino. The Senate Watergate Committee had named Rebozo, along with Nixon's two brothers, as witnesses who obstructed its work.

Unlike many presidents, Nixon had never been suspected of being a philanderer. He had offered to support Marianna Liu, a former hotel hostess he had met in Hong Kong in the sixties, when she sued over press reports about their relationship. Liu, who had lived in Nixon's hometown after moving to the United States, visited his grave sometime after the funeral.

The Saudi millionaire arms dealer Adnan Khashoggi had cultivated Nixon before he became president, met with him while in office, and was said once to have given him a million-dollar campaign contribution, illegal because it came from a foreign donor. Khashoggi was at the funeral, seated in a privileged spot close to the relatives. There too was the former Empress Farah Diba, widow of the shah of Iran, with whom Nixon had an unusually close friendship and to whom—with almost no consultation within the U.S. government—he granted access to an almost unlimited amount of U.S. arms.

Those who extolled Nixon when he died almost all cited his achievement in extracting the United States from the Vietnam War. "The greatest honor history can bestow," read the inscription on his black granite tombstone, "is the title of peacemaker." The line was taken from the president's first inaugural address.

Of the total of more than fifty-eight thousand Americans who died in Vietnam, almost twenty-one thousand were killed during Nixon's presidency—before the agreement that he said brought "peace with honor." During his time in office more than six hundred thousand Vietnamese combatants also died, and an unknown number of civilians. There are no reliable figures for the number of deaths in Cambodia and Laos.

Tens of thousands more Vietnamese died in the short time that remained until South Vietnam collapsed, less than a year after Nixon's resignation. The ousted former president of South Vietnam, Nguyen Van Thieu, was not at the funeral.

New research strengthens the suspicion that in 1968, on the eve of the election that brought him to the White House, Nixon manipulated the Vietnam War for selfish political ends. Did he, fearful that impending peace negotiations would swing vital votes to his Democratic opponent, covertly urge Thieu to boycott the talks? The prominent Republican Anna Chennault, who met secretly with Nixon and acted as a go-between with the South Vietnamese, claims he did. She eventually came to despise Nixon and stayed away from the funeral.

Asked what would be found written on his heart when his life ended, the former president had told an intimate, "That's easy. One word: Pat!" Nixon was buried next to his wife, and there were touching testimonials at the funeral about their fifty-three-year marriage. Other memories told a sadder story: of prolonged marital difficulty, of physical abuse, of threatened divorce. One of the few times Nixon broke down in public had been a year earlier, at Pat's funeral. As he struggled to compose himself, he had clutched the hand of a man few outsiders recognized, a trusted psychotherapist, Dr. Arnold Hutschnecker.

Hutschnecker watched Nixon's burial on television on the other side of the continent, reflecting on the patient who had first come to him with his troubles four decades earlier. Some at the funeral, and others not present, recalled a Nixon who sometimes cracked under the pressures of public office. There had been myriad minor incidents, the slapping of a campaign worker who had criticized him, the time he sat kicking the back of a car seat like a child until an aide walked away in disgust. During the presidency, much more seriously, there had been times when he had seemed uncoordinated, rendered unstable by fatigue, alcohol, and medication. He had reportedly ordered acts of war that aides had chosen to ignore, even slept through a crisis meeting when a heightened stage of nuclear alert was ordered in his name. At the end, a message had gone out to the military that instructions from the White House were to be ignored unless cleared by a senior member of the cabinet.

In the fifties, after he had begun treating then Vice President Nixon, Dr. Hutschnecker had begun urging that "mental health certificates should be required for political leaders." In private he had expressed concern at the possibility that Nixon should hold high office.

Haldeman likened the former president to a "multifaceted quartz crystal. Some facets bright and shining, others dark and mysterious. And all of them constantly changing as the external light rays strike the crystal . . . some smooth and polished, others crude, rough, and sharp. . . ."

Henry Kissinger has written of the "Walter Mitty dimensions of his personality . . . the absence of any sense of proportion. His self-image of coolness in crisis . . . distorted by the dogged desperation with which he attacked his problems. . . . The titanic struggle among the various personalities within him."

At the funeral, the former secretary of state quoted *Hamlet:* "He was a man; take him for all in all." In these pages we seek the "all in all" of Richard Nixon, including the parts of him that he and his supporters have preferred to conceal.

1

*He belongs to the world,
but he is also still very much mine.*

—Richard Nixon's mother in 1960,
when he was forty-seven years old

He was a dark-haired boy of six, scrubbed and smart in starched white shirt, black bow tie, and knee pants, walking each morning to the Yorba Linda elementary school. In mild weather, like other local children, he made his way along the unpaved road barefoot.

Richard Milhous Nixon had been born on January 9, 1913, in the do-it-yourself Sears, Roebuck house his father had built on the twelve-acre site in Southern California that he hoped would become a profitable lemon grove. He was the second child born to Frank and Hannah Nixon, the second of five sons, and it was obvious from the start that he was special. "Please call my son Richard and never Dick," his mother told the teacher. "I named him Richard."

"He was one of those rare individuals," recalled that teacher, Mary George. "He just never had to work for knowledge at all. He was told something and he never forgot. He was a very quiet, studious boy . . . a solemn child who rarely ever smiled or laughed. His mother was a wonderful person. You always knew she was right there with you, because of the work she would do with Richard at home."

More than half a century later, with his wife and his own grown children at his side, President Nixon would spend his last minutes in the White House making a farewell speech to his staff—and a battery of television cameras. He would not speak of affairs of state, nor would he apologize for his actions. His face wet with perspiration and tears, his voice quavering, he launched into a disquieting stream-of-consciousness discourse. He asserted that he was not educated, that he had no personal wealth. He claimed he had barely managed to pass his bar exam to become a lawyer. He recalled Theodore Roosevelt, who had overcome his grief over his wife's death and gone on to become president. He made no reference to his own wife, who had been steadfast for so long. Instead, he eulogized his father and mother, long since dead.

"I remember my old man," Nixon told his audience. "I think they would have called him sort of a little man, common man . . . he had a lemon ranch. It was the poorest lemon ranch in California. . . . He sold it before they found oil on it. And then he was a grocer. But he was a great man, because he did his job. . . .

"My mother," the president went on, "was a saint. And I think of her two boys dying of tuberculosis, nursing four others in order that she could take care of my older brother for three years in Arizona, and seeing each of them die . . . she will have no books written about her. But she was a saint."

In this outpouring, delivered at what seemed like the end of a wrecked career, lay the key to its beginnings—and to much else about the man. First, and perhaps above all, it was less than truthful.

Of course Nixon had been educated. He had attended college and gone on to law school at a respected university, from which he was graduated with highest honors. Far from struggling through the bar exam, he had passed easily. As for his wealth or lack of it, a subject that is still the subject of controversy, suffice it to say here that Nixon was affluent in 1974 and would remain so. It was not true that his father suffered a loss by selling his land, only to have others strike oil on it. In fact, no oil was ever found on the Nixon property.[1] Two of the Nixon boys did die tragically young, as he asserted, but only one of them is known to have suffered from tuberculosis. The other died of a brief illness that was never satisfactorily diagnosed.

Richard Nixon's life was shot through with lies great and small, whether outright lying, skirting the truth, or embroidering it. It was his lying that most damaged him during Watergate. Yet Nixon even lied to the man to whom he entrusted his fate in his time of crisis, his Watergate lawyer Fred Buzhardt. Buzhardt later remembered the president as "the most transparent liar he had ever met."

This same man sometimes championed the truth, not least on the ground that in the long run lying usually backfires. He liked to cite the example of his own first great victory, in seeing to it that Alger Hiss was convicted for lying under oath. "If you lie," he said, reflecting on Hiss's fate, "you go to jail for the lie rather than the crime. So believe me, don't ever lie."

"Let us begin," Nixon exhorted Republicans as he accepted the 1968 nomination for the presidency, "by committing ourselves to the truth, to see it like it is and to tell it like it is, to find the truth, to speak the truth and to live with the truth. That's what we will do." In the event, not so.

Some of the untruths Nixon told as president mattered little. There was the claim, convenient when meeting a group of athletes, that he had met his wife at a football game. By all other accounts, including his own, he met her when both auditioned for parts in a play. There was his assertion, useful when addressing French reporters, that he had "majored in French." In fact his college major had been history. There was his written instruction to his staff—an unusually careless lapse—to find some chopsticks, and any chopsticks would suffice, to display in an exhibit commemorating his breakthrough visit to China. He did so in the knowledge that the authentic ivory chopsticks, used at dinner with Mao Zedong, had not been preserved. "That doesn't make any difference," he wrote. "We undoubtedly have some chopsticks, ivory or otherwise."

Other untruths and deceptions mattered greatly, whether or not they constituted outright lies. These included encouraging the notion that he had what the press called "a secret plan to end the war" at a time, during the 1968 campaign, when the Vietnam conflict was the crucial election issue; assuring the nation that there were no U.S. combat troops in Laos—a lie; most notoriously, denying in a national television address that the United States had been bombing Cambodia, a lie that oddly, Henry Kissinger later recalled, Nixon added unnecessarily to the draft of his speech.[2]

Nixon's master plan to regain credibility during Watergate was dubbed Operation Candor. Yet he lied to the nation, to congressional colleagues, to his closest aides, and to his own attorneys, insisting as late as a year into the scandal that he was "the one person that's totally blameless in this. . . ." "I have nothing to hide," he insisted to Senator Hugh Scott, the Senate minority leader, "and you are authorized to make that statement in my name." "The danger in this whole thing," recalled Senator Barry Goldwater, who thought the president was losing his mind and who eventually led a deputation to urge him to resign, "was his constant telling lies."

Saddest of all, perhaps, the president lied to his own family, denying that he had had any part in Watergate or the cover-up. "We have every reason to believe him," his daughter Tricia told an interviewer, "because he has never lied. . . . Richard Nixon is a man who has never lied, not even a white lie, to his family or to the American people. . . ."

In private, Nixon sometimes dropped all pretense at honesty. Lying as a political ploy, he would say, was just part of the game. "One time," recalled John Sears, a former deputy counsel, "we were going up to see the Mormon elders at the Mormon cathedral. And we got halfway up the steps, and the band was playing, and the people were watching. And all of a sudden he stopped and said to me, 'Whatever I say in there, don't you believe a word of it . . .'"

Len Garment, Nixon's law colleague before the presidency and later a senior aide, remembered what Nixon told him in a relaxed moment at the Drake Hotel in New York. "He was alone, stretched out on the bed, a phone in one hand and a highball in the other. Nixon, by then reasonably well oiled (it didn't take much to do the trick . . . it was kind of truth serum in this instance), . . . said, 'You're never going to make it in politics, Len. You just don't know how to lie.' "

Out of office, Nixon declared on national television that in his view, "dissembling" and "hypocrisy" were necessary to win and hold public office, arguing that there was "a very fine line" between not being candid and "lying in an immoral sense." Not telling the truth can eventually become as confusing to the chronic liar as it is misleading to his audience, and so it was for Nixon. On occasion, Kissinger thought, the president convinced himself that his distortion of a fact was actually the true fact. "I doubt if he knows himself when he's not telling the truth," said presidential aide John Ehrlichman.

To focus on Nixon's lying and—if it can be judged a lesser sin—on his dissembling is not undertaken here to prejudge the man, but rather to point up an inherent difficulty faced by anyone who strives to write about him. In many ways Nixon has left his biographers much more to work with than most politicians. His autobiographical work is massive and illuminating, as are the books produced by those who knew him well. Some of those writers, however, are themselves prone to lying; their number includes convicted perjurers. Then there is the unique bounty of the White House tapes. They are priceless raw material, but they too are shot through with Nixonian lies—not all of them easy to identify even now.

Truth is always elusive for a biographer. It is generally more accessible, though, in the smaller body of material left behind by leaders considered to have been fundamentally honest—a Truman, a Ford, or a Carter—than in the extensive record that is the legacy of a man known to have been a chronic liar. To travel Richard Nixon's life requires, more than for most subjects, a careful passage through a minefield of lies, lies of varying degrees of seriousness, lies self-serving but in the end self-defeating.

John Ehrlichman made his observation that Nixon may have lost touch with the truth in 1978, when Nixon's two-volume autobiography was published. He referred in particular to what the former president had written about his own family. "Read that description of his family," Ehrlichman told the writer Paul Theroux. "They're all perfect, right? But what man can say his family's perfect? Those people are human . . . he makes them into waxwork dummies . . . if he doesn't come clean about them, how can he come clean about anything else?"

———————

The picture of Richard's boyhood and family life comes down to us, as must most such memories, largely from the family itself and, above all, from the adult Nixon and his mother, Hannah. Their interviews, even the earliest ones, were given with an eye to generating favorable propaganda for a budding politician.

The acknowledgments page of one early biography, by Bela Kornitzer, gushes with thanks to Nixon and his "great and dedicated" mother. Hannah Nixon cheerfully joined in propagating the yarn about the missed fortune in oil supposedly discovered under the family property after it had been sold. "It's been a campaign ever since he was born," she admitted. "All his life, I've been his campaigner." In years to come, incongruous in an otherwise simple decor, a massive, translucent, three-dimensional color photograph of Richard—illuminated at the touch of a button—hung in her house.

For his part, Nixon forever extolled Hannah's virtues, which included her pie-making ability—reporters noted that the pies he claimed his mother had gotten up at 5:00 A.M. to bake changed from apple to lemon, and from lemon to cherry, as he moved from one rally to another. Aides were struck by how often Nixon spoke of Hannah even when he was not in the public eye. He was still going on about her, tears welling in his eyes, as he approached his eightieth birthday. "My mother taught me about hard work, endurance, and patience. . . . She sacrificed everything for us. She worked like a dog, through pain and tears and you name it. She was so strong because she put it all in God's hands. She never gave up. . . . I always knew that women were the stronger sex."

Hannah Milhous Nixon—Richard was the only one of her sons to bear her maiden name—came from a long line of Quakers. Her ancestors were Germans who migrated first to Ireland, then in the eighteenth century to what was to become Pennsylvania, and then from one community of Friends to another until they finally settled in California. Hannah was one of nine children born to a prosperous rancher and his wife. Her father's generation was a tight-knit family of "thee and thou"-ing Quakers, staunch in adherence to tradition, stern in their discipline, and so fiercely clannish that they conceded only reluctantly the biological necessity of marrying outside the Milhous bloodline.

Hannah was regarded as a quiet, dutiful daughter, who talked of becoming a teacher until, at the age of twenty-three, she dropped out of college to marry Frank Nixon. Frank, then twenty-nine, was of humbler stock. He was one of five children of an impoverished Ohio family, Methodists with combined English, Irish, and Scots roots. He had left school at fourteen to earn a living wherever he could find it. When he was twenty-seven, a job as an omnibus motorman ended after he suffered frostbite while driving at night on an open platform. He led fellow workers in a struggle for better conditions, then left for the warmer climate of Southern California. He roomed in a boardinghouse run by Quakers where, at a Quaker Valentine's party in 1908, he met Hannah Milhous and wooed and wed her in less than four months.

The bride not only was "marrying below her station," as one local put it, but—as a woman who had never once gone out with a man before—had fallen for a fellow who, by his own boast, was currently seeing five girls at once. Frank was to be remembered as a "hot man," a pincher and a squeezer of females, a "horny bastard," according to a local lawyer, who would later give up dancing because he became "instantly aroused . . . when his arms went around a woman."

Hannah married Frank in the face of her parents' opposition. Her teenage sister Olive, reflecting the outrage of the family and local Quakers, carved the words "Hannah is a bad girl" on a pepper tree in the yard. Relations eventually improved, however. Hannah's father provided the couple with a parcel of land to launch them, and the babies soon started to arrive.

There were to be five children, all boys: Harold, born a year after the wedding; Richard, born during a freak cold snap four years later; Donald in 1915; Arthur in 1918; and Edward—a surprise late arrival—in 1930, when Hannah was forty-five. All but Donald were named after English kings of history or legend. In Richard's case, Hannah was to explain, she had in mind King Richard the Lionheart, warrior hero of the Crusades.

As Hannah recounted it, it was tough growing up in the Nixon family. She recalled having had nothing to serve but cornmeal, night after night. Richard once told a reporter of "going to bed many nights after eating only a slice of bread covered with tomato sauce, of knowing what hunger was." "We were poor," he said on another occasion. "We had very little." On other occasions he came closer to the probable truth. "It's been said our family was poor," he told the columnist Stewart Alsop, "but we never thought of ourselves as poor. We always had enough to eat, and we never had to depend on anyone else."

The Nixons did not start without resources. For all his reservations about Frank, Hannah's father advanced him three thousand dollars—the equivalent of some fifty-two thousand dollars today—to build their first home and start the lemon grove at Yorba Linda, thirty miles from Los Angeles.

The lemons never did flourish, in part because the land was unsuitable, in part because Frank Nixon refused to take advice on how to improve it. Over the years he took on other work, and Hannah worked in the SunKist fruit-packing plant. Life for her was hard not least because the life she had left behind when she married Frank had been, by contrast, so comfortable. She could and sometimes did, moreover, return for a while to the comfort of her parents' home.

Boyhood hardships, the grown Nixon was to say, meant Harold having to forgo having a pony because the money went toward groceries and shoes for the younger siblings. Richard claimed he yearned for "an automatic train, not an electric train, but just one that would wind up," but never got one. (Hannah, however, said the boys did get an electric train, a luxury toy in those days.) Their father owned not only a tractor, a necessity on the land, but also a car, as early as 1919. In Yorba Linda, where many families struggled to make ends meet, the Nixons were seen by neighbors as "well-to-do," even "just a shade above what you might want to call the middle-income bracket."

Matters improved materially in 1922, when just after Richard's ninth birthday the Nixons gave up on the lemon grove, sold the land, borrowed five thousand dollars—about fifty-one thousand at today's values—from the bank, and moved to Whittier to start a grocery and gas station business. Home was now a modest house behind the store with a living room, kitchen, and one bedroom downstairs and another bedroom over the garage for the children. Hannah prepared her famous pies at a kitchen table covered with an oilcloth. Neatly ironed antimacassars shielded upholstered chairs in the living room, and an upright piano stood in the corner. Hannah liked to play it, and by the age of three, we are told by the Nixon Library, little Richard could pick out a simple tune.

"My father," Nixon recalled in middle age, "was a scrappy, belligerent fighter, with a quick, wide-ranging raw intellect. He left me with a respect for learning and hard work, and the will to keep fighting no matter what the odds. . . . My father had an Irish quickness both to anger and to mirth. It was his temper that impressed me most as a small child. He had tempestuous arguments with my brothers Harold and Don. . . . He was a strict and stern disciplinarian. . . . "

Frank Nixon had been beaten as a child, and he in turn used the ruler and the strap on his sons. Was Richard a target of his punishment? Mostly, he claimed that while his brothers were beaten, he dodged the strap by following the rules. Other times, he said he too got strapped and, "Father would spank us sometimes; my mother never." Other memories paint a darker picture, of not only a violent, punitive father but also of a mother not the sweet creature she has been portrayed.

Once, when Harold was being whipped by his father, his screams could be heard in nearby houses. The boys' playmates, who feared getting a Frank Nixon thrashing themselves, thought him "an awful rough guy." A family friend said he was "hard . . . beastly . . . like an animal." Once, when he caught Richard and one of his brothers swimming in a nearby canal, he hauled them out and then threw them back in again, hollering, "You like water? Have some more of it!" Richard's cousin Jessamyn West, later a prominent writer, witnessed the incident with her aunt Elizabeth. Fearing the boys would drown, the aunt screamed, "You'll kill them, Frank! You'll kill them!"

Jessamyn West recalled her own father's shock when, in later years, the Nixon boys spoke bitterly about Frank Nixon in front of others. "They could be so cruel, so loud-mouthed, so critical of their father. . . . [My father] couldn't understand it, unless they got it when they were young and now they were paying their father back."

Richard himself never spoke of such tensions. "It is the love beneath his brusque and bristling exterior that I remember best," he said of Frank Nixon. Likewise, he never mentioned any friction between his father and mother. Yet Dr. Arnold Hutschnecker, the psychotherapist Nixon consulted for many years, had a harsh impression of the marriage, one he could have received only from his patient. "Nixon's father was brutal and cruel," he said in 1976. "[He] brutalized the mother, and this is of enormous importance." Nixon was still alive at the time, and Hutschnecker offered no details.*

Richard himself never spoke ill of his mother, whom he called "the gentlest, most considerate woman." Some friends described her as a "wonderful . . . kind, gentle-spoken" woman with "the quiet stillness of a nun, saying little in a low, sweet voice." Yet Hannah's personality generated its own tensions. "She had a temper too," said her youngest son, Edward, "but controlled. She knew how to throttle my dad if he was hurting one of us unintentionally. . . . "

Helene Drown, a friend so loyal that she usually found no fault in the Nixons, also remembered Hannah's temper, remarking, "She was not a 'holy-holy saint.'" One neighbor saw her as "cranky and puritanical." Another thought her "hard . . . pure steel, pure steel."

Hannah did not leave corporal punishment to her husband. "We never paddled him," she claimed when discussing Richard with one reporter, while admitting to another, "I may have paddled him a little." She encouraged one neighbor to spank Richard if he got out of line, and another recalled seeing her seated on the piano stool next to Richard, switch in hand, as he practiced.

"One day," Nixon's aide John Sears learned, "Hannah Nixon baked some cookies. Little Richard saw those cookies and ate one of them. And she said, 'Richard, did you eat that cookie?' He didn't know any better than to say yes, and she beat the daylights out of him, or maybe his father did when he came home. But Richard Nixon learned one thing from that: He would probably still have gotten the daylights beaten out of him if he'd said no. But when he'd admitted it! He was now just totally rejected. That was a lifelong lesson to him."

It was Hannah's tongue, though, that the boys feared most. "She would just sit you down," Richard recalled, "and she would talk very, very quietly and then, when you got through, you had been through an emotional experience." "Tell her to give me a spanking," little Arthur said once, when he was in trouble, "I can't stand it, to have her talk to me."

Arthur's offense that day was serious; he had been caught smoking cigarettes behind the house—at the age of five!—cigarettes he had taken from his parents' store. His reason for doing it, Richard thought, was to "show the world he was a man." Frank and Hannah had been hoping for a daughter when Arthur was born in 1918. When he turned out to be a boy, they at first told his brothers that there "was a little doll over at the hospital for us, a real live doll." For the first few years of his life they treated him as much like a girl as possible, until poor Arthur begged to have a boy's haircut.

Another story about Arthur reveals the tenor of the emotional life of the

*Nixon first visited Dr. Hutschnecker in 1951 and consulted him sporadically as patient and friend until shortly before he died. The true nature of their relationship was long obscured, by the doctor as well as by Nixon. Dr. Hutschnecker gave the author access to his unpublished writing on Nixon and extensive interviews for this book. His involvement with Nixon is fully reported in chapter 10.

Nixon family. Once, when he was seven and Richard had been away, Arthur rushed to greet him on his return. Then, shyly, he said, "Would it be all right if I kissed you?" This was an event. Arthur had had to ask his mother in advance for permission to kiss his own brother.

Richard Bergholz, former political editor for the *Los Angeles Times,* once watched Nixon and his mother greeting each other after a long separation. "I couldn't believe my eyes. . . . Here was a guy who hadn't seen his mother in . . . I don't know how long, and all he could do was shake her hand; he couldn't show any form of affection. It bothered me. . . ."

In old age Richard declared himself "nauseated" by the custom of hugging and kissing children and loved ones. His mother, he said, "could communicate far more than others could with a lot of sloppy talk and even more sloppy kissing and hugging. . . ." She never kissed him, ever.

"In her whole life," Nixon said of Hannah, "I never heard her say to me or anyone else, 'I love you.'" He said she had not needed to. "No one projected warmth and affection more than my mother. . . . Only one of those rather pathetic Freudian psychiatrists would suggest that her love of privacy made her private even from her sons." Dr. Hutschnecker, the psychotherapist Nixon trusted with his confidences for years, suggested almost exactly that in interviews for this book. He concluded—again, the basis for that conclusion must certainly have been what his patient told him—that Hannah was "not really close to Richard. . . . No woman ever gave Nixon the support he really needed."

Hutschnecker thought Nixon "an emotionally deprived child" who grew up to become a "person who regarded love and physical closeness as a diversion that would drain him, deplete him, make him less manly. Love . . . never had priority in Nixon's life, for he always convinced himself that he didn't need to be loved as a human being, only respected as a man."

The tensions in the Nixon family were twice compounded by tragedy. First his brother Arthur died in 1925, when Richard was twelve. The boy was just seven years old, and the cause of his death cannot be determined for certain. The first writer to interview the adult Nixon about it reported that Arthur fell ill after being hit on the head by a rock thrown in the schoolyard. A nurse who tended him also mentioned the incident. Edward Nixon, the surviving brother, remembers hearing about it, as does Richard's nephew Donald. He recalls that in the fifties, when he was growing up, he was forbidden to throw rocks or earth when playing because, as his father explained, Arthur had died after being "hit by a clod on the back of the head."

The death certificate, however, attributed Arthur's death to "encephalitis or tubercular meningitis," and in later years Richard went with the theory that the root cause was tuberculosis. TB was the scourge of his youth and the health nightmare of his family, having killed his paternal grandmother, an aunt, and a cousin. When Arthur died, according to Hannah, Richard sat in a big chair, "staring into space, silent and dry-eyed in the undemonstrative way in which, because of his choked, deep feeling, he was always to face tragedy." He said he cried every day for week. Soon TB was to start killing his elder brother, Harold, painfully slowly.

Harold was sixteen when Arthur died. He was handsome, keen on girls, the proud adolescent owner of a stripped-down Model T Ford, and he was not doing well at school. With the grocery and the gas station flourishing, the Nixons decided to send him off to an expensive boarding school in Massachusetts. Harold came back a few months later coughing, in the first stages of his illness.

His father had invited such disaster, Richard claimed after his parents were dead. Frank Nixon had scoffed at safety measures like the pasteurization of milk, insisting that the family drink milk straight from the cow. For a while Richard was seriously ill with undulant fever, a form of brucellosis that can be contracted by consuming animal products. Richard and Don both had TB scares when X rays showed shadows on their lungs.

Harold's tuberculosis was a family ordeal that lasted six years. Because his father was too proud to send him to a public clinic, he began the first of a series of stays in expensive private sanitoriums. To pay for his care, the Nixons' comfortable existence was disrupted by costs that Richard remembered as "catastrophic." Whatever exaggerations may have been made about the family's earlier days, this period was genuinely difficult. Richard, barely sixteen, regularly rose at 4:00 A.M. to drive the fourteen miles to Los Angeles to buy fruit and vegetables for the store, then returned to set them up in a display, all before leaving for school. Even in the family's straitened circumstances, he remained fastidious. He insisted that his shirts be perfectly ironed and that his mother check him for halitosis each morning by smelling his breath—"to make sure he would not offend anyone. . . ."

Richard's work in the store spawned an anecdote suggesting that integrity was not his finest point, even then. "One day," his cousin Merle West recalled, "when Richard was helping Don in the meat department, making hamburgers, he cut his finger badly and it bled into the meat. Don said they had to throw the bled-on meat away, but Dick said, 'No way! That's the freshest-looking meat on the counter. Leave it there. . . .'"

Hannah Nixon's crusade to save Harold took her away from the family for long periods. She hung her hopes on the possibility that his health would improve in the drier climate of Arizona, four hundred miles away, and they traveled there for extended stays over a period of more than two years. Richard, who joined her in the summers of 1928 and 1929, found himself in a community of TB sufferers, sick people drifting about in pajamas and robes, sputum cups in hand. He felt afraid, even of his own brother. Meanwhile he took summer jobs, plucking chickens and working as a pool boy at a posh country club and as a barker at a carnival, where he had his first exposure to gambling. His Quaker mother reportedly turned a blind eye to the latter activity.

In happier days Richard and Harold had fooled visiting salesmen at their father's store by concocting phony radio advertisements and broadcasting them over a speaker system Harold had rigged up. Richard, a relative remembered, excelled at faking the broadcasts. In Arizona, Harold figured out a method of intercepting a girlfriend's phone conversations with a rival suitor, which was probably Richard's first experience of wiretapping.

All the while Richard watched as his mother tended Harold and the other tuberculosis patients she took in as paying guests, emptying bedpans and washing bloody sheets. Death came for Harold in 1933, at home in Whittier, on his mother's birthday. "Richard sank into a deep, impenetrable silence," Hannah remembered. "From that time on, it seemed he was trying to be three sons in one, striving even harder than before to make up to his father and me for his loss. . . . I think Richard may have felt a kind of guilt that Harold and Arthur were dead and he was alive."

Frank Nixon had judged Harold, of all the boys, "the flower of the family." "Why is it," he asked Jessamyn West's father, "that the brightest and strongest, handsomest and best, get taken first?" Jessamyn suspected her cousin Richard had been made to feel "a substitute, a man on the second team."

When Arthur died, Frank Nixon had decided he was being punished for keeping his store open on the Sabbath, and he closed it on Sundays thereafter. After Harold's death Hannah vowed never to celebrate her birthday again, and banned parties or presents for the rest of her life. She and Frank accepted their son's passing as yet another expression of God's will.

The Nixon children were steeped in religion. Of the two Quaker meetinghouses in their hometown, the family attended the one that followed an evangelical tradition, which had very different practices from the original Quaker concept of silent prayer. Evangelical Quakers were more given to music, singing, and passionate sermons.

"We regularly went to church four times on Sunday," Richard recalled, "Sunday school and a worship service in the morning, a young people's meeting called Christian Endeavor, and another worship service in the evening. . . . We never had a meal without grace. Usually it was silent. Sometimes each of us would recite a verse of scripture." At home, Hannah Nixon preferred her religion quiet. She followed Jesus' instruction "Enter into thy closet when thou prayest," actually going into a clothes or broom closet to pray each night. Religion, said her sister Jane, "was just really her life."

Frank Nixon, the convert from Methodism, was a prominent Sunday school teacher, remembered as a "firebrand" with flaming cheeks and trembling voice. After Arthur's death he would rise from his seat at the meetinghouse to shout, "We must have a reawakening! We have got to get people back to God!" He began driving his family to Los Angeles for revival meetings, and at one of them the thirteen-year-old Richard surged forward with other devotees to commit himself to Christ.

At twenty, however, within months of Harold's death, Richard was questioning the foundations of his religious faith. "My beliefs are shattered," he declared in a series of college essays titled "What Can I Believe?" He rejected the infallability of the Bible and its miracle stories and drew up a chart that mapped his concept of how factors like "Will" and "Self-Organization" interacted with "Spiritual Energy" and other drives. He concluded that although his thinking was now "revolutionized," he remained "a believer in God as Creator and in the philosophy of Christ."

Nixon professed to be a Christian for the rest of his life, but swung from admiration of one church to another. He told Walter Trohan of the *Chicago Tribune*, one of the few journalists who became an intimate, that he would not have stayed a Quaker, except for Hannah; instead, he said, he would have become a Presbyterian. In the sixties, when out of office, he was often seen attending the services of the Reverend Norman Vincent Peale, the conservative minister of *The Power of Positive Thinking* fame. One of that book's chapter titles is "I Don't Believe in Defeat."

Nixon announced at the start of his presidency that he was going to hold nondenominational services at the White House every Sunday. Billy Graham, spiritual confidant to every president since Truman, was a regular preacher. On a retreat with Graham, Nixon spoke of his youthful "conversion"—presumably a reference to his experience at the Los Angeles revival meeting—and told Graham, "Pray for me. I'm a backslider."

Presidential aide John Ehrlichman, at that time a committed Christian Scientist, regarded the Sunday services and the Billy Graham connection as "a lot of window dressing." He maintained that "Nixon was not a motivated Christian. Sometimes he reverted to Quaker beliefs, telling me about his mother's teachings, and how the Quaker ceremony was very simple, more authentic. Other times he'd say, 'You know, if I were ever to embrace a religion, it would be Catholicism, because they're so well disciplined in their dogma, so well defined.' Nixon picked Claude Brinegar as secretary of transportation because he thought he was a Catholic, though he turned out to be Episcopalian. He told him, 'I want you to be secretary because I want you to be my liaison with the cardinals.' That was hilarious, because Brinegar just looked at him and said, 'Well, the L.A. Rams are my team, Mr. President.'"

According to Charles Colson, the aide who later turned to God and became a lay minister, Nixon had considered converting to Catholicism before the 1972 election, having come to be convinced that Catholics represented "the real America." To traditional Quakers like his mother, Catholicism is anathema.

Nixon stopped holding Sunday services at the White House during Watergate and for months did not attend church at all. "Bob," he confided to Chief of Staff H. R. ("Bob") Haldeman the day he fired him, "there's something I've never told anybody before, not even you. Every night since I've been President, every single night before I've gone to bed, I've knelt down on my knees beside my bed and prayed to God for guidance." He told Colson the same thing, recalling later that before making any difficult decisions, he prayed at the table at which Abraham Lincoln had signed the Emancipation Proclamation.

As his resignation approached, Nixon turned for help to a rabbi, Baruch Korff, and attended about two dozen "pastoral sessions." He had been able to withstand the "vilification and savagery" to which he had been subjected, he explained to Korff, because of the "peace at the center" instilled in him by his Quaker mother. On his last day at the White House, Nixon told Korff he believed he was being "punished by God," much as his father had felt after Arthur's death.

According to Billy Graham, he and Nixon prayed together at San Clemente after the resignation. They discussed the Bible and perused a leather-bound *Life of Christ* that had belonged to Nixon's Quaker grandmother. A few months later Watergate Special Prosecution Force attorneys were nonplussed when, having been handed a borrowed Bible to take the oath, the former president whipped out a pen, autographed the Bible as if he were an author at an autograph session, then solemnly handed it back.

In old age, Nixon said, he regularly consulted his own well-thumbed King James Bible, and his library shelves were crowded with books on religion and philosophy. He still admired Catholicism, having come to believe that ritual and ceremony were essential to religion, yet continued to declare himself a Quaker. "I believe that Richard is an intensely religious man," his mother said in 1960, "but he shuns even the restrained rituals of his faith. I am sure other Quakers understand my son." While Nixon's old church in California spoke up for him after Watergate, most Quaker groups repudiated him.

Some observers thought that the tenets of the Quaker faith—especially the doctrine that each member of the church has access, individually, to God's Inner Light—became skewed in Nixon. "We spent a great deal of time arguing about it," said the *Chicago Tribune*'s Trohan, "and I tell you frankly: Nixon's great trouble was his religion. Quakers don't have anybody to deal with God except themselves, and that can make them loners. He didn't consult people. . . ."

Dr. Hutschnecker, the psychotherapist in whom Nixon confided for years, agreed. "He was a victim of the rigidity of his religious training. His indoctrination was that you must help yourself . . . he had been brought up to do everything by himself." For Hutschnecker, it was Hannah, the mother Nixon obsessed about and called a saint, who was ultimately responsible for that isolating independence. "A saint is someone you cannot pray enough to, improve enough for, beg enough to. He felt he had to prove to his mother that he didn't need anybody."

"Fear," Hutschnecker came to believe, "was a virus that infected Nixon's life, that he never recovered from—the fear that he would be regarded as weak. What would Mama think? What would Daddy say? . . . I believe that the image of the saintly but stern face of his mother defeated him more than any other factor. . . . His mother was really his downfall."

2

---

*One man may have opportunities that others
do not . . . what counts is whether the individual
used what chances he had.*

—*Richard Nixon, 1962*

In 1933 Richard Nixon fought a tough campaign, won a presidency, and subsequently went to jail. The presidency was that of the student body at Whittier College, the liberal arts school in his hometown, and he won it by promising to fight for the removal of a prohibition on student dances. No matter that he himself was no dancer or that his parents thought the ban should continue. "He's a real smart politician," said the candidate who lost the election. "He knew what issues to use to get support."

The scrape with the law came a few months later, when Nixon and some fellow students snake-danced into town and burst into a movie theater without buying tickets. When the police hauled the group off to jail, Nixon got them out by phoning a Whittier alumnus who happened to be a judge. A year earlier, as chairman of a committee organizing the annual bonfire, he had more than fulfilled the traditional obligations of that post. The chairman was expected to supply a large wooden privy to top the heap. A one- or two-seater privy was considered satisfactory, but Nixon distinguished himself by producing a four-seater. He and a few confederates had broken into a rancher's premises at night, disconnected the privy from its sewer pipes, and escaped unseen.

At twenty the man who as president claimed to have had no education was flying high in academe. All his young life he had been an exemplary student. "He absorbed knowledge of any kind like a blotter," elementary school teacher Mary George remembered. "He just never had to work for knowledge at all. . . ." Nixon would claim he had learned to read before starting first grade. Although Miss George thought not, she did recall wondering, that year, how he managed to read "no less than thirty or forty books, besides doing all of his other work."

"My mother spent countless hours," he wrote by way of explanation in old age, "encouraging me, helping me with homework and challenging me to learn." When relatives saw a light burning late at the Nixon house, they would say knowingly, "Richard is studying, and Hannah is with him." His mother said: "Richard always seemed to need me more than the four other sons did. He used to like to have me sit with him when he studied."

Because of his good grades, Nixon was advanced into classes with children older than him. He scored steady As in all subjects except math and geometry. In fifth grade he was top of the class the entire year. At eleven he was devouring the book *How to Win Friends and Influence People,* by Dale Carnegie. At twelve he was sent away for six months to stay with his aunt Jane, a professional music teacher, and came home able to play the Grieg piano sonata. Music aside, however, he proved inept at any work that involved hand-eye coordination. He was hopeless at woodwork or anything that required mechanical aptitude and as an adult was known as a total klutz.

In 1930, his last year at high school, Nixon won the Harvard Club of California's award for the "best all-around student" in the state. The prize was a stepping-stone to a Harvard University scholarship, and by one account he was offered one. There was also talk of Yale, but he wound up attending neither. Perhaps the family finances would have been overstretched by an Ivy League tuition, as Nixon explained. Yet, as he also admitted, with Harold's drawn-out illness, the arrival of new baby Edward, and a shortage of help in the store, he was needed at home.

So it was that Nixon applied for a Milhous Scholarship to help him attend Whittier College, a scholarship he could hardly fail to win. It was funded by fifty thousand dollars left to Whittier by his own maternal grandfather and specifically designed to pay for the education of Milhous family members. One of Nixon's uncles supplied his letter of reference. Whittier College was—and is—an entirely respectable seat of learning, but it was not a name to conjure with. "I had dreamed of going to college in the East," Nixon wrote in his memoirs. Once that dream had ended, and for the rest of his life, he indulged an obsession about entitlement and social class.[1]

In the early thirties, with the national economy shuddering, most Whittier students were children of the affluent minority in the local community. The majority of young men in this group aspired to join the Franklins, a literary club that had become a pretext for the sorts of dinners and balls at which tuxedos were de rigueur. As one student put it, the Franklins were the "aristocrats of the campus." Even though he was a member of the Milhous family, Nixon was not invited to join the Franklins. He agreed at once, therefore, when asked to help form a rival society. He became president and founding member of a group of students who called themselves the Orthogonians, a name taken from the Greek word meaning "upright."

Membership of the Orthogonians was made up, in Nixon's words, of men who "had to work their way through college." Most were football players, with skills that Nixon famously aspired to in vain. Though he made the team, he was remembered as having "two left feet" and sat out most games on the bench.

It was he who chose the society's French motto, *Ecrasons l'infâme,* or "Let us crush infamy," adapted from the philosopher Voltaire's call to do battle with the Roman Catholic Church. Nixon claimed to have written the society's song, although according to a contemporary student newspaper account, someone else was actually responsible. Nixon did select its mascot, a wild boar, and its "4 Bs" slogan, standing for Beans, Brains, Brawn, and Bowels. He was also one of those who dreamed up the society's induction rite, a test of manhood that involved being stripped naked, chastised with a wooden paddle, and digging up the corpse of an animal and eating its decaying flesh. As a founding member Nixon was exempted from this ritual, which was later banned by the college after a student was seriously injured.

"They were the haves," Nixon said of the rival Franklins, "and we were the have-nots." The truth, however, was that by local standards *he* was perceived as one of the haves. It was not just that he had a scholarship to Whittier. It was that as the Depression tightened its grip, his family's fortunes actually improved. The grocery never failed to show a profit. His cousin Jessamyn West thought it ludicrous to suggest Richard was poor at that time. "By some," she said, the Nixons "were considered rich." Nixon's first girlfriend, Ola Welch, said in 1996 that she considered the Nixons "middle-class." Nixon's principal college professor, Dr. Paul Smith, believed class was a key factor at Whittier in the thirties, in a way that impinged on Nixon in a special way. "His family," Smith said, "wasn't looked down upon, but the Frank Nixon family was in no way regarded at the social level of the Milhouses." The mother's name stood for something, while his father was just a belligerent fellow who ran a store.

By Nixon's junior year, at a time when only a handful of students at Whittier had cars, he was the proud owner—with his cousin—of a 1930 Model A Ford. The vehicle cost $325, more than most students' annual fees. While the Franklins wore formal dress for group photographs, the Orthogonians posed in open-necked shirts—to signal their everyman status and, as one member put it, "because none of us owned a tux and didn't have the wherewithal to rent it. . . ." Nixon, however, owned a tuxedo throughout his time at college and in his senior year even owned two.

Nevertheless the boy with two tuxedos harped on his supposedly humble origins for the rest of his life. James Bassett, Nixon's press secretary and adviser in the fifties, called it his "poor boy complex." As a budding vice president Nixon told Bassett that his wife had to tell him which fork to use at dinner. "My dad was a grocer," he later said, playing up to Hubert Humphrey in a speech. "You came up the pharmacy way." He urged a law firm colleague to seek out young lawyers who were "not children of the elite but people who had fought to make their way in the world . . . like you and me." As president Nixon told his cabinet that only he and the secretary of labor, Peter Brennan, had "come from the working class."

His desire to portray himself as such ultimately contributed to a vengeful neurosis. In the White House, Nixon was soon exhorting staff to destroy the "Eastern Establishment." He recoiled when Robert Bork, who became his solicitor general, was introduced to him as a professor from Yale, one of the universities Nixon had not been able to attend. In a tape-recorded Oval Office conversation he raged against members of the administration who "start sucking around the Georgetown set. . . . They're disgusting."

"The President has said he wants to screw the universities," a White House contact reported in 1973 to Admiral Elmo Zumwalt, a member of the Joint Chiefs, "especially Harvard, by cutting back research and development money." Likewise Nixon ordered George Schultz, then running the Office of Management and Budget, to cancel all funding for the Massachusetts Institute of Technology: "All money stops by Friday. I don't want a nickel to go to MIT!" Schultz ignored the instruction.

Nixon flew into a rage when he learned that the president of Harvard, Dr. Derek Bok, was visiting. Told that the professor was a member of the White House Preservation Committee, and that he was meeting with Pat, he was not placated. "He asked me once," his aide Alexander Butterfield remembered, "'Did one of those dirty bastards ever invite me to his fucking men's club or his goddamn country club? Not once.' He was shaking. . . . The hatred was very deep-seated. He didn't just not like them; he hated them."

Even after his resignation Nixon continued to carry on about liberals, intellectuals, and journalists. "They'll never let up, never," he told Ken Clawson, his former communications director, "because we were the first threat to them in years. . . . What starts the process, really, are laughs and slights and snubs when you are a kid . . . [but] if you are reasonably intelligent and if your anger is deep enough and strong enough, you learn that you can change these attitudes by excellence, personal gut performance, while those who have everything are sitting on their fat butts."

The irony in Nixon's obsession with class was that he had himself managed to break into the establishment long before becoming president. By the early sixties he had been welcomed to membership in exclusive Manhattan clubs like the Metropolitan, the Links, and the Recess and had been accepted by two fashionable country clubs, Blind Brook in New York and Baltrusol in

New Jersey. In truth Nixon enjoyed consorting with the elite he habitually scorned.

"He'd love to get people like David Rockefeller in, to call him 'Mr. President,'" recalled William Watts, staff secretary of the National Security Council in the first Nixon presidency. "He loved to have all those real old-core rich around, that had to defer to him. I felt like I was sitting in the throne room. It was very odd."

At Whittier College, ironically, the future conservative president was considered a liberal, and an energetic one. He pushed for changes in old-fashioned rules and for student rights, and he got a black man into the society he had founded. He involved himself in myriad campus activities and was forever working. "Dick lived somewhat abnormally," a fellow student recalled. "He studied a great deal *and* worked in the store. It wasn't uncommon for him to work himself ill.

"Dick was not universally popular," said the same contemporary. "He was not what you would call a real friendly guy. Many felt Dick was above them in thinking and that probably he didn't care to associate with them." Others thought him "stuck-up," with "a ruthless cocksureness," a "wheeler-dealer . . . a big-time operator." One student, remembering Nixon's "incredible combination of enthusiasm and energy," said he "used to wonder if it was wholly genuine and, if not, how much was real and how much was simulated for the benefit of all present."

Dr. Albert Upton, who taught Nixon English and literature, urged him to read Tolstoy, and Nixon later claimed to have plowed through most of his massive oeuvre, including *War and Peace, Anna Karenina,* and much else, during the course of a single summer. Nixon's favorite was *Resurrection,* the story of a nobleman's crisis of conscience when he realizes he is responsible for destroying another person's life and his decision—after studying God's laws—to give up his wealth and his position in society so that he can regain his self-respect.

"He just didn't do bad things," Upton said of this perfect student. "It makes you wonder if there wasn't something wrong." As the college drama coach, Upton also directed Nixon in several plays in which he displayed "a deep voice and an old man's face" beyond his years and an ability to weep to order. "I taught him how to cry," said Upton. "I told him, 'Dick, if you just concentrate real hard on getting a big lump in your throat, I think you can cry real tears.' He did too—buckets of tears. . . . The tears rolled down and dropped off his nose."

Nixon starred on the Whittier debating team, traveling with other students—on occasion in a roomy Packard automobile driven by his father—throughout the West. He achieved success by doing his research in advance, changing tactics as the debate developed, and learning to keep his temper in public. Debate was the nearest thing in student life to politics, and some judged him a brilliant public speaker. Others were troubled.

Years earlier his high school debating coach had been disturbed by Nixon's "ability to slide round an argument, instead of meeting it head-on. . . . There was something mean in him," according to Mrs. Clifford Vincent, "mean in the way he put his questions, argued his points." "To get his point across," said Mildred Johns, one of his mother's friends, "he wouldn't hesitate to twist the truth."

A few years later, when Nixon had attained political prominence, a number of people remembered the "dirty debating techniques" of his school days. At Whittier College a fellow student spotted Nixon cheating during a debate. "I remember it well," said Lois Elliott, the editor of the college newspaper. "I sat in the gallery, and I saw—when Nixon spoke in his rebuttal—that he was quoting from a blank sheet of paper. It was all against regulations and very cunning."[2]

When he was thirteen, Nixon's grandmother had given him a picture of Abraham Lincoln and a handwritten verse from Longfellow's "The Psalm of Life" to hang over his bed:

> Lives of great men all remind us
> We can make our lives sublime,
> And, departing, leave behind us
> Footprints on the sands of time.

At twenty-one, having graduated second in his Whittier class of eighty-five, Nixon was poised to make his first footprints on the road to fame.

Richard had announced at the age of twelve that he wanted to be a lawyer one day. His aunt Jane said it was the result of his reading about Teapot Dome, the scandal over corrupt oil deals by government insiders. "I remember Richard lying down on the floor, down on his stomach with the newspapers spread out in front of him. He didn't like what he was reading. He said, 'When I grow up, I'm going to be an honest lawyer so things like that can't happen.' . . . He was really serious. . . ."[3]

The account is plausible, for Frank Nixon regularly raged about the "crooked lawyers" involved in Teapot Dome, and another aunt gave him a book glorifying the legal profession. His grandmother had declared, when he was a baby, that his noisy crying marked him out as a future lawyer—or preacher. At college, however, Nixon rejected his mother's suggestion that he consider going into the church. And the law might be his means to an end—politics. For already, politics fascinated him.

Nixon's cousin Merle West remembered listening, bored and uncomprehending, when Richard, at the age of seven, stopped on Main Street to extol the virtues of Warren Harding, the Republican candidate in the 1920 presidential election. There too the boy was under the influence of his father, who was soon cursing the "crooked politicians" in the Harding administration involved in Teapot Dome. Frank Nixon, originally a Democrat, had switched to the Republican party after William McKinley stopped to compliment him on his horse. The formative influences on his son were more sophisticated.

Richard Nixon admired Abraham Lincoln the way every American did, but additionally so because his grandmother virtually idolized him. He admired Woodrow Wilson, whom his mother had voted for—against her husband's wishes—because he tried to keep the United States out of World War I. On his own first day as president Nixon would request that Wilson's desk be brought to the Oval Office. When told later that it had in fact belonged to *Henry* Wilson, who had been vice president under Grant, he was reluctant to let the truth be made public.

Nixon's favorite former president was to be Theodore Roosevelt, who, he believed, combined idealism and pragmatism and "would compromise all over the place" when he wanted something accomplished. He would quote Roosevelt's speeches time and again, and not least his lines about the "man in the arena" who, if he fails, "fails while daring greatly."

The first prophecy that Nixon would one day become president is said to have been made by a Yorba Linda Sunday school teacher when he was nine. The story sounds apocryphal, but the source, usually reliable, was his cousin Jessamyn West. His father was soon making the same forecast. By the time Nixon reached college, he was telling students at a meeting that he "wanted to go into politics . . . felt the field was dominated by too many unscrupulous politicians." He first mentioned the aspiration even earlier, in a school essay written after Arthur's death: "I would like to study law, and enter politics for an occupation, so that I might be of some good to the people."

The fall of 1934 found Nixon crossing the continent on a scholarship to Duke University Law School, in North Carolina. Her son's winning the scholarship had given his mother what she later recalled as "the proudest day of her life," more so even than the day he became vice president.

The three years at Duke, however, turned out to be a tough, lonely period for the young man. Three thousand miles from home, after years as a shining academic star in his hometown, Nixon found himself up against real competition for the first time. "I don't believe I can ever stay up top," he groaned to an acquaintance, then proceeded to work prodigiously hard. To earn extra cash, he also took paying jobs. As did many students, Nixon lived in makeshift accommodations, at one point sharing a cabin in the woods with three other young men.

He was remembered as a solitary figure around campus, sloping around in patched gray flannels and an old purple sweater that he wore day after day. Some remembered decent things Nixon did. In an era when there were few facilities for the disabled, he regularly helped carry a crippled student up the steps to the lecture hall. As a newcomer to the South from California, he was shocked by racial bias and spoke out about the need for change.

Yet Nixon was considered somewhat strange, even by those who got on with him. One classmate thought him "shot full of rectitude . . . industrious, reverent, all of that." A law professor, Lon Fuller, remembered him as "what today we'd call uptight. There was a suggestion of an intellectual inferiority complex." Bradley Morrah, a contemporary, saw him as "slightly paranoid. . . . He was odd, something of an oddball." Ethel Farley, one of the few women at Duke, found him "dour and aloof. . . . We disliked his 'holier than thou' attitude. He was not unmoral, just amoral. He had no particular ethical system, no strong convictions. . . . He was there to advance himself personally."

And so he did. In June 1937 Nixon's entire family—mother, father, two surviving brothers, and eighty-eight-year-old Milhous grandmother—squeezed into a Chevrolet sedan and drove across the country to see him graduated. The oddball had come in third in his class of twenty-six, with an 80.49 average, qualifying for a prestigious national legal honor society. He had, moreover, been president of the Duke Bar Association.

Some thirty years later, when he was president of the United States, the details of a shabbier episode in Nixon's law school career were examined by a North Carolina newspaper. At the end of their second year Nixon and two friends—Freddie Albrink and Bill Perdue—had broken into the dean's office.

While the miscreants' later accounts differ in detail, the raid went more or less as follows: The three tried the door and found it locked. Then, with a helping heave from his accomplices, one of them clambered in through the open transom and let in the others. They rifled desks and file cabinets, found what they were after in a drawer of the dean's own desk, and made their getaway.

Rumors about the raid circulated on the campus for years. According to the perpetrators, their motive had been to get an advance look at their grades. The dean's office was late in posting them, and Nixon especially was anxious. (Indeed, as he feared, his grades that year were not as good as he had hoped.) Some later suggested the intruders had more sinister motives: that their purpose was to change the grades, not just to check them. By another report they had broken in earlier, to sneak an early look at examination questions.

The escapade did not weigh on Nixon's conscience. He would be the first to brag about it, telling a writer during the buildup to the 1960 election that he—as the thinnest of the three—had been the one to go through the window. He had "moved with the finesse of a cat burglar" once inside, he boasted. The incident shows that long, long before the scandal that would cost him the presidency, Richard Nixon was prepared to take a risk for little or no gain.

Unlike the Duke affair, of course, the Watergate burglary was discovered and the subsequent cover-up exposed. Yet even months after the Watergate arrests, when discussing with Haldeman and White House counsel John Dean how to obtain the tax files of political enemies, President Nixon would unhesitatingly suggest a break-in. "There are ways to do it," he would say into the Oval Office microphones. "Goddamnit, sneak in in the middle of the night. . . ."

In the summer of 1937, as Nixon celebrated his graduation, disgrace was unimaginable. No one then could foresee a day when Duke would turn its back on Richard Nixon. The first occasion was in 1954, when he was vice president and faculty members, objecting that he was an unscrupulous "red-baiter,"[4] voted down a plan to award him an honorary doctorate. In 1973, students and some professors would sign a petition calling for his impeachment. Still later there was an uproar over an aborted plan to site the Nixon Library at Duke. Nixon's portrait, removed from its place of honor during Watergate, had by that time been consigned to obscurity in a storeroom.

During his last months at Duke, Nixon started looking for a job. He applied to prestigious New York law firms and to the FBI for a job as an agent, but nothing materialized. Dean Horack, who knew Nixon dreamed of a political career, offered some advice. "Don't go to New York," he said. "If you're interested in politics, go home. Practice law at home. You may not get as much money, but that's the only way if you want to do anything in the political arena."

Nixon crammed into his father's car at the end of the family's graduation trip and headed back with them to Whittier. Soon he passed the California bar exam and—at his mother's urging—began work with a family friend, a partner in one of the two established law firms in his hometown. He was twenty-four.

A few years earlier, during the Christmas holiday, a teenager with a talent for fortune-telling had read Richard Nixon's palm. "I got quite a shock," she recalled. "What I saw in his palm was a path of incredibly brilliant success and then the most terrible black cloud like a disaster or accident or something. I told him what I read, but in a toned-down version . . . he was such a serious sort of guy that the full version would have made him distraught. He wouldn't have known how to cope. . . ."

Perhaps not. As president Nixon would react with real fright when told that a prominent astrologer was predicting an attempt to assassinate him. The youthful Nixon did probably listen politely, however, to Dorothy Welch, the girl who read his palm. For she was the sister of the young woman he was planning to marry.

Richard Nixon was in love.

3

Sometimes I think I never really knew him,
and I was as close to him as anyone . . .
he was a mystery.

—Ola Florence Welch,
Nixon's first love

Females and femininity had made Nixon uneasy as early as those childhood days when his mother—disappointed when her baby turned out to be yet another boy—tried to make Arthur look like a girl. Richard would pull down the blinds when he had to do the washing up at home because it was not "man's work." At school he was punished for blowing in girls' faces—after first stuffing his mouth with raw garlic.

Was this something more than the "boys hate girls" and "girls hate boys" phase most children go through? "He used to dislike us girls so!" recalled Harriet Palmer. "He would make horrible faces at us. As a debater his main theme in grammar school and the first years of high school was why he hated girls."

Harriet had dismissed Nixon as a goody-goody when he stopped her, at thirteen, from going on a roller coaster against her mother's instructions. Later girls found him "stuffy," and "too aloof to be much fun." "He didn't know how to be personable," said a contemporary. "I felt a kind of amused affection for him, like 'Oh, Dick, come off it.'" "He didn't have the glamour about him that attracts the opposite sex," said another former female student. "He wasn't sexy."

Teenage male friends had to push Nixon to come up with dates for social events. A female cousin who was fond of him reported glumly on his reaction, or lack of it, when she got him to take her for a drive. He was "the slowest driver in the world," and he talked on and on—about politics.

In their last year of high school the daughter of the Whittier police chief, Ola Florence Welch, wrote in her diary, "Oh, how I hate Richard Nixon!" After playing the queen of Carthage to Nixon's Trojan Prince Aeneas in the 1929 Latin class play, however, she changed her mind. His onstage "tender embrace" had drawn hoots of derision from the audience. Yet that night, before Ola had her makeup off, Nixon delivered the opening lines of their real-life romance. "He insisted," she remembered, "that I must come and meet his folks immediately."

Nixon was Ola's first real date, and she his. They were sixteen and beginning a stormy relationship that was to last more than six years. "I've tried to figure out why I'm so cracked about you," he wrote in the first of a stream of letters. "These are the reasons. You are not a boy chaser. You use your brains to good purposes. You never show your anger to anyone . . . and most of all, 'You are just you.' . . . Love from Dick Nixon."

"Would you think," Nixon had asked his cousin Merle earlier, "it would be wiser to marry a pretty girl or a smart girl?" In Ola he found a girl who was both intelligent, an A student, almost as active as he in student affairs, and attractive too. Ola, for her part, thought him "the smartest man that ever was . . . tremendously interesting and engrossing"—and "quite handsome" too.

Soon there were trips together to the movies and the beach, walks in the hills, and expeditions in the Ford Nixon shared with Merle. His mother professed to know what went on, or rather did not go on. "He talked not of romance," she claimed years later, "but about such things as what might have happened if Persia had conquered the Greeks or what might have happened if Plato never lived. At least, this is what I have been told by boys who double-dated with Richard."

About that time Nixon ventured with Merle into a Los Angeles burlesque joint to watch the bump and grind of "a stripteaser who didn't strip too far." His cousin thought him "very normal" so far as girls were concerned, as did Ola, while insisting fifty years later that there had been "no hanky-panky." She added, though, that he was "never comfortable with women."

As the pair moved on from school to college, they were increasingly seen as a couple, to the point that friends assumed they would get married. Yet all was not well. It was not just that Ola's parents disliked Nixon or that her sister thought him "a real pill." Nor was it only that they argued constantly about politics; she liked Franklin Roosevelt, of whom he disapproved. Ola discovered that the boy she had admired as "so strong, so articulate" had a weaker side. "Deep down," she reflected recently, "he had this insecure side to him."

Four years into the relationship, as the couple turned twenty, it began to fall apart. When Nixon was running for president of the student body and became afraid he was going to lose, he became depressed. Then he turned to Ola for support. Once he had won the presidency, though, he treated her shabbily. "He started dating other girls," she remembered, "and I was left thinking, 'Maybe now he's president he's changed.' I began to feel that I wasn't good enough for him."

"He was so disloyal . . . " said Ola's sister. "He two-timed her. . . . He would take her to a party and then go home with someone else, so that my mother had to come out and pick Ola Florence up. Mothers don't like that." Mrs. Welch, who already disapproved of Nixon because of the imperious way he sounded his car horn when he picked Ola up, now refused to speak to him.

Nixon patched up the rift with a salvo of letters—Ola still kept some three dozen under lock and key as late as 2000—that she considers "so apologetic they would probably fascinate a psychologist." For a while the couple seemed reconciled, and in 1933, after a friend's wedding party, Nixon told Ola he loved her. "He had never said that before," she recalled. "Everything about that night was so beautiful: the flowers, the music, the atmosphere. Dick was really moved. . . . He became soft and tender . . . we sat and talked for hours.

She agreed to marry him that night, and they started saving. "Whenever we had a date and there was some change left over, Dick would pass me a quarter, a dime or whatever it was, saying 'That's for the ring.' " A measure of the communication between mother and son is that when asked about the relationship years later, Hannah said she thought there had been "nothing to it."

Soon things went wrong again. Nixon seemed to have no male friends and did not get on with Ola's girlfriends. They had bitter, frequent quarrels. "He didn't know how to mix," she remembered. "His face would cloud. . . . He'd be harsh, and I'd cry." A friend who knew them thought Nixon "combative rather than conciliatory," with no warmth. He exhibited a "nasty temper."

Nixon went on seeing other young women behind Ola's back. When they went to a dance together, he ignored her and spent the evening chatting with other men. They fought, and again a humiliated Ola called her mother for a ride home. Then, seizing the opportunity offered by a dance to which the females could invite the males, she took revenge by asking another fellow, a handsome young man from a prosperous family, to be her escort.

From then on, a friend recalled, Ola favored the new man in her life "while keeping Richard on the string." Yet Nixon went off to law school in the Southeast assuming she was still his girl. He stopped seeing other women altogether and kept a stream of letters—"real love letters," she remembered—flowing back to California. He was behaving as though marriage to Ola were just a matter of time.

When Nixon arrived home on vacation after a nine-month absence, he called her at once, only to hear Ola reveal that she was now going with the rival of the previous summer. Indeed, she said, the other suitor was at that moment in her living room. Enraged, Nixon shouted, "You'll never hear from me again!" and slammed down the phone. On the next day, though, he was again talking of marriage; back at law school he went on writing as though nothing had happened. The letters did not stop even six months later, when Ola wrote to tell him she planned to marry the other young man. Nixon finally accepted defeat only two weeks before the wedding.

In all his time at Duke University, even in the months after learning that he had lost Ola forever, Nixon never said a word about her to students he knew well. He did not mention her in early interviews about his personal life. Decades later, when he was president and Ola came to a White House reception with other Whittier alumni, he is said to have behaved as if he did not know who she was. There is a reference to her in his memoirs, but not a hint that this was a woman he once loved and planned to marry.

Those who knew Nixon after the breakup and far into the future had theories about the effect the breakup had on him. "She broke his heart," said Hubert Perry, a Whittier contemporary and son of the family friend who later helped launch Nixon in politics. Bryce Harlow, a longtime friend and senior White House adviser, believed that in his youth Nixon had been "hurt very deeply by somebody he trusted . . . hurt so badly he never got over it and never trusted anybody again." Harlow guessed that this person had been a friend, or a parent, or a lover.

If there were such wounds, the deepest and most lasting were surely inflicted as much by a parent as by a sweetheart. When Ola Welch had at last written begging Nixon to stop his letters, he replied as follows:

February 2nd, 1936

Dear Ola Florence,

Finally I have become wise! And although I regret having embarrassed you with my letters, I don't regret the feeling I've had towards you for the past year. In the year and a half I've been at Duke, *I've realized more than ever the perfection, the splendor, the grandeur of my mother's character. Incapable of selfishness she is to me a supreme ideal.** And you have taken your place with her in my heart—as an example for which all men should strive. Old memories are slowly fading away. New ones are taking their place. But I shall always remember the kindness, the beauty, the loveliness that was, that is, and shall forever be Ola Florence Welch.

Your friend,
Richard Nixon

What can Ola have thought of this, a "last" letter from a lover faced with losing her to another man, that focused on his *mother*?

If Ola's rejection affected Nixon so greatly, it may have been because he had dared to utter to her the words he was to report—approvingly—that his

---

*Author's emphasis.

mother had never spoken to him: "I love you." For any man or woman to say those three words aloud for the first time is, or should be, a large step. For Nixon, coming from a home where affection was never shown physically and where "love" went unspoken, it must have been a giant one.

Sadly, his "I love you" had failed to convince Ola. She told an interviewer years later that she thought Nixon "may have been playacting" when he spoke of his feelings.[1]

Nixon's six-year romance with Ola had begun when they were actors in the make-believe world of a school play. His next relationship with a woman also began on a stage, but this one would endure.

In the month he turned twenty-five, January 1938, Nixon auditioned for a part in a Whittier amateur production of a melodrama titled *The Dark Tower*. He had recently played an attorney in another play, after a colleague told him that portraying a stage lawyer might help bring in clients to his real-life law firm. Now, as he read for the part of Barry—a "faintly collegiate, eager blushing youth"—a young woman was waiting to try out for the part of Daphne, which called for "a tall, dark sullen beauty of twenty wearing an air of permanent resentment." In the play Daphne is wooed by Barry.

Pat Ryan, a slight, fair twenty-six-year-old teacher, got the part—and Richard Nixon for life. "That night," he recalled, "a beautiful and vivacious young woman with titian hair appeared whom I had never seen before. I found I could not take my eyes away from her. . . . For me it was a case of love at first sight."

Nixon drove the young woman home, along with her friend Elizabeth Cloes, who had suggested she do the audition. "On the way," Nixon was to claim, "I asked Pat if she would like a date with me. She said, 'I'm very busy.' I said, 'You shouldn't say that, because someday I am going to marry you!' . . . I wonder whether it was a sixth sense that prompted me to make such an impetuous statement."

Cloes recalled the anecdote differently, saying that Nixon began his talk of marriage only after the third rehearsal, when Pat refused even to sit next to him in the car. Pat's response, however, is not in dispute. "I thought he was nuts," she said years later.[2] The Nixon version of course made better copy for the newspapers in future years, as did another harmless fiction.

"Her name was Patricia Ryan, and she was born on St. Patrick's Day," Nixon was to tell a television audience of millions in his Checkers speech in 1952. This was a cozy line, handy for wooing the Irish vote, but it was not true. Nor had Pat been born in 1913, as was claimed in early handouts, conveniently making her the same age as her husband. These were fibs, like the claim—useful for a football audience—that they had met not at the audition but at a Rose Bowl game. On the one hand, Nixon thought it "silly" that he attracted criticism when caught out in such minor untruths. Yet he could also insist, at a later press conference, "We must not permit even a little lie."

Her birth certificate shows that the woman Nixon was to marry was born in March 1912, making her almost a year his senior. She was born not on St. Patrick's Day, March 17, but the previous day, March 16.* The baby's registered name, moreover, was Thelma Catherine, and Thelma she was called by most people during her childhood. The exception was her father, who, with his Irish roots and the proximity of her birth to the Irish patron saint's day, called her Pat as a pet name. She took the name Pat only after his death, in part because she loathed her given names. Far into the future the White House chief of staff H. R. Haldeman, with whom she did not get on, referred to her as Thelma behind her back as an expression of derision.

Whatever the deceits about her birth and name, the future Mrs. Nixon came from a background of genuine deprivation and tragedy. She was born in a shack in a Nevada mining town to Will Ryan, a former seaman turned prospector, and Kate, the widow of an engineer killed in an accident. When circumstances in Nevada proved unpromising, they moved to try their luck in Artesia, California—eight miles from Whittier, where Richard Nixon had just been born.

Life in Artesia was hand to mouth. A family of six crowded into a two-bedroom bungalow with no plumbing or electricity. Will Ryan made a meager living as a vegetable farmer. For the children, happy memories of the outdoor life would be outweighed by harsh realities at home. Their father, a hot-tempered drinker, fought regularly with their mother.

When Pat was fourteen, her mother died of kidney disease and liver cancer, and the burden of feeding her father and brothers and keeping house now fell on her. At seventeen, in addition to her other duties, she took on a part-time job as a cashier at the local bank, where one dramatic afternoon she found herself confronted by a holdup man. When she was eighteen, her father died of tuberculosis.

With both her parents dead, Artesia did not hold Pat for long. At nineteen, offered a job chauffeuring an elderly couple to the East Coast, she seized the opportunity to leave. In New York an aunt found her a job as a secretary at a Catholic hospital for TB patients. While the work could be distressing, there were compensations, among them a busy social life.

As an attractive woman in a hospital filled with bachelor doctors, Pat was much in demand. One man, an Irish doctor in his thirties, wooed her assiduously. According to the 1986 biography of Pat, written by her daughter Julie, he courted in vain. "When he hinted about marriage," according to Julie's ac-

---

*Long after this detail was known, Nixon's handouts—and the approved biography of Mrs. Nixon—sought to explain that the baby had been born "near midnight" on the sixteenth and been celebrated by the happy father as his "St. Patrick's Babe in the morning" when he got home from working the late shift. This yarn too runs counter to the evidence of the birth certificate, which indicates the birth occurred at 3:25 A.M. on the sixteenth.

count, "she responded by continuing to accept invitations from other men. She felt the need for the freedom to go where she liked, when she liked. . . ."

This may be accurate, but a little mystery eddies around the future Mrs. Nixon's time in New York. During the 1960 presidential campaign it was rumored that she had been briefly married before. *Washington Post* reporter Maxine Cheshire even obtained the name of the alleged first husband. "When I called him," she recalled, "he denied it in such a way that I didn't know whether to believe it or not." Some thirties-vintage documentation, which should have included Pat Ryan's marital status, seemed to have gone missing.

The notion of an undisclosed first marriage may not be as preposterous as it sounds. The fact that President Ford's wife, Betty, had been married before was unknown until a *Time* magazine reporter dug into her background in 1974. Did the future Mrs. Nixon have a similar secret? The question may now be unanswerable, not least because of the needle-in-the-haystack nature of hunting down old marriage records in New York State.[3]

By the time Pat Ryan met Richard Nixon, in early 1938, she had been back in California for three years. She had completed her education, earning a B.S. degree in merchandising from the University of Southern California. She had worked at various jobs, including a stint at a department store and—more glamorously—as an extra in a couple of Hollywood movies. Then, putting aside plans for a business career, she decided to become a teacher. So it was that Pat found herself teaching secretarial skills, and dabbling in amateur dramatics, in Nixon's hometown.

Nixon's own life was not yet living up to the promise of his high-flying school years. Within days of joining Wingert and Bewley, a local law firm specializing in probate casts, he had been assigned a role in a bad debt case. Out of his depth, the new law graduate promptly made a blunder that resulted in his firm's being sued for negligence by the client and in Nixon's getting a drubbing from a municipal court judge.

By one lawyer's account, he had merely done "a very stupid thing," but according to two others Judge Alfred Paonessa rebuked him as follows: "Mr. Nixon, I have serious doubts whether you have the ethical qualifications to practice law in this state of California. I am seriously thinking of turning this matter over to the Bar Association to have you disbarred."[4] Readers of Nixon's memoirs will find no mention of this episode.

While working for Wingert and Bewley, Nixon joined two local businessmen in a frozen orange juice venture, an innovative idea at the time. He set up the company, became its president, even labored in shirtsleeves at night at the plant, all in vain. They never got the packaging right, and the project ended messily when a consignment of frozen juice bags exploded in a refrigerated railroad boxcar. Nixon's savings were wiped out and some angry investors wound up, as his boss Tom Bewley put it, "hating his guts."

Working as an attorney also meant handling lurid divorce cases. Evlyn Dorn, Nixon's secretary, remembered his embarrassment when a witness described catching a couple having sex in the open air. Nixon himself recalled with a shudder the day a "good-looking girl, beautiful really, began talking to me about her intimate marriage problems. . . . I turned fifteen colors of the rainbow."

Nixon was still a virgin, a fact he confided to a fellow officer during World War II, and remained so until his marriage at age twenty-seven. In 1938, at twenty-five, he continued to live at home. Two years after the breakup with Ola he regularly received dinner invitations from hopeful mothers with available daughters but still had no girlfriends. When he met Pat Ryan, he launched into an almost desperate courtship, so desperate that it is surprising he let so many of its details become public in his lifetime.

Pat fended Nixon off from the start, yet—as once he had with Ola—he engineered a meeting between his parents and her even before having a proper date with her. He insisted they come to the play in which he and Pat were appearing, then invited Pat home afterward. His mother was noncommittal, and never really hit it off with Pat.

For all of Nixon's promise, and for all of Pat's experience outside California, these were hometown young people in a hometown situation. Even though their families had not previously known each other, their worlds had intersected. Nixon's father had helped build the brick fireplace in Pat's childhood home. He and Pat's father had purchased adjoining plots at the cemetery.

Yet Pat did not wish to see herself in those terms. During the four years she had been teaching in Whittier, she spent not one weekend there but headed instead for Los Angeles, where for a long time after meeting Nixon, she continued to date other men. Once, when Pat explained to him that she had a date in the city, Nixon asked if he could "have her company" by acting as chauffeur. Sometimes, having driven her to Los Angeles, he would just kill time waiting to drive her back to Whittier again.

When Nixon showered Pat with flowers and poems, she told him she could not return his love and tried to fix him up with one of her girlfriends. Nixon responded with the sort of abject devotion that invites rejection. When Pat begged off seeing him, claiming pressure of work, he settled for helping mark her students' papers. When she refused to go for a walk with him, he wrote describing what it had been like to take the walk alone. "I know I'm crazy," he wrote, "and I don't take hints, but you see, Miss Pat, I like you!"

Nixon's love letters, published in Julie's biography of Pat, reveal a man prostrating himself in the face of rejection. Months into the one-sided relationship, after Pat had shown him the door one night, Nixon wrote a confused, pathetic letter:

Dear Patricia,

Please forgive me . . . I appreciated immeasurably those little rides and hats. I hope that you survived them without too much mental worry over the problem "what shall I do to get rid of him before he falls?" . . . May I tell you now what I really thought of you? You see, I too live in a world of make believe—especially in this love business. And sometimes I fear I don't know when I'm serious and when not! But I can honestly say that Patricia is one fine girl, that I like her immensely, and that though she isn't going to give me a chance to propose to her for fear of hurting me! and though she insulted my ego just a bit by not being quite frank at times, I still remember her as combining the best traits of the Irish and the squareheads [Germans]—

Yours,
Dick

Pat kept Nixon at arm's length for months. For a while, when his novice's blunder in the bad debt case was becoming a crisis, she broke off contact altogether. Still, he was persistent, and a year after their first meeting was seeing her regularly. Pat liked dancing, and Nixon—a famously poor dancer—muddled along with her. She was a good ice skater, an activity at which Nixon was also hopeless, and he was once spotted staggering around the rink alone, his face bloodied from falls, doggedly preparing for a skating date. Nixon, not known for his sense of humor, kept Pat laughing. At one party he had her in stitches during an impromptu performance of "Beauty and the Beast," in which he played the Beast.

Pat liked having fun, and Nixon suggested they visit a Los Angeles club with another couple, all of them dressed in weird outfits. He wore a tight-fitting raccoon coat that had belonged to his mother. One of their companions, Curtis Counts, recalled how a stripteaser "came on strong, taking off her clothes and swinging her fanny all over the place, until some guy in the front seat touched her butt with a lighted cigarette. . . . I'll never forget how much we laughed, including Dick."

Eighteen months into their relationship Pat had relented enough to send him notes from a vacation trip. A postcard to Nixon's business address bore only the sardonic three-word message "Love from mother." In another note, signed "Lots of luck," she admitted to feeling "sorta lonesome."

At the time Nixon needed some luck. While pining for Pat, he was presiding over the collapse of the orange juice venture, single-handedly opening a new branch of his boss's law firm, and plunging into a whirl of activity with local business groups. While president of a young businessmen's club, the 20-30's, he indulged in the bachelor's fallback, a fair amount of drinking.

Alcohol was banned in the Quaker town in which Nixon had grown up, and he had encountered it only at nineteen, when he sipped a Tom Collins in a San Francisco bar. At law school in North Carolina, a dry state, drink was routinely smuggled in for student celebrations. "Those parties were real blasts," he remembered in 1990. "Most of us drank a lethal concoction of sloe gin and grapefruit juice. The next day we all awoke with terrible hangovers."

In Whittier, when he became an assistant city attorney, Nixon ostentatiously pursued businesses that broke the local prohibition. Meanwhile in private he cheerfully broke the rules with his friends. Philip Blew, an old college contemporary, recalled a night on which a business meeting turned into a booze-up. Nixon got so drunk that his friends had to drive him home. "We got him on the back porch," said Blew, "took off his shoes . . . and instructed him to tiptoe into bed and not let his father hear him . . . we had to pour Dick into bed."

In 1995, when the Oliver Stone movie *Nixon* appeared with scenes suggesting Nixon had problems with alcohol, the loyalists cried foul. Yet he was to have such problems, before the presidency and during it.

In early 1940 Nixon's long wooing of Pat Ryan seemed to be nearing success. That February, in a letter marking the second anniversary of their meeting, he felt safe in addressing her as "Dearest Heart." "Nothing so fine ever happened," he wrote, adopting the old Quaker usage, "as falling in love with Thee. . . ."

So persistently had he asked for Pat's hand over the months that she had imposed a three-month ban on proposals. In March that year, though, Nixon drove at sunset to a promontory looking out on the Pacific Ocean and a beach the couple had come to love, a place they were one day to make famous as the site of the Western White House, San Clemente. He proposed once more, and this time Pat said yes. Even as she did so, she admitted years later, she had lingering doubts.

They were married on June 21, 1940, in a Quaker ceremony at a Spanish-style inn near Whittier. The wedding was held in the presidential suite, apparently not because it had housed three presidents over the years but because it was the least expensive room available. The president of Whittier College officiated, and Nixon's mother provided the cake. Only two dozen guests attended the reception. Oddly, in this heavily documented life, no photographs of the wedding have surfaced. Afterward the bride and groom headed off by car for a two-week honeymoon in Mexico.

Marrying Pat marked the start of a gradual separation from the narrow world in which Nixon had grown up and a lifelong marathon of travel. Their first year together brought trips around the United States, to Canada, and then—on a United Fruit Company vessel—a cruise to Panama, Costa Rica, and Cuba.

Cuba was then the kingdom of the dictator Fulgencio Batista, its capital, Havana, a gambling mecca run by American mobsters.[5] Nixon took a liking to the place and, when he returned home, told his secretary he might move there to practice law. It was the genesis of a long fascination with the Latin world, one that would eventually draw him, as it would John F. Kennedy, into the quicksand of confrontation with Fidel Castro.

Nixon had needed special permission from the draft board to travel outside the United States. War was sweeping across Europe, and during the Nixons' cruise news had arrived that Hitler had invaded Russia. Six months later came Pearl Harbor, bringing America into World War II. For the next four years the war determined the course of Nixon's life, as it did that of so many other Americans.

His first wartime job was in the Office of Price Administration. It meant a move to Washington, D.C., but he soon tired of negotiating the complexities of tire rationing. In April 1942 he applied to join the U.S. Navy against the wishes of his mother, who knew that as a Quaker he could easily have avoided active service. After officer training and some dull months in Iowa, he sailed for the South Pacific.

Nixon's war record was honorable but unheroic. He worked as a ground operations officer processing supplies and men, moving from island to island as the Japanese fell back. In his first political campaign Nixon would pose in naval uniform and speak of his time "in the foxholes." He reminisced about his experiences "when the bombs were falling," while taking care not to embellish too much. The best research suggests that Lieutenant Nixon, known to his unit as Nick, was rarely in danger.[6]

Nick's Snack Shack, the beer and hamburger stand he ran at the airstrip on Green Island, was later remembered by veterans as a catering miracle. "Some of the stuff," one of Nixon's men said, "was, shall we say, liberated . . . but Nick could swap anything. If you ever saw Henry Fonda in *Mr. Roberts,* you have a pretty good idea of what Nick was like."

Nixon, navy comrades noted, could curse a blue streak. Some discovered to their cost that he played a mean game of poker, which he had been playing since his days at Duke. "Nixon was as good a poker player as, if not better than, anyone we had ever seen," said fellow officer James Udall. "Sometimes the stakes were pretty big, but Nick had daring and a flair for knowing what to do. . . . I once saw him bluff a lieutenant commander out of fifteen hundred dollars with a pair of deuces." According to one intimate, Nixon returned from the war some ten thousand dollars richer—the equivalent of ninety-five thousand dollars at 2000 rates.[7]

He also found time for poker in his political career, even in the White House. In retirement Nixon regaled guests with stories of the "big pots" he had won while president. In the fifties, when vice president, he played regularly with a group of senators and representatives. Tip O'Neill, later Speaker of the House, was unimpressed. "Nixon thought of himself as a good poker player," O'Neill recalled, "but he talked too much and didn't follow the cards. Moreover, he used to take advantage of the fact that he was the highest-ranking person at the game by asking the other players how many cards they had drawn. . . . Every time he lost a few bucks, which was often enough, he'd holler and complain. . . ."

Every single day during his service in the Pacific, according to their daughter Julie, Richard Nixon wrote to his wife. Every day she wrote him as well. These were happy contacts, full of affection and yearning. Nixon begged his wife to say, "I love you," in each letter: "I always look for that first. . . ." Pat sent a letter smeared with lipstick. "Sweet," she wrote shortly before he came home, "you'll always have to love me lots and never let me change my feelings for you. . . ."

Down the political decades to come, the world would be invited to believe the Nixons had a happy marriage, a union for the American century— "Pollyanna going steady with Horatio Alger," as *Time* magazine described it thirty years later. Yet while outsiders can never assess the love of others with absolute certainty, a mass of evidence indicates theirs was no idyll.

4

*They tried to love each other, but the gulf remained,
a kind of black hole that sucked into it the good
feelings that might have made Nixon a more human,
more stable President.*

—Margaret Truman in 1995,
on the marriage of Richard and Pat Nixon

There were fault lines in the relationship from the start. On the eve of Nixon's wedding, when he had to fill out the marriage license, he had realized he had never learned his wife's real name; "Pat" had never told him she had been born Thelma Catherine. There was, as he later discovered, much else that Nixon did not know about his wife-to-be. "Pat never told me," he recalled with astonishment in old age, "about what she had done, where she had been, what she had been through . . . she had never told me about some of her family problems, the tragedy of her mother who died . . . or her father who died when she was sixteen."* In their two-and-a-half-year courtship, after all the walks on the beach together, all the drives in his car, all the spaghetti dinners, he had learned virtually nothing of the background of the woman he was marrying.

He was, too, still fettered by the inhibitions his mother had instilled in him. Six years into their relationship, anticipating his return from the war, Nixon found it necessary to write: "Hundreds of times I have pictured our first meeting again. . . . I'm going to walk right up to you and kiss you—but good! Will

*In fact, she was eighteen at the time.

you mind such a public demonstration?" Pat did not mind, and at the airport she rushed to hug him, a greeting she would offer again and again in the years that followed. Mostly, Nixon would avoid her embrace.

Evlyn Dorn, his longtime secretary, saw her boss reach out to touch his wife only once—and then merely to steady her as they stood in the back of a car. "He had a way of ignoring her," she said. "I never saw him touch Pat's hand," recalled Tom Dixon, a broadcaster who acted as an aide during elections in the late forties. "I have never seen quite so cold an arrangement."

Public affection was not forbidden to Quakers, who upon meeting often kissed on each cheek, French-style. Yet in 1952, when Pat reached up to kiss her husband as he accepted the nomination for the vice presidency, Nixon turned away. His public rejections clearly hurt her.

"Both were shy," their daughter Julie wrote, by way of explaining her parents' apparent coldness. "Both would find it difficult to break through their reserve and discuss their deepest feelings." She attributed it to memories of their hot-tempered fathers and marital strife in their childhoods. The Nixons avoided scenes, she said, "at the cost at times of candor." As a loyal daughter Julie did not discuss the long-term cost.

There were occasional scenes, when Pat had finally been pushed too far, and outsiders glimpsed the extent of her unhappiness. Once, during the vice presidency, a priest was greeted at the door by a Pat Nixon who was clearly furious, temporarily estranged from her husband; another story from the same period claimed that Nixon came home one evening to find his clothes scattered across the lawn, where Pat had thrown them. Once, when a reporter suggested during an interview that she had a good life, Pat raised her eyebrows and simply replied: "I just don't tell all."

As this unfolding story will show, there are reports that Richard Nixon on occasion even abused his wife physically.

It was the political life she had to live, whether she liked it or not, that Pat resented most. "She didn't want politics, ever," said Earl Mazo, a family friend as well as a Nixon biographer. "Her friends were never political friends. She hated the idea of ever facing another campaign. Every time Nixon entered one, she was in despair." In 1960, at the start of the race against John F. Kennedy, she said: "I've given up everything I ever loved. The people who lose out are the children," she continued on the verge of tears. "Any of the glamour or reward in it comes to the grown-ups. It's the children who really suffer."

Usually, though, Pat carefully hid such feelings. "She is," social secretary Lucy Winchester said after the collapse of the presidency, "the proverbial Iron Butterfly." "Pat is a far stronger man than Dick," thought Dr. Paul Smith, Nixon's former teacher at Whittier College. "She's much the stronger of the two, a real Hercules. I don't know of anyone who has so disciplined herself to endure a life she does not like."

In an attempt at humor Nixon once told female members of the White House press corps that were she always to accompany him on trips, Pat would just be "excess baggage." Some women journalists had been thinking along just those lines, and for quite a long time. "They never seemed to talk to each other on the plane, nor do I think they sat together," said Gloria Steinem, who followed the Nixon campaign in 1968. "There was never, ever, ever, ever, any sign of affection whatsoever," recalled Kandy Stroud, who specialized in covering Pat for *Women's Wear Daily*. "I rode in the limousine with them, the first time I was alone with them together. He did all the talking, she did none. She just sat there . . . like a staff member . . . the entire ride and he didn't refer to her, or defer to her."

John Ehrlichman, who worked for Nixon through four campaigns as well as in the White House, thought the couple seemed remote from each other even in private. "They had essentially separate lives," he said. "He resented her interference, and they had conflicts. She might criticize the schedule as unworkable, and she was often right. But when Pat made a suggestion, Nixon would brush it off. . . ."

"You get a little insight when you work, as I did, on their estate plan," said White House counsel John Dean. "He excluded Pat from knowledge of what he was going to do. He didn't want her involved in those decisions, and I was instructed not to speak with her about it at all. When the papers were completed, she was summoned to the Oval Office like an aide virtually, and told to sign on the dotted line. . . . He didn't seem to trust her."

"He was so cold it could be funny," said Kissinger aide William Watts. "When the shah of Iran was in Washington, I watched Nixon going around the room shaking hands with a group of women. And as he came to each one, he would say, 'Hello, I'm Richard Nixon.' And he came to another one, and I heard him say again, 'I'm Richard Nixon'—and it was his own wife. She just replied, 'Yes, dear, I know. I'm Pat. . . .'"

Hugh Sidey, who covered the presidency for *Time* for more than twenty years, reached a harsh conclusion. "She kind of followed along with him, and he used her in campaigns," he said, "but once he got in the White House that was the end of it. . . . Between Nixon and his wife I don't think there was any kind of human bond. There had to be something, but I don't understand it."

They did have one element in common, albeit a negative one. Nixon of course forever complained about the rich eastern elite, and his wife shared that attitude. "The moneyed class," Pat had written to a relative while working in the Los Angeles department store at the age of twenty-three, "come in and ask us to do their shopping. . . . They sit in luxurious chairs while we go all over the store and gather things for them. . . . I drape the lovely velvet robes etc., around me, grin at the fat, rich customers and pff! they buy. . . ."

"Richard and Pat Nixon were bonded as two outsiders," said Gloria Steinem, reflecting on the interview during which—in a rare achievement—she found chinks in the iron butterfly's armor. "They were together in their resentment of glamorous people who'd had it easy. . . . She just let go about this to me, like a long accusation, saying, 'I never had time to dream about being anyone else. I had to work. I haven't just sat back and thought of myself or what I wanted to do. . . . I'm not like all you . . . all those people who had it easy.'

"I could see," Steinem said, "that Pat thought of me as an adversary, someone who'd led a very privileged life. I tried to explain that it wasn't so: My father made an insecure living, and after my parents divorced, my mother and I lived in a factory neighborhood in a house that had been condemned by the health department. . . . But Pat Nixon just didn't want to listen."

When she talked with Steinem about her husband, Pat did not just trot out the usual campaign platitudes. "I got the distinct feeling," Steinem recalled, "that she didn't *respect* him very much. . . ."

To suffer for so long, constantly hiding her feelings, took a massive toll on Pat Nixon. Robert Pierpoint, a CBS White House correspondent through six presidencies, had known her back in Whittier when she was a high school teacher and he a student. Then, he remembered, she had been vivacious, enthusiastic, even sexy. When he met Pat little more than a decade later, on one of Nixon's vice presidential trips, he was shocked. "I could scarcely believe she was the same woman," he said. "I was immediately struck by her tension, nervousness, and drawn appearance . . . she seemed so totally remote."

A few years later a British reporter interviewed her at the U.S. ambassador's residence in London. "Mrs. Pat Nixon, face to face, is like a Republican Coppélia. She chatters, answers questions, smiles and smiles, all with a doll's terrifying poise. There is too little comprehension. Like a doll, she would be smiling when the world broke. Only her eyes, dark and strained, signal that inside the black suit and pearls there is a human being. . . . One grey hair, one hint of fear, one golden teacup overturned on the Persian carpet, and one could have loved her."

Pat Nixon claimed she used neither cigarettes nor alcohol. In fact, she smoked almost all her adult life and was to die of lung cancer. By the time her husband was president, she was chain-smoking the moment she stepped out of the public eye. "She smoked incessantly aboard Air Force One," said chief pilot Ralph Albertazzie. "That was one of the little secrets she shared with the crew. Sometimes, after a flight, the stewards counted the butts. . . ."

Drink was a sensitive subject too. "I once saw a tray of sherry aperitifs being passed around," said veteran White House correspondent Helen Thomas. "She reached out for a glass, saw the newspaperwomen looking at her, and pulled her hand back." According to a former Secret Service agent who spoke out in 1993, "Pat Nixon had a problem. . . . I think at one point she was almost an alcoholic. She had to have counseling, arranged through her friends. . . . It was during the second term."[1]

Late in the second term, according to *Washington Post* journalists Bob Woodward and Carl Bernstein, Pat was "more and more reclusive, and drinking heavily." They told of staff members finding her in the White House kitchen in the early afternoon, trying in vain to hide a tumbler of bourbon on the rocks. Her daughter Julie and former aides hastened to deny the story.

———————

As for Nixon, marriage did not resolve his problems with the opposite sex. "When I worked for him, he was still shy and afraid of women," said Alexander Haig, his last White House chief of staff. "He wouldn't sit alone in a room with Imelda Marcos, I remember, or with Indira Gandhi—or even Golda Meir!"

Two years later, as president, Nixon ordered the acclaimed Philip Roth novel *Portnoy's Complaint,* with its masturbation theme, removed from the White House library. The reporters' perception of Nixon's sexuality was summed up in a spoof question a *Newsweek* man put to the White House press secretary. "What," Karl Fleming asked, "does Nixon do on the occasion of his semiannual erection? The consensus is that he smuggles it to Tijuana. . . ." The press secretary did not smile.

As if to compensate, CBS's Dan Rather noted, Nixon was prone to locker room talk and obscenities, usually at inappropriate moments. In the fifties he was asked to meet and thank the flight attendants on his campaign aircraft. "Mr. Vice President," said columnist Art Buchwald, "these are our stewardesses. They've been so nice to us. I'd like to introduce them." Nixon replied: "Stewardesses? I thought they were B-girls." He moved on, oblivious of the fact that the women were looking nonplussed. ("B-girl," in those days was the term used to describe slinkily dressed bar hostesses, many of whom were, by common knowledge, whores.)

Campaign aide John Sears recalled a nocturnal episode before the 1968 election and a welcome flash of more subtle humor. "He often didn't sleep well and would venture out into the hallway in his blue bathrobe to pace back and forth. It was quite late when he encountered a member of his staff going back to his room with a young lady. Without breaking stride, Nixon said, "Mike, we don't have to get those votes one at a time, you know."

As president Nixon told a gathering of male staffers that he would help them conceal extramarital affairs. "If you ever have to say you are working late, I'll cover for you."

In 1972, during a working session on Air Force One, Nixon gave Haldeman an odd instruction. Henry Kissinger was working too hard, he said. Haldeman was to call a friend and "have him give Henry all of his phone numbers of girls that are not over thirty." The following year, as Kissinger began a briefing for congressional leaders on the Yom Kippur War, Nixon interrupted. "Ah . . . we had trouble finding Henry," he said. "He was in bed with a broad." As the secretary of state tried to continue, the president giggled and rolled his head around. "Henry," he insisted, "which girl were you with? It's terrible when you have a girl and the Secret Service has to break in on you."

As he left a Miami restaurant with Kissinger one night, tipsy on martinis, Nixon accosted an attractive woman, a total stranger. "She looks like she's built for you, Henry," he said with a leer, then told the woman she could have a job at the White House.

––––––––––––

Kissinger, who found much to admire in Nixon, made a sad observation years later. "Can you imagine," he said, "what this man could have been had somebody loved him? Had somebody in his life cared for him? I don't think anybody ever did, not his parents, not his peers. He would have been a great, great man had somebody loved him." Kissinger did not mention Pat Nixon in the context of these remarks, but the implication seems clear.

Nixon did discuss his relations with Pat, and with women in general, with Arnold Hutschnecker, the New York psychotherapist he first consulted a decade into his marriage. The conversations were difficult because as Hutschnecker told this author, Nixon was "so very inhibited." Hutschnecker concluded that "no woman ever gave Richard Nixon the support he really needed. I'm reluctant to talk about his marriage. But let me put it this way. What the average American man wants [in a wife] is a mother; they often even call her Mom. Most put their mothers on a pedestal but eventually free themselves from that. Nixon couldn't free himself. That's it in a nutshell. He was totally devoted to his mother. He had been brainwashed, if you will. . . ." Once, tellingly, when Nixon and Pat quarreled in the prepresidential days, the grown man called on his mother for help. His wife was not speaking to him, he told her. So Hannah Nixon flew to Washington as peace broker.

"Nixon depended on Pat because he trusted her, and she stayed with him," said Dr. Hutschnecker. "But that was for politics. The truth is, his only passion was politics."

5

Ma-chi-a-vel-lian-ism n : *the political theory of Machiavelli;* esp: *the view that politics is amoral and that any means however unscrupulous can justifiably be used in achieving political power.*

—*Webster's New Collegiate Dictionary*

"I was about thirty stories up . . . there he came, with his arms outstretched and his face up to the sky. Even from where I was I could feel the impact of his personality. . . ." It was June 1945, and Richard Nixon was standing in the window of an office building high above Manhattan, tearing paper into little pieces to shower on the returning hero passing below. He was one of thousands saluting General Dwight D. Eisenhower, victorious supreme commander of Allied forces in Europe and the man who—seven years later—Nixon was to serve as vice president.

Even as the cheers rang out and the troops returned from the war, America entered an era of fear, suspicion, and uncertainty: fear of nuclear warfare, suspicion of the Soviet Union and the supposed legions of Communists within the United States, and pervasive economic uncertainty. Thirty-two-year-old Richard Nixon, now Lieutenant Commander Nixon, had come home with his poker winnings. Now, with a newly pregnant wife, he was serving out his final months in the navy, shuttling among Washington, Philadelphia, New York, and Middle River, Maryland (near Baltimore), winding up contracts with civilian companies. It was at Middle River in September that he received a letter from California asking if he wanted to run as a Republican candidate for Congress in the 1946 elections.

"The idea that I might play even a minor part in practical politics," Nixon would insist years later, "never previously occurred to me." Like much else claimed about Nixon's start in politics, the assertion was not true. Politics was of course what he had had in mind from childhood, what he had been yearning for since leaving law school. He had started running, really, in 1940 while he was courting Pat, when he made a series of speeches as a move toward winning a state assembly seat. The opportunity did not materialize, but later the same year he had put himself before the public with speeches supporting the Republican presidential nominee.

Pat, for her part, would also insist years later that she and her husband never discussed the possibility of a career in politics. Before their wedding, though, he had written to her: ". . . We shall realize our dreams . . . It is our job to go forth together and accomplish great ends and we shall do it too . . ." Even earlier, within weeks of meeting Nixon, Pat had told friends he was going to be president some day. It is unlikely she would have said such a thing had Nixon himself not told her it was his ultimate ambition. He had shared the same aspiration with male friends.

The call to arms from California in 1945 came from Herman Perry, a family friend and the manager of the Whittier branch of the Bank of America. He had been deputized to sound out Nixon on whether he would be interested in running for Congress against Jerry Voorhis, a wealthy Yale-educated Democrat who had held his seat through five elections. Voorhis's peers in Washington had voted him the hardest-working man in the House and the second most diligent in putting the national interest above political gain. The press in turn had named him the representative with most integrity. To the frustration of California Republicans, Voorhis seemed almost unbeatable—until Richard Nixon was asked to take him on.

The details of the subsequent struggle between the two men were to become political legend. Nixon flew to Los Angeles, addressed the selection board in his officer's uniform, and convinced them—if the members needed convincing—that he was indeed their man. He received his discharge from the navy, came home to Whittier, and began devoting every waking minute to the fight. He researched his opponent's record in minute detail, went incognito to watch him speak, and filled yellow legal pads with copious notes—a practice that was to become familiar to colleagues for the rest of his life.

Nixon made polished speeches as he began campaigning, but for a while his efforts seemed to be going nowhere. Then, for $580 a month, Nixon's backers brought on board a tough lawyer and public relations consultant, Murray Chotiner, to handle publicity. Chotiner was renowned and feared, even by some of those who worked alongside him, for his ruthless tactics. His campaign philosophy was summed up by one who knew him as "Hit 'em, hit 'em, and hit 'em again."

Nixon proceeded to hit Voorhis again and again until he was fatally crippled. Supported by a barrage of scathing advertisements and press coverage orchestrated by Chotiner, he succeeded in creating the impression that his opponent was a tool of the Communists. The accusation took advantage of a growing mood of hysteria, with FBI Director J. Edgar Hoover warning in a California speech that tens of thousands of Communists were "at large in the country," with the U.S. Chamber of Commerce releasing a report on Communist "infiltration" of the nation, and with the Republican Women of Southern California portraying the election alternatives as "Americanism or Communism."

Voorhis himself had actively opposed communism, but he was a New Deal Democrat who once, during the Depression, had registered as a Socialist. In Nixon's hands, the taint of this alleged communism was his undoing. Voorhis came off looking tired and second best in a series of debates and went down to humiliating defeat on election day. He left politics forever, and Nixon went off to Washington and a famous future.

Pat had been at his side throughout the election effort. Their first child, a baby daughter they named Tricia, was born at the start of the campaign. Within hours of her delivery, according to Nixonian lore, Pat was sorting through political papers. Within weeks she was out working with her husband, taking notes during speeches, shaking hands, typing letters in the office. She stopped smoking in public because in Whittier it was not acceptable for women. She patiently accepted the criticisms of Republican matrons, who carped at everything from her shyness to the color of her fingernails.

Simultaneously Pat had to deal with the callousness of her own husband. Broadcaster Tom Dixon and his then wife, Georgia, who accompanied Nixon on the campaign trail, saw the earliest signs of trouble in the Nixon marriage. "He would always hold the door for me," said Georgia, "but would walk through in front of Pat as if she wasn't there." Tom Dixon remembered Nixon's behavior when his wife walked into a room while he was preparing for a broadcast. "He flared at her like a prima donna and said, 'Haven't I told you never to bother me when I'm working? . . . Now get out.'"

Nixon banished his wife, Dixon said, "with as little ceremony as he would have a dog. If he had been doing a brand-new speech, I could have understood it, but this speech he knew by heart. . . . I've never heard any wife cut off in public so curtly without giving a rejoinder, not even a dirty look. . . . But she just backed off. She was kind of a saint."

On the night of his victory Nixon said his greatest satisfaction was for his wife and his parents. He took them along that evening to receive congratulations from Norman Chandler, publisher of the *Los Angeles Times*. Offered a drink, they asked for glasses of milk. Nixon followed suit, then slipped into the hall with Chandler's wife. "Could you get me a double bourbon?" asked the thirty-four-year-old new member of Congress. "I don't want Mother and Father to see me take a drink." Fourteen years later, when Nixon was nearing fifty, Hannah had still never seen her son drink alcohol. He likely hid his drinking from her until she died.

The campaign in 1946 was a first glimpse of Nixon's political style, of his sense of expediency, and of his attitude to political foes. Nearly thirty years later, during the uproar over the Watergate burglary, Pat Nixon would say that in the Nixon-Voorhis campaign someone had broken into her husband's office to steal—and presumably destroy—a large batch of pamphlets. "No one cared," she complained, "when it happened to us in '46!"

This was one of those Nixon stories the details of which changed according to circumstances. Pat's first version of the story, told soon after the Voorhis campaign, described a lesser dirty trick. Then she merely said that Democratic opponents had posed as supporters to pick up large batches of pamphlets, only to destroy them. There was no mention, in the original version, of any break-in.

In 1946 few cared about Nixon's misfortunes, perhaps because of the ferocity and cynicism of the onslaught he had unleashed on the Democrats. Republican tactics ranged from the trivial to the dastardly. Local citizens were urged to say, "Nixon for Congress," whenever their phones rang during the campaign. If the call was from Republican headquarters, they would be entitled to buy from a wide selection of electrical appliances like irons and toasters—items in short supply after the war. Those who did so emerged with leaflets promising a plentiful supply in the event of a Republican victory.

False stories about both candidates were circulated: that Voorhis had voted in the House to increase the ceiling price on Florida oranges but not on those from California (there had been no such vote); that he was sponsoring a bill to stop the production of beer and liquor, a grotesque twisting of the facts; that Nixon's work record including "farming" and "fruit grading," references to chores he had done when he was less than ten years old.

At one debate with Nixon, Voorhis realized that the Republicans had planted people in the audience armed with specific questions. At another meeting he recognized Nixon supporters who had booed and heckled him at an earlier gathering miles away.

Businessmen were warned by banks that should they put their names to press notices supporting Voorhis, their credit lines would be cut off. One bank admonished its staff not to vote for the Democrat. Just before the election a leaflet appeared claiming that Voorhis was the spokesman for "subversive Jews and Communists" who aimed to "destroy Christian America and our form of government." Nixon's people may not have been responsible for the leaflet, but they neither disowned nor denounced it.

The taint of communism, though, was the blunt instrument most effective in felling Voorhis. The attacks had begun four months before the election, when Nixon claimed publicly that Voorhis had been endorsed by the "PAC."

Nixon's supporters had for months been promoting the notion that Voorhis was a tool of the PAC (Political Action Committee) of the CIO, the Congress of Industrial Organizations, which, while not Communist-based, undeniably included Communists and fellow travelers in its ranks.

The charge, however, was simply not true. On the contrary, the left had specifically prevented a PAC endorsement of Voorhis, after whom a 1940 anti-communism act had been named and who was a member of the House Un-American Activities Committee. There was, however, also a group called the National Citizens' PAC—the NCPAC—a nonlabor organization weighted with literary, academic, and entertainment figures, churchmen, politicians, and jurists. Its membership did include Communists. Unbeknownst to Voorhis, a committee of the NCPAC had made a recommendation, though it was never adopted, that Voorhis be endorsed.

Having learned of this motion, Nixon discovered that it had been committed to paper as an internal bulletin, and waited to pounce. At a key debate he produced the document itself, brandishing it in the air—in a scene eerily prefiguring Joe McCarthy's waving of a paper supposedly showing there were 205 Communists in the State Department—and thrust it into the hand of his astonished opponent. The document proved nothing at all, but Voorhis, caught off guard, floundered around ineffectually in response. THE TRUTH COMES OUT. VOORHIS ADMITS PAC ENDORSEMENT, Nixon's advertisements were soon shouting. Voorhis had admitted no such thing; but by then the truth was utterly obscured, and the Democrat never recovered.

In the last days before the election came the cheapest trick of all, a fusillade of anonymous telephone calls to potential voters. "Did you know," a mystery caller would ask, "that Jerry Voorhis is a Communist?" Nixon and his supporters later denied such calls had been made or authorized. Yet they were apparently made, according to one source by people specifically hired to do so, working from a bank of telephones at Nixon headquarters in Alhambra.[1]

"Of course," Nixon was to admit later in private, "I know Jerry Voorhis wasn't a Communist. . . . I suppose there was scarcely ever a man with higher ideals than Jerry Voorhis, or better motivated. . . . But . . . I had to win. That's the thing you don't understand. The important thing is to win."

The key to understanding how Nixon broke into politics, and how he remained there, is to identify his power base. After the election the Nixons painted a homey picture of a campaign fought on a shoestring. "We drew on our savings," Pat said, "and rented a little office in one of the oldest buildings in Whittier. Dick's mother contributed an old leather sofa. . . . We found a battered desk, and a friend lent us a typewriter. Another contributed a throw rug for the floor."

Nixon wrote in his memoirs that he and his wife themselves financed the campaign in its early stages. At one point, Pat claimed, they were "so broke that I wept because at a critical moment there wasn't any money to buy stamps. . . ."

This tale of hardship is somewhat less than credible, given that Nixon's old law firm had reportedly created a position for him that provided a salary for the duration of the campaign.

Apparently forgetting the campaign poverty yarn, Nixon later recalled having arrived in Washington as a U.S. representative with his wartime savings intact. Even had he had to dip into them to underwrite the campaign, he would not have had any serious concerns about his future financial stability. Earl Adams, a key supporter in Los Angeles, had promised him a job in his prestigious law firm should he fail to win the election.

In the official accounting for the preprimary stage of the 1946 campaign, Nixon reported having spent only $555 of his own money. At least another $11,000, and more, had come from outside sources. The total expenses for the whole campaign, formally reported later, were supposedly $17,774, as opposed to $1,928 for Voorhis. Years later Nixon supporters admitted having in fact spent between $24,000 and $32,000, but even those figures are improbably low. One backer, interviewed for this book, said he alone contributed $10,000.[2]

Who financed Nixon? In his telling, his backers were "typical representatives of the Southern California middle class: an auto dealer, a bank manager, a printing salesman, and a furniture dealer." He insisted that "no special vested interest" was behind him. Voorhis thought otherwise. A year before the election, he alleged, an unnamed "representative of a large New York financial house" made a trip to California to hold talks with "a number of influential people." The emissary exhorted his contacts to see that Congressman Voorhis, "one of the most dangerous men in Washington," was ousted.

Why? According to Voorhis, it was because he had worked "against the monopoly and for the changes in the monetary system." He "had advocated the purchase of the Federal Reserve System," asserted Merton Wary, a college contemporary of Nixon's. "So the bankers decided to get rid of him."

Voorhis had made enemies in big business with such talk. Three years before the elections that destroyed him, moreover, he had exposed a shady deal that gave Standard Oil exclusive drilling rights—and massive profits—on a federally owned oil field in California. He had gone on to displease the petroleum industry on a number of key issues, the major insurance companies by opposing their exemption from antitrust regulation, and the liquor industry by proposing that grain be diverted from alcohol production to wartime famine relief.

But were such shadowy enemies responsible for plotting Voorhis's removal, as he believed? Very possibly. Nixon's name was actually first put forward not, as generally assumed, by Whittier bank manager Herman Perry but rather by somebody else in the local Republican fraternity, according to Murray Chotiner. Perry himself said a "wealthy business friend," whom even twenty-five years later he would not identify, had promised money as early as 1944 to fund the unseating of Voorhis. Financial support came in regularly from then on from this unnamed friend and was made available for each campaign until 1952.

"There was a lot of material I had in documentary form," Voorhis wrote in an unpublished draft of a 1947 book, "which would have shown how the Nixon campaign was a creature of big Eastern financial interests . . . the Bank of America, the big private utilities, the major oil companies, were resolved to beat me. I never used it." While Nixon supporters insisted that "not a nickel of oil money" found its way into the campaign, Willard Larson, who carried the "political proxy" for Standard Oil, the company Voorhis had most angered, had sat in on the selection meeting that picked Nixon as a candidate.

Nixon's campaign manager later conceded that he had worked "very closely" with Richfield Oil's local man during the early stages of the contest. While historians have differed on if or how much Signal Oil contributed, surviving correspondence shows that Nixon was in touch early in 1946 with J. Paull Marshall, a contact from wartime days at the OPA who was on the staff of the Republican National Committee. Marshall suggested that Nixon meet with Harry March, a Signal Oil president reputed in California political circles to be "the man with the black bag."

A firsthand glimpse of how Nixon was financed, and of Nixon's political ethics, comes from William Ackerman, the former financial officer of Gladding McBean, a senior management company. Its chairman, Atholl McBean, was a director of Standard Oil and the husband of the heiress to the Newhall Oil fortune. The company's board included William Crocker of the Crocker Bank and other top-rank business leaders.

"I know how it started in 1946," Ackerman said of Nixon's political beginnings in a 1979 letter, "because, in retrospect, I was then a bagman for Nixon." Citing a journal he had kept in 1946, Ackerman said a meeting of seventy-five executives took place in the spring of that year at The Inn in Ojai, north of Los Angeles. At the final session, he said, McBean president Fred Ortman talked about Richard Nixon.

"The fellows down at the California Club," Ackerman quoted Ortman as saying, "have lined up a young man fresh out of the Navy. Smart as all get out. Just what we need to get rid of Jerry Voorhis. If he makes it, they think he has what it takes to go all the way. He says he can't live on a congressman's salary. Needs a lot more than that to match what he knows he could make in private law practice. The boys need cash to make up the difference. We're going to help."

Ortman had long made it clear, Ackerman said, that the legality of the group's contributions was of no concern to him. The important thing was not to get caught. The money for Nixon from Gladding McBean, Ortman decreed, was to be raised by every executive's stumping up a hundred dollars—that would be about nine hundred dollars today. "Send it to my office in cash. You tell the key people. Tell them to pass it on to their own group. This . . . deal will give everybody a big enough expense account to hide it. Taxis, Entertainment. This and that. We're all experts at it. Gotta get at least five thousand. . . . We just gotta get rid of that pinko Voorhis."

Decades later Ackerman was still astonished by the notion that one company alone had raised five thousand dollars, the equivalent of forty-four thousand dollars today, for Nixon in 1946. He recalled thinking of the wider pool from which Nixon's backers could draw, "a pot big enough to engulf the world." Over the years Ackerman was neither especially for nor against Nixon himself. "Instead," he said, "I reserved my contempt for those who, while parading themselves as pillars of society, fertilized the soil in which to grow Nixons for their own gain."

One of the McBean directors, insurance magnate Asa Call, was a link to a crucial fertilizing element, the power of the press. Call, and other men in the group that picked Nixon, gave him a vital connection to the most influential paper in Southern California. By the spring of 1946 Nixon had been looked over and approved by Kyle Palmer, the grizzled former racing tout who had long been political editor of the *Los Angeles Times*.

Palmer, aptly known as the Little Governor, functioned as much more than a political editor. "Anyone who wanted to run for political office," said Robert Hartmann, a sometime *Times* bureau chief and future counsel to President Ford, "had to clear it with Kyle." Before television ended the print press monopoly on political influence, Palmer was a kingmaker. When he looked upon Nixon, he recalled, he saw a dream candidate: clean-cut but a gutter fighter, "an old head on young shoulders." He brought him to the *Times*'s publisher, Norman Chandler, who said: "He looks like a comer. He has a lot of fight and fire. Let's support him."

The *Times* accordingly gave Nixon blanket benediction. Fair play had never been a factor in the paper's political coverage. Twelve years earlier Palmer and the *Times* had created phony news photos of tramps, supposedly streaming into the state to live off the handouts that would be available should Upton Sinclair, a Democratic candidate, become governor. The "tramps" in the *Times*'s pictures had been actors. In 1946, using a shortage of newsprint as its excuse, the *Times* limited the Voorhis campaign to small advertisements. The Nixon side was allotted more space. Palmer meanwhile wrote some of Nixon's speeches.

In later years, when he began to complain about his treatment by the press, Nixon also railed at his old mouthpiece. For after 1962, after Palmer died and Norman Chandler's son Otis had taken over the paper, the *Times* became more evenhanded. "Things would be a lot different if Kyle were alive," Nixon would say during his losing 1962 campaign for governor of California, and he went on saying it well into the seventies. So enraged was he by the change that as president, the White House tapes show, he ordered the IRS and the immigration authorities to investigate the entire Chandler family.

"We're going after the Chandlers," he told Attorney General John Mitchell, "every one, individually, collectively, their income tax . . . starting this week. Every one of those sons of bitches." He ordered the immigration people to find out whether the *Times* was hiring illegal immigrants. "I don't want any argument about it," he said. "I want you to direct the most trusted person you have in the Immigration Service that they are to look over all of the activities of the *Los Angeles Times*—all. . . . Otis Chandler—I want him checked with regard to his gardener. I understand he's a wetback. Is that clear?"

Early in his career, Nixon fully appreciated how indebted he was. "I would never have gone to Washington in the first place," he told Chandler in a 1960 letter, "had it not been for the *Times*." In the breakthrough campaign against Voorhis, Nixon also had a patron in Jim Copley, who owned the *Union* and *Tribune* in San Diego, along with a string of smaller dailies. A mass of correspondence shows that for decades to come Copley put what he called his organization—as well as cash contributions—at Nixon's disposal.

Nixon also benefited repeatedly from the expertise of Herbert Klein, a senior Copley editor who took long periods of "leave" to serve as Nixon's press secretary. During the presidency, Klein was named director of communications. Klein has claimed he did not know Nixon well during the 1946 campaign, when he was news editor of the *Alhambra Post-Advocate,* but one of Nixon's campaign managers had a different memory. "Herb helped us," said Frank Jorgensen, "let's put it that way—on publicity and writing."

Perhaps the most flagrant misuse of the press in the 1946 campaign against Voorhis was the phony news trick. "Nixon's campaign managers," said W. E. Smith, then a reporter on the *San Gabriel Valley Press-Times,* "reached an agreement with our publishers. . . . Nixon bought front-page space in the *Press-Times* papers. He had an agreement for so much space per week—not for ads, but for planted news stories and pictures."

If the Nixon campaign did invent news stories, there cannot be little doubt who was behind them. The prime suspect was a man who, one way or the other, was to remain close to Nixon throughout his political life.

6

*Organized crime will put a man in the White House
someday, and he won't even know it
until they hand him the bill.*

—Ralph Salerno, congressional consultant
on organized crime

He was something of a prodigy, the paid press adviser to that first Nixon campaign. The son of a cigar maker, born in Pittsburgh, reared in Los Angeles, Murray Chotiner left school at fifteen yet at nineteen obtained a law degree, the youngest graduate Southwestern Law College ever produced. At twenty-three he was working on Herbert Hoover's campaign for the presidency and at thirty-three masterminding Earl Warren's campaign for the governorship of California. In spite of his campaign expertise Warren soon threw Chotiner out of his office, apparently because his zeal was untempered by principle. Richard Nixon was to trust and rely on him for his entire political career.

Chotiner was a plump, diminutive figure who favored white suits, loud silk ties, and shirts with clock-face cuff links. He called himself Murray M. Chotiner, presumably because he believed it sounded more impressive; in fact he had no middle name.

In Chotiner, as Nixon's later adviser Len Garment put it, he "met his Machiavelli, a hardheaded exponent of the campaign philosophy that politics is war." According to the fourth of his wives, Nancy, "Murray was not beyond doing anything he could possibly do in a campaign, within the law, to rattle the cages."

He rattled the cages for Nixon from the moment he set eyes on him at the selection meeting for the Voorhis campaign. In the years that followed he managed the 1950 campaign that defeated Helen Gahagan Douglas and took Nixon to the Senate. It was he who picked the color for the notorious "pink sheet" flyer that falsely implied Douglas was a Communist sympathizer. It was he who ran the 1952 campaign that took Nixon to the vice presidency, he who was the driving force behind Nixon's defense when he was accused of corruption that year. He was manager again in the 1954 midterm elections, during which—resorting to a tried and true tactic—Nixon referred time and again to supposed documentation of his charge that the Democrats were under Communist influence.

In 1956, with another presidential election due in the fall, controversy suddenly arose around Chotiner. When parts of a lecture he had given at a "campaign school" for leading Republicans were leaked, Democrats expressed shock. It was, they said, "a textbook to hook suckers." So it was, but that worried Chotiner not at all. As Len Garment has said, this was a man who "didn't mind accepting the fact that politics is shabby most of the time, filled with lies and deceptions."

Chotiner did grow concerned, and was nearly torpedoed, by discoveries made about him that spring by a Senate subcommittee investigating bribery and influence peddling. The Democrats had of course been looking for a way to get at Chotiner and, through him, at Nixon. The opportunity came by chance when Carmine Bellino, a legendary accountant and congressional investigator, was poring over canceled checks paid out on behalf of a New Jersey uniform manufacturer convicted of stealing from the federal government. One five-thousand-dollar check had been made out to "M. Chotiner" and deposited in a Los Angeles bank. When first contacted by Robert Kennedy, the youthful chief counsel of the Senate Subcommittee on Investigations, Chotiner had no immediate explanation. At a later meeting he came up with a story that sounded convincing—until Bellino slipped out to call a contact who had inside information. "The informant," he recalled, "stated that Chotiner had been engaged because of his friendship with Nixon and Deputy Attorney General William Rogers, and he was expected to help in connection with the tax case then being considered for possible prosecution by the Department of Justice. . . ."

Chotiner tried every possible tactic to avoid testifying to the committee. First he promised to appear voluntarily, insisting there was no need to issue a subpoena, but then failed to turn up. When he was eventually obliged to do so, he gave little away. To divulge what services he had rendered, Chotiner argued, would violate the lawyer-client relationship. He denied he had ever used Nixon's name to seek favors for a client.

Senator Joe McCarthy declared the probers were wasting time, that they had produced no evidence of misconduct by Chotiner, a favor for which Nixon later thanked him at a private lunch. The committee's chairman finally suspended the hearings in light of the impending election, but by then Chotiner's reputation had been gravely damaged.

Most seriously, his name was now linked publicly with organized criminals. The uniform scam had involved a number of notorious mobsters. One of the men Chotiner had represented, formally described as a "uniform contractor," was actually a Mafia chieftain from Chotiner's home state of Pennsylvania, Marco ("The Little Guy") Reginelli.

An attorney can of course legitimately represent anyone he chooses. Chotiner and his partner, his brother Jack, however, had handled no fewer than 221 California bookmaking cases in one four-year period prior to the investigation. Bookmaking had subsequently been identified by the California State Crime Commission as "the most menacing racket in the entire field of organized crime." As this chapter will show, the bookmaking connection impinged directly on the early career of Richard Nixon.

Nixon and Chotiner both scrambled to limit the damage of the 1956 probe, with Nixon claiming through an aide that he had had "nothing to do with Chotiner for a long period of time." For his part, Chotiner insisted: "I have had no contact with the Vice President whatsoever since the day he was elected, as far as any contact with his office is concerned."

Neither statement was true. Chotiner had paid the Washington hotel bill for Nixon's guests when he was inaugurated as vice president, and as late as March 1956 he had been signing letters "on behalf of the Vice President." According to reporter Howard Seelye, a Chotiner friend and Republican campaign adviser, Chotiner regularly left phone messages asking to be called back through the White House. On a visit to Chotiner's office just weeks before the scandal broke, a reporter noticed letters addressed to Nixon in a pile of Chotiner's outgoing mail.

Despite his claims of innocence, the Republicans were forced in 1956 to act as if they were dropping Chotiner. Officials informed the press that he would not travel with Nixon during the campaign and would not attend the convention. Both men spoke thereafter as though their relationship had ended. "It was a tragedy," Nixon said piously, that Chotiner "had to get involved in the kind of law business that does not mix with politics." In 1960, when he himself ran unsuccessfully for Congress, Chotiner once pointed to an empty spot on the wall where, he said, Nixon's picture had formerly had a place of honor.

The supposed estrangement, however, was largely a pretense. Investigator Bellino remembered what Nixon staffers told him privately: "They stated [Nixon] was a man without guts. One of them mentioned how he had urged that Nixon break his association with Chotiner. But Nixon felt he couldn't do it."

Chotiner was a presence behind the scenes that year, advising Nixon during his losing campaign for the presidency against John F. Kennedy. He was available with advice during Nixon's bid for the governorship of California in 1962. "I was asked to deliver something," Dwight Chapin, later a close White House aide, recalled of a campaign chore in Los Angeles. "The door opens and the room is filled with cigar smoke, and there are Vic Lasky* and Murray Chotiner—like a classic picture of the Tammany Hall back room." Chotiner, almost alone that year, forecast that Nixon would one day recover from his shattering defeat.

In the 1968 campaign, when Nixon undertook his successful fight for the presidency, Chotiner was quietly entrusted with serving as liaison with the states where it was crucial to garner maximum votes—again discreetly and out of public view.

The day after Nixon's victory Chotiner claimed his reward, demanding the chairmanship of the Republican National Committee. When he was turned down—other Nixon advisers regarded him as too high risk for such a prominent post—Nixon created a job for him despite a routine FBI background check that suggested Chotiner had links with organized crime. The job description was curious—general counsel in the obscure Office of the Special Representative for Trade Negotiations—but a special executive order ensured he would be well paid. Few took much notice, a year later, when he was named special counsel to the president.

In his voluminous memoirs Nixon made only a handful of references to Chotiner, characterizing him merely as "brilliant . . . ever resourceful." He altogether omitted mentioning Chotiner's activities during the presidency. Chotiner remained a constant factor in Nixonian intrigue. He was involved in White House crimes and misdeeds in numerous spheres: representing Nixon in contacts with an operative for billionaire Howard Hughes, whose secret gifts of cash may be the key to Watergate; overseeing the extortion of millions of dollars from the heads of the dairy industry, an old connection for Chotiner and Nixon that dated back twenty years; secretly threatening a troublesome Greek exile with deportation and likely imprisonment or even death should he reveal what he knew about Nixon's illegal acceptance of funds from the Greek military junta; directing the secret payouts to congressional candidates known as the Townhouse Operation; providing lists of political enemies for investigation by the IRS; spying on Democratic presidential candidate George McGovern, at one point paying Lucianne Goldberg (the woman who in 1998 would play a key role in exposing President Clinton's sexual activity) to pose as a journalist on Senator McGovern's plane; taking charge of a delivery of cash from renegade financier Robert Vesco, reportedly laundered through a casino in the Bahamas; serving on a secret committee that arranged for construction union officials, including convicted criminals and one full-fledged mafioso, to visit Nixon in the White House; intervening in the federal investigation of Teamsters Union leaders in a twelve-million-dollar building scam (those in-

---

*Victor Lasky, author and Nixon intimate.

volved were dealt with more leniently); and playing a leading role in arranging the release of jailed Teamsters leader Jimmy Hoffa, reportedly in return for huge secret payments either for Nixon personally or for his 1972 campaign. In a file on those negotiations, which involved an associate of Mafia boss Carlos Marcello, Chotiner was referred to by the code name Mr. Pajamas.

By the time of the Watergate burglary, Chotiner would have departed from the White House and returned to private practice. Yet his law offices were one floor above those of CREEP, the Committee for the Re-Election of the President, and he still maintained a White House telephone. At least one woman working on White House dirty tricks operations was carried on the payroll of his firm.

"There is a person who goes all the way back through this thing," Nixon aide Chapin reflected in 1994, "and that is Murray Chotiner. He was in the White House . . . he leaves; the break-in happens. Murray was the operator for Nixon on God only knows what. . . ."

Nixon had known as early as 1946 that Chotiner was a shady character. He ignored Pat when she voiced her disapproval of the man, yet he knew the connection was better kept hidden. When Nixon saw the draft of the first campaign press release, bearing the letterhead "Murray M. Chotiner and Associates," he scored the letterhead through in blue ink, noting "Do not use—R.N."

If Nixon was aware even then that to be linked to Chotiner was synonymous with being linked to organized crime, it was precisely because he was himself similarly involved. That first campaign involved a relationship that has been little reported and never analyzed. At the very start of his political career, Nixon had met with a leading criminal and taken his money. Years later, seated in the governor's office in Alcatraz prison, Mickey Cohen, the man who had once dominated the mob scene in Los Angeles, signed a statement detailing his role in two Nixon elections, for the House in 1946 and for the Senate in 1950.

Cohen was a flamboyant gangster who had originally been sent to California in the early forties to join Benjamin Siegel—the infamous Bugsy—in the effort to take over the rackets in the West. Siegel and Cohen, both Jews, worked uneasily and often violently alongside the Italian criminals already in place. By 1945, when Siegel began to open up Las Vegas, Cohen was already established, as he put it, as a "power" in Los Angeles. When Richard Nixon was picked as the Republican candidate for the Twelfth District, an area Cohen regarded as his territory, a meeting was arranged. It took place, Cohen said, at Goodfellow's Grotto, "a little fish house where the politicians met and where they pull the screens across the booths for these kinds of talks. . . . The meeting was arranged by Murray Chotiner.

"It was a matter of one situation leading to another," as Cohen explained, "Like somebody would say, 'Well, ya ought to get together with Dick' or 'You ought to know Dick.' He was just starting to get his foot into the door, and Orange County, where he was from, was important to my bookmaking program. I think all I really said to him was something like 'We got some ideas, we may put some things in motion.'"

For his House campaign, Cohen gave Nixon a check for five thousand dollars—that would be about forty-four thousand dollars today—an amount he had negotiated with Myford Irvine of the Irvine Ranch, a huge agricultural concern in Orange County. "The contribution," according to Cohen, "was important for me and for the County. . . . Irvine was powerful, in as far as he was instrumental and a part and parcel of me running out there. So when he asked, I gave . . . I think a bigger amount was asked, but I Jewed him down to $5,000. . . . Irvine was my man in Orange County on certain propositions."

Cohen's connection with Nixon did not end in 1946, for Chotiner sought his help again four years later, during the 1950 Senate race. "I was again asked by Murray Chotiner to raise funds," Cohen recalled ". . . we had to. . . . See, Chotiner had a brother, Jack, that was a lawyer, one of the guys with the programs with the bookmakers, that also defended some of my guys. . . . I reserved the Banquet Room in the Hollywood Knickerbocker Hotel for a dinner meeting to which I invited approximately two hundred and fifty persons who were working with me in the gambling fraternity. . . . Everybody from around here that was on the pad naturally had to go to the dinner. It was all gamblers from Vegas, all gambling money; there wasn't a legitimate person in the room."

Among those present, Cohen said, were Joe and Fred Sica, George Capri, Hy Goldbaum, and Jack Dragna. The Sicas were Cohen henchmen. George Capri and Hy Goldbaum ran Las Vegas casinos, representing respectively the interests of Meyer Lansky and the Cleveland mob. Jack Dragna, once known as the Al Capone of Los Angeles, was running the local rackets in reluctant collaboration with the eastern syndicate.

"There was a certain figure we had to raise for that night," Cohen recalled, "$75,000, a considerable piece of money in those days.* . . . I'm sitting at the affair with a group of my guys from Vegas when my business manager, Mike Howard, says, 'Mick, we didn't raise the quota. We're short $20,000.' I said, 'Tell ya what ya do, Mike.' There were three entrances to this banquet room. I says, 'Close them.' Then I got up and I said, 'Lookit, everybody enjoyed their dinner, everybody happy? Well, we're short for this quota, and nobody's going home till this quota's met.'"

According to Cohen, the mobsters quickly rediscovered their generosity. "All the guests seen the doors were being closed, so the quota was met over and above, and that was it.[1] Then Nixon made a speech. He made a hop, skip, and jump speech . . . [but] the guy that really done all the speaking was Murray Chotiner.

*About $660,000 at today's values.

"In addition to helping Mr. Nixon financially," said Cohen, "I made arrangements to rent a headquarters for Nixon in the Pacific Finance Building at Eighth and Olive Streets in Los Angeles. . . . My attorney, Sam Rummel, leased the space, but I put up the bankroll, all the money for the printing material and everything. . . . We posted Nixon signs and literature. . . ."[2] Cohen said he continued to make large contributions to the Nixon campaign, sometimes through the notorious liquor industry lobbyist Art Samish.

However damning, is this account by a criminal really credible? Did Nixon and Chotiner ask one of the leading mobsters in Los Angeles, a man notorious for his crimes even then, for cash contributions—and in not one but two election campaigns?

The Cohen story was first aired by the columnist Drew Pearson, best known as originator of "Washington Merry-Go-Round," the nationally syndicated feature carried on in recent times by Jack Anderson. Given its authors, some might argue it was false propaganda, circulated to discredit Nixon and to benefit his Democratic opponents. Pearson, for decades a scourge of corrupt politicians, primarily targeted conservatives and often harried Nixon in the fifties and sixties.

In the spring of 1956, when Chotiner's links to organized crime were emerging in the Senate hearings, Pearson touched on the Nixon-Cohen connection in his regular radio broadcast. In a one-minute segment he said Cohen had "collected money from the underworld" for Nixon, with Chotiner as the contact man. In a 1959 broadcast he repeated the allegation.

It was in October 1962, only weeks before incumbent California Governor Pat Brown was to face Nixon in the gubernatorial election, that Cohen gave his long statement in prison—the statement from which much of the account in this chapter is taken—to an attorney named Richard Rogan. Rogan was the chief deputy attorney general at the time, as well as a leading Democrat close to the Kennedy brothers. In his autobiography, published in the mid-seventies, Cohen claimed Rogan's visit was approved in advance by President Kennedy himself. The Democrats, Cohen said, wanted to use his information to discredit Nixon and help Brown. As it turned out, they did not use his statement that year, and Nixon of course lost that election anyway. Pearson got hold of the information, though, and ran it at length in 1968, just before the election that took Nixon to the White House.

The fact that the story was valuable to Nixon's political enemies does not necessarily make it untrue. But what of the mobster's own motives? His memoir makes it clear that while he had no use for Nixon—Cohen characterized him as being "like the newspapers stigmatized him . . . a used-car salesman or a three-card monte dealer . . . a hustler"—he also thought Bobby Kennedy was a "vicious little bastard." The pragmatic Cohen believed that one used whichever politician appeared to offer "the best of what you've got going." In 1968 he hoped his statement would help him obtain parole if the Democrats won, as of course they did not.

The breaking of the story cannot be attributed to any vengeful motive on Cohen's part. Pearson's earliest information, in 1956, came not from Cohen but from an informant who in turn had heard it from one of Cohen's friends, Luis Saldana. Saldana apparently never cooperated with Pearson, nor at the time did Cohen, who refused to tell his story to the press and resisted testifying to the Senate committee that year, claiming, "I don't know what it's all about. . . . I've never been mixed up in politics." Even earlier, in 1952, he would not discuss the episode with Democratic emissaries because, he said, it would be like "ratting."

Finally, to gauge the truth about the relationship between Cohen and Murray Chotiner, one must consider what happened when—after Pearson's 1959 broadcast—Chotiner demanded a retraction from him and threatened to sue. The columnist's private files, examined by the author, reveal that the worried Pearson telephoned Cohen and pressed him for more details. The mobster declined to help but said he thought Chotiner was foolish to be mentioning a lawsuit. "I'll talk to him," promised Cohen, "and tell him to forget about it." The very next day the mobster called back to say that he had indeed spoken with Chotiner, who agreed to drop the matter. Chotiner never did sue—even when Pearson ran Cohen's full statement in 1968.

Mickey Cohen's support operation on Nixon's behalf was no philanthropic initiative undertaken by Cohen alone. The orders came, he made clear in his memoir, from "the proper persons from back East." The "proper persons," he explained, were Frank Costello and Meyer Lansky, the men who founded the national syndicate, the emperors of American organized crime.[3]

To Costello and Lansky, the ability to corrupt politicians, policemen, and judges was fundamental to Mafia operations. It was Lansky's expertise in such areas that established him as the nearest there ever was to a national godfather of organized crime. As reported later in these pages, Lansky encountered Richard Nixon—as he encountered John F. Kennedy—early in his career, probably even before the 1946 election that gave Nixon his start.

"If you were Meyer," Walter Sheridan, the renowned Senate rackets investigator, once said, "who would you invest your money in? Some politician named Clams Linguini? Or a nice Protestant boy from Whittier, California?"

"I want you to know," Nixon told a cheering crowd during the Voorhis election, "that I am your candidate primarily because there are no special strings attached to me. I have no support from any special interest or pressure group." Whatever the extent of his links to organized crime, it is clear that Nixon was very much tied to the world of big money, the banks, and the oilmen. Harry Schuyler, a prominent businessman and mayor of East Whittier, who knew the young Nixon and his backers well, was clear about the relationship. Nixon, he said, was "a natural" for the moneymen who picked him. "The minute he became available he was told in no uncertain terms of what he was offered, a political life that he must accept."

Osmyn Stout, who had gone to Whittier College with Nixon and watched him being launched in politics, put it another way. "I could see who the Republican committee were," said Stout, "and I knew he had sold his soul."

7

Intrigue was second nature to him,
an exercise he went through without thinking.

—*William Safire, Nixon speechwriter*

"He looks like the boy who lived down the block from all of us," a *Washington Times-Herald* columnist enthused in January 1947, soon after freshman Representative Richard Nixon had been sworn in. "He's as typically American as Thanksgiving." Nixon's face stared from the page in an idealized portrait next to the report, which praised the "clean" campaign that had brought him victory.

George Reedy, the UPI's congressional correspondent,* saw another aspect of Nixon. Invited for drinks, he found the congressman sitting with his feet on the desk, coat off, sleeves rolled up. This was rare informality in a man who in the future seemed inseparable from his dark suits, who wore business shoes even for walks on the beach. "It was a very uneasy feeling," Reedy recalled. "He sort of pulled himself up, as though he had rehearsed the gesture, then told some masculine story—No. 347 out of 500 stories appropriate for all occasions. Not dirty—Pat was standing there with her very tight-lipped smile. It wasn't an unpleasant afternoon, but there was something weird about it. . . . It was a feeling that we weren't talking to a human being. Seeing him walk and hearing him talk was like watching a doll, like a Barbie doll. . . ."

The *Chicago Tribune*'s Walter Trohan, the conservative journalist who became close to the Nixons—close enough to help with the baby-sitting—experi-

*Later press secretary to President Johnson.

enced a similar unease. "From the very beginning," he said, "I found Nixon more calculating than warm, more self-centered than outgiving, more petty than generous, and more inclined to say what a listener might want to hear than frank enough to reveal his own stand."

The authorized version of Nixon's Washington debut is straightforward enough: An earnest young couple drives across the continent and finds an apartment in the suburbs. They wrestle with social etiquette, discovering the hard way that on Capitol Hill "informal" means tuxedo and ballgown. Pat becomes pregnant with their second and last child, another daughter, Julie, born in July 1948. She begins to "despair" that her husband's work means the early joys of married life are a thing of the past. Richard's mother and father meanwhile follow him east. Retired and in their sixties, the Nixons take on a Pennsylvania dairy farm. Frank Nixon names his cattle after movie stars, Dorothy Lamour, Loretta Young, and Gary Cooper. Hannah is once again within driving distance of their successful son.

Nixon is ensconced in an office called the attic, a bit of a hike from the chamber, but a sumptuous suite. "I suppose I feel elated," he says, when fellow freshman John F. Kennedy asks his reaction to having toppled Jerry Voorhis. He tells a writer he has "a lost feeling." Asked if he has a pet project, he replies, "No, nothing in particular. I was elected to smash the labor bosses. . . ." He is given a job on the Education and Labor Committee, and champions a bill to curb unions.

While most newcomers were appointed to only one committee, Nixon was also named to the House Un-American Activities Committee.* He was reported to have struggled with himself over whether to accept the appointment to such a controversial body, "pacing up and down, lighting one cigarette after another, talking to the ceiling." Within a month of joining the committee, though, he had become a zealous HUAC activist. His maiden speech was a demand for a contempt of Congress citation against a German Communist active in the United States, Gerhart Eisler. Sentenced to a year in jail, Eisler jumped bail and fled to East Germany. His name has long faded from public memory, but he was a peripheral character in the affair that shot Nixon to national prominence, the Alger Hiss case.[1]

The Case, as it is known to some aficionados, is a pivotal episode of twentieth-century American history. Anyone with a grounding in modern politics is familiar with its basic elements: Hiss, a handsome forty-three-year-old lawyer and State Department official, was publicly accused in 1948 by Whittaker Chambers, a rumpled former Communist turned *Time* journalist, of having been not only a secret Communist in the late thirties, but also a Soviet spy.

Chambers claimed Hiss had removed documents from the State Department, had his wife type copies, and then passed them to him for transmission

*Hereafter referred to as HUAC.

to the Soviets. To support his charges, Chambers produced papers and micro-film—some of it from a hollowed-out pumpkin, hence the popular name Pumpkin Papers—that seemed to be damning evidence against Hiss. They included sixty-four pages that had apparently been copied from 1938-vintage State Department documents by someone using the Hiss family typewriter. Chambers asserted that while he had passed many such packages on to the Russians, he had kept these back by way of insurance against the future.

Because the statute of limitations in the case had expired, Hiss could no longer be tried for espionage. He was charged instead with perjury, for allegedly having lied to a grand jury when he denied both having known Chambers at the relevant time and having supplied him with documents. Although a first trial ended with a hung jury, in 1949, Hiss was found guilty at a second. Sentenced to five years in jail, he remained adamant that he was innocent. He fought to clear his name until his death in 1996, at the age of ninety-two.

For the right, The Case vindicated the notion that domestic communism was a potent danger, a threat to the country's security by the Soviet foe. For the left, it marked the start of the period one historian dubbed the Great Fear, infamous for Senator Joseph McCarthy's crusade against American Communists, real or imagined. Central to the left's mindset was the theory, believed or at least suspected by millions, that Alger Hiss had been the victim of a diabolical frame-up.

It was the young congressman Richard Nixon who spearheaded the pursuit of Hiss. Headline after headline built up the image of the principled crusader who stayed on the trail when others concluded it was leading nowhere, who fought on relentlessly until Hiss was shamed, ruined, and imprisoned. Without The Case, the McCarthy nightmare might have been stillborn, and Nixon, to whom it brought lasting fame, might have remained a relatively obscure politician. It is at the very least highly unlikely that he would have advanced from freshman congressman to vice president in only six years.

After Hiss had been sentenced, Nixon made a four-hour victory speech in the House. He gave it the title "A Lesson for the American People," and it was a lesson he returned to for the rest of his life. He picked The Case as the opening chapter, the first crisis, of his 1962 book *Six Crises*, his eulogy to himself. As president, a decade later, he would instruct at least six senior White House aides to read the book. Haldeman, who said he had already read it, was told to read it again. "How he loved that case!" Haldeman recalled. "He was able, somehow, to compare every tough situation we ever encountered, even Watergate, to his handling of the Hiss case." Charles Colson was to claim he had read *Six Crises* fourteen times. Nixon referred to the case three times in one conversation with John Dean in 1973, during Watergate. "I conducted that investigation . . ." Nixon told Dean. "We broke that thing without any help."

Nixon's role in the Hiss case raises many issues, but one question is rarely addressed: Why, so soon after becoming a congressman, did he focus almost exclusively on matters involving espionage and intelligence? Just possibly, the answer lies in his distant past.

———————

A decade earlier, when Nixon was about to graduate from law school, he had gone job hunting in New York. Of the several prestigious law firms he visited, two had partners who were to reach the pinnacle of U.S. intelligence. William ("Wild Bill") Donovan, the founding partner of Donovan, Leisure, Newton, and Lombard,* was a leading Republican who in the coming war headed the OSS (Office of Strategic Services), forerunner of the CIA. Donovan favored recruiting individuals like bankers, industrialists, and lawyers for intelligence work. He met with Nixon personally when he applied for a job and later asked him back for a second interview. According to Nixon, he declined the opportunity.

Nixon's "highest hope" on that New York trip, he later said, was to win a position at another Wall Street firm, Sullivan and Cromwell. The panel that interviewed him there included John Foster Dulles, a senior partner and future secretary of state in the Eisenhower-Nixon administration. It is not clear if Dulles's younger brother, Allen, was present. Allen Dulles, also a Republican stalwart, was a former Foreign Service officer who had for years provided what his biographer describes as "very particular services" at Sullivan and Cromwell. He became a top operative for the OSS during the war and the director of Central Intelligence under Eisenhower.

David Wise, a veteran writer on intelligence, has raised a question about Nixon's next sojourn in the New York area, when as a navy officer home from the Pacific in 1945 he was transferred to the East Coast. According to Nixon, he spent that time winding up naval contracts, and his wife recalled his going to work at the "Bureau of Aeronautics." Wise, noting that there were no references to the period in Nixon's official biographical sketches, thought there was "something of a mystery."

If there is indeed such a mystery, another writer on intelligence believes he has solved it. John Loftus, a former prosecutor with the Justice Department unit investigating Nazi war crimes, claims that one of Nixon's assignments at the time involved the review of captured Nazi documents. Citing interviews with retired intelligence officers, at least one of whom worked in the same area as Nixon, Loftus makes a startling suggestion. "Allen Dulles," he writes, ". . . told [Nixon] to keep quiet about what he had seen and, in return, arranged to finance the young man's first congressional campaign, against Jerry Voorhis."[2]

What could Dulles have wanted Nixon to keep quiet about? According to some chroniclers, the Dulles brothers had links to the Nazis dating back to pre-

*Later Donovan, Leisure, Newton, Irvine.

war business contacts. Loftus, who had access to contemporary records, claims Allen Dulles maintained such contacts even during the war and that proof of the ties lies in captured German documents, still classified to this day.[3]

Dulles had returned to the United States, his war service over, in the late fall of 1945, the same period that Nixon accepted the invitation to run for Congress against Voorhis. At the time Voorhis said he discovered that a mysterious "representative of a large New York financial house" had traveled to California to urge that he be ousted. The reader will recall the firsthand account by an executive of Gladding McBean, the Californian company that levied money from its staff to pay Nixon the money he demanded, over and above his congressional salary, if he was to serve as representative.* One of the company's directors, Herman Phleger, was to serve Allen Dulles as legal adviser at the CIA.

Whatever the genesis of their relationship with Nixon, the Dulles brothers were to be his long-term political allies. Although they were Ivy League products of the elite Nixon professed to deplore, they shared the same worldview and became his friends and regular dinner companions. Allen had befriended Nixon in 1947, when both were in Europe on a postwar fact-finding mission, one of several trips Dulles used to nurture his contacts and to do some "quiet recruiting." Nixon met with the brothers early in his drive, the following year, to expose Alger Hiss as a traitor.[4]

The connection to the Hiss case of the OSS and its successor, the CIA, reportedly involving both William Donovan and Allen Dulles, has been little probed. As it happened, the OSS had had reason for an early interest in Hiss: At one stage he had been, ironically, at the top of a list of candidates for the post of its general counsel.[5] In 1945, though, when it seemed possible that Hiss might become the first secretary-general of the United Nations, Donovan warned the State Department that Hiss had been charged by OSS sources with being a traitor.

In July 1948, days before HUAC started its Hiss probe, the fledgling CIA reportedly ensured that Nixon, the committee's youngest member, would be given inside information. Its intelligence, passed to him through Thomas Dewey, Republican candidate in that year's presidential election, was that Hiss was indeed a Communist.

The following month, as HUAC faltered in the face of Hiss's denials, Nixon received confirmation that Hiss had indeed known Chambers. It came, according to CIA sources, from Allen Dulles.[6] Dulles, who had a run-in with Hiss years earlier,[7] was at this time in close touch with his former chief, Donovan, and was entirely likely to be privy to whatever the OSS had learned about Hiss.

———————

Nixon also had assistance in the Hiss case from the domestic guardian of U.S. security, the FBI. The genesis of this connection is, again, something of a puzzle.

*See p. 47.

In 1937, within weeks of looking for a job as a lawyer in New York, Nixon had applied to join the FBI. He filled out the forms and supplied a list of references—including Whittier Police Chief Guy Welch, father of his former sweetheart Ola—and his application was supported by a personal letter to Hoover by the dean of Duke Law School. The surviving FBI file indicates that Nixon did well in the initial interview process and was recommended for employment but was then dropped.

A handwritten notation in the Nixon file reads, "Not Qualified," and the appointment, which had already been passed to the Justice Department for approval, was canceled by Hoover's closest aide, Clyde Tolson. Years later, embarrassed at having turned down a future leader of the United States, Hoover and his aides concocted various explanations for the rejection: that Nixon was unsuitable because he was already practicing law (he was not) and that budgetary factors were involved.

Two FBI assistant directors, one of them future domestic intelligence chief William Sullivan, said Nixon's application was ultimately set aside because he was judged "lacking in aggression," a characterization that runs counter to remarks in the FBI file. By another account, the problem was a report prepared by John Vincent, agent in charge in Charlotte, North Carolina, the FBI office responsible for the area that included Duke Law School. It was there that a year earlier Nixon had broken into the dean's offices. Hoover's fact checkers may also have turned up the fact that Nixon had once been briefly under arrest following a student prank at Whittier College, despite his assertion on his application form that he had never been arrested.[8] The FBI investigated as well Nixon's claim to have worked during vacations as Richfield Oil's "manager" of the service station next to his father's store. A Richfield representative said Nixon had only "done odd jobs for him from time to time." Not for the last time Nixon had been caught bending the truth.[9]

In 1947, when Nixon arrived in Washington, Hoover had access to all file material concerning the incoming representative, for his staff routinely provided him with detailed briefs on all new congressmen. Apparently nothing Hoover learned then about Nixon, however, troubled him. During Hoover's appearance before HUAC that year, when Nixon asked the director several questions, an attorney accompanying Hoover leaned across to offer him a piece of information: Nixon, he said, had used dirty tricks to beat Voorhis in the recent election. "I know all about that," Hoover replied, "but it looks to me as if he's going to be a good man for us."

Nixon met with Hoover that year, and—after some initial misunderstandings[10]—a long collaborative relationship began. Five years later, when Nixon ran for vice president, the supposedly apolitical Hoover hosted a fund-raiser for him. They were seen together at the races and at baseball games. Hoover also secretly supplied Nixon with negative intelligence about other politicians. After the 1960 election had swept Nixon into the wilderness, Hoover was a sympathetic houseguest.

Like many others, Nixon feared what compromising information the director might have about him—so much so that when he was president and Hoover had become senile, he did not dare fire him. On balance, though, the FBI connection was a huge long-term asset. "Hoover," Nixon said ruefully after the director had died and Watergate was dragging him down to disgrace, "was my crony."

In 1948 that crony had a motive to encourage the congressman's pursuit of Alger Hiss. Hoover was frustrated by what he saw as the Truman administration's failure to fight domestic communism, and he wanted vindication for the FBI's work against subversives. Like Dulles, he was committed to seeing President Truman defeated in the presidential election.

Truman of course surprised everyone by beating Thomas Dewey in November. Years later Truman would insist he knew what the Hiss case had really been about. "What they were trying to do, all those birds," he said, "they were trying to get the Democrats. They were trying to get me out of the White House, and they were willing to go to any lengths to do it. . . . They did do just about anything they could think of, all that witch-hunting. . . . The Constitution has never been in such danger. . . ."

Hoover's assistance to Nixon on the Hiss case proved crucial. Although rumors about Hiss had been circulating since 1939,[11] the FBI had taken action only in 1941, when his name appeared on a list of alleged Communists. The bureau began intercepting his mail that year. A few months later Chambers named Hiss as a Communist during an interview with FBI agents.

By 1945 the flow of allegations had increased. A Soviet defector in Canada, a code clerk, described a spy within the State Department in terms that pointed directly to Hiss. Hiss was also implicated by a former Communist courier, Elizabeth Bentley, and Chambers told a State Department security officer that Hiss had been one of the "top leaders of the underground." Hiss had been a junior figure in the department when the rumors started, but by war's end he had risen to become a close aide to the secretary of state, an adviser to President Roosevelt at the Yalta Conference with Stalin and Churchill, and secretary-general of the founding convention of the United Nations. Claims that such a highly placed figure was a Communist had to be taken seriously.

In late 1945 the FBI had begun tailing Hiss wherever he went, as well as tapping his phone and resuming interception of his mail. Hiss was ultimately eased out of the State Department, but not fast enough for Hoover. In late 1946 the FBI director began orchestrating a series of leaks to friends of the FBI, key press contacts, and members of Congress—among them Richard Nixon.

Nixon was to claim later that the first he heard of Hiss was in August 1948, when Whittaker Chambers testified before the Un-American Activities Committee. "The FBI," he insisted, "played no role whatever in the Hiss case. . . ."

The facts suggest otherwise. Within a month of taking office, Nixon had accompanied a fellow congressman to a meeting with Father John Cronin, a

Catholic priest who had informed on Communists while working with labor unions during the war. The bureau now used him as a conduit for deliberate leaks. In a report prepared for the Catholic hierarchy, drawing on what the FBI had told him, Cronin had named Hiss as the most influential Communist in the State Department. He later recalled having shown Nixon that report and having discussed Hiss with him. "Nixon," Cronin claimed, "was playing with a stacked deck in the Hiss case."[12]

Once the HUAC probe of Hiss got under way, Cronin said, "the really hard-core material was given to me—uh, informally . . . by my friends of the FBI." One such friend, Agent Ed Hummer, supplied daily reports of progress in the ongoing bureau investigation. Hummer, Cronin said, would "tell me what they had turned up. . . . I told Dick, who then knew just where to look for things and what he would find." By the time the HUAC probe became serious, Nixon was on the phone late at night with one of Hoover's top aides, Louis Nichols, and meeting in his hotel room with former FBI agents.

One of HUAC's key investigators on the Hiss case was a former FBI agent, Lou Russell, who by one account had been the initial investigator of the committee's interest in Whittaker Chambers. Russell spent an enormous amount of time with Nixon, traveled with him, and stayed in touch by telephone outside working hours; he reported Nixon's thinking back to Hoover. Russell was a Democrat, but one said to have used the word "liberal" as though it were synonymous with "radical." First and foremost, though, he was an operator, one who would crop up again in the unfolding story of Nixon's life. Two decades later, he would be a mystery figure at the scene of the Watergate burglary.

8

They're trying to prove . . .
my entire career was built on a fraud.

—Richard Nixon in 1992,
on a report that Soviet archives showed
Alger Hiss to have been innocent

"I am a graduate of Harvard Law School," said the debonair witness. Then, after a pause, he asked, "And I believe yours is Whittier?" Thus did Alger Hiss, at their first Un-American Activities Committee encounter, slyly trigger Richard Nixon's neurosis about the East Coast elite. "It absolutely ripped Nixon apart," remembered HUAC's chief investigator Robert Stripling. "I realized from that moment on that he could not stand Hiss."

Hiss himself took a dispassionate view of the man who effectively destroyed his career and put him in jail. "Nixon," he said years later, "I always regarded as an opportunistic politician. . . . And I knew enough about politicians to know what political ambitions sometimes lead people to do."

Stripling too questioned Nixon's motives. "Nixon had his hat set for Hiss," he said. ". . . It was a personal thing. He was no more concerned about whether Hiss was [a Communist] than a billy goat." Having at first had the impression Nixon was even tempered, Stripling soon saw an immoderate side. "I was surprised one day, sitting in his office. . . . He said to me, 'Hiss, that son of a bitch is lying . . . lying, lying, lying!" Recalling how Nixon pounded the table during this outburst, Stripling said it was "more than, you know, just somebody saying, 'I don't believe this guy.' He was just *outraged*. Of course, I knew nothing about him being briefed. . . ."

Nixon assiduously cultivated Whittaker Chambers early in the investigation, making repeated trips to Chambers's home in the Maryland countryside. Hiss, concerned by a news story describing one of the visits, questioned Nixon about it at a HUAC executive session. When he made a minor error, asking Nixon if it was true that he had just spent the weekend at Chambers's farm in *New Jersey*—as distinct from Maryland—Nixon denied it.

Suspicious, he explained, of Hiss's initial denials that he even knew Chambers, Nixon turned detective, searching for compelling evidence that the two men had indeed been associates. Chambers knew myriad details about Hiss and his family life—more, surely, one might add today, than could have been proved to him by FBI agents armed with the fruits of the bureau's surveillance of Hiss. Eventually, at a confrontation with Chambers orchestrated by Nixon and Lou Russell, Hiss conceded that he had known Chambers, albeit under another name.[1]

Hiss claimed that he had been friendly with Chambers for only a brief period in 1935. Yet he had provided Chambers and his wife with accommodations—first in his own home and then in a furnished apartment—and had given him a used car as a present. Evidence in a real estate agent's files also indicated that in 1936 and 1937 both men had negotiated to buy the same remote farmhouse, a fact that seemed beyond coincidence.

Most reasonable people would conclude from the accumulated evidence[2] that Hiss did know Chambers, and for longer than he admitted, and that he did associate with leftists and Communists before the war. There was no crime in that. What, then, was Hiss hiding? That his relationship with Chambers was one of spy working with fellow spy? Or was it something less serious, some embarrassing personal secret?

Twenty-five years after the Hiss affair, in a converation with a senior congressman aboard the presidential yacht, Nixon would reveal what he called "the true story of the Hiss case"—namely, that Chambers and Hiss had been "queers." He repeated the allegation to others.

Chambers, who was married with children, admitted to numerous homosexual encounters. Once, according to the other man involved, he tried to force himself on a colleague in their rooming house. His homosexuality, Chambers told the FBI, was his darkest secret, and his active homosexual phase had corresponded precisely with the period in which he knew the Hisses. According to one report received by the FBI, he had had relations with Hiss's stepson, Timothy, then in early adolescence.[3] The last time he had seen Hiss, Chambers told Nixon, was an evening when Timothy "wanted him to stay overnight." Mrs. Hiss objected, and he had left.

Chambers denied having had any sexual involvement with Alger Hiss but told Nixon that Hiss had been his "closest friend." He revealed an attachment to things linked to Hiss that bordered on fetishism, keeping—years after their association ended—numerous items that once belonged to the Hisses, including a wing chair, a table, and a broken love seat. More than a decade later he produced a carefully folded piece of cloth, explaining that it was the fabric that once had covered the wing chair. He had removed it, had it dry-cleaned, then carefully preserved it.

Hiss suggested that Chambers had framed him because of unrequited sexual passion. His accuser had never made any homosexual advances, he said, but "His attitude to me, and his relations, were strange . . . he had a hostility to the point of jealousy about my wife. . . . My guess is that he had some obscure kind of love attachment . . . about me." Perhaps there was an emotional foundation to Chambers's attitude toward Hiss, and perhaps it did turn to hatred; but if so, it does nothing to explain the hard evidence that put Hiss in jail: Chambers's hoard of documents and microfilm.

Hiss's accuser produced his first surprise—copies of State Department documents, stored until then in a dumbwaiter shaft, in November 1948, having insisted until then that although Hiss had been a fellow Communist, no espionage had been involved. When word of the material reached HUAC, at a time the Hiss probe seemed moribund, Nixon reacted oddly. Far from being excited at what seemed a big break in the case, he seemed nervous and irritable. When investigator Stripling suggested driving at once to see Chambers, Nixon talked instead of leaving with Pat the next day on an ocean cruise.

"I'm so goddamned sick and tired of this case," he told Stripling in early December, "I don't want to hear any more about it, and I'm going to Panama. And the hell with it, and you, and the whole damned business!" Hours later, after Nixon did agree to go to see Chambers again, the witness intimated that he had a second bombshell. Surely, Stripling asked Nixon, he would now postpone his vacation plans? Nixon retorted, "I don't think he's got a damned thing. I'm going right ahead with my plans."

He left on the cruise the following morning, having grudgingly told Stripling to subpoena Chambers for any documents still in his possession. Within twenty-four hours, with flabbergasted HUAC staffers standing by, Chambers produced several rolls of microfilm of State Department documents from the famous hollowed-out pumpkin. Informed by radiogram aboard ship, Nixon decided to return to Washington at once. He did so in theatrical fashion, transferring from his liner to a coast guard seaplane, then flying to Florida to be met by a posse of reporters.

The photograph of the young congressman emerging from the seaplane, accompanied by his declaration (made before he had even seen the new evidence) that Chambers's cache would "prove once and for all that where you have a Communist you have an espionage agent," was flashed across the nation. Back in Washington, after only a cursory look at the latest discoveries, Nixon announced to the press they were "conclusive proof of the greatest treason conspiracy in this nation's history . . . proof that cannot be denied."

Two factors may explain Nixon's odd behavior, and the truth may embrace both. His overwrought condition before the trip may have been in part a reaction to too much pressure and a marriage under strain. After a canceled summer vacation, he said, he had promised Pat he would not postpone another. "He was so exhausted," his secretary asserted, "that we talked him into a vacation."

Other information, however, suggests that the interrupted vacation scenario was in fact staged. Nixon had phoned one of Director Hoover's closest aides late the night before his departure, to ask the FBI to stay away from the new development, as he would be holding hearings in two weeks. Telling Stripling he would be back after Christmas, he also tried to put HUAC on hold. Yet it seems he already knew he would be back far sooner than that.

In the early hours of the day he was to leave on his cruise, Nixon had happened to meet the House doorkeeper, William Miller, in a corridor of the House of Representatives. To the congressman it was a casual conversation with a lowly functionary, unlikely ever to be reported. Unfortunately for Nixon, though, Miller later wrote a memoir in which he recalled that as they greeted each other in the corridor, Nixon said: "I'm going to get on a steamship, and you will be reading about it. I am going out to sea, and they are going to send for me. You will understand when I get back. . . ." The puzzled Miller thought the congressman looked "very elated and keyed up, as if he were dancing on wires."

Three days later, with Nixon on his way back to Washington, Miller recalled, "Finally I knew what he meant about the trip. The [newspaper] story said he had been aboard the steamship when the call came to return to Washington. I thought to myself, 'That clever guy—he knew all the time.' . . . I had been in on the start of something very peculiar." Coast guard logs also reportedly suggest that arrangements for Nixon's return had been made even before his ship left harbor in New York, which would confirm suspicion that the trip was a charade to ensure maximum publicity.

With the Pumpkin Papers in hand, however, things moved apace. Concerns about Chambers's credibility were put aside, and by Christmas Hiss had been indicted for perjury. The big issue now was the need to link Hiss to the copies of the compromising documents with hard evidence. "Attempt," Chambers had told HUAC investigator Stripling, "to locate the typewriter . . ." And they did find a typewriter.

When Hiss came to trial in the summer of 1949, an antiquated office machine sat on a table in the courtroom in full view of the jury. Its keys clacked noisily as an FBI agent demonstrated that it still functioned. The Woodstock machine, vintage circa 1929, serial no. N230099, became one of the prosecutor's "imutable witnesses" against Hiss.

"It had a powerful psychological impact," the accused man remembered long afterward, ". . . sitting there like a murder weapon." "The typewriter evidence," Nixon said, "was a major factor in leading to the Hiss conviction."

Document examiners for both sides judged that the purloined State Department documents had been retyped on the same machine as old letters known to have been typed on the Woodstock the Hisses had once owned. They had given the machine away, however, and just when they did so it became a crucial issue in the case. For if the Woodstock had been no longer in the family's possession before the earliest date on the papers in Chambers's hoard, then Hiss was surely innocent.

The Hiss defense team and the FBI hunted eagerly for the family's old typewriter, tracking the chain of possession from person to person. The Hiss group found it first—or believed they had—when they recovered Woodstock N230099 from a junk dealer. However, its discovery brought the defense no comfort, for again experts for both sides were in agreement: The type on the salvaged Woodstock matched that on both the stolen government documents and the Hiss family correspondence, hard evidence that appeared to be devastating.

"It is the contention of the government," the trial judge was to conclude as he summed up the evidence, "that this is the typewriter upon which the Baltimore exhibits were typed." In fact, the prosecution had carefully contended no such thing. It was not just that there was ultimately uncertainty about whether the Hisses were still in possession of their machine at the time the State Department documents were purloined and copied, for the evidence on that issue has always been hopelessly muddled. There was also serious doubt about whether the Woodstock produced in court was really the old Hiss family machine. Its serial number, N230099, almost certainly indicated that it had been manufactured too late to be the Hiss typewriter. While the FBI had that information when the case went to trial, the defense did not.

Hiss spoke only two sentences in court after he had been found guilty. The first was to thank the judge. The second was to assert that one day in the future it would be disclosed how "forgery by typewriter" had been committed. "Even his most ardent supporters could not swallow such a ridiculous charge," Richard Nixon scoffed in response to Hiss's claim as late as 1976. "A typewriter, is, as you know, almost the same as a fingerprint. It is impossible, according to experts in the field, to duplicate exactly the characteristics of one typewriter by manufacturing another one."

Nixon was wrong. Contrary to his claim, typewriters have been expertly forged, and with the government's blessing, in a very relevant time frame. By 1941, as part of World War II liaison between American and British intelligence, operatives had developed machines that, according to one of the British officers involved, "could reproduce faultlessly the imprint of any typewriter on earth." One successful anti-Nazi operation achieved precisely that by rebuilding an old Italian typewriter.

Who, though, might have performed such a feat in the Hiss case? And who else, then, might have had the means, motive, or opportunity to frame Hiss with a counterfeit typewriter? Who would have had access to the original typewriter in order to do so?

The machine was apparently recovered by the defense team a full five months after Chambers had produced his cache of documents.[4] There are some indications, though, that it was actually retrieved much earlier than that—by HUAC, or by the FBI, or by HUAC and the FBI working together. Just a month after Chambers released the papers, the *New York World-Telegram* cited congressional investigators as saying they had found the machine "with the assistance of the FBI." Similarly, HUAC's final report credited the FBI with "the lcoation of the typewriter." A HUAC congressman, John McDowell, wrote that committee investigators and the FBI deserved the credit for "finding the typewriter."

The FBI's future domestic intelligence chief, William Sullivan, served in Washington in 1948 and his work included the Hiss case. Interviewed years later, he was quoted as saying that "to the best of my knowledge . . . the FBI did have the typewriter before it was found by the Hiss defense. . . ."[5] He was not certain "whether it had been located by the FBI or brought to the Bureau labs by Nixon."

To the delight of Hiss's defenders, moreover, Nixon also repeatedly drew suspicion on himself regarding the typewriter. In his book *Six Crises,* he noted: "On December 13, 1948, FBI agents found the typewriter.* . . . On December 15 an expert from the FBI typed exact copies of the incriminating documents on the old Woodstock machine. . . ."

Pressed for an explanation when *Six Crises* was published, Nixon offered only a superficial explanation for the discrepancy. His spokesman claimed the passage was all a researcher's mistake based on the *World-Telegram* story and—ludicrously—insisted that Nixon had not been close to the case at the time.[6]

Yet Nixon again seemed to implicate himself in an Oval Office conversation he had with senior aides on March 10, 1972, recorded on a tape released in 1996 and monitored during research for this book. The subject was the uproar over a press story that International Telephone and Telegraph had committed a huge cash donation to the Republicans, a payoff for government intervention in an antitrust suit against the company. The story was based on a typewritten memo written by an ITT lobbyist, and Nixon wanted the memo declared a forgery. In the course of the discussion, the tape shows, Nixon harked back to the Hiss case and the Chambers documents, and stated: "*I found* the typewriter . . . [author's italics]."[7]

John Dean's memoir, *Blind Ambition,* has given Hiss loyalists their choicest morsel of all. The White House counsel quoted what, he said, Charles Colson told him after another talk in which Nixon drew a parallel between the ITT matter and the Hiss case. "The typewriters are always the key," the president told Colson, in Dean's version. "We built one in the Hiss case."

---

*December 13 was also the date that the *New York World-Telegram* reported the bureau had located the typewriter.

When Dean's book was published, Colson protested that he had "no recollection" of Nixon's having said the typewriter was "phonied," and Nixon
himself characterized the claim as "totally false." Dean, however, insisted that
his contemporary notes confirmed that Colson had quoted the president as he
indicated and seemed serious when he did so.

Can we take seriously the notion that Hoover and the FBI or Richard
Nixon, separately or in alliance, might have framed Hiss by forging a typewriter? In this author's view, only an intelligence organization would have had
the resources and the experience to carry out such a plan. The World War II
feat of forgery described earlier in this chapter was part of a joint British-FBI
operation. Hoover himself had visited the secret installation in Canada where
typewriter fabrication and similar acts of wizardry were perfected. (The operation was sited there to facilitate easy access by FBI agents and OSS staff.)

If forgery was used to ensure that Hiss was found guilty, there may have
been a rationale more powerful, more historically compelling than Hoover's
obsession with the Red menace or his frustration about foot-dragging on the
part of the Truman administration.

New information, reported in the pages that follow, suggests that by 1948
Hoover and other U.S. intelligence chiefs may have received information on
Hiss from Soviet cable intercepts that seemed to leave no doubt that the man
was guilty. Coupled with the flow of data about Hiss that had been reaching
the intelligence agencies for several years, it may have seemed the clinching
piece of evidence.

The existence of such evidence, though, could not be revealed because the
very fact that the United States had broken the Soviet cipher was one of the
most closely kept secrets of the century. Yet other parts of the government's information on Hiss also had come from secret sources. Could there have been
some twisted reasoning along the lines that since Hiss was now apparently
clearly guilty, but the real proof of it had to remain concealed, it was justifiable
to fabricate another sort of "proof"?

The one substantive piece of information indicating typewriter forgery features the OSS and its chief, William Donovan. In late 1948, when the Hiss defense and the FBI began the protracted hunt for the Woodstock typewriter, a
man named Horace Schmahl joined the Hiss defense team as an investigator.
Schmahl had worked for either the OSS or army intelligence during the war,
then joined the Central Intelligence Group, the organization that operated in
the period between the closedown of the OSS and the inception of the CIA.[8]

After his stint for the Hiss side, Schmahl defected to the prosecution team.
Still later, after Hiss had been jailed, his lawyer received a tip that "Schmahl
was implicated with the typewriter." An investigator who had worked with
Schmahl, Harold Bretnall, subsequently told the lawyer that Schmahl had been
involved in forging the Hiss typewriter. "Hiss," Bretnall said, "was framed."

Tracked down in 1973 in Florida, Schmahl admitted to a Hiss investigator
that he had been a "consultant" on the typewriter forgery. He said that the

OSS had set Hiss up—just when was not clear—and that the orders had come through Donovan's New York law firm, Donovan, Leisure. (Schmahl later retracted his statements and declined further interviews.)

There the trail ends. The Schmahl lead never was officially investigated. Is it plausible that either the FBI's Hoover or Nixon would have been prepared to frame Hiss or to remain silent had they learned of it? The answer, the records suggest, is yes.

The damaging information on Hoover comes from his own files. A decade later, asked by the agent in charge in New York if the FBI laboratory could assist with the framing of a leading U.S. Communist, Hoover expressed no disapproval. He merely insisted that the job be well done—to "avoid embarrassment to the Bureau"—and added some advice. "To alter a typewriter to match a known model," he counseled, "would require a large amount of typewriter specimens and weeks of laboratory work." In the Hiss case in 1948 there were a great many specimens—and many weeks in which to achieve a forgery.

"Had Nixon asked the FBI to manufacture evidence to prove his case against Hiss," opined former FBI Assistant Director Sullivan, "Hoover would have been only too glad to oblige." As for whether Nixon would actually have gone as far as to frame Hiss, the later record includes disquieting instances of forgery or planting false information.

In 1971, for example, after announcing publicly that the American involvement in Vietnam was instigated by the Kennedy administration and by U.S. "complicity in the murder of [South Vietnamese President] Diem," Nixon called for the examination of the files on the episode. When his aide Charles Colson found no hard evidence in State Department cables about Diem's death, Colson asked Howard Hunt to "improve" on the record. Hunt did so, using scissors and paste and a Xerox machine to fabricate a message "proving" that President Kennedy had effectively approved the murder. He and Colson then tried to get the forgery published in *Life* magazine.

Recently released White House tapes feature Nixon's telling John Ehrlichman, when this forgery was revealed at the height of Watergate, that no one had informed him of the scheme. "I'm not so sure that you weren't," responded Ehrlichman, ". . . my recollection is that this was discussed with you." Soon after, Haldeman noted in his journal, Nixon admitted he was really "the guilty one . . . he was the one that started Colson on his projects. . . . Apparently Ehrlichman told him he had evidence that the P [Haldeman's usual abbreviation for 'President'] knew about the fake cable about Diem, and that the P was really the one who ordered all these acts. . . ." Ehrlichman later wrote: "I was aware of the Nixon-Colson-Hunt effort to produce the *Life* piece."

A similar such incident occurred during the 1972 presidential campaign, after Alabama Governor Wallace had been shot in an assassination attempt. As reported in detail later, Nixon would at that time discuss with Charles Colson the notion of planting false evidence in the would-be assassin's apartment—

material that would smear him as a radical leftist. He appeared to approve the idea.

Would not the Richard Nixon who connived at such deceptions as president have been prepared, as a young, zealous congressman, to plot the framing of Alger Hiss? This scenario seems plausible if, as seems possible, he had already been assured confidentially but authoritatively that according to impeccable sources that could not be disclosed, Hiss was indeed guilty.

In years to come, as Nixon's fortunes rose and disastrously fell, and as Hiss continued to pursue his crusade to prove his innocence, both men knew the ultimate key to the case rested in a place that was inaccessible, the files of Soviet intelligence. If Hiss had been a Soviet agent, then Soviet intelligence should have a record of it. So it was that after the Soviet Union collapsed, at a time both men knew their own days were numbered, Nixon and Hiss each relayed messages to Moscow.

In 1991, seeking definitive corroboration of what he had long believed, Nixon sent an emissary to General Dmitri Volkogonov, an adviser to President Boris Yeltsin and the chairman of the commission on the KGB and military intelligence archives. The director of the Nixon presidential library, John Taylor, followed suit, as, some months later, did Alger Hiss. In October 1992 Volkogonov wrote to Hiss with what sounded like an unequivocal response. "Not a single document—and a great amount of material has been studied—substantiates the allegation that Mr. A. Hiss collaborated with the intelligence services of the Soviet Union. . . . You can tell Alger Hiss that the heavy weight should be lifted from his heart."

The *New York Times* featured the story on its front page, and it was covered prominently by the international media. "It's what I've been fighting for for forty-four years," said Hiss, by then nearly ninety years old. Nixon, at home in New Jersey, refused to speak to the press, but privately he exploded. "Hiss was a goddamned spy, and they still don't want to admit that I was right." He remained furious for weeks.

Dimitri Simes, the Russian affairs specialist who had delivered Nixon's original letter, hurried back to confer with Volkogonov. A month later the general issued new statements conceding that his search had perhaps not been thorough enough. By then, however, the media was taking little notice, leaving Nixon to splutter that "they put the lies in headlines, but the truth they bury back in corset ads."

Before Nixon died, however, there came what appeared to be a measure of vindication. Even as Hiss was triumphing in his "not guilty" headlines, a historian was turning up damaging information about him in Hungarian secret police files. These documents recorded the responses under interrogation of Noel Field, an American who had known Hiss and worked with him at the State Department and whom Chambers had also linked to Communist espionage. Field had fled behind the Iron Curtain after the war, only to spend five years in prison on charges that he was an *American* spy. According to the Hungarian files, he told his captors Hiss had confided that he was "working for the Soviet secret service" and had tried to recruit him "for espionage." Field insisted that he had demurred, explaining that he was already working for Soviet intelligence.

Are these assertions credible, given that they were made in jail, where Field claimed he was starved and beaten, and at a time when he was desperate to prove that his loyalties had always been to the Soviets?[9] Perhaps not. Field's claims seem to dovetail with similar statements made in 1948 by Hede Massing, a courier for a Soviet spy ring and one of Field's associates.[10] They are also consistent with messages reported by Allen Weinstein, a veteran writer on the Hiss case, to have been located recently in previously unseen Soviet files.

Weinstein, the author of *Perjury: The Hiss-Chambers Case,* followed up on the Volkogonov fiasco by seeking access to old files of the NKVD, a forerunner of the KGB. After help from the current Russian intelligence service and its former director, Yevgeny Primakov—later Russia's prime minister—Weinstein discovered at least ten messages purportedly sent from the United States to Moscow and vice versa in 1936 and 1938.[11] All appear to refer to Hiss.

One, sent by Massing, tells in detail how Hiss had asked Field to gather information for the Soviets. The name Hiss appears here in clear text—as it does in two other messges sent by an NKVD agent. Others, referring to "Lawyer," said to have been one of the code names for Hiss,[12] debate the problems caused by Hiss's contacts. Still another message discusses the risk that a recent recruit "might guess that Hiss belongs to our family." Yet another refers to Hiss as having first been "implanted" into the State Department and "sent to the Neighbors later." ("The Neighbors" is accepted code for the GRU, Soviet Military Intelligence. Chambers had testified that he and Hiss worked specifically for the GRU.)

In 1990 and 1994, although without supporting documentation, two former Soviet intelligence operatives further implicated Hiss. Oleg Gordievsky, a senior KGB defector who had worked on an in-house history of the agency, wrote that Hiss had been a Soviet agent. Pavel Sudoplatov, who held high positions in Soviet intelligence in the Stalin era, claimed in a memoir that Hiss had been "close to . . . our active intelligence operators in the United States" but that "there was no indication that he was a paid or controlled agent." Sudoplatov too suggested Hiss was linked to the GRU.[13]

Such claims by the former Soviet agent, however, cannot be relied upon. In a 1996 memoir, another former Soviet intelligence officer, Vitaly Pavlov, decried Gordievsky's claims about Hiss, dismissing them as "the pure fabrication of a traitor." Pavlov said Hiss was not a Soviet agent.

In 1996, after Nixon's death but while Hiss was still alive, the National Security Agency in Washington released a series of long-withheld intercepts of Soviet messages, known by the code word VENONA. One, deciphered by the Army Security Agency, was sent from Washington to Moscow. Dated March

30, 1945, it reports on a conversation with someone named ALES, who, with his relatives,[14] had been working for the GRU since 1935, concentrating on military information. The report quotes ALES as saying that on a visit he paid to Moscow after the Yalta Conference, the deputy Soviet foreign minister had passed on the GRU's gratitude. ALES and his fellow traitors had, moreover, been awarded Soviet decorations. (See facsimile, p. 493.)

A footnote, appended by a U.S. intelligence analyst, reads: "ALES: Probably Alger Hiss." By the time this document was made public, the aged Hiss had only months to live. Speaking through his son, he said he was not ALES. Yet two additional reports, said to be from NKVD files, were published by historian Weinstein. They too refer to ALES, are in the same time frame, and contain details that may be consistent with the idea that ALES was Hiss. Weinstein also noted that of the four State Department officials who had flown to Moscow from Yalta, only Hiss has ever come under suspicion of espionage.

"Alger Hiss was most likely a Soviet agent," a *New York Times* editorial intoned in 1998. Had he lived to hear of these developments, Richard Nixon would doubtless have been delighted. As things stand, however, the newly available data from the old Soviet Union are not proof that Hiss was rightly convicted, at least not the sort of proof that history requires.

The identification of ALES as Hiss is suggestive but must for now be regarded as tentative. We have not yet been able to examine copies of the NKVD reports that appear to be so damaging, and Weinstein reportedly never saw the originals for himself. The one person who apparently did have access to them was Weinstein's coauthor for the book in which the reports are published, Alexander Vassiliev, and he was a retired KGB officer. The supposed NKVD reports were produced as the result of a cash-for-documents deal between Weinstein and his publisher and the association of former KGB officers. Weinstein did not respond to repeated attempts to make contact during the writing of this book.

It can be argued that the identification of ALES as Hiss is less than convincing. John Lowenthal, a lawyer who has long been a student of the subject and who maintains Hiss was innocent, has noted that—unlike the ALES of the 1945 message—Hiss was never accused of betraying "military" information. As he reads it, moreover, the syntax of the message refers not to ALES as having gone to Moscow from Yalta, but a Soviet official. Finally, in an article due to be published in the fall of 2000—and shared with the author—Lowenthal produced a new denial from a Russian official source that Hiss had ever worked for Moscow.

Meanwhile many other important files remained closed, including other Soviet records, and ironically—even though the House Un-American Activities Committee is long defunct–HUAC's own documents. These were sealed, in 1976, for an additional fifty years. Until we have full access, the Hiss controversy will continue to be debated.

A fascinating question, still unresolved, is whether Nixon's secret sources—J. Edgar Hoover, Allen Dulles, or other OSS/CIA contacts—were aware by

1948 of the deciphered VENONA messages—and of the ALES cable in particular—that seem to point to Hiss's guilt. It is not clear, as of this writing, just when the possibly compromising ALES message was first decoded by U.S. intelligence. A new release of the document, provided to the author in the summer of 2000, appears to establish that the basic text had been cracked at least by 1949. We know, too, that the first breakthrough in decoding the VENONA material had come as early as 1946—well before Nixon began pursuing Hiss.

The Army Security Agency severely restricted access to VENONA—it seems that even President Truman was not allowed in on the secret. FBI Director Hoover, however, apparently was in the know, for his agents were working alongside the ASA staff as they gradually broke the code.

According to the available record, the fledgling CIA was not in the immediate loop on VENONA. The chairman of the Joint Chiefs of Staff, Omar Bradley, however, had authority to brief "anyone else in authority" at his discretion. We do not know if this included the former OSS chief, William Donovan, whose organization had by then been disbanded. Yet because of his eminence and not least because it was he who had provided the army with the tool that enabled it to start cracking the Soviet cipher in the first place—a partially burned Soviet codebook salvaged from a World War II battlefield—Donovan may have been kept apprised of the findings.

If Donovan was privy to compromising VENONA information on Hiss, then Allen Dulles may well have learned of it too.[15] If he did—and if as reported he briefed Nixon on the case—then therein may perhaps lie the explanation for Nixon's confidence in his pursuit of Hiss. Heavy hints from the world of U.S. intelligence, along with the information he was receiving from the FBI, may have led Nixon to feel he could safely press the matter beyond what the publicly available evidence seemed to justify.[16]

Whether Nixon was being manipulated by others, or driven by his own overweening ambition, the Hiss case was a paradigm for his entire career—in which several themes were paramount:

❖ Delusion, of himself and others. While the affair brought him fame, he could not resist exaggerating his own role in it. "Pure bullshit!" Robert Stripling, HUAC's chief investigator, said of the *Six Crises* account, "Mr. Nixon did not break the Hiss case." Nixon's intimate journalist friend, Walter Trohan, said Nixon did not develop information in the affair; rather, "It was handed to him."

❖ An addiction to intrigue. "He developed a weakness for playing cops and robbers in the Hiss case," Trohan reflected in 1974 in a letter to an FBI friend. "Maybe this led him to countenance Watergate."

❖ A vengeful desire for retribution against those who failed to do what he wanted. Nixon pilloried Samuel Kaufman, the judge in Hiss's first trial, which ended with a hung jury, and pressed for an inquiry into his fitness to serve on the bench. He also wanted the foreman of the jury prosecuted for alleged left-wing bias.

❖ The obsession with the Ivy League elite that he saw as his perennial enemy. "They couldn't bear," he said, speaking of a posh dinner party he attended during the case, "to find one of their own, like Hiss, being involved in this kind of thing. . . . Those attitudes were all crap, but that was what I had to fight against."

❖ A perception of himself as a marked man. "Those sons of bitches are out to get me," he said during the 1952 campaign. ". . . [T]hey tried to get me, and they'll try to get anybody that had anything to do with the Hiss case." Meanwhile he himself would repeatedly be out to get others, from Adlai Stevenson to Edward Kennedy.

❖ A tendency to fly into a rage and to blame others when things went wrong. "This is all your fault!" he had shouted at Nicholas Vazzana, an attorney hired to assist investigation on the Chambers side of the case, when for a while it seemed that the Pumpkin Papers were about to be exposed as a fraud. "What are you going to do about it?" Nixon's language turned abusive, and both Vazzana and Stripling thought him almost hysterical.

❖ Driving himself beyond his limits, putting himself and his family under intolerable pressure. Even early in the Hiss case, Nixon admitted later, "I was spending as much as eighteen to twenty hours a day at my office. I deliberately refused to take time off for relaxation or a break. . . . I was 'mean' to live with at home and with my friends. I was quick-tempered. . . . I lost interest in eating and skipped meals. . . . Getting to sleep became more and more difficult." During the Hiss case, for the first time but not the last, Nixon started using sleeping pills.

His mother remembered a weekend when he and Pat came to stay at the elder Nixons' new home, the farm in Pennsylvania. "He wouldn't even come in and eat supper. He just walked from one corner of the yard to the other. I went to him and told him that if he didn't give up this whole Hiss question, he was not going to be on earth very long. I will never forget his pale face and his gaunt look. . . ."

Even thirty years later, her daughter Julie found when writing a book about her mother, Pat Nixon spoke only reluctantly of the Hiss episode. She had found in her husband's involvement "an absorption that was almost frightening." She, and even Nixon's parents, had repeatedly accompanied Richard on visits to Chambers and his family, starting a relationship that endured throughout the Nixon vice presidency. Chambers was entertained at the Nixons' home in Washington, and Nixon and Pat trekked out to the farm to dispense, as Chambers put it, "some loving care for us." To the Chambers children, their father recalled, Nixon in time became " 'Nixie,' the kind and the good."

Yet while Chambers long regarded Nixon as his champion, recently released correspondence shows that he also perceived his faults. He thought Nixon lacked real political conviction or vision and believed he was less than loyal to old friends. "I rather pity him," was Chambers's final verdict.

The Hiss affair was an episode that marked the Nixons, a time of unimagined success yet one that presaged a dark future. Pat recalled it as "a difficult time for us." Even before her husband plunged into the Hiss case, she told Julie, she had already felt "deep discontent" at the way their married life was going. Soon the Nixon marriage would be in crisis. Within three years, Nixon would be seeking help from a psychotherapist.

9

Whenever a man has cast a longing eye on offices,
a rottenness begins in his conduct.

—*Thomas Jefferson, in 1799*

In February 1950, on Lincoln's Birthday weekend, a drunken man climbed onto a plane in Washington, D.C. In his briefcase he carried a bottle of whiskey and the rough draft of a speech. Senator Joseph McCarthy was on his way to address the Ohio County Women's Club in Wheeling, West Virginia, the only campaign speaking slot the Republican National Committee could find for him. The good ladies of Wheeling were expecting him to talk about social issues. What they got instead was the infamous speech claiming that the State Department was riddled with Communists, the allegation that launched the American Inquisition. Passages in it were lifted virtually verbatim from a speech on Hiss made in the House two weeks earlier by Richard Nixon. McCarthy said: "One thing to remember . . . is that we are not dealing with spies who get 30 pieces of silver to steal the blueprint of a new weapon. We are dealing with a far more sinister type of activity because it permits the enemy to guide and shape our policy." In his speech, Nixon had warned: "The great lesson . . . is that we are not just dealing with espionage agents who get 30 pieces of silver to obtain the blueprint of a new weapon . . . this is a far more sinister type of activity, because it permits the enemy to guide and shape our policy."

Challenged by reporters to reveal what hard information he had, McCarthy responded characteristically. "Listen, you bastards," he bellowed, "I'm not going to tell you anything. . . . I've got a pailful of shit, and I'm going to use it where it does me the most good." Although his charges were mostly reckless and hopelessly inaccurate, McCarthy was soon riding high as the right's champion hunter of Communists.

Nixon stated in his memoirs that he had found McCarthy "personally likeable, if irresponsibly impulsive. At the end I felt sorry for him, as a man whose zeal and thirst for publicity were leading him and others to destruction." In *Six Crises,* published when McCarthyism was still a raw issue, Nixon did not mention McCarthy once. It is true that as McCarthy was gradually being exposed as an alcoholic and a fraud, Nixon—by then rising to a prominence that required him to appear responsible—prudently distanced himself from the senator's excesses. Historically, though, the two men will remain forever joined.

Bobby Baker, Lyndon Johnson's future aide, first became acquainted with McCarthy as a Senate page, and the two became friendly enough to go to the races together. Baker also picked up information through his wife, Dorothy, who worked both for Nixon and for Senator Pat McCarran, a fanatical rightwinger much courted by McCarthy. Baker concluded that McCarthy was one of Nixon's "real hard-core buddies." Nixon went out of his way to campaign for the man he called "my good friend" in the 1952 elections, when it had long since become apparent that McCarthy's rampage was no more than a witch-hunt. Senior journalists like Stewart Alsop, Eric Sevareid, and Walter Cronkite reached much the same conclusion—namely, that as Cronkite put it in 1996, Nixon was "in the same ideological league as McCarthy and his followers." Even Nixon's ally Tom Dewey characterized him as "a respectable McCarthy."

As vice president Nixon attended McCarthy's 1953 wedding. In private, even in the face of McCarthy's evident malfeasance, his loyalty did not waver. The psychotherapist Nixon was seeing by then, Dr. Arnold Hutschnecker, recalled in 1995 how his patient had remonstrated with him—at the height of the McCarthy period—when the doctor expressed disapproval of the senator. Nixon seemed stunned and insisted, "But McCarthy's a friend of mine."

It was only in 1953 that Nixon moved publicly to criticize McCarthy— and that at President Eisenhower's behest. The senator's sidekick Roy Cohn thought Nixon's posture on the matter that of an ambitious opportunist. "When they finally decided to do McCarthy in," he said, "Nixon was the fellow they selected, and he was perfectly willing to turn on his conservative friends and cut their throats—one, two, three. . . . Nixon was a superb hatchet man."

A similar comment on the Nixon-McCarthy relationship comes from a leader of the Soviet Union, but it was perceptive even considering the source. "When McCarthy's star started to fade," Nikita Khrushchev told an American visitor in the sixties, "Nixon turned his back on him. So he was an *unprincipled* puppet, the most dangerous kind."

In 1954 Nixon asked a colleague, James Bassett, to dine with him at a favorite Washington restaurant, La Salle de Bois. He downed three gins, followed by white wine with oysters, guffawed at a dirty joke, and then said brusquely of McCarthy: "It's probably time we dumped him." In the same conversation, Bassett noted in his journal, "RN said he's 100% for the President, and will do anything needed. But anything!" Even so, as presiding officer when the Senate finally brought McCarthy's antics to an end a few months later, Nixon used his prerogative to sweeten the pill, striking out the word "censure" from the wording of a motion condemning McCarthy. He also was among the mourners at the funeral when McCarthy died of drink in 1957.

One day in 1950, a congresswoman from California found herself being warned about Nixon by the venerable Speaker of the House, Sam Rayburn. Rayburn, who thought him "the next thing to McCarthy in the United States," warned his colleague "not to make any mistakes." The warning was timely, for the congresswoman was Helen Gahagan Douglas, then about to battle Nixon for a seat in the U.S. Senate.

Nixon's run for the Senate was a virtual replay of the 1946 campaign against Voorhis—this time with even cruder use of dirty tricks and inflammatory rhetoric. His tactics reflected the fact that he knew precisely why he had decided to run against Representative Douglas. "The House," he told a friend, "offered too slow a road to leadership, and I went for broke."

Kyle Palmer, the power broker at the *Los Angeles Times,* claimed it was he who first pitched the Senate idea to Nixon, and certainly the *Times* and most of the California press gave him unconditional support. Of twelve papers in the state, nine backed Nixon. The *Times* did not run a single picture of Douglas during the campaign. The press baron who ran most of the other papers in the state, William Randolph Hearst, arranged for the planting of pro-Nixon articles. Orchestrated "letters" were placed in the correspondence columns. A search began for any photographs of Douglas that might help brand her as a leftist.

Douglas, a forty-nine-year-old former Broadway star and opera singer, had begun her political career as a left-wing Democrat. She was both a supporter of the New Deal and a friend of Eleanor Roosevelt. While outspokenly anti-Communist, she was also—to her detriment—in favor of reining in big business, not least the oil industry. She proved no match for the Nixon operation, once again managed by Murray Chotiner.

Along with his other functions, Chotiner masterminded a public relations blitz similar to the one during the congressional campaign of 1946. Skywriting planes traced out Nixon's name over California's beaches. A blimp pelted the Los Angeles city streets with leaflets promising voters that if they answered the phone with the magic mantra "Vote for Nixon," and if the call came from Nixon headquarters, then they could win:

PRIZES GALORE!!!

Electric clocks, Silex coffee makers with heating units—General Electric automatic toasters—silver salt and pepper shakers, sugar and creamer sets, candy and butter dishes, etc., etc.

The Republicans were especially proud of a four-page ad that resembled a photo spread in *Life* magazine. "Practically nothing but pictures," said a grinning Chotiner. Nixon was sold aggressively as "an ardent American," "the perfect example of the Uncommon Man."

The *Los Angeles Daily News* had dubbed Douglas the Pink Lady, and more than half a million of Nixon's anti-Douglas leaflets were printed on pink paper. In public Chotiner was to claim that the color of the paper had been fortuitous, that pink had been the only choice available. In private, in the company of fellow Republicans, he would say, "It just seemed to appeal to us." Then he would smile sardonically.

Nixon's people seized Douglas's own flyers by the thousands and dumped them in the ocean. Meanwhile they produced phony Douglas propaganda purporting to have been issued by the "Communist League of Negro Women," a surefire way to alienate white middle-class voters.

Flying squads of pickets pursued Douglas at her speaking engagements, heckling her at every stop. During a speech at the University of Southern California "students" let fly with water siphons, drenching the Democrat. One of the ringleaders was reportedly Patrick Hillings, a young man soon to become Nixon's close associate; another, Joe Holt, later joined Nixon's staff. At times the contest turned violent. Douglas's San Diego organizer was forced off the road by other drivers. She herself was pelted with red ink, and even stones, and began traveling with bodyguards.

The Democrats also resorted to questionable tactics, but they occurred late in the campaign and were primarily an effort to strike back. A student named Dick Tuck, who later became a specialist in anti-Nixon pranks,[1] posed as an advance man for a Nixon speech and ensured that only a handful of people turned up. Pat Nixon, who again went on the stump with her husband, claimed he was often prevented from speaking by labor union members. Enraged Douglas workers once overturned a Nixon campaign car.

Douglas eventually tried to lash back at Nixon by "Red-baiting" *him*—a nonsensical ploy that failed—and by talking about Republican "young men in dark shirts," evoking fascism. Such efforts were not only wrongheaded but pointless, for nothing the Democrats could muster could outdo the scale of the propaganda pumped out by the Nixon side.

According to Douglas supporters, the last days of the campaign brought an onslaught of anonymous phone calls to voters, just as in the Nixon push against Voorhis. "Did you know that Helen Douglas is a Communist?" a caller would ask, then hang up. It was later claimed that this was a massive, statewide operation allegedly involving more than half a million calls.

Pat Nixon's account of the campaign, published later in a homey story in the *Saturday Evening Post,* suggested, without stating it directly, that her husband had been short of funds. "A friend who is an automobile dealer lent us a used station wagon," she wrote, "and we painted it with big signs . . . and with it we covered California." The Nixons did have a station wagon, in which they drove massive distances, but the vehicle was only a few months old and came with a chauffeur. The friend who provided it, Henry Kearns, was one of Nixon's wealthy backers.

Once again, Nixon had heavy financial backing from power brokers in the oil business—Nixon was pushing for the oil policy that best favored their interests—and from big industry, real estate, and banking. One supporter, another car dealer, was Henry Haldeman, father of Nixon's future White House chief of staff.

To fund this campaign, the net was also cast outside the state, among the oil tycoons of Texas. Two of them, Clint Murchison and Sid Richardson, soon welcomed Nixon to Del Charro, the luxury California resort Murchison owned. "They spoke to Nixon like he was an office boy," recalled the resort's manager, Allan Witwer.

Serving on Nixon's finance committee was Dana Smith, heir to a lumber fortune and a Pasadena attorney who within two years would be at the center of the furor that nearly cost Nixon the vice presidency, the scandal over behind-the-scenes cash supplied to Nixon by California businessmen.

There was, too, illicit money: five thousand dollars funneled to Nixon, against Senate rules and through a crooked fixer, by Senator Owen Brewster of Maine, and seventy-five thousand dollars strong-armed out of the gambling fraternity by the mobster Mickey Cohen.*

There is no knowing now how much money was poured into the Nixon campaign. Figures available at the Nixon Library suggest that it received more than two hundred thousand dollars. This, however, may be a fraction of the true amount. Billboards alone, by Chotiner's reckoning, cost "around $50,000." Some estimates suggest that the real expenditure may have been between $1 million and nearly $2 million, fabulous sums by the standards of the time, whichever was correct. The Nixon people had generated so much money that they gave away cash to Republican candidates in other contests. The Douglas campaign, by contrast, was impoverished, so much so that at one point it had no money to pay printers for brochures.

In such a situation, in the anti-Communist ferment of 1950, with the Korean War in its first months and American casualties mounting daily, the "Pink Lady" was doomed. Yet Nixon did not behave as though he expected to triumph. On election day he sat on the beach in the drizzle with Pat, then went to the movies by himself. He emerged "sure that we were licked," only to learn that he had won a fabulous victory.

*As described in chapter 6.

Nixon made light in his memoirs of the fact that the Senate fight earned him the nickname that stuck with him for the rest of his life, "Tricky Dick."[2] He made no mention of the huge funding, the one-sided media barrage, or the organized heckling by his supporters. Instead, he wrote plaintively of Democratic heckling, casting himself as the offended party.[3]

Nixon himself bore ultimate responsibility for the campaign against Douglas. Chotiner recalled him as having been "a perfectionist . . . a general who demanded absolute precision and carefully planned coordination in every move. . . ." "Nixon knew everything that was going on," said Tom Dixon, who as in the past traveled with him as radio announcer and warm-up man. Interviewed in 1997, Dixon and his wife recalled a Nixon who demanded that an audience be "screaming ecstatically" before he would go onstage. Occasionally he had to delay facing the audience until he had recovered from tantrums so violent he seemed "out of control" to Dixon. In 1946 Dixon had voted for his employer. In 1950 Nixon's conduct of the campaign so disillusioned him that he voted for no one.

Further testimony suggesting that Nixon personally favored malicious attacks on Douglas comes from a memoir by the press aide who traveled with him during the campaign, William Arnold. Arnold recalled his employer's reaction when told that his opponent had made "somewhat unflattering" remarks about him in a speech. "Did she say that?" Nixon asked. "Why, I'll castrate her." Arnold commented sardonically that such retribution would be difficult, since Douglas was a woman. "I don't care," riposted Nixon. "I'll do it anyway."

It was Nixon who lowered the already abysmal tone of the contest by telling audiences that Douglas was "pink right down to her underpants." He even resorted to a sexual smear, insinuating that she had slept with President Truman. Nixon was careful to make such pronouncements at gatherings away from the press or at least from the tiny portion of the press that opposed him. He was equally guarded about ethnic slurs. Douglas's husband, the actor Melvyn Douglas, had been born Hesselberg, of a Jewish father. When an extremist, Gerald Smith, goaded Douglas for being married to a Jew, Nixon disassociated himself.

The Nixon anonymous phone call campaign did however include "Did you know?" messages that whispered about Douglas's Jewish connection. Nixon also sometimes referred to his opponent disingenuously as Helen Hesselberg, a name that neither she nor her husband used. He would then correct himself, as though it had been an unintentional slip. He did this at his sole platform appearance with Douglas, but only after his opponent had left the meeting.

As the campaign went into top gear, during a brief visit to New York, Nixon had sat drinking whiskey into the small hours with the columnist Murray Kempton. Kempton was to recall Nixon's saying how he hated having to end Helen Douglas's political career, because he admired her so much. Years later, asked by the British publisher David Astor to explain his campaign tactics, Nixon reportedly "cast down his eyes with a look of modest contrition" and explained, "I want you to understand. I was a very young man."[4] In 1950 he was thirty-seven and a veteran of four years in the House of Representatives.

And now he was a U.S. senator, and his star continued to rise. Yet for all his success, or perhaps because of it, Nixon was starting to lose his balance.

10

*His fragile masculine self-image always
drew him to the strong and the tough—
and the ultimate power of the presidency.*

—Dr. Arnold Hutschnecker, psychosomatic medicine specialist
and psychotherapist consulted by Richard Nixon

The strain on Nixon had started to show long before he reached the Senate.
There had been the twenty-hour workdays during the Hiss case, the
skipped meals, the refusal to take time out for relaxation. It made him quick-
tempered with colleagues, as well as "mean" with his family. When he had
trouble sleeping, he resorted to sleeping pills. The campaign against Helen
Douglas had only driven him to greater limits.

As a senator he continued to work obsessively. When his secretaries left for
the day—Nixon had nine—their boss regularly went on working into the
evening. He often did not get home for dinner, if at all. "Many times," said
Earl Chapman, a friend in whom Pat confided, he worked "until the small
hours. . . . Maybe if he gets through early enough he'll come back home, but
many times he'll curl up on the couch and get a few hours' sleep. Then he'll get
a little breakfast and shave, and go right down to the Senate chambers. . . ."

A month or two into this punishing schedule Nixon began to be plagued
with persistent back and neck pain. The first doctors he consulted were no
help, and he found himself perusing a book on psychosomatic illness pressed
on him by the outgoing senator from California, Sheridan Downey. The book
was *The Will to Live,* by Dr. Arnold Hutschnecker, an easy-to-read best-seller

written for people "in the grips of acute conflict." It emphasized "the interaction of the human psyche and bodily reactions."

Hutschnecker was described by one academic as "a sort of Pavlovian and Freudian synthesizer." He himself professed that he "treated my patients as if they are my children." Famous clients over the years reportedly included the actresses Elizabeth Taylor, Celeste Holm, and Rita Hayworth and the novelist Erich Maria Remarque. An Austrian emigré who graduated in Berlin soon after World War I, he had been working in New York City since 1936.

While he practiced internal medicine, he had early in his career been interested in the way mental and emotional disturbances affect health. By 1951, this topic had become the primary focus of his work. He dropped internal medicine completely by 1955, to specialize exclusively as a psychotherapist engaged in what he called "psychoanalytically oriented treatment of emotional problems."[1]

Dr. Hutschnecker had, in the words of one interviewer, "a touch of the missionary zeal of a Billy Graham, of the cheery optimism of a Norman Vincent Peale, of the psychic beliefs of a Jeane Dixon, and an accent a bit reminiscent of Peter Sellers as Dr. Strangelove." Nixon, as we have seen, publicly associated himself with both Graham and Peale, and, according to one close aide, credited the prophecies of Dixon, the popular astrologer.

In *The Will to Live*, Hutschnecker dealt with a range of human complaints: chronic fatigue, hypertension, ulcers, insomnia, the inability to love, aggression, impotence in men and frigidity in women. On reading it, Nixon took a step that was to lead to a long and trusting relationship with the doctor—as well as to future political embarrassment. He asked one of his new secretaries, Rose Mary Woods, to telephone Hutschnecker and ask if he would take on a new private patient. Woods, just starting the loyal service to Nixon that would one day give her a notorious role in the Watergate saga, told Hutschnecker her boss was "really interested in something in *The Will to Live* that related to himself."

So it was that, probably in the early fall of 1951, Nixon went to New York and presented himself at Dr. Hutschnecker's imposing office at 829 Park Avenue. The doctor's wife, acting as his receptionist that day, entered the inner sanctum to announce that the young senator had arrived—and looked "very tense." He was to see Hutschnecker several times that first year and in the four years that followed.

From 1952, when he became vice president, Nixon arrived for his consultations—five that year—openly, in the official limousine, and with a Secret Service escort. In 1955, though, when Hutschnecker began to specialize solely in psychotherapy, Nixon became worried about publicity. After Walter Winchell had made a snide reference to the visits in one of his columns, he began taking his physical ailments to a military doctor in Washington.

By that time he and Hutschnecker had established a close relationship and met privately whenever Nixon came to New York. "I remember going to his suite in the Waldorf," the doctor recalled, "and hearing him singing so happily in the shower. And I said to myself, 'Aha, my treatment is working.'"

The discreet meetings continued throughout the fifties. When Nixon called, said Hutschnecker, "He'd never say: 'I have a problem.' He'd say, 'Could we have breakfast?' And I'd go." "He needed me. It was what we call a transference, a trust. He came to me when he had decisions to make. Or when something was pending, and it troubled him."

Nixon did not always reveal what was on his mind. After one 1952 visit Hutschnecker was astonished to learn from the press of his patient's possible selection as Eisenhower's vice presidential running mate. It must have been the matter uppermost in Nixon's mind during the consultation, yet he had failed to mention it. Later the same year, however, when enmeshed in allegations of having taken under-the-table money—the fund scandal*—Nixon tried frantically to reach the doctor.

"I went out for a while one day, and when I came back, my wife said, 'Where were you? The senator's office was calling every ten minutes.' They had been holding the plane, and the last call had been just a few minutes before, but Mr. Nixon could not wait any longer. . . . I learned later about the secret fund charges."

The psychotherapist also made a number of trips to see Nixon in his Washington office. During one lunch he astonished the senator by declaring that he considered both Joe McCarthy and Secretary of State John Foster Dulles mentally disturbed. "Dr. Hutschnecker . . ." Nixon wrote in a 1959 note to Rose Woods, "I want to have him come down . . . check with me as to whether I want it before we go on vacation." The following year, during the campaign against John F. Kennedy, there was another summons.

In early 1961, within weeks of the Republican handover of the White House, Nixon was back at the doctor's office. The following year he consulted Hutschnecker before his disastrous bid for the governorship of California, having ignored the doctor's advice not to run. A journalist who happened to live next door to the building that housed Hutschnecker's Park Avenue offices, Harriet Van Horne, recalled seeing Nixon's "grim visage" passing beneath the canopy. "I once asked a building employee," Horne recalled, "'Does Mr. Nixon visit friends at 829?' 'Naw,' came the reply. 'He comes to see the shrink.'"

During the presidency, however, Nixon's aides saw to it that the link to Hutschnecker was virtually severed, though he would make two visits to the White House, the first to discuss violent crime and the second after the U.S. incursion into Cambodia in 1970. The doctor had long hoped that Nixon would swiftly get the United States out of Vietnam, and a friend quoted him as saying, "Pavlovian technique had been helping him brainwash Nixon into becoming a

*See page 118.

better person." He believed he could "remake the man into a dove" on South-east Asia. But the second trip was to misfire. As reported in context later, Nixon would end the meeting in frustration after a few minutes. There were a number of other meetings outside the White House, though, but only when Nixon felt he could avoid detection—not only by the press but, the doctor implied, by his own aides.

Later, after the resignation, the doctor would visit Nixon at San Clemente. By then he seemed, Hutschnecker thought, "like a confessant." They met for the last time in 1993, when Nixon asked the doctor to accompany him to Pat's funeral. He was seated, at Nixon's request, in the area allotted to the family. The doctor did not attend the former president's own funeral the following year because, as he put it, there was no one left for him to help.

A few cautious comments aside, Dr. Hutschnecker did not speak publicly about his patient over the years. He avoided putting Nixon's name on prescriptions, kept his name out of the appointment book, and apparently did not ask for payment. Although he is said to have been less guarded in private—snippets of his dinner party asides leaked out on occasion—the doctor was careful to shield Nixon as medical ethics required.

In 1995, however, he gave the first of three lengthy interviews for this book. Toward the end of the former president's life, Hutschnecker said, he had written authorizing him to write about their relationship, assuming Hutschnecker would survive him. It must have seemed a reasonable gamble that he would not, for the doctor was nearly ninety at the time. Yet Nixon did die first, and Hutschnecker wrote the draft of a manuscript about his experiences with his patient, though he kept it at home unpublished. He had felt constrained, he said, to "leave out a lot."

Astonishingly sprightly at ninety-seven and living testimony to his own advice on how to achieve longevity, Dr. Hutschnecker received his interviewer at his home in sylvan northern Connecticut. He answered questions in a study cluttered with the bric-a-brac of a long professional life, including a photograph of Richard Nixon—inscribed in 1977 "in appreciation of friendship"—and a Nixon gift of ivory elephants. Later, on the veranda, over tea laced with Irish whiskey, he talked on in his heavily German-accented English about the politician to whom he had had such exclusive access.

Restricting himself to what he felt ethically acceptable, Dr. Hutschnecker said little of Nixon's first visit, in 1951. His patient's initial complaint, he said, had been of feeling "a little nervous, irritable, and not sleeping so good. I gave him a mild sedative and told him to come back in two weeks."

Nixon, however, did not travel from Washington to New York merely to obtain a prescription for insomnia. In a brief response to a question posed by *Newsweek*, Hutschnecker once let slip that "Nixon wondered if there was an emotional cause" for what was bothering him physically. Nixon, for his part, said years later that he always believed there was a direct relation between physical and mental health.

One aspect of Nixon's problem, the doctor revealed years later, was depression. Pat Nixon spoke of her husband's having been "more depressed than she ever remembered" early in the election year of 1956. The eminent *New York Times* journalist Harrison Salisbury recalled a meeting in early 1960, the year of the Nixon-Kennedy campaign, with a businessman who had served with Nixon in the war, who, like other acquaintances in the service, knew him as Nick. "Say," the businessman asked Salisbury, "is Nick still seeing that shrink of his in New York?" He then explained to a surprised Salisbury that Nixon "had severe ups and downs, and it was not easy to pull him up when he fell into depression"— as he had, the businessmen said, at the time of the conversation with Salisbury.[2] Len Garment, a Nixon colleague from the mid-sixties—himself no stranger to the malady—said Nixon suffered from "powerful depression."

Hutschnecker told the author that his patient had at first been reluctant to talk about himself but gradually became more open. As the doctor put it, he prided himself on being able to "lure patients into therapy." He eventually built up enough trust that—some four years into their relationship—Nixon "said he could really tell me everything. It was safe." The doctor never did get Nixon to accept a full course of psychotherapy, but they seem to have found some sort of mutually acceptable middle ground.

As early as the end of the second session, Hutschnecker said, he was certain his patient's sharp intellect and outward self-confidence masked "deep-seated inhibitions." He thought "Nixon was an enigma, not just to me but to himself. And I . . . had to try to understand what motivated his superdrive, and—paradoxically—his inhibitions."

As other information suggests, Hutschnecker believed that Frank Nixon had been a "brutal and cruel" man who had beaten his sons and "brutalized" his wife. While the doctor viewed this as an enormously important factor in Nixon's makeup, the heart of the problem, he believed, was Hannah herself. "Clinically," Hutschnecker said, "it started with the mother. Nixon's mother was *so* religious he was trapped in many ways. I wouldn't say that he was really religious but he was totally devoted to his mother—like a robot if you want. Even to the last, you know, he was kneeling down to pray every day. He was completely smothered. His mother was really his downfall."

While Nixon's father died in 1956, Hannah lived on until 1967, passing away just a year before her son was elected president. In 1960, during his losing fight against Kennedy, she had still been very active. Hutschnecker thought Nixon's performance in the televised debates then—as well as earlier, in his self-revealing 1952 TV speech answering charges about illicit funds—was affected by the notion that his mother could see him. "I was convinced," he said, "of the connection between being in front of the camera and being in front of his mother. . . . Multiply the singular face of a critical mother watching the flaws, to the flaws seen by millions, then one can better comprehend the telegenic awkwardness of Nixon. . . . I believe that the image of the saintly but stern face of his mother defeated him more than any other factor. . . . He wanted his mother to believe him perfect. That was his problem."

Looking back, Hutschnecker suspected Nixon had "guilt feelings" for having pursued politics in the vindictive style of his father rather than on the "saintly" path of his mother. Nixon's fervent wish, the doctor felt, was that someday he would be able to say to Hannah, "Mother, I have made peace. Now I am worthy of you."

In the course of discussing Nixon's relationship with his mother, the author raised the possibility that he had suffered at some point from sexual impotence. According to James Bassett, who from 1952 became unusually close to Nixon as a press aide—and drinking companion—this was the case.

Hutschnecker denied having treated Nixon for impotence. He said, however, that his patient would "become fourteen years old, red-faced, and stammer" when matters of sex were raised. The doctor did speak a little about Pat Nixon. He had learned from her directly "how much she detested politics. She wanted a simple life . . . wanted to be a housewife. But he couldn't. He liked to be in the thick of things." On the one hand, Hutschnecker regarded Pat as "a wonderful lady . . . loyal . . ." who gave her husband limitless support and encouragement. On the other, he said Nixon viewed her as "his sun"—to a degree that was not entirely healthy. "He was devoted," said the doctor, "but that was like the relationship with his mother . . . one-sided. He became very dependent on her."

Pressed again on the alleged impotence problem, Hutschnecker hesitated. "Every boy," he said, falling back on a psychiatric staple, "has the imprint of his mother as an ideal. And unless he drowns out that ideal woman, he cannot do sex." Asked if he was applying that principle to Nixon's relationship with Pat, Hutschnecker responded, "I cannot say it," but he then added, "If someone was like a mother and was a saint, you don't have sex. That far I can go." He would say no more on the subject.

In *The Will to Live,* the book that first encouraged Nixon to consult him, Dr. Hustchnecker suggested that the late twentieth century should be named the Age of Ambivalence. In psychiatry, he wrote, "ambivalence" is a term meaning "the simultaneous existence within us of opposite emotions towards the same object or person." For Hutschnecker, it explained the darkest, most destructive side of man. Were modern man to understand this, he maintained, he would no longer have an excuse for "emotional immaturity."

The ambivalence concept, said the doctor, dealt at one blow with the constant references to the notion that there was an "old Nixon," and "a new Nixon." For Hutschnecker, it explained "the contrasting behavior of an almost puritan Nixon with the Nixon of uninhibited language and angry outbursts. It is a direct reflection of the opposing parental personalities. . . . We all judge what we see, but what could not be seen was the Quaker boy who had a 'saintly' mother and an angry father, filled with the unknown hungers and conflicts of his inner self that would become his remarkable 'sense of mission.'"

Somewhat less charitable is the view Hutschnecker shared with dinner companions one loquacious night in 1965, according to the lobbyist Robert Winter-Berger, who was present. "Nixon is happiest," the doctor said then, "either when he has no responsibility or when he has it all. When he has no responsibility, he can't be criticized for anything and he can relax and be a little boy. When he has all the responsibility, he feels he has the right to exercise it as he alone sees fit, and he can't bear to be criticized for anything at all. That's when he says or does shortsighted things, and I get a call."[3]

So it was that, although Nixon shied away from therapy, he continued to use the doctor as a kind of medical life preserver, to be consulted at times of crisis.

Hutschnecker's 1955 decision to narrow his practice to psychotherapy alone alarmed Nixon. He was well aware that should the press start probing, the fragile pretense that he was consulting the doctor purely for physical complaints was unlikely to hold up. "It is safer for a politician to go to a whorehouse than to see a psychiatrist," Hutschnecker himself once said mournfully. To protect himself, Nixon went out of his way to decry psychiatry in public and in private. "People go through that psychological bit nowadays," he told a writer in 1966. "They think they should always be reevaluating themselves. . . . That sort of juvenile self-analysis is something I've never done."

Roger Ailes, a television producer hired to make seemingly spontaneous Nixon interview programs for the 1968 campaign, remembered calling a Nixon aide to tell him the makeup of the panel for one of the shows. All was going well, Ailes reported—they had a black man, a newsman, and other professional people—until Ailes said he had booked "a Jewish doctor from Philadelphia, a psychiatrist." The aide, Len Garment, immediately rejected the idea. "Jesus Christ!" Ailes told a companion when he hung up. "You're not going to believe this, but Nixon hates psychiatrists. He's got this thing apparently. They make him very nervous. You should have heard Len on the phone! . . . Did you hear him? If I've ever heard a guy's voice turn white, that was it. He said he didn't want to go into it. But apparently Nixon won't even let one in the same room." Ailes dropped the psychiatrist and went out to look for a cabdriver to appear on the show in his place.

Three years earlier, in a late-night conversation with Garment, Nixon had said that he "would do anything to stay in public life—'except see a shrink.'" To Garment this "was a sure sign, in Nixon-speak, that despite himself, he had indeed seen a shrink." Garment learned only later about Dr. Hutschnecker.

Nixon remained concerned about the "shrink" taint even after the resignation. According to the doctor, Nixon was concerned to conceal the nature of their meeting at San Clemente. "Just say," Nixon advised him conspiratorially, "that you came to visit an old friend."

Exposure of their relationship, Nixon impressed on Hutschnecker, would lead to people's believing he "must be cuckoo" or "nuts." The irony of course is that even without knowledge of the relationship, precisely this thought did cross the minds of a good number of people. The comments that follow, many of them by men who could hardly be considered Nixon's enemies, constitute a stunning chorus of misgiving, surely not comparable with assessments of the mental state of any other president in American history.

George Christopher, a former mayor of San Francisco and senior Californian Republican, recalled that "Nixon would be depressed long before the 1962 election—kind of moody and withdrawn. There was nothing to hate about the guy at such times. He was just in a terrible state of mind, in which I think another man might have done away with himself."

Kenneth O'Donnell, John Kennedy's close confidant, was more blunt. "JFK," he said, "never trusted his mental stability." A key supporter, *San Diego Union* publisher James Copley, was troubled when he saw Nixon debating Kennedy on television. "Dick's expression was very studious," he wrote to a colleague, "but to the point where it looked almost like he was mad or disturbed."

Journalists also perceived the instability. Eric Sevareid, writing in 1960, referred to Nixon's "black spells of depression. These moods may last for an hour, or even days, when he feels 'circumstances' are against him." "At times," wrote Walter Cronkite, "he actually seemed unbalanced. I was a guest at a state dinner on one occasion when I noticed his eyes fix on the molding at the edge of the ceiling. Then they began following the molding across that side of the room, then across the adjoining side, even to the side behind him, and back along the next wall to the starting place. One would assume that he was following an intrusive beastie in its circumnavigation of the room, but I could see nothing there. . . ."

Robert Greene, senior editor of *Newsday,* spoke of "Hamlet-type moments," adding, "There was some kind of quality, or lack of quality, in Nixon in terms of his mental stability, that would have him go off into these off-drift things where nobody existed around him. . . ." *Newsweek*'s John Lindsay regarded Nixon as a "walking box of short circuits."

During the Watergate crisis the concern reached a crescendo. "He was acting so strangely," thought John Herbers of the *New York Times,* "acting obviously so deeply troubled and so weird in his actions, that it just brought on speculation." Henry Hubbard, of *Newsweek,* said that at one point most of the White House press corps believed the president had gone "off his rocker." As reported in detail later, Tip O'Neill—the House majority leader—and Special Prosecutor Archibald Cox privately had the same concern.

One of the men who lived closer to Nixon than anyone except his immediate family, a White House Secret Service agent, found him "very depressed." Deep Throat, the anonymous source quoted by the *Washington Post*'s Woodward and Bernstein, reportedly told Woodward Nixon had been "having fits of dangerous depression."

"What the men in the White House were involved in was the management of an unstable personality," concluded Theodore White. "Here was the leader of the free world in an almost shattered condition," Attorney General Richard Kleindienst recalled of the meeting at which his resignation was decided. "His sobs and distraught manner were, to me, profound and genuine. . . . Richard Nixon was President of my country and he was imperiled. If he was imperiled, my country was endangered."

Kleindienst's successor, Elliot Richardson, was said by Vice President Spiro Agnew to have believed Nixon was "losing control, emotionally and mentally." William Saxbe, who followed Richardson as attorney general, thought Nixon's actions were not those of a "reasonable man."

Alexander Butterfield, cabinet secretary and senior factotum, was struck early by Nixon's obsession with detail that seemed utterly out of proportion. It did not seem reasonable that on a trip to Yugoslavia Nixon took time to dictate a letter about "the lousy restroom facilities we had around the Mall." Butterfield characterized it as "abnormal" behavior, in "the strangest man I'd ever met . . . a strange, strange fellow."

Even Haldeman, the keeper of the gate, later agreed that Nixon was "the strangest man he ever met." As for John Ehrlichman, he told the Senate Watergate Committee in 1973, "From close observation, I can testify that the President is not paranoid, weird, psychotic on the subject of demonstrators, or hypersensitive to criticism." Three years later, asked if he would still make the same assessment, he replied curtly, "No, I would not," adding, "There was another side," he said of the man he served loyally for so long, "Like the flat, dark side of the moon."

Henry Kissinger, initially national security adviser and later secretary of state, has written of Nixon in his memoirs with compassion, yet the odder aspects of Nixon's nature surface time and again. "Nixon seemed driven by his demons," Kissinger recalled, in a description of the 1973 ceremony at which he was elevated to secretary of state. "His remarks at the swearing-in ranged from the perfunctory to the bizarre." Among other things, Nixon had relentlessly pursued the topic of Kissinger's hair, going on and on about how he was the first secretary since World War II who did not part it. At other times Kissinger emerged from his office after a phone call with Nixon—he had his staff monitor such calls—rolled his eyes, and asked, "Did you hear what that madman said?"

Just months before he joined the Nixon administration, in 1968, Kissinger had been a dinner guest at the home of Fawn Brodie, professor of history at the University of California at Los Angeles and author of an acclaimed book on

Thomas Jefferson. At the dinner, Brodie recalled, he "electrified our guests by telling them that Richard Nixon had had four years 'on the couch.'"

A decade later, when Brodie came to write her book on Nixon,[4] she asked Kissinger for an interview, reminding him of his comment about Nixon's supposed sessions with an analyst. By that time, however, having served eight years at the pinnacle of government, Kissinger no longer wished to discuss such topics. Others, including the longtime press aide James Bassett and Herbert Katcher, an attorney for the New York Psychoanalytic Association, also referred to Nixon's having received treatment from a psychoanalyst. Katcher certainly was referring to a therapist other than Dr. Hutschnecker. Did Nixon, then, at some point overcome his fear of analysis? If so, who was the psychiatrist involved?

The sketchy evidence on the subject suggests the other doctor was a woman. Dr. Hutschnecker himself recalled having heard as much but said he never learned the analyst's identity. Robert Finch, Nixon's aide and friend from early days in Congress, said that he too had heard Nixon had been treated by a "woman psychiatrist in New York." Sources differ on whether the city involved was New York or Los Angeles. The suggestion, though, is that the treatment occurred after Nixon's defeat in the 1962 gubernatorial elections, the lowest ebb of his prepresidential career. The chronology, and what we know of his use of Dr. Hutschnecker, also indicates that—if he did see an analyst—it was at that time, when he was based in Los Angeles.

Professor Foster Sherwood, a former dean of UCLA, has recalled a woman psychoanalyst's asking his advice on depositing her files on Nixon. Interviewed for this book at age eighty, he said he could not remember the analyst's name. Other information suggests the analyst died in the late sixties. Katcher revealed the analyst's identity to his brother Leo, but swore him to secrecy. Both Katcher brothers are now dead, and there the trail ends—except for one last detail. While refusing to reveal the woman analyst's name, Leo Katcher said she had been "deeply troubled" at the possibility that Nixon might one day achieve great power.[5]

Although he never expressed them publicly, Dr. Hutschnecker allegedly made similar comments about Nixon. That he had such concerns of course does not imply that he considered Nixon mentally ill. "He didn't have a serious psychiatric diagnosis," the doctor told the author, "Nixon wasn't psychotic. He had no pathology. But he did have a good portion of neurotic symptoms."

Six months into the presidency, in 1969, after a story in the press about the consultations by his famous patient, Hutschnecker responded with a long article in *Look* magazine. "During the entire period that I treated Mr. Nixon," he wrote, "I detected no sign of mental illness in him. . . . After his election as President, I felt confirmed in my belief . . . that Richard Nixon had not only the strength but the imagination and clarity of goal that I thought were prerequisites for a successful leader."

It may be that the doctor was damning with faint praise. The title of his *Look* piece was "The Mental Health of Our Leaders," and its message—repeating an old Hutschnecker theme—was that "a kind of mental health certificate" should be required of all young adults, as a precondition for their seeking any responsible political job.

Curious though this suggestion may sound, even in the year 2000, Hutschnecker was not alone in holding this view. Dr. Lawrence Kubie, a former president of the New York Psychoanalytical Society, said in 1972 that he favored "a careful medical screening of every candidate for important office, including psychological screening. . . . Perhaps the National Institutes of Health and the National Institute of Mental Health or an organization like the New York Academy of Medicine, or some of our major and presumably incorruptible schools, could be assigned to the task."

In the *Look* piece, Hutschnecker returned to a favorite formula, derived from Pavlov's experiments on dogs, that identified four personality categories in terms of reaction to stress:

1) The strong, excitatory type
2) The lively
3) The calm-imperturbable
4) The weak, inhibitory

Applying those categories to humans, Hutschnecker said, Types One and Four were "the most likely to break down under stress. Therefore, they become a risk in social and certainly in political positions of responsibility. Men of Type Two represent the most desirable leaders because they show a controlled reaction when exposed to stress."

Nixon, Hutschnecker wrote hopefully in 1969, "may turn out to be a Type Two leader, the controlled, adjusted personality. . . ." In 1995, in his interview for this book, Hutschnecker conceded that Nixon had in fact been a Type One, a person who "released his aggression so as to feel better." This was "healthy for an individual who cannot live with inner tension, but mature it was not." In *The Drive for Power,* a book published after the president's resignation, the doctor wrote that, in spite of the pressure of office, Nixon had not had a "nervous breakdown."

How did Hutschnecker account for Nixon's role in Watergate and the collapse of his presidency? "I am in no position to give an answer," wrote the doctor, who is not known to have seen his patient for many months. "I wish to express my hope that at some point in history all can be told."

The Hutschnecker-Nixon story probably never will be fully told. The doctor was still alive, age 102, as this book went to press. He had, however, become wheelchair-bound and without the power of speech, following a fall at his home in Connecticut. Records relating to Nixon's contacts with Hutschnecker in the fifties, stored at the National Archives, are properly withheld on the grounds of doctor/patient privilege. If there are signficant records for a later period, and if they are held at the Nixon Library, it is unlikely that they will be released in the foreseeable future.[6]

Some astute observers, men who followed Nixon from start to end of his career, have wondered if any man who drives himself to the peak of power in America can arrive at his goal and remain entirely—however inadequate a word—normal.

"The awful burden of the presidency does things to the mind," said Dr. Paul Smith, former president of Whittier College. "I know that the thinking process can be frightfully inhibited by mental overload. . . . Maybe Nixon was mistreated, I don't know. Maybe he mistreated himself. . . ."

A presidential candidate, John Ehrlichman thought, "is not like ordinary Americans. The aspiration demands enormous sacrifice. . . . Candidates are hybrid humans, from whom are plucked the normal joys, emotions and experiences of life, that they may single-mindedly run the race. . . . Then, when one of them is elected, we wonder at the man in the White House who is so strangely different from the rest of us. . . . It doesn't lead to a well-rounded individual."

"They've nearly all been strange," said Len Garment. "I mean, they are the *strangest*. Just to go through all that to become President of the United States. With the exception of most of those who sort of inherited the office—George Washington, Harry Truman, and Gerald Ford, who turned out to be men of exemplary character and (for politicians) decency, courage, and common sense—so many of them were very weird. Those who campaigned for the presidency have to have been among the strangest of Americans. Their life is a combination of lying and cheating, nobility and patriotism, and cowardice. There's a sort of presidential gene, a predilection in people who become President that makes them very strange. And Richard Nixon just happened to be one of the strangest of a very strange crew."

"Deep down," commented Henry Kissinger, "one could never be certain that what one found so disturbing in Nixon might not also be a reflection of some suppressed flaw within oneself."

Former Attorney General Elliot Richardson had no difficulty, years after his own bruising experience during Watergate, in reconciling Nixon's talent and intellectual capacity with his human fragility. "You could well say he never would have been president," said Richardson, "if he hadn't had that basic core of insecurity. You could say that, except by chance, no totally healthy human being is likely to become President of the United States. . . ."

11

Bebe Rebozo is a man
of great character and integrity.

—*Richard Nixon, in his memoirs*

P art of Dr. Hutschnecker's early prescription for Nixon was a vacation in the sun. Nixon headed for Florida and there began a relationship that, in the words of Bob Finch, "provided therapy for relief of tension." It was a relationship Nixon maintained until he died, so discreetly at first that no coverage of it appeared in the *New York Times* for nearly twenty years. As former congressional reporter George Reedy was still saying long after the presidency had ended, it has remained "the most important unsolved mystery in Nixon's life."

The new friend was Charles Gregory ("Bebe") Rebozo, American-born Cuban property speculator and wheeler-dealer and—for Nixon—much else besides.

The friendship began, apparently, with an emergency phone call from the Florida Democratic senator George Smathers to former Miami city manager Richard Danner. "Dick," said Smathers, calling from Washington, "is on the verge of a nervous breakdown. We're all concerned about him."

Smathers had been elected to the House at the same time as Nixon, and both subsequently moved up to the Senate. He was on the right wing of the party, sufficiently so to have sent Nixon tips on how to defeat his fellow Democrat Helen Douglas, and was also prominent on the Washington social scene, known as Gorgeous George for his success with women. When an exhausted Nixon turned to him for help, Smathers packed him off on a train to Florida.

Danner, one of the friends Smathers assigned to look after Nixon, recalled his arriving in Miami wearing a heavy raincoat, "like a northern hick." Danner took him for treatment by an osteopath, who in his turn recommended sun and sea air. So it was, apparently in December 1951,[1] that Nixon first stepped aboard the boat of another pal Smathers had lined up, Bebe Rebozo.

This encounter did not go well. "Bebe wrote me a letter after that visit," Smathers recalled, "saying, 'George, don't ever send that dumb son of a bitch Nixon down here again. He's a guy who doesn't know how to talk, doesn't drink, doesn't smoke, doesn't chase women, doesn't know how to play golf, doesn't know how to play tennis. . . . He can't even fish.'"

The "son of a bitch," however, was back in Florida within three months, and by then Rebozo had warmed to him. "I don't want to say that Bebe's level of liking Nixon increased as Nixon's position increased," Smathers said dourly, "but it had a lot to do with it." From that point on the pair invariably vacationed together. Although Pat was often along, and Rebozo became an uncle figure to the Nixon girls, Nixon increasingly spent time with Rebozo alone.

The friend from Florida was there to support Nixon at all the milestones on his political trail: in Florida after the 1952 election that made him vice president, after the major Republican setback in 1958, and at the Ambassador Hotel in Los Angeles in 1960, when news came in that he had lost to John F. Kennedy. In 1962, when Nixon ran for the governorship of California, Rebozo was there to comfort him in defeat. He traveled around the world with Nixon during the wilderness years of the mid-sixties and celebrated with him after he reached the White House in 1968. Nixon wrote his inaugural address while with Rebozo in Florida, and a rough calculation indicates that Rebozo was at his side one day in ten for the duration of the presidency.

The friendship had grown so close that Rebozo effectively had the run of the White House and his own phone number there. He flew on Air Force One, donning the coveted flying jacket bearing the presidential seal, cruised on the presidential yacht with Nixon and Kissinger, and picked movies for Nixon to watch at Camp David.

Despite his intimacy with the president, Rebozo long managed to keep a relatively low profile. Then came Watergate, and he was suddenly at the center of allegations about misuse of campaign contributions, gifts of jewelry for Pat Nixon, and secret presidential slush funds. Still he stayed close to Nixon, whenever possible under deep cover. He slipped into the White House without being logged in by the Secret Service and, using a false name, into Nixon's hotel suite during a trip to Europe.

Rebozo was one of the first to advise Nixon it was probably best that he resign.[2] Afterward he frequently joined him in his exile in California, remaining a close companion through Nixon's years of rehabilitation until, by one account, he sat at Nixon's bedside during his final illness in 1994.

"I say to myself," Rebozo recalled of the occasion he advised Nixon to resign, "'What's a punk kid like you, Bebe, doing talking to the President of the

United States that way?'" That remains a valid question. Who was Bebe Rebozo, and what accounted for the closeness he achieved with Richard Nixon, a man almost notorious for his lack of close friends?

Born Charles Gregory Rebozo the same year as Nixon, he never used Charles Gregory except as a cover name for business operations. He was Bebe from infancy, after one of his nine siblings had trouble pronouncing the word "baby." (Everyone pronounced it "Be-be" except Nixon, who called him Beeb.) The youngest child of Cuban immigrants living in Tampa, he had Latin good looks—they won him the "best-looking boy" vote at high school—but, as he came to adulthood in the Depression, little else to launch him in life.

While wealthier classmates went on to college, Rebozo worked for a year as a steward with Pan American Airways, flying Caribbean routes. Then he pumped gas and chauffeured tourists before embarking on his first business venture, Rebozo's Service Station and Auto Supplies, at the age of twenty-three. After branching out into the lucrative retread tire trade during World War II, he emerged in 1945 as a man of some substance.[3]

By 1951 the substance had grown considerably, for Rebozo had established a self-service laundry chain and begun buying and selling land. The land speculation had started in a small way at the gas station, where he papered the bulletin board with real estate notices. Then he formed syndicates with friends, buying up undeveloped tracts that he sold at huge profits as Miami expanded. Rebozo also ran two finance companies at a time when Florida law permitted the charging of exorbitant interest. He was a hardheaded businessman: A 1953 writ of attachment showed that he repossessed a baby car seat, a tricycle, and a toy truck from a couple unable to repay a $150 debt.

By now Rebozo had also broken into Miami society. A woman who knew him after the war recalled an occasion when Rebozo was asked to make up the numbers at a posh party. The nervous hostess, who had expected him to look "as if he worked in a garage" or like "a flashy gigolo," was relieved to find him immaculately turned out, with "nice instincts." Later, when Nixon was president, he had Rebozo buy clothes for him. "Blue suits," said one of Rebozo's neighbors, "are a badge of respectability for both of them. Bebe is Nixon's class of people."

Behind the success, though, Nixon's friend had a sad personal story. His love life had started disastrously and long continued in that fashion. In 1931, at the age of eighteen, Rebozo had followed "an intense friendship" with Donald Gunn, a well-heeled young man, by rushing into marriage with Gunn's teenage sister Clare. She agreed to the union, she explained four years later at the annulment hearing, only after endless badgering by Rebozo and on the understanding that he would never reveal it and never live with her as man and wife. The marriage, she said, was never consummated.

In the early forties, Clare remarried and had two children, but Rebozo remained a bachelor. When she returned to Miami alone, her husband having been killed in the war, he pressed his suit again. Again they married, and again the marriage failed, with Rebozo moving out after only two years, "Who knows why?" said one who knew them both. "Maybe Bebe was too unctuous, too fawning. Clare was very domineering. . . . Maybe, having finally made it with Clare, Bebe believed he had proved himself, and that was all he wanted."

Clare took yet another husband but then died young, and the faithful Rebozo hurried to pay a last visit to her when she was on her deathbed. He shied away from remarriage until middle age, when he formalized what *Newsweek* called an "antiseptic" relationship with his lawyer's secretary. She was said to have been a "reincarnation" of his former wife.[4] Clare's sister-in-law, who stayed in touch with Rebozo, said in 1996, "I have been told not to talk about these things."

In 1951, when the two men first became friendly, Rebozo was fresh from his second divorce from Clare and Nixon was perennially exhausted and troubled. Accounts of their early times together suggest a curious relationship. Their boat trips, which continued throughout the years, were notable mainly for the silences. "Nixon would go out on Bebe's boat," said George Smathers, "get off in a corner with a yellow pad, and sit there making notes. He might never fish, never say a damn thing. He was really sort of a screwball."

Rebozo's old schoolmate and business partner Sloan McCrae recalled joining Nixon and Rebozo for a three-hour cruise up the inland waterway to Fort Lauderdale. Nixon spent the entire journey in silence, his head in his hands. When at last the visitor tried to start a conversation, Rebozo swiftly cut in. "Shhh!" he whispered. "He's meditating." The trip ended without another word's being said. "We'd have barbecues at Bebe's house," said McCrae. "He'd be entertaining mostly men. Everyone would be drinking and talking, and it was not unusual for Nixon just to go into another room and play piano. He wanted to be by himself. He was very involved in himself. . . ."

Hoke Maroon, a banker who worked on numerous deals with Rebozo, once arrived at his home when Nixon was visiting. He and his wife had met Nixon before, and said hello. Nixon did not acknowledge their presence and sat silently, facing away from them, until they left nearly an hour later.

As time passed, and Nixon began to be seen more and more alone with Rebozo—at the Jamaica Inn and the English Pub on Key Biscayne—rumors started. The notion that they had a homosexual relationship persisted, in part because they were two men in a close relationship, in part because, as newscaster Dan Rather put it, Rebozo "transmitted the sense of great sensuality. . . . [He was] magnetic . . . [with] beautiful eyes."

Gossip about Rebozo spanned the decades. An airline steward who once worked with him reportedly claimed to have had a long sexual relationship with him. An elderly Miami resident said Rebozo had "definitely" been a member of Miami's homosexual community. But Rebozo and Nixon? General Alexander Haig, the president's last chief of staff, is said to have mimicked Rebozo's "limp wrist" manner and to have joked that the pair had a homosexual relationship.

In fact, a good deal of information suggests the opposite was the case. Norman Casper, who investigated tax abuses for the IRS, recalled testing the rumors by sending a woman to Rebozo. She came back reporting firmly that he was not homosexual. Antoinette Giancana, daughter of the mobster, recalled Rebozo's asking her out on a date. "We had a few drinks," she recalled, ". . . and then it was up to his suite in the hotel." One of John F. Kennedy's lovers, Joan Hitchcock, told an interviewer she had been to bed with Rebozo.

The newspaper morgue is filled with clippings about Rebozo, the "ladies' man," "squiring beautiful women," "seen with a variety of statuesque women at Miami night spots." Stories of bacchanalia in luxury villas on secluded islets, hosted by Rebozo, percolated to Washington. "Bebe was rather notorious," said George Reedy, "for throwing wild parties with lots of women and liquor. Scenes that have been described to me sounded like orgies in the time of Lucullus."

For both Nixon and Rebozo, however, sex seems to have been more a matter of chat and practical jokes than of action. Still-withheld White House tapes reportedly feature Nixon talking bawdily with hospitalized male friends about their nurses' curves. He asked his Secret Service agents—and more famously his interviewer David Frost—if they had "done any fornicating" over the weekend.

In a rare television interview Rebozo told how he and Nixon tricked a friend by obtaining a pair of inflatable legs—"skin-colored and all"—and leaving them protruding from under a bed sheet. They then photographed the friend as he hovered in amazement beside the bed. In another version of the story, one Rebozo did not discuss publicly, the joke involved a full-size blowup woman, complete with vagina.

A Secret Service agent who traveled with Nixon in retirement recalled watching him and Rebozo chatting up a young woman at a Caribbean resort. The woman would "come out of her cabana topless. She would place herself at a discreet distance from Nixon, but close enough so he could still ogle her. He and Rebozo were out in the water, it was only waist-high, so they got down so their noses were at water level. And they were like alligators, using the water as cover so they could stare at this girl on the beach. . . . I listened to them talking afterwards, and they couldn't admit to each other they'd been looking at her tits, at her body. They talked instead about how she could speak six languages or something, they couldn't be real with each other." To John Lindsay, the *Newsweek* political correspondent, such stories suggested that Nixon and Rebozo were "arrested adolescents" as far as sex was concerned.

Sexuality aside, the degree of intimacy between the two men was really remarkable. Bobby Baker, Lyndon Johnson's confidant, knew Rebozo and his friends. Intending no sexual innuendo, he described Nixon and Rebozo as having been "close like lovers."

To Herb Klein, who knew them for many years, the relationship was like "a boyhood bond." The talk in the Nixon White House was that after Nixon's most ignominious defeat, in the California gubernatorial election of 1962, he and Rebozo "held hands and pledged eternal friendship no matter what happened." Once, at a Washington dinner party, a woman journalist who sat near them bent below table level to retrieve a dropped fork and was astounded to see that Nixon and Rebozo were clasping hands, an intimacy rare indeed in males in the Western world.

To many observers, however, the relationship seemed, as John Ehrlichman put it, "unilateral." The comedian Jack Paar, who often saw them together, thought of Rebozo as Nixon's devoted Tonto or Sancho Panza. The woman Rebozo eventually married, Jane Lucke, said—not entirely in jest—"Bebe's favorites are RN, his cat—and then me." Jake Jernigan, another intimate, thought: "He loved Nixon more than he loved anybody. He worshiped Nixon. Nixon was his God . . . his Little Jesus." William Safire added context to this interpretation. "Bebe worshiped Nixon," he said, "and hated Nixon's enemies."

Others, including Pat Nixon, took a more caustic view of Rebozo's idolatry. "Bebe's like a sponge," she said in a rare blunt comment. "He soaks up whatever Dick says. . . . Dick loves that." Charles Colson dismissed Rebozo as just "the dog you talk to when you feel like talking."

As late as 1970, flying home aboard Air Force One after a visit to Ireland, Nixon was in conversation with his cousin, the writer Jessamyn West. He peered out the window, brooding. Then, she recalled, "In a calm voice, stating a fact, not complaining or asking for pity, he said, 'I haven't a friend in the world.'" West asked: "Not Rebozo?" Rebozo, Nixon replied, was just "a golfing partner."[5]

"Anyone who has known me," Rebozo said during Watergate, "knows that I am not a mystery man. I'm just a private person. . . . My relationship with politicians has been truly a social one. . . . I do not offer advice to the President on any political matter." In fact, whatever the truth about Rebozo's relationship with other politicians—he also cultivated numerous U.S. senators, including the future presidents Kennedy and Johnson—he took a highly political role in Nixon's career.

The precise detail of Rebozo's involvement can never be established, but we have glimpses of his activities. In 1960 political foes made efforts, unsuccessful at the time, to destroy John F. Kennedy's wholesome family man image, and Rebozo fed sexual dirt on him to the Nixon campaign. This included sending Nixon documents suggesting that his opponent was concealing an earlier marriage to a Palm Beach divorcée. Kennedy, Nixon recalled, "was so careless . . . just like Clinton."

"In the background, straddling a chair behind Nixon," an aide recalled of a 1968 strategy meeting on Long Island, "sat a swarthy, smiling man who was not introduced . . . Charles Rebozo." The previous Christmas Nixon had flown alone to Florida to decide whether to run for the presidency. He made his decision in the company of two men, the evangelist Billy Graham and Rebozo.

Richard Danner, one of those who initially brought Nixon and Rebozo together, gave a sworn deposition during the Watergate investigation. A hundred and fifty pages long, it was devoted in large part to Rebozo's wheeling and dealing and describes a politically savvy fund-raiser who operated—not least with respect to contributions from the billionaire Howard Hughes—with Nixon's knowledge and authority.

Nixon's two most senior aides remembered Rebozo's pervasive influence. "Bebe was unselfish but not entirely selfless," said John Ehrlichman. ". . . I began by thinking of him as a potted palm, standing in the corner. He was a great deal more than that—he had political influence." "Nixon once sent Bebe Rebozo to lecture me," Bob Haldeman recalled. "Over coffee . . . Bebe got down to business. The President felt I would do better in my job if I were more circuitous, more diplomatic, less straight-ahead . . . a whole string of Dale Carnegie homilies."

Recently released White House tapes reveal that Rebozo suggested a person who would commit to a huge campaign contribution—"a quarter of a million at least," Nixon thought—in return for an ambassadorship. Nixon used Rebozo as go-between with a caller who had offered to provide "the goods" on 1972 presidential contender Edmund Muskie. Rebozo was also asked to make a secret approach to the George Wallace camp.

Nixon listened to Rebozo's thoughts on Vietnam War policy and on at least one telephone call, transcribed by secretaries, used Rebozo to pass on his views to Henry Kissinger. The president himself sounded drunk at the time. Rebozo had long involved himself in Caribbean politics—he was linked to at least two of the Cubans who took part in the Watergate burglary[6]—a connection that troubled the secretary of state. Rebozo "hated Castro with a fierce Latin passion," Kissinger wrote, and Nixon's friendship with him "guaranteed that he would constantly be exposed to arguments to take a hard line; he would never want to appear weak before his old friend." Rebozo's presence at Nixon's side, Kissinger observed, "did not usually make for the calmest reflection."

In the White House, Haldeman noticed, Nixon was "always edgy" when Rebozo's name was mentioned. Well he might be edgy, for Rebozo was much more than a golfing partner, much more than a social friend. He was dangerous to know, in part because of the way he helped enrich Nixon, in part because of his links to dubious characters—including members of organized crime.

"While I have never had the urge to accumulate wealth," Nixon wrote in old age, "I have great respect for those who do, because I can see the worthwhile things many rich people do with their money. . . . I never wanted more wealth than I needed to provide a comfortable life for myself and my family."

Rebozo, for his part, described his friend as "a man to whom money means nothing" and adding that he thought Nixon had never signed a check himself. James Bassett said Nixon "had a disregard for money but liked to live well. . . . He had no real consciousness of where it came from . . . that didn't concern him. Nixon was naive to the nth degree about money." Bassett noted, though, that Rebozo was "a damn shrewd operator . . . [and that] as Bebe's fortunes enhanced, so did his need for government considerations." Another colleague noted that Nixon relied on friends for advice on investments. Only two such advisers were cited, one of them Rebozo.[7]

In the fifties, when he was vice president, the Nixon the world saw was a man who went to Florida merely in search of relaxation. He and Rebozo dined at Don Julio's in Miami or had a beer or two out of personal tankards engraved with their names at the English Pub. Behind the scenes, though, as Rebozo began to expand his interests, he reportedly cut Nixon in on some of the deals.

According to a law enforcement source and an FBI informant, the two men jointly invested in interests in pre-Castro Cuba. According to Rebozo's banker colleague Hoke Maroon, they also shared in the ownership of a Coral Gables motel, with Rebozo fronting for Nixon on the ownership documents. Maroon told a hilarious tale of the night the pair stood in the parking lot counting cars, because Rebozo suspected the manager of lying about how much business he was doing.

When press stories like this appeared during the presidency, stories for which Maroon seemed the most likely source, Nixon's office ordered two undercover men—future Watergate burglars Howard Hunt and Bernard Barker—to look for derogatory information on Maroon. They found instead that the banker was regarded by the financial community as a man of "unimpeachable integrity," while Rebozo was "not well thought of." This was not the report the White House wanted.

In 1958, during a scandal about high-level Republican corruption,[8] Rebozo told the Florida papers how "selfless" Nixon was, that he always insisted on paying his own bills. "They'll never get anything on that boy," he asserted. "In my view," said George Smathers, "Nixon never made a dishonest dollar in his life."

In 1960, after losing to Kennedy and going into political limbo, Nixon reckoned his personal worth at a mere $50,000, made up mostly of his house and his federal pension plan. A year or two later, as a prosperous lawyer, he told a friend with delight that he had enough to donate $11,000 to charity in one twelve-month period. Eight years later, when he was elected president, property and investments—plus his salary as an attorney and his income as an author—had left him by his accounting worth $307,141—about $1.5 million at today's values.

Meanwhile, down in Florida, Rebozo had become seriously rich. In 1964 he had started his own financial institution, the Key Biscayne Bank. Nixon, as former vice president, wielded a golden shovel at the groundbreaking (for the bank's parking lot) and held Savings Account No. 1. The bank became a Nixon shrine, with photographs of him on its walls and a bust of him sitting benignly on the teller counter. It was a small bank, housed in a nondescript brick and glass building, and well-off locals tended to pad in on bare feet, while the staff doled out popcorn and lollipops to children.

Sometimes Rebozo himself—chairman, president, and principal stockholder—could be seen working in his office at the end of the lobby. On the outer wall of the office, facing the public, hung a red, white, and blue plaque representing the American flag, with the inscription "This is our flag, be proud of it." He drove to work in a large green Lincoln Continental—license plate "Miami 1"—bearing a bumper sticker that read: "The only issue is America."

In spite of the folksy welcome it offered, Key Biscayne Bank was not a place for the man in the street to go to obtain a loan. A survey later showed that it was last but one of the 687 banks in Florida in the number of loans it issued. Rebozo's bank was primarily a place that held money or assisted in the movement of money.

By the time the bank opened, Rebozo's specialty had long since become real estate speculation, with a particular interest in the islets and cays dotting the ocean off Miami and in the Caribbean archipelago. "Bebe loved property," said Smathers. "He never saw an island he didn't fall in love with." One that especially took his fancy was Fisher's Island, some two hundred acres of speculative investment off Miami Beach. Nixon started buying shares in Fisher's in 1962 at a dollar each, and by the time he became president he owned 185,891 of them.

"After the 1968 election," Nixon wrote in his memoirs, "I decided to sell all my stocks. . . . I thought it would be worth going the extra measure to avoid even the appearance of a conflict of interest." Rebozo proposed that Nixon be bought out at three dollars per share and was furious when Hoke Maroon, the largest single shareholder in the venture, initially offered only the dollar Nixon had originally paid. Nixon settled for two dollars a share, which at the time made him the only shareholder to double his investment.

By his own later account, the president put most of the money from the sale of his stocks into buying "two houses in Florida and a house in California." These were the palatial residences that became famous as the southern and western White Houses, the presidential compound in Rebozo country, Key Biscayne, and San Clemente in Southern California.

Rebozo organized the purchase of the Key Biscayne complex and was a silent partner in the investment company that purchased San Clemente. The twenty-eight-acre estate had been much too costly for Nixon to finance alone, so Rebozo and a second friend, aerosol tycoon Robert Abplanalp, looked after the matter. A complex series of sales, mortgages, and resales left Nixon technically owning the luxury villa, its outbuildings, and some six acres, though he had the use of the entire property. Rebozo also bought a house in an exclusive Washington suburb, again involving labyrinthine financial arrangements, for the use of Nixon's daughter Julie and her husband. The couple would not reveal the rent they paid, beyond describing it as "reasonable."

Early in Nixon's first term, John Ehrlichman recalled, Rebozo expressed concern that the president's personal finances were not being well managed. Close aides objected to Rebozo's overseeing them completely, but he was soon in control of all Nixon's money. "If there's something I think he should have," Rebozo told probers later, "I might just go ahead and do it without even him knowing about it. He just doesn't concern himself with financial problems; never has."

Ehrlichman also noted that Nixon repeatedly asked him to "help Bebe with his personal problems": assistance at the Department of the Interior over a real estate problem here, a little help for his relatives there. Should anyone complain about favoritism, Nixon blandly directed, aides should point out that "Bebe is different: he handles the President's personal affairs."

For a while, even when the presidency became suspect under the impact of Watergate, the president's friend seemed unassailable. Then, when an unrelated IRS investigation led to the discovery of a hundred-thousand-dollar cache, held in hundred-dollar bills in a safe-deposit box at Rebozo's bank, the carefully cultivated image of the innocuous, apolitical friend was shattered. Every aspect of Rebozo's affairs was relentlessly scrutinized, with the focus on misappropriation of campaign contributions, acceptance of money in exchange for favors by the Justice Department, distribution of Watergate hush money, and alleged diversion of campaign funds to Nixon's brothers and personal secretary.*

As the Senate stated in its formal report, Rebozo obstructed its official investigation, at one point even leaving the country to avoid further questioning. Nixon meanwhile tried to subvert IRS inquiries. An IRS intelligence supervisor, Andy Baruffi, said in 1996 that his team concluded that the IRS investigation "was being manipulated by the White House." Called to a meeting at the office of the director of IRS intelligence in Washington, he and his lead agent expressed the view that at least two of Nixon's own tax returns had been fraudulent. Baruffi never forgot his shock at the reaction of his superiors, who simply left the room. Attempts to resume the conversation were met with blank stares and pointed silence.

A more senior IRS source, also interviewed for this book, confirmed the shameful way the Rebozo case was blocked. "I was assigned to review the entire case file. We had Rebozo primarily on a straight up-and-down provable false statement charge. It was a dead-bang case. I believe a deal was made with the White House to kill the investigation."

Senate hearings on the Rebozo matter were likewise aborted. The special prosecutor eventually decided, at the end of a trail littered with promising

---

*The hundred thousand dollars, which had come from the billionaire Howard Hughes, is a key factor in the Watergate saga and will be reported more fully later.

leads and frustrating dead ends, not that Rebozo was innocent but—in the careful words of the published report—that "the evidence would not support an indictment." Rebozo escaped prosecution, and the former president claimed in his memoirs that his friend had been "exonerated." He had "endured a modern-day Star Chamber of political persecution," Nixon wrote. "His crime was that he was Richard Nixon's friend."

A number of salient facts and leads give context to the friendship that paralleled Nixon's rise and fall. Some are small but cumulatively significant. There was Rebozo's ability to obtain business favors by devious means, starting in 1962, when he wanted a federal loan to help pay for a real estate deal. Having been repeatedly rejected by the Small Business Administration (SBA), and for good reason, Rebozo's application suddenly was approved. Strings had been pulled in Washington and Miami. The official involved in Miami wound up owning lots on Fisher's Island and—when Rebozo's bank started up, holding stock in that business. This was the first in a series of such breaks, culminating in the extraction of government money to develop a shopping center for Cuban refugee merchants.

One of the SBA directors recalled Rebozo's conduct at a 1967 meeting about the planned shopping center. He described him as "having an extremely quick temper and being a name-dropper," one of the names dropped being that of his "close friend" Richard Nixon. Rebozo and his partner won the deal and profited nicely. The man he brought in to organize the shops, the former Batista cabinet minister Edgardo Buttari, headed the Cubans for Nixon lobby in the 1968 election and was later appointed to a highly paid job in the Department of Health, Education, and Welfare.

Early in the presidency, when the government was buying up islands in Biscayne Bay that had been zoned as a national monument, Rebozo demanded and got a higher price than other landowners. An Army Corps of Engineers official involved said he had been told Rebozo was "an intimate of people in high places," to be "treated with kid gloves." Rebozo's brother-in-law remained caretaker of one of the islands, on a federal salary.

When a business group not connected to Rebozo applied to open a second bank on Key Biscayne, again during the presidency, it was twice turned down by the federal agency that regulates banks. Rebozo had let it be known that he objected. When a group of *his* associates applied to open a savings and loan institution, however, it was given an approval.

More sensational, but much harder to substantiate, were the allegations about the amount of money Nixon accumulated with Rebozo's help, where it came from, and where it ended up. The public learned during Watergate that the president's net worth, $307,000 when he took office, had tripled during his first five years in the White House to nearly $1 million. In the same period Rebozo's net worth—reported as $673,000 in late 1968—had increased nearly sevenfold, to $4.5 million.

There was suspicion, though, that Nixon had more money than was publicly acknowledged. That Rebozo did hold funds for Nixon, over and above what is known, seems certain, on the basis of scraps of surviving correspondence and Nixon's own comments to aides, some of them preserved on the White House tapes.[9]

In an interview shortly before his death Nixon's longtime campaign treasurer, Maurice Stans, revealed: "Bebe told me: 'I've set up a trust fund for Richard Nixon's family from my own and the bank's money to take care of the family. It's money I have set aside.' It was Bebe's generosity." Stans said he did not know the eventual extent of the fund, which he learned about in 1968.

In another incident, proof emerged that Nixon used $4,652 from 1968 campaign funds, maintained and moved about by Rebozo, to buy Pat diamond-studded platinum earrings from Harry Winston, the New York society jeweler. Nixon devoted a passage in his memoirs to an outraged rebuttal of corruption claims, but remained silent on that one. There was no denying it.

Both Nixon and Rebozo did vociferously deny a story published by the columnist Jack Anderson, suggesting they had hidden money in Switzerland. Nixon called the account "totally false," and Rebozo dismissed it as "just about as accurate as most of the other things I've heard about Mr. Anderson's writing." In fact, much of what Anderson dug up about Nixon over the years turned out to be true or at least close to the truth. New information suggesting that Nixon did indeed keep such funds abroad will be revealed in this book.

An even more questionable aspect of the Rebozo connection, however, was the pervasive presence of organized crime. Although the bane of many investigative books is the assigning of guilt by association—"so-and-so-knew-and-so-and-so-connects-to-so-and-so"—in this case the connections deserve examination.

––––––

The pattern was evident early on. The man who brought Nixon to his first meeting with Rebozo, Richard Danner, is usually referred to merely as a former FBI agent or former Miami city manager. He had held both those jobs, but there were smudges on his record. Danner had also worked for the Miami Beach Hotel Owners Association at a time when several large Miami hotels were controlled by the mob—notably Meyer Lansky and his brother Jake, out of New York, and Joe Adonis out of Detroit—and was especially close to the association's president, gambler Abe Allenberg. He had been dismissed as city manager, accused of "playing both ends against the middle," in the wake of a gangland dispute over control of the local police. Soon afterward Danner was alleged to have taken a mob bribe while managing George Smathers's congressional campaign.

Smathers arranged for Nixon to stay during the early Florida trips at oceanside villas on Key Biscayne owned by the Mackle family, who at the time were coinvestors in land development with associates of Meyer Lansky's, including Trigger Mike Coppola. Nixon remained friendly with the Mackles over the years.

A decade into the Nixon-Rebozo friendship, when Nixon was temporarily out of politics, an intelligence report filed at the Miami Police Department cited a mob informant as saying Rebozo was running a numbers racket out of one of his coin laundry businesses. He was, the informant claimed, "fronting in this operation for ex–Vice President Nixon." The report was uncorroborated, but it forms part of a larger picture. Organized crime figures were a presence in Rebozo's real estate and banking ventures.

Walter Frederich, a stockholder in the corporation controlling Fisher's Island, where Nixon bought land, was a convicted sugar bootlegger. Rebozo was a coowner of another island, close by Fisher's, along with a gambler called Richard Fincher. A former Florida state senator, Fincher was said by law enforcement sources to have fronted for a Meyer Lansky associate in national gambling operations.[10] His phone records in later years revealed calls to associates of mob bosses Carlos Marcello and Santo Trafficante. "Bebe," Fincher boasted, "is a very close friend of mine."

To finance his Fisher's Island purchases, Nixon borrowed money from Rebozo's bank and an additional hundred thousand dollars from City National Bank of Miami. A prominent director of City National, Max Orowitz, was referred to in a Justice Department memo as having taken millions of dollars, through the Bank of Miami Beach, on behalf of Lansky. He was convicted of securities fraud, involving Swiss banks, the year Nixon was elected president.

That same year, when Rebozo organized the development of the Cuban shopping center in Miami, he picked the Polizzi Construction Company to build it. Alfred ("Big Al") Polizzi, who headed the company, had been a top mobster in Prohibition days. He had headed the Cleveland mob, holding such seniority that according to an FBI report, he was on the Mafia Grand Council, a predecessor of the Commission. He too worked with Meyer Lansky and had been jailed in 1943 for smuggling liquor between Cuba and the United States, for violation of war price controls, and for tax evasion. In the fifties Polizzi was summoned before the Kefauver Committee because of his ownership of the Sands, one of the Miami Beach hotels then controlled by the mob. He was also associated with drug trafficking and named by the Bureau of Narcotics as late as 1964 as "one of the most influential members of the underworld in the United States."

In 1952 Rebozo's sister-in-law Eleanor signed an unsuccessful petition to get Polizzi a federal pardon. She, along with the other signers, stated that she had always considered Polizzi "a person of good moral character." In 1965 Rebozo tried unsuccessfully to obtain a zoning permit for another gas station. Polizzi was one of only seven citizens who signed a petition supporting his bid, at a time he was still very much in the mob loop. A contemporaneous FBI bug overheard another top mafioso insisting the only way to sort out an internal dispute was to see Polizzi.

In 1967, as Nixon prepared for the campaign that was to make him president, Rebozo got him to pose for a publicity photograph with Donald Berg, a customer of Rebozo's bank and a real estate developer and owner of Key Biscayne's Jamaica Inn, where Nixon often dined. Nixon had known Berg since he first came to the area and was aware that the photograph was intended to boost efforts to sell plots for Berg's Cape Florida Development Company. The picture was circulated around the country and proved useful to them both. Nixon "exposed the product like soap on TV," said Berg. "All of a sudden people came down and discovered Key Biscayne was an island paradise." Nixon, for his part, was able to buy two Cape Florida plots for half the price of two lots close by. Rebozo got a tract at a bargain as well.[11]

Both Nixon and Rebozo delayed recording their purchases of two of the Berg plots until several years later. Nixon finalized his registration only two years after becoming president, for it took that long for one of the plots to come clear of previous mortgages held by an associate of Lansky and Teamsters leader Jimmy Hoffa. He ultimately disposed of the land in 1972, following unwelcome publicity about the arrangements, and stopped eating at Berg's Jamaica Inn, reportedly at the request of the Secret Service after it had received a report on Berg's background.[12] He remained friendly with Berg, however, as late as 1994, the year of his death.

Rebozo and his bank were embroiled in a securities case in 1968 that raised further questions about his integrity. The affair concerned the handling of IBM stocks lodged with him as collateral for a loan, stocks, it turned out, that had been stolen from a New York brokerage firm. The thieves and con men involved included associates of Tony "Fats" Salerno and Gil "The Brain" Beckley, known accomplices of the now familiar name of Meyer Lansky.

Rebozo's role in the deal raised a number of troubling questions. Why had he promptly offered the loan to a would-be customer who was a stranger from another state, without asking for any credit history? There were routine ways to conduct such checks. Yet, when he finally did place two calls, they were to the chairman of Resorts—the man who ran Paradise Island in the Bahamas—and to Nixon's businessman brother Don.

Why, even after he had been visited by FBI agents making inquiries about the stock, did Rebozo write a warm note to the man who provided them as collateral: "Everything thus far has worked out well for both of us . . ."?

Why, when an insurance investigator tried to tell Rebozo the stock was stolen, did Rebozo respond so strangely? He initially claimed he was too busy to see the investigator and canceled two appointments. When they did meet, Rebozo aroused great suspicion. "I do not believe," the investigator wrote in his report, "that Mr. Rebozo was giving me all the information. . . . This would appear to me to be a shady deal, and I suspect that Mr. Rebozo is aware of this."

Did Rebozo falsely tell the investigator that he had already sold on the stock when in fact he sold the balance of shares more than a week after the meeting?[13]

Finally, why was the litigation in the case settled in a way that avoided further complications for Rebozo? A civil suit against the bank was terminated after one day by a U.S. district court judge, James King, who had recently been appointed by President Nixon.

A Washington-based gambler jailed during the Nixon presidency for transportation of stolen securities, Alvin Kotz, was interviewed in prison for this book. Kotz asserted that the true role of Rebozo and his bank was common knowledge in criminal circles, long before publicity about the stolen stocks case. "Bebe and Bebe's bank were an outlet for these things. It was a well-known thing in organized crime circles."

Vincent Teresa, at the time the only high-ranking mafioso to have turned government informant, later admitted having taken part in the IBM stock scam. He told the Watergate Special Prosecution Force that he had used Rebozo's bank to cash the proceeds of another batch of stolen stock. A convicted stock swindler, Louis Mastriana, testified to the Senate Subcommittee on Investigations that the publicized stolen stock case had been "brought in by Teresa." He said he himself had been to the Key Biscayne Bank and had dealings with Rebozo. Asked whether Rebozo was aware of his mob connections, he said: "I don't know. I understand he would take a hot stove, too, if you gave it to him."

Mastriana acknowledged in his testimony having worked with Washington mob figure Joe Nesline, with whom Kotz was closely associated, as well as with Vincent ("Jimmy Blue Eyes") Alo, the senior surviving longtime associate of Meyer Lansky's. Questioned about Rebozo in a rare 1997 interview, Alo used the same metaphor as had Mastriana. "Everyone," he said, "knew Rebozo would take a hot stove," later adding that he "was the one who picked up the money for Nixon."*

William Gallinaro, a senior investigator with the Senate Subcommittee on Investigations, recalled: "We were preparing to subpoena Bebe Rebozo and to go to his bank. . . . We were going after him. He was keeping stock in there that was fraudulent, stolen. . . . When we started making inquiries about this, somebody tipped him off to watch himself. And next thing we know he sold the stolen stock. That's a crime in itself, and he should have been arrested and gone to prison for that. Bebe Rebozo was a friendly banker when it came to the mob."

Sometime in the sixties those monitoring organized crime in the Department of Justice and the FBI developed designations for criminals, fringe criminals, and their associates. A former FBI agent who specialized in organized crime in the Miami area, Charles Stanley, identified Rebozo as a "non-member

*The Lansky factor is covered in chapter 12.

associate of organized crime figures." This designation applied to individuals determined to have significant, witting association with "made members" of La Cosa Nostra.[14]

Having been so close to Rebozo for so long a period, Nixon cannot have been totally ignorant of Bebe Rebozo's connections and cannot surely have been unaware of his friend's proximity to the world of organized crime, a world he promised to combat with the full power of the presidency. Still, he chose Rebozo as his closest intimate.

Some of the material on Rebozo in this chapter was first probed in late 1971 by the Pulitzer Prize–winning investigative team for the East Coast paper *Newsday*. As the journalists prepared the series, they found doors slamming in government agencies and that FBI agents had reached interviewees before them. Both FBI and Secret Service agents ran surveillance on *Newsday* reporters.

The paper suffered severe reprisals after publishing the results of its investigation. Its White House correspondent was ostracized by the president's press secretary and prevented from covering the groundbreaking visit to China. Behind the scenes, orders went out for tax probes of its publisher and senior editors. The president himself was behind such measures. "Nixon's reaction," thought William Safire, the former Nixon speechwriter, "was worse than foolish. . . . Nixon could not take it when it came to an attack on Bebe."

Later still, when the Cronkite *Evening News* ran reports on Rebozo, a White House aide said Nixon bitterly resented the coverage. The aide said he saw nothing wrong with Rebozo's behavior.

Other presidents of course have relied on confidants. Roosevelt had Harry Hopkins, Truman had Harry Vaughan, and both of them had the company of George Allen. Eisenhower and Kennedy had their brothers. The men at their side served as advisers and court jesters and often just patiently listened. None, though, has left behind so little sense of substance or so strong a sense of the furtive, of criminality, as Bebe Rebozo.

"When you were dealing with Bebe and Richard Nixon," said George Smathers, "you were dealing with two of the most secretive, reserved, fearful people you could ever know." Robert Finch regarded Rebozo as "one of the silentest men in U.S. history." According to another White House aide, "Bebe would endure having his nails pulled out one by one, rather than reveal anything but commonplaces about the President."[15]

By 1952, as his relationship with Rebozo was growing closer, Nixon had become consumed with political ambition, ambition advised less and less by the strict precepts of his upbringing. He was becoming mired in shabby secrets that could not be told, and that made Rebozo, in the most unfortunate way, the right friend for him. "Bebe," as William Safire has said, "was never going to blab."

12

*All you have got to do in this country of ours
is just to tell the people the truth,
and not hide anything from them*

—*Richard Nixon, September 1952*

"For Richard Nixon," wrote Stephen Hess, an aide in both the Eisenhower and Nixon presidencies, "the end is power." Not content with having become a representative at thirty-three and a senator at thirty-seven, the political comer from California did not pause in his rush to rise higher.

Legislative activity was evidently not a priority. No sooner had Nixon taken his seat in the Senate than he began crisscrossing the nation making speeches—forty-nine of them in 1951, and only three of those in his home state. On the tour he projected an image, as Earl Mazo saw it, of part revolutionary hero and part doomsday preacher. Nixon explained the purpose of these travels in a letter home to Herman Perry, the Whittier bank manager who had first urged him into politics: "A few friends in other states may prove to be of considerable value in the future."

In fact, national power brokers by now had come to see in Nixon a man who could spearhead the Republican party's comeback from two decades of drift and defeat. The currents of history were about to whirl him to the center of the stream, beside the man whom just six years earlier, as a junior naval officer, Nixon had watched parading through Manhattan as the conquering hero of World War II.

General Dwight Eisenhower, now supreme commander of NATO, had been courted by American big business interests since 1948. Eisenhower had met secretly with Nixon two years earlier, for a briefing on the Hiss case and the extent of domestic communism. Nixon had been present in 1950, when Eisenhower auditioned at Bohemian Grove, one of those curious gatherings in the California redwoods at which wealthy patrons inspect politicians with promise. When they met again in Paris, six months into Nixon's Senate tenure, they discussed matters on which they were unlikely to disagree. Nixon felt a certain "aloofness" in the general and in time was to feel he was "just Ike's prat boy."[1] For now, though, a connection had been made.

Two months before the 1952 Republican convention, New York Governor Thomas Dewey summoned Nixon to Manhattan's Roosevelt Hotel. Dewey, a two-time presidential contender, had looked favorably on the younger man for a long time; now he was the party's senior kingmaker.

In his suite on the twenty-fourth floor, Dewey revealed to Nixon that there was "a possibility of him becoming the Vice President." Earlier that evening, after Nixon had made a rousing speech at a political dinner, Dewey had taken his trademark cigarette holder from his mouth, reached for the younger man's hand, and exhorted him: "Make me a promise. Don't get fat, don't lose your zeal, and you can be President someday." The two men never divulged the finer details of their conversation that night, but later speculation suggested that Dewey had tempted Nixon with the vice presidency on condition that he woo the California delegation over to Eisenhower at the convention. To do so would involve treachery, but Nixon complied.

Weeks before the meeting with Dewey, Nixon had signed a legally binding pledge to support California Governor Earl Warren for the presidential nomination. But now he proceeded to mail to twenty-four thousand Californians a cunningly phrased questionnaire, the cost of which, about one thousand dollars, was charged illegally to the government—inquiring whom they would prefer as the Republican presidential candidate. The questions in the mailing were worded to suggest strongly that Warren's candidacy was doomed. At the convention in Chicago, Nixon and Murray Chotiner, well aware of the damage they were doing to Warren, intrigued busily on Eisenhower's behalf.

Warren behaved with dignity at the time, but never forgot the disloyalty. "He hated Nixon," said Californian John Rothmann, keeper of the finest private archive of Nixonia and for a long time a Nixon supporter. "The most distasteful moment in Warren's career would come in 1969, when as Chief Justice he had to swear Nixon in as President." "Tricky," Warren said in old age, when he was no longer concerned with party niceties and when Nixon was sinking beneath the waves of Watergate, was "despicable . . . a cheat, a liar, and a crook . . . he abused the American people."[2]

When the 1952 convention ended with Eisenhower emerging as the candidate for the White House, the nominee wrote down a list of six potential vice presidents, with Nixon's name at the top. After a smoke-filled room session and with key support from Tom Dewey, Nixon was picked as the running mate. He was lying in his shorts in his hotel room when the news reached him and was said to be "surprised as hell."

The previous night he and his wife had argued into the small hours over whether he should accept the nomination. Pat was voicing "second thoughts," and Chotiner was enlisted at 4:00 A.M. to change her mind. "I guess," she said when Chotiner had finished talking, "I can make it through another campaign." But she dreaded the prospect.

Pat was to claim that she too was surprised to hear the next day, over lunch, that her husband had been nominated. "The bite of sandwich popped right out of my mouth," she recalled. She joined her husband on the victory platform, with instructions to be sure to smile for the cameras. That night in Washington photographers burst into the Nixons' home, brushed past the baby-sitter, and insisted on waking their sleeping daughters to pose them for photographs.

The Eisenhower-Nixon ticket did not begin auspiciously. As the crowd acclaimed the general, Nixon had grabbed the older man's wrist and pulled his arm above his head as though he were some pugilist's manager. It was not Eisenhower's style, and the expression on his face showed it. The incident marked the beginning of a long and chilly relationship.

The following week a smiling, idealized picture of Nixon was featured on the cover of *Time* magazine, the first of a staggering fifty-six such appearances. He had been picked for the candidacy, readers were told, because he was young and a proved vote getter and because he had "fought government corruption." A series of scandals concerning tax fraud, kickbacks, influence peddling, and lax prosecution of top Democrats had plagued President Truman's administration, giving the Republicans a ready-made election issue. "When we are through," Eisenhower told voters, "the experts in shady and shoddy government operations will be on the way back to the shadowy haunts in the shadowy sub-cellars of American politics from which they came." Then, within two months of the convention, a corruption scandal exploded around Nixon himself.

The allegations first appeared in a story by Leo Katcher, in the *New York Post* in mid-September, with a headline charging, SECRET RICH MEN'S TRUST FUND KEEPS NIXON IN STYLE FAR BEYOND HIS SALARY. Katcher and three other journalists had conducted an investigation based on an original tip from embittered supporters of Earl Warren. They established that wealthy California supporters had supplied Nixon with thousands of dollars to supplement his Senate pay. Dana Smith, the corporation attorney who had raised the money and kept it in a Pasadena bank, was to say it amounted to about eighteen thousand dollars.[3] The money, Smith explained, had been used to compensate for Nixon's "personal lack of funds," office expenses—including the mailing of twenty-five thousand Christmas cards—production of material for radio and television broadcasts, airfares, and hotel costs.

Notified of the story before it broke, Nixon had responded with apparent nonchalance. Rumors of impropriety, he said, were "all wrong"; the money was just a "political fund . . . used to pay expenses." He did not know the contributors' names, he claimed, and none of them had enjoyed any special favors. He put the reporter who interviewed him, the conservative columnist Peter Edson, in touch with fund organizer Smith.[4] Nixon had told his colleagues privately that the charges were "nothing to worry about."

As it turned out, the Katcher story caused a sensation. In a campaign in which the Republicans were trumpeting their probity in contrast with Democratic corruption, it was an incendiary revelation. Within days, as Eisenhower and Nixon moved about the country on separate campaign trains—in those days a factor that made communication difficult—it became a full-fledged scandal impossible to ignore.

Eisenhower did not rush to Nixon's defense but instead instructed him to make an immediate and fully documented disclosure of how much money he had received and how he had spent it. The Republicans, he added at a press briefing, must be "as clean as a hound's tooth."

Halfway across the country Nixon claimed the whole affair was a Communist smear and, when heckled, blamed "the Alger Hiss crowd." Eisenhower in turn found himself confronted by pickets, and some papers began calling for Nixon to withdraw from the election. Four days into the crisis, from New York, Dewey informed Nixon that most of the general's advisers thought he should resign.

Late the same day Eisenhower himself called Nixon and urged him to appear on national television to tell the public "everything there is to tell." Would the general then announce his own view on the matter? Nixon asked. "Maybe" was the most Eisenhower would promise. Nixon had been alternately angry or despairing for days, and now he lashed out. "General," he burst out, "there comes a time in matters like this when you've either got to shit or get off the pot. The great trouble here is the indecision." Eisenhower remained cool in the face of the insolence. Go on the television show, he repeated, and then he would decide.

On September 23, five days into the scandal, Nixon went to the NBC studios in Los Angeles to deliver the make-or-break performance of his career, the Checkers speech. He was scheduled to speak for half an hour at prime time, immediately after *The Milton Berle Show,* from the theater that was normally home to *The Colgate Comedy Hour* and *This Is Your Life.*

Long after the event he was to insist there had been no rehearsal, no run-through of movements or facial expressions. A witness, however, reported that—prompted by a professional director and advertising executives—he had practiced poses and smiles. In a later talk to broadcasting executives, Nixon acknowledged that he had delayed the broadcast for two days in order to "build an audience."

Sixty million Americans, linked by more than eight hundred television stations, watched and listened that night. Not a cent of the disputed eighteen thousand dollars, Nixon said during the speech, had gone to his personal use, only to political expenses. The fund had not been secret. No contributor had received "any consideration" he would not have received as an ordinary citizen. Independent accountants and attorneys had formally reported that Nixon had neither profited nor broken any law. Nixon next appealed to the hearts of ordinary people. He offered his version of his life, of a childhood spent in modest circumstances, of his hardworking "Mother and Dad," and of "the best thing that ever happened to me," his marriage. Pat sat close by throughout the broadcast, her face immobile whenever the camera cut away to capture her reaction. Her eyes were fixed on Nixon as he told the nation, "Pat doesn't have a mink coat. But she does have a respectable Republican cloth coat, and I always tell her she looks good in anything." He cataloged their apparently insignificant income, the mortgages on their homes in Washington and California, their 1950 Oldsmobile.

Then came the pull on the heartstrings that gave the speech its familiar name, when Nixon admitted that the family had accepted a gift after the last election, a cocker spaniel sent to his daughters by a man in Texas. It was black and white, and Tricia had named it Checkers. "And you know," he went on, "the kids, like all kids, loved the dog. And I just want to say this, right now, that regardless of what they say about it, we are going to keep it."

As he approached the final part of his address, Nixon turned to a quote from Abraham Lincoln: "God must have loved the common people—he made so many of them." (Nixon later said he had fortuitously remembered the quote, when in fact he had earlier phoned two of his former Whittier College teachers to request a number of Lincoln samples.) That reference led him on to politics: to the fund enjoyed by Eisenhower's opponent, Adlai Stevenson, a man who had "inherited a fortune" and was thus clearly not one of the common people; to Truman, who had failed to clean up corruption and expose the Communists and who was not fit to be president; and finally, back to his own predicament. "I don't believe I ought to quit, because I am not a quitter. And, incidentally, Pat is not a quitter. After all, her name was Patricia Ryan and she was born on St. Patrick's Day,* and you know the Irish never quit."

Then came the conclusion: "But the decision, my friends, is not mine. . . . I am submitting to the Republican National Committee tonight through this television broadcast the decision which is theirs to make. Let them decide. . . . Regardless of what happens, I am going to continue this fight. I am going to campaign up and down America until we drive the crooks and the Communists and those that defend them out of Washington. And remember, folks, Eisenhower is a great man. Folks, he is a great man, and a vote for Eisenhower is a vote for what is good for America."

*Not quite. See p. 28.

Nixon was still talking, his hands spread and reaching out to the viewers, as the picture faded. Realizing the program was over, he stumbled into a camera, began stacking his notes, then hurled them to the floor and buried his head in the stage drapes. "I was a failure," he muttered to his television adviser. "I loused it up. . . . Let's get out of here and get a fast one. I need it."

But a failure it was not. In response to the speech, some four million telegrams flooded in, the vast majority of them in Nixon's favor. Many were euphoric, describing him as "a great man," "dynamic," even "a modern-day Lincoln." Both he and Pat were eulogized. A woman with two fur coats offered Pat one of them. Another sent twenty-five dollars she had saved toward a new coat for herself.

Nixon had struck a valuable populist chord. He had "stripped himself naked," one columnist reported, "for all the world to see, and he brought the missus and the kids and the dog and his war record into the act. . . . The sophisticates sneer, but this came closer to humanizing the Republican Party than anything that has happened in my memory."

Eisenhower had watched the speech with his wife, Mamie, at his Cleveland, Ohio, hotel. Mamie, like so many others, was weeping by its end. The general realized how effective it had been and sent Nixon a congratulatory telegram, which ironically was temporarily lost in the torrent of cable traffic. He went out to tell supporters he admired Nixon's courage and would decide about keeping him on as running mate as soon as they could get together.

In Los Angeles, hearing of this new delay, Nixon exploded with rage and wrote a letter of resignation, which Murray Chotiner intercepted and tore up. Mollified only by a series of wheedling phone calls from Eisenhower's staff, he agreed to fly to meet the general in West Virginia. On his arrival Nixon was rewarded by Eisenhower's coming on board his plane to greet him in person with a firm handclasp and the greeting "You're my boy." The crisis was over, and that night the Republican National Committee endorsed Nixon once again as its vice presidential candidate and "a truly great American."

Reporters watched and cameras clicked as Nixon burst into tears and hid his face on the shoulder of a fellow U.S. senator.[5] Back in Whittier his old drama coach remembered how he had once taught Nixon the trick of crying "buckets of tears" by concentrating on getting a lump in the throat. "I was inclined to say to myself, 'Here goes my actor!' But it was a sincere performance," the teacher hurried to add. "There is nothing perfidious or immoral about being a good actor."

"Overnight," Nixon's friend Bryce Harlow said thirty years later, "he turned an extreme negative into a positive. How many people do you know who could have pulled it off? He was amazing."

Even Checkers became a hero in his own right. For weeks after the speech dog lovers swamped the Nixons with collars, hand-woven dog blankets, and enough dog food to last a year. The cocker spaniel lived on, first as a pet for Tricia and Julie and then, even after he had been laid to rest in New York's

Bide-a-Wee cemetery, as an enduring symbol of Nixon's triumph. In 1997 it was reported that the dog was to be exhumed and reburied near the tomb of the former president and his wife, on the grounds of the Nixon Library.

Eisenhower can hardly have had Checkers in mind when, during the fund crisis, he declared that the Republicans had to be as "clean as a hound's tooth." Nixon surely did, however, when he agreed a few days later to a suggestion that members of his entourage who had lived through the crisis should form a group called the Order of the Hound's Tooth. Pat was to be president and he vice president. Nixon later sent each member a key ring sporting a sliver of ivory symbolizing the immaculate canine tooth and a photograph of himself, signed and inscribed cryptically "I.N.C." The abbreviation stood for the order's secret motto in pseudo-Latin: "Illegitimis non carborundum," which translates as "Don't let the bastards grind you down."

Every year, to his dying day, Nixon would remind people of the anniversary of his victory in 1952. In 1992, when Democratic candidate Bill Clinton was scheduled to appear on 60 Minutes to respond to allegations of marital infidelity, some likened the appearance to the Checkers speech. Nixon disagreed. "Any comparisons," he said, "are misleading. . . . I had the truth on my side."

But did he? The fund crisis was in some measure resolved in Nixon's favor because of the emotional appeal of his speech, and the fact that the press had not properly covered the original allegation. A survey of seventy daily newspapers in forty-eight states revealed that all but seven delayed running the fund story after it had broken in the New York Post and, when they did finally run coverage, at first devoted little space to it. The Los Angeles Times, which had boosted Nixon politically from the start, featured the story with a headline and copy slanted to favor Nixon's denials. The vast majority of papers likewise tended to back the Republican side uncritically.

Nixon's response to the allegations that had been made, moreover, were less than accurate. It was not true that "not one cent" of the fund money had gone to his personal use. One of the contributors, interviewed by the press, revealed that the appeal for funds had been pitched in part on the grounds that the Nixons needed a larger home and were "so poor they haven't got a maid." Nixon had indeed put twenty thousand dollars down on a forty-one-thousand-dollar Washington house soon after becoming senator, and had hired an interior decorator to refurbish it in style. He even admitted to one reporter that without the fund he could not have made the down payment. (The Nixons had also acquired a full-time maid.)

Later reports commented archly on the apparent increased prosperity of the extended Nixon family, including the fact that Nixon's brother Donald—by now running both his parents' former grocery and a drive-in restaurant—was talking of setting up another restaurant on land owned by a contributor to Richard's fund.

In the Checkers speech Nixon had also made much of the claim that every cent of fund cash had been spent on items he thought should not be charged to American taxpayers. This defense ignored the fact that the money had gone toward purchases that could not legally have been charged to the taxpayers in any case. He had told a newsman that while in Washington he had no income except his Senate salary. This was not true: Money from the fund aside, Nixon had earned $6,611.45 from speech-making fees—about $44,000 at today's rates and about half as much again as a senator's salary in those days—in 1951 alone.

The fund money admitted by Nixon and formally audited may in fact not have represented the only fund in existence or all the money. When journalists first interviewed fund organizer Dana Smith before the story broke, one of them spotted on his desk a sheet of paper headed "Nixon Fund No. 2." Another journalist discovered that Smith had paid a bill for Nixon using checks on two accounts: the trust fund and a special account. Later still it was reported that *three* separate funds were involved.

These leads were never investigated, nor was the remark made by one of the fund's contributors to a journalist that "we've been paying his expenses for sometime now." No one knew then that as revealed in this book,* Nixon had let it be known to his supporters as early as 1946 that he could not live on a congressional salary and needed "a lot more than that" to match what he could expect to make as an attorney. The response of his big business backers, as described by corporation financial officer William Ackerman, had been to make a long-term financial commitment.

In 1952, as in the past, the driving force behind Nixon's campaign was Murray Chotiner. Years later Chotiner admitted that the fund had been his idea, with Dana Smith. He saw it as "a necessary source of the money Nixon needed to advance his career."

The seventy-six known fund contributors were as the *New York Times* put it, "an abbreviated Who's Who of wealthy and influential southern California business figures." Most reportedly were big-league millionaires, the majority being from the world of real estate, followed by oil magnates and manufacturers.

Why did they reach into their pockets? Smith, the fund's organizer, was disarmingly open about their motives when he first met with reporters before the scandal broke and damage control began. "We realized," he said of Nixon, "that his salary was pitifully inadequate for a salesman of free enterprise for his people in California. . . . [Earl] Warren never has gone out selling the free enterprise system. But Dick did just what we wanted him to."

No one seriously questioned another of Nixon's assertions: that none of the fund contributors had ever asked for or received a special favor in return. Again, that representation was less than the truth.

*See p. 47.

Solicitations for money had begun within a week of Nixon's election to the Senate. Two of the oilmen who responded were Tyler Woodward and William Anderson, who had been unsuccessfully trying to get clearance to drill for oil on government land in California. A dairy industry man who contributed, Alford Ghormley, wanted continued restrictions on European cheese imports. Others, including savings and loan executive Joseph Crail, Morgan Adams (chairman of a mortgage corporation), and the Rowan brothers (real estate brokers), all were vocal campaigners against public housing.

Within months of arriving in the Senate, Nixon had introduced a bill designed to allow precisely the sort of oil exploration that Woodward and Anderson wanted. He voted for strict limits on dairy trade with Europe, in contrast with his usual record of support for aid to the Continent. He was outspoken in opposing an increase in public housing, and voted for an amendment to a tax bill that favored building and loan associations.[6]

"Never, so far as the people that contributed to this fund are concerned," Nixon said in the Checkers speech, "have I made a telephone call for them to an agency." Here, again, he was skirting the truth. In February 1952 he had reportedly telephoned the secretary of the air force, Thomas Finletter, to arrange an interview for the head of Hammond Manufacturing. Hammond's bid for a half-million-dollar contract, previously rejected, was accepted soon afterward. The manufacturer was not known to have contributed to the Nixon fund, but he was a registered client of the law firm of which Dana Smith was a partner.[7]

Smith was a friend of Nixon's, and had often played host to him in his home. Not only did he manage the fund, but he and his law partner were contributors. He had also received two favors from Nixon, both of which place in doubt Nixon's claim that he had never phoned or "gone down to an agency" on behalf of his financial supporters. One of these episodes is an instance of questionable behavior, while the other suggests serious deception.

Not six months into Nixon's Senate term Smith had written to him asking for help with a long-standing tax problem, a wrangle with the IRS involving more than half a million dollars. The letter got results, including a meeting with Nixon in Washington and a phone call by Nixon's administrative assistant to arrange a half-hour interview with an IRS attorney. The outcome was "progress" for Smith with his tax problems, and eventually a settlement was reached.

In early August 1952 Nixon had written on Smith's behalf to the State Department, a curious intercession given that the matter concerned a gambling debt, a mob-run casino in Havana, Cuba, and controversy about the involvement not only of Smith but of Nixon himself.

Nixon's letter, according to the State Department, stated that Smith was "a highly respected member of his community" and that "the Senator would appreciate anything which the Embassy might be able to do to assist Mr. Smith in his problem." The enclosure, a letter from Smith himself, explained the nature of the problem. The previous April, on a visit to Havana's Sans Souci casino, he had lost forty-two hundred dollars—more than twenty-five thousand dollars in modern terms—while playing a dice game. He had then written a check to cover the losses, but subsequently put a stop on it. The casino management was considering legal action to recover the money.

Since it came from a senator, Nixon's request received attention. In Havana it was handled by the ambassador himself, who ordered local diplomats to respond immediately, within hours if possible, and department records show that they did so. They obtained a legal opinion from an outside attorney to answer Smith's queries as to whether the game in question was legal in Cuba and whether Smith would be held liable for the debt under Cuban law. The attorney responded with a yes on both counts.[8]

Later, when it emerged that Nixon had pressed the government to help his friend, his staff downplayed the story. An aide acknowledged that he had written the letter, while insisting that it had been a "routine service for a constituent." Later still his office claimed that the letter had in fact been written and signed by a secretary—an odd procedure, if true—and that Nixon did not know it had been sent or indeed anything at all about the case. The senator's staff was doing everything possible to disassociate him from Smith's run-in at the Sans Souci, and for good reason.

On October 30, a month after Nixon had survived the fund crisis and just days before the presidential election, the *St. Louis Post-Dispatch* added an intriguing detail to the affair: Nixon, it said, had been with his friend Smith at the Havana casino the night of the gambling incident.

While "in Miami on a combined holiday and political trip" and staying at the exclusive Quarter Deck Yacht Club on Pirate's Key, the paper reported, the two men had "decided to visit Havana," an hour's trip away by airplane. To take care of the embarrassing matter, Smith had since been trying to settle the dispute by offering to pay half the sum owed. The casino operator, Norman Rothman, was insisting on full payment.

When others in the media picked up this story, Nixon demanded an immediate retraction. He had not been in Havana, he maintained, in the past ten years, a reference to his 1941 vacation trip with his wife.* At the time in question, he was later to claim, he had been in Hawaii.

While Nixon's denial cited his whereabouts for the period "from March 14 through April," it is not clear exactly when Smith got into trouble in Havana. The *Post-Dispatch* story did not specify the date any more closely than "March or early in April." Moreover, the information as to when Smith wrote his check and when he stopped it is conflicting.[9]

Fresh study meanwhile indicates that the evidence that Nixon *was* in Havana with Smith cannot be easily dismissed. The reporter who wrote the *St.*

*See p. 32.

Louis Post-Dispatch story, Theodore Link, was a distinguished journalist with thirty years' experience and relevant qualifications. His articles on corruption in the IRS had recently led to the resignation of President Truman's attorney general and won his paper a Pulitzer Prize. He had been praised by the Kefauver Committee on organized crime for providing vital leads on "the underworld, conniving politicians, and corrupt law enforcement." He also had extensive contacts in the criminal world of Miami, the segment of the mob primarily involved in running Cuba's casinos.

Information now available reveals that before writing his story, Link interviewed the manager of the Quarter Deck Yacht Club, Warren Freeman. Freeman confirmed that he and Richard Danner, Nixon and Bebe Rebozo's mutual friend, had "squired" Nixon and Smith during their visit; Nixon was known as a freeloader who habitually let others pick up the tab. Freeman confirmed to Link that Nixon had indeed accompanied Smith to Havana.

Separately Link located five witnesses who said they had seen Nixon at the Sans Souci with Smith. He had not gambled or drunk to excess, while Smith had been "lurchingly drunk."

After Nixon complained about the stories that placed him in Havana, moreover, the *Post-Dispatch* sent Link to interview the man himself. Nixon, he said, proved to be "chiefly sore at two other newspapers which had intimated that the gambling trip involved some girls. We had made no mention of any women. Nixon agreed that all the facts we printed were correct."

Mercifully for Nixon at the time, the published facts did not include the ominous element at the heart of the Cuba trip story, organized crime.

Two years after the 1952 election, when Nixon was well into his first term as vice president, Sans Souci operator Rothman met with a Pennsylvania district attorney, Horace Culbertson, and stated "categorically" that Nixon had indeed been in Havana at the time of the Dana Smith episode and had been gambling. Later still, in other interviews with law enforcement officers covering a range of matters, Rothman said that while Smith had written the offending check, on a 1950 Nixon campaign account, it had been Nixon who actually lost money that night.

Even more troubling was Rothman's assertion that he had covered up for Nixon, falsely telling a journalist in 1952 that Nixon had *not* been with Smith. In the months that followed, he claimed, he had shielded Nixon by avoiding giving testimony in the lawsuit against Smith. In response, he said, Nixon had sent him a message of thanks through a fellow member of Congress.[10]

Norman Rothman was a significant player in the organized crime apparatus that ran gambling in Havana. The casino he ran, the Sans Souci, was Cuba's classiest gaming palace, located in the heart of the Country Club district, home to the capital's elite families. Just weeks before the Dana Smith incident, the dictator, Fulgencio Batista, had returned to power. The American mafiosi who owned him, and filled his Swiss bank accounts, had already been flourishing. Now they virtually controlled Cuba.

If the likes of Dana Smith or Richard Nixon wanted to sample Havana's swankiest nightlife, the Sans Souci and the Hotel Nacional were the places to visit. Patrons of the Sans Souci, most of them Americans over from Florida on brief excursion trips, dined, danced, and gambled on a twenty-five-acre spread set with lush tropical vegetation enhanced by thousands of towering palm trees. Rothman ran the place for the Mannarino brothers of Pennsylvania, who were associated loosely with Florida mobster Santo Trafficante, but always in thrall to the organization's business brain, Meyer Lansky. Lansky, through his brother, Jake, was the power at the Hotel Nacional.

In Cuba and much farther afield, Lansky had become the most influential figure in moving organized crime away from the old-style extortion and mayhem to the penetration and sophisticated control of legitimate businesses and officialdom. In probing Nixon's possible links to gambling and to Cuba—and specifically to the Dana Smith embarrassment—Lansky's name crops up again, as it has repeatedly in connection with Bebe Rebozo.

The most authoritative study of Lansky was written by the Israeli journalist Uri Dan, working with two colleagues in the seventies, when Lansky was living in enforced exile in Tel Aviv. In their book, which drew on exclusive interviews with Lansky and his longtime intimate Joseph Stacher, they cast new light on the Dana Smith affair that would have pleased neither Nixon nor his fund organizer. Lansky, they learned, knew Smith "very well," well enough to contact him years later, during the earliest discussion of assassinating Fidel Castro.[11] The authors were also told that Nixon had been one of a group of men who accompanied Smith to Havana the year he hit a losing streak. One of the group was Rebozo's associate Dick Danner, and other information suggests Rebozo himself was on the junket.

"The really close friendship between Nixon and Rebozo," said former IRS operative Norman Casper, "began in Cuba." Casper, a Republican supporter who met Rebozo in the relevant time frame and on occasion did background checks for him, gained that impression from a conversation with a gambler friend who often visited Havana during the Batista period. The gambler, Arch Horner, told of seeing Nixon and Rebozo together in Havana at the Hotel Nacional in the early fifties. "I think Horner was either at the same table or at one nearby," Casper recalled in a 1999 interview, "because he described watching Nixon. Nixon was gambling pretty heavily. And, from a relative who worked in the cage, Horner said he learned that Nixon lost thousands of dollars—I think he said fifty thousand dollars—and Bebe picked up the marker on it. Bebe bailed Nixon out."

Newly released testimony appears to dispel doubt that Nixon, the strictly raised Quaker, indulged in gambling. In 1967 Max Courtney, one of three notorious bookmakers known to have worked for Lansky, appeared before a commission probing gambling in the Bahamas—in connection with Lansky's attempt to re-create his lost Cuban casino empire in the islands. Courtney had been hired by a Lansky associate to run a Nassau casino, he said casually, because of the extensive U.S. clientele he had, "from the ex-Vice President down." In 1967 "ex-Vice President" could mean only Nixon.

In a recent interview a second former investigator offered further allegations about Rebozo's background as well as a startling claim about Nixon and Lansky's people in Cuba.

"Rebozo," said Jack Clarke, a former OSS operative and a source of information on organized crime in the period, "was involved in Lansky's gambling. Lansky ran gambling illegally in Harlandale, Fort Lauderdale, and the areas east of Miami, and Rebozo was involved. He was tight with Lansky. . . . In 1951, when I was doing an investigation in the Miami area, Rebozo was pointed out to me at the racetrack by one of the hotel owners. He said, 'He's one of Lansky's people. We try to keep the Jews [Jewish criminals] out of Lauderdale. Rebozo's a pimp for them.' . . . When I checked the name with the Miami police, they said he was an entrepreneur and a gambler and that he was very close to Meyer."

An FBI document released in 2000 cites an informant who emphasized Rebozo's involvement, with Nixon and others, in business ventures in Cuba during the Batista period. "Rebozo," according to the informant, "fronted for the Italian money."

Later in the fifties, Clarke recalled, he stumbled upon Nixon's name while doing a black bag job, pilfering documents in an office at Havana's Hotel Nacional in connection with an unrelated investigation. "I was in the accounting office, looking for something on a fellow whose name began with *P* and going through the file alphabetically. I couldn't find it, and I went back further and came up with 'Nixon.' I took a quick look and snatched it. It showed that when Nixon stayed at the Hotel Nacional, which Lansky owned, they comped the whole deal—paid his bill. And it was the presidential suite, before he was really anything. The guy that signed the register, that authorized comping him, was Jimmy 'Blue Eyes' Alo."[12]

Vincent Alo, known always as Jimmy, came out of New York, as did Lansky, and became Lansky's trusted henchman. The criminal fraternity quickly learned that when Alo issued an order, it came from Lansky himself. Interviewed in Hollywood, Florida, in 1997, Alo, still sprightly at ninety-four, said he had handled money for Nixon. Alo was involved in the management of the Hotel Nacional. What of the suggestions that Nixon had a relationship with Lansky? "He met him in Havana," Alo acknowledged, "in the old days," by which, he explained, he meant the fifties. He would say no more.

Using his mob contacts, veteran organized crime specialist Hank Messick was told only that Lansky was "impressed" by the Havana gambling incident involving Nixon and Dana Smith. In 1948, said his close associate Joseph Stacher, Lansky and Charles "Lucky" Luciano "had hoped fervently that Tom

Dewey would win the presidency for the Republicans." "Meyer and Charlie," said Stacher, "were certain Dewey would accept financial support from them, and in return they would be allowed to operate their gambling without much interference." "In evaluating Nixon," Messick wrote, "Lansky could not fail to note that it was Governor Dewey of New York—having abandoned his own ambitions—who sponsored Nixon for Vice President in 1952."[13]

No more is known of Lansky's attitude to Nixon, for he did not elaborate in his interviews with his Israeli biographers, the only writers in whom he confided. We do have a notion, though, of another top mafioso's judgment as the 1952 presidential election approached. In Chicago, Sam Giancana, then a rising power in the national crime syndicate, had been observing the race closely. Asked if he was supporting the Democratic candidate, Adlai Stevenson, he merely laughed, as Giancana's brother Chuck recalled. "I like a winner," Giancana said then. "I like Ike. But I like his running mate, Nixon, even better. . . . I'm hedging my bets. We got campaign contributions to both sides: Our guys out in California are backing Nixon, and [Jake] Arvey's* handling Stevenson."

This sort of talk is reminiscent of FBI wiretaps of gangsters' conversations about their political preferences at the time of the 1960 election and about what they hoped for from John F. Kennedy. In 1952 the leaders of both parties knew the smear potential of information that would link their opponents to mob backing. In 1952 Adlai Stevenson learned that Nixon had received funding in California from the very start of his political career through gangster Mickey Cohen, who answered to Lansky.† According to an FBI report, Stevenson "sent an emissary to Cohen to try to get the story for use in the campaign, but Cohen refused to give it on the grounds that it would be like 'ratting.'" He would not be so coy later, as reported in an earlier chapter, when he was in jail and hoping for leniency under a new adminstration.

Nixon and some of his biographers have argued that he survived that year thanks not to luck but simply because he was an innocent man, the victim of vicious smears by the Democratic National Committee. True, the Democrats took every opportunity to slander his reputation, suggesting especially that he was susceptible to bribery. While they may on occasion have done so without good evidence, information now available, information that appears well sourced and not politically motivated, indicates that Nixon was indeed corrupt.[14]

---

*Jake Arvey was a Chicago political fixer with close links to organized crime and, in Las Vegas, to Lansky.

†See p. 54.

13

The top officials of both parties should set
an example of propriety and ethics which goes
beyond the strict minimum required by law.

—*Richard Nixon, October 1951*

On November 2, 1952, two days before the presidential election, Nixon's perennial foe Drew Pearson threw out two last-minute barbs in his television broadcast. Both questioned Nixon's ability to tell the truth. The first was trivial, pointing out that to court the Irish vote, the candidate had falsely claimed that his wife had been born on St. Patrick's Day. The second, a much more serious allegation that was soon to be lost in the excitement of the Republican victory, concerned Nixon's connection to a dubious Romanian exile named Nicolae Malaxa.

Malaxa, a diminutive fellow with a great line of patter, was a business wizard and a political Houdini. Before the war he had been his country's Alfred Krupp, a steel tycoon with interests ranging from oil pipelines and railroad locomotives to long-range cannons, munitions, and explosives. He had come to the United States in 1946, emerging from postwar Europe and the Communist takeover of Romania to reclaim his assets in the United States and get back into major international business. For him to operate effectively, it had been essential to obtain permission to remain in the United States, a requirement that proved to be a major hurdle and eventually brought a curious intervention by Richard Nixon.

Although many official files on Malaxa are still withheld, what is available makes it clear that there was widespread concern about admitting him to the United States. This is reflected in reports generated at the CIA, the State Department, and the General Services Administration (GSA) and eventually in no fewer than twenty file drawers at the Immigration and Naturalization Service (INS). In the words of a GSA special inquiry report, he had a "very unsavory reputation in his business dealings. He is described as a political opportunist . . ." said to have "made large-scale financial contributions to the [Romanian] Communist Party, and bribed several Romanian government officials prior to his entry into the United States . . . [and] his attitude toward the United States is strictly colored by his financial interest here."

Nor did the concern focus only on his business reputation. The GSA report also noted dryly that Malaxa had been "sympathetic toward the Nazis while they were in control in Romania." He was reportedly associated with both Hitler's number two, Hermann Göring, and his brother, Albert. Worse than that, according to a captured German wartime cable, he had been "the financial mainstay of the Legionnaires—the Iron Guard."

Romania's Iron Guard movement, which was supported by the foreign intelligence branch of the German SS, was a feared anti-Jewish terrorist organization. A witness who had once worked at its headquarters told the INS that Malaxa had indeed been a major source of funds for the guard. According to other sources, his mansion had been used by the guard as a base when it attempted a coup in 1941, a coup in which thousands of Jews were killed, some after suffering unspeakable torture.[1]

One August afternoon in 1951, in the United States, as Malaxa strove to obscure his past—he frustrated immigration officials by refusing to answer their questions—one of his New York lawyers placed a call to Whittier, California, to Thomas Bewley. Bewley was the attorney and Nixon family friend who had taken Nixon on at his law firm directly out of law school in 1937 and had backed his political rise since then. Malaxa needed California representation for a pipeline factory he was setting up in the state, the lawyer explained, and asked Bewley to handle the work. The choice of the one California law firm linked to Nixon, it was later claimed, was pure chance.

Although Nixon himself had not been active as an attorney since before the war, the firm was still called Bewley, Knoop and Nixon. Even when the firm did drop his name, it provided him with an office in the Bank of America Building for use when he was on the West Coast. Malaxa's new pipeline company, the Western Tube Corporation, was soon also listed as based in the same office suite, in room 607. The Romanian appointed both Bewley and Herman Perry, another Nixon family friend, to the board of Western Tube.

Western Tube never set up a plant or produced a single pipe. Even Tom Bewley later admitted that the venture amounted to no more than "paper shuffling." According to California Congressman John Shelley, years later, the company seemed "to have been a complete fraud, a springboard for entry to the United States." It was Nixon himself who put that springboard in place.

Even before the Malaxa approach to Bewley, Nixon had unsuccessfully introduced a private bill that would have allowed the Romanian to stay in the United States. Months later, as the Western Tube initiative got under way, Nixon wrote under his U.S. Senate letterhead to the head of the Defense Production Administration arguing that support for the project was "important, strategically and economically, both for California and the entire United States." A week later the administrator gave formal approval, ensuring the company and Malaxa preferential treatment and massive tax advantages.

Nixon continued to go to great lengths to help Malaxa with his immigration difficulties. He personally telephoned senior INS official Howard Blum and, with his friend Pat Hillings, now a congressman, again pushed for special legislation to ensure that the Romanian was granted permanent residence. When Malaxa was refused readmission to the country following an absence abroad, Attorney General William Rogers, another close Nixon associate, overruled the immigration authorities and allowed him back in.[2]

As a senator Nixon had access to the best information and the most authoritative sources. Why, in the case of Malaxa, did he go to such great lengths to help a rich foreign businessman with so dubious a reputation? The explanation now at hand, never aired publicly during Nixon's lifetime, is that Malaxa had purchased Nixon's favors with a massive bribe.

Drew Pearson's old working files, some of them typed and some in the form of sheets of scrawled notes, have survived among the journalist's papers at the Lyndon Johnson Library. They reveal that Pearson was probing the roles in the affair of Frank Wisner, who had worked in Romania as an agent for the OSS (forerunner of the CIA) at the end of the war, and Alexandre Cretzianu, a former Romanian diplomat. Close by, in a typed note, was the name of Constantin Visoianu, who had served as Romania's foreign minister.

Also in the file, in answers prepared for use in a libel suit brought by Malaxa, which never came to trial, Pearson noted that he had access to a CIA report during his work on the investigation. "I received," he added in the same document, "an anonymous message that Nixon had received $100,000 as a political campaign contribution from Malaxa. . . . I was not able to establish this to my satisfaction, and therefore did not include it in any column."

Pearson's lead, damning to Nixon if true, lay unseen and unpublished for more than thirty years, in records opened only in response to a request by this author. Today, in light of contemporary knowledge of U.S. intelligence activity and recent interviews with an elderly retired CIA officer, the clues the columnist was pursuing begin to seem plausible indeed.

Malaxa's modus operandi appears to have been based primarily on the power of the bribe. Soon after coming to the United States, he reportedly bought two Cadillacs and twelve thousand dollars' worth of jewelry at Cartier's in New York. One of the Cadillacs was shipped to Communist Romania's minister of communications and public works and the other to the head of the Romanian delegation in Washington. The jewels were a gift to Ana Pauker, the Romanian minister of foreign affairs. By one account, his very entry to the United States was achieved on the promise of a payment to a senior OSS officer.

Whether or not such inducements played a role, it is likely the OSS and later the CIA were involved with Malaxa. Wisner, the OSS officer mentioned in Pearson's notes, was a passionately committed cold warrior who upon his return to the United States after World War II headed his own covert action empire within the CIA. United States immigration laws barred the entry of war criminals, but Wisner quietly arranged exemptions for émigrés he believed he could manipulate in the fight against communism. According to a former CIA official, it was he who made use of Nicolae Malaxa.

Others in the CIA did have scruples about resorting to such a man.[3] In 1952, in the months before the presidential election, they included several officers on the Balkan Desk. Its branch chief that year was Gordon Mason, a veteran of postwar intelligence work in Romania, who was supplying several leading Romanian exiles with funds, among them Cretzianu and Visoianu, the former diplomats whose names appear in columnist Pearson's old notes. It was from them, Mason informed the author in 1999, that the CIA learned Malaxa had bribed Richard Nixon.

According to Mason, the bribe was the sum of one hundred thousand dollars—precisely as Pearson had been told by his source decades earlier. Malaxa had paid it, almost fatally for Nixon, with a check deposited in Nixon's account in Whittier, California, almost certainly at the Bank of America branch in the building where he, the Bewley law firm, and Malaxa's pipeline company all shared the same address.

Depositing the check nearly proved disastrous, Mason explained, because one of the tellers at the bank was a Romanian émigré in contact with exile leaders Cretzianu and Visoianu. The two former diplomats loathed Malaxa and, tipped off by the teller, got him to provide them with a photographic copy of the check. They relayed it to Mason at the CIA, who wrote a report for his division chief, who in turn took it to Wisner. With a "Jesus Christ! We'd better see Allen Dulles," Wisner sent the report on up the line.

Allen Dulles, newly appointed deputy director for operations, was of course a staunch Nixon backer. He did not block the report, however—the CIA is a bureaucracy, with automatic processes much like those of other bureaucracies—and the incendiary document was submitted to the man at the very top, Director of Central Intelligence Walter Bedell Smith.

As the author of the report Mason was summoned to a meeting in the director's office. Smith, "Beetle" to his colleagues, had served Eisenhower as chief of staff during World War II, and Mason never forgot his explosion of rage when confronted with the incriminating evidence of the Nixon bribe. "Smith was a man who could cuss in three languages and in almost every sentence. He also had a violent temper, and he acted as though I personally was trying to scuttle Eisenhower. He demanded that Herman Horton [the Southern Europe division chief] and I bring every copy of every item on this case to him personally, and he waited in the office while we went back and collected it all. It was obvious he was going to take over from there. And it was going to go nowhere. The story was cleaned from the books."

According to Mason, none of the material—not least the copy of the check—was ever seen again. Neither he nor his boss, Horton, had made duplicates. "I guess," Wisner later told Mason, "Beetle just flushed it all down the toilet."

Wisner said too that President Truman had learned of the episode and phoned Bedell Smith to ask about it. Mason concluded that the story had probably made its way to Truman as the result of a leak by the Balkan desk's Romanian exile operatives, frustrated that their ploy—from their point of view designed to trap Malaxa, rather than Nixon—had failed. Without the paper proof, however, the information was useless, a bomb without a detonator.

Can this story be confirmed, or as Nixon claimed of corruption accusations throughout his career, is it another cruel calumny? Mason's superior, Herman Horton, is dead, as are Wisner, Dulles, and Bedell Smith. Mason's two Romanian exile operatives, Visoianu and Cretzianu, are also dead. Visoianu's widow, contacted in 1999, remembered only that her husband had discussed "the Malaxa problem."

Mason, who seems a credible witness, offered one further detail. There were, he said, actually two checks involved. The hundred thousand dollars, as he understood it, were purportedly to be used to help finance a new venture for Nixon's brother Donald. The second check, a much smaller sum of five thousand dollars, was a contribution to Nixon's 1952 campaign. Mason dismisses the notion that the hundred thousand dollars may really have been intended for use by Donald. "I don't think Malaxa even knew Nixon's brother. . . . These were gifts to Nixon for his influence."

If Donald was indeed involved in the Malaxa affair, the episode eerily prefigured the $205,000 "loan" that the billionaire Howard Hughes would make—again supposedly to help Donald Nixon—in 1956.* This was a huge sum in the fifties, and would become a vast embarrassment for Nixon in two future election campaigns. Other Hughes contributions, supplied covertly before and during the Nixon presidency, would prove to be one of the most damaging elements in Watergate.

The hundred thousand dollars allegedly paid by Malaxa—more than half a million in modern terms—came perilously close to exposure in 1952. Had Drew Pearson been able to substantiate his anonymous tip, he might have run the story. Coupled with the allegations about the fund, it would surely have caused Eisenhower to drop Nixon as his running mate—even if, as remains possible, the charges were not true.

*See p. 154.

As for Nikolae Malaxa, he avoided deportation and lived on in the United States, ensconced luxuriously at a Fifth Avenue address, until the late sixties. Nixon made no mention of him in his memoirs.

———

On November 4, 1952, election day, Nixon cast his vote in his hometown of Whittier, climbed into a policeman's car, and vanished for the day. It was later revealed that, as he had two years earlier with Pat, but this time accompanied only by future Secretary of State William Rogers, he spent the time on the beach. They had bought swimming trunks and a ball and joined up with a group of marines from Camp Pendleton to play touch football.

That evening Nixon was wakened from a nap to learn that the voters had given the Eisenhower-Nixon ticket a historic landslide victory. The campaign, *Time* magazine later said, had been fought and won on "transcendent issues of morality." Within days, as the cheering ebbed away, Nixon and Pat headed for Florida and a vacation hosted by Bebe Rebozo.

They visited, once again, the Quarter Deck Yacht Club, the jumping-off point the previous spring for Nixon's alleged gambling trip to Cuba. The only embarrassment on this trip, however, came when house photographers snapped pictures of the vice president fishing in the ocean. In some of the shots he appeared to be struggling to land a huge fish—in fact, a stuffed trophy removed from the clubhouse wall and attached to his line as a joke. Soon afterward Rebozo scurried to retrieve both copies and negatives. Nixon was now "important," a man to be treated with decorum.

In forcing the pace to become a big political fish, though, he had made lasting enemies, some of whom loathed him with an intensity unusual even in the world of politics. Two years earlier, after observing at close hand Nixon's tactics against Helen Douglas, Democratic presidential aide Averell Harriman had been revulsed. Realizing Nixon was a fellow guest at a Washington dinner party soon after, he had declared, "I will not break bread with that man!" and wheeled around to leave. Persuaded to stay by the hostess, he had switched off his hearing aid and sat through the meal without uttering a word. Two decades later, when Harriman was an elder statesman, the perennial topic at his dinner table would be the importance of unseating Nixon.

Nixon's conduct in 1950 had offended both age and youth. "I have no respect," said Eleanor Roosevelt, "for the kind of character that takes advantage and does something they know is not true. . . . Anyone who wanted an election so much he would use those means did not have the character that I really admire in public life." The young John F. Kennedy had been friendly with Nixon in Congress and had contributed to his campaign in 1950 even though he represented the opposing party. "I did donate to Nixon," he acknowledged later, "the biggest damnfool mistake I ever made."

While Democratic criticism was predictable, the virulence of its expression was unusual. "He would double-cross and destroy the reputation of anybody," said Roger Kent, the Democratic chairman in Nixon's home state, "if it seemed to serve his interest." Adlai Stevenson characterized "Nixonland" as "a land of slander and scare, of sly innuendo, of poison pen and anonymous phone call and bustling, pushing, shoving—the land of smash and grab and anything to win." Emanuel Celler, the veteran congressman from New York, thought Nixon "naive, inept, maladjusted," a fellow who could not muster enough character references to join the local library.

Unlike the millions swayed by the Checkers speech, the powerful columnist Walter Lippmann had considered it "the most demeaning experience my country has ever had to bear." George Ball, the future undersecretary of state, dismissed it as an "emetic sciamachy," a string of absurdities likely to induce vomiting, a toilet reference echoed by others. He deplored Nixon's "sanctimonious pose of self-pity, seeking to associate himself with other beleaguered Americans burdened by debt and family anxieties."

The speech "was the cleverest demagogic ham I've seen," thought Florida's Congressman Claude Pepper. "It was almost frightening to think how dangerous he is and what a reception he got with it. It was full of holes but they were cleverly concealed." Norman Redlich, future dean of New York University Law School, read the Checkers speech as a "Handbook for Demagogues" based on low precepts. "Above all," he wrote in *The Nation*, "never discuss the actual thing for which you were called to task by the American people. . . . Never raise the question of whether it was right to take money from people who have a stake in the way you vote. Create your own ethical standards and then point out how rigidly you adhere to them. . . . And if the people are really as dumb as you think they are, you may someday be President of the United States."

One of Nixon's taunts at the outgoing president, Harry Truman, was never forgiven. In Arkansas, shortly before the election, Nixon had lumped the president, Adlai Stevenson, and Secretary of State Dean Acheson together as "traitors." Precisely what he said remained disputed. Nixon insisted that he stated that the three were traitors not to their country but to "the high principles in which many of the nation's Democrats believe."[4] Whatever the truth, it was the very word "traitor," uttered in a time of high ferment about national loyalty, that rankled Truman. In another speech, moreover, Nixon had dared call him "one of these crooks" and then tried to back away from it as he had from the "traitor" remark. Truman told his biographer that he rarely carried personal grudges but that Nixon was one of the only two men he could not stand.[5] "You can't very well forget things of that kind, and that's why I don't trust Nixon and never will. . . . Nixon is a shifty, goddamn liar, and people know it." Truman was not sure if Nixon had ever read the Constitution. "But I'll tell you this," he added. "If he has, he doesn't understand it."[6]

Justly or not, Nixon was held in contempt by very many Americans by the time he became vice president. Such citizens shrank away from him because he was already established in their minds as representing something politically abhorrent, unclean. "Like more than a few Americans of my generation," wrote

New York Times theater critic Frank Rich in 1994, when he was in his mid-forties, "I learned to despise Richard Nixon around the time I learned to recite the Pledge of Allegiance."

As he habitually did, Nixon dismissed the charges leveled against him in 1952 as malicious smears. "My instinct was to fight back," he wrote years later. "I quickly came to feel a kinship with Teddy Roosevelt's description of the man in the arena 'whose face is marred by dust and sweat and blood.'" He used the quotation often during his career, and liked the image of himself as the hard-pressed gladiator fighting massive odds.[7]

But at the height of his troubles during the 1952 campaign, in a room at New York's Barclay Hotel, Nixon had seemed more plaintive—paranoid even—than brave and gladiatorial. "Strip," he had told his former Hiss-hunting aide Robert Stripling, "those sons of bitches are out to get me. . . . They tried to get me, and they'll try to get anybody that has anything to do with the Hiss case." Behind the strident speechmaking, Nixon was not standing up well under pressure.

"The hotter the political fighting," Pat told a magazine that fall, "the cooler he seems to get. . . . Dick seldom loses his temper." In fact, the contrary was true. Nixon admitted to volatility, inherited, he said, from his father. He called it blowing his stack, and aides recalled "Black-Irish" stack blowing after every crisis.

It was the aides who took the brunt of such rages. Herb Klein and Pat Hillings long remembered Halloween night 1952, when they saw, as Klein put it, "the full display of his quick anger."

At an event in Hollywood, Nixon had noticed that the stadium was only half full. Major stars like John Wayne and Jane Russell were there, but hundreds of seats remained empty. Back in his hotel Nixon exploded. "Goddamn you! Goddamn you! How the hell could you embarrass me like this?" he shouted at Hillings. "You could lose us the election like this, Goddamn you!" Murray Chotiner, who was present, had seen such outbursts before; Nixon had behaved much the same after the Checkers speech. To Klein he appeared "as angry as any man I have ever seen." To Hillings he seemed frighteningly close to violence.

A leader, Nixon said, had "an obligation not to lose his temper in public," and his rage usually erupted behind closed doors. After a rally in Southern California, however, when he recognized a Democratic party activist who had long plagued him, he reportedly strode over and slapped her in the face.[8] The press missed the episode, and horrified aides hustled him away.

During the 1952 campaign Nixon's followers sometimes did resort to violence. In Oregon fighting broke out as his campaign train pulled away, immediately after an angry speech made in the face of pickets suggesting Nixon was corrupt. "The crowd surged over with fists flying," recalled Charles Porter, later a Democratic congressman. "I was mad because we had a right to be there and express our opinion. This is what Nixon had done."

Two days before the election, at Long Beach, Nixon threatened vocal critics with jail. A "gang of roughnecks" in his entourage reportedly beat up hecklers carrying anti-Nixon signs. The local press ran an account of "roughhouse tactics" used by an eight-man "strong-arm squad" traveling with the candidate. Democratic official Richard Rogan complained of incidents in three towns: a Stevenson driver manhandled at Burbank, a placard holder worked over at Glendale, a man handing out leaflets punched and kicked at Pasadena.

For obvious reasons it was rarely possible to link Nixon himself to his supporters' strong-arm tactics. When he lost his temper publicly, though, his direct involvement was often clear. "When we're elected," he yelled at one heckler, "we'll take care of people like you!" He then ordered, "Okay, boys, throw him out!"

Several years later, when he was vice president, a similar situation occurred. When a heckler shouted, "Tell us the dog story, Dick!" identifiable members of Nixon's party surrounded him. When he raised his voice again and moved toward the podium, Nixon became "white with anger" and instructed police and Secret Service agents to detain the heckler, James Heavey, while he harangued him in front of the audience for ten minutes. Then once again, he gave, reportedly screamed, the command "Throw him out!" Heavey later brought a civil suit, alleging public humiliation, battery, and bruising to his arms and body.[9] Such incidents escaped national attention, as did violent episodes in the future.

Anger and on occasion a penchant for violence alternated with depression and fits of weeping. The well-documented seven days of the fund crisis featured numerous instances of seesawing emotion. On day one, seeing the first headlines while aboard the campaign train, Nixon had slumped in his chair so physically stricken that he had to be helped back to the privacy of his compartment. "He almost needed intensive care," said a companion. "They almost had to take him off the train." In the early hours of day three, by his own account, he was feeling "the full weight of fatigue and depression." Hours later he seemed "completely shaken and despondent . . . edgy and irritable." On day four he was dejected, "ready to throw in the sponge." To Jack Drown, a longtime friend, he appeared to "age a lifetime." Worried campaign managers thought it was "conceivable he could blow up."

Later the same day a telegram from Hannah Nixon—HAVE FAITH, MOTHER—left him sobbing openly. "When I brought him that yellow paper," Hillings recalled, "he broke down and cried. I thought I had better leave the room and give him time to compose himself. . . . When I opened his door again, Dick was sitting in a huge leather armchair, his arms stretched out, his hand dangling in that characteristic way of his. . . . I knew I was in the presence of total despair."

From then on Nixon surrendered to tears: tears after making his Checkers speech, tears on board his plane in front of embarrassed reporters when Eisenhower came on board to say, "You're my boy," and the famous public tears on Senator William Knowland's shoulder an hour or so later.

"Frankly," Chotiner said later, he had been "more worried about Dick's state of mind than about the party." As he prepared to fly to Los Angeles to make the Checkers speech, Nixon had tried frantically to reach Dr. Hutschnecker on the telephone.[10]

Pat had been supportive of her husband throughout the campaign, in spite of her misgivings, playing the good wife for him in the way the fifties public expected. She prattled dutifully about the details of domestic life, of his wardrobe and hers, of sewing classes and trips to the zoo, of Sunday family picnics on the floor of her husband's office. As for campaigning, she said meekly, "I go around with him and talk to the women." She claimed to "really love" the work, and that a future in politics "terrifically thrilled" her.

When the fund crisis hit, according to Nixon, it was she who urged him not to resign but to go on fighting. Just before the speech, when he felt he could not go through with it, it was she who insisted, "Of course you can," and led him to the microphone, she who told him afterward that it had been "great." When it was all over, though, after the conciliatory meeting with Eisenhower, she had driven back to the hotel with her husband in total silence.

The crisis had only multiplied Pat's previous doubts. "Why?" she had sobbed. "Why should we keep taking this?" Jack Drown's wife, Helene, who comforted her, thought she looked "like a bruised little kitten." Three decades later, when Pat's daughter Julie asked her to discuss the fund, she turned her face to the wall for long minutes before replaying. "There was so much pain in her eyes," Julie recalled, "that I could not bear to look at her."

"I knew," Nixon wrote in the seventies, "how much it had hurt her, how deeply it had wounded her sense of pride and privacy. I knew that from that time on, although she would do everything she could to help me and help my career, she would hate politics and dream of the day when I would leave it behind. . . ."

And then there was Mother. Hannah Nixon played an unusual role in the fund crisis, one that most adult sons would surely have regarded as an outrageous intrusion. She had been in Washington baby-sitting the girls, then aged six and four, when the story broke in the newspapers. Her husband, Frank, like his son, had been reduced to bouts of weeping. Hannah began a series of long-distance calls to Pat and, along with the telegram to her son, composed another to General Eisenhower himself. It read:

I AM TRUSTING THAT THE ABSOLUTE TRUTH MAY COME OUT CONCERNING THIS ATTACK ON RICHARD. WHEN IT DOES I AM SURE YOU WILL BE GUIDED ARIGHT IN YOUR DECISION TO PLACE IMPLICIT FAITH IN HIS INTEGRITY AND HONESTY. BEST WISHES FROM ONE WHO HAS KNOWN RICHARD LONGER THAN ANYONE.

HIS MOTHER, HANNAH NIXON

Eisenhower read the telegram aloud in public the night he welcomed Nixon back into the fold.

Four months later, on January 19, 1953, as the Nixon family gathered for a private dinner on inauguration eve, Nixon's mother took him aside and handed him a small piece of paper bearing the following message:

> To Richard
> You have gone far and
> we are proud of you always—
> I know that you will keep
> your relationship with your
> maker as it should be
> for after all that, as you
> must know, is the most
> important thing in this life
> With Love Mother

"I put it in my wallet," Nixon wrote of the note, "and I have carried it with me ever since." Soon enough it was joined there by a brief memorandum to himself that Nixon wrote at Pat's request. He would retire from politics, he was to promise her, at the end of his first term as vice president, in 1956. He had put the assurance in writing, as if to emphasize that it was unbreakable. "But," as Pat said years later, "things took a different turn."

––––––––––

Nixon used an ancient family Bible, an heirloom brought along by his mother, at his inauguration as vice president. As a Quaker he had the right to substitute the word "affirm" for the word "swear"—Quakers have a religious objection to swearing any oath—but he chose the standard phrasing and, with his Quaker parents close by, intoned: "I, Richard Nixon, do solemnly swear that I will support and uphold the Constitution. . . ."

His hand rested on a passage from the Sermon on the Mount—"Blessed are the peacemakers: for they shall be called the children of God"—which may have been intended as a nod to the Quakers' guiding precept of Peace at the Center. Certainly, in the years that followed, Nixon was to assert that his life's deepest desire was to bring peace between nations. In the eight years he served Eisenhower as vice president, he was to travel the world more than any American leader had done before, building up a breadth of knowledge on international affairs unequaled in his time.

At forty Nixon was the youngest vice president in nearly a century. On that January day of his first inauguration, the head of his Secret Service detail thought, the look on his face was one of "exaltation."

Yet even then there were portents. Some of those who would feature in his future disgrace had already crossed his path. A few months earlier, as Nixon arrived at the studio to make the Checkers speech, one of the Young Republicans cheering him on had been twenty-five-year-old H. R. Haldeman. His father, car dealer Henry Haldeman, had been a contributor to the fund. During the campaign a teenager called Lucy Steinberger had had the chutzpah to ask Nixon for an interview when he visited her high school in Virginia; under her married name, Lucianne Goldberg, she would become better known. The revelation of her work as a sex spy for the Nixon White House gave her a bit part in the Watergate saga. In 1998, in a not dissimilar function, she orchestrated the exposure of President Clinton's sexual adventures with Monica Lewinsky.

It was also probably in 1952 that Nixon met a much more significant Watergate player, E. Howard Hunt. Then a young CIA officer, he had come over to Nixon's table at Harvey's restaurant in Washington, discussed politics for a while, and left his calling card. "My wife and I," Hunt scrawled on the back of the card, some twenty years before he was to lead the raid on the Democratic party headquarters in the Watergate building, "want to thank you for the magnificent job you're doing for our country." *[11]

In his function as vice president, Nixon would soon officiate at the swearing in of a new U.S. senator for North Carolina, Sam Ervin. He was the man whom President Nixon, on the Watergate tapes, would characterize as an "old shit," the man who, as the magisterial chairman of the Senate Watergate Committee, earned the affections of millions when he presided over the ruin of Richard Nixon.

Back in the fifties Ervin had felt "Somewhat cool" toward the young man officiating at the ceremony. He did not like what he had heard about his election tactics.

*See facsimile on following page.

E. Howard Hunt, Jr.
Attaché
Embassy of the United States of America
Mexico City

(over)

My wife and I want to
thank you for the
magnificent job you're
doing for our country.

Howard Hunt

14

Handsome and kind, Handsome and kind,
Always on time, Loving and Good.
Does things he should, Humerous, funny
Makes the day seem sunny, Helping others to live,
Willing to give his life, For his belovd country,
That's my dad.

—Julie Nixon's poem for her father, written in 1956,
when she was eight and he was vice president

One evening in 1954, after martinis and steak at Duke Zeibert's Restaurant in Washington, Nixon slumped back amid the plush and gold plate of his official limousine. "This," he said wearily, patting the upholstery, "is the only thing about the goddamn job I like. Except for this, they can have it. . . ."

Eighteen months into his term of office his exaltation about the vice presidency had turned to despond. His companion in the limousine that night was James Bassett, the political journalist on loan from the *Los Angeles Mirror* who was to manage his press relations and scheduling for years to come. Bassett, a bespectacled navy veteran just three months older than Nixon, served as adviser, political sounding board, and drinking companion. His letters home to his wife, Wilma, offer a rare, intimate glimpse of the private Nixon.

Bassett had thought Nixon "quietly intense" but "affable" when he first met him six years earlier and had jokingly used his minuscule seniority to address Nixon as "son." Now, he reflected, he barely recognized him. Nixon, he wrote his wife, had become "the oldest young man I ever saw. . . . Sometimes I feel like a doggoned kid when I'm around him."

Nixon preferred to do his real work not in his ceremonial headquarters or in his staff suite in the Senate complex but in P-55, a remote room in the Capitol building that few knew how to find. While Bassett had always respected his "judgment and ability," he thought he had grown more intense than ever. "The man never rests, relaxes—I guess he takes politics through his pores, the way a leaf gets chlorophyll."

Nixon told Bassett he was one of those politicians with "ice water in our veins," but he sometimes showed a "subliminal sentimental streak." "I'd met him for lunch somewhere in uptown Washington," Bassett wrote, "and he was carrying with him a clumsily wrapped paper parcel. 'It's a doll,' he explained, although I hadn't asked. 'For Julie and Tricia?' 'No," Nixon frowned. 'It's actually for a little crippled kid I happened to read about in the paper this morning. She's in a charity hospital. It said she wanted a doll. So I'm going to take this out to her after we've finished.' "

Ever the PR man, Bassett thought the gift would make good press. But Nixon would have none of it. "If you ever leak this to the newspapers," he threatened, "I'll cut your balls off."

Nixon seemed to Bassett to be a loner with a tendency to "retreat deeper into that almost mystic shell." He rarely went home in the evening and, because Bassett was living in Washington away from his own wife and family, would call him on the spur of the moment to suggest dinner. In these, his "lonesome lost moods," Nixon shed some of his "grimness and glacial determination" and did some companionable drinking.

Bassett's account establishes that Nixon's somewhat pious writing about drink in later years and loyalists' protestations that he rarely drank are hypocritical. Himself no stranger to liquor, Bassett recalled their bibulous nights. "We ordered extra dry Gibsons (with Nixon darkly muttering it was a 'great mistake'). Then a second round. Then RN, having relaxed enthusiastically, briskly demanded a third, all his darkling fears apparently gone. Then a sound California Inglenook white Pinot, oysters and baked pompano. . . . In RN's fabulous Cad, we tooled out to a place called Martin's in old Georgetown, a saloon-type café, where we feasted on corned beef, cabbage, and great drafts of Michelob. . . . We had Scotches. RN took two of them fast, heavy and straight, thereby heightening his curious mood."

Sometimes the drinking was a feature of the working day. Bassett again: "We'd arrived earlier for lunch than usual, and prowled through his desk for a jug of Scotch, but finding only a platoon of very defunct soldiers; then RN arriving with Rose Woods in tow, and she laden with a small box in which nestled the necessaries of any decent midday confab."

In 1952, the year *Time* reported the official line that Nixon "rarely takes a drink," the Democrats' financial wizard Carmine Bellino had visited him. "At about 5 P.M.," he recalled, "Nixon stated it was cocktail hour. He pulled open his desk drawer, took out a bottle of scotch, and called Rose Woods to bring three glasses. After pouring scotch into the glasses, he offered us a drink without ice. . . ."

Elmer Bobst, the pharmaceutical tycoon, advised Nixon in the fifties to put a bottle of scotch in his briefcase if he wanted to avoid losing it. "Scotch, or perchance gin," he wrote, "are [sic] wonderful catalysts blending together memory and briefcases." Nixon apparently did develop a liking for gin. Bobst recalled how they once both pretended to order plain tonic water to avoid offending an accompanying cleric; that the well-trained barman would add gin to it.

In 1954, the year Bassett spent the most time with Nixon, an article based on a personal interview with the vice president reported that he "won't drink at all if he's tangling with a problem." However, Bassett's accounts suggest that like other mortals, Nixon used alcohol precisely when he was confronting a difficult issue.

Drink affected him easily and perhaps more so as time passed. Bassett remembered spending "a most curiously interesting couple of hours" with his boss in the late fifties, when he "let his thinning hair way down over a few Scotches." Bassett reported, as did others, that "after two Martinis he'd be very garrulous . . . two drinks and he's off to the races."

Nixon on occasion became obviously the worse for wear in lofty company. "Nixon had a glass or two more than he should have done," Pat Hillings recalled of an evening with the Eisenhowers shortly before the start of his vice presidency. "It didn't really show until he came down in the elevator, but then he startled everyone by giving the wall a smack and saying at the top of his voice, 'I really like that Mamie. She doesn't give a shit for anybody—not a shit!'"

Nixon may have genuinely liked Mamie, but his relationship with Ike remained ambivalent.

———————

At the start of the Eisenhower administration some dubbed Nixon "Ike's errand boy." The sneer was not unexpected because the post of vice president of the United States had traditionally been one with an imposing name but no real power. Eisenhower needed Nixon to keep the Republican right on his side and, not least, to help contain the erratic Joe McCarthy. At sixty-three, he also needed a younger man to carry the burden of hard campaigning and foreign travel. Nixon took on all those responsibilities, and his marathon trips abroad were the foundation of the foreign policy expertise that remains his most positive legacy. What Eisenhower did not want, however, was for Nixon to be perceived as playing the role Life magazine proposed early on: "Assistant President."

While the two men were publicly civil to each other, Eisenhower went out of his way to keep Nixon at arm's length. Lyndon Johnson, then a rising power in the Senate, recalled Eisenhower's resentment when Nixon tried discreetly to influence policy. According to James Reston, the *New York Times* journalist, Eisenhower "simply was not interested in Nixon's view of things." He reportedly found him "immature" and would still be describing him as such as late as the sixties, after Nixon had turned fifty.

Some at the White House thought Nixon more liability than asset, and the scorn was reciprocated. In private, drinking with Bassett, Nixon spoke contemptuously of the "tea drinkers" surrounding the president. He dismissed the cabinet as "dumb." When he went on television to help distance the White House from Joe McCarthy, though, he smiled for the camera as Eisenhower had urged him to.

Shortly before that speech, while quaffing bourbon with Bassett, Nixon had made a remark that today resonates with irony. "He said wistfully," Bassett recalled, "that he'd love to slip a secret recording gadget into the President's office, to capture some of those warm, offhand, greathearted things the Man says, play 'em back, then get them press-released. . . ." Curiously enough, two decades before Nixon was to install secret recording equipment in his White House, Eisenhower had recording equipment set up in the Oval Office, a device he activated with the flip of an unseen switch under his desk.

With Nixon present, Eisenhower urged senior colleagues to tape their phone calls. "You know, boys," he said, "it's a good thing, when you're talking to someone you don't trust, to get a record made of it. There are some guys I just don't trust in Washington, and I want to have myself protected so that they can't later report that I said something else." According to one Nixon biographer, Eisenhower "nearly always remembered to turn on the machine when he was talking to Nixon."[1]

The transcript of one such recording, made in June 1954, shows Eisenhower castigating his vice president for a speech in which he had attacked Democratic foreign policy. The president bluntly told Nixon that he was wrong on his facts and was compromising White House efforts to build bipartisan support. Having promised to be more circumspect in future, Nixon was so depressed afterward that Bassett thought him "lower than a snake's belly." In his memoirs Nixon would suggest he had had a collegial relationship with Eisenhower. Privately he told Haldeman that he "saw Dwight D. Eisenhower alone about six times in the whole deal. . . ."

Political issues aside, Nixon suffered many small humiliations. Eisenhower loved golf and often played at the exclusive Burning Tree Club in the Maryland countryside. Nixon, usually more spectator than sportsman, now took up golf energetically. While he reportedly played with "furious dedication," he lacked skill or finesse. It was even reported that he cheated on occasion, by throwing the ball out of the rough back onto the fairway.

Once, on an excursion with Bassett, Nixon went to Burning Tree on a day Eisenhower was playing. "Nixon fired off the tee first—a wobbly shot into the woods. He hit six in all. Then the others, and by this time Ike and his party were breathing on our group's necks. So, after some slight Alphonse and Gastoning, the presidential group went through. . . . We lunched at one of the long communal tables. . . . The president sat at the adjoining table, grinning, laughing and joking, with *his* foursome."

"Nixon complained to me," recalled Walter Trohan, "that Ike didn't have him in to play golf—I guess his game wasn't good enough. Ike played with pros."[2] Nor were invitations extended to play bridge with the president or to attend social evenings in the private quarters of the White House.[3] Four years into the presidency, out at the president's Gettysburg farm, Nixon watched as Eisenhower escorted other guests indoors. "Do you know," he told a companion bitterly, "he's never asked me into that house yet."[4]

Nixon spoke to Dr. Hutschnecker, the psychotherapist, about his resentment. According to the doctor, "Eisenhower was always telling Nixon to straighten his tie or pull back his shoulders, or speak up or shut up."

The conservative writer Ralph de Toledano thought Eisenhower was a "complete sadist" toward Nixon. "He would cut him up just for the fun of it. . . . Nixon would come back from the White House and, as much as he ever showed emotion, you'd think he was on the verge of tears."

Not only the president spurned Nixon at this time. In the spring of 1954 he was rebuffed by both the educational institutions at which he had once excelled. The Duke University faculty, in its first ever such action, turned down a trustees' proposal that Nixon be awarded an honorary Doctorate of Laws. When officials called a second meeting, in hopes of getting the decision reversed, Nixon was again rejected. Weeks later, when he gave the commencement address at his alma mater, Whittier College, students formed two reception lines: one for those who refused to shake Nixon's hand, one for those willing to greet him. Only two were in the latter group, and Nixon's mother declared herself "pained."

In Washington, meanwhile, Nixon was making few friends. At a party the Nixons gave, CBS reporter Nancy Dickerson recalled, "he was an uncomfortable host, disappearing from time to time, only to return to urge guests to have another drink, with a vigorous show at being friendly. Being a host did not come easy for him."

Patricia Alsop, the English wife of columnist Stewart Alsop, found the Nixons "wooden and stiff . . . terribly difficult to talk to" when she invited them to one of her soirees. "Nixon danced only one dance, with me. He was a terrible dancer, and Pat didn't dance at all. They stayed only half an hour. It was like having two little dolls—or as if the school monitor had suddenly appeared at the dance. I couldn't wait for him to go."

Stewart Alsop noted that Nixon often sparked an almost allergic dislike in people, including many Republicans. Those who did not think Nixon worthy of a halo, the columnist observed, tended to ascribe to him cloven hooves and a tail. Alsop coined a term for this condition, one that remained chronic for forty years to come: Nixonophobia.

By the end of the 1954 congressional campaign Nixon was at a low ebb. "I am tired, bone tired," he said privately. "My heart's not in it." He told Chotiner he was "through with politics" and assured Pat that he would retire when his term as vice president ended. Bassett bet him ten dollars that he would run again, and he took the bet. Then came a sudden, unexpected event that changed his mind.

Nixon had just returned home from a Washington wedding reception on a September afternoon in 1955 when he learned that he might become president of the United States within hours. In far-off Colorado, after a day of travel, work, and twenty-seven holes of golf, Eisenhower had suffered a heart attack. Informed by phone, Nixon responded, "Oh, my God! How bad is it?" and then fell silent for so long that the aide thought he had been cut off. When he finally spoke, Nixon pointed out that many people made full recoveries from coronaries. He agreed to stay near the phone and await more news.

To ascend to the presidency had always been the logical goal of Nixon's struggle. Now that the prospect was upon him, at the age of forty-two, he was stunned. "For fully ten minutes I sat alone," he recalled, "and to this day I cannot remember the thoughts that flowed through my mind. The only accurate description is that I probably was in a momentary state of shock. . . . I realized what a tremendous responsibility had descended upon me. It was like a great physical weight holding me down in the chair."

In Nixon's version, he quickly gathered his wits and faced the crisis. Friends thought his reaction less poised. "His voice was hoarse and charged with emotion. 'It's terrible, it's terrible!' he said over and over. . . . [He] was trying to keep his composure, but he was in semishock. His eyes were red and his face drawn and pale. . . . he aged the equivalent of quite a few years during those three months—in his own estimation, as well of those with whom he worked."

Eisenhower did recover, of course, but it was nearly two months before he returned to Washington, and Nixon meanwhile presided over meetings of the cabinet and the National Security Council.

Eisenhower's chief of staff, Sherman Adams, asserted that Nixon "leaned over backward to avoid any appearance of assuming presidential authority." John Foster Dulles's biographer, on the other hand, concluded that Adams and the secretary of state strove "to retain control in trusted hands and to avoid delivering political power to an ambitious Richard Nixon." Adams was reportedly "doing everything he can to cut Mr. Nixon down to size."

There were two more Eisenhower health crises during his presidency: an intestinal operation the following year and in 1957 a minor stroke that affected the president's speech. Nixon "did not preside very well," noted economic adviser Clarence Randall after a cabinet meeting the vice president chaired during the second hospitalization. "He let the discussion get way out of hand. . . ." Another participant passed a note to a colleague during the same meeting. "I shall pray harder than ever," it read, "for the President's recovery."

It was the situation created by Eisenhower's 1955 heart attack, Nixon noted, that made him hesitate about quitting politics. For if Ike did not run for a second term, he figured, "I would be next in line for the presidential nomination." The prospect appalled many. Asked what the Republicans would do should Eisenhower die, party chairman Leonard Hall replied with black humor: "We would run him anyway. There is nothing in the Constitution that says the President must be alive."

As the recovering Eisenhower pondered whether to face a reelection campaign, he had a long conversation about political successors with his press secretary, James Hagerty. Nixon did not feature on a shortlist of four people he deemed "mentally qualified for the presidency." "The fact is," he told speechwriter Emmet Hughes, "I've watched Dick a long time, and he just hasn't grown. So I just haven't been able to believe that he *is* presidential timber."

Should he run again, Eisenhower later told Nixon at a face-to-face meeting, he thought it might be better for Nixon to take a cabinet post rather than be his running mate. While some later insisted that Eisenhower was merely offering Nixon a better long-term stepping-stone to power, it may be that he simply had other preferences. Notes of a meeting with Len Hall reflect discussion about "getting Nixon out of the picture" and end with the president's instructing Hall to see Nixon but "be very, very, gentle." In fact, Eisenhower remained noncommittal for months to come.

Nixon and those close to him variously described his reaction to Eisenhower's ambivalence as "agonizing," "absolutely indescribable anguish," "one of the greatest hurts of his entire career," and "fury." Pat Nixon said the episode made her husband "more depressed than she ever remembered."

An additional reason for Eisenhower to be hesitant about having Nixon on the ticket again emerged at an April meeting when Nixon, according to contemporary notes, tackled what he called "another matter . . . the Murray Chotiner case." Nixon's close associate's criminal links had first emerged four days before Eisenhower suggested that Nixon might quit the vice presidency for a cabinet post and more revelations followed, some of them leading to the involvement of the FBI. There was a furor over an article labeling Chotiner "Dick Nixon's Secret Link to the Underworld," and the *Washington Post* reported Chotiner's untrue claim to have had no contact with Nixon since he became vice president. A congressional probe was getting under way.*

Nixon's fund scandal had threatened not only Nixon but the entire Republican campaign, and the Chotiner revelations must have filled the president with foreboding. Eisenhower wanted Nixon's assurances that the charges had no basis, and he needed the record to show that those assurances had been given. With that accomplished, he cleared Nixon to announce to the press that he would again be on the ticket.

*See full coverage in chapter 6.

Bassett had won his ten-dollar bet, and Nixon was running again. Again he bore the brunt of the campaign, this time setting out on a whirlwind marathon run with efficiency and flair. He covered forty-two thousand miles, barnstorming thirty-six states in less than two months. His use of a campaign plane, a DC-6B dubbed the Dick Nixon Special, was an innovation. While traveling between cities, Nixon hunched in his private cabin, working with his briefing sheets to tailor the Speech—the boilerplate text used throughout the tour—to suit the next destination.

Some campaign days began at 7:00 A.M. and ended at 3:00 A.M. the following day, only to start again at 7:00. Pat, described by the press as "always cheery, never weary," traveled with her husband. She packed for him, readers were told, making sure he had a plaid smoking jacket to work in—"to keep his suits unwrinkled for the day's appearances." When Nixon got a throat infection, he pushed on with the help of antibiotics and a cortisone throat spray. When he lost his voice, Pat stepped up to the mike and finished a speech for him.

A tour manager, press aides, and secretaries with typewriters and a duplicating machine manned the work area in Nixon's flying headquarters. A corps of advance men ranged ahead, preparing the way at each new stop. One of them was a thirty-year-old advertising man on leave of absence from J. Walter Thompson, Bob Haldeman. It was now, he would recall, that the future chief of staff began to be "closer to Nixon than just a casual constituent."

As the Republicans rode to victory that November, Murray Chotiner had virtually disappeared from the scene. Forced from public view since the negative headlines in the spring, he was to function for years to come strictly from the shadows.

Even as Nixon managed to escape the taint of the Chotiner connection, he was stepping into another snare. This time the stakes—and the dollar figures—were higher than ever before. So were the risks, and the long-term damage would be horrendous. Still, Nixon seemed especially beguiled by this new association and would return to it until it inflicted one of his most grievous wounds at Watergate. The fatal attraction in this case was the helping hand, and the money, of the man one of America's most accomplished historians has called "the most powerful and dangerous fat cat of them all"[5]: Howard Hughes.

In 1956, as Eisenhower dithered over whether Nixon should again be given the vice presidential slot, Hughes had just turned fifty. The spoiled heir of a Texan who had invented a revolutionary oil-drilling tool, he was afflicted with deafness, was hypochondriacal, drug-addicted, bisexual, and—it was evident even then—eccentric to the point of being mentally disturbed. He was also brilliant, a record-breaking flier, a prolific filmmaker, the owner of Trans World Airlines, and a major government defense contractor operating principally out of California. He had a fortune somewhere in the range of $350 million, making him one of the richest men on the planet.

Howard Hughes was also utterly unscrupulous, concerned above all with getting his own way. Senate investigators, probing his squandering of millions of dollars in government money during World War II, had uncovered massive evidence of influence buying. One of Hughes's targets had been President Roosevelt's son Elliott. In 1944, when Vice President Harry Truman was on the campaign trail for the ailing FDR, Hughes had himself gone to the Biltmore Hotel in Los Angeles to give Truman a cash contribution. Four years later he sent an emissary to New York with twenty-five thousand dollars in cash for Truman's Republican opponent, Thomas Dewey.

Hughes was passionately anti-Communist but otherwise apolitical. His senior aide for thirty-two years, Noah Dietrich, never learned whether his boss considered himself a Republican or a Democrat. Party affiliation mattered little to Hughes, so long as he could bend politicians to his will.

"I can buy any man in the world," he boasted, and operated on that principle. "He figured he could buy his way to favor," Dietrich said years later. "'Everybody has a price,' he always said. And he was willing to offer that price. . . . He financed Los Angeles councilmen and county supervisors, tax assessors, sheriffs, state senators and assemblymen, district attorneys, governors, congressmen and senators, judges—yes, and vice presidents. . . ."

"I never met Hughes," Richard Nixon said in a taped interview in 1988, admitting only that he had twice spoken with the billionaire on the telephone. He had made the same claim in 1972, to Bob Haldeman, adding that one of the phone calls concerned Hughes's suggestion that Nixon use a 707 Superjet to impress the Soviets on his 1959 visit to Moscow.

Nixon was almost certainly lying about the extent of his relationship with Hughes. Adela Rogers St. Johns, a veteran writer who supported and advised Nixon in the fifties, said she introduced the two men. Her association with Nixon dated back to the time that the young Nixon had delivered groceries to the ranch near Whittier owned by St. Johns's first husband. Nixon's nephew Don, son of his brother Donald, said in 1996 that Hughes was "an old buddy of my dad's." He remembered, as a boy, meeting Hughes. "He was a strange-looking guy, tall, quiet, drove a white, two-door Chevy. . . . My dad used to meet him in parking lots, places like that. . . ."

Herb Klein, the longtime Nixon press aide, told the author that Richard Nixon first "personally encountered" Hughes in either the forties or fifties. If there had ever been documentation of the relationship, though, it has long since been been removed from available files. One telltale memo, however, survives in the records of the Nixon vice presidency at the National Archives. (See facsimile on following page.) Written on January 23, 1959, by Nixon's military aide Don Hughes (no relation to Howard), it reads: "I spoke with Howard Hughes and relayed your message. He was most happy and enthusiastic over seeing you in California. He cannot come East at this time. I'll arrange an appointment when your California plans are firm."

OFFICE OF THE VICE PRESIDENT

WASHINGTON

January 23, 1959

file

MEMORANDUM

TO: RN

FROM: JDH

    I spoke with Howard Hughes and relayed your message.

    He was most happy and enthusiastic over seeing you in California.

    He cannot come East at this time. I'll arrange an appointment when your California plans are firm.

"I don't remember what it was about," General Hughes said in a recent interview. "As I remember it, Howard Hughes called the vice president. They talked, and the boss put me on the phone, and introduced me to him. The vice president said, 'Anytime you want to get ahold of me call Don Hughes.' . . . I got three or four calls from Howard Hughes. He would call using the name Mr. Thomas. . . . He was very, very polite, had a high, whiny voice, very low-key, very solicitous. . . . I think Hughes wanted to feel that he could reach out whenever he wanted. . . ."

Noah Dietrich, certainly the closest person to Hughes at the time, said the billionaire had supported Nixon as early as the 1946 run for Congress and contributed to every subsequent campaign. He also provided large sums for the personal use of Nixon and members of his family. Nixon, for his part, went out of his way while serving in the Senate to praise Hughes for the measures he was taking against filmmakers he believed to be Communists. "Hughes' stand," he said, "deserved the attention and approval of every man and woman who believes the forces of subversion must be wiped out."

By 1954, according to Chuck Giancana—brother of the Chicago mob boss, Sam—Hughes was telling associates that he had Vice President Nixon "eating out of his hand." The first detailed evidence of Hughes's help and financial largess, though, dates from 1956, during the long period of uncertainty over whether Nixon would again be Eisenhower's running mate.

In July that year Harold Stassen, former Minnesota governor and assistant on disarmament to the president, held a press conference. A specially commissioned poll, he announced, had indicated that Governor Christian Herter of Massachusetts would be a far more attractive vice presidential candidate than Richard Nixon. Stassen urged the Republican party to support Herter and asked Nixon to back out. His initiative gave rise to what became known as the Dump Nixon movement.

Years later Nixon made light of this effort, saying it was the work of "wishful thinkers" from whom he "could afford to remain aloof." At the time, however, he was not at all aloof. "He was running scared," recalled Patrick Hillings. A push to rally support for Nixon was soon under way, boosted by a secret operation financed by Howard Hughes.

Soon after the Stassen press conference the telephone rang in the Washington office of Robert A. Maheu Associates, a company that offered "private investigations," that catchall term for a multitude of shadowy services. Maheu, aged thirty-nine, had been an undercover agent for the FBI during the war and was now on a monthly retainer for the CIA. He said later that his role was to perform "impossible missions." (His exploits, indeed, are said to have inspired the TV series *Mission: Impossible.*)

The agency assigned Maheu the sort of tasks it needed to keep "deniable," activities that ranged from providing sex services for some foreign statesmen to the sexual compromising of others, illegal wiretaps, and assassination planning. He had also worked, at Nixon's bidding, on an undercover operation against the Greek oil tycoon Aristotle Onassis.* For some time now, too, Maheu had been handling assignments for Howard Hughes.

The Hughes work had begun prosaically enough. The billionaire had asked for an investigation of the first husband of the woman he was soon to marry, the actress Jean Peters. Soon afterward came instructions to snoop on Ava Gardner to find out who she was seeing. Then, following Maheu's successful handling of a would-be blackmailer, Hughes phoned to express his satisfaction. "From that point on," as Maheu put it, "I was Howard's man," eventually replacing Dietrich and serving Hughes for fifteen years. First, though, came the assignment of ensuring that Stassen would fail to unseat Nixon as Eisenhower's running mate.

The operation to block Stassen was bankrolled by Hughes after a request by unnamed "leading Republicans." Maheu responded by hiring an undercover man to pose as a volunteer and infiltrate Stassen's headquarters. He thus learned that Stassen was planning to unveil a new opinion poll at the convention. It was to be a phony poll, Maheu has claimed, heavily stacked against Nixon. To preempt Stassen's plan, Maheu used Hughes money to conduct a poll of his own, with results showing that far from lagging behind as a vote getter, Nixon was far ahead.

The penetration of Stassen's office, meanwhile, yielded even more ammunition. "There was a 'cover' placed on Stassen's wastepaper basket," Maheu said in the seventies, "and the results of that cover . . . well, let's say it turned the tide." Asked what information was found in the basket, Maheu shook his head. "It wouldn't," he said, "be in anyone's best interests to discuss it." Stassen, for his part, was still insisting years later that "the whole story cannot yet be told."

The 1956 convention ended in total victory for the Nixon forces. The climax came when, minutes after Stassen had regaled the press with the poll unfavorable to Nixon, a U.S. senator made him look foolish by announcing the opposite findings provided by Maheu. Stassen capitulated and wound up being forced to second Nixon's nomination in the name of party unity.

"Nixon knew what I had done for him," Maheu said in 1996, "but he expressed no gratitude. . . . I saw him the day after we defeated the Stassen threat; he never even said thank you." Hughes, for his part, was delighted that Nixon had been so well looked after. "It wasn't that he thought Nixon was doing such a good job," Maheu reflected. "It was more that he felt the vice president was malleable."

In December 1956, just weeks after Eisenhower and Nixon were returned to the White House, Hughes provided a different sort of assistance. While the Stassen episode remained a secret for nearly twenty years, this new intervention soon leaked, causing incalculable damage to Nixon's political hopes and

*See p. 195.

long-term reputation. According to Noah Dietrich, he brought the disaster on himself.

It began, Dietrich said, with a call to Hughes's Los Angeles headquarters by one of the millionaire's lawyers, Frank Waters. "Look, Noah," Dietrich quoted Waters as saying, "Nixon keeps approaching me. . . . His brother, Don, is having financial difficulties with his restaurant in Whittier. The Vice President would like us to help him."

"Help him in what way?" Dietrich asked.

"He needs some cash. Actually, he needs two hundred and five thousand dollars."

Even Dietrich, long used to Hughes's excesses, balked at this figure: $205,000 in 1956 was the equivalent of more than $1.25 million today. "That," he said, "is something I'm not going to take the responsibility for." Although he regularly disbursed some $500,000 per year for political purposes, it typically went out in relatively small amounts, never as such an enormous amount for a single individual. Dietrich explained that Hughes himself would have to authorize such a huge payment, and he subsequently did. "Hughes called me the next morning. . . . He said, 'I don't give a darn about the size of it. I want to do it, because it's a chance to cement a relationship.'"

The only relationship Hughes had any motive to cement was the one he had with Richard Nixon. There would have been no gain whatsoever in committing such a sum to *Donald* Nixon, an ebullient and overambitious middle-level businessman who was forever embarking on grandiose schemes. He was president of Nixon's Inc., a business consisting of a drive-in restaurant featuring a sandwich called the Nixonburger, the grocery store that had once been his parents', and a coffee shop—all in Whittier—and was building another Nixon drive-in at Anaheim. He also had major debts and faced bankruptcy if he failed to obtain major financing.

As Dietrich put it, "The whole thing had a bad smell to it." He was even more troubled when told that the $205,000 was to be accounted for as a loan. The Hughes Tool Company was not in the habit of making loans, let alone to businessmen totally unconnected to the oil or aviation business. The proposed loan, moreover, was to be secured with the deeds of a vacant lot and a gas station lease worth less than half its value. A transaction of this sort with the brother of the vice president of the United States, by a company holding major government contracts, would look highly suspicious.

Dietrich, who liked Nixon and had voted for him, was so worried that he flew to Washington with a warning. "I feel compelled to tell you," he informed Nixon, "if this loan becomes public information, it could mean the end of your political career." Unfazed, Nixon replied, "Noah, my family comes ahead of my political career, and Don wants this and he's got to have it to survive."

The loan duly went ahead, but under conditions of extraordinary secrecy. On paper it was made not by Hughes Tool but by Hughes's attorney, Frank Waters, a former Republican politician and a friend of both Nixon brothers.

Waters gave the money to Nixon's mother, who in turn made a loan to Nixon's Inc. Months later, to bury the transaction even deeper, the paperwork was moved out of Waters's name into that of an accountant not on the Hughes payroll.

Hughes's massive cash outlay disappeared within weeks of reaching Donald Nixon. Whatever happened to the money—it was supposedly used to service old debts—Nixon's Inc. was still drowning in a sea of red ink. Dietrich made a last-ditch effort to save it from going under, first asking Richard Nixon's approval to bring in accountants to reorganize the business. When Donald resisted their suggestions, Dietrich again traveled to Washington to see the vice president. Richard Nixon rebuffed him, saying, "Pull 'em off. . . . my brother wants to run it his way." Nixon's Inc. did go under two weeks later, just as the accountants had predicted.

The Hughes loan might well have remained secret forever were it not for the very measures taken to conceal it. By 1960, when Nixon and Kennedy were battling for the White House, the accountant holding the deeds had fallen out with Hughes officials. A Democrat, he leaked the story to the Kennedy camp, which ensured the press heard about it. Nixon would never again be free of the Hughes loan scandal. It was to be investigated and reinvestigated—in 1960, 1962, 1968, and 1972.

When questioned, Nixon tried either to make light of the loan or to claim he had not been involved. "I had nothing to do with making that loan," he told one journalist. "It was to my brother. . . . My mother deeded the property to the lenders. She lost everything she had. . . ." There is no evidence that Hannah Nixon "lost everything she had." Although the vacant lot used as collateral was eventually transferred to Hughes's proxies, she retained her house and other properties. Indeed, the conditions of the Hughes loan waived "all rights to assert any claim or deficiency against Hannah Nixon."

As for Richard's insistence that he had played no role in the transaction, signs to the contrary abound. The signatory on the lease on the vacant lot, executed shortly before the loan was made, was notarized by one William Ridgeley. This was an employee of the disbursing office of the U.S. Senate in Washington, where the vice president's office was then located. Nixon, moreover, covered up not only his exchanges with Dietrich but other compromising details. During a meeting about the loan a Hughes lawyer had gone out at one point to "call Dick" and returned saying he had spoken with "an aide to the vice president." Thereafter Nixon was referred to in Hughes reports and correspondence in code as the Eastern Division or just plain East. "There was never any confusion," one of the accountants said long afterward. "It was the vice president."

Nixon later flew to California to discuss conveyancing of the property provided as security for the loan, "to establish a capital gains situation for his mother." It was his old law partner Thomas Bewley who drew up the documents that ensured Hannah Nixon would pay no tax on the transaction. Finally the corporation commissioners' office in Los Angeles contained a list of proposed stockholders in Nixon's Inc. One of the names on it was Richard M. Nixon.

Who profited from the transaction? When Donald Nixon's business was floundering, Dietrich said, he suggested a linkup with the Carnation Milk Company. When it finally collapsed, Donald was appointed to a lucrative post as PR executive for Carnation. The company's president, Alford Ghormley, had been a contributor to the Nixon fund, and then Senator Nixon had been responsive to his pressure on milk quotas.*

Did Nixon personally profit from the Hughes loan?

Contacted in 1996, Hughes's attorney Frank Waters refused to be drawn on whether the $205,000 went not to Donald's business but to his brother, the vice president. "I won't answer," he said. "He is dead. He is gone. And I hope he is in the arms of the Lord."

A different reply came from Arnholt Smith, the munificent San Diego millionaire who knew Nixon from childhood and was long one of his most generous backers. "I think it was really for Richard," Smith said, "to help him live. He was a relatively poor man."

Some of Nixon's Democratic foes speculated in private about where at least a portion of the money had gone. Within a month of the Hughes loan's being approved, Nixon bought a grand new house in Washington, once the property of former Attorney General Homer Cummings. He reportedly paid seventy-five thousand dollars for a sixteen-room Tudor-style château, set in leafy grounds overlooking a park. Nixon maintained he purchased it solely thanks to a mortgage. Yet he was reportedly able to do so before selling his existing house.

Was Howard Hughes rewarded for his largess? Some observers believed so. The Internal Revenue Service had been blocking the billionaire's efforts to have his Hughes Medical Institute declared a charity and therefore granted tax-exempt status. The institute, announced as providing millions of dollars to "combat disease and human suffering," was a tax dodge, 84 percent of its vast income going not to medical research but to Hughes. Two months after Hughes made the Nixon loan, the IRS reversed its decision. Because IRS files are so tightly held, there is no way of determining what caused the change of course.

In the months before the loan, moreover, and against the advice of his senior executives, Hughes had committed his company to the largest airplane order in aviation history: more than four hundred million dollars for new passenger jets and equipment. The massive outlay, which represented more than the value of the company's assets, was made at a time when the Hughes airline, TWA, was losing ground to its competitors and showing a loss. In the month of the Hughes loan the Civil Aeronautics Board gave TWA permission

*See p. 124.

to raise huge loans, in a manner contrary to its usual restrictions. In the months that followed, the airline was granted new domestic and international routes and long-delayed fare increases. The new president of TWA, appointed soon after, was one of Nixon's financial backers.

Did Richard Nixon influence these developments, or were they just lucky breaks for Hughes? Dietrich, for one, found the IRS reversal on the Medical Institute ruling curious. "Did Howard get a bargain?" he asked. ". . . You can draw your own conclusions." Hughes "was definitely not a philanthropist. . . . In the back of his mind, there was no question it was to put the vice president of the United States under his obligation."[6]

Even after the disaster of the 1956 loan, however, Nixon was unable to resist accepting financial favors from Hughes. It was a folly as great as that of President Clinton in the nineties, engaging in a silly sexual dalliance long after he had been pegged as a womanizer, and with the knowledge that his enemies saw his philandering as his Achilles' heel. Yet while Clinton survived the Monica Lewinsky affair, Nixon's lasting need for Hughes's money was to be a major factor in his downfall.

"I, Richard Milhous Nixon, do solemnly swear that I will support and defend the Constitution of the United States. . . ." In January 1957, as he again intoned the inauguration pledge to the American people, Nixon's promise to his wife not to run had been broken—for the first time but not the last. Since he had made it, their marriage had inexorably changed.

The Pat the public saw loyally continued to uphold the image of the devoted spouse. She accepted all the titles bestowed upon her: Outstanding Homemaker of the Year, Mother of the Year, the Nation's Ideal Wife. She indeed had been a rock, ever supportive, ever at Nixon's side. She took part in trivial activities without looking bored, shook a thousand hands, handed out ballpoint pens inscribed "Patricia Nixon." She shared with the press absurd facts: that her campaign wardrobe consisted of five dresses, four suits, two pairs of shoes, and eight hats, but no briefcase, because she was only the wife. "She had the characteristics of a great actress," Nixon told his daughter Julie years later, "being at her best when onstage."

Privately Pat was ever more frustrated. "I would like to do part-time work," she wrote her friend Helene Drown, "rather than all the useless gadding I am expected to do." She let slip, at the 1956 convention, that she could think of "any number of things I prefer to politics." Nixon was aware of her resentment and had even confided in Eisenhower that he had "a serious problem with his wife." If Pat did not reconcile herself to staying in Washington, he told the president, "I will have difficulty in doing *anything*."

Two years had passed since CBS's Robert Pierpoint, shocked at how remote Pat had grown, had seen in her a "deep-seated terror" of doing anything that might impede Nixon's ambitions. Now she began to lash back. Visitors spoke of having witnessed Pat "blowing her stack," and insiders commented on her "rare but furious temper." Nixon's go-between with the FBI during the Hiss case, Father Cronin, had become his principal speechwriter in 1956. Once, when Nixon delivered a speech badly, Cronin recalled, "Pat chewed the hell out of him in front of the staff.

"One day," Cronin said, "Dick sent me to his home in the suburbs to get some papers he needed in a hurry. I knew the family well, had been there to dinner, and liked the daughters. But when I knocked, Pat opened the door and said, 'Oh no! He can't get back in by sending a priest!' I went back and said, 'What did you get me into?' He said, 'Oh, I didn't think she'd say anything to *you*. We're just having a little problem now.' But I noticed then that Nixon was not going home at night. He kept a hotel room in the District. . . . And he was just living there."

It was probably during this period that—as Nixon's cousin Jessamyn West learned—Hannah Nixon flew across the continent to the rescue. She came not to be with her son but with Pat, who "wasn't speaking to him."

"Pat is in one of her moods," James Bassett told his wife in a letter home. "Nobody else in the U.S. would believe it." Bassett observed the couple on the campaign plane. "They would always sit across the aisle from each other, or still further apart. Then, as the plane circled for landing, they would get together and put on their 'Pat and Dick' smiles. He would put his arm around her for the photographers."

In late 1956 Nixon returned from a trip to Europe with the suggestion that they adopt a refugee child. Pat refused.

Months later Bassett came upon Nixon, a senior cabinet colleague, and a bevy of six young women in a secluded Maryland restaurant. The colleague disappeared with one of the women. Nixon, who was very drunk, refused Bassett's offer to take him home. He said the girls would look after him.

Bassett thought Nixon looked on women as "a different species . . . an extra appendage," that he had "a total scorn for female mentality." Nixon had a repertoire of smutty jokes, and a favorite—one his staff knew well—concerned a stud who prevailed on his wife to have sex a dozen times a day. When at last she protested she was too tired for more, went the punch line, her sneering husband would call her "Deadass!" One morning on the campaign train, Bassett recalled, Nixon emerged from his compartment with Pat on their way to breakfast. Then, in front of aides, he looked at Pat "with a curious glint in his eye, and said: 'Deadass!'" No one laughed.

During that same 1956 campaign, Nixon's once-fierce father fell seriously ill. At seventy-five, suffering from kidney disease, arthritis, and bleeding ulcers, Frank Nixon sent word from Whittier that he wanted to see his son. Nixon was unable to go to California at first but, on a secretary's advice, managed a "Dear Dad" letter instead of his usual "Dear Mother and Dad." Then, during the Republican convention, his father suffered a rupture of the abdominal artery and went downhill rapidly.

Fresh from his nomination for vice president, Nixon hurried to the dying man's bedside. "I shall always remember the last time I saw him," he wrote years later. "He asked me to shave him, because he was too weak to do it himself. When I had finished, he said he felt better. I told him, 'I will see you in the morning.' 'I don't think I'll be here in the morning,' he replied. 'Dad, you've got to keep fighting,' I said. His last words to me were, 'Dick, you keep fighting.' The next day he died. . . ." During the deathwatch, Nixon's mother had welcomed sympathizers with a request they sign a visitors' book and inspect a square of red carpet on which her son had stood when he took the oath as vice president in 1953. He had sent it to her himself, she said. When Hannah let the press in, at her son's suggestion, Nixon told them she had risen at dawn to bake them apple pie.

Sitting with Nixon that weekend as his father suffered upstairs, Bassett thought his boss seemed oddly detached. "I could hear the strangled breathing, a crackling noise," Bassett remembered. "It didn't seem to bother Dick, but it bothered me. He was busy planning his campaign. . . ."

After Frank Nixon died, on September 4, Nixon forbade photographers to take pictures of the grieving family at the funeral. This, he let it be known, was "strictly personal sorrow." Within weeks, though, back on the stump, he was courting the sympathy vote without a qualm.

In Buffalo, New York, on October 16, Nixon opened his speech with "My father . . ." Then, after a catch of the breath as if to master his emotions, he continued: "I remember my father telling me a long time ago—'Dick, Dick,' he said, 'Buffalo is a beautiful town.' It may have been his *favorite* town!" Moving on to the city of Rochester, and then to Ithaca—three political rallies in twenty-four hours—Nixon reportedly began each speech with the same line about his father's "favorite town," changing only the name of the city.

While in Ithaca, Nixon had exploded with rage after taking questions from Cornell University students on a television show. "Get me away from these little monsters!" he hissed to an aide, and rushed off the set. So upset was he that, back at the airport, he vomited at the edge of the runway before boarding the plane. Once airborne, he lost control completely, ranting in front of the press and threatening—it was a line he often used—to "cut off the balls" of the staff who had set up the program. "You son of a bitch!" Nixon shouted at Ted Rogers, the loyal TV aide who had masterminded his fund appearance four years earlier. "You put me on with those shitty-ass liberal sons of bitches; you tried to destroy me. . . !" He flung himself on Rogers and had to be pulled off by one of the reporters. During the same tour Nixon allegedly punched another man in the face.

Any political candidate is exhausted by the end of a campaign. Nixon, though, seemed abnormally disoriented. In Kentucky he kept referring to the time as "tonight" when it was early morning. Hours later, in Illinois, he thought he had just arrived from Texas. In Ohio, boarding a plane at a deserted airstrip, he turned to wave at a nonexistent crowd. James Reston noted in the

New York Times that reporters had been "psychoanalyzing" Nixon since the convention.

Watching Nixon at the convention, Bob Haldeman had been shaken. "Before gray-colored draperies in a San Francisco hotel room," he recalled, "Dick Nixon stood among a group of Republican delegates. I moved closer and listened in dismay. My first thought was that he had been drinking. His sentences were almost incoherent; his monologue rambled on circuitously while everyone around him looked at each other, wonderingly. . . ."

Slurred rambling was typical of Nixon when he was fatigued and stressed, whether he had been drinking or not. It worried Bassett, who by now knew Nixon very well indeed. "What scares the hell out of me," he had told Nixon the night he ran amok after the Ithaca television show, "is that you would blow sky-high over a thing as inconsequential as this. What in God's name would you do if you were president and got into a really bad situation?"

Nixon said he would consider the question. It was just a few months since he had learned that Dr. Hutschnecker, his New York medical consultant, had decided to specialize solely in psychotherapy. The news had distressed him, because it meant that future appointments with the doctor might prove embarrassing. His meetings with Hutschnecker would now be less frequent and usually at a private location.

"I have a feeling," Nixon had written to Bebe Rebozo as the campaign went into high gear, "that I might be applying for one of the famous Rebozo 'rest cures' after the battle is over." And so he did, heading down to Key Biscayne right after the election.

There was always Rebozo.

15

Does a man "enjoy" crises? . . . I find it especially difficult to answer the question.

—Richard Nixon, in 1962

By the summer of 1957 visitors to the Nixons' new home were shown a cornucopia of foreign wonders: pictorial scrolls from Japan on the living room wall, copper candelabra from Korea on the table. A third-century Buddha in Richard's study, courtesy of the king of Afghanistan. A teak chest inlaid with mother-of-pearl; "Madame Chiang Kai-shek gave it to me," said Pat. A fine rug in the dining room, a gift from the shah of Iran, an early token of a generosity that would be extended for years to come. Two lacquer coffee tables from a land not yet familiar to Americans, named Vietnam.

The gifts, Pat told guests, were diplomatic tokens of esteem from forty nations. The number of countries would exceed fifty before the vice presidency ended, and by then the Nixons would have traveled twice around the world. They visited countries where no American president or vice president had set foot before. They were "superambassadors," an idea conceived by Dwight Eisenhower.

"What are you doing this summer?" the president had asked in 1953, and then suggested a trip to the Far East. Nixon had accepted the task eagerly and took his mission seriously. Every stop of the journey was preceded by meticulous briefings, the record of every potentate on the route thoroughly analyzed. In each country diplomats were urged to get the vice president off the cocktail circuit and into meetings with ordinary citizens, ranging from businesspeople and intellectuals to laborers and peasant farmers.

Nixon was to recall that tour as his first step in gaining the foreign expertise that years later, when the rest of his reputation was squandered and gone, might enable him to claim the mantle of "great statesman." It also presaged, in country after country, what many now consider Nixon's future policy errors and personal folly.

In Indonesia, Nixon and Pat banqueted—he would remember—"off gold plate to the light of a thousand torches, while musicians played on the shore of a lake covered with white lotus blossoms." President Sukarno's gifts to Nixon included ivory ornaments embossed with the Kuwaiti coat of arms, perhaps received by the Indonesian president as presents from the Emir and then recycled to his American guest.

Nixon later said that Sukarno's "corrosive vanity" offended him, although his own concept of grandeur would one day raise eyebrows in his own country. The splendor of his escort's regalia on a visit to India would inspire him as president to order Ruritanian uniforms for the attendants at the White House. In India in 1953, Nixon got on neither with Prime Minister Nehru nor with his daughter, future Prime Minister Indira Gandhi. Nehru's verdict, when Nixon followed a visit to Pakistan by endorsing U.S. military aide to the Pakistanis, was to call him "an unprincipled cad." Nixon got on well, on the other hand, with the general soon to become leader of Pakistan, Ayub Khan.

Nixon's comments as president about Indira Gandhi were, as Henry Kissinger was to say, "not always printable." He despised her, and he distrusted Indian policy statements. Nixon was to favor Pakistan in the 1971 war between India and Pakistan—even after a million Bengalis had been killed and more millions left homeless in a genocidal rampage by Pakistan's army. Before the war ended, he would consider using nuclear weapons in the event China and the Soviet Union were drawn into the conflict.

A vital underlying issue for Nixon in 1971 would be the opening to China, in which Pakistan was an intermediary. In 1953 the young Nixon had visited the Chinese Nationalist island of Taiwan, as the honored guest of Generalissimo Chiang Kai-shek. He said then that Red China would not be recognized and encouraged the impression that the United States backed Chiang's hopes of reconquering the mainland. Soon, though, at a Christmas party in Washington, he would be heard to say, "Someday I'll go to China . . . mainland China." Two decades later, the Chinese breakthrough was to be his undeniably fine achievement as president.

In 1953 Nixon also went to Iran, where he met the shah, His Imperial Majesty Mohammad Reza Pahlavi. Although he quickly became, in Nixon's words, a "personal friend," Pahlavi is referred to only once and briefly in the Nixon memoirs. There is no mention of the fact that their meeting came within months of the shah's return to the throne with the assistance of Operation Ajax, a CIA-orchestrated coup designed to bring oil-rich Iran firmly under Western influence. Nor does Nixon discuss the way that following a personal visit as president, he would anoint the shah (a repressive ruler with a brutal secret police) the guardian of Western interests in the entire region. Nixon armed the Kurds at the shah's request and gave the ruler extraordinary access to the latest U.S. weaponry, without prior consultation with the Joint Chiefs of Staff or the State Department. Former Undersecretary of State George Ball likened this to "giving the keys of the world's largest liquor store to a confirmed alcoholic." The negative consequences are still reverberating today.

Least of all would the Nixon memoirs mention the extent of the shah's personal largess. Gifts to American leaders by foreign heads of state must by law be turned over to the government. After Nixon left office, at least a dozen such gifts from the shah were listed as "missing." The shah also reportedly contributed hundreds of thousands of dollars—by one account more than one million dollars—to Nixon's 1972 campaign.

There is little in the memoirs about the Philippines, also on the 1953 itinerary, and not a single reference to the later president of the Philippines, the robber baron–dictator Ferdinand Marcos. Marcos and his wife, Imelda—she of the myriad pairs of shoes—are variously reported to have contributed either $250,000 or $1 million to Nixon's political campaigns. Marcos's motive was simple. As historian and Nixon specialist Professor Stanley Kutler has said, he was "buying influence"—as was the shah.

There was a good reason, Nixon argued years later, for the United States to maintain alliances with such dictators. "Do you want communism out there?" he replied when asked about the relationships with the shah's Iran and Marcos's Philippines. "Those are authoritarian states, but they don't threaten their neighbors, and they are our friends. Totalitarian Communist states do threaten their neighbors and they are not our friends."

The serious political business of the 1953 Nixon tour was to determine how best to stop the forward march of communism in Asia. Whatever their differences, Eisenhower and Nixon shared the belief that America could not be insular, that it was essential for it to contain hostile powers, and in the fifties that meant Communist powers. For Nixon, however, the effort involved more than simply containment. He had long been preaching that to avoid another world war and bring "peace and security in our time," the United States had to "go on the offensive in the ideological struggle." The battle with communism topped the agenda as Nixon's air force Constellation flew around Asia, to Korea—just starting to settle into the uneasy stalemate that passed for peace—to Malaya, to Laos, to Cambodia . . . and to Vietnam.

At that time, few Americans could have located Indochina on a map. The war being fought there was someone else's conflict, and few foresaw that the French colonial forces would soon go down to humiliating defeat at the hands of Ho Chi Minh's guerrillas. Nixon remembered sitting with Emperor Bao Dai in a grand villa north of Saigon, as "barefoot servants padded in noiselessly carrying silver trays laden with fresh fruit and cups of tea." "If Vietnam is divided," Bao Dai correctly prophesied, "we will eventually lose it all."

On a field trip in northern Vietnam, dressed in battle fatigues and helmet, Nixon told French officers and Vietnamese conscripts that they were "fighting on the very outpost of freedom," that the American people "supported their cause and honored their heroism." He flew home believing that should the French leave Vietnam, it and its neighbors "would fall like husks before the Communist hurricane." He uncritically accepted the domino theory, the theory that—fatally for thousands of Americans and millions of Vietnamese—would drive his nation's foreign policy far into the future.

Soon after Nixon's return to Washington, when America faced its first serious decision on Vietnam, he was a strong advocate of drastic action. Ten thousand crack French troops were cut off in a shrinking enclave at Dien Bien Phu, under the unrelenting attack of a large Communist force. With the United States funding 80 percent of the cost of the French war effort, and providing some two hundred advisers,[1] Eisenhower came under pressure to use U.S. force to relieve the French force. "The boys," he recalled, referring to his senior aides, "were putting the heat on me." Lacking the support of Congress or of America's allies, however, the president did not intervene.

In April 1954, during a speech to the American Society of Newspaper Editors, Nixon was asked his opinion of what the United States should do if the French were to withdraw from Vietnam. He replied that the plight of the free world was desperate, and retreat in Asia unthinkable. He continued: "If in order to avoid it we must take the risk now by putting American boys in, I believe that the executive branch has to take the politically unpopular position of facing up to it and doing it, and I personally would support such a decision."

With those words Richard Nixon had become one of the very first senior elected politicians, even possibly the first, to speak out in favor of putting American ground troops into Vietnam.

Although the remarks had been made on an off-the-record basis, the European press identified Nixon as their source. U.S. papers soon followed up with major headlines. Given the controversial line Nixon had taken and the fact that his audience has been made up of journalists, he could hardly have expected otherwise. Some assumed the vice president was floating a trial balloon on Eisenhower's behalf, to test public reaction. Yet the record suggests the comments reflected his own view. A letter written the next day by his aide James Bassett, moreover, shows Nixon came to him "wanting his hand held" after his "very forthright talk." Nixon "knew this would cause an uproar," Bassett told his wife, and "did it deliberately (as he told me on the phone just now) to 'stir up some thinking. . . .'" Nixon's talk of sending U.S. troops to Vietnam was "strictly his own baby."

Behind the scenes Chairman of the Joint Chiefs Admiral Arthur Radford had suggested coming to the aid of the French with air strikes flown by U.S. bombers. The plan was designated Operation Vulture and included a special option, the use of three tactical nuclear weapons. Eisenhower's reaction to that idea, he recalled, was: "You boys must be crazy. We can't use those awful things against Asians for the second time in less than ten years. My God . . ." Nixon, and others, including Air Force General Curtis LeMay, who would later advocate bombing North Vietnam "back to the Stone Age," supported the nuclear option.

As the days passed and a French defeat at Dien Bien Phu looked inevitable, Nixon talked on in private about the need for "inculcating some real *guts* into people." Eisenhower continued to take a cooler view. "The sun's still shining," he said at a White House meeting. "Dien Bien Phu isn't the end of the world . . . it's not that important."

At Duke Zeibert's with James Bassett, during an evening of "vast hair-letting down" over liqueurs, Nixon argued that the best hope now was a Pacific alliance—"even without the laggard British"—and use of Nationalist Chinese troops if Red China made threats. "Then, by God, we'd have to employ the atom bomb. Mark my words. . . ."

After Dien Bien Phu had fallen, after Eisenhower had notified France that the United States would not intervene, and after Vietnam had been divided in two by the Geneva agreement, Nixon was one of those who continued to promote an invasion involving amphibious landings and ground troops. Eisenhower would later write that he had thought unilateral U.S. intervention "nothing less than sheer folly." Seven years were to pass before John F. Kennedy was to commit thousands more "advisers" to South Vietnam, the first act in the protracted tragedy of America's Vietnam War, a war that Nixon would long support.

───────────

Nixon continued to go out of his way meanwhile to show that he personally had "the guts" to face down Communists. His 1958 tour of Latin America, billed as a goodwill mission, nearly cost him his life. The plan called for him to visit eight countries, with Pat at his side, at a time of growing agitation encouraged by Moscow. After a decade of tilting at the idea of communism in the United States, Nixon would now have to deal with the real thing.

At first, in Uruguay, he faced nothing worse than student heckling, signs reading FUERA NIXON! ("Get out, Nixon!") and IMPERIALIST! and claims that he was a warmonger and friend of dictators. Then, after he had trumped the protesters by debating the issues and—in Alfredo Stroessner's Paraguay—calling for political freedom, Communist leaders elsewhere decided to be confrontational.

Warned that demonstrators intended to prevent him from visiting Lima's San Marcos University, Nixon decided to meet them head on. Accompanied only by his interpreter and lead Secret Service agent, he left his car and advanced on a throng of two thousand angry students. "I would like to talk to you," he shouted. Then, over the roar of abuse that encountered him, he asked, "Why are you afraid of the truth?" Rocks began flying, one breaking one of the Secret Service men's teeth and glancing off Nixon's shoulder. When they retreated to their open car, Nixon stood up, hands over his head like a victorious prizefighter, shouting, "Cowards! . . . You are the worst kind of cowards!" as the vehicle pulled away.

Later, as he returned to his hotel, people threw fruit and small stones. A man he remembered as a "weird-looking character . . . [with] bulging eyes" spit full in Nixon's face. On receiving a sympathetic message from Eisenhower, Nixon replied that the only casualties were "a couple of Ben Freeman's suits which I will be unable to wear again."

After that, Nixon recalled, he was "hailed as a hero by the citizens of Lima." He deemed the episode a victory and flew into a rage when told that State Department officials thought he had embarrassed the host government, with U.S.-Peruvian relations suffering as a result.

The real drama, though, came in Venezuela. From the moment the Nixons emerged smiling from their plane, it was clear the Communists intended a massive onslaught. As the couple stood to attention for the Venzuelan national anthem, a mob on a balcony began showering them with spit. "It fell on our faces and our hair," Nixon remembered. "I saw Pat's bright red suit grow dark with tobacco-brown splotches." They stood and took the abuse, then struggled to their separate limousines for the motorcade into the city.

In the capital's roughest suburb the Communists had prepared a series of ambushes. What followed, one reporter said, was "like a scene from the French Revolution." First came a shower of rocks, then a crowd of ragged people brandishing placards and clubs. The Nixon motorcade found a way through, only to run into another barricade to make another short-lived escape, and again be blocked. The chanting this time was not "*Fuera Nixon!*" but "*Muera Nixon!*"—"Death to Nixon!"—and it came close to that.

> The inside of the car, [Nixon remembered] made me think of a tank, battened down and ready for combat. . . . The Venezuelan and U.S. flags were ripped from the front of our car. . . . I could see that we were really stuck. . . . Out of the alleys and side streets poured a screaming mob of two or three hundred, throwing rocks, brandishing sticks and pieces of steel pipe. . . . A large rock smashed against the shatterproof window and stuck there, spraying glass into the Foreign Minister's eye.
>
> This crowd was out for blood. . . . It made me almost physically ill to see the fanatical frenzy in the eyes of teenagers—boys and girls who were very little older than my twelve-year-old daughter, Tricia. My reaction was a feeling of absolute hatred for the tough Communist agitators who were driving children to this irrational state. . . . One of the ringleaders—a typical tough thug—started to bash in the window next to me with a big iron pipe.

The man with the pipe, Nixon said later, looked to him like a combination of Gerhart Eisler, Eugene Dennis, and other Communists he had seen in the past. He had of course seen Eisler and Dennis, both American leftists, in the more tranquil ambiance of a congressional hearing room.[2] In Caracas the thug with the pipe succeeded in punching a hole in the car window. Flying glass wounded Nixon's interpreter, hit a Secret Service agent, and nicked Nixon in the face. The iron stave began poking at him through the hole in the window.

"Then we heard the attacker shout a command," Nixon recalled, "and our car began to rock. I knew now what was happening. It was a common tactic for mobs throughout the world to rock a car, turn it over, set it afire. For an instant, the realization passed through my mind—we might be killed. . . ."

They indeed might have been had not a Venezuelan security detachment cleared the roadblock and made it possible to drive on.[3] With its wipers flapping—to clear the waterfall of spit on the windshield, Nixon's limousine pulled away.

No one had been seriously hurt. The car carrying Pat Nixon had also come under attack, but she was uninjured. Six cars back secretary Rose Woods had been superficially cut by flying glass. On the advice of his Secret Service aide and the interpreter, a U.S. Army lieutenant colonel, Nixon abandoned plans for a wreath-laying ceremony and headed for the U.S. ambassador's residence. The party were soon relaxing over gin and tonics and canapés courtesy of the American ambassador's wife.

Intelligence later established that had Nixon gone on to the wreath laying he would have faced being bombed with Molotov cocktails, four hundred of which had later been found neatly stacked near the tomb of Simón Bolívar. "I don't think the American people realize how close to death Mr. Nixon and his wife came," Secret Service chief U. E. Baughman wrote years later. "He damn near got creamed," said the CIA's Caracas station chief, Jacob Esterline.

That evening an alarmed President Eisenhower ordered Operation Poor Richard, the movement of a thousand marines, paratroopers, six destroyers, a cruiser, and an aircraft carrier toward Venezuela. They were not needed. Nixon traveled to the airport the next day in a heavily armed convoy and flew home to a hero's welcome in Washington. The president, the cabinet, senior members of Congress, and a cheering crowd greeted him at the airport.

The placards Nixon now saw carried statements like DON'T LET THOSE COMMIES GET YOU DOWN, DICK and COMMUNIST COWARDICE LOSES—NIXON COURAGE WINS. Soon, in the spirit of the Hound's Tooth group formed to celebrate his fund crisis, Nixon would found a club for veterans of the Latin American trip. He called it the Rock and Roll Club, presumably referring to the attempt to overturn his car. Members serenaded him at the first reunion with a song, to the tune of "Frère Jacques," that knocked Venezuela and Peru—"Abajo Venezuela!" ("Down with Venezuela!")—and hailed their leader with "Viva Nixon!"

The trip had put Nixon in the man of action's "arena" he so often evoked. Having emerged unharmed, he seemed to indulge the notion that all had worked out well in the end thanks to him, that *he* had been in control at all times. Witnesses agreed that Nixon did show courage. Whether he demonstrated real control or the sort of wise judgment and self-control a citizen would hope for in a leader is another question. In part the answer lies is in his own compulsive comments about the tour.

"I slept very little," Nixon said of the night before he confronted the Peruvian rioters. "I knew this necessary period of indecision was far more wearing than tomorrow's action would be. This was part of the crisis syndrome. . . . A man is not afraid at a time like this because he blocks out any thought of fear by a conscious act of will. . . ."

"I felt the excitement of battle," he said of the moment he chose to abuse the protesters as cowards, "but I had full control of my temper as I lashed out at the mob." "It was a terrible test of temper control," he recalled, of the time a demonstrator spat full in his face. In a tough situation, Nixon said he remained "analytical and cold." "When someone is trying to damage you, the way to hurt him is not to become angry, but to handle him with detachment."

Yet by his own contradictory account, Nixon had been far from "cold." "I felt an almost uncontrollable urge," he said of the spitter with the bulging eyes, "to tear the face in front of me to pieces." Only the intervention of a Secret Service agent, he admitted, prevented him from striking the man. Even then, he said, "I had the satisfaction of planting a healthy kick on his shins. Nothing I did all day made me feel better."

Nixon lost his temper several times during the trip. The first occurred in Peru, when he summoned two State Department officials—half dressed, because they had been preparing for a state dinner—to chastise them for suggesting privately that his actions might prove diplomatically damaging. In Caracas, as his car ran the gauntlet of the mob, he let the Venezuelan foreign minister "have it with both barrels" for trying to explain his government's policy on demonstrations. Later, his military aide Don Hughes recalled, he gave other government leaders "the most godawful dressing down." He "exploded in fury" when told Eisenhower was mobilizing American troops for a possible rescue, because the White House had not consulted him first. (It could not have done so, in fact, because communications had been temporarily cut off.)

The "detachment" Nixon ascribed to himself extended also to his attitude to the long-suffering Pat. He had made no move to shield her as they stood through the playing of the Venezuelan national anthem in a shower of spit. He had then insisted that Pat's car drive immediately behind his, breaking the Secret Service's cardinal rule that only agents travel in the follow-up car. "One remark made by Mr. Nixon stayed with me from this terrible episode," said Secret Service chief Baughman. "The agent inside Mr. Nixon's car said to the Vice President after the motorcade had started to roll again: 'I hope Mrs.

Nixon gets through.' To which Mr. Nixon replied, 'If she doesn't, it can't be helped.'"

Nixon would claim it was he who made the "command decision" for the maneuver that brought the motorcade out of the moment of greatest danger, and that he then made "another command decision" that avoided further trouble at Bolívar's tomb. Other accounts, however, indicate he had nothing to do with the first decision and acted on advice for the second.

Nixon used similar military language to describe how the incidents affected him. "Once the battle is over," he wrote, "a price is paid in emotional, mental, and physical fatigue." In Peru he felt "worn out" after an experience lasting just two hours. He was "wrung-out" after the Caracas episode and took his "first afternoon nap in twelve years of public life." "My reaction to stress, a challenge, some great difficulty," he explained, "is sort of chemically delayed. . . . After a crisis like that is over, I feel this tremendous letdown, a fatigue, as though I'd been in battle."

The irony, one that was to have parallels throughout Nixon's life, was that he had brought the Latin America ordeal upon himself. "It was entirely avoidable," the Secret Service's Baughman said of the close call in Caracas. "I'd had a report on just how bad things were, and I didn't want the Vice President to make the trip. It was like talking into a barrel." Nixon's experiences "did not seem to temper his indiscretion."

The man who supplied the advance intelligence on Caracas, CIA station chief Jacob Esterline, had tried almost desperately to have the visit canceled. Weeks earlier surveillance had produced "incontrovertible proof," captured on tape, that local Communists were planning to kill Nixon. On his own initiative Esterline had flown to Washington to brief Director of Central Intelligence Allen Dulles and to warn Nixon. Dulles said: "It's a political decision. Nixon's going and that's that." A Nixon aide told Esterline to "keep your damn nose out of it."

On the eve of the trip, when Nixon was already in Bogotá—the stop before Caracas—Esterline had tried one final time to stop the visit.[4] Dulles, a Nixon friend, again told Esterline Nixon had gone ahead "for his own political purposes." "It soured me on Nixon," recalled Esterline, "I realized that he was driven above all by his ambition, his single-minded ambition to become president."

Neither grave risk to the lives of others nor the questionable effect the tour had on U.S. foreign relations was, surely, justified by Nixon's demonstration of his bravery. "The possession of guts," Stewart Alsop pointed out, "obviously does not in itself qualify a man for the presidency." "As an exercise in national self-bamboozlement," James Reston wrote less gently, "the reaction to Nixon's trip was a classic." "A national defeat has been parlayed into a personal political triumph. . . ." Nixon had virtually incited disorder in pursuit of political victory, a pattern he would play out in his future career.

During the 1960 presidential campaign, he would order the Secret Service to limit crowd control measures in Greensboro, North Carolina, in a way that—in the words of Secret Service chief Baughman—"rendered our protective strategy useless." The result, a field agent reported, was that "orderly crowds immediately deteriorated into an ever-growing, mad mauling melee."

In 1970, before a rally in California, reporters were tipped that there was likely to be trouble. As if in a deliberate re-creation of the Lima confrontation, Nixon climbed onto the hood of his car and gave the V sign to a crowd of students protesting the Vietnam War. Stones and missiles began flying, and the president's aides were jubilant. "It looked like he deliberately provoked that crowd," said James Wrightson, editor of the *Sacramento Bee*. "It was like Caracas, which he liked to brag about."

————————

On July 23, 1959, Nixon flew into another foreign airport, one where the "ominous unfriendliness" reminded him of his arrival in Caracas. This time, though, no crowd had assembled to scream abuse; in fact there was no crowd at all. The motorcade sped into town through almost empty streets, and the few passersby barely turned their heads. At the U.S. ambassador's residence Nixon was briefed in a small sitting room, the only place deemed free of hidden microphones. He had arrived in Moscow, on the most significant mission of his vice presidency.

For the Americans on the trip, as President Eisenhower's brother Milton put it, this was a journey of "hope, mystery, and fear." Since the end of World War II and the fall of the Iron Curtain across Eastern Europe, the Soviet Union had become not only a military threat but also a land unknown and virtually inaccessible to Americans. For years the two countries had been rattling their nuclear weapons and fighting a protracted war of espionage and propaganda.

Less than three years earlier, after Moscow's bloody suppression of the Hungarian uprising, Eisenhower had sent Nixon to neighboring Austria to report on the refugee crisis. He had traveled in a hay wagon right up to the border, seen the misery of the refugees, and called Soviet Prime Minister Nikita Khrushchev the Butcher of Budapest. Now, although the occasion for the Moscow trip was to open an exhibition displaying American products, a breakthrough in itself, the real challenge was to be his encounter with Khrushchev.

Characteristically Nixon was to remember having felt "keyed up and ready for battle." Before leaving Washington, he had had lengthy briefings from the CIA and the State Department and had spoken to everyone he could find who had met the Soviet leader. He had perused the works of Marx, Lenin, and Stalin and even—along with Pat—learned a little Russian. In Moscow, the night before the first meeting with Khrushchev, he could not sleep.

Contemporary headlines and the folklore that followed have portrayed the encounter between the aging Bolshevik and America's leading anti-Communist as a furious, chest-thumping confrontation. Khrushchev did do some crude blustering and famously did wave his finger in Nixon's face, and Nixon answered back. In one of their first exchanges the Russian ranted on about the U.S. Congress's Captive Nations resolution, which called for support for all peoples under Soviet rule. "It stinks like fresh horse shit," he said, "and nothing smells worse than that!" Nixon replied that he knew from experience that pig shit smelled worse. Khrushchev retorted that he had shoveled the human version.

The polemics continued, for public consumption, at the American Exhibition. At an exhibit featuring the wondrous development of videotape, the two men sparred in front of a TV camera. Khrushchev boasted that the Soviet Union would overtake the United States technologically within seven years. "You don't know anything about communism," he told Nixon, "except fear of it." He browbeat his opponent, even—although only a few of the Americans present heard it—bad-mouthing him with a contemptuous "Go fuck my grandmother. . . ." Sweating profusely, Nixon found no effective way to respond and felt he had lost the round.

The vice president regained his composure in the kitchen of the "typical American house" exhibit, a visit engineered by a young press agent named William Safire, later to become a prominent columnist and—during the Nixon presidency—a White House speechwriter. The Soviet press had been ridiculing the exhibit, claiming it was no more typical of a worker's home than England's Buckingham Palace or India's Taj Mahal. Nixon scotched Khrushchev's argument, then lectured him on the futility and peril of one nation trying to impose its will on another.

Photographs of the scene showed Nixon gesturing sternly and jabbing a finger in the Soviet leader's chest. No longer did he seem on the defensive, let alone browbeaten. Overall, thought Harrison Salisbury, one of the few reporters present who spoke Russian and understood what Khrushchev was saying, "It was a remarkably able presentation by each man of his viewpoint. . . . I was surprised at how well Nixon handled himself."

A few nights later, in American company, he disgraced himself. Milton Eisenhower, the president's brother, recalled his behavior upon his return from making a broadcast on Soviet television. "He came back terribly upset, terribly nervous. . . . So he drank about six martinis before we sat down for dinner. . . . As soon as we sat down, he started going around the table to see what everyone thinks about the speech. And he'd keep interrupting the person: 'Did you hear me say this? Did you hear me say this?' Then he began using abusive—well, not abusive, but vulgar swearwords in this mixed company. . . . He was a strange character."

"The fact that he had a couple of extra drinks didn't bother me," recalled U.S. official Vladimir Toumanoff, "so much as the fact that . . . he was vicious . . . riddled with anger and hostility and self-praise and arrogance." That Nixon drank and could not hold his drink was a concern. That he crumbled under pressure did not bode well in a man with presidential ambitions. When Milton Eisenhower returned to Washington, he reported to his brother what he had seen that evening.

The public Nixon, though, had done himself no harm in the Soviet Union. Khrushchev might disdainfully recall him as "a typical middle-class American businessman," a "son of a bitch," and claim that he later did what he could to help John F. Kennedy defeat him the following year. Many Americans, on the contrary, thought that Nixon's showing on the Soviet trip won him votes.

In a letter before he left for Moscow the wealthy Elmer Bobst had written to advise him that his primary purpose on the trip should be "to stick your fist under Khrushchev's nose and become President of the United States." For Nixon, poking his finger at the Soviet leader may have been the result as much of advance planning as of spleen.

Other elements of the Moscow visit were contrived, and some of those who participated were significant to Nixon in ways outsiders could not appreciate. Nixon had acted on the telephoned suggestion of "Mr. Thomas," aka the helpful millionaire Howard Hughes, that the latest American airliners, including one of his own TWA 707 jets, carry the U.S. contingent on the journey. The TWA plane set a new speed record for the Moscow flight and received massive publicity in return.*[5] Also along was TWA's president, Charles Thomas, who had contributed to Nixon's fund.

Not mentioned in Nixon's account of the Moscow visit was his initiative on behalf of PepsiCo Inc. Donald Kendall, head of Pepsi's overseas operations and a Nixon friend, had asked him beforehand to bring Khrushchev over to the company stand at the trade exhibit. "I had to get a Pepsi in Khrushchev's hands," Kendall remembered. "I had to get a picture."

Nixon duly obliged. Kendall served the Soviet leader Pepsi, asking whether he preferred a bottle of the drink as produced in New York or one made using local Moscow water. Khrushchev said, predictably, that he preferred the local version. Kendall meanwhile had thus obtained his coveted photograph of the leader of the Communist bloc clutching a drink symbolic of "decadent" American society. The picture was disseminated around the world, to become a major feature of Pepsi's advertising campaign. It not only represented a victory over the company's market rival, Coca-Cola, but also massively boosted Kendall's career—he soon moved up to become Pepsi's president—and sealed a mutually beneficial long-term bond with Nixon.

———————

The Khrushchev encounter had been a benchmark in the maturing of Richard Nixon. He had stepped onto the world stage with the leader of America's most feared enemy and had held his own. The words he had spoken embodied the

———————

*See p. 151 on the Howard Hughes call.

thinking that was to direct his policies for years to come, defining attitudes that shaped the foreign policy of his presidency and his country in the last half of the century.

Just before flying to Moscow, Nixon had issued a stern edict to his speechwriters that they must never use the statement "We endorse the principle of coexistence." "Tell all of them," he wrote his national security aide Robert Cushman, "it is never to be used again . . . whoever does it will be shipped [out] on the next plane."

Before leaving Russia, in an unprecedented broadcast by an American politician to the Soviet people, he explained his position. "To me," Nixon said, "the concept of peaceful coexistence is completely inadequate and negative. Coexistence implies that the world must be divided into two hostile camps with a wall of hate and fear between. What we need today is not two worlds but one world, where different peoples choose the economic and political systems which they want. . . . Let us have peaceful competition."

"Mr. Khrushchev predicted that our grandchildren would live under Communism. . . . We do not object to his saying this will happen. We only object if he tries to bring it about. And this is my answer to him. I do not say that your grandchildren will live under capitalism. We prefer our system. But the very essence of our belief is that we do not and will not try to impose our system on anyone else. . . . You and all other peoples on this earth should have the right to chose the kind of economic and political system which best fits your particular problems, without any foreign intervention. I pledge to you that in the years to come I shall devote my best efforts to the cause of peace. . . ."

When he was selected to run for the presidency a year later, Nixon rearranged the verbiage for domestic consumption. "When Mr. Khrushchev says our grandchildren will live under Communism," he now told fellow Republicans, "let us say his grandchildren will live in freedom." Absent, then, would be the assurance that Washington had no wish to impose its system on any other nation. Gone too was the promise of "no foreign intervention."

Although Nixon may have been more or less sincere when he addressed the Soviet people, there were key exceptions to the assurances he gave them. Foremost among them were the nations of Latin America and the Caribbean, a region the United States regarded as its own backyard. In those countries what Washington could not be seen to do by open intervention it sought to achieve by pressure, intrigue, and, when necessary, covert action.

Five years before the Moscow visit a young CIA agent named Howard Hunt had been briefed on a new mission by the agency's psychological warfare chief. He "swore me to secrecy," the future Watergate burglar recalled, "and revealed that the National Security Council under Eisenhower and Vice President Nixon had ordered the overthrow of Guatemala's Communist regime." The Guatemalan government, which some argue was not in fact Communist but which had had the temerity to seize some of the vast holdings of the United

Fruit Company, the American-owned banana corporation,[6] had duly been toppled by the CIA in the early summer of 1954.

It had been a cunning operation, achieved with a great deal of bluff and comparatively little bloodshed. President Eisenhower had been pleased and summoned senior agency officers to the White House to brief him on how they had accomplished the task. That morning, when the lights were turned off for a slide show, one of the officers had an odd encounter.

"A door opened near me," recalled propaganda specialist David Phillips. "In the darkness I could see only the silhouette of the person entering the room; when the door closed, it was dark again, and I could not make out the features of the man standing next to me. He whispered a number of questions: 'Who is that? Who made that decision?' I was vaguely uncomfortable. The questions from the unknown man next to me were insistent, furtive. . . . The lights went up. The man moved away. He was Richard Nixon, the vice president."

Six years later Phillips, Hunt, and other members of the Guatemala team would convene again in Washington, this time at a shabby CIA building opposite the Lincoln Memorial. They knew a new project was underway, but had not yet been told what it involved. Given three guesses, though, as to why they had been summoned, Phillips had a ready response. The explanation, he said, was: "Cuba, Cuba. And Cuba."

Fidel Castro had come to power in Havana on New Year's Day 1959. His revolution, he promised in his victory speech, would not be like the events in 1898, "when the North Americans came and made themselves masters of our country." When Castro visited Washington four months later, the senior official Eisenhower chose to meet with him was Nixon. From that time on, Nixon remembered, he became "the strongest and most persistent advocate" of efforts to overthrow the new Cuban regime and replace it with one acceptable to Washington.

Those efforts of course ultimately led to the botched invasion at the Bahía de los Cochinos, the Bay of Pigs. That military fiasco, performed by ill-starred Cuban exiles but orchestrated by the CIA, would occur in 1961 at the start of President Kennedy's term. Its prelude, though, took place during a year of messy machinations under the auspices of the Eisenhower-Nixon administration. Just what role Nixon played in those machinations has remained uncertain. Not least among the uncertainties has been the question of whether he was involved in the plotting at the dark heart of the Cuba story: American state-sponsored attempts to murder Castro.

16

Cuba was a neuralgic problem for Nixon . . .

a raw nerve.

—Henry Kissinger

"Obsession," said James Schlesinger in 1996, "may be the correct word." Nixon's second CIA director was attempting to describe the persistence with which Nixon, as president, was to press the agency for its records on the Bay of Pigs. As soon as he assumed office, according to Bob Haldeman, Nixon demanded "all the facts and documents the CIA had . . . a complete report on the whole project." He was "really distressed" when nothing was forthcoming.

Two years later he renewed his efforts with even greater intensity. The White House tapes alone indicate that Nixon demanded the Bay of Pigs documents—"for me personally"—four times in as many weeks. In September 1971, frustrated and angry, he ordered John Ehrlichman to press the CIA for the material. "Get started right in on this. . . . I don't want to discuss it. We are entitled to the facts. . . . I'm going to have it."

In his handwritten records of White House meetings, Ehrlichman referred to the president with the Greek letter π (*p*). His note on this instruction read:

Bay of Pigs—
   π order to CIA
π is to have the *full* file
or else
Nothing w/held

Richard Helms, director of central intelligence in the early part of the Nixon presidency, could hardly send over the agency's thirty-thousand-page archive on the Cuba project. Nor did he produce either of the two bulky internal studies that had been generated within the CIA since 1961.[1] What he did do, on a visit to the Oval Office, was hand Nixon a slender report by a marine colonel who had been seconded to the CIA at the time of the Bay of Pigs. The president complained in his memoirs that what Helms had given him was "incomplete. . . . The CIA protects itself, even from presidents."

That may be an accurate assessment, but the question remains precisely why Nixon was so keen to examine what the agency had on the Bay of Pigs. One reason is that he wanted access to anything that might reflect badly on the Kennedy brothers. As early as 1968 Nixon had said that Robert Kennedy's presidential bid that year offered "the chance to indict the whole JFK-LBJ tenure, right back to the Bay of Pigs."

In 1971, when Nixon urged aides to unearth material likely to damage his predecessors' reputations, the Bay of Pigs topped his priority list.[2] Two years later, as Watergate engulfed him, he demanded the file again. Meanwhile his lawyer Fred Buzhardt went out at dead of night to try to get a journalist to part with other Bay of Pigs information supposedly compromising to the Kennedys.[3]

Close study, however, suggests there was more to Nixon's persistence than presidential malevolence. Nixon's memoirs, which sometimes reveal more about him than he may have intended, refer to his "imperative need" to get the facts on the Bay of Pigs. Why was it so vital to see the files, a decade after a military failure for which President Kennedy had after all publicly accepted responsibility? What was the basis for the "preoccupation" and "concern" that John Ehrlichman noted?

Haldeman recalled how in 1969, during the first attempt to wrest the records out of Helms, Ehrlichman burst into his office to report a bizarre development. "The Mad Monk," Ehrlichman said, using his favorite nickname for Nixon, "has just told me I am now to *forget* all about that CIA document. . . . I am to cease and desist from trying to obtain it. " The sudden turnaround had come soon after Nixon had had a "long, secret conversation" with Richard Helms. What made him retreat so suddenly?

A White House tape made in 1971 suggests that what concerned him was material in the Cuba reports that could prove damaging to him. "The matter . . . is going to arise without question as time goes on—the Cuban thing," he told Haldeman, Ehrlichman, John Mitchell, and Charles Colson. "Tell Helms . . . I want this . . . in order to protect ourselves in the clinches." Weeks later, after sitting in on the meeting at which Helms surrendered some material, Ehrlichman noted: "Purpose of presidential request for documents: must be fully advised in order to know what to duck. . . ." Why did Nixon believe "the Cuban thing" was bound to come up? What was there that he needed to protect himself from, or to be ready "to duck"?

Ehrlichman was still puzzled about the matter when interviewed in 1997. He had always felt there was a secret but never figured out what it was. His note of the conversation in which Nixon told him to get back after Helms, however, offers a hint: "was involved in Bay of Pigs . . . deeply involved. . . ."

"Apparently," Haldeman wrote in his memoir, "Nixon knew more about the genesis of the Cuban invasion than almost anyone." He also remembered Helms's reaction after Watergate, when Nixon had him try to persuade the CIA director to help obscure the White House role in the break-in on the ground that it might somehow be linked to the Bay of Pigs.* There was "turmoil in the room," Nixon's chief of staff recalled, "Helms gripping the arms of his chair, leaning forward and shouting, 'The Bay of Pigs had nothing to do with this. I have no concern about the Bay of Pigs.' . . . I just sat there. I was absolutely shocked by Helms' violent reaction. Again I wondered, *what was such dynamite* in the Bay of Pigs story?"[4]†

Six years before the Bay of Pigs invasion, in January 1955, Nixon had written to Bebe Rebozo, thanking him for Christmas gifts—"Rum Zombies, Rum Coke, and guava jellies"—and promising to forward the schedule for an upcoming trip to Havana. Nixon had long had a special interest in Cuba. He had been there first with Pat soon after their marriage and liked it so much he talked of moving to Havana to practice as an attorney. Then there had been his alleged visit, or visits, to the island's Mafia-operated gambling casinos before he became vice president. Once, as reported in these pages, the crooks who ran one of the casinos are said to have paid his bill.‡

In 1955, as on Nixon's previous visits, the man who held power in Cuba was Fulgencio Batista. Three years earlier, after a period in exile in Florida, the fifty-four-year-old dictator had seized power again. He had suspended constitutional guarantees, dissolved political parties, and promised the people order and honesty. In the event, his seven remaining years in power were a time of tyranny and economic misery for the majority of Cubans. To maintain Batista's hegemony, his police and army murdered at will. Thousands reportedly died.

The most glaring feature of Batista's rule was corruption, on a colossal scale. The per capita income in the countryside was pathetically low, and the Cuban treasury virtually emptied, while the dictator banked untold millions abroad. Much of that fortune came from the U.S. Mafia, headed in Havana by Meyer Lansky. Lansky and Batista had a mutually beneficial business deal. The American criminals got to run their casinos and nightclubs, extracting millions from the pockets of junketing Americans, while in return, once a month at

---

*This ploy, covered in a later chapter, was the subject of the "smoking gun" tape of June 23, 1972. Its discovery was the final straw that led to Nixon's resignation.

†Haldeman's italics.

‡See p. 32 and p. 128.

noon, a Lansky courier is said to have delivered a briefcase containing $1,280,000 to the side entrance of the presidential palace. Batista and Lansky, recalled the mob boss's lawyer, were "very, very close—like brothers."

"Batista's continuance in office," read the brief Nixon received before his 1955 trip to Havana, "is probably a good thing for the United States." He "is friendly . . . admires the American Way of Life, and believes in free enterprise." The brief noted that American businesses—the legitimate sort—had more than six hundred million dollars invested in Cuba. As the U.S. naval attaché at the time put it, "Batista was a dictator. But he was our dictator."

Before he left, Nixon also received an impassioned letter from fifty prominent Cubans who had fled Batista's "tyrannical fury" to live in the United States. They begged him not to close his eyes to the more than a million unemployed, to try to visit political prisoners and talk with the wives and mothers of those who had been murdered. "Please, Mr. Nixon," they wrote, "be a sort of speaking trumpet of justice."

Instead, once Nixon arrived in Havana, his friendliness toward Batista seemed to exceed even the standard diplomatic niceties. He announced that he was pleased to be in a land that "shares with us the same democratic ideals of peace, freedom and the dignity of man." In the privacy of a cabinet meeting on his return home, Nixon gave no hint of disapproval of the regime, telling Eisenhower and senior colleagues that the dictator was "a very remarkable man . . . older and wiser . . . desirous of doing a job for Cuba rather than Batista . . . concerned about social progress. . . ."

Nixon said Batista had impressed him too as "self-educated . . . a voracious reader." The dictator had perhaps told him he was in the middle of reading *The Day Lincoln Was Shot,* his favorite opening gambit to all American visitors. His real reading staple was the daily "novel" prepared by aides, the juicier bits of recent telephone wiretap transcripts. In the evenings Batista liked to watch Boris Karloff and Dracula movies.

Batista, Nixon reported to the cabinet, claimed he would "deal with the Commies." Two years earlier a twenty-seven year old lawyer named Fidel Castro and his brother Raúl had been jailed after a bungled assault on an army barracks. After the Nixon visit, made more confident by the strength of his U.S. backing, Batista released them.

Less than a year later the Castro brothers and Che Guevara, starting with a band of just twelve men, embarked on the grueling guerrilla campaign that ended with the collapse of Batista forces on New Year's Eve 1959. Batista fled in the night with his family and closest henchmen and, according to the CIA agent who reported his flight, "a vast array of suitcases stuffed not with clothes but money." Fidel Castro entered Havana a few days later and, having said in his first marathon speech that he would know when to leave, began the iron rule that was to last more than forty years.

In all accounts of the Cuba story the roles of two men have remained little documented and sketchily reported. Both wanted Fidel Castro dead from the moment of his rise to power. At different stages both urged or actively plotted his assassination, an act that, when perpetrated by one nation's leaders against those of another, is, in the words of a U.S. Senate committee, "short of war, incompatible with American principles, international order, and morality." What we can piece together of their actions suggests that both influenced or sought to influence Richard Nixon.

The first man is Meyer Lansky, long said to have been linked either to Nixon or to Bebe Rebozo.* Lansky and the other top mobsters active in Cuba were infuriated by the Castro takeover. The gambling empire that they had worked painstakingly to create over many years was now lost to them, and in a manner that made Lansky especially enraged.

While the victorious revolutionaries had at first closed down the casinos, Castro later negotiated with the mobsters and then allowed gambling to resume. Months later he briefly jailed Lansky's brother and several associates before expelling them from the country. Gambling continued for some time, but under strict supervision and with the mob's control and profits effectively destroyed. Finally the casinos were shut down once and for all.[5] The way Lansky saw it, Castro had two-timed him, an offense that in the Mafia culture is punishable by death.

Legend has it that Lansky placed a million-dollar bounty on Castro's head. Years later, when questioned about this by a journalist, he refused to elaborate. "A number of people came to me with a number of ideas," he said, "and of course I had my own suggestions to make. . . . I don't think I should go into details. . . ." A longtime intimate, Joseph Stacher, provided some of the missing details. "Meyer indicated to the CIA," he said, "that some of his people who were still on the island, or those who were just going back, might assassinate Castro. . . . He tried hard to convince the CIA agents that he could have Fidel removed."

The CIA, hedging its bets, had acted benignly toward Castro in the months before the revolution. It had facilitated the guerrillas' arms supplies and even sent an agent to join them in the mountains.[6] During Castro's first year in power, too, Washington had yet to become convinced that he was a Communist. That being the case, according to Stacher, the agency turned down Lansky's early murder proposal. FBI files show that the bureau, likewise, ignored the mobster's warning about the growing Communist threat in Cuba. Meanwhile Lansky tried another approach: contacting Vice President Nixon.

He went about it in a logical way, Stacher said, by calling in a favor. Lansky sought access to Nixon through Dana Smith, the California gambler who had gotten into trouble while at Havana's Sans Souci casino—reportedly with

*See earlier Lansky references.

Nixon—a few years earlier. He also contacted Senator George Smathers, mutual friend of Nixon and Rebozo. A Lansky message passed through either man, he knew, would go straight to Nixon.[7]

The other individual enraged by the Castro takeover was a very different sort of character. A wealthy, high-ranking former diplomat with instant access to President Eisenhower, to the CIA at the highest level, and to Nixon, this was William Pawley, a sixty-three-year-old veteran of international intrigue. After making one fortune in Florida real estate and another in the airline business in Cuba and China, he had held high office in the Defense and State departments, twice serving as ambassador in Latin America. A staunch right-wing Republican, Pawley had contributed to both Dwight Eisenhower's and Nixon's political campaigns and counted CIA Director Allen Dulles a personal friend. His customary apparel of white suit and broad-brimmed straw hat—suggested a plantation owner of another era.

Pawley had grown up in Cuba, spoke excellent Spanish, owned the Havana bus system and gas company, and had made it his business to foster personal relationships with both President Batista and the dictator of the neighboring Dominican Republic, Rafael Trujillo. Not far into the future Pawley would choose Bebe Rebozo as his companion on a journey to try to persuade Trujillo to abdicate power. Just days before Batista fled, Pawley had flown to Havana—after discussions with President Eisenhower and the CIA's Western Hemisphere Division chief, J. C. King—to urge him to step down.

At that point the objective had been damage containment. As events spiraled out of control, Pawley had hoped Batista could be replaced by a military junta, or by any viable right-wing alternative to Fidel Castro. Pawley would claim that he had discovered Castro was a Communist years earlier, and although his story of how he discovered that was probably untrue, facts did not much concern him when it came to anticommunism.[8] Pawley had been involved in the disinformation campaign that accompanied the CIA's Guatemalan coup of 1954; and afterward he served on a panel that recommended the creation of "an aggressive covert psychological, political and paramilitary organization more effective and, if necessary, more ruthless than that employed by the [Communist] enemy."

After the Cuban Revolution an outraged Pawley began talking about having Castro killed. "Find me one man, just one man," he told a Miami acquaintance, "who can go it alone and get Castro. I'll pay anything, almost anything." In the months and years that followed he was to be, as Pawley's niece told the author, "up to his eyebrows" in U.S. efforts to topple Castro. One of his key contacts in that endeavor was Richard Nixon.

———

One rainy April weekend in 1959 Nixon and Castro met in Washington. The Cuban, just three months in power and still acclaimed by most as the guerrilla hero who had ousted a cruel dictator, had been astonishing America since his arrival. The beard, the ten-inch cigar, and the army fatigues had bewitched thousands. A cheering throng estimated at thirty-five thousand had welcomed him at a rally in New York's Central Park. To the general public Castro seemed like an amalgam of George Washington, Billy Graham, and Barnum and Bailey. To the capital's politicians, bureaucrats, and businessmen, he was as yet still a puzzle.

Before leaving Havana, Castro had perceived a dilemma in the possibility of a meeting with President Eisenhower. He hoped to see him yet worried that it would appear as though he—just like the sort of Latin American potentate he despised—was "selling out." In the event, Eisenhower remained pointedly out of town, and Castro had to make do with the vice president. "The president of the United States didn't even invite me for a cup of coffee," Castro grumbled later. "They sent me Nixon. . . ." The Cuban had refused an invitation to meet Nixon at his home and settled for the vice president's office at the Capitol. Nixon later claimed there was nothing he had wanted less that weekend than to meet "the new Cuban dictator."

Given the prolonged conflict to come, the encounter between America's most prominent anti-Communist and the suspect revolutionary was historic. They sat talking for three hours beneath a chandelier that had once hung in Jefferson's White House—alone, because Castro had decided that his English was good enough to allow him to get by without interpreters.

The vice president thought Castro seemed "nervous and tense," "looked like a revolutionary, and talked like an idealistic college professor. . . ." For his part, Castro found Nixon oddly young, almost "a teenager, not in appearance but in behavior . . . a bit superficial," though not hostile. Nixon said he spoke to Castro "like a Dutch uncle," severely but kindly. His long report to Eisenhower and Dulles, written soon afterward, suggests he lectured the Cuban in the paternalistic way that perennially offended Latin American visitors to Washington.

"That son of a bitch Nixon," Castro was to complain, "he treated me badly," explaining what he meant in a conversation that night with the lawyer who represented Cuba in the United States, Constantine Kangles. "Nixon didn't look me in the eye," Castro said; "he looked up in the air, at the wall, all over, but not at me. I didn't ask for money, but I did say we needed help. He told me I'd been a fine fellow, put in plenty of good reforms. Then he said that in about six months we could meet and talk again. Six months! He knew Cuba was broke, that Batista had looted the treasury. What he was effectively telling us to do was to go and starve to death."

"Castro didn't believe Nixon was interested in helping," Kangles remembered in 1999. "He thought Nixon wanted economic catastrophe to hit Cuba, so that the people would overthrow Castro. He thought Nixon just wanted to see him toppled."

The pair emerged from their meeting "with their arms around each other's shoulders," said Bob Stephenson, a State Department official who had waited outside. Dean Rusk, then heading the Rockefeller Foundation, recalled seeing them on television and hearing Nixon say, "We're going to work with this man."[9] Behind the scenes Nixon took a different stance. Slapping his knee, he told Stephenson that Castro had no understanding of democracy. Closeted with his own aides Herb Klein and General Hughes, he said Castro was an "outright Communist and he's going to be a real danger." He told Jack Drown, a close California friend, that Castro was a "dedicated Communist, who's going to be a thorn in the side of us all."[10]

In a conversation with the former Costa Rican president José Figueres, Nixon commented that Castro had made a "terrible impression" on him. He "characterized Fidel as a lunatic," Figueres recalled. "He was scared as hell; I could see it in his eyes."

Castro meanwhile succeeded in convincing others in the government, including the CIA's senior expert on communism in Latin America, Gerry Droller, that he was not a Communist. "Castro," Droller announced delightedly after meeting him, "is not only not a Communist, but he is a strong anti-Communist fighter."

Whether Castro was committed to communism at that point remains a question to which only he knows the answer. There is some evidence that at the time he met Nixon he was attempting to go his own way, at odds with avowed Communists like his brother Raúl. Cuban leftists had even told Soviet contacts they suspected Castro was a tool of the *Americans*. In the nineties a former Soviet diplomat insisted that Castro made no approaches to Moscow until the year after his meeting with Nixon.

Some have argued that Castro merely sought to use communism as a vehicle for his personal style of one-man rule. He was neurotically anti-American, but that is not necessarily the same thing as being a Communist.

"The one fact we can be sure of," Nixon wrote in his report about Castro to Eisenhower, "is that he has those indefinable qualities which make him a leader of men. . . . He seems to be sincere, he is either incredibly naive about Communism or under Communist discipline—my guess is the former. . . . But because he has the power to lead . . . we have no choice but at least to try to orient him in the right direction."

"We will check in a year," Eisenhower scrawled on another report about the Castro visit. In the months that followed, Castro—assisted by William Pawley, Allen Dulles, and Nixon—made up his mind for him. The Cuban leader soon seized American businesses in Cuba, businesses representing a billion-dollar investment, and started to arm rebels in other Latin countries. Nixon began urging the National Security Council that it was time to "find a few dramatic things to do . . . to indicate that we would not allow ourselves to be kicked around. . . ."

According to a former cabinet secretary, Robert Keith Gray, "There were no executive secrets between Eisenhower and Nixon." In part because of how he had functioned during the president's illnesses, Nixon now saw himself as the president's deputy. He attended two hundred NSC meetings and presided over twenty-six of them. His assistant for NSC affairs, Brigadier General Robert Cushman, brought him a full intelligence briefing every morning.

Nixon, CIA officials had discovered when he sat in for Eisenhower, was an "apt and eager" student of intelligence matters. One of them recalled that he had a "vicarious interest in the supposedly romantic side of spying . . . like a child who wants to know what lies behind a magician's illusions. Technique and detail were Nixon's interests . . . how to open and reseal a letter without leaving any marks, or how to detect, move or install a bug. . . ."

The agency had come to treat the vice president as its "friend at court" and made certain he received a regular flow of intelligence. This would explain why, when NSC deputy executive secretary Marion Boggs tried to carry out his duty of briefing Nixon's staff, he found they often "didn't see fit to talk to us very much." Nixon's more direct line to U.S. intelligence made such conversations unnecessary.

At the NSC meeting on December 16, CIA Director Dulles said it was time to do "a number of things in the covert field" on Cuba. Behind the scenes, Nixon was also listening to advice from William Pawley, who had argued from the start that Castro should be killed. Pawley's friend at the top at CIA, J. C. King, had just days earlier sent Dulles a list of four "recommended actions." One of them, which Dulles approved, proposed "Thorough consideration be given to the elimination of Fidel Castro. . . . Many informed people believe that the disappearance of Fidel would greatly accelerate the fall of the present government." It was the first recorded official reference to the assassination track. The notion of murdering certain other foreign leaders was to come up in National Security Council sessions, although always veiled by euphemisms. "Removal" or "dispose of," for example, would be used, but never the word "assassination."

Eisenhower let the dogs of covert war loose against Castro, in a more general way, at a meeting in March 1960. Dulles told him there was no hope of living with the Cuban leader, and the president approved a plan the CIA had been working on for months. It called not for an invasion—that was to come later—but for the creation of a paramilitary force made up of exiles, a resistance network inside Cuba, and the formation of a moderate leadership capable of replacing the Castro regime once it was overthrown. The agency called the scheme Operation Pluto, after the Roman god of the dead. Castro was allotted a cryptonym, AM/THUG.[11]

To Nixon, Pluto was a potential stepping-stone to the goal that motivated him more than the overthrow of any Caribbean dictator, the presidency. Thomas McCoy, a CIA man offered an assignment on the project, was told there was "substantial pressure coming from the White House to get the thing settled by October of 1960, so that this would not be an issue that Nixon had to deal with in the presidential campaign."

As Nixon viewed it, the anti-Castro effort could work either for or against him. Unresolved, it could be detrimental to Republican chances. Successfully handled, and at the right time, it would be a highly effective vote getter. In spite of Eisenhower's admonition that Pluto should be held in utmost secrecy, Nixon spoke of the plans with four of his staff. He told his press aide, Herb Klein, that the toppling of Castro would be "a real trump card." "He wanted it to occur in October, before the election," Klein said in 1997. "The only people who knew his role exactly were himself and his aide General Cushman."

Some commentators have resisted the notion that Nixon was a prime mover in the Cuba project, let alone a party to plots to murder Castro. "By no stretch of the imagination," CIA historian Jack Pfeiffer wrote in an in-house report, "was Nixon the architect of the Bay of Pigs." Perhaps not, but Pluto did not evolve into an invasion plan until the last months of the Eisenhower presidency. Pfeiffer did note that Nixon and Bob Cushman attended dozens of meetings on Operation Pluto. "The Vice President," he said, "had a great interest in the Agency's progress in organizing the ouster of Castro."

The last U.S. ambassador to Cuba, Philip Bonsal, stated flatly that Nixon was "one of the earliest sponsors . . . in a sense the father of the operation" to topple Castro. In private, apparently, Nixon claimed it was his initiative. President Figueres of Costa Rica, whose country the CIA hoped to use for covert training, was often in Washington in 1960. "Nixon," he said, "told me he had told the CIA to prepare for an invasion of Cuba. He called Allen Dulles and said, 'Castro has to be overthrown. You try the best you can.' . . ."[12] A senior CIA veteran, Sam Halpern, has said he had the impression Nixon "more or less" became the White House action officer on Cuba. "It's my understanding," Alexander Haig said in 1998, "that Nixon was Eisenhower's point man. . . ."[13]

The agency officer who directed Operation Pluto was Jacob Esterline, who two years earlier had encountered Nixon during his Venezuela trip. He found the vice president a "heavy monitor" of CIA activities, through his aide Cushman. Howard Hunt, the CIA's liaison with Cuban exile leaders, has recalled a luncheon meeting with Cushman and Esterline in the summer of 1960. According to Hunt, Cushman described his boss as the "chief architect . . . the honcho" of the project. He stressed that Nixon wanted nothing to go wrong, telling Hunt to call him day or night should he need "high-level intervention."[14]

It became obvious to many that summer that Nixon was growing impatient with the delay in dealing with Cuba. "How the hell are they coming? How are the boys doing at the Institute?" he would ask Cushman, referring to the CIA. "What in the world are they doing that takes months?" Nixon, with no significant military experience, talked as though the Pluto operation involved little more than some "rifle training." Eisenhower, the veteran professional, urged caution. "He knew the perils," Cushman said dryly later. "Nixon didn't."

By September a top man on the CIA's Cuba project, Tracy Barnes, would find himself confronted by a colleague asking, "What's the hurry? . . . Why are we working our asses off on this?" Barnes knew, as did Cushman, that it was Nixon, focused on his presidential ambitions, who was applying the pressure.

To the frustration of the CIA planners, who hoped to replace Castro with democratically minded Cubans, Nixon took advice on the matter from William Pawley. The conservative Floridian, who also had Eisenhower's respectful attention, kept promoting the idea of using the far-right exiles. "Ike, Nixon, and Pawley . . . don't know it, " joked Richard Bissell, the overall head of the CIA's Cuban effort, "but we're the real revolutionaries." His men stalled the exile extremists, who complained to Pawley, and he in turn pressed their case with Nixon.

Nixon became involved in one of the rightist intrigues, in a way that suggests a penchant for hands-on skulduggery that went far beyond what was permissible in an elected official—economic sabotage on the grand scale and later, allegedly, conspiracy to murder. It brought Nixon together with Mario García Kohly, a middle-aged exile who had been a prominent financier and politician before Batista's fall. Kohly placed a special emphasis on disruption of the Cuban economy, a position entirely in line with that of Nixon, Pawley, and the CIA.

CIA Director Dulles had been avidly interested in a suggestion made at a Washington dinner party by Ian Fleming, author of the James Bond spy novels. One way to destabilize Castro, he said, would be to flood Cuba with fake currency. Soon, at a National Security Council meeting, Nixon was urging economic warfare. Failing swift action, he said, the United States would soon be known not as Uncle Sam but as Uncle Sucker.

Kohly gravitated naturally toward Nixon. By one account, his first patron on arriving in Florida had been none other than Bebe Rebozo, himself a Cuban-American who—Henry Kissinger would one day note—"hated Castro with a fierce Latin passion." According to Kohly's son, Mario, Jr., his father was in touch with Nixon within months of his arrival.[15]

The pivotal contact came in July 1960, engineered by former Senator Owen Brewster, a conservative Republican who had once been investigated for supplying Nixon with illegal campaign funding. Also involved as go-between was Marshall Diggs, a Washington lawyer and former Treasury official who had long been in touch with Nixon on intelligence matters. Nixon met with Kohly, then put him in touch with Allen Dulles. A series of contacts with CIA agents followed.

Kohly was to organize the printing of huge sums in counterfeit Cuban pesos, with the assistance of powerful accomplices. In the summer of 1960 Nixon's aide Bob Cushman found himself on a plane with Dulles, flying down to Florida to discuss "a scheme to print Cuban bonds" with Pawley.

The CIA operatives trying to forge a united anti-Castro leadership, however, saw Kohly as a handicap. He had delusions of grandeur, saw himself as "president-in-exile," and was too right-wing to be compatible with the moderates the CIA wanted in its exile alliance. Nixon disagreed, describing Kohly as "a red-hot prospect to lead the Cubans." He would remain enthusiastic about him three years later, when Kohly's counterfeiting eventually got him into trouble with the law.

Nixon was to ensure that Kohly received free legal advice, and would write to the judge in the case pleading for leniency. Rather than send the exile to prison, he was to tell a colleague, "they should give him a medal." According to one witness, Nixon even told Kohly that "everything would be all right" if he could just hold up court proceedings by jumping bail and going into hiding for a while. Kohly did jump bail, but was eventually picked up and jailed anyway.

Nixon may have helped Kohly not least because he feared exposure of his own role in a matter that did not come up in court—namely, conspiracy to murder. Kohly's son has recounted an extraordinary episode that took place in October 1960—after the CIA had steered Nixon away from Kohly and when U.S. policy was shifting from support of guerrilla action to plans for outright invasion. Kohly, Jr., told of a telephone conversation with his father, conducted for security reasons on predesignated pay phones, in which his father described a meeting with Nixon at the Burning Tree Club in Maryland.[16]

According to an affidavit sworn by Kohly's son, Nixon agreed at the meeting to "the elimination of the leftist-approved Cuban [exile] leaders at a time when the island would be invaded by the exile groups trained under the direction of the CIA. This promise was made if my father would guarantee the use of his underground organization inside Cuba and his 300–400 man armed guerrilla force in the Escambray Mountains."[17] Interviewed in 1996, the younger Kohly repeated the allegation, saying it was clear that Nixon had sanctioned the executions of any exile leaders Kohly deemed leftist. "The way I recall it was that Nixon okayed it, saying, 'When you go into Cuba, if you have to get rid of a bunch of Communists, go ahead and do it. If there's leftist leaders there, kill them and let it be known that they fought to the last man. . . .'"

Kohly, Jr., said it was also understood "absolutely" that Fidel Castro, his brother Raúl, and Che Guevara were to be killed in the event of an invasion. "Part of Washington went along with this," he said, "the Nixon part. Many in the CIA were against it."

The details of U.S. plots to kill Castro have emerged in dribs and drabs ever since their existence was revealed by a Senate committee in the midseventies. Much of the focus has been on whether President Kennedy and his brother Robert were privy to the assassination plans, and to what extent. But was Nixon also involved? Was he even aware of the plots? It is a key question, and one until now much neglected.

17

The determination to kill a foreign leader . . .
is not only a sign of moral and political impotence,
but an arrogant assertion of one nation's right
to control the destinies of all humanity.

—Harry Rositzke, career CIA officer

Trying to determine who authorized the CIA's attempts to murder foreign leaders, said Walter Mondale after a 1975 Senate Intelligence Committee investigation, was "like trying to nail Jell-O to the wall." He thought "the system was intended to work that way, that things would be ordered to be done that—should it be made public—no one could be held accountable."

The Intelligence Committee did nevertheless establish the outlines, albeit fuzzy, of the agency's murder plots against three foreign leaders. Poisons were sent to the Congo in 1960 to kill Prime Minister Patrice Lumumba, although he eventually met his death at the hands of his own countrymen. Weapons were sent to the Dominican Republic in 1961 to dissidents seeking the overthrow of the dictator Rafael Trujillo, and may have been used in his assassination. As for Castro, the CIA tried repeatedly to have him murdered over a period of five years, starting under Eisenhower and Nixon in 1960.

By the time the Intelligence Committee did its work, none of the presidents who had served during the relevant periods remained alive to answer questions. The committee made no formal finding "implicating presidents." In spite of denials by Eisenhower's intimates, however, the senators heard testimony suggesting that he approved the plan to kill Lumumba.[1] The former executive secretary of the National Security Council, Marion Boggs, said in an interview for this book that Eisenhower also discussed the possible assassination of Castro. The president eventually rejected the idea—but on purely pragmatic grounds. "Eisenhower's view," Boggs explained, "was always: 'Why should anyone assassinate the head of Cuba, Castro? Because we'd only get his brother instead, who's worse.'"[2]

Allen Dulles, the head of the CIA at the time the death plots were initiated, maintained in his memoirs that the agency "never carried out any action of a political nature . . . without appropriate approval at a high political level in our government *outside the CIA*."* Other senior CIA officials have maintained the same. "Authorization outside the CIA for a Castro assassination," the Senate committee concluded, "could, according to the testimony, only have come from President Eisenhower [or] from someone speaking for him . . ."[3]

The CIA official in charge of anti-Castro operations, Deputy Director of Plans Richard Bissell, told the committee he never discussed the assassination plots with any administration official, having relied on Director Dulles to do that, and to obtain authorization.[4] "What happened above his level," he said years later, "I never knew precisely and didn't particularly inquire. . . . No one would have expected to get an affirmative, an explicit approval from the president."

Dulles, like Eisenhower, had died by the time of the committee investigation. The responses of CIA chiefs who did testify, like Bissell and Helms, rested on the opaque principle that where assassination was concerned, the CIA related to the White House on the basis of the nod and wink rather than direct authorization. "I think we all had the feeling," Helms said, "that we were hired out to keep those things out of the Oval Office." With that proviso he testified that the Castro death plots were known "to almost everybody in high positions in government."

Only one man who had served at the highest political level and had had a special involvement in Cuban matters, the year the murder plots began, was alive and available for testimony in 1975. Richard Nixon, forced out of office the previous year, was by then ensconced at San Clemente in California. Yet the committee was unable to question him on the subject.

The senators had certainly sought to have Nixon testify in full. In months of negotiation, however, Nixon insisted on his right not to answer certain questions, by invoking the Fifth Amendment against self-incrimination and the principle of executive privilege. He also objected on the ground of ill health to having to come to Washington to be interrogated, even though he had recently been photographed playing golf. In the end Nixon was only persuaded to respond, in writing, to a number of agreed-upon questions. None of them dealt with Cuba or specifically with the Castro plots.

---

*Dulles's italics.

The committee lawyer who carried the questions to San Clemente, Joe Dennin, said in 1996 that the arrangement was "the compromise between the perfect, which would have meant that Nixon testified like other people and sat for eight hours of questioning under oath, which wasn't going to happen, and a grudging agreement to written interrogatories. . . . This was eleventh-hour stuff for the committee. They were ready to go to print, and there was tremendous pressure, a sign up on the wall in jest reading: 'If you can't get it right, get it written.'"

"Nixon should have been questioned," said former Senator Gary Hart, who served on the committee. "But this was a man in exile, and we had no real belief that under oath or not, he was going to tell us what he knew. . . . There was a kind of fatalism about it, that even if we went through the motions, we probably wouldn't get Nixon to admit culpability. . . ."

One of the negotiated questions did touch on whether national security considerations could justify breaking the law, if that was ordered by the president or a high official. Nixon answered in a way the committee chairman thought "pernicious and dangerous." Certain actions that would otherwise be unlawful were legitimate if undertaken by "the sovereign," Nixon asserted, evoking a peculiarly Nixonian concept of presidential authority. "Assassination of a foreign leader," he went on, "might have been justified during World War II as a means of preventing further Nazi atrocities."[5] But assassination of a foreign leader, he claimed, was "an act I never had cause to consider."

In spite of his long-standing interest in Cuba, Nixon made no reference in his memoirs to the Castro plots, even though their discovery made headlines not long before the book came out. Thus, obviously, he avoided having to make any denial that he had played a part in them. Only in 1986, in a little-noticed magazine interview, did he refer directly to the matter. "I was amazed," he stated then, "to hear that they had the assassination plots. I really was. Maybe that's the way they operate . . . it's a strange world, isn't it?" Strange indeed, given what one can now piece together about the way that the 1960 Castro conspiracies interconnected with Nixon's Cuban involvements.

The historian Fawn Brodie was verbally briefed in 1978 by Dr. Jack Pfeiffer, then the CIA historian, following his review of agency files on Nixon and Cuba. Brodie's notes indicate that in January 1960, just after Western Hemisphere Division chief, J. C. King, first proposed Castro's "elimination," Nixon's aide General Cushman asked at a meeting, "If you need to get some goon squads into Cuba, why don't you do it?"

That March Nixon was personally briefed on the use of "goon squads." What the squads were to do is not stipulated in the notes, but the dictionary definition of "goon" is a man "hired to . . . eliminate opponents."[6] That same month, and on later occasions, Nixon's friend William Pawley discussed with the head of the CIA's exile-training program the killing of an unnamed "somebody" inside Cuba.

Also in March, at the dinner party at which he had proposed flooding Cuba with forged currency, the author Ian Fleming offered a solution to the Cuban problem gentler than murder. Ridicule, he reckoned, would be as good a way as any to destabilize Castro. If bombarded with propaganda warning of radioactive residue that would linger in their beards and render them impotent, Castro's followers—and El Líder Máximo himself—would hasten to shave. With its best-known symbol gone, the revolution would wither away.

On the heels of this wacky suggestion, the CIA began its most fatuous anti-Castro schemes. CIA technicians seriously considered how a woman's depilatory, one that worked either orally or by absorption through the skin, might be administered to him. Would it work to dust it into the Cuban leader's shoes, in powder form, when the footwear was left out for shining during a foreign trip? We shall never know, because Castro canceled the trip in question.

The agency's boffins also turned their attention to how to impregnate Castro's food—or a box of his favorite cigars, Montecristo No. 1 brand—with a chemical that would leave him disoriented and looking foolish during one of his marathon speeches. A CIA in-house history says Nixon was briefed on these famously silly plots. Soon, though, the ludicrous turned to the lethal when the CIA's Office of Medical Services was asked to contaminate a box of Montecristos with a botulin toxin "so potent that a person would die after putting one in his mouth." By the time the poisoned cigars were ready, it was established policy that Castro was to be murdered.

Howard Hunt made four recommendations in an April report to his CIA superiors. The first was: "Assassinate Castro before or coincident with the invasion (a task for Cuban patriots)." Hunt later denied knowing if the CIA had taken up this suggestion. "I myself never heard of the plots until the Church Committee revealed them," he told the author in 1996. According to Nixon's aide Charles Colson, however, Hunt had informed him of the efforts to kill Castro much earlier. Also, in 1974, in an internal memo purloined by a CIA source from G. P. Putnam's Sons, then about to publish Hunt's second volume of memoirs, Hunt was quoted as saying he "recommended *and planned* assassination/Castro operation."*[7]

In his 1996 interview Hunt confirmed that his proposal that Castro be killed had been discussed at his June meeting with Nixon's aide General Cushman. He had raised the topic, he said, "like dropping it into a well." It is logical to conclude that Cushman would have passed the information on to Nixon; it was after all his responsibility to do so.

The CIA file on William Pawley, who also wanted Castro dead, includes a document filed just two weeks after the Hunt-Cushman meeting. The heavily censored message, sent to Allen Dulles, reports an offer by a Cuban contact of Pawley's to collaborate in Castro's assassination. Five days later, on July 18, Pawley wrote to Nixon: "I'm in touch with Dulles' people almost daily and

*Author's italics.

things are shaping up reasonably well. The matter is a very delicate problem and every care should be taken to handle it so as not to affect our Nation adversely, nor our political campaign."

"For a secret assassination," a CIA training manual had advised in the fifties, "the contrived accident is the most effective technique." Two days after Pawley's letter to Nixon, CIA headquarters responded to a suggestion by an Air Cubana pilot that he might be able to arrange an "accident" to kill Castro's brother Raúl. "Possible removal top three leaders is receiving serious consideration at HQS," a cable notified the CIA's Havana station, promising the pilot a ten-thousand-dollar reward should he succeed in killing Raúl. A few hours later a second cable rescinded the message, in part perhaps because it had flouted another provision in the agency manual: that "assassination instructions should never be written or recorded."

This aborted plot had in fact been ordered by Pawley's friend division chief J. C. King and by Tracy Barnes, the number two headquarters man on Cuba and a key figure in the fake peso operation to which Nixon was privy. The Operation Pluto field chief liaising with Nixon's office, Jacob Esterline, was also told about it.

Meanwhile, also in 1960, a more exotic plot was hatched. A close Pawley associate, Alexander Rorke, spent months cultivating a dark-haired young woman, just twenty years old, named Marita Lorenz. The daughter of a German sea captain and an American mother, Lorenz had unique qualifications to take part in a Castro murder conspiracy. The previous year, on a visit to Havana aboard a cruise liner skippered by her father, she had met Castro, then thirty-three. Soon afterward, summoned back to Cuba, she had done office tasks for him and become his lover. Within weeks she was pregnant—by Castro, according to Lorenz[8]—but the romance ended soon and unhappily. Lorenz wound up back in New York, recovering from a bungled abortion and badgered by U.S. agents determined to get her to become what one reporter later called "the Mata Hari of the Caribbean Cold War."

Pawley's friend Rorke, a former FBI agent now apparently in cahoots with the CIA, filled Lorenz with notions of religion and sin, ending up by persuading her, in her words, that "if I eliminated Fidel, I could make myself right with God." In Florida that summer, she has claimed, she met a CIA officer known to anti-Castro fighters as Eduardo. This was the name Howard Hunt used, and years later Lorenz would claim she was certain that Eduardo had been one and the same as the man who organized the Watergate break-ins.

Rorke also introduced her to Frank Sturgis, likewise to win notoriety as a Watergate burglar. A former marine who had once fought alongside Castro in the mountains, Sturgis was now his avowed enemy. It was Rorke and Sturgis, said Lorenz, who convinced her to return to Havana—apparently in the spring of 1960— armed with two poison capsules. Her mission was to slip them into one of Castro's drinks. The poison was odorless and tasteless, the plotters assured her, and death would come quickly.

The operation went wrong, as would all the Castro murder plots, in a manner straight out of movie melodrama. Afraid she would be searched at the airport, Lorenz hid the capsules in a jar of cold cream. Reunited with Castro in his suite at the Havana Libre, the old Hilton Hotel, she felt "torn by feelings of love and obligation." Behind the closed bathroom door she dug the capsules out of the cold cream only to find them glutinous and greasy, in no state to slip unnoticed into Castro's coffee. The frightened young woman flushed them down the drain and returned to the room to watch her lover sleeping. She returned to Miami the next morning, to face the rage and scorn of her American mentors.

Sturgis, who had told Lorenz that her mission was a CIA-backed operation, confirmed years later she had indeed been sent to Cuba with the poison. In an October 1960 memo, moreover, FBI Director Hoover warned the CIA that word had leaked of an impending operation to kill Castro, an operation that called for "a girl, not further described, to drop a 'pill' in some drink or food of Castro's."[9]

The Lorenz fiasco, too, turns out to have a Nixon connection. CIA records released in 1994 include material on June Cobb, an American woman who had worked in Cuba alongside Lorenz and had known of the young woman's abortion. In the spring of 1960 a CIA agent induced Cobb to return to the United States, where she was questioned and then surveilled as she met and talked with people immersed in the Cuba intrigues. They included Marita Lorenz and Rorke, not long before Lorenz left on the murder mission to Havana. Related documents appear in the CIA file on William Pawley. The routing on another, dated a week after the CIA brought Cobb out of Cuba, shows that it originated in Nixon's office, on the desk of General Cushman.

When she worked in Castro's office, Cobb had worked as assistant to its director, Juan Orta. Orta was to be the man at the heart of the next and best-documented of all the Castro murder intrigues, the CIA-Mafia plots.

In August 1960, as the Senate Intelligence Committee's probe established, the CIA began conspiring with U.S. Mafia bosses to murder Castro—with the knowledge and authorization of Director Dulles, according to two of the senior officials involved. The key contacts on the Mafia side, Sam Giancana of Chicago and Santo Trafficante of Florida, both had interests in Havana's gambling and crime rackets. The casinos in Cuba were still operating at that point, although under severe restrictions, and Trafficante regularly traveled to the island from Florida. After meeting with a senior CIA officer—Giancana introduced himself as Sam Gold and Trafficante as Joe, the courier—the mobsters agreed to try to locate someone in Castro's entourage to carry out the killing.

CIA technicians worked to perfect the poison of choice—botulin again, this time in a form that would dissolve in a drink and produce a "firmly predictable end result." The gangsters settled on Orta as the best candidate for the role of assassin. As head of Castro's office he had the necessary access, or so they believed, and he was known to be corruptible, having taken kickbacks from casino bosses in the past. It was not until February 1961, early in the Kennedy presidency, that the pills would finally reach Orta, by which point he would have been fired.[10]

Next, poison pills were supplied to Antonio de Varona, a former prime minister and now a key figure in the exile leadership, whose financial backers included Meyer Lansky and Santo Trafficante. Varona claimed to have a contact in a Havana restaurant that Castro frequented but—in another absurd setback for the plotters—the Cuban leader stopped eating there. As his long-term survival was to prove, Castro had a charmed life, and very good security. The CIA-Mafia plots would be revived the following year, but this was the last assassination conspiracy initiated while Nixon was vice president.[11]

Varona consulted regularly with Howard Hunt, and both he and the CIA officer involved in the Mafia operations were in touch with William Pawley. Hunt and Pawley of course were regularly in contact with Nixon or his staff. Other clues, some tentative and some specific, also suggest a Nixon connection to the CIA-Mafia conspiracies.

It is likely that the earliest murder proposals had come to the CIA from the mob.[12] Varona said he met in summer 1960 with Lansky, the real brain behind the Cuban rackets and the mobster said to have suggested Castro's assassination immediately after Batista's fall. Other initial contacts with the CIA were reportedly made by the man who had operated the Sans Souci casino, Norman Rothman. As described in a previous chapter,* Rothman had earlier played a central role in the gambling scandal involving Nixon and one of his friends and claimed he had covered up for Nixon. In his view, Nixon owed him a favor.

Scattered among Nixon's vice presidential papers are fragments of semi-coded exchanges, apparently about Cuba. They include, for example, a note from Pawley referring to the "problem we are having south of Miami," and one file contains a letter to Nixon from Marshall Diggs, the vice president's go-between with the exile leader Mario Kohly. Dated July 29, 1960, it speaks of keeping "in close contact with the General regarding the Caribbean situation. . . . Senator Brewster and his associates are thoroughly familiar with everything that has been done. They are prepared if the possible out can be found." Nixon's reply said Diggs's suggestions had been "passed to the responsible officials for their consideration."

On August 1 Diggs's secretary wrote to General Cushman introducing "Mr. C. H. (Jim) Pulley," who "enjoys a highly confidential relationship with both former Senator Brewster and Mr. Diggs on the matters they have discussed with you and Vice President Nixon."

A search of Brewster's papers turned up empty envelopes bearing the name Pulley—the former senator is said to have sanitized his papers before his death—but research has failed to discover just who Pulley was. According to a former CIA operative, however, he served as a "Washington mob liaison man

*See p. 126.

for Lansky and Trafficante." If that is true, the date of Pulley's introduction to Nixon's aide on Cuban matters takes on significance. It was written days or at most weeks before the CIA began the process that led to contacts with Mafia boss Trafficante about killing Castro.[13]

Over and above these suggestive clues, however, there exists a far more direct connection. Nixon had long known one of the key men involved in the CIA-Mafia plotting and had even directed him in an earlier secret operation. This was Robert Maheu, former FBI agent turned private investigator, in the employ of both Howard Hughes and—when called upon—the CIA.

Maheu, once described as having the demeanor of W. C. Fields playing a con man, was used as the agency's go-between with the mafiosi. It was he who made the initial mob contact in the Castro plots, organized and attended meetings over a protracted period, and handed over bundles of cash and poison pills. Maheu had more overall knowledge of the plots than anyone else involved. He also shared information about these activities with Howard Hughes, who thought the CIA-Mafia scheme "a pretty good idea."

Maheu had multiple connections to Nixon. The full name of his firm, which covered public relations and management consultancy as well as investigations, was Maheu and King Associates Inc. The King in the partnership referred to Bob King, another former FBI man who had been on intimate terms with both Richard and Pat Nixon since World War II. King was a specialist in counterintelligence, had lobbied for Nixon to play a major role on the National Security Council, served as his senior assistant during the vice presidency—for "protection," as he put it—and had been a key aide in the 1956 campaign. Nixon on occasion described him as his "alter ego," a place of pride usually reserved for Bebe Rebozo, to whom King was also close.

Even when he formally left Nixon's office to join Maheu, King had continued working for Nixon. He was back on the campaign trail with him in 1960 and was therefore both allied with Maheu—and close to Nixon—at the time of the anti-Castro plots.

Maheu's other link to Nixon had been his undercover work four years earlier, on Hughes's orders but on Nixon's behalf, in torpedoing opposition to Nixon's reselection as Eisenhower's running mate.* Earlier still, and significantly in terms of the Castro plots, he had undertaken secret work at Nixon's direction, a successful operation against Greek shipping magnate Aristotle Onassis.

In July 1954 National Security Council minutes had noted that President Eisenhower had asked "whether it was not possible, with all the power of the United States, to 'break' Onassis." His concern arose from a pending Onassis agreement with the king of Saudi Arabia, one that would have put him in control of almost all Saudi oil shipments. The NSC decided on "all appropriate measures" to wreck the deal.

*See Harold Stassen episode, p. 153.

Maheu and a colleague, John Gerrity, found themselves summoned to the vice president's office. "Nixon came in," Gerrity recalled, and "gave us the whole *Mission: Impossible* bit. 'I know you'll be careful,' he said, 'but you have to understand that while this is a national security matter of terrific importance, we can't acknowledge you in any way if anything should go wrong.' ... I could tell that Nixon enjoyed saying it. He loved these kinds of operations."[14]

There followed a series of dirty tricks. Working out of a suite in the National Republican Club, a team of Maheu operatives placed phone taps on Onassis's New York headquarters.[15] The shipowner was harried with lawsuits and branded a liar, cheat, and traitor in stories planted in the world's press. After a trip by Maheu to Jidda to persuade the king that one of his high officials had been bribed in the deal, the Saudis tore up the Onassis contract.[16]

In 1992 Maheu added a chilling postscript to the episode. After briefing him, he recalled, Nixon had made a final remark about Onassis. "If it turns out we have to kill the bastard," he said in hushed tones, "just don't do it on American soil." In retrospect, Maheu suggested that Nixon may have said this merely as "something to say, something that sounded tough. . . . "

As for the Castro plots, Maheu asserted that he "had no reason to believe" Nixon knew about them; his partner, Bob King, "drew a blank" altogether when interviewed for this book. Both men, however, spoke in the knowledge that two of the mobsters involved in the scheme died violently while it was being investigated. The body of one of them was found dismembered, floating in an oil drum.[17] "I'm one of the last people left who knows what really went on during the operation to assassinate Fidel Castro," Maheu has explained. "I'm not sure how I want to go, but I am certain I want my body to be in one piece when I do."

In the magazine interview in which he declared himself "amazed" to learn about the assassination plots, Nixon also declared himself astonished by "all this stuff about the poison shtick."[18] Yet to believe Nixon's claim to have known nothing about assassination plans in 1960 requires our accepting too long a string of improbabilities—that he was not informed of any of the Castro plots by any of those involved with whom he or his aide General Cushman had some form of contact: Allen Dulles, William Pawley, Howard Hunt, J. Edgar Hoover, Howard Hughes, Mario Kohly and his accomplices, the handlers of Marita Lorenz and June Cobb, and, above all, Bob King and Robert Maheu.[19]

Those still unpersuaded that Nixon was privy to the murder plots may reconsider in light of a new piece of information. If what the author was told in 1997 by President Kennedy's former press secretary Pierre Salinger has validity, Nixon not only was aware of the CIA-Mafia plots but authorized them.

In 1968, said Salinger, he had lengthy conversations with Maheu while soliciting his boss, Howard Hughes, for a contribution to Robert Kennedy's presidential campaign. "I knew Maheu well," Salinger said. "He told me then about his meetings with the Mafia. He said he had been in contact with the

CIA, that the CIA had been in touch with Nixon, who had asked them to go forward with this project. . . . It was Nixon who had him [Maheu] do a deal with the Mafia in Florida to kill Castro."

Nixon's frantic insistence, as president, on obtaining the CIA's Bay of Pigs material, now begins to make sense—especially in light of events never before laid out in sequence for the public. It includes discoveries originally made by Terry Lenzner and Mark Lackritz, senior counsel on the Senate Watergate Committee, but not further pursued.

On January 18, 1971, halfway through Nixon's first term, papers across the country carried a sensational story. The columnist Jack Anderson, Drew Pearson's successor, offered remarkably accurate revelations about the Castro plots. He named Maheu directly and reported that the murder plans had begun under Eisenhower and Nixon and continued until shortly before the assassination of President Kennedy. Then Anderson raised a chilling possibility: Some of those privy to the plotting, he wrote, suspected that the plans to murder Castro had provoked the Cuban leader into retaliating in kind, by having Kennedy killed.[20]

On the same day, at the White House, Bob Haldeman wrote an internal memo requesting information on Howard Hughes, Maheu, and Maheu's contact with Democratic National Committee Chairman Lawrence O'Brien, who had been working as a Hughes consultant.[21] The following afternoon, after publication of a second Anderson article on the plots, the attorney general, John Mitchell, placed a call to Maheu.

At the time Maheu was under pressure to appear before a grand jury in connection with a Las Vegas gambling prosecution. He had so far denied knowledge of the Castro plot story but, as he has put it, thought things might "very easily get out of hand" with the grand jury and the press. Maheu came to Washington and, in private, told Mitchell "the entire Castro story."[22] Mitchell, he remembered, was "shaking" by the time he finished. The attorney general forthwith offered him a deal: Instead of going before a grand jury on the Vegas matter, Maheu would merely be interviewed by senior Justice Department officials. In this formal session he did not expound on his work for the CIA. "I assured them," Maheu recalled, "I intended to keep my word and maintain the secrecy of the mission."

Meanwhile, Assistant Attorney General Will Wilson was quickly assigned to review whatever the Justice Department might hold on the CIA-Mafia contacts. The Nixon White House, he would later tell Watergate investigators, was hoping to turn up proof that it was the Kennedy brothers who had tried to kill Castro, news that could damage the surviving Kennedy brother, Edward, should he run for the presidency in 1972. Maheu's information, though— along with anything that might be found in the files—posed a threat as much to the sitting president, Nixon, as to the Kennedys.[23]

Within three days of Maheu's initial phone conversation with Mitchell, White House investigator John Caulfield filed the first in a series of cautionary memos. Caulfield, a former policeman who had first met Nixon while working security during election campaigns, had been charged with responding to Haldeman's demand for information on Hughes, Maheu, and the Democrats' O'Brien.

In his first memo Caulfield pointed out that Maheu and O'Brien had been close since "pre-Kennedy" days. In the second he warned that Maheu's "tentacles touch many extremely sensitive areas of government, each one of which is fraught with potential Jack Anderson type exposure. . . . Before any action is taken . . . we should authorize an in-depth analysis of all (CIA, FBI, IRS) information available. . . . There is a serious risk here of counter scandal."

A further Caulfield memo, sent within days of Maheu's meeting with Mitchell, raised the issue of "Maheu's covert activities . . . with CIA in the early Sixties." There were "significant hazards in raking over the matter," Caulfield emphasized, and the risk that pursuit of O'Brien "might well shake loose Republican skeletons from the closet." Three years later, questioned about this by Senate Watergate Committee counsel Lenzner and Lackritz, Caulfield first asked to go off the record. After discussion in private, he conceded that his reference to "covert activities" related to the Castro plot revelations.

Lenzner and Lackritz were pioneers at the time of the Watergate investigations. After stumbling onto the Castro plots, known publicly at the time only through the allegations in the Jack Anderson articles, they quickly found themselves stalled. When they asked the CIA for information they were given none. When they asked Senate Watergate Committee chairman, Sam Ervin, to let them subpoena key witnesses, he turned them down. The attorneys were left frustrated, able only to guess at the implications of what they had found.

Nixon had good reason to fear exposure of his part in the Cuban intrigues. The information marshaled here shows starkly why it was that in 1971, in the wake of the Anderson articles and the Maheu scare, he renewed his demands for the CIA's files on the Bay of Pigs. He hoped, to be sure, that they contained embarrassments for the Kennedys. At the same time, he knew the agency's records probably contained material compromising to himself. Nixon needed to see them, as he explained to Ehrlichman, in order to know what to "duck," to "protect" himself.

Four years after the collapse of the presidency Haldeman would add a dramatic new dimension to the puzzle of Nixon's worry about "the Bay of Pigs." "It seems," Haldeman wrote in his memoirs, "that in all those Nixon references to the Bay of Pigs, he was actually referring to the Kennedy assassination."

Researchers have pored over this passage in the Haldeman memoirs as though it were a newfound parchment in the Dead Sea Scrolls.[24] It was probably no more than its author's speculation—but provocative nonetheless. In subsequent paragraphs Haldeman suggested that, in his exchanges with the

CIA about the Bay of Pigs, Nixon may have been goading the agency over the fact that after Kennedy was killed, it failed to inform the Warren Commission about the Castro plots.

If the Cuban leader decided to retaliate, Haldeman surmised, then the U.S. plots to kill him "may have triggered the Kennedy tragedy." The CIA, he suggested, "desperately wanted to hide that dark possibility." What Haldeman did not say, but what is likely, is that Nixon was equally desperate to keep the Castro plots secret.

Nixon's right-hand man made one further observation, which appeared in his book immediately after his supposition about the meaning of Nixon's Bay of Pigs references. Haldeman recalled how Nixon reacted, on their arrival in the White House, when he suggested using the power of the presidency to reopen the investigation into Kennedy's death. "I felt we would be in a position to get all the facts," Haldeman wrote. "But Nixon turned me down."

Was Nixon weighed down by "survivor's guilt"? Very possibly, even if he had merely been privy to the early Castro plots, let alone instrumental in them. Ehrlichman once spoke of Nixon's "Kennedy fixation." "There was something about Nixon and the Kennedys," Harrison Salisbury of the *New York Times* thought "not rational." Not rational, perhaps, but understandable in a man so haunted.

18

I felt crushed by the sense of the really awful burden
he was inviting in the office he wants. . . . If he were
a great, vital man, I think I should have felt: "Yes,
he must have it. . . . " I did not have this
feeling. . . . I felt dismay and growing pity.

—Whittaker Chambers, *after lunching with Nixon*
before the 1960 presidential campaign

It had been thirteen years since they had met, Nixon and Kennedy, at a cocktail party for the freshmen congressmen of 1947. Kennedy, tanned and tousle-haired, had breezed over to greet the dapper newcomer from California. Nixon was "the star of the show" then, thanks to his upset victory over Jerry Voorhis. Kennedy, his road to the House of Representatives smoothed by his father's millions, was a star act born and bred.

They were "like a pair of unmatched bookends," in Nixon's description, separated by background but at that point not by politics. They agreed on the imperative of crushing domestic communism. Appointed to the Labor Committee together, they soon found themselves on the same podium, addressing fractious steelworkers in Pennsylvania. Afterward they talked baseball over a meal at a local diner, then reminisced about their navy days in a shared sleeping compartment on the train back to Washington.

The moderator of that evening's debate had been struck by what appeared to be their "genuine friendliness." The pair began meeting to compare notes, once talking far into the night at the home of one of Kennedy's sisters. Nixon kept two books his colleague gave him at that time, inscribed "To Dick from his friend John F. Kennedy."

"In those early years," Nixon recalled, "we saw ourselves as political opponents but not political rivals. We shared one quality. . . . He was shy, and that sometimes made him appear aloof. But it was shyness born of an instinct that guarded privacy and concealed emotions. I understood those qualities because I shared them."

Not enough, however, to deal easily with one Kennedy gesture that was not at all shy. Before Nixon left on his first trip to Europe, the congressman from Massachusetts dropped by with the phone numbers of three young women in Paris. Nixon, his secretary remembered, was "too embarrassed" to take the numbers with him.[1]

When a contribution came in the other currency the Kennedys had in plenty, hard cash, Nixon accepted. At the bidding of his conservative father, Kennedy walked into Nixon's office in 1950 with a donation to the campaign to unseat Senator Helen Gahagan Douglas. Nixon later denied having received the money but admitted in his memoirs that Kennedy gave him an envelope containing $1,000. To have helped Nixon's political advance, John F. would one day admit, had been "the biggest damnfool mistake."

Meanwhile, the chumminess seemed genuine. To Nixon's aide William Arnold they appeared to be "fast friends." Kennedy sent a handwritten note to wish Nixon "all kinds of good luck" when he was picked as Eisenhower's running mate. Nixon wrote sponsoring his "personal friend" Kennedy for membership in the Burning Tree Club. Kennedy invited Nixon to his wedding to Jacqueline Bouvier. By the late fifties they occupied offices 361 and 362 in the Senate Office Building, facing each other across a corridor.

For Kennedy, however, the relationship had little meaning beyond cordiality. In 1958, at a background-only dinner for selected journalists, he assessed Nixon carefully as "a man of really enormous ability . . . at heart more conservative than the pose he adopted . . . for reasons of expediency." An oral history interview with former Senator George Smathers, who was close to both men, offers a clue to what he really thought of his colleague.

"Nixon," Smathers began by saying, "had a greater admiration for Kennedy than Kennedy had for Nixon. . . ." The lines that follow were once blanked out in the transcript available to researchers, but have been reinstated after application to the Kennedy Library by the author. The uncensored passage reads: "Nixon told me several times he admired Jack, and I happen to know the feeling was not particularly mutual. I don't think Jack ever thought too highly of Nixon, either of his ability or of him as a man of great strength of character. . . . He felt that Nixon was a total opportunist."

In a 1959 conversation with a journalist, speaking for background only, Kennedy added another observation about Nixon. "It seems," he said, "he has a split personality, and he is very bad in public, and nobody likes him."

Nixon by contrast set aside his antipathy toward Ivy League elitists when it came to the Harvard-educated Kennedy. He seemed almost transfixed by the representative from Massachusetts. "When Jack started to talk" at a congressional hearing, Kennedy aide Ted Reardon remembered thinking, "Dicky-boy sort of looked at him . . . with a look between awe and respect and fear." Theodore White, chronicler of four presidential campaigns, considered that Kennedy exerted over Nixon "the same charm that a snake charmer exerts over a snake."

Raised to avoid displays of emotion, Nixon was visibly moved when Kennedy became seriously ill. Chronic back trouble, combined with an adrenal deficiency not yet alleviated by medication, made him a semi-invalid in the early congressional days.[2] In 1954, after an operation on his spine, the doctors feared for his life. Nixon, unaware of the gravity of the situation, arrived at the hospital to learn that Kennedy had been given the last rites. He hurried back to the vice presidential limousine and slumped in his seat in tears. "That poor young man is going to die," Nixon sobbed to a Secret Service agent. "Poor brave Jack is going to die. Oh God, don't let him die!"

When Kennedy recovered, Nixon made certain a basket of fruit with a "Welcome home!" message was on Kennedy's desk when he returned to work. Nixon's official suite, slightly closer to the Senate floor than Kennedy's office, was placed at his disposal. "He really admired Jack," Reardon thought. Jack Drown, Nixon's longtime friend, said he "really liked Kennedy." "He loved him," Nixon's brother Edward observed in an interview with the author.

In 1960 the man who loved Kennedy was to confront him on the battlefield of politics, playing for the highest stakes of all. After the struggle that was to follow, love would be replaced by disillusion and resentment—and something as close to hatred as is possible in one who has once loved.

"The powers that be in California—and they are really powerful, especially the publishers—have determined that nothing shall stand in the way of putting Tricky Dick Nixon in the White House." Thus read a Drew Pearson diary note, written three years before Nixon ran for the presidency, after a chat with Jim Bassett, a Los Angeles newspaper editor when not on loan to Nixon for campaigns. The "powers" to which Pearson referred included Norman and Dorothy ("Buff") Chandler, publishers of the *Los Angeles Times*. It was to the Chandlers, who had always backed him, that Nixon turned for advice in 1959. Should he do as everyone expected and make his run for the White House?

"I've got to decide," Nixon told the Chandlers over drinks, and they discussed the issue for hours. The alternative, Nixon said, was to get out of politics and make some real money. By 3:00 A.M. politics had won. "I've got to do it," Nixon declared. "The time is right." Pat was at his side as they talked, Pat who had remained supportive, who had traveled three hundred thousand miles at his side during the vice presidency, who yearned for more quality family time. "I wish you wouldn't run," she said now. According to Buff Chandler, Nixon "paid no attention to her at all."

Nixon had decided to run, but his mood was strange for a man about to launch on a great endeavor. "He went into a slump," recalled Father Cronin, a confidant and speechwriter since the Hiss days. "He was practically unavailable to anybody, including myself, for over six months. There was something wrong there, and you could say he was afraid of winning. I suspect probably the answer is going to be that there's a schizophrenic personality there, maybe not in the technical sense, but in the loose sense."

In July 1960, fifteen years after having been chosen to run for Congress as a young navy veteran, Nixon arrived in Chicago to hear his party select him as its candidate for the White House. Pat was there, her doubts long since dutifully suppressed. Nixon's mother, now seventy-five, looked proudly on. She had for weeks been giving interviews extolling her son's virtues—to interviewers approved by Nixon. Now Hannah perched like a tiny bird on her chair in the old Stockyards Convention Hall, waiting for Nixon's big moment.

In the three days of policy wrangling that preceded the nomination, Nixon had had virtually no sleep. Hearing loud music late one night, former Republican Committee Chairman Len Hall had entered Nixon's room to find him in a trance, conducting to the trumpets and thundering drums of the *1812 Overture*. Soon afterward, nominated by an overwhelming majority, he made the speech he came to consider the most effective of his career. Apart from the rhetoric about "building a better America," Nixon accurately prophesied the collapse of the Soviet Union. "When Mr. Khrushchev says our grandchildren will live under Communism, let us say his grandchildren will live in freedom." In a time of heightened world tension, the globe-trotting vice president presented himself as the man of experience on whom Americans could rely.

Eleven days earlier, facing west into the sunset at the Los Angeles Coliseum, John Kennedy had made his acceptance speech to the Democratic National Convention, his call to the New Frontier of the sixties. Across the continent in Washington, watching on television, Nixon realized he had underestimated his opponent. "Kennedy's got no chance," he had forecast months earlier, before a poker session with former Speaker Tip O'Neill. "I'm running against [Lyndon] Johnson. You're not going to be able to stop him." Kennedy had stopped Johnson, who was now—controversially—his running mate. "We just didn't think Kennedy was a heavyweight," Nixon adviser Pat Hillings would recall ruefully. "We didn't think he would work that hard. . . ."

Nixon was seriously shaken when Kennedy tore ahead in the primaries, thanks to his charisma and the ruthless disbursement of his father's money. "Dick is really worried about K winning the Democratic nomination," Ruth Buchanan, wife of the White House chief of protocol, wrote in her diary. "He's sure that's who he'll have to beat, and he doesn't feel too easy about it." "Anyone who does not recognize that we are in for the fight of our lives," Nixon soon admitted, "must be smoking opium."

The fight that ensued was to be more about style than issues. Nixon did well in the situations he understood best, the small towns where the locals enjoyed the colorful pageantry, the fluttering parading of the Stars and Stripes, and the "Nixon Girls," young women in pretty dresses shipped in from stop to stop. Even on friendly turf, though, it hardly worked for Nixon to push the notion that all was well with America as the Eisenhower years ended. James Reston noted that he seemed to be saying, "Buck up, old cheese, everything's approximately wonderful. . . . The only trouble is that his basic theme adds up to a picture of the world that no well-informed man would seriously consider for a moment." The nation had been in a major recession for the past two years.

A presidential campaign is a barbaric marathon that drives even fit young men to their physical and mental limits. It quickly became obvious that Nixon had lost weight and looked haggard and exhausted. Kennedy, who had once been a semi-invalid, stayed the course far better.

Press-ganged by Nixon's team into a starring role, Pat appeared thinner than usual and sapped with fatigue. Jackie Kennedy, rarely on the campaign trail because she was pregnant, smiled from the pages of the nation's magazines, radiating youth and charm. It did not help Nixon's cause, Theodore White noted, that the public saw Pat's "drawn, almost wasted face" as she followed her husband "with stoic weariness." Observing Nixon, his head sagging with exhaustion, "the mouth half-opened in tired slackness," White came to feel only "sorrow for the man and his wife."

The *New York Times*'s Harrison Salisbury had been impressed by Nixon in Russia but was now more critical. "At home the crowds tensed him up," he wrote. "I watched him ball his fists, set his jaw, hurl himself stiff-legged to the barriers at the airports and begin shaking hands. He was wound up like a watch spring. . . . No ease."

"I have been heckled by experts," Nixon snarled at a rowdy group of pickets in Michigan, "so don't try something on me, or we'll take care of you. . . . I didn't hire you, so stay right out of here, OK?" Later, on no evidence, he ordered press aide Herb Klein to declare that the protesters had been "goons" from the auto workers' union. Some reporters believed they had in fact been hired by the Nixon camp to undermine Kennedy's labor support. Luckily for Nixon, his "we'll take care of you" remark, with its implied threat, failed to appear in the newspapers.

While Kennedy never lost his temper in public, Nixon was by now known for his tantrums. Nixon's "fiery temper," wrote Willard Edwards of the *Chicago Tribune*, "is an awesome spectacle." On the road in Minneapolis he began an answer about civil rights calmly. Then, *Baltimore Sun* correspondent Philip Potter recalled, he suddenly "blew his stack . . . lips trembling and face livid."[3]

The Secret Service agent closest to Nixon, Jack Sherwood, said he "would snap when the campaign became too much." Bob Haldeman recalled a day when Nixon became frustrated over a poor schedule while touring Iowa by car. "Don Hughes, Nixon's military aide, was in the seat directly in front. Suddenly, incredibly, Nixon began to kick the back of Hughes's seat with both feet. And he wouldn't stop. . . . The seat and the hapless Hughes jolted forward jaggedly as Nixon vented his rage. When the car stopped at a small town in the middle of nowhere, Hughes, white-faced, silently got out of the car and started walking straight ahead, down the road and out of town. He wanted to get as far away as he could from the Vice President. . . ."[4]

Nixon would sit hunched and alone in the back of the campaign plane, trying to avoid conversation with other politicians and his own staff, scribbling endlessly on his yellow pads, writing and rewriting speeches. While he would recall with pride having worked on the talks himself, his aides thought it a wasteful use of able speechwriters. "He reduced us all to clerks," one said bitterly.

After appointing a board of seasoned advisers, Nixon ignored them and insisted on making the smallest decisions himself. "He wanted to be horse and jockey," said Jim Bassett, now planning director. For no good strategic reason, Nixon promised to campaign in every single state of the Union, a commitment that was to leave him rushing off to sparsely populated Alaska just two days before the election. The advisers told him the trip was pointless, worth only three electoral votes, but Nixon would not listen. "Dick has painted himself and all of us into an impossible corner," Bassett wrote his wife, Wilma.

Bassett also remembered "horrible temper" outbursts after which Nixon would go and "hole himself up in his room." "I don't even want to set down on paper all my thoughts about this campaign," he wrote his wife. "We've done so many things wrong, wasted so much time, and blown our lead so. . . . From the top down, it's agreed that the one guy responsible, perhaps the only guy, is the candidate himself. When loners insist on loneness and shun advice, even reject it out of hand, then, by golly, they must suffer all the penalties. . . . And when his brain tires and his temper shortens, then the aloneness is magnified rather horribly. It's a little scary, isn't it?"

The self-inflicted blow that most damaged Nixon was his decision to debate Kennedy on television. One-to-one encounters on the air were possible for the first time in 1960, following a change in the broadcasting law. Kennedy promptly accepted when the networks pressed for debates after the Democratic convention—he saw television as "the one way to break through." For that very reason, his opponent's advisers wanted to reject the idea. Nixon agreed with them at first, telling campaign chairman Len Hall, "No damned debates!"[5]

Then, without a word of notice to his colleagues, he changed his mind and publicly announced that he would debate Kennedy. Press aide Klein "almost fell over" on hearing the news. "The boo-boo," as Bassett called it, "was handed down to the troops like an edict from the Almighty." When Len Hall asked Nixon to explain, he "just looked up at the sky and didn't answer. The rain started coming down . . . he still stood there looking up at the sky."

Nixon did have a reputation as an effective debater, dating back to his school days. "I can take this man," he had reportedly remarked after hearing Kennedy's convention speech. "Kennedy speaks over people's heads. . . . I did pretty well with Khrushchev. I'll murder Kennedy." Nixon's only hesitation, he told Bassett, was that "he might clobber that kid Kennedy too tough on the first debate, and thus womp up a 'sympathy factor' for the guy. . . ."

Too late, Nixon dithered and tried to change course, sending aides to propose to the Kennedy side "conditions they won't accept." The tactic did not work; Kennedy had given his negotiator Leonard Reinsch "one directive, and only one directive: 'Make sure the Republican candidate doesn't get off the hook.'" Weeks of haggling later, Nixon found himself committed to not one but four debates, to begin in late September.

Poor judgment in the negotiations over the debates was followed by bad luck, illness, then more poor judgment. Nixon ignored Secret Service advice on crowd control and one day on the campaign trail found himself in what a senior agent reported as a "mad, mauling melee." Moving into another crowd, and shoved hard against the door of his limousine, Nixon injured his leg. A few days later, during a television appearance, he visibly flinched when interviewer Jack Paar put his hand on his knee. Soon after, doctors at Walter Reed hospital diagnosed a virulent infection, so serious that Nixon faced amputation if he did not submit to intensive medication and two weeks in bed. To lose even a single day of a presidential campaign is a setback; to be out of the game for two weeks is a candidate's nightmare.

The president did not help. Asked at a press conference to name a Nixon idea that he had adopted, Eisenhower responded with: "If you give me a week I might think of one. I don't remember." It was just a slip, at worst facetious, but it led to terrible press for Nixon.[6] The president phoned to apologize but found a "lack of warmth" in his vice president when he visited him in the hospital. Eisenhower did later endorse Nixon's candidacy but on medical advice campaigned little on his behalf. His heart was playing up again.[7]

As late as 1991 Nixon was still complaining that Eisenhower had been "a tough son of a bitch. . . . He didn't endorse me in 1960 until he absolutely had to. That was pretty devastating to my campaign. . . . It wasn't really the most loyal thing to do." Eisenhower, for his part, had been scornful of Nixon late in the 1960 campaign, exclaiming afterward: "Goddammit, he looks like a loser to me! . . . When I had an officer like that in World War II, I relieved him."

Once released from the hospital, Nixon again ignored advice and threw himself into a nonstop travel marathon—only to come down with a raging fever and chills nine cities later. Ehrlichman, who first worked for Nixon that year, said he sometimes "resorted to pills or liquor" to help him sleep. One night he was found slumped in a chair, sleeping so deeply that an aide feared he was in a coma. It was reported that at forty-seven Nixon suffered from high blood pressure and elevated cholesterol levels. His doctor denied it, saying his only ailment was hay fever.

On Sunday, September 25, the Nixon caravan careened into Chicago with the crucial first television debate with Kennedy, one that was to reach seventy million citizens, scheduled for the following evening. Closeted in a suite at the Ambassador East Hotel, Kennedy held a strategy meeting all morning, relaxed over lunch, slipped out to give one untaxing speech, took a nap, then presided over a final planning session from his bed. Shortly before airtime Kennedy reportedly devoted fifteen minutes to a session with a prostitute.

Nixon, by contrast, spent most of the day alone in his room at the Pick-Congress Hotel. While he later claimed to have studied briefing notes for five hours, senior adviser Bob Finch said he "totally refused to prepare. We kept pushing for him to have some give-and-take with somebody from the staff . . . anything. He hadn't done anything except to tell me he knew how to debate. . . ." Jim Shepley, a future president of *Time* who prepared the research for Nixon, recalled that "he didn't even look at the stuff." Nixon did speak with William Rogers, the attorney general, who suggested he play the "good guy" toward Kennedy in the debates. He brushed off advice from his TV consultant, Ted Rogers, that he should wear makeup. Then, on the way to the studio, he banged his bad knee on the car door again.

CBS producer Don Hewitt, later to achieve distinction as the head of the *60 Minutes* team, greeted Kennedy when he arrived for the debate. The Democrat was tanned, fit, and well tailored, the image of "a young Adonis." Nixon, on the other hand, looked terrible. He had lost ten pounds while hospitalized, and his clothes hung loosely on him. His complexion was as gray as his suit, which turned out to be the wrong color for the backdrop.

On hearing Kennedy refuse makeup, Nixon again declined. Then, when Kennedy accepted talcum powder to tone down his ruddy complexion, Nixon sent out for some Lazy Shave to lighten his five o'clock shadow. It merely accentuated the ghostly pallor of the rest of his face. When he noticed Robert Kennedy staring at him, Nixon asked whether he looked all right. The candidate's brother replied with a smile "Dick, you look great! Don't change a thing!"

Nixon's aversion to makeup, he had recently told a BBC executive, had begun after "some amateur makeup artist dabbed the powder puff in his eye and nearly blinded him." A military aide had fended off makeup artists thereafter, occasionally administering a little something himself.[8] Press aide Klein, meanwhile, has offered a specific explanation for the fateful refusal of September 1960. Kennedy, Nixon had heard, had recently mocked fellow Democrat Hubert Humphrey for wearing heavy makeup on television. "To Nixon," said Klein, "this made it look like [Humphrey] lacked macho, and Nixon was a very macho man."

As airtime approached, Kennedy fazed the man who thought of him as a friend, simply by ignoring him. As the pair posed for photographs, producer Hewitt quipped, "I assume you guys know each other." The rivals shook hands without warmth. While Kennedy retired to another room, Nixon paced nervously about the stage. He barely glanced at his opponent when he returned.

The startled reactions began as soon as the program got under way. "Why, Nixon has lost this thing!" exclaimed columnist Doris Fleeson. "He's sat there spraddled out almost as if his fly were open." "Probably no picture in American politics," Theodore White would reflect later, "tells a better story of crisis and episode than that famous shot of the camera on the Vice President as he half slouched, his Lazy Shave powder faintly streaked with sweat, his eyes exaggerated hollows of blackness, his jaw, jowls and face drooping with strain."

Nixon's foes reacted with amazement and glee. Kennedy aide Richard Goodwin saw "a man strangely severed from his own shrewd reasoned discourse. . . . Lips occasionally forced into a smile unrelated to his words, Nixon looked more like a losing football coach summoned before the board of trustees than a leader of the free world." "My God!" exclaimed Chicago's Mayor Richard Daley, "They've embalmed him before he even died."

Friends were no less shocked. "It almost looked like he was mad or disturbed," press tycoon Jim Copley wrote Klein the following day. Nixon's mother telephoned a shocked Rose Woods, her son's secretary, and asked, "Is Richard ill?" Pat, saying she "couldn't imagine why he looked that way," took the next plane to Chicago to join her husband.

An hour later the debate was over, and Nixon drove back to his hotel with Klein. He was exhausted and silent but seemed to believe he had done well. "None of us disillusioned him that evening," said Klein. Pat did that, later.

In the Democratic camp, as aides rejoiced, Kennedy just smiled. "It was all right," he said quietly. In private, on the phone to pollster Lou Harris, he exulted: "I know I can take 'im! I know I can take 'im!"

Some who heard the debate on radio, rather than seeing it on television, thought Nixon had been a success or even bettered Kennedy. In a Gallup poll, though, 43 percent of respondents thought Kennedy had come out on top, with only 23 percent for Nixon.[9] As Russell Baker later wrote, "That night, image had replaced the printed word as the natural language of politics."

The tide of the 1960 election had perceptibly turned. Crowds began turning out for Kennedy in unprecedented numbers. In the remaining three debates, with good makeup and fortified by four milk shakes a day—on doctor's orders, to restore his weight—Nixon performed effectively.[10] The damage, however, had been done. "That son of a bitch," running mate Henry Cabot Lodge had said after watching the initial debate, "has just cost us the election."

Nixon flew into Memphis the day after the first confrontation to encounter a seemingly sweet old lady standing near the front of the crowd. Wearing a large NIXON button and a welcoming smile, she stepped forward to embrace him.

1. Nixon's father Frank and his mother Hannah, on their wedding day in 1908. Richard described her as a "saint."

2. Richard, age nine, *(standing at left)* at play with three of his four brothers—two were to die young.

3. Richard was a star student at school and at college, and later when he studied at Duke University.

4. Richard *(left)* with his mother and brothers Harold and Donald. Of the latter, only Donald was to survive.

5. With his first love, Ola Welch—she left him to marry another man.

6. Pat Ryan, soon after her 1940 marriage to Nixon—theirs would be a rocky relationship.

7. A First Family-to-be. Nixon with Pat and their two daughters, Tricia *(right)* and Julie *(left)*, in the early days in Washington.

YOUR VETERAN CANDIDATE

Dick Nixon is a serious, energetic individual with a high purpose in life—to serve his fellow man. He is a trained scholar, a natural leader and a combat war veteran. He has acquired the "human touch" the hard way—by working his way through college and law school; by sleeping in fox-holes, sweating out air raids; by returning from war confronted with the necessity of "starting all over again."

There is in Richard Nixon's background much that is typical of the young western American. There are the parents from the mid-west, the father who has been street car motorman, oil field worker, citrus rancher, grocer. There is the solid heritage of the Quaker faith; the family tradition of Work—and Service.

The effects of this background show in Richard Nixon. He has worked in a fruit packing house, in stores, as a gas station attendant. He has made an outstanding success of his law practice. He played college football ("not too successfully," he says); maintains an intensive interest in sports.

Of course, the No. 1 Nixon-for-Congress enthusiasts are Mrs. Richard Nixon, born Patricia Ryan on St. Patrick's Day, and six-months-old baby daughter Pat. Mrs. Nixon is a public servant in her own right, having worked for the government as an economist while her husband was fighting for his country in the South Pacific. Like so many other young "war couples," the Nixons resumed civilian life on a financial foundation comprised solely of War Bonds purchased from the savings of the working wife and sailor husband.

Mr. and Mrs. Richard Nixon have been very busy this year. Individually or jointly, they have (1) been looking for a place to live; (2) practiced law; (3) been taking care of their little girl; (4) been active in veterans' affairs, particularly those relating to housing for Whittier College veteran-students and their families; (5) been looking for a place to live again; and (6) they have been campaigning to ELECT RICHARD NIXON TO CONGRESS.

New, Progressive, Representation in Congress

VOTE FOR
RICHARD M. NIXON
ON NOVEMBER 5

MR. AND MRS. RICHARD M. NIXON AND PATRICIA

ELECT
RICHARD M.
NIXON
WORLD WAR II VETERAN
YOUR
CONGRESSMAN

8. The campaign propaganda that helped win the first election.

9. Murray Chotiner (*left*), Nixon's election strategist—his guiding principle was "hit 'em, hit 'em, hit 'em again."

10. Mobster Mickey Cohen (*left*). He met with Nixon and, he claimed, raised money from the criminal fraternity in two election campaigns.

11. Meyer Lansky (*right*). "If you were Meyer, who would you invest in? Some politician named Clams Linguini? Or a nice Protestant boy from Whittier, California?"

12. Alger Hiss. A Communist traitor who committed perjury, or the victim of a frame-up?

13. After the Pumpkin Papers were produced, Nixon made a dramatic return from a sea cruise. The Hiss case gave him national prominence.

14. In 1950, on the way to a seat in the U.S. Senate.

15. Dr. Arnold Hutschnecker, the Park Avenue psychotherapist. Nixon's people obscured the truth about their relationship.

16. Nixon at ease. Bebe Rebozo's home territory, on Key Biscayne, became the site of the "Florida White House."

17. Best friends to the end. Nixon said Rebozo was a man of "great character." In fact, he had criminal connections.

18. The Checkers speech, in 1952—a plea to the nation to believe he was innocent of financial wrongdoing.

19. Nixon weeps on a senior colleague's shoulder on learning that he will remain Eisenhower's running mate.

20. Nixon with Ike—he became vice president at forty.

21. A close call in Caracas. Nixon narrowly escaped a leftist mob.

22. With Cuban dictator Batista, 1955. "He admires the American way of life."

23. A talk with Fidel Castro four months after the revolution. Nixon would soon be White House point man, planning Castro's overthrow.

24. Debating John F. Kennedy on television—a public relations calamity.

25. Narrowly defeated by Kennedy. Nixon believed the election had been stolen, and a long-burning resentment of the Kennedys began.

26. The second defeat, in the election for California governor in 1962. "You won't have Nixon to kick around anymore."

27. The family afterward. Away from the cameras, it is alleged, he got drunk and physically abused Pat.

28. Climbing back. Nixon became a top-flight New York attorney, but was already planning a political recovery.

29. During the wilderness years, in Hong Kong with Hilton Hotel hostess Marianna Liu—the only woman, other than Pat, with whom he has been linked.

30, 31. Howard Hughes. The billionaire loaned $205,000 to Nixon's brother Donald *(right)*. Was he, in fact, buying influence with the vice president?

32, 33. The toll bridge at Paradise Island— a source of secret income for Nixon? James Crosby *(right)*, the mob-linked owner of the island, became a key contributor to the 1968 campaign.

34. At the Raspoutine Restaurant in Paris—the friends included Saudi entrepreneur Adnan Khashoggi. Khashoggi has admitted to having given jewelry worth thousands to Nixon's daughters. Did he also donate $1 million for the 1972 campaign?

35. A contentious *Life* magazine photograph taken in Florida in 1969. Is the man behind Rebozo *(arrowed)* a gold and silver dealer who claimed he made millions for Nixon and the Republican party in an insider dealing scam? Or a Secret Service agent?

Perfidy over the Vietnam War?

36. Anna Chennault said Nixon asked her to carry messages to South Vietnam's President Thieu during the 1968 campaign.

37. President Johnson received Nixon at the White House after the election, but reportedly believed he had sabotaged the peace initiative.

38. On the way to victory in 1968—the trademark pose.

39. January 1969: inaugurated as the thirty-seventh president of the United States.

Then, as the cameras rolled, she said loudly and waspishly, "Don't worry, son, he beat you last night, but you'll win next time. . . ."

The scale of the debate disaster had yet to register with Nixon, and this was the last thing he wanted to hear in public and on television. He looked shattered and puzzled until he spotted a familiar face in the crowd, that of Dick Tuck, a Kennedy campaign researcher. Armed with a tape recorder, he openly followed the Republican leader around and fed information back to the Kennedy team. No one objected to that. At the same time, though, Tuck was forever plotting mischief in the form of political pranks designed to embarrass and enrage Nixon. The pranks, he has insisted, were done entirely on his own initiative.*

"What we should have," Kennedy press aide Salinger had told his Republican counterpart, Herb Klein, "is a very honest campaign and no sleaze on either side." Klein concurred, talked with Nixon, and as Salinger tells it, both parties agreed to behave fairly.

In fact, both sides pulled dirty tricks, ranging from the droll to the sinister. Before the second debate Republican organizers devised a way to avoid having Nixon appear covered in sweat again. When the Democratic team arrived for the broadcast, Salinger recalled, "You needed a parka, a fur coat, in the goddamn joint . . . the Nixon people had tried to freeze the studio!" Kennedy aides rushed to the basement, browbeat a janitor into giving them access to the thermostat, and turned the temperature up as high as possible. By the second half of the debate, Nixon was mopping his face with a handkerchief.

Nixon's public persona that year gave many the impression that deliberately or not, he never took the gloves off, that this was a "new" Nixon, no longer the political "alley fighter" of old. Kennedy, for his part, came across as a Sir Galahad, the good knight of the New Frontier. The true picture was murkier.

Both sides played the spying game, even against members of their own parties. John Ehrlichman, on the road for the first time, played chauffeur to Nixon's Republican rival Nelson Rockefeller before the convention, as a cover for gathering intelligence.

"The Kennedy fellows were really much better at the dirty stuff than we were," Ehrlichman recalled. "The Nixon campaign staff always felt a bit outclassed." Nixon claimed in his memoirs that he had been faced "by the most ruthless group of political operators ever mobilized for a presidential campaign."

"The dirtiest trick of all in 1960 was the manner in which the Kennedys manipulated the 'religious issue' for their political benefit," wrote Victor Lasky, a self-described "freelance writer" who was in fact a longtime Nixon friend and front man.[11] Kennedy was of course a Catholic, and no one of that faith had ever before been elected president. Nixon, as a Quaker himself and

---

*For more Tuck exploits, see Chapter 9, Note 1.

member of a minority faith, was to declare his pride in having resisted all efforts to exploit the religious factor. The Kennedys, he claimed, "repeatedly made religion an issue even as they professed that it should not be one" in order to woo voters who were fellow Catholics.

The allegation of Democratic chicanery was later attached to a flood of anti-Catholic hate mail sent out anonymously to Catholics. Robert Kennedy said the Nixon side spent a million dollars on such anti-Catholic propaganda. Lasky and Nixon countered that the mailings were, rather, organized by "one of Bobby's hatchet men," an agent provocateur working to trigger Catholic sympathy for Kennedy.[12] From Texas meanwhile came a claim that as in 1946 and 1950, Nixon supporters were making anonymous phone calls. Before hanging up, callers would ask: "Would you vote for a Catholic?" or "Do you want the pope to boss the president?"

If Nixon's own public stance on the religious issue was impeccable, the same cannot be said of two prominent Protestant leaders who were his close associates. The conservative minister Norman Vincent Peale, with whom Nixon had been friendly since World War II, attached his name to a statement expressing serious reservations about electing a Catholic president. Responding to this on the television program *Meet the Press*, Nixon said that he did not believe religion should be a "substantial" issue, criticizing Peale's action. "I decided," he wrote later, "it would be unfair for me to attack him personally."

Peale had endorsed Nixon and urged the evangelist Billy Graham, a Nixon golfing buddy and long-standing supporter, to do the same. In his memoirs Graham was equivocal about the way he dealt with this "complication," admitting only to having made "veiled allusions" to his preference and having participated in a Nixon rally. In fact, when publicly rejecting a Kennedy request that Graham sign a pledge not to make religion an issue, his spokesman drew attention to a bizarre claim that Catholics in Spain had prayed that Graham's plane would crash. Two days later, speaking from Europe, the evangelist declared that religion would indeed be a "major issue," adding that no one should vote on the basis of which candidate "is more handsome or charming," a less than subtle reference.

Months earlier Graham had called Nixon "probably the best-trained man for President in American history, and he is certainly every inch a Christian gentleman." Billy Graham would reassess Nixon after Watergate. "I wonder," he was to write then, "whether I might have exaggerated his spirituality in my own mind."

On another front, each side dug for information on the opposing candidate's sex life. It was in 1960 that rumors first reached the press that Pat Nixon had been married before.* The Democrats looked for bedroom dirt on Nixon, with little success but one hilarious result.

*See p. 29.

Lloyd Cutler, the future White House counsel under President Clinton, recalled having done "a little volunteer investigative work" with Bill Baggs, the editor of the *Miami News* and a Kennedy associate. Baggs, said Cutler, "was especially interested in the weekend parties that Richard Nixon used to attend at Bebe Rebozo's house in Key Biscayne. . . . Bill found some call girls in Miami who claimed to have been at these parties. It was all going to make a very good story about Richard Nixon until we learned that among the people who were frequently in the house was Senator Kennedy, so we dropped the story. We never did find out whether Mr. Nixon had gone upstairs. . . ."

The most damaging revelations, as the world is now aware, would have been about Kennedy. "I knew some of it at the time . . . " Nixon said in 1992. "Bebe told me more later. . . . But of course we couldn't use it." It was no accident that Nixon knew "some of it." An FBI document reveals that an aide to his friend William Rogers, the attorney general, had specifically asked FBI Director Hoover for sex information on Kennedy.

Hoover, who had long treated Nixon as his protégé, complied by adding sexual allegations to the political research material he was already supplying. One item was the durable allegation that Kennedy had been briefly and secretly married to a wealthy young Florida divorcée before his marriage to Jacqueline. Nixon aide Robert Finch thought the story "documentable," and many years later, in 1997, the author Seymour Hersh produced a witness, one of Kennedy's closest friends, who stated flatly that the wedding did occur. Had Nixon's people been able to confirm the rumor in 1960, the revelation would have ended the Kennedy bid for the White House in minutes.[13] The Hoover file contained much other information on Kennedy's busy sex life, from a World War II dalliance with a woman who had supposed Nazi connections to more recent adventures, including an affair with a Senate secretary and his use of prostitutes.

When Kennedy learned that details of his private life might be exposed, he sought out former Eisenhower cabinet secretary Maxwell Raab. "Nixon and the Republican National Committee are doing a job on me," Raab recalled an angry Kennedy saying. "They're trying to destroy me, and Jackie's all upset. . . . It's got to be stopped." He asked Raab to tell the Republican side to "stop spreading the word that I'm philandering." When Raab went to see him, Nixon denied any involvement, claiming the culprit was campaign chairman Len Hall. Nixon later said his team decided not to release the sex charges because they would have been "counterproductive." Another account holds that he was in fact eager to leak the stories but relented after Hoover and Barry Goldwater convinced him it would be a mistake. (Ironically, women were to vote in greater numbers for Nixon in 1960 than for his handsome opponent.)

Two other areas of dirty trickery foreshadowed Watergate. Intruders broke into the offices of both of Kennedy's New York doctors, presumably searching for proof that he suffered from Addison's disease. The incidents occurred at a time that New York Republican William Casey, later to be CIA director under President Reagan, was looking into Kennedy's health status on behalf of the Nixon people. According to a former Republican aide, James Humes, the Nixon campaign office was also raided shortly before the election. Files were stolen but, Humes said, the press dismissed the story as just "part of the game."

Electronic eavesdropping was the other alleged abuse of the 1960 campaign, according to Nixon supporters. It is, however, an allegation with a serious weakness, for the Republican side made the claim only after Watergate, at a time when Nixon's men had themselves been caught bugging Democratic phones. In July 1973, when Watergate had already broken wide open, Republican National Committee Chairman George Bush was to make a long statement suggesting that key figures in his party had been "under surveillance and spied upon" in 1960. The spying, the future president asserted, had been directed by a "Kennedy man . . . Carmine Bellino." Bellino was now nothing less than chief investigator of the Senate Watergate Committee.

Bush based this allegation on the statements of five private detectives who claimed knowledge of Bellino's activities back in 1960, when he had worked for Robert Kennedy. One of them, John Leon, said Bellino had had him surveil a senior official of the Republican National Committee, Albert Hermann, "utilizing an electronic device known as 'the big ear,' aimed at Mr. Hermann's window from a nearby vantage point." Leon quoted an associate, Ed Jones, as stating he had tapped the phones of three Protestant ministers suspected of distributing anti-Catholic literature.

In the most dramatic claim of all, Leon recalled a conversation with colleagues the day after the first Nixon-Kennedy debate. They had agreed, he said, that Kennedy "had the debate all wrapped up," that he was "extremely well prepared." He concluded from the conversation that Jones and another member of the group, former FBI agent Oliver Angelone, "successfully bugged the Nixon space or tapped his phones prior to the television debate."

Jones, an electronics specialist, admitted having worked for Bellino on two surveillance operations during the 1960 campaign but denied any bugging. Angelone quoted Bellino as saying the Protestant ministers had been bugged but denied having taken part in the operation. He denied it again in 1999, when interviewed for this book.[14] Bellino, for his part, admitted having ordered physical surveillance but not bugging or wiretapping.

The truth can probably no longer be determined. A Senate subcommittee that probed the allegations found no proof of electronic eavesdropping. As president, however, Nixon repeatedly declared himself "convinced that wiretapping had been a key weapon in the Kennedy arsenal during the campaign of 1960." In old age he still talked of how he had been "victimized by all kinds of dirty tricks." Robert Kennedy, he said, "was the worst. He illegally bugged more people—and started it—than anyone. He was a bastard."

Both Kennedy and Nixon had been touched by the tentacles of the Mafia. Kennedy's father had made much of his fortune by conniving with gangsters during Prohibition, and compelling information indicates that he and his politician son used the mob connection as a stepping-stone to power in 1960. Chicago Mafia boss Sam Giancana would be overheard on an FBI wiretap discussing the "donations" the gangsters had made during the vital primary campaign. John Kennedy's lover Judith Campbell alleged years later that Kennedy took outrageous risks to enlist Giancana's help, covertly meeting with him in person at least twice.

Kennedy's game was especially dangerous because his brother Robert was committed to the pursuit of organized crime and in particular to the downfall of Jimmy Hoffa, the crooked Teamsters leader. When he continued that pursuit as attorney general, the mob chieftains were so furious that some—including the House Assassinations Committee—would come to suspect the Mafia was behind the 1963 assassination.

Nixon was also vulnerable. Before the 1960 campaign started, the author was told, an informant passed documentation to Robert Kennedy indicating that Meyer Lansky's people had footed Nixon's bill on a visit to Cuba.* The candidate's brother made no use of the information, probably because his brother had himself been compromised in Cuba when Lansky fixed him up with women there. Florida mob boss Santo Trafficante, who was aware of that episode, despised Kennedy and favored Nixon. "Santo," recalled his attorney Frank Ragano, "viewed Nixon as a realistic, conservative politician who was 'not a zealot' and would not be hard on him and his mob friends. The Mafia had little to fear from Nixon."

"We'll contribute to Nixon, too. . . . We'll hedge our bets. Just like we did out in California when Nixon was running for senator. . . . You don't know what the hell Jack'll do once he's elected. With Nixon, you know where you stand." So said Giancana before the 1960 election, according to his brother Chuck.[15] "Marcello and I," Giancana allegedly added, "are giving the Nixon campaign a million bucks."

Carlos Marcello, Mafia boss of New Orleans and much of the southern United States, did reportedly make a massive donation to Nixon that year. According to a man who said he was present when the money exchanged hands, Marcello did so in September, at a meeting in Lafayette, Louisiana. "I was right there, listening to the conversation," said the witness. "Marcello had a suitcase filled with five hundred thousand dollars cash, which was going to Nixon. . . . The other half was coming from the mob boys in New Jersey and Florida." Five hundred thousand dollars, at today's values, would be around three million dollars.

The suitcase containing the money was handed to Teamsters leader Jimmy Hoffa, and the witness who said he saw the transaction was Edward Partin, a

*See page 128.

close Hoffa associate who later turned informant and became the Justice Department's principal prosecution witness against Hoffa. He told of the Marcello donation first to department investigator Walter Sheridan and later—on tape—to Michael Ewing, a congressional staffer and specialist on organized crime.[16] The mob leader hoped, according to Partin, to exact a pledge that a Nixon administration would not deport him, something that Robert Kennedy would indeed attempt the following year.

Hoffa's alleged involvement meshes with other information, only too well for Nixon's reputation. It brings into troubling focus exchanges that had taken place in previous months between Nixon, a former congressman friend from California, and Hoffa. The onetime congressman, Oakley Hunter, had met with Hoffa at the Americana Hotel in Miami Beach just before Christmas 1959. In the privacy of Hunter's room—both men having removed their coats to show that neither of them was wired—they had discussed the Teamsters' "program for political action."

The two men spoke circumspectly, as Hunter afterward explained to Nixon in a "Dear Dick" letter. He told Hoffa that Nixon "did not have the knife out for him, and bore no preconceived prejudices against him." He agreed that no person "could be elected President of the United States without substantial support from the rank and file of labor." Then he asked Hoffa what he "expected of the government" and what he "might do for political candidates whom he favored."

In reply, Hoffa complained that the Department of Justice, then under close Nixon associate Attorney General William Rogers, was harassing him with "nothing more than nuisance suits." He asked that the judge in a corruption case against him be removed. Then he said he could best help Nixon in 1960 by generating endorsements from local Teamsters officials and by harshly criticizing leading Democrats.

Hoffa did precisely that, attacking Kennedy as soon as he announced his candidacy. After a further meeting with Hunter, at the Republican National Convention, he hammered away at him for the duration of the campaign, especially in the weeks after he had passed on to Nixon's people the five-hundred-thousand-dollar Mafia donation. "You may be assured," a senior Nixon aide told a correspondent at exactly that time, "that neither the Vice President nor the Republican Party will ever ally themselves with men like Mr. Hoffa." Behind the scenes, almost coincident with the Marcello donation, the Eisenhower-Nixon Justice Department abruptly stopped the indictment process in the corruption case Hoffa had raised with Hunter. It was to be reactivated after the Kennedy election. Attorney General Rogers, thought investigator Sheridan, "obviously did not want to leave behind him what might appear to be a fixed case for Jimmy Hoffa. Thus Richard Nixon's political debt to Jimmy Hoffa remained unpaid."

It would be paid, however, during the Nixon presidency, when Hoffa was in prison, sentenced to thirteen years for his crimes. Then, following more alleged payoffs, Nixon would order Hoffa's release after he had served only five years.

In 1960 no reports ever surfaced about help from organized crime for either candidate. Instead, thanks to yet more bad luck and bad judgment, another skeleton came rattling out of the Nixon closet. Six weeks before the election, while campaigning for his brother in California, Edward Kennedy received a call from an attorney who said he had "something hot" to impart. Days later, at a meeting at the Los Angeles airport, the man handed young Kennedy a single sheet of paper, a draft agreement under which the Kennedys were asked to pay half a million dollars for access to "research" about a "feebly disguised loan." The information, said the attorney, "might affect the election." Kennedy replied, "I don't know whether we would use this or not," pocketed the draft agreement, and left. The Hughes Loan, the $205,000 gift the millionaire Howard Hughes had made four years earlier—ostensibly to Don Nixon but with his brother Richard's connivance*—was about to surface.

Word of the airport rendezvous reached a second attorney, James McInerney, a close Kennedy friend, who was also, as fate would have it, lawyer for the accountant who had acted as proxy to hide Hughes's involvement in the loan. Perhaps by chance, perhaps not, the accountant had recently come into possession of the entire bulky folder on the matter.[17] He now made it available to McInerney, who passed it to the Kennedys, who in turn passed it to a newspaper friendly to them, the *St. Louis Post-Dispatch*.

A comedy of errors followed. A *Post-Dispatch* reporter, in California checking the story, left a briefcase containing documents on the loan in a photographer's studio, and photocopies were soon being circulated all over town. The material eventually reached *Time* magazine, which put five men on the story. The Kennedy people made certain it also found its way into the hands of Nixon's perennial nemesis, Drew Pearson.

Howard Hughes meanwhile ordered his crack troubleshooter Robert Maheu to help rescue Nixon from "tremendous embarrassment." Sequestered in the Bel-Air Hotel with the Hughes' copy of the records, Maheu thought he saw a solution. He went for "the sympathy angle," showing *Post-Dispatch* reporters portions of the file that indicated Nixon's mother had pledged all her worldly possessions as security for the loan. If the story was printed, Maheu said, Hughes would be forced to take all this "poor lady's assets."

Influenced not only by this argument but also by concern about printing such incendiary information late in the campaign, editors hesitated. They did not run the story, might never have run it, had Nixon himself not subsequently panicked. "Nixon naively believed he could control the 'spin' on the story if he was the one to release it," Maheu recalled. Nixon decided—and it was a unilateral decision, press aide Klein confirmed—to give a doctored account of the

*See p. 154.

loan to Peter Edson, the same friendly reporter used years earlier to preempt revelations of secret funding by wealthy supporters.

"They made a sucker out of me," Edson acknowledged later. The story fed to him was a total distortion, one that made no mention of either Hughes's involvement in the loan or of Richard Nixon's. Provoked, Drew Pearson promptly went to press after all, naming both men. Then, while Nixon was still denying the charges, his brother Donald admitted Hughes was the source of the money. The accountant in the case, meanwhile, said the major decisions on the arrangement for the loan had been made by Richard Nixon. All this emerged on November 1, with only six days to go before the election.

Nixon was to tell Haldeman and Bebe Rebozo that he believed the Hughes furor had been a major factor in his defeat at the hands of John Kennedy. Robert Kennedy thought so too. As for John F. Kennedy, by the closing weeks of the campaign he shed all pretense at feelings of friendship for his old congressional colleague. Speechwriter Richard Goodwin heard him say of Nixon, "He's a filthy, lying son of a bitch, and a very dangerous man."

As quickly as the Hughes scandal flared, it died away. The Kennedy people had sensed only a brief surge in their fortunes and George Gallup of Gallup poll fame declared the election too close to call or, as *Time* magazine put it, "as close as a boy with an ice-cream cone." After a last lap of grueling travel, the quixotic trip to Alaska, Nixon finally came home to Whittier for election day.

As soon as he and Pat had voted and smiled for the cameras, Nixon eluded reporters and sped south down the Pacific Coast Highway to Mexico, where he lunched on enchiladas and beer in the border town of Tijuana. He is said to have prayed on the way back at what he called "one of my favorite Catholic places," the mission chapel at San Juan Capistrano.

That evening Nixon sat in the Royal Suite of Los Angeles' Ambassador Hotel, monitoring what turned out to be a cliff-hanger of an election. He isolated himself in front of the television, accepting occasional visits from Pat and his daughters and a select few associates, including Murray Chotiner and Rebozo.

By 11:00 P.M. California time Nixon deemed his chances of winning "remote." At 11:30 he prepared to make a statement, telling his daughter Tricia, "I'm afraid we've lost, honey." At 12:15, in front of the cameras in the hotel bedroom, he announced to supporters that "if the present trend continues," Kennedy would win. He never did verbally and publicly concede defeat.[18]

Millions of viewers had watched Pat, standing beside Nixon as he spoke, struggle to keep from crying. Then she broke, the tears flooding down her face. As they walked away, out of sight of the cameras, she darted from her husband's side and ran for the privacy of her separate bedroom. Jim Bassett's wife, Wilma, recalled how soon after, as she walked along the hall, Pat's door opened and "a long, bony arm reached out and drew me in." "Now," Pat sobbed as Wilma tried to comfort her, "I'll never get to be First Lady." She had not wanted her husband to run but was distraught at the prospect of defeat.

Nixon meanwhile prowled the corridors far into the night. There was still a chance he might win.

The result, when it came, was too close for any man to bear with equanimity. Kennedy became president with 49.71 percent of the popular vote to Nixon's 49.55 percent, with 303 electoral votes to 219 for Nixon. Translated into voter numbers, Kennedy had won by a tiny margin of a mere 113,057 votes out of a turnout of nearly 69 million people. If 28,000 Texan voters had cast their ballots differently, along with 4,500 in Illinois, they would have shifted enough electoral votes to Nixon to elect him president.[19]

There was the immediate suspicion of election fraud, and those who questioned the outcome focused on Illinois, one of the last state tallies to come in. A shift of just 4,480 votes from Nixon to Kennedy there would have left neither man with an electoral majority and thrown the decision on who was to be the victor to the House of Representatives.[20] From Illinois came rumors of legitimate voters' having been denied a vote, of votes cast by nonexistent voters, of manipulation of the count, even photographs of voters being slipped money after voting. "With a little bit of luck and the help of a few close friends," archetypal power broker Mayor Daley of Chicago had told Kennedy by telephone when the vote hung in the balance, "you're going to carry Illinois."

As documented once and for all in Richard Mahoney's masterful 1999 study of the Kennedys, *Sons and Brothers,* the "friends" were the local mafiosi. "If it wasn't for me," Chicago mob boss Giancana would brag later, Kennedy "wouldn't even be in the White House." While that was an overblown boast, the Mafia chief's brother Chuck has recalled how "guys stood menacingly alongside the voting booths, where they made it clear to prospective voters that all ballots were to be cast for Kennedy . . . more than a few arms and legs were broken before the polls closed." "I know that certain people in the Chicago organization knew that they had to get Kennedy in," claimed Mickey Cohen, who had ties to the Chicago mob. "The presidency really was stolen in Chicago, without question, by the Democratic machine." Even Notre Dame law professor Robert Blakey, who once worked in the Kennedy Justice Department, has used the word "stolen" to describe the Democratic victory in Illinois.

The situation was not entirely one-sided, however. Republicans may also have cheated in the election, though obviously not with the same happy result as the Democrats'. "The point," the *New York Times'* Tom Wicker wrote years later, "is not that the election was stolen from Nixon but that it *might* have been, since it was so close. Republicans had ample reason to think it *had* been stolen."

For several anxious days, the Democrats worried that Nixon would challenge the result. He did not, and later claimed he chose not to do so because he felt he "could not subject the country to such a situation." Although some considered this Nixon's "finest hour," his friend writer Ralph de Toledano claimed the opposite was true. "Nixon was bitter," he said. "I discussed it with him. . . . *He* pressed for the investigation, and it was Eisenhower who said,

'No, it will tear the country apart.' At the time, Nixon and the people around him were absolutely furious at Eisenhower." To have taken the credit for not challenging Kennedy's victory, said de Toledano, was "the first time I caught Nixon in what you might call a lie."

In private Nixon never did accept that Kennedy had defeated him. "I lost," he started to say at the age of eighty, then added hurriedly, "Well, not really . . . everyone around me, including Mrs. Nixon, believed that the election had been stolen and that I should have demanded a recount." At the time he was shattered. "He started to sob, and he couldn't stop . . . he had to be led out of the room," recalled campaign chairman Len Hall. Days later, in Florida, Herb Klein thought his boss "completely depressed. . . . Nixon found it difficult even to speak."

His spirits lifted somewhat when Kennedy, urged by his father to mend fences in the name of national unity, helicoptered in from Palm Beach to see him. Later he would claim Kennedy had offered him a post abroad and that he had turned it down, a story that Kennedy denied. In private the president-elect just shook his head and said, "It was just as well for all of us that he didn't quite make it." "If I've done nothing for this country," he told an old friend, "I've saved them from Dick Nixon."

For Nixon, it was the bitter start to a resentment that festered for the rest of his life. "I had the wisdom and wariness of someone who had been burned by the power of the Kennedys and their money . . ." he was to write. "I vowed that I would never again enter an election at a disadvantage by being vulnerable to them—or anyone—on the level of political tactics."

One longtime aide, however, took a different view. "Dick didn't lose this election," he told Theodore White off the record. "Dick blew this election." Another said thoughtfully "Maybe Dick was never cut out to be a top banana, from the very beginning."

Two years before the 1960 election, the author Margaret Halsey had written a strangely prescient article for the *New Republic,* looking ahead to the day when Nixon might become president. In that event, Halsey wrote, "Many people will automatically develop a sort of selective morality. They will have one set of ethics—the one they were taught as children and have been used to all their lives—for judging themselves and their friends. They will have another, and a much lower one, for the President of the United States."

Soon after Watergate, Charles Colson ran into former Kennedy aide Kenneth O'Donnell at an airport. "How did you ever stand working for Nixon?" O'Donnell asked. "JFK never trusted his mental ability." According to former *Washington Post* editor Benjamin Bradlee, Kennedy came to regard Nixon as "sick," "mentally unsound." Less harshly, he said he thought his former opponent "did not know who he was."

Kennedy's comments had probably been based on more than just personal observation, for Nixon's use of the New York psychotherapist Dr. Hutschnecker had come close to exposure in 1960. Joseph Kennedy told a female friend that his people had "a whole dossier" on the matter. Frank Sinatra, who was in touch with Kennedy Sr. and campaigning for his son, tried to get publicity for a private investigator's report revealing that Nixon was Hutschnecker's patient. Gossip columnist Walter Winchell ran veiled references to that effect. Two days before the election, sitting at home with his wife, the doctor took a call from an Associated Press reporter wanting to know if Nixon was "in good health." Hutschnecker fended him off.

Those who watched Nixon that year worried about his ability to cope with pressure. "It was this lack of an over-all structure of thought, of a personal vision of the world that a major statesman must possess," wrote Theodore White, "that explained so many of those instances of the campaign when he broke under pressure." "The presidency, of course," Nixon's own mother said, "is such a great responsibility that I often wonder whether any man could survive under the pressure of that office. I have, however, faith in Richard. . . ."

Nixon found the day of Kennedy's inauguration, in January 1961, "one of the most trying days in my life." He sat through his former opponent's speech, then went home. That night, knowing that he had the use of his official limousine for only a few more hours, he asked his driver to take him on a last tour around Washington. Nixon no longer had a Secret Service escort. When he tried to enter his Senate office, to take a last look out the window at the view down the Mall, he found it locked. The prestige and power of the vice presidency, such as it was, were already passing.

"I opened a door," Nixon remembered, "and went out onto the balcony that looks out across the west grounds of the Capitol. . . . It never seemed more beautiful than at this moment. The Washington Monument stood out stark and clear against the luminous gray sky, and in the distance I could see the Lincoln Memorial. . . . I thought about the great experiences of the past fourteen years. Now all that was over. . . ."

Then he was driven home through the snow-shrouded streets, clogged with traffic taking guests to inaugural balls celebrating another man's victory, the victory Nixon believed should have been his.

On the last day of the contest, aboard his campaign plane, John Kennedy had been asked by a journalist how he expected he would cope were he to lose. "I'll tell you one thing," he had replied, "I won't take it nearly as hard as Nixon will." Because Nixon did not have much "inner resource," Kennedy thought, it would be a "terrible blow."

Even before the campaign started, a more sympathetic observer had weighed the same prospect. "Suppose he misses it," Whittaker Chambers had written in a letter to a friend. "I cannot imagine what such a defeat will do to him."

19

*He can't help it. He must always have a
crusade. . . . So I said to our dog Checkers this
morning, "Well, Checkers, here we go again. I am
once more a candidate's wife and proud to be one."*

—Pat, in 1962, weeks before her husband reportedly beat her up

The damage from Richard Nixon's loss in the 1960 presidential election
went beyond politics. In 1961, journalists in search of a "human interest
story" got more than they bargained for. On the day the moving van was being loaded for the family's return to California, Pat suddenly came rushing out
of the house. She was "screaming like a banshee," recalled Washington *Daily
News* reporter Tom Kelly, "completely out of control. Her hair was disheveled,
her face red, and her eyes were wild."

Kelly and an Associated Press colleague quickly discovered that it was they
who were the targets of Pat's rage. She stood cursing them, claiming that a hostile press had caused her husband's defeat, until Nixon himself appeared. "She
had just snapped," Kelly said. "Nixon had to lead her back into the house,
apologizing to us all the while. . . ."

This was a Pat the public had never seen, a Pat embittered by the experience of the previous year. "I've given up everything I loved," she had said even
before the campaign, referring to the loss of privacy and family time. "Mother
took the defeat even harder than he did," her daughter Julie would recall.
Years later Pat, like her husband, would still be insisting, "We won in 1960,
but the election was stolen from us."

The months afterward, Julie said, marked a "turning point in my mother's attitude toward politics. 1960 disillusioned her beyond redemption." What Julie did not reveal was what other intimates noted: that much of Pat's rage was directed against her husband, the husband who had ignored her appeals to quit politics. Even when Nixon had been in the hospital after the knee injury, Pat had not exuded sympathy. "Pat, who seems to feel that Dick is having a wonderful jolly time in the hospital," Jim Bassett noted in a letter home, "is in one of her 'moods.' . . . nobody else in the U.S. would believe it, would they?"

In early 1961 before leaving the capital, the couple took a vacation in the Bahamas, planned to last a month but cut short by Nixon after two weeks. "The shallow talk, the lack of interest in subjects of importance," he remembered, "grew more and more boring. . . . I could hardly wait to get back to work."

Pat and the children spent the next six months in Washington, "in limbo," as she put it, while Nixon began work with a Los Angeles law firm. "To be alone," he would recall, he rented a "small bachelor apartment" in which he learned to fix TV dinners—not mentioning the fact that the apartment was at a very exclusive address across from the Ambassador Hotel.

When the rest of the family reached California, they lived first in a borrowed mansion, then in a house they built in Bel Air. The new home had a panoramic view of the city, four bedrooms, a library, guest and servants' quarters, a swimming pool, and a bathroom for every day of the week. The Nixons' new neighbors included Groucho Marx, Dinah Shore, and the actor Cesar Romero.

More interesting than the house itself was the property's cost and ownership background. The regular listed price for the lot had been $104,250, about $600,000 at today's rates, but Nixon paid only $35,000 because, the real estate agent explained, "he was a celebrity who would spur sales."

The development on which the property was located was owned by Texas oil tycoon Clint Murchison, a campaign contributor who had long wooed Nixon with gifts and hosted him at his luxury retreat south of Los Angeles. Murchison had purchased the development with financing from the Teamsters Union pension fund, soon to be the subject of a criminal probe. Only months before Nixon bought the house, of course, Teamsters leader Hoffa had been the conduit for a massive Mafia contribution to Nixon's campaign chest.

"After eight years in Washington," Nixon was to tell Charles Colson, "I left the White House with $38,000 in my savings account and a four-year-old Oldsmobile. Don't you make that mistake." If that accounting was true, Nixon improved his financial situation rapidly. Back in 1946 Earl Adams, senior partner in a top Los Angeles law firm and one of his original supporters, had guaranteed him a job should he fail to win a seat in Congress. Now that Nixon had missed the most glittering of all political prizes, Adams made good on the promise, handing Nixon a position worth one hundred thousand dollars a year. Nixon was also given a large percentage of any business he brought to the firm and also had income from writing contracts. The first contract alone was worth forty thousand dollars.

These were riches indeed in 1961. After twelve months, having installed a butler named Reeves—a moniker as close as a man could wish to Jeeves—at home and having purchased a sleek new convertible to convey him around Los Angeles, Nixon was able to give his family even better news. He had made $350,000 that year, the equivalent of $2 million today, more than the total of all his earnings as a politician since 1946. Pat's response was to throw up her hands and cry "Hallelujah!"

On the surface all seemed well with the Nixons in the late summer of 1961. Friends said they had never seen Pat so relaxed and apparently happy. One close friend, however, the writer Adela Rogers St. Johns, overheard a searing quarrel between husband and wife. "If you ever run for office again," the Nixons' old confidante recalled Pat threatening, "I'll kill myself."

As one who had been close to the family for years, St. Johns thought the threat sounded genuine. Yet running for office again was exactly what Nixon intended.[1]

Nixon had never truly abandoned politics, nor politics him. Within twenty-four hours of leaving the vice presidency, when he had left for the vacation in the Bahamas, his hosts had been a former assistant secretary of defense and a property magnate. Nixon named them in his memoirs as Perkins McGuire and Lindsay Hopkins, without identifying them. In fact, McGuire owned Southern Air Transport, a "spook airline" that had for months been flying CIA missions in the secret war against Castro, while Hopkins was a director of Zenith Technical Enterprises, the main dummy company that provided cover for the CIA's massive anti-Castro operation in Florida.

Three months later, over drinks at Nixon's Washington house, a distraught Allen Dulles told him that the Cuba project was about to end in disaster at the Bay of Pigs. Nixon's daughter Tricia, now fifteen, left a message by the telephone in the hall the following day: "J.F.K. called. I knew it! It wouldn't be long before he would get into trouble and have to call on you for help.

We have only Nixon's account of what passed between the two men when they discussed Cuba later in the Oval Office. A biographer who saw his contemporary notes reported that Nixon wrote at the top of the page that Kennedy had "said 'shit' six times!" The president was furious at what he viewed as the useless assurances he had been given about the invasion and called the debacle "the worst experience of my life."

Nixon's published account of the meeting makes no mention of matters that must surely have been covered, including the exile politics in which Nixon had dabbled and the CIA activity to which he had been privy. Least of all did he mention the plots to kill Castro, of which both men were probably aware.

After leaving the White House, Nixon made numerous calls to fellow Republicans, cajoling, even threatening them, not to attack Kennedy over the Bay of Pigs. It is not likely he did so in a burst of fellow feeling. Nixon well knew that a full exposure of the poor decisions, misadventures, and conspiracies that had led to the Bay of Pigs would indicate that all had had their genesis in the previous administration and that he had been involved.

Whatever the potential risk, however, Nixon himself would soon enough find an opportunity to criticize Kennedy's Cuba policy. In the short term he contented himself with declaring publicly that the United States "should not start things in the world unless we are prepared to finish them." Later he would shift to, "Jack handled Cuba badly." In his memoirs he would insist it was Kennedy who "doomed the operation" by withholding air support. As late as 1992 he would be lashing out at the dead president on the subject in a bizarre way yet to be explained. "Do you think he ran the Bay of Pigs plan past Congress?" he asked. "Or his plans to knock off Castro? Money changed hands on that score, don't fool yourself."

After Eisenhower's death Nixon would heap blame on him as well, reportedly telling Henry Kissinger in a 1970 memo that Eisenhower had "let Cuba go down the drain." He was to state six years later that he would have gone in with whatever force was necessary to win, "probably in the last month of 1960. . . . I was hard line on Cuba and would have wanted to go ahead without delay."

The only way to have provided "the force necessary to win" by December would have been to mount a full-scale American invasion—probably some sixty thousand troops strong—and advance planning for such an operation would have to have started many weeks earlier.[2] For a multitude of political reasons, this option seems to have been rejected—except perhaps by Nixon. He later recalled telling Kennedy after the Bay of Pigs that had he been president, he would have found "a proper legal cover"—namely, a pretext—to invade Cuba. Kennedy replied that he could not have risked provoking the Soviet Union with such an action.

Criticism of Kennedy's management of the Bay of Pigs is said to have been especially strong within the CIA. It is instructive, then, to discover that the man who headed the CIA's preparations, Cuba Task Force head Jacob Esterline, assigned the blame not so much to Kennedy as to Richard Nixon.

"It is very wrong to pick too much on Jack Kennedy," Esterline said in 1975 in a taped interview for a CIA in-house history. Both then and in a 1998 interview, the former task force chief faulted Nixon for having put selfish political motives above operational priorities. "It came down to us by way of Dulles," Esterline explained, that it was Nixon who had "canceled the timetable." In the weeks before the Nixon-Kennedy election, in November 1960, CIA trainers had still been working on the insertion of guerrilla teams into a region of Cuba where they were likely to have strong popular support and where it was hoped that they could start a groundswell of counterrevolution to topple the Castro regime.

"It might not have worked," Esterline said, "but it would not have been a major disaster. It would just have been another little thing. . . . But I am told Nixon thought, 'Well, they had better wait until the election before they mounted anything of the sort.' . . . Nixon may have thought that, with the action taking place—especially if not successful—the resultant fallout might negatively affect his presidential aspirations. . . . And after he lost the election, they felt they didn't know whether they wanted to do it or not. The end was that it just kept escalating and turning into the nightmares that became the Bay of Pigs, which they then dumped on Jack Kennedy's lap."[3]

"Of course," Nixon was still complaining in rancorous old age, President Kennedy "was never held accountable" for the Bay of Pigs. Nor of course was Nixon himself. History may one day change that if the full CIA record has been preserved. Until we know more, the "Bay of Pigs thing" Nixon was to fret about as president must mark his reputation as least as much as it did that of John F. Kennedy.[4]

The perks of life as a top-flight attorney had rapidly palled for Nixon. "I found it difficult to concentrate," he recalled, "almost impossible to work up much enthusiasm." Nixon missed Washington, so much so that he commissioned a weekly report on goings-on in the capital. As titular head of the Republican party he crisscrossed the country making speeches. He also set about writing a book.

This was *Six Crises,* Nixon's personal account of his political career, from the Hiss case to his defeat at Kennedy's hands, presented as the self-portrait of a battler against life's tough odds. Producing the book, he claimed in its introduction, was such a great ordeal that it rated as "the seventh major crisis of my life." Told of a weeklong session during which Nixon "barricaded himself with groceries, long yellow pads, a tape recorder and reels of tape," one reporter wrote in awed tones of his "fierce self-discipline."

In a new 1990 edition of *Six Crises,* Nixon credited two colleagues with "editorial and research assistance" but gave the impression that most of the writing had been his. One of these colleagues, his former special assistant Alvin Moscow, said in 1998, "I was hired, I wrote the first five chapters, of the total of six. Nixon didn't want to go over each one. . . . Between you and me I thought I'd been had. He waited until I'd written the whole thing, and then he went back and put in a lot of his Nixonian expressions. . . . The sixth chapter he did write, the one on the election of 1960."

Nixon's friend Adela Rogers St. Johns also claimed to have done much of the writing. Years later, when the author Seymour Hersh asked Nixon for an advance blurb on one of his books, a spokesman phoned with regrets. "Mr.

Nixon," he said, "only comments on his own books, the ones written for him."

Six Crises was not written merely for the financial reward—Nixon received an estimated advance of $345,000 in 1962 dollars, which he agreed was "too much, really"—but with a shrewd eye to timing. The book was to be published in the spring of 1962, touted as "the mature wisdom and courage of a great American statesman," and sent to political writers throughout California just as Nixon embarked on a new political campaign. Dropping any pretense that the attorney's job was more than a stopgap, he had begun running for governor of the state against the Democratic incumbent, Edmund ("Pat") Brown.

If Nixon was to return to politics at that point, the California race was his only viable option. Given recent historical precedent, a sitting president was likely to be reelected, so it would have been folly to plan another run against Kennedy in 1964. The gubernatorial contest in the nation's most populous state, which had voted by a small margin for Nixon in 1960, was the one race on the horizon worth his running.

Nixon had mentioned the possibility of running for governor during his vacation after Kennedy's inauguration. The pharmaceuticals tycoon Elmer Bobst had warned him then, as they cruised in the Caribbean aboard Bobst's yacht, that the race would do nothing to help him reach his ultimate goal, the presidency. Yet Nixon came home to a letter from Whittaker Chambers—the last one, as it turned out, for Chambers died that summer—that urged him to run. Tom Dewey, the old warhorse, also encouraged him. Longtime colleagues were divided on the subject.

Herb Klein cited polls indicating Nixon would beat Brown. Jim Bassett told him he would be "out of his mind to run," that in California he would get tripped up by local issues while his expertise was in foreign affairs and that the Democratic legislature would "cut [his] balls off." Nixon did not heed the warnings. The thought that he might lose, Bassett said, seemed not to have occurred to him.

"As nearly as I can define my attitude," Pat Nixon said later, "it was: 'Let's not run! Let's stay home. Let's be a private family.' " Her feelings changed, she recalled, when fifteen-year-old Tricia put her arms around her father and said, "Daddy, come on—*let's show 'em!*" No mention was made publicly, of course, of the Pat who had said she would commit suicide should Nixon return to politics. The nearest a relative came to expressing that sentiment was her brother Tom, when he said: "Pat told me that if Dick ran for Governor she was going to take her shoe to him." Nixon merely remembered Pat's promising, "If you run, I'm not going to be out campaigning with you. . . ."[5]

There are varying versions of her reactions during dinner at a restaurant in late September 1961, the night Nixon publicly announced he would run. Bob Finch's wife, Carol, recalled Pat's saying suddenly, "I'm trapped. Which way can I go?" Another account had her fleeing to the rest room in tears.

Nixon's opponent, in contrast, relished the contest that faced him. "I welcome the opportunity," Governor Brown said when Nixon declared, "to confront Richard Nixon in a campaign that once and for all will return him to private life." Whatever Brown's own merits, he was to benefit from his challenger's mistakes. Nixon ranted on about the perils of domestic communism, a war cry that by now sounded dated. He campaigned largely on the strength of his international experience, while Californians cared most about state matters. He spoke of the "mess" in state government when few could see much wrong with it.

Word got around that Nixon disdained the "little people" of his home state. "That's what you have to expect from these fucking local yokels," he told a reporter commiserating with him when attendance was poor at a rural rally. Advised to drop in to talk with representatives of a local newspaper, he responded, "I wouldn't give them the sweat off my balls." As the editor of the *Sacramento Bee* put it dryly, "This kind of thing turned people off."

Democrats and Republicans alike indulged in dirty tricks and personal slurs both petty and serious, sometimes disinterring ancient charges. The Democrats harped on about a covenant Nixon had signed when buying one of his homes, a racist pledge binding him not to sell it to "negroes, . . . Armenians, Jews, Hebrews, Persians, and Syrians. . . ." The clause was indefensible, but commonplace enough at the time. Leading Democrats had signed similar agreements. The press meanwhile questioned the circumstances of Nixon's purchase of his new house in Bel Air, pointing up the Teamsters' involvement in the development.

President Kennedy threw his clout behind Pat Brown by campaigning for him. Behind the scenes his people helped dig out Nixonian dirt relevant to California. It was now that, apparently armed with Kennedy's authorization, a Brown official gained access to Mickey Cohen in Alcatraz. The gangster signed a statement admitting that mob money had helped elect Nixon in past campaigns.[6]

The campaign also returned to the matter of the Hughes Loan. Although Kennedy Justice Department officials had investigated but discarded the possibility of bringing prosecutions over the billionaire's handout to Nixon's brother, California Democrats now found ways to use it against Nixon. At a Chinatown rally, when the Republican candidate posed with Chinese children holding signs reading WELCOME NIXON in English, he was helping in his own ambush. Beneath the greeting, in Chinese characters that the locals could understand, was a very different message: WHAT ABOUT THE HUGHES LOAN? The photograph, plus the translation, duly appeared in the newspapers. Dick Tuck, the ubiquitous Democratic prankster, was up to his tricks again.

When Tom Braden, a Brown appointee on the Board of Education, raised the Hughes issue before a group of newspaper executives, Nixon challenged his rival to "stand up as a man and charge me with misconduct." "Do it, sir!" he cried, apparently hoping for a repeat of the Checkers speech effect. Brown did not respond, and Nixon found himself forced to discuss the matter again a few days later on *Meet the Press*.

Nixon would eventually conclude that the Hughes Loan had been one of his biggest handicaps of the election, while Brown thought that it had given him a key advantage. Years later, after Nixon had become president, the impertinent Tom Braden would himself being audited by the Internal Revenue Service year after year. He did not think it was a chance occurrence.

Governor Brown publicly denied having "ever said anything" about the Hughes matter "other than in casual conversation." That was not true, according to an electronics expert, interviewed in 1999, who had direct contact with Brown on the subject. The expert has requested anonymity because he still sometimes works for federal agencies, but has long proved a reliable source.[7] By 1962 his clients had included the military, politicians, and several large companies, including the Hughes organization. "Probably in the late summer of that year," he recalled, "I got a call from a top man on Brown's campaign. He set up a meeting at the Biltmore Hotel in Los Angeles and before we talked introduced me to Governor Brown himself. Brown told me: 'You come well recommended. I want you to know that talking to him is like talking to me.'

"Then Brown went off, and the campaign official and I talked. They wanted dirt on Nixon and specifically wanted me to get them to whoever at Hughes had firsthand knowledge of Nixon's involvement in the Hughes loan. I said there could be stiff fees involved. And he said, 'I've got twenty thousand dollars right here, and I can go up another twenty—no, make that fifty.' "

What Brown's people did not know was that the electronics man was at that very time conducting "defensive" operations on behalf of Richard Nixon and some of his closest aides. He had met Nixon at Republican headquarters on Wilshire Boulevard and swept the office—and Nixon's home in Bel Air—for bugs almost every day.

Far from assisting the Brown campaign, the specialist informed Hughes executives of the Democratic probe. By the time Brown's people discovered his true loyalty, it was too late: A key Hughes man privy to the Nixon Loan had been spirited out of town. "The people around the governor," the specialist remembered, "were furious that I'd pulled the wool over their eyes."

In his work for the Republicans, the electronics man discovered their suspicions were justified: that the Nixon headquarters was indeed being bugged, not by local Democrats, but under the direction of Robert Kennedy.

"There was a phone box on the side of the Republican building," the specialist recalled in the 1999 interview, "and when I checked it from time to time, I'd leave one screw slightly raised or something, a sign for myself so I could see at a glance if anyone else had tampered with it since my last visit. One day I saw that it had been opened, and I found the transmission equipment right away. There were a couple of bugs, one of them on Haldeman's phone."

Former campaign aide Alvin Moscow has confirmed that the Republican phones were checked, under the supervision of Nixon's friend John Davies, an executive with Pacific Telephone and Telegraph. Moscow also remembered that a bug was found.

"We spotted the guys who were doing the bugging," the electronics man said. "They were monitoring the transmission from a car. For a while we used the bug to feed them a whole lot of false information, just bullshit. Then we were able to follow them when they flew back East; I figured they had their tapes with them. We were able to tail them on the plane, and there were guys waiting for them in Washington with a car. Then we tailed them right to Bobby Kennedy's place in Virginia, saw them going through the gates."

Nixon and his senior staff ruled that this Democratic snooping was not to be made public. "Although we had a good deal of proof," the electronics man said, "Murray Chotiner thought the last thing they needed was to get into a public fight with the Kennedys. The Kennedys were very popular then, remember."

The electronics man recalled his frustration over his discoveries being hushed up in 1962. "The dirty shit that was done to Nixon during the Kennedy presidency! We knew the Kennedys were bankrolling this, putting money behind a load of smear stuff against Nixon. . . . But we couldn't use any of it. What an irony, looking back now! Here were the Kennedys bugging Nixon in 1962, and in 1974 Nixon's going to go down the tubes for bugging. . . . No wonder he was so bitter. . . ."

"We were bugged in '62 running for governor," Nixon would one day claim in a recorded Oval Office conversation. "Goddamndest thing you ever saw!" The electronics man's account is the first credible corroboration of that claim.

On the same White House tape, Nixon quoted Senator Barry Goldwater as having put Watergate in context when he said, "For Christ's sake, everybody bugs everybody else!" As late as 1994, aged eighty-one, Nixon would still be complaining that he had been "victimized by all kinds of dirty tricks—everything from being wiretapped by Bobby Kennedy and Johnson and having my tax returns audited by Kennedy—I understood how the game was played."[8]

The assertion that "everybody does it" is of course no justification for such surveillance. In 1962, moreover, Nixon had good reason not to try to expose the fact that he had once caught the Democrats bugging him, for he and his aides had also been playing the "game" in other ways.

The men who were to become notorious during Watergate were gathering around Nixon in 1962: Haldeman had been promoted to campaign manager. John Ehrlichman, who had worked temporarily as an advance man in 1960, was now fully on board. Nixon's finance chairman was Maurice Stans, who after Watergate would plead guilty to campaign finance violations. Herb Kalmbach, who would one day go to jail for finance irregularities, was brought in to manage the southern part of the state. Ron Ziegler had been hired as a press aide for the first time. Rose Woods was by now formally billed as Nixon's Girl Friday. And Chotiner was back on the team as a "volunteer"—though in fact, he functioned as the key strategist—presumably in the hope that his role in the 1956 Senate influence-peddling probe had been forgotten. A constituent wrote to warn Pat Brown that in private Chotiner talked of starting "a hate movement against the governor."

The first dirt to fly in the campaign, though, was internecine, from within Republican ranks. Former Governor Goodwin Knight accused Nixon of secretly trying to get him out of the race by promising him the chief justiceship of California should Nixon win. When Nixon denied the charge, Knight produced witnesses who said they had heard the offer being made by a Nixon emissary. "I don't want to call Mr. Nixon a liar," Knight told the press, "but he is not telling the truth."

Underhanded tricks against Brown involved false propaganda accusing him of being soft on communism. Nixon was able to disown one pamphlet, which featured a doctored photograph showing the governor kowtowing to Khrushchev, as the work of an extremist. It remained available, though, in Republican outlets.

Another photograph, purporting to show Brown applauding a call for Communist China's admission to the United Nations, was cropped from a picture that in fact showed him watching a crippled child's attempt to walk. This ploy was the creation of a group formed and financed by Nixon's people. (In fact, Brown was on record as opposing China's admission to the UN.) When the Democrats went to court on the matter, a judge stopped distribution of the pamphlet in which the photograph appeared.

Another massive illegal fabrication was exposed and stopped late in the campaign. The Republicans had created a fake Committee for the Preservation of the Democratic Party in California and mounted a mailing campaign designed to persuade conservative Democrats to vote for Nixon. It did so by maligning a genuine Democratic organization, the California Democratic Council (CDC), which supported the reelection of all Democratic officials, including Governor Brown. The mailer spoke of a "left-wing takeover of California's political leadership" and claimed falsely that nine out of ten registered Democrats rejected the CDC and were pouring in funds to fight it.

By the time the Democrats discovered the ruse and again got a judge to stop it, half a million copies of the mailing, of a planned total of nine hundred thousand, had been sent out. The Republicans evidently judged it an important weapon, for the cost of the effort, seventy thousand dollars, was its largest single reported item of expenditure. What no one knew at the time was the extent of Nixon's personal involvement in the scam.

A year later, under questioning during a Democratic suit over the mailings, Haldeman was asked if Nixon had reviewed the plan. He replied: "I don't think so." The head of the public relations company involved in producing the material, however, recalled having gone over the proofs with Nixon and Haldeman at Nixon's house in Bel Air. The judge determined that Haldeman had lied under oath, as he would after Watergate. He declared in his judgment that the mailing had been "reviewed, amended and finally approved by Mr. Nixon personally."

Neither Nixon's complicity nor Haldeman's perjury received public attention at the time, because the Republicans quietly negotiated a settlement. The Democrats' state chairman, Roger Kent, accepted the deal because of the high cost of pursuing the case. Nixon, for his part, felt no shame. Speaking of the matter at the height of Watergate, the White House tapes show, he said of Kent: "Do you remember in '62? . . . the little asshole sued us. . . ."

Nixon's fraudulent mailings had involved a poll for recipients to fill out and mail. Getting caught in 1962, however, would prove no deterrent to trying similar tricks in 1972. Another White House tape shows the following exchange between Nixon and Charles Colson:

> COLSON: Well, we did a little dirty trick this morning.
> NIXON: Of course, everybody should say, "We expect the Harris Poll to show a ten-point closing." Is that what you did?
> COLSON: What we did is we had someone . . . phone Gary Hart and tell him that the spread is going to be [nineteen] points, and it's great news for McGovern because he's gaining rapidly. I hope he will go out and have a press conference and talk about it just before the damn thing hits Monday showing. . . .

This exchange was followed by laughter, and then:

> COLSON: It'll sandbag him. Jesus, it'll sandbag him.
> NIXON: Sandbag them always, that's right.

In 1962 Nixon's old foes Nikita Khrushchev and Fidel Castro contributed indirectly to Governor Brown's election victory. Khrushchev's dispatch of missiles to Cuba, the act he called "throwing a hedgehog at Uncle Sam's pants," triggered the world's worst nuclear crisis and pushed coverage of the Nixon-Brown confrontation off the top of the front page of the newspapers.

Nixon had in fact been edging closer to Brown in the polls. Now, on October 22, as he sat in Oakland's Edgewater Inn watching the televised broadcast of Kennedy's address to the nation, he decided his campaign was doomed. On election day morning two weeks later, when speechwriter Stephen Hess asked if he still thought he was going to lose, he said, "Yes." Hess suggested he might be mistaken. "I'm not wrong," Nixon replied.

He sat up most of election night watching the returns come in at Los Angeles' Beverly Hilton Hotel, in the same presidential suite where Truman,

Eisenhower, and Kennedy had all once stayed. He wore a robe, which at first glance gave the impression of relaxation, but under it his shirt and tie, buttoned up tight. "We had," he wrote later, "to play the dreary drama through to its conclusion."

The outcome was clear enough by midnight, and at 4:00 A.M. Nixon went to bed. When he woke and called for coffee at about 8:00, he learned he had indeed lost by 297,000 out of 6 million votes cast. Press aide Herb Klein went in to see him with a draft concession statement and thought Nixon looked "haggard . . . bad."

Told the press was waiting to see him, Nixon just stared and then simply said, "Screw them." When aides told him he ought to make the traditional admission of defeat, he said it again and again, adding with finality: "I'm not going down there. To hell with those bastards!" It was agreed that Nixon would leave from the hotel's rear entrance while Klein spoke to the reporters. "He was," Klein remembered, "in no shape to do anything else."

Nixon's friend Pat Hillings recalled what happened next. "Suddenly the figure of Richard Nixon came hurtling into the room and practically pushed Klein off the platform. He was angry. It was quite apparent. . . ." Haldeman had urged him to tell the press "where the hell to get off," and Nixon now launched into the rambling speech that no one was ever to forget, the one with the famous "last point." It was now that he told startled reporters: "You won't have Nixon to kick around any more because, gentlemen, this is my last press conference. . . ."

"All the members of the press," he declared, were delighted that he had lost. From that he swung to the assertion that he "had no complaints about press coverage." From that, via meandering references to defense contracts, Cuba, the economy, and Governor Brown, he circled back to the "fun" the press had had attacking him over the past sixteen years. He said he hoped his speech would lead the media to "put one lonely reporter on the campaign who will report what the candidate says now and then."

Nixon had been angry at the press in 1960, even though the vast majority of papers that did endorse a candidate had backed him. He was especially miffed in 1962 because the *Los Angeles Times*, long his mouthpiece, had changed its policy and become more evenhanded. His press aide Herb Klein, himself a senior newspaperman, did not think the overall coverage unfair to Nixon that year. His fund-raiser Maurice Stans, looking back on the incident in 1997, thought the attack on the press had been "ridiculous."

"What unnerved the reporters," the *New York Times*'s Gladwin Hill thought, "was an uncomfortable feeling of being involuntary viewers of an appalling act of self-revelation, of a convulsive venting of a long-dammed bitterness towards many people. Although Nixon appeared to be lucid—his words were unslurred, his syntax orderly—his fifteen-minute monologue was a patchwork of schizoid contradictions. . . ."

"I gave it to them right in the ass," Nixon muttered to Klein when it was over. "It had to be said, goddammit." Then he stepped into the waiting car and went home to Bel Air, only to drive off alone again soon after. Nobody knew why he had left or where he had gone. "Desperately we alerted friends," Klein recalled. "He finally wandered back."

At that "last" press conference local reporter Jack Langguth had thought Nixon looked like "someone you'd see if you went into a bar on Eighth Avenue in New York at seven in the morning, talking almost to himself, so exhausted but too tired to sleep." He and fellow journalists concluded that Nixon had been drinking, although they decently omitted from their reports anything about his physical condition.

Years later Gladwin Hill attributed the performance to "the perversely stimulating effects of tranquilizing pills on top of some drinks." Loyal aides admitted only that Nixon had had "one or two scotches" the previous night and a "watered-down drink" in the morning.

John Ehrlichman was more forthright. He knew his boss "occasionally resorted to pills or liquor," and on the night of the election he learned from colleagues that this was such an occasion. "Nixon had begun greeting defeat with lubrication but without grace," he recalled. "Haldeman and the others had decided that in view of his deteriorating condition there would be no Nixon interviews for the TV cameras. . . . As the evening wore on I gathered that our candidate was good and drunk." Nixon's lecture to the press, Ehrlichman said, came "after a night of drinking, sleeplessness, remorse. . . ."

Insomnia was a long-term problem for Nixon. Even at the start of the campaign, he admitted, "I was more tired than I had been at the end of the 1960 campaign . . . and I became short-tempered at home." Just how short-tempered was not revealed while he was alive. Research for this book, however, suggests that Nixon physically attacked his wife after his loss in 1962.

As Pat once again stood tearfully at her defeated husband's side, many had felt sympathy for her. Betsy Cronkite, wife of the CBS newsman, found herself at lunch the next day with a group of Republican women friends. One said, "I felt so sorry for Pat last night." Betsy Cronkite responded: "I feel sorry for her every night."

At the start of the campaign John Ehrlichman had spent time with Pat and the girls on a yacht cruise through the San Juan Islands, off Vancouver. "We talked about a lot of things," he recalled. "We were at close quarters, and I think I got a fairly good read of the dynamics of them. She wasn't happy about his running, was dragging her feet about the campaign. She was talking about how a settled life, the house and kids in school, was her desire."

Ronald Ziegler, protective of the Nixons' memory, also remembered "tension" between them during this period. Howard Seelye, who had known Pat years earlier in Whittier, found himself sitting next to her at lunch that year. "I'll never forget," he said recently, "how she said, 'I just hate politics.' In the early days she had thought it was great. But things had got tough." In public Pat acted out her role, "bubbling with excitement" and telling reporters, "Our hearts are in politics, and we are glad to be back in the thick of it."

Nixon called Pat his "secret weapon" and, in an allusion to her namesake Pat Brown, dubbed her the new Pat, destined soon to reside in the state capital. Watching as she went through the motions, the *Los Angeles Times*'s Richard Bergholz thought her "just a stick of furniture sitting there, someone who smiled and had that adoring look on her face when she'd heard the same speech for the fiftieth time . . . she was obviously on edge, and we all suffered when she suffered. He abused her perpetually."

Word spread about an ugly moment during a plane trip from San Francisco. Pat, sitting apart from her husband while he talked with others, had asked if she might join them for a drink. The answer, reportedly, was a snarled "Keep your fucking mouth shut."

In the blur of Nixon's defeat, when he was drunk in his suite at the Beverly Hilton, aides were preoccupied with preventing him going downstairs. Pat reportedly sat alone, sobbing quietly, in an adjoining room. Just as the press coverage after his exit omitted to mention Nixon's hung-over condition, so too there was no mention of another episode involving Pat.

This concerned a prizewinning *Los Angeles Times* reporter, Jack Tobin, who had opened a recent article with a reference to Nixon's house in the Trousdale Estates and the estates' link to the Teamsters. Now, as her husband finished his harangue and the cameras ceased turning, Pat "went berserk." In a reprise of the scene on the day she moved out of her Washington home, Tobin recalled, she "began to scream obscenities at me, and kept saying, 'You caused this!' "[9]

As the car whisked Nixon and his wife away at last, home to the Trousdale house, Pat is said to have sat slumped silently in the back seat. From that point on, the precise sequence of events is unclear. It was soon afterward, according to press aide Klein, that Nixon slipped out of the house, climbed into his car, and vanished for several hours. This apparently was in the time frame that his then fourteen-year-old daughter Julie would one day describe in her book about her mother.

Pat, Julie was to write, was watching television in the den when the television ran the "kick around" speech. At the point where Nixon attacked the press, she shouted, "Bravo!" When her father came home, Julie recalled, "We were waiting tearfully in the hallway at the front door. Mother spoke first. She said brokenly, 'Oh, Dick.' He was so overcome with emotion that he brushed past and went outside to the backyard. That afternoon was the first and the only time my parents gave way to their emotions simultaneously, and it bewildered Tricia and me. . . ."

Domestic life for a top politician is rarely what most families would consider normal. What happened to bewilder the children that sad Wednesday in November 1962, however, may have been something they never learned of as children.

Future cabinet member Bob Finch, Nixon's intimate for many years, once admitted cautiously that he had sometimes witnessed Nixon in a rage, a rage "irrational in that it was much broader than the incident that provoked it." Speechwriter William Safire would write of Nixon's capacity for "deep, dark rage." Pat had a temper too.

Another aide remembered a night in the sixties when Nixon was enjoying a couple of vodka martinis. "God," he said, "these martinis are great. But you mustn't have more than two of them."

"Why not?" asked the aide.

"More than two," Nixon replied, "you fight with your wife."

Nixon's offhand remark may have been more than just the exaggeration of a common cliché, for rumors that he had physically abused Pat circulated in Washington for years. Two investigative reporters stumbled on such stories, but none were at the time well enough sourced to publish. While writing *The Final Days* with Carl Bernstein, their account of the end of the Nixon presidency, Bob Woodward was told of an incident in which Nixon supposedly hurt his wife badly enough to put her in the hospital.[10] Seymour Hersh, while working on his study of Henry Kissinger, *The Price of Power,* learned from sources of three alleged wife-beating incidents.

Soon after resigning the presidency, Hersh was told, Nixon attacked Pat at their home in San Clemente. According to the source, she had to be taken to a nearby emergency room. The doctor who treated her, Hersh told the author, corroborated the story.

The most compelling account of such abuse, however, relates to the 1962 defeat and comes from several sources. Governor Pat Brown said years later, "We got word at one stage of the campaign that he kicked the hell out of her, hit her." A senior Brown aide, Frank Cullen, used the same language, saying he heard Nixon had "beat the hell" out of his wife after his defeat.

A former Los Angeles area reporter, Bill Van Petten, years later told of his experiences while covering the gubernatorial campaign. Nixon, he said, had been a "terrible, belligerent drunk, mean when drunk, and would become obnoxious at night when in hotels on the road." Either during the night before the "kick around" speech or—much more plausibly, in this author's view—after it, Nixon "beat Pat badly . . . so badly that she could not go out the next day."

"This had happened before," Van Petten was told, "and aides like Haldeman, Robert Finch, or Ehrlichman would on occasion have to go in and intervene. On this particular night there was a lot of commotion at an ungodly hour, and one or some of the aides had to run in and pull him off Pat. She had bruises on her face. Everyone was shaken up."

Van Petten is dead, and his account as related here comes from a friend to whom he spoke in the early eighties. Elements of it, however, mesh with comments later made by John Ehrlichman that Nixon's drinking left him "very much troubled." Alcohol, he said, made his boss "more susceptible to inebriation than the average male." "I was in no position to ask him to stop," he was to say a few years later. "But I didn't want to invest my time in a difficult campaign that might well be lost because the candidate was not fully in control of himself. . . . If he wanted me to work for him he would lay off the booze."

During the writing of this book the first credible corroboration of the 1962 beating allegation was provided by John Sears, a former Nixon aide who went on to political distinction. Sears, now in his early sixties, came to the future president's notice as a young lawyer sometime after the California gubernatorial. He was to be a key figure in the Nixon comeback in 1968 and would join the Nixon White House as a political strategist under Ehrlichman. He later served as Ronald Reagan's campaign manager, then worked as a lobbyist.[11] As a younger man Sears looked on Nixon almost as a father, and in 1997 still discussed his former boss with considerable admiration.

By the time he met the couple, Sears recalled in a 1997 interview, the marriage seemed to him "peculiar." He thought Pat "a strong woman. Her overriding political view was that she hated politics. He would have run for anything."

Then Sears related what he had learned of Nixon's physical abuse. "The family lawyer," he said, "told me that Nixon had hit her in 1962 and that she had threatened to leave him over it. . . . I'm not talking about a smack. He blackened her eye. . . . I had heard about that from Pat Hillings [Nixon's longtime friend and associate] as well as from the family lawyer." Sears identified the "lawyer" as the late Waller Taylor, who in 1962 had been a senior partner at Adams, Duque and Hazeltine, the firm Nixon had joined after his defeat by John F. Kennedy.

Taylor, the son of a president of Union Oil, was certainly close to Nixon. His father, Reese, had been one of Nixon's original political supporters. After the infamous Hughes Loan to Nixon's brother, Reese had built a Union Oil service station on the plot Hannah Nixon provided as collateral, greatly increasing the land's value. He had also provided a private plane to fly Nixon to one of the ritual gatherings of political power brokers at Bohemian Grove, in Northern California.

Waller Taylor, the son, was responsible for bringing Nixon together with the youthful Donald Segretti, later notorious for his involvement in Watergate. During the presidency he also reportedly served as a bagman, delivering sixty-five thousand dollars in cash from a wealthy contributor who hoped to buy himself an ambassadorship.[12]

A 1960 letter, revealing that he provided Nixon with intelligence on the Democratic National Convention, establishes that Taylor knew Pat. The prominent journalist Lou Cannon, who gained extensive knowledge of Nixon during his years in California, said Taylor was "the man to talk to" about trouble in the Nixon marriage. "He knows Pat, and he would know about that."

As Sears understood it from Taylor, the 1962 beating was not an isolated incident. Spousal abuse, indeed, is almost always repetitive. A psychologist consulted by the author listed characteristics typical of those who abuse their partners. They are usually, but not always, men. Abusers tend to have belief systems that are "rigid, impersonal and inadequate to deal with stress" and "values that respect rigid sexual stereotypes." They believe "aggression is a means of survival" and resort to physical abuse when they feel "backed into a corner and unable to control the situation." They "expect others will blame, judge, or reject them."

It is fair to say that Nixon conformed to this profile, to one degree or another—respect for rigid sexual stereotypes included. (As late as 1970 he publicly rebuked a distinguished woman member of the White House press corps for wearing trousers rather than a skirt.) As the *New York Times*'s Tom Wicker wrote of Nixon at the height of the 1962 campaign: "He is more reserved and inward, as difficult as ever to know, driven still by deep inner compulsion toward power and personal vindication, painfully conscious of slights and failures, a man who has imposed on himself a self-control so rigid as to be all but invisible."

———————

In her memoir of her mother Julie Nixon recalled how the day after the 1962 election ended. "Mother lay on her bed, the room darkened by closed shutters, and cried in front of us for the first time we could remember. Tricia and I sat on the floor by the bed and cried also."

That evening close family friends took both the Nixon daughters away to their home for a few days. "When we returned," said Julie, "my parents seemed fine." But "There was a sadness," as Tricia told Nixon himself later when he asked for her teenage memories of the 1962 race, "and the sadness went on for years."

San Diego entrepreneur Arnholt Smith, one of Nixon's earliest supporters, remembered a melancholy evening in the early sixties when Nixon was holding a meeting and asked him to get Pat out of the way. "Pat was not feeling well physically, and even worse . . . mentally," Smith said. "Dick sent word, 'Could I please take her and hide her from the public so to speak, let her rest her mind and what have you.' "

Smith took Pat to dinner that night on the *Chito,* a yacht that had once belonged to the president of Mexico. "Arnie," she burst out, as they sat at the long table in the wood-paneled dining room, "is it ever going to stop?" "She felt pounded," Smith said, "in the sense that when they pounded Nixon, they pounded her."

Pat now even talked of divorce. "I think she would have divorced him," Smith went on, "if he had not agreed to stay out of politics. But Nixon wanted to go on, and without her it wouldn't work. He'd got to have the wife, the whole nine yards. She'd have to sacrifice her feelings to go forward."[13]

John Sears recalled family lawyer Taylor telling him about divorce discussions, beginning after the alleged beating in 1962. "She may have just put some space between them, but they came to some sort of accommodation . . . the way married people do. But the idea was that she would have a break. They would live this other life for a while. She wouldn't object, she'd go along if he wanted to run again, so long as nothing like that happened again. But it did. . . ."

It was about this time, James Bassett told friends, that Nixon "sought out therapy in New York" because "he was in a depression . . . his sex life had diminished to such a point that he went for help." One cause of the depression, Bassett reportedly said, was impotence. Nixon was reportedly seen entering the office of his psychotherapist Dr. Hutschnecker during that period. In 1995, pressed as to whether his patient had sexual problems, the doctor at first denied it and then equivocated at length.*

Nixon's appointments with Dr. Hutschnecker were made by his secretary, Rose Woods. Then in her early forties, she was fiercely dedicated to her boss, intolerant of anyone who did not believe in his political destiny. One evening, Bassett said, she and Nixon were found together in his office, a table laid for dinner and a candle burning. "Rose," said Bassett, was sitting on the sofa "all dressed up," and Nixon "was really making up to her."

This sad little scene almost certainly signified nothing more than mutual loneliness. Murray Chotiner's wife, Nancy, recalled hearing that Woods had once been in love with Nixon. She thought it just "the kind of thing that happens to anybody who works for one person for a long time." Bassett, too, agreed the relationship remained platonic, "the vestal virgin working for the high priest."

———————

"This man will never be president," Eisenhower had said privately. "The people don't like him." In November 1962 *Time* magazine decreed that "barring a miracle, Nixon's public career has ended." Two years earlier Nixon had been close to becoming president. Now, said the *New York Times,* he was "unelected and unmourned, an unemployed lawyer." "He was shot down and left for dead," was the way his friend Bryce Harlow expressed it.

President Kennedy gloated over the news of Nixon's defeat. Aboard Air Force One en route to Eleanor Roosevelt's funeral, the journalist Mary McGrory watched Kennedy as he sat with Chief Justice Earl Warren, an old Nixon foe. "They had their heads together over the clippings," she recalled, "and were laughing like schoolboys."

"You reduced him to the nuthouse," Kennedy told the victor, Governor Brown, in a phone call taped at the White House. "You gave me instructions," Brown replied, "and I follow your orders." "God," said the president, "that last farewell speech of his . . . it shows he belongs on the couch."

*See p. 93.

237

Brown agreed. "This is a very peculiar fellow. . . . I really think he is psychotic . . . an able man, but he's nuts . . . like a lot of these paranoiacs."

"Nobody," the president had said after hearing Nixon's "kick around" speech, "could talk like that and be normal."

Nixon too believed his career was over. "It's finished," he told Billy Graham. "After two straight defeats it's not likely I'll ever be nominated for anything again, or be given another chance." Murray Chotiner, who had known him from the beginning, was a lone voice predicting otherwise. "It would be hard for me," he said, "to visualize Nixon's removal from the American scene."

As Chotiner spoke, Nixon was on vacation in the Bahamas, at first without Pat but with his pal Bebe Rebozo. Her other miseries aside, his wife had been complaining to him about their financial situation, remembering perhaps a promise Nixon had made years earlier, when they were courting. In response to a birthday present Pat had given him, he had sent her a thank-you note promising to pay her four billion dollars "when I'm fifty, or before if you'll let me."

Now, at forty-nine and at his lowest ebb, Nixon would begin to pay serious attention to his bank balance. According to a number of sources, the place he chose for his 1962 vacation would become the seed ground for his future, an island called Paradise.

20

I was accused in the media of . . . stashing away piles
of cash . . . these charges were false. . . . I have never
had the urge to accumulate wealth. . . .

—*Richard Nixon, 1990*

It is a narrow strip of land, some six hundred acres in all, separated from the Bahamian capital, Nassau, by a mere five hundred yards of water. For two hundred years it was mostly scrub, a neglected place designated by British colonialists as an execution site. They grazed pigs there too and so called it Hog Island. By the mid-1960s it had become a flawed jewel in the Caribbean, a tawdry vacation spot with a casino and a high-rise hotel. In the American underworld some called it Meyer's Island, after mob boss Meyer Lansky, who viewed the Bahamas as an ideal locale in which to revive the gambling fiefdom lost to Fidel Castro. Officially, though, its new name was Paradise Island, and it had become the dream and folly of one of America's richest men.

Huntington Hartford, the A&P grocery chain heir, had decided around 1960 to turn the island into a tropical vacation wonderland. At fifty he was a sad, spoiled roué, but as a famed patron of the arts he wanted to transform Paradise with exquisite taste.

Twenty-five million dollars later the island had a little hotel the color of strawberry ice cream, surrounded by fish pools and shaded by palm trees. There was a gourmet restaurant, the Café Martinique; a golf course; a riding stable; and tennis courts. A medieval Spanish cloister, which had originally been shipped to Florida by William Randolph Hearst, had been painstakingly reconstructed atop a small hill. Visitors were greeted by statues of Hercules, Napoleon's wife Josephine, President Theodore Roosevelt, the explorer David Livingstone, and Faust in the company of the devil.

It was to this odd resort that Nixon, accompanied by Bebe Rebozo, came in November 1962 after his defeat in California. (Also along for the trip, less predictably, was the rotund figure of John Davies, the phone company executive who had helped detect Democratic eavesdroppers during the campaign.) Huntington Hartford greeted the group at the airport and ferried them over to Paradise Island in his launch.

The millionaire had been told these guests needed privacy, a request easy to accommodate because his hotel had no guests. It was so exclusive, and at the time so inaccessible, that it was proving hopelessly unprofitable. Yet Nixon and his friends were never given a bill.

Davies would later recall that Nixon spent much of his time on Paradise alone, "deep in thought." Others said he was very obviously sunk in despair.

The Nixon party continued to have the hotel to themselves until Pat came with the children at Thanksgiving. Then the television personality Jack Paar arrived with his family, on a free trip organized by Hartford's public relations people. Paar, who had interviewed Nixon in the past and hoped to again, remained silent for twenty years before describing the Nixon he had encountered on Paradise Island.

"He was a sad, depressed man," Paar recalled, "as pathetic a national figure as I had ever seen. He was drinking heavily, and my heart went out to his family. . . . Nixon would sit and brood and occasionally utter a few words of profanity. . . ."

Hartford's general factotum Sy Alter, under orders to see that Nixon was well looked after, found him "morose. . . . I pride myself on being a pretty good amateur comedian, but I couldn't get a laugh out of him."

Nevertheless, Nixon later sent Hartford an engraved silver cigarette box by way of thanks. He would return to Paradise in a cheerier mood five years later in December 1967, in the company of a group of businessmen, aristocrats, and fashion models flown in for a lavish celebration, and then again for a similar bash a few weeks later, striking an incongruous figure amid a bevy of what the tabloids used to call the beautiful people.

Much had changed on Paradise in those five years. The parties Nixon attended were to publicize the opening of an opulent new hotel and casino. Guests no longer arrived by boat but in limousines, across an elegant bridge spanning the channel between the island and Nassau. Hartford made an appearance, but he was not in the lineup at the ceremonial opening. Nixon told nothing of this occasion in his memoirs and indeed did not mention the island at all, for good reason.

Hard-eyed, dubious businessmen had taken over from the eccentric millionaire by 1967. The new casino, some would claim, was not unconnected with Meyer Lansky. Even the ownership of the bridge to Paradise involved a shadowy Swiss bank. There was more than a suspicion of criminality about the island, a suspicion that would soon fall on Nixon and Rebozo and fascinate and frustrate those who investigated Watergate.

It is now established historical fact that gambling and its associated sins were brought to the Bahamas by the U.S. Mafia following the Castro revolution in Cuba. Lansky had in 1962 met with confederates—his brother Jake, Charles ("Charlie the Blade") Tourine, Michael ("Trigger Mike") Coppola, Dino Cellini, Max Courtney, and Frank Ritter—at the Fontainebleau Hotel in Miami to discuss starting a casino on Grand Bahama Island.

To overcome the fact that gambling was illegal in the Bahamas,[1] Lansky had offered a two-million-dollar bribe to the chairman of the islands' development board. A lawyer by profession, the chairman "refused," only to accept approximately that sum in "legal fees" for arranging an exemption.[2]

Once the casino in Grand Bahama opened, a Justice Department informant reported, it was soon clear it was being managed mob-style:

> MM T-2 advised that small, thin gold cigarette lighters having a false bottom in which a magnet is placed, are being used by croupiers to control the wheel. . . . These lighters are also used in the dice games. . . . The dice will be loaded. . . . "Dusty" Peters is in the counting room every hour, and when the bank gets low Peters issues orders to all dealers to start "taking" the players.

Soon, with two casinos flourishing, U.S. agents had begun trailing Dan ("Dusty") Peters as he flew twice weekly from the Bahamas to Miami. On each trip he would proceed to a Miami Beach bank, deposit around three hundred thousand dollars, then meet with one of the Lansky brothers at the Fontainebleau. So much money was being generated by the businesses that by 1967 it was being mailed to the banks, parcel post, in cardboard beer cartons.

On Paradise Island, 150 miles across the ocean to the south, Huntington Hartford had been furious when he learned that gambling had been approved on Grand Bahama. His own resort being a financial disaster, he too had applied for a gambling license and a permit to bridge the channel between his island and Nassau. The islands' corrupt development chief, however—the same man who had allowed the mob-backed casinos—had turned Hartford down.

A license to operate a casino on Paradise was finally approved in 1966, but only under new business arrangements that sidelined Hartford. The development chief gave the go-ahead only when Wallace Groves, a convicted swindler with links to the Lansky mob, was brought into the operation. He was to share the majority of the profits with a company run—and this is a very relevant factor in terms of the Nixon connection—by an American businessman named James Crosby.[3] Crosby was also to build the bridge to the island, essential to get the gamblers to the casino.

A Georgetown University graduate and the son of a former U.S. deputy attorney general, Crosby seemed respectable enough when he moved into the Bahamas to start the operation that later became Resorts International, a hotel and casino empire. Careful examination, however, raises questions about his associations. While he saw to it that Groves was removed from the Paradise operation, Crosby did so only after Groves's mob connection had been exposed in *Life* magazine. Meanwhile, he quietly pursued a real estate project with another Lansky man.[4]

Crosby's career has been studied most thoroughly by Alan Block, a professor in the administration of justice at Pennsylvania State University.[5] "The funds amassed to finance the Paradise Island ventures amounted to about $33 million," Block concluded. "Of that sum at least 63 percent appeared to come from or through 'funny money' sources, some directly related to organized crime. . . ."

Even years later lawyers for New Jersey's Gaming Enforcement Division would oppose the granting of a gambling license to Crosby and his company, citing "links with disreputable persons and organizations," and specifically their record on Paradise Island.[6]

As the island changed hands in 1966, a Justice Department official had expressed his view in a now-celebrated memo. "The atmosphere," he wrote, "seems ripe for a Lansky skim." It certainly looked that way.

The first Paradise casino director was Eddie Cellini, who was eventually banned from the islands by the Bahamian government. Crosby's company had transferred him to Florida by then, but again only after he had received adverse publicity. Company officials claimed Cellini was an innocent, vilified only because of his brother Dino, a known Lansky lieutenant. Yet Eddie Cellini had himself worked at two Lansky casinos in Cuba and been indicted during a gambling cleanup in Kentucky.

Six months after Nixon attended the Paradise casino opening, Lansky and Dino Cellini were indicted by the IRS for directing gambling junkets to the island. The first high-ranking mobster to break the Mafia's code of silence, Vincent Teresa, testified that Lansky and Dino Cellini were involved with the Paradise casino as late as 1971. (It was Teresa who styled Paradise "Meyer's Island."[7]) An inspector at the Paradise casino and a former FBI agent specializing in casino crime said Lansky's henchmen "still dictated" to Crosby's people as late as 1973.

—————

Precisely when Nixon became involved with Crosby and the Caribbean gambling milieu is unclear, but he had featured in a Crosby promotion as early as 1960, when he was running for president and Crosby was promoting a new advertising technique. Crosby used a device called the Skyjector to project a mammoth picture of Nixon and a Pepsi bottle cap—in the unlikely company of French film star Brigitte Bardot—onto the side of a Manhattan skyscraper.

Lansky's fixer in the Bahamas, Lou Chesler, contributed cash to the Nixon campaign that year and traveled with the candidate. The pilot who flew Nixon during the campaign went on to work for Chesler. As for Sy Alter, the Hartford aide who looked after Nixon on Paradise Island after the 1962 defeat, he was much more than a mere caretaker and had more than a passing acquaintance with both Nixon and Rebozo.

Frank Smith, a former career FBI agent sent to clean up the Bahamas casinos, described Alter as a "mob guy" linked "back to the Meyer Lansky group from the old days. . . . [He was] Eddie Cellini's man." Professor Block, the expert on Bahamas crime, has written that Alter "had a deserved reputation as a corrupter."

Alter had met with Lansky, the month before Nixon's arrival on Paradise, in connection with the efforts to get a license for a casino on the island. He was already in trouble in the United States at the time, for offenses that would one day lead officials to oppose his working in a casino. Cited for liquor law violations at a store he ran in New York, Alter tried to evade the charges by bribing officials, including a judge. He also attempted to get to U.S. Senator Jacob Javits of New York, in hopes of using Javits's "political influence in the Republican Party."

Far from distancing themselves from such a character, Nixon and Rebozo began a relationship with him. They visited him at his New York liquor store within weeks of the 1962 trip to Paradise Island and while he was still in trouble with the law. Alter saw Nixon in the years that followed, and Nixon took time to call him when he was in the hospital. Alter's relationship with Rebozo became so close that Alter would be admitted to the Florida White House—the Nixon-Rebozo compound—at the height of Watergate.

At the Rebozo bank in Key Biscayne, where Alter conducted numerous transactions, he received special attention. "Alter is a friend of ours," Rebozo told a senior aide. "Treat him well."

Rebozo's solicitude is understandable, both in terms of favors owed and concern about confidentiality. According to the former FBI agent Frank Smith, "both Rebozo and Nixon were in on the negotiations" for the Paradise Island casino license. If true, it was a dubious role for a man harboring presidential ambitions.

The Paradise Island connection was to provide crucial funds for Nixon's successful White House run in 1968. Alter, who stayed on after the Crosby takeover of Paradise, took the initiative. "I knew a lot of people," he recalled. "I felt I could introduce Nixon around. I talked to Crosby and I said, 'I think this wouldn't be a bad deal for you.' I called Bebe and said, 'Crosby may be interested in this campaign.' We set up a meeting, and Crosby met with Bebe at Bebe's place, after closing hours."

Nixon himself then met Crosby, and the casino owner contributed one hundred thousand dollars to the 1968 campaign. At least as much, and perhaps more, came in from Crosby's friends.[8]

Nixon found time that summer to return to Paradise Island to dine with his benefactor. He later attended a party on the *Cosa Grande*, a luxury yacht Crosby placed at the party's disposal during the Republican National Convention.

During the presidency Nixon would personally escort Crosby through the White House. The casino boss, meanwhile, announced that James Golden, who had served Nixon as special assistant and security chief, had joined his staff. Company insiders came to know Golden as "Nixon's man." Ehrlichman recalled "a lot of back and forth" in the Oval Office about helping Crosby's company out, with Rebozo acting as go-between.

Rebozo and White House aides visited Paradise Island during the presidency, but Nixon apparently did not, on the advice of the Secret Service. "Presidents of the United States," as *Barron's* magazine tartly put it, "did not hang out at gambling spots." Instead Nixon met with Crosby on another Bahamian island.[9]

In 1968, at the gala opening of the Paradise casino, Nixon remarked that the island "could be one of the most significant pieces of American investment abroad." It may also have proved a lucrative source of income for him.

"Nixon was a charming man, who—along with Jim Crosby—ended up giving me the shaft." So claimed Huntington Hartford, who wound up years later suing Crosby for depriving him of his slice of Paradise. He sued, in particular, over the profits from the toll bridge linking the island to the mainland, and thereby hangs a mystery.

At $2 a crossing—an exorbitant charge at the time—the bridge was producing significant revenue. It paid for itself by 1969 and from then on brought in $1 million to $1.5 million a year. If one takes the lower figure it was generating, at today's values—nearly $5 million.[10]

It later emerged that 80 percent of the shares in the bridge were held by a group made up of Crosby himself, a colleague linked to the Florida-based company Benguet Consolidated, and an Anglo-Canadian banking concern. The remaining 20 percent was owned by "a number of individuals," represented by a Swiss bank.

Huntington Hartford said early on that he had "reason to believe" that one of those individuals was "a close friend of President Nixon." Privately, he claimed knowledge of massive deposits Nixon had made in a Swiss bank. Crosby, for his part, denied that Nixon or Rebozo were hidden investors in the bridge but refused to identify the unnamed shareholders. Information now available suggests that Hartford's claim was more than the wild allegation of a millionaire who believed he had been bilked.

Former FBI agent Frank Smith, who tied Nixon and Rebozo to the planning of the Paradise Casino, said they were also party to the negotiations over the bridge. As former special assistant to the president of Benguet, Smith was well placed to have such knowledge.

So was Allan Butler, founder of Butler's Bank in Nassau and for some time a partner of rogue financier Robert Vesco. Vesco had reason to be familiar with the affairs of Paradise Island: He tried to buy it. One of the banks that owned the bridge, Butler said, was acting as nominee for Nixon, Rebozo, and a third party. Oral questions to the Nixon White House about these assertions met with flat denials, and a written inquiry went unanswered.[11]

An interviewer had better luck in 1987 with former Attorney General John Mitchell, who had been one of the former president's closest associates. Asked if he knew of offshore holdings owned by Nixon, Mitchell said he was aware of only "whatever he received from his interest in the Paradise Island Bridge." The astonished interviewer asked if he was joking, but Mitchell shook his head. "No," he said slowly. "Nixon had the bridge."

The Nixon story is permeated with rumors of ill-gotten gains. Those who probed Watergate were bombarded with them. "We're not talking about twenty a week," recalled Carl Feldbaum, a Watergate Special Prosecution Force attorney. "We're talking about twenty a day." Even working around the clock, there was not enough time or money to follow up on everything. One such lead, a serious financial allegation, remained unresolved even though, as Feldbaum reported to his boss, it seemed to form "a sound basis for investigation." Fresh research today has uncovered an extraordinary story.

It began on a balmy day in Florida, just weeks after Nixon's 1969 inauguration, when the new president was cruising Biscayne Bay on Rebozo's boat *Cocolobo*. Rebozo had told yacht club members he feared "someone would snap a picture while Nixon was aboard," and the fear proved justified: *Life* photographer George Silk was hidden belowdecks on one of the boats in the harbor, his camera hidden in a sail bag.

As Nixon stepped ashore with several companions, Silk stood up and began taking pictures. Seconds later Secret Service agents came running with guns drawn. It was a frightening moment, the photographer recalled in 1997, but the result was a rare picture of Nixon in casual clothes—and perhaps something much more interesting, something Silk could not have guessed at.

Four years later, in June 1973, a *Seattle Post-Intelligencer* reporter named Michael Buckley received a phone tip about a precious metals dealer, David Silberman, whom the caller alleged to be "involved in large gold transactions with officials of the Committee to Re-elect the President and the White House." Among Silberman's papers, the caller claimed was "a *Life* magazine of February 21, 1969, that included several photographs . . . one of these showed Nixon, Rebozo and Silberman walking along a dock."

Buckley investigated for months. Silberman, he learned, was a known smuggler moving gold and silver across the Canadian border. When tracked down, Silberman admitted having worked for politicians of both parties but denied knowing the president or Rebozo. Confronted with the *Life* photograph, he excused himself and went to the telephone. On his return Silberman said he had never seen the photograph in his life.

Then in his midthirties, Silberman was a commodities dealer by profession with his own company, American Metals Inc. Intimates knew that he lived on the fringe and delighted in taking risks, breaking the rules. Silberman's wife would remember how he once laid a pile of gold bars out in the form of a pyramid on the kitchen table. His secretary was aware of her boss's trips to Swiss banks, trips Silberman would not discuss in detail. His daughter later found a list of twenty-five Swiss bank account numbers among his things.

A number of Silberman's associates, some with their own questionable backgrounds and hence reluctant to speak on the record, have spoken of his links to Las Vegas casinos and mobsters and to a Florida bank tied to Meyer Lansky.

Silberman's wife, Elsie, meanwhile, believed her husband had "a code of integrity of his own." "He was an enigma," said secretary Dee Anne Hill. "Extremely intelligent, secretive, devious, yet possessing a social charisma and a gentle caring for people. Yet, naïve as I was, I felt I should always watch my back." Seven years after Watergate, Silberman would be sent to prison for life, convicted of killing the female companion of a former local Republican official who claimed he had cheated him over a gold deal.

Silberman was himself a Republican, who decades later still spoke of Nixon with admiration. One associate, who counts a close relative of the former president as a friend, told the FBI that "Silberman was given a large amount of cash by [Nixon attorney and fund-raiser] Herbert Kalmbach, for conversion into gold certificates. . . ." Another said he learned, though not from Silberman directly, that Silberman had a "business relationship with Rebozo."

Those once close to Silberman recall that he displayed two framed pictures. One, a signed photograph, showed him with Nixon at some unknown function. The other, which he put up behind the bar at his home with other collectibles, was a copy of the photograph taken at Key Biscayne in 1969 and published in *Life*. It clearly shows Nixon, wearing a windbreaker, with Rebozo at his side in black, walking along the dock. Behind them are three men, two in white polo shirts, one in an open-neck white shirt and dark blazer (see photograph number 37).

Two of Silberman's friends, interviewed for this book, remembered his pointing out the photograph and saying casually that it had been taken at Key Biscayne and that he was one of the men behind Nixon. He did not elaborate, and one of the friends was not especially surprised. "He was open about some things," said Jack Cassinetto, a former colleague, "and very secretive about others."

Elsie Silberman remembered him getting the picture framed. She and their daughter, Kathy, thought it looked like him, and Silberman's own mother believed it was her son. His secretary too saw the likeness. Assuming correctly that two of the men at the rear of the photo were part of the Secret Service escort, the author contacted former Secret Service agent Art Godfrey, who had been head of the detail. Godfrey knew about the photograph, for he too had it framed on his wall.

Godfrey said that he was the man to the left rear of Nixon, that the man in the white to his right was fellow agent Bob Jameson, and—flatly—that the man in dark glasses and blazer was a third agent, Earl Moore. Reached at his home in Florida, Moore insisted that he was indeed the fellow in the blazer.

Yet Moore behaved oddly. Having first agreed to forward a photograph of himself taken during the same period, he abruptly changed his mind. Contacted again, he refused once more and hung up on the interviewer. Godfrey, for his part, had been unusually close to both Nixon and Rebozo. After retiring in 1974, he had visited the disgraced president at San Clemente and watched the Grand Prix with him at Long Beach. Rebozo even asked Godfrey to work for him. As late as 1994 Godfrey was a member of the February Group, an association of diehard Nixon loyalists.

The escutcheon of the Secret Service, rightly admired for its members' courage and efficiency in the physical protection of presidents, was not uncontroversial during the Nixon presidency. Its best-known hero, Rufus Youngblood, decorated for valor during the Kennedy assassination, departed angrily accusing Nixon's close aides of bending the service to their will "like Disneyland." The service allowed itself to be used for political and private purposes, such as spying on Nixon rivals like Edward Kennedy and George McGovern, or surveilling his own brother Donald.

The *New York Times* would write of Nixon's "perversion of the Secret Service" and of "troubling signs that the agency has come to put service to his person ahead of any tradition of public service." Former White House deputy counsel Edward Morgan has claimed that Nixon tried to convert the Secret Service into his personal "secret police." "I was concerned about it," John Ehrlichman recalled. "The Secret Service turned the President down very seldom. They were very willing to please."

The service's loyalty to presidents can persist long after they are gone and in areas remote from its official function. As late as 1992, shown a press picture of himself with President Kennedy in Chicago, a former senior agent suggested ludicrously that the photograph might be a fabrication, in which his head had been pasted onto another person's body. The context, in that interview, was a question about Kennedy's activity with one of his mistresses.[12]

Within this context, one need not unquestioningly accept the assertions of former Secret Service agents about the photograph that allegedly shows Nixon with gold smuggler David Silberman—particularly when a document in the FBI file on the case states flatly that Silberman is indeed the man in the picture.

In 1997 the author was able to interview him, by now a frail, stooped figure looking far older than his fifty-eight years, at the California prison where he was serving out his life sentence.[13] Silberman had at first been reluctant to speak at all, insisting that he was not "into digging up dirt." A woman friend remembered that he had resisted talking to reporters who pressed him in the past, because he had not wanted to hurt Nixon. Also, he seemed nervous about discussing Rebozo. Yet there was a story to be told, he said, one "more interesting than you could ever dream of."

At last, seated in the prison visitors' room, Silberman did talk. He had indeed been on the Florida dock with Nixon when the *Life* photograph was taken, he said, and he explained how the meeting had come about. Silberman had traveled to Florida at the request of Alfred Selix, a wealthy San Franciscan he knew through his father. They had flown to Miami and gone on to Key Biscayne for a luncheon meeting with Nixon and Rebozo. He recalled how, after Selix had introduced him as Mr. David Silberman, he had said nervously, "You can call me Dave." Nixon replied with a straight face, "And you can call me Mr. President." Everyone laughed.

After lunch, alone with Silberman for a while, Rebozo brought the conversation around to money. "I hear you're in banking," he said, making quotation marks in the air around the word "banking." Rebozo evidently knew Silberman laundered money and indicated knowledge of a specific deal in which Silberman was involved. That aside, though, he said nothing further to explain why he or Nixon might be interested in their visitor.

Soon after, accompanied by Secret Service agents, the pair rejoined Nixon for a trip on Rebozo's boat. Silberman remembered the photographer appearing as they came ashore and that his presence caused brief alarm. One of the agents passed him a pair of sunglasses to wear, apparently to make him less recognizable. Then the visit was over.

Nothing compromising had been said that day, and a puzzled Silberman returned to San Francisco. Selix said later that Nixon and Rebozo had been "impressed" with him and he would hear from them.

Two full years later, in the summer of 1971, Silberman said, he received a message asking him to meet the recently retired Republican governor of Nevada, Paul Laxalt, at Harrah's hotel casino in Reno. Silberman agreed, and in the course of their discussion Laxalt asked, as if the question were hypothetical, what Silberman thought might happen if the United States closed "the gold window."

Simply stated, such a step would mean the United States ceased to exchange gold for dollars with other countries at the fixed price. This would be a drastic measure, designed to rescue the dollar as a currency at a moment of potential disaster. It was also, predictably, a move sure to trigger a massive hike in the price of gold on the public market. Silberman told Laxalt that someone who had advance knowledge of such a decision and knew how to operate in that area of finance would have the opportunity to make a fortune. Laxalt revealed that he had such advance knowledge, and asked Silberman to come up with a plan to take advantage of it.

Events then moved swiftly. At a second meeting, Laxalt handed Silberman a satchel containing $215,000 in cash: $180,000 to invest in the gold scheme and $35,000 as a fee for his services. Within days Silberman began buying gold futures through a Canadian bank at a time when, with the gold price virtually static, it seemed a pointless investment. When the gold window did close, however, in August of that year, the opposite proved true: Silberman went to Canada and collected more than $10 million.[14]

Following instructions he had been given in advance, he claimed, he transported the cash to the United States packed in cardboard boxes in the back of a Dodge van. He crossed the border at Peace Arch State Park, in Washington State, and was waved through the customs point—the easiest crossing he had ever experienced. At a prearranged spot north of Seattle he switched vehicles with another driver who was waiting for him. He later learned, he said, that the money "got to where it was supposed to be," which he has always believed was the Republican party.

Silberman had no proof of his story. There is no documentary trail, and he would not reveal who gave him the detailed instructions regarding the border crossing and the cash handover. Paul Laxalt, who later became a U.S. senator and an intimate of President Reagan, responded to a letter from the author in 1999. A spokesman for Laxalt said the former governor "did not recall" having met Silberman and characterized the claim about a cash handover as "absolute fiction."

Allegations have been made in the past linking Laxalt to organized crime. He played a role in an early effort to deliver a secret cash donation to Nixon from the millionaire Howard Hughes, and within months of the episode alleged by Silberman he made a personal appeal to Nixon for the release of the jailed Teamsters leader Jimmy Hoffa, whom he termed a "political prisoner."

Silberman's story ended as it had begun, with direct references to Nixon. In late 1973 or early 1974, he said, he was asked to travel to San Clemente to meet with Nixon. The summons came at a time when Nixon's presidency was sliding to disaster in the welter of Watergate revelations and—as the files show—after the phone tips to the FBI about Silberman. The smuggler recalled driving to the "Western White House," being escorted from the gate, waiting awhile, then seeing Nixon in his study. He remembered the room as having been smallish, with shutters, probably brown, facing the ocean. Nixon, who looked "beat," told Silberman there was a "problem." There might be trouble, and Silberman might be questioned. "About what?" Silberman said he asked. "I don't know anything." It was apparently the right answer, for Nixon thanked him for his services and said "the party" would be grateful.

According to Silberman, he met Nixon one final time, after the fall. In 1976 or 1977 he was asked to attend a small supper gathering at San Clemente. Among the guests, perhaps a dozen of them, was Laxalt. Silberman and Nixon exchanged only small talk, but Nixon amazed him with his recall of personal details: Silberman's wife's name, how many children he had. At the close of the evening he returned home.

How credible is Silberman's story? The closure of the gold window, a measure that could be taken only under an executive order by the president, is a matter of historical record. The possibility had been rumored for some time, and Nixon took the decision against the advice of some of his top advisers. As treasury undersecretary Paul Volcker had forecast at a meeting with the president, gold speculators seized on the moment "to make a mint." The price of gold did indeed shoot up as a result.

Silberman urged the author to contact Alfred Selix, the businessman who, he claimed, took him to his first meeting with Nixon. Selix, however, had died, and his widow said she was not aware of any contact he had had with the president. She confirmed, however, that her husband knew Silberman, as did a mutual woman friend of both men.[15]

Nixon was indeed at San Clemente in late 1973 and early 1974, the period referred to by Silberman.[16] A former senior aide has confirmed that the president's study was laid out as described, brown shutters included, a detail not located by this author in any book.

As for the second alleged visit, another former woman friend of Silberman's recalled—apparently without prior discussion with Silberman—that he had asked her to join him at a social occasion at San Clemente, again during the relevant time frame. She declined because of another commitment, she said, but remembered Silberman describing the evening later and saying Laxalt had been present.

Three witnesses tracked down by the author—the former secretary, a cousin, and another woman friend—recalled Silberman's alluding to contact with Nixon and Rebozo, and a money deal, as early as 1974 and again in the years that followed. If Silberman's account is untrue, he was telling fragments of it in private long ago.

There this particular trail ends, but the story does not stand as an isolated incident.

———

Just months before the Silberman scam, across the continent in Florida, a wealthy divorcée named Elizabeth Newell, whose family owned a newspaper in Indiana,[17] moved into a high-rise apartment on Key Biscayne. From the windows of her new abode, with the island laid out before her, she could see Bebe Rebozo's Key Biscayne Bank. "I decided to move my money there," she recalled in 1998. "With the president of the United States' best friend running it, how could it be anything but safe? What could possibly go wrong?" Newell was, as she put it, "a good Republican."

As it turned out, much was to go wrong for Newell. A large part of her capital was to vanish irretrievably, and she would find herself encumbered with information about the president it would have been safer not to know.

At the bank her business was placed in the hands of the vice president in charge of the Trust Department, Franklin DeBoer. He had landed this senior post, he later told investigators, purely on the basis of answering an advertisement in the local newspaper. Rebozo, he said, thought him "the most honest man I have ever met."

In fact, DeBoer's wife had known Rebozo for twenty years, and he himself had met Rebozo a year before he got the job.[18] It may not be irrelevant that he was also acquainted with James Crosby, the Rebozo friend who ran the Paradise Island casino, and his principal partner, who had been DeBoer's college roommate. He had first met Crosby, he admitted, "in days gone by when I was on Wall Street." Both Crosby and his partner had accounts at Key Biscayne Bank.[19]

In New York, less than a year before he had been hired by Rebozo, the Securities and Exchange Commission had barred DeBoer from working as a broker on charges that he had sold unregistered stock and appropriated to himself more than three hundred thousand dollars from a public company.[20] Two years earlier the New York Stock Exchange had expelled him for making false statements and refusing to give testimony. He would eventually be jailed for filing false registration documents in Florida.

Not long after becoming a client at the bank, Elizabeth Newell started seeing DeBoer socially. "He was personable and fairly good-looking," she recalled ruefully. "I was single, and I assumed he was. We began meeting for dinner two or three times a week. He was kind of a bore, not the romantic type. But when he drank, he became more talkative. He'd talk too much."

When he became loquacious, DeBoer had startling things to say. "We were at a restaurant in Miami," Newell remembered. "He was sort of bragging that he would tell me what was going on in the bank. He said, 'They hired me because what they wanted done; they knew I knew how to do it.' He told me he could tell me what was going on in the bank concerning Nixon, and the illegal funds, the money that was coming in for Nixon. At the beginning it was illegal campaign funds filtered through the Bahamas. Later it was going straight to Nixon's portfolio."

Newell was frightened by what she heard or, rather, by the potential danger she felt she might be placed in by being privy to it. After her newspaper executive nephew urged her to share the information with some reputable person as soon as possible, she spoke on condition of anonymity with a trusted ABC Television reporter and—later—with Watergate investigators. Her name has remained secret until now, as have her contemporary notes, which she supplied to the author.

Encouraged to keep up the contact, Newell went on seeing DeBoer. He talked of direct phone lines from the bank to the White House, of secret contributions to Nixon: an unnamed sum from Howard Hughes, five hundred thousand dollars from *Reader's Digest,* three hundred thousand from Pepsi-Cola. She got the impression that the supply of money for Nixon was "endless."

The coffers were filled with illegal funds, according to DeBoer, by contributors who traveled to Paradise Island and "lost" money at the casino, which would then be brought back to the United States. Those who transported the money, he said, included the casino boss, James Crosby, and Sy Alter, friend of Nixon and Rebozo since 1962.

The Paradise PR man, Ed Woodruff, said it was "his information and belief" that "large sums of money from the casino were transferred to Bebe Rebozo's bank." The casino's cashier, Richard Stearns, recalled meeting Alter at the bank after hours so that he could exchange twenty-dollar bills for larger denominations.[21] All dealings with Alter, Stearns said, took place on Rebozo's personal instructions. Rebozo's guidance on how to handle Alter, DeBoer told investigators, was: "There are lots of things you don't ask questions about. Just let him to do what he wants." DeBoer categorized Alter as "a bagman."

At the request of her ABC-TV contact, Newell conducted some of her final conversations with DeBoer with a tape recorder under the coffee table—and a bodyguard close by.[22] Her efforts to get him to repeat some of his contentions resulted in the following exchange:

> DEBOER: You do step across the line a little too much. I have to push you back, all right? . . . I happen to work for Mr. Rebozo, Mr. Abplanalp,[23] and Mr. Nixon.
>
> NEWELL: You work for Mr. Nixon?
>
> DEBOER: Yes, I work for Mr. Nixon—which is rather none of your business. I happen to draw a substantial salary outside the bank from them, for doing this. That's obviously what those bastards are trying to prove.
>
> NEWELL: What do you work for, for Mr. Nixon?
>
> DEBOER: Who do you think runs the private portfolios for these people at the bank? . . . If you do this for people—you know—I have a salary substantially more than the bank pays me, from fees from them.

With such a salary, DeBoer said, "I don't go out and piss in their face." Stressing that he was sworn to secrecy, he asked: "When two people I'm directly involved with say this is the policy I wish to have adhered to, what would you do? Go out there and say, 'Fuck thee, Nixon.'"

As the pressure of the Watergate investigation mounted on Rebozo, on the bank, and on himself in particular, DeBoer grew nervous and urged Newell to forget everything he had told her. Were she to be questioned, he advised, "Always say you 'don't recall.'" Later, confronted privately by investigators with what Newell quoted him as saying, he would claim it had all been a fabrication. "Don't ask me," he said, "why I said it."

"If they find out about it all," DeBoer had told Newell, "Rebozo will go to jail and Nixon will have to resign." But, he added, "It's all buried so deep they'll never find it."

"Burying money deep" usually means caching it in a secret bank account, often abroad, and is by definition beyond discovery by the U.S. tax authorities. "I have no foreign bank accounts, had none, don't have any," Nixon would tell interviewer David Frost in 1977. "I have no foreign assets at all." Yet even before he was engulfed in scandal, evidence that he did have assets abroad flickered briefly into view.

It came about as the result of Operation Tradewinds, a twelve-year-long IRS investigation that targeted individuals who hid their money in the Bahamas. The project was spearheaded by Richard Jaffe, a Florida-based agent of the IRS Intelligence Division commended by Robert Kennedy for his work against the Mafia and—as late as 1988—by the future U.S. attorney general, then a Florida state attorney, Janet Reno. For Tradewinds Jaffe set up an intricate information network, one that was to finger mafiosi, drug smugglers, casino developers, Hollywood figures, and crooked bankers.

One day in autumn 1972, at the end of Nixon's first term, one of Jaffe's key operatives, fifty-one-year-old Norman Casper, gained access to a suspect financial institution in Nassau. Casper was an experienced informant, known in the IRS at the time as TW-24, "TW" for Tradewinds. The financial institution in question was Castle Bank and Trust Company, on Frederick Street.

Castle Bank had come under suspicion because a narcotics violator was using it to hide money. Cash deposits had been flowing into a Miami bank without any name identification, then on into Castle's closed vault in the Bahamas. IRS headquarters wanted a list of the bank's other account holders, a tall order indeed. Informant TW-24, however, delivered.

Thanks to a cunning use of his contacts and a pretext that hid his IRS connection, Casper found himself ushered into a small conference room at the bank and left alone to peruse documents related to his ostensible request. He scanned the shelves not very hopefully in search of his real target, and then, right at his feet beneath a pile of folders, he spotted a "brand-new IBM printout of customers' names, approximately four inches thick, perforated and folded over as it comes out of the machine. I looked at the door, and it was closed. . . . I reached down and leafed through it."

Worried that a bank official might come in any moment, Casper ran his eye down the hundreds of names on the list. Many of them were companies. Others, like that of Las Vegas racketeer Moe Dalitz, were known criminals. Then came a total shock. "One of the first names I saw," Casper recalled, "was the name of Richard Nixon. . . . Lo and behold! That name kind of took the wind out of my sails. When that happened, I think I sat there, got a little bit quiet. . . ." The entry was troubling not least because it was complete with middle initial—"Richard M. Nixon," as well as an account number.

Casper reported the discovery verbally to his employer, agent Jaffe, and the wider investigation continued. Jaffe now wanted a copy of the full customers' list, and soon—by dint of a cloak-and-dagger trick that involved separating a bank official from his briefcase while he dined with an attractive woman—Casper managed that too. The document was photographed, page by page, by IRS agents.

There were more than three hundred names on that copy and on another that surfaced later. They included *Playboy* publisher Hugh Hefner, *Penthouse*'s Bob Guccione, the actor Tony Curtis, members of the rock group Creedence Clearwater Revival, and Leonard Hall, former chairman of the Republican party and long a Nixon intimate. Of "Richard M. Nixon" himself, however, there was no longer any trace.

An internal IRS report suggested that since the initial sighting, the entry had been "purged from the Castle records or otherwise concealed." The probe established that at various stages records were indeed transferred or shredded. As Casper observed, it was surely madness for Nixon's name to have been openly listed in the first place. With Watergate making news in the months after Casper's penetration of the records, to remove it would have been an obvious precaution.

The story did briefly surface publicly much later, well after Nixon's resignation and then only in an oblique sort of way.[24] When it did, the Castle Bank manager, faced with indictments and extradition proceedings, said it was "unlikely . . . in fact, impossible" that Nixon's name had been on the list the IRS had obtained. (No one, of course, had ever claimed that it had been.) The former president of the bank, which lost its license and closed in 1977, tried another tack in an interview with the author. "I am absolutely positive," Samuel Pierson said, "that the Nixon the idiot read about was a black Bahamian."

That intriguing notion does not stand up to scrutiny. The name Nixon is not uncommon in the Bahamas, but thorough research involving old voters' lists, telephone directories, and personal interviews has turned up no Richard M. Nixon.[25] Bahamian citizens, moreover, were prohibited by law from holding accounts in offshore institutions like Castle Bank.

A 1972 article in a Nassau newspaper confirms that as the IRS operative recalled, Castle Bank was transferring its records to a new computer at the very time Casper spotted the Nixon name and account number. The man responsible for that process, a Canadian named Alan Bickerton, said in 1997 that he had been aware of the identity of all the bank's customers. Asked if one of them had been *the* Nixon, however, he declined to answer. "I'm not prepared to discuss it at all," he said. "It wouldn't matter if it were Richard Nixon or the prime minister of Canada. I wouldn't discuss it with you. . . ."

Never satisfactorily resolved, the matter was lost in a troubling upheaval within the IRS.[26] Higher-ups suspended the Jaffe probe, blowing its cover in the process. There was a protracted internal row, with dark hints about the fact that IRS Commissioner Donald Alexander was a Nixon appointee and that his old law firm's name appeared on an index card at the Castle Bank office. Alexander denounced such attacks as the smear tactics of "faceless liars."

A final odd twist is the reaction of the man who stumbled upon Nixon's name in the first place, and his experiences afterward. Far from trumpeting his discovery when testifying to a House committee probing IRS practices, former informant Norman Casper ventured the opinion that the name might have gotten onto the list because someone "had too many martinis . . . got to playing." The explanation is implausible but should be interpreted in the context of the fact that the printout especially disturbed Casper because, he told members of the committee, "neighbors of mine were involved."

What he meant by "neighbors" emerged in a 1996 conversation with the author, as Casper, a decent man highly respected by his IRS colleagues, gradually relaxed his guard. His full story is filled with ironies. A resident of Key Biscayne long before he became an IRS operative, Casper knew Nixon and Rebozo personally. He had met Nixon when he came to stay at the Key Biscayne Hotel, and the Nixon girls had even looked after Casper's daughters at the beach. He had met Pat Nixon and admired her greatly. Casper was in fact a conservative Republican, active enough at one point to have served on the local Republican committee.

Casper likewise characterized Rebozo as "a pretty good friend." The men had met in the early fifties, and Casper had even run background checks on prospective employees of the Key Biscayne Bank. He had worked for Rebozo as recently as 1969, not long before he was hired by the IRS. For Casper, finding Richard M. Nixon's name on the Castle Bank customers' list was the one blemish on an otherwise triumphant operation. It was the last thing he had expected, or wished, to find. As he told the author, "I didn't want to believe it."

After Casper had testified in Washington, Rebozo's secretary called to say her boss wanted to see him urgently. He consulted with IRS colleagues, then agreed to meet Rebozo at his office. The president's friend wanted to know if Casper had actually seen a Nixon *account* at the Castle Bank. Casper replied that he had seen only the customers' list. Rebozo then told him that a Nixon attorney had been to the Bahamas and found "incontrovertible proof" that there was no such account. He produced the lawyer, who had been waiting in a nearby room, and got Casper to tell his story again.

Nixon was "very angry," Rebozo told Casper, and then asked him about the state of his own finances. When Casper replied that they were not flourishing, Rebozo expressed "dismay" and said he "hoped the situation would improve." A week later he called about nothing in particular and said again that he hoped Casper's financial situation "would improve in the near future."

Casper promptly reported these conversations orally and in writing to his IRS contact, a record of which has survived.

If Nixon did have offshore holdings, what were they worth? The original Castle customers' list of course showed only a name and an account number. Although the briefcase later "borrowed" from a bank official contained the list on which Nixon's name did *not* appear, it also held records of Castle's bank and brokerage accounts, copies of ledgers, and extensive correspondence showing how investments were being managed.

Casper, who was present as IRS photographers took pictures of the papers, was provided with copies of some of them for his work. They included this document, which Casper has provided to the author. It has never been published before:

```
Cosmos, Zurich.  Acct. #479 326 08 ZRA
Acct. in name of Zepher Group. (N&R)

DEPOSITS:

10/21/71 :   3,772,423
 4/10/72 :  10,427,920
 6/11/72 :  21,682,727
 4/23/73 :   6,962,275


All funds came through the Bahamas


Good luck

          m
```

Taken at face value—and there is no reason to doubt what Casper says about its origins—the document appears to be a typed note summarizing four deposits in the Cosmos Bank in Switzerland. It does not indicate whether the sums listed represent U.S. dollars or Swiss francs. If in dollars, then the total of the Swiss bank holding was the immense amount of $42,845,345. If, as more likely, the reference was to Swiss francs, then the dollar equivalent was $11,157,642.[27]

The annotation, stating that the funds deposited had flowed through the Bahamas, appears to be a note between bank officials. The "Good luck" is unexplained, and the identity of the writer, "m," uncertain.[28]

Interest in the document of course turns on only one question: Do the initials in parentheses, N & R, refer to Nixon and Rebozo?

The use of initials is consistent with two of Rebozo's other business arrangements. A real estate partnership with banker Sloan McCrae was titled R & M Properties. A company Rebozo formed with Nixon's friend Bob Abplanalp became B & C Investments, *B* apparently for Bob and *C* for Charles (Rebozo's rarely used given name).

According to Casper, the N & R document was one of the many items from the Castle briefcase shared with Herschel Clesner, the chief counsel of the House Commerce and Monetary Affairs Subcommittee. Clesner, who had developed contacts in the Swiss banking community, believed it did signify a record of massive Nixon and Rebozo holdings in a foreign bank.

Casper at first seemed to regret having shown the author the Cosmos document and became highly defensive of Nixon. "I'm not going to clarify a goddamn thing," he said, sitting in the living room of his modest Florida home. "Nobody got killed. Let it go. The man has enough problems. Some things are better forgotten." Now in his seventies, Casper made it clear that he was going to take the story with him "to the crematorium."

Later, however, Casper admitted that a Castle Bank source had "indicated" to him that the "N & R" did refer to Nixon and his best friend. When Casper raised the matter with another staff member, he said, "she clammed up like you wouldn't believe."

The Swiss bank document, or most of the information in it, matches that provided by another source. In the 1980s, during a meeting with a reporter in his Manhattan home, the A&P heir Huntington Hartford produced a piece of paper with the same Cosmos Bank account number and three of the four deposit amounts that appear on the document seized by the IRS from the briefcase.

In 1996, elderly and ill, Hartford would not discuss the matter. "Do you want to blacken Nixon's name?" he asked. "Don't do it. I didn't think he was so bad. Why would I care if Nixon had an account in a Swiss bank?"

Hartford almost certainly came by his information on the deposits from investigators working on the lawsuit he brought against his Paradise Island partners.* Available information strongly suggests a Paradise Island connection with both Castle Bank and Cosmos.

Some of the stock of James Crosby's company, which bought the island from Hartford, was held at Castle Bank. Cosmos Bank subsidiaries, meanwhile, owned 20 percent of the shares in the Paradise Island bridge, the bridge said to have been partly owned by Nixon.[29]

In the year of the briefcase seizure Cosmos Bank was a well-established Swiss *Privatbank* operating from an inconspicuous fourth-floor office just off the Bahnhofstrasse, in Zurich. While it revealed little about its dealings, its main activities were described as "business with the United States." One of Cosmos's early directors had been Robert Anderson, a secretary of the treasury

---

*See this chapter, p. 244.

under Eisenhower, later convicted on charges connected with yet another off-shore bank.[30] Cosmos had subsidiary offices in New York, on Park Avenue, and in the Bahamas.

The author's investigation into this matter led him to visit the legendary district attorney of New York County, Robert Morgenthau. As U.S. attorney in the sixties Morgenthau had been the scourge of organized crime, a particular foe of Meyer Lansky's and the first senior U.S. law enforcement figure to probe the arcane secrets of Swiss bank accounts. It was a course that eventually cost him his job.

At nearly eighty, pacing his vast cavern of an office in lower Manhattan, Morgenthau recalled how, during the investigations of several cases, "Nixon's name kept coming up."[31] "We were looking at Paradise Island," said Morgenthau, "and that led us to Nixon. We didn't have an open investigation of him, but we were going to open one." When the author shared with Morgenthau the document showing the "N & R" accounts at the Cosmos Bank, the district attorney reacted strongly. He had never seen it before, but his probe had led him in exactly that direction. He had information on a visit Nixon had made to a Paris attorney, an expert in helping people set up Swiss bank accounts. "I have no doubt," Morgenthau said, "that he used Cosmos. He may have used something else too. But he certainly used that bank."

When Nixon became president, New York's U.S. attorney was working with the House Banking and Currency Committee to formulate a new law that would have made it much harder for U.S. citizens and corporations to operate secret accounts abroad. Long before it materialized, however, Nixon removed Morgenthau from office—over the protests of senior Republicans as well as Democrats. The new law curbing the use of foreign bank accounts was eventually passed, in 1972, but in attenuated form.

The author's interview with Morgenthau brought him once again to the issue of Nixon's alleged financial interest in the Paradise Island toll bridge. "We had Cosmos people, the American branch of Cosmos, before the grand jury," said District Attorney Morgenthau, "and they were asked who owned the 20 percent investment in the Paradise Island bridge. They said, 'We own it.' We said: 'Have you ever made another direct stock investment?' And they could not tell us of any such investment they'd ever made. I don't have any doubt they were holding that for Richard Nixon. Could I prove it? No. Am I sure of it? Yes."

Cosmos Bank failed in 1974, and chronologically the trail ends there—except for an item District Attorney Morgenthau received through the mail in 1997, a single sheet of paper sent anonymously.[32] It reads:

NIXON'S SWISS BANK ACCOUNT
BANK CANTRADE, BLEICHERWEG 30, ZURICH 8039
051-36 23 60 AS OF EARLY 70
SUBSIDIARY OF UBS
BAERWALD & DEBOER FLORIDA (REBOZO)

"UBS" stands for Union Bank of Switzerland, the largest Swiss bank, specializing in investment management for private clients. Bank Cantrade, which is part of it, advertised—as late as 1998—"absolute loyalty towards our clients . . . trust discretion, performance, and continuity."

Even though this was an anonymous communication, the reference to Baerwald & DeBoer is interesting. That was the securities firm that had been run by Franklin DeBoer, the trust officer at Rebozo's bank and the man who said he managed "private portfolios" for Nixon and Rebozo.

This account of Nixon's alleged secret funds has thus come full circle. If the late nineties communication received by Morgenthau was mere fiction and mischief, it was put together by a cognoscente. The DeBoer connection is an obscure one, not exposed at length anywhere until publication of this book.

Finally, the man who raised funds for Nixon through three election campaigns, and a staunch loyalist, let slip an interesting detail shortly before his death. "Rebozo," said Maurice Stans in a 1997 interview, "was a very nice guy, a sweet fellow. . . . He told me, 'I've set up a trust fund for Richard Nixon's family—to take care of the family.' The only money set aside for Nixon was through Bebe's generosity. Bebe told me that."

Stans said the fund, which he believed was started in 1968, never became public knowledge, and he himself never learned of its extent.[33] It was therefore initiated years before the first of the large deposits made in Zurich's Cosmos Bank in the names of "N & R," according to the document seized by the IRS.

A Swiss hotelier, Raoul de Gendre, met Nixon while he was working in the United States. He later returned to Switzerland, to become manager of the Dolder Grand Hotel in Zurich. A fan of Nixon, whose photographs cover the walls of his present place of business, de Gendre has fond memories of their further encounters. He has recalled that throughout the eighties, sometimes accompanied by Pat, often by Rebozo, Nixon traveled to Zurich every single year.

21

*He has been vaporized by political nukes half a dozen
times and resurrected by his own hand. He has
breathed into his own mouth.*

—Bryce Harlow, Nixon friend and adviser

Whatever his future fortune was to be, Nixon claimed enduring financial
hard times after the 1962 defeat. Pat was "nagging him about their
plight," according to a source close to the family, and wanted to get out of California. It was a plan that suited Nixon well, even as he once more promised
her that he would never run for public office again. Within a month of his loss
to Pat Brown, Nixon had met with intimates in a suite at New York's Waldorf-
Astoria to discuss how to keep himself politically in play. New York in fact
seemed the one place where resurrection might be possible.

To that end, Nixon wanted an attorney's job in Manhattan, one that
would pay $250,000 a year and leave him free to use his time as he liked. "He
had to have his cake, money," said one aide, "and eat it too—pursue his interest in foreign policy."

One account suggested it was Rebozo, working with DuPont heir Ed Ball
and World War I flying ace Eddie Rickenbacker, who landed him such a position. Another—the version Nixon perpetuated—held that pharmaceuticals tycoon Elmer Bobst arranged it. In any event, Nixon became a senior partner of
a New York law firm, thenceforth to be known as Nixon, Mudge, Rose,
Guthrie and Alexander.

The Wall Street firm was a long-established champion of big business, de-

scribed by *Life*'s Hugh Sidey as a place where "the faces inside are commanding but for the most part unrecognizable . . . the talk about corporations and
dollars." Its lawyers served their clients by guarding their money from taxa-
tion, negotiating bond issues, and administering estates. The company existed
primarily for the manipulation of big money.

Lucrative job offer in hand, the Nixons found a home to suit their stature,
a $135,000 Upper East Side apartment with a view of Central Park and Gov-
ernor Nelson Rockefeller as a neighbor.[1] With their daughters and Manolo
and Fina Sanchez, the Spanish valet and housekeeper who had become permanent members of the household[2]—and their now geriatric dog Checkers—they
moved east in June 1963. No one in California gave them a going-away party.

Pat was to describe their time in New York as a "six-year vacation." She
decorated the apartment in "French provincial," all pastel yellows and golds,
and remodeled the twin-bedded master bedroom. Her "Republican cloth
coats" were now joined in the walk-in closet by a mink. She sent her daughters
to Chapin, the fashionable private school for girls, and in due course would
launch them as debutantes. In spite of such conformity with the social requirements, Nixon was not readily welcomed into the bastion of the eastern establishment. "They just didn't want to go to dinner with Nixon," recalled an
acquaintance of one attempt to corral guests for a dinner party.

Nixon applied for and obtained admission to the New York bar, respond-
ing to one question with praise for the Constitution's safeguards against the
misuse of power. He worked from a twenty-fourth-floor office at Nixon,
Mudge, Rose, seated at an antique desk adorned with a vice presidential ash-
tray and a pen set Eisenhower had given him. As the new "name" partner,
Nixon brought the firm prestige. Powerful backers, Pepsi's Don Kendall and
Bob Abplanalp of Precision Valve, now moved their legal business to Nixon,
Mudge, Rose.

The firm and its clients were attuned to Nixon's politics. Milton Rose, a
senior partner, had led the promotion of U.S. business in Latin America after
the riots during Nixon's vice presidential tour. The firm had represented
shipowner Stavros Niarchos during the tussle with Aristotle Onassis over oil
shipping routes, directed from Washington by Nixon.* Corrupt San Diego
banker Arnholt Smith, a Nixon contributor, would use Nixon, Mudge, Rose to
fight a case for him. It may not be incidental that during Nixon's tenure the
firm had as a client the government of South Vietnam.

From the office on Broad Street, Nixon wrote to a judge requesting leniency for Mario García Kohly, the rightist exile—now in trouble on counterfeiting charges—whom he had once pressed on the CIA as the potential leader
of free Cuba. He also worked to recover the millions of dollars claimed by relatives of the assassinated Dominican Republic dictator Rafael Trujillo; thirty

*See p. 195–.

million dollars had reportedly vanished in a plane crash that killed Kohly's primary financial backer.[3]

It would be the firm's business that put Nixon in Dallas on the day that John Kennedy was assassinated. Public courtesies aside, their feelings about each other had remained suffused with rancor. "It makes me sick," Kennedy said privately of *Six Crises,* deprecating the saccharine way Nixon had woven his family into the text. "He's a cheap bastard." "Bastards" was the description Nixon used of the Kennedys, too, as he smarted over tax audits he believed they had ordered.

Five months before the assassination, both men had happened to be in Rome at the same time. Both had appointments to meet the newly elected pope, Paul VI. On learning that the president's visit had lasted thirty minutes, Nixon contacted the U.S. consul general to insist that his audience be "exactly as long as the one Kennedy had." Before ending his state visit, the president telephoned Nixon at his hotel. "He just wanted to say hello," Nixon recalled. The two men never spoke again.

Early on the morning of November 22, Nixon was in a suite at Dallas's Baker Hotel, winding up two days' work for Pepsi at a bottlers' convention.[4] In a city seething with anti-Kennedy feeling, he had not been able to resist mixing politics with business, telling local journalists, "I am going to work as hard as I can to get the Kennedys out." Kennedy was reportedly irritated by this comment, the latest of several Nixon outbursts, as he scanned the newspapers that last morning. He may or may not have noted that along with the criticism, Nixon had expressed the hope that Dallas would give Kennedy a "courteous reception."

Nixon flew out on a commercial flight just two and a half hours before Kennedy arrived in Dallas aboard Air Force One. By the time he arrived in New York, the president would be dying. Unaware of the assassination, Nixon threw out more anti-Kennedy barbs to a group of reporters at the airport, posed cheerfully for photographers, and hailed a cab. On the way into town the cab was stationary at a red light when a man rushed up to ask if the driver had heard the news: Shots had been fired at the president. At Nixon's home in Manhattan a weeping doorman told him Kennedy was dead. He rushed into the apartment to find his daughters watching the tragedy unfold on television.

The writer Stephen Hess, arriving minutes later, found Nixon "very shaken. He took out the Dallas morning paper, which had a story about the press conference he had had the day before. He had talked about how the people of Dallas should have respect for their political adversaries. . . . He was saying to me in effect, 'You see, I didn't have anything to do with creating this.' He was very concerned then that Kennedy had been assassinated by a right-winger and that somehow Nixon would be accused of unleashing political hatred."

As Hess listened, Nixon placed a call to FBI Director Hoover, who told him that he believed the alleged assassin Lee Harvey Oswald was in fact a leftist, leaving Nixon "somewhat relieved." His reaction, Hess recollected, was "There but for the grace of God go I."[5]

That night Nixon wrote to Jacqueline Kennedy recalling that he and her husband had been "personal friends." He attended the funeral in Washington[6] with Pat at his side. A year later, in an article for *Reader's Digest,* he would praise his former rival's "keen intelligence, his great wisdom and vitality."

The sourness, however, remained. In the eighties he attributed the nation's sense of loss at Kennedy's death to "mythology" and argued that Kennedy's achievements were "not so much what he did, but the man, the style." Haldeman said Nixon had "neither respected nor liked" the slain president.

When Nixon in turn reached the White House, a former Secret Service agent recalled, "It sometimes seemed that he went out of his way to take his place as a martyr beside Jack Kennedy. In his first term Nixon's favorite limo was said to be SS 100X, the restored midnight blue eight-thousand-pound Lincoln Continental that Kennedy had been shot in."

The tragedy had one important ramification for Nixon. "History intervened," his colleague Len Garment noted. "John Kennedy's death had the ironic consequence of restoring Richard Nixon to life as a national political figure." Nixon had sensed his opportunity immediately. Stopping by at his apartment again the morning after the assassination, Hess found him huddled with key Republicans, "already assessing how this event would affect or re-create the possibilities of Nixon running for president."

"I never wear a hat," Nixon would respond, when asked on *The Arthur Godfrey Show* whether he planned to run in 1964, "so it must always be in the ring."

"If all I had was my legal work," Nixon was soon telling friends, "I would be mentally dead in two years and physically dead in four . . . there was no other life for me but politics. . . ."

On a visit to the New York World's Fair, his daughter Julie recalled, a Republican companion was warned in advance to "not bring up politics with my mother." However, as soon as Pat and the girls were packed off to Europe for a month, Nixon immersed himself in the 1964 campaign.

While his declared role was one of neutrality, he initially tried to position himself as an alternative to Barry Goldwater. When that scheme failed, he made a highly successful convention speech. Even as the red, white, and blue balloons floated down upon Goldwater, nominated but on his way to the worst Republican defeat in thirty years, Nixon was once again being spoken of as a future leader.

The political machine was running again, and Nixon already knew which image of himself he would present to win over his countrymen. It was the image that he hoped would be his legacy: that of world statesman par excellence.

On a night flight to Europe, after several martinis, Nixon had a prompt response for a friend who wondered why in the world he would want to run for president again.

"Because I know the fucking Commie mind," he replied. "But they don't know mine. I really think I could do something. I really believe I could make a contribution to peace."

Nixon's law firm colleague Len Garment had previously been a Democrat and "reflexive Nixon denigrator." Now, though, he joined the Nixon camp. One night in Florida in 1965, in a rare intimate interlude, Nixon seemed to open his heart to Garment.

After dinner with Elmer Bobst, the two men headed for a newly built house that had been placed at their disposal. Then, fearing the developers might use his presence for publicity purposes, Nixon ordered the driver to return to the Bobst estate. The gates were locked—it was after midnight—and Nixon and Garment got in by climbing over the wall.

"We didn't want to wake up Elmer," Garment remembered, "so we found the pool house, where there were two camp beds. There Nixon was, with his big head sticking over the covers. The lights were off, but he couldn't sleep—he never could—and he just kept talking. He talked for what must have been an hour, sounding sad and determined, about the things that meant a lot to him. If he couldn't live in politics, he said, how was he to live? We had been talking about him running for president. And he said that if he couldn't play a real role, on that front or otherwise, he'd be dead very soon.

"It was a soliloquy," said Garment. "He was talking himself to sleep." Nixon declared himself driven "by his pacifist mother's idealism and the profound importance of foreign affairs. . . . He would do anything, make any sacrifice, to be able to continue using his talents and experience in making foreign policy."

As the historian Michael Beschloss has noted, Nixon was "a romantic and ardent champion of the great man theory of politics." Of all the world leaders whose careers he studied, he revered one above all others, Charles de Gaulle. When he announced his move to New York, Nixon had said Paris was to be his secondary base of operations. Within weeks he made a trip there, paying court to de Gaulle, whom he had first met in Washington in 1960. The general was now five years into his extraordinary eleven-year rule, a period during which he wielded more power over his nation than any French leader since Emperor Napoleon III.

Seated with Nixon on the terrace of the Élysée Palace, de Gaulle held forth on world affairs. He said the United States should negotiate with China, urged that it improve relations with the Soviets, and introduced Nixon to a term he had not heard before, détente. Most important of all, de Gaulle raised his glass in a toast his guest never forgot. Nixon, he declared, would someday return to serve his country "in an even higher capacity."

The older man's confidence won his guest's lasting devotion. Nixon gazed admiringly on de Gaulle at John F. Kennedy's funeral, visited him on every trip to Paris while out of office, sent an emissary to him during the 1968 run for the White House, and made an audience with him the high point of his first European trip as president.

Henry Kissinger believed that the respect was mutual. General Vernon Walters, who interpreted for them, said de Gaulle treated Nixon "as an equal." Nixon was, however, as Haldeman put it, "in awe" of de Gaulle. Writing about the French president, Nixon referred to him by his full name, Charles André Joseph Marie de Gaulle. It resonated, Nixon thought, with echoes of Charlemagne, the eighth-century emperor Charles the Great, and of Roman Gaul—"grandeur, glory, greatness."

Nixon noted without demurring that the Frenchman had no use for the parliamentary system, that he thought "Members of parliament can paralyze action, they cannot initiate it."[7] "Authority," he quoted de Gaulle as arguing, "derives from prestige . . . there can be no prestige without mystery."

No book in Nixon's library reportedly was more well thumbed or more densely annotated than de Gaulle's 1960 memoir, *The Edge of the Sword*. He underscored passages like: "Powerful personalities . . . frequently lack that surface charm that wins popularity. . . ." Also, "Great men of action . . . have without exception possessed to a very high degree the faculty of withdrawing into themselves."

As early as 1960, the year he met de Gaulle, CBS's Nancy Dickerson watched the Nixons board an airplane "as if they were traveling royalty on an imperial state visit." She believed Nixon had even then "studied de Gaulle and was already trying to emulate him." Robert Finch thought the same, as did Bob Haldeman.

"He feels he should be more aloof, inaccessible, mysterious, i.e. de Gaulle . . ." the chief of staff would note after a session with Nixon after arriving in the White House. And soon after de Gaulle died: "We discussed the general P.R. question . . . especially since the death of de Gaulle we have a real opportunity to build the P as *the* world leader. . . ."

On a state visit to Paris Nixon publicly extolled his mentor as "a giant among men." Defense Secretary James Schlesinger, who agreed that Nixon tried to imitate de Gaulle, suggested dryly in a 1997 interview that therein lay the difference: Nixon was "a shrewd, calculating figure, but no giant. He would have liked to have been more giant than he was. He was not capable of being de Gaulle."

To establish himself as a master world statesman, Nixon began an extensive program of travel. In 1963, during what was supposed to be a family vacation, he saw, in addition to de Gaulle, Spain's Franco, President Nasser of Egypt, Italy's defense minister, the British foreign secretary, and West Germany's Adenauer.

Touring East Berlin behind its newly erected wall, he filed a news report on the excursion in breathless tabloid tones. "As we were walking along the street searching for a taxi, a shadowy figure walked up to us and said, 'Do you have a cigarette?' . . . The man looked around and said, 'Our only hope is with the Americans.'"

Nixon's guide in the Eastern sector, BBC correspondent Charles Wheeler, recalled how Nixon leaped out of the car on Stalin Allee to hand out visiting cards inscribed "Vice President of the United States of America," a post he had not held for nearly two years. To the bemused Wheeler, Nixon seemed "weird . . . Totally mad."

Two years later, while in Finland, he decided on a whim to make the twenty-hour train journey to Moscow. A Canadian journalist, David Levy, came upon him there dining at the Sovietskaya Hotel, "seated at a long table groaning with jellied sturgeon and Georgian wines." Learning that Levy knew the private address of Nikita Khrushchev, ousted and "unpersoned" six months earlier, Nixon asked to be taken at once to see the man he had once famously confronted.

When the *babushka* at the door of Khrushchev's apartment building proved uncooperative, Nixon made do with leaving a scrawled note. On the following day he engaged in a dialogue—fatuous, according to Jules Witcover, a usually evenhanded biographer—with an official at Moscow University. He also "accosted a policeman with stupid questions."[8] American reporters present thought his behavior ludicrous but reported it all anyway. Nixon achieved what he wanted: publicity back home.

He continued his circuit of the world for five years, taking in Europe, Latin America, Africa, and Asia—especially Asia, where the United States was becoming mired in the Vietnam War. He covered 225,000 miles and on one of ten flights to Japan contracted phlebitis, the inflammation of a vein in his leg that—as president and afterward—would come close to killing him.

Nixon was to claim later he had been "running the whole operation on a shoestring, traveling sometimes on coach flights with only one person with me and sometimes none at all. . . . As far as privacy was concerned I just took the inside seat and put whoever was riding with me on the outside, opened my briefcase and became deliberately oblivious. . . ."

This was a misrepresentation. The companion on many of the flights was his best friend, Bebe Rebozo, and much of the travel was paid for by *Reader's Digest* or Pepsi, which he represented as VIP attorney at bottle plant openings. Neither company was a mean patron, and Pepsi certainly got a return on its investment. In Rome, Nixon addressed the press while conspicuously sipping the soft drink. During a television appearance a waiter reached past Nixon to turn a Pepsi bottle so that the label faced the camera.

Globe-trotting for Pepsi, however, was hardly the Gaullist grandeur to which Nixon aspired. "Nobody paid any attention to him," said *Life*'s Hugh Sidey. "Some of my bureau chiefs said he would come into town—a former vice president—and ask to see the head of state, whether he was in Kuala Lumpur, Algiers, or some faraway place. In many cases they wouldn't see him. He was a has-been; they didn't like him very much.

"He didn't care. . . . When he got to the White House, he knew virtually every leader of every country in the world because someplace along the line he'd ended up as a reject with the guy. . . . Six or twelve years later this fellow would be elected president or prime minister, and he'd be Nixon's pal. . . . It paid off in the end."

Behind Nixon's desk in his New York office stood a second desk, holding serried ranks of signed photographs of the high and the mighty. The monarchs had pride of place: the queen of England, the kings of Belgium and Thailand, the emperor of Ethiopia, the shah of Iran. There were poses of Nixon at Eisenhower's side and—somewhat unexpectedly—a portrait inscribed with *"bonnes pensées"* from Albert Schweitzer in his West African leper colony. A book about the Quakers was left lying where visitors could not miss seeing it.

"This," an aide reflected later, "was Nixon's carefully set stage for winning over the skeptical."

Sheer hard work, more than his attempts at window dressing, is what ultimately brought Nixon real rewards. During one forty-eight-hour period in the fall of 1966 the man who was not a candidate appeared before the Supreme Court in his legal capacity, flew to San Francisco to give television interviews, drove north to Oakland to address a political meeting, south to Palo Alto for a planning meeting, then—after three hours' sleep—there was more television, a fund-raising breakfast, an airplane flight, a press conference, a rally for a fellow Republican, another flight, another press conference, more TV, another flight and another rally, yet another airplane hop, and then—after another short night—the long haul back to the East Coast.

Nixon had sallied forth to breathe fire into the Republican faithful in the midterm elections, to bring the party back from the ignominy of 1964, and he delivered a smashing victory. On election day, with most of the results in, he celebrated with colleagues at El Morocco, the New York nightclub. "I never heard him sound happier," said Herb Klein, whom he called that night. "It was clear that he knew he now had a launching pad for another try at the presidency."

Nixon had been refusing even to discuss the possibility of running in 1968. He remained noncommittal even after the big win and a Thanksgiving break with Rebozo, and after political intimates said they wanted to organize a Nixon for President committee. The following year, as other contenders—George Romney, Nelson Rockefeller, and a former actor by the name of Ronald Reagan—entered the lists, Nixon watched and waited. In nearly two hundred years no man defeated in a run for the U.S. presidency and denied renomination on the following attempt had ever been nominated again, let alone elected.

In September 1967 Nixon's mother Hannah died. She had languished in a rest home, giving no sign that she recognized visitors, since suffering a stroke four years earlier. According to Nixon, his last conversation with her had taken place in the hospital in 1962, after she had been through a serious operation and he had been defeated by Pat Brown. Then, he recalled, he had leaned over her bed to urge: "Mother, don't give up." She responded, he claimed, by pulling herself up and telling him: "Richard, don't *you* give up. Don't let anyone tell you you are through." Her advice was almost identical to what, as Nixon told it, his dying father had told him in 1956: "Dick, you keep fighting."

Three months after Hannah's death, according to Nixon, he sat down in front of a fire and made notes on whether or not to run for president. His first line supposedly read: "I have decided personally against becoming a candidate." Then, after a listing of reasons not to run, he wrote: "I don't give a damn."[9]

That Christmas, Nixon said, he consulted the family and gave "great weight" to what they thought. Nineteen-year-old Julie told him, "You have to do it, for the country," and twenty-one-year-old Tricia said, "If you don't run, Daddy, you really will have nothing to live for." "Daddy," Julie has recalled, citing her contemporary diary, "was very depressed. I had never known him to be depressed before. . . ."

We cannot know what Pat really thought. She later told an interviewer of the "horror" she had been through in the past, that she felt she could not go through it again. According to Julie, though, life as a New York matron was beginning to pall somewhat for her mother. She sometimes grew restless, she confided to a friend. On a stroll along Madison Avenue, Julie remembered, she and her father agreed that "Mother needed something to do."

Pat's resolve to avoid politics had already been broken in 1966, when, as "Miss Ryan," she had quietly worked a campaign telephone. Was she, Pat asked her daughters that year, "a failure to Daddy"? A few months later, though, she was telling Julie "flatly, almost tonelessly" that she could not face another presidential race.

Nixon had recently discussed his marriage with his younger brother Ed. "There's never been anybody but Pat," he had said, "never needs to be." In fact, Nixon the proper family man had recently been letting his standards slip a little.

During the 1964 convention, while drinking with a group of Republicans in his suite at the St. Francis Hotel, Nixon had become, in John Ehrlichman's words, "loudly celebratory." At the end of the evening, when most of the others had drifted away, he made "clumsy passes" at a campaign staffer in her twenties. "He was drinking hard, and he lost it," Ehrlichman recalled. "She was very embarrassed; we were all embarrassed." The young woman finally escaped Nixon's advances and left.[10]

Arnholt Smith, who had known Nixon from childhood, recalled an episode during another party in California. "I was looking for my wife and—jeez!—I couldn't find her. Apparently Dick had maneuvered her into the john, and they were drinking highballs. I finally found out where they were and had to jerk her out. He was high as a kite, and he said, 'We're not doing anything, we're not doing anything!' . . . When he got to drinking, Nixon was really something.

"Pat," said Smith, "was a wonderful woman, but very straitlaced. She was Queen Victoria. I think he sought a change from that. . . . He sometimes wandered."

During this period Nixon took an interest in a Chinese woman in her early thirties, a relationship that remained hidden from the public until 1976, when the *New York Times* revealed that the FBI had investigated a reported "affair" between Nixon and Marianna Liu, a former hostess at the Hong Kong Hilton. The *National Enquirer* gleefully assigned a team of reporters to dig further and later ran two lengthy stories.

The situation had begun to surface with a security flap in 1967. "One of my contacts in another U.S. agency," former FBI Hong Kong representative Dan Grove told the author, "came to see me one morning and said one of his sources, Marianna Liu, was seeing Nixon. He thought I should be aware of this. . . . He said he knew Nixon had had a top secret briefing on the People's Republic of China, and that made his contact with Liu a risk."[11]

According to Liu's attorney, FBI records confirm that her contacts with Nixon triggered an alarm and that Nixon himself came under surveillance in Hong Kong, to the point of being photographed through his bedroom window with infrared cameras. Grove believed the work was carried out by the British—Hong Kong was then a British colony—at the request of the CIA.

Early press accounts suggested the pair had first met in the late fifties, when Nixon was vice president and Liu was visiting Washington with a group from Hong Kong. They certainly met repeatedly between 1964 and 1967, when Nixon was making annual trips to Hong Kong. Liu told the *New York Times* she thought she saw him on all but one of the visits. In 1967, when she was hospitalized, Nixon sent flowers.

Later, when he was president, Liu not only moved to the United States but lived initially in Nixon's hometown, Whittier. Her sponsors for residence included a businessman with whom Nixon had stayed in Hong Kong and a Nixon-era immigration official. By one report, Liu saw Nixon twice at the White House.

The *National Enquirer* quoted Liu as telling of "many dates" with Nixon in Hong Kong and of dancing with him on a yacht. "I knew he cared for me," she was reported as saying, "because despite my constant warnings he still insisted on seeing me and being alone with me. . . . We had many opportunities to make love—we were alone in his hotel room at least six or seven times—but I wouldn't let it happen . . . he had an important career and a wife and family to think of. . . ."

Liu later sued the *Enquirer* over aspects of its story, and the paper settled out of court. Her own attorney, she has said, had advised her not to pursue the case, warning her that the paper's reporting was "true."[12] Tracked down in 1996 in Los Angeles, where she was working as a waitress, Liu offered the following account of the relationship.

Her narrative, in broken English and Chinese, was delivered in brief sentences and monosyllables, and with obvious reluctance. She told how after fleeing Communist China in her late teens, she had worked her way up to become chief hostess in the Opium Den, one of several bars at the Hong Kong Hilton. It was there, she said, that local businessman Harold Lee introduced her to Nixon.

In her interview for this book, Liu told of only two Nixon encounters. "He was nice, quiet," she recalled with a smile. "I'll just say he was smooth and nice. . . . Not jump all over, you know. . . . He was not that handsome; one side of his face was bigger than the other! . . . He gave me a bottle of Chanel No. 5. And he gave me his card. He tell me to come to New York and see him. . . ."

Nixon and the bar hostess were photographed together in 1966 by the Hilton's publicity office. The second meeting, a private one, occurred when Nixon—in town with Rebozo—invited Liu and a hostess named Theresa to his suite at the Mandarin Hotel.

"We finished work and went to the hotel," Liu said. "We went to their room, and they have a bar there. We had a drink and a snack. They had martinis or something. I don't drink; I had Coke. Mr. Rebozo was very quiet, don't talk much. We left there around two A.M., I think. We had to catch the last ferry. . . ."

Liu's contact with Nixon, she asserted in this recent interview, was "just talking" and involved neither sex nor a love affair. "I don't want to think about it," she said, and then—as was obvious—insisted, "I don't want to talk about it." She had not attended the funeral when Nixon died yet, surprising perhaps in someone who claims so minimal a connection to the man, she later went to visit his grave.[13]

There are no further details to add to this account, except to note that Nixon both publicly and privately expressed an appreciation of Chinese women. At dinner at the Annenbergs',[14] according to Mickey Ziffren, a Los Angeles social acquaintance, he "had too much to drink and began talking about the beauty of Chinese women and how they were really much more beautiful. He was doing this in front of Pat and kept going on about the particular qualities he appreciated. . . ."

In December 1967, when Nixon made "to run or not to run" the subject of a Christmas Day family debate, Pat declared she was "resigned to helping out." "Whatever you do, we'll be proud of you," she added later, according to Nixon. In the months that followed, when he did start running, Pat kept her word, offering the standard trite comments to the media. Pat was "a volunteer," "running the office for him," "having a marvelous time." *Newsweek* puffed her as "the public man's dream, a seemingly selfless, super-efficient helpmeet . . . her looks and taste classic Middle American . . . country, family, loyalty and discipline."

The campaign was as usual an endurance test for Pat, a time of going through the motions, frozen between bad memories and hope for the future. When a television show audience applauded her, she was seen to be glassily clapping herself. At some rallies she was merely an appendage, not even introduced by name.

Some perceptive journalists saw through the facade. Pat looked as if she hated campaigning, thought the *New Republic*'s John Osborne. "Mr. Nixon publicly gave her reason to hate it. . . . On a platform near Los Angeles, in a fashion so crass it could not be missed, he ignored her presence. . . . At Saginaw, Michigan, she didn't hear him when he called her back to a makeshift platform, and jumped as if she had been flicked with a whip when he roared, 'Pat!' "

Esquire's Garry Wills observed pityingly as Pat, asked how it felt to be on the road again, answered: "I love it; one meets so many old friends." "But," Wills recalled, "I watched her hands as she said it; the freckled hands were picking at each other, playing with gloves, trying to still each other's trembling."

Very occasionally the mask slipped. "I tell them what their readers want to hear," Pat said wearily of the scores of required interviews with women's magazines. On a flight from Denver to St. Louis she tried hard to say nothing to Gloria Steinem, on assignment—as reported earlier—for *New York* magazine. Steinem, however, pressed for more than the usual bland answers. Had Pat really liked all the stories written in past campaigns? "Yes, of course," she replied. "I don't object to what's been written . . . most of you have been very kind." In that case, Steinem recalled telling her, she was "the only person I'd ever met, including myself, who liked everything written about them." There was a flicker of annoyance behind the hazel eyes; the first sign of life.

"No, she was never bored with campaigning. . . . She liked the theatre, especially *My Fair Lady*, and had seen *Hello, Dolly!* three times . . . 'I feel there's enough seriousness in the world without seeing it in the theatre.'

"There is no Generation Gap in our family," Pat went on. "Why, only the other day, Tricia and Julie didn't go to one of their parties. I said, 'Aren't you going out?' And they said, 'No, we'd much rather have dinner with you and Daddy.'" "Mamie Eisenhower was the woman in history she most admired, Pat said, 'because she meant so much to young people.'"

As she probed Pat's platitudes, Steinem was briefly rewarded with "a stream of anger and resentment": resentment about her disadvantaged youth, and resentment of Richard Nixon. "There were things she said about her husband that I couldn't figure out a tasteful way to use," Steinem remembered, "but she wanted me to say them. She didn't like doing what she was doing, she *didn't* like campaigning. She didn't like the world in which she was, the world he had created. . . ."

22

*I am inclined to believe the Republican operation
in 1968 relates to the Watergate affair of 1972. . . .
As the same men faced the election of 1972, there were
memories of how close an election could get and the
possible utility of pressing to the limit—or beyond.*

—Walt Rostow, Special Assistant
for National Security to President Johnson, 1973

Months before Nixon announced he was running for president in 1968, his aides were using a code name for their leader in office communications. Their designation—DC—was a straightforward statement of certainty about his ultimate destination.

From early in the year of the election Nixon ran hard and brilliantly. A Nixon for President headquarters had long since opened its doors, in an old bank building in Washington. The real heart of the operation, though, was the candidate's New York law office. Throughout the previous year it had served as recruiting office for his troops, including advisers, speechwriters and aides, all waiting to be unleashed.

Even before Nixon formally announced, the press carried a picture of a group of bright young men in suits, the "New Nixon team." Absent were Bob Haldeman and John Ehrlichman, still on the West Coast waiting for the serious action to begin; Murray Chotiner, a key player but one whom it was prudent not to publicize; and the new power at the center, John Mitchell.

Mitchell, of jowly face and trademark pipe, had become a multimillionaire as an attorney specializing in municipal bonds. His clients had been the bond sellers, while the Nixon firm had been the underwriters, and it was this mutual interest that had led the two partnerships to merge. (Perhaps not incidentally the new partnership thus formed had contact with Franklin DeBoer, the broker who later claimed he handled a secret Nixon portfolio at Rebozo's bank.[1] Rebozo, DeBoer revealed, used Mitchell to buy bonds in New Jersey.)

Mitchell's public finance expertise gave him a useful entrée to the political world. He was tough but soft-spoken and so understated that even after 1968 the press would characterize him as "a blank." Billing him as "our leader against crime and lawlessness," Nixon would later appoint Mitchell attorney general of the United States, in which capacity he would preside over the initial planning of the Watergate break-in and later be sentenced to prison for perjury and obstruction of justice.

Nixon went into the New Hampshire primary with surgical skill, entering in late January at the last possible moment, and won with more votes than any candidate in any presidential primary in the history of the state. He then triumphed in five other states, the last of them a critical win over Ronald Reagan in Oregon.

Ehrlichman, who came on board in the Oregon race, was impressed and relieved by the candidate's performance. In the past, as reported earlier, he had been concerned about Nixon's drinking, which he thought serious enough to "cost him any chance of a return to public life." He agreed to join up in 1968 only if Nixon promised to abstain. Nixon responded by taking a "solemn pledge," which Ehrlichman never saw him break during the campaign.

The "New Nixon" of whom the pundits were writing seemed easier in his skin, relaxed with the press, less angry, less obviously driven. He presented himself not just as a candidate but as a confident man claiming a well-deserved crown. "Nixon," thought Theodore White, "has the weight and presence. It is visible. . . . He runs as President."

Nixon was watching on television in Oregon when Robert Kennedy declared his candidacy. According to speechwriter Richard Whalen, he repeated two or three times, "We can beat the little S.O.B." As Ehrlichman recalled, he shook his head for a long moment, then said: "We've just seen some very terrible forces unleashed. Something bad is going to come of this."

"Why does Bobby get to be so mean," Nixon grumbled as the Kennedy effort got under way, "and why do I have to be so nice?" In fact, he welcomed the prospect of Robert's becoming the Democratic nominee, believing it offered an opportunity to indict the Democrats "right back to the Bay of Pigs." And as Whalen recalled, "He wanted to beat a Kennedy."

The ultimate "something bad" that Nixon had foreseen came in June, with Kennedy's assassination in the kitchen of Los Angeles' Ambassador Hotel, two months after the murder of Martin Luther King. Nixon had attended King's funeral but worried afterward that it had been "a serious mistake" that would cost him crucial southern white votes. Robert Kennedy's death was "tragic" for Nixon, according to his brother Ed. He also went to that funeral, and then headed for the Bahamas and relaxation with Rebozo and the owners of Paradise Island.

Two months later, in a regal arrival ritual timed to coincide with prime time television, he flew into Miami for the Republican National Convention. "Nixon's the One!" sang the campaign girls gathered at the entrance to the Hilton, and soon he was.

Once nominated, Nixon had to pick a running mate. One outsider was a young Texas congressman named George Bush. The senior House Republican, Gerald Ford, thought he was being seriously considered.[2] Nixon, however, had long been focused primarily on Spiro Agnew, the governor of Maryland.[3] Gasps of disbelief went up from the convention floor when the choice was announced.

Agnew's only apparent qualification was that he was a centrist, a moderate, though some thought "mediocre" a more apt description. The Democrats quickly capitalized on the curious selection by running derisive commercials, with the sound of prolonged laughter over the slogan "Agnew for Vice President." Nixon would admit years later that he had opted for Agnew knowing that his running mate was corrupt, the flaw that would eventually force Agnew's resignation.

Nixon made an acceptance speech filled with patriotic sentiment, featuring calls for reconciliation at home and peacemaking abroad. Its best-remembered element, though, would be his allusion to the dream of a child—Nixon himself—the son of a hardworking father and a "gentle Quaker mother," on his way to achieving the American dream. (Two passages from the speech were not included in the excerpts reprinted in Nixon's memoirs. "Respect for law," he told his followers, "can come only from people who take the law into their hearts and their minds. . . ." and "Let us begin by committing ourselves to the truth, to see it like it is, to find the truth, to speak the truth and to live the truth. That's what we will do.")

Between the convention and election day the public continued to see a self-assured, effective Nixon backed by meticulous organization. The campaign was to spawn a book by Joe McGinniss titled *The Selling of the President,* and sold Nixon was—by a New York advertising agency, two television producers with long experience at CBS, and a "creative supervisor" from J. Walter Thompson.[4] Bob Haldeman, of course, came from the J. Walter Thompson stable.

Nixon at first spoke more readily to the press, dismissing television as a gimmick. "He was afraid of television," thought McGinniss. "He half expected it was an eastern liberal trick: one more way to make him look silly." The TV men converted him, however, and print journalists found themselves relegated to "three-bump interviews," the time between the campaign plane's landing approach and its arrival at the terminal.

Nixon's television team, McGinniss concluded, "controlled him, controlled the atmosphere around him. It was as if they were building not a President but an Astrodome, where the wind would never blow, the temperature never rise or fall, and the ball never bounce erratically. . . ." They left no chance that the horrors of the 1960 debates with Kennedy would be repeated, and—when a televised appearance had to be live—Nixon's managers made sure it was rigidly circumscribed.

Control was exerted right down to the party symbol, the elephant. A Republican rally in 1960 had been spoiled when an inconsiderate pachyderm defecated pungently in front of the speaker's platform. In 1968 a printed manual instructed Nixon advance men to see to it that all performing elephants had preemptive enemas.

While the Democratic candidate, Hubert Humphrey, was also represented by a Madison Avenue ad agency, the difference was in the funding. The Nixon side had vastly more money to spend on propaganda—twice as much, in fact, as the Democrats. "The response" of the public, Nixon aide Ray Price remarked, was "to the image, not the man. . . ."

"I was ashamed of being in the company of mediocre merchandisers," speechwriter Whalen wrote ruefully later. To him, the men around Nixon were "a bunch of second-raters and automatons, dangerous men without serious political convictions." Whalen quit, but he was an exception.

"With Nixon there are good manners and white shirts and thin-line briefcases," Hugh Sidey reported after a ride on the *Tricia*, the lead plane in Nixon's three-jet flotilla. "The candidate is combed, shaved, tanned, pressed and serious. . . . Nixon resides, both physically and emotionally, just above the battle."

By contrast, Sidey wrote, "Humphrey sweats and removes his coat and shouts back at the yippies and dodges tomatoes and grapples at every stop with the problems of race and war and lawlessness. It is steamy and sordid and yet it is real."

Walter Cronkite had an audience with another Nixon, a Nixon who lay back on a sofa with a drink and talked "the language of the streets, sprinkled with profanities." This was a Nixon few outsiders would ever see or hear—at least not until years later, when transcripts of the Watergate tapes appeared peppered with the notation "expletive deleted."

Sidey did notice occasional public slips, as when Nixon "smiles too quickly and for a fleeting moment doesn't seem to mean it." "None of us," Whalen had thought, "could say with confidence what, if anything, Nixon felt passionately about. . . . We were like bootleggers serving a client of unpredictable taste and thirst; all we could do was leave samples on his doorstep."

Oddly, Nixon seemed to scorn the voters, the very people who could guarantee his victory. "It hasn't changed in twenty years," he complained in private. "You still have to put out a folder saying what you're for and against, where you stand on the issues. Women particularly like it. They don't have the slightest idea what it means, but the voter's been taught to expect it." Whalen thought the candidate aimed no higher than "the least assailable middle ground."

Some tactics had not changed. The public Nixon urged an audience to give protesters a hearing because they "may have something to say worth listening to." The private Nixon meanwhile told staffers: "Kick the weirdos and beardos on the college campuses. I want to see the violent ones expelled."

"We would go in and infiltrate the opposition," recalled advance man Ron Walker. "I was the one that grew the beard and put the wig on and went into these meetings and incited. . . . I'd cause all kinds of problems. . . . I would get a mimeograph machine, and in the middle of the night I was in my bathroom printing opposite material that would fuck them up."

Walker was in the lead car of a Nixon motorcade in New Jersey when a radio call came warning of possible "difficulty with demonstrators." Humphrey supporters up ahead were brandishing posters picturing a large black pregnant woman and the legend "Nixon's the One!"—a mocking play on the Republican campaign slogan.

"I wanted those signs down before Nixon got there," Walker explained. "We simply went in and pulled them down. All the black ladies came falling to the floor. . . . And the people were sitting there, their signs were down and they were pulling splinters out of their hands for a week. . . . I don't call that dirty tricks as much as, you know, guerrilla warfare."

Nixon's solution to the protesters problem, Ehrlichman remembered, "was to order me to have the Secret Service rough up the hecklers." When informed that the Secret Service, which had been placed at each candidate's disposal since the Robert Kennedy murder, would have none of it, Nixon had a fallback plan. "He wanted me to create some kind of flying goon squad of our own," Ehrlichman said, "to rough up the hecklers, take down their signs and silence them. . . . He approved of strong-arm tactics."

Advance man Walker recalled another confrontation, also in New Jersey, when opponents were disrupting a rally. "I said, 'Let's take them out!' And I had ushers who were off-duty policemen and firemen that were on our side, and there were hard knocks and stuff. And we moved the people out of our entrance so our guests could get in." The Nixon team sometimes even paid cash to have opponents forcibly silenced.

Meanwhile they also went on the offensive. Busloads of pro-Nixon hecklers followed Humphrey from rally to rally, trying to drown out his speeches, and there were other, more subtle deceits. Three times a day a TWX wire machine on the Nixon plane clattered into life, transmitting messages from a spy in the Humphrey camp. The Humphrey people knew him as Hearst journalist Seymour Freidin, a friendly fellow who played a mean game of poker and spoke little about his job. In reality Freidin, a veteran CIA informant, was receiving thousands of Republican dollars to phone reports on the Democrats to a secretary in Murray Chotiner's office. Chotiner edited the messages, then wired them to Nixon's plane.

Freidin's 1968 code name, as it would be in 1972, was Chapman's Friend. Republican kingmaker Tom Dewey had used the designation for covert contacts with Nixon as early as 1952. At the start of the 1968 campaign, to hide from the press, Nixon himself had registered at a hotel under the name Chapman. The spy in the Humphrey camp was his spy.

The man who promised truth to the nation talked privately as though his stock-in-trade were deception. There was the occasion when, on the way into a meeting with Mormon Church elders, Nixon told John Sears not to believe a word of what he was about to say—it was merely for the Church leaders' consumption. On another occasion, "reasonably well oiled," he had some advice for Len Garment. "You're never going to make it in politics," he told the younger man. "You just don't know how to lie."

"The money matters," Nixon announced bluntly at a meeting early in the campaign, and of course it did matter—seriously so. The issue of campaign contributions—what is legal and what is illegal, what is ethically acceptable and what is not—remains a controversial issue, perhaps the most controversial issue, of U.S. elections to this day.

By its own accounting, the Nixon side spent $36.5 million on the 1968 campaign. It was the largest expenditure ever for a presidential contest and gave the Republicans a fundamental advantage. The Humphrey side probably had less than half as much money at its disposal.

Nixon behaved as though it did not matter who donated the money, whether it was given in expectation of future favors, or how it was delivered. He claimed he "refused always" to accept contributions himself. W. W. Keeler, the president of Phillips Petroleum, however, admitted that in 1968 he delivered a package containing fifty thousand dollars "personally to Nixon at his New York City apartment." This revelation emerged only after the presidency, in the course of a stockholders' suit against Phillips filed on the ground that this donation—and twice that sum in the 1972 election—contravened the law banning corporate contributions.

It was early in the 1968 campaign, when the coffers were empty, that Nixon accepted a hundred thousand dollars from Paradise Island casino owner James Crosby. In spite of the dubious source, finance chairman Maurice Stans recalled, "Nixon was ecstatic" and merely ordered that the money be delivered in thirty-four separate personal checks to thirty-four different campaign committees, to observe the legal requirement that individual donations to local committees be limited to five thousand dollars. At the same time, of course, the ploy camouflaged the real donor's identity.

Arnholt Smith, the San Diego banker, remembered by Pat Nixon as "one of our first supporters," reportedly personally donated $250,000 in 1968, and the contributions he generated totaled four times that. An associate of his, bookmaker John Alessio, gave $26,000. On election night Smith would be part of the Nixon inner circle at the Waldorf Towers.[5] (Both Smith and Alessio would later go to prison for tax evasion, but only after secret efforts by the Nixon White House to intervene on their behalf.[6])

Bebe Rebozo, not surprisingly, also served as personal fund-raiser, financial cutout, and bagman. It was he who organized the Crosby donation. When the Davis brothers of the Winn-Dixie grocery chain contributed seventy-five thousand dollars, it was to Rebozo's home that the envelope containing the first cash installment was delivered.

Months before the campaign started, Rebozo had accompanied Nixon to England and joined him on a visit to J. Paul Getty's stately home, where they admired the billionaire's collection of Rubenses, Titians, and Renoirs. Rebozo wrote afterward to say how "enthralled" everyone had been, what a wonderful dinner party Getty had given. Later, when Nixon sought a contribution from Getty, and Rebozo was the go-between, Getty duly obliged. Rebozo was also the key intermediary for cash payments that Nixon should by now have known better than to accept, from Howard Hughes.

———

"You must remember," Hughes told his lieutenant Robert Maheu, "that I, Howard Hughes, can buy any man in the world. . . ."

He presented his 1968 agenda in a neatly written memo (see facsimile below): "I am determined to elect a president of our choosing this year and one who will be deeply indebted. . . . Since I am willing to go beyond all limitations on this, I think we should be able to select a candidate and a party who knows the facts of political life." "If we select Nixon," Hughes wrote later, "then he, I know for sure, knows the facts of life."[7]

Sequestered in a suite atop the Desert Inn in Las Vegas, the eccentric billionaire was now sixty-two. Long since a recluse, he was seriously disturbed and addicted to prescription drugs, yet remained as manipulative as ever.

Hughes was not particular about where he bestowed his financial largess. He cleared Maheu that year to offer Lyndon Johnson a million dollars (Maheu saw the president but decided not to risk offering the bribe) and to take fifty thousand dollars to Hubert Humphrey (Maheu claimed he made the delivery, though Humphrey denied it). Hughes' favorite, however, was Nixon. "I want you to go see Nixon as my special confidential emissary," he wrote after Nixon's first primary win. "I feel there is a really valid possibility of a Republican victory this year. . . ."

When he sent Maheu to Johnson, Hughes had instructed him to focus on two primary demands. To recoup the huge losses he had suffered from disastrously budgeted helicopter production, he wanted the Vietnam War to continue. He also sought an end to atomic testing in the Nevada desert, one of his saner obsessions. Hughes's demands varied over time, but his baseline requirement remained unchanged: He wanted whoever became president, as Maheu put it, to be "in his debt."

How much Hughes paid in cash directly to Nixon, how it was transmitted and by whom and when, are questions so permeated with deceit and confusion as to be beyond discovery.[8] One of the few certainties in the matter is that even before Hughes started doling out money, Nixon had approached him for financial support. The man he assigned to make the contact was Richard Danner, the former Miami city manager who years earlier had brought Nixon and Rebozo together. Danner's diary for 1968 indicates constant contact with both men, by telephone and in person. At one early meeting, he later testified, they asked him to approach Hughes.

Hughes laughed out loud when he received the request, then ordered Maheu to arrange a delivery of fifty thousand dollars cash—almost a quarter of a million dollars at today's values. Long delays followed, however, because both Rebozo and Nixon became nervous. Rebozo backed away from one handover fearing that one of the intermediaries, who happened to be a Democrat, might reveal the plan.

Soon after the election Maheu flew by private jet to Palm Springs with the money, hoping that Nevada's Governor Laxalt would be able to arrange for him to see Nixon at a reception. Nixon, however, sent word that he had "no time" for a meeting. Whatever his reason, he would certainly have avoided the encounter had he known that, as Maheu's son remembered it, the Hughes people wanted a signed receipt for the contribution.

Maheu and Danner finally accomplished their mission, sometime into the presidency, by making deliveries directly to Rebozo. Danner described how, after he had been handed ten batches of hundred-dollar bills—fifty thousand dollars—Rebozo "laid the bundles out on the bed and counted them . . . didn't fan them or break down the amounts [but] put them back in the envelope and put them in his handbag." Each packet came secured by a Las Vegas bank wrapper, for the source of the cash was a Hughes casino. When the transaction was completed, Rebozo and Danner strolled off for a chat with Nixon.

Maheu also admitted to having given Rebozo a second payment of fifty thousand dollars, which involved an arrival by chauffeured limousine and a wordless exchange of the cash, followed by gin martinis on the rocks and a lavish dinner at a local restaurant. Neither he nor Rebozo, he said, mentioned the reason for the meeting.

If the deliveries were executed with all the finesse of a B movie, the participants' subsequent accounts of them—during the Senate's Watergate probe—played as pure farce. They could not get their stories straight as to when the payments were made, whether they were handed over at San Clemente, at Rebozo's bank, or at his home, or precisely who was present at which delivery.

Investigators noted with interest the timing of the donations. One seemed to dovetail with Hughes' purchase of Air West, a deal that required approval ·by the Civil Aeronautics Board and—because of the foreign routes involved—by President Nixon himself. Hughes had said he relied on Maheu's "political ability" to get the decisions ratified.

Danner, it emerged, also met three times during the first presidency with John Mitchell, who as attorney general was in a position to grant or withhold clearance for Hughes to acquire yet another Las Vegas hotel. This was an antitrust issue, and Mitchell gave his consent against senior staff advice. It was after one of these meetings that Hughes gave the order to deliver the second fifty thousand dollars to Rebozo—with the explanation that "certain political obligations had to be met."

What was the money used for? Future probes would uncover an entry in Danner's diary, dated just after the election, reflecting a call from Rebozo about a "house project." More calls followed, apparently on the same matter, though Danner claimed he could not recall to what the notation "house project" referred. As it happens, however, the calls to Hughes' bagman coincided with early plans for Nixon to buy a house next to Rebozo's at Key Biscayne, the so-called Florida White House.

Extraordinary efforts by Senate investigators to discover the fate of the Hughes money led to suspicion that it had been used to pay for such items as architects' fees, remodeling, a swimming pool, and even—at $213.57—an "Arnold Palmer Putting Green." The labyrinthine trail petered out when Rebozo refused to produce financial records.

Nixon's attorney Herb Kalmbach recalled Rebozo's having told him that some of the Hughes money had gone to Nixon's brothers, Donald and Edward, and to his secretary Rose Woods. The brothers and Rebozo denied it, and Rose Woods said she had nothing to do with her boss' business affairs. Rebozo claimed he never touched the Hughes money and eventually returned it.[9]

While investigators had firm evidence of only the two fifty-thousand-dollar Hughes cash payments, some suspected the real total was much higher. In

March 1970, at a meeting in New York, Maheu was asked to call a Hughes aide from a pay phone. Moments later, hunched in a nearby booth, he listened in amazement as the aide read out, or rather whispered, a message from Hughes. "Go to Key Biscayne," it said, "and offer Nixon through Rebozo one million dollars." Hughes's hope, Maheu recalled, was that a bribe of that size—the same figure Hughes had had in mind two years earlier for President Johnson—would be persuasive enough to convince Nixon to stop atomic testing in Nevada.

This latest mission was so outrageous, Maheu has said, that he and Danner simply went through the motions. They flew to Florida, stalled for days pretending that Rebozo was unavailable, and waited until Hughes's attention turned to other topics.

Another former Hughes employee, John Meier, claimed recently that a million-dollar delivery to Rebozo did take place, in 1969. Meier said he saw the money, "made up of $100 bills . . . stacked neatly on edge—two rows, five thousand bills in each," in a colleague's large briefcase. Rebozo made the pickup from a room at Miami's Airport Hotel, then, alarmed that more than one witness was present, abruptly left.

Both Maheu and the man named as the courier have denied this episode took place.[10] True, Meier is not a reliable witness. Fired after a compromising business involvement with Nixon's brother Donald, he fled to Canada, a fugitive from an IRS tax fraud charge. Yet the question remains: In this gallery of corrupters and corrupted, men who suffered convenient memory lapses or simply lied, whose account *can* be deemed reliable?

"There is evidence," the Senate report on these matters would one day say dryly, "suggesting that there may have been more than two deliveries from Danner to Rebozo. The only way much of the conflicting testimony can be reconciled is to conclude there were more than two deliveries of funds."

To avoid the Senate committee's most awkward questions, Rebozo would eventually flee the country for a while in 1974. "Mr. Rebozo," said the report, "persisted in his refusal to make records controlled by him or his bank available . . . and placed himself beyond the reach of the committee by traveling to Europe. . . ." By the time he returned, as Rebozo well knew, the committee would have run out of time to issue further subpoenas.

"Unfortunately," the committee also observed, "the President did not avail himself of the opportunity to clarify or explain the matters arising out of his dealings or his relationship with Rebozo."

———

The evidence suggests that Rebozo's hand was in everything that was dubious and touched on Nixon and money—not least the forbidden territory of foreign money.

One such area involved Nixon and Adnan Khashoggi, the hugely wealthy Saudi businessman. Usually characterized as an "arms dealer," he once said he preferred to be known as a "connector." In 1997, interviewed at his Paris home, Khashoggi recalled that his relationship with Nixon began in the wilderness years—they were introduced by an associate of Paul Getty—and lasted through the presidency and Nixon's fall, with meetings continuing until shortly before Nixon's death.[11]

Khashoggi had courted Nixon in 1967 by putting a plane at his disposal to tour the Middle East after the Six-Day War. Soon afterward, using a proxy, he opened an account at Rebozo's bank in Florida. He did so, he explained to Watergate prosecutors, hoping to "curry favor with Rebozo," to get an entrée to the man who might become president, and to pursue business deals. Khashoggi also told the prosecutors he thought Rebozo "not very smart and not nearly well-informed enough to serve as an effective spokesman." He said to the author, by contrast, that he found Rebozo "very fine, very secretive, you know, the type you can trust. . . ."

Rumors of Khashoggi's largess proliferated after Watergate, but prosecutors were "cautious" in their questioning because of the witness' high-level connections in the Saudi government. Khashoggi asserted that he contributed forty-three thousand dollars in 1968, not as a cash contribution but to fund production of a recording of a Nixon speech. He also admitted to having sent a further fifteen thousand dollars through an intermediary. "I was afraid," he told the author, "to spoil our relationship with money.

"I know it looks suspicious," Khashoggi remarked of two separate unexplained hundred-thousand-dollar withdrawals from his account at the Rebozo bank during the 1972 election campaign. The proxy account holder had reported that his financial records for that year—and only those for that year—had been stolen in a burglary five days before Nixon resigned as president.

"If Nixon asked me for a million dollars," Khashoggi said in the seventies, "I would have given it to him." He added, however, that neither Nixon nor Rebozo ever asked him for money. The author mentioned these denials to former Democratic aide Pierre Salinger, who had an affable relationship in later years with both Nixon and Khashoggi and whom the author happened to interview within hours of meeting the Saudi.

According to Salinger, a million was exactly what Nixon received in 1972. "Adnan showed up in Washington and had a secret meeting with Nixon," Salinger said, "and later on, he told me, he'd given a million dollars to help with the campaign. . . ."

Khashoggi is known to have met with Nixon on Rebozo's houseboat in Florida after the 1968 election and attended both Nixon inaugurals. When his first wife, Soraya, divorced him, her lawyers tried to subpoena Nixon to ask about "gifts of jewelry to members of Nixon's family." Khashoggi said in 1997 that he had given jewelry worth sixty thousand dollars to Nixon's daughters and later donated two hundred thousand dollars to the Nixon Library. If true, it did not earn him a single mention in Nixon's memoirs.[12]

Nixon should have avoided Khashoggi not just because he was a questionable character but because to have accepted money or gifts from him during a campaign, or even to come under suspicion of having done so, was dangerous since it was against the law. It was, and is, a crime for an American politician to solicit or accept contributions from a foreign citizen, government, or political party. Yet whatever the truth about the Khashoggi relationship, Nixon appears to have committed precisely that crime—in inadmissible circumstances—in 1968.

Seated beside Pat Nixon and her daughters at the 1968 convention, silent and expressionless, had been a man few recognized. This was sixty-eight-year-old Thomas Pappas, a vastly wealthy Greek-American with strong international connections and great generosity for those he favored.

Pappas was an immigrant who, like Nixon, had started his career in the family grocery store, built a vast supermarket and food import business, and then returned to Greece to found an oil, steel, and chemical empire. He had been raising funds for the Republican party since the twenties and had known Nixon since the Eisenhower days. Photographs autographed by Nixon adorned his office wall. He was a regular guest at White House dinners, attended Tricia's wedding, and donated fifty thousand dollars for a box in Tricia's and Julie's names at the Kennedy Center for the Performing Arts.

As Nixon would describe him on the White House tapes, he was "good old Tom Pappas." That would be during Watergate, when Pappas was producing hush money for the burglars and referred to in White House telephone code as the "Greek bearing gifts." In fact, Pappas had delivered a massive financial gift much earlier, as cochairman of the 1968 finance committee, but not without receiving a favor in return.

As we have seen, Nixon's choice of Agnew as running mate seemed incomprehensible at the time. In a celebrated editorial the *Washington Post* surmised that it would go down in history as "perhaps the most eccentric political appointment since the Roman Emperor Caligula named his horse a consul." Now that more has been revealed about the Pappas connection, however, the decision seems less inexplicable.

Agnew's Greek father had also been an immigrant, born Theodoros Anagnostopoulos, whose family came from a village in the Peloponnese close by Pappas's own. The millionaire said he "put in a good word for Spiro" at the convention, and Nixon himself admitted that Pappas influenced his selection. It was a decision that played well with the Greek-American community in the United States, and also in Greece itself.

Why, though, pick Agnew over all the more likely candidates? The answer almost certainly lies in a conjunction of events in Greece; the political responses of Nixon, Agnew, and Pappas; and—once again—dirty money.

In the spring of 1967, a military junta had seized power in the birthplace of democracy. It suspended civil liberties and political parties, imposed press censorship, and imprisoned dissenters. Many of those jailed were tortured, some at a facility just steps away from the U.S. Embassy, and for many nations this brutal regime became a pariah to be shunned. The Johnson administration had maintained relations, for strategic reasons, but cut back on arms shipments.

The junta hoped for more overt acceptance under a Nixon administration, and it was Spiro Agnew who sent the first signal that this would be the case. The way he did that, however, hastened the discovery of a secret, one that—had it been revealed at the time—might have prevented Nixon's election as president. That the secret did come close to exposure was a result of the outrage and determination of a single Greek exile.

Elias Demetracopoulos, today in his early seventies, had worked all his life as a journalist, for American newspapers as well as for the Greek press. Then and since, having often reported critically on senior American officials, he has come under aggressive investigation, but always emerged with his reputation unscathed.[13] In Washington political figures on both the right and the left came to hold him in respect, as did numerous fellow journalists. "His data is meticulously accurate," the columnist Robert Novak has commented. "I find him a triple A source."

By the time Nixon and Agnew became candidates in 1968, Demetracopoulos had been in the United States for nearly a year, having fled Greece rather than be silenced by censorship there. Based in cramped quarters at Washington's Fairfax Hotel, he was working single-mindedly to overthrow the junta. With a Greek-American running for vice president, it was obviously important to him to learn what Agnew's attitude toward the regime would be, and at first there seemed no cause for alarm.

Demetracopoulos had been introduced to Agnew by Louise Gore, owner of the Fairfax and, as chairman of the Nixon-Agnew campaign in Agnew's home state, a Republican of impeccable credentials. There were three meetings with him in late 1967 and 1968, all of them encouraging to Demetracopoulos. In January, Agnew said he hoped soon to see an elected government back in power in Greece. When Gore and Demetracopoulos saw him about two months before the election, he assured them that—as a vice presidential candidate—he intended to remain neutral. Then suddenly, the very same week, he made a public statement sympathetic to the junta.

The turnabout was shocking, especially so because of the powerful encouragement it gave to the Greek dictatorship. "What happened?" Louise Gore wrote to Demetracopoulos. "Why did Agnew tell us one thing one day and say something else the next? . . . What made him change his mind—or rather *who!* What are you going to do?"

What Demetracopoulos did, after a quick blast at Agnew the next day, was what he did best: use his network of contacts to find out what was going on. What he learned was hugely compromising to Nixon.

The exiled journalist's sources told him that between July and October the Nixon campaign had received large sums of money from the Greek dictatorship. There had been three separate payments totaling $549,000, nearly $2.75 million at today's values, and Demetracopoulos discovered exactly how they had been made.

The funds, he learned, originated with the secret Greek intelligence agency, the KYP,* an organization founded, trained, and organized by the CIA. The payments, ordered by KYP Deputy Director Mikalis Roufogalis, were passed in cash, in large bills issued by the Central Bank of Greece, to Thomas Pappas, an active supporter of the renegade regime.[14] Pappas personally transported the money to the United States.

The accuracy of Demetracopoulos' information was confirmed years later by a future KYP chief, Kostas Tsimas, and by Henry Tasca, whom Nixon would appoint ambassador to Greece.[15] The details of exactly how the payments were processed, which Demetracopoulos supplied to a House committee, are still withheld in congressional archives.

Uncovered just weeks before the 1968 presidential election, this information was potentially politically devastating. Demetracopoulos contacted the parties most likely to have an interest in exposing the scandal: the Humphrey Democrats. Through Nixon's old foe in California, Governor Brown, he arranged an appointment with Democratic National Chairman Lawrence O'Brien. O'Brien met twice with the Greek exile, his staff as many as five times.[16] They were impressed by the quality of his information, but uncertain how to handle it.

O'Brien wanted corroboration, and that could be obtained only by sending aides to Greece to interview Demetracopoulos' contacts or by bringing the contacts to Washington. In the frantic final days of the campaign neither course seemed feasible. O'Brien did brief Democratic candidate Hubert Humphrey on the matter. The president in turn was briefed by O'Brien.

The Democrats' hope was that Johnson would ask CIA Director Richard Helms, with his direct line to Greek intelligence, to confirm that the dictatorship was indeed funding Nixon. Yet Johnson took no action, and O'Brien made do with a half measure. Citing a newspaper report—also seeded by Demetracopoulos—that junta money had been reaching Nixon through Pappas, O'Brien issued the following press statement: "Mr. Nixon and Mr. Agnew should explain their relationship with Tom Pappas, and let the American people know what's going on." In the clamor of the countdown to the election, the statement was barely noticed. Nixon and Agnew responded by not responding.[17]

Yet in the months and years that followed, and in spite of attempts to silence him, Demetracopoulos would persist in trying to get the story out. Nixon had given another hostage to fortune.

*Kentriki Yperesia Pleroforion, or Central Intelligence Service.

Historians have speculated as to why Johnson did nothing about the information O'Brien brought to him about the junta funding. A persuasive explanation is that the president was at that very time preoccupied with a weightier matter, his struggle to extricate the United States from the Vietnam War. On the very day that O'Brien publicly challenged Nixon about Tom Pappas Johnson was confronting intelligence on Vietnam that, if accurate, was even more damaging to Nixon and Agnew than the Greek scandal.

Nixon's involvement with Vietnam went far back and is replete with mystery—some merely intriguing, some as serious as it is possible to be.

23

How many American soldiers
Died in this land?
How many Vietnamese
Lie buried under trees and grass . . .
Now the wineglass joins friends in peace.
The old men lift their glasses.
Tears run down their cheeks.

—Poem by former Viet Cong guerrilla Van Le, given
to CBS correspondent Morley Safer, 1989

Sergeant Hollis Kimmons, a helicopter crewman, was not one of the more than fifty-eight thousand Americans who died in the Vietnam conflict.[1] When he returned home, after service with the army's 145th Aviation Battalion, he rarely talked about the war. Both his former wives, however, have recalled that he mentioned an encounter with Richard Nixon. It had been a "mission," he said, but would not discuss the details.

In 1984, at home in Oregon with his second wife, Gaby, Kimmons noticed an ad in the paper. An autograph dealer on the East Coast, he read, was willing to purchase signatures or letters written by famous people. "I have something," Kimmons told his wife, and dug out a page from an old notebook. On it, scrawled in faded green ink, was the following:

To Hollis Kimmons

with appreciation for his protection on my helicopter ride in Vietnam

from
Richard Nixon

Kimmons responded to the autograph dealer, and eventually, after the dealer judged the handwriting to be genuine, sold his scrap of paper for a hundred dollars. In the process he told the dealer a remarkable story. Nixon had signed the notebook, the former soldier said, during an April 1964 trip to South Vietnam. Kimmons had been one of a helicopter crew of four assigned to fly him around during the visit, in the course of which, according to Kimmons, something most unusual happened.

The crewmen had been briefed by the unit commanding officer, Lieutenant Colonel Hughes, and by Major Schreck, who was to pilot the Nixon helicopter. Kimmons and his fellow fliers were told the mission was secret and not to be revealed for twenty years, which was exactly how long Kimmons waited to tell his story.

Before 8:00 A.M. on the morning of the second day of the trip, Kimmons said, Nixon had boarded the helicopter dressed in army fatigues bearing no nametags. Escorted by two other machines, they had first flown to Phouc Binh, a provincial capital northwest of Saigon. There Nixon had met with "a Catholic priest named Father Wa." Wa, according to Kimmons, was "a unique individual who had contact with the Viet Cong. . . . He was the go-between and arranged the exchange of gold for U.S. prisoners . . . a meeting place was arranged for the following day."

The next day, Kimmons said, Nixon was flown first to An Loc, a town near South Vietnam's border with Cambodia, and then on to a jungle clearing. There, Kimmons told the autograph dealer, "Nixon met with a Viet Cong lieutenant and established a price for the return of five U.S. prisoners. The location for the exchange was agreed, and the crew departed for Saigon. . . ."

Later that day, according to Kimmons, the helicopter took on board a box loaded with gold—in those days very much a currency in Southeast Asia—and flew to "Phumi Kriek," inside Cambodia.[2] "At the exchange point five U.S. servicemen were hustled out of the jungle accompanied by several armed soldiers. The box of gold was unloaded and checked by the VC lieutenant and the exchange was made. The crew and rescued prisoners immediately departed for Saigon where [the ransomed prisoners] were sent to the hospital."[3]

Nixon did indeed visit South Vietnam in April 1964. Old press clippings report a stay of two days, from April 1 to 3, on what he said at the time was "a private business trip" for Pepsi-Cola across Asia. In fact, as he later acknowledged in his memoirs, it was a political fact-finding trip, one of the many he made while out of office. But is there any truth to the account of U.S. prisoners, the Viet Cong, and gold bars?

The autograph dealer who bought Kimmons' scrap of paper with Nixon's signature, Mark Vardakis, has said that he tried repeatedly—through Nixon's office—to get him to confirm or deny the story. In the past, on another matter, Nixon had been helpful to Vardakis, but this time the dealer's phone calls and letters went unanswered. "I got the cold shoulder," Vardakis told the author, "got no cooperation at all."

In 1985, when the Forbes Collection acquired the note for its collection of presidential autographs, a story on the alleged incident appeared in the *New York Times*. The *Times'* reporter, in turn, received no assistance when he contacted Nixon's office. Nixon himself was eventually asked about the matter by the historian Herbert Parmet. Responding to questions submitted in writing in advance, he at first replied, in contradiction of his own assertion at the time, "The trip was purely political. I never took a trip to Vietnam for business purposes." Then, when pressed on the specific allegation: "It's a marvelous story, but totally apocryphal . . . I've heard of it."[4]

Parmet was not sure what to believe. "Remember," he reminded the author, "Nixon was a master of dissembling. . . . Everything has to be treated with caution."

A hard look at the crewman's story fails to disprove it. While in Vietnam in 1964, Nixon was flown by helicopter—five heavily armed machines were involved—to see villages outside Saigon.[5] They were not the locations named by Kimmons, but nothing in the available record excludes the possibility that he had the covert meetings claimed by Kimmons.

Evidence exists, moreover, of a dispute between U.S. diplomats and army officers about Nixon's travel that day. A National Security Council memo written soon afterward referred to "the unfortunate episode of Nixon and the helicopters." A footnote to the memo, published by the State Department in 1992, states that the deputy commander of U.S. forces in Vietnam at the time, General William Westmoreland, "escorted Nixon . . . apparently by unauthorized use of helicopters."

Other records indicate that Henry Cabot Lodge, the U.S. ambassador to South Vietnam and Nixon's former running mate in the 1960 election, had ordered a senior aide to "keep an eye" on Nixon during the visit. He told the aide, Mike Dunn: "Get on the helicopter with him. I don't want him ever alone with anybody unless you are there to hear what he is told and what he says." Dunn, who failed to join the group on the helicopter, was quoted as saying Westmoreland had turned him away.[6] Why he really became separated from the Nixon party was never fully resolved.

Notes written by Major Paul Schreck, one of the two officers named by Kimmons as having briefed the helicopter crews, show that he did pilot Nixon. They do not refer to the secret operation Kimmons described, and Schreck could not be interviewed; like Kimmons, he died in the early nineties. However, the second officer named, Lieutenant Colonel John Hughes, was alive and provided tantalizing information.

The battalion commander recalled meeting Nixon and ferrying him around on a "milk run," the overt part of the trip.[7] Hughes said he assigned his "best people" to the job, including Kimmons, who served either as crew chief or door gunner. He had no direct knowledge of the story Kimmons told—of the meeting with the Viet Cong and the prisoner exchange—but he was aware that a part of the mission had been a secret operation.

"That was run by the Green Berets," Hughes said carefully. "All I know about it is that the Green Berets took Nixon on a mission. . . . That was all classified, and I didn't have access to it. I knew he was going out on something unusual. . . . I didn't care for the idea of his doing that. He came out of it alive. Nobody got shot. No holes in the bird. I bellied up real close to the Berets, and I'm not going to tell you everything we did. . . ."

The famed Green Berets—more formally, the U.S. Army's Special Forces—were deployed in strength across South Vietnam at the time of the Nixon visit, with two camps near the Cambodian border in the area of the prisoner exchange that Kimmons described. They were working with other services that year under the umbrella of the Special Operations Group (SOG), answerable directly to the Pentagon. A new program of clandestine missions, approved by President Johnson two months earlier, involved what were politely described as "destructive undertakings"; using Vietnamese and Chinese mercenaries to run commando raids into Cambodia, North Vietnam, and Laos.[8]

General Westmoreland, who accompanied Nixon on at least part of his helicopter tour, was one of a handful of senior non-SOG officers briefed on those operations. The go-between, remembered by Kimmons as Father Wa, almost certainly refers to a gun-toting soldier-priest by the name of Nguyen Lao *Hoa*, celebrated for organizing resistance to the Viet Cong under the patronage of Edward Lansdale, the legendary CIA operative who pioneered covert actions in Southeast Asia. Lansdale was on close personal terms with Nixon.

Research has also unearthed an order to the U.S. Special Forces, dated the day of Nixon's arrival, instructing units to "cease activities within 5km. Of VN [Vietnam]/Cambodian border." The command originated with "Maj. Gen./Prime Minister of RVN"—South Vietnam's prime minister, Major General Nguyen Khanh. Khanh and his foreign minister met Nixon for dinner during the visit. Were the U.S. Special Forces being ordered to avoid combat to keep a former vice president out of harm's way—as much as possible—during a secret negotiation?

U.S. personnel did go missing in those early days of the war. Yet published government records, subjected to intense scrutiny in the nineties because of claims that U.S. prisoners remained alive in enemy hands, reflect no prisoner exchange in 1964.[9] The chief of analysis for the Defense Intelligence Agency's office on POW/MIA affairs, Sedgwick Tourison, in 1999 judged Kimmon's account "farfetched."

How then to account for the several components of the episode that seem to fit Kimmons's claims? Would Kimmons have named Major Schreck and his former commanding officer, Lieutenant Colonel Hughes, both alive when he made his allegations, had he known they were likely to challenge his story? Why did Colonel Hughes agree in his interview for this book that the Green Berets did take Nixon on a "classified" mission?

At the time of Nixon's 1964 visit Vietnam had still been a small war in a distant country remote from day-to-day concerns in the United States. That year 146 Americans died there, and 1,039 were wounded. Four years later, with the 1967 U.S. death toll at nearly 1,000 a month and rising, it had become the key issue of the presidential election.

For Nixon, almost certainly facing his last chance of capturing the White House, the national crisis posed a difficult question. As the candidate presenting himself as an expert on foreign affairs, as the veteran of more trips to Southeast Asia than any other politician, what cogent Vietnam policy could he offer the nation?

Nixon had always supported the line U.S. leaders from Truman to Johnson had taken, namely that support for the South Vietnam regime was justified by the notion that its collapse would be followed by the loss to the Communists of the entire region. Fourteen years earlier Nixon had been one of the first to urge that the government "take the risk now by putting American boys in." Then, he had even shown himself open to using nuclear weapons in Vietnam.[*]

As late as 1992, Nixon would maintain that President Kennedy had been right to commit sixteen thousand "advisers" with air and naval backup, which represented the first step into the quagmire.[10] The United States, Nixon urged at the time, should allocate all possible resources to achieve victory. In those gung ho days, before the casualties started to mount, he was not alone. Robert Kennedy too had been confident his country was "going to win."

In 1964, after the trip to Vietnam on which he allegedly negotiated the release of American prisoners, Nixon had called for "nothing less than victory." As American deaths climbed into the hundreds, he charged that the Johnson administration lacked "the will to win . . . win for America and win for the Southeast Asians."

By 1965 Washington raised its commitment to two hundred thousand men, including combat troops for the first time, and undertook the first strategic bombing of North Vietnam. Nixon now called for "victory over the aggressors," arguing that U.S. forces could not be withdrawn until the South became capable of defending itself. On the ideological front, he claimed, "we have already won." He opposed talk of a negotiated settlement, again insisting there could be "no substitute for victory."

In 1966, with troop levels expanded to four hundred thousand and increased bombing failing to have the desired effect, Defense Secretary Robert

*See p. 165.

McNamara was assailed by doubt regarding the government's strategy. He advised Johnson to "level off military involvement for the long haul while pressing for talks." The leader Nixon so admired, President de Gaulle, publicly called for American withdrawal, as he likewise urged Nixon privately both then and later.

The tycoon Elmer Bobst, so close a confidant to Nixon that he was Uncle Elmer to the Nixon girls, thought the war "an unmitigated disaster." "We must stop this war," he would write Nixon, "because of the uselessness of having to keep on killing and maiming thousands of human beings who have the right to live. We will have to face up to the world and state that for reasons of humanity alone we wish to bring this godless war to an end, without having to thrust further hundreds of Vietnamese into the earth."

It was during that year, when staying with Bobst, that Nixon told Len Garment he was "driven by his pacifist mother's idealism." On yet another trip to Vietnam, however, he called for not just "a marginal number [of troops] . . . but more than enough. . . ." He seemed to swing from one policy to another, on one day apparently calling for troop increases, on another warning of the risk of "going overboard" and sending too many soldiers. The Vietnam conflict, Nixon repeatedly said, would be remembered as "the war that had to be fought to prevent World War III."

In 1967, the year before the election, more than eleven thousand Americans were killed in the war, along with an estimated hundred thousand Vietnamese combatants. Some fifty thousand civilians were also killed or wounded. The U.S. troop strength would rise to nearly half a million by year's end.

Defense Secretary McNamara decided at this point that "escalation threatened to spin the war utterly out of control." U.S. efforts had hurt the Communists, he told Johnson, but they were still able to keep up their attacks. The enemy showed no sign of breaking under the bombing. McNamara suggested reining in the military and adopting a more flexible bargaining position. At the same time CIA Director Richard Helms told Johnson that the risks of accepting failure in Vietnam were "probably more limited and controllable than most previous argument had indicated."

McNamara reported moreover, that the "other war," the struggle for the hearts and minds of the Vietnamese population, was also going badly. Corruption was rampant, the population apathetic. Such concerns appeared not to bother Nixon. On another visit to Saigon that year he responded cynically when an American official asked for his help in encouraging that genuine elections be held in South Vietnam. "Oh sure, honest, yes, honest, that's right," said Nixon, *so long as you win.*" Then he winked and slapped his knee.

Unlike McNamara and many others in Washington, Nixon remained effusively optimistic about the war's outcome. "It can be said now," he declared, "that the defeat of the Communist forces in South Vietnam is inevitable. The only question is, how soon?" When U.S. bombers hit targets inside the buffer zone along the Chinese frontier, an area previously out of bounds, Nixon said the time was right for "massive pressures."

"Most Americans," McNamara told Johnson, "do not know how we got where we are. . . . All want the war ended and expect their President to end it. Or else." At home mass protest was beginning in earnest—twenty thousand people marched on the Pentagon in the fall of 1967. Nixon had already called for limits to protest, supporting a call for dismissal of a professor who said he would welcome a Communist victory. By now even many formerly hawkish Republicans were having grave doubts about the conflict.

No politician could safely ignore such a groundswell of popular opinion. Nixon listened in September 1967, when speechwriter Richard Whalen advised him not to visit Vietnam again if all he was going to do was come back continuing to voice support for the war. Nixon canceled the trip. "Flexibility," he told Whalen, "is the first principle of politics."

From then on until the election Nixon became not so much flexible on Vietnam as opaque, ambiguous. In conclave with Whalen, he pondered ways to make his pitch on the war sound different from Johnson's. He thought he should stop talking about seeking "an honorable end to the war," exclaiming: "What the hell does that mean?" Yet "peace with honor" would ultimately become Nixon's long-term theme, and more than five years later, as president, he would claim to have achieved precisely that.

If he were in the White House, Nixon told Whalen in private, he would be prepared to threaten the North with nuclear weapons. In the meantime, though, he wanted his speechwriters to produce something that had a "hopeful note, an upsweep of optimism," language that signaled flexibility. Whalen and his colleague Ray Price turned out draft after unused draft. When Whalen submitted a memo suggesting that the war was a "gross failure," that the nation stood "imprisoned in a gigantic mistake," Nixon did not reply.

Instead, he again publicly called for tougher tactics against North Vietnam "in our national interest" and characterized the latest Communist onslaught, the Tet offensive, as "a last-ditch effort." He again raised the possibility that the Vietnam conflict could lead to World War III. Then he took a position that startled everyone, including his own staff.

"If in November this war is not over," Nixon announced to an audience in March 1968, "I say that the American people will be justified in electing new leadership, and I pledge to you that new leadership will end the war and win the peace in the Pacific." "Nothing lay behind the 'pledge,' " speechwriter Whalen wrote later, "except Nixon's instinct for an extra effort of salesmanship. . . ."

The *New York Times*'s David Halberstam recalled that Nixon used this ploy repeatedly, "touching his breast pocket as if the plan were right there in the jacket—implying that to say what was in it might jeopardize secrecy." As Halberstam's colleague Neil Sheehan put it, Nixon gave the public the impression he had such a plan—and that was what counted.[11]

For a while after the "pledge" speech, it seemed to his aides that Nixon was about to say something meaningful about Vietnam. Feet propped on a desk at campaign headquarters, he told Whalen he was going to start talking "substantively" about "this stupid war." He said that it was vital to restrain China and to persuade the Soviets—who with China supplied North Vietnam with arms—that an American defeat would embolden Beijing and heighten the risk of a superpower confrontation.

As a Nixon speech was being drafted along these lines, President Johnson changed the political landscape. He announced a peace initiative in the form of a limited bombing halt and, astonishing almost everyone, said he would not be running for reelection. Nixon canceled his own speech, explaining he would refrain from comment on the war while hopes of a peace breakthrough lasted.

Dispirited, Whalen concluded that on Vietnam as on many other issues his boss was guided less by conviction than by centrism, "the pragmatic splitting of differences along a line drawn through the middle of the electorate. . . . Nixon's aim was to find the least assailable middle ground."

Nixon's withdrawal into silence, couched to look like patriotic support of the president, seemed to Whalen to be nothing more than "a brilliantly executed political stroke—and a cynical default on the moral obligation of a would-be president to make his views known to the people. But politics imposed no sanctions on maneuvers that worked, and Nixon's worked superbly."

"I've come to the conclusion," Nixon told Whalen and colleagues privately, "that there's no way to win the war. But we can't say that, of course. In fact, we have to seem to say the opposite, just to keep some degree of bargaining leverage."

That summer of 1968, during a stroll beside the ocean with Haldeman, Nixon talked of frightening North Vietnam into taking part in peace talks. "I call it the 'Madman Theory,' Bob," he said. "I want the North Vietnamese to believe I've reached the point where I might do *anything* to stop the war. We'll just slip the word to them that, 'for God's sake, you know Nixon is obsessed about Communists. We can't restrain him when he's angry—and he has his hand on the nuclear button'—and Ho Chi Minh himself will be in Paris in two days begging for peace."[12]

In a 1984 interview Nixon claimed not to remember having made such a remark. Yet Charles Colson likewise recalled Nixon, as president, instructing Kissinger to warn Soviet Ambassador Anatoly Dobrynin that "the President has lost his senses, that you don't know if you can restrain him, that Nixon might start using serious weapons in North Vietnam and dramatically escalate the war."

Nixon "sat in the Oval Office chuckling," said Colson, "while Kissinger carried out the mission." This account corresponds to an episode described by Kissinger in his memoirs. Nixon, he said, told him in the fall of 1969 to "convey to Dobrynin that the President was 'out of control' on Vietnam." Kissinger claimed that he regarded the order as too "dangerous" to carry out and so said nothing to Dobrynin about Nixon's supposed instability.

Three months earlier, however, Kissinger had sent that very same message by proxy when he instructed Len Garment, about to leave on a trip to Moscow, to give the Soviets "the impression that Nixon is somewhat 'crazy'—immensely intelligent, well organized and experienced to be sure, but at moments of stress or personal challenge unpredictable and capable of the bloodiest brutality." Garment carried out the mission, telling a senior Brezhnev adviser that Nixon was "a dramatically disjointed personality . . . more than a little paranoid . . . when necessary, a cold-hearted butcher."[13] The irony, the former aide reflected ruefully in 1997, was that everything he had told the Russians turned out to be "more or less true."

Within weeks of the "Madman" chat with Haldeman, Nixon changed his tune totally when he spoke with Republican Senator Mark Hatfield, a committed opponent of the war. "He gave me assurances," a satisfied Hatfield wrote afterward in a letter to a concerned citizen, "that he saw this war not as a military threat . . . but rather as an outgrowth of the misery and injustices of life in South Vietnam . . . that the real thrust against Communism will not be made with hand grenades and guns alone but with a more effective battle against social, economic and political injustices that deny people their basic right to adequate food, living conditions and human dignity. . . . I concluded that Richard Nixon represented the greatest hope for peace."

Heartened and convinced by their discussion, Hatfield announced that Nixon was his candidate for president, for he found him to be a man with "a reliable believable peace alternative." Nixon told Haldeman he was "the one man in this country" who could end the war, a task he would accomplish in his first year as president. Earlier he had informed a visitor he would do it in six months.

In the late spring of 1968, though, Nixon told an interviewer, "There is no alternative to the war's going on. We have to stop it with victory, or it will start all over again." Did he really believe victory was possible? His first defense secretary, Melvin Laird, told the author in 1998, "I think he started out that way. He felt he could win. . . ."[14]

If Nixon had a cogent notion of how he could win the war or even end U.S. involvement in Vietnam, the American people never got a chance to consider it. As the countdown to the election began, Senator Hatfield worried that the candidates' real positions on Vietnam remained unclear. "In the democratic process," he said, "voters should not be forced to go to the polls with their fingers crossed; they should not be forced to rely on blind faith that the men they vote for will share their views on the most important issues of the election."

That was very much the dilemma voters found themselves facing in November. Only insiders knew that in the very last days before the election President Johnson had been presented with damning intelligence suggesting that Nixon and his running mate Agnew were playing politics with the lives of hundreds of thousands of men, American as well as Vietnamese. Had this information been made public at the time, it would surely have destroyed Nixon's presidential hopes in a single stroke—then and forever.

This is a story that has long hung between the shadows of Nixon's past and the disgrace of his presidency, half reported on partial evidence, often exploited by partisan sources, yet never fully resolved. He escaped full opprobrium for his behavior while he was alive, yet the evidence implies a sin and a cynicism worse than any of the offenses that would later make headlines.

The episode in question turns on the attempt by President Johnson, in the weeks before the 1968 election, to convince the Communists and the South Vietnamese to attend peace talks that might end the war. To achieve that would mean overcoming the complex objections of both sides. Would the Communists sit down with the South? Would the South sit down with both the North and the Viet Cong, theoretically an independent guerrilla movement but dismissed by the South as the creature of the northerners?

In the fall, after marathon diplomatic efforts, Johnson was persuaded that a formula had been found. Overcoming his own doubts, and with the support of U.S. commanding General Creighton Abrams, he at last decided to take the step essential to secure North Vietnam's cooperation. On October 31, in spite of evidence that South Vietnam might not come into line, he ordered a halt to the bombing of the North.

Had the talks actually gotten under way there was a chance—impossible and pointless now to debate how good or slender a chance—that the Vietnam War would soon have ended. The talks did not start, however, because two days later South Vietnam's President Thieu announced his government would not take part.

Thieu had a slew of reasons not to attend, not the least of them being the likelihood—unpalatable and usually unacknowledged in those days—that his regime had virtually no chance of long-term survival were the Americans to disengage.[15] Whether and when the Americans would disengage, however, would depend on who was in the White House.

President Johnson, nearing the end of his term, would soon be an irrelevance. Hubert Humphrey, his would-be Democratic successor, was a poor prospect from Thieu's point of view. He had already told South Vietnam's president bluntly that prolonged U.S. aid was just "not in the cards." Humphrey had also publicly promised to stop bombing the North and spoke of reducing the number of U.S. troops. With Nixon, on the other hand, as Thieu had told a close assistant, his regime would have "a chance."

In the weeks preceding the election, Nixon postured as a candidate who put the issue of the war above partisan politics. "In the spirit of country above party," he said before the bombing halt, the peace effort had his full support. "The pursuit of peace," he told voters, "is too important for politics as usual."

Pointing to Agnew, seated near him at a rally in Madison Square Garden, Nixon assured the nation that neither of them would make any remarks that might disrupt the negotiations. "Neither he nor I," he told the crowd, "will destroy the chance of peace."

Neither Nixon or Agnew of course did say anything publicly to derail the talks. It is what they did in secret that matters. It now seems clear that with John Mitchell, through one or more go-betweens, Nixon not only encouraged President Thieu to believe he would get a better deal from a Nixon administration but actually urged him to boycott the talks. They were apparently still doing so just three days before the election, when hopes for peace, boosted by Johnson's bombing halt announcement, sent Humphrey surging ahead in the polls.[16]

Stephen Ambrose, professor of history at the University of New Orleans, has stated the charge succinctly. "In private," he wrote, "Nixon made contact with President Thieu in an effort to scuttle the peace prospects." Clark Clifford, who had replaced McNamara as secretary of defense, thought Nixon's action "probably decisive in convincing President Thieu to defy President Johnson."[17]

At the time, to dispel rumors about his role, Nixon sent word to Johnson through Senator George Smathers that there was "not any truth at all in this allegation." In his memoirs he dealt with the accusation by leaving it out entirely.

The facts about the incident have emerged only gradually. Not until 1995 did researchers gain access to the "X" Envelope, a redacted collection of sensitive documents on the affair deposited at the Johnson Library, originally with the recommendation that it remain sealed for fifty years. Relevant FBI documents were released to the author only in 1999. With these documents, the first scholarly studies, and new interviews with a key protagonist, a fuller picture has emerged.[18]

The key protagonist in the episode was Anna Chennault, the Chinese-born widow of the American World War II hero Claire Chennault.[19] By 1968, when she was forty-three, she was established as a wealthy Washington hostess, living in a new apartment block named Watergate. She was deeply involved in Southeast Asian affairs and had regular access to regional leaders like Taiwan's Chiang Kai-shek and the Philippines' Ferdinand Marcos. A 1966 letter examined by the author suggests that she may that year have had some contact with the CIA.[20]

Chennault had joined the Republican cause in 1960 and by 1968 had become vice-chairman of the Republican National Finance Committee and cochairman of Women for Nixon-Agnew. She and Nixon had first met in the early fifties, when he visited Taiwan as vice president. In the wilderness years, as Vietnam became a dominant American issue, they stayed in touch.[21] Chennault had contacts at the top levels of the Saigon government and tough views on how to deal with Hanoi. Her line, as surviving letters to Nixon show, was that an increase in bombing was the way to get the North to "bow down for peace."

The intrigues of 1968 really began the previous year. While Chennault was traveling in Asia, she received a spate of telegrams asking her to visit Nixon in New York. Robert Hill, a Republican foreign policy specialist, met her at the airport and escorted her to Nixon's Fifth Avenue apartment. While Hill waited in another room, Nixon introduced her to John Mitchell.

Chennault agreed that day to provide Nixon with advice on Vietnam in the coming months, working through Hill and Texas Senator John Tower. "When we do things," Nixon told her as the meeting ended, "it'll be better to keep it secret." He seemed even then, Chennault recalled, "conspiratorial."

In July the following year, as the election drew nearer, Chennault went to the Nixon apartment with South Vietnam's ambassador Bui Diem—a visit documented by both their diaries. A surviving internal staff memo addressed to "DC," Nixon's campaign pseudonym, pointed out that it "would have to be absolute [sic] top secret." "Should be," Nixon replied in a scrawled notation, "but I don't see how—with the S.S. [Secret Service] If it can be [secret] RN would like to see. . . ."

Nixon had told Chennault he wanted to "end this war with victory," a sentiment he now always repeated at the meeting with her and Bui Diem. "If I should be elected the next President," Chennault recalled his telling Bui Diem, "you can rest assured I will have a meeting with your leader and find a solution to winning this war." Nixon had met with Thieu in Saigon the previous year. Now, he told Thieu's ambassador that Chennault was to be "the only contact between myself and your government. If you have any message for me, please give it to Anna, and she will relay it to me, and I will do the same. . . ."

According to Chennault, she met more than once that year with President Thieu in Saigon. He complained about the pressure the Johnson administration was putting on him to attend peace talks and told her: "I would much prefer to have the peace talks after your elections." He asked her to "convey this message to your candidate." She did. From time to time President Thieu also sent her word through Ambassador Diem. He also used other messengers, including a colonel on his military staff, apparently because he did not entirely trust his own ambassador.[22]

In the weeks that followed Chennault had several more meetings with Nixon and Mitchell in New York. They told her to inform Saigon that were Nixon to become president, South Vietnam would get "a better deal." "The message," she told the author, "was relayed."

Asked if Nixon and Mitchell were trying to cut a deal to help win the election, Chennault nodded. "They worked out this deal to win the campaign," she said. "Power overpowers all reason."

"It was all very, very confidential," in Chennault's description. The air of intrigue was pervasive. At the July meeting Bui Diem remembered, Mitchell had been "silent, didn't say a word." Chennault noted that he worried constantly about wiretapping and kept changing his private telephone number. Chennault meanwhile told Nixon she could always be reached through Robert

Hill, the party official who had arranged the first meeting, Rose Woods, or another prominent Republican, Patricia Hitt.

In the weeks before the election, with growing signs of an impending bombing halt and the acceptance of peace talks, Nixon publicly voiced support for President Johnson. Privately, he admitted years later, he seethed with resentment. Today any objective reading of the notes and minutes of Johnson's meetings that fall reveals a president sometimes too hesitant in going forward for the taste of his own aides but genuinely devoted to the cause of peace. Nixon, however, was convinced the peace initiative was at least in part a political ploy, designed to swing the election to Humphrey.

Chennault stoked this resentment, apparently flying to Kansas City to meet with Nixon on October 16, the very day that Johnson briefed Nixon and the other candidates on his Vietnam plans, urging discretion in their public statements.[23] She bore with her a long written presentation that deplored the rumored bombing halt and recommended a long-term approach to the conflict. The same day Agnew received a briefing on the coming halt, originating with unnamed sources. Two days later Chennault saw the South Vietnamese ambassador again. A few days after that there was another meeting with Mitchell.

She and Mitchell were now in touch by phone almost daily. "Call me from a pay phone. Don't talk in your office," he would urge her. When she joked about possible wiretaps, he was not amused. Mitchell's message, she said, was always the same: If peace talks were announced, it was vital to persuade President Thieu not to take part.

In the last week of October Thieu's ambassador, Bui Diem, sent two encrypted radio messages from Washington to Saigon. The first, he wrote in his memoirs, noted: "Many Republican friends have contacted me and encouraged us to stand firm. . . ." The second—again, this is Bui Diem's account—mentioned that he was "regularly in touch with the Nixon entourage."

The former ambassador repeatedly told the author he would let him see the full text of those messages, but never produced them. His published version of the second cable, it seems, was almost certainly an exercise in damage limitation. The actual message was more troubling, according to the former State Department executive secretary, the late Benjamin Read.

Read's notes cite Saigon's ambassador as reporting that he had "explained discreetly to our partisan friends our firm attitude" and "plan to adhere to that position." "The longer the impasse continues," Bui Diem told Saigon, "the more we are favored," and Johnson would "probably have difficulties in forcing our hand." The ambassador also advised Saigon that if elected, Nixon would send an emissary to see President Thieu and consider visiting Saigon himself before the inauguration.

John Mitchell's concern about electronic surveillance was more justified than he knew. The National Security Agency was intercepting and deciphering South Vietnam's cable traffic—hence the State Department's access to the true text of the ambassador's message about "partisan friends." The CIA meanwhile was tracking the ambassador himself and had tried to install bugs in his office and living quarters.

In Saigon the agency had successfully placed a device in Thieu's own office at the presidential palace. The same week the intercepted embassy messages were sent, he was overhead saying: "Johnson and Humphrey will be replaced and then Nixon could change the U.S. position."

President Johnson was subsequently briefed on both the embassy intercepts and the transmission from the bug in Thieu's office. But more was to come. In the dawn hours of October 29, after an all-night meeting at which he finally decided on a bombing halt, came appalling news: President Thieu was backing out, raising pretexts to avoid committing Saigon to the peace talks.

Fifteen minutes later the president informed his most senior advisers—the secretaries of state and defense, the chairman of the Joint Chiefs of Staff, and the director of the CIA—of another development, something that could "rock the world."

In addition to the South Vietnamese cable intercepts, Johnson now had fresh information from a human source about Nixon's "conniving"—Johnson's characterization—with the Thieu regime. From Alexander Sachs, an eminent Wall Street banker who had once counseled President Roosevelt, came word that Nixon was "trying to frustrate the President, by inciting Saigon to step up its demands." He was "taking public positions intended . . . to block. They would incite Saigon to be difficult."

"It all adds up," President Johnson snapped to the assembled advisers. Through the grueling hours and days to come, amidst rising anger, the White House frantically tried to get Saigon back on board while simultaneously attempting to pin down precisely what the Nixon side was doing. Johnson ordered FBI wiretaps and physical surveillance of the South Vietnamese Embassy and a day later, after she had been seen entering the mission, surveillance of Anna Chennault.

On the evening of the thirty-first, during a conference call to the presidential candidates to brief them on the bombing halt, Johnson dropped a heavy hint that he was aware of the machinations to undermine his efforts. Nixon merely joined the opponents in promising the president his full support.

Behind the scenes, however, panic and pantomime gripped the Nixon camp. Mitchell went through the motions of interrogating campaign staffers—none of whom was in the know—asking if they had been "in touch with any embassies." Then he "reassured" administration contacts that his people had not been talking to the South Vietnamese.

Chennault suddenly found she could no longer get through to Mitchell. Certain now of the wiretapping he had always feared, Nixon's closest aide was avoiding direct contact with her. That night, however, as she was finishing dinner at the Sheraton Park Hotel, Chennault was called to the phone.

It was Mitchell, tension in his voice, asking her to call back on a safer line. When she did, he picked up on the first ring. "Anna," he said, "I'm speaking on behalf of Mr. Nixon. It's very important that our Vietnamese friends understand our Republican position, and I hope you made that clear to them. . . . Do you think they really have decided not to go to Paris?"

Realizing that the administration was working around the clock to change Thieu's mind, Nixon's man wanted to make sure he remained firm in his refusal.[24] Thieu duly obliged. On November 2, only three days before the election, he announced publicly that his country would not take part in peace talks under present conditions.

In the United States meanwhile Nixon found a devious way to insinuate that the bombing halt had been premature, designed purely as a ploy to help the Democrats win the election. He did so by getting a senior aide to make the accusation and then claiming the aide's views were at odds with his own. It was a barefaced lie; reporters on the campaign plane had actually seen Nixon briefing the aide who made the remarks.

As President Johnson grew angrier, his national security assistant, Walt Rostow, reminded him that there was still no really hard evidence that Nixon personally was involved in the chicanery with President Thieu. (The FBI agents watching Anna Chennault, for example, knew nothing of Mitchell's late-night call to her at the Sheraton Park. While they had seen her enter and leave the hotel and had trailed her home that night to the Watergate, they had no way of knowing about the compromising conversation held on secure phones.) So far as the public was concerned, that is how things have remained ever since: a very strong suspicion of perfidy but—Anna Chennault's statements aside—no conclusive proof.

With the release of the FBI file in 1999, however, the situation changes, for two key new documents bring fact and context to old rumor—and culpability much closer to Nixon and Agnew.

On November 2, the wiretapping of Ambassador Bui Diem's phone finally paid off. Chennault, the FBI's Washington field office reported (see p. 303):

CONTACTED VIETNAMESE AMBASSADOR BUI DIEM, AND ADVISED HIM THAT SHE HAD RECEIVED A MESSAGE FROM HER BOSS (NOT FURTHER IDENTIFIED), WHICH HER BOSS WANTED HER TO GIVE PERSONALLY TO THE AMBASSADOR. SHE SAID THE MESSAGE WAS THAT THE AMBASSADOR IS TO "HOLD ON, WE ARE GONNA WIN" AND THAT HER BOSS ALSO SAID "HOLD ON, HE UNDERSTANDS ALL OF IT." SHE REPEATED THAT THIS IS THE ONLY MESSAGE[.] "HE SAID PLEASE TELL YOUR BOSS TO HOLD ON." SHE ADVISED THAT HER BOSS HAD JUST CALLED FROM NEW MEXICO.

Spiro Agnew had made a campaign stop at Albuquerque, New Mexico, that day—and within the time frame that corresponded to Anna Chennault's movements.[25]

Days later, when things quieted down, Johnson would order the FBI to check all calls made by the Agnew party. He was unfortunately ill served. Director Hoover, a long-term Nixon supporter on cordial terms with Chennault, had already warned her she was being surveilled. As much as possible, he told her, the bureau was merely "making a show" of obeying Johnson's orders.

When it came to the Albuquerque calls, Hoover and his aide Cartha De-Loach ensured investigation was cursory and incomplete. Eventually, realizing he was being stalled, the president himself called to tell DeLoach: "Get me the information, and make it damned fast."

Out of the mess, and the still partially censored files, come two salient facts. The first is that phone records show that an Agnew aide in Albuquerque,

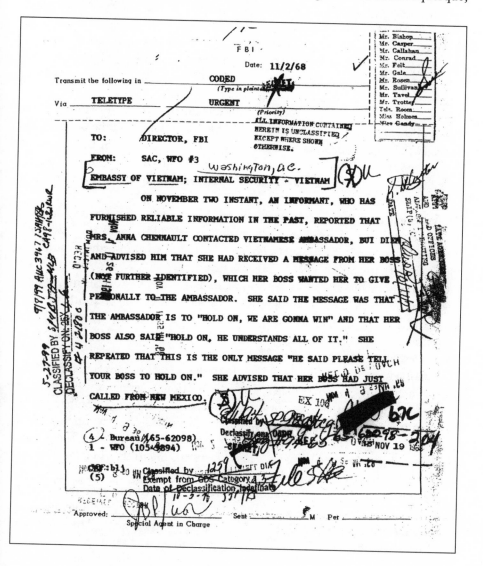

the very aide responsible for briefing Agnew on Vietnam, had made a call during the stopover to a "Mr. Hitt" at Nixon-Agnew headquarters.

Robert Hitt, an official of the Republican National Committee, was paymaster to the wireman Nixon used during the campaign to sweep for bugs and who conducted offensive bugging during the presidency. Hitt would also be named during the Watergate probe in connection with questionable cash transactions. His wife Patricia, cochairman of the campaign committee and a trusted Nixon friend from Whittier days, was as noted earlier one of the people Chennault earlier named as a potential go-between should Nixon wish to pass her messages.

The most important discovery, though, was relayed to the president by National Security Assistant Rostow when all the facts were in, ten days after the Albuquerque stopover. In a brief memo, referring to Chennault as "the Lady" and to Agnew as "the gentleman in Albuquerque," Rostow reported that there had been a call placed to Chennault.[26] Moreover, contrary to an earlier analysis, Agnew himself had had ample time to make the call.

The new information suggests a logical sequence to the events of those days. Following Thieu's announcement that he would not join the peace talks, as the Nixon side had hoped, he faced renewed pressure from the outraged Johnson administration. In the wake of the announcement, word came to Chennault from Agnew in Albuquerque that she should urge the South Vietnamese to remain resolute.

As revealed by the wiretap on the South Vietnamese Embassy, she duly relayed the message to President Thieu that he should "Hold on," because "we're gonna win": Nixon was going to win the election and would, as promised, give the South Vietnamese a better deal.

With whom did the message originate? Early on Rostow surmised in a report to the president that Agnew was "acting" on behalf of another party. While the report is still partially censored, the security assistant's supposition is clear enough. Agnew and Chennault barely knew each other; Nixon's running mate acted for no one but Nixon.[27]

Finally, wiretaps previously unknown to the public do connect Nixon himself to Chennault. On November 7, after the election, Chennault was overhead on the FBI's taps in a conversation with the South Vietnamese Embassy. She called initially the ambassador to say she had "made contact already" and would phone later. Then, speaking with the ambassador's secretary, she passed word that she had talked to "him," had been "talking to 'Florida,'" and has to make a few other calls before she can move."

Chennault and the ambassador apparently lunched together that day at Washington's Le Provençal restaurant and then talked on the phone again in the evening. She now told Bui Diem the message from President Thieu to "our boss" was "alright" [sic]. Then, the FBI report noted, she said:

THE PERSON SHE HAD MENTIONED TO DIEM WHO MIGHT BE THINK-
ING ABOUT "THE TRIP" WENT ON VACATION THIS AFTERNOON AND
WILL BE RETURNING MONDAY MORNING AT WHICH TIME SHE WILL
BE IN TOUCH AGAIN AND WILL HAVE MORE NEWS FOR DIEM. . . . THEY
ARE STILL PLANNING THINGS BUT ARE NOT LETTING PEOPLE KNOW
TOO MUCH BECAUSE THEY WANT TO BE CAREFUL TO AVOID EMBAR-
RASSING YOU, THEMSELVES, OR THE PRESENT U.S. GOVERNMENT.

Chennault had not named her "boss," but his identity is clear. The message from Thieu was a message of congratulation for the president-elect, who had indeed left for Florida to relax after the rigors of the campaign. Chennault's boss was Nixon himself.

Three days before the election, not all this damning evidence had been uncov-ered. What President Johnson did have in hand, however, was enough to make him furious.[28] Learning of his rage, Nixon phoned late at night with adamant denials. Anna Chennault, he insisted, had been acting on her own. At the end of the conversation, it was later reported, "Nixon and his friends collapsed with laughter. . . ."

The laughter was premature. "Johnson was certain in his own mind," re-called his aide Joe Califano, "that Nixon had betrayed his country. . . . Nixon's denials did nothing to undermine the President's conviction. . . . It was hor-rendous. . . . At last now, in the final hours, Johnson desperately wanted Humphrey to win the election."

To help Humphrey sustain his last-minute surge in the polls, Johnson now gave him the chance to expose the Chennault affair by personally briefing a Humphrey aide on the Nixon side's activity. When Humphrey was in turn in-formed by the aide aboard a campaign flight, he became uncharacteristically enraged. "By God," he roared, "when we land I'm going to denounce Thieu. I'll denounce Nixon. I'll tell about the whole thing." "What kind of a guy," he growled to a colleague, "could engage in something like this?"

As things turned out, however, neither he nor Johnson revealed what they knew. Humphrey worried that the raw intelligence was not sufficiently clear— at the time he got it—to make a convincing case. Aides also warned him that to go public with the information might look like an electoral ploy and back-fire. Humphrey accordingly deferred to Johnson, telling him he might "want to consider that you have an obligation to disclose this to the American people."

As late as election eve the word from the White House was that the Chen-nault matter might "very well blow the roof off the political race yet." In the end, though, Johnson's advisers decided it was too late and too potentially damaging to U.S. interests to uncover what had been going on. If Nixon should emerge as the victor, what would the Chennault outrage do to his viability as an incoming president? And what effect would it have on American opinion about the war? "You couldn't surface it," recalled Johnson's assistant Harry McPherson. "The country would be in terrible trouble."

There was another reason the lid stayed on. Three days after the election Johnson was still considering whether to "blow the whistle" on Nixon. Instead, Rostow recalled, the president "actively sought and obtained Nixon's cooperation . . . in delivering the word that the President-elect wished the South Vietnamese to proceed in moving towards a negotiation with Hanoi."

As so often in his career, Nixon's desperate need was to avoid exposure. Therefore, as both Johnson and Humphrey had predicted he would, Nixon now double-crossed President Thieu. He sent "strong word" to Saigon that it should reverse course and attend peace talks after all.

Anna Chennault was "flabbergasted" to find herself asked to accept Nixon's new line. "What makes you change your mind all of a sudden?" she asked John Mitchell.

"Anna, you're no newcomer to politics," Mitchell responded. "This, whether you like it or not, is politics."

Chennault stormed out in disgust, only to be harried with phone calls from other Nixon aides. At first she was urged again to send the changed signal to Saigon. When it became clear she would never agree, Nixon's people began to fear that she might disclose the true story.[29] A string of emissaries was sent to beg her not to talk to the press.

Chennault fended off reporters' inquiries for a long time thereafter, in part, she claimed, because she feared for her safety.[30] Later, at a White House function, Nixon thanked her effusively for her help in the election. "I've certainly paid dearly for it," she replied curtly. "Yes, I appreciate that," he responded. "I know you're a good soldier."

In Vietnam meanwhile, the real soldiers fought on. In the final five weeks leading up to the election 960 Americans had died. Vietnamese casualties, though less well documented, as always far exceeded U.S. losses.

Nixon cannot be held responsible for the collapse of the Johnson peace initiative. President Thieu would very probably have balked at attending talks anyway, even without the Republican pressure. The fact that Nixon covertly intervened, though, deliberately flouting the efforts of the American authorities, was indefensible. The way in which he involved himself remains to this day undefended.[31]

Richard Holbrooke, today U.S. representative to the United Nations, was in 1968 a young diplomat with Washington's Vietnam negotiating team in Paris. More recently, he investigated the Chennault episode while coauthoring former defense secretary Clifford's memoirs. "What the Nixon people did," he said in 2000, was "perhaps even a violation of the law. They massively, directly and covertly, interfered in a major diplomatic negotiation . . . probably one of the most important negotiations in American diplomatic history. There was no excuse for it. . . ."

According to his aide Califano, Johnson concluded from the experience that Nixon was "a man so consumed with power that he would betray the country's national security interests, undermine its foreign policy, and endanger the lives of its young soldiers to win office."

In Saigon, President Thieu sat hunched in front of a television watching the election returns. Nixon's victory was reportedly toasted in South Vietnamese government circles in French champagne. "We did it," one official bragged. "We helped elect an American president."[32]

The intrigues of the previous weeks, though, had a tragically insidious consequence: Thieu felt that Nixon was now in his debt and there had to be a payback. Ironically, moreover, South Vietnam's president would later defy Nixon, much as he defied Johnson in 1968. He would stall at the critical moment, denying Nixon a peace agreement in advance of the 1972 presidential election.

According to a former close aide, Thieu attended his first meeting with Nixon as president seeking "some acknowledgment of his role in helping Nixon win." He got it, even though Nixon was already talking publicly about troop withdrawals. The man who had spoken of ending the war within six months to a year privately offered reassurance. "He promised me eight years of strong support," Thieu recalled, "four years of military support during his first term in office and four years of economic support during his second term."

Under Nixon the Vietnam War was to burn on for four more agonizing years. A second country, Cambodia, would be secretly drawn into the conflict, eventually to be overwhelmed by the cataclysm of a revolution that was to take close to two million lives. Nixon would repeatedly punish North Vietnam with bombing more prolonged and devastating than any that had gone before.

Under Nixon, and in the name of the quest for an honorable peace, 20,763 more Americans died—more than a third of the total killed during the entire period of U.S. commitment. 111,230 Americans were wounded, and 109,230 South Vietnamese soldiers died, as did some 496,260 of the Communist enemy—and unknown thousands of innocent civilians.

Some commentators—Nixon included—have argued that his extension of the conflict was justified, that the struggle prevented other Southeast Asian countries from falling to communism. In old age Nixon persistently made the case that had Congress not eventually withdrawn funding and support, the Thieu government could have survived.

The case for the contrary seems equally compelling. To innumerable men and women who served in Vietnam or who observed the war as diplomats and journalists, the corrupt southern regime never deserved the sacrifice that was made in democracy's name. In the field, thousands of miles from the talking shops of Washington, many, including this author, by 1969 had rated Vietnam's prospects of ever surviving on its own as practically nil.

To such critics, the shame is not merely that the struggle was to no avail. It is that the peace with honor "won"—as Nixon put it—was in no meaningful way any more worthwhile than the settlement that seemed possible had the 1968 Johnson peace initiative succeeded.

There was something else, as grave a betrayal—if it is true—as the undermining of the peace effort. Henry Kissinger, soon to find fame as national security adviser and secretary of state, offered a cynical assessment of the administration's position a few months after meeting Nixon. "I agree that the war is a mistake," he reportedly told a visitor. "I think it is clear now that we should never have gone in there, and I don't see how any good can come of it. But we can't do what you recommend and just pull out, because the boss's whole constituency would just fall apart; those are his people who support the war effort: the South; the blue-collar Democrats in the North. The Nixon constituency is behind the war effort. If we were to pull out of Vietnam, there would be a disaster, politically, for us here, at home."

For Nixon, in November 1968, political disaster was far off. What he had, at last, was political victory—if just barely.

24

*This really is the American dream, where people
from humble circumstances can, through
sheer hard work, go up the ladder.*

—Pat Nixon, 1968

The people of the United States fulfilled Nixon's need to win in November 1968, but grudgingly. The last Harris poll, on election eve, put Humphrey ahead by three points. Neither man could hope for a clear majority.

Aboard the campaign plane, as he headed for New York to wait out the count, Nixon shocked Pat and the girls by acknowledging, "We could lose." He lunched with Bebe Rebozo, then closeted himself in his private compartment for the rest of the journey.

Fearing the election would be stolen from him, as he believed it had been stolen in 1960 by John Kennedy, Nixon had mounted Operation Eagle Eye, designed to thwart trickery in Chicago by the Democrats' Mayor Daley. A former FBI assistant director ran Operation Integrity, monitoring the national scene. Now, in the final hours, Nixon was still anxious. When word came in of a holdup in the count in Texas, he deputed Haldeman to "find out what the hell was happening."

Nixon sat alone in his suite at the Waldorf Towers, high above Manhattan, far into the long night. Refusing to watch the television and its yammering pundits, he relied on tallies brought to him every quarter of an hour by Haldeman. He scribbled calculations on his yellow pads and smoked his way through five cigars.

So insecure was Nixon that he had urged Humphrey to agree that should the outcome be so close that it had to go to the House of Representatives for a decision, the winner of the popular vote should get the support of the loser. Humphrey replied dryly that he would "stand by the Constitution." The journalist Tom Wicker thought Nixon's proposal foreshadowed "what the nation was later to see in Watergate—an impatience with constitutional procedures and a willingness in some cases to circumvent them.[1]

In the dawn hours, with the numbers suggesting he had won but with Illinois yet to report, Nixon tried to steamroller his opponent. He sent word to "tell Hubert to quit playing games. We've won Illinois, so let's get this thing over with." It was a breach of custom and etiquette, and the Humphrey camp was outraged.

In their suite down the hall Pat and the Nixon daughters had sat through the returns isolated and ignored. During the Illinois standoff, overwhelmed by nervous tension, Pat rushed to the bathroom and threw up.

Then it was over. Illinois did declare for Nixon, and Humphrey did concede. Nixon had won by an infinitesimal margin: 43.40 percent of the national vote to Humphrey's 42.72 percent, with Alabama's George Wallace and marginal candidates taking the rest. Even though four million more Americans had voted than in 1960, Nixon received more than two million votes fewer than he had against Kennedy. But he had won.

Bebe Rebozo summoned Billy Graham to Nixon's suite that morning. Nixon, Pat, Tricia, Julie, and the evangelist stood in a circle holding hands as Graham gave thanks for "God's plan for the country" and "the spiritual heritage of Nixon's mother."

Then it was down to the Waldorf ballroom, weary family at his side, secretary Rose Woods weeping with relief, to address the crowd. Nixon said his great objective as president would be to "bring the American people together." He did not mention Vietnam but told Graham privately that the United States was "on the verge of victory"—so long as the bombing continued.

At home that afternoon, as the women packed for a break in Florida, Nixon retreated to his study. Soon, through the double doors, came the blare and brass of one of his favorite records, the Richard Rodgers theme for *Victory at Sea*. Later, as he and Pat boarded the plane, he swung her around in a pirouette. His staff noticed that the aircraft, provided by President Johnson as a courtesy, was Air Force One, the same jet that five years earlier had carried John F. Kennedy home from Dallas in a coffin.

The trappings of office were already in evidence. People accustomed to addressing him as Mr. Nixon or Dick started trying out Mr. President. To the Secret Service detail guarding him, its number now doubled, Nixon was now known by the code name Searchlight. Pat was Starlight.

This was what Nixon had yearned for so long. Yet, Haldeman thought, watching and listening to his boss, that "he felt it was very strange that he could get elected."

The days and weeks that followed were not exactly as the public was led to believe, and they were full of portents.

"Baloney!" exclaimed Ehrlichman, recalling press reports that the president-elect was ensconced with his staff and "with bulging briefcases, doing a lot of work. We did have a couple of meetings, but basically we were left on our own to compose the government. . . . How did Nixon pick the White House and other personnel? The answer to that question is: 'Not very well.' The personnel process during our transition from Johnson was a shambles."

Scorning the free offices that had been made available to them in Washington, the Nixon people installed themselves in Manhattan's Pierre Hotel. Campaign treasurer Maurice Stans, soon to be secretary of commerce, was shocked by "the lavish facilities and the extravagant costs," a million dollars more than the federal allowance.

When a prepared file on possible appointees proved useless, Nixon approved a farcical scheme. Letters went out to every single person listed in *Who's Who,* some sixty thousand individuals, soliciting recommendations on how to fill two thousand government jobs.

The selection process began oddly. Less than twenty-four hours after the election, Nixon casually offered John Ehrlichman the post of attorney general. Ehrlichman, who had had limited experience as an attorney, thought the notion "ridiculous." He became instead White House counsel, in which job, he later recalled, "I didn't do one single legal chore." He advised, rather, on domestic policy.

The attorney general job went to campaign manager John Mitchell. Nixon's patron Thomas Dewey had sniffed that Mitchell "may be the best bond lawyer in New York, but he's no politician." He served however—as one reference book has it—as Nixon's "political right arm—arm-twister and lightning rod, counselor and confidant. . . ."

Mitchell had not immediately joined Nixon and other staff in Florida after the election, explaining tearfully that he had to go "take care of some things with Martha." His mercurial wife, whom Nixon could not stand and whose indiscretions were to help blacken his name, was already having problems with alcohol.

In picking Bob Haldeman as White House chief of staff, Nixon had in mind advice Eisenhower had once given him: that every president needs "his S.O.B." At forty-two, having earned his stripes as a superefficient campaign organizer, Haldeman became by his own account his boss's "pluperfect S.O.B."

Beguiled at first by the chief of staff's quiet manner, Theodore White thought him an "absolutely outgoing, fine guy." Before leaving J. Walter Thompson to follow Nixon, Haldeman had supervised the accounts of 7-Up, Sani-Flush, Blue Chip Stamps, and Walt Disney Productions. His "great dream," even after 1968, was that he would one day become head of the Disney empire. By staying with Nixon, White later concluded, he became a man who "swam too far out, beyond his natural depth."

The cliché would later be that with Ehrlichman, Haldeman was one of Nixon's "Nazis."[2] While he was the aide closest to the throne, Haldeman had an odd nonrelationship with Nixon in human terms. In the thirteen years of their association, the two men dined informally together, with their wives, only once. "He didn't see me as a person, or even, I believe, as a human being," Haldeman said years later. "To this day he doesn't know how many children I have or anything else about my personal life. He never asked. . . .

"Shortly after it came out," Haldeman said, "I saw the movie *Star Wars*: there is a robot, a metal machine clanking along doing what it's told by a computer-like mind. From Nixon's viewpoint, that's what I was. And I was a good machine." Nixon would eventually designate Haldeman his "Lord High Executioner." The "good machine" inspired terror in White House colleagues.

Having won the presidency, Nixon rid himself of many old friends and retainers. Herb Klein, remembered as one of the most decent figures in the entourage, was passed over as press secretary in favor of Ron Ziegler, a much younger man from Haldeman's old ad agency. Ziegler—"Zigzag" to reporters because of his talent for obscuring the facts—would remain loyal to the end and beyond.

On Haldeman's orders, but with Nixon's acquiescence, even the faithful Rose Woods was relegated to a basement room far from the Oval Office. At one stage after hearing this news, she refused to speak to Nixon, even allowing herself an outraged "Go fuck yourself!" She made her point and, while Haldeman got the office adjacent to the president, she wound up with one close by.

One after another, White House posts were filled with clean-cut, upright-seeming young men approved by Haldeman. A cosmetics businessman, Jeb Magruder, was brought in as a special assistant. Another J. Walter Thompson product, Dwight Chapin, would work the Oval Office phones and tend to Nixon's personal needs. He believed his boss would become "the greatest president in history." A lawyer completing a hitch in army intelligence, Tom Huston, was recruited to the domestic security committee. A young attorney with the Nixon law firm, Gordon Strachan, became Haldeman's personal assistant.

Later arrivals would include attorney Charles Colson, an ex-marine who became a Nixon intimate and, in his own words, a "flag-waving, kick-'em-in-the-nuts, anti-press, anti-liberal Nixon fanatic"; and John Dean, the counsel Nixon was to describe as "a Judas and a turncoat . . ." when he spilled the Watergate beans to a Senate committee.

Colson's father considered his son "viciously loyal," and colleagues recall Dean's initial eagerness to "please the boss." Huston would later speak—one assumes with hyperbole—of the unquestioning readiness of Nixon's young men to follow orders. "If Nixon told them to nationalize the railroads," he said, "they'd have nationalized the railroads. If he'd told them to exterminate the Jews, they'd have exterminated the Jews."

Haldeman and Ehrlichman would later come to view such unconditional obedience as the key to the scandals that would one day destroy them all. Nixon, Ehrlichman said, was given to issuing "rhetorical instructions . . . excesses . . . you just simply had to know the difference. . . . There were people around who didn't know the difference, such as the Marine Corps types. They saluted and went out and did whatever they were told." The implication was that unlike some of their colleagues, he and Haldeman knew when to ignore Nixon's more foolhardy orders.

Nixon's announcement of his cabinet was promoted as a major public relations event, but in the event it excited no one. His priority was to transform foreign policy, and the cabinet appointments, even that of secretary of state, had little relevance to that. Nixon thought domestic policy "a bore." "I've always thought this country could run itself domestically without a president," he had said the previous year. "All you need is a competent Cabinet to run the country at home. You need a president for foreign policy. . . ."

Daniel Patrick Moynihan, appointed assistant for urban affairs, came away from a first meeting with Nixon amazed at his ready admission of the huge gaps in his knowledge. As even his strongest critics must agree, however, the opposite was true of Nixon's knowledge of geopolitics. He intended to make foreign policy himself, and that meant giving priority to the appointment of assistant for national security affairs, to which he named forty-six-year-old Henry Kissinger.

The collaboration of the politician and the professor was a historic one, but had improbable beginnings. As a lecturer heading Harvard's Defense Studies Program, Kissinger had declared a special abhorrence of Nixon. While he dismissed Humphrey during the campaign as a "clown," he deemed the Republican party "hopeless" and Nixon "the most dangerous, of all the men running, to have as President." He was "not fit to be President," a "disaster," who if elected would bring national catastrophe. Kissinger expressed such views despite a first meeting with Nixon the previous year at which he had found Nixon "gentler . . . more thoughtful" than he had expected.

Kissinger had cannily played both sides against the middle in the months before the election. He contacted Humphrey's foreign policy adviser, Zbigniew Brzezinski, saying he "hated" Nixon and offering to make "shit files" on him available to the Democrats—a proposal on which he never delivered. Soon afterward, according to Nixon and his campaign foreign policy adviser, he leaked what he knew of the Vietnam peace talks to the Republicans.

Shortly after the election Kissinger called the journalist Gloria Steinem to ask whether he should work for Nixon if invited. Was it better he wondered, to "try to make things less bad by working from the inside?" Steinem got Kissinger to agree to write a piece for *New York* magazine entitled "The Collaboration Problem." He never followed up on the assignment because Nixon did offer him a position, which he accepted.

Soon Kissinger would be on his way to morning meetings at the White

House, growling, *"Guten Morgen, Herr Haldeman!"* Haldeman would respond with "And a *guten Morgen* to you, Heinz!" Ahead lay the drawn-out entanglement of the Vietnam negotiations, the breakthrough to China, a complex relationship with Nixon—and lasting fame.

FBI Director J. Edgar Hoover also trekked to the Pierre Hotel to be confirmed in the job he had held for forty-four years and to play on Nixon's fears. During the probe of Republican interference in the Vietnam peace initiative, Hoover claimed to Nixon, President Johnson had ordered the FBI to bug Nixon's campaign plane. There is no evidence that the instruction was carried out, and former Hoover aide Cartha DeLoach has said his boss deliberately embellished the facts. Nixon, however, believed what he was told. He would raise the matter time and again during Watergate, in the hope of demonstrating that the Democrats were as guilty of electronic abuses as his own people.

In similar vein, Hoover admonished Nixon not to make calls through the White House switchboard. "Little men you don't know," the FBI director warned, "will be listening." He claimed that presidential communications, which were overseen by the Army Signal Corps, were insecure and said "the President should know that if he talked on those lines he would probably be monitored."

Since the discovery of a bug in his 1962 campaign headquarters,* Nixon had been perennially anxious about electronic surveillance. A veteran wireman had been on duty throughout the campaign, checking for bugs in Nixon's law office in New York, at aides' offices, at the Republican convention, and at every hotel the candidate used around the country.[3]

Concern about bugs preoccupied Nixon even when on nonpolitical business—if one can say he was ever so detached. "Let's get off in a corner someplace and make sure we're not bugged," he had told a Pepsi vice-president on a trip to Cairo a year or so earlier. His friend Pat Hillings recalled Nixon's anxiety after visiting the Johnson White House in 1966. "We got into the White House limo to travel to the airport, and I asked Nixon what had happened upstairs. He said, 'Shh! Shh!' and pointed to the car roof, indicating it was bugged, so we said nothing until we got into the airport."

A meeting with Johnson after the election confirmed all such fears. "Johnson was so obsessed with all the recording crap," Nixon said in 1991. "I will never forget the day he had me to the White House after I won. . . . One of the first things he did was to show me the recording contraptions that Kennedy had installed under the beds. Johnson got down on the floor, lifted the bedspread, and waved his hand under the bed. 'Dick,' he said, 'they are voice activated.' Johnson was obsessed with recording everything. He had every room taped."

*See p. 227.

The wiring of the White House was not new. It had begun as early as 1940, when Roosevelt had his office space and phone rigged with primitive recording devices. Truman did not use the equipment, but it stayed in place. Eisenhower, indulging a penchant for covert recording that dated to his army days, used a concealed Dictaphone machine to record some meetings.

John F. Kennedy had the Secret Service install multiple microphones in the Oval Office, the Cabinet Room, and elsewhere, feeding back to recorders in a locked storage room. The phone in the president's bedroom was wired, but the most recent study of the subject makes no reference to the voice-activated mikes "under the beds" that Nixon described.

Kennedy's recording apparatus was dismantled hours after his assassination, but Lyndon Johnson moved in a formidable new system of his own. According to a former director of the White House Military Office, Bill Gulley, Hoover's warning to Nixon about its potential was fundamentally accurate.

"Johnson had an extensive, really extensive taping system," Gulley said. "He had it installed by the White House Communications Agency, which is under the Military Office. . . . It was a very professional job. . . . The Military Office handled the secret bugging of the Oval Office and Cabinet Room, and installed taps on his telephone and those of his staff members."

"As any new tenant, I inspected the fittings," Haldeman would recall of his arrival in his quarters adjoining the Oval Office. "I opened the door of a closet in the wall connecting my office to the President's suite, and found myself staring at a mountain of gleaming electronic components jammed in that closet, obviously for the use of the previous tenant to tape or monitor LBJ's conversations."

According to Haldeman, Nixon made a snap decision after his meeting with Hoover in November, 1968. "We'll get that goddamn bugging crap out of the White House in a hurry," he said. So they would. But toward the end of Nixon's first term, as all the world now knows, microphones would again be sown around the presidential quarters—this time with devastating results.

"As 1968 came to a close, I was a happy man," Nixon was to write in his memoirs. "In Key Biscayne a wreath hung on the front door and a beautifully trimmed Christmas tree stood in the living room. . . . Those were days rich with happiness and full of anticipation and hope."

Nixon had achieved his goal, was about to take possession of the prize that only thirty-six men had won before. Yet he did not seem to be a man at ease with his destiny. At the Hotel Pierre, Kissinger had thought Nixon's greeting "a show of jauntiness that failed to hide an extraordinary nervousness. . . . His manner was almost diffident; his movements were slightly vague, and unrelated to what he was saying, as if two different impulses were behind speech and gesture. . . . While he talked, he sipped, one after another, cups of coffee that were brought in without his asking for them."

The previous months had been hellishly tough, as is any campaign for an American presidential candidate, but Nixon's condition worried close aides. "I would call for him at his hotel in a small Midwestern city in the morning," Haldeman remembered, "and find he was missing. Some time in the early dawn he had gotten out of bed and slipped away, with a nervous Secret Service man tailing him. We'd search all over town until we found the candidate looking haggard and wan in a flea-bitten coffeeshop."

Nixon suffered from chronic insomnia. "A month before the election," Len Garment recalled, "I would get a call, three or four times a week, somewhere between midnight and three A.M. I was at home, in New York. The phone would ring, and my wife and I would look at that phone. Usually it would be John Ehrlichman, and he'd say: 'The Old Man wants to talk to you.' It was always the same thing. He would start off with 'How are things back there? How's it going with John Mitchell?' But manic, manic, and depressive. . . . He'd go from all the assertive, confident things to 'Are we gonna be all right?'"

Once reassured, Nixon would seem to drift off, murmuring memories of the forties and fifties. "He would become blurred and slightly incoherent, then more so, like talking to somebody who was very drunk. I'd be getting worried about what was happening, and then it would just end, click."

Years later Ehrlichman told Garment how it had been at his end of the line. "He would talk to political people," Ehrlichman remembered. "Then, for the last call, he would say, 'Get me Len.' By that time we would have given him his Seconal and a good stiff single-malt scotch. And he'd get on the phone with you until the phone dropped from his fingers and he fell asleep. Then I'd pick the phone up very quietly, and hang up."

"I was the disembodied presence," Garment recalled, "to whom Nixon could unload his daily deposit of anxieties until he was finally carried away by alcohol, sedation, and exhaustion into the Land of Nod . . . cries and whispers . . . I worried over these calls."

Nixon's public stance at the start of the race was that he seldom drank anything. "When I'm campaigning, I live like a Spartan," he declared even as he was nursing a whiskey. Once again where the subject of Nixon and drink was concerned, the issue was one of propaganda versus reality.

Nixon told Theodore White that he realized that once in office he "couldn't take a drink again, couldn't party it up. You can't drink and think clearly . . . two drinks and your mind isn't quite sharp, and you may not be able to think clearly when that phone rings at night . . . you've got to be ready. . . . No more drinking, no more late hours. . . . I felt I knew what Jefferson meant when he said the presidency was a 'splendid misery.'"

Returned to spontaneously, twice in the course of a single interview, these were the words of a man who recognized that he had a weakness. Meanwhile, what of Ehrlichman's reference to Seconal? What of Nixon's use of prescription drugs?

By his own account, Nixon first used sleeping pills in the late forties. His fellow Republican in the 1962 California race, George Christopher, thought he used "some pills to ease his mind a bit. Dispassionate pills to cool down. He was under great, great pressure." "There may have been some medication to reduce stress," Nixon's brother Edward agreed in 2000, "but he was not one who wanted to do anything like that habitually. . . ."

In fact, as it became clear during research for this book, Nixon consumed large quantities of one particular drug over a long period, apparently without a prescription or proper medical supervision. The drug was Dilantin, the brand name of an anti-epileptic medication known to pharmacologists as Phenytoin, and the circumstances in which Nixon came to start taking it were alarmingly casual. He heard about the drug, probably soon after being elected president, while dining at Key Biscayne with Bebe Rebozo and the millionaire founder of the Dreyfus Fund, Jack Dreyfus, Jr.

Dreyfus, who had contributed to the Nixon campaigns in both 1960 and 1968, had no medical qualifications. Having credited Dilantin with relieving him of chronic depression almost overnight, he had become the leading advocate of it as a panacea for all manner of ailments. He poured millions of dollars into promoting the drug, which he considered a "gift from God" with properties that could bring almost miraculous relief from disorders ranging from heart problems and asthma to leprosy and arthritis—beliefs he still held at age eighty-six in the year 2000.

At their 1968 meeting in Key Biscayne, as Dreyfus told the author, "Nixon said, 'Why don't you give me some Dilantin?' So I thought, 'What the heck, he's [going to be] president of the United States. I can't get in trouble. . . .' So I went out to the car and got a bottle of a thousand and gave it to him. A few days later he called me and said, 'Is it all right if I take two a day?' I said, 'Yes, I think so.' Later on when I went to see him at the White House, he asked me if he could have some more. I gave him another large bottle. . . ."

Asked what Nixon wanted the Dilantin for, Dreyfus was vague. Nixon, he said, had "a lot of things . . . worries." At one point, when Dreyfus suggested that the president should perhaps get the medication from a doctor, Nixon said, 'To heck with the doctor.'" The president likely had little to worry about on that front. John Ehrlichman remembered the White House physician, Dr. Walter Tkach, as a compliant doctor who would do exactly as a patient asked. "You'd go to him and say, 'I'm going to Turkey tomorrow and I need inoculations.' And he'd say, 'Here, give me your book,' and he'd stamp all the inoculations and say, 'There! That ought to immunize you. . . .'"

Dr. Tkach, moreover, had used Dilantin himself and enthused over it. When asked later by Dreyfus if his eminent patient was still taking the drug, Tkach merely said airily: "I don't know, but the amount of pills in the bottle in his bathroom is reducing in size, so I suppose he is."

Neither Nixon's cavalier use of Dilantin, nor Tkach's style of doctoring, is reassuring to those who like to assume the president makes prudent use of medication under the direction of the most meticulous of physicians. Dilantin is, moreover—to the frustration of Dreyfus and like-minded converts—a medication approved by the Food and Drug Administration only as an anticonvulsant to counter epileptic seizures. While it is also effective in pain relief and may be prescribed at a qualified doctor's discretion, it can have serious side effects.

Dreyfus has conceded that should dosages not be well calculated and observed, the user can become what he termed "a little disjointed-feeling . . . dizzy . . . [with] a drunkish feeling." The *Physicians' Desk Reference*, used by doctors nationwide, lists numerous known adverse reactions to Dilantin. They include "slurred speech, decreased coordination, and mental confusion, dizziness, insomnia, transient nervousness. . . ." Dr. Lawrence McDonald, a Washington physician consulted by the author, was alarmed at the notion of anyone's—especially a person in a position of high responsibility—using Dilantin in uncontrolled doses or combined with other medications or alcohol.

"If such a user of the drug were the president of the United States," Dr. McDonald said, "I would be very nervous. Mental confusion is not something you want in a leader. Dilantin certainly could impair someone of that caliber from making correct and timely and appropriate judgments. It's a potential time bomb, waiting to happen."

Nixon did use alcohol and did use sleeping pills. His longtime speechwriter Ray Price recalled how even a single drink could make him appear drunk "if he had a sleeping pill." As if the drinking, the sleeping pills, and the Dilantin were not troubling enough, Rabbi Baruch Korff—a Nixon apologist late in the presidency—said he learned that "at times he resorted to amphetamines." Amphetamines, of course, are stimulants, the opposite of the relaxing medications mentioned by other associates.

Billy Graham, a longtime confidant, offered a startling verdict on the cause of Nixon's ultimate downfall. "I think," he said in 1979, "it was sleeping pills. Sleeping pills and demons. I think there was definitely demon power involved. He took all those sleeping pills, and through history, drugs and demons have gone together. . . . My conclusion is that it was just all those sleeping pills, they just let a demon's power come in and play over him. . . ."

The evangelist's notional demons aside, Nixon's tenure of the White House was to bring times when it was obvious all was not well with the president. Observers who heard the slurring of the voice or saw the disjointed gestures were to wonder about his use of drink or drugs.

On the eve of the 1968 election, another highly sensitive aspect of Nixon's private life had come perilously close to exposure, his use of a new York psychotherapist.

———

On the morning of October 29, exactly a week before voting day, while President Johnson was grappling with the Republican sabotage of the Vietnam peace talks, the phone rang in the Park Avenue office of Dr. Arnold Hutschnecker. It was the columnist Drew Pearson calling with a stunning double-barreled question. Was it a fact, Pearson asked, that Hutschnecker had been giving Nixon "psychiatric treatments"? If so, was it true that the doctor was concerned as to whether his patient was "the right man to have his finger on the nuclear trigger"?

Although the columnist was working largely from old information—a private investigator's report prepared in 1960 in the hope of embarrassing Nixon during the contest with Kennedy.[4] Hutschnecker, however, did not know what evidence Pearson had. Caught off guard, and with a patient in his office, he confirmed that he had treated Nixon. It was a "delicate matter," he added, one he was "reluctant to talk about." Would the columnist please call back in the afternoon?

The telephone hummed in the hours that followed. It was ironically Pearson's colleague Jack Anderson, phoning Nixon headquarters for a comment, who tipped the Republicans to the threat of disastrous publicity. With Nixon and Humphrey running so closely, a story about Nixon's receiving psychotherapy could prove critically damaging.

"We felt we had to be ready to react immediately," press aide Herb Klein recalled. "We had friends on a few newspapers ready to alert us if they received advance copies of such a column. . . . We wanted to be ready to deny the story in a way that editors would be cautious on the use of the material. . . . One damaging column could have tipped the close election." As another precaution, Klein put in a check call of his own to the psychotherapist.

At 4:00 P.M., when Pearson called back, Dr. Hutschnecker squelched the story. He had treated Nixon "for a brief period" while he was vice president, he said, "but only for problems involving internal medicine." Pearson wondered why at a time when Nixon was Washington-based, he would have traveled all the way to a doctor in New York for routine physical problems. Not satisfied with Hutschnecker's account, he continued digging.

Word soon reached Republican Congressman Gerald Ford, the House minority leader, that Hutschnecker was chatting socially about his call from Pearson. The Nixon damage control operation went back into action, and the doctor received separate visits from both Klein and Murray Chotiner.

Voting day came and went without Pearson's running the story. A week later, though, the columnist used the forum of an address to the National Press Club to reveal his unwritten information. He now knew, he said, that Hutschnecker had "confirmed to others that he had treated or advised Mr. Nixon over psychiatric problems. And he had expressed some worry privately that Mr. Nixon had problems—or did have a problem—of not standing up under great pressure."

When Nixon's press secretary dismissed this allegation as "totally untrue," Pearson riposted in print. Several of Hutschnecker's patients, he said, had spoken with him about Nixon's visits. One, who agreed to be quoted by name, said it had been "common knowledge" that Nixon received "psychotherapeutic treatments" during his vice presidency. Dr. Hutschnecker, asserted this witness, had "expressed some concern that such a man should occupy the important post of vice president."[5]

Press aide Herb Klein would state in his memoirs that at the time of the early Hutschnecker treatments, the only ones the Nixon side would admit to, the doctor had merely been "studying psychiatry" and that Nixon had seen him primarily because of "severe headaches." In 1997, interviewed for this book, he was more forthright. Nixon had gone to the doctor, Klein revealed, because "he was feeling depressed."

During the 1968 flap the journalist Gloria Steinem joined the procession to Dr. Hutschnecker's office and kept him talking for more than three hours. The doctor remained evasive but dropped a number of hints. "He didn't deny and he didn't confirm," she recalled. "He wasn't forthcoming about Nixon per se, but he energetically put forward his belief that all leaders, including candidates for the presidency, should have some vetting by mental health experts. And when he told me his view about examining would-be presidents, he was responding to questions I had asked about Nixon."

In his interviews for this book the doctor said Nixon gave him to understand that should he be elected president, he would appoint Hutschnecker his personal physician. That was not to be, however, because Haldeman and Ehrlichman, whom the doctor categorized as "goons" or "gangsters," insisted that using the doctor would be "the kiss of death . . . would destroy the presidency."

Keeping his distance from Hutschnecker did keep the threat of the "shrink" connection at bay. Other Damoclean swords, weapons of his own making, however, were already pointed at Nixon's head.

Bryce Harlow, who had been associated with Nixon for many years, knew some of the man's dangerous secrets. As early as the Pierre Hotel transition period he warned younger aides of the perils ahead, predicting that the new administration "would attract scandal like a dog would attract fleas."

Four of these potential scandals were especially worrisome: the original assassination plots against Fidel Castro, the cash connection with Howard Hughes, the massive recent campaign contribution from the dictatorship in Greece, and the recent offense that was still being actively hushed up, the sabotage of the Vietnam peace talks.

While there were various ways these secrets might surface, one man especially, a man on the wrong side of the political spectrum, knew too much. This was Lawrence O'Brien, fifty-one, leading light of the Democratic party's Irish Mafia and master political strategist. A veteran of the Kennedy and Johnson administrations, it was O'Brien—he had taken over in late summer after the murder of Bobby Kennedy—whose expertise had brought Hubert Humphrey from almost certain defeat to almost defeating Nixon.

Within hours of the younger Kennedy's death, issuing orders from his penthouse suite in Las Vegas, Howard Hughes had come up with a characteristically perverse scheme. As the latest ploy in his effort to turn the nation's top politicians into his personal puppets, he set out to hire "Kennedy's entire organization." That being an unrealistic goal even for Hughes, he reached out for O'Brien.

Several weeks later, after negotiations with Hughes's aide Robert Maheu, O'Brien accepted a post as the tycoon's Washington consultant, for an annual fee of $180,000. The previous year, hints that there had been assassination plots against Castro appearing in the press for the first time had been characterized as ethically inadmissible, "a political H-bomb." The initial report had pointed the finger only at the Kennedy brothers. Yet Maheu, now in close touch with O'Brien, well knew that the first anti-Castro conspiracy, involving the Mafia, had started in 1960, when Nixon was White House point man on Cuba. How much did O'Brien learn about Nixon's role in the assassination plots? How much, once his Hughes consultancy got under way, was he going to learn about Hughes' money flowing to Nixon?

Lawrence O'Brien also knew about the Greek dictators' contributions to the Nixon campaign, a subject on which he had been briefed by exile activist Elias Demetracopoulos. It was O'Brien who had issued the press statement four days before the election, challenging Nixon to explain his relationship with Tom Pappas, the go-between with the Greek regime.

If Nixon also feared that O'Brien had knowledge of the Republican interference in the Vietnam peace process, he feared correctly. Records show that, logically enough, Hubert Humphrey had informed his campaign manager of the gist of what he had learned from President Johnson.

There was something else. The night before the voters went to the polls, when the result hung in the balance and there was little more he could do to advance his cause, Nixon—and a large proportion of the voters—had watched on television a Democratic party commercial that Theodore White called Humphrey's "high moment of identification." There was Senator Edward Kennedy, the last remaining brother, walking the sands of Hyannis Port. In earnest conversation with him, as the wind off the Atlantic blew their coats up in swallowtails, had been that repository of secrets so dangerous to Richard Nixon, Lawrence O'Brien.

Nixon fretted about O'Brien and about the potential threat from the last of the Kennedys. In the White House, ever insecure and determined to win a second term with a truly convincing victory, he would plot against them both. It would be the plotting against O'Brien, later elevated to the chairmanship of the Democratic National Committee, that was to result in Nixon's destruction and disgrace.

At a bone-chilling noontime on January 20, 1969, as dignitaries shivered under their temporary canopy, Richard Nixon stepped out of a limousine in front of the great dome of the Capitol.

He tripped as he took his place on the dais for his inauguration so that, as the ambassador from Ecuador noted, the last word he uttered before the ceremony was "Oops!" Pat, in rosy red outfit and fur hat, held out two family Bibles dating back to the nineteenth century. Her husband placed his left hand upon them as Earl Warren, the chief justice who loathed him, administered the presidential oath.

Nixon was now the thirty-seventh president of the United States. Billy Graham intoned a prayer, and the new leader of more than two hundred million people launched into his seventeen-minute inaugural address. He spoke rapidly but evenly of winding up the war in Vietnam, ending the cold war with the Soviet Union, and bringing the divided nation together.

Both Bibles had been opened to Isaiah 2:4, the passage about beating swords into plowshares. The keystone sentence in Nixon's speech was a Quaker sentiment from his own pen that was destined to be chiseled into his tombstone: "The greatest honor history can bestow is the title of peacemaker." On the drive to the White House afterward he could see antiwar protesters lobbing sticks, stones, and beer cans and hoisting a huge placard reading BILLIONAIRES PROFIT OFF G.I. BLOOD!

That night at the inaugural balls, throngs of Republicans from across America—huge contingents of them from Nixon's native California and much-favored Florida—crowded so close that few could dance. Bebe Rebozo was there of course, as was the Saudi entrepreneur Adnan Khashoggi, whose beauteous wife missed what Nixon was saying because a man behind kept pinching her.

Also present was Anna Chennault, the intermediary in the operation designed to sabotage the Vietnam peace talks. Patricia Hitt, whom Chennault had named as a possible go-between in her contacts with Nixon, hosted a party of her own. As assistant secretary at the Department of Health, Education and Welfare, she now held the highest government position of any woman in the new administration.

Noting that one of the featured bands was Guy Lombardo's, Nixon recalled having danced to Lombardo's music with Pat the night World War II ended. Around 2:00 A.M., when the Nixons got back to 1600 Pennsylvania Avenue, they walked from room to room turning on all the lights.

"He seemed exultant," Henry Kissinger would say of the inauguration, "as if he could hardly wait for the ceremony to be over so that he could begin to implement the dream of a lifetime." Nixon's friend Bryce Harlow, however, had doubts. "When Dick was finally elected President," he said, "he attained eighty percent of all his goals in life. He has no idea of what he will do after he is sworn in."

On his first working day in office Nixon invited a thousand campaign workers to the White House. He told them: "This is your house, too. We'll get up early and work late so this will always be a happy house. And your home will always be a happy home. . . ."

It had begun.

25

The office neither elevates or degrades a man. What it does is to provide a stage upon which all his personality traits are magnified and accentuated.

—*George Reedy, President Johnson's press secretary*

"**D**on't you dare call me Dick. I am the president of the United States. When you speak to me you call me Mr. President." So commanded Nixon, early in the presidency, at a meeting with Florida banker Hoke Maroon, a man he had known for years. "He was as obsessed with the office as any president has ever been," his old friend Bob Finch ruefully recalled. "He gloried in it, night and day."

The outward signs were quickly obvious. Before the Nixons moved into the White House, the message they had conveyed to the public was that it did not need refurbishing. That opinion soon changed, however, and a massive remodeling program, costing millions, was begun.

Military planes were dispatched to Italy to bring back green watered silk for just one medium-size room. An ornate four-poster bed for Nixon cost six thousand dollars, its draperies ten thousand. The next presidential couple to occupy the White House, the Fords, thought it unbelievable, "something Marie Antoinette would have slept in," and promptly had it removed.

Whereas Lyndon Johnson had maintained three Boeing passenger jets, Nixon had three Boeings, eleven Lockheed Jetstars, and sixteen helicopters at his exclusive disposal. The existing Air Force One was refurbished at a cost of $800,000, with the emphasis on the First Family's accommodation. Later, when a new plane was delivered—with a layout the Nixons did not like—another $750,000 went toward the alterations.

The fleet was not used solely for government business. Nixon's extended family, including in-laws, availed themselves of the planes. When a troubled official reported that senior aides were taking Air Force One on transcontinental flights to and from vacations, Nixon signed off on them. An Air Force Jetstar was once used to ferry a package from Florida to Camp David for senior aides, at a cost of five thousand dollars in fuel alone. Its contents: ten pounds of crabs from Joe's Stone Crabs in Miami Beach.

The White House and the Camp David retreat were not sufficient for Nixon. He bought houses on Key Biscayne—the complex to be known as the Florida White House—and at San Clemente, the fourteen-room house and estate in California styled the Western White House. Nixon himself purchased the properties, with a massive financial assist from Rebozo and aerosol tycoon Abplanalp. The government, however, was to spend more than ten million dollars—more than forty-four million dollars at today's values—to install special features not only at Nixon's out-of-town homes but also at houses he frequented, like Abplanalp's in the Bahamas.

A helicopter pad at Key Biscayne cost $418,000, and communications equipment there $307,000. "The bottom line for military expenditures at Key Biscayne came close to two million dollars," recalled Military Office head Bill Gulley. "Then we did it all again at San Clemente." Camp David was also revamped. A swimming pool next to the presidential "cabin" was built at an expense of $500,000, because the chosen site stood atop an underground nuclear shelter.

Nixon had nine offices for his personal use: the Oval Office, a hideaway in the Executive Office Building, a room in his private quarters, two at Camp David, one at the Key Biscayne house, another at Abplanalp's Caribbean home, and two at San Clemente. All required sophisticated communications systems, installed at public expense. A former Budget Bureau official would calculate that, by four years into the presidency, Nixon's household expenses had added up to a hundred million dollars.

Nixon spent more than one in three nights away from the White House in the first eighteen months of his term. While the days of absence included foreign trips, there were also forty-two trips to Camp David, fourteen to Key Biscayne, and nine to San Clemente. The California stays tended to last two or three weeks.

Before assuming office, Nixon had repeatedly pressed Ehrlichman to "capitalize upon the work habits of the President-elect—long hours of work, delayed dinners, eighteen-hour days, late reading, no naps. . . ." That was not the routine Nixon's assistant Alexander Butterfield observed, however. He was struck by the fact that his boss "had so much leisure time. There were many days with no appointments at all. Every now and then he would work like a Trojan. . . . But generally he allowed plenty of time to sit and kick things around. . . . And every afternoon Nixon took a nap. . . ."

For the women in the family, pride in Republican cloth coats was a sentiment long since abandoned. Pat Nixon arrived at the White House with a new Persian lamb coat to supplement her mink, and both daughters had acquired expensive coats of real fur. Julie had married President Eisenhower's grandson David a month before the inauguration, a ceremony at which she bent custom a little by kissing her father first rather than her new husband.

The junior Nixons had long since assigned each other joke initials, parodies of what the trio viewed as their hilarious billing in the press. Julie, who was to graduate from Smith College, was N.C.P.D.—for "No Cream Puff Deb." David was T.C.C. for "Teen Carbon Copy"—of his famous grandfather. Tricia was F.P., for "Fairy Princess."

In the White House, Tricia soon acquired the reputation of being a spoiled princess. Then twenty-three, she spent entire days shut up in her Louis XV bedroom, surrounded by a collection of Dresden and Meissen figurines. Her favorite featured two little girls on a seesaw with a spotted dog, a gift from her father that he called "Tricia and Julie with Checkers."

Tricia did not endear herself to Nixon's staff. Ehrlichman thought her a "tough and troubled cookie." She once reported an Air Force One steward for allegedly staring at her legs. An usher who had been told to bring pillows to the garden for Tricia and a friend was then expected to lift the friend's outstretched legs to create a hassock. Secret Service agents, who dubbed Tricia Goody Two-shoes, objected to being instructed to water her plants while she was away on a trip. They carried out the mission, one agent claimed, by urinating on them.

When Britain's Prince Charles came visiting, Nixon tried to pair Tricia off with him, to no avail. Tricia was to marry Edward Cox, an Ivy League law student descended from one of the framers of the Declaration of Independence. Their wedding in the Rose Garden, in the third year of the presidency, would be staged as a television spectacular reportedly seen by sixty million viewers. CBS's Dan Rather thought it "the closest thing Americans have, or want, to a royal occasion."[1]

Early in his travels as president, Nixon was greeted in Brussels by royal guards in operatically grand uniforms. In India he was escorted by outriders in British Empire–vintage scarlet coats. One of these trips reportedly inspired the outfitting of the White House police in similarly outlandish uniforms. The new outfits, high-necked white tunics with gold epaulets, first appeared on public view a year after the inauguration. They were topped by tall military caps with blue and gold visors, reportedly paid for by Nixon himself.

After early critics noted how plump the uniforms made their wearers look, the policemen were ordered to diet. Then, following a national chorus of ridicule, the regalia was withdrawn altogether. The tunics were eventually sold off to high school bands in Iowa, and the caps reappeared at an Alice Cooper rock concert.

"The President," Haldeman said by way of explaining the uniforms, had "wanted something more formal." Peter Flanigan, Nixon's political adviser, thought the livery an attempt to emulate the "grandeur" his boss admired in Charles de Gaulle. De Gaulle himself fell from power, then died soon after Nixon took office. By that time Nixon had established his own self-important style.

Four days after the inauguration the president dictated the following memo to Pat, referring to himself in the third person, rather as the queen of England affects the royal "we" on formal occasions,

> To: Mrs. Nixon
> From: The President
> In talking with the GSA [General Services Administration] with regard to RN's room, what would be most desirable is an end table like the one on the right side of the bed which will accommodate *two* dictaphones as well as a telephone. RN has to use one dictaphone for current matters and another for memoranda for the file which he will not want transcribed at this time. In addition, he needs a bigger table on which he can work at night. The table which is presently in the room does not allow enough room for him to get his knees under it.

Nixon sought to preserve everything that related to his tenure, however trivial. "He saves everything," Rose Woods would one day tell investigators, "place cards, menus. Even one Halloween we were at Camp David and he and Mrs. Nixon invited me to dinner and a steward put a colored mask on each of the three plates—I know Mrs. Nixon put hers in the wastebasket, and I did mine. But his came down to be filed. . . ."

"Things got more and more regal," recalled Traphes Bryant, the presidential kennel keeper. "Nixon decreed that even workers like me had to get all prettied up for official functions. The White House had suits tailored for any electrician or carpenter who might be around during a party or official function. Several times I had to go to a Georgetown haberdasher to be measured for my black suit, which was almost like a tuxedo. . . ."

"Problems with signals," Haldeman noted in his diary after a morning meeting with Nixon. "Dinner last night . . . served just champagne when should have had cocktails, 12 in black tie." *White* tie and tails, long out of fashion, were at first de rigueur at Nixon White House occasions.[2] At dinners the small round tables favored by the Kennedys and the Johnsons were replaced by long banquet-style tables with seating that indicated to all present just who was and was not "above the salt." For cabinet meetings Nixon replaced Johnson's reclining chair with a high-backed chair, higher—for that was the point—than those his colleagues used.

The pomp and circumstance of a typical Nixon airport arrival gave *Life*'s Hugh Sidey pause: "Acres of automobiles parked on the landing field. Men, women, and children in luxurious coats and sweaters . . . wives of the dignitaries elegant in furs, jewels sparkling in the sun. Agnew . . . flawlessly tailored, combed, manicured, polished. There was about him the smell of power, position and possessions. . . . There were ruffles and flourishes from the army's special heraldic trumpets, followed by 'Hail to the Chief.' A journalist next to me turned away. 'My God,' he muttered, as Nixon appeared at the airplane door, 'it's like the arrival of the King.'"

The Nixons seemed almost oddly attracted to royals, even exiled ones. "White tie, decorations to be worn" invitations were sent out for a dinner for the duke and duchess of Windsor, who had hosted Nixon while he was out of office. When the duke sent apologies—he did not have his decorations with him—bemedaled guests were asked to shed their badges and ribbons at the door.

On a flight to Europe with the First Family the writer Jessamyn West, Nixon's cousin, recalled a telling interview with Pat. "I wanted to hear about her early struggles," West remembered. "She replied: 'How can you present me as being other than perfect?' She was giving me statistics about how many crowned heads they had served in the White House. . . ."

Investigations would eventually reveal that Pat and her daughters accepted lavish gifts of jewelry from Middle Eastern royalty. Saudi Arabia's King Faisal gave Pat a shoulder-length pair of earrings set with marquise diamonds and cabochon rubies, as well as, reportedly, a strand of pearls, worth as much as a hundred thousand dollars at seventies values.

From Saudi Deputy Prime Minister Prince Fahd, Faisal's half brother, Pat received a matching diamond and emerald ensemble—necklace, bracelet, ring, and brooch—worth $52,400. Defense Minister Prince Sultan, another half brother, presented a diamond bracelet to Pat and brooches—in diamonds, rubies, and sapphires—to Julie and Tricia.

Upon her marriage, according to her cousin Donald, Tricia was given a diamond and emerald brooch by the shah of Iran. The emperor of Ethiopia, Haile Selassie, sent a silver vase. Donald told the author he thought such gifts were "the way various people Uncle Dick had helped throughout the world thanked him. . . ."[3]

The official roster of Britain's nobility, *Burke's Peerage,* pronounced Nixon one of thirteen U.S. presidents able to claim royal ancestry. The grocer's son from Whittier was supposedly a direct descendant of King Edward III (d. 1377) and thus distantly related to Queen Elizabeth II and Sir Winston Churchill. While thousands of people can claim similar bloodlines, one should perhaps not assume this was totally irrelevant to Nixon.

"I often felt that inwardly the president secretly wanted to be considered an English lord," said his close associate Herb Klein, "someone who, like Jack Kennedy, would be praised for upgrading the social dignity of the White House. . . . he longed for this elite social distinction."

Nixon himself denied such notions. "The Imperial President," he wrote, "was a straw man created by defensive congressmen and by disillusioned liberals. . . ." One such critic was future Speaker Tip O'Neill. "After he became President," O'Neill recalled, "Nixon seemed to change. He no longer played cards with our group, and I doubt he played with anybody. Unlike Truman, Kennedy and Johnson, Nixon didn't pal around much with his old friends . . . he became aloof and imperial."

Even some Republican stalwarts had similar thoughts. "I could not detect a touch of humility in his demeanor or in his facial expression," Federal Reserve chairman Arthur Burns said of the inauguration. "That troubled me very much. That, combined with his attitude when he took me through the White House and talked about its splendor. . . ." "I don't know what's happened to Dick," grumbled Tom Dewey, "He just doesn't listen anymore."

He behaved "like Napoleon," said the entrepreneur Arnholt Smith, who had known Nixon since childhood. "I mean, he was very imperious, gave you a feeling you were almost traveling with God." Former Republican party chairman Len Hall thought Nixon became "regal, kinglike. . . . He loved power, power to sit in that Oval Office and just issue orders. . . ."

———

Under Nixon, according to an early brief, Nixon cabinet officers were to be considered "Deputy Presidents who run their own departments." That concept was rapidly forgotten, however. "Nixon never intended the cabinet to be a board of directors," said Haldeman. "He never took a vote and would have cared less concerning the result; he didn't make any pretext of seeking consensus."

"I remember one occasion during the energy crisis," Defense Secretary James Schlesinger recalled. "Nixon said to the cabinet at large, 'I don't know whether the energy crisis will ever end.' I leaned over to him and remarked that we were in close negotiations with the Saudis about ending the embargo. He turned to me and whispered, 'I know that, Jim, but I'm not going to say that in front of these clowns.'"

"We began to get these long soliloquies about how tough it was to be president surrounded by idiots," said Ehrlichman. "You began to get instructions from him. 'Get rid of that fellow Allen over at HEW!' 'Call Finch today and fire him! He is going around saying we favor busing; we don't favor busing. Don't they understand?' More and more, as we proceeded through the first year, he began taking back all those delegations of absolute authority that had been rather frivolously handed out at transition time. . . .

"It got so bad that in about the third year we learned of a rump session of the cabinet. They actually held a meeting over at [Housing and Urban Development Secretary] George Romney's conference room to discuss economic problems, because they couldn't get any discussions at the cabinet table. . . . It was a minirevolt. . . . Nixon was terribly upset that they would call such a meeting behind his back. . . ."

"Nixon never trusted anyone in the Executive Branch," said CIA Director Richard Helms. "Here he had become president of the United States and therefore the chief of the executive branch, and yet he was constantly telling people that the State Department was just a bunch of pin-striped, cocktail-drinking diplomats, that the agency couldn't come up with a winning action in Vietnam, that the Interior Department was full of 'pinkos.' It just went on and on."

Nixon once exploded in rage, a tape of a telephone call reveals, because too few aides called to congratulate him on a nationally televised address about Vietnam. "Screw the Cabinet and the rest!" he told Kissinger. "From now on, they come to me. I'm sick of the whole bunch. The others are a bunch of goddamned cowards. The staff, except for Haldeman and Ehrlichman, screw them. The Cabinet, except for [cabinet secretary] Connally, the hell with them!"

Nixon was the first president in more than a century to have to work with an opposition Congress, and he did not have the patience for the task. "He simply didn't want to spend the kind of time that was required to cultivate these folks," Ehrlichman said. Congressional liaison Bill Timmons would scrawl, "ASK FOR HIS VOTE," on talking papers when Nixon was about to meet with a member of Congress, but he never did so. "I think he felt it was somehow demeaning for the president to ask a member for his vote," Timmons said. "It was not in his personality to do it."

Nixon's ploys to circumvent congressional authority ultimately alienated the nation's elected representatives. He blocked bills, impounded funds when he knew his veto would not work, and eroded the power of the Senate in the field of foreign policy. Kevin Phillips, himself a former Nixon aide, noted that Nixon was moving toward government by an "unprecedented, unreachable elite managerial cadre." One man in particular, a veteran U.S. senator, was increasingly troubled by the tone of the government. This was Sam Ervin, who was to be Nixon's nemesis during Watergate. "Divine Right," Ervin would growl then, "perished in America with the Revolution."

Relations with the press were similarly contentious. Six years after his "kick around" speech, Nixon's scorn and resentment toward the media were undiluted. A senior aide to Spiro Agnew had tellingly expressed the administration's tone only minutes after the victory announcement. "Why don't we all get a member of the press and beat them up?" he said. "I'm tired of being nice to them." After the election, in conversation with Theodore White, Nixon dismissed the media as "that fucking bunch of crew cut boy scouts."

The "boy scouts" failed to please. Four months into the presidency Nixon issued an edict that was patently impractical: There was to be no more White House contact with the *New York Times*—one of whose editorials had annoyed him—the *Washington Post*—had broken news of an upcoming meeting he had hoped to announce himself—or with the *St. Louis Post-Dispatch*, which had run an inside account of the administration's problems.

A few weeks later, when U.S. astronauts returned from the first moon landing, Nixon told the British prime minister that, should rocks they brought back turn out to be laden with lethal germs, he would dole them out as presents to journalists.

At first it seemed that the new president might be making an effort to improve conditions for the press. On Nixon's personal initiative the old and filthy White House press room was replaced with grander quarters. More than half a million dollars were spent on a briefing room and lounge in the style of an English club, with plush chesterfield sofas and stylish prints on the walls. The room had been moved, however, to a new location—one that prevented reporters from observing the movements of key personalities. "You cannot see who is coming and going to see the President," Hugh Sidey observed. "The whole purpose is to cut the press off from the flow of visitors to the White House."

Nixon held no televised press conferences in his first eight months as president and only thirty-one in his first four years. Kennedy had held more than twice as many in less than three years, and Johnson four times as many in his five.

Nixon claimed to be indifferent to what the press said about him. It was he, however, who put Agnew up to making his infamous tirade against television's "small band of network commentators and self-appointed analysts." The commentators' offense in question was "instant analysis," deemed impertinent criticism, of a Nixon speech on Vietnam.

Covering the White House by talking to its staff, Sidey decided, was pointless. "It's a non-news operation, a laborious waste of time. . . . This crowd came in like an occupying army. They took over the White House like a stockade. . . . They have no sense that the government doesn't belong to them, that it's something they're holding in trust for the people."

———————

"Without the Vietnam War," Haldeman came to think, "there would have been no Watergate. Without a Vietnam War, Richard Nixon might have had the most successful presidency since Harry Truman's. . . . But the Vietnam War destroyed Nixon. . . ."

On his first morning at the White House, while shaving, Nixon remembered a safe Johnson had shown him after the election, a small security box concealed in the bedroom closet. It turned out to contain only a single document, the most recent tally of U.S. dead and wounded in Vietnam. Nixon perused the figures, then returned the folder to the safe "until the war was over."

His campaign promises of bringing a swift end to the war were now a thing of the past. "Who knows?" Nixon said airily to Theodore White within weeks of the election. "One year, two years, six months? I can't put any time limit." "Peace cannot be achieved overnight," he told the nation in May, 1969, "cannot be settled at a single stroke."

As indeed it would not be. The North Vietnamese kept up their attacks. The South's President Thieu, believing Nixon to be in his debt for having blocked the Democratic peace initiative on the eve of the election, came away uneasy from their first meeting of the presidency. Asked to agree to the withdrawal of twenty-five thousand American troops, he worried that it might be the start of a full-scale pullout. Nixon insisted that the pullout was only "symbolic," a "public opinion ploy," to help him placate domestic opponents of the war. "Strong support," he promised, "would continue for years."

Nixon withheld from Thieu the fact that Kissinger was about to open secret talks with the North. Not that it made any difference. Kissinger was to liken dealing with the two Vietnams to being an animal trainer cracking a whip to get two obstinate tigers to sit on stools. "When one is in place, the other jumps off."

Nixon did brief Thieu on Vietnamization, the push to make South Vietnam capable of surviving on its own. The French colonialists had used the same term, and critics claimed that the policy was a fallback: using Vietnamese to fight Vietnamese. Others argued that it was a maneuver not to accelerate peace but to buy time to keep the war going. Meanwhile, behind the meetings and the public rhetoric, another clandestine scenario was developing.

Within two months of becoming president, Nixon approved a massive B-52 bombing strike, code-named Breakfast, on an area around and beyond Vietnam's border with Cambodia. Breakfast was to be followed by Lunch, Dessert, Snack, Supper, and Dinner, an extended series of strikes over a period of fourteen months, under the umbrella designation Menu. Menu's purpose was to pulverize enemy concentrations and arms dumps near the frontier, in areas from which Communist forces had previously launched attacks with impunity.

Intrinsic to Menu, though, was a problem. Cambodia was a neutral country, and the bombing campaign marked a significant expansion of the war. On Nixon's personal instructions, therefore, it was carried out under conditions of extraordinary secrecy. A few press leaks aside, the truth about Menu would not emerge for nearly five years. When it did, at the height of Watergate, outraged critics would accuse the president of having exceeded his constitutional powers.

One congressman, Robert Drinan, was to characterize the bombing as "presidential conduct more shocking and more unbelievable than the conduct of any president in any war in all of American history." Nixon would retort that the strikes had had the effect of saving the lives of U.S. soldiers and hastening the peace settlement. Twelve members of the House Judiciary Committee, on the other hand, would deem them a "deception of Congress and the American public," serious enough to add to the articles of impeachment.

While that proposal was ultimately voted down, the fact remained that

Nixon had publicly lied. In a solemn speech during the election campaign he had spoken of the people's "right to know," of a president's duty to "lay out all the facts." "Only through an open, candid dialogue with the people," he had declared, "can a President maintain his trust and leadership."

During the period of the bombing he had reassured the nation that he was presenting the facts on the war "with complete honesty." In another speech, referring directly to the Cambodian border area, he said the United States had never "moved against these sanctuaries because we did not wish to violate the territory of a neutral nation." This assertion was made after some three thousand B-52 sorties had been flown and a hundred thousand tons of high explosives had been dropped.

Nixon's mood, as much as tactical planning, was a factor in the bombing. He ordered the attacks initially while aboard Air Force One, en route to Europe. He then twice rescinded the order, on Kissinger's advice, before finally giving the go-ahead. He ordered a second phase of the bombing, in Kissinger's view, "because of an event far away . . . in North Korea. . . . Nixon looked for some other place to demonstrate his mettle. There was nothing he feared more than to appear weak. . . ."

The faraway event in question was the shooting down of a U.S. spy plane by a North Korean jet fighter, on April 14, 1969. All thirty-one American crewmen on board were killed. According to a Haldeman diary entry, Nixon at first wanted a "strong reaction." When aides advised prudence, he held back, "suppressing his instinct for a jugular response," as Kissinger put it. A few days later, however, he ordered the Lunch bombing of the Cambodian border.

Nixon's private language about Vietnam remained bellicose. Behind their back, he reportedly referred to anyone he thought dovish as "sweet-ass." He used extreme verbal threats to illustrate how he would make North Vietnam submit. "I'll turn Right so goddamn hard it'll make your head spin," he told Kissinger in a recorded phone call. "We'll bomb the bastards off the Earth."

Nixon professed shock when, in late 1969, the horrific story of the worst atrocity in modern U.S. military history broke in the press. The previous year, it emerged, troops of the Eleventh Light Infantry Brigade of the Americal Division had slaughtered at least 350 unarmed Vietnamese civilians. American soldiers and junior officers had shot and bayoneted old men, women, and children, even babies. Some of the women had been beaten and raped before being killed. All dwellings had been burned to the ground, the carcasses of the villagers' cattle tossed into wells to poison the water.[4] The massacre, in and around the village of My Lai, had been carried out without provocation. There had been much enemy activity in the area, but the brigade had met no hostile fire that day.

Nixon had his press spokesman declare the mass murder "abhorrent to the conscience," promising that it would be "dealt with in accordance with the strict rules of military justice." Behind the scenes he ordered the army to spy on the young veteran who had exposed the atrocity by writing to Nixon and other politicians about it. The president griped to an aide about the negative publicity for hours, saying, "It's those dirty, rotten Jews from New York who are behind it."

While twenty-five soldiers were eventually charged with involvement in the attack, the focus of attention was Lieutenant William Calley, the twenty-four-year-old platoon leader who admitted to having played a leading role. Calley was charged with the deaths of 109 civilians and was convicted of the premeditated murder of 22. He told the judge he thought it had been "no big deal."

When Calley was sentenced to life imprisonment, Nixon ordered that he be released pending an appeal and said he would personally review the case before any sentence was carried out. Calley was eventually confined for only three years, spent mostly in a comfortable apartment at Fort Benning, Georgia, with permission to receive visits from a girlfriend. A record entitled "The Battle Hymn of Lieutenant Calley," sung to the tune of "The Battle Hymn of the Republic," proved immensely popular. A publisher paid the soldier a hundred thousand dollars for his life story.

The military prosecutor in the case, Captain Aubrey Daniel, sent Nixon a four-page letter protesting his intervention. The president's action, the prosecutor wrote, had enhanced Calley's image as "a national hero" and "damaged the military judicial system." The White House declined to comment.[5] In his memoirs, Nixon defended his decision on the ground that he had acted on the advice of others.

Within weeks of the first My Lai story appearing in the press, Nixon was presented with a budget proposal to cut spending on the provisional reconnaissance units, small American-led teams that targeted the Viet Cong infrastructure. Their activity is better remembered today as the Phoenix program, under which between twenty and forty thousand Vietnamese were killed.[6] National Security Council aide Laurence Lynn recalled the president's reaction to the proposed reduction to the Phoenix funding. "Nixon went into his reverie," Lynn said, "that strange reverie. It may have lasted for thirty seconds. 'No,' Nixon said. 'We've got to have more of this. Assassinations. Killings. That's what they're doing [the other side].'" The allocation for Phoenix was maintained.

According to a report never officially investigated, the U.S. military in Saigon was told in early 1969 that there was "exceptional interest" at the "highest levels of government" in a plan to send a U.S.-trained team to assassinate Cambodia's head of state, Prince Sihanouk. The prince, whose ambiguous diplomatic position had kept Cambodia out of the Southeast Asia conflict, was ousted, though not killed, the following year.[7]

"Highest level," of course, is a time-honored code for a national leader or his most senior associates. The possibility that Nixon may have been involved in plotting against the Cambodian head of state again raises the question of his attitude to political assassination, probed earlier in connection with the Castro murder plots. It demands a brief diversion from Southeast Asia to an event that was to take place on the other side of the Pacific.

In the fall of 1970 democratic elections had brought the Marxist Salvador Allende to power in Chile. He would remain in office for three years, then die violently in a military coup. That Nixon ordered the CIA to oppose and obstruct Allende is a matter of historical record, but exactly what actions he authorized and whether the United States was implicated in Allende's death are issues that remain unresolved.

Nixon's personal effort to thwart the Chilean president began at the urging of his old supporter Donald Kendall, the head of PepsiCo and a key member of a business group known as the Council on Latin America. It was the day after meeting with Kendall and a Chilean associate, a newspaper magnate, that Nixon ordered CIA director Helms to act against Allende.

Trying to reason with Nixon on Chile, Helms recalled in 1999, was "like talking into a gale." One of the director's senior colleagues characterized the president's mood as "furious." Another called his instructions "aberrational and hysterical." What exactly did Nixon order, then or at a future date?

Five years later, according to verbatim notes of a conversation with President Ford, Kissinger said that William Colby, by then heading the CIA, was "blackmailing me on the assassination stories. Nixon and I asked Helms to look into the possibilities of a coup in Chile in 1970. Helms said it wouldn't work. . . ." The next two lines of Kissinger's remarks remain censored.

All sources agree that Nixon's ukase triggered a dual approach toward Allende. Track I authorized political maneuvering and propaganda designed to prevent Allende's election from being confirmed by the Chilean Congress. Track II, which was kept top secret, involved using the CIA to provoke and assist a military coup that would oust Allende.

Nixon "wanted something done," Helms was to tell the Senate Intelligence Committee, "and he didn't much care how. . . . This was a pretty all-inclusive order. . . ." Asked by a senator if assassination was included, Helms replied, "Well, not in my mind. . . ."

In his written response to the committee's questions after his resignation, Nixon distanced himself from any coup planning. Eleven times he claimed not to remember key points. He offered a brief, vague account of the affair in his memoirs, not stating clearly whether Track II was ever stopped or not.[8]

Allende's overthrow and death in 1973 would follow an assault on the president's palace by forces under the command of General Augusto Pinochet. United States senators were told by a State Department official days later that the Nixon White House had had advance warning of the coup but decided on a "hands off" policy.

Recently released documents establish that the administration was immediately sympathetic to the new regime, and offered economic assistance. Nixon received its first ambassador only two months after the coup, by which time Washington well knew that Pinochet's forces had begun "severe repression." This was the reign of terror, including summary executions and torture, that a quarter century later would lead to an international effort to put the general on trial.

Nixon dealt with Allende's death in his memoirs in two lines, saying merely that "according to conflicting reports," Chile's leader "was either killed or committed suicide during the coup." The reports do indeed conflict. Pinochet's people alleged that Allende "shot himself once in the head with an automatic weapon that was a gift from Premier Fidel Castro of Cuba. . . ." The president's widow, however, said there were also "several bullet wounds" to the stomach, and she believed he had been "murdered."

Vague reports have long circulated of American involvement on the day of the coup, of a U.S. electronic intelligence airplane relaying communications for the plotters, of U.S. naval ships off the Chilean coast, of liaison during the coup planning between a Chilean admiral and a Marine Corps officer. The marine, Colonel Patrick Ryan, denied this. His own report on the coup, however, released in 1998, is a triumphalist account of a "close to perfect" operation by Pinochet's soldiers, among whom he counted one senior friend. The report ends in a paean of praise for the new regime.

The author here contributes two items of related information. A former CIA officer and undercover agent, David Morales, whose career background was established during a congressional probe, reportedly confided after he had retired that "he was in the palace when Allende was killed." Morales, described by a former House Assassinations Committee investigator as a "hit man for the CIA," had worked closely with David Phillips, the CIA officer assigned to run the Nixon anti-Allende project at its inception.

Phillips was also head of the CIA's Western Hemisphere Division, which supervised operations in Chile at the time of Allende's overthrow. Later, as a result of his congressional testimony on another matter, he became a controversial figure. Two chief counsel doubted the truth of his testimony, and staffers wanted him charged with perjury. His specialty, during his rise in the CIA, had been black propaganda and disinformation.

Phillips asserted in his memoirs that the Track II effort on Chile had been closed down long before Allende's death. In a public letter to the Chilean president's widow, he stated that accusations of CIA involvement in the death were "untrue and the evidence tainted." Whatever the truth of that claim, the former Western Hemisphere chief admitted in a previously unpublished interview that the full truth about Chile had yet to be told. His comments about Nixon's role were startling. "The Senate Intelligence Committee left an imperfect record," Phillips said. "There was no question . . . to those of us in the trenches that the Nixon administration wanted a violent coup, since all previous efforts—the elections—had gone bad. . . . This meant Allende's death by supportive Chilean military officers.

"There was no doubt they would kill him in any coup attempt. There was never a time then in which we were not in very friendly contact with officers who wanted to assassinate him. . . . With the pressure on Helms from Nixon and Kissinger, there was no doubt that we were to give the green light to whoever in the military could carry out such a coup. . . . They wanted Allende removed and were fully aware that would entail his murder. . . . The people who would do it would not take him alive. They probably would not have taken him alive even if we had asked for that, which we did not.

"And the National Security Council knew that. . . . There was no squeamishness in Richard Nixon on that score."

As reported earlier, in the account of the Castro assassination plots, Nixon told the Senate Intelligence Committee—on oath—that assassination of a foreign leader was "an act I never had cause to consider."

Chile, though the subject of prolonged plotting, was a sideshow compared with Vietnam, which remained the nation's agony and the president's preoccupation. Haldeman, who kept a scribbled record of every meeting with Nixon, made this note in 1969:

> VN [Vietnam] enemy
> Misjudges 2 things
> —the time—has 3 years + 3 mo
> —the man—won't be 1st P to lose war

However strong his resolve, "the Man," as aides sometimes referred to the president, found his military and diplomatic efforts constantly frustrated. Secret contacts with the North Vietnamese seemed to lead nowhere. Attempts to negotiate through the Soviets, who were supplying Hanoi with arms, did not bring a breakthrough, nor did a deliberate leak, designed to make the enemy believe Nixon was considering invading the North. In his memoirs Nixon pinned the blame for the impasse on those known in the Oval Office as "the bad guys," the domestic opponents of the war.

In the fall of the first year two massive demonstrations were held in Washington. During the first, in October 1969, a quarter of a million people took to the streets. "Don't get rattled—don't waver—don't react," Nixon scribbled in a note to himself. *Time* magazine reported that the president seemed "unconcerned and aloof from it all."

His public posture notwithstanding, Nixon was in fact consumed by both the war and the domestic opposition to it. With another huge demonstration looming, he decided to address the nation. "Three of us worked on a first draft," recalled National Security Council aide William Watts. "The line we took would have had us out of Vietnam in six months. Then, voom, it was gone. The speech he gave had nothing to do with what we wrote."

Nixon made a note to himself to "talk softly and carry a big stick." In early November, after days of writing and rewriting, on one occasion working through the night, he went on national television to ask for the support of "the great silent majority of my fellow Americans" to fulfill the U.S. commitment in Vietnam. The route to peace, Nixon insisted, was to continue fighting. He would not be deflected by the protesting "minority."

In a White House staffed at the top by advertising men, Vietnam policy was largely conceived and measured in public relations terms. "The important thing" in rallying Republican support, Haldeman aide Larry Higby had said in a recent memo, was to get out a headline reading WORLD WIDE ACCLAIM FOR NIXON'S PEACE INITIATIVES. The big speech more than achieved that—or so, until very recently, it seemed.

"The White House switchboard," Nixon wrote in his memoirs, "lighted up from the minute I left the air. . . . More than 50,000 telegrams and 30,000 letters poured in, and the percentage of critical messages among them was low. . . . For the first time, the Silent Majority had made itself heard."

Nixon claimed he had barely slept the night he made the speech, so "keyed up" was he over what the reaction might be. Only in 1999 did Alexander Butterfield, the aide who handled the flow of paper in the Oval Office, reveal the truth: The positive reaction, he maintained, was "largely contrived. It was manufactured."

Weeks before the address, Butterfield said, he was told "to make damn sure that the response was fantastic." A high proportion of the telegrams and letters was generated in advance by contacting Republican state chairmen, the American Legion, the Veterans of Foreign Wars, and the like. Future presidential candidate Ross Perot, then a billionaire businessman mustering support for Nixon's war policy, promised a trainload of mail and did not fall far short of his pledge.

"Everything," Butterfield said, "was spring-loaded." Yet Nixon responded with frenetic excitement, calling Haldeman twenty times between 10:00 P.M. and 1:00 A.M. on the night of the speech, with instructions to counterattack critical comments on television, orders to fire off cables, and orders to get reaction and, again, to manufacture it. Nixon pleaded, a Haldeman note shows: "If only do one thing get 100 vicious dirty calls to *New York Times* and *Washington Post* about their editorials (even though no idea what they'll be)."

Nixon was so "elated," Kissinger recalled, "he kept the congratulatory telegrams stacked on his desk in such numbers that the Oval Office could not be used for work, and for days he refused to relinquish them."

Basking in his apparent success, the president hosted a dinner for Britain's Prince Phillip and deluged Haldeman with yet more calls saying how marvelous everything was. "You heard a lot about those of us who screened Nixon from reality," Ehrlichman would say years later. "Well, Nixon shielded Nixon from reality."

Two days after the address, feet up on the desk, Nixon told aides: "We've got those liberal bastards on the run now. . . . Floored those liberal sons of bitches . . . never let them get back on their feet."

In fact, the "liberal bastards" swarmed into Washington again the following week in even greater numbers—by one count, as many as 325,000 people. At Nixon's request, three hundred soldiers armed with rifles and machine guns were concealed in the basements of the White House and the neighboring Executive Office building, ready for possible action.

Monitoring the demonstration from a helicopter, Haldeman looked down on what was becoming a familiar scene, a White House marooned, cordoned off behind a barricade of buses. At the Justice Department, Attorney General Mitchell stood with aides on a balcony watching the demonstrators, chewing on his pipe and sending orders to U.S. marshals to use more tear gas. Later, over scotch, he said all the demonstrators should be deported to Russia. "It was like St. Petersburg in 1917," he told Nixon.

The president had long since ordered an in-depth CIA analysis of the "Communist factors" behind the protests. When the CIA found evidence of no such involvement, he merely ordered further investigation. "There was nothing we could do to convince him," CIA Director Helms recalled.

Nixon's reaction to the November protest was pure farce. When the young people began to march past, a single file of candle carriers with placards bearing the names of the fallen, he at first ignored them. "P not interested," Haldeman noted. "Spent two hours at the bowling alley." The following evening, with the demonstration continuing, Nixon offered "helpful ideas, like using helicopters to blow their candles out."

"Of all choices," Kissinger thought, Nixon "was probably the least suited for the act of grace that might have achieved reconciliation with the responsible members of the opposition. Seeing himself in any case the target of a liberal conspiracy to destroy him, he could not bring himself to regard the Vietnam War as anything other than a continuation of the long-lived assault on his political existence."

In the first twelve months of his presidency, 11,527 more American servicemen had died in Vietnam.

On January 20, 1970, the anniversary of his inauguration, Nixon was alone in the Oval Office as the evening shadows lengthened. Summoned into the presence, Haldeman and Rose Woods found him sitting in the dark in his overcoat, fiddling with a silver music box. Nixon lifted the lid, which bore his name and the presidential seal. Then the three of them listened as the box tinkled out a tinny, cheery rendition of "Hail to the Chief."[9]

He let the little box play on until the mechanism wound down and the music slid painfully into silence. Then, murmuring, "Been a year," Nixon walked out through the French doors like an actor making a meaningful exit. No one could have guessed at the nightmare action that was to follow. The stage, though, had been set.

26

You talk about a police state. Let me tell you what happens when you go to what is really a police state. . . . You can't talk in your bedroom. You don't talk on the telephone . . . you can't even talk in front of a shrub.

—*Richard M. Nixon, 1971*

Months earlier, in the summer of 1969, a short gray-haired man had arrived outside the house at 3021 N Street in Washington's fashionable Georgetown district. Dressed and equipped like a telephone company repairman, the man clambered up a telephone pole and attached a small battery-powered transmitter to one of the lines. From then on every call made on that line was taped, on a recorder concealed in the trunk of a nearby parked car.

The victim of the surveillance was Joseph Kraft, one of the nation's most prominent syndicated columnists. The "repairman" was John Ragan, the wireman who had done duty for Nixon throughout the 1968 campaign by checking for bugs in his office and at hotels.[1] He was by now, effectively, the president's personal wireman.

As cover while installing the Kraft tap, Ragan was also equipped with a bogus telephone company card. It had been supplied to him by former phone company executive John Davies, the White House "tour director," who had been close to Nixon as early as 1962.[2]

Ragan had met with Nixon repeatedly during the campaign. He was one of those to whom Nixon later presented a framed map of the United States marked with crisscross lines, a memento of the arduous route traveled on the way to victory. Ragan and his wife had been invited to the inauguration and the inaugural ball and to breakfast at the White House the following day.

Officially Ragan was employed during the first Nixon presidency by the Republican National Committee as "security director" at a salary of thirty-four thousand dollars. He would later describe the bulk of his work as "defensive," but the claim is suspect. During the Nixon effort to unseat President Allende, Ragan was sent to Chile by ITT (International Telephone and Telegraph) ostensibly to teach antibugging techniques. He met Allende during the trip and supposedly swept the presidential palace and residence for bugs.[3] Given Ragan's connections and Nixon's malign intentions toward the Chilean leader, it is possible he also planted some.

Ragan is known to have investigated a member of the Democratic National Committee and—a long-ignored fact that has never been adequately explored—to have had advance knowledge of the activities of the Watergate burglars.

The actual order to bug columnist Kraft had been issued by a former New York police detective, John Caulfield, also now working for the White House. Caulfield had worked security for Nixon during his presidential campaigns, at Nixon's personal request, and was especially close to Rose Woods. His White House function was to provide "investigative support."

Caulfield in turn received his instructions to bug Kraft from John Ehrlichman. When he assigned the job to Ragan, Caulfield told him the orders originated with "the top man." Correctly, Ragan took this to mean Nixon himself.

"I want no climate of fear in this country," Nixon had insisted to Theodore White within days of his inauguration, "no wiretapping scare." He claimed he had instructed Attorney General Mitchell to control wiretapping with an iron hand. Yet within three months he was secretly issuing orders to initiate electronic surveillance of numerous journalists and administration officials.

The bugging was triggered by Nixon's fury at the "crew cut boy scouts" of the press and specifically at the *New York Times*. It began in April 1969, when the *Times* ran a report suggesting there might be a unilateral withdrawal from Vietnam, and got under way in earnest when the paper revealed the secret bombing of Cambodia. Haldeman remembered the reaction to that story: "We were in Key Biscayne. . . . That morning, at breakfast by the pool, Henry [Kissinger] had been reading the morning newspapers. Suddenly he stood up, shaking. He showed me the offending story and said that the President must be informed at once."[4]

Nixon was "enraged," and Kissinger immediately phoned FBI Director Hoover with instructions to find out who was leaking to the press. There followed two years of FBI snooping on seventeen targets: journalists, some of whom considered themselves Kissinger's confidants; members of Kissinger's and Nixon's staffs; and State and Defense Department officials. The wiretap of columnist Kraft was carried out by White House operatives, Nixon said in his memoirs, because the FBI at first failed to cooperate.

Despite the extent of the operation, none of the bugging produced useful information. "The taps," Nixon was to tell counsel John Dean, "never helped us. Just gobs and gobs of material; gossip and bullshitting. . . ."

He and Kissinger later tried to blame each other for the operation. "Henry ordered the whole goddamn thing," the president said during the Watergate crisis. "He ordered it all, believe you me. He was the one who was in my office jumping up and down about 'This and that got out,' and buh, buh, buh got out. I didn't give a shit . . . but he did. . . . He read every one of those taps until the very last one. . . . I never saw a one, never. . . ."

Other information suggests that Nixon's version of the events was simply not true. "The overall program was approved by the president, and I was aware of that from the outset," said Alexander Haig, who cited the "highest authority" when he transmitted some of the earliest bugging orders to the FBI. Bureau documents indicate the wiretap logs at first went "only to the President" and later were delivered directly to Haldeman, who suddenly found himself living a cloak-and-dagger existence. "Every now and then, on my way into the office or in a hotel corridor on a trip, a man would suddenly jump out of a dark doorway, thrust an envelope in my hand, then disappear. . . ." Nixon, he insisted, "was one hundred percent behind the wiretaps."

A friendly interviewer later asked Nixon whether, given that press leaks are a fact of political life, he had perhaps overreacted in ordering the taps. "You're being too kind," came the unusually candid reply. "I was paranoiac, or almost a basket case, with regard to secrecy. . . ."

Nixon recognized that exposure of the bugging would be disastrous. When FBI Assistant Director William Sullivan, who had custody of the wiretap records, warned that Hoover might use them as blackmail material, Nixon ordered the file transferred to the White House at once. But he was soon worrying about Sullivan himself. "Will he rat on us?" he asked sharply when Ehrlichman reminded him that Sullivan, recently fired from the FBI, had "executed all your instructions for the secret taps." "It depends on how he's treated," Ehrlichman replied, and Nixon suggested Sullivan be found a new job. He was duly appointed head of the new Office of National Narcotics Intelligence.

The wiretapping was to be a key item when, in 1974, the House Committee on the Judiciary drew up its articles of impeachment. "In violation of his constitutional oath . . . and in disregard of his constitutional duty," the article stated, Nixon had "repeatedly engaged in conduct violating the constitutional rights of citizens. . . ."

The full extent of the surveillance will probably never be known. Electronic measures aside, FBI agents lurked outside the home of former Ambassador Averell Harriman to try to identify his visitors. Others covertly took photographs of meetings between journalists. The congressional doorkeeper, William Miller, was taken aback one day to discover Signal Corps technicians wiring the Speaker's dining room before a luncheon to be attended by Nixon, the Speaker, the majority and minority leaders, and the party whips.

"I believe that for possibly three years in a row the room was bugged," Miller said. "Nixon must have had a record of what the congressmen were saying about him even before his arrival . . . or what they might have been saying about him on the other side of the table, where they thought he couldn't hear. . . . Maybe I should have made a fuss about it."

Men as disparate as Nixon's old friend Bob Finch, secretary of health, education and welfare, and Colonel Ralph Albertazzie, captain of Air Force One, strongly suspected their phones were tapped. Both had the disquieting experience of having had what they assumed to be private conversations, then discovering soon afterward that a third party appeared fully informed on what they had said. Finch considered raising the matter with the president but, like others, wound up doing nothing.

———————

Nixon's own beliefs about how extensive his surveillance powers should be emerged behind the scenes in July 1970 after a series of traumatic political events.

In response to a temporary U.S. invasion of Cambodia, an action that drew that country inexorably into the Vietnam conflict, student unrest erupted at campuses across the land. Arsonists burned buildings at three universities, and a bomb exploded at an army teaching center in Wisconsin, killing a physicist and wounding others. Four students were shot dead and nine injured when national guardsmen opened fire at Kent State University in Ohio. At Jackson State University, in Mississippi, police killed two students and wounded twelve.

Nixon's response to the mayhem was maladroit and disastrously timed. Three days before the Kent State shootings, in emotional comments to a group of Pentagon employees, he spoke of the "bums blowing up campuses" and of the nation's students—"the luckiest people in the world"—in the same breath. After Kent State, he managed only a tut-tutting statement that "when dissent turns to violence, it invites tragedy" and offered not a word of sympathy in public for the dead and wounded. He urged that a story that the guardsmen had not been justified in shooting be knocked down, and another—a baseless allegation that the guardsmen had been targeted by a sniper—promoted.[5] Leafing through photographs of the Jackson dead, Nixon asked: "What are we going to do to get more respect for the police from our young people?"

Soon afterward, following another massive protest in Washington, Nixon directed the heads of the FBI, the CIA, the Defense Intelligence Agency, and the National Security Agency to discuss how to combat the "hundreds, perhaps thousands, of Americans . . . determined to destroy our society." The resulting plan, drawn up by a Nixon aide, would cause an outcry when eventually made public. Senator Sam Ervin would denounce it as a "Gestapo" scheme. More soberly, in the words of the Senate Intelligence Committee, the plan would have meant that: "With presidential authority, the intelligence community could at will intercept and transcribe the communications of Americans using international telecommunications facilities; eavesdrop from near or far on anyone deemed to be a 'Threat to the internal security,' read the mail of American citizens, break into the homes of anyone tagged as a security threat."

The plan never went into effect, and some of the measures described were not even really new. Its historical significance is that Nixon, apparently convinced he had the authority to break the law, approved it and believed he had the power to do so.

"When the President does it, that means that it is not illegal," Nixon explained years later, when asked about the plan by British interviewer David Frost. There were, he suggested, circumstances in which a president could justifiably order crimes like break-ins. He did not reject outright the possibility that a president might be within his rights to order murder.

The abortive 1970 operation had been one of the earliest of what John Mitchell came to call the "White House horrors." For although it was shelved, Nixon's frustration with what he saw as the failures of the agencies remained, frustration that soon enough would lead him and his aides to plot break-ins and buggings of their own.

By that time, and fatally for the presidency, he had also decided to bug himself.

"Mr. President," Haldeman aide Alexander Butterfield said one evening in February 1971, "the taping system that Bob said you wanted is in place now. It works fine, and I would like to brief you on the locations of the microphones."[6]

Nixon at first gave Butterfield a blank stare and mumbled: "Oh, hmm, ah, hmm, ah, oh, well," as if reluctant to discuss the matter. Then at last he asked, "How does it work?" and Butterfield explained. The White House tapes had started rolling and were to roll on for more than two years.

The desire to record his own conversations was not a novel idea for Nixon. During the 1962 campaign in California he had made an unusual request of the electronics specialist employed to debug his office. "One of the first things I was asked to do," the technician remembered, "was to put microphones and a recorder in his office. He just wanted a record of *everything*. . . . I put in a nice system."

At the beginning of the presidency, as reported earlier, Nixon had ordered most of President Johnson's recording equipment removed. Although he was skittish about a system that was not of his own making, he remained preoccupied with the notion that a record had to be kept.

Haldeman provided two reasons for this: Nixon wanted to be able to rebut anyone who might quote him inaccurately, and he wished to have a complete record for the writing of his memoirs. Elliot Richardson, his second secretary of defense, had an elegant theory about this desire to keep a record. Nixon was fascinated by Robert Blake's biography of the nineteenth-century British prime minister, Ben Disraeli, a book, Richardson thought, that one put down "with the sense that this extraordinary, exotic, even bizarre creature remains elusive." As a result, Richardson believed, Nixon decided that only an exhaustive record could provide the "indispensable tool whereby *his* biographers would gain the insights denied to Blake."

Butterfield, a military man, had a different interpretation. "You assume that when the president is busy behind the closed door, great affairs of state are being discussed," he said later. There was, however, "a lot of leisure time," during which Nixon pondered other matters, which included a number of "typical items" that Butterfield recalled.

"The President," he testified, "often was concerned whether or not the curtains were closed or open, the arrangement of state gifts, whether they should be on that side of the room or this side of the room . . . social functions . . . he debated whether we should have a U-shaped table or round table. . . . He was very interested in whether or not salad should be served . . . the details of the drive up the walkway [to the South Portico] . . . whether or not the Secret Service would salute during the Star Spangled Banner and sing . . . the plants in the south grounds and whether or not we should retain the tennis court or move it. . . .

It was in this testimony that Butterfield recalled the peculiar memorandum the president had dictated while in Yugoslavia, pointing out the poor standard of the restroom facilities on the Mall back in Washington. "I thought it strange that he would dictate a letter from Belgrade about the lousy restroom facilities. . . . And the dog [Nixon's red setter, King Timahoe]—a lot of time with the dog and when the dog was going to have his hair cut, all that sort of thing. . . .

"He seemed to me," Butterfield said, "to be preoccupied with his place in history, with his presidency as history would see it . . . the concept is normal, but the preoccupation is not. My honest opinion is that it was a bit abnormal."

To satisfy his desire for a thorough record, Nixon at first tried using note takers. Senior staff members, however, ordered to prepare long notes on every meeting, failed to capture what Haldeman called "the human intangibles, the subtle nuances." The chief of staff then asked the assistance of Nixon's old interpreter, General Vernon Walters, whom the president considered the "perfect" scribe. The general pushed his medals under Haldeman's nose and declared: "I am a commander of troops. I am not a secretary to anybody."

According to Nixon, he eventually opted for the taping system on the advice of his predecessor. "Johnson said the recordings of his conversations had proved to be exceedingly valuable in preparing his memoirs," Nixon recalled. "He urged that I reinstall the recording devices."

Others ascribed less lofty motives for the taping, among them Nixon's concern that Henry Kissinger would steal his thunder. "Haldeman once explained to me," Ehrlichman recalled, "that Nixon had particularly wanted the White House taping system installed in order to demonstrate that the foreign policy initiatives of his presidency were in fact his own, not Henry's. At times he despaired of Henry."

Nixon obsessed about making a record of everything, everywhere, for its own sake. "Great consternation," Haldeman noted early on when Nixon complained after making a speech, "because it wasn't recorded." It was against that background that the new system was installed at the White House in 1971.

Seven microphones were placed in the Oval Office, five embedded in the president's desk and one in each of the wall lamps beside the fireplace. Two were concealed beneath the table in the Cabinet Room. Not long afterward four more were hidden in Nixon's hideaway office in the Old Executive Office Building. Others were later planted in his study at Camp David.

The phones were wired, too, in all the rooms that were miked and in the Lincoln Sitting Room. The tape recorders, Sony 800B reel-to-reel models, were sited elsewhere—at the White House the collection center was a locker room in the basement—and engaged automatically each time a phone was picked up and a conversation begun.

That feature was the crucial, and in the long term so damaging, difference between the Johnson system and Nixon's. Johnson's recorders had gone into action only when he turned them on via a switch. Except in the Cabinet Room, where the device had such a switch, the Nixon microphones were voice-activated, and recording began the moment a person spoke.

"Haldeman asked me to make it voice-activated," Haldeman's aide Larry Higby said, "because the president was an absolute klutz when it came to things mechanical." Without a control system, however, the mikes simply picked up *everything*, including material that no man could sensibly wish to preserve for posterity. Nixon had created a monster that preserved his every word, words that one day, when publicly revealed, were to sweep him away on a wave of self-incrimination.

This was a covert, furtive arrangement. "Nixon said I was to tell nobody about the existence of the tapes," Haldeman recalled. "I say things in this office that I don't even want Rose to hear," Nixon told him. Woods was not informed, nor were Pat and the girls. Pat was said to have been "appalled" when news broke of the recordings' existence. She would insist they were "like private love letters, for one person only," meaning of course her husband.

But were the tapes really heard by one person only? Haldeman noted in an early diary entry that his boss feared that the "White House [switch]board may be tapped, or operators listen in." Nixon had not forgotten Hoover's warning that the phone system, run by the White House Communications Agency, a military unit, might not be secure. When the taping system was put in place, orders went out to "Have anyone but WHCA do the project." The installation of the devices, their day-to-day maintenance, and the changing and storage of the tapes, was handled instead by the Technical Services Division of the Secret Service.

As reported elsewhere information exists suggesting that the tapes were not secure even in Secret Service custody. Some even suspected that Butterfield, the former air force colonel who oversaw the taping system, was a CIA stool pigeon.[7]

Only four aides are supposed to have had any knowledge of the tapes: Haldeman, his assistants Higby and Butterfield, and Butterfield's successor, Stephen Bull. Ehrlichman, who covertly recorded some of his own conversations, was not made aware of the taping until shortly before his resignation. Kissinger was also excluded from the secret—by his account, until the spring of 1973.[8] Even though he had been a party to the wiretapping of the journalists, and had his staff make notes of many of his own phone conversations, he was taken aback when he learned of the Nixon procedures.

"We are going to look perfect fools when all of the tapes are released," Kissinger was to warn Ehrlichman. "Nixon will be heard delivering one of his tirades, saying all sorts of outrageous things, and we will be sitting there quietly, not protesting or disagreeing. You and I know that's how we had to do business with him, but we will be judged harshly. . . ."

Some Oval Office visitors guessed their conversations were being recorded, among them Sir Alec Douglas-Home, then Britain's foreign secretary. When he noticed at a meeting that no one was taking notes, Douglas-Home recalled, he "immediately drew the obvious conclusion, that every single word was being taped. . . ." Sir Alec had figured out what Kissinger missed when, about the time the taping commenced, he received a memorandum informing staff that they need no longer "pay too much attention to substantive details in our records of presidential conversations."

House Majority Leader Tip O'Neill caught on when, during a discussion of Vietnam with the president and Kissinger, he asked if a certain development was Kissinger's doing. Nixon cut in with "I'll answer that one, Henry." Then, O'Neill recalled, he "did something very strange: he paused, raised his voice, and looked up at the ceiling. I looked up too, to see who he was talking to, but the only thing up there was the chandelier. 'I want you all to know,' he announced, 'that as President of the United States, this was *my* decision. . . .'" From the bizarre declaiming and from the way Nixon craned his head, O'Neill guessed there were hidden microphones.

Conversations that had made no sense at the time fell into place, Kissinger was to say, once he learned of the taping. "I could see occasions," he said, "when I was set up to prevent my dissociating myself from some course, or to get me on record supporting some complicated design."

Nixon claimed he soon became oblivious to his own recording devices, and happily for posterity, he clearly often was. It is equally clear that the claim was at least partly disingenuous, for he undoubtedly also used the system to ensure he got something on the record. Yet sometimes, leery of his own microphones, he tried to hide from them.

With Watergate in full flood, but the tape system still undiscovered, Republican Senator Howard Baker asked Nixon if Mitchell was vulnerable. "Nixon suddenly lowered his voice and sort of turned away," Baker recalled, then whispered that Mitchell might indeed have "a problem of some proportions." Baker suddenly suspected that the meeting was being taped, and ended the conversation as swiftly as possible.

The president's lapses into whispering occurred often enough to be noticed by all manner of people. Even the White House dog keeper, Traphes Bryant, guessed at bugging. Charles Colson, the ultimate Nixon loyalist, would remember "moments when I should have been suspicious: the time at Camp David when he walked from his office to the corridor to whisper to me sensitive information about another staff member. Then once, during a telephone conversation, there had been a clicking sound. . . ."

White House counsel John Dean was to notice Nixon "posturing" during a key Watergate conversation, "always placing his own role in an innocuous perspective. . . ." "I wondered if the meeting was a setup," Dean wrote later. "Was he recording me?" His suspicion deepened when Nixon got up and walked away a few steps before saying something compromising to himself in "an almost inaudible tone."

When some of the tapes were finally surrendered to Congress, they not only bolstered Dean's credibility but suggested he had been right about the president's odd Oval Office performance. "You never heard a more programmed conversation in your life," Judiciary Committee member Jerome Waldie noted in his diary after hearing one of the Nixon-Dean recordings.

Nixon claimed in his memoirs that he was "not comfortable with the idea of taping people without their knowledge. . . ." Yet one taped transcript, of a 1971 meeting with dairy industry chiefs, demonstrates strikingly that this was not true. With the hidden tapes rolling, Nixon made the remark ". . . this room is not tapped. Forgot to do that. . . ." The milk industry men guffawed at the apparent joke, yet Nixon had to know he was lying. The meeting occurred just a month after the first installation of the microphones, at a time when he could not possibly have forgotten their existence. It took place, moreover, in the Cabinet Room, where the microphones had to be manually switched on.

Every head of state, every senator or representative, and every colleague who believed he was having a private conversation with the president, on the phone or in person, was wrong.[9]

_____

From the day of his downfall until his death Nixon would struggle to prevent public access to the four thousand hours of tape recordings, and the forty-two million pages of documents, generated during his time in office. Immediately after the resignation he would try to have the tapes shipped to his home in California. A truck and a plane were standing by when, at the last moment, the transfer was halted. Recognizing that letting Nixon have the tapes would be seen as "the final act of cover-up," President Ford blocked shipments to San Clemente of anything except Nixon's clothing and that of his family.

After the twenty years of legal wrangling that followed, and further delays caused by Nixon's heirs since his death, comes a fact of which many remain unaware. As of the year 2000, the public has access to only about 864 hours of Nixon recordings.

Only 60 hours were provided to the Watergate Special Prosecution Force, after a legal battle that went all the way to the Supreme Court. Of those 60 hours, only 12½ were made accessible to the public—and that only in edited transcript form—until six years after Watergate. After stiff resistance a further 851 hours of recordings were released during the nineties, some of them under a congressional mandate requiring release to the public of the "full truth" on matters defined by the archivist of the United States as "abuse of governmental power." Under the current agreement, some 2,765 hours of tape are scheduled to be released in the next five years or so.

In his memoirs Nixon quoted a passage taken, he said, from his daughter Tricia's diary. "Daddy," the cited entry read, "has cautioned us that there is nothing damaging on the tapes. . . ."

"Imagine your own feeling," Haldeman was to write, "if you were to open your Monday morning paper and find that someone had taped all the conversations in your home over the weekend—then selected the very worst segments and printed them in the paper. That's just about what happened to us."

As late as 1997 Nixon Library archivist Susan Naulty condemned those who, she claimed, had tried to perpetuate the "false caricature" of Nixon as "villainy incarnate." Accusations that the available tapes reveal "felony wrongdoing" or serious character defects, Naulty argued, are unfair.

It is true that those of the tapes that have been made available are merely a small portion of the total, and that their audio quality is sometimes poor. Yet they remain riveting historical documents, not least because of the style and tenor of the material. "Here's this voice you've heard all your life," Congressman Waldie noted, "and it starts in stammering and stuttering. . . . Rarely is a thought expressed coherently, and a lot of it is covered up with obscenities . . . [or] some unintelligible grunt from the President."

Nixon was so bothered by his own swearing and blaspheming on the tapes that when he authorized a partial release, he ordered the recordings sanitized. Published transcripts were interrupted often by the words "expletive deleted."

One historian did a computer analysis demonstrating that Nixon's most common swearwords were "Damn," "Goddamn!," and "Jesus Christ!" Nixon had attempted to have the "goddamn" in the transcripts changed to a mere "damn." "Little shits," another perennial, was the phrase most often deleted. On occasion, recent releases show, the president also used the word "fucking."

What is more interesting, though, is the fact that Nixon seems to have used different personas with different people. Rebozo, predictably, claimed the president "never" used a "bad word." Others—Finch, Kissinger, General Cushman, speechwriter Ray Price, and Stephen Hess—did not remember him as having been foulmouthed. Yet even Nixon's mother said her son swore "like a sailor" when tense. Nixon's friend Earl Mazo claimed he did so only among friends.

In fact, a witness who heard Nixon at a diplomatic dinner party as early as 1956 had been taken aback by his foul language. Butterfield remembered him, in the White House, aiming the word "fuck" at Transportation Secretary John Volpe behind his back. Nixon called Canada's prime minister "fucking Trudeau" and Richard Kleindienst, his second attorney general, a "motherfucking cocksucker" during an angry phone call. Ed Rollins, a Republican political consultant, recalled that when they first met—as late as 1979—Nixon used three obscenities in his first sentence.

"All Presidents swear," Nixon protested in old age. Indeed, Abraham Lincoln had a reputation for using expletives, and Truman, Kennedy, and Johnson all used swear words. The difference between Nixon and them is in the hypocrisy. Nixon, although himself a habitual swearer, deprecated the cursing of other politicians. He publicly condemned Truman for having used "gutter language"—he had come out with a "go to hell"—and said piously that as president he intended to avoid such talk—"as a responsibility to the children of this country."

Alcohol may have been partly responsible for Nixon's use of expletives. In 1962, on Paradise Island, Jack Paar had noted Nixon's profanity while "drinking heavily." A *Washington Post* report observed that it was "plain from his slurred syllables that he had been drinking" when on a 1973 tape he came out with "Goddamn it, I'm never going to discuss this son-of-a-bitching Watergate thing again. Never, never, never. . . ."

Spiro Agnew recalled Nixon worrying aloud, that same year, about "how the tapes would be used to embarrass him and affect his future place in history . . . he had the look of a frightened man." Public response to the tapes' content would matter much more than disapproval of the swearing, and Nixon knew it.

His natural allies appreciated how devastating the tapes were as soon as they were released. William Randolph Hearst, Jr., wrote a column blasting Nixon as a man "with a moral blind spot." The president and his aides, he said, sounded like "a gang of racketeers talking over strategy in a jam-up situation."

Billy Graham wept as he perused the published transcripts and reportedly vomited afterward. The evangelist said he had a "real love" for Nixon, had looked upon him as the nation's best hope. "But then the way it sounded in those tapes—it was all something totally foreign to me. He was just suddenly somebody else."

"The spider got entangled in its own web," Kissinger concluded. "Even had Watergate not occurred, the tapes would have damaged Nixon's reputation severely. . . . Had the tapes trickled out posthumously, Nixon would have managed the extraordinary feat of committing suicide after his own death."

Just weeks before the taping system was installed, Nixon had sat alone in the Lincoln Room, writing of his need to create a "definite image." He listed the character traits he hoped would be the foundation for such an image, a list so long that only a few of the items can be included: "compassionate, humane, fatherly, warmth, confidence in future, optimistic, upbeat, candor, honesty, openness, trustworthy, boldness, fights for what he believes, vitality, youth, enjoyment, zest, vision, dignity, respect, a man people can be proud of. . . ." And so on for as many words again, all contributing to the "visible presidential leadership" Nixon wanted his public relations to convey. If such a Richard Nixon existed, he does not appear on the White House tapes thus far released.

The tapes that we have are, rather, a unique opportunity to glimpse the public man in private, rarely obviously cheerful, often moody, ever resentful of apparent slights, ever scheming and fighting, and habitually subject to self-pity.

Recent tape releases also reveal a man with a penchant for ethnic and sexist slurs. In 1999, as the legal contest between government attorneys and the Nixon estate dragged on, the dead man's voice boomed out again in a Washington courtroom.

Women in government, he said, were "a pain in the neck, very difficult to handle," and he doubted they were "worth the effort." The problem with Mexicans, Nixon told colleagues, was finding one who was honest. "Italians," he added, "have somewhat the same problem."

House Judiciary Committee Chairman Peter Rodino, angered by a Nixon tape he heard in 1974, called in Tip O'Neill to listen along with him. "They're not, we, ah, they're not like us," Nixon said of Italians. "Difference is they smell different, they look different, they act different . . . trouble is, you can't find one that's honest. . . . I've got to deal with the Germans and the Italians and all those shit-asses . . ." he said on another tape. (Before becoming president, Nixon had voted for the Immigration and Nationality Act, a measure some criticized as being designed to prevent Italian immigration.)

"The President," the chief of naval operations, Admiral Elmo Zumwalt, was informed, "castigates every ethnic group in the U.S. as being against him—the Jews, the blacks, the Catholics, the Wasps etc. . . ."

Was Nixon anti-Semitic? He did after all appoint Kissinger, a Jewish immigrant, to the second most powerful post in his administration. Another Jew, Arthur Burns, was named chairman of the Federal Reserve, and yet another, Herb Stein, headed the Council of Economic Advisers. Murray Chotiner was a Jew, as was Nixon's counsel Leonard Garment.

"Show me a Christian, or for that matter a Jew who does not have some traces of anti-Semitism in his or her soul," Garment has said, "I will show you a human being whose body contains no germs." On an anti-Semitism scale of one to one hundred, Garment placed Nixon "somewhere between fifteen and twenty—better than most, worse than some, much like the rest of the world." Rabbi Baruch Korff, a Nixon champion in the final days, said he thought there was "not an ounce of prejudice" in the man.

Kissinger disagreed. "You can't believe how much anti-Semitism there is at the top of this government," he said, "and I mean at the top." "Nixon would talk about Jewish traitors," Ehrlichman recalled, "and he'd play off Kissinger. 'Isn't that right, Henry? Don't you agree?' And Henry would respond, 'Well, Mr. President, there are Jews and there are Jews.'"

The tapes and the contemporary record tend to support Kissinger's view. Nixon once wanted to know, Haldeman noted in his diary, why "all the Jews seem to be the ones that are for liberalizing the regulations and marijuana." Urging a revival of the House Un-American Activities Committee to investigate spies, Nixon told Haldeman: "You know what's going to charge up an audience, Jesus Christ, they'll be hanging off the rafters. . . . going after all these Jews. Just find one that is a Jew, will you?"

Nixon once ordered an aide to investigate a "Jewish cabal" at the Bureau of Labor Statistics, according to contemporary notes, and two Jewish bureau officials were transferred within weeks. An entry in the Haldeman diary cites him as identifying "our enemies" as "youth, black, Jew." Nixon objected to "having a Rabbi again" to conduct the White House church service. In 1970, as he nagged Ehrlichman to ensure the tax affairs of Democratic contributors be investigated, he zeroed in on ". . . the Jews, you know, that are stealing . . . [next phrase hard to hear on tape]."[10]

Days later Nixon was begging Haldeman: "[P]lease get me the names of the Jews, you know, the big Jewish contributors. . . . Could we please investigate some of the cocksuckers?" The IRS, he insisted, was "full of Jews," and he demanded the firing of a California Immigration Service official, "a kike by the name of Rosenberg. He is to be out. . . . Transfer him. . . ."

"This is national security," Nixon said in 1973, while trying to justify illegal White House activity. "We've got all sorts of activities because we've been trying to run this town by avoiding the Jews in the government, because there were very serious questions."

"Jews are all over the government," the president complained at an Oval Office meeting, adding they should be brought under control by putting someone "in charge who is not Jewish." "Most Jews are disloyal," he told Haldeman, ". . . generally speaking, you can't trust the bastards. They turn on you. . . ."

No one, surely, could maintain that such remarks are permissible from a president, even in private. Yet some of his defenders have continued to argue that Nixon was not an anti-Semite, citing the fact that, long before he became president, a leading Jewish group defended him against charges of anti-Semitism. They point, also, to his role in helping Jews emigrate from the Soviet Union and the perception of him as a friend of Israel.

There seem to have been two Nixons where minorities were concerned: the private man, spewing the abuse evident on the tapes, and the candidate, concerned above all about garnering votes. In a somewhat more complex way, the same went for Nixon and blacks.

"With blacks you can usually settle for an incompetent," the president said, discussing hiring policy on an early tape, "because there are just not enough competent ones. And so you put incompetents in and get along with them, because the symbolism is vitally important. You have to show you care." Such private scorn on racial matters, leavened by necessary public gestures, was an ambiguity that had a long history with Nixon.

A Quaker great-grandfather in Indiana is said to have helped smuggle escaped slaves to freedom, and Nixon's own mother welcomed black employees to her dinner table. At college Nixon was instrumental in getting the only black youth on campus into the social club. At Duke Law School in North Carolina, where racial prejudice was deeply ingrained, he raised his voice against it.

As vice president Nixon took a black Senate attendant to baseball games in his limousine. As president he made a point of chatting with the lone black technician on a television crew. He even made the occasional trip to the White House basement to drink with a black employee. "My feelings on race," Nixon told Ehrlichman, "are ultra-liberal."

Martin Luther King, who met him during the vice presidency, thought he had "a genius for convincing one that he is sincere . . . he almost disarms you with his sincerity. . . . I would conclude that if Richard Nixon is not sincere, he is the most dangerous man in America." Years later, though, with her husband dead and Nixon in the White House, King's widow, Coretta, decided he had "not evolved from racist reflexes."

Solicitor General Robert Bork, no liberal, thought Nixon "had the usual country club prejudices against blacks." Former aides have said he referred to blacks as "niggers," "jigs," "jigaboos," and "jungle bunnies." This last epithet, John Ehrlichman said, was picked up from Bebe Rebozo.

Nixon told Haldeman there had "never in history been an adequate black nation, and they are the only race of which this is true. . . . Africa is hopeless. . . ." He had spoken out during the 1968 campaign in support of the Ibos in Nigeria, then fighting for independence. Once he was in office, however, his administration virtually ignored the problem while hundreds of thousands starved. His policy toward white supremacist South Africa was to be vocal in opposition to apartheid while relaxing economic restrictions against the country. "Let's leave the niggers" to the State Department, Nixon reportedly told Kissinger; "we'll take care of the rest of the world."

"He presented different sides to different people," Ehrlichman said. "He was the Queen of Hearts in *Alice in Wonderland*. . . . There were things he said to me that he never would have said on the record, for example, that blacks are ethnically inferior. . . ." According to researchers at the National Archives, describing as yet unreleased tapes, Nixon spoke of blacks as being "just down from the trees."

Again according to Ehrlichman, Nixon thought "blacks could never achieve parity—in intelligence, economic success or social qualities. . . . He would do his best for them by getting them a place at the starting line." Nixon's "best" included urging desegregation and greatly increasing the federal budget for civil rights enforcement. His administration also appointed the first black assistant secretary of the navy, a black admiral, and a black head of the Federal Communications Commission.

Yet many critics excoriated Nixon for not doing enough in this area, especially regarding his adamant opposition to the busing of schoolchildren. Repeatedly, Haldeman noted in his diary, Nixon said he wanted "nothing more done in South beyond what law requires," for as he viewed it there was "No political gain for us."

When Kissinger was preparing a foreign policy speech, Nixon exhorted him to "make sure there's something in it for the jigs." He reminded Haldeman, on the other hand: "We do *not* make votes playing to Negroes."

Nixon resorted to deceit to avoid alienating white voters with his racial policies. Ehrlichman, deep in negotiations over busing in Michigan, was startled to discover that another White House aide was in the state making inflammatory antibusing speeches. The president denied having ordered the second aide into action, but Ehrlichman was sure he was lying.

When it came to winning votes, the tapes show, the president was utterly cynical on the race issue. With the 1972 election on the horizon, he discussed a plan to funnel five million dollars secretly to a black candidate, but only as a device to siphon votes away from the Democrats. Aides initially put forward the names of Congresswoman Shirley Chisholm and civil rights activist Julian Bond as potential puppets.

A few weeks later Jesse Jackson's name was suggested as a possible stooge. Haldeman proposed mailing the preacher thousands of one-dollar bills, to fool him into thinking large numbers of blacks supported his candidacy. Then,

Haldeman hoped, the White House could strike a deal with Jackson. "The payoff is afterwards. Give him about $10,000 per percentage point. He gets 20 per cent of the vote, he gets $200,000. That's a personal payment, after the election."[11]

Nixon welcomed the underhanded scheme. "Put that down for discussion," he responded when it came up, "not for discussion but action." Politics, as ever, had taken precedence over principle.

The tapes were rolling on the morning of May 5, 1971, as Nixon and Haldeman discussed the latest wave of Vietnam War protest. Demonstrations had continued unabated for weeks, and not all of those on the streets were students. Seven hundred veterans had gathered in front of the Capitol to throw away their decorations in disgust. Police and troops had arrested eight thousand people in Washington alone.

Today, Haldeman told the president, there would "very likely" be more trouble. "Good," came Nixon's response. ". . . These people try something, bust 'em." As the tapes silently rolled, the two men discussed ongoing dirty tricks: sending food to the demonstrators, purportedly from one of Nixon's Democratic opponents but in fact from the White House, as a ploy to smear the Democrat as an extremist sympathizer; and using "hard hats and [American] Legionnaires to provoke fights with the demonstrators."

Then came the following conspiratorial dialogue:

> HALDEMAN: What I suggested . . . and I think that they can get away with this. Do it with Teamsters. Just ask them to dig up those, their eight thugs.
> PRESIDENT NIXON: Yeah. . . . They've got guys who'll go in and knock their heads off.
> HALDEMAN: Sure. Murderers. Guys that really, you know, that's what they really do. Like the Steelworkers have and—except we can't deal with the Steelworkers at the moment.[12]
> PRESIDENT NIXON: No.
> HALDEMAN: We can deal with the Teamsters . . .
> PRESIDENT NIXON: Yeah.

Both men had reason for confidence that they could "deal" with the Teamsters, for they were already doing so. The union's acting president, Frank Fitzsimmons, had been at the White House just a week earlier meeting with Charles Colson. Already, the White House had been pressuring the Justice Department to ease up on prosecutions of crooked Teamsters, as a way to ensure the union's backing in the coming presidential election. Now the president and Haldeman discussed with confidence how the Teamsters could deal with the war protesters:

HALDEMAN: . . . It's the regular strikebuster types . . . they're gonna beat the shit out of some of these people. And, uh, hope they really hurt 'em. You know, I mean go in with some real . . . and smash some noses . . . some pretty good fights.

The president, brought up to espouse nonviolence, had not demurred but enthused.

The conversation then turned to the TV coverage of the protest, and the ringleaders:

HALDEMAN: I think getting Abbie Hoffman and . . . the other . . . they got . . . Uh [tape noise] . . . but they got him. . . .

PRESIDENT NIXON: Aren't the Chicago Seven* all Jews? . . . Hoffman, Hoffman's a Jew. . . . About half of these are Jews.

HALDEMAN: They got one shot of a policeman clubbing a guy. . . . It doesn't do us any good. But, you know, you can't avoid that. . . .

PRESIDENT NIXON: . . . inevitable, Bob. How the hell do you expect the poor goddamned policemen? . . .

The tape of this conversation lay undiscovered for ten years. When it finally surfaced, with its talk of smashing noses and knocking heads off, so did other information: Two days before the Oval Office conversation Abbie Hoffman's nose had been broken. He had suffered multiple fractures of the nose and a split lip, during a confrontation with the police near Washington's Dupont Circle.

"We were attacked," he said, "by about half a dozen guys. At least two were dressed as policemen. Some were in plainclothes. They picked me out and they chased me through a parking lot into an alley. One held my arms and I was beaten, and at the culmination of this beating I was hit about the face with a billyclub. . . ." "He was jumped by two plainclothesmen." Hoffman's widow said in 1998, "At first it looked like they were right-wing demonstrators. . . . That's when his nose was broken."

The injury was genuine, as news photographs of the bandaged nose show. It was initially treated by pediatrician Benjamin Spock, who had also been arrested that day. Hoffman said he later had to undergo surgery as a result of the attack.[13]

Haldeman declined to comment on the "thugs" tape. The CD-ROM of his diary, transcribed from tapes he made each evening, reflects a gap ascribed to garbled recording. The former chief of staff noted merely that he and the president had spoken about "demonstrations—danger of caution."

---

*Leaders of the protests during the Democratic National Convention of 1968, prosecuted by the Nixon Justice Department and convicted on charges of incitement to riot. Most of the convictions were overturned on appeal. The defendants were more properly known as the Chicago Eight.

The May 5 tape meanwhile suggested that recruiting thugs was a strategy that had been used before. "Do it with Teamsters," Haldeman had said casually. "Just ask them to dig up their eight thugs." The president just replied with a "Yeah." The exchange prompts a reexamination of another violent episode, one that had taken place a year earlier.

On May 8, 1970, in New York City, young people protesting the Kent State shootings had been set upon by construction workers brandishing American flags and chanting, "All the way, U.S.A! Love it or leave it!" They beat the young people with their fists and their hard hats, and some of the victims ended up in the hospital.

The counterprotest had been well organized. Workers had been briefed by their shop stewards the previous day "to go and knock the heads of the kids who were protesting the Nixon-Kent thing." One worker, who did not join the group, said employees were offered a bonus as an incentive.

During the assault, another worker said, he saw "men in business suits with color patches in their lapels . . . shouting orders." A businessman, watching from his office window through binoculars, saw "two men in gray suits and hard hats . . . directing the construction workers with hand motions."

Two weeks later, after demonstrations in support of the war by tens of thousands of construction workers and longshoremen, Nixon received their leaders at the White House. The union bosses presented him with a hard hat of his own inscribed "Commander in Chief," as a symbol of "freedom and patriotism." One member of the deputation, Biagio Lanza of the Plasterers Union, was a known mafioso, and another, a Glaziers Union official, had recently been convicted of extortion.[14]

Peter Brennan, the union leaders' spokesman and organizer of the march, was president of the Building and Construction Trades Council of New York. The council was mob-linked, and Brennan routinely carried a loaded gun and traveled with bodyguards. Nixon later appointed him secretary of labor. "Pete Brennan's people," Nixon said, "were with us when some of the elitist crowd were running away from us. Thank God for the hard hats!"

Was the New York violence triggered by orders from the Nixon high command? "There aren't many spontaneous acts in politics," former White House aide Richard Howard chuckled when asked that question in 1997. "It's all for the media." Ehrlichman said he always assumed the White House had "laid on" the hard hat demonstrations.

Nixon's response on the "thugs" tape, when Haldeman told him trouble was expected, had been a mere "Good!" Today it is clear that he and his people actually welcomed violence, in hopes of making opponents look bad. Consider the rally at San Jose, California, five months after the New York unrest, when the president's motorcade was pelted with rocks and eggs.

It was said to have been the first ever such attack on a president in his own country, a scene from which neither side emerged with credit. Nixon climbed onto the hood of his limousine to give the V sign, and was heard to comment,

"That's what they hate to see." Rose Woods was quoted as saying it was "just like Caracas." The slightly damaged limousine was displayed to reporters, and Nixon followed up with a speech. "No band of violent thugs," he said, "is going to keep me from going out and speaking with the American people. . . ."

The San Jose protesters' abuse, and their missiles, had been real enough, yet some journalists suspected a setup. The "so-called riot has been exaggerated," asserted the city's police chief.

Twenty-four years later, with publication of Haldeman's diary, came confirmation that Nixon had actually sought out trouble. "We wanted some confrontation," Nixon's chief of staff said into his tape recorder that evening, "and there were no hecklers in the hall, so stalled departure a little so they could zero in outside. . . . Made a huge incident, and we worked hard to crank it up. . . ."

Not long before the "thugs" conversation on the White House tapes, the Quaker president apparently even lost patience with a Quaker protester. Monroe Cornish, a Maryland schoolteacher and maverick political candidate, was maintaining a prolonged peace vigil in Lafayette Park within sight of the White House windows. He had a ten-foot banner, and Nixon sent word that it had to come down. Dwight Chapin, the appointments secretary, told a colleague he was "going to get some 'thugs' to remove that man. . . . it would take a few hours to get them, but they could do the job."

In the event, the thugs were not needed: The offending man moved away a short distance, out of the president's line of sight, after a police warning. Later the Quakers' Washington headquarters would be ransacked, one of numerous break-ins that went unnoticed during the Watergate furor. The intruders left valuables untouched but rummaged through the files.

Also in 1971, when Nixon was to appear at a Billy Graham Day in Charlotte, North Carolina, an advance man sent Haldeman a briefing memo. There would be demonstrators, the aide reported. ". . . They will be violent; they will have extremely obscene signs. . . . It will not only be directed towards the President, but also toward Billy Graham . . . the Charlotte police department is extremely tough and will probably use force to prevent any possible disruption of the motorcade or the President's movements."

Haldeman wrote, "Good," beside the line in the memo warning the protest would be violent. He scrawled, "Great!" beside the forecast that the abuse would also be aimed at Graham. "Good" appeared again beside the prediction that the local police would use force.

As it turned out, the meeting took place without significant violence. The discovery of the memo, however, shocked the Senate Watergate Committee. "What mentality," asked Senator Lowell Weicker, "is in the White House that goes ahead and indicates 'good' when the word 'violence' is mentioned, when 'obscene' is mentioned, which violence and obscenity is [sic] to be directed against the President of the United States?"

When the first sketchy outline of these abuses emerged, the columnist

Mary McGrory offered her personal impression of them. Nixon, she thought, "sounded rather like a demented monarch, totally removed from reality, calling down vengeance on his enemies . . . a man as incapable of the presidency as he was unworthy of it."

A hard look at the record raises serious questions as to whether Nixon was sufficiently balanced, or emotionally stable, to be president.

27

Was Nixon "sick of mind"? . . . I agree with the senior Nixon assistant who concluded that the President must have been suffering from some mental defect that long preceded Watergate.

—*John Osborne, in the* New Republic, *1975*

"What do we do with him?" H. R. Haldeman had asked rhetorically even before Nixon took office. "He knows he needs to relax, so he comes down to Florida. He likes to swim, so he swims for ten minutes. Then that's over . . . he doesn't have a hobby. His best relaxation is talking shop, but he knows he should not be doing that, because that doesn't seem to be relaxing. So what do we do with him? It's a problem."

Senior aides noticed the tension in Nixon early on. Even a press conference, Kissinger observed, left him "so drained that he sought to avoid stress for days afterward . . . sustained efforts, especially on routine matters, exhausted him physically and made him extremely irritable." Just months into the presidency, Arthur Burns worried privately about how the president was withstanding the pressure of office in what was perhaps the most pressured job in the world.

By the late spring of 1969, Burns said, Nixon was already in "a mood of frustration . . . angry." He talked for a while as though the problems he faced as President were too big to be solved, then seemed to recover. "We were quite concerned abut him," Burns recalled.

In the fall, ushered in to meet Nixon on joining the staff, new aide Jeb Magruder was startled by the way his new boss' hands shook. "When he drank coffee," Magruder remembered, "there was an embarrassing rattle of cup against saucer."

Years earlier, in *Six Crises,* Nixon had written of the need to exercise self-mastery, to keep impulses firmly under control. Those who observed him closely early in the presidency, though, saw public and private flashes of untoward fury. Kissinger remembered Nixon's reaction on learning that diplomats and CIA operatives in Southeast Asia were not obeying instructions promptly: "He flew into a monumental rage. On the night of April 23, 1970, he must have called me at least ten times. . . . As was his habit when extremely agitated he would bark an order and immediately hang up the phone. . . . In these circumstances it was usually prudent not to argue and to wait twenty-four hours to see on which of these orders Nixon would insist after he calmed down."

What Kissinger was seeing in Nixon, as a mass of evidence indicates, was a president of the United States losing his sense of proportion and his emotional balance, while directing events of great military and political significance.

Early that same month Nixon had a private viewing of the film *Patton,* George C. Scott's portrayal of the World War II general who played a key—and famously aggressive—role in the Allied conquest of Germany. He would watch the movie again within weeks and cajoled Kissinger to see it twice also. Secretary of State William Rogers thought Nixon was behaving like "a walking ad for that movie" at a time Nixon was set on a strike of his own: an attack by U.S. troops inside Cambodia.

The actual decision to invade took place in late April in an atmosphere within the White House of confusion, scorn, and truculence. After a meeting with the president, Kissinger told one of his staffers, William Watts: "Our peerless leader has flipped out."

The same day, asked by Kissinger to listen in on a conversation with Nixon, Watts found himself witness to a shameful exchange. "They were on the helicopter to Camp David, and Nixon was talking to Henry. His voice was slurred, like a person who'd had too much to drink, and he said, 'Hold on, Bebe has something to say to you.' Rebozo came on and said, 'Henry, the president wants you to know that if this doesn't work, it's your ass.' "[1]

An Ehrlichman minute written the following day suggests that to some degree an ignoble imperative lay behind the Cambodia initiative. Kissinger phoned, Ehrlichman noted, to say that Nixon's "leadership quotient [is] very low and he's not gaining on domestic side—needs a bold stroke. . . ." The midterm elections were a few months away, and a military success would help the Republicans.

Nixon had been rebuffed that month by the Senate, which for the second time rejected his choice for a new Supreme Court justice. William Watts, again instructed to listen in on an extension, was startled to hear the president speak of the Cambodia plan as a way to spite the Senate. "We're going into Cambodia," he told Kissinger, "and I'll show those fucking senators who's tough."

Nixon told Kissinger of his decision to go into Cambodia while swimming in the pool at Camp David. They then flew back to Washington for a cruise on the presidential yacht, the *Sequoia*. "The tensions of the grim military planning," Kissinger recalled, "were transformed into exaltation by the liquid refreshments, to the point of some patriotic awkwardness when it was decided that everyone should stand to attention while the *Sequoia* passed Mount Vernon—a feat not managed by everybody with equal success." Nixon viewed *Patton* again that evening and is said to have seen it as many as five times in all.

The directive for the attack into Cambodia was issued the next day, and the president signed the order twice—once, with an imperial flourish, with just "RN," and then with his full name. Three days later he stayed up all night crafting a TV address to announce the invasion. During the broadcast he slurred his words and sweated as he spoke of America's bold stand against "the forces of totalitarianism and anarchy." Nixon made much of his role as "commander in chief."

The public response to the speech, said to have been overwhelmingly favorable when measured in terms of calls to the White House, turned out to have been largely manufactured by presidential PR men. As for the military action on the ground, which this author covered as a journalist for the British Broadcasting Corporation, its results were at least questionable.

"The president's unbridled ebullience and his obvious expectation of spectacular results," Army Chief of Staff General Westmoreland recalled of a Pentagon meeting on the first day of action, "required some adjustment to reality."

Protest over the invasion was almost instantaneous. "Everyone misunderstands me," Nixon said tearfully as he downed scotches with an aide. He seemed to know he was in fragile shape, for that week he summoned Dr. Hutschnecker, the psychotherapist he had consulted in the years before the presidency.

Hutschnecker, who had once reportedly worried that his patient might not be the right man to have his finger on the nuclear trigger and might not hold up well under pressure, had seen little of Nixon since he became president. Haldeman and Ehrlichman are said to have blocked his visits, and the doctor had gained an audience only once, to discuss the causes of violent crime and his utopian notions of how the United States could achieve world peace.

Now, furtively and without having had to sign the White House gate log, Hutschnecker was ushered in for a meeting with the president. The doctor, who had not realized that this time Nixon wanted him for a consultation, instead launched into another pitch for his world peace plans.

His "old intimacy" with Nixon, the doctor felt, seemed absent that day. The president listened for a while, then abruptly ended the meeting. Two days later, with a wave of protest engulfing the nation and the White House under virtual siege—aides were overheard discussing having machine guns set up on the lawn—Nixon called a press conference. He seemed composed enough as he defended his Vietnam policy, though Kissinger thought he was in fact "on the edge of a nervous breakdown."

NBC's Nancy Dickerson had cause to remember that night. "I had the strange feeling that he would have liked to slap me," she recalled of the way Nixon glared when she asked a pointed question. Then his mood and facial expression abruptly changed, and ludicrous though it seemed, he now appeared to be flirting with her.

A little after one in the morning, when Dickerson and her husband were in bed asleep, the phone rang. It was Nixon, opening the conversation with "This is Dick." He complained about the way the conference had gone, saying he wondered what the media's problem was. Then, plaintively, he said, "I'm the best thing they've got—I'm the only president they have." He talked about the student protesters, then asked Dickerson if she would be attending the White House church service that weekend. When she said she had not been invited, the tone of Nixon's reply left her disconcerted.

"Oh! I can take care of that," Nixon said with a bravado, Dickerson thought, that "would have been more fitting if he were announcing his ability to bomb Hanoi . . . it was almost like a small boy bragging about his physical prowess." "That man has not been drinking," she observed to her husband when the call ended, "but I would feel better if he had been."

The call to Dickerson was one of no less than forty-six made by Nixon between 9:30 P.M. and 2:00 A.M. that night. There were seven to Henry Kissinger, the White House log shows, seven to Haldeman, one to Ehrlichman, two to Rebozo, one each to Pat and Tricia, and four to Rose Woods. Two preachers, Billy Graham and Norman Vincent Peale, received one each.

After this flurry of telephoning, Nixon slept for an hour and a quarter—soundly, he said in a memo to Haldeman a few days later. Then he went to the Lincoln Sitting Room, adjacent to his bedroom, to listen to classical music. He took care to specify in the memo that his selection included "an Ormandy recording with Entremont at the piano playing a Rachmaninoff album for piano and orchestra." Next, having woken a few more people with phone calls, he summoned his valet, Manolo Sanchez. Minutes later astounded Secret Service agents were rousted out to escort Nixon on an excursion that has become legendary, the dawn visit to talk with protesters at the Lincoln Memorial.

Nixon had long since told Haldeman he wanted nothing to do with "the hippie college-types."[2] That night, however, in the bizarre phone call to Nancy Dickerson, he had mentioned going out to see the student demonstrators. "I really love those kids, I really do," he insisted. Now, as the pink light of dawn crept into the sky, the president of the United States and Sanchez, his valet, stepped out of a limousine and climbed the steps to the great brooding statue of Abraham Lincoln.

They were just yards away from the site where the ebony marble Vietnam

Wall stands today, a memorial that Nixon would in old age dismiss as too "mournful" and decline to visit. After giving Sanchez a brief guided tour, the president walked over to a group of people gathering for the day's protest against the war.

Later, in his memo to Haldeman—and with an eye to a possible press story—Nixon would offer his version of what "actually took place" at the Lincoln Memorial. He described a wide-ranging and serious talk, but young people quoted in the next day's newspapers were not favorably impressed.

"I hope it was because he was tired," said Joan Pelletier, a twenty-year-old sophomore from Syracuse University, "but most of what he was saying was absurd. Here we had come from a university that's completely uptight, on strike, and when we told him where we were from he talked about the football team. When someone said he was from California, he talked about surfing."

Some were alarmed as much by Nixon's manner as by what he had to say. "He didn't look anyone in the eyes," said Lynn Schatzkin, also from Syracuse. "He was mumbling. When people asked him to speak up he would boom one word and no more. As far as sentence structure, there was none."

"He looked like he had a mask on," Pelletier remarked. "He was wearing pancake makeup. He looked scared and nervous like he was in a fog. His eyes were glassy."[3] "The vibrations in the air were scary," thought her companion, Ronnie Kemper.

Nancy Dickerson, remembering Nixon's call that night, understood what the students meant. "If he talked to the students the way he talked to me," she said, "they had reason to be taken aback and even a little scared." She thought Nixon was suffering a "dislocation of personality."

The president made one further stop during that strange outing. A lone White House aide, thirty-year-old Egil Krogh, had joined the president's group at the memorial, keeping his distance because Nixon had specifically asked that no one but the valet and the Secret Service accompany him. He had followed in another car when Nixon ordered his limousine to head for the Capitol.

It was a Saturday, still not yet six o'clock in the morning. "We went to the House of Representatives," Krogh recalled in 1997. "There was a charwoman there, an older black woman, mopping up the floor. They got talking about the Bible. She had hers with her, and I think he signed it, and he talked about his mother to the charwoman, saying: 'My mother was a saint.'"

Then, after getting a janitor to unlock the House chamber, Nixon headed for the seat that he had occupied as a young representative in the forties. As Krogh, White House doctor Walter Tkach, and the Secret Service agents stood by, he told his valet to step up to the Speaker's chair and make a speech.

"I watched this extraordinary tableau unfold before me," said Krogh. "Richard Nixon, exhausted, his face drawn, like a man running on adrenaline . . . sitting there by himself telling the valet, 'Manolo, say something!' Manolo was embarrassed—he was a dear, sweet man—but he did try to talk a little. And Nixon started to clap. *Clap, clap, clap,* echoing in the chamber. I tell you, at that moment I wasn't quite sure what was going on . . . what really was the matter here. This was very bizarre to me. . . . I did question his mental stability."

The House visit over, Nixon was "upset" to discover he could not gain entrance to the Senate chamber. Then Haldeman appeared and the party headed off again in the limousine. Nixon insisted on stopping for breakfast, hash with an egg on it at the Mayflower Hotel. "Very weird," Haldeman noted in his diary. "P completely beat and just rambling on."

Next, with demonstrators starting to throng the streets, the president insisted on trying to walk back to the White House. "The president kept walking," Krogh remembered, "and the car was sort of moving along trying to keep close to him. Haldeman hissed, 'Stop him!' and I kind of grabbed Nixon by the arm. He pulled his arm away and glowered, and then he got in the back of the car. We drove back to the White House. . . ."

"The weirdest so far," Haldeman noted that day. "I am concerned about his condition . . . there's a long way to go and he's in no condition to weather it."

It was decided to clear Nixon's schedule and get him away to Florida as soon as possible. "This whole period of two weeks of tension and crisis," Haldeman wrote, "has taken its toll . . . is not getting enough sleep, is uptight etc. . . . Could be rough if a new crisis arises, because he's not ready to handle it." Kissinger thought the Lincoln Memorial episode "only the tip of the psychological iceberg."

A day into the four-day break Nixon's aide was still worrying. "The unwinding process is not succeeding . . ." he recorded in his diary. The next day: "More of the same." According to one of Dr. Hutschnecker's associates, the psychotherapist was summoned to Key Biscayne that weekend in "an emergency housecall," intended "to piece together Nixon's shattered ego."[4]

The president seemed removed from reality. While in Florida he asked Bebe Rebozo's woman friend and future wife, Jane Lucke, to do some sewing for him. Then he held an odd little ceremony. "In plane on way back," Haldeman recorded in his diary, "P had me up . . . then Ehrlichman . . . and Kissinger and said the three of us had borne the brunt these past few weeks and we deserved an award like the Purple Heart, so he had devised a new award, the Blue Heart, for those who were true blue. Then gave us each a blue cloth heart made by Jane Lucke, and said the honor was to be kept very confidential."

The president did relate the Blue Heart episode in his memoirs. In the contemporary memo to Haldeman, he even mentioned the visit with his valet to the House of Representatives. He omitted that incident from the autobiography, however, presumably realizing his readers would find it bizarre.

Less than two weeks after the rest period in Florida, Nixon flew to San Clemente. He was still "recovering from the ordeal" of defending the Cambodia decision, Kissinger recalled, and having trouble sleeping. After another phone conversation with Billy Graham, the president asked Kissinger to join him on a remarkable trip. The former adviser remembered:

> He had his heart set on showing Rebozo and me his birthplace in Yorba Linda. So we set off in a brownish unmarked Lincoln . . . we could not possibly share the emotion that obviously gripped him . . . suddenly Nixon noticed that two cars had followed us; one was filled with Secret Service agents, the other contained the obligatory press pool . . . standard procedure. . . . But Nixon lost his composure as I had never seen him do before or after.
>
> He did not want company. He was President and he was ordering privacy for himself. The orders were delivered at the top of his voice—itself an event so unprecedented that the Secret Service car broke every regulation in the book and departed, followed by the press pool.

Nixon seemed to relax for a while as he showed Rebozo and Kissinger the gas station his father had run—he told them the false story about how the family had missed out on a later oil find on the property[5]—and his alma mater, Whittier College. When he could not find the way to the Los Angeles house he had lived in just a decade earlier, however, he again became "agitated, nervous."

It was more than a week before Haldeman could record that his boss was "back to a fairly full schedule . . . generally simmering down. Will coast along for a bit, then we'll be ready for the next crisis. . . ." But the fact that all was not well and that there was no physical reason to explain Nixon's behavior had not gone unnoticed. The veneer of the supposedly self-possessed Nixon, carefully nurtured by his public relations men, had cracked.

While he was in San Clemente, the Associated Press had run a story on the remarkable amount of time he was spending away from Washington. UPI's Helen Thomas noticed during the Cambodia crisis that he "looked like a man in a daze." Nancy Dickerson thought he had become "mentally erratic" and told her bureau chief as much. Like most other journalists, though, the bureau head did not pursue the matter, for it was inconceivable to run a story suggesting the president of the United States was unstable.

The White House correspondent of the *New Republic,* John Osborne, was an exception. One of Washington's most respected journalists, he came closer than anyone, and as early as 1970, to writing what he actually believed.

"Things that have never happened before at the Nixon White House kept happening in early May," he wrote, "and the President's people kept saying that it didn't mean anything." He described Nixon's "alternating moods of anger and euphoria," his increasingly frequent slips of the tongue. "The staff habit of denying Mr. Nixon ever loses his cool, tires himself beyond the limits of prudence," he noted, "suddenly went out of fashion."

Interviewed by Henry Brandon of the London *Sunday Times,* the president at first "created the impression of feeling that he was on top of the world, in control of the situation." Yet something about Nixon bothered Brandon. "However reassuring his words," he remembered, "his refusal to look one straight in the eye was disturbing to me. He either looked straight ahead of himself or at my lapel. . . . His eyes looked as cold as ever, often shooting cruel flashes. He had virtually no eyelashes, and under his eyelids was a redness that betrayed fatigue. I also had the feeling, throughout the interview, that here was a man who constantly tried to observe himself, how he was doing and how he sounded."

Reflecting on the Nixon presidency years later, Osborne would state openly what he had long been hinting. "Even in the first years of his presidency," he wrote, "reporters who followed and observed Nixon as closely as I tried to did so in part because, way down and in some instances not so far down in their consciousness, there was a feeling that he might go bats in front of them at any time."

The president was "letting himself slip back to the old ways," Haldeman confided to his diary. The "old ways" were the symptoms that had bothered him and Ehrlichman after the 1962 campaign: exhaustion combined with chronic insomnia and the problem with alcohol.

Nixon increasingly had trouble sleeping. Tormented by the barking of his own dogs, he sometimes abandoned his grand bedroom at the White House to seek slumber in the room assigned to his daughter Julie, now married and often out of town.

There had been a scare when Nixon visited Romania early in the presidency. After a marathon journey around the world, Air Force One had brought him into Bucharest to a rapturous welcome. His first visit to a Communist country as president, at a time of tension with Moscow and the first tentative feelers toward Beijing, was going brilliantly well. He had met with the Romanian dictator Nikolai Ceaucescu, who impressed him very favorably, smoked a cigar, and had gone to bed feeling ebullient.

Around 1:00 A.M. Nixon phoned speech writer Raymond Price from his room. He sounded ebullient, "savoring the triumph, basking in it," Price thought. "Then, as I finished my answer to one of his questions, there was no response. The phone line was still open. But where a moment earlier I had been talking with the president of the United States . . . now suddenly there was no president on the other end."

Before the sudden silence Nixon had sounded slurry and repetitive. It was a scenario Price remembered from the campaign trail, when sudden fade-outs had been triggered by the combination of beer and a sleeping pill. Worried, he alerted the Signal Corps switchboard operator, and a Secret Service agent was soon rushing to the president's suite. He found him propped on a pillow, out to the world, the phone still resting on his shoulder.

The standard line from the White House was that Nixon drank "little more than an occasional sip of light wine." This was not true, and alcohol had alarming effects even when he drank little. Researchers at the National Archives, listening to the White House tapes in years to come, heard time and again the clink of glass on glass, followed by slurred, rambling speech.

The truth was known to some even during the presidency. "I got a call one afternoon after I had written a piece about Vietnam that he liked," *Life*'s Hugh Sidey recalled. "Nixon called me about three o'clock in the afternoon. He said, 'I just want to tell you that's a great piece. Come on down for the weekend . . . we're going out to the Virgin Islands' . . . obviously he had been drinking, since he couldn't talk very well."

Some officials who served Nixon were also aware of the problem. "He was given to exploding," said Deputy Assistant Secretary of State William Sullivan, "particularly in the course of the evening if he had had a few drinks. He would call up [Secretary of State] Bill Rogers or somebody else and say, 'Fire this man' . . . Bill said Nixon would forget this the next morning. . . ."

"Two glasses of wine," Kissinger recalled in 1999, "were quite enough to make him boisterous, just one more to grow bellicose or sentimental with slurred speech. Alcohol had a way of destroying the defenses he had so carefully constructed to enable him to succeed. . . ."

Determining what Kissinger really thought, on this, as on other subjects, is difficult. Nixon's drunken episodes, Kissinger has written, "occurred rarely, always at night and almost never in the context of major decisions. The few of us who actually witnessed such conduct never acted on what he might have said; we felt we owed the President another chance to consider whatever the issue was."

Kissinger has also said that others' descriptions of Nixon's drinking himself into incoherence are absurd. Former members of Kissinger's staff, however, throw doubt on this assertion.

Roger Morris, a senior National Security Council aide early in the presidency, said Kissinger referred to Nixon as "our drunken friend." Morris was one of a handful of staffers entrusted with collating Kissinger's daily diary notes. "We caught glimpses of Nixon, Laird, Rogers, and Kissinger in action," he said. "Nixon drank exceptionally at night, and there were many nights when you couldn't reach him at Camp David. . . . There were many times when a cable would come in late and Henry would say, 'There's no sense waking him up; he'd be incoherent.' "

The *Washington Post*'s Watergate reporters Bob Woodward and Carl Bernstein wrote of learning about a call in which the president "drunkenly related to Dr. Kissinger the Vietnam military policy of his friend Bebe Rebozo. . . . During another call, Kissinger mentioned the number of American casualties in a major battle in Vietnam. 'Oh, screw 'em,' said Nixon."

At Key Biscayne, according to a Secret Service source, Nixon once lost his temper during a conversation about Cambodia. "He just got pissed," the agent quoted eyewitnesses as saying. "They were half in the tank, sitting around the pool drinking. And Nixon got on the phone and said: 'Bomb the shit out of them!'"

"People who knew about the slurred voice and the nights beyond reach," Roger Morris said, "seem to have a range of contrasting motives for silence. It was, after all, they told themselves, only an occasional problem. Its revelation might invite Soviet recklessness or some other action that would not have happened otherwise. Patriotism, fear, admiration for Nixon's potential greatness, shame, personal fear, or desire for power—all had a part in a covenant of silence about the other side of Richard Nixon."

For many years Kissinger spoke only to colleagues in private about one particularly outrageous episode that occurred in the first year of the presidency. The last weekend of August 1969, Haldeman's diary shows, started early for Nixon. He had been at San Clemente for much of the month, a good deal of that time taken up with relaxing and entertaining. On the Friday afternoon, he had spent two hours on the beach with Rebozo before hosting a party for "old friends." The next day was scheduled to be a day off, with another visit to the beach and a trip to a football game.

Meanwhile, more than seven thousand miles away in the Middle East, Palestinian terrorists had hijacked a TWA airliner with more than a hundred passengers on board and forced the pilot to fly to Damascus. The hijackers were demanding the release of comrades held in Israeli prisons.[6]

Kissinger, also in California that week, swiftly briefed the president on the situation. His response, described by Kissinger publicly for the first time in 1999, was startling. "I reported to Nixon," Kissinger recalled, "who was in San Clemente with his two friends Charles 'Bebe' Rebozo and Robert Abplanalp. Obviously trying to impress his pals, Nixon issued a curt-sounding order. 'Bomb the airport of Damascus.'"

Even had that order not been rash and ill considered, a bombing operation is not simply a matter of carrying out a sudden command. Targets have to be plotted, diplomatic measures prepared, and many other steps taken. Mercifully, no U.S. aircraft carrier was then within range of the Syrian capital, a factor that proved helpful to Kissinger as he decided how to respond.

Certain the order "would not survive the night," Kissinger worked out with Defense Secretary Laird a way to avoid outright disobedience while blocking the president's order at the same time. "Laird and I decided to carry out the letter of the order by implementing the first steps and leaving the other measures for the morning."

The two U.S. aircraft carriers on station in the Mediterranean, the *Saratoga* and *John F. Kennedy,* were instructed to sail toward a potential launch position, but no further orders were given. When Nixon came on the line with badgering phone calls—he did so "hourly" that night—Kissinger mollified him with reports of the naval movement. Laird, for his part, stalled the president with the excuse that bad weather was hampering operations.

The following morning, when Kissinger informed him of the carriers' progress, Nixon asked innocently, "Did anything else happen?" "When I replied in the negative," Kissinger recalled, "the President without moving a facial muscle said, 'Good.' I never heard another word about the bombing of Damascus."

The weather pretext was needed again a year later, when Palestinian terrorists hijacked several airplanes to the Jordanian desert. "The president wanted to hit an airfield in Jordan," Laird recalled, "and I said: 'Just tell 'em [the White House] we had bad weather.' Because we're not going to hit that airfield."

Ten days later fighting broke out in Jordan between Palestinian forces and King Hussein's army. It was a conflict that threatened to spread, with the possibility of a U.S.-Soviet confrontation. Perhaps with some exaggeration, Nixon was to remember the period as being "like a ghastly game of dominoes, with a nuclear war waiting at the end."[7] In the context of previous episodes, Haldeman's diary entry for the day the war began, September 17, is interesting:

> "K [Kissinger] woke me at 2:00 this morning with call that war had started in Jordan. . . . Possibility Israel will go in. . . . K wants to take position that he notified P tonight and act on basis of P orders. *We agreed no need to call P, no decisions needed* . . . [author's italics]."

Nixon's "tough guy orders," Kissinger has said, were less common on foreign affairs issues than in the domestic area. "I was able," Kissinger commented, "to distinguish between what he intended to be carried out immediately and what he deserved to be given an opportunity to reconsider."

The notion that cooler heads prevailed is comforting, but begs the question of what might have happened had no cooler heads been available. "It wouldn't have been a good day for something bad to happen, would it?" a source had remarked to the *New Republic*'s John Osborne in May 1970, after Nixon's dawn peregrinations to the Lincoln Memorial and the House of Representatives. Less than two weeks later the president, remembered today for opening relations with China, responded impetuously to a call from Mao Zedong for the people of the world to "Unite and Defeat the U.S. Aggressors and All Their Running Dogs."

Although the chairman's exhortation was clearly just a propaganda blast, Nixon ordered all available naval forces into the Taiwan Strait, without waiting for Kissinger's analysis. His command specified "Stuff that will look belligerent. I want them to know we are not playing this chicken game. . . . I want you to call [Chief of Naval Operations] Moorer that it's an order from the

Commander-in-Chief. . . . There's no recourse. I want them there within 24 hours."

Kissinger said years afterward this was yet another of "those orders that close associates had come to recognize would better serve the public welfare if not implemented for twenty-four hours." No action was taken, and Nixon later "thought better" of his plans.

"If the president had his way," Kissinger growled to aides more than once, "there would be a nuclear war each week!" This may not have been an idle jest. The CIA's top Vietnam specialist, George Carver, reportedly said that in 1969, when the North Koreans shot down a U.S. spy plane, "Nixon became incensed and ordered a tactical nuclear strike. . . . The Joint Chiefs were alerted and asked to recommend targets, but Kissinger got on the phone to them. They agreed not to do anything until Nixon sobered up in the morning."[8]

As reported earlier, Kissinger has written of Nixon "suppressing his instinct for a jugular response" after North Korea downed the spy plane but without mentioning drink as a factor in the incident. Kissinger's close associate Lawrence Eagleburger, however, told a friend the following week. "Here's the president," he said, visibly upset, "ranting and raving, drunk in the middle of a crisis."

This particular allegation of flirting with nuclear weaponry is not an isolated one. Nixon had been open to the use of tactical nuclear weapons in Vietnam as early as 1954 and as president-elect considered striking "a blow that would both end the war and win it." A Kissinger aide who moved over to the White House, David Young, told a colleague "of the time he was on the phone [listening] when Nixon and Kissinger were talking. Nixon was drunk, and he said, 'Henry, we've got to nuke them.'"

Nixon's aggressive posturing was brought to bear as much as if not more to domestic politics. On another cruise down the Potomac on the *Sequoia*, in the spring of 1971, he would again lead his guests to the foredeck to stand at attention as the yacht passed George Washington's tomb. His companions this time were Haldeman, Ehrlichman, Kissinger, and Charles Colson, the lawyer and former marine he had brought to the White House as a political strategist. As the president looked ahead to election to a second term, Colson had risen swiftly from obscure newcomer to trusted intimate.

Nixon drank scotch and soda, then wine over dinner, as the talk turned to his domestic opposition. "Chuck" he told Colson, "your job is to hold off those madmen on the Hill long enough for Henry to finish his work in Paris . . ."—a reference to the Vietnam peace negotiations. "Then we go for the big play—China, Russia." The "madmen on the Hill" were the senators and representatives who opposed Nixon's war policy and were now talking about domestic repression.

"The President's finger circled his wine-glass slowly," Colson remembered. Then he said: "One day we will get them—we'll get them on the ground where we want them. And we'll stick our heels in, step on them hard and twist— right, Chuck, right? . . . get them on the floor and step on them, crush them, show no mercy."

"And so on the *Sequoia* this balmy spring night," Colson would one day write, "a holy war was declared against the enemy. . . . *They* who differed with *us,* whatever their motives, must be vanquished."

28

*He hated with a passion, and I don't know
if anyone has quite captured it yet.*

—Alexander Butterfield, former assistant to the President, 1994

For Richard Nixon, enemies were everywhere. Americans who never knew or who have forgotten the details of the Nixon scandals still remember the "enemies list," which drew outrage across the political spectrum.

William Buckley thought the creation of the list an "act of proto-fascism . . . ruthless in its dismissal of human rights . . . fascist in its automatic assumption that the state in all matters comes before the rights of individuals . . . fascist in tone, the stealth, the brutality, the self-righteousness."

James Kilpatrick declared that the list could be understood "only in terms of corruption . . . an abuse of office, an arrogance of power, that goes beyond mere scandal . . . vindictive and vile. . . ." He did insist, though, "There is no proof whatever that Richard Nixon initiated these lists or knew of their existence."

There is no such proof, if it requires a presidential signature as validation. Yet the sorry history of the lists—for there were several—leads back directly to the Oval Office. It began early in the presidency, when Nixon asked Deputy Counsel Clark Mollenhoff, ironically the ombudsman responsible for dealing with abuses by public officials, to arrange "access to tax returns. . . ." The ostensible reason for the order was to "avoid any Internal Revenue scandals."

Mollenhoff spoke with top IRS officials, but little came of it. Then he began getting specific requests from Haldeman and others for tax information on politicians, and Murray Chotiner, now a presidential counsel, began seeking data on particular individuals.

"Chotiner dropped by the office," Mollenhoff recalled, "with a list of people he said had been making contributions to the Democrats and were believed to be illegally dipping into business expenses to reimburse themselves. . . ." Chotiner said the request had come to him from Haldeman. Leery of "Chotiner's political sophistry and Haldeman's devious *modus operandi*," Mollenhoff asked Haldeman directly whether this was something the president himself wanted. Whenever he called, Nixon's senior aide replied, "it was always for the president."

Mollenhoff made contact with the IRS commissioner—the first of three during the Nixon administration, for the president found they bent insufficiently to his will—Randolph Thrower. Interviewed for this book, Thrower recalled having received "two or three" lists of people the White House wanted investigated, each presented as carrying presidential authority. He blocked the requests, however, saying he would act only if shown justification. He asked to see the president, but Haldeman said Nixon "did not like such conferences." Thrower then offered to resign.

Discussing a successor to Thrower, Nixon made his requirements clear. "I want to be sure he is a ruthless son-of-a-bitch," he said into the White House microphones, "that he will do what he's told, that every income tax return I want to see I see, that he will go after our enemies and not go after our friends." He raged about the "stinking little bastards" at the IRS and what they had allegedly done to him during the Kennedy administration. "When the Christ," he wanted to know, "are they going to go after some Democrats? . . . It's a matter of using the law to its full—to our benefit rather than someone else's."

That tape was recorded in May 1971, just weeks before Thrower was replaced and five days after Nixon's conversation with Colson about crushing political enemies. By mid-June Colson aides had prepared a priority list for "activity" and forwarded it to presidential counsel John Dean.

Haldeman and Colson would later claim this document merely contained the names of people who were not to be extended privileges or invited to White House parties. In fact, it was comprised of twenty Democratic politicians and journalists and included annotations like "He should be hit hard," and—of a black congressman—"Has known weakness for white females."

The best-known statement of the administration's goals in this area, written by Dean and headed "Dealing with Our Political Enemies," came two months later. It addressed "the matter of how we can maximize the fact of our incumbency in dealing with persons known to be active in their opposition to our administration. Stated a bit more bluntly, how can we use the available federal machinery to screw our political enemies?"

Weeks later, the White House tapes show, Nixon himself considered that question in the Oval Office. "John," he said to Ehrlichman, "we have the power, but are we using it to investigate contributors . . . are we going after their tax returns?" A new IRS commissioner was now in place, the president said, and he wanted him used.

The new man, Johnnie Walters, would recall being summoned by Dean and handed an envelope containing a long list of enemies. Instead of responding to it, however, he and Treasury Secretary George Shultz agreed to take no action. The commissioner merely locked the list away in his office safe.

"The man I work for," Dean had said when it was clear that cooperation was not forthcoming, "doesn't like 'no' for an answer," and the White House tapes reflect Nixon's eventual rage. "We've got to kick Walters' ass out," he exploded, "he's finished. . . . Believe me. Out." Walters left a few months later.

"Shultz," Nixon blustered, "is to see that any order or list that he gets comes directly . . . be sure it's done. . . . He didn't get Secretary of the Treasury because he's got nice blue eyes." The last sentence of Nixon's taped comment on Shultz has not been released, but according to John Dean, who was present, he added "candy ass" to the "nice blue eyes." Shultz, however, survived almost to the end of the presidency.

The Senate Watergate hearings would ultimately identify more than two hundred citizens who had been on the Nixon enemy lists, including thirty-one politicians, fifty-six people from the media, fifty-three from the world of business, fourteen labor leaders, twenty-two academics, and eleven celebrities, along with newspapers and organizations. Among them were the actress Carol Channing of *Hello, Dolly!* fame, Paul Newman, Barbra Streisand, Gregory Peck, Steve McQueen, and New York Jets quarterback Joe Namath.

According to Dean, the president would instruct him also to "keep a good list of the press people giving us trouble, because we will make life difficult for them after the [1972] election." One of the latter was *New York Post* columnist Harriet Van Horne, who had reported Nixon's visits to New York psychotherapist Arnold Hutschnecker.

Although IRS commissioners behaved with integrity, the White House had alternative methods of getting the tax information it wanted. "We have to do it artfully," Nixon was to say; "there are ways to do it. Goddamn it, sneak in in the middle of the night." Two lower-ranking officials were also apparently helpful—one of them a close contact of the detective working directly for the Oval Office, John Caulfield.

When the lists were finally exposed, several prominent journalists noted that they had been subjected to unusual IRS attention, among them Mary McGrory, Carl Rowan, Rowland Evans, and Tom Braden. *Newsday* editor Robert Greene, who had headed his paper's series on Bebe Rebozo, was audited after the IRS received an anonymous letter. The letter followed liaison between Nixon's man Caulfield and his contact inside the IRS, and the White House tapes show Nixon was fully aware of the reprisals.

"The guy that's running that Rebozo investigation," Haldeman told the president, "the New York IRS office has opened a check on him and they think they may have something. . . ."

At the same time that he targeted his "enemies" Nixon fulminated about perceived attacks on his friends. He had told Haldeman of a complaint he had received from Billy Graham. "The IRS is battering the shit out of him. Some sonofabitch came to him and gave him a three-hour grilling about how much he, you know, how much his contribution is worth. . . . Say now, goddammit, are we going after some of these Democrats or not?"

They were indeed going after the Democrats, on many fronts and on Nixon's personal instructions.

A Haldeman diary entry and a recently released White House tape reveal a significant milestone on the road to Watergate. On May 28, 1971, at the very time the "enemies" operation was under way, Nixon and Haldeman held their morning meeting in the Oval Office.

The subject that day, Haldeman noted discreetly, was "the general political situation." The politics in fact were highly personal, for the president had been brooding on the ways John and Robert Kennedy had once supposedly committed abuses against him by bugging (likely true) and by probes of his tax affairs. Now, annoyed by carping at his daughter Julie's being awarded a new teaching job, he fretted that the "attack" might have a "partisan source."[1] He wanted it "tracked down."

"That led him to thinking," Haldeman wrote in his diary, "that we should put permanent tails on Teddy and Muskie and Hubert on all the personal stuff, to cover the kinds of things they hit us on in '62: personal finances, family, and so forth."

It is almost comically ironic that a perceived slight against the president's daughter may have been the wellspring for Watergate, yet in a sense it was that, the start of a fatal slide. ". . . I want more use of wiretapping," Nixon said in hushed tones, perhaps briefly remembering the hidden microphones. Then: "Are we dealing adequately with their candidates, tailing them and so forth?"

Surveillance was sporadic, Haldeman replied, and Nixon cut in, "Well, it should not be on and off. I mean, that's something we can afford. . . . Maybe we can get a scandal on any, any one of the leading Democrats."

As his chief of staff warmed to the idea, Nixon wavered. "I don't know," he said, "maybe it's the wrong thing to do. But I have a feeling if you're gonna start, you got to start now."

The president wanted the surveillance pursued energetically—with one condition. "Can't do that out of the White House," he cautioned. The covert activities should go forward, but they must not be traceable to him.

The burglaries of the Democratic party headquarters were a year away, and the election that would win Nixon a second term just a few months more.

Nixon wanted "permanent tails" placed on "Teddy"—Edward Kennedy—"Muskie"—Senator Edmund Muskie, the likely Democratic front-runner—and "Hubert"—Humphrey, the former vice president Nixon had narrowly defeated in 1968.

Muskie and Kennedy were on the Enemies List along with George McGovern, who would in fact emerge as the Democrats' candidate for 1972. However real the threat posed by the last Kennedy brother, Nixon still obsessed about the Kennedy legacy.

"Nixon was ill at ease," Kissinger recalled of a 1969 visit to Berlin, "worried that the turnout would be compared unfavorably with that for Kennedy in 1963. Only after he was assured repeatedly that no unfavorable comparisons could possibly be drawn did he relax."

Although Edward Kennedy had recently been elected assistant Senate majority leader, his presidential hopes had been severely compromised in the summer of 1969 by the tragedy—and international sensation—of Chappaquiddick.

Nixon "called me over to tell family about Teddy Kennedy's escapade," Haldeman recorded in his diary, ". . . late last night in Martha's Vineyard, drove his car off a bridge into a pond, left girl in it to drown. . . . Lots of peculiar possibilities . . . . [President] wants to be sure he doesn't get away with it . . . *very* interested . . . feels it marks the end of Teddy."

If Nixon was confident that Chappaquiddick spelled an end to Kennedy's career, his actions belied it. At the president's behest, Ehrlichman sent one of his permanent undercover men—retained on a twenty-two-thousand-a-year salary paid by Nixon's personal attorney—to the scene of the drowning within hours.[2] He stayed there for days, posing as a *Philadelphia Enquirer* journalist and reporting back several times daily to the White House.

A week later Nixon was in the middle of the Pacific Ocean, welcoming the Apollo astronauts back from the first moon landing. The mission was the fulfillment of a dream first articulated by President Kennedy, and the president now called it "the greatest day since the Creation." His mind, though, was still on the car wreck in a Massachusetts pond.

Nixon reached Ehrlichman by radiotelephone, aboard a train, for an update on Chappaquiddick. Later, when Kennedy presented his version of the accident in a nationwide broadcast, an aide in Washington held a phone to the radio so that Haldeman could listen in Guam. "P still very interested," Haldeman noted, "has a lot of theories."

Nixon would claim in his memoirs that he felt "deeply sorry" for Kennedy over Chappaquiddick. Two weeks afterward, following a meeting at the White House, he took him aside to say he "understood how tough it was. . . ." The record contains nothing to indicate he was genuinely sorry, however, and a former aide thought he was actually "overjoyed" at Kennedy's plight.[3]

The desire to produce dirt on Kennedy consumed Nixon. The detective sent to Chappaquiddick obtained phone records and later a restricted transcript of the inquest for the woman who drowned, Mary Jo Kopechne. The phone at Kopechne's Washington home, which she had shared with friends, was reportedly tapped as well.

Reports of the detective's findings went to Chotiner, Bebe Rebozo, and the president himself. The sleuthing reportedly cost one hundred thousand dollars in the first six months, with no significant discoveries. Nixon never ceased fearing that Kennedy would rebound politically.

In 1970, with midterm elections coming up, the president and Charles Colson schemed to get the *Lil Abner* cartoonist, Al Capp, to run against Kennedy in Massachusetts. Although that notion failed, Capp seemed to do the White House a service by speaking out publicly against the anti-Nixon press bias. His usefulness ended abruptly, however, when he was charged with sexually assaulting a female college student. Panic at the White House was followed by a covert word with the prosecutors, a sordid end to hopes of using Capp to oppose Kennedy the womanizer.

Nixon's aim in hurting Kennedy, Haldeman and Colson recalled, had a simple focus: His orders, Haldeman recalled, were "to catch him in the sack with one of his babes."

They tried hard. In Paris for the funeral of President de Gaulle, Kennedy was surreptitiously photographed dancing into the dawn hours with an Italian princess. Nixon was delighted with the pictures, especially when Colson—on his orders—got one of them printed in the *National Enquirer*.

But the tactics were to no avail: The polls in the spring of 1971 suggested Kennedy could be the Democratic front-runner for the next year's presidential election. "Nothing on Teddy?" Nixon asked when aides reported no compromising material had been found. Then ". . . goddammit, there ought to be a way to get him covered," he insisted, as the Oval Office tapes ran on. "You watch. I, uh, predict something more is going to happen." Told a man had been assigned to spy on Kennedy, Nixon worried that one snooper was insufficient.

One of Colson's men tried yet again to find something new and incriminating on Chappaquiddick. He later retailed inaccurate information that Mary Jo Kopechne's body had been without underwear when recovered, along with a theory that a second woman had been in Kennedy's car at the time of the accident.[4]

Another White House operative decorated a Manhattan apartment in red plush, reportedly to entrap a woman who had been at the party that preceded the accident. Nixon's men hoped she would succumb to a seducer, then reveal useful information while hidden microphones recorded her every word.

In spite of the president's orders that he be watched around the clock, Kennedy failed to perform as hoped.[5] A lead suggesting two Las Vegas showgirls could produce damaging testimony failed to pan out. A detective trailed the senator all the way to Hawaii only to report: "No evidence to indicate that his conduct was improper." Nixon was disappointed.

When evidence failed to materialize, the White House tried fabricating it. The press was tipped that Kennedy had recently been arrested for drunken driving and released without charge. The truth, discovered in time, was that an incident along those lines had indeed taken place, but years earlier.

By the end of 1971 a Gallup poll would show Kennedy within three points of the president. "Do you think Kennedy's going to run?" bemused National Archives researchers would one day hear Nixon ask Colson on a tape of a phone call. Then his voice trailed off, and Colson was left saying: "Mr. President? Mr. President?" into a void. Nixon had once again fallen asleep in mid-conversation.

After Kennedy had publicly announced that he would not run, and even after George McGovern had been nominated at the Democratic convention, Nixon would still continue to insist that his aides poll Kennedy's popularity. Eight weeks before the 1972 election, when asked to provide Kennedy with Secret Service protection, the president saw a fresh opportunity to gather dirt.

"Plant one, plant two guys on him," Nixon said at an Oval Office meeting. "A big detail," he insisted hours later, "one that can cover him round the clock. . . . I want to make sure that he is followed." Although the Secret Service has denied it, Alexander Butterfield has maintained that its agents were used to spy on the senator.

Nixon also urged aides to ensure that Kennedy's latest rumored liaison was given widespread coverage.[6] "Just might get lucky," he said hopefully into the hidden microphones, "catch this son of a bitch and ruin him for '76."

Nixon presumably forgot the existence of his taping system during that conversation. A year later, though, in a conversation with John Dean, he would appear to be trying to use it to cover himself. "You recall," Dean would say, "that right after Chappaquiddick somebody was up there to start observing, within six hours."

"Did we?" the president asked. "I didn't know that."

———

If Edward Kennedy was pursued with lip-licking relish, other leading Democrats were also the subject of predatory attention. Before being diverted to Chappaquiddick, Ehrlichman's field investigator tried to prove Hubert Humphrey was guilty of financial impropriety. His brief came from Nixon's secretary, Rose Woods.

In the period before the election a private detective in the employ of the White House would work his way onto Humphrey's campaign staff. Once in place, he caused as much disruption as possible without risking exposure.

A second operative, directed by Nixon's appointments secretary, Dwight Chapin, distributed thousands of bumper stickers reading: "Humphrey: He started the war. Don't give him another chance!"[7] Haldeman persuaded Nixon to "lay off," but only after the Humphrey campaign had collapsed.

Another candidate who posed a more potent threat was savaged accordingly. As early as two years before the election, Nixon had marked Edmund Muskie, along with Kennedy and Humphrey, for "all-out attack." When polls in early 1971 revealed that he was capable of defeating Nixon, intense efforts were initiated to stop him by underhand means.

Nixon repeatedly ordered false propaganda, "lib" mailings purportedly backing Muskie but designed to alienate conservative voters. Nixon investigators trawled Maine for "scandals or other skeletons" in Muskie's closet. The result was disappointing—Nixon learned his opponent was "monkish" with a "big family. Six kids . . . ordinary type of life." Documents from Muskie headquarters, "borrowed" by an infiltrator and photographed surreptitiously in the back of a car, were delivered to Haldeman aide Gordon Strachan.

Appointments secretary Chapin again orchestrated harassments designed to wear Muskie down, picketing and distribution of false and misleading literature, some of it on counterfeit Muskie stationery. Nixon told aides to "get a massive mailing in Florida . . . on the basis that it came from [Muskie], see?"

Thousands of Floridians received a scabrous letter under the Muskie letterhead, exhorting them to vote for Muskie while noting "several facts" about his Democratic rivals: that Humphrey had been arrested for drunken driving in the company of "a well-known call-girl" and that another contender, Scoop Jackson, had fathered an illegitimate child by a seventeen-year-old girl. For good measure, Jackson was also accused of having been arrested twice on homosexuality charges. No evidence was ever found to substantiate these "facts."

The sex smear letter reportedly especially pleased Chapin, who had copies of the propaganda sent to his home address in Washington. The strategy, as one of those involved explained, was to set the Democrats at one another's throats. In Muskie's case, the specific aim was to goad the short-tempered senator to lose control. Handed a report that Muskie had "proved he can keep his cool," Chapin scrawled a note in the margin: "We really missed the boat on this—obviously the press now wants to prove EM can keep his temper—let's prove he can't."

According to one aide involved, Nixon personally approved an effort to take votes away from Muskie in the first and key primary, New Hampshire. White House operatives using false names plotted a write-in campaign for Kennedy, whose name was not on the ballot.

They were also likely behind the creation of another false letter published in the press less than two weeks before voting day, which implied disrespect by Muskie for French Canadians, an especially vicious slur in an area close to the border with Canada.[8] They certainly were behind a hurtful piece in the local paper about Senator Muskie's wife, Jane, suggesting she smoked and drank to excess.

The White House undercover men hoped that this last blow would push Muskie over the emotional edge, and it did. Standing on a flatbed truck in the snow, trying to make a speech, he broke down in tears. The lapse threw public doubt on the senator's emotional stability, and his campaign never recovered. He withdrew from the race weeks later.

Even afterward, on being told damaging information might be available on Muskie, Nixon urged Bebe Rebozo to check it out. If it could be used, the White House tapes recorded his saying, "We tear him to pieces." Later still, when the falsity of the smears against Muskie and Jackson began to emerge, he was unfazed. That sort of activity, he said, was "chickenshit."

———

Nixon never ceased worrying about the man with real power to hurt him—in his words, "the one we had to take most seriously." George Wallace, the segregationist governor of Alabama, had proved a serious threat in the close-run fight of 1968, when he had taken 13.6 percent of the vote. He was still a potent third force, a figure with an appeal not only to southern racists but to conservatives and blue-collar voters across the land. The votes he won were likely to be votes lost to Nixon, in numbers potentially large enough to cost the president reelection.

Nixon made his first move against Wallace early on, in a bid to destroy the governor in his home state. In March 1970 the president's personal lawyer stepped into the lobby of New York's Sherry-Netherland Hotel with an airline bag containing a hundred thousand dollars—a million at today's values—to rendezvous with a man for whom he had no name, only a description. "Are you from Pennsylvania?" the lawyer asked. When the stranger responded as required, "No, pal, I'm from Miami," the lawyer handed over the money and left.

Thus was Nixon channeling funds to Wallace's opponent in the Alabama gubernatorial election, funds that ultimately amounted to some four hundred thousand dollars. A later White House tape and Haldeman's diary establish that it was the president who authorized the payments. Simultaneously, the White House ordered an IRS probe of Wallace and his brother Gerald, then leaked a preliminary audit indicating widespread corruption. The source of the leak is today rather clear; the damaging tax information had been provided to Nixon himself.

Despite the sabotage, Wallace was to regain the governorship and remain a threat to Nixon's reelection hopes for a full year to come. The White House maintained the pressure with the IRS probe and the odd dirty trick.[9]

———

By the start of Nixon's third year in office, it was becoming increasingly clear that his was a Jekyll and Hyde presidency. "Can you believe this?" Nixon asked the nation in the spring of 1971, as the U.S. involvement in Vietnam was coming to an end. Pointing to the steady reduction in the number of U.S. troops and casualties, he said Americans could indeed believe it.

The president emphasized that he would end the war "nobly" without abandoning the South Vietnamese. In fact, no settlement would be reached for almost two years. In the meantime Nixon's negotiators were secretly laying the groundwork for a settlement that would leave North Vietnamese troops in place on South Vietnamese territory—a presence that could spell doom for South Vietnam's regime. In the same April speech Nixon spoke respectfully of the sincerity of those who questioned his policies. Just weeks later, as reported earlier, he would be discussing the use of "thugs" to beat up demonstrators.

As the domestic and foreign chicanery continued behind the scenes, Nixon offered the American people pomp, ceremony, and romance. White House servants were preparing frenetically for Tricia's June wedding to Edward Cox, an opportunity for a public display of what the president had called a "First Family you can be proud of."

The wedding cake was seven feet high. More than a hundred chefs, florists and seamstresses, painters and calligraphers prepared a dazzling wedding party for four hundred guests—and sixteen hundred journalists. Rarely at ease socially, Nixon sent out a memo asking staff to submit jokes he could make in the receiving line.

All went well on the day of the ceremony, June 12. "The President's diminutive ethereal blond daughter," bubbled one reporter, "finally walked down the curving staircase on her father's arm." Tricia married her groom, "tall, fine-boned and handsome," in a dainty white pavilion specially erected in the Rose Garden. Nixon, in gray swallow-tailed suit with striped trousers, ascot, and stiff wing collar, danced with his wife—apparently for only the second time in twenty years. A radiant Pat on his arm, he confidently made the OK sign for the photographers.

But all was not OK, as Nixon discovered next morning on the front page of the *New York Times*. "In the top left-hand corner," he recalled in his memoirs, "there was a picture of me standing with Tricia in the Rose Garden. . . . Next to the picture was another headline: VIETNAM ARCHIVE: PENTAGON STUDY TRACES 3 DECADES OF GROWING U.S. INVOLVEMENT."

This was the first installment of a series of reports that *Times* managing editor Abe Rosenthal was to characterize as "the biggest damn story in the world." For the past three months, at one point holed up in a Manhattan hotel suite, his reporters had pored over a seven-thousand-page, forty-seven-volume study dryly titled "United States–Vietnamese Relations, 1945–1967," what the world rapidly came to know as the Pentagon Papers.

Prepared in the final months of President Johnson's administration, the papers were an official history—complete with copies of original documents—of how the United States had become enmired in Vietnam and of the often less than noble or intelligent thinking that had kept it there.

Publishing the papers neither endangered the lives of U.S. fighting men nor caused any specific damage to national security. The history covered no events later than 1968, and according to Defense Secretary Laird, 98 percent of the material could have been declassified. The very fact that the material *was* classified, however, triggered a reaction in high places that had unimaginable consequences.

By the time of the collapse of the presidency three years later it would become clear that Nixon lied and that many of the men around him lied, sometimes to save their leader, sometimes themselves. Of those convicted of crimes after Watergate, five, including four of the President's closest aides—Haldeman, Ehrlichman, Mitchell, and Chapin—would be sentenced for perjury.

To re-create accurately, then, the aftermath of the publication of the Pentagon Papers involves picking a way through a landscape strewn with falsehoods and half-truths. Sometimes the White House tapes and the documented record signpost the truth, yet even they can be misleading. The president's tapes are but a partial record, and some of what Nixon said into the White House microphones may have been spoken deliberately to deceive. A false paper trail may have also been created, and many documents are known to have been destroyed.[10]

The available record suggests that Nixon's initial reaction to the Pentagon Papers' publication was fairly cool, for he perceived their potential for damaging the reputation of his predecessors Johnson and Kennedy. Nevertheless, although no one yet knew who was responsible for the leak, the president urged his staff to "get the story out" on Leslie Gelb, the man who had directed the study. Gelb was now working at the Brookings Institution, a liberal Washington think tank closely associated with the Democrats.

Most of Nixon's immediate ire, though, was directed at the *New York Times* for its "clear disloyalty" in publishing the material. No facilities, he ordered, were ever again to be granted to the nation's newspaper of record. "No contact and no interviews," the president ordered, "never in the office, never on the pool, never on the plane." Any White House staffer who spoke with the *Times* was to be fired. "He wants to be sure," Haldeman noted, "that we do everything that we can to destroy the *Times*." Nothing in his presidency would give him more pleasure, Nixon stormed.

Nixon's initial anger turned to unbridled rage, sparked and fueled by Henry Kissinger. The security adviser had called the president from out of town on the day the first installment of the papers appeared, fulminating about the damage to the conduct of foreign policy. Those with whom he was involved in delicate diplomacy—the Chinese, the Soviets, the North Vietnamese—might, Kissinger said, conclude that the United States was "too unsteady, too harassed, and too insecure to be a useful partner."

Expressed calmly later in Kissinger's memoirs, the concern seems reasonable, but at the time the adviser was enraged. "These leaks," Colson quoted him as shouting, "are slowly and systematically destroying us." Kissinger pounded his hand palm down on the antique Chippendale table, rattling the coffee cups. To Colson he seemed to be "going through the ceiling . . . almost irrational."

The culprit behind the leaks turned out to be forty-year-old Daniel Ellsberg, a Rand Corporation consultant who had used his privileged access to copy the papers. Once an ardent supporter of the U.S. intervention in Vietnam, Ellsberg was now convinced the conflict was futile. He dismissed Nixon's Vietnamization policy as a "bloody, hopeless, uncompelled and surely immoral prolongation" of the war, "mass murder." Ellsberg hoped that "by revealing over twenty years of secret plans for escalation, lies to the public, plans to violate treaties, and plans to basically enlarge the war . . . the public would draw from that that the current President might be doing the same . . . it would be just as serious if it became known that he was lying as it would have been for Johnson. So he had to try to shut me up."

While Nixon did try but failed to stop further publication of the papers by taking the *New York Times* to court, his pursuit of Daniel Ellsberg became a vendetta. Kissinger, who knew Ellsberg, fed the president's spleen with a torrent of allegations. Ellsberg may have been "the brightest student I ever had," he told Nixon, but he was "a little unbalanced." He supposedly "had weird sexual habits, used drugs" and, in Vietnam, had "enjoyed helicopter flights in which he would take potshots at the Vietnamese below." Ellsberg had married a millionaire's daughter and—Kissinger threw in for good measure—had sex with her in front of their children.

The accusations were over the top, but they reached their mark.[11] A man with an Ivy League background who had married into money, indulged in far-out sex, and took drugs was a ready-made Nixon target. In the days that followed, the president would remind his staff frequently of his glory days pursuing another Harvard man, Alger Hiss. Kissinger also touched another nerve certain to prompt a reaction from Nixon. If the president failed to respond, the adviser dared suggest, it would show he was "a weakling."

That meeting with Kissinger, with Haldeman and Ehrlichman sitting in, raised more than the spector of Ellsberg. Nixon had long since ordered aides to bring him the file on the 1968 "bombing halt episode," President Johnson's election eve effort to get peace talks started by calling off bomb strikes against North Vietnam. If the files revealed that the cessation of bombing had been merely a vote-getting ploy at election time, as the Nixon side had always maintained, they might be used against the Democrats.

"You can blackmail Johnson on this stuff," Haldeman suggested, "and it might be worth doing." Nixon of course had another reason for wanting to obtain the file. As reported earlier, he had actively worked to sabotage the 1968 peace talks, and the records in question might actually prove more damaging to *him* than to President Johnson.

When Haldeman explained that the material had likely been lodged at the

Brookings Institution, Nixon seized on the possibility of getting hold of it. "I wanted it . . . right now," he would recall in the memoirs, "even if it meant having to get it back surreptitiously."

A tape released in 1996 reveals that Nixon ordered a break-in of Brookings. He reminded Haldeman of the 1970 domestic intelligence plan that had featured burglary as a component—a plan he had approved and later aborted—and then said: "Implement it. . . . I want it implemented. . . . Goddammit it, get in and get those files. Blow the safe and get them."

The notion that this was merely an impetuous command, one he did not expect to be carried out, is belied by the evidence.[12] Less than two weeks later, on June 30, the tapes show, Nixon again insisted on action at Brookings.

> PRESIDENT NIXON: The way I want that handled, Bob is . . . I want Brookings . . . just *break in, break in* and take it out. Do you understand? . . . You're to break into the place, rifle the files, and bring them in.
>
> HALDEMAN: I don't have any problem with breaking in . . .
>
> PRESIDENT NIXON: Just go in and take it! Go in around 8:00 or 9:00 o'clock.
>
> HALDEMAN: . . . Make an inspection of the safe.
>
> PRESIDENT NIXON: That's right. You go in and do an inspection. I mean clean *it out*.

The next morning, meeting with Haldeman and Kissinger, the president again raised the subject of Brookings.

> PRESIDENT NIXON: Now you do it and wake them up, get them off their goddamn dead asses. . . . We're up against an enemy, a conspiracy, they're using any means. [*Then, with separate emphasis on every word*] We—are—going—to—use—any—means. Is that clear? Did they get the Brookings Institute raided last night? . . . No? Get it *done*. I want it *done*. I want the Brookings Institute safe cleaned out. And have it cleaned out in a way that it makes somebody else look . . . [*next word unintelligible, perhaps "guilty"*].

And two hours later:

> PRESIDENT NIXON: Who's going to break into the Brookings Institute? . . . Henry . . . He's a little afraid. He's got some friends over at Brookings . . . he told me he was for it. . . . You've got to get this stuff from Rand and Brookings.

Then, to Ehrlichman:

PRESIDENT NIXON: John, you mop up. You're in charge of that. And
I want it done today. . . .

The following day, more:

PRESIDENT NIXON: I really meant it when I, I want somebody to go
in and crack that safe. Walk in and get it. . . . They've got to do
it. . . .

They did try to do it, more than once, and over a period of months. One
of the detectives used for earlier undercover jobs, including the pursuit of Edward Kennedy, recalled being assigned by Charles Colson to raid the Brookings Institute. Colson, he testified, suggested a way to go about it: Nixon
operatives would set fire to the Brookings building, and the file would be
grabbed during the ensuing commotion.

This witness, former policeman John Caulfield, thought the scheme "asi-
nine" and asked White House counsel John Dean to intervene. Dean did so, he
would testify, by flying to San Clemente to see Ehrlichman. The president's
aide, apparently unsurprised by the report of the fire-bombing plan, merely
looked over his half-glasses and said, "Well, maybe we should call it off." Then
he called Colson to say, "Chuck, that Brookings thing. We don't want it anymore. . . ."

By that time, Dean was to tell investigators, Colson's men had already
"cased the joint." A veteran guard at Brookings, interviewed years later, did recall an evening visit by two suspicious strangers. When he blocked their way,
they made their excuses and left.

According to another of the detectives on contract to the White House, a
second reconnaissance was carried out later. Other operatives were at work by
that time, devising a variant on the original scheme. Brookings was still to be
set on fire, but the first fire engine to arrive would be a phony, an old, used
model purchased expressly for the operation. Its "crew" would "hit the vault,
and then get themselves out in the confusion of other fire apparatus arriving."

The dangerous caper was scrapped, said the former operative who described it, only because the fire engine was "excessively expensive."[13] While
Colson later tried to deny his alleged role, Ehrlichman acknowledged having
called it off. He said too that Nixon knew about the fire-bombing plan in advance. If true, that is surely the most astonishing feature of the whole mad
episode.

That Nixon was in earnest about the Brookings plot is evident, and not
only because the tapes reveal his insisting it be carried out. They have also preserved the conspiratorial moment when—just for a moment—he evidently remembered the hidden microphones. On June 30, as he urged Haldeman to see
the plan through, Nixon paused to warn: "Don't discuss it here. . . ."

To break into Brookings, Haldeman had pointed out, they would need "somebody to do it." The president had someone in mind. "You talk to Hunt," he said. Hunt. E. Howard Hunt, the man who exactly a year later would lead the Watergate break-in.

As reported earlier, Hunt had first met Nixon some twenty years earlier as a young CIA officer.[14] It was then that, already an admirer, he had gone up to Nixon's table in a Washington restaurant to congratulate him on his pursuit of Alger Hiss. Out to dinner with Pat, the young politician had asked Hunt and his wife to join them at their table.

Six years on, when Hunt was serving in Uruguay and Nixon stopped there en route to Caracas, they talked again. Later still, when both men were embroiled in early efforts to overthrow Fidel Castro, Nixon's military aide Robert Cushman told Hunt to call on the vice president for help if necessary.

That was the extent of the relationship prior to the Nixon presidency, Hunt said in a 1997 interview. Nixon mentioned nothing of the earlier meetings in his memoirs—and one passage could be taken to mean that he had not heard Hunt's name until as late as 1972.[15] "You know," he was to tell Ehrlichman on the White House tapes, as his presidency began to implode, "Colson never told me about Hunt, that he knew Hunt, until after the Watergate thing."

It was not true. If the earlier meetings were insignificant and understandably forgotten, Hunt's name had at least been floated past the president by June 30, 1971. On that day, the tapes show, he had mentioned Hunt's name as a candidate for the Brookings break-in. The following morning Colson briefed the president in detail, praising Hunt as "a very close friend of [Senator] Jim Buckley's . . . hard as nails . . . a brilliant writer . . . just got out of the CIA, fifty, kind of a tiger." Colson knew Hunt because they had socialized before the presidency as members of the Brown University alumni club.

Haldeman also discussed Hunt with the president as a potential recruit, on two occasions. Colson praised him again a month later, recommending Hunt as "a first-rate analyst who spent his whole life in subversive warfare . . . an admirer of yours since the Alger Hiss case." Hunt's name, he later recalled, was at the bottom of a list of six men he put forward for the job of countering leaks like the Pentagon Papers. It was, however, Hunt whom Nixon picked.

Haldeman had noted in his diary that week that the president wanted a "dirty guy" to go after the "conspiracy" against him. Now he had one. "I want to alert you," Ehrlichman said in a call to Cushman, by now a senior CIA official, "that an old acquaintance, Howard Hunt, has been asked by the President to do some special consultant work on security problems. He may be contacting you sometime in the future for some assistance. . . . You should consider he has pretty much carte blanche."

Sitting in the sun on the terrace at San Clemente, a week after Hunt had joined up, Nixon proceeded from the hiring of one individual to the establishment of a secret investigative unit that would respond directly to the Oval Office.

The new group, composed of five men, would soon be working out of a room in the half basement of the Executive Office Building, with a sign on the door reading MR. YOUNG, PLUMBER. Young was David Young, the unit's joint leader. "Plumber" described their mission: to plug the leaks that infuriated the president.

Nixon had personally briefed the other man assigned to run the outfit, Egil ("Bud") Krogh, the young aide who had witnessed his bizarre dawn visit to the House of Representatives the previous year. Krogh was, and is—as the author learned in extensive interviews—one of the most decent of those who served on the White House staff. He was at that time also somewhat inexperienced or, by one friend's account, "the kind of guy who, if you put him in charge of a big wedding . . . wouldn't have known how to get a couple of cops to help with the traffic." As such, he was not, perhaps, an ideal choice to head the president's crack undercover unit.

Also drafted were Howard Hunt and the strange character with whom his name would be forever linked, Gordon Liddy. A former FBI agent, then aged forty, Liddy had a particular interest in Nazi Germany. The music of the Third Reich stirred him, made him feel "strength inside." He was also, by his own account, preoccupied with guns, violence, and the elemental power of the human will.

Liddy liked to discuss methods of killing—such as how to dispatch a victim with one thrust of a sharp pencil just above the Adam's apple—and acquired a CIA 9 mm parabellum pistol "for use in the event Bud Krogh or other of my White House superiors tasked me with an assassination." It was perhaps not an irrelevant potential asset, as these pages will show.

"Gordon's a cowboy," said one who knew him then, and the description would remain apt far into the future. In the year 2000, at seventy, he was a hectoring talk-show host with a "LIDDYPage" Web site featuring himself with his "formidable Lingenfelter modified '94 Corvette ZR–1," his "Boss-Hoss" motorcycle, and his role in the TV series *18 Wheels of Justice*. The site also included an ad for the "G. Gordon Liddy Stacked and Packed Calendar Featuring America's Most Beautiful Women Heavily Armed." This was the man who, in 1971, became field operations coordinator for the president's special unit.

Soon after becoming a Plumber, Liddy would brag later, he would earn Nixon's praise for writing "the best memo he's seen in years. . . ." The reference was to a report he had submitted summarizing why it was time for FBI Director Hoover to retire, an argument of which Nixon was already persuaded. Hoover had long been an ally, but now he wanted him gone.

The president had been having trouble with the director, most recently over the pursuit of Daniel Ellsberg. "Notwithstanding the president's agitation," Ehrlichman recalled, "Hoover assigned a very low priority to the project." Nixon was frustrated by the apparent indifference, so much so that he phoned Hoover to say he was "having to resort to sending two people out there."

The "two people" were Hunt and Liddy, and "out there" was California. Disappointed by an initial psychiatric profile of Ellsberg provided by the CIA, the Plumbers had proposed, in writing, a "covert operation" to "examine all the medical files" in the office of Ellsberg's Los Angeles psychiatrist. Ehrlichman approved the idea, again in writing, on condition the mission could be carried out in a way that was "not traceable."

As the world would learn during Watergate, Hunt and Liddy duly flew to the West Coast. Equipped with silly disguises provided by the CIA and assisted by Cuban exile accomplices, they broke into the doctor's office, found nothing, and left the place a mess to give the impression that their motive had been to steal drugs. The crime achieved absolutely nothing except—one day in the future—to imperil further Nixon's presidency.

In a 1973 broadcast to the nation, after the break-in had been exposed, Nixon would explain that his brief to the Plumbers had been that the Ellsberg matter was "of vital importance to the national security." He was more forthright in the memoirs, insisting that Ellsberg's "views had to be discredited." In other words, the sort of charges Kissinger had alleged against Ellsberg were to be corroborated and made public. "He can be painted evil," as Colson told Nixon; or "neutralized," Hunt put it in a memo.

Whether Nixon ordered the break-in or knew of it in advance is a question that has long been debated. Krogh, who sent Hunt and Liddy on their mission, told the author Nixon had given him general "authority" for the assignment but no specific break-in order. Ehrlichman quoted Nixon as having given the go-ahead for "direct action" by Hunt and Liddy.[16]

Recently released White House tapes fail to clarify the matter. "I briefed Ehrlichman on it today on the investigative side," Nixon told Colson during a discussion of the Pentagon Papers. This conversation took place at the very time, and probably on the very day, that Ehrlichman signed the memo approving the mission.

Days after the break-in, however, Ehrlichman withheld specific details about it from the president, telling him only that there had recently been "one little operation. It's been aborted out in Los Angeles, which, I think, it's better you don't know about." Ehrlichman later testified that he opted not to communicate to his boss what had happened, after the fact—because "there wasn't anything the President could do about it."[17]

Likewise Nixon's later conversations with aides reveal no certainties as to the level of his involvement. "Goddamn to hell," he would complain to his press spokesman, Ron Zeigler, in the midst of Watergate. "I didn't tell them to go fuck up the goddamn Ellsberg place." Two days later: "I am stuck with, and have to be stuck with . . . approving this plan, which I did. I didn't check whether there were burglaries and all that. God to hell, we didn't even think of such things!"

As the tapes clearly demonstrate, Nixon certainly had considered similar actions. He had repeatedly ordered a break-in of the Brookings Institution only two months before the burglary of the psychiatrist's office. Another exchange makes it clear what his primary motive was as scandal engulfed him. "I believe somehow," he told colleagues, "I have to avoid having the President approve the break-in of a psychiatrist."

In the 1973 broadcast Nixon did categorically deny involvement, insisting he "did not authorize and had no knowledge of any illegal means." In private, days after his resignation, he was less assured. "Did I know about it?" he asked former Plumber Egil Krogh, one of the first visitors to San Clemente after Nixon had left Washington.[18]

Two years later, Nixon expressed the same uncertainty to Bob Haldeman. "I was so damn mad at Ellsberg in those days," he said. "I've been thinking— and maybe I did order that break-in."

According to Ehrlichman, two aides who worked with Nixon in exile told him Nixon eventually did take responsibility. "Nixon now admits what he formerly denied," Ehrlichman claimed. "He knew of the [Ellsberg psychiatrist] break-in before it occurred, and he encouraged it."[19]

In the memoirs Nixon resorted to vagueness. "I do not believe I was told about the break-in at the time," he wrote, ". . . but I cannot rule it out." The equivocation enraged Ehrlichman, for while Nixon was never held to account, he and Krogh had served time in jail in large part because of their role in the break-in of the psychiatrist's office.

Ehrlichman went to his grave believing that Nixon did authorize the crime, through Charles Colson. Colson has denied involvement, yet the paper record proves he was privy to the idea from the moment it was proposed.[20] He features too in another, more pathetic possible explanation for Nixon's apparent amnesia on the matter.

"It would be hard to know what [Nixon] did—or didn't—know," said Haldeman's eventual replacement, Alexander Haig. Colson "would get President Nixon in the bag—when I say 'in the bag,' all Nixon needed was one scotch. His toleration of alcohol is zero—and he could get pretty high. . . . The real éminence grise of all this was Colson."

It was unbelievable, Nixon was to grumble as Congress's investigation began, that he had to put up with "this horse's-ass crap" about his operatives' covert activity. A skein of information, however, suggests that more such activity had been undertaken, even by late 1971, than Watergate probers ever were able to investigate.

Argument on whether Nixon personally plotted the break-in of the psychiatrist's office seems academic in the context of what we now know of other plotting. The taped evidence, and not just that recording his insistence on a burglary of the Brookings Institution, indicated that theft, to him, was easily justified.

A week after the break-in of Ellsberg's doctor's office, Nixon conspired with Ehrlichman about how to purloin documents from the National Archives, the nation's most revered repository of historical records. As in the Brookings scheme, the aim was to get access to files on the Vietnam War, records deposited by former Johnson officials on condition that only they could authorize access.

"I am going to steal these documents out of the National Archives . . . and photograph them . . ." Ehrlichman told the president on September 10, 1971. Nixon merely asked, "How do you do that?" and Ehrlichman explained his plan. He would arrange through a Nixon appointee in the General Services Administration to have the archivist of the United States leave town. Then, he said, "we can get in there and [the Nixon appointee] will photograph, and we'll reseal them." At a later meeting, they discussed how the job could be carried out without disturbing the seals.

The photographic work, Ehrlichman told the president, would be done by staff sent over from the Pentagon by one of their own, Defense Department counsel Fred Buzhardt. Two years later, as Nixon's Watergate counsel, Buzhardt would warn Nixon there were likely to be "rumors of additional burglaries . . . they won't know by whom. . . ."

Nixon responded by claiming he knew of none. Henry Kissinger, however, has recalled being told by another Nixon attorney that there had indeed been "other break-ins sanctioned from the White House for several different purposes, some as yet unclear . . . [it was] a 'sordid mess.'"[21]

A study by one of the most thorough students of the period suggests there may have been as many as a hundred "political" break-ins during the Nixon administration. "Although the evidence linking the government to these break-ins is largely circumstantial," U.S. Senator James Abourezk told colleagues, "it is both striking and persuasive . . . virtually all the victims were objects of administration concern . . . the attacks against them followed a consistent pattern."[22]

The intruders in the cases studied were no ordinary burglars. They stole little or nothing of value and targeted instead correspondence, financial records, and tapes. Consider some of the suspicious break-ins that occurred during the first presidency.

Three months after Nixon's men made their way into the office of Daniel Ellsberg's psychiatrist, unidentified burglars entered the New York office of the psychoanalyst who had treated Ellsberg's wife. The file cabinet containing her records received special attention. The study also noted a burglary of the New York offices of the NAACP Legal Defense Fund, which had been fighting the administration's race policies. It occurred twenty-four hours after the break-in of Ellsberg's doctor's quarters, and Hunt and Liddy are know to have traveled to New York that day.

Another Nixon investigator was ordered to reconnoiter the offices of Potomac Associates, a policy research group run by the dissident former

Kissinger aide William Watts. Potomac had published a study suggesting the country was sliding into a crisis under the Nixon administration. The investigator reported that "a penetration is deemed possible if required," and a Haldeman aide asked to be updated. A break-in was eventually attempted.

The offices of pollster Lou Harris were broken into not once but three times, following publication of an unfavorable poll result on public reaction to the Cambodian invasion.

One of two burglaries at the Washington home of Mortimer Caplin, who had been IRS commissioner during the Kennedy administration, was especially suspect. Whoever was responsible had ignored watches, jewelry, and government bonds and taken instead a case of documents. Caplin had that month supported a Democratic party complaint about the monitoring of tax returns by the Nixon White House. His name had also appeared on one of the Enemies lists.

Of the numerous other mysterious incidents that occurred in the months that followed, only the most glaringly pertinent can be covered in these pages. Few of them attracted much attention at the time; they are relevant, though, for they suggest that the Nixon White House abuses may have taken place on a greater scale than ever publicly recognized.

"The Fourth Amendment," Republican Senator Lowell Weicker observed of the more famous wiretaps and break-ins, "guarantees the 'right of the people to be secure in their persons, houses, papers, and effects, against unreasonable searches and seizures. . . .' It was expressly violated." Weicker judged the eventual "intelligence activities" of Nixon's White House to have been its "greatest distortion of the political system."

"Let us be sure," the president said at a staff dinner to celebrate the beginning of his fourth year in office, "that nothing was left undone that could have been done to make this a more decent country. . . ."

On the foreign front a moment of deserved glory was imminent. The pearl of Nixon's international diplomacy, the breakthrough to China, would culminate weeks later in his spectacular trip to Beijing to meet with Chairman Mao Zedong. Not long afterward Air Force One was to carry the president to Moscow for momentous discussions with Leonid Brezhnev. Real progress was made on control of nuclear weapons. The war in Vietnam continued, but soon all but sixty-nine thousand American troops returned home. These were key achievements, golden assets for the coming election, the election Nixon hoped would deliver—at last—an overwhelming victory.

That Christmas of 1971 television brought the nation heartwarming pictures of the First Family. Julie took CBS viewers inside the private quarters of the White House to show that it was "like any home in the United States." Nixon, Haldeman noted in his diary, "did his bit" by the Christmas tree.

The president had in fact wanted to avoid the holiday festivities, according to an earlier Haldeman entry. He had hoped to "drop all our services in December, skip the Christmas 'Evening at the White House,' schedule several weekends in Florida. . . . Also he wants the White House Christmas parties all scheduled during the time he's going to be gone, so that he won't have to attend them."

Nixon did head off to Florida and Bebe Rebozo's "Christmas boat parade," but not until after Christmas and after attending at least one of the White House parties. One of those present, with his family in tow, was Howard Hunt. "I passed through the line," Hunt recalled in 1997, "and Nixon recognized me. He said, 'How nice to see you!' I said, 'I'm working for Chuck Colson now.' And he said, 'Oh yes, I know about that. . . .' "

On New Year's, FBI Director Hoover sat in a parked limousine in Florida with the local agent in charge, Kenneth Whittaker. He was about to fly back to Washington with the president aboard Air Force One, and it was his birthday. Yet the old man was gloomy. "He wasn't high on Nixon," the agent remembered. "He said, 'Let me tell, you, Whittaker, Pat Nixon would make a better president than him.' "

Back in the capital Hoover asked a journalist he trusted, Andrew Tully, to join him for lunch in his private dining room. "I have some things to say," he told Tully, "but I don't want you to publish it until I'm dead." The reporter agreed, and Hoover held forth.

He was scathing about the men around Nixon. "Some of those guys don't know a goddamned thing about due process of law. They think they can get away with murder. I told the President I hoped I'd live long enough to keep those people from getting him into bad trouble."

Hoover dismissed Nixon's advisers one by one. John Mitchell: "Never been in a courtroom . . . not equipped to be Attorney General." Ehrlichman, Haldeman, and Ziegler: "They don't know anything except how to sell advertising." John Dean: "Doesn't know law . . . son of a bitch." The president's "kindergarten," the director warned, kept "coming up with half-baked schemes."

Then, with uncanny prescience, he effectively predicted the coming disaster. "By God," he growled, "Nixon's got some former CIA men working for him that I'd kick out of my office. Someday that bunch will serve him up a fine mess."

Hoover would not live to save the president from catastrophe. The Watergate break-in was less than six months away.

29

*We are lucky it was Watergate, because if it
hadn't been that, it would have been something
much worse, the way things were going.*

—Bryce Harlow, presidential counsel, recalling a
conversation with Henry Kissinger after Watergate

"Jesus God!" Nixon had exclaimed in the summer of 1971. "We need *two*
million dollars . . . at least two million. . . ." He had asked how much
money was stashed away for special operations, and Haldeman had told him
"about $1,000,000," around four million dollars at today's values.[1] Fantastic
campaign wealth was to enrich the coffers further, and large portions of it
would be spent on dirty tricks.

An early indicator of just how much money was generated for Nixon's
1972 campaign came to investigators in the form of "Rose Mary's Baby," a list
of secret contributors that had been kept in the desk drawer of the president's
secretary and escaped post-Watergate shredding.

The Committee to Re-Elect the President—properly CRP but since known
universally as CREEP—would eventually acknowledge having collected more
than sixty million dollars, almost twice the amount available for the 1968 campaign.

Both parties are perennially guilty of financial abuses. The money flow to
the Nixon side in 1972, however, was fantastic. Much of it came in cash, delivered not by the bag but by the suitcase. Huge sums were of doubtful origin,
and some of the donations were plainly illegal.

The shah of Iran, visited by Nixon that year and given carte blanche to buy any American conventional weapon he wished, provided hundreds of thousands of dollars, perhaps more than a million, reportedly delivered through the Swiss Bank Corporation and the Banco de Londres y Mexico in Mexico City. Having tracked the course of the money, one dogged journalist found his inquiries to the Iranian Embassy answered in person, and blocked, by the president's close associate William Rogers.

Another donor at that time, as he has acknowledged privately, was Saudi businessman Adnan Khashoggi, who gave a million dollars.[2] "We Arabs," said the influential Egyptian editor Mohammed Haykal, "were almost the most zealous contributors to Nixon's campaign." From the Philippines, President Ferdinand Marcos reportedly came through once again. Then, as now, contributions by foreign governments or their agents were illegal.

Domestically, money was gathered by dint of strong persuasion and virtual extortion. Top business leaders were invited to a conference, ostensibly to hear Nixon speak on the year's financial prospects. Commerce Secretary Stans, who convened the meeting, resigned while it was in progress to become CREEP's chief fund-raiser. Corporate chiefs were taken aside and told the president was putting together "a coalition of voters and campaign techniques that will keep Nixon and his chosen successors in power at least through 1990."

Companies were promised "a friendly climate in Washington"—if they came through with gifts for CREEP. Corporate donations to political campaigns were illegal, however, and many big concerns, including Phillips Petroleum, Ashland Oil, Occidental, Goodyear Tire and Rubber, Braniff, and American Airlines, would eventually find themselves being prosecuted.

Oilmen alone gave five million dollars. Officials of Gulf Oil, one of the companies later fined, recalled having been informed just how much the company was expected to provide. "I certainly considered it pressure when two cabinet officials asked me for funds," said one. "It's different from someone collecting for the Boy Scouts." Another recalled having withdrawn money in hundred-dollar bills from a Swiss bank and handing the cash to Stans stuffed in an envelope.

A Grumman Corporation chief would tell how a White House aide urged him to make a million-dollar contribution in return for Nixon's "assistance" in arranging an aircraft sale to Japan. The aide argued that the profits to be made on the E2C, a reconnaissance plane, justified that amount. The president was due to meet with Japan's prime minister soon after the conversation took place.

An order to McDonald's, canceling an unauthorized price increase levied on its quarter-pounder cheeseburger, was reversed—after the company's chairman had donated $255,000. Smaller companies had less luck. A New York architectural firm found its bid for a government contract withdrawn when its senior partner decided not to contribute. His reason for not donating, he had incautiously told CREEP representatives, was that he thought Nixon "wasn't a good character."

"If you're thinking of coming in for under a hundred thousand dollars," Nixon's personal attorney told American Shipbuilding chairman George Steinbrenner, "don't bother. We work up to a million around here. You do a lot of business in Washington. You'd do well to get in with the right people." Afraid to decline, Steinbrenner paid as instructed.

"Anybody that wants to be an ambassador," Nixon told Haldeman in a recorded conversation, "wants to pay at least $250,000 . . . from now on, the contributors have got to be I mean . . . big. . . . I'm not gonna do it with quote, 'political' friends and all the rest of this crap . . ." The president was aiming a little high, but the thirteen noncareer ambassadors he was to appoint after his reelection did donate an aggregate of more than $700,000. Walter Annenberg, who alone gave $250,000, was given the London embassy.[3]

Bebe Rebozo, whose advice Nixon heeded on ambassadorships, took delivery of fifty thousand dollars in cash (in bundles of hundred-dollar bills) from a supermarket chain head at a Key Biscayne bar. Albert ("Toots") Manzi, a fund-raiser for former Massachusetts Governor John Volpe, reportedly gave Nixon five hundred thousand dollars in the hopes that Volpe might be chosen for the vice presidency in the second term.[4] "I made the kitty," a witness in an extortion case quoted Manzi as saying, "and the kitty was presented to Mr. Nixon."

Even today the true nature of the Nixon connection with Robert Vesco, the financier at the center of what the Securities and Exchange Commission called "one of the largest securities frauds ever perpetrated," remains unclear. In the year 2000, as he remained in Castro's Cuba, in jail for fraud and other offenses, pending charges against Vesco in the United States included an indictment for an illegal two-hundred-thousand-dollar contribution to Nixon's 1972 campaign.

"Vesco is a crook. I never met the man," Nixon is heard to say on one of the White House tapes. In fact, the two men had been introduced at a VIP dinner soon after the 1968 election, which Vesco had backed with a twenty-five-thousand-dollar contribution. Vesco's longtime private pilot told the author that his boss sat with Nixon, then president-elect, at the Rose Bowl game a few weeks later.

In a muddle of evidence, some facts stand out. Just as fund-raising for 1972 was getting under way, Vesco was arrested in Switzerland on charges of fraud and embezzlement. Nixon's attorney general, John Mitchell, intervened personally, ordering U.S. diplomats in Berne to bring "all possible pressure" to secure his release.

Soon afterward a senior Nixon campaign aide suggested to a Vesco associate that the financier might want to contribute to CREEP. A month or so later a Vesco aide flew to the States with a briefcase containing two hundred thousand dollars.[5]

The younger of the president's two brothers, Edward Nixon, described by CREEP's deputy director as a "presidential surrogate," helped arrange the delivery of the Vesco cash. His elder brother Donald had been a conduit for Vesco's 1968 donation. Donald's son, Donald, Jr., worked for Vesco as a personal aide during the presidency.

In 1974 Walter Cronkite would interview the financier in Costa Rica, his then country of refuge. Asked if he had spoken with Nixon personally about the money he donated in 1972, Vesco paused for a full half minute and then said, "Let's go to the next question. . . . I didn't quite hear the question too clearly. And I'm sure if you said it ten times, I still couldn't hear it. . . ."

Vesco did reveal one detail of substance. The person who told him his campaign contribution should be in cash, he said, had been Nixon's longest-serving retainer, Murray Chotiner. It was Chotiner who, with Charles Colson, played a key role in an episode that, had even its bare outline become known at the time, might have been as great a scandal as Watergate itself.

———————

"The P," Haldeman noted in his diary in December 1971, "apparently met with the Attorney General yesterday and agreed to pardon Hoffa." Jimmy Hoffa, the Teamsters leader, had been jailed for tampering in 1967 after a long pursuit by Robert Kennedy. Nixon nevertheless decided to free him, with nine years of his sentence still to run. How that came about is a complex tale with links to the 1972 election.

The previous year Haldeman had sent Colson the following instruction: "The President wants you to take on the responsibility for working on developing your strength with the labor unions. . . . He feels this must be done by picking them off one by one . . . we have to pick them as individuals. . . . The President has specifically in mind the Teamsters. . . . There is a great deal of gold there to be mined."

Colson was ordered to work closely with businessman Curtis Counts, a friend of the Nixons' from Whittier days, whom they had known for more than thirty years.[6] Counts, now a labor mediator, had recently introduced Nixon to Frank Fitzsimmons, who was standing in for Hoffa during his imprisonment and was intent on seizing the union leadership for himself. Nixon colluded in this scheme and began a long-term alliance with Fitzsimmons, one sealed with hard cash.

Even before the instruction to Colson, word of a darker element had reached White House aide Clark Mollenhoff, a decent man opposed to such shenanigans. He had been informed that Nixon was going to spring Hoffa and that Chotiner was "handling it with the Las Vegas mob."

The following year, in an internal memo marked SECRET, Colson had reported that "substantial sums of money, perhaps a quarter of a million dollars, available for any . . . purpose we would direct" could be generated by "arrang[ing] to have James Hoffa released from prison."

When Hoffa was eventually released, it was done in a way designed to benefit both Fitzsimmons and Nixon. For Fitzsimmons there was a stipulation that Hoffa would be barred from union activity for a decade to come. For Nixon there was a Teamsters Union endorsement—and allegedly huge payments involving organized crime.

Seven years after Nixon's fall a *Time* magazine investigation reported on a purported 1972 "meeting between Nixon and Fitzsimmons in one of the private rooms of the White House. [Attorney General] Kleindienst had been summoned to the session and ordered to review all investigations pending against the Teamsters and to make sure that Fitzsimmons and his allies were not hurt. The meeting supposedly occurred after Nixon's 1972 re-election campaign, to which the Teamsters contributed an estimated $1 million."

The *Time* article drew on IRS agents' interviews with Fitzsimmons and some of his Teamsters colleagues, who had cooperated in hope of avoiding prosecution on other matters.[7] Fitzsimmons and the cronies involved have since died, but the informant who acted as their go-between with IRS intelligence, Harry Hall, spoke with the author in 1997.

"A large amount of money was given by the Teamsters to the Committee to Re-Elect the President," Hall said. "Fitzsimmons figured he'd found an ally in Nixon. The Teamsters would help him financially, and Nixon ate that up. . . . I was told they gave money to Chotiner that was to go to Nixon. I think it was close to five hundred thousand dollars."

According to Hall, the president's brother Don received twenty-five thousand dollars. The half million was separate from the sum donated to CREEP and intended for Nixon personally.

Two leads on the "Las Vegas mob" connection suggest a link to the White House.[8] When hush money was required during the Watergate scandal, Colson would travel to Las Vegas at the same time as a mob courier. It was then, allegedly, that another five-hundred-thousand-dollar payment was made to Nixon's people at Fitzsimmons's request. Later still, after Colson resigned from the White House, Fitzsimmons would retain him as an attorney at a fee of one hundred thousand dollars a year.

Questions also arose over alleged trips to Las Vegas by the two leading figures in the operations that would culminate in the Watergate break-in, Howard Hunt and Gordon Liddy.[9]

"For God's sake keep it to yourself," Liddy confided excitedly to Hunt in late 1971. ". . . Get this: The AG [Attorney General Mitchell] wants me to set up an intelligence organization for the campaign. It'll be big, Howard. . . . They don't want a repetition of the last campaign; this time they want to know everything that's going on. . . . There's plenty of money available—half a million dollars for openers, and there's more where that came from."

There was indeed, and involved in its disbursement were figures at the very top of the administration. A surviving Talking Paper prepared for Haldeman on October 1, 1971 shows that a budget of "800–300 [thousand dollars]" for "surveillance" was on the agenda for a meeting with Mitchell.

Weeks later, Mitchell and John Dean discussed an improved "political intelligence capability," with Liddy, no longer a humble Plumber, now transferred to CREEP with the exalted title of general counsel.

Along with Hunt, Liddy's principal operational colleague was to be another former CIA man, a new recruit named James McCord, who was to be CREEP's "security coordinator," in charge of defensive security. Soon, though, McCord would be briefing Liddy on offensive surveillance or, simply stated, bugging.

Nixon himself knew CREEP now had an "intelligence branch," and he was impatient for it to start getting results. The president would sit drumming his fingers on the desk, Haldeman remembered, asking again and again: "When are they going to *do* something over there?"

On January 27, 1972, Liddy walked into the Justice Department, passing beneath the frieze that reads: "NO FREE GOVERNMENT CAN SURVIVE THAT IS NOT BASED ON THE SUPREMACY OF LAW," for a meeting with Attorney General Mitchell. Also present were CREEP's deputy director, Jeb Magruder, and presidential counsel John Dean. The plan they had assembled to discuss was blatantly criminal.

"Smart, isn't he? . . . must be as conservative as hell," Nixon had remarked of Liddy after reading his memo on getting rid of J. Edgar Hoover. Now, using charts set on an easel, Liddy laid out for the attorney general, one of Nixon's closest associates, his proposal for the project he called GEM-STONE.

One part of the operation, code named DIAMOND, outlined methods of dealing with "urban guerrillas" expected to disrupt the Republican convention. They were to be identified in advance, kidnapped, drugged, and held incommunicado in Mexico until after the convention. The men selected for the job, Liddy told Mitchell, included "professional killers who had accounted between them for twenty-two dead so far . . . members of organized crime."

Another component, RUBY, was a scheme to infiltrate spies into the Democratic camp. COAL was designed to feed money clandestinely to black Congresswoman Shirley Chisholm, in line with the plan to divide the Democrats that Nixon had approved earlier.[10] EMERALD called for a pursuit plane to bug radiotelephone transmissions from the aircraft carrying the Democratic candidate.

Under CRYSTAL, Liddy proposed leasing a large houseboat moored "within the line of sight" of the Fontainebleau Hotel in Miami Beech, where the Democratic convention was to be held. It was to have a dual function, doubling as a nerve center for bugging and as what intelligence people like to call a honeytrap.

Under SAPPHIRE, the bedroom on the "opulent barge" would be furnished with a king-size bed. "I'll use prostitutes," Liddy explained, "to go out and seduce into the houseboat high campaign officials." He was already seeking out females who could pose as "idly rich young women, so impressed by men of power they would let themselves be picked up at parties and bars by Democratic staffers."

Liddy went on to brief his colleagues on OPAL, for clandestine entries to place bugs; TOPAZ, for photographing documents; and GARNET, for mounting sham pro-Democratic demonstrations carried out in a way that would repel voters rather than attract them.

There was also TURQUOISE, which would undertake sabotage at the Democratic convention. A "commando team" was to destroy the air-conditioning system of key buildings, making conditions intolerable for delegates in the July heat. Finally, Liddy presented the budget, which he called BRICK, set at around a million dollars.

Although Mitchell would later claim that he thought the GEMSTONE plan "beyond the pale," he did not fire Liddy, as one might have expected of the nation's senior law officer. Rather, he merely dismissed the project as too expensive and urged Liddy to come back with "something more realistic." Haldeman's diary entry for the following day, January 28, records that Mitchell met with Nixon to discuss "the overall political plan." It was agreed that Mitchell would soon leave the Justice Department to run CREEP full-time.

Mitchell was present that same evening when Nixon gave a white-tie dinner in honor of DeWitt Wallace, founder of *Reader's Digest*. (The Wallaces would sleep in the Lincoln Bedroom that night, beneficiaries of precisely the perk for which a later Democratic president, Bill Clinton, would come under attack by the Republicans.) The *Digest* had long promoted Nixon, and Wallace personally gave him more than a hundred thousand dollars for the impending campaign. According to one account, the magazine company gave much more, funneled in covertly through the Bahamas. The *Digest*'s editor personally brokered another huge cash contribution—from a prominent businessman—that was placed in Nixon's personal White House safe, then quietly returned after Watergate.

The white-tie banquet that January was for people Haldeman had designated "major political backers"—memospeak for fabulously wealthy supporters. It was especially galling, then, when one of the entertainers, a singer backing Ray Conniff, interrupted the performance with a protest against the Vietnam War. Looking directly at the president, she stepped to the microphone in the middle of "Ma, He's Making Eyes at Me," pulled out a banner reading STOP THE KILLING, and appealed to Nixon to halt the bombing. She ended her action with a cry of "God bless Daniel Ellsberg!" As the singer left the stage to shouts of "Throw her out," the president sat "speechless . . . smiling a sickly smile." Just before the dinner, he had dictated an angry memo demanding a coordinated attack on opponents of his war policy.

Meanwhile Gordon Liddy had gone back to the drawing board. What exactly he had planned, and what targets were finally authorized and when are questions that were to become the subject of bitter controversy. The one issue that matters, amid the bickering, is what the president—or his most senior aides, who should have kept him informed—knew, and when.

Dean has always claimed that, after a second inconclusive meeting with Liddy in Mitchell's office, he recommended to Haldeman that the White House should have nothing to do with the project. If true, Dean's assertion means that Haldeman knew about the scheme by early February 1972.[11] There is no doubt, at any rate, that word of GEMSTONE did reach the president's orbit in that same period.

Impatient because the project remained stalled, Liddy got Hunt to introduce him to Nixon's confidant Charles Colson. Colson immediately phoned CREEP's Magruder, indicating, according to Magruder, that "the president wanted—he always used 'the President'—to get this thing off the dime, get it going."

Nixon by now had reason for confidence about his showing in the election. Muskie still looked quite good in the polls but was faltering in the face of the White House counteroffensive. The president thought the liberal Senator George McGovern, though steadily moving up, would be an easy opponent to beat. He was not complacent, however. George Wallace, whom all of Nixon's maneuvering had failed to remove from the race, was running well enough to erode the Republican vote.

This time around, however, it was not sufficient that Nixon merely win. As Colson has expressed it, "We wanted a coronation; we wanted the power that went with the biggest landslide in history."

On March 30, in a house owned by Bebe Rebozo on Key Biscayne, Magruder attended another planning meeting with John Mitchell. There, according to Magruder, Mitchell gave the go-ahead for a scaled-down version of the Liddy plan.[12] The project was then memorialized in a Political Action Memorandum and was on the agenda when, only days later, Mitchell met with Haldeman.

The president's closest aide, it now seems certain, was notified that the project had been authorized. A document that surfaced only in the nineties, a Talking Paper written to prepare Haldeman for the meeting with Mitchell, includes a paragraph headed "Intelligence" that begins: "Gordon Liddy's intelligence operation proposal ($300)* has been approved. Now you may want to cover with Mitchell who will be privy to the information."

Not long after the Mitchell meeting, moreover, Haldeman ordered that Liddy was to shift his "capability" away from Muskie to the Democrat now gaining ground, McGovern.

*This means $300,000. It was the latest cut-back budget.

It seems more than possible that Nixon too knew about the Liddy project. Haldeman's diary and White House logs indicate that Mitchell saw the president, as well as Haldeman, on the very day the Talking Paper featuring the "intelligence operation" was to be discussed.

One copy of the document is marked with a ringed letter that may be a *P* at its top right-hand corner. If the original bore such a *P*, Haldeman's regular abbreviation for the president—with a check mark through it—that would indicate that Nixon almost certainly read or discussed it. We do not have the original, however, because it was one of the documents consigned to the shredder, on Haldeman's orders, at the onset of the Watergate crisis.[13]

Nixon was later to deny that CREEP's intelligence plan was discussed at the meeting, and the tape of the relevant Oval Office conversation contains no reference to it. He also insisted, on another White House recording: "I didn't talk to Mitchell about this matter. . . . I never met with him alone." That statement has been disputed by Alexander Butterfield, whose job required him to be privy to Nixon's White House movements hour by hour. Butterfield recalled that during the campaign "the president met with John Mitchell almost every night, over in the Executive Office Building."

Microphones had been installed in Nixon's office at the EOB, but Mitchell spoke privately of campaign discussions with the president that occurred in locations where there were none. "I usually met with the President in his living quarters or talked to him on a secure line," he told Rabbi Baruch Korff, one of Nixon's most vocal supporters during the Watergate struggle.

Many of the meetings in the spring of 1972, Mitchell said, were held in the solarium and kitchen of the White House. "No one was present—no one was allowed." Even family members, and Nixon's valet, were warned to keep their distance. "I never did anything," Mitchell added, "without his approval."

The exchange with Mitchell, Korff recalled, reminded him of something odd Nixon was to say to him after the resignation, a curious question reminiscent of Nixon's musings to Haldeman and Egil Krogh on whether he had after all ordered the break-in at the office of Ellsberg's psychiatrist's office. "Don't you think," he was to ask Korff, speaking this time of Watergate, "that everyone agrees now that I didn't know beforehand of the burglary?"

"That was the moment," Korff, so long Nixon's loyal defender, reflected in 1995, "I realized that if he told the whole truth, he might never recover, privately or publicly."

According to three key witnesses, discussion of Liddy's "intelligence project" included talk of breaking into the Democratic National Committee offices almost from the start. As of March, it also included plans to make "entries" at the Fontainebleau Hotel in Miami, site of the Democratic convention, and at the headquarters of whichever candidate the Democrats picked.

The priority target, though, was the Democratic National Committee headquarters in the Watergate building.

Hunt and Liddy had been frantically busy with nefarious projects since the start of the year. There had been a handful of break-ins, in Washington and farther afield, that none would connect with them until long afterward.[14] They had also been recruiting foot soldiers, a motley all-purpose crew from Miami. All were anti-Castro Cuban exiles except for one, Frank Sturgis, an ex-marine deeply involved in the exile cause.

On May 2 the foot soldiers were summoned to action in the streets of Washington. FBI Director Hoover had died in his sleep, a loss that Nixon would come to regret. At the time, however, he is said to have greeted the news with a prolonged silence, followed by "Jesus Christ! That old cocksucker!" Then, having ordered a display of national mourning, he followed up with a truly bizarre command.

For several weeks now the president had been raging about the new Communist offensive in Vietnam. "The bastards have never been bombed like they're going to be bombed this time," he had told Haldeman and Mitchell. He ordered ever mightier strikes, and his behavior at times seemed especially erratic. Once he burst into a meeting in the White House press office, kicked press spokesman Ron Ziegler's desk, and demanded that the North Vietnamese always be termed "the enemy." "The Old Man's really high again," Ziegler had murmured, as the door closed behind him.

As the flags drooped at half-mast, and Hoover's body lay in state in the Rotunda of the Capitol, word came that an antiwar demonstration was to take place on the Mall. The cursed Daniel Ellsberg would be in attendance, and a Viet Cong flag would be flying. A ludicrous directive now issued forth from the Oval Office, in the form of a call from Colson to CREEP's Magruder, passed down the line to Gordon Liddy.

"The president is really pissed about the Viet Cong flag" was how Liddy recalled the message. ". . . Do you think your guys could break [the rally] up and get it?" The flag was to be seized, he was told, and presented to Nixon as a trophy.

The following evening, as demonstrators intoned the names of the Vietnam dead, a group of strangers erupted on the scene, fists flying and shouting abuse. Hunt's Cubans had been flown from Miami to Washington, first class, and then briefed. Shown a picture of Ellsberg, they were told: "Our mission is to hit him, call him a traitor, and punch him in the nose. Hit him and run."

The Miamians did manage to provoke a melee. Two were briefly arrested but then released when a man in civilian clothes had a word with the police. Although a man close by him took a punch, Ellsberg was unharmed. The president never got his Viet Cong flag, for there was none to capture.

As Nixon readied for a groundbreaking trip to Moscow, the first ever by an American president, a new proposal came to Howard Hunt. On May 15, while campaigning in a Washington suburb, George Wallace was shot by a revolver-toting gunman wearing a red, white, and blue shirt and a campaign button. The assailant, an apparently deranged twenty-two-year old named Arthur Bremer, was seized at the scene. Wallace, his spinal cord severely damaged, was paralyzed for life.[15]

Nixon's public posture was one of sympathy and concern. He was to write in his memoirs that the news was "terrible and stunning," and he offered a lump-in-throat description of a hospital visit to his gravely wounded opponent. The president's conversations behind the scenes, however, were utterly cynical and triggered the summons to Hunt.

Reconstructing the events from several sources, including recently released Nixon tapes, the following scenario emerges: Nixon was "agitated" when informed of the shooting, and "voiced immediate concern that the assassin might have ties to the Republican party or, even worse, to the President's Re-election Committee." Were that to have been the case, Colson was to note, "it could have cost the President the election."

Within three hours, before any details about the assassin were clear, a White House aide announced to the press that papers found in Bremer's Milwaukee apartment linked him to "leftist" causes, perhaps to the campaign of Senator McGovern. "What matters for the next 24–48 hours is the story," Nixon would tell colleagues the next morning, according to Haldeman's diary. "Don't worry about doing it all by the book. The problem is who wins the public opinion on it. It's all P.R. at this point."

His real view was in fact even blunter. The president recalled that day that he had recently told the new attorney general, Richard Kleindienst, that there were "times when it's best that the Justice Department not know . . . we'll tell you what we think you need to know." Now was one of those times, and the president urged aides to use the acting FBI director, Pat Gray, as "an accomplice." Meanwhile he exhorted them: "Use Colson's outfit, you know, to sneak out things. I mean, he'll do anything. *I mean, anything!*"

Nixon spent the hours after the Wallace shooting drinking and dining with Colson, pestering the FBI for half-hourly updates, and plotting ways to bend the truth. "We sat there for a couple of hours," Colson recalled, "Nixon having a cocktail, he's sitting there with his feet back, we're waiting for the FBI to call . . . he would say, 'Wouldn't it be great if they had left-wing propaganda in [the assassin's] apartment? . . . Too bad we couldn't get somebody in there to plant it. . . .'"

Attributing the idea for this mischief to the president may have been buckpassing on Colson's part, but it is clear that the pair colluded in the matter. A snatch of the evening's exchanges between Nixon and Colson, taped off Nixon's telephone, recorded this dialogue between the president and his trusted aide:

PRESIDENT NIXON: Is he a left-winger, right-winger?

COLSON: Well, he's going to be a left-winger by the time we get through, I think.

PRESIDENT NIXON: (chuckling) Good. Keep at that. Keep at that.

COLSON: Yeah. I just wish that, God, that I'd thought sooner about planting a little literature out there.

PRESIDENT NIXON: Hah! Ha, ha, ha!

COLSON: It may be a little late, although I've got one source that maybe . . .

PRESIDENT NIXON: Good.

COLSON: You could think about that. I mean, if they found it near his apartment that would be helpful.

That evening, Colson later told the FBI, he placed a call to the man he had in mind for the task, Howard Hunt. Hunt was to fly to Milwaukee, where the would-be assassin had lived, and penetrate Bremer's apartment. To obtain entry, Colson suggested, Hunt could "bribe the janitor or pick the lock." According to Hunt, he pointed out that it was too late, that the apartment would now be sealed and virtually impenetrable. Colson called off the mission the following day.[16]

The president's entire election strategy, a senior colleague recalled, had been based on whether Wallace ran or not. That spring, Theodore White observed, "With the needle sticking at 43% of the vote for Nixon, the President was still vulnerable—until, of course, May 15 and the shooting. Then it was all over."

Wallace's effective removal from the race was so decisive, in Nixon's favor, that some serious commentators later considered the possibility that the attempt to kill him was—as *Washington Post* managing editor Howard Simons put it—"the ultimate dirty trick," that the assassin might have been put up to the deed by Nixon's men. There were indeed troubling aspects to the case, and Wallace himself harbored suspicions until his death in 1998.[17]

The notion that the White House sanctioned murder cannot be dismissed out of hand as a melodramatic conspiracy theory. A man since convicted of the murder of a Massachusetts policeman, William Gilday, has claimed since 1974—in communications with the *New York Times* and others, including this author—that Nixon aides had asked him and a crony as early as 1970, in Boston, to take part in schemes ranging from dirty tricks to murder.

Those he was incited to kill, Gilday has said, included Senator Edward Kennedy and George Wallace. The aides in question are unnamed here for legal reasons, but Gilday has appeared to have knowledge of corroborating details—their nicknames, for example—and has provided reconnaissance photographs he said were taken with Kennedy's murder in view.

In one of Nixon's most conspiratorial taped conversations, recorded after Watergate, he discussed with Colson the mistakes that had been made in mounting operations that were "very close to me."

"I did things out of Boston," Colson replied. "We did some blackmail and . . . my God, uh, uh, uh, I'll go to my grave before I ever disclose it. But, uh, we did a hell of a lot of things and never got caught . . . you had one of the men who was in line at your Christmas tree lighting reception who ran 15 or 20 black projects in Boston, and that'll never be traced. No way. And I could under oath say I didn't know how it happened . . . that's the way to do it." Nixon listened without demur.

Only years later did it become known that Hunt and Liddy had had detailed discussions on how to get rid of the columnist Jack Anderson. Anderson, successor to Nixon's perennial critic Drew Pearson, had repeatedly enraged the president with his revelations: of secret payments to Nixon from Howard Hughes; of settlement of an antitrust suit against International Telephone and Telegraph, apparently in return for a huge cash contribution to fund the Republican convention; of Nixon's support of Pakistan in its recent conflict with India over Bangladesh—a war in which the United States was supposedly neutral—in which an estimated million Bengalis died and many times that number became refugees.

Anderson and Pearson, Ehrlichman observed, were Nixon's "deadliest foes" in the media. Only in 1975, when official inquiries were winding down, would information reach Watergate investigators that the president's fury had led to talk of murder.

"They charged us with the task: 'Come up with ways of stopping Anderson . . .'" Liddy has said. "We examined all of the alternatives and very quickly came to the conclusion the only way you're going to be able to stop him is to kill him. . . . And that was the recommendation."

According to Liddy, he and Hunt debated ways of killing Anderson at a meeting with a CIA physician in early 1972. The options included a covertly administered dose of LSD that would cause Anderson to crash his car, a deliberate collision designed to be fatal, and "aspirin roulette," the placing of a poisoned tablet in the appropriate bottle in the journalist's medicine cabinet. It was agreed after some debate to recommend that Anderson "should just become a fatal victim of the notorious Washington street-crime rate." Eventually, however, word came down that murder was "too severe a sanction."

Hunt has never publicly acknowledged the murder planning but said in an affidavit that Colson settled "on a concept that would have Anderson appear to be drunk or incoherent during one of his TV or radio appearances." "It would be great," Colson had exclaimed, "to make it look as though he's blown his mind." The discussion with the CIA doctor about covert drug doses, Hunt maintained, had been pursued not with murder in mind but with the idea of discrediting Anderson by making him appear insane. Hunt said in passing that he had proposed the same treatment for Daniel Ellsberg.

Both Ellsberg and Anderson escaped unscathed, but some CIA staffers reportedly believed that Edmund Muskie had not. The public breakdown that wrecked the senator's campaign, some officials suspected, had been caused by "Howard Hunt or his henchmen spiking his drink with a sophisticated form of LSD."

The truth of that rumor may never be known. A disquieting possibility, though, emerges from Hunt's affidavit on the meeting that set him off on a search for ways to silence Jack Anderson. "Colson seemed more than usually agitated," Hunt recalled, "and I formed the impression that he had just come from a meeting with President Nixon."

By May 1972 Nixon had cause to be more confident than ever about winning the election. The polls showed him pulling strongly ahead of McGovern, the surviving Democratic front-runner. With Wallace crippled and soon to be out of the race, there was little real competition.

Behind the scenes, though, the "political intelligence" operation trundled on, some of its schemes relatively harmless. In line with other CREEP propaganda, phony polls, and trumped-up letters and telegrams, Liddy had Miami Cubans stage a demonstration backing Nixon's latest bombing in Vietnam.

After the abortive attempt to beat up Daniel Ellsberg, Hunt and Liddy had driven around Washington one night on a reconnaissance mission with three of their men. The bright lights around Senator McGovern's headquarters, Liddy had remarked, would have to be dealt with before any break-in was attempted. (He was to shoot them out later with a pistol.) Then the group had headed down Virginia Avenue, past the Democratic National Committee offices in the great curved complex called Watergate. "That's our next job," Liddy said, pointing.

Preparations for two bugging operations were already well in hand. The electronics man, McCord, had reconnoitered the McGovern building on the evening of the day Wallace was shot. There were problems there, so the team concentrated first on the Watergate. His masters, Liddy confided, were especially eager to target the office and nearby apartment of Nixon's old foe, DNC Chairman Lawrence O'Brien.

Early in May there was an unexplained break-in of offices in the Watergate two floors above the Democratic headquarters. Another occurred, within the complex but in another building, at law offices used by four leading Democrats, two of them on Nixon's Enemies list.[18]

McCord meanwhile brought on board two new men. Former FBI agent Alfred Baldwin was used first as a security guard for John Mitchell's wife and then for a little spying on Capitol Hill offices, pending bigger assignments. The second recruit, whose name to this day remains virtually unknown to the general public, had a link to the president himself.

Louis Russell was yet another former FBI man. Two decades earlier, as a congressional investigator, he had worked closely with Nixon on the Hiss case. In the fifties he was recruited for the operation Nixon sanctioned while vice president against shipping tycoon Aristotle Onassis. In the late sixties he had been hired by another member of the coterie of Washington investigators, one with links to key Nixon associates, Caulfield, Chotiner, Colson, and Mitchell.

A year into the presidency, having requested an appointment with Nixon himself, Russell had visited with Rose Woods at the White House. He wanted a job, and Woods wrote to the White House personnel department on his behalf. A report on Russell was later sent to Attorney General Mitchell, and the former agent lunched with William Birely, a Washington stockbroker who had long been friendly with Nixon and his secretary.

Russell worked on the continuing White House probe of Chappaquiddick and, according to his daughter, was used as a courier to carry large sums of cash. Then, in 1972, he began working for CREEP. His known responsibilities included running staff security checks, researching leftist newspapers, and— the latest stage of what had now become a White House preoccupation— investigating the columnist Jack Anderson.

This operative with a personal connection to the president, however, had a special qualification. It can hardly be a coincidence that before joining CREEP, Russell had worked for the security service that protected the Watergate.[19]

On the night of May 22 Richard Nixon was in Moscow, keyed up in anticipation of tough negotiations with the Soviets. Sleep eluded him, and the hours before dawn found him wandering the enclosed courtyards of the Kremlin. During the ten-day trip abroad, and in spite of the momentous foreign policy issues he had to wrestle with, the president was to hold regular meetings on the situation at home. "He never loosened his grip on White House operations," a senior correspondent reported.

In Washington that same night six of Howard Hunt's Cubans were settling into the Manger Hamilton Hotel, a dozen blocks from the Watergate. Four days later, as Nixon and Kissinger struggled through the last phase of a complex arms negotiation, the Cubans moved to rooms at the Watergate Hotel— directly behind the Democratic National Committee's offices.

Hunt's men were now posing as businessmen and using aliases. Across Virginia Avenue, at a Howard Johnson's, McCord's man Alfred Baldwin waited with equipment that picked up radio transmissions from bugs. "We're going to put some units across the street," McCord had told him, "and you are going to be monitoring."

No bugs were planted in the Democrats' phones that night or the next, for Hunt and his burglars twice failed to get in. On May 28 they finally made a successful entry. Hunt's Cubans photographed papers on O'Brien's desk, and McCord, according to his later testimony, placed bugging devices, miniature transmitters, on two telephones, one in the office of Spencer Oliver, head of the association of Democratic state chairmen, the other on the phone of O'Brien's secretary, on a line she shared with her boss.[20]

Five thousand miles away in Moscow, Nixon would later note without a hint of irony, he refrained from his usual daily dictation of his diary "because of the pervasive bugging." "The Soviets were curiously unsubtle in this regard," he wrote in his memoirs. "A member of my staff reported having casually told his secretary that he would like an apple, and ten minutes later a maid came in and put a bowl of apples on the table. . . ."

As Nixon began his homeward journey, via Iran and Poland, Baldwin sat in the Howard Johnson's listening to the first bugged conversations transmitted from the DNC. The logs of these conversations, which were passed on to Liddy, were deeply disappointing. No transmissions had been picked up from the device McCord said he had placed on O'Brien's office phone. The conversations intercepted on Oliver's phone, meanwhile, apparently contained little or nothing of political value.

The high-risk, expensive venture was so far a virtual failure, a result that was met with irritation. Although smartly typed up on GEMSTONE stationery and presented in envelopes marked "SENSITIVE" and "EX DIS"—for executive distribution only—the executive recipients greeted the edited logs with derision.

Magruder, backed up by testimony from his assistant, later said he showed the material to John Mitchell. "This stuff," Mitchell reportedly grunted, "isn't worth the paper it's printed on."[21]

Magruder also asserted that, deeming the logs "too sensitive" for the internal mail, he had Haldeman's aide Gordon Strachan come over to CREEP's office to peruse them. Later Liddy faced criticism over their contents. "Strachan called me to the White House," he recalled, "and told me that the original submissions from the electronic surveillance were unsatisfactory. I assumed he was speaking for Haldeman."

For Haldeman to have admitted any knowledge of the bugging would have brought the responsibility for Watergate too close to himself and by implication to the president. "To the best of my knowledge," Nixon's chief of staff said on oath before the Senate Watergate Committee, "I did not see any material produced by the bugging. . . ." It was a carefully qualified denial and, when asked in court if he had known of espionage against the Democrats before June 1972, he refused to reply "on advice of counsel."

Under cross-examination, though, Haldeman slipped up. Immediately after the Watergate arrests, he testified, he told Strachan to check the file to see "whether any result of bugging the Democratic National Committee had been provided to us." Unfortunately for Haldeman's credibility, at that time only the burglars themselves and their controllers had any *idea* there had been a break-in, or any bugging, that could have produced a "result."

Haldeman had lied under oath for Nixon before, during the lawsuit over operations against the Democrats in 1962. He had all the more reason to lie over prior Oval Office knowledge of the Watergate bugging.[22]

The president had returned from his foreign trip four days after the planting of the bugs. He was still fretting about the election, even though new polls showed him now way ahead of McGovern, by 54 percent to 38 percent. At a meeting at Camp David Haldeman received fresh campaign orders from his boss: "We need savage attack lines. . . . Get McGovern tied as an extremist." The Nixon tapes show that the president urged Colson at this time to get the Secret Service to spy on McGovern. Confidential information was subsequently picked up by an agent on the senator's detail and passed to the White House.

Another idea, Nixon suggested, was to hire a tame reporter that "just covers the son of a bitch like a blanket." "That business of the McGovern watch," he insisted, "it just has to be—it has to be, now, around the clock."

That conversation took place on June 13. The previous day Liddy had promised CREEP's Magruder that he was planning to "hit McGovern headquarters" within days. Magruder, for his part, wanted another entry to Watergate, to rifle the files and to get the defective bug fixed or replaced.

John Mitchell would later deny having known anything about bugging by the organization he headed. Colson's testimony, however, suggests otherwise. That same week, Colson said, he and Mitchell sat speculating about what strategy would emerge from a meeting of top Democrats at a New York hotel. "Tell me what room they are in," Mitchell said with a half-smile, "and I will tell you everything that is said in that room."

On June 15, at a meeting with Mitchell, Liddy handed over the accumulated logs; some two hundred calls had by then been monitored by the bug that was functioning. He promised new action to deal with the faulty device said to have been planted in O'Brien's office. "The problem we have," he told the man running Nixon's election campaign, "will be corrected this weekend, sir." Mitchell just nodded.

But the question remains: Why? Why, especially, was Lawrence O'Brien being targeted?

30

My God! The Committee isn't worth bugging in my opinion. That's my public line.

—Richard Nixon, in the first-known recorded White House conversation
after the Watergate arrests, June 20, 1972

Despite all the official probes, the trials of the miscreants involved, and the massive efforts of scholars and reporters, no one has ever convincingly established the motive for the Watergate break-ins.

Determining precisely why Nixon's men went into the Watergate, U.S. District Court Chief Judge John Sirica was to assert when the burglars' trial got under way, was "the basic issue." "To this day," Haldeman was still claiming in the late eighties, "I still don't know why that was done."

One might have expected the burglars themselves, the men charged with the mission, to have known what their goal was when cameras at the ready, they made their furtive way into the Democratic offices. "We were looking for both general and specific information," Howard Hunt was to say. "The specific information was the contribution lists. By going through these we hoped to find, and tracing back the names, a source of foreign funding."

That was their mission, according to Hunt and some of his accomplices. The Democratic candidate-to-be, Senator McGovern, was pressing for a normalization of relations with Castro's Cuba—anathema to Nixon and his supporters—and CREEP had received intelligence "that the Cuban government was supplying funds to the Democratic Party campaign."[1] It was a strange notion, but would be catastrophically damaging to McGovern if it could be proved.

This explanation has been dismissed as merely a ruse, fed to the burglars to fire up their anti-Castro zeal. But would it not have been pointless to instruct them to seek out something so specific had it not been the real target? There is evidence, moreover, that they searched for precisely that.

"One of the things we were looking for," Frank Sturgis was to recall, "was a thick secret memorandum from the Castro government, addressed confidentially to the Democrats' platform committee. We knew that this secret memorandum existed—knew it for a fact—because both the CIA and the FBI had found references to it. . . . But we wanted the entire document . . . it was more than one hundred thirty typed pages, according to our information. . . . We looked high and low . . . and although we found a piece of it one night at another office, we never did find the entire thing."[2]

The elusive document, Sturgis explained, not only was valuable as the proof of an alleged Castro deal with the Democrats but was prefaced by "a long, detailed listing of all the covert espionage and sabotage the CIA and the DIA [Defense Intelligence Agency] and the various joint operations groups have launched against Cuba . . . the complaints were especially bitter about the various attempts made to assassinate the Castro brothers."[3]

Therein does lie a compelling motive. As reported earlier, the columnist Jack Anderson had in 1971 published sensational revelations regarding the assassination plots against Castro, stories stating that the murder plans had been initiated during the Eisenhower administration. They had stopped short, though, of exploring Nixon's hidden role. At the White House meanwhile, as reported earlier, Nixon had repeatedly asked to see the CIA's files on the "Bay of Pigs." That was when Ehrlichman had noted, significantly, that the president wanted to know what he might need to "duck" for purposes of self-protection.

At one point it had seemed possible that Robert Maheu, the CIA's go-between with the mobsters used in the plots, might tell what he knew. John Mitchell, however, had quietly ensured his silence.[4] If Maheu had dangerous secrets, though, so did Johnny Rosselli, one of the key gangsters involved in the plots. And Rosselli was talking—to the columnist Jack Anderson.

The Watergate prosecutors were to interrogate Rosselli, and their line of questioning—his attorney Leslie Scherr believed—indicated clearly what they believed to be the motive for the operation. The break-ins occurred "because Nixon or somebody in the Republican Party suspected that the Democrats had information as to Nixon's involvement with the CIA's original contact with Rosselli. [The Republicans] felt that a document existed showing Nixon was involved with or knew what was going on with the CIA and the assassination of Castro . . . they wanted to try to get this information that Nixon suspected they were going to try to use against him."

In his first efforts to prevent a serious investigation of Watergate, in discussions recorded on the White House tapes, the president would allude repeatedly to the Bay of Pigs. His aides, he said, were to have the CIA tell the FBI: ". . . Hunt . . . that will uncover a lot . . . you open that scab there's a hell of a lot of things in it that we just feel that this would be very detrimental to have this thing go any further. . . . When you get [the CIA] people in say, 'Look, the problem is that this will open the whole, the whole Bay of Pigs thing, and the President just feels that'—without going into the details—'that we wish for the country, don't go any further into this case, period. . . .'"

Later the same day, still discussing how Haldeman could approach the CIA, Nixon would suggest telling the agency: ". . . very bad to have this fellow Hunt, ah, you know . . . he *knows* too damn *much* and he *was* involved, we happen to know that. . . ." As a CIA officer in 1960 Howard Hunt had been one of the very first to suggest the murder plotting against Castro in which Nixon was implicated.[5]

Senate Watergate Committee counsel Terry Lenzner also thought the Cuban angle was probably the key to Watergate. "The obsession of the administration in keeping tabs on Larry O'Brien in 1971 and 1972," he theorized in a memo, "was in part motivated by fear that Maheu would impart some of his sensitive information about the plot to O'Brien. Alternatively the objective was to discover if there was any information about the plot that might be damaging to the Democrats."[6]

Lawrence O'Brien knew Howard Hughes aide Maheu because he himself had worked as a consultant to the Hughes organization early in the Nixon presidency. That connection made Nixon vulnerable in yet another way. What might O'Brien have learned from Maheu of the sums that had flowed to Nixon from Hughes since 1968? What of the favors apparently done for Hughes in return for his largess?[7]

In his memoirs Haldeman reconstructed a conversation with Nixon that, he suggested, had occurred immediately after the Watergate arrests. As he recalled it, Nixon had said: "Colson can talk about the President, if he cracks. You know I was on Colson's tail for months to nail Larry O'Brien on the Hughes deal. Colson told me he was going to get the information I wanted one way or the other. And that was O'Brien's office they were bugging, wasn't it? Colson's boy, Hunt. Christ."

Nixon's people had in fact been on O'Brien's tail for far longer than six months. Two years before Watergate a Haldeman memo had referred to "Operation O'Brien," designed to "keep the heat on the DNC and O'Brien." Murray Chotiner reported that he was making checks on O'Brien in nine states, checks too sensitive, he told Haldeman, to put in writing.

In January 1971, with little to show for such efforts, Nixon himself had dictated this memo aboard Air Force One:

MEMORANDUM FOR H. R. HALDEMAN
FROM THE PRESIDENT:

It would seem that the time is approaching when Larry O'Brien is held accountable for his retainer with Hughes. Bebe has some information on this although it is, of course, not solid but there is no question that one of Hughes' people did have O'Brien on a very heavy retainer for "services rendered" in the past. Perhaps Colson could make a check on this.

It was soon afterward, following some initial investigation, that an underling reported that "forced embarrassment of O'Brien" might well backfire and "shake loose some Republican skeletons."[8]

One of those skeletons had already rattled—namely, the Castro plot scenario as published by Jack Anderson. The columnist would soon bring forth another, publishing the first story on the Hughes handout that was later to lead to a huge investigation. A hundred thousand dollars, according to the Anderson reports, had been "siphoned off" from the Silver Slipper casino in Las Vegas and passed to Bebe Rebozo.

Nevertheless, Nixon never let up in the targeting of O'Brien. "I said: 'Get the word out down to the IRS that I want them to conduct field audits,'" he admitted long afterward, "and I suggested that one they ought to look into was O'Brien. . . ." O'Brien later recalled having been "attacked by the IRS . . . subjected to a series of audits in 1971 and 1972 . . . and concluded I was stuck in the computer. I was to learn otherwise. . . . What the President had engaged in was to misuse the power of the Internal Revenue Service."

No irregularities of any significance emerged from the IRS investigation of O'Brien. Meanwhile, a familiar distressing message went back to the White House. A probe of the Hughes operations, an IRS official reported, had turned up instead "possible wrongdoing by Mr. Rebozo and Mr. Nixon, the President's brother or brothers. . . ."

The months before the Watergate break-in brought new trouble due to the Hughes connection and covert attempts to counter it. "Attorney General called today about the Howard Hughes problem," Haldeman noted in his diary in January 1972. The "problem" had been the publication of one of several books dealing with the Nixon-Hughes relationship, all of them embarrassing.

The infamous Clifford Irving "as told to" portrait of Hughes was ultimately exposed as a fake and canceled, but only after having generated headlines on the Nixon side of the story that came perilously close to the truth. The work of another author on Hughes, Benjamin Schemmer, never got beyond the manuscript stage for very different reasons.

First, someone broke into Schemmer's office and stole tape recordings of key interviews. Then his publisher, Grosset and Dunlap, canceled the book as it was going to press, a decision Grosset's attorney attributed to "White House pressure." A Hughes executive told Schemmer: "Attorney General Mitchell has seen and read your book. The problem is at the White House."

In May, Mitchell and Ehrlichman received a long memo about yet another book, this one just published, titled *The Nixon-Hughes Loan*. It had been sent to them by Gordon Liddy, just two weeks before Liddy's team broke into the offices of the Democratic National Committee for the first time.

In 1987 Liddy's former boss at CREEP stated publicly that it was indeed the Hughes connection that was the motive for Watergate. "It was a planned burglary," Jeb Magruder told a Hofstra University conference. "As far as I know the primary purpose of the break-in was to deal with information . . . about Howard Hughes and Larry O'Brien, and what that meant as far as the cash that had supposedly been given to Bebe Rebozo and spent later by the President possibly."[9]

That claim corresponds to what we now know Magruder said in private as Watergate began to drag Nixon down. Quoting Magruder, Haldeman scrawled this note: "Plan hatched here—Hunt, Liddy & Cols[on]. Cols[on] called Jeb twice—to get on this thing. Specifically L. O'Brien info re. Fla [Florida] dlgs [dealings]." "[Florida] dealings" is understandable here only if it refers to the cash that Rebozo, in Key Biscayne, had received from a Hughes emissary. Liddy, citing Magruder's orders for the second—fatal—break-in, later claimed the objective was "to find out what O'Brien had of a derogatory nature about us, not for us to get something on him or the Democrats."

It seems they did find something of relevance during the break-in at the Watergate. In a 1973 conversation with Nixon on the White House tapes, Colson responded to a suggestion by the president that "we didn't get a goddamn thing" from the operation. "Well, apparently we did, of course," said the aide, "mainly Hughes. . . ."

Was the Hughes information, then, the reason for the operation that was to destroy Nixon? More likely, taking all the evidence together, CREEP's motivations were multiple and catholic. The raids were both offensive and defensive and targeted a number of political vulnerabilities. That general concept brings us to the wild card in the pack of possible motives: sexual scandal.

From the start of the Nixon presidency, as one of the White House operatives was to testify, "background checks" were conducted on individuals' personal lives, to find out if they were heavy drinkers, what sort of sex lives they had. The same tactics were a factor in Watergate. The man who monitored the functioning DNC bug, Alfred Baldwin, told prosecutors that his orders were to monitor "all telephone calls . . . including personal calls." Special attention, he said recently, was to be given to those of a "sexual" nature.

Precisely what Baldwin actually overheard in this regard cannot be established, in part because of court restrictions imposed to protect those whose privacy the bugging had invaded.[10] Soon after the Watergate arrests, though,

Baldwin would confirm that some of the conversations he eavesdropped on concerned "personal matters." "With several secretaries and others using the phone, apparently in the belief it was one of the more private lines," he said in an interview, "some conversations were explicitly intimate."

The prosecutor in the Watergate break-in case, Earl Silbert, concluded on the basis of Baldwin's description while under interrogation that the conversations had been "extremely personal, intimate, and potentially embarrassing." Who made the calls? "I don't know if you had one very active secretary or you had ten," Baldwin said recently. "I don't know if you had one very active male or if you had ten . . . there were a lot of calls of a sexual nature."

The phone on which the conversations took place was in the office of thirty-five-year-old Democratic official Spencer Oliver. CREEP's Jeb Magruder, who saw Baldwin's logs, brought up Oliver's name when John Ehrlichman questioned him during the Watergate crisis. Ehrlichman's handwritten notes of the meeting include the name "Oliver" followed closely by "sex."

"What they were getting," Ehrlichman told Nixon the same afternoon, "was mostly this fellow Oliver phoning his girlfriends all over the country lining up assignations."[11] Oliver, today a top official with the Organization for Security and Cooperation in Europe, was a prime mover in ensuring that the content of the bugs was not revealed in court.

The woman at the DNC who in recent years has drawn the most attention is Maxie Wells, at the time Oliver's twenty-three-year-old secretary. By her account, she was "completely naïve and innocent," a music major from a small town in Mississippi. Months after Watergate, when she had left the DNC and the Democrats brought a civil suit against the burglars for invasion of privacy, she would write to a girlfriend:

> I've developed a crisis. . . . I'm flying up tomorrow to talk to
> Spencer and the DNC lawyers. . . . It appears that the Republicans
> are going to try to discredit Demo. witnesses on moral grounds . . .
> I am really upset and nervous. . . . I may have to bare (or bear) all
> in court . . . better get rid of this, I shouldn't write, but must confide
> in someone. . . . If you talk to God in the next few days remind him
> about your friend who needs help keeping her nose clean.

> *Love, Max*

Testifying in 1997, in a more recent lawsuit, Wells said that while working at the DNC, she thought her life "pretty wild by the standards of where I grew up. Living in a house with five men, dating several different people, working for a man who was rumored to have numerous affairs, and gossiping on the phone about it with my friend."

Wells said she was "kind of appalled by a lot of the romantic and sexual behavior I saw going on at the DNC. . . . People were just sleeping with each other kind of indiscriminately, I thought, not real relationships, but one-night stands and things like that. That was pretty wild stuff to me." So she gossiped, she said, especially on the internal phone with her friend Marty Sampson, who worked in an office a few floors below. "I bet," she said, "we gossiped about every single person we knew at the DNC . . . it was kind of crude sometimes. . . . Marty and I gossiped about adultery."

Her own chatter aside, Wells said, other secretaries took advantage of the fact that the phone in question was in a room that was often unoccupied to "[talk] to their sweeties on the phone."

Was that all that took place, then, on the infamous bugged phone at the Democratic headquarters? Conversation about personal relationships and secretaries' gossip? Some suspect not, noting that when arrested, one of the Watergate burglars would have with him a key to a drawer in Maxie Wells' desk. Reasonably enough, such researchers have concluded that her desk was a specific target for the burglars.[12]

Phillip Bailley, a former Washington lawyer convicted in 1972 of pimping, has claimed that a secretary at the DNC was used as a go-between with prostitutes based at the Columbia Plaza, the huge apartment complex nearby. This secretary, he said, would provide would-be customers with photographs of available whores. Then, unknown to Oliver, a phone in his office was used to set up specific assignations.[13]

As reported earlier, one element of Gordon Liddy's "intelligence" plan had envisaged the employment of prostitutes. Everyone privy to the plan admitted later that he hoped to put into action, as John Mitchell put it, "the call girl bit," the houseboat at the Democratic convention, wired for sound, to which classy-looking women would lure leading Democrats and try to get information out of them.

A madam he had located in Baltimore, Liddy told colleagues, promised "girls who can be trained and programmed," and there was later discussion— after the houseboat plan had been shelved—of using prostitutes in Washington. Howard Hunt later told one of his accomplices that he feared "accusations about prostitutes" would come out at his trial.

While one aide has said that Nixon's top men were too straitlaced ever to have approved such antics, another—one of Ehrlichman's assistants—stated in an interview that Nixon and Haldeman both had "perverted interests in their surveillance activities."

Prostitutes did operate in the apartment complex near the Watergate, a fact confirmed by police arrest records, interviews with former policemen, and by former Assistant U.S. Attorney John Rudy, who investigated call girl operations in the spring of 1972.

The author, for his part, located Barbara Ralabate, a former madam once known in the trade as Lil Lori. Ralabate's criminal history reflects several prostitution-related arrests, one of them just before CREEP's burglars turned their attention to the Watergate. Now a middle-aged woman living far from the capital, she readily acknowledged having managed call girls operating at different times out of apartments 204 and 901 at the Columbia Plaza.

Her professionalism would not allow Ralabate to divulge clients' names, and she would say only that they included both Republicans and Democrats. "I'd give them nicknames, and I knew them by voice," she said. "If I knew their voice they could come . . . that's how secretive I was. It kept me out of trouble because so many people were political. It's a political town."

"That's the way business was done," said Ralabate, when asked if it was plausible that a DNC phone had been used to make appointments. "That's the way politicians are, and every other business. Attorneys, they entertained their clients in those days too, especially in the Nixon days. . . . They were spending big money to entertain this politician or that politician to get things done. That's just the way it was."

Pressed on whether she herself had a special arrangement with the DNC, Ralabate replied with a smile, "I wouldn't tell you if I did." She did admit, however, that she had had "good friends . . . customers" among the Democratic staff. "There was a lot of business done at that place. . . . These people were good to me, trusted me."

Former Assistant U.S. Attorney Rudy, who investigated links between the Columbia Plaza prostitution and the DNC, was told Democrats were involved. He was also informed that a woman at the DNC "arranged for liaisons." Most startlingly, he revealed that some of the prostitutes' operations were filmed or tape-recorded.

A number of customers, Rudy learned, knowingly performed in front of a movie camera or with sound tapes turning because they wanted a record to keep for their own later pleasure. The police meanwhile had "phone taps . . . pursuant to a court order," and "perhaps other agencies . . . involved in some type of intelligence operations. I mean, it was a ball of wax." The ball of wax, Rudy added, included "people who were having illegal taps."

One of Rudy's sources was Lou Russell, the former FBI agent who had once worked with Nixon on the Hiss case and was employed by CREEP at the time of Watergate. Russell was on close terms with several Washington whores and their madams—he said specifically that he knew Ralabate— and by his own account made covert recordings of conversations between the Columbia Plaza girls and the DNC. An associate who came to know him in the months after Watergate, Robert Smith, actually listened to one of the tapes.

"I had three or four meetings with Russell," Smith told the author, "and among other things he claimed—and I have no reason to doubt it—that there was a tape recorder operating against a couple of prominent Democratic leaders. They were picking up these conversations in which they were making dates with women over the phone . . . for sexual liaison purposes." Russell told Smith and other associates that one of the senior Democrats involved was

DNC Chairman Lawrence O'Brien. He also named a prostitute O'Brien allegedly frequented.

Ralabate, the former Columbia Plaza madam, admitted in 1997 that she knew people involved with the Watergate break-in. She declined to elaborate but told of a visit by a senior Democrat at the height of the Watergate crisis. "I remember him talking with me on the balcony," she said. "He wanted to know what I was going to say when I was questioned, if I was questioned. I said: 'What I'm going to say is I don't know what anyone is talking about.' . . ."

Whatever the truth about the occupants of the Democratic offices and their neighbors the whores, the sex angle came up in the Oval Office a few months after Watergate. As Nixon sat discussing the situation with Haldeman and colleagues, John Dean briefed him on the lawsuit the Democratic National Committee had brought against CREEP. The burglars' attorney, Dean told the president, was "getting into the sex lives of some of the members of the DNC . . . he's working on an entrapment theory that they were hiding something or they had secret information, affairs to hide."

Three days earlier, in a memo to Haldeman headed "Counter Actions (Watergate)," Dean had written: "NOTE: Depositions are presently being taken of members of the DNC by the defense counsel in the O'Brien suit. These are wide ranging and will cover everything from Larry O'Brien's sources of income while Chairman of the DNC to *certain sexual activities of employees of the DNC. They should cause considerable problems for those deposed* [author's emphasis]."

The lawyer representing the burglars, Henry Rothblatt, has since died, but Liddy's attorney, Peter Maroulis, well remembered the nature of the sex activities Rothblatt hoped to use against the Democrats. "The Democrats," his fellow attorney had told him, "were using call girls."[14]

Potential embarrassment about prostitution, however, could cut both ways, as the Nixon White House well knew in the months before Watergate. In the fall of 1971 Charles Colson had received a tip from a *Life* magazine contact about a breaking story in New York. Bugs installed in a Manhattan brothel had led to exposure of a police protection scam. Now political scandal also loomed.

In a note to Colson, the *Life* reporter summarized what he had heard from the electronics man who had installed the bugs: "He said: 'I know a lot about that operation. There were a lot of politicians mixed up in it, even the White House.' I said: 'What are you talking about?' And then he brought up Mosbacher's name. . . ."

Emil Mosbacher was Nixon's chief of protocol, and the allegation was that he had taken prostitutes from the brothel by limousine to service clients elsewhere. The *Life* reporter believed his source was telling the truth.

Alerted by Colson, John Dean began making inquiries. Even before they were completed, however, the *New York Times* featured a story with an ominous headline: POSSIBLE BLACKMAIL OF NIXON OFFICIALS CHECKED HERE. "At least two high-ranking officials in the Nixon administration," ran the lead, "are among the people the Manhattan District Attorney's Office intends to question about the possibility that they were blackmailed because of their association with an East Side brothel."

The woman who had run the brothel, Xaviera Hollander, surfaced soon afterward with her book *The Happy Hooker,* an instant worldwide best seller. It contained no revelations about the Nixon White House, but allegations got into the press again, this time about "one of the hierarchy of the White House." In the spring of 1972, just weeks before the first Watergate break-in, Hollander was deported to Europe. The wiretapper who claimed his tapes proved a White House connection also left the country.

"Thank you, Tricky Dicky," Hollander wrote in the next edition of her book, for the pressure to deport her had apparently come from the top levels of the government. "The White House got her kicked out to stop her making a noise," said the author Robin Moore, who listened to the brothel tapes and worked with Hollander while ghosting her book. "The Nixon administration had been using the Hollander outfit to entertain foreign dignitaries, especially Arabs. It was organized by Nixon's press secretary, Ron Ziegler. It was taped. . . ."

Sometime after Nixon's resignation, in a report suppressed officially but leaked to the press, the House Intelligence Committee would reveal that the CIA had provided foreign heads of state with "female companions." Several leaders, including King Hussein of Jordan, had so benefited.

Watergate Special Prosecution Force attorney Carl Feldbaum, who had access to highly classified material, told the author in 1997 that documents he saw established that the Nixon administration "understood the CIA had a capability to provide hookers . . . when Emperor So-and-So, or a king or a president or premier comes to town and made known the creature comforts he was used to—whether he liked them tall and dark, blonde and petite or whatever his taste was. . . ."

Ron Ziegler has insisted he had nothing to do with providing sex for foreign guests. The very suggestion, he said, is "absurd." John Dean, however, recalled Ziegler going "white as a sheet" when asked if he had "anything to fear from Xaviera Hollander's address book." He replied, "I'll deny it," according to Dean, and over the weeks that followed frequently called the counsel's office asking for further developments.[15]

Protocol chief Mosbacher, whose primary responsibility was to look after foreign guests, resigned within days of the Watergate break-in, and has since died. So too has assistant protocol chief Nick Ruwe, the veteran aide Nixon placed in charge of all White House social events. Neither, obviously, could be interviewed for this book, but it seems Ruwe might have been a key source. "What do you do as deputy protocol chief?" Republican lawyer William Bagley once asked him during the presidency. "Well," he replied, "we have ten

Arabs coming to town, and they've ordered twenty prostitutes—none of them Jewish. . . ."

"Nick Ruwe," a longtime Nixon aide told the author on condition of anonymity, "was himself the biggest cocksman this town ever saw. He was a bachelor at the time. When our families were out at San Clemente, we'd go over to his place. And before the night was over, he'd have girls in there, and those of us that were frail and sissies would leave, and they'd party."

Comments by this source and by Nixon's top advance man, Ron Walker, along with other leads, suggest the White House indeed had secrets of a sexual nature to hide in early 1972. These were secrets much more directly damaging than those involving the Xaviera Hollander prostitution outfit in New York.

Walker was aware of the brothel next to the DNC at the time, he said in 1997. "I knew it from the Advance Office. I had colleagues that used call girl rings." One such colleague, said the aide who requested anonymity, was deputy protocol chief Ruwe, who "was always using those call girls at the place next to the DNC."

How the whores were employed—whether to provide sex for government guests or for personal pleasure, or both—remains uncertain. Depositions in a recent libel case focused on Heidi Rikan, a flashy German-born blonde, who graduated from striptease dancing at Washington's Blue Mirror Club to a social life that by 1972, when she was thirty-four, included friends ranging from gamblers to White House counsel John Dean and his girlfriend—later wife—Maureen.

Before her death in 1990, Rikan said in a conversation with her maid that she had once been a call girl. Explaining that a call girl was "a lady that meets men, and men pay them"—the maid had grown up in the country and knew nothing of big-city sins—she added, tantalizingly: "I was a call girl at the White House."[16]

Exactly a week before the Watergate break-in, John Dean again had to follow up on a prostitution story. The June 9 banner headline in the *Washington Evening Star* was: CAPITOL HILL CALL GIRL RING UNCOVERED. "The FBI," its opening paragraph read, "has uncovered a high-priced call girl ring allegedly headed by a Washington attorney and staffed by secretaries and office workers from Capitol Hill and involving at least one White House secretary, sources said." Among the clients of the call girl operation, the *Star*'s sources also claimed, was a "lawyer at the White House."

The president's aide and personal friend Peter Flanigan, the *Star* reported, had called the U.S. attorney's office to "find out if there was a chance of embarrassment to the Nixon administration."[17] The following day, the *Washington Post* reported, courthouse sources said that "the White House had shown a special interest in the case and was exerting pressure on the prosecutors not to comment on it."

Now that the story was in print, there was an immediate reaction from the Oval Office. "There was a big folderol," recalled Dean's lawyer colleague Pete

Kinsey. "I remember John having to question each one of us, on the instructions of Haldeman. They were looking for the identity of the 'White House lawyer,' for damage control."

Assistant U.S. Attorney Rudy found himself in Dean's office within hours, explaining the investigation and showing him materials seized from Phillip Bailley, the man indicted in the call girl case. Dean thumbed through one of Bailley's address books, comparing it with a roster of White House personnel. He had his secretary copy the book and paid particular attention to one photograph of a naked woman.

The woman, a young attorney in her twenties, was not exactly a White House lawyer. She did work in the Executive Office Building Annex, however, and was summarily fired.[18] It is not known if internal inquiries identified others compromised by the probe, but the case clearly had too many links to the Nixon White House for comfort.

Protocol chief Mosbacher's alleged connection to the Xaviera Hollander ring, if revealed, would have triggered disastrous publicity.

Nick Ruwe, said to have "used" the Columbia Plaza women—for whatever purpose—was also very close to the president. He had worked for Nixon since 1960, had been his personal aide in 1962, and was to serve as his senior assistant and traveling companion long after the resignation. Had Ruwe been associated at the time with the Columbia Plaza whores, as a colleague has alleged he was, the scandal would have come embarrassingly close to the president.

In the late summer of 1972, Assistant U.S. Attorney Rudy has recalled, he was ordered to "ice" his investigation into linkage between the Columbia Plaza prostitutes and the Democratic headquarters, to close it down. "The directions that I received," he said, "were that the DNC should not be pursued, that it was a political time bomb. It was very politically sensitive. . . . It was a time that was very highly politically charged about what Republicans might have done. I worked for a Republican administration, and I was told that was no longer a subject matter to be looked into."

CREEP's Gordon Liddy, writing of Xaviera Hollander's appointment books, observed that they "were useless to either Democrats or Republicans, because so many prominent members of both parties were represented in them they would cancel each other out in a political 'balance of terror.' . . ."

———————

However potentially damaging such evidence might be, the final fateful break-in of the Democratic headquarters was not driven solely by the prostitution angle. Had the target been only the desk of one secretary, it would have made no sense to commit eight men with varied criminal specialties to the task. One, at most two, burglars would have sufficed.

There is indeed no need to try to explain Watergate by a single motive. "We were really after anything . . ." Magruder would tell Ehrlichman. That, in the end, was the burglars' brief.

"We were looking for *everything*," Sturgis emphasized in his detailed account. "Our orders were to sweep the entire file system of the Democrats. Our assignment was to photograph two thousand documents. We had very efficient photo gear, and an efficient system. . . . we had done other assignments, successfully, and as we went along, we improved our techniques."

It is, however, apparent that two full years after the start of Operation O'Brien, the chairman of the Democratic party remained a primary target. His Washington apartment was also twice burglarized, and documents taken. There were two attempts to break into his home in New York City. He and his wife concluded that their private phones were tapped both in the capital and in New York. Spies, one of them a known member of the Watergate operation, trailed O'Brien around the restaurants of both cities, trying to find out with whom he was dining. Howard Hunt was in Miami before the final Watergate break-in, preparing "an alternate plan" for the bugging of O'Brien's suite at the Democratic convention.

The DNC leader himself concluded that on the evidence, the overall motive had been to get "information that CREEP, President Nixon and his associates, could use against me, in the hope of embarrassing me. . . . The political realities and the facts show conclusively that the objective of Watergate was to secure all possible information that would help destroy the Democratic Party and its chairman. It is as simple as that."

That and, as Liddy and Sturgis were to say, to discover what the Democrats might have on Nixon and his colleagues. "We knew the Democrats had a shit file of damaging rumors about Republican leaders," Sturgis said. "We dug for that everywhere." Nixon had reason to fear what O'Brien knew or might know of an array of guilty secrets: the Castro plots; the Howard Hughes money; the illicit funding by the Greek colonels; the sabotage of the 1968 Vietnam peace initiative. If revealed, any of these issues would have been capable of sinking Nixon in the coming election.[19]

One of the two attorneys most concerned with defending Nixon during Watergate, Leonard Garment, had no doubt who and what was behind the crime. "These people," he said in the nineties of the CREEP operatives, "had an assignment: What the president wants is information about Larry O'Brien. O'Brien had him spooked for decades. He thought: 'Why can't you guys get the stuff for me that I know is there?'

"It was Richard Nixon who said: 'I'm not going to risk this campaign; it was too close last time. There are people who have information I want. . . .' If anybody can believe that it wasn't made clear what this was all about, then they really do believe in Santa Claus."

Early on Gordon Liddy had characterized his "intelligence" project against the Democrats as "war." It had been, until then, a secret vendetta, but on Friday, June 16, 1972, it was about to be secret no longer.

31

Watergate has done for the politician what the Boston Strangler did for the door-to-door salesman.

—Nixon's friend and colleague Robert Finch,
addressing the California Republican League, 1973

At noon on Friday, June 16, 1972, Nixon sat in the Oval Office waiting to take part in a commemorative ceremony. Though rarely noted in accounts of the day that would lead to his downfall, the occasion evoked all the tensions that had riven the presidency: the Vietnam War, its heroes, its opponents, and those Nixon saw as traitors.

At Arlington Cemetery that morning politicians, generals, and former colleagues had gathered to bury John Paul Vann, the nearest the United States had to a great charismatic leader in Vietnam. A symbol of the struggle for America to prevail in Southeast Asia and the inspiration for Neil Sheehan's *A Bright Shining Lie,* that brilliant study of the conflict, Vann had died in a fiery helicopter crash the previous week. Now, the burial over, his widow and four sons had arrived at the White House. Nixon was about to present them with the Presidential Medal of Freedom, the posthumous honor he was awarding Vann.

The atmosphere was shadowed by ambiguity and bitterness. One of the mourners at the funeral had been Vann's friend and Nixon's foe Daniel Ellsberg. Vann had been torn over his friend's exposure of the Pentagon Papers. On one hand, he had given advice to Nixon aides on the best way to prosecute Ellsberg. On the other, he had promised to testify on his behalf at his trial.

Jesse, Vann's twenty-two-year-old son, was a draft resister. At the graveside in Arlington he had resolved to make a gesture he believed his father would have understood, "the gift of his own honesty." He had torn his draft card in two and laid one half of it among the flowers on the coffin. The other piece he planned to give to Nixon instead of shaking hands.

Word of Jesse's intention spread from his family to the White House staff, and an aide scurried to warn Nixon. When the aide reemerged, he told the young man to abandon his plan or see the ceremony canceled. The young man relented, out of deference to his mother, and the family filed into the Oval Office.

Nixon did not impress the Vanns. He irritated them when he announced he could not award the dead man the nation's highest award, the Congressional Medal of Honor, because Vann had no longer been in the army at the time of his death. The excuse was legitimate, but the family thought Nixon's explanation overly complicated and disingenuous. He smiled too much and failed to look them in the eye.

This awkward scene ended Nixon's official schedule for the day. He flew alone to the Bahamas that afternoon, for a weekend in the sun with Bebe Rebozo and Bob Abplanalp. There was time to swim and inspect the island turtles before dinner.

As the president headed south, Howard Hunt's Cubans had been on their way north. Once in Washington, they checked into the Watergate Hotel and dined sumptuously on lobster. Then, after a briefing session with Hunt and Liddy, they waited for the all-clear to start their second break-in of the Democratic headquarters. It wasn't until after midnight that the last lone campaign worker was seen to put down the phone, relieve himself in a planter on the terrace, switch out the lights, and leave. Sometime after that the burglars moved in.

Hunt and Liddy remained in the hotel, watching an ancient film on television. Baldwin, in his room with a view from across the street at the Howard Johnson's, had instructions to keep an eye on the Watergate. (The other eye apparently was trained on a movie called *Attack of the Puppet People*.)

The burglars, along with CREEP security director McCord, went about their felonious tasks inside the DNC for about an hour. They searched through files and broke into Lawrence O'Brien's office. "I personally checked O'Brien's desk," one recalled. "All I could find were bottles of liquor. . . ."

At 2:10 A.M. plainclothes police officers in cruiser 727 received a radio call from their dispatcher. A guard at the Watergate building was reporting a probable break-in in progress, just weeks after a previous burglary. The police responded promptly, and the burglars were caught in the act, arrested, and taken to headquarters.

Hunt and Liddy, who had been sitting out the action in the Watergate Hotel, got away that night, as did Baldwin, the lookout in the Howard Johnson's. So too did Louis Russell, Nixon's former investigator on the House Un-American Activities Committee, who later admitted privately what he denied to the FBI: that he too had been "watching." Like the others, he managed to skulk off, never to be fully unmasked.[1]

Police Inspector Thomas Herlihy caught the essentials of the story in the six-page report he wrote the following day. Five men had been arrested in the DNC with electronic equipment, Minolta cameras, and dozens of rolls of film. One of them, posing as "Edward Martin," had been identified as "James McCord, Security Director, Committee to Re-Elect the President." In the search that followed the arrests, moreover, police had found a check signed by "E. Howard Hunt . . . holder of a White House pass and employed as a Special Consultant to Charles Colson, on the President's staff." "It is reported," wrote Inspector Herlihy, "that Hunt was used as a consultant by the White House on highly confidential matters."

The slow collapse of Richard Nixon's presidency had begun.

———————

When and how the president first learned of the arrests is a matter shrouded in contradiction. He would tell the nation he found out from news reports within hours, on Saturday, June 17. In his memoirs, though, he claimed he did not become aware of them until the next day, Sunday, after flying back to the mainland from the Bahamas. He heard the news, he said, over coffee in the kitchen of his house on Key Biscayne while scanning the *Miami Herald*.

Nixon's two companions that weekend later offered their own versions of the discovery, which merely increase suspicion that the truth was concealed. Abplanalp, his host in the Bahamas, supported the Sunday Key Biscayne version, claiming he was with Nixon at Key Biscayne that day when Haldeman phoned with the news. Yet the official record of the president's movements on Sunday, and the helicopter manifests, indicate that Abplanalp did not fly back to the mainland with Nixon and Rebozo.

Rebozo in turn maintained that Nixon got the news on Key Biscayne on Saturday—at a time the president was in fact still in the Bahamas. The detail Rebozo added, moreover, suggests the three friends concocted a story and then muddled it. "I was with him when he got word," Rebozo said. "We were swimming in front of my house. . . . They came out and told him." That scenario was totally at odds with both of Nixon's versions.

How did Nixon react? "Hell, I was with him in the room," Abplanalp asserted, remembering the call from Haldeman. "I heard him say, 'They did WHAAT?' . . . He was so astonished he was practically shouting. He came off the phone shaking his head." Rebozo, on the other hand, said Nixon just "sat down and laughed about it. He said two or three times, 'What in God's name were we doing there?'"

Haldeman, who spent the entire weekend in Florida, in accommodations not far from the president's, said he heard the news on Saturday. His first reaction, he claimed, was to think: "Good Lord, they've caught Charles Colson." That fear was assuaged, he said, when he spoke with Nixon on Sunday. The president, Haldeman observed, "wasn't concerned at all by the break-in. In fact, he was amused."[2]

Colson, whom the president called twice on Sunday, painted a different picture. He recalled Nixon's saying he had reacted in a manner unlike the calm described by Rebozo and Haldeman. "He was so furious," Colson gathered, "that he had thrown an ashtray across the room."

"I had seen Nixon blow up in towering rages," Haldeman observed when he learned of this episode, "but never throw anything. Why did he telephone Colson so angrily, yet hide that emotion from me and everyone else?"

All these years later the question hangs there still.

Whether he was "amused" or "furious," Nixon exercised control over the situation from the start. "Track down Magruder and see what he knows," he had ordered Haldeman when he called on Sunday. Haldeman did so, and immediately conspired with CREEP's deputy director on how to mislead the press with the first official statement on the break-in. "Idea," read a line in Haldeman's notes of the conversation, "to get it as confused as possible."

The cover-up and the destruction of evidence began at once. Gordon Liddy had been at the shredder within hours of the arrests, while others organized little domestic bonfires.

Papers McCord kept at the office were removed by his secretary for burning, while others were destroyed by his wife in the living room fireplace. Howard Hunt also burned documents at home. John Dean and a colleague, wearing surgical gloves to avoid leaving fingerprints, picked over the contents of his White House safe. Potentially incriminating papers they found, including material on Ellsberg and Edward Kennedy, would eventually be burned by Nixon's compliant acting FBI director, Pat Gray.

"Maybe you ought to have a little fire at your home," Magruder was to quote John Mitchell as suggesting, and his GEMSTONE material duly went up in flames. Mitchell himself would destroy his campaign correspondence with Nixon and Haldeman.

Having flown back to Washington with Nixon, Haldeman called a Tuesday morning meeting with Ehrlichman, Mitchell, Richard Kleindienst (Mitchell's successor as attorney general), and John Dean. They discussed how to handle Watergate, and afterward Haldeman saw his aide Gordon Strachan. When the aide, "scared to death," showed his boss the compromising political action memorandum of early April memorializing approval of Liddy's plan, Haldeman ordered: "Make sure our files are clean."* Strachan headed for the shredder.[3]

While his closest colleagues debated damage control that morning, Nixon sat alone for more than hour, neither making nor receiving calls. Then he met with Ehrlichman. Watergate was discussed, although no tape of the conversa-

*See page 402.

tion has ever been produced. The tape of the president's next meeting that morning, with Haldeman, became known around the world not for what it contained but for what was obliterated.

Visitors to the National Archives today may don a pair of headphones and listen solemnly to what remains of the part of that morning's conversation that, according to Haldeman's skeletal notes, dealt with Watergate. They will hear no words, however, but only more than a quarter of an hour of audio buzz. This is the infamous eighteen-and-one-half minute gap.

"It looks a very serious thing, Your Honor," Nixon's principal Watergate lawyer would admit to Judge Sirica during the legal fight for the tapes. ". . . It doesn't appear from what we know at this point that it could have been accidental." The president had assigned his secretary Rose Woods to transcribe the tape in late September 1973 and it was she who was ultimately blamed for its destruction. There ensued the ludicrous reenaction scene for prosecutors in which—equipped with tape recorder, earphones, and foot pedal—Woods tried to convince the court she could have erased part of the recording by accident, while distracted by the telephone.

Experts, approved by the White House as well as the prosecutors, would later conclude that the tape's long stretch of buzzing, clicks, and pops reflected a series of overlapping erasures. Someone had manually set the machine to erase at least five times, suggesting the tape was intentionally wiped.[4] Who was that someone? Woods herself insisted that, at worst, she was responsible for the loss of only five minutes of dialogue.

When Woods had rushed into the Oval Office to explain that she had erased a portion of the June 20 recording, she testified the president had merely said casually, "Don't worry about it." At some point in the court furor, it seems, she began to feel she was being made the scapegoat. On the phone to an old friend, former press secretary James Bassett, that most loyal of Nixon retainers, declared she was "being framed."

Nixon did personally review critical tapes during the Watergate crisis, and Woods said in testimony that at Camp David he had "pushed the buttons on her recorder back and forth." Was he, then, responsible for having created the eighteen-and-one-half-minute gap? Several people believed so.

"Most likely it was the president," the prosecuting attorney who interrogated Woods in court, Jill Wine-Banks, said in 1999. Special Prosecutor Leon Jaworski offered a less qualified judgment. "Only the President," he noted, "had access to both the tape and the machine [at the likely time of the erasure] . . . what was on the tape, and what portion might be incriminating. . . ."[5]

Having struggled to recall precisely what was said during the erased phase of the conversation, Haldeman later suggested Nixon had worried aloud about what might come out about Charles Colson. "I know one thing," Haldeman's reconstruction had Nixon asserting, "we can't stand an FBI interrogation of Colson. . . . Colson can talk about the President, if he cracks."

As for his other conversations with Haldeman and Colson that first Tuesday, Nixon was to refuse to release the relevant tapes. If we examine the two that have since become available, it is obvious why.

Nixon met with Colson for more than an hour after lunch that day and—although the sound quality is poor—the audible portion of the recording is a curious mix of concern about Watergate, mutual back scratching, and insistence that political spying is routine. "A lot of people think you oughta wiretap . . ." said Nixon, and most people "knew why the hell we're doing it, and they probably figure they're doing it to us, which they are."[6]

If this discussion did not include an admission of involvement in Watergate, it involved none of the flat denials that Nixon was to spout in public and private for the rest of his life. After Colson departed, Nixon had another meeting with Haldeman, at which they spoke of the Democrats' reaction to the arrests: O'Brien had promptly brought a suit for wiretapping and invasion of privacy. The available transcript contains two deletions in quick succession for privacy reasons, one of them after a Nixon reference to the "bizarre" aspects of the story. Was this an allusion to the sex activity the CREEP bugging had picked up?

At another point Haldeman remarked that "this financial thing" may have justified the bugging of the DNC. CREEP's spies, he said, "thought they had something going on that." Was the "financial thing" a reference to O'Brien and Howard Hughes's money? Or perhaps to illicit funding from the Greek colonels? Nixon's laconic response—"Yeah, I suppose"—certainly suggests that he knew exactly what his aide was talking about.

By now the game plan was clear. The president's "public line," he told Haldeman, was going to be that the DNC was not worth the effort of bugging. Also, he had told Colson, "We are just going to leave this where it is, with the Cubans." The Cubans had to plead guilty, he and Haldeman agreed, explaining that their espionage had been to expose "crazy" McGovern's "sellout to the Communists." It was, Nixon thought, "a very nice touch."

Early that evening Nixon spoke on the telephone with John Mitchell, the first-known contact between the two since the Watergate arrests. Nixon's lawyer would later explain that there had been no record made of the conversation because the call had been placed on a line from the president's private quarters, one that was not hooked into the recording system. Later still, it emerged that Nixon had made a note of the conversation on the Dictabelt machine on which he recorded his daily diary. While the transcript of this recording includes nothing of import, it is significant for another reason: There is a forty-two-second break in the dictation, followed by an unintelligible remark: "[T]he Dictabelt," a Watergate Special Prosecution Force document states, "appears to have been tampered with."[7]

We have no tapes of four further calls Nixon received that evening from Haldeman and Colson, even though three of them were made from an office where recording was automatic.

During one of the evening calls, according to Haldeman, the president told him Watergate might now be "under control" because of the Cuban involvement. "A lot of people think the break-in was done by anti-Castro Cubans. . . . I'm going to talk to Bebe and have him round up some anti-Castro Cubans. . . . Those people who got caught are going to need money. . . . I'm going to have Bebe start a fund for them in Miami. Call it an anti-Castro Fund, and publicize the hell out of the Cuban angle. That way we kill two birds with one stone. Get money to the boys to help them, and maybe pick up some points against McGovern on the Cuban angle."

Bebe Rebozo's name kept being mentioned on the tapes over the next few days, in a way that suggests Nixon was nervous about his friend's vulnerability. At one point, while discussing the fact that Howard Hunt's name had turned up in two of the burglars' contact books, he suddenly asked an odd question:

PRESIDENT NIXON: Is Rebozo's name in anyone's address book?
HALDEMAN: No . . . He told me he doesn't know any of these guys.
PRESIDENT NIXON: He doesn't know them?

Here the released tape features another "privacy" deletion. Nixon was evidently concerned, and with reason: We now know that there was a degree of connection between two of the burglars, Bernard Barker and Rolando Martinez, and Rebozo. Martinez was vice president of a real estate firm with which Rebozo had extensive dealings, and one of the firm's directors was on the board of Rebozo's bank. The firm had also brokered the purchase of Nixon's house on Key Biscayne. Both Martinez and Barker, moreover, were leading lights in a second real estate company, Ameritas Inc., which had been used by the burglars as cover when they came to Washington to break into the Watergate.

On Thursday, June 22, in his first press conference since the arrests, Nixon made his first misleading public statement on Watergate. The White House, he insisted, "has had no involvement whatever in this particular incident." He would not comment further, he said in tones of respect for due process, because the police and the FBI were investigating the matter. Yet, behind the scenes, he and his closest aides had already been puzzling how to get the FBI "turned off."

Nixon's taped comments over the months about covering up and lying are confused and confusing. "You can't cover this thing up, Bob," he would tell Haldeman two weeks after the arrests. "The worst thing a guy can do, the worst thing," he would remark two weeks after that, "two things and each is bad. One is to lie and the other one is to cover up. . . . If you cover up, you're going to get caught. . . . And if you lie you're going to be guilty of perjury . . . basically, that was the whole store of the Hiss case."

"The *cover-up* is what hurts you, not the issue," he would assert several weeks later in a conversation with Colson. "It's the cover-up that hurts." As the crisis deepened, he would comment, again to Colson: "A cover-up is, is the main ingredient." When Colson agreed, he added: "My losses are to be cut. . . . The President's losses got to be cut on the cover-up deal."

Nixon was well aware that involvement in a cover-up could bring him down. Yet it is utterly clear, with the advantage of access to the tapes released since his death, that he connived in such a deception from the very beginning. He is implicated in page after page of the transcripts, sometimes directly and sometimes by nuance. Even without the new tapes, however, that conclusion is unavoidable from the recording of a meeting with Haldeman just over a week after the Watergate arrests.

On that day, Friday, June 23, Haldeman learned the FBI was only a short step away from discovering that CREEP was the source of the cash that had been found on the burglars and in their hotel rooms. It was now indeed urgent to turn off the FBI investigation.

In his discussion with Nixon that morning, Haldeman offered a solution. Because it had established that some of the money involved had been laundered through a Mexican bank, the FBI was wondering if it had stumbled across a CIA covert operation. The bureau could almost certainly be persuaded to stop pursuing the Mexico angle, or at least change course, if the CIA so requested. He and Ehrlichman, Haldeman suggested, could call in CIA Director Richard Helms and Deputy Director Vernon Walters, an old Nixon associate, and get them to make the request.

"All right, fine," Nixon responded to this proposal to obstruct the course of justice. He again said, "Right, fine," and then yet again, "All right, fine." Then: "You call them in. Good. Good deal. Play it tough. . . ." Then, in two other conversations that day, he proceeded to offer his own ideas on the best way to pressure the CIA.

It was at this juncture, as reported earlier, that the president urged his aides to warn the CIA chiefs that further inquiry would expose their own former agent Howard Hunt. It would also likely "blow the whole Bay of Pigs thing, which we think would be very unfortunate for the CIA and for the country."[8] Any exposure of early anti-Castro operations, of course, would also likely have been unfortunate for Nixon himself, and a study of that day's taped conversations may reflect that. One tape, examined repeatedly on the author's behalf, appears to contain at least six unexplained erasures.[9]

Helms and Walters were summoned that afternoon, and for the time being the ploy worked. The agency did intervene with the FBI, and key interviews were stalled.[10] "No problem," Haldeman was soon reporting to Nixon. The president and his men had bought a delay, but at immeasurable cost.

"The thing that bothers me about this thing," Haldeman observed days later, "is that it's a time bomb." It was indeed, and one of Nixon's own making in more than one respect. On his first day in the office after the arrests at

40. The palace guard, in the Oval Office. Bob Haldeman is in the foreground, John Ehrlichman at the far end of the table. Dwight Chapin *(standing)* thought his boss would be "the greatest president in history."

41. The president with Attorney General John Mitchell, his "political right arm."

42. An ally, and a deal. Nixon with Teamsters Union leader Frank Fitzsimmons. Fitzsimmons got a (conditional) pardon for his jailed predecessor, Jimmy Hoffa, while Teamsters money flowed to the Nixon White House.

43. Hard hats on a table in the White House—there was a special one for Nixon—during a 1970 visit by construction workers' leaders. Their members had recently attacked antiwar demonstrators.

44. In 1971, Nixon and Haldeman discussed using Teamsters thugs to beat up antiwar demonstrators and "smash some noses." Two days earlier assailants had broken the nose of Abbie Hoffman. ". . . they got him . . ." Haldeman now told the president.

45, 46. Nixon visited South Vietnam to encourage U.S. troops. At home, in 1970, he rushed out in the middle of the night to meet with demonstrators at the Lincoln Memorial, then had his valet make a speech in the deserted House of Representatives.

47, 48. Nixon's crowning achievement was the breakthrough to China, marked by the meeting with Mao Zedong in early 1972. Months later, he became the first American president to visit Moscow. At the first of three meetings with Leonid Brezhnev, he concluded a historic arms limitation agreement.

49. Henry Kissinger, national security adviser and later secretary of state, was the helmsman of Nixon's foreign policy. He saw "Walter Mitty" dimensions in the president's personality.

50. Chile's President Salvador Allende, shortly before he was found shot dead on the day of his overthrow by General Augusto Pinochet. "The Nixon administration wanted a violent coup," according to a senior CIA official.

51, 52. The president and *(left to right)* Haldeman, Kissinger, and Stephen Bull midway through his first term. Determined to win reelection, Nixon put his trust increasingly in covert operations run by special assistant Charles Colson. "We did a hell of a lot of things," Colson said, "and never got caught."

54. Gordon Liddy made the plans.

55. Howard Hunt recruited the burglars.

53.

Break-in at the Watergate, spring 1972

56. James McCord testified that he planted bugs.

57. Louis Russell, who had worked with Nixon on the Hiss case, admitted he was "watching" that night.

59. *Secret 1:* Republican sabotage of peace talks, using Anna Chennault, in 1968.

60. *Secret 2:* Nixon had taken money from the Greek dictatorship, through his friend Thomas Pappas.

58.

What was the motive for the break-ins? Democratic Party chairman Lawrence O'Brien had knowledge of several matters that could damage Nixon.

61. *Secret 3:* The reclusive billionaire Howard Hughes had not been seen or photographed for years. Yet he still aspired to control politicians, and Nixon had taken his money.

62. *Secret 4:* Heidi Rikan said she had been "a call girl at the White House." Both Democrats and Republicans had reportedly used a brothel near the Watergate.

63. The mighty fallen. Haldeman and Ehrlich-man—convicted on obstruction of justice, conspiracy, and perjury charges—went to jail.

64. The Watergate grand jury's evidence went to the House Judiciary Committee in two locked briefcases. The jury named the president as an "unindicted coconspirator."

65. Nixon's secretary, Rose Woods, demonstrated how, she claimed, she might accidentally have erased a key Watergate tape. Special Prosecutor Jaworski believed the culprit was Nixon.

66. A president out of control. At New Orleans, in the fall of 1973, Nixon grabbed press secretary Ron Ziegler, whirled him around, and shoved him toward reporters. His speech and gestures that day led to press speculation that he was either drunk or drugged.

67. End game, 1974. The House Judiciary Committee voted three articles of impeachment, charging Nixon with offenses warranting trial and removal from office. He avoided facing the charges by resigning.

68, 69. Supporters and opponents took to the streets.

70, 71, 72. As Nixon's presidency collapsed, there were unprecedented fears and precautions. Defense Secretary James Schlesinger *(below left)* ordered that any military orders emanating from the White House were to be checked with him. Air Force General George Brown told the Joint Chiefs *(above)* there were fears of "some sort of coup." Nixon's aide Alexander Haig *(below right)* said he feared improper action only by the Congress, not the armed services.

73, 74. Resignation, August 9, 1974. Pat held back her tears as Nixon made a rambling speech to the staff about his father and his mother—and the importance of never giving up. He bade farewell, in defeat, with the *V* for Victory sign.

75. In his first months of
"exile," Nixon came close
to death when a blood clot
moved from an inflamed
vein in a leg to one of his
lungs. He was thus spared
from appearing as a witness
at the Watergate cover-up
trial.

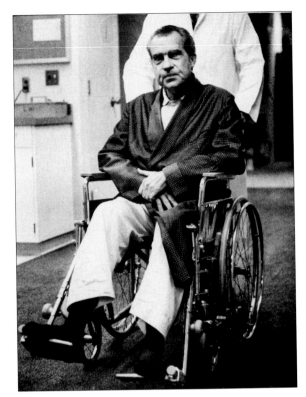

76. He remained isolated in
San Clemente, with only a
handful of aides, for many
months afterward.

77. Over the years, Nixon gradually recovered from his disgrace, remaking himself in the image of an elder statesman. He thought his White House meeting with President Clinton, in 1993, "the best I have had since I was president."

78. When Pat died in June 1993, her husband's grief was obvious. Holding his hand at one point on the day of the funeral, unrecognized by the press, was the psychotherapist Dr. Hutschnecker.

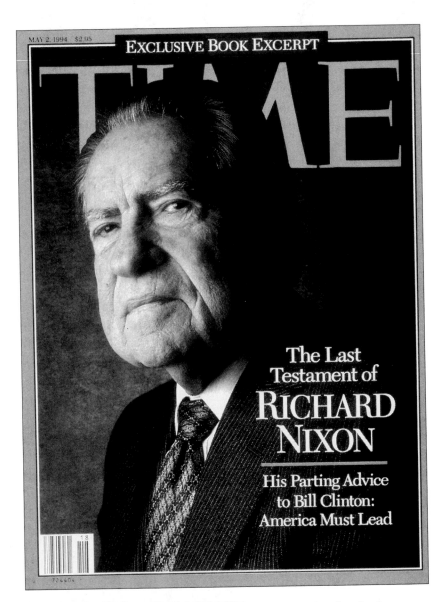

MAY 2, 1994 $2.95

EXCLUSIVE BOOK EXCERPT

T**I**ME

The Last
Testament of

RICHARD
NIXON

His Parting Advice
to Bill Clinton:
America Must Lead

RICHARD NIXON
1913 – 1994
THE GREATEST HONOR HISTORY CAN BESTOW
IS THE TITLE OF PEACEMAKER

79, 80. After his death at age
eighty-one, in April 1994,
Richard Nixon made the
cover of *Time* for the fifty-
sixth time. He had made a
final strenuous journey, to
Russia, the previous month.
The gravestone honors him
as he would have wished, as
a peacemaker.

the Watergate, the president had worried briefly about the hidden microphones and the recorders whirring away in a nearby closet. The recording system, he had told Haldeman thoughtfully, "complicates things all over." Haldeman assured Nixon the tapes were "locked up . . . super-secure—there are only three people that know." The moment of disquiet ended, and the talk moved on to other things.

Twenty-five months were to pass before Nixon would confront the cost of having said, "That's fine" to Bob Haldeman. With the existence of the recording system exposed and with the Supreme Court ordering him to surrender key tapes, those two words alone would become the bullet in the "smoking gun." They were proof that the president was guilty of criminal obstruction, evidentially lethal.

The months ahead would be a time of not only political crisis, but also personal collapse.

The president was to recall that when the news of the arrests reached him in Florida, he had been "trying to get a few days' rest" after his visit to Moscow. He had returned from Russia, though, more than two weeks earlier and for nearly a week of that time he had been at Key Biscayne or Camp David. In July, when Nixon spent three weeks at San Clemente, aides blamed his fatigue on the China trip of four *months* earlier.

"According to associates who see him in his private moments," a senior correspondent reported carefully, Nixon had for some time shown increasing signs of needing rest. The recollections of two Secret Service agents suggest this was an understatement. One evening either just before or after the fateful break-in, in a rerun of his bizarre 1970 nocturnal adventure, the president suddenly decided he wanted to visit the Capitol.

The senior man on duty, Agent Dennis McCarthy, recalled how Nixon emerged through the White House's diplomatic entrance, then "stood staring out toward the Washington Monument. Finally, I opened the door and said, 'We're ready anytime you are, sir' . . . he seemed to have forgotten why he was waiting. . . ." Nixon was waiting, as it turned out, for his dog, an Irish setter named King Timahoe. The dog was loaded into the limousine alongside him, and off they headed to Capitol Hill.

As in 1970, both houses of Congress were locked and barred, and the Secret Service had to get a policeman to open the building. Nixon then walked in, past the marble statues of statesmen long gone, through the dimly lit hallways, to the office he had used when vice president. No one could find a key so, silent and apparently lost in thought, he returned to the White House.

A former officer with the uniformed branch of the Secret Service, the Executive Protection Service, also observed odd behavior in that period. "I used to see the president outside the Oval Office or outside the Executive Office Building," said Lou Campbell," and he would just sit there and stare off into space, for thirty to forty-five minutes at a time. You could cut the tension with a knife."

Often genial with those who guarded him, Nixon could also be irrationally unpleasant. "Right after Watergate," Campbell recalled, "he was coming from the Oval Office to the steps to go to the EOB, and I was standing there. He walked by, and looked right at me, and I said, 'Good evening, Mr. President.' If looks could kill, I'd have been dead. There was such arrogance on his face, such disdain. And the next morning a memo arrived for all Secret Service personnel, saying, 'You will no longer address the president by anything like "Good morning" or "Good evening." Keep contact to a minimum.'"

Whatever his emotional state or his other preoccupations, Nixon had his hand firmly on the helm of the election campaign. Nothing was to stand in the way of an overwhelming victory, and not even the Watergate arrests had given him pause so far as that goal was concerned.

Although it is hard to conceive of now, for months Watergate made barely a mark on the public consciousness. Gallup estimated as late as the fall that only half the electorate had heard of the break-in. Two young *Washington Post* reporters named Woodward and Bernstein, however, were already boring toward the truth. So too were the *Los Angeles Times'* Jack Nelson and the *New York Times*'s Seymour Hersh—never to get sufficient recognition for their Watergate work. Most of the media, however, long remained supine.

"In terms of the reaction of people," Nixon had said within days of the arrests, "I think the country doesn't give much of a shit . . . most people around the country think that this is routine, that everybody's trying to bug everybody else . . . it is not going to get people that excited . . . because they don't give a shit about repression and bugging and all the rest."

To "the average guy," he would still be insisting months afterward, "whether or not the Republicans fuck the Democrats doesn't mean a goddamn thing." Even a year later, with his presidency beginning to founder, the president would still be calling Watergate "chicken shit."

As few are aware, the criminal plotting continued. Just two weeks after the arrests, again in the Oval Office with the tapes running, Nixon and Colson twice discussed the notion of faking a break-in at his own party headquarters to make people think the Democrats were as guilty as the Republicans of this sort of activity. "There should be a rifling . . . missing files," Nixon said, "something where it's really torn up, where pictures could be taken."[11]

No such phony break-in ever took place, but a similar one may have done. Three months later, in an apparent break-in at the office of the president's California physician, Dr. John Lungren, cash was ignored, but a file containing Nixon's patient records left disordered on the floor. Haldeman and an aide then called the FBI at the highest level fifteen times, urging that the bureau issue a press release on the case.

Assistant Director Mark Felt turned down the request, saying it was a matter for the local police. Such was the persistence of Nixon's men, though, that

Felt came to suspect someone at the White House, fearing news of the break-in of Ellsberg's psychiatrist's office would surface sooner or later, "wanted to be able to show that President Nixon had also been a victim of such tactics."[12]

At a more serious level, covert operations against the Democrats and Larry O'Brien continued unabated even after the Watergate arrests. CREEP's Jeb Magruder recalled Haldeman asking him to "get someone into McGovern's headquarters in July, so that we could get his schedule further in advance than the press release was telling. . . . Even with the problems of the break-in, they were still talking in those terms."

According to the state's attorney for the Miami area, Richard Gerstein, the abuse went much further than simply tracking down schedules. His investigators concluded that the Fontainbleau Hotel, headquarters for the Democratic convention, was bugged from a listening post established in a nearby apartment building. The groundwork for the operation had been laid by Watergate burglar Howard Hunt before his arrest and carried out nonetheless.

Gerstein and his staff had been probing local Watergate angles from the start because most of the burglars were Miami-based. Their own office had been broken into within weeks.

There had also been a break-in at the Texas home of Lawrence O'Brien's close colleague Robert Strauss. The house had been ransacked, but jewelry worth thousands of dollars left untouched.[13]

"Go gung-ho on O'B—& the others," read a Haldeman note of an instruction from Nixon in the late summer of 1972. "What, if anything, is being done on the Democratic candidate?" Nixon said into the Oval Office mikes around the same time. "I mean for example on his income [tax], on O'Brien. Have we got anything further on that, Bob? . . ." As for McGovern, he hoped the candidate "might have feet of clay . . . kick him again . . . keep whacking, whacking, whacking . . . on O'Brien . . . if you could dirty up O'Brien."

"Get everything you possibly can," Nixon demanded in the early fall. "Any little crumb or lead involving anyone. I don't care. O'Brien, another senator. Anything that involves a Democrat . . . Goddamn it." His aides tried, hard, unlawfully bullying the IRS to get compromising financial information on O'Brien, by then heading the Democratic campaign. "I wanted them to turn up something and send him to jail before the election," Ehrlichman would admit later. Nothing materialized; O'Brien's records were in order.

After the election Nixon would direct his public relations staff to prepare propaganda pointing out that he had run "one of the cleanest campaigns in history."

In the end, all the undercover operations would prove to have been unnecessary. By mid-July there was virtually no question who was going to be president. The Democratic convention had been a disastrous, chaotic affair guaranteed to alienate vast numbers of party members. The television coverage had shown viewers an explosion of disaffected youth and wild-looking advocates of every fashionable demand for freedom: "women's lib," abortion rights, rights for homosexuals, black militancy, freedom to smoke marijuana. The picture the public saw was of a party and a culture out of control.

McGovern's chances plummeted even further after the convention when it emerged that his running mate, Senator Thomas Eagleton, had been hospitalized three times for psychiatric care that had included electroshock treatments for depression. McGovern eventually dropped Eagleton but only after damaging prevarication. Nixon's response, by his account, was compassionate and he would later quote in his memoirs a long handwritten letter of sympathy that he had sent to the humiliated senator's son. The truth may have been shabbier.

"Supposing," McGovern aide Frank Manckiewicz asked Eagleton early in the crisis, "Chuck Colson has the [psychiatric] records before him, and he's going in to tell the President. . . ." That dire possibility was then merely an imagined horror, but it may have been prescient. The *Washington Post*'s Bob Woodward was told by "Deep Throat," his mysterious inside source, that the exposure of Eagleton involved Nixon's undercover operatives.[14]

CREEP had had a plant in the McGovern camp at the Democratic convention, a private detective who later admitted having overheard a discussion about Eagleton's personal history. There was a report too, again in the *Washington Post*, that not long before the senator's medical records were leaked to the press, they were in John Ehrlichman's possession.

"Bob Haldeman once intimated to me," Nixon's aide Alexander Butterfield revealed recently, "that they had stuff on Eagleton: that electroshock therapy. They were just waiting to spring it, waiting for the right time. They knew it would be explosive."

As for Nixon's professed sympathy, a recently released tape indicates that just as the news was breaking publicly, he discussed with Haldeman how best to exploit the Eagleton revelations. It would be a fine idea to plant hecklers at Eagleton meetings, the pair agreed, to badger him with accusations of dishonesty.

The Republican convention, in mid-August, presented an image the very opposite of that of the Democratic shambles. "Everything was scheduled and organized," observed journalist and Republican aide James Cannon, "not for the delegates in the hall but for middle America, to convey a sense of order at home and the promise of peace in the world. The Republicans arrived united in the cause of four more years for President Nixon."

Theirs was a convention that followed a script written and produced by Bob Haldeman, staffed by bland men in blue suits and ties carrying walkie-talkies. The young people in attendance, a different species entirely from those who had thronged to the Democrats' gathering, were praised by Ehrlichman as individuals who had "come here spontaneously, sometimes at great hardship, to support Nixon." The truth was that a party committee had subsidized their attendance, and a cheerleader orchestrated their chants.

A television audience of some sixty million Americans, it was calculated, was treated to packaged movies tracing the high points of Nixon's presidency, from grandeur in the White House to the Beijing and Moscow summit meetings. At the crowning moment the president himself appeared in triumph on a podium designed by the art director of the program *The Dating Game,* its floor constructed to rise or fall at the flick of a switch, to ensure that no other speaker could appear taller than Nixon.

"I ask everyone listening to me tonight," he said in his acceptance speech, the fifth in two decades, "Democrats, Republicans and independents—to join our majority. . . ." It was already becoming clear that that majority would be massive. A Gallup poll in the wake of the convention gave Nixon 64 percent to McGovern's 30 percent.

The election, when it came, was the predicted landslide. Of people who identified themselves as Democrats, more than a third voted for Nixon, a defection without precedent in American political history. With George Wallace out of the race, moreover, Nixon even carried the South. In the final tally he won more than 60 percent of the national vote, only marginally less than Lyndon Johnson's massive majority of eight years earlier.

The victory was not quite as impressive as it first seemed, however, for almost half the electorate had chosen not to vote at all. "Americans, numbed by words, headlines and TV shows, cross-analyzed by canvassers, telephone banks and statisticians," noted Theodore White, "simply drew in on themselves." Also, the people returned a Congress in which the Republicans remained a minority, a factor that was to prove pivotal for Nixon in the ordeal that was coming.

For a man who now had the "coronation" he had so long desired, Nixon seemed joyless on the night of his election. He appeared "preoccupied, somber instead of elated, and somewhat sad" to a reporter who encountered him hours later, walking alone in the White House precincts. The cap on one of the president's front teeth had snapped off, and some attributed his melancholy to that.

Nixon spent most of the evening in the Lincoln Sitting Room, listening to *Victory at Sea* again and some light classical music. Later, at 2:00 A.M., he was ensconced in his room in the Executive Office Building with Haldeman and Charles Colson. Nixon ordered a scotch and soda, downed most of it in one swallow, and soon called for another. Haldeman also seemed surly, angry almost. "The picture was out of focus," thought Colson. "If this was victory, what might these three men have looked like in defeat?"

By the next day the sourness had spread. "The good feeling was shattered within twelve hours," Henry Kissinger recalled. "The White House staff had been asked to assemble at 11:00 A.M. in the Roosevelt Room. At the dot, Nixon strode in. He was grim and remote as if the more fateful period of his life lay ahead. Nothing in his demeanor betrayed that he was meeting associates from perilous and trying times; he acted as though they were from a past now irrevocably finished."

The president said a few words and quickly departed, leaving Haldeman to announce to the staff they were—all of them—to submit their resignations at once. The cabinet received the same instructions soon afterward. Although some would be reappointed, and Nixon had supposedly meant to administer a short, sharp shock of fresh energy, few saw it that way. Kissinger thought the move "degrading . . . political butchery," delivered in a manner that was "almost maniacal."

Nixon spent much of the month that followed sequestered at Camp David, seeing old and new appointees. Colson found the atmosphere there "something right out of *1984* . . . like one of those secret hideaways in a James Bond movie—eerie." Back at the White House, there was pervasive bitterness.

In December Nixon embarked on the Christmas bombing of North Vietnam, the final brutal drive to get the United States out of the war. United States troop levels had fallen to about twenty-five thousand, and few of them were combat troops. American casualties had been reduced to very small numbers, and it had seemed in October that a settlement was imminent. "We believe peace is at hand," Kissinger had said dramatically two weeks before the election. Now there was a new stalemate, with the North again intransigent, and the South's President Thieu stubbornly blocking a deal he thought fatal for his regime.

Nixon, however, desired a resolution before the start of his second term. "He now wanted the war over on almost any terms," according to Kissinger. ". . . The North Vietnamese committed a cardinal error in dealing with Nixon: They cornered him. Nixon was never more dangerous than when he seemed to have run out of options."

The president responded by mounting the most concentrated air offensive of the entire conflict, which he set in motion on Monday, December 18. Haldeman had noted in his diary: "The P said I would rather bomb on Monday, unless you think we really need to do it on Sunday. He didn't like the idea of having a Sunday church service while we were bombing." This domestic squeamishness aside, Haldeman observed, Nixon "wanted to appear to be the tough guy all the way through."

An armada of some two hundred airplanes—more than half the Strategic Air Command's B-52s—flew nearly three thousand sorties, bombing Hanoi and Haiphong virtually around the clock. The North Vietnamese suffered serious losses—estimates of casualties and destruction vary wildly—and twenty-six American planes were shot down. Except for a break Nixon allowed on Christmas, the assault continued for twelve days.

When he ordered the bombers in, the president told the chairman of the Joint Chiefs that the air offensive was a chance to "win this war." Won it was not, but North Vietnam accepted a deal with the United States within two weeks, in time for Nixon's sixtieth birthday. "Brutality is nothing," he told Kissinger when South Vietnam's Thieu at first declined to fall into line. "You've never seen it if this son-of-a-bitch doesn't go along." Thieu soon yielded, for he had no choice.

A peace agreement was duly signed in late January, and Nixon told the nation that "peace with honor" had been achieved. To "have it break within a year or two," the president would recall having observed to Kissinger, "would leave us nothing to be proud of. . . ."

Yet that is precisely what was to happen. The Nixon settlement offered more to the North Vietnamese, in a real sense, than had been foreseen in the Geneva accords of 1954. Then, the Communists had agreed to withdraw to the North. The arrangement Nixon accepted in 1973 permitted some 148,000 North Vietnamese troops to remain in the South, posing a grave threat to Saigon from the outset.[15] That, he admitted in old age, was the "biggest flaw" in the agreement.

North Vietnamese attacks began again almost immediately, attacks that were to culminate in 1975 with total victory over the South and the ignominious departure of those Americans left in Saigon.

Nixon would insist to his dying day that American military force could and should have been used again to rescue the South Vietnamese regime. The new attacks would have been summarily stopped, he argued, had his presidency not been weakened by Watergate, had the "stupid and shortsighted" Congress not set itself firmly against further military involvement. It is an argument, however, that fails to take into account the utter determination of the northerners to prevail.

"We won the war," Nixon would still be claiming in 1992, "but lost the peace." It was mere verbiage, as was his claim that the United States had achieved "peace with honor in Vietnam." What the Christmas bombing of 1972 really achieved was to blast open an escape route from a predicament that, from the American point of view, had long since ceased to be tenable.

To bomb during the holiday season, Nixon was to say, had been "the most difficult decision I made during the entire war . . ." "I suppose all the decisions are hard," he had written in his diary, "but this one was heartrending."

The president had Winston Churchill on his mind during this period, and on Christmas Eve his diary entry had been positively Churchillian:

> This is December 24, 1972—Key Biscayne—4 A.M. The main thought that occurred to me at this early hour of the morning the day before Christmas, in addition to the overriding concern with regard to bringing the war to an end, is that I must get away from the thought of considering the office at any time a burden. . . . I think the term glorious burden is the best description.
>
> On this day before Christmas it is God's great gift to me to have

the opportunity to exert leadership, not only for America but on the world scene. . . . this really begins a new period and this tape concludes with that thought—a period of always reminding myself of the glorious burden of the presidency.

Within months, in an address to the nation that was really an attempt to talk his way out of Watergate, Nixon would be using the Christmas air campaign as the banner of his personal suffering: "my terrible personal ordeal of the renewed bombing of North Vietnam."

His ordeal took place in private, mostly in the peace and sunshine of Key Biscayne. Haldeman had no contact with the president for a full twelve days, an unprecedentedly long gap. He himself took a vacation in California, as did other senior staff, including for a while Henry Kissinger. So far as the press was concerned, as the UPI's White House correspondent Helen Thomas has recalled, the president was "in hiding." He made no public appearances for eleven days, watched a lot of football on television, and took in six movies.

Nixon's true condition at that time can only be guessed at. His silence on the bombing, he was to claim, was out of a concern not to jeopardize negotiations. "But I also think," Kissinger was to write later, "there were other, more complex reasons. Nixon was still seized by the withdrawn and sullen hostility that had dominated his mood since his electoral triumph."

Others had more damning interpretations. Anthony Lewis of the *New York Times* accused the president of acting "like a maddened tyrant." The *Washington Post* said millions of Americans were wondering at "their President's very sanity." Republican senator William Saxbe thought Nixon had "left his senses on this issue."

The *New York Times*'s James Reston called the bombing offensive "war by tantrum"—and perhaps on good evidence. His colleague William Beecher, the *Times*'s military correspondent, had filed a dispatch reporting that in the course of demanding renewed bombing, the president had been "throwing stuff against the wall."[16]

At dinner on the first night of the attack, Nixon had talked in an astonishing vein in front of the chairman of the Joint Chiefs, Admiral Moorer, Henry Kissinger, Teddy Roosevelt's daughter Alice Longworth, Pat and Julie, and the columnist Richard Wilson. He said, Wilson recalled, that he "did not care if the whole wide world thought he was crazy in resuming the bombing. If it did, so much the better. The Russians and Chinese might think they were dealing with a madman and so had better force North Vietnam into a settlement before the world was consumed in a larger war. . . ."

It was the Madman Theory again, four years after Nixon had first proposed frightening the Communists with the notion that the man with "his hand on the nuclear button" could not be restrained "when he's angry."[17]

———

Two months earlier, before the November landslide, Haldeman had made a remarkable diary entry following a meeting with the president. Nixon, he noted, had "made the interesting point that after the election we will have awesome power with no discipline, that is, there won't be another election coming up to discipline us."

One item on the agenda was revenge. "I want the most comprehensive notes on those that have tried to do us in," Nixon had told John Dean. ". . . they didn't have to do it . . . they are asking for it and they are going to get it. . . . We have not used the power in this first four years. . . . We have never used it . . . things are going to change now."

There were also grandiose plans for the future. Early in December, Nixon ordered immediate action on three political projects. He wanted his brother Edward to run for Congress in Washington State; Tricia's husband Edward Cox to run in New York; and Julie's husband David Eisenhower in Pennsylvania. Was he attempting to emulate the Kennedys and found a dynasty of his own?

During the Christmas recess Dean met for lunch with the chief counsel of the House Judiciary Committee, Jerome Zeifman. What did Zeifman think, Dean inquired, of Nixon's chances of persuading Congress to repeal the two-term limit on the presidency? "Sometimes," Zeifman responded, "I wonder if your boss is demented."

Life's Hugh Sidey, an authority on the presidency, reported that after the election Nixon had gone "to the mountaintop at Camp David and read Arnold Toynbee for ideas about how to carry his administration to greater heights. He mused about how he might wage a campaign to rescind the 22nd Amendment and run for a third term."

Should Nixon not succeed in extending his presidency, Jeb Magruder was to write, he intended to "control the Executive Branch of the government by establishing 'a perpetual presidency.' He was so convinced that his kind of administration was better for the country than anything the Democrats could offer, that he wanted to be able to pick his successors."

Nixon's choice as his heir, he told several people, was former Texas governor John Connally.[18] With him in the White House, Nixon hoped, he himself would retain effective control of foreign policy.

Such great expectations were nonetheless shot through with anxiety. "In the Oval Office that December of 1972 I saw a very troubled man," recalled James Keogh, summoned by Nixon to discuss his appointment as director of the United States Information Agency. "I left the office concerned because I could see that he was troubled . . . he, as a perceptive man, already knew how serious the road ahead was for him."

The president's fears, like those of his namesake who had reigned over fifteenth-century England, were driven by dreams and portents. Late in 1972, Ehrlichman remembered, "a strange shudder—a premonition?—went through the people near the President. . . . He had been getting messages via Rose

Woods from Billy Graham and Jeane Dixon, among others, that his life was in danger. . . . the soothsayers had him worried."

As early as a month after the Watergate arrests, Nixon himself had glimpsed the future and turned away. "I had a strange dream last night," a recently released tape shows he confided to Haldeman. "It's going to be a nasty issue for a few days. I can't believe that—we're whistling in the dark—but I can't believe that they can tie the thing to me. . . ."

32

We kept one step ahead of the sheriff . . .
that's what we're doing.

—President Nixon, as Watergate broke on him with full force, April 1973

It did not rain on the inaugural parade, but the day was cold and damp. "We shall answer to God, to history, and to our conscience for the way in which we use these years," Nixon proclaimed in his address. He seemed upbeat, and the theme was triumphal.

The Philadelphia Orchestra crashed out Beethoven's Fifth Symphony at the celebratory concert, its opening four notes the Morse code for *V*, as in "victory." It closed, at the president's personal request, with the bells and kettle-drum cannons of the *1812 Overture.*

On the evening of the inauguration Nixon took to the floor at all five balls, astonishing everyone. A song written for the occasion promised "A Wonderful Day Coming for a Wonderful U.S.A." He danced with Pat to the tune of "People Will Say We're in Love."

The undertones of the occasion were less festive. "Pat did not kiss me," Nixon recalled of the swearing-in ceremony. "I am rather glad she didn't. I sometimes think these displays of affection are very much in place. . . . Other times, I don't think they quite fit." Robert Bork, soon to be solicitor general, thought Pat looked deeply unhappy that day, her face "a death mask."

As the presidential limousine rolled down Pennsylvania Avenue, Secret Service agents had batted away garbage thrown from the crowd. "Some jerk broke through the police lines of the parade and charged at my car," Nixon snarled to John Dean afterward. "I want the bastard prosecuted, you understand?" Told the man had been harmless, Dean did nothing.

One group of spectators had watched the parade from an unusual vantage point. These were the jurors in the Watergate break-in trial, sequestered in the U.S. District Courthouse and peering from a designated window.

All the burglars, soon to be convicted, had until then kept their mouths shut. One of them, though, CREEP electronics man James McCord, was mulling an explosive decision. Before sentencing, he was to tell the judge that perjury had been committed during the trial, that his comrades had kept quiet because of "political pressure."[1]

A key component of controlling them had been hush money—first paid within weeks of the break-in—funneled by Nixon's personal lawyer Herbert Kalmbach to one of the White House detectives and from him on to the burglars. The detective, Tony Ulasewicz, made the deliveries in standard pulp fiction style, using code names for communications. Hunt was "the writer"; his fellow burglars were "the players"; the money was "the script." Ulasewicz stashed an envelope containing twenty-five thousand dollars and hid in a phone booth nearby until it was safely collected. He left forty thousand dollars in a locker at an airport, with its key taped under a ledge. More than four hundred thousand dollars—over one and a half million dollars at today's rates—were paid out in the first eight months after the arrests.

Nixon would claim as late as 1990 that the notion that he "personally ordered" the hush money payments was a "myth." As president he stated flatly that he knew nothing of such payments until mid-March 1973.[2] His representations were untrue, as documented by the dialogue on a recently released tape, dated six weeks after the Watergate arrests:

> HALDEMAN: It's worth a lot of work to try to keep it from blowing.
> PRESIDENT NIXON: Oh, my, yes . . .
> HALDEMAN: . . . everybody's satisfied. They're all out of jail, they've all been taken care of. We've done a lot of discreet checking to be sure there's no discontent in the ranks, and there isn't any . . . Hunt's happy.
> PRESIDENT NIXON: At a considerable cost, I guess?
> HALDEMAN: Yes.
> PRESIDENT NIXON: It's worth it.
> HALDEMAN: It's very expensive. It's a costly . . .
> PRESIDENT NIXON: Well . . . they have to be paid. That's all there is to it.

Another tape, also unknown during the Watergate investigation, is equally incriminating. "Goddamn hush money," Nixon exclaimed in a January 1973 exchange with Colson. "How are we going to . . . how do we get this stuff?"

In fact, obtaining it was no problem. Later, when John Dean told him further hush money payments might amount to a million dollars, the president replied: "We could get that . . . you could get it in cash. I know where it could be gotten . . . no problem. . . . The money can be provided."

A good deal of the money, the tapes indicate, came from the Greek-American millionaire Thomas Pappas, and Nixon and Haldeman discussed how convenient it was that Pappas was "able to deal in cash." To keep the tycoon sweet, the president cheerfully acquiesced to his request that a U.S. ambassador sympathetic to the Greek dictatorship stay on in Athens. He worried nonetheless that Pappas's role might be discovered, for exposure of Pappas might in turn bring exposure of the illegal funding Nixon had received from the Greek colonels in 1968.[3]

As the president sought to wriggle off the Watergate hook, he alluded repeatedly to another murky episode: the Republican subversion of the Vietnam peace talks in 1968. Time after time, the tapes reveal, he brought up the fact— or what he initially believed to be a fact—that President Johnson had had his campaign plane bugged on the eve of the election.

Citing what FBI Director Hoover had told him, Nixon claimed "Johnson knew every conversation I had . . . you know where [my plane] was bugged? In my compartment . . . every conversation I had for two weeks Johnson had it."[4] Twice, before the 1972 election and again in early 1973, Nixon tried to get proof of the alleged eavesdropping. He seemed to hope that, armed with such proof, he could either get it exposed in the press or, covertly, bring pressure on the Democrats to cut off investigation of Watergate.

He first tried to get information out of Johnson through George Christian, a former aide who had since come to favor the Republicans. Johnson responded in conciliatory fashion, denying the alleged bugging and indicating that it was best to let lie the matter of whatever either side had done in 1968.

In early 1973, with Watergate an ever-increasing threat, Nixon tried again to approach Johnson on the subject through Cartha "Deke" DeLoach, the former Hoover aide who had personally handled Johnson's order to probe the sabotage of the 1968 peace initiative. This time the former president's reply was curt and contained a warning, as a handwritten Haldeman note makes vividly clear: "LBJ got very hot & called Deke deL . . . J said to DeL if people play w/ this—direct threat he'd release intercepted cable from Emb. To Saig saying our side asking things be done. . . ."

Haldeman's diary entry, expanding on the notes, repeats that this was "a direct threat from Johnson." If Nixon persisted in his inquiries, Johnson intended to make public a cable sent in October 1968 from the South Vietnamese Embassy in Washington to President Thieu in Saigon and intercepted by U.S. intelligence. It would be a message showing that the Nixon side had encouraged Thieu to boycott the peace talks.[5]

The threat of exposure was serious but became moot when Johnson died two weeks later. A month after that, when Ehrlichman was looking for ways to frustrate congressional investigation, Nixon returned to the idea of using the alleged Democratic bugging to counterattack. Too late.

The staff of the House Banking Committee had been on the trail of the money found on the burglars within days of the arrests. Under the committee chairman, seventy-nine-year-old Wright Patman, they had made quick progress. Nixon, fearing their discoveries might damage him before the election, had demanded that Republican congressmen, including a "very smart fellow" named Gerald Ford, "get off their asses" and stop the Banking Committee. Its investigation had indeed been blocked, not only by predictable Republican votes but also—mysteriously—by six Democrats from whom Patman expected support. White House work behind the scenes, including bribery, was suspected but never proved.

For a while it seemed that the *Washington Post,* still plugging away on the Watergate story, might be all the president had to fear. The *Post* was "going to have damnable, damnable problems," Nixon fulminated, and Bebe Rebozo and other Nixon supporters would scheme—not for the first time—to ensure that the newspaper lost its valuable Florida television franchises. *Post* publisher Katharine Graham, as John Mitchell put it in a late-night conversation with Carl Bernstein, was "going to get her tit caught in a big fat wringer. . . . " Soon Mrs. Graham's neck was adorned with a tiny model of a clothes wringer and a small silver breast, and the *Post,* pressed on undaunted.

In the Senate, meanwhile, Edward Kennedy and his Judiciary subcommittee had begun a preliminary probe of Watergate, what he called "a holding action." "I know the people around Nixon," he told Bernstein. "They're thugs."

Two Senate veterans, Majority Leader Mike Mansfield, aged seventy, and Senator Sam Ervin, seventy-seven, met after the election to discuss what could or should be done. Then Mansfield announced that he was asking Ervin to form a special committee of investigation.

"I don't see how the Senate can destroy us," Nixon told Ehrlichman as the probe got under way. Recently released tapes show that he deprecated Ervin as an "old fart," a "senile old shit," "unpatriotic," a "slick southern asshole," an "old ass." For all his quivering jowls and flyaway eyebrows, the senator in fact proved highly effective. In a time of confusion he seemed a rock of fairness and old-fashioned morality.

Nixon quickly concluded that the senior Republican senator on the committee, Howard Baker, was "off the reservation," not ready enough to fight in the president's corner. "Baker may not realize it," he said vengefully, "but by getting on the wrong side of this we will destroy . . . his chances ever to move into a leadership position."

Baker was a loyal Republican, but he was also inconveniently interested in discovering the truth. Nixon denounced him in private as "a simpering asshole" with a "character flaw," who would "never be in the White House again, as long as I am in this office. Never, never, never . . . "

Nixon dismissed Baker and another Republican member of the committee, Lowell Weicker, as men who "run around in the social set, and want to be hotshots." When Weicker began charging that higher-ups were involved in Watergate, the tapes show, Nixon urged the same sort of action against the senator as he had against Democratic foes. "We've got to play a tough damn hard game on him," he told Haldeman. ". . . Is his income tax being checked yet?"

During a week in which the president raged in this vein day after day, there was a break-in at Weicker's office. In the now-familiar pattern, documents were tampered with but valuables left untouched.

The "only good friend" on the Senate committee in Nixon's estimation, was Edward Gurney, a Florida senator whose financial supporters that summer included Bebe Rebozo, Murray Chotiner, and Charles Colson's best friend and law partner. Gurney would try to discredit key witnesses and insist that the hearings were damaging the presidency and the nation.

Committee chairman Ervin meanwhile set a high moral tone. "If the many allegations made to this date are true," he declared, "then the burglars who broke into the headquarters of the Democratic National Committee at the Watergate were in effect breaking into the home of every citizen of the United States. And if these allegations prove to be true, what they were seeking to steal was not the jewels, money or other precious property of American citizens, but something much more valuable—their most precious heritage: their right to vote in a free election."

As the senators worked on, Nixon's world began to implode. The spring of 1973 saw his once-buoyant coterie of aides fall one after the other. John Dean, fatally for Nixon, defected.

It was Dean, as White House counsel, who had implemented the cover-up, devising legal strategies, liaising with the Justice Department, coordinating cover stories, supervising hush money payments. The president had praised him to his face as "very skillful" for "putting your fingers in the dikes every time that leaks have sprung . . ." "Dean," he told Haldeman in a fine oxymoron, "is an absolutely innocent accomplice . . . he gave good advice. . . . He was holding the pieces together. . . ."

In April 1973, realizing the danger in which his complicity had placed him, Dean went to the prosecutors seeking immunity. He was to testify before the Senate committee at vast length and with myriad details, damaging Nixon more than any other witness. "Goddamn him," the president now raged, ". . . one disloyal President's counsel . . . we must destroy him." Dean was now "a Judas and a turncoat" who had "deceived us all."[6]

As his own position was increasingly threatened, however, Nixon himself proved to be no pillar of loyalty. "We can't let Mitchell get involved," he had said of his steadfast colleague early in the year. "It just can't be done. We have to protect him." Yet two months later, when Ehrlichman suggested Mitchell be told "the jig is up," that he step forward and admit he is "both morally and legally responsible," the president just said, "Yeah." John Mitchell should assume responsibility, he told Haldeman.

By the spring of 1973 Mitchell's patience had been strained to the limit. His inebriate wife, Martha, had been prone to sensational outbursts since the Watergate arrests, hinting to reporters that she was privy to dark secrets, claiming her husband was being made a scapegoat. So bizarre a figure did she cut, though, and so well known was her weakness for the bottle, that she caused only limited damage.

In April, John Mitchell had a scotch-laced conversation with White House correspondent Winzola McClendon, one she did not publish at the time. "Richard Nixon," Mitchell said, "is lucky she [Martha] hasn't blown it all the way." Ehrlichman, he went on, had run "a whole espionage operation." Dean was an honest man whose function had been merely "to protect people in the White House." It was a rare lapse, never repeated. Mitchell would die in 1988 without having betrayed Nixon.

On April 17 the president offered the Senate committee some partial concessions. There had been major developments in the case, he said, and no one should be granted immunity from prosecution. He would allow White House staff to testify. As Nixon spoke, a reporter noted, his hands were shaking.

The gravest blow to the administration, and to Nixon's confidence, was now imminent. The advice from the Justice Department was that the available evidence compromised both Haldeman and Ehrlichman and that they should resign. The president "knew by now that he had no running room left," Len Garment recalled in 1997. "He described his feelings to me, rehearsing what he was going to say to Bob and John, that losing them was like losing his right and left arms. . . ."

Nixon's two closest aides were brought up to Camp David by helicopter and given the news separately. Nixon looked in "terrible shape," Haldeman thought. He "began crying uncontrollably" in front of Ehrlichman.

The president came closer to accepting his culpability that day than he ever would again. He said he was "really the guilty one," Haldeman's diary entry shows. "He said he's thought it all through, and that he's the one that started Colson on his projects. He was the one who told Dean to cover up, he was the one who made Mitchell Attorney General and later his campaign manager and so on. And that he now has to face that and live with it. . . ."

As he and Haldeman stood on the terrace of Aspen Lodge, Nixon seemed to share a deeply personal confidence. "You know, Bob," he said, "there is something I've never told anybody before, not even you. Every night since I've been President, every single night before I've gone to bed, I've knelt down on my knees beside my bed and prayed to God for guidance and help in this job. Last night before I went to bed I knelt down, and this time I prayed I wouldn't wake up in the morning. I just couldn't face going on."

At the time Haldeman was touched. Later, when he compared notes with Ehrlichman, he learned that Nixon had delivered precisely the same speech to him. He was hurt, for he had believed he had a unique emotional bond with the president. "Now," Haldeman observed later, "I see that this was just a conversational ploy—a debater's way of slipping into a different subject—used on both of us."

It is a measure of Nixon's discomfort in human relationships that, when he shook Haldeman's hand that day, his closest aide realized that in seventeen years he had never done so before. Nixon and Haldeman would have occasional contact with each other in the future. Ehrlichman received one phone call from Nixon the following Christmas but never heard from him again. He was sent a signed copy of his former boss's memoirs in 1978, but was less than delighted. "My name was misspelled," Ehrlichman told the author, "the ultimate insult."

Nixon appeared on television on April 30 to announce to the nation that his top aides, as well as Attorney General Kleindienst and John Dean, were resigning. He accepted responsibility, but no blame, for the Watergate abuses. They had been concealed as much from him, he claimed, as from the public. Then he rambled on about how most people in politics were good people, how he loved America and wanted his remaining days in office to be the best in American history, and how he hoped everyone would pray for him.

The president appeared wan and shaken, tearful as he stepped off camera. When he retreated to the Lincoln Sitting Room, some heard him say, as he had to Haldeman and Ehrlichman, that he hoped he would not wake up in the morning.

Less than an hour later, however, he was on the phone complaining to Haldeman that only one cabinet member, Caspar Weinberger, had called to praise his speech. Nixon slurred his words as he said: "Goddamn it, I'm never going to discuss this sonofabitching Watergate thing again. Never, never, never, never." Then, as the slurring grew more pronounced, he told Haldeman he loved him. He loved Ehrlichman too. He hoped his having ended the speech with "God bless America" had gone over all right.

Nixon placed other similar calls that night, and the sound of his voice on the tape suggests he was either drunk or perhaps mixing alcohol with pills. When Dean had visited him one night earlier that month, he had smelled liquor on the president's breath and seen him reach down into his desk drawer for a pill bottle. He had trouble getting the cap off, Dean noticed. Just weeks earlier, Nixon had received a visit from Jack Dreyfus, who had introduced him to the drug Dilantin. That may have been the occasion when, as Dreyfus told the author, he provided the president with another batch of a thousand pills.

Those who closely observed Nixon had been concerned about his condition for some time. The UPI's Helen Thomas had noted that "his eyes seemed not to see us" during an interview. Checking a press conference transcript against a tape recording, John Osborne had written "tremor" beside ten passages. Secret Service agent Dennis McCarthy, escorting Nixon back to the family quarters after the April 17 address, found himself with a man in distress.

"We had walked only a few feet," McCarthy recalled, "just far enough to be out of sight of the office, when he abruptly stopped, leaned against one of the columns, and began to cry . . . his shoulders heaved as he sobbed, and he took a handkerchief from his pocket and held it against his eyes. He stood there for at least a full minute, until he seemed to get control of himself, straightened up, and walked on without ever saying a word to me. . . ."

Days earlier, sounding "highly agitated," Nixon had phoned Henry Kissinger and asked if it was time to "draw the wagons around the White House." Kissinger murmured something noncommittal. Two weeks later the president made a strange remark to press aide Ziegler. "Good God Almighty," he said, decrying the attacks on him, ". . . the whole hopes of the whole goddamned world, of peace, Ron, you know where they rest? They rest right here in this damned chair. . . . The press has got to realize that . . . whatever they think of me, they've got to realize I'm the only one at the present time in this whole wide blinking world that can do a goddamn thing, you know. Keep it from blowing up . . ." "Yes, sir," Ziegler tactfully responded.

The firing of Haldeman and Ehrlichman, Ziegler thought, was Nixon's lowest emotional moment. "He looked out of the window and said, 'Ron, it's over.' And I knew he was referring to himself and the presidency." The next day, when the president saw an FBI agent posted in front of Haldeman's office door to prevent unauthorized removal of documents, he physically shoved the man. Then he summoned an immediate cabinet meeting.

"No sooner had the President sat down," recalled Kleindienst, then in his last hours as attorney general, "than he began pointing his finger at me in an agitated manner." Nixon was still raging about the guard he had found posted outside Haldeman's office, and wanted someone to blame. When the tirade continued, Kleindienst walked out.

Nixon headed for Key Biscayne after the resignations of Haldeman and Ehrlichman. He reportedly spent his days there sitting silently with Rebozo and his nights, away from Pat, in a converted office some distance from the house.

He seemed in good form a few weeks later, at a White House dinner for prisoners of war recently released from captivity in North Vietnam. Behind the backs of the freed servicemen, though, Nixon is said to have made disparaging remarks. He threw away gifts they had brought him.[7]

During the election campaign the previous year, according to one of a fifteen-strong team of CIA psychologists, all but one had concluded that the president "lied in public most of the time." He had continued to lie, liberally, in 1973. In March he had authorized Senate Republican leader Hugh Scott to say in his name that the White House had nothing to hide. The tapes show he gave a similar false assurance to Billy Graham.

"I don't give a shit what happens," Nixon had said to Mitchell on March 22. "I want you all to stonewall it, let them plead the Fifth Amendment, cover-up or anything else, if it'll save it. . . ." He had proffered the sly lawyer's advice on how to avoid telling the truth without actually committing perjury: ". . . just be damned sure you say 'I don't remember; I can't recall. . . .'" He coolly informed Assistant Attorney General Henry Petersen: "I don't lie to people." Then, the very next day, he told Haldeman that Magruder was "supposed to lie like hell" before the grand jury.

John Ehrlichman likened the Nixon of early 1973 to "some sea anemone which recoils and closes when it is threatened. I began to feel that he didn't know what the truth was. He didn't know what he had said, didn't know what he had done, and the fact was whatever he was saying was truth at that particular moment."

Nixon actually spoke of resigning that spring, sixteen months before the final fall. "Maybe," he told Kissinger during one after-dinner phone session, "we'll even consider the possibility of, frankly, just throwing myself on the sword . . . and letting Agnew take it. What the hell." Kissinger told him not even to consider it.

Two weeks later, when speechwriter Ray Price was working on the Haldeman-Ehrlichman resignation speech, the president again floated the notion that he too could quit. If Price agreed, Nixon said as if past caring, he should just "write it into the next draft." The president seemed "unraveled . . . distraught," Price recalled. ". . . I was very concerned about his state of mind."

Nixon brought up the subject of resignation twice more in the weeks that followed, both times with his family. Pat urged him to fight on, as did his daughters, arguing that the country needed him.

Nixon wavered between despair and defiance. Ehrlichman, who had dared mention the possibility that he might be impeached, recalled his reaction as having been flat, "like dropping a dead cat into the Kool-Aid."[8] Weeks later Nixon would be claiming to Alexander Haig, Haldeman's replacement, that he, the president, was "the one person who is totally blameless in this. . . ." "I wouldn't give a damn," he told Kissinger, "if they proved red-handed that I was there in the Watergate, you know, and wearing a red beard, collecting the evidence. Hell, I wouldn't even consider—the President of the United States isn't going to resign . . . not over this chicken shit stuff."

The atmosphere at the White House was by now growing increasingly surreal. "I came away feeling very comfortable," said one senior member of Congress after a meeting with Nixon in the Cabinet Room. "It was obvious that he was trying too hard to appear normal, as if nothing had gone wrong."

Kissinger noticed in early April that the president was no longer paying proper attention to business. Gone were the plethora of annotations he had habitually appended to memorandums. Once, presented with a document that required him to indicate his preferences, Nixon checked *all* the boxes.

Kissinger considered what he was seeing nothing less than "the disintegration of a government that a few weeks earlier had appeared invulnerable. The President lived in the stunned lethargy of a man whose nightmares had come true. . . . Like a figure in Greek tragedy, he was fulfilling his own nature and destroying himself."

A year to the day after the Watergate arrests, when John Dean was about to testify before the Senate, Nixon received the Soviet leader Leonid Brezhnev. He had insisted on going ahead with the summit, Kissinger believed, because "to concede that his ability to govern had been impaired would accelerate the assault on his presidency." Yet the fact was, in Kissinger's view, that Watergate had "deprived him of the attention span he needed to give intellectual impetus to SALT,"—the arms control talks.

As Nixon was seeing Brezhnev off at an air base in California, the Soviet leader wandered away unexpectedly to chat with the press. Instead of taking this in stride, Nixon snapped angrily that his counterpart had surely said all he needed to already. It was a gesture of considerable rudeness, a diplomatic discourtesy.

"By the end of the visit," Kissinger gathered from Soviet Ambassador Anatoly Dobrynin, "the Soviet party understood that the summit had been overshadowed by Watergate. . . . More gravely, the summit began to convince the Soviet leaders that Nixon's problems might turn out to be terminal." This perception of U.S. weakness at the top, Kissinger has suggested, encouraged the Soviets to risk acting as boldly as they would less than four months later, when war erupted in the Middle East.

The "domestic passion play," as Kissinger called Watergate, now threatened to enfeeble the nation, not only the man.

———

By the early summer of 1973, Nixon's ultimate fate was no longer really in his hands. Two considerable forces were now moving inexorably forward on the Watergate investigation, and a third was stirring. The Senate committee which was hearing witnesses in the glare of constant publicity, had been joined in the field by Special Prosecutor Archibald Cox, appointed at the insistence of the Senate Judiciary Committee because of the perception that the White House had been interfering with the course of justice. Cox's Prosecution Force, unlike a congressional committee, could bring people to trial, though not—it was thought—the president of the United States.

The only process by which a sitting president can be forced from power is impeachment. The House of Representatives is the prosecutor, the Senate the judge and jury. The ultimate penalty is removal from office, and there is no appeal. Only one president, Andrew Johnson, had ever faced impeachment before, in the mid-nineteenth century, and he had been acquitted.[9]

Impeachment was a virtually unthinkable remedy, but senior men in the Congress were now thinking about it. "The time is going to come," House Majority Leader Tip O'Neill had said months earlier at a private meeting with Speaker Carl Albert, "when impeachment is going to hit this Congress." Peter Rodino, the House Judiciary Committee chairman, had thought at the time that O'Neill was wrong. In June 1973, however, he told his chief counsel, Jerry Zeifman, to start preparing for the process—"just in case."

On July 12 Ervin's seven senators gathered to discuss a problem: Nixon had sent a letter refusing to produce documents relevant to the investigation, claiming "executive privilege." The committee decided to respond both by writing to the president, explaining that his position could cause a "fundamental constitutional confrontation," and requesting a telephone conference between him and Ervin.

Nervous jokes were made as the senators gathered in Ervin's office to await the telephone call. "Should we all stand when the telephone rings?" one joked. Another responded that they should indeed, and "all sing 'Bail to the Chief.'" Then the president came on the line.

"We could hear Ervin's side of the conversation," chief counsel Sam Dash recalled in 1997. "He was talking respectfully about working out some arrangement about the documents and how perhaps he and Senator Baker could go and see Nixon. . . . And then suddenly the senator was saying: 'But, no, Mr. President, we're not out to get you, Mr. President. We're just trying to do our duty.' Then again: 'No, we're not out to get you, Mr. President. . . .'"

Ervin concluded the conversation a quarter of an hour later looking flushed and troubled. Nixon had been "shrieking" and "hysterical," the senator told his colleagues, "emotionally distraught."

When word came that evening that the president had been taken to the Bethesda Naval Hospital, some of Ervin's staff assumed he had suffered a mental breakdown. In fact, he had pneumonia, which was to keep him in the hospital for eight days. Meanwhile, within twenty-four hours, came the revelation that doomed him. The Senate committee learned about the existence of the White House tapes.

Twice that spring, in conversations with Haldeman, Nixon had expressed concern about the taping system. "Frankly," he had said one April morning, "I don't want to have in the record discussions we've had in this room on Watergate." He and Haldeman agreed that the recording system would henceforth be activated only when the president switched it on. It was a sensible, if belated, precaution, but the taping of compromising conversations continued.

A week later, when Nixon asked if the system was still in place, he was informed it was. Should the tapes be preserved? On balance Nixon seemed to think they should, but he was nervous. "I don't think it should ever get out that we taped this office," he told Haldeman in one of their last taped conversations. "Have we got people that are trustworthy on that? I guess we have."[10]

It got out in July as the president lay in the hospital, aptly enough on Friday the thirteenth. That day, three Senate staffers sat in the Dirksen Office Building interviewing Haldeman's former aide Alexander Butterfield, who had recently moved on to a new job.

Ironically it was a Republican, deputy minority counsel Donald Sanders, whose questioning brought the breakthrough that sealed Nixon's fate. Sanders had two leads to go on. Investigators had come by a White House summary of Nixon's version of his meetings with Dean, a summary that seemed almost unnaturally detailed and complete—unless it had been prepared from a recording. Dean, moreover, had told how Nixon had behaved oddly at one of their meetings, moving away to a corner and speaking in a virtual whisper. Dean had wondered at the time, he testified, whether the president was secretly taping him, hoping to set him up.

Sanders, a former FBI agent, asked Butterfield if he knew why Nixon would have behaved as Dean had described. "I was hoping you fellows wouldn't ask me that," Butterfield slowly replied, then went on to reveal the existence of the president's recording system. The White House and Camp David, he told his questioners, were positively riddled with microphones.

The investigators knew at once what they had. Staffers of both parties rushed to notify colleagues, and the Republicans made sure the White House was warned that the secret was out. Nixon, delivered the news in the hospital, was appalled. Rose Woods called Butterfield to say: "You dirty bastard. You have contributed to the downfall of the greatest president this country has ever had."

Unsurprisingly the taping system was shut down almost at once. Democrats hastened to claim that no president of theirs would ever have made such secret recordings, as in fact, several had, if not on the scale of the Nixon operation. Meanwhile a preemptive damage control operation got under way at the Kennedy Library. "Sensitive" tapes were hastily erased, according to Edward Kennedy's aide Richard Burke.

At the same time, Nixon's men headed to the hospital to discuss what he should do with his. Some advised destruction, but the lawyers warned that would be obstruction of justice. The president himself reportedly at first suggested having the tapes stored under his bed at the White House. So vast was the accumulated body of recordings, however, that the tapes would not have fitted in the room, let alone under the bed. Given the unfeasibility of that option, Nixon was of two minds as to what to do. "Should have destroyed the tapes after April 30," he scribbled on the notepad at his bedside. Yet he told Alexander Haig, "I know what I did and didn't do. I don't think I knowingly committed any crime. I need those tapes to protect me."

Today, with the release in recent years of several hundred hours of tape, including many categorized by the archivist of the United States under the heading "Abuse of Power," it is astonishing that Nixon imagined they might exonerate him.

The Senate committee quickly subpoenaed recordings likely to have evidentiary relevance, as did the special prosecutor. Nixon refused to submit any at all, again claiming executive privilege. A long, long struggle had begun, during which the president's lawyers were to argue that he had "absolute power to decide what may be disclosed." "Unlike a monarch," the special prosecutor was to counter, "the president is not the sovereign." The Supreme Court would eventually rule that the only thing that was absolute was Nixon's obligation to obey the law—but that decision was still a year away.

Even before the legal battle began, Special Prosecutor Cox had shared another concern with James Doyle, his aide and spokesman. "Do you think," he asked, "the president is mentally ill?"

Nixon's behavior in public on occasion fueled such concerns. At an appearance on a Florida college campus, *Newsweek*'s Washington bureau chief Mel Elfin reported, the president did a walkabout that "seemed spontaneous but was guided by staff and Secret Service men with radioed stage directions. 'Turn him right there and have him go to the faculty,' and Mr. Nixon turned and went to the faculty. 'Have him wave.' Nixon waved."

This was not just the normal management of a chief executive. The president had seemed "zombie-like," Elfin was to recall. So oddly, indeed, had he acted that the reporter consulted doctors to ask if the symptoms were consistent with the taking of any particular drug.

In August, arriving at New Orleans' Rivergate Center to address the Veterans of Foreign Wars, the president at first appeared "relaxed and confident." Then, suddenly, he objected loudly to the presence of newsmen, grabbed Ron Ziegler by the shoulders, spun him around, and propelled his own aide with a hard push toward the photographers.

When Nixon launched into his speech, something was evidently wrong with him. "What was remarkable," the *New York Times* correspondent thought, "was his manner on the stage. He paced about, smiling and gesturing in an exaggerated way. He stumbled over his words. . . . His voice fluctuated in volume and speed."

Some in the audience thought the president was drunk, others that he was on "uppers," which made him look like "Ed Sullivan on speed." A spokesman told reporters he was not using any medication. Today, armed with the knowledge that Nixon used Dilantin, it seems more than likely that drug was the culprit. The symptoms are consistent with having taken too high a Dilantin dosage.

The word at the *New York Times* was that Nixon was seeing a psychiatrist. The therapist they had in mind was Dr. Hutschnecker, with whom Nixon had been in contact since the fifties, and reporters armed with his photograph for identification began looking for him wherever Nixon went. The doctor had in fact written to the president just weeks earlier, expressing deep concern and offering to see him. It is not clear whether Nixon accepted Hutschnecker's suggestion, but his letter was found in Nixon's desk after the resignation—a year later.[11]

The same week that he wrote to Nixon, an op-ed article by Hutschnecker had appeared in the *New York Times*. Its headline was direct: A SUGGESTION: PSYCHIATRY AT HIGH LEVELS OF GOVERNMENT. The article cited the sins of Watergate in light of the doctor's long-held theory that potential leaders should be given clean bills of health in advance by psychiatrists as well as physicians. Hutschnecker wrote sorrowfully of how men charged with protecting the people's rights had betrayed their trust and done something Americans usually associated with foreign dictatorships, "spying on one another."

Suitably trained doctors, he urged, should be available in government at all times, to "raise their voice when human ambition and greed or drives for an uninhibited use of power seem to be getting out of control." It was time, the psychotherapist wrote, to "explore possibilities other than purely political to secure that our best and brightest leaders are also our mentally and morally healthiest and soundest."

Few informed people can have missed the article's message or failed to note its timing. Week by week the Nixon presidency was irretrievably losing something at its core, the dignity that is intrinsic to the office. After the New Orleans episode, Nixon was referred to with a disrespect hitherto unimaginable.

"Millions of us," wrote Nicholas von Hoffman, "saw El Flippo on TV grab Ziegler by the arms, whirl him around and, with an expression on his face both frightening and frightful, shove him. . . . Who can forget the picture of a President so out of control of himself that he expresses it by laying angry hands on a member of his staff in public? . . . [T]he impression is gaining that Nixon is becoming dysfunctional, and the fear is growing that he may do something we'll be sorry for."

The *Washington Star-News*, meanwhile, published an extraordinary piece about what would happen should a U.S. president become mentally ill. The Twenty-fifth Amendment to the Constitution, it pointed out, provided a mechanism for the transfer of power in the event of incapacitating illness. The procedure was straightforward enough if the president was capable of recognizing and acknowledging his condition. "But," writer Smith Hempstone asked, "what happens if the President becomes physically or emotionally incapacitated and is unable or unwilling to recognize that incapacity, as might well happen in the case of a mental breakdown? . . . that prospect is too horrible to contemplate."

According to his biographer, Senator Ervin had discussed just such a possibility with Majority Leader Mansfield before they decided on the Watergate probe. It had been, even then, "that thing which was the main fear and therefore the prime issue. Which wasn't whether or not Nixon was a crook. Millions had been talking on both sides of that issue for more than a quarter century now. Everyone knew what the prime issue was. A certain thumb moving awkwardly towards a certain red button, a certain question of sanity. . . . Query: if the man who holds the thumb over the button is mad. . . .' "

Such fears, harbored by men not known for paranoia, were now very real.

"Al Haig is keeping the country together, and I am keeping the world together," Kissinger had been heard to say as summer ended. He had recently become secretary of state and, retaining his post as security adviser, now had more independence of action than ever. Nixon did not bother to attend National Security Council meetings and reportedly often initialed documents without reading them.

On October 6, just six weeks after the president's alarming behavior in New Orleans, a red-button moment arrived. Soviet-backed Arab armies, performing militarily better than ever before, struck at Israel, and for a while it seemed they might triumph. Israel was able to contain and reverse the threat thanks to a massive American airlift, but before the guns stopped firing, a moment of nuclear peril would put the entire world in danger. At that unsafe moment, and during the three weeks the war lasted, the president of the United States gave it less than adequate attention.

He did not attend a single formal meeting on the conflict during the first week of the conflict. He was clear on the essentials, Kissinger recalled, not least on the fact that a massive airlift of arms supplies was essential to Israel's survival. Yet he remained "preoccupied with his domestic scandals . . . deflected from details." In private, at the time, the secretary of state was more forthright.

At lunch with the columnist Max Lerner during the war Kissinger took a telephone call at the table. "I could hear some muttered words about the president and saw his face change color," Lerner recalled. "For a moment he was silent, and then—as we rose from the table—he said, almost under his breath but quite clearly, 'That anti-Semitic bastard!' "

While they ate lunch, Lerner had asked the secretary about Nixon. "Kissinger was in effect carrying the burden of the presidency," he concluded, "seeking to salvage by his prestige whatever shreds of legitimacy the executive still had. He knew how Nixon was coming apart, as a mind, and as a man."

Nixon spent much of the conflict's fourth day preoccupied with the fate of his vice president. Spiro Agnew, accused of having received thousands of dollars in kickbacks on building contracts, had hoped the president would come to his rescue. Nixon, however, had long since wanted to be rid of Agnew, and under the strictest scrutiny as the result of his own crisis, he could not appear to be interceding on behalf of his vice president in a criminal case. Agnew pleaded no contest on a tax charge and resigned.

Nixon wrote his departing colleague a placatory letter, declaring his sadness and "great sense of personal loss." Agnew, however, believed the president had become his "mortal enemy." While he was still resisting resignation, he had received a final message from the White House, reminding him curtly that "the President has a lot of power." Agnew had interpreted it as a physical threat. He feared he would be killed, he was to write years later, should he refuse to "go quietly."

His concern sounds exaggerated today, but it is worth recalling how deeply Watergate spread the poison of fear. "Everyone's life is in danger," Bob Woodward was warned by his source Deep Throat. He and Bernstein briefed their editor and took a few precautions, but pressed on with their work.

A threat to kill John Dean, meanwhile, caused the Senate Committee to arrange around-the-clock protection for Nixon's former counsel. Senator Ervin's life was also threatened, as was that of Special Prosecutor Cox.

There was concern too that one or more of the Watergate burglars might be murdered to ensure their silence. A caller had phoned a bomb threat to the home of James McCord days after the arrests. "If the administration gets its back to the wall," a White House messenger warned him later, "it will take steps to defend itself." Like Agnew, McCord took the assertion as a threat to his life. Louis Russell, the former Nixon investigator who had been "watching" on the night of the Watergate arrests, died of an apparent heart attack during the summer, after alleging he had been poisoned. The claim may well have been baseless, but it was symptomatic of the rotten atmosphere of Watergate Washington.[12]

Early on the morning of the day Agnew resigned, with the war in the Middle East in its fifth day, the congressional leadership went to the White House for a briefing. It proved a disconcerting experience. While Kissinger attempted to present a situation report, Nixon kept interrupting with bad jokes about the secretary of state's supposed sex life. "President," Tip O'Neill scrawled on his notepad, "is acting very strange."

Two days later, October 12, Nixon chose a curious way to name Agnew's successor. The televised announcement of his choice, Gerald Ford, featured red-coated marines playing violins. At a time when only understatement would have been appropriate, the occasion was raucous and celebratory. The *Times*'s Anthony Lewis thought it the "most repellent American public ceremony in memory. . . . There was not the slightest sense of responsibility for what had passed, not the least reference to the grisly reason for this occasion." Ford aide Robert Hartmann thought Nixon was "visibly wallowing in his stellar role."

Behind the scenes the president denigrated his own appointee. "Can you imagine Jerry Ford sitting in this chair?" he reportedly sneered to Nelson Rockefeller. Nixon sent one of his attorneys a pen he had used to certify the Ford nomination, with a note reading: "Here is the damn pen I signed Jerry Ford's nomination with." For Kissinger, the naming of Ford stilled, if only briefly, "the worry about the future of a country with a visibly disintegrating executive authority."

Nixon was about to take a disastrous step, the removal of the man he called "the viper in our bosom," Watergate Special Prosecutor Cox. The stated reason for firing him was to be that Cox had rejected the president's proposed compromise on the tapes—an offer of White House "summaries" rather than the tapes themselves. To Nixon, though, the prosecutor was more than an obstinate public servant insisting on full compliance. For Cox's background combined two elements sure to raise the president's ire: He was a Harvard professor, and he was favored by the Kennedy clan.[13] "Now that we've taken care of Agnew," Nixon had said in the hearing of his attorney general, Elliot Richardson, "we can get rid of Cox."

On the night of October 20, around nine o'clock, Judiciary Committee chief counsel Zeifman received an anguished call from a special prosecution force attorney, Philip Lacovara. "The FBI has just entered our office, and they are armed," Lacovara shouted. "This may be the end of the Republic. You've gotta do something."

The Saturday Night Massacre was under way. Rather than obey Nixon's order to fire Cox, Richardson resigned. When his deputy, William Ruckelshaus, refused the same command, he in turn was fired. Solicitor General Robert Bork, however, temporarily promoted to acting attorney general, obediently sent the letter of dismissal. It had been composed by Nixon's lawyer and typed on Justice Department stationery that had been transported from Richardson's office to the White House by chauffeured limousine.

As Cox awaited the letter at home, his staff hurried to the office to secure records as best they could. Three reels of tape were spirited away, stuffed down the pants of an attorney's wife, just as the FBI arrived to seal the building. Provided secretly to the prosecutors just days earlier, they contained the covertly recorded conversations of Rebozo bank vice president Franklin DeBoer, saying he managed Nixon's "buried" financial portfolio.[14] On the money front, the investigation was getting dangerously close to the president. Ten days earlier Rebozo had admitted receiving one hundred thousand dollars in cash from Howard Hughes on Nixon's behalf.

"Constitutional crisis," "dictatorship," "Brownshirt operation," "act of desperation": The media's condemnation of the Saturday Night Massacre was immediate and universal. Nixon was "acting like a madman, a tyrant," "crazy." A Gallup poll showed that the president's approval rating had sunk to a nadir of 17 percent. He would admit, years later, that dismissing Cox had been a "serious miscalculation."

The situation in the Middle East remained grave, with the successful Israeli counterattack bringing new risks and uncertainties. Kissinger, on a trip to Moscow to negotiate a cease-fire agreement, phoned the White House on an urgent matter—only to have Alexander Haig tell him, "Get off my back . . . I have troubles of my own."

Back in Washington, on the evening of October 24, the secretary of state found himself faced with the possibility that the Soviets might send forces to the war zone. At 7:05 P.M. he interrupted a phone confrontation with Ambassador Dobrynin to take a call from the president. Nixon was "agitated and emotional," and his principal concern was himself. Congressional leaders, he insisted, must be told how indispensable he was to the management of the Middle East crisis. The politicians, Nixon told Kissinger, were attacking him "because of their desire to kill the President . . . they may succeed. I may physically die. . . . It brings me sometimes to feel like saying the hell with it." Kissinger thought his boss "in the paralysis of an approaching nightmare."

It was on that night that the red-button moment occurred. Kissinger's conversation with Dobrynin, resumed after he had spoken with Nixon, convinced him that Moscow was intent on sending in Soviet troops. He worked the phone for two hours, then called Haig at 9:30 P.M. only to be told that Nixon had already "retired for the night." At a moment that he and Haig agreed might herald the presidency's "most explosive crisis," the leader of the free world was unavailable.

Roger Morris, a former Kissinger aide, has quoted the secretary of state's senior assistant, Lawrence Eagleburger, and other colleagues as saying Nixon was "upstairs drunk . . . slurring his words and barely roused when Haig and Kissinger tried to deal with him in the first moment of the crisis." Haig, the principal relevant witness, has said the president was merely "tired."

Minutes after his call to Haig, Kissinger heard from Dobrynin again, this time to read a peremptory warning from Brezhnev to the president. "I will say it straight," the crucial sentence read, "if you find it impossible to act jointly with us in this matter, we should be faced with the necessity urgently to consider the question of taking appropriate steps unilaterally." The letter demanded an immediate response.

Intelligence reports confirmed suspicious Soviet air and naval movements that seemed to suggest that insertion of an airborne force was imminent. The appropriate response, Kissinger reasoned, was to shock the Soviets into abandoning such plans. At 9:50 P.M. he called Haig again. "I asked whether I should wake up the President," Kissinger recalled. "He replied curtly: 'No.' I knew what that meant. Haig thought the President too distraught to participate. . . ."

After more phone calls and a warning to Dobrynin, the Washington Special Actions Group, made up of top Defense Department, intelligence, and military chiefs, was summoned to the White House Situation Room. Kissinger again discussed with Haig whether to wake up the president. There was no vice president to summon because Ford had yet to be confirmed by the Senate.

Most U.S. forces at that time were normally at an alert status known as DEFCON (defense condition) IV. DEFCON I is war. That night the military went to DEFCON III, or Flash III.

At U.S. air bases, B-52s loaded with nuclear weapons lined up nose to tail. In missile silos, launch commanders buckled themselves into their chairs. Nuclear-armed submarines sped to secret positions off the Soviet coast, prepared to launch. In case those steps were not sufficient to put the Soviets on notice, two aircraft carriers were ordered to move closer to the conflict, amphibious ships were ordered to leave port in Crete, B-52s in the Pacific headed for the United States, and the 82nd Airborne was placed on alert. A stern reply to Brezhnev's letter, telling him that unilateral Soviet action would among other things be contrary to the Agreement on Prevention of Nuclear War, went out at dawn. It was sent in Nixon's name.

Nixon seemed "clearheaded and crisp" when Kissinger briefed him at 8:00 A.M. Forty minutes later, however, when congressional leaders arrived to be brought up-to-date, they were once again confronted with bizarre behavior.

As Tip O'Neill recalled, "Kissinger had barely opened his mouth when the President interrupted him and started talking to us about the history of communism in the Soviet Union. He rambled on for almost half an hour about the czars and the revolution, about Marx and Lenin, and even the assassination of Trotsky in Mexico. Nobody could understand what, if anything, all this had to do with the Middle East war."

When Kissinger managed to resume speaking, he was interrupted by Nixon with another twenty-five-minute history lecture. With the House due to convene at ten o'clock, the members of Congress eventually excused themselves and left. On the way back to the Hill, O'Neill discussed Nixon's demeanor with George Mahon, chairman of the Appropriations Committee, and Thomas Morgan, chairman of the Foreign Affairs Committee. Morgan, the only practicing doctor in the Congress, said the president seemed to him "paranoid . . . in real trouble."

A new letter from Brezhnev came in within hours, written as though the threat of the previous night had never been made. The crisis evaporated, and Nixon—"elated," according to Kissinger—went off to Camp David. From there he called again to ask that the press be informed how indispensable he had been.

Whether or not the president had been drunk, the fact remains that the world had been on the brink of a nuclear crisis while he was asleep. Haig, who would remain at Nixon's side until the resignation, has said he took the threatening Brezhnev message to the president, that Nixon called it "the most serious thing since the Cuban Missile Crisis" and called for action. Later, told of the decision to hold an emergency meeting, Nixon "expressed no enthusiasm for attending. . . . As usual he preferred to let others set the options. . . . With a wave of the hand, he said, 'You know what I want, Al, you handle the meeting.'"

The account of another senior participant suggests this is not the full story. Admiral Elmo Zumwalt, the chief of naval operations, recalled being summoned on the night of the alert, along with the other Joint Chiefs, to a 2:00 A.M. meeting with Defense Secretary James Schlesinger and William Clements, Schlesinger's deputy. Nixon's name was not mentioned when they discussed the alert, and Zumwalt was told it had been initiated without the president's involvement.

"We had to go on nuclear alert without his permission," the admiral recalled in 1997. "The reason we had to do that was because he could not be awakened. Nixon obviously had too much to drink. . . . I was told at the time that they were not able to waken him."

Zumwalt said he was given this information as the meeting ended, by the chairman of the Joint Chiefs, Admiral Moorer, and by Clements, quoting Schlesinger. The former defense secretary, whom the author interviewed several times, was circumspect in his replies. If Nixon was unwakable, he said, "Haig put up a good performance, going out to consult with him two or three times. . . . I felt that it was unusual that he should be absent throughout what was a major point of confrontation between ourselves and the Soviet Union." Schlesinger could think of no other president of modern times who would not have been present during such a momentous meeting.[15]

In the watches of that dangerous night, faced with what appeared to be a deliberate Soviet provocation, Nixon's closest advisers had wondered if the crisis would have occurred at all had he been a "functioning" president.

The year ended miserably and in humiliation. In November, at an Associated Press managing editors' meeting in Orlando, Florida, Nixon made gaffe after gaffe as he responded to a volley of sharp questions: on missing tapes; on the tiny income taxes he had paid; on the rumors that Rebozo kept a secret trust fund for him.

The locale was Disney World, and it was there that he notoriously delivered the line "I welcome this kind of examination, because people have got to know whether or not their President is a crook. Well, I am not a crook."

On the short flight back to Key Biscayne afterward, Nixon had several stiff drinks. As he left the plane, he confided to the captain of Air Force One, Colonel Albertazzie, that he had had "a couple of good belts." At the foot of the aircraft steps, where a general was waiting to greet him, the president bowed—in Albertazzie's words—"from the waist, grandly, magnificently, with great flourish." He was very obviously drunk.

The parlous state of the man was increasingly obvious to visitors to the White House. At a cabinet meeting Robert Bork saw the president's hands trembling and observed the difficulty he had controlling his voice. The new FBI director, Clarence Kelley, heard Nixon's rambling speech and concluded he was "breaking down." Treasury Deputy Secretary William Simon was reminded of a "wind-up doll, mechanically making gestures with no thought as to their meaning."

In December, Senator Barry Goldwater was one of a group of nine invited to dine at the White House. "The President entered after we were assembled," he recalled. "He was quite animated, even garrulous. . . . Unexpectedly, his mind seemed to halt abruptly and wander aimlessly away. . . . I became concerned. I had never seen Nixon talk so much, yet so erratically—as if he were a tape with unexpected blank sections."

As the president jabbered on, Goldwater felt he was witnessing "a slow-motion collapse of Nixon's mental balance." "I drove home," the senator recalled, "and dictated these words for my files: 'I have reason to suspect that all might not be well mentally in the White House. This is the only copy that will ever be made of this; it will be locked in my safe. . . .'"[16]

The following week, at a routine conference with the Joint Chiefs of Staff, Nixon ignored the subject of the meeting, the defense budget, and launched, as Admiral Zumwalt recalled, into "a big rambling monologue, which at times almost seemed to be a stream of consciousness, about the virtues of his domestic and foreign policy. He repeatedly expressed the thought that the Eastern liberal establishment was out to do us all in and that we should beware. . . . It was clear that he perceived himself as a fighter for all that was right in the United States, involved in mortal battle with the forces of evil."

The next part of the Nixon diatribe, however, shocked the admiral. "'We gentlemen here,' he told them, 'are the last hope, the last chance to resist . . .' I got the impression he was sort of testing the water with us, to see whether there would be support—any nodding of heads—at some of these things. One could well have come to the conclusion that here was the Commander-in-Chief trying to see what the reaction of the Chiefs might be if he did something unconstitutional. . . . He was trying to find out whether in a crunch there was support to keep him in power. . . ."

Stunned by what he had heard, Zumwalt consulted afterward with General Creighton Abrams, who had been his superior officer and close colleague in Vietnam. The general said he had decided to act as though the episode had never happened. Zumwalt, for his part, wrote a record of the conversation and deposited it in Pentagon archives. It will remain classified, he told the author before his death in 2000, for twenty years.

Nixon spent Christmas Day at the White House with his family, which was by now in increasingly low spirits. Tricia and Julie both had suffered on their father's behalf that year. When Tricia and her husband had visited Yankee Stadium, a barrage of boos had broken out when the scoreboard flashed the greeting "Welcome Tricia Nixon."

Julie had made 150 public appearances over the past months, speaking out for her father often. "Anyone thinking that Nixon deserved a better fate from Watergate," George Will was to write, "should remember his silence as his brave daughter Julie crisscrossed the country defending him against charges he knew to be true."

After the holiday Nixon and Pat headed for San Clemente, where they remained for seventeen days. He had so far spent only four of the forty-four weekends of his second term in Washington. To outsiders, Pat had seemed to be withstanding the turmoil better than her husband. "Amazing," a visiting African diplomat had observed. "I could see his hands shaking, and he looks gray. But she has such control."

The control had been less evident behind the scenes. According to Ehrlichman, Pat had also been drinking too much during the long crisis and once had to be rescued by the Secret Service from an overflowing bathtub.[17] On another night, according to an Executive Protection Service officer, agents had been obliged to rush to Pat's aid for another reason. As he allegedly had years earlier, after the 1962 defeat in California, Nixon had struck her.

Bebe Rebozo joined the Nixons during the stay at San Clemente, and when they were alone together on New Year's Eve, the president asked if he should resign. "No," Rebozo responded, "you have to fight."

"Do I fight all out," Nixon wrote on his bedside notepad in the early hours of New Year's morning, "or do I now begin the long process to prepare for a change, meaning in effect, resignation?" Then he wrote the answer: "*Fight.*"

A few nights later, at 5:00 A.M., he composed another note: "Dignity, command, faith . . . act like a winner. Opponents are savage destroyers, haters. Time to use full power of the President. . . ."

33

I suppose it was inevitable that a time would come when this constant accumulation of power would have to be checked, in a manner clearly understood not only by the President in office at that particular moment in history, but by presidents yet to come.

—Representative Jerome Waldie, House Judiciary Committee,
in his "impeachment journal," on the eve of Nixon's resignation

There is little likelihood that during his 1974 New Year's vacation the president of the United States looked up the meaning of the word "power" in *Webster's Dictionary*. Had he done so, he would have read that it means "possession of control, authority, or influence over others" and would hardly have quibbled with the definition. That surely was the very essence Nixon meant to use to the full, as his January diary note suggested.

The long Watergate crisis inspired the writer Jimmy Breslin to propose an alternative definition for the word. Power, Breslin suggested, was really no more than "mirrors and blue smoke. If somebody tells you how to look, there can be seen in the smoke great magnificent shapes, castles and kingdoms. . . . Power is an *illusion*." Part of the illusion is that power exists only so long as others believe you have it. Once they stop believing, it rapidly disappears.

Early that year, a passage in his memoirs suggests, Nixon figured that if he could just find a way to realign the mirrors, to make the smoke swirl in the right formations again, the public would go on believing, and he would survive as president. "I convinced myself," he wrote, "that although the *case* was badly flawed . . . the *cause* was noble and important."

The cause, for Nixon, was preserving "the nature of leadership in American politics . . . if I could be hounded from office because of a political scandal like Watergate, the whole American system of government would be undermined and changed. I never for a moment believed that any of the charges against me were legally impeachable. . . ."

At the end of January, Pat at his side, the president made his way to Congress to deliver his fourth State of the Union address. He spoke of the matters of which presidents speak—of world peace and the economy, of health care and welfare reform—and he was well enough received. After twenty-two thousand words he finally turned to the topic about which everyone in the hushed chamber was really thinking: Watergate.

It was time to move on, Nixon urged, on and away from the scandal to the real issues. He had, he claimed, provided the special prosecutor with "all the material that he needs to conclude his investigations. . . . I believe the time has come to bring that investigation and the other investigations to an end. One year of Watergate is enough."

Yet far from coming to an end, the investigations were gathering momentum. Cox's replacement as special prosecutor, Leon Jaworski, had not turned out, as some had feared and Nixon loyalists had hoped, to be amenable to manipulation. On the contrary, the evidence he had examined so far merely made him determined to press for more.

Nixon had by now reluctantly surrendered a few White House tapes, and Jaworski was stunned by the tenor of the conversations he heard on them. They left him, he told aides, with the impression that Nixon was a man who "wanted psychopaths around him . . . ," that there was "something missing in his make-up." The tapes also convinced the prosecutor, for the first time, that the president had been "culpably involved." Informed that White House attorneys believed there was no criminal case against Nixon, Jaworski disagreed. He told Alexander Haig that the president should "get the finest criminal lawyers he could find."

The Senate committee, now assembling its massive thirty-volume report, was preparing the ground for the process Nixon had most to fear. Impeachment had ceased to be a talking point and was now being actively pursued. The House Judiciary Committee had funds and a special staff—among whom was an attorney in her mid-twenties named Hillary Rodham[1]—and would shortly have full powers, voted by a massive majority, to investigate whether "grounds exist for the House of Representatives to impeach Richard M. Nixon, President of the United States of America."

All this had been under way well before Nixon left for his New Year's vacation. Yet in public and in private, like some King Canute of old hoping the tide would fail to come in if so commanded, he acted as though it would all go away. At Alice Longworth's ninetieth birthday party in February, the president's show of confidence was disquieting. "I found myself asking him how he stood up under all the pressure," CBS's Nancy Dickerson recalled. "He gave a broad sweep of his hand, indicating that it was water off a duck's back. At first he was convincing, but then I realized that he was speaking as if about some other person rather than about himself. He was totally detached from the realities, and it was eerie."

But by now the realities—realities personal, political, and judicial—continued to come rushing unabated at Nixon. Most of the old guard had left or were on the way out. Haldeman and Ehrlichman were facing trial on multiple charges. Herb Klein and Melvin Laird, honorable men, had both departed. Bryce Harlow, who had been Nixon's first political appointee as president, was about to step down.

The longest-serving retainer of them all, Murray Chotiner, had died in the hospital at the turn of the year, aged sixty-four, following a car crash. One of the vehicles involved in the collision had been driven, by odd coincidence, by a man named McGovern. The accident had occurred, moreover, outside the home of Edward Kennedy, and the senator himself had summoned the paramedics. Nixon went to the funeral, mourning his "ally in political battles, trusted colleague . . . friend."

With his staff decimated, Harlow recalled, Nixon was "almost incommunicado. He dealt with General Haig, Ron Ziegler, Rose Woods, his counsel . . . stopped seeing anyone else." In part this was because few could now bear to spend time with him, so distracted was his manner. Even Ziegler, the eager young press aide, reportedly often tried to avoid Nixon's phone calls.

Many of those who had served him were already being brought to justice. Krogh, sentenced for his role in the burglary of the office of Ellsberg's psychiatrist, had been first to go to jail. Nixon's attorney, Kalmbach, would be next, convicted on a corrupt practices charge of offering an ambassadorship in return for an election contribution. Nixon aides high and low were facing terms in jail: Colson, for obstruction of justice; Magruder, for obstruction of justice and conspiracy to intercept wire communications unlawfully; Mitchell, for conspiracy to obstruct and perjury; Chapin, for lying to the grand jury; Dean, for conspiracy to obstruct justice; Haldeman and Ehrlichman, for conspiracy to obstruct and perjury. By the end fourteen associates were to serve time behind bars.

The day Nixon delivered his State of the Union address, the federal grand jury probing the Watergate cover-up wrote asking him to testify. He refused, citing the independence of his office and the pressure of work. The jurors, though, were not overawed by the fact that they were dealing with the presidency. Several of them revealed later that even on the basis of the evidence available at that early stage, they had wanted to indict the president along with the other defendants. The straw vote they held on the issue was so conclusive as to be hilarious. "We all raised our hands about wanting an indictment, all of us," recalled former juror Elayne Edlund. "Some of us raised both hands." A four-count indictment was duly prepared.

Prosecutor Jaworski opposed taking this course, evoking passionate dissent from some of his own attorneys. "The facts described to you," four of them told him in a twenty-one-page memorandum, "constitute clear and prima facie evidence of the President's participation in a conspiracy to obstruct justice . . . it is essential that this simple primary truth emerge from the action we and the grand jury take: that but for the fact that he is President, Richard Nixon would have been indicted."

A compromise was eventually reached: When indictments were presented against Haldeman, Ehrlichman, and company, Nixon's name was joined to the list of the accused as an "unindicted coconspirator."[2] The documentation handed to the district court, which included White House tapes, filled two bulky locked briefcases.

Few Americans knew then that the grand jury had wanted to send their president to trial for bribery, conspiracy, obstruction of justice, and obstruction of a criminal investigation. That fact was kept secret and, when finally reported in the press in midsummer, was lost in the onrush of events. The jurors and the prosecution force, however, had ensured that their work would not be wasted. The evidence in the two briefcases was to be passed, as the jury had requested, to the real arbiter of Nixon's fate, the House Judiciary Committee. It was to form the core of the evidence for the impeachment of the president.

On March 6 a reporter dared ask Nixon if he considered that the crimes alleged against the indicted defendants, if applied to himself, were impeachable offenses. "Well," he responded, taken unawares, "I have also quit beating my wife."

For Pat and the girls, maintaining their composure was getting harder with every week that passed. Julie insisted early in the year that her father "hasn't done anything wrong." By the spring, though, the strain was obvious. "She seemed emaciated, bewildered, grasping at straws," the president's fervent supporter Rabbi Korff wrote in a note to himself after seeing her at lunch. "I turned from Julie, unable to look at her sans breaking down in pity and sorrow for what this fragile creature must endure."

"We do believe in Daddy as ever," Tricia told an interviewer in April. "He has never lied. . . . He is the most honest man we know."

Pat, for her part, on occasion betrayed obvious distress. "Nixon came out with some Secret Servicemen," a neighbor recalled of a visit to Key Biscayne. "He was heading back to Washington, and Pat was standing there. A tear came down her cheek, and she kind of shook her head. Nixon looked like the weight of the world was on his shoulders. He was slumping, shuffling along."

Observed close up on a trip to Latin America, Pat seemed suffused with pain and rage. Asked how she was coping, she declined to reply. A happy moment, however, seemed at hand when—in Nashville en route home—she had a public reunion with her husband at the opening of the Grand Old Opry.

It was Pat's sixty-second birthday, and her face glowed as Nixon took to the piano to play "Happy Birthday." "At the last chord," her assistant Helen McCain Smith remembered, "Pat rose from her chair and moved toward her husband . . . he rose, turned, stepped brusquely to center stage—and ignored Pat's outstretched arms. I shall never forget the expression on her face."

At the White House one day, Pat and her daughters ate alone while Nixon lunched with Norman Vincent Peale and his family, Rose Woods, and former Eisenhower aide Robert Keith Gray. "He never ate a thing, just stared at his food," Gray recalled. "The Peales talked to me and to Rose, and Nixon never said a word. He was obviously too much in agony to have company, yet also too much in agony to be alone."

It was the tapes that were to prove the coup de grâce, and the president knew it. "Any more tapes," he noted just before midnight on April 20, "will destroy the office." More tapes, though, were precisely what the special prosecutor and the Judiciary Committee insisted on having. "The people have been patient for a long, long time," committee chairman Peter Rodino said that month. "But the patience of this committee is wearing thin." He now imposed a deadline for their production.

Nixon's response was to make a show of compliance. White House stenographers typed up the dialogue on the subpoenaed tapes, and the Government Printing Office produced a thousand-page volume of transcripts. Then the president appeared on television against a backdrop of gold-embossed binders—not the official Printing Office version—which made the material he was releasing look more substantial than it really was.

It was a masterful, composed performance, with none of the strange gestures or slurring that had marred other appearances. Nixon assured the nation that "those materials, together with those already made available, will tell it all."

The story they told, however, was not the complete one. The transcripts had been edited, under the active supervision of the president himself. While it mattered little that they were peppered with the phrase "expletive deleted," the version he offered was incomplete. The Judiciary Committee was swiftly able to establish that fact, for the transcribed conversations included several that the committee had already received in audio form. A comparison of the versions revealed troubling discrepancies, as in the following:

Transcript for March 22, 1973, as released by Nixon	*Judiciary Committee transcript*
PRESIDENT: Well, all John Mitchell is arguing then, is that now we use flexibility in order to get off the cover-up line.	PRESIDENT: but now—what—all that John Mitchell is arguing, then, is that now, we, we use flexibility. DEAN: That's correct. PRESIDENT: In order to get on with the cover-up plan.

A twenty-five-hundred-word segment had also been deleted from the transcript of the same tape, one that included the now-infamous passage in which Nixon had ordered: "I want you all to stonewall it . . . cover up, or anything else." The deletion was made at his personal behest.

The effect of the release was wholly negative. Ford, the new vice president, had previously come out strongly on Nixon's behalf. Now he declared, "The time has come for persons in political life to avoid the pragmatic dodge which seeks to obscure the truth."

The Republican leader in the Senate, Hugh Scott, called the released material "deplorable, disgusting, immoral." Senator Goldwater underscored a glaring sin of omission. "The thing that hurt the American people," he said, "is that no place in these tapes does the President bang on the desk and say, 'Gentlemen, this has to stop, and stop now.'"

The Judiciary Committee, meanwhile, told Nixon bluntly that he had failed to comply with its subpoena and issued new ones. When he turned them down, they warned that his continued defiance "might constitute a ground for impeachment." On May 9, in room 2141 of the Rayburn House Office Building, the committee's thirty-eight members took their seats and began to hear the evidence. The countdown to the end of the Nixon presidency had begun.

———

As the country grew jittery rumors flew, some of them baseless. Word went around Washington that the president had visited a psychiatric hospital while on a visit to Phoenix. When he summoned Gerald Ford to a private meeting, resignation was deemed imminent. Nixon failed to oblige. When the yacht *Sequoia* became stranded short of its dock, and Nixon used the tops of submerged pilings to cross to dry land, wags observed that he could walk on water.

In June, when Nixon left Washington on a grueling five-nation trip to the Middle East, it was difficult for him to walk at all. On a stopover at Salzburg, Austria, Haig found him alone in his bedroom with his swollen, discolored left leg resting on a chair. He was suffering from a resurgence of phlebitis, the painful inflammation of a vein he had suffered in the Far East a decade earlier. Painful, and also dangerous, for the ailment can result in a blood clot's breaking loose and causing a fatal embolism. Nixon was flouting medical advice in traveling at all.

"I thought I would be buried in the shadow of the Pyramids," he later admitted to Dr. Hutschnecker, the psychotherapist. Dr. Tkach, his personal physician, who was at his side in Egypt, worried not only about his patient's phlebitis but about his reckless behavior. He plunged into crowds and rode in open cars in one of the most dangerous, volatile regions of the world. "You can't protect a president," one of the Secret Service agents on the trip commented dryly, "who wants to kill himself."

Skeptics criticized the journey as "impeachment diplomacy," an attempt to distract attention from the deepening trouble at home. Kissinger thought Nixon was "beyond hoping that it might deflect his critics. . . . Deep down, he must have realized that matters were out of control." The reception Nixon received in the Middle East was tumultuous and lavish, but he was dogged by depression. John Osborne observed a moment when "Mrs. Nixon and President and Mrs. Sadat stepped away from Mr. Nixon and he was alone upon a terrace, his back to the Pyramids. . . . We saw him, but he didn't see us. His gaze and his thoughts were far away, and sadness was all about him."

Kissinger, for his part, discerned the diplomatic downside. "We sensed in the exaggerated solicitude of our hosts," he recalled, "the pity that is the one sentiment a head of state can never afford to evoke." Kissinger realized that lame as Nixon was politically as well as literally, "he could not provide what was most needed: a reliable guide to the long-term thrust of American foreign policy."

After the briefest return home, the president set off to the Soviet Union. At a stopover in Brussels, reporters heard he was being visited at the Hilton by a mysterious Mr. Christopher. It turned out to be Bebe Rebozo, smuggled into the hotel by a back entrance. Rebozo's recent advice to Nixon, he had told the press days earlier, was that he should resign: "It's like a fight manager saying, 'You betta get outta there, they're beating your brains out.' " In fact, Rebozo swung back and forth on the resignation issue.

The Soviet trip, Nixon's third summit meeting with Brezhnev, bordered on the surreal. He stayed in the sumptuous Kremlin apartments that had once housed the czars, huddled with the Soviet leader at his grand residence on the Black Sea coast, and—in a rare break in the schedule—found time to dine alone in the moonlight with Pat.

"Since she was a very little girl," Nixon would recall Pat telling him that night, "when she looked at the moon, she didn't see a man in the moon or an old lady in the moon—always the American flag. . . . She pointed it out to me and, sure enough, I could see an American flag . . . of course, you can see in the moon whatever you want to see. . . ."

During the Black Sea phase of the trip, the UPI's Helen Thomas became certain there was something "seriously wrong" with the president. "He walked slowly, pacing himself as if he were in a daze. All the life seemed to have drained out of him. He appeared to be only going through the motions."

"No mention of Watergate was ever made during the discussions," Viktor Sukhodrev, Brezhnev's former interpreter, said in the nineties. "Nixon was clutching at the [sic] straw, trying to show that he alone could really talk to the Soviets, trying as hard as he could to prove that he was the real expert in foreign affairs."

The president understood, Kissinger thought, "that the biggest obstacle to serious negotiation was the Soviet conviction that if he survived politically he would lack authority, but that in all likelihood he would not survive."

Nixon fumbled statistics and had trouble concentrating. He failed on occasion to observe the special vigilance that any politician, businessman, or journalist had to exercise in those days in the Soviet Union. As an old hand, he knew it was essential to be alert to the likely presence of hidden microphones.

One night, he recalled, he did remember the drill and made a point of meeting with Kissinger and Haig in his car, "where we could talk without being bugged." At other times, according to former KGB Colonel Oleg Gordievsky, he was careless, so loose-lipped that the Soviet agents responsible for surveilling him were decorated after the summit. The last of the Nixon tapes ultimately may be not those generated in the White House but those preserved in the archives of Russian intelligence.

Foreign affairs expertise had been Nixon's greatest talent, and the slippage in 1973 and 1974 was in professional terms the most significant aspect of his fall. Two significant events had occurred in the space of a few weeks that spring, a left-wing army coup in Portugal and India's first nuclear test. United States intelligence had failed to anticipate either, a fact that should have aroused presidential ire and a demand for action. Yet the CIA director of the day, William Colby, recalled no response from Nixon at all.

Nor did Nixon pay any serious attention when, two weeks after his return from Moscow, a major problem erupted in southern Europe. A coup in Cyprus was followed by a Turkish invasion. Then democratic forces toppled the government in Greece—the junta Nixon had long favored. Turkey next mounted a second invasion of Cyprus, establishing a new statelet that remains internationally unrecognized to this day.

This grave crisis would persist for weeks and involve complex decisions about the status of American nuclear weapons in the region. Yet Nixon remained in retreat at San Clemente, paying insufficient attention. He spent only six days of his last six weeks in office at the White House.

While in California he found time to express sadness over the death of Dizzy Dean, the former baseball star, and to address by telephone a Washington meeting in support of himself. The State Department, though, found communications with the Western White House blocked—priority was being given to heavy traffic on Watergate. The president was preoccupied with his personal crisis, as Kissinger saw it, and "in no position to concentrate. . . ."[3]

The last moment of good cheer for the Nixon family, in Tricia's judgment, was a dinner party with old friends in Bel Air on July 21. "Ever since," she wrote in her diary, "something was lost. . . . At times it was like being in the eye of a hurricane . . . quite calm, quite still. . . . You recall a time without 'Watergate' or when Watergate simply meant a rather extravagant place to live. An isolated moment. But then your eyes open and the darkness you see is the darkness of the storm."

Far away in the capital, the Senate Committee's final report was issued. Twenty-three-hundred damaging pages long, it called Watergate "one of America's most tragic happenings," reflecting "an alarming indifference displayed by some in high public office or position to concepts of morality and public responsibility and trust."

The House Judiciary Committee subsequently released five volumes of evidence, amounting to 3,888 pages. It presented a stark chronology, without comment, of a widespread abuse of power.

Nixon, no longer discussing the substance of Watergate, had begun doing his arithmetic, counting Judiciary Committee heads. Would key Republicans, and southern Democrats effectively controlled by George Wallace, vote his way? On July 23, when news came that the southern Democrats were defecting, Nixon called Wallace. "George," he said to the man who, we now know, suspected Nixon's men might have played a role in the 1972 attempt to assassinate him, "I'm just calling to ask if you're still with me." "No, Mr. President," Wallace replied, "I'm afraid I'm not."

The numbers were against him, and Nixon acknowledged as much to Haig. There remained one other crucial unknown. How would the Supreme Court rule on the special prosecutor's demand for sixty-four further White House tapes? At midmorning on July 24 the justices announced their unanimous decision in the case of *United States of America v. Richard Nixon, President of the United States:* He was to turn over the sixty-four tapes "forthwith."

It was shortly after 9:00 A.M. in California when Haig gave him the news. Woken from sleep, Nixon reacted at first with apparent calm. Later he reportedly "exploded," cursing Warren Burger, whom he had named chief justice, and his other Supreme Court appointees.

When Haig called Watergate counsel Fred Buzhardt, Nixon took the phone for a moment. "There is one tape in particular that I want your opinion on," he told the lawyer. "It's the one for June 23, 1972. I want you to listen to it right away, then call Al and tell him what you think." The June 23 recording was the one on which Nixon had told Haldeman—three times and just a week after the Watergate arrests—that it was "fine" to get the CIA to pressure the FBI to stop key Watergate inquiries.[4]

Buzhardt did call back after listening to the tape, with a blunt message. "This is the smoking gun," he said, clear evidence of obstruction of justice. Haig remembered how seven weeks earlier Nixon had emerged from listening to the tapes on his own with the curt instruction "No one is to listen to these tapes. No one—understand, Al? No one. Not the lawyers. No one. Lock 'em up."

Haig had suspected their potential even then. "I was overwhelmed by feelings of doubt and apprehension. Something fundamental had changed. There was something bad on the tapes, and Nixon had discovered it. . . . I had no idea what it might be."

Now he understood. Nixon had *known*. He had long known that this was evidence that could destroy him, and had hidden it even from his own people. He had been found out, and it was only a matter of time until all the world and—most to the point—the members of Congress who would vote on his impeachment, realized the truth.

Visiting Nixon two days after the Supreme Court's decision, Kissinger was appalled by the change in him. "His coloring was pallid. Though he seemed composed, it clearly took every ounce of his energy to conduct a serious conversation. He sat on the sofa in his office looking over the Pacific, his gaze and thought focused on some distant prospect eclipsing the issues we were bringing before him."

Except for attending one dinner party, the president had not left the compound since arriving two weeks earlier. He had spent much of that time staring at the ocean and reading a biography of the ill-fated Emperor Napoleon. Nixon was on the beach, changing after a swim, when a new phone call came in—the call that conclusively spelled his own fall from power.

In Washington the House Judiciary Committee had voted on the first of five articles of impeachment. It charged that Nixon had violated his constitutional oath, "prevented, obstructed and impeded the administration of justice . . . acted in a manner contrary to his trust . . . to the great prejudice of the cause of law and justice and to the manifest injury of the people of the United States."

The representatives on the committee had passed the resolution by a majority of more than two to one. They would also vote for Article II, stating that Nixon had "repeatedly engaged in conduct violating the constitutional rights of citizens . . . misused the Federal Bureau of Investigation, the Secret Service . . . to conduct or continue electronic surveillance or other investigations for purposes unrelated to national security . . . unlawfully utilized the resources of the Central Intelligence Agency . . . knowingly misused the executive power."

Article III, charging Nixon with obstructing the work of the House of Representatives by disobeying its subpoenas, also passed. Two other charges, related to the secret bombing of Cambodia, tax evasion, and personal corruption, failed.

As a result of the conduct described in Articles I, II, and III, the resolutions decreed that "Richard Nixon warrants impeachment and trial, and removal from office."

Nixon had always fought, always wanted his name to be synonymous with never giving up. Would he fight now and allow his case to go forward to the Senate for a prolonged trial?

On seeing the state of the man the day after the Supreme Court decision,

Kissinger and Haig quietly agreed that the end of the presidency was inevitable. Nixon should resign, but they knew it would be folly to push him.[5]

Nixon flew back to Washington with Pat on July 28. The next day, alone in his office in the Executive Office Building, he phoned to ask John Mitchell his advice. "Dick," said Mitchell, himself facing trial for Watergate crimes, "make the best deal you can and resign."

The next day, Tuesday, Nixon sat listening to the June 23 tape again, still convinced—he said—that he had done no wrong. His attorneys, however, told him he was mistaken. Unable to sleep that night, Nixon rose at 4:00 A.M. and sat scribbling down his options. "There were strong arguments against resigning," he was to write, the first of them being that he was "not a quitter." He could not face "ending my career as a weak man. . . ."

On the other hand, Nixon mused, perhaps he should resign for the sake of the country and the Republican party. In the end, though, he turned the notes over and wrote: "End career as fighter." It seemed "the right thing to do."

Hours later the president asked Haig in turn for his view on the June 23 recording. "Once this tape gets out," the general told him, "it's over." Summoned to the presence again the next day, Thursday, Haig found Nixon looking "thin, battered, like a stroke victim." He now agreed he would resign, and soon. Haig was to "tell Ford to be ready."

As Haig met with the vice president, Nixon went back to the tapes. That evening, during a river cruise on the *Sequoia* with Bebe Rebozo, he again said he planned to resign. "You can't do it," Rebozo retorted now. "It's the wrong thing to do. . . . You just don't know how many people are still for you." Nixon promised "one last try to mount a defense" and said he would consult the family.

He told Julie first, not Pat, that he expected to resign. When she sought out her mother afterward, Julie recalled, "A look of alarm spread across her face, and she asked, 'But why?'" Pat wept, but only for a moment. Then she canceled plans to buy new china for the White House and started packing.

That night, in conclave with Rebozo and his family in the Lincoln Room, Nixon handed out transcripts of the June 23 recording. After they had read it and sat silently around him, he asked if the experience of the presidency had been worthwhile. They assured him that it had.

Pat, however, told him after the others were gone that she—like Rebozo—favored "fighting to the finish." "Quite late that night," Haig recalled, "he called me at home and told me that he had changed his mind. . . . 'Let them impeach me,' he said. 'We'll fight it out to the end.'"

So it went through the weekend of August 3 and 4. More advice came from the daughters, and reportedly from their husbands, to fight on. Haig and the presidential speechwriters struggled to draft Option A and Option B speeches. The incriminating June 23 transcript was publicly released on the Monday, to predictable outrage. Nixon took another cruise on the presidential yacht, with the family this time, then called a cabinet meeting for the following morning. He had another sleepless night.

Tuesday, August 6. Nixon's account of the cabinet meeting differs from that of others who were present. In his version he opened by discussing Watergate, offered his gratitude for his colleagues' support, and asked their opinions on whether he ought to resign. In fact, others agree, he first held forth on "the most important issue confronting the nation": inflation.

When he did turn to the topic of Watergate, he said he had rejected the notion of resigning. "What he sought," thought Kissinger, who was seated to the president's right, "was a vote of confidence . . . a show of willingness to continue the fight. . . . All he encountered was an embarrassed silence."

Then Vice President Ford spoke up, politely making it clear that he expected soon to be president. Nixon replied with more discussion of the economy. Attorney General Saxbe and, even more forcefully, future president George Bush, at the time Republican National Committee chairman, interrupted to say it was time to end the crisis.

After the cabinet had dispersed, Kissinger returned to tell the President directly, in the Oval Office, that he owed it to the country to resign. "Nixon had never sought my views. Nor did he do so now," the secretary of state remembered. "He said he appreciated what I said. . . . He would be in touch. Then there was silence."

Haig called later that day and told Kissinger that Nixon was, after all, "tilting toward resignation. But it would be a close call; in the evening his family might change his mind again."

The only thing that was clear about the situation, at that moment of awesome historic and personal confusion on August 6, was that nothing was yet clear. It was made even less so, and more frightening, by a phone call Tricia's husband, Edward Cox, made that afternoon.

Cox, a New York attorney, had flown down to join the family conference over the weekend and then returned to his office in New York. From there he placed a call to the Republican party whip, Senator Robert Griffin. He and Julie's husband, David, he said, disagreed with their wives and thought their father-in-law should resign. On the *Sequoia* the night before, however, the president had insisted that he intended to hang on.[6]

Cox added more disturbing information. Nixon was drinking, and his mental condition was troubling. He had been "walking the halls" in the White House, "talking to pictures of former presidents, giving speeches and talking to the pictures on the wall." Finally, Cox confided, he was worried Nixon might commit suicide.

Nixon would insist in old age that killing himself at that juncture had never crossed his mind. Yet there had been a disquieting moment that same afternoon, Haig was to recall, when the president had said he envied the soldier's way out: "Leave a man alone in a room with a loaded pistol." Haig thought the president was speaking figuratively, but he worried nonetheless. "I told the

White House doctors," he revealed in 1995, "if Mr. Nixon had any pills to take them away. . . ."

David Eisenhower had similar worries. He too reportedly feared his father-in-law might take his life, and for months he had been "waiting for Mr. Nixon to go bananas."

Anthony Lukas, one of the most reliable of Watergate chroniclers, quoted a White House aide who compared Nixon in the last days to Captain Queeg in Herman Wouk's *The Caine Mutiny:* "given to sudden rages, to wild speculations, terrible doubts. . . ."

Suspicion and doubt sow suspicion and doubt. The uncertain days of August 1974 sparked unprecedented precautions, the logical outcome of months of anxiety about the president's mental stability.

The concern had been mounting since the firing the previous year of Special Prosecutor Cox, followed within days by the nuclear alert over the Middle East War.

"A new element crept into our calculations about the effect our actions might have on the president," Assistant Prosecutor Ben-Veniste remembered. "If there was a streak of instability there, then it meant we would have to be extra careful to keep from pushing Mr. Nixon over some invisible line into disaster—maybe disaster for all of us."

Leon Jaworski, Cox's successor, had a variant of the same worry when he warned grand jurors against indicting the president. "He gave us some very strange arguments," deputy foreman Harold Evans recalled. "He gave us the trauma of the country, and he's the commander in chief of the armed forces, and what happens if he surrounded the White House with his armed forces?"

By the summer of 1974 the apprehension had spread to Congress, focusing on two issues in particular. Was the president so disturbed that he might start a war? Also, might he attempt to use the military to keep himself in office? A group of legislators, headed by Jacob Javits, the Republican senator from New York, even consulted the director of the National Institute of Mental Health, Dr. Bertram Brown.

"I had breakfast with a half dozen senators," Brown recalled. "It was to talk about these issues, whether he would lose his cool. . . . Whether he was going crazy, becoming psychotic, whether he would start a war. I gave them some clues on what to watch out for. The clues were irrational statements, disappearing—not knowing where he was—and not eating."

Alan Cranston, senator from California, had become alarmed when, as the impeachment process got under way, Nixon began courting members of the House, inviting them on his yacht. The president had spoken, Cranston heard, of how he could press a button and in twenty minutes fifty million Russians would be dead, and—after that—how many Americans?

Senator Harold Hughes of Iowa, who was on the Armed Services Committee, worried that Nixon might use the army to seal off the Capitol. "He made sure there was somebody in the office twenty-four hours a day," Hughes's legislative aide Margaret Shannon recalled. "It was sort of like before World War Two. You knew something was coming down the pike. You just had no idea what Nixon would do. . . ."

As early as June, when Nixon was en route to the Middle East, Gerald Ford's aides had begun considering how a transfer of power might work—or not work. Close Ford associate Philip Buchen and Clay Whitehead, director of the White House Office of Telecommunications, held one such conversation in a car to ensure privacy. What if Nixon was impeached and convicted in the Senate but refused to give up power? What if he lost his mind and tried to use the military to stay in office? The two men wondered if they should raise these dire possibilities with the secretary of defense, James Schlesinger.

In fact, the secretary was already alert to such fears. His attention had been drawn to the president's state of mind by a phone call a few months earlier from Joseph Laitin, the public affairs spokesman of the Office of Management and Budget, based in the Executive Office Building, just across from the White House.

In an interview with the author Laitin vividly recalled the encounter with Nixon in the spring of 1974 that prompted him to phone Schlesinger. "I was on my way over to the West Wing of the White House to see Treasury Secretary George Shultz," Laitin said. "I'd reached the basement, near the Situation Room. And just as I was about to ascend the stairway, a guy came running down the stairs two steps at a time. He had a frantic look on his face, wild-eyed, like a madman. And he bowled me over, so I kind of lost my balance. And before I could pick myself up, six athletic-looking young men leapt over me, pursuing him. I suddenly realized that they were Secret Service agents, that I'd been knocked over by the president of the United States."

Laitin was so shocked at Nixon's appearance that he postponed the meeting with Shultz and returned to his office. "I sat there stunned," he said, "and I thought, you know, 'That madman I have just seen has his finger on the red button.' I had a number for Schlesinger, a phone that only he would answer. I called him, and I asked him if the president could order the use of atomic weapons without going through the secretary of defense. I said, 'If I were in your position, I would want to know who the nearest combat-ready troops were who would respond to the president's wishes to surround the White House. I would want to know what the next nearest combat-ready division was, which would not only be able to overcome them but also respond only to the chain of command. That's what I have to say.' Then there was just a click at the other end, as the secretary of defense hung up."[7]

A single call from a friend, describing a president apparently gone momentarily berserk, would not on its own have prompted Schlesinger to take any precautions. Yet his position placed him in line of a constant flow of information from all manner of sources. The chief of naval operations, Admiral Zumwalt, had told him of Nixon's bizarre diatribe to the Joint Chiefs the previous Christmas, when he had seemed to be feeling them out, to determine "whether in a crunch there was support to keep him in power."[8]

Given his own access to the president, Schlesinger also had firsthand experience of his behavior. More than once, according to Zumwalt, Schlesinger himself said privately that Nixon was behaving in a "paranoid" way.

Around the time of the Laitin phone call the secretary had begun to make certain he stayed more than usually informed of the goings-on in the Oval Office. Then, in late July, he asked for a meeting with the chairman of the Joint Chiefs, Air Force General George Brown.

"I told him," the former secretary recalled in an interview with the author, "that every order that would come from the White House had to come to me directly, immediately upon receipt. . . . The message had to be gotten through that there were not to be any extraordinary measures taken. The message did get through."

General Brown later confirmed that the conversation with the defense secretary had taken place. Schlesinger had asked "if the House voted impeachment and the Senate trial process was long and drawn out and going unfavorably for the president, could the president get an order down to the end of the military establishment without our knowing it?" Brown thought that the "normal process would prevent any such happening because troop orders must go to a high Pentagon command center. . . . I would have it in two minutes, and I'd be in the secretary's office in thirty seconds."

After the conference with Schlesinger, the general briefed the Joint Chiefs. Admiral James Holloway, who had recently succeeded Zumwalt as chief of naval operations, recalled the scene. "Brown's hands were shaking. He told us, 'I've just come from the office of the secretary of defense. I made some notes. I want to read them to you.' What the secretary wanted was an agreement from the Joint Chiefs, all of them, that nobody would take any action or execute any orders, without all of them agreeing to it."

"General Brown said they were afraid of some sort of coup involving the military," a former member of the Joint Chiefs told the author on condition of anonymity. "We almost fell off our chairs. If anyone was thinking of a coup, it was not anyone in uniform. None of us wanted to conjecture on 'What if we get a screwy order from the president?' We knew it would take care of itself. We had in the JCS five people with an average of forty years' experience, and they are picked for their good judgment. . . . They would have found a way to make sure the right thing happened."

The "right thing" under the circumstances was to abide by the provisions of the National Security Act, which required that the president transmit all military orders through the defense secretary, who in turn would relay them to the chairman of the Joint Chiefs. "I did assure myself," Schlesinger has said of the episode, "that there would be no question about the proper constitutional and legislative chain of command. And there never was any question."

The secretary was also concerned to ensure that the system not be circuited, that "no idiot commander somewhere was misled." He wondered in particular about the air force, in part because of admiration for Nixon among its ranks for his role in effecting the release of U.S. prisoners of war in Vietnam. Most had been downed pilots.

As he considered how steady or otherwise senior officers of the various services might be, Schlesinger wondered in particular about General Robert Cushman. As a brigadier general during Nixon's vice presidency Cushman had been his national security adviser. During the presidency, as deputy CIA director, he had been involved in providing agency facilities to Watergate burglar Howard Hunt.[9] By the summer of 1974 he was commandant of the U.S. Marine Corps, an appointment that, unusual for the corps, was seen as a political appointment. In that capacity he now served on the Joint Chiefs of Staff.

"General Cushman was a pleasant but weak man," Schlesinger is said to have commented privately. "He might have acquiesced to a request from the White House for action. The last thing I wanted was to have the marines ordered to the White House and then have to bring in the army to confront the marines. It would have been a bloody mess."

Schlesinger also found himself calling for answers to the questions his friend Laitin had asked in the spring. The nearest significant troop concentrations to the White House, he learned, were marine units under Cushman's command, one at a barracks on the outskirts of Washington—at Eighth and I streets SE—another at a facility in Quantico, Virginia.

The secretary was also interested in the mobility of the army's 82nd Airborne Division, which had been secretly brought in to protect the White House during antiwar demonstrations early in the presidency. How swiftly could the 82nd move troops to Washington from its base at Fort Bragg, North Carolina? A significant force, Schlesinger learned, could be in the capital in about five hours.

When Pentagon correspondents first reported the gist of these precautions, soon after Nixon's fall, President Ford would move quickly to squelch them. "No measures were actually taken," a spokesman claimed. During research for this book, however, the author was told otherwise by a former army operations intelligence specialist named Barry Toll.

A much-decorated veteran, Toll was in 1974 serving on one of the battle staff units, known in the military as doomsday teams, on permanent standby to brief the president and top commanders in the event a military crisis should "go nuclear." In August 1974 he was based at Langley Air Force Base in Virginia, with the Worldwide Military Command and Control System.

"The last week or so of the Nixon administration," Toll said in 2000, "we received a top secret, 'eyes only,' limited distribution order effectively instructing us not to obey the president—on anything, not just nuclear, until further notice. The order came in as topmost priority, Flash Override. It was signed, at the Joint Chiefs' insistence, as I understood it, by not one but two cabinet officers. The names I recall as having signed were Secretary Schlesinger and Secretary Kissinger. There had been similar orders in the past, up to five that I saw over the months, at times when, as I understood it, the president had been drunk."

While Toll testified on elements of these events to a Senate committee, his account remains uncorroborated.[10] Information from Henry Kissinger, meanwhile, indicates that consideration was given to using the 82nd Airborne in the last tense week of the presidency.

"Haig was in touch with me every day," the former secretary of state has written. "Usually I started my day at the White House in a brief meeting with him. On Thursday, August 1, he said matters were heading towards resignation, though the Nixon family was violently opposed. On Friday, August 2, he told me Nixon was digging in his heels; it might be necessary to put the 82nd Airborne Division around the White House to protect the President. This I said was nonsense; a presidency could not be conducted from a White House ringed by bayonets. Haig said he agreed completely . . . he simply wanted me to have a feel for the kinds of ideas being canvassed."

"The end of the Nixon presidency was an extraordinary episode in American history," former Secretary Schlesinger said in 2000. "I am proud of my role in protecting the integrity of the chain of command. You could say it was synonymous with protecting the Constitution."

In his dry way the chairman of the Joint Chiefs agreed that Schlesinger had acted correctly. "I think," General Brown later commented, "the secretary had a responsibility to raise these sort of matters."[11]

Mercifully, nothing untoward happened.

Wednesday, August 7. Alexander Haig was feeling simultaneously relieved, worried, and angry: relieved because the president had been speaking as though he were really going to resign; worried, because he had received word that Barry Goldwater and other Republican leaders were about to confront Nixon in person and "demand" that he resign; and angry about what he viewed as dark machinations within Congress.

"Do you know where the coup was coming from?" Haig was still saying in outraged tones two decades later. "The legislature! The Congress! Not from the military."[12] In August 1974 Nixon thought so too and might yet have balked at resignation if pressured.

"Senator, you simply cannot let this [congressional maneuver] happen," Haig told Goldwater at a hastily arranged meeting. "This is a banana republic solution. . . . If the President goes, he must go on his own terms, by due process of law, as the result of his own uncoerced decision." Goldwater promised that he and his eminent associates would not so much as mention the possibility of resignation when they met with Nixon.

Consequently, when Nixon received Senator Goldwater and two colleagues, no one mentioned the real reason for the meeting. "We sat there in the Oval Room," Goldwater remembered, "and the president acted like he just played golf and had a hole in one. You'd never think the guy's tail was in a crack."

Nixon put his feet up on the desk and prattled on about Lyndon Johnson and Dwight Eisenhower and what fine men they had been. Then, almost casually, he asked "how things stood in the Senate." The senators told him the numbers in an impeachment vote were likely to go decisively against him. The president stared up at the presidential seal on the ceiling and murmured that he seemed to have run out of options. The senators then left.

Nixon was now prepared to utter the word others had so scrupulously avoided—to Rose Woods. It was she who was to tell the family that he had "irrevocably" decided to resign. Only an hour had passed since Edward Cox had again called Senator Griffin. His mother-in-law Pat, he said, had told him the president was still "not talking about resignation." The family, he added, continued to worry about Nixon's mental condition.

Now at last though, the troubled mind had fixed its course, and the oft-told denouement began. After the senators had left, the Nixons ate a final family supper in the White House. "We spoke only of light things," Julie would recall. Her father had decreed that "we not talk about it anymore." Nixon had, however, arranged for the house photographer to come in. Teary, fixed-smile pictures were taken over Pat's protests.

Later there was a distraught, agonized session, alone with a compassionate Kissinger. Strong drink was taken, by Nixon's account from the same bottle of brandy from which they had once toasted the breakthrough to China. The two men knelt to pray together, Nixon was to claim, though whether they actually got on their knees was a detail lost to Kissinger's memory.

Later still, more nocturnal phone calls, including one that Kissinger's aide Lawrence Eagleburger thought "drunk . . . out of control." Yet the president's loyal speechwriter Ray Price thought the three calls he received "absolutely rational." The last one came around 5:00 A.M.

Thursday morning, the 8th. A things-to-do list for Haig, some last business with a piece of legislation—Nixon insisting on vetoing the agricultural appropriations bill. Some judges to appoint, resignations to accept. Business as usual was best, Haig thought—at a time when nothing at all was usual. The next step was a meeting with Gerald Ford, to say "I know you'll do a good job."

In the afternoon, with possible prosecution in mind, Nixon forced jollity in a conversation with Haig. "Lenin and Gandhi did some of their best writing in jail." The same lines, fatalistically this time, in a talk with attorney Fred

Buzhardt. And worry, one more time, on a familiar theme: "I've never quit before in my life. . . . *You don't quit!*"

"There'll be no tears from me," the president had assured Goldwater the previous day. Yet he had cried, reportedly, with Kissinger, and now he cried with the representatives and senators who came to make their farewells. "I just hope," he managed to say, "I haven't let you down."

A half hour later Nixon appeared on television to tell the nation he would go at noon the following day. He was composed and fluent and closed with a benediction: "May God's grace be with you in the days ahead." No apology, however. With his family afterward, embraces. "Suddenly I began to shake violently," he recalled, "and Tricia reached over to hold me. 'Daddy!' she exclaimed. 'The perspiration is coming clear through your coat!' I told them not to worry."

Hearing noise from the street, Pat drew her husband to a window. Her elder daughter, recognizing the chant as "Jail to the Chief," tried to drown it out by talking loudly. From outside, the Nixon women were seen drawing curtains that had never been seen closed before, not even after the Kennedy assassination.

Nixon was back on the phone that night. He had an apology for Len Garment, the Democrat who had switched allegiance to him, who had camped with him in Elmer Bobst's pool house, listened to him say he would do anything to stay in public life—"except see a shrink."

"Sorry, I let you down," the president said now. What would the special prosecutor do about him? Would he be indicted? Garment said he thought not. Then: "Well, it's not the worst thing in the world. Some of the best writing's been done in jail." For the third time that day, a reference to Gandhi. No good night. Just a click, and the line going dead.

Friday, August 9. Morning found Nixon in the Lincoln Sitting Room, memoirs of past presidents piled in front of him. Haig brought him a letter addressed to Henry Kissinger. The political death warrant, requiring signature.

Dear Mr. Secretary,

I hearby resign the Office of President of the United States.

Sincerely,
Richard Nixon

Time running out. In the elevator on the way down to the East Room, an aide explained precisely where family members were to stand for the television cameras. "Oh, Dick," Pat said in anguished tones, "you can't have it televised."

But he did, rambling on emotionally before the assembled cabinet and staff and the watching nation. Disjointed, unconnected sequences about money (the lack of it), his father, and his mother, who "was a saint."

Nixon quoted Theodore Roosevelt on the death of his young wife: "And when my heart's dearest died, the light went out of my life forever." Another man's personal grief, borrowed to evoke the loss of the presidency.

From the inappropriate to the almost inevitable—recourse once to TR's line about the man in the arena who fails while daring greatly.[13]

Then: "We think that when we suffer a defeat, that all is ended. . . . Not true. It is only a beginning, always. . . ."

By the time he finished, many of those present were weeping. Those at center stage held back the tears. Ford's wife Betty said, "Have a nice trip, Dick." Then Nixon was walking with Pat to the helicopter that would take them to Andrews Air Force Base, to Air Force One, and so on to California.

Looking back at the White House, at the door of the helicopter, the man who had failed greatly smiled hugely, made the V for Victory sign with both hands, arms spread wide. As the plane took off, Pat murmured, "It's so sad. It's so sad."

Technically the presidency remained Nixon's until noon eastern standard time. Air Force One was somewhere over Missouri when Gerald Ford took the oath of office and told the nation, "Our long national nightmare is over." Nixon was sipping a martini as the new president spoke, with not Pat but Ziegler at his side.

At that moment of transition Air Force One lost its presidential call sign. Protocol had already changed. As Nixon boarded the plane, he had been seen off not by a saluting general, as was customary, but by a mere colonel. It rankled, and a complaint was sent to a high-level Defense Department official as the aircraft flew west.

Then there was the matter of the "nuclear football," the "black box"—in reality a briefcase—that then, as now, remained close to the president at all times. On the ground it was chained to the wrist of an army warrant officer. In flight aboard Air Force One, it was stored in a safe just forward of the president's compartment. The black box had traveled with Nixon to China, to the Soviet Union, and everywhere else he had gone.

It contained the nuclear launch codes, in those days printed on plastic-encased rectangles the size and shape of playing cards. When bent, and the plastic popped open, the cards would reveal the digits that authenticated presidential approval for a nuclear strike. Given the other precautions Defense Secretary Schlesinger had taken, it seems possible that Nixon's black box had probably been effectively disarmed for some time. Alexander Haig reportedly confided as much to the special prosecutor.

Nixon apparently was not aware of that precaution. The night before he left the White House, it is said, he had told his visitors from Congress that the black box would travel with him as usual on the flight to California. It had not. The secure briefcase was not on board, not resting in the safe a few feet away from the man sipping a martini in the presidential compartment.

The power had gone from Richard Nixon. When Air Force One set down at El Toro Marine Air Station, near San Clemente, a sizable crowd was waiting. As the fallen president walked over to shake hands, a humming—at first indistinct, hesitant—began to arise from the throng. Gradually it became clearer, more confident.

The people were singing, "God Bless America."

———

Two decades later, a seventy-three-year-old man sat at the piano in the embassy of the United States in Moscow, giving an impromptu rendition of that same tune. Everyone sang along. The pianist was Richard Nixon, on a "private visit" that included meetings with Soviet leader Mikhail Gorbachev.

Two months earlier, *Newsweek* had run a cover story on him headlined, "HE'S BACK: THE REHABILITATION OF RICHARD NIXON." The feature was a public endorsement of the recognition President Jimmy Carter had long since given him by quietly consulting him on foreign affairs. Every president that followed—Reagan, Bush, and Clinton—did likewise. After the scandal of Watergate, Nixon had found for himself a role of eminent respectability, that of the nation's elder statesman. Once again he had achieved a degree of resurrection, if not a full return from the political dead.

The story of that remarkable, carefully paced recovery is not the subject of this book. As one observer put it, the disgraced leader of the United States spent the years that remained to him "running for the ex-presidency." If proof was needed that he had achieved that goal, it came at his death in 1994, when all his successors saw him to his rest as a national hero.

A month after Nixon's resignation, President Gerald Ford had granted his predecessor a blanket pardon for all crimes he had committed or possibly committed during the presidency. There had been a real likelihood he would be prosecuted, and the foreman of the Watergate grand jury has recalled ruefully that Ford's action "shortcircuited our efforts to get to the bottom of the thing." "This is justice?" asked another.

Nixon's former aide Egil Krogh, himself just recently released from jail, had visited San Clemente before the pardon came through. "Do you feel guilty, Mr. President?" he had asked. Nixon answered, "No I don't. I just don't." When Ford required him to issue a statement of contrition, he offered only "regret and pain" at the anguish his "mistakes and misjudgments" had caused. Later, laying the ground rules for the writing of his memoirs, he told his staff, "We won't grovel, we won't confess, we won't do a *mea culpa*."

It is said that Nixon once admitted to a Quaker pastor, in private: "I did wrong, but I'll live with it." Publicly, he never offered a clear-cut apology. Watergate, he had assured Charles Colson in a letter before the resignation, would become "only a footnote in history." Asked by ABC television's Barbara Walters whether he thought history would be kind to him, he responded with a quotation from Winston Churchill: "History will be very kind to me, because I intend to write it." Nixon had by that time already written his memoirs, a thousand pages long and with the imperial title *RN* inscribed on its cover with a grand flourish. Eight more books were to follow.

In retirement in North Carolina, former Senate Watergate Committee Chairman Sam Ervin had a characteristic comment on the autobiography. Nixon, he declared, had "obeyed Mark Twain's injunction in writing about Watergate: 'The truth is very precious; use it sparingly.' "

One of Nixon's own, who had himself served time in prison for perjury, sounded a warning note even before the memoirs came out. "Someday," Jeb Magruder wrote, "Richard Nixon and his apologists will try to rewrite history, claiming that this tragic president was betrayed by his underlings and railroaded out of office by his enemies. When that time comes . . . it would help to have the record at hand."

"If there was any dominant sentiment," historian Barbara Tuchman recalled of the first phase of Watergate, "it was reluctance to believe ill of the President and a desperate desire to sweep all the horrid doings under the rug and let him maintain his fiction of untainted rectitude. Americans have an over-developed tendency to president-worship. The public *wants* to believe the president—any president—is good . . . we put worship where the power is, which is an unwise arrangement."

Since Tuchman wrote those words, and because of what they learned at Watergate, Americans are perhaps today less ready to trust blindly in their leaders. This may be a positive outcome of a melancholy time. The downside, however, is that Richard Nixon's abuses and deceptions may have led many citizens not to trust their leaders at all.

Author's Notes

See list of abbreviations on pages 609–610.

Chapter 1

1. Nixon claimed more than once that his father sold the Yorba Linda land only to learn later that "oil that would have made us millionaires" was discovered on it. His mother made the same claim. In 1970, on a drive with Henry Kissinger, Nixon said oil had been found after his parents sold the Whittier property they had operated as a store and gas station from 1922 until the forties. In fact, oil was found only on a site Nixon's father considered, but decided against, purchasing in 1922. (*FB*, p. 30–; *Good Housekeeping*, June 1960; Kissinger, *Years of Upheaval*, op. cit., p. 1185; *MO*, p. 6–; Earl Mazo, op. cit., p. 14 fn.)
2. Nixon's statements on the Vietnam War and related issues will be assessed in chapter 23.

Chapter 2

1. Exactly what he had dreamed of and when is not clear. The Jonathan Aitken biography, which had Nixon's full cooperation, cites an eighth-grade school essay in which Nixon said he hoped to attend Whittier College, then do a postgraduate course at Columbia University, in New York. A reference a few pages later cites the same essay as indicating merely that Nixon longed to "go East" for his university education. (*Pat*, p. 85; *JA*, p. 30, and see *MEM*, p. 14.)
2. The Lois Elliott story seemed uncertain when first mentioned in a 1970 *Life* article. Later, by interviewing Elliott for his book *Nixon vs. Nixon*, Dr. David Abrahamsen was able to verify it. (*Life*, Nov. 6, 1970; Abrahamsen, op. cit., pp. 111, 250, line 1.)
3. Hannah Nixon claimed he made this remark to her. She dated it, however, to 1922 and in Yorba Linda. Yet the long-running investigation of Teapot Dome did not start until late 1923, and the family was living in Whittier by that time. Nixon's aunt Jane Beeson was certain he made the declaration to her, in her house, and she was probably right. Nixon's mother, who told the story as political propaganda for her son, may have thought it would play better as a "mother-son" conversation. (Kenneth Harris int. of RN, *SF Chronicle*, Nov. 24, 1968; *Good Housekeeping*, Gardner, op. cit., p. 24–; *FB*, p. 523, n. 13; *MO*, p. 881, n. 83.)
4. Duke University proposed the honorary doctorate again in 1961. Still smarting from the previous rebuff, however, Nixon declined to accept. (*Durham Morning Herald*, June 15, 1961.)

Chapter 3

1. Ola Welsh did marry the man for whom she left Nixon, Gail Jobe, and was still married to him when interviewed for this book in 1996. She quoted Nixon as saying he loved her in an interview for Jonathan Aitken's biography of Nixon. Roger Morris's biography, however, reports that she could not remember if he ever said, "I love you." Ola told Dr. David Abrahamsen she could not recall if he even said he liked her. The author has credited her remarks on the subject to Aitken, who appears to have interviewed her most extensively. (*JA*, p. 61; *MO*, p. 169; Abrahamsen, op. cit., p. 107.)

2. Pat Nixon also said Nixon proposed that first night. Nevertheless, while one might expect the couple themselves to have the story right, the author believes in this case that Elizabeth Cloes's account is more likely to be credible. (Mazo, op. cit., p. 31; Kenneth Harris int. *Miami Herald,* Jan. 19, 1969.)

3. In letters home Pat Ryan was specifically referring to herself as *not* married as late as February 1934. If there was a first marriage in the New York period, it was almost certainly not to Dr. Francis Vincent Duke, the Irish-born suitor mentioned in this chapter. There is no reference to a first marriage in Dr. Duke's 1965 obituary, and unlike the putative husband interviewed by Maxine Cheshire, Duke never lived in New Orleans. It is clear that Pat dated several different men while in New York. She returned to California in August 1934. (Duke: *NYT,* March 24, 1965; *Journal of the American Medical Association,* June 21, 1965, p. 1115; NY dates: *Pat,* p. 38.)

4. The case was *Schee v. Holt,* a family dispute case that began in the fall of 1937, when Marie Schee sued to get back money she had lent to her uncle, Otto Steuer. She was awarded judgment, with the right to demand the sale of Steuer's house, a sale that went wrong under Nixon's supervision. As a result, Schee found herself liable to lose all she had won and sued Wingert and Bewley for malpractice. The firm settled out of court. The process dragged on until 1942. (The most detailed coverage of the case is in *FB;* David Abrahamsen, op. cit., p. 123–, and *MO,* p. 189–; case files are listed at *FB,* p. 527.)

5. American organized crime, in the person of Meyer Lansky, had taken over Havana's two casinos and its racetrack in 1938. According to sources interviewed for this book, including Lansky's close associate Vincent Alo, Nixon met Lansky in Cuba, perhaps initially on the 1941 visit. This alleged connection will be probed in chapter 12. (Robert Lacey, *Little Man,* Boston: Little, Brown, 1991, pp. 108–, 469, n. 23; Charles Rappeleye and Ed Becker, *All American Mafioso,* New York: Doubleday, 1991, p. 144; ints. Vincent Alo, Jack Clarke.)

6. Nixon's Navy record indicates that he went to the South Pacific in the spring of 1943 and served first in New Caledonia and then in Vella Lavella, not under Japanese attack at the time. He was transferred to the Northern Solomons in January 1944. His first posting there, the island of Bougainville, was largely in U.S. hands when he arrived. Fighting did continue for a month or so, though it was not concentrated on the area where Nixon was stationed. In his memoirs Nixon mentioned a Japanese assault during which he had to shelter in a bunker. There were some bombing raids on Green Island, his next posting, but fewer than at Bougainville. One of Nixon's friends said, "The only real danger was the possibility of a banyan tree falling on you during a storm." Nixon's lasting memory was of the carnage when a B-29 bomber exploded on landing. Two authors, Fawn Brodie and Dr. David Abrahamsen, have critically examined Nixon's war record. Although Brodie, like Abrahamsen, was generally unfriendly toward Nixon, she argued convincingly that he was not guilty of intentionally fabricating his military experiences during his early political campaigning. Rather, he "blurred and embroidered and failed to correct exaggerations he encouraged among friendly biographers and journalists." On the available evidence, this author agrees with Brodie's view. (*FB,* ch. XII; Abrahamsen, op. cit., ch. 8; *MEM,* p. 28.)

7. Steward Alsop, writing in 1960, cites an intimate as saying Nixon saved ten thousand dollars from his wartime winnings. A fellow officer, Jim Stewart, said: "I know for a fact he sent home sixty-eight hundred dollars, from Green Island." Nixon's daughter, citing one of his last letters home, suggested it was only one thousand dollars. In his memoirs Nixon said both his skill and his winnings had been exaggerated. He added that Pat and he wound up with some ten thousand dollars at the end of the war, taking together his pay, her salary, and his poker winnings. (Stewart Alsop, op. cit., p. 144; *JA,* p. 108; *Pat,* p. 85; *MEM,* pp. 29, 34.)

Chapter 4

1. Secret Service agents usually prefer to remain anonymous. The author accepts that this interview, conducted by the experienced former *Washington Post* reporter and author Ronald Kessler, is authentic. (Int. Ronald Kessler.)

Chapter 5

1. According to a Voorhis worker in Alhambra, Zita Remley, she arranged for a relative to apply for paid work in the local Nixon office as a ploy to learn what the Republicans were up to. The relative, she said, reported back that "they had a whole boiler room with phones going all the time." She was told to dial numbers and ask just one question: whether the person answering knew Voorhis was a Communist. Nixon defender Irwin Gellman, a history professor at Chapman University in Orange, California, claimed recently that such accounts were "tales"—not to be relied upon. (Remley: Bullock, op. cit., p. 276; "tales": Gellman, op. cit., p. 84–.)

2. C. Arnholt Smith, the San Diego banker and entrepreneur, who knew Nixon as a child and supported him until as late as 1972, told the author before his death in 1996 that he contributed ten thousand dollars to Nixon's first campaign.

Chapter 6

1. In his 1975 memoir Cohen said the required figure was seventy-five thousand dollars, while his 1962 prison statement gives a figure of twenty-five thousand. The higher figure is used here because the 1975 memoir is a long, detailed account given to an experienced coauthor. On the other hand, the more formal 1962 statement may be more accurate; there is no way to know now. Similarly, the 1962 statement suggests Cohen could not recall for certain whether the Knickerbocker Hotel fund-raiser took place in 1950 or during the 1948 congressional election. The 1975 memoir places it firmly in 1950. The latter is surely the correct date; the Republicans spent a fortune on the 1950 campaign against Helen Gahagan Douglas, by one estimate perhaps as much as two million dollars, while the 1948 election was a walkover for Nixon. (1950 estimate: *MO*, p. 616.)
2. Cohen gives the address as Eighth and Olive in his 1962 statement but as Ninth and Hill in his 1975 memoir, in which he also names the building as the Guarantee Finance Building (as opposed to the Pacific Finance Building). The most authoritative source on the 1950 campaign, Roger Morris's book (see Bibliography), refers to a Nixon campaign headquarters in the "Garland Building at Ninth and Spring." Confusion over the address need not diminish belief in Cohen's claims; he said he paid for a Nixon office for only "three or four weeks." The author guesses he helped out in this way during an early stage of the twelve-month 1950 campaign. (Garland Building: *MO*, p. 536.)
3. After his defeat by Nixon, former Congressman Voorhis recalled, he was told that "organized liquor interests [in New York] were claiming credit for my defeat. It was some satisfaction to have the right people against me." Mickey Cohen, who had begun his mob career in bootlegging days, was close to Art Samish, the mob's political front man in California. Samish had links to underworld liquor and racing interests dating back to Prohibition and was still involved with the Schenley liquor tycoon, Lewis Rosenstiel. Rosenstiel had long been close to Cohen's ultimate gangster masters, Lansky and Costello. His right-hand man, from 1958, was former FBI Assistant Director Lou Nichols, later an adviser to Nixon in the 1968 campaign. ("liquor interests": Voorhis, op. cit., p. 346; close to Samish: Cohen, op. cit., p. 2–; Samish, Rosenstiel: Fox, op. cit., p. 229–; Rosenstiel, Lansky: Summers, *Hoover,* op. cit., p. 248; Nichols: ibid., p. 369.)

Chapter 7

1. Depending on which source one credits, Eisler was either a leading Soviet agent in the United States or a lowlier figure. His former wife, Hede, who with her next husband, Paul Massing, also had links to Soviet espionage, told the FBI she had known Hiss as an active Communist operative in the mid-1930s. See later references. (*PERJ*, p. 176–.)
2. According to Loftus, the allegation came to him in interviews with former members of the U.S. Army Counter-Intelligence Corps and of Military Intelligence. He also cites interviews with members of the Strategic Services Unit, the Central Intelligence Group, and the Office of Policy Coordination. (John Loftus and Mark Aarons, *The Secret War against the Jews,* New York: St. Martin's Press, 1994, pp. 221, 557; ints. John Loftus.)
3. Peter Grose's biography of Allen Dulles, published in 1994, the same year as the Loftus and Aarons book, appears to reject suggestions that Allen Dulles was less than honorable in his relations with his German contacts. (Grose, op. cit., p. 264–, and see refs. in Townsend Hoopes, *The Devil and John Foster Dulles* Boston: Little, Brown, 1973.)
4. With Representative Charles Kersten, a HUAC colleague, Nixon met the Dulles brothers to discuss the Hiss case at the Roosevelt Hotel in New York, on August 11, 1948. Foster had previously backed Hiss but later testified for the government, in court. See also Note 10, below. (Allen Weinstein article, *Esquire,* Nov. 1975, p. 79, and *MO*, p. 414.)
5. Whittaker Chambers, for his part, had done work during the War for ONI, the Office of Naval Intelligence. (Ralph de Toledano, ed., *Notes from the Underground: The Whittaker Chambers–Ralph de Toledano Letters: 1948–1960,* Washington, D.C.: Regnery, 1997, p. 18.)
6. According to the journalist Howard Kohn, citing CIA sources, Dulles gave Nixon this confirmation at their meeting in New York on August 11, 1948. (See Note 4, *supra.*) That meeting has long been public knowledge, but it was characterized by Nixon purely as one at which he laid out the known facts and persuaded the Dulles brothers that Hiss was a liar. However, that Allen Dulles was privy to information on Hiss, and that he shared it with Nixon, is entirely plausible. (Howard Kohn article, *Rolling Stone,* May 20, 1976, and see limited retraction, *Rolling Stone,* Apr. 28, 1983; *MEM*, p. 57.) Kohn is a former staff writer for *Rolling Stone,*

and bureau chief of the Center for Investigative Reporting. He wrote the book *Who Killed Karen Silkwood?*, which exposed unsafe practices at the nuclear fuel plant where Silkwood worked and was the basis for the movie *Silkwood*.

7. Dulles and Hiss had encountered each other in the thirties, when Hiss was on the staff of a congressional committee. Dulles had accused Hiss of betraying a trust by revealing private papers of former Secretary of State Robert Lansing, for which Dulles was responsible. (Grose, op. cit., p. 297 fn.)

8. Nixon's role in the break-in would not surface publicly until many years later. Not least since it involved accomplices, however, it very likely was known about on the law school grapevine. While there is nothing on it in the surviving FBI file, it is precisely the sort of activity agents pursuing a bureau "character investigation" would have pounced on had they learned of it from contemporaries.

9. Nixon's father's gas station was leased by W. Q. Dietrich, who later operated another station for Richfield Oil. It would be interesting to learn whether this was Will Dietrich, brother of Noah Dietrich, a close aide to Howard Hughes who was to organize the notorious Hughes Loan while Nixon was vice president. According to Nixon's nephew Don, the family connection with Hughes dated back many years. (G. J. Ross report on RN, Aug. 3, 1937, p. 6, FBI 67-102459; Noah Dietrich and Bob Thomas, *Howard, the Amazing Mr. Hughes*, Greenwich, Conn.: Fawcett, 1972, p. 26; int. Don Nixon.)

10. Former agents reported to Hoover that Nixon spoke alternately as though he wanted to embarrass Hoover and to praise him, leading Hoover to scrawl on one report, "This fellow Nixon blows hot and cold." (Ladd to Hoover, Dec. 9, 1948, Hiss FBI file in FBI Reading Room.)

11. In September 1939, literally on the eve of World War II, Chambers, in the wake of his defection from the Communist party, had told his story to President Roosevelt's security adviser Adolf Berle. He mentioned Hiss and his wife and brother as belonging to a group of American Communists. Roosevelt, informed of the allegations during a croquet game, is said to have dismissed them as another attempt to discredit the New Deal. Berle, he supposedly said, should tell Chambers to "go fuck himself." Sometime later, early in the war, the U.S. ambassador to France, citing the French prime minister and French intelligence, told a State Department friend that Hiss was either a Communist or a fellow traveler. (Berle: *Navigating the Rapids* [journal of Adolf Berle], eds. Beatrice Berle and Travis Jacobs, New York: Harcourt Brace Jovanovich, 1973, pp. 24, 582, 598; *PERJ*, p. 291–; Roosevelt: *MO*, p. 388, but see Ralph de Toledano, *J. Edgar Hoover, The Man in His Time*, New York: Manor, 1974, p. 222; French intelligence: *PERJ*, p. 311; Levitt, op. cit., p. 267.)

12. In his 1993 biography Jonathan Aitken claimed Nixon denied having discussed the Hiss case with Cronin or having received information from the FBI until *after* mid-August 1948. Aitken claimed too that in a 1990 interview Cronin conceded that Nixon was right and that his "stacked deck" remark was unfair. Was Cronin capable of making any such remark in 1990? In January 1991, when approached for an interview, the elderly Cronin was in a home for the aged, deaf, and in a wheelchair and unable to hold a cogent conversation. In addition, Cronin said in 1959—and in subsequent interviews—that he discussed Hiss with Nixon as early as February 1947. Cronin's FBI file, released in 1999, reportedly shows that Director Hoover was concerned in 1946 because Cronin "talks too much." It may later have suited the FBI to feed him information precisely because he was a talker. Certainly he had an on-going relationship with the bureau. (Aitken claimed: *JA*, p. 155 and see Gellman, op. cit., p. 234; Parmet, *Nixon*, op. cit., p. 166–; 1991 approach: visit to Cronin by Robbyn Swan for this author, Jan. 10, 1991; perjurer: *Irish Times*, Jan. 20, 1999; 1959: int. Cronin in Kornitzer, op. cit., p. 172, and see Mazo, op. cit., p. 51; subsequent ints.: Lowenthal script, *supra.*, p. 39–; *Esquire*, Nov. 1975; FBI file: *New England Journal of History*, Vol. 56, Winter 1999/Spring 2000, p. 24.)

Chapter 8

1. Hiss said he recognized Chambers as a man who had used the name George Crosley at the time he knew him. In *Six Crises*, Nixon wrote, "In the entire history of the case . . . no one could be found who could remember George Crosley—except Priscilla Hiss." [Hiss's wife]. The implication was that Hiss had lied and fabricated the name. In fact, Chambers said the Hisses had never known his last name and had never heard the name Whittaker Chambers. He did use aliases, however, and admitted it was "possible" he had used the name George Crosley. One witness, a publisher named Samuel Roth, said Chambers had submitted poems to him for publication asking that they be printed under the name George Crosley; (Nixon, *Six Crises*, op. cit., p. 39; Levitt, op. cit., p. 17–; *PERJ*, p. 126; Roth: ibid., p. 40–.)

2. The book *Perjury*, by Allen Weinstein, published in 1978 and reissued in an updated form in 1997, was received as the most powerful assembly of evidence against Hiss. While it per-

suaded many previous skeptics that Hiss was guilty on all counts, it has many critics. Victor Navasky, editor of the *Nation,* responded to publication of *Perjury* by checking back with several of Weinstein's sources. One replied that his interview comments had been distorted. Another said he had been quoted out of context. Both these subjects and two others gave Navasky accounts that conflicted with what they allegedly told Weinstein. (One of the interviewees, Sam Krieger, sued Weinstein and his publisher and won a settlement; an erratum slip was inserted in subsequent copies of the book.) When Navasky published a major article, including the interviewees' remarks and other criticisms, Weinstein riposted in the *New Republic.* The paper war has sputtered on ever since. (*Nation,* Apr. 8, June 17, 1978, Nov. 3 1997; *Newsweek,* Apr. 17, 1978; *New Republic,* Apr. 8, 1978, and see the 1976 edition of Weinstein's *Perjury,* published by Random House, and *Nation,* Jan. 4 and 11, 1993, Nov. 3, 1997; *Commentary,* Apr. 1993.)

3. In 1945, when he was twenty-two, Timothy was discharged from the navy "on emotional grounds related to homosexuality." He later married. (*PERJ,* pp. 359, 482.)

4. Allen Weinstein has written that Hiss's brother Donald and Raymond Catlett (son of Hiss's former maid) had "traced" the Woodstock in February 1949, months before it was actually found, and were thus the only two people in a position to have replaced it with a planted Woodstock. There is no evidence that Donald Hiss and Catlett actually laid hands on the typewriter in February or had anything to do with typewriter substitution. (*PERJ,* pp. 349–, 518.)

5. In response to a call from Hiss, Sullivan "tried to back away" from this statement. He also said the typewriter "was not made in the FBI Lab" and that the bureau would not have been capable of fabricating a typewriter. As described earlier, however, it is now known that Allied intelligence had indeed forged typewriters successfully during World War II. (Sullivan, op. cit., p. 95.) The journalist who interviewed Sullivan was Peter Irons, writing for *The Real Paper.* Historian Allen Weinstein believed Sullivan had confused the FBI's identification of Mrs. Hiss's typing with the finding of the typewriter. This is only Weinstein's interpretation. (*New York Review of Books,* May 27, 1976, p. 38; *Real Paper,* March 12, 1975.)

6. The reference to the typewriter's having been found in December 1947 does not appear in later editions of *Six Crises.* The 1968 and 1990 editions carry a footnote referring obliquely to "rumors" and to the *World-Telegram* article. Attorney General Robert Kennedy, who looked into the matter in 1962 in light of the furor over the first edition, reportedly found nothing in the files to indicate that the FBI ever had the typewriter. (Nixon, *Six Crises,* op. cit., p. 64, and 1990 ed. New York: Simon & Schuster, 1990, p. 60; Kennedy: Fred Cook, "The Ghost of a Typewriter," *Nation,* May 12, 1962, p. 421.)

7. Previous writers have also noted the White House tape of February 28, 1973, in which Nixon discussed the Hiss case with John Dean. In the first transcript released, which cheered those who championed Hiss, Nixon is rendered as saying, "We worked that thing. We then got the evidence, *we got the typewriter* [author's italics]." A later transcript, however, made by the Watergate Special Prosecution Force, reads: "We got *Piper* [author's italics]," which makes no sense. In *Perjury,* Allen Weinstein suggests that "Piper" may have referred to Hiss's attorney at the time Chambers produced his documents, William Marbury of Piper and Marbury. This is reaching. Having listened to the tape again and again during research for this book, the author finds it more likely that Nixon said, "We got the *typer* [again, author's italics], a remark that might make some sort of sense if Nixon meant to refer to Mrs. Hiss who, according to Chambers, typed the copies of the documents her husband brought home. (Feb. 28 "first transcript": Gerald Gold, ed., *The White House Transcripts,* New York: Bantam, 1974, p. 71; "later transcript": WHT, Feb. 28, 1973, 9:12–10:23 A.M.; Weinstein: *PERJ,* p. 492; "for this book": monitored for the author by researcher Robert D. Lamb, Dec. 9 and 12, 1998.)

8. The activities of Schmahl and his associates were to intersect with those of the CIA—and of Nixon—in the decade that followed. In 1954, as vice president, Nixon directed the former FBI agent Robert Maheu in a secret operation to thwart shipping tycoon Aristotle Onassis's bid to gain a virtual monopoly over Saudi Arabian oil traffic. Lou Russell, Nixon's former HUAC aide, was assigned to place taps on Onassis's phones, but Schmahl reportedly took over the job. In 1956 Schmahl was questioned in connection with the disappearance and reported murder of Professor Jesús de Galindez, a political enemy of Dominican Republic dictator Rafael Trujillo. Schmahl was questioned in connection with Galindez's abduction, as was another Maheu operative. After Trujillo was assassinated in 1961, Nixon, by then a practicing attorney, handled attempts to recover Trujillo's fortune for the dictator's family. In 1961, when running his Florida boatyard, Schmahl was involved in the CIA's anti-Castro operations, for which Nixon had been White House liaison while vice president. (Schmahl: Hougan, *Spooks,* op. cit., p. 289–; Levitt, op. cit., p. 203; Nixon, Trujillo: Murray Kempton, "How Nixon Endures," undated clip, DPP.)

9. The Hungarian interrogation transcripts were seen in 1992 by a Hungarian historian, Maria Schmidt, and presented in a paper to New York University's Center for European Studies the

following year. Schmidt found Field's statements about Hiss convincing. Attorney Ethan Klingsberg, who examined the same material later, warned that "uncritical readings of Communist secret police files . . . does [sic] not serve the interests of truth." Field's statements must be treated with caution, while it is acknowledged that they seem consistent with other evidence. (*New Republic, Nation,* Nov. 8, 1993.)

10. See chapter 7, Note 1, *supra.* Massing was the former wife of Gerhart Eisler.

11. So far as the author has been able to ascertain, Weinstein did not see the actual documents. He did not respond to letters or messages from the author.

12. Historian Weinstein asserts that Hiss was allotted the code name Lawyer in the mid-1930s, presumably because he had trained as a lawyer and worked in a New York firm, on the legal staff of the Agricultural Adjustment Administration, on a Senate legislative body (the Nye Committee), and then—before joining the State Department in 1936—at the Justice Department. Another individual identified as a member of the U.S. Communist underground, Harry Dexter White, was also supposedly code-named Lawyer at one stage. (Weinstein and Vassiliev, op. cit., pp. 7, 165.)

13. Sudoplatov's book, written by his son and two journalists, one of them a former diplomatic editor of *Time,* caused a storm because of its claim that leading scientists on America's wartime atom bomb project fed information to the Soviets. Based largely on taped interviews with Sudoplatov, the book was criticized by some reviewers for its lack of documentation. The present-day Russian Foreign Intelligence Service called it a mosaic of "truthful events, semi-truths and open inventions." Others praised the book, *Le Monde's* reviewer thought it "the most important historical testimony to appear since the death of Stalin." It devotes three pages to Alger Hiss, apparently drawn directly from the Sudoplatov interviews. Sudoplatov indicated that much of what he said was based on a 1993 conversation with a former colleague who had been a GRU agent in New York and London. The former colleague believed Hiss was chosen by President Roosevelt for secret contacts with the Soviets in the knowledge "that he had contacts and was pro-Soviet." (Sudoplatov, op. cit., p. 227–, *New York Review of Books,* June 8, Sept. 22, *WP Book World,* May 1; *NYT,* May 6, 1994; *WP,* Sept. 27, 1996.)

14. In the United States Chambers had from the very start cast suspicion on Hiss's wife, Priscilla, and his brother, Donald, who also worked at the State Department. Their names appear with Alger's in the notes and journal entries made in September 1939 by President Roosevelt's security adviser Adolf Berle after Chambers had spent the evening with him. (See chapter 7, note 11.) "I think," Berle wrote in a later diary entry, on August 9, 1949, "that when we get to the bottom of this we will discover the true Communist in the Hiss family is the wife either of Alger or Donald Hiss." Priscilla Hiss's role in the case remains somewhat unclear, and there has been speculation that Hiss deceived questioners in order to protect her. (Notes: *MO,* pp. 388, 911 [n. for 388]); journal: Berle and Jacobs, eds., op. cit., pp. 249, 583.)

15. Not only was Dulles still in regular touch with Donovan, but he had his own connection to the Hiss scenario. In the course of his OSS work in Europe, he had had extensive dealings with Hiss associate Noel Field and been duped by him. Dulles reportedly took revenge in 1949 by feeding the Soviets information that Field had all along been an American spy; thus Field wound up spending eight years behind the Iron Curtain in a Communist jail. (Mosley, op. cit., pp. 276, 506–; Stuart Steven, *Operation Splinter Factor,* New York: J. B. Lippincott, 1974, pp. 85–, 97–.)

16. As of this writing, there are no certainties as to how much progress had been made in decoding the VENONA documents by August 1948, when Nixon's probe of Hiss got under way. The FBI's Robert Lamphere said in an interview for this book that the ALES message (see facsimile, p. 493) was not broken until 1955. Yet an FBI document copied to Lamphere in May 1950 refers to the message—saying it likely refers to Hiss. A CIA spokesperson told the author that the available documentation indicated that the message had probably been decoded in the spring of 1950. Both these responses are clearly wrong. A rendering of the message obtained under the Freedom of Information Act provided to the author bears the legend TOP SECRET COPSE—and a notation that this was a code word for the VENONA material used only in 1949. According to the author Nigel West, writing in 1999, one of only two deliberate excisions in the modern publication of the declassified documents is "the consistent removal throughout of all references to the first date of circulation [within the intelligence community]" (Lamphere int.: Robert Lamphere, Belmont to Ladd, May 15, 1950; FBI doc. provided to author; CIA spokesperson: int. Anya Guilsher, CIA press office, after consulting staff who reviewed VENONA decrypts; "COPSE": March 30, 1945 message Washington–Moscow, obtained under the Freedom of Information Act and provided to the author by John Lowenthal—a notation reads "The codeword COPSE was in use in 1949 only.")

TOP SECRET ~~VENONA~~

MGB

From: WASHINGTON

To: MOSCOW

No: 1822

3ʃ March 1945

Further to our telegram No. 283[a]. As a result of "[D$ A.'s]"[i] chat with "ALES"[ii] the following has been ascertained:

1.   ALES has been working with the NEIGHBORS[SOSEDI][iii] continuously since 1935.

2.   For some years past he has been the leader of a small group of the NEIGHBORS' probationers[STAZhERY], for the most part consisting of his relations.

3.   The group and ALES himself work on obtaining military information only. Materials on the "BANK"[iv] allegedly interest the NEIGHBORS very little and he does not produce them regularly.

4.   All the last few years ALES has been working with "POL'"[v] who also meets other members of the group occasionally.

5.   Recently ALES and his whole group were awarded Soviet decorations.

6.   After the YaLTA Conference, when he had gone on to MOSCOW, a Soviet personage in a very responsible position (ALES gave to understand that it was Comrade VYShINSKIJ) allegedly got in touch with ALES and at the behest of the Military NEIGHBORS passed on to him their gratitude and so on.

No. 431

VADIM[vi]

Notes: [a]   Not available.
Comments:
  [i]   A.: "A." seems the most likely garble here although "A." has not been confirmed elsewhere in the WASHINGTON traffic.
  [ii]   ALES: Probably Alger HISS.
  [iii]   SOSEDI: Members of another Soviet Intelligence organization, here probably the GRU.
  [iv]   BANK: The U.S. State Department.
  [v]   POL': i.e. "PAUL," unidentified cover-name.
  [vi]   VADIM: Anatolij Borisovich GROMOV, MGB resident in WASHINGTON.

Chapter 9

1. Over the next two decades Tuck earned the sobriquet clown prince of U.S. domestic politics. Although Nixon and his aides held him up during Watergate as an example of Democratic dirty tricks, Tuck's japes were very different from Republican operations during the Nixon presidency. While irritating to the Republican side, his antics were essentially humorous. Nixon communications director Herb Klein considered his work "legitimate intelligence," his activities more amusing than sinister, and thought of Tuck as a friend. During the 1956 campaign, when Nixon was in San Francisco, Tuck went out at night and affixed Nixon placards to road signs designed to guide garbage trucks. Daylight revealed that they now read, DUMP NIXON! In 1968 Tuck hired a group of obviously pregnant women to carry signs reading NIXON'S THE ONE. Nixon was not Tuck's only target; he once persuaded a flight attendant on Barry Goldwater's plane to offer the candidate a choice of "coffee, tea, or hemlock." ("clown prince": Boston *Globe*, Sept. 30, 1973; Nixon, aides: *WP*, June 17, 1997, and "An Evening with Dick Tuck," broadcast tape available at Library of Congress; 1956: ibid., David Halberstam, *The Unfinished Odyssey of Robert Kennedy*, London: Barrie & Jenkins, 1968, p. 71; Klein: Klein, op. cit., pp. 139, 145; women: Halberstam, op. cit., p. 72; Goldwater: ibid.)
2. The nickname Tricky Dick was coined in the spring of 1950 by a small newspaper, *Independent Review*. It did not catch on until late September, when the paper used it again in an editorial, and it was subsequently adopted by Douglas supporters. (Mitchell, op. cit., p. 184–; Douglas, op. cit., p. 328.)
3. A heavily researched account of the 1950 campaign is that of Roger Morris, in his book *Nixon, Rise and Fall of an American Politician*. His work on the entire period, from Nixon's birth to his inauguration as vice president, is also valuable. This is so notwithstanding the challenge to aspects of Morris's work in 1999 by Professor Irwin Gellman of Chapman University, Orange, California, in his book *The Contender*. While Gellman's book was published only when this author's research had already proceeded too far for exhaustive followup, his criticisms of Morris seem strident and somewhat inconclusive. A truly scholarly comparison of the two studies would be a welcome addition to the literature. See Bibliography for details of both books.
4. Nixon's spokesman later said there was "no basis in fact" to what Astor had written (*AMI*, p. 459, *MO*, p. 617.)

Chapter 10

1. Dr. Hutschnecker has said that his concentration on psychosomatic theory began at the Charitee, the hospital of the Friedrich Wilhelm University in Berlin, where he trained as a doctor. In the United States any medical doctor could specialize in psychotherapy. To be certified by the Board of Psychiatry and Neurology of the American Psychiatric Association, however, required a two-year residency in psychiatric medicine. Hutschnecker did not have that certification. He was a member of the American Medical Association, a member of the American Psychosomatic Society, and a fellow of the Academy of Psychosomatic Medicine. (Author's research; *WP*, Nov. 20, 1973; Roger Rappoport, *The Superdoctors*, Chicago Playboy Press, 1975, p. 155.)
2. Salisbury came to know Dr. Hutschnecker well but apparently only after the 1960 encounter. (Hutschnecker, *Drive for Power*, op. cit., pp. 18, 182–, 267.)
3. In testimony to the Senate Rules Committee in 1973, after Winter-Berger's account of the doctor's alleged table talk was published, Dr. Hutschnecker excoriated Winter-Berger, dismissing his comments as a "deliberate attempt to hurt people." However, the doctor does seem to have been rather loquacious about his Nixon connection—at times he believed he was speaking privately—and the author (who has met Winter-Berger) tends to believe the lobbyist's account. (Hutschnecker, *Drive for Power*, op. cit., citing Rules Committee testimony, p. 20–.)
4. Fawn Brodie's book *Richard Nixon: The Shaping of His Character* was published posthumously, in 1981, after Brodie's death from cancer earlier that year. It was much criticized for its overemphasis on psychiatric interpretation of Nixon's life. Yet the book contains valuable research, and Brodie's files, preserved at the University of Utah, Marriott Library, remain an indispensable tool for any scholar working on Nixon. (Fawn Brodie, *Richard Nixon: The Shaping of His Character*, New York: Norton, 1981.)
5. This quotation is taken from historian Fawn Brodie's notes of her interview with Leo Katcher, brother of the source, Herbert Katcher. Leo indicated the analyst was a woman. A more alarming version came to Brodie from Daniel Ellsberg, the protagonist in the Pentagon Papers case. Ellsberg, apparently citing Leo Katcher at one remove, suggested Nixon's analyst had called him an "extreme paranoid megalomaniac, very well controlled but far out— [who] feared his being in the seat of power." Absent corroboration, the author has used the version Leo Katcher gave to Brodie. Leo Katcher had a special interest in psychiatry, he held a Ph.D. in psychology from Columbia University. As a journalist he also had direct

experience with Nixon; he had been one of several journalists who developed the fund story in 1952 and was investigated by the FBI afterward. "For twenty-five years," he said in 1975, "that man has to some extent possessed me. He stands in the same relationship to morality as a color-blind man stands to color." (FB notes of ints. Daniel Ellsberg and Leo Katcher; *FB*, p. 275.)

6. Nixon makes no reference to Dr. Hutschnecker in his memoirs, in spite of the evidence not only of the doctor's medical care but also of the long friendship between the two men. Nixon does write, dismissively, of the fact that some journalists concluded he was starting to go "off [his] rocker" during Watergate and asked "whether I was under psychiatric care." (*MEM*, p. 961–.)

Chapter 11

1. There is some doubt about the date. In his memoirs Nixon placed it in 1951, and a thank-you letter in his vice presidential papers, the first-known note of its kind, is dated January 9, 1952. Interviews with Rebozo, Danner, and another member of the circle of friends, Sloan McCrae, also place the first Nixon-Rebozo meeting in the early Senate period, 1950 or 1951. Yet the author's interviews with Smathers and 1972 interviews with Danner and another friend, a former FBI agent, John Madala, suggest the Miami visits began as early as 1948, when Nixon became overwrought during his pursuit of Alger Hiss, or even earlier.

   According to Danner and Madala, there were several such early trips, during which Nixon went on boat outings with Rebozo and Tatem Wofford, a hotelier. The journalist who conducted the 1972 interviews, Jeff Gerth, concluded that the later date for the initial visit, 1951, was concocted to conceal the fact that Nixon was in Miami and associating with men linked to organized crime in the late forties, a period when, as revealed by the Kefauver Committee and prominently reported, some top Miami hotels were controlled by mobsters. One of them, Gerth points out, was the Wofford Hotel. Research for this book, however, does not indicate that Tatem Wofford was involved with the Wofford Hotel; it was owned, rather, by John and Olive Wofford.

   Not least because of Nixon's January 1952 letter of thanks, the author inclines toward dating the first Nixon-Rebozo meeting to late 1951. This is not to deny that Nixon had Florida connections that placed him unhealthily close to organized crime; these are covered later in this chapter. (Memoirs: *MEM*, p. 247, and *MO*, p. 655; Rebozo: *Miami Herald*, Nov. 1, 1973; Smathers: ints. George Smathers; Danner: deposition, Sept. 4, 1973, Box B56, E files, NA; McCrae: int. Sloan McCrae; Danner, Madala: article by Jeff Gerth, *Sundance*, Nov.–Dec. 1972; Kefauver: Special Committee to Investigate Organized Crime in Interstate Commerce, U.S. Senate, 81st Cong., Washington, D.C., U.S. Govt. Printing Office, 1950, Interim Report, p. 7–; obituary of Olive Wofford: *Miami News*, Oct. 11, 1978, and listing for Tatem Wofford [of Tatem Surf Club] in 1953 city directory.)

2. Rebozo told the *Miami News* in mid-June 1974 that he had advised Nixon that it would probably be better to resign. Yet according to the president in his memoirs, Rebozo was still trying to persuade him *not* to resign as late as August 1, by which time the situation was even less tenable than it had been earlier. (*Miami News*, June 18, 1974; *PAT*, p. 398; *MEM*, p. 1058.)

3. There was strict tire rationing at the time because of the acute wartime rubber shortage, and big profits were made by those who found a way around the regulations. Several people linked to Rebozo—including George Smathers's father, Frank—administered rationing in the Miami area, contrary to the rules. The regulations were enforced by the Office of Price Administration in Washington, where in the same year Rebozo expanded to become the largest tire retread operative in the area, Nixon was acting chief of interpretations of the department covering tire rationing. Researchers have sought without success to prove some linkage between Nixon and Rebozo at this time, and many relevant OPA records have long since been routinely destroyed. (During the war Rebozo served as a civilian navigator flying for Army Transport Command, leaving the gas and tire business to be managed by one of his brothers.) (*MO*, p. 237; Weisman, op. cit., p. 255–; *Sundance*, Nov./Dec. 1972, p. 35; *Life*, July 31, 1970.)

4. This is Jane Lucke, who worked for Rebozo's attorney and business partner Thomas Wakefield. A divorcée, she lived with her mother and two sons, who often came along on her dates with Rebozo. She got to know the Nixons, visited the White House, and was supportive of her husband and the president. She survived Rebozo on his death in 1998. (Ints. Jake Jernigan, Don Berg, Sloan McCrae; *Boston Globe*, Oct. 4, 1970; *Ladies' Home Journal*, Nov. 1973 *supra.*; *Miami Herald*, Oct. 7, 1971, Oct. 14, 1973; *Nation*, Nov. 12, 1973.)

5. Nixon made oddly few references to Rebozo in his memoirs, given the amount of time they spent together. He did, though, acknowledge him as his "friend" several times, and at one point as "one of the kindest and most generous men I have ever met . . . a man of great character and integrity." (*MEM*, pp. 247, 967, 964.)

6. As early as 1961 Rebozo accompanied former Ambassador William Pawley on a secret mission to see Dominican Republic dictator Rafael Trujillo shortly before he was assassinated. A *Newsday* probe suggested he was involved in covert operations prior to the Bay of Pigs invasion. Two of the Watergate defendants, Bernard Barker and Eugenio Martinez, were officers of real estate firms that acted in property deals for Nixon and Rebozo. Three days after the break-in Nixon told Haldeman he was going to call Rebozo and have him round up some anti-Castro Cubans to raise money for "the boys" who had got caught. (Trujillo: William Turner and Warren Hinckle, *The Fish Is Red,* New York: Harper & Row, 1981, p. 192; *Newsday:* Oct. 6, 1971; defendants: Scott, Hoch, and Stetler eds., op. cit., p. 372–; William Turner, "Richard Nixon's Vendetta and the Old Boy Network," unpub. ms., p. 61; RN, Haldeman: Haldeman, *Ends of Power,* op. cit., p. 24.)
7. The other friend was Robert Abplanalp, the millionaire who developed the aerosol valve and founded the Precision Valve Corporation. Abplanalp became close to Nixon after the 1960 election, hired him as an attorney during the sixties wilderness years, and regularly welcomed him to his Bahamian island hideaway. Abplanalp's role in the property deals involved in the purchase of San Clemente was investigated during Watergate. He did not respond to requests for an interview for this book. (Summers to Abplanalp, Dec. 30, 1996, Feb. 18, July 31, Oct. 17, 1997; *NYT Magazine,* Jan. 13, 1974, p. 12; Ron Kessler, "Abplanalp Hired Nixon as Lawyer," *WP,* undated clip.)
8. This was the scandal surrounding President Eisenhower's close aide Sherman Adams, driven from office in 1958 because of accusations that he had intervened on behalf of a textile manufacturer in exchange for gifts and favors. Vice President Nixon, one of Adams's few supporters, may have felt obliged to back him; Adams had first been touched by corruption charges during a Senate probe of influence peddling by Nixon's own close friend, Murray Chotiner. (Associations: Piers Brendon, *Ike, His Life and Times,* New York: Harper & Row, 1985, pp. 519–, 361; Herbert Parmet, *Eisenhower and the American Crusades,* New York: Macmillan, 1972, p. 519–.)
9. Nixon told Bob Haldeman and John Ehrlichman, when about to fire them, that money could easily be produced for their legal fees: "There's a way we can get it to you . . . two or three thousand dollars, huh? . . . No strain . . . I never intended to use the money . . . I told Bebe . . . 'Be sure that people . . . who have contributed money . . . are, uh, favored.' And he's used it. . . . " (*NM,* p. 366, citing *WHT,* Apr. 17, 1973; Haldeman, *Ends of Power,* op. cit., p. 348, and see RN version, *MEM,* p. 827.)
10. The Lansky associate in question was Gil Beckley, whose name appeared in Fincher's coded address book in 1966. Two years later some of Beckley's mob colleagues were convicted in a major stolen stocks case in which Rebozo featured controversially, as reported later in this chapter. (Moldea, *Interference,* op. cit., p. 292–; Sifakis, op. cit., p. 314.)
11. Berg was quoted by *Newsday* in 1971 as saying Nixon "got a substantial discount." The company's vice president, Francisco Saralegui, said he thought Nixon should have been given the sites for nothing. In his interview for this book Berg denied that Nixon got a special deal. (*Newsday,* Oct. 13, 1971; int. Donald Berg.)
12. Berg acknowledged negotiating with a Lansky associate, Lou Chesler, about a planned deal in the Bahamas. See reference chapter 20 and chapter 20, Note 4. (Berg acknowledged: *Newsday,* Oct. 13, 1971.)
13. Rebozo sued the *Washington Post* for a story on the stock theft case that asserted, quoting insurance investigator George Riley, that Rebozo had cashed $91,500 of the stock even after the investigator had notified him that it was stolen. Rebozo denied the investigator had told him that, and alleged libel. He demanded ten million dollars in damages. The case ended, after ten years of litigation, with a settlement under which both Rebozo and the *Post* donated undisclosed sums to the Boys' Clubs of America. The *Post* published a statement clarifying its "intentions" in publication of the article. Rebozo won no damages. (*WP,* Oct. 25, 1973; *Miami Herald,* Nov. 6, 1983; int. Ron Kessler.)
14. A 1973 FBI report asserted that the bureau had "no derogatory information" about Rebozo. One should take into account, however, that Rebozo had long since engaged in unctuous correspondence with Director Hoover—Rebozo signed himself "Bebe"—and was a "close personal friend" of Miami special agent in charge Kenneth Whittaker. For reporting on the attitude of Hoover's FBI to organized crime, see *Official & Confidential, The Secret Life of J. Edgar Hoover,* by this author. ("no derogatory": SAC Miami to acting director, May 30, 1973, FBI 62-112974-4; Rebozo, Hoover: corr. Jan. 14, 20, 1959, Dec. 2, 11, 1964, July 14, 1969, FBI 9436880-1, 62-109811-4185, 62-112974-3; SAC "friend": SAC Miami to acting director, *supra.*)
15. In 1996 and 1997 the author wrote to Rebozo asking for an interview in connection with this book. He had already suffered a stroke and sent a message declining. In 1971, when fit, he had refused to speak with reporters preparing the *Newsday* series cited in this chapter. Bebe Re-

bozo died in 1998. (Author's letters to Rebozo, May 25, 1996, Feb 20, 1997, and Rebozo office phone message to author, March 7, 1997.)

Chapter 12

1. As in one who takes a pratfall. Nixon probably meant that he had to take the rap.
2. Four months before his death in 1974, Warren told Alden Whitman of the *New York Times* he thought Nixon "the most reprehensible" president in the nation's history, one who had abused not only the office but the American people. In 1974, after Warren died, it was reported that in his last illness he had been denied admission to Bethesda Naval Hospital, which has traditionally cared for the nation's most distinguished citizens. According to Associate Justice Arthur Goldberg, Nixon's "inaction" may have been responsible for this. As a retired justice Warren needed White House approval to be received at Bethesda. (Miller, ed., *Breaking of the President*, op. cit., p. 536.)
3. Smith told the journalists it was $16,000. The figure later used, and reviewed by accountants and lawyers hired by the Republicans, was $18,235, almost all of which had been supplied to Nixon and spent. A further $11,000 had been collected since the convention and was still on deposit. (Price Waterhouse report, *U.S. News & World Report*, Oct. 3, 1952.)
4. In his memoirs Nixon mentions having told Edson to phone Smith, as though to indicate that, as Edson put it in his article, he had "nothing to hide." One of Nixon's principal reasons for allowing publication of this information at this time," Edson wrote, "is to offset rumors about his finances." Since such rumors had been current for months, Nixon may have prepared Smith in advance to receive such a call, as a ploy to preempt stories by less friendly journalists. He was to praise Edson's story as "objective," as against the *New York Post*'s "bombastic fantasy." Edson would be manipulated in exactly that way ten years later, when he was fed the Nixon version of an impending story on Howard Hughes's $205,000 loan to Nixon's brother Donald. Then Nixon aides characterized him as "a friend." According to press aide Herb Klein, "Nixon decided [it was] the best way to defuse such a story." (*MEM*, p. 93; Nixon, *Six Crises*, op. cit., p. 754; *Chicago Daily News*, Sept. 18, 1952; Mazo, op. cit., p. 106–; Klein, op. cit., p. 415; Maheu and Hack, op. cit., p. 84.)
5. The senator was California's William Knowland.
6. On August 21, 1951, Nixon voted for the basing point bill, which the oil companies wanted, and the following month he voted against cutting the oil depletion allowance from 27 percent to 14 percent. As in the past, he energetically championed the oil companies' efforts to get access to tidelands (offshore) oil. So far as the dairy industry is concerned, one should note that by voting the way contributor Ghormley and other dairymen wanted, Nixon did not oblige Danish-born contributor Thomas Knudsen, who had hoped the United States would lift the quota on Danish cheese imports. (Oil: Drew Pearson column text, Box G 281, DPP, *New Republic*, Sept. 29, 1952; Knudsen: Kornitzer, op. cit., p. 189–.)
7. Nixon was to deny having telephoned Finletter, but Drew Pearson noted privately that his research confirmed that the call was made. (Thomas Harrington telegram to DP, including message from RN, Nov. 3, DP to Harry Hoyt, Nov. 4, 1952, Box G281, DPP.)
8. The casino management, however, was to fail in its suit against Smith in the United States. He claimed that the debts were uncollectable under U.S. law and, contrary to the advice of the embassy's attorney, under Cuban law. (*NYT*, Jan. 30, 1963; *MO*, p. 941; DP memo, Sept. 26, 1952, Box G 281, DPP; Pearson column, Oct. 29, 1962.)
9. The denial, cited in *Look* magazine, did not detail the documentation that was supposedly available. Published references to the Hawaii trip do not settle the matter, although it is clear that Nixon arrived in Honolulu on April 4. The author has been unable to establish how long he stayed. Meanwhile available information on Smith's canceled check does not pin down the date of the Havana visit. The *St. Louis Post-Dispatch* indicated it was written on April 15, while the *New York Times* quoted Smith as saying he stopped it on April 4, an obvious chronological impossibility. It is not even clear that the check was written by Smith while he was in Havana; one document suggests he may have done so later, in Florida. In the absence of full documentation of Nixon's movements and given the rather strong human testimony that he was in Havana, it is reasonable to conclude that he could have been there in either March or April. (*Look: Look*, Feb. 24, 1953; Hawaii: *Honolulu Advertiser*, Apr. 5, 1952, *JA*, pp. 198, 529, n. 19, citing Jack Drown letter of Apr. 30; and *PAT*, p. 112; check: *St. Louis Post-Dispatch*, Oct. 30; *Miami Herald*, Sept. 26, 1952, and *NYT*, Jan. 30, 1953; check written in Florida?: Thomas Gaddis to DP, Sept. 28, 1952, Box G 281, DPP.)
10. Rothman names the member of Congress only as "Johnson." Representative Justin Johnson, a Republican from California, served from 1943 to 1957. (Rothman named: Norman Rothman, Internal Security—Cuba, June 26, 1961, in FBI Cosa Nostra files supplied to House Select Committee on Assassinations, released 1998, JFK Collection, NA.)

11. According to his close associate Joseph Stacher, Lansky was one of the first to propose the assassination of Castro and discussed it with CIA contacts as early as 1959. It was at this time, Stacher said, that Lansky reached out to Dana Smith and Senator Smathers, in the hopes of getting the administration to "accept his assassination plan." In 1960, according to exile leader Antonio de Varona, Lansky discussed "destroying Castro" at a meeting in Miami. Norman Rothman, for his part, said that he too was involved in discussions about killing Castro. (First: Eisenberg, Dan, and Landau, op. cit., p. 257; Varona, Rothman: House Select Committee on Assassinations, vol. X, pp. 171, 183 and corr. Michael Ewing; int. Gerry Hemming.)

12. In his interview for this book, Clarke did not recall the date on the document he filched. Before the 1960 election, at a time he was doing work for Democrats and Republicans alike, he provided it to Robert Kennedy. The document showed Nixon had stayed at the Nacional, expenses paid, according to Clarke. Kennedy did not use the information.

13. Dewey had made his name as a crime-fighting special prosecutor in the thirties. This author has seen no evidence demonstrating that he was ever corrupt. He did, however, have a long-term social relationship with the liquor millionaire Lewis Rosentiel, who was involved with the Mafia and specifically with Lansky. Later Dewey was reportedly involved in efforts to help crooked Teamsters leader Jimmy Hoffa get out of jail. (Not corrupt: Block, op. cit., p. 189; Rosenstiel: Dewey-Rosenthiel corr., Series 5, Box 163, Dewey Papers, University of Rochester, and Summers, *Official & Confidential,* op. cit., p. 248; Hoffa: Block, op. cit., pp. 133, 310.)

14. Before the 1952 election the *New York Post* was passed a letter purportedly written by a Union Oil vice president, referring to an alleged 1950 payment to Nixon of fifty thousand dollars. The money had supposedly been provided by the oil industry and its associates. The *Post* could not authenticate the document and printed nothing, while Drew Pearson referred to it obliquely after the election. A Senate subcommittee later concluded that the letter was forged. *Look* magazine linked the affair to an alleged campaign of "forgeries, false charges, innuendoes" in which President Truman had himself participated. (*NYT,* Feb. 10, 12, 1953; *Look,* Feb. 24, 1953; copies of documents in Box G 281, DPP; Abell, ed., op. cit., pp. 237, 238, 239.)

Chapter 13

1. Columnist Drew Pearson failed to get representatives of the Anti-Defamation League to back the claim that Malaxa was anti-Semitic. In the course of a long-running libel suit against Pearson, however, Malaxa admitted on oath that he had paid one of the ADL leaders, Rabbi Paul Richman, to help with his immigration problems. When the case was called for trial, Malaxa's lawyers withdrew the action against Pearson and agreed to pay his legal costs. (Pilat, op. cit., p. 17–; Pearson memo to editors, June 5, 1962, Box G 192, 2/3, DPP.)

2. Nixon's benign attitude to Romanian exiles with unsavory war records was not limited to Malaxa. In 1955, as vice president, he invited an émigré named Viorel Trifa, who at the time styled himself a bishop in the Romanian Orthodox Church in exile, to offer the opening prayer in the U.S. Senate. According to the Simon Wiesenthal Center, Trifa was tied to the Nazis and involved in the murder of Jews in Romania in World War II. The Institute for the Study of Genocide described him as a "prime mover" of the 1941 massacre of Jews, the pogrom in which Malaxa had also been implicated. Trifa was eventually deported from the United States in 1984 because of his background. (Trifa prayer: Blum, op. cit., p. 116; Wiesenthal Center: Aaron Brietbart, of Wiesenthal Center to author, May 26, 1999; background: origins of the Institute for the Study of Genocide, by Richard Korn, Korn Archive, Web site, 1997; "10th Anniversary of the Death of Archbishop Valerian," ed. Rev. Vasile Hategan, Jan. 14, www.roca.org; Loftus and Aarons: op. cit., p. 224; Hazard, op. cit., p. 203, Blum, op. cit., p. 114–; deported: *NYT,* Feb. 2, Aug. 15, 1984.)

3. Lyman Kirkpatrick, who had been chief of operations under Frank Wisner in the CIA's Directorate of Plans, would formally advise the INS that Malaxa was "considered entirely unscrupulous . . . a dangerous type of man. . . . " (*WP,* Nov. 16, 1979; John Ranelagh, *The Agency,* New York: Simon & Schuster, 1986, p. 191.)

4. According to an AP dispatch on October 2, 1952, Nixon did say Truman, Acheson, and Stevenson all were three "traitors of [sic] the high principles in which many of the nation's Democrats believe." He claimed that a tape recording confirmed this, although the author has been unable to locate such evidence. Truman's biographer Merle Miller made the point that in the absence of such electronic proof, what Nixon really said must remain as uncertain as Joseph McCarthy's precise words in February 1950, when he made claims about Communist penetration of the State Department. "No matter really," wrote Miller. "*Traitors* was the operative word"—and Truman never forgave Nixon for using it. (Miller, *Plain Speaking,* op. cit., p. 178, fn.; *MEM,* p. 112.)

5. The other man Truman said he could not stand was former Missouri Governor Lloyd Stark, who had fawned on him to get his support, then turned on him during a Senate campaign. (Miller, *Plain Speaking,* op. cit., p. 178.)

6. Truman refused even to enter the Senate while Nixon was present and was still lambasting him in speeches in 1960. Backstage at New York's Shubert Theater, at Christmas 1963, Nixon made his way to Truman and shook his hand. Truman accepted the gesture but said, "The hell with it," when a photographer asked for a repeat performance. He did allow Nixon to bring him a drink at a Gridiron Dinner in Washington some months later. In 1969, when Truman was eighty-four and Nixon president, Nixon came to the Truman Library in Missouri to present the former president with the piano his predecessor had once used in the White House. He then sat down at the piano to play "The Missouri Waltz," perhaps unaware that Truman hated the tune. When Nixon finished playing, the old man turned to his wife and in a loud stage whisper asked, "What was that?" (Truman refused to enter Senate: UPI, Oct. 28, 1958; 1960: *Houston Post,* Oct. 11, 1960; handshake: *Newsweek,* Jan. 6, 1964; AP photo, Dec. 1963; drink: *Kansas City Times,* Apr. 28, 1964, Robert Ferrell, *Harry S. Truman,* Columbia, Mo.: University of Missouri Press, 1994, p. 392; "Waltz": ibid., and Miller, *Plain Speaking,* op. cit., p. 358.)

7. The struggle "in the arena" was an image Nixon used in public and in private over a long period: in a late-night dialogue with Len Garment; at a dinner honoring Mamie Eisenhower; in his farewell talk at the White House when he resigned the presidency. He quoted the Theodore Roosevelt reference at length in the frontispiece to his 1990 book, entitled *In the Arena.* (Garment, op. cit., p. 85; Remarks at 75th Birthday Dinner Honoring Mamie Doud Eisenhower, Sept. 27, 1971, cited in *Public Papers of the Presidents, 1971,* Washington, D.C.: U.S. Government Printing Office, 1973; *MEM,* pp. 1076, 1089; Nixon, *Arena,* op. cit., and see Safire, op. cit., p. 364.)

8. The activist Zita Remley had been a perennial anti-Nixon whistle-blower since 1946, when she reportedly learned of an anonymous phone call offensive on Nixon's behalf during the congressional campaign. In 1952 she plied the columnist Drew Pearson with tips, one of them a claim that Nixon had made a false statement in order to obtain a veteran's tax exemption. Pearson published the story, only to issue a retraction when it seemed that another couple called Richard and Pat Nixon had applied for the exemption. Nixon was still angry enough to tell the story in his 1978 memoirs. Remley, for her part, was still telling the story in 1980; she said it had come to her directly in her work as a deputy assessor for Los Angeles County. (Anonymous calls: chapter 5, Note 1, above; tips: Remley to DP, Oct. 7, 1952, Box G 281, DPP; exemption: *MEM,* p. 109; *FB,* p. 236; int. Zita Remley by FB, FBP.)

9. The outcome of the suit is unknown to the author.

10. In 1952 Nixon also frequently turned for "counsel and support" to Whittaker Chambers, his star witness in the Hiss case. It was an odd choice considering that Chambers was a notoriously unstable personality. (De Toledano, ed., *Notes from the Underground,* op. cit., p. 87, *MEM,* p. 102; unstable: see Weinstein, *Perjury,* op. cit., especially re: suicidal tendencies.)

11. In at least one Nixon biography it has been suggested that Hunt, who served in Mexico City from about 1950 to 1953, gave Nixon his card when he visited Mexico as vice president in late 1952. Copies of the card, bearing the handwritten notation "RN saw in Mexico 1952?," are in both the Mexico visit and Howard Hunt correspondence files in the vice presidential papers at the National Archives. Hunt, however, said in an interview for this book that he passed the card to Nixon somewhat earlier: at the meeting in Harvey's Restaurant. (Mexico trip and Hunt corr. files, VP, NA; int. Howard Hunt, and Hunt, *Undercover,* op. cit., p. 127, and see *MO,* p. 865.)

Chapter 14

1. Eisenhower's Oval Office recordings, made on Dictabelts, are apparently of poor quality and often incomprehensible. Only one intelligible conversation with Nixon, the one referred to in the text, has been reported. (AP, Oct. 24, 1979; *AMI,* p. 334, fn; and corr. Sandra Feldstein/Dwight Standberg, Archivist, DDEL, Aug. 1999.)

2. According to Earl Mazo, Eisenhower did occasionally invite Nixon to join him on the course. Another writer who knew Nixon well, Frank Holeman, however, said otherwise. It seems they played together once in a while during Eisenhower's second term. (Mazo: Mazo, op. cit., p. 196; Holeman: Sevareid, ed., op. cit., p. 140, and see *AMI,* p. 428.)

3. Nixon does refer in his memoirs to visiting the family quarters in early 1956, but this was apparently as part of a group. (*MEM,* p. 168.)

4. By one account, Eisenhower became aware of Nixon's resentment. On his wife's initiative, the Nixons were then given a perfunctory tour of the Gettysburg house. (Costello, op. cit., p. 230.)

5. The historian was Herbert Parmet, author of seven political biographies, including *Richard Nixon and His America* (Boston: Little, Brown, 1990), especially p. 402. As in the past, the author is indebted to Professor Parmet for his help.

6. For a discussion of the loan that argues against the suspicion that it was a quid pro quo for Nixon's intervention on Hughes's behalf, see Stephen Ambrose's biography of Nixon. (*AMI,*

p. 597–; and Justice Dept. statement, Oct. 27, 1960, Nixon-Hughes Loan file, Campaign Numerical file 804, Box 92, WSPF, NA.)

Chapter 15

1. The figure rose to about seven hundred during the Eisenhower presidency. (Manchester, op. cit., p. 918, but see Karnow, op. cit., p. 267.)
2. Eisler and Dennis both appeared before the House Un-American Activities Committee, and the two were cited for contempt of Congress, Eisler at Nixon's personal urging. (Caute, op. cit., pp. 90–, 210; re: Eisler: see p. 60 *supra*.)
3. Nixon wrote scornfully in his memoirs of the Venezuelan security effort, crediting the driver of the press truck with effecting the escape from the crowd. His army interpreter, Lieutenant Colonel Walters, said he did not know who moved the roadblock, composed of vehicles parked across the highway, out of the way. Former CIA station chief Jacob Esterline said in 1998 that Venezuelan security chief Jorge Moldonado, acting on his own initiative, organized the extraction. Earl Mazo, who was present, noted that "soldiers" came to the rescue. So did Secret Service agent Dennis McCarthy, citing a colleague who was on the Caracas detail. (Nixon, *Six Crises,* op. cit., p. 219; *MEM,* p. 191; Walters: Walters, op. cit., p. 332; ints. Jacob Esterline; Mazo, op. cit., p. 235; Dennis McCarthy and Philip Smith, *Protecting the President,* New York: Morrow, 1985, p. 46.)
4. Nixon would later acknowledge having received both early and last-minute warnings but said security decisions were "outside my domain." It is clear the decision to go to Caracas was entirely his own. (*MEM,* p. 186; Nixon, *Six Crises,* op. cit., pp. 186, 210–; Rufus Youngblood, *20 Years in the Secret Service,* New York: Simon & Schuster, 1973, p. 69.)
5. TWA and its aircraft were plugged five times in one newspaper alone, the *New Orleans Times-Picayune. (Times-Picayune,* Aug. 8, 9, 17, 19, 20, 1959.)
6. Evan Thomas, in his 1995 book on early CIA chiefs, presents both views: that Guatemala's president Jacobo Arbenz considered himself a Communist and harbored Communists and that he was merely a reformer who posed no security risk. Christopher Andrew, in his 1995 book on intelligence, took the latter view. (Thomas, op. cit., pp. 112, 370, n. 7 and n. 8; Andrew, op. cit., p. 206.)

Chapter 16

1. In the memoirs Nixon said Helms "refused to give Ehrlichman the agency's internal reports." There are four principal postmortem style reports on the efforts to overthrow Castro. CIA Inspector General Lyman Kirkpatrick's Survey of the Cuban Operation was closely held until its 1998 release following a Freedom of Information suit by the National Security Archive. The 1967 Report on Plots to Assassinate Fidel Castro, also from the inspector general's office, was declassified in 1994. A history of the Bay of Pigs, compiled by CIA house historian Jack Pfeiffer in the mid-seventies, is still withheld, although some of Pfeiffer's interviews with CIA personnel are available. CIA Director Helms could have produced the Kirkpatrick report and the Castro assassination study for President Nixon had he chosen to or had Nixon persisted. According to Helms, "Nixon never told me later that he hadn't received what he wanted." (Reports: *MEM,* p. 515, Kornbluh, op. cit., and Thomas, *The Very Best Men,* op. cit., p. 344–, reference the reports thoroughly; Helms: Powers, op. cit., p. 327, and int. Helms, and Ralph Weber, *Spymasters,* Wilmington, Del.: SR Books, 1999, p. 270.)
2. The start of the 1971 pressure coincided with a memorandum from Charles Colson to Haldeman. Colson reported that Howard Hunt, who as a CIA agent played a major role in the Bay of Pigs project, had told him that "if the truth were ever known, Kennedy would be destroyed." A few days later Hunt began working at the White House, with assignments that included digging for dirt on President Kennedy. One of his exploits involved the forgery of cable traffic to suggest the Kennedy administration had been behind the 1963 killing of Vietnamese President Ngo Dinh Diem. ("If the truth . . . ": Colson to HRH, July 2, 1971, memo extract released Nov. 1994, NA, E, vol. VII, p. 700; assignments: WHT, Sept. 18, 1971, and Hunt, *Undercover,* op. cit., p. 147; Diem: ibid., p. 179.)
3. Greek émigré journalist Elias Demetracopoulos, whose January 1961 interview with Admiral Arleigh Burke had upset President Kennedy, told the author of a late-night visit to his apartment by Buzhardt in June 1973. Fearful of bugs, Buzhardt persuaded Demetracopoulos to come out and talk while walking around the block. He wanted Demetracopoulos's file on Burke because Burke had been chief of naval operations at the time of the Bay of Pigs. Demetracopoulos declined to help. (Int. Elias Demetracopoulos.)
4. Helms has recalled Haldeman's bringing up the Bay of Pigs but has denied shouting. His biographer Thomas Powers thinks he probably did lose patience. He had after all been badgered on the subject over a long period. (Powers, op. cit., p. 476, n. 57.)

5. Earlier, before seizing power, Castro told *Paris-Match* correspondent Enrique Meneses that he would allow gambling to continue, but only for foreign tourists. In a radio broadcast before the revolution, however, he said he was "disposed" to deport the casino operators or even shoot them. (Meneses, op. cit., p. 58; Lacey, op. cit., p. 252.)
6. Former CIA agent Ross Crozier, interviewed in 1996, says that both Castro and Che Guevara knew he was with the agency. Crozier was told—he thinks reliably—that no less a figure than J. C. King, CIA's Western Hemisphere Division chief, himself flew in to meet and assess Castro. Later, as described in this chapter, King favored Castro's assassination. (Int. Ross Crozier, but see Dorschner and Fabricio, op. cit., p. 94.)
7. Smathers has said he discussed Castro's assassination with President Kennedy in 1961. Kennedy disapproved of the notion, he told a Senate committee. Smathers told this author in 1994 that Kennedy in fact approved of the idea and that his brother Robert was aware of the later CIA/Mafia plots. (U.S. Senate, *Assassination Plots*, op. cit., p. 123–; Summers, *Not in Your Lifetime*, op. cit., p. 188.)
8. Pawley claimed he had heard the young Castro talking as though he were a Communist in 1948, in a radio broadcast during the violent uprising in Colombia known as the Bogotazo. An official probe, however, found no Communist involvement in those disturbances. (Broadcast?: Mario Lazo, *American Policy Failure in Cuba*, New York: Twin Circle, 1968, p. 144; untrue?: Geyer, op. cit., p. 94.)
9. The journalist Andrew St. George, who knew Castro and wrote extensively about Cuba, was present as they left Nixon's office. He too recalled Nixon's saying words to the effect that the United States would be able to work with Castro. (Int. Andrew St. George.)
10. Those cited indicate Nixon felt sure Castro was a Communist once he had met him. As in his report to Eisenhower, however, he suggested in a private letter to the editor of the *Miami News* that he thought it "possible" Castro might "change his attitude." (*AMI*, p. 516.)
11. Howard Hunt claimed in a 1973 book that the CIA did not use the code name Pluto—and surmised that it was perhaps, rather, a name used by the Pentagon. The name Pluto, however, was still being used in the context of CIA usage in 1986—by the author John Prados. (Hunt, *Give Us This Day*, op. cit., p. 214; Prados, op. cit., p. 178–.)
12. Figueres said this in 1977 in a taped interview with the politics editor of the *New Republic*, Ken Bode. He added that he "came to believe that Eisenhower actually did not know about Nixon ordering preparations. . . ." Obviously the president did know about the plans, at least in a general executive sense. Conversations with Bode lead the author to infer that Figueres meant Eisenhower did not fully understand the hands-on nature of Nixon's involvement. (*New Republic*, Apr. 23, 1977.)
13. Haig became involved in Cuban matters, and with relevant military and intelligence personnel, somewhat later. As military assistant to the secretary of the army he worked with returning members of the Cuban exile force that had been defeated at the Bay of Pigs. Later still Haig served as President Nixon's last chief of staff.
14. In corroboration of Hunt's account, CIA historian Pfeiffer also referred to this meeting. Pfeiffer placed it in late June, Hunt in July. (Notes of Pfeiffer int. by FB, FBP.)
15. Kohly, Jr., who himself became an exile activist, said his father got Nixon to intercede on his behalf in 1959, when he was having trouble obtaining a U.S. visa. The visa came through within twenty-four hours of his father's meeting with Nixon. (Int. Dr. Mario Garcia Kohly, Jr.)
16. Nixon did use the Burning Tree Club golf course, which, coincidentally, would also one day be the setting for the very first attempts to cover up Watergate. (Klein, op. cit., p. 360; Liddy, *Will*, op. cit., p. 344.)
17. Another affidavit to the same effect was signed by Robert Morrow, who claimed to have been a CIA contract agent. Morrow was arrested for counterfeiting in 1963 along with Kohly, and later pleaded nolo contendere. Morrow later spun his story into books that expanded his involvement to supposed knowledge of alleged plotting in the John F. Kennedy assassination. The author does not find Morrow's books credible in that respect. Morrow's appendices, however, are a useful source for relevant public documents. (Ints. the late Robert Morrow, Professor John Williams; Robert Morrow, *Betrayal*, New York: Warner, 1976 and *First Hand Knowledge*, New York: S. P. I. Books, 1992.)

Chapter 17

1. The committee took into account the testimony of Robert Johnson, a former National Security Council staffer, who recalled Eisenhower's saying something at an NSC meeting that "came across to me as an order for the assassination of Lumumba." Later in the testimony Johnson seemed to retreat from this statement, but he also emphasized the "profound moral dilemma" he had in discussing matters he had learned under conditions of secrecy. In an interview for this book he reiterated his belief that Eisenhower had ordered or at least agreed to

the killing of Lumumba. CIA officials, for their part, said they believed the Lumumba plotting was authorized by the president or "at the highest levels," which tends to mean the same thing. Beyond what is covered in the main text, next to nothing is known of Eisenhower's position on the Castro plotting. Jacob Esterline, the CIA officer who directed Operation Pluto and thus had to authorize disbursement of operational funds exceeding $50,000, recalled challenging two 1960 requests for $150,000. The colleague making the requests swore him to secrecy and explained that the money was for a Castro assassination project, authorized by "the President of the United States." Esterline had no way of knowing if his colleague was telling him the truth. (Johnson: int. Robert Johnson; U.S. Senate, *Assassination Plots,* op. cit., p. 55–; "highest levels": ibid., p. 65–, and see also Stephen Ambrose with Richard Immerman, *Ike's Spies,* Garden City, N.Y.: Doubleday, 1981, p. 293–; Esterline: int. Jacob Esterline by Gus Russo, 1998.

2. Many now accept that the Kennedy brothers, both doomed to be assassinated, authorized later plotting to kill Castro. There has been enduring speculation that President Kennedy's murder was somehow linked to the Castro plots. Lyndon Johnson, who apparently learned of the plots after succeeding Kennedy, died not long before the Senate committee began its probe. In 1974, at a meeting of *New York Times* editors, President Ford said he expected the forthcoming Rockefeller Commission on the CIA might come upon matters that could "blacken the reputation of every president since Truman." "Like what?" asked the *Times* managing editor, A. M. Rosenthal. "Like assassinations!" Ford replied, "That's off the record!" The *Times* observed the restriction, but word soon leaked out. Noting that "every president since Truman" would clearly include Nixon, the author wrote to former President Ford asking if he knew whether Nixon had been privy to Castro assassination plans while vice president or whether he was aware of any assassination plans made while Nixon was president. Ford replied:

1) I do not specifically know of any knowledge President Nixon may have had of assassination plans.
2) I do not know whether President Nixon as Vice President under President Eisenhower was privy to plans to assassinate Fidel Castro or other Cuban leaders.
3) When I became President, I did not become aware of any specific plans made during the Nixon presidency.

The author asked for clarification. Ford replied saying, "I was very precise in my wording. I do not intend to revise or add. Please accept my response as final." This may suggest that, while Ford knew nothing of the situation during the Nixon vice presidency, he did gain nonspecific knowledge of assassination plans or operations during the Nixon presidency. (For the Kennedys' apparent involvement in the Castro plots and the possible ramifications, see, inter alia, this author's articles on Judith Exner in the *New York Daily News,* Oct. 6, 7, 8, 1991, and in *Not in Your Lifetime,* op. cit., pp. 187–, 247–, 305–; Ford: Daniel Schorr, *Clearing the Air,* New York: Berkley, 1978, p. 144; Ford-author corr.: author's letters, Dec. 6, 1996, Apr. 1, 1997, Ford letters, March 4, Nov. 26, 1997.)

3. The Senate report notes that authorization could also have come from the Special Group (or 5412 Committee), a body consisting of "designated representatives" of the president and the secretaries of state and defense assigned to study and agree on proposed operations. At least on occasion Nixon was briefed on the Special Group's deliberations. (Special Group: Andrew, *For the President's Eyes Only,* op. cit., p. 212; RN briefed: notes of Jack Pfeiffer int. by FB, FBP.)

4. In testimony to the Senate Intelligence Committee, Bissell said he believed Dulles had "probably" talked to Eisenhower about the CIA-Mafia plots and "guessed" the president had given authorization, "perhaps only tacitly," based on his knowledge of Dulles's mode of operations. This conflicts with a *Newsweek* report of a Bissell interview that cites him as saying he was "certain" Dulles told no one at the White House. (U.S. Senate, *Assassination Plots,* op. cit., p. 111; *Newsweek,* Dec. 11, 1995.)

5. A year later, interviewed for television by David Frost, Nixon suggested that had President Roosevelt ordered Hitler's assassination before World War II, the act would have raised a "tough call" for constitutional authorities. (Frost, op. cit., p. 185.)

6. *Webster's New Collegiate Dictionary* (1980) says "goon" also refers to someone hired to "terrorize" an opponent, the sense intended by John Ehrlichman when he described Nixon's order to hire "goon squads" during election campaigns to rough up hecklers. In relation to agents sent to Cuba, however, the word surely referred to "elimination" of opponents rather than the mere scaring of them. (Ehrlichman, op. cit., p. 33; int. John Ehrlichman.)

7. The journalist Tad Szulc, Hunt's biographer, has reported that Hunt took part in a later, (1964) Castro assassination plot. According to Szulc, Hunt was at one stage assigned to the office of Allen Dulles and was asked to help him with his memoirs. Dulles was aware of the

anti-Castro plots. (Szulc: Tad Szulc, *Compulsive Spy*, New York: Viking, 1974, pp. 97, 95; Dulles aware: Grose, op. cit., p. 552.)

8. According to June Cobb, who worked alongside Lorenz in Castro's Havana office, it was not Castro but a senior military aide, Captain Jesús Yánez Pelletier, who fathered Lorenz's child. Castro, she said, spent intimate time with Lorenz, but never had sex with her. According to a document in a CIA file, citing notes by Alexander Rorke, Cobb was instrumental in Lorenz's having the abortion. Cobb said in a recent interview that she opposed the abortion. (Cobb, abortion: John Newman, *Oswald & the CIA*, New York: Carroll & Graf, 1995, p. 110–, citing CIA documents and Cobb int. by John Newman; Rorke notes: CIA Domestic Contacts Division report to chief, Jan. 22, 1964, JFK files, Jan. 1994 release, p. 2, NA.)

9. Researching the Lorenz story poses multiple difficulties, not the least of them the fact that Lorenz herself is one of those rococo figures in the Cuba saga who has expanded her story over the years to include elements that, to most investigators, are not credible. Most notably she has spun a tale linking key figures in her story to the assassination of President Kennedy. The scenario covered in this text, however, is backed by evidence. That Lorenz had some sort of relationship with Castro is supported by photographs of the two of them together and by the statements of June Cobb and Frank Sturgis. The first reporter to report the Lorenz assassination mission, Paul Meskil of the *New York Daily News*, found her account believable. Gaeton Fonzi, a meticulous investigator for the Senate Intelligence Committee, believed Lorenz to be truthful on many points while not so on others. The deputy chief of the CIA's Security Analysis Group, Jerry Brown, treated her story seriously in a six-page report. He was struck by the similarity between Lorenz's account and FBI Director Hoover's October 1960 memo to the CIA referring to leakage of a plan to use a girl to poison Castro's drink. (Expanded story: Fonzi, op. cit., p. 93–, and Lorenz, op, cit.; photographs: *New York Daily News*, June 13, 1976, Lorenz, op. cit., and Fonzi saw relevant documents; Meskil: *New York Daily News*, Apr. 20, 1975, June 13, 1976; Fonzi: Fonzi, op. cit., conv. with author and partial transcript of int. Marita Lorenz by Fonzi, Feb. 3, 1976, NA; Brown: undated [late seventies] report to chief of Security Analysis Group, no. D02016, Box 2, 1993 CIA release, NA.)

10. Orta took refuge in the Venezuelan Embassy in early April 1960 and finally received a safe passage to leave Cuba in late 1964. (CIA Inspector General, *Plots to Assassinate Castro*, op. cit.)

11. Varona was used again when the CIA-Mafia plots were revived in 1962. He was supplied with poison pills and weapons, but again with no result. The real reason Castro survived the poison plots may be that the intermediary, mob boss Trafficante, duped the CIA. "The CIA had all this crazy talk about poisoning," Trafficante's attorney Frank Ragano quoted him as saying in 1967. "Those crazy people. They gave me some pills to kill Castro. I just flushed them down the toilet. They paid us a lot of money and nobody intended to do a damn thing. It was a real killing." (Varona: CIA Inspector General, *Plots to Assassinate Castro*, op. cit.; "real killing": Frank Ragano and Selwyn Raab, *Mob Lawyer*, New York: Charles Scribner's, 1994, p. 209.)

12. As the CIA inspector general admitted in his opening sentence, his report on the Castro murder plots was "at best an imperfect history." When and how who first proposed what to whom will probably never be known. Doris Mirage, a CIA secretary, recalled that the overall head of Cuban operations, Richard Bissell, "got calls from the Mafia, but he wouldn't take them. I don't even know how they got his inside number." An offer to kill Castro, in writing, mysteriously arrived from one of the Mafia bosses, Joe Bonanno. While he reportedly recoiled from these direct contacts, Bissell wrote in his memoirs, posthumously published, that "the Mafia seemed a reasonable partner." ("imperfect": CIA Inspector General, *Plots to Assassinate Castro*, op. cit., p. 1; Mirage: Thomas, op. cit., p. 234; "reasonable": Richard Bissell, *Reflections of a Cold Warrior*, New Haven, Conn.: Yale University Press, 1996, p. 157.)

13. "Pulley" appears spelled variously in the Diggs correspondence file, the Brewster papers, and in Robert Morrow's books, as "Pulley," "Pullay," and "Polley." "Pulley" is probably correct, as rendered in the letter of introduction to Cushman. A file on Pulley in the Nixon vice presidential records indicates contact in 1959, and one note is written under an Americans for Constitutional Action letterhead. The ACA, a conservative group, included on its board of directors the chairman of United Fruit, the U.S. company loathed by Caribbean revolutionaries. The late Charlie McWhorter, a Nixon aide who processed some of the relevant correspondence, told the author he did not remember Pulley. Robert Morrow, who was arrested with Mario Garcia Kohly in the Cuban peso–counterfeiting case, was asked about Pulley shortly before his death in 1998. He said "Pulley" was an alias and seemed to link the name with Myron "Mickey" Weiner, a lobbyist from New Jersey. Weiner featured in a 1964 Senate probe of former Majority Secretary Bobby Baker, in connection with suspect payments and the services of "party girls" for government officials. A Rules Committee report spoke of Weiner's "unrestrained and unpoliced wrongdoing." A March 30, 1961, letter from Diggs to Brewster just

before the Bay of Pigs invasion is worth noting. It refers to "Mario," who was "ready to roll," and to asking for help from "your friend Joe." It seems likely that the Mario in question was Diggs's client Mario Garcia Kohly and conceivable that "Joe" referred to Trafficante, who used that name in contacts with the CIA. (See sourcing for main text for location of Diggs and Brewster material; Weiner: *WP*, Dec. 4, 1964, and *WP, NYT,* and *Washington Evening Star,* July 1, 1965.)

14. It is not clear to what degree the anti-Onassis operation was driven by the U.S. government, the U.S. oil companies, and by Onassis's business competitor Stavros Niarchos. Maheu's associate Gerrity claimed Nixon "ran the thing, but he was never more than a front for the multinational oil companies. You have to remember, one of his main jobs was to raise campaign contributions for the Republicans." According to Drew Pearson's sources, Nixon had received massive backing from U.S. oil interests in the 1952 campaign. (Pearson: Abell, ed., op. cit., p. 228–.)

15. One member of the team was Lou Russell, who had worked with Nixon during the Hiss case and who would one day be linked to the Watergate break-in. Another was Horace Schmahl, the intelligence-linked investigator who reportedly admitted having been involved in setting up Alger Hiss, see p. 73. (Undated Washington field office document, FBI 105-20653, Report of Agents Morgan and Kellogg, Oct. 23, 1958, number censored.)

16. Ironically, Onassis would in 1970 give a substantial contract to Nixon's brother Donald, then with the Marriott Corporation, for in-flight catering on Olympic Airlines aircraft. That deal was brokered by Nixon's friend Thomas Pappas, who had also arranged for an illegal Greek cash contribution to the Nixon campaign in 1968. Pappas failed, however, to persuade Onassis to contribute to the 1972 campaign. (Donald contract: *NYT,* June 4, 1970, *WP,* Feb. 16, 1972; Pappas, 1968: Kutler, *Wars of Watergate,* op. cit., p. 205–, and ints. Elias Demetracopoulos; Onassis, 1972: Gratsos to Dorsen, Dec. 7, John Doukas to William Mayton, Senate file, Box 11 [Pappas, Onassis], WSPF.)

17. Sam Giancana was found shot dead in 1975, when he was due to be questioned by the Senate Intelligence Committee. Santo Trafficante, whom some suspected of ordering his murder, died of natural causes in 1987. When Maheu referred to dismemberment, he was speaking of John Rosselli, whom he had used to bring the CIA, Giancana, and Trafficante together. Rosselli's corpse, its legs sawn off, was found crammed in an oil drum in 1976, soon after he had given testimony to the Intelligence Committee. He had been due to testify again. Rosselli's attorney Leslie Scherr believed that the Watergate Special Prosecution Force, which also questioned his client, suspected the Watergate break-in was sparked by fear that the Democrats had learned of Nixon's involvement in the Castro plots. (Deaths: Summers, *Not in Your Lifetime,* op. cit., p. 365; Scherr: Rappeleye and Becker, op. cit., p. 307.)

18. As quoted in *Newsweek* (May 19, 1986), Nixon referred to "poison *sticks.*" This makes no sense. The author guesses that he actually used the Yiddish word *shtick,* which has come to mean "stuff" in colloquial American.

19. Robert Geddes Morton, who headed Pepsi-Cola's bottling operation in Cuba, was reportedly not only a key contact in the CIA's invasion plan but also involved in the Castro plots. Morton, a British subject, was jailed by the Cuban regime but released in 1963 after diplomatic intervention. Since Morton was a Pepsi vice president, Nixon's friend Donald Kendall, head of Pepsi's overseas operations, probably knew something of this. He too may therefore have discussed the plots with Nixon. (Louis and Yazijian, op. cit., p. 171; Martino, op. cit., p. 139, et al.)

20. Anderson got his information from John Rosselli, the California mobster Maheu had used to contact the Mafia bosses. Under heavy pressure from law enforcement and immigration authorities, Rosselli had decided to get the story of the plots out, with emphasis on his own "patriotic" role, in the hope of forcing the powers that be to remove some of the pressure on him. He met with Anderson on January 11. The CIA did later try to intervene on Rosselli's behalf. The mobster was not deported, as seemed possible, but he did go to prison for nearly three years. The judge reduced the jail term after hearing pleadings about Rosselli's part in the CIA plots. As mentioned in Note 17, above, the mobster was savagely murdered in 1976, after testifying about the plots. (Rappeleye and Becker, op. cit., p. 296–.)

21. Because of his own compromising relationship with Howard Hughes, Nixon had earlier been concerned that an IRS matter involving Hughes should *not* be pursued. In parallel, however, Nixon had pushed for information on Lawrence O'Brien, the former close aide to John F. Kennedy, whom he regarded as the most effective Democratic political operator. Most recently, on January 14, he had told Haldeman it was time to hold O'Brien "accountable for his retainer with Hughes." Haldeman reacted by passing on the president's message, virtually word for word, to the White House counsel John Dean. (Summary of RN previous concern: Emery, op. cit., p. 28–; RN, Jan. 14: RN to HRH, Jan. 14, 1971, HRH Box 140, NA.)

22. As officially reported, Justice Department files on the Castro plots consist of reports arising from a 1960 wiretap episode involving Giancana and Maheu and its sequel, involving CIA objections to prosecutions and a 1962 briefing of Attorney General Robert Kennedy. (U.S. Senate, *Assassination Plots*, op. cit., pp. 77–, 130–.)

23. Maheu was involved throughout the first phase of the CIA-Mafia plots, which lasted from August 1960 to March 1961. According to the CIA inspector general's report, Maheu "knew nothing" of the second phase of the plotting, which began in April 1962. (U.S. Senate, *Assassination Plots*, op. cit., pp. 74–, 83–; CIA Inspector General, *Plots to Assassinate Castro*, op. cit., p. 120.)

24. Oliver Stone used Haldeman's notion that "Bay of Pigs" was code for the Kennedy assassination in his 1995 movie *Nixon*. Soon afterward the writer Christopher Matthews reported that Haldeman had disowned the theory. When terminally ill, Matthews said, Haldeman claimed the theory had been not his but that of Joseph DiMona, his collaborator on the book. The disclaimer was repeated by *Newsweek*'s Evan Thomas, in a cover story critical of the Stone movie. Haldeman, however, wrote in a special note for the paperback version of his book that he and DiMona "worked on it together from the beginning up through the final version. The writing style is DiMona's. The opinions and conclusions are essentially mine." DiMona has insisted that Haldeman *was* responsible for the controversial passage. "It is preposterous," he wrote, "to think that Bob Haldeman, of all people, would allow any writer to 'invent' information or erroneous theories, to be published in a book under his name . . . the 'theory' survived no less than five drafts of the most meticulous editing known to man, during which Haldeman made extensive changes of every kind, as well as minutiae. If untrue, why wasn't the theory deleted?" DiMona accounts for the disclaimer by noting that having been highly critical of Nixon in his 1978 memoir, Haldeman spent the rest of his life "disavowing" the negative parts. This author can contribute to the dialogue, having himself spoken with Haldeman in 1989. After a long formal interview focused on my project at the time, a book on J. Edgar Hoover, I raised some points that had long interested me, including the Bay of Pigs interpretation. Then Haldeman did not disown the passage but made it clear that it was merely his speculation and that as for Ehrlichman, Nixon's insistence on obtaining the CIA's Bay of Pigs material remained a puzzle to him. It does seem improbable that Haldeman, ever insistent on detail, would have allowed the insertion of material with which he did not agree. His interest in accuracy was obvious during my exchanges with him. My view that the Haldeman passage amounts merely to informed speculation is bolstered by the analysis of the scholar Paul Hoch, who, like Haldeman, had discussed the issue with former CBS correspondent Daniel Schorr. (Stone: Eric Hamburg, ed., *Nixon: An Oliver Stone Film*, New York: Hyperion, 1995, p. xv; Mathews: *San Francisco Examiner*, Dec. 6, 21, 1995; Thomas: *Newsweek*, Dec. 11, 1995; paperback: H. R. Haldeman and Joseph DiMona, *The Ends of Power*, New York: Dell, 1978, p. 422; DiMona: int. Joseph DiMona by Julie Ziegler for author, and Dec. 8, 1995, fax shared with author by Dr. Gary Aguilar; see also *WP*, Feb. 15, 1978, citing DiMona years earlier as saying: "you don't write anything *for* Haldeman. He changed my book right down to the end. He rewrote, revised, edited . . . "; Hoch: letters to David Marwell, Assassination Records Review Board, Dec. 6, and to Dr. Aguilar, Dec. 23, 1995, provided to author.

Chapter 18

1. As described elsewhere, Nixon would be supplied with sexually compromising information on Kennedy during the 1960 campaign and reportedly hoped to use it. As president, the White House tapes show, he tried persistently to catch Edward Kennedy with a woman not his wife. "Jack," he said in old age, of the late president's womanizing, "was the original sexual harasser," "Kennedy got away with it; I don't think Clinton can. Although he has that same . . . —here a pause and an attempt at a Massachusetts accent—'viga.' " (tried persistently: Haldeman and DiMona, op. cit., p. 60; "harasser": Crowley, *Nixon in Winter*, op. cit., p. 329; 'viga': Monica Crowley, *Nixon Off The Record*, New York: Random House, 1996, p. 33.)

2. Kennedy suffered from Addison's disease, a chronic affliction that would likely have proved fatal had it not been brought under control by then-new medication. While long rumored, the fact that Kennedy was an Addison's sufferer was kept from the public until many years after his death in 1963. (Summers, *Not in Your Lifetime*, op. cit., p. 9.)

3. Edwards added that Nixon sometimes swore "like an army sergeant." The candidate, whose swearing on the Watergate tapes would one day create a furor, said in the 1960 campaign that presidents should never use "gutter language." (*Kansas City Times*, Oct. 13, 1960.)

4. Hughes confirmed in 1996 that this incident happened as described. (Int. General Don Hughes by Gus Russo.)

5. In *Six Crises* and in his memoirs, Nixon wrote as though he never doubted the need to debate Kennedy and made no reference to the vacillation reported by others involved. His surprise announcement that he would do so may reflect the influence of Arthur Burns, Eisenhower's economic adviser and a Nixon confidant, who suggested he debate Kennedy—but "just once, and thus finish off that nice young man from Harvard. . . . " "I couldn't have given him worse advice," Burns said in the eighties. Other aides, including Murray Chotiner, counseled Nixon not to take part. (RN wrote: Nixon, *Six Crises*, op. cit., p. 323; *MEM*, p. 216; "just once": int. Arthur Burns in Miller Center, eds., op. cit., p. 151; Chotiner: Katcher, op. cit., p. 165.)
6. Asked to comment on the Eisenhower comment during the first debate with Kennedy, Nixon said it was "probably a facetious remark." The journalist Walter Trohan, however, said Nixon told him privately it was the "unkindest Eisenhower cut" of all. ("facetious": RN-JFK debate transcript, Sept. 26, 1960, transcript in Senate Committee on Commerce, Final Report, *supra.*, p. 81; "humor": Robert Finch Oral History, Columbia University, p. 58; "unkindest": Trohan, op. cit., p. 368–.)
7. A 1992 study of the health problems of U.S. presidents tended to support Nixon's account in his memoirs that in 1960 he was urged by Eisenhower's personal physician and his wife Mamie to influence the president against campaigning on his behalf. The diary of the physician, Dr. Howard Snyder, shows that Eisenhower was suffering serious heart rhythm and blood pressure problems at the time and that Snyder was concerned about the additional stress of campaigning.
   During the 1968 campaign, when Eisenhower was seventy-seven and in ever poorer health, Nixon worried that the former president might die without having endorsed him. He got word through to him, however, and Eisenhower, by then in the hospital, made a generous statement of support before the convention. (Illness 1960: *MEM*, p. 222; Robert Gilbert, *Mortal Presidency*, New York: Basic Books, 1992, p. 115, citing Snyder's medical diary on Eisenhower—but see Satire, op. cit., p. 623; endorsement 1968: Goldwater, op. cit., p. 216; AP, July 18, 1968; endorsement text, JFRP; *PAT*, p. 242.)
8. Nixon had submitted to being made up as early as 1954, and his office was issuing his makeup type, a blend of shades 22 and 23, to reporters as late as 1957. By the following year, however, when he visited London, he was resisting makeup. He refused the services of BBC makeup staff, saying his military aide would look after it if necessary, until told he might cause a strike by TV technicians. (1954: Bassett unpublished ms., *supra.*, March 13, 1954; 1958: int. and corr. Leonard Miall.)
9. Of those polled, 29 percent thought the candidates had come off even, and 5 percent were undecided. (*TW60*, p. 294.)
10. After the disaster of the first Kennedy debate, Nixon took expert advice on makeup, although he still preferred his Lazy Shave. He even wore makeup to a friend's wedding when he learned it was being televised. Before the 1968 campaign he said he wanted to hire talk show host Johnny Carson's makeup man. As president, according to congressional doorkeeper William ("Fishbait") Miller, he wore pancake makeup to the Capitol for his State of the Union address. "I would feel sorry for him," Miller wrote, "because he would be nervous and the sweat would just pour over his top lip . . . he would lick it off rather than use a handkerchief." To minimize his perspiration, Nixon had the air conditioning turned up to the maximum when he gave televised "fireside" addresses from the White House. "Put him on television, you've got a problem," said his 1968 TV adviser Roger Ailes. "He's a funny-looking guy. He looks like somebody hung him in a closet overnight." "If the country wants a new face," Nixon told Irv Kupcinet in 1968, "I'm dead." (Took advice: Wise, *Politics of Lying*, op. cit., p. 376; preferred Lazy: *Saturday Evening Post*, Feb. 25, 1967; wedding: int. Norma Mulligan by FB, FBP, re: wedding of William Rogers's son; Carson: *Saturday Review*, Dec. 16, 1967; at Capitol: Miller, op. cit., p. 342; "fireside": Halberstam, *The Fifties*, op. cit., p. 731; Ailes: Wise, *Politics of Lying*, op. cit., p. 377; RN, Kupcinet: *Look*, March 5, 1968.)
11. Lasky is best known for his books *JFK: The Man & the Myth* and *It Didn't Start with Watergate*, published in 1977, which trumpeted "the many sins—by his enemies—against Richard Nixon." Behind the facade of regular journalist, Lasky was on "Dick" terms with Nixon from as early as 1949, during the Hiss episode. Dwight Chapin recalled finding him in 1962 in a cigar smoke–filled office with Murray Chotiner, "like a classic picture of the Tammany Hall back room." The Rockefeller brothers put up sixty thousand dollars to underwrite a controversial biography of Supreme Court Justice Arthur Goldberg when he was running for governor of New York in 1970. "If nobody else will print it, Lasky will," Haldeman said on a 1971 White House tape. Many White House memos referred to the planting of stories with Lasky, and Nixon's 1972 reelection committee offered him twenty thousand dollars to write speeches. In January 1975, as Nixon made his first tentative moves to emerge from the obloquy of Watergate, Lasky was one of those who flew to California to celebrate his birthday. It was through Lasky that Lucianne Goldberg, who found notoriety in 1998 for her role in the

Clinton sex exposé, became a Nixon spy in the Democratic camp. ("Many sins": Lasky, op. cit., back cover; "Dick": Levitt and Levitt, op. cit., p. 135, and see *MO*, p. 491; de Toledano, ed., op. cit., p. 13; Chapin: Strober, eds. *Nixon*, op. cit., p. 340; Goldberg: Miller, ed., *Breaking of the President*, op. cit., p. 503; "If nobody": HRH to Mitchell-Nixon, July 6, 1971, WHT; 1972 Tittle-Kicklighter memo, June 6, 1973, FBI WFO 139 166; planting stories: Schorr, op. cit., p. 183; 1975: unidentified June 17, 1975, Vera Glazer clip; Lucianne Goldberg: *WP*, Feb. 4, 1998; Michael Isikoff, *Uncovering Clinton*, New York: Crown, 1999, p. 191.)

12. Citing an article in the *National Review*, Lasky said a first wave of mailings, during the primary campaign, had been organized by a Kennedy worker named Paul Corbin. Nixon repeated the allegation in his memoirs. Corbin was described by Kennedy biographer Arthur Schlesinger as a "raffish and outrageous rogue . . . a fixture in Robert Kennedy's political operations . . . prone to reorganizing the truth." While the author has not attempted to verify the *National Review* article, it seems Corbin was capable of perpetrating such abuses. Readers should note, though, that the mailings in question were directed not at Nixon but at a fellow Democrat, Hubert Humphrey, during the primary phase of the campaign. (Lasky, op. cit., p. 35; *MEM*, p. 775; Schlesinger, *RFK*, op. cit., p. 196–.)

13. The "first marriage" claim—that Kennedy married a Florida socialite named Durie Malcolm in 1947—arose from an entry in a privately printed history of Malcolm's family. It stated flatly that among her several husbands was "John F. Kennedy, son of Joseph P. Kennedy, one time Ambassador to England." There is conflicting evidence on whether this information first reached FBI Director Hoover in 1960 or during the Kennedy presidency, in 1961. In 1997 John Kennedy's close friend Charles Spalding told author Seymour Hersh the marriage to Malcolm had indeed occurred and that he had "removed the marriage papers" at Kennedy's request. Malcolm has denied that she married Kennedy. While there were problems with Spalding's account—he was seventy-nine when interviewed and had short-term memory lapses—other evidence persuaded Hersh the story was credible. (Hersh, op. cit., p. 326–.)

14. The statements about the alleged Democratic surveillance and eavesdropping are elements of a tangled tale. The two detectives not cited in the main text were former federal agent John Frank and former Washington police inspector Joseph Shimon. Frank said Bellino did run investigations for the 1960 Kennedy campaign committee and that he was given assignments by him but that he could not remember what they were. Shimon said Angelone asked him for help in a bugging operation against Nixon supporters based in Washington's Wardman Park Hotel. It is interesting to note that Frank was an associate of Horace Schmahl, the private investigator who allegedly claimed he helped frame Alger Hiss. Shimon was a witness to the CIA-Mafia Castro assassination plots. Bellino had once shared an office with Robert Maheu, a central figure in the CIA-Mafia plots and an aide to Howard Hughes. The interconnections of the characters in the 1960 eavesdropping allegations are curious, and the truth about their actions and motivations will probably never be fully known. The White House tapes show that Haldeman and Nixon discussed the exploitation of "some allusions to some probable Kennedy wiretapping in 1960" as early as February 1973, months before the claims by the alleged participants surfaced. (Frank-Shimon: report and affidavit, Box 120, Korff Papers, Brown University; Frank-Schmahl: see p. 73, chapter 8, Note 10; Shimon, plots: int. Joseph Shimon; Hougan, *Spooks*, op. cit., p. 279; Maheu-Bellino: Maheu, op. cit., p. 40; RN-Haldeman: WHT, Sept. 6, 1973, *AOP*.)

15. According to the 1992 book *Double Cross* by Giancana's brother Chuck and his nephew (and godson) Sam, Giancana said words to this effect in late October 1960, at Meo's Norwood House restaurant in Chicago. *Double Cross* attracted justified criticism for its claims about the Kennedy assassination, but an interview with Sam Giancana (the nephew and coauthor) encouraged the author's feeling that core parts of the book reflect the authentic memories of Chuck Giancana. (Ints. Sam Giancana.)

16. Michael Ewing, longtime staff assistant to Senator Harold Hughes of Iowa, interviewed Partin in 1977 on the recommendation of Walter Sheridan. Partin's account remained consistent with what he had told Sheridan in the sixties, with the exception that Sheridan quoted him as originally having named a figure less than five hundred thousand dollars. Also present at the meeting when the money was handed over, according to Partin, was Washington lobbyist Irving Davidson. Davidson, who later denied that Marcello even knew Hoffa, had arranged the meetings between Hoffa and Oakley Hunter (see p. 214); Sheridan said he later located information confirming the Marcello donation while working in the Kennedy Justice Department. (Int., corr. Michael Ewing: Moldea, *Hoffa Wars*, op. cit., pp. 108, 260.)

17. The accountant, Phillip Reiner, had been chosen in 1957 as the front man behind whose name the true origin of the loan could be concealed. Then, he had shared office space with the Hughes law firm of James Arditto and Frank Waters. By 1960 the Arditto-Waters partnership had been dissolved, and Reiner and Arditto were at loggerheads. In August 1960, according

to Reiner, full documentation of the loan to Don Nixon was delivered to his home with other files he had left behind in the Arditto office. Arditto, for his part, told the police that his office had been burglarized. His widow speculated in 1996 that Reiner had purloined the material to sell it to the Kennedy team. (*Reporter*, Aug. 16, 1962; int. Clare Arditto.)

18. Nixon's concession was expressed in a wire to Kennedy the next morning. (Nixon, *Six Crises*, op. cit., p. 398.)

19. For the best analysis of the figures, see Appendix A in Theodore White's *The Making of the President: 1960*.

20. There were also allegations of vote fraud in Texas. A shift of a mere 4,491 votes in Missouri, or minor changes in the count in New Mexico, Hawaii, and Nevada, could also have changed the result. For a study of the possible permutations, see Wicker, op. cit., p. 251–.

Chapter 19

1. St. Johns had known Nixon from childhood. In 1962 he described her as having been a "close friend and adviser" since 1947. (See p. 151, and Nixon, *Six Crises*, op. cit., p. xi.)

2. The CIA's Cuban exile force gathered by April 1961 for the infantry-style Bay of Pigs landing numbered only fourteen hundred men—this to confront Castro's army of thirty-two thousand plus a two hundred-thousand-man militia. In mid-December 1960 it numbered only about five hundred. The decision to switch from guerrilla training to an infantry invasion had been made only a month earlier. (Exile strength Apr. 1961: Kornbluh, ed., *Bay of Pigs*, op. cit., p. 277; Castro forces: Trumbull Higgins, *The Perfect Failure*, New York: Norton, 1987, p. 70; mid-December 1960: Wyden, op. cit., p. 55; decision to switch: Kornbluh, ed., *Bay of Pigs*, op. cit., p. 277.)

3. In a 1998 chronology, based on the latest official releases, U.S.-backed action against Cuba developed as follows in the latter part of 1960. Talk of shifting from guerrilla warfare plans to a possible amphibious operation began in late summer, as did the first documented CIA-Mafia plots to kill Castro. A cable from CIA headquarters to the field first described a plan for a fifteen-hundred-man invasion on October 31. Four days later this was followed by an order to change training operations in line with the new concept. The change was relayed to Eisenhower's Special Group on November 8–9, coincident with election day. As president-elect Kennedy was briefed by CIA Director Dulles and Deputy Director Bissell on November 18 and by outgoing President Eisenhower on December 6. Training and recruitment for the proposed invasion were stepped up in January 1961, in the weeks before Kennedy's inauguration.

   Nixon had been enraged when less than a month before the election Kennedy repeatedly attacked the Republican administration for giving insufficient aid to the anti-Castro exiles. Nixon later charged that Kennedy had deliberately put him at a disadvantage, making an unfounded allegation when he well knew from secret briefings that plans were in place to overthrow Castro and knew too that Nixon could not rebut the charge without breaching national security. Instead, in his final television debate with Kennedy, Nixon told the American public Kennedy's proposals for toppling Castro were "most dangerously irresponsible" and would risk a dangerous confrontation with the Soviet Union. Even allowing for electioneering license, this was a real liberty with the truth since operations to overthrow Castro were precisely what were under way. In *Six Crises* Nixon defended this strategy as a necessary step to protect the government's secret plans. In a later interview he said it was the "only *political* position that was salvageable...." At the time, press aide Herb Klein revealed in 1995, Kennedy's charges on Cuba made Nixon "so angry it was difficult to prepare him for the debate." He was still fulminating on the subject in private as president eleven years later, the White House tapes reveal. Just what Kennedy knew about in advance of the plans to topple Castro, and from whom, remains the subject of debate. Nixon's accusation that the CIA debriefed Kennedy on the Cuba plot may, ironically, have been misplaced. There is evidence he got his knowledge from another source. In any case, the CIA's plans were hopelessly insecure. (1998 chronology: Kornbluh, ed., *Bay of Pigs*, op. cit., p. 275–; RN rage: Nixon, *Six Crises*, op. cit., p. 353– [paperback version]; MEM, p. 220; Nixon article, *Reader's Digest*, Nov. 1964, and see Wicker, op. cit., p. 232; Klein, op. cit., p. 94; "only political": *Washington Star*, Apr. 26, 1978; "so angry": *San Diego Union-Tribune*, Dec. 19, 1995; still fulminating: June 23, 1972, WHT (retranscribed for author by Robert Lamb), and see July 5, 1971, WHT, AOP, p. 23; what JFK knew: Strober, eds., *Kennedy*, op. cit., p. 325; Hersh, *Camelot*, op. cit., p. 175–; Weber, op. cit., p. 17; Grose, op. cit., p. 507, *San Diego Union*, March 25, 1962.)

4. Nixon never got over his preoccupation with Cuba. On becoming president in 1969, he promptly ordered the CIA to step up covert action against Castro at a time it was being wound down. He sought legislation to prevent Americans from helping the Cuban economy. In 1970, when U.S. reconnaissance detected the apparent construction of a Soviet naval base in Cuba, a genuine concern, Nixon demanded an immediate CIA briefing on "*any* kind of action which will irritate Castro." In 1971 the CIA supplied a consignment of African swine fever virus to

anti-Castro operatives, who then smuggled it into Cuba. An outbreak of the disease followed six weeks later, requiring the slaughter of half a million pigs to avert an epidemic. The same year Nixon posed for photographs with the family of a Cuban exile whose ship had been attacked and captured by a Castro gunboat. Testimony suggests that, also in 1971, the CIA was involved in a plot to assassinate Castro during a visit to Chile and that Howard Hunt, former CIA agent turned White House Watergate conspirator, told associates another "assassination team" was being readied in Spain. Fellow Watergate burglar Bernard Barker said Hunt "mentioned something about planning for the second phase of the Bay of Pigs around the beginning of Nixon's second term." (RN, step up: Raymond Garthoff, *Detente & Confrontation,* Washington, D.C.: Brookings Institution, 1985, p. 88, n. 37; legislation: Ehrlichman, op. cit., p. 142; "*any* kind of action": Kissinger, *White House Years,* op. cit., p. 142; swine fever: *Newsday,* Jan. 9, 1977; *Nation,* March 9, 1998; Fidel Castro speech to 68th Inter-Parliamentary Conference, Sept. 15, 1981 [Cuban government release]; RN posted: Fonzi, op. cit., p. 137; Hunt on "team": notes of int. Howard Liebengood and Frank Saunders, Jim Hougan papers, provided to author; Hunt "mentioned": memo re: Barker int., Sept. 13, 1973, Box 99, WSPF, NA; ints. Bernard Barker and Howard Hunt [the latter a denial].)

5. The Nixons' accounts of this family discussion are not entirely consistent one with another.
6. See chapter 6. The Nixon-Cohen story was leaked to the columnist Drew Pearson in 1962, but he did not use it until 1968.
7. The author has been in touch with this source for nearly twenty years. Cross-checks have confirmed his background and expertise, and the author has come to believe he is a man of integrity. Professional concerns aside, he shuns publicity.
8. Referring to taps conducted by the FBI (as distinct from freelance eavesdroppers), Nixon told Kissinger in 1973: "Bobby Kennedy was the greatest tapper of all.... Hoover told me . . . 'Bobby Kennedy had me tapping everybody.' I think, incidentally, I'm on that list." This is one of many such references to Democratic bugging, including Nixon's insistence—again citing J. Edgar Hoover—that his campaign plane had been bugged in 1968. ("greatest tapper": June 1, 1973, entry, *AOP,* p. 561, and see ibid., p. 92; 1968 campaign plane: e.g., ibid., p. 198.)
9. The late Jack Tobin, whom the author knew, was a skilled investigative reporter, working throughout that period, with colleague Gene Blake, on a *Times-Mirror* probe of Teamsters Union leader Hoffa's West Coast activities, in particular Hoffa's abuse of the union pension fund. Nixon's home purchase had been the lead to the *Times* story of May 17, 1962. The very sight of Tobin, when they met again years later at an airport, triggered another outburst of shouting and swearing by Pat.
10. The information was omitted from *The Final Days,* probably because the reporters had insufficient sources on the matter at that time. Scott Armstrong, who worked both as a staffer on the Ervin Committee and on research for *The Final Days,* said in a 1980 interview that he too had been told that "Nixon beat Pat up." (Ints. Bob Woodward, Carl Bernstein, and David Obst, and notes of int. Scott Armstrong by FB, FBP.)
11. Sears did not get along with Attorney General John Mitchell, who apparently believed he leaked information to the press. He decided to leave the White House after only nine months, in October 1969. It later emerged that Sears was wiretapped and surveilled during that period, probably because of Mitchell's suspicions. (Ehrlichman, op. cit., p. 27, n; Wise, *American Police State,* op. cit., p. 56–.)
12. The contributor was Francis Kellogg, a mining magnate. Washington lobbyist Robert Winter-Berger recalled accompanying Taylor to Kellogg's office and collecting sixty-five thousand dollars in cash; Taylor said forty-five thousand dollars of it was going directly to Nixon. Kellogg wanted an ambassadorship in Africa but made do with a post as special assistant to the secretary of state for refugee and migration affairs, which reportedly carried an ambassadorial title. (Winter-Berger, op. cit., p. 249–.)
13. In *The Final Days,* Woodward and Bernstein reported that Pat had wanted to divorce Nixon after the 1962 defeat and wrote of her "rejection of his advances since then." (Woodward and Bernstein, *The Final Days,* op. cit., p. 173.)

Chapter 20

1. Prior to the sixties only two "clubs" were allowed to operate casinos, and those only during the high tourist season. One, the Bahamian Club, was on the outskirts of Nassau; the other was on Cat Cay. Nixon showed interest in visiting Cat Cay in 1959, and Bebe Rebozo was to buy the island in 1983. Nixon subsequently vacationed there. (Only two: Mahon, op. cit., p. 60; RN 1959: RN to Elmer Bobst, Dec. 18, 1959, corr. files, Series 320, Box 90, VP; *Report of the Commission of Inquiry into the Operation of the Business of Casinos in Freeport and Nassau,* Nassau, Bahamas: 1967, p. 65; Rebozo: *Miami Herald,* May 14, 1984; int. Jake Jernigan; RN vacationed: *Nassau Tribune,* Jan. 28, 1986.)

2. The Development Board chairman, Sir Stafford Sands, a leading white Bahamian, testified to the 1967 commission of inquiry into Bahamas gambling operations that Lansky visited him in 1960 or 1961, offering a certified check for two million dollars if Sir Stafford could get for him a casino permit. Sir Stafford said he turned Lansky down. He later had meetings with Lansky associates involved in the management of the mob-run casino that did open in 1962 with his approval—and to his great profit in legal fees (see text). Sir Stafford liquidated his Bahamian holdings and moved to Spain after the casino business and his role came under investigation. (*Nassau Tribune*, Aug. 25, 1967; Hank Messick, *Syndicate Abroad*, London: Macmillan, 1969, p. 224.)

3. The company Crosby headed when he bought into Paradise Island was Mary Carter Paint Inc. He sold it in 1968 and founded Resorts International. Resorts later sued *Rolling Stone* magazine for libel over an article by Howard Kohn titled "Strange Bedfellows—The Hughes-Nixon-Lansky Connection: The Secret Alliance of the CIA from World War II to Watergate." *Rolling Stone* eventually later published a retraction, stating that "Based on the evidence now available," the magazine was "satisfied that Resorts was not a front for either Meyer Lansky, organized crime or the CIA, and did not permit gaming revenues to be skimmed by underworld operatives, and did not funnel money to Cuban counterrevolutionaries or otherwise launder funds for covert operations." None of the substantive information used in this chapter is drawn from the *Rolling Stone* article.

   A CIA document released in 1998, on the subject of Resorts International Inc. and dated August 18, 1976, states: "Resorts International Inc. was of interest to Cover and Commercial Staff, DO, in 1972 and 1973." It also notes that Wallace Groves, initially a partner with Mary Carter Paint in the purchase of Paradise Island, was "the Subject of OS file 473 865" and "of interest to the Office of the General Counsel for the utilization of Groves as an advisor or possible officer of one of the Project WUMUTUAL entities. Additional information in this file would suggest that Groves was connected with Meyer Lansky." Other CIA documents show that a "Covert Security Approval" was applied for in respect to Groves in December 1965, shortly before the Mary Carter and Groves purchase of Paradise Island. It was approved and not canceled until April 1972. (Mary Carter became Resorts: Resorts International Stockholders Report, undated [1969?], Block Collection, and see Mahon op. cit., p. 77; suit and retraction: *Rolling Stone*, Apr. 28, 1983, referring to article, ibid., May 20, 1976; Mahon, op. cit., p. 42; CIA document 1998: Jerry G. Brown, deputy chief, Security Analysis Group, to chief, Security Analysis Group, Aug. 18, 1976, CIA Record No. 104-10408-10212, JFK series, released under FOIA; other CIA documents on Groves: CI/Operational Approval & Support Division, Office of Security documents, "Subject: Wallace Groves," Dec. 30, 1965, Jan. 26, Apr. 8, 1966, Apr. 12, 1972, Block Collection; Groves and Mary Carter Paint: *NYT* Jan. 17, 1979.)

4. The real estate scheme, which eventually collapsed, involved a plan to build condominiums on Paradise Island. The "Lansky man" involved in the project was Lou Chesler, a Canadian associate of Groves. Chesler's involvement with gangsters dated back to the early forties, and he met with Lansky to plan Bahamas casino operations. See also chapter 11, Note 12. (Real estate: Mahon, op. cit., p. 208; "Lansky man": Block, op. cit., p. 43–; Messick, *Syndicate Abroad*, op. cit., p. 130; met Lansky: *Nassau Tribune*, Apr. 18, 1967.)

5. Professor Block has been an adviser to the New York Senate Select Committee on Crime and editor in chief of a criminology journal. He has written nine books on organized crime, including *Masters of Paradise: Organized Crime and the Internal Revenue Service in the Bahamas*, New Brunswick, N.J.: Transaction, 1991. He was interviewed for this book and made his files available to the author.

6. James Crosby's brother Peter was an officer of the company listed in courthouse records as the holding company for James Crosby's Mary Carter Paint. Peter Crosby, who had mob associates, was convicted and jailed in 1960 on charges of mail fraud, securities fraud, and the sale of unregistered securities. Similar cases followed in 1969 and 1971, when he was again convicted, this time of conspiracy to violate the Small Business Corporation Act. He vanished while free on appeal bond and was listed as a fugitive. He was living in New Jersey at the time of his brother James' death in 1986. Mob stock swindler Louis Mastriana testified in 1973 that he and John Lombardozzi, brother of a New York Mafia boss of that name, had met with Peter Crosby in the Bahamas to discuss one of the frauds for which Crosby was indicted. As reported in chapter 11, Mastriana was one of those who said he had dealings with Nixon's friend Rebozo. Doubts about Rebozo's integrity were raised because of his handling of stolen stocks. In that case Rebozo named James Crosby as one of the people he consulted about the stocks. The other was Donald Nixon. (Holding company: *Miami Beach Sun*, Jan. 29, 1970; offenses: Jonathan Kwitny, *The Fountain Pen Conspiracy*, New York: Knopf, 1973, pp. 98, 294; and *Manhattan Inc.*, Feb. 1987; Mastriana testified: *Hearings, Permanent Subcommittee on Investigations, Committee on Government Operations, (Organized Crime: Securities,*

Thefts, and Frauds), U.S. Senate, 93d Congress, 1st Session, Pt. 2, Sept. 18, 1973, p. 146–; and see also Patsy Lepara testimony in Pt. 3, pp. 454, 472; Rebozo consulted James Crosby: *WP*, Oct. 25, 1973)

7. While a Resorts official tried to brand Teresa a liar, government counsel Edward Harrington, later U.S. attorney in Boston, declared him a credible witness. Twenty defendants were convicted on the basis of Teresa's testimony. (Mahon, op. cit., p. 233.)

8. One such friend, New York promoter Richard Pistell, donated seventeen thousand dollars. Pistell, who helped form Crosby's casino operation, was later sued for fraud by the Securities and Exchange Commission. In the early seventies he was first to interest the financier Robert Vesco in buying Paradise Island. (Donation: *NACLA Latin America & Empire Report*, Oct. 1972; helped form: *Wall Street Journal*, Oct. (?) 5, 1972; sued: Robert Hutchison, op. cit., p. 260; Block, op. cit., p. 55; Vesco: Hutchison, op. cit., p. 264.)

9. Henry Kissinger visited Paradise Island, as did press aide Ron Ziegler. Crosby traveled with Kissinger to meet with Nixon on Grand Cay, owned by the president's friend Robert Abplanalp. Abplanalp frequented the Paradise casino and reportedly lost large sums on the gaming tables there. (Kissinger: *NYT*, Jan. 21, 1974; undated memo, Warren Adams to John Sablich, *Fidelifacts report*, supra, p. 545, citing Paradise Enterprises PR director Ed Woodruff; Ziegler: ibid.; Crosby, Grand Cay, Abplanalp: *NYT*, Jan. 21, 1974.)

10. A 1977 article in *Barron's* magazine cited the bridge's annual income as "around a million." Sy Alter, who ran the bridge in 1967, gave the author the same figure, while Paradise security director Paul Shealy said the bridge grossed up to eighteen thousand dollars over a three-day weekend. (*Barron's*, Sept. 26, 1977; int. Seymour Alter; memo to file, IRS Informant TW-24 [known to be Norman Casper], Nov. 7, 1973, Casper Papers, and research for author by Nassau researcher Catherine Kelly.)

11. The third partner, according to Butler, was Senator George Smathers, mutual friend of Nixon and Rebozo's. Nixon's last chief of staff, Alexander Haig, has recalled being told by the president to issue denials to *Time* or *Newsweek*. A written inquiry about Nixon and the ownership of the bridge, addressed to the White House by Robert Hutchison (an authority on the Vesco affair) elicited not even a pro forma response. (Smathers: Hutchison, op. cit., p. 282; Haig: int. Alexander Haig in Strober, eds., *Nixon*, op. cit., p. 427; Hutchison: Hutchison, op. cit., p. 282.)

12. The former agent, Gerald Behn, had accompanied Kennedy on a visit to Chicago in April 1961. He was asked about the visit in 1992 because the president's former mistress, Judith Exner, had said Kennedy met secretly on that occasion with the local Mafia boss, Sam Giancana. Behn claimed not only to know nothing of the Giancana allegation but even to have forgotten the visit itself. He went on to become head of the Kennedy White House detail and later president of the former Secret Service Agents' association. The association censured four former agents for having discussed Kennedy's private life with the journalist Seymour Hersh. (Research supplied to author by Mark Allen.)

13. There were many phone interviews with Silberman, two prison visits, and extended correspondence, from 1996 to 2000.

14. This seems an outlandish sum to the layman. Obviously, even though the price of gold tripled in the year following the closure of the gold window, a simple tripling of the initial $180,000 investment would have meant a profit of $360,000, not the astonishing figure of $10 million claimed by Silberman. The explanation is in Silberman's reference to buying gold "futures." According to an investment adviser consulted by the author, a return on this scale is indeed plausible when commodities futures are traded. A "future" is an agreement to buy or sell a fixed quantity of a fixed asset at or by some fixed future date at a price agreed to on the day of making the agreement. A buyer, however pays not the full price but an agreed "margin," a form of deposit. Silberman could have made a margin payment of as little as a dollar an ounce, thus securing for himself, from the massive increase in the gold price that followed—as he knew it would when the gold window closed—a massive profit on the margin paid when he made the agreement. (Int. and corr. Peter Metcalf.)

15. Silberman said he believed that Selix, who owned a chain of formal men's wear shops, had visited China at the same time as Nixon. Selix is not on the list of those who accompanied Nixon to China on the famous 1972 visit, and it has not been possible to check on the participants in the subsequent trip during the Ford presidency. Selix's widow said she knew nothing of her husband's having accompanied Silberman to Florida to meet Nixon. Silberman meanwhile indicated that he received instructions from a go-between, yet declined to identify who that person was. After repeated questioning of Silberman, the author came to suspect he was using Selix's name as a decoy to avoid identifying a real go-between. (China 1972 list: Anne Collins Walker, *China Calls*, Maryland: Madison Books, 1992, p. 411.)

16. Nixon was at San Clemente from December 26, 1973, to January 11, 1974. Official logs for the stay include no reference to Silberman, but that record is not conclusive. Entries contain

notes like "We received no record of the President's activities after 12:39 P.M." or "he took a ride with Mr. Rebozo yesterday afternoon. . . . I do not think Pres. wants reported." (Rebozo was evidently present much of the time.) Ladislas Farago, a possible candidate to write an authorized Nixon biography, recalled having been asked to use a pseudonym when on a visit to San Clemente early in Nixon's exile period. (President's daily diary and schedules, WA, end int. Ladislas Farago by FB, FBP.)

17. The *Kokomo Tribune*, serving central Indiana.

18. There may also have been a link between DeBoer and Nixon himself that dated to before the presidency. As a New York attorney in the mid-sixties Nixon recommended several clients to the Italian financier Michele Sindona. Sindona was represented in New York by DeBoer's security firm, Baerwald & DeBoer. Sindona offered a million-dollar contribution to Nixon's 1972 campaign, a sum that was supposedly not accepted. He oversaw efforts to get Nixon the Italian-American vote. Said to have been the Sicilian mob's head banker, Sindona later drew a U.S. jail term for fraud, was convicted in Italy on narcotics and murder charges, and died of cyanide poisoning while in custody. (RN recommended: Luigi DiFonzo, *St. Peter's Banker*, New York: Franklin Watts, 1983, p. 152; Sindona, DeBoer: Stephen Haberfield to Hughes-Rebozo file, Jan. 10, 1974, Campaign Contributions Task Force, Int. folder 804, WSPF, NA; Judith Denny to files, Aug. 15, 1975, DeBoer folder, Box 98, WSPF, NA; million-dollar: Stans, *Terrors*, op. cit., p. 186; oversaw: Penny Lernoux, *In Banks We Trust*, Garden City, N.Y.: Anchor Press, 1984, p. 188; crimes, death: Scheim, op. cit., p. 321.)

19. The partner was I. G. ("Jack") Davis, then president of the Crosby company. (DeBoer Executive Session testimony, E, NA, Aug. 8, 1973, p. 52–.)

20. DeBoer later repaid the money, according to the SEC. He consented to the commission's findings, without admitting the allegations. (*WP*, Oct. 3, 1973.)

21. Alter claimed later that his money movements related solely to the finances of his gift shop on Paradise Island. (*NYT*, Jan. 21, 1974.)

22. Newell has the receipt for three tapes given by her to the Watergate Special Prosecution Force and the record of the disposition of the tapes as of December 1973. The story of how the tapes were smuggled out of the offices of the Special Prosecution Force after the Saturday Night Massacre is told in chapter 32. (Oct. 13, 1973, receipt signed by Carl Feldbaum, in Newell file supplied to author, and John Galus to Feldbaum, Dec. 10, 1973, and receipt signed by Arthur Quinn, Feb. 3, 1975, Box 6, Huges-Rebozo files, WSPF, NA.)

23. The reference is to Robert Abplanalp, the aerosol tycoon and a Nixon friend and supporter for many years.

24. Casper's discovery emerged in fragments in the 1975 House Oversight Hearings into the Operations of the IRS, cited earlier.

25. The Bahamian voters' list for 1972 did turn up two Nixons with Richard as one of their first names. The first, an upholsterer named Henry Richard Nixon, died in 1981. His son knew nothing of his father's having had a Castle account but oddly recalled that his father had once been photographed in the company of *the* Richard Nixon. The upholsterer signed himself "Henry R." and never used the "Richard." There was also a King Richard Nixon, a former servant to a British naval officer. He recalled that his employer opened an account for him at a bank he at first thought might have been Castle, though a friend believed it had been the Bank of New Providence, in the same building. This Nixon account, however, had been opened in the fifties, when neither bank yet existed. His employer, moreover, could not have opened the account in either bank since he had left the Bahamas before they started business. This Nixon signed himself "King Richard Nixon" or "King R. Nixon." There are no other possible candidates in the Bahamas. While it is not easy now to determine how many people by the name of Richard M. Nixon lived in the United States in 1972, an indicator of the name's prevalence may be gained from a 1999 check, which located eleven. (Bahamian Nixons: research and ints. by Nicki Kelly; 1999 check: www.switchboard.com.)

26. A closing memo to the Watergate special prosecutor deemed the allegation of a Nixon account at Castle Bank "probably unfounded." The force's examination of the matter, however, was cursory and incomplete. Neither Casper nor key bank official Michael Wolstonecraft would cooperate, and the prosecutor's staff avoided even looking at the purloined documents on the ground that they had been obtained illegally. (Paul Michel to Henry Ruth, Oct. 16, 1975, pp. 91, 235–, WSPF [H-R], NA.)

27. Whether the sums mentioned as deposited in the name of "Zepher Group. (N&R)" are in U.S. dollars or in Swiss francs—the latter is more likely—there is no way now of discovering how the sums were held. If they were merely managed by the bank, as opposed to being used by the bank in the normal way for loan purposes, they would not show up in the bank's published statistics. (Int. and corr. Peter Metcalf.)

28. "m" could conceivably have been Michael Wolstonecraft, vice president and secretary of Castle Bank and the man in whose briefcase the Cosmos document was discovered.

29. Cosmos Holding AG, Zug, Switzerland, held ten shares, while Cosmos President H. U. Rinderknecht held three. Cosmos Equities Corporation of New York held nine. (Stockholders' List, Paradise Island Bridge Co., Box B78, E, NA.)

30. Anderson was sentenced in 1987 to a month in prison and five months' house arrest for tax evasion and operating an illegal offshore bank in the Caribbean. Just before becoming treasury secretary, in 1957, he completed a deal with a group of oilmen that was designed to bring him nearly a million dollars and that would influence his policy in office. Eisenhower, however, admired Anderson and reportedly would have preferred him to Nixon as a presidential candidate in 1960. (sentence: *NYT*, Aug. 16, 1989; oil deal: *WP*, July 16, 1970; Sanford Ungar, *FBI*, Boston: Little, Brown, 1975, p. 272; Charles Ashman, *Connally*, New York: Morrow, 1974, p. 83; Ike preferred: *FB*, pp. 351, 355.)

31. Morgenthau referred to Max Orowitz, who was convicted on securities offenses involving a Swiss bank. Entwined in his case were Lou Chesler, Lansky man and Nixon contributor, and Max Courtney, the Lansky bookmaker who casually testified that one of his eminent customers was Nixon. It was Morgenthau, too, who convicted Peter Crosby, brother of Paradise Island casino boss James Crosby—heavy Nixon contributor and friend of Rebozo—for stock fraud. (Orowitz int.: Robert Morgenthau; Waller, op. cit., pp. 91–, 118; *Newsday*, Oct. 11, 1971; Block, op. cit., pp. 37, 43, 123, 189; Chesler/Courtney: ibid., and—re. Courtney—see p. 127.)

32. The sending of the anonymous note, as late as July 26, 1997, was doubtless triggered by a *New Yorker* piece on Morgenthau. The article quoted Morgenthau as saying, "I always thought he [Nixon] had Swiss bank accounts." (*New Yorker*, July 28, 1997; int. James Traub.)

33. Jonathan Aitken, a biographer to whom Nixon gave unusual access, refers without explanation to the former president's benefiting in 1978 from payments "into the 'silent partner's' bank account" at Rebozo's bank. (*JA*, p. 543.)

Chapter 21

1. Another source priced the apartment at $425,000. (Troy, op. cit., p. 178.)

2. The Sanchez couple was Spanish-born but had lived in Cuba until becoming exiles after the Castro takeover. They had started working for the Nixons in 1961 and were to remain in their service until long after Nixon's resignation. In 1968 Nixon would interrupt his hectic campaign schedule to appear as their sponsor when they applied for U.S. citizenship. After the Sanchezes retired to their native Spain, around 1980, they were succeeded by a Chinese couple. (Raymond Price, *With Nixon*, New York: Viking, 197, p. 14; Bryant with Leighton, op. cit., p. 251; int. Edward Nixon; Spanish: *MEM*, p. 291; Chinese: *New York*, June 9, 1980.)

3. A wealthy Florida contractor, Louis Berlanti, perished in a plane crash in August 1963, reportedly while carrying more than half of the $53 million siphoned to him by Trujillo. Berlanti had funded Kohly's Cuban peso-counterfeiting scheme. (Hinckle and Turner, op. cit., p. 201.)

4. Nixon was to tell the FBI and the Warren Commission that he had been in Dallas for two days before the assassination, omitting to mention that he had still been there on the morning of the day itself. It was a curious Nixonian obfuscation, inviting black humor when the facts came out and, to those with a paranoid turn of mind, suspicion. (FBI Assistant Director John Malone report of RN int., Feb. 28, 1964, FBI NY 10538431, and see Warren Commission Exhibit 1973, Matthews, op. cit., p. 247, citing RN letter to commission, Aug. 4, 1964.)

5. Later, in statements to the FBI and the Warren Commission, Oswald's widow Marina would claim her husband had earlier intended to kill Nixon. Her account of the episode was hopelessly confused, however, and Nixon had not been in Dallas at the time in question, April 1963. While the Warren Commission deemed the story of "no probative value," Nixon repeated it as if it were fact in his 1978 memoirs. (Scott, op. cit., p. 289–; Sylvia Meagher, *Accessories after the Fact*, New York: Vintage, 1976; *MEM*, p. 252.)

6. Nixon printed the full text of his letter to Jacqueline Kennedy and a facsimile of her reply in his memoirs. In 1971, while he was president, Pat Nixon invited Jacqueline and her children to a private viewing at the White House of new Kennedy portraits. Kennedy's widow was moved by the warmth of the Nixons' welcome. (*MEM*, p. 502; *AMII*, p. 416; Matthews, op. cit., p. 293.)

7. "Richard Nixon," John Ehrlichman said, "simply didn't want to spend the kind of time that was required to cultivate these folks [the Congress]." Nixon would also disdain his cabinet, calling them "clowns." He "never took a vote," Haldeman recalled, "and would have cared less concerning the result." "Screw the Cabinet and the rest," he is heard to say on a tape revealed in 1998. ("simply didn't want": int. John Ehrlichman, in Miller Center, eds., op. cit., p. 133; RN, cabinet: eds. Strober, *Nixon*, p. 88–; *WP*, Dec. 27, 1998.)

8. Nixon returned again to Moscow and to Sokolniki Park, site of his 1959 encounter with Khrushchev, in 1967. His purpose was unclear. (Witcover, op. cit., p. 194.)

9. The author writes "supposedly" because researchers must take it on trust that Nixon's contemporary notes, or the personal diary he sometimes referred to, are as cited in his memoirs. Nixon Library archivist Susan Naulty told the author in 1998 that "the diaries are the private property of the President's Estate, and there are no plans at present to release them to the public." Given Nixon's less than perfect record for truthfulness, the author notes the possibility that purported citations may not be authentic. (Susan Naulty to author, March 23, 1998.)

10. According to Ehrlichman, the woman concerned was Shelley Scarney, a veteran Nixon campaign worker and later White House receptionist who went on to marry Nixon aide and future presidential candidate Pat Buchanan. Contacted in 2000, Mrs. Buchanan said she did not recall the incident. (*NYT*, Feb. 21, 1971; Patrick Buchanan, *Right from the Beginning*, Washington, D.C.: Regnery Gateway, 1990, pp. 9, 259.)

11. The FBI aspect of this story, including Director Hoover's alleged use of the episode to bring pressure on Nixon as president, is covered at greater length in the author's book on Hoover. (Summers, *Official & Confidential*, op. cit. pp. 371–, 376, noting document, Director to SAC San Francisco, Aug. 18, 1976, FBI 105-40947-8.)

12. The author interviewed several of those who, in 1976, were involved in the *Enquirer* coverage. Al Coombes, now a lawyer, and Gerry Hunt recalled their joint interview with Liu. "I read it back to her," Coombes said, "and she agreed that that was what she said." Coombes conducted several interviews with Liu. Hunt recalled that initially Liu spoke "freely." (Ints. Al Coombes, Gerry Hunt, Dick Saxty, Brian Wells, Malcolm Balfour, Bernard Scott, Shelley Ross, John Cathcart, John South, and Robert Smith.)

13. In conversation with Liu's attorney, Nixon too denied any sexual involvement. He said he knew Liu "casually." (*SF Examiner* & *SF Chronicle*, Feb. 8, 1981.)

14. The publishing magnate Walter Annenberg, who served as U.S. ambassador to London in Nixon's presidency, was a longtime personal friend. (*Fortune*, June 1970, MEM p. 977.)

Chapter 22

1. Under questioning by the Senate Watergate Committee, however, DeBoer denied contact with Mitchell personally. (DeBoer testimony, Executive Session, Aug. 8, 1973, p. 5, Box C-28, E, NA.)

2. Nixon had also considered Ford as running mate in 1960. (Int. Robert Finch; Miller Center, eds. op. cit., p. 259.)

3. As early as May, on a flight to Portland, Oregon, he had fed the *Washington Post*'s David Broder the notion that if he were nominated, his running mate would be Agnew. (Crouse, op. cit., p. 91.)

4. *The Selling of the President* (New York: Simon & Schuster), by Joe McGinniss, was first published in 1969. The TV producers were Frank Shakespeare and Roger Ailes; the "creative supervisor" was Harry Treleaven.

5. Press aide Herb Klein has queried whether Smith was with Nixon on election night. In his interview with the author, however, Smith insisted that as news reports have stated, he was present. (Klein, op. cit., p. 37; int. Arnholt Smith.)

6. Former IRS Special Agent David Stutz, later a deputy district attorney in San Diego, recalled receiving a call from John Caulfield at the White House. Saying he was phoning on behalf of Ehrlichman, Caulfield asked Stutz to fly to Washington with all the information he had on Alessio and Smith—without informing his superiors. Stutz took the call with a colleague listening in and told Caulfield to put the request in writing. The line then went dead. (Int. David Stutz, *Ramparts*, Oct. 1973.)

7. Hughes's memorandums, later circulated and cited in scattershot fashion, are best accessible in Michael Drosnin's book *Citizen Hughes*. For this author, however, the most authoritative account is *The Hughes Papers*, by Elaine Davenport and Paul Eddy, because it relies almost entirely on sworn testimony and exhibits. (See Bibliography.)

8. The secret cash payments aside, Hughes made one legitimate donation in 1968: Fifty thousand dollars, routed through Governor Laxalt, was distributed in seventeen checks paid to seventeen campaign committees, as a device to circumvent the limit on individual contributions to any one committee. Donald Jackson, a Nixon campaign official, had formally asked for financial assistance in March that year. The fifty-thousand-dollar donation was paid in October. (Legitimate donation: Stephen Haberfield to Hughes-Rebozo file, Aug. 20, 1974, Campaign Contributions, file 804, WSPF, NA; formally asked: Donald Jackson to Robert Maheu, March 4, 1968, file 804, Box 111, WSPF, NA.)

9. During the Watergate investigation, Rebozo would produce a hundred thousand dollars in cash from a safe deposit box and say it was the Hughes money, and that it had been undisturbed and unused in the box since he had received it. A complex study of the banknotes involved led the Senate Watergate Committee to doubt this claim. (E, Report, p. 944–; FBI 62-112974.)

10. The Hughes man alleged by Meier to have delivered the million dollars was Ken Wright, head of the Howard Hughes Medical Institute. (Meier, op. cit., p. 46.)

11. Two men appear to have been involved in the first introduction: Getty associate John Pochna and Nixon friend John Shaheen, also in the oil business. (Int. Adnan Khashoggi, and see Paul Michel to Files, Aug. 13, 1975, re: int. Khashoggi, Box 95, WSPF.)

12. Jonathan Aitken, favored Nixon biographer and former British Conservative MP (jailed for perjury in 1999), reported that Khashoggi was one of several entrepreneurs who explored "private business deals overseas" with Nixon after his resignation. (Aitken, it should be noted, has a connection with Khashoggi's family: He fathered a child by Soraya Khashoggi.)(One of entrepreneurs: JA, p. 540; perjury: *NYT*, *Times* [London], June 9, 1999; fathered child: London *Sunday Times*, Jan. 10, 1999.)

13. In the United States Demetracopoulos sustained himself principally not as a journalist but as a consultant for a Wall Street stockbrokerage. He has told the author of his run-ins with both Greek and U.S. officialdom over the years, backing up his claims with copious documentation. Concern about him in the Nixon administration and attempts to silence him are covered in Chapter 30, Note 20. At least two overt smears of Demetracopoulos were demonstrated to be false, first when columnist James Kilpatrick published a humiliating retraction in 1972 and later when a 1977 story by David Binder of the *New York Times* proved baseless. Binder cited a CIA source and CIA records, but after a battle by Demetracopoulos to clear his name the agency admitted that the information was inaccurate. (Kilpatrick: *Washington Star*, July 30, Aug. 10, 1972; Binder: *NYT*, Dec. 6, 1977; London *Guardian*, Jan. 5, 1978; *WP*, Jan. 5, 1978; Sept. 3, 1979; *Newsday*, May 7, 1984, and see Hearings and Appendices, House Permanent Select Committee on Intelligence, Subcommittee on Oversight, 95th Congress, 1st and 2d Session, Dec./Jan./Apr. 1978, and see Joseph Goulden, *Fit to Print*, New Jersey: Lyle Stuart, 1988, p. 292–.)

14. His Greek contacts aside, Pappas made no secret of the fact that he collaborated with the CIA. His Pappas Charitable Trust of Boston was identified in early 1967 as a conduit for CIA money into Latin America. "I have worked for the CIA anytime my help was requested," he told a pro-junta Greek newspaper in the summer of 1968. (Trust: *Boston Globe*, Oct. 31, 1968; "I have worked": *WP*, July 16, 1975, referring to a Pappas int. in *Apogevmatini*, July 18, 1968.)

15. Tasca, whom Nixon had known for years, regularly entertained Pappas and was close to the junta. In 1975, when Nixon had fallen and Tasca was no longer ambassador, he was interviewed by an attorney for the House Select Committee on Intelligence, primarily on other matters. In the course of the interview, the attorney told the author, Tasca said that "the Colonels were nervous by 1968 that the Democrats would win and that American policy would be set against them. They wanted to contribute to the Nixon campaign. How to do it? It had to be filtered, and that's what Pappas did—and in doing so cemented his own relationship with the Nixon administration. "Nixon's people," Tasca told the House attorney, "were happy to have the money." Further corroboration of the allegation that junta money went to Nixon was obtained by the author Seymour Hersh in an interview with a senior State Department official. (Tasca background: Kutler, *Watergate*, op. cit., p. 206; *Boston Sunday Globe*, Nov. 14, 1971; State Dept. Source: Seymour Hersh, *The Price of Power*, New York: Summit, 1983, p. 138–; author's conv. Seymour Hersh.)

16. The O'Brien aide most involved in the exchanges, according to Demetracopoulos, was Ira Kapenstein. He was present at the two meetings with O'Brien and, in part as a precaution against telephone taps, repeatedly visited Demetracopoulos at the Fairfax Hotel.

17. In 1975, in the wake of renewed press allegations, Agnew denied knowing of any contributions to the 1968 campaign by the Greek junta. He offered to testify to the Senate Committee on Intelligence but, reportedly because of pressure over the entire matter by Secretary of State Henry Kissinger, never did. In interviews in 1988 and 1989 Agnew claimed he did not know Demetracopoulos or anything about Greek money for the 1968 campaign. In the 1989 interview he did admit having met Demetracopoulos. (*NYT*, Aug. 1, 2, 1975; *Miami News*, Aug. 2, 1975; *NYT Magazine*, Oct. 26, 1975; Stanley Kutler notes and transcripts of ints. Spiro Agnew, Kutler Papers; int. Demetracopoulos.)

Chapter 23

1. Latest available figures indicate there were 47,357 U.S. battle deaths and 10,796 nonbattle fatalities: 58,153 U.S. dead in total. The wounded in action numbered 153,303. A spokesman for Vietnam's Washington embassy cited his government's report of 1996 as giving "more than 3,000,000" as the figure for Vietnamese war dead. Reuters suggested "about 3,000,000." (Spencer Tucker, ed., *Encyclopedia of the Vietnam War*, vol. III, Santa Barbara, Calif.: ABC-Clio, 1998, p. 1093, and figures supplied by National Archives, Defense Dept., and Vietnamese embassy, Washington, D.C.)

2. The Cambodia location was rendered in the autograph dealer's catalog as "Phumi Kriek." The spelling on maps seen by the author is "Phumi Krek."

3. This citation is from the fullest version of the Kimmons story, compiled by autograph dealer Mark Vardakis from his conversations with Kimmons. Along with the original of the Nixon inscription, it is available at the Forbes Gallery in New York. Vardakis paid Kimmons one hundred dollars for the inscription, sold it for five hundred dollars to another dealer, Paul Richards, who sold it to the Forbes Gallery for twenty-five thousand dollars. (Ints. Mark Vardakis, Gabrielle Kimmons [second wife], and Gerard Stodolski, colleague of the late Paul Richards.)

4. In response to a written inquiry enclosing the *New York Times* report on the matter, the Nixon Library told the author in 1998 there was "no confirmation of [the] report in files available here." (Archivist Susan Naulty to author, Feb. 2, 1998.)

5. Nixon visited two villages in the Mekong Delta near Saigon, Tan Anh and Phu My (Not to be confused with the Phu My many miles north of the capital). (*LAT*, Apr. 3, 1964; *Pacific Stars & Stripes*, Apr. 5, 1964.)

6. It is not clear just what did happen when Dunn sought to board the helicopter with Nixon on April 2. Dunn, a lieutenant colonel with an otherwise unblemished career record, was later charged with telling Lodge "with intent to deceive" that Westmoreland had refused to let him join the Nixon party. The army inspector general cleared him of this and another unrelated allegation. Westmoreland's memoirs and Dunn's correspondence indicate that Lodge forbade the army command to take reporters by helicopter to cover the overt Nixon visits to villages. It is clear there were serious differences between U.S. officials and senior army officers at the time. (Dunn charges: Lodge to Dunn and Advice to Dunn on Rights under Article 31b; Lodge to General Harold Johnson, July 2, Lodge to Dunn, July 2, Dunn to Lodge, Dec. 16, 1964, Colonel Victor Baughman to Lodge, undated, General Johnson to Lodge, Feb. 26, Lodge to General Johnson, March 10, Lodge to Dunn, Nov. 30, 1965; Zalin Grant, *Facing the Phoenix*, New York: Norton, 1991, p. 213; ints. Mary Dunn [widow] and Alan Dunn [son], and Oral History int. John Michael Dunn, LBJL; row over press: Henry Cabot Lodge Papers, Massachusetts Historical Society; William Westmoreland, *A Soldier Reports*, Garden City, N.Y.: Doubleday, 1976, p. 67; differences: ibid., p. 67–; Karnow, op. cit., p. 341.)

7. Hughes recalled pinning on his flak jacket an old 1960 Nixon-Lodge campaign button he happened to have with him in Vietnam. He and Nixon joked about it, as pilot Paul Schreck also recalled in his notes about the episode. (Int. John Hughes; Paul Schreck's draft account, supplied by his son Terry.)

8. Out of OPLAN-34A, issued by Defense Secretary Robert McNamara in December 1963, grew the largest clandestine military unit since World War II's OSS. It operated as the Special Operations Group, or SOG, an acronym it kept for security reasons when its name was changed to the euphemistic Studies and Observations Group. (Plaster, op. cit., p. 23.)

9. According to Defense Department records, sixty-two Americans went missing in Southeast Asia between 1961 and April 1964. While some returned alive over the years and some bodies were recovered, the published records list no prisoner handover between January and May 1964. One man who did get out alive is listed as an "escapee." (Dept. of Defense Prisoner of War, Missing in Action Office Reference Document, *U.S. Personnel Missing, Southeast Asia*, March 1998.)

10. While he may privately have approved Kennedy's decision to send advisers to Vietnam, Nixon did his best as president to blame Kennedy for the U.S. involvement. In September 1971 he said at a press conference that "the way we got into Vietnam was through overthrowing Diem and the complicity in the murder of Diem." He told Billy Graham, a recently released White House tape shows, that Kennedy "started the whole damn thing. He killed Diem, and sent the first 16,000 combat people there himself. . . . You see, Billy, the key thing here was Kennedy's, and—I must say—our friend Lodge's agreement to murder Diem. That's what opened the whole damn thing."

Nixon's comments were typical of his spleen against the Kennedys but distorted the facts. President Ngo Dinh Diem, who had been maneuvered into office by the CIA in 1954, had been supported by the Eisenhower administration, which sent in the first 700 U.S. military advisers. The Kennedy administration also backed Diem initially, but the 16,000 military advisers were not combat troops, and only 195 had died by 1963. No combat troops were deployed until 1965. The burden of the evidence, reflected in most of Kennedy's public statements on the subject, is that he wished to avoid further U.S. involvement and bring the advisers home. In the fall of 1963, with South Vietnam slipping into chaos and the autocratic Diem losing control, Kennedy aides concluded the United States could no longer work with him. President Kennedy and Ambassador Henry Cabot Lodge did collude with the Vietnamese generals who toppled him on November 2, 1963. In a tape intended for his memoirs, released in 1999, Kennedy admitted that "we must bear a good deal of responsibility." He deplored the way he and his colleagues had handled recent contacts with Saigon. There is no evidence that Kennedy approved or encouraged the *murder* of Diem and his brother, news of which left him shaken and dismayed.

Nixon, whose Whittier College classmate John Richardson was CIA station chief in Saigon at the time, was outraged by news of the coup. In September 1971, just days after the outburst on the subject reported above, Nixon's confidant Charles Colson began trying to get *Life* magazine to run a story on Diem's murder. *Life* was never sufficiently convinced by the evidence to do so, but its reporter was shown "cables" suggesting Kennedy gave orders refusing Diem asylum, effectively sealing his fate. The cables were in fact fakes concocted by White House consultant, later Watergate burglar, Howard Hunt. Nixon later disclaimed all knowledge of the forgery attempt, but a recently released White House tape shows Ehrlichman disagreed. "My recollection," he told Nixon, "is that this was discussed with you." ("the way we got into Vietnam": Schlesinger, *The Imperial Presidency*. op. cit., p. 262, citing *NYT*, Sept. 17, 1971; "started whole damn thing": *WP*, Dec. 27, 1998, citing WHT, March 8, 1971; maneuvered by CIA: Sheehan, op. cit., p. 134; Eisenhower support: ibid., and Karnow, op. cit., p. 235; and John Newman, *JFK & Vietnam*, New York: Warner, 1992; advisers: Manchester, op. cit., p. 918, but see Karnow, op. cit., p. 267; 195 dead: Dept. of Defense statistics, NA; combat troops: Karnow, op. cit., p. 431 [they were two Marine battalions, deployed to defend Da Nang airfield]; JFK's intentions: Newman, op. cit.; Robert McNamara with Brian VanDeMark, *In Retrospect*, New York: Times Books, 1995, p. 86; Kennedy aides, coup: ibid., p. 41–; Wise, *Politics of Lying*, op. cit., p. 175–; Ball, op. cit., p. 370; Henry Cabot Lodge, *The Storm Has Many Eyes*, New York: W. W. Norton, 1973, p. 208–, and see especially fresh account at Grant, op. cit., p. 191; JFK admitted: *San Francisco Examiner*, Nov. 29, 1998; JFK memoir entry, Nov. 4, 1963, Cassette M, Side 2, Pres. Recordings, JFKL; Kennedy dismayed: ibid.; McNamara and VanDeMark, op. cit., p. 84; Karnow, op. cit., p. 326; Richardson: Prados, op. cit., p. 246; RN outraged: Postscript to RN to Dwight Eisenhower, Nov. 5, 1963; Post-Presidential Special Names Series, Box 14, DDEL; *Reader's Digest*, Aug. 1964; *AMII*, p. 30–; Colson, *Life*: E, Final Report, p. 125–, and Vol. 9, p. 3672; *WP*, July 19, 1974; Nixon insisted: May 8, 1973; *AOP*, p. 416, and see *MEM*, p. 844; Ehrlichman disagreed: *WHT*, Apr. 28, 1973, AOP, p. 371.)

11. Nixon did make the "pledge" remark, to a New Hampshire audience. A memorandum in Republican National Committee files indicates that he also told a reporter, "I have a plan to end the war." The allegation that he said he had a "secret" plan was apparently made in a UPI report out of Boston. (See analysis at Parmet, *Nixon*, op. cit., p. 506–.)

12. The historian Joan Hoff has questioned whether Nixon really discussed a Madman Theory with Haldeman, surmising that the term originated with Kissinger. Hoff's doubt seems overdone, given Haldeman's characteristic precision and the further testimony along these lines cited in the next paragraphs of this book. Note meanwhile that Seymour Hersh misdates the Madman Theory exchange in his book *The Price of Power*. Haldeman made it clear in his memoirs, and later in an address to a discussion group, that the exchange occurred in the summer of 1968. (Hoff, op. cit., pp. 177–, 398; Hersh, op. cit., p. 52; Haldeman and DiMona, op. cit., p. 121; int. H. R. Haldeman in Miller Center, eds., op. cit., p. 82.)

13. Nixon noted in his memoirs, with apparent approval, that he was told by a returning U.S. prisoner of war that "the North Vietnamese really thought that the President was off his rocker—was totally irrational. He said that it was absolutely essential for them to think that." (*MEM*, p. 864.)

14. Laird told the author that at the start of the presidency, Nixon believed he could win the war "without Vietnamization." Nixon "had no program at all," Laird said, adding that he convinced Nixon to press ahead with Vietnamization in March or April 1969. (Int. Melvin Laird, and see *AMII*, p. 277.)

15. Thieu's reasons for eschewing involvement in the 1968 talks are neatly summarized by Professor Stephen Ambrose in the second volume of his Nixon biography. Nixon, and Henry Kissinger, would strive to make the case that the Thieu regime could have survived—even after the 1973 settlement and the American pullout—if only the U.S. Congress had not vetoed the use of American power and cut back on military aid. (Ambrose: *AMII*, p. 215; Nixon-Kissinger case: *MEM*, p. 889; Kissinger, *White House Years*, op. cit., p. 1470; Kissinger, *Upheaval*, op. cit., ch. 8.)

16. Gallup gave Nixon a 44 percent to 36 percent lead over Humphrey on October 21. By November 2, two days after the bombing halt, his lead had fallen to only two points, 42 percent to 40 percent. According to the Lou Harris poll, Humphrey actually overtook Nixon at this point. (*TW68*, p. 445–; *AMII*, p. 212; but see *TW68*, p. 446.)

17. In his memoirs Johnson would write that he had "no reason to think that Republican candidate Nixon was himself involved in this maneuvering, but a few individuals active in his campaign were." The author agrees with historian Herbert Parmet, who believes Johnson was

"dissembling" because he "knew more than he would or could, let on." To be forthright, the former president would have had to have revealed what he had learned from intelligence sources, some of which remains secret to this day. In 1971, when the memoirs were published, to have exposed Nixon would have been to expose a sitting president himself still wrestling with the Vietnam impasse. ("no reason": Johnson, op. cit., p. 518; "dissembling": Parmet, *Nixon*, op. cit., p. 521.)

18. The most thorough study is "Woman of Two Worlds: Anna Chennault and Informal Diplomacy in U.S.-Asian Relations, 1950–1990," a 1997 doctoral dissertation by Catherine Forslund, then at Washington University, St. Louis, Missouri. *A Tangled Web*, the 1998 book by former Assistant Secretary of State for East Asian Affairs William Bundy, was also groundbreaking. The contents of the "X" envelope were referenced by Professor Robert Dallek in his 1998 biography of Lyndon Johnson, *Flawed Giant* (New York: Oxford University Press). (Bundy: William Bundy, op. cit.; ints., corr. Bundy; FBI documents: FBI 190-HQ-1204905, released with redactions, Dec. 1999.)

19. Lieutenant General Claire Chennault in 1941 founded American Volunteer Group, the corps of American fliers known as the Flying Tigers, who helped defend China and Burma against the Japanese. The group merged in 1942 with the China Air Task Force, which eventually became the U.S. 14th Air Force under Chennault's command. In retirement after the war, the general had an honorary role with the Flying Tiger freight line. His wife, Anna, was the line's vice president of international operations.

20. In a 1966 letter from Hong Kong, Anna Chennault wrote that when asked by State Department contacts about her "job," she had replied that she was a tourist. A subsequent inquiry by her "U.S. connection," however, had "made 'The Agency' very unhappy." (The CIA is widely referred to by cognoscenti as the agency.) In a recent publication and in a conversation with the author, Chennault recalled that her late husband had a relationship with the CIA. She denied, however, ever having worked for the CIA herself. (1966 letter: Anna Chennault to "Tom" [almost certainly Thomas Corcoran, Washington political fixer and Chennault's constant companion], Aug. 10, 1966, obtained by author; husband: *World Journal* (Taiwan), Apr. 21–26, 1994.)

21. According to his friend Pat Hillings, Nixon tried to fend Chennault off during a Taiwan visit as late as 1967. Yet he kept up the contact in 1967 and 1968 and in September 1968 was writing to her in "Dick-Anna" terms. The authoritative scholar on Chennault, Catherine Forslund, speculated in her study that Nixon sometimes disparaged Chennault as a political maneuver. (Hillings: *JA*, p. 365; Forslund, op. cit., p. 14–; "Dick-Anna": ibid., p. 28.)

22. A blind memo in the "X" Envelope, probably written by Walt Rostow, read: "The damage was done via Thieu in Saigon, through low level Americans." There is evidence elsewhere in this redacted material that the White House ordered investigations of Americans other than Chennault. Chennault told historian Herbert Parmet that "the full story was far from known, that more confidential messages went from Washington to Saigon through couriers and not through Ambassador Diem. . . . Asked to name the other couriers, however, Chennault refused." (Blind memo: Nov. 4, 1968, "X" Envelope, *supra*.; story far from known: Parmet, *Nixon*, op. cit., p. 522.)

23. It was previously thought that Chennault merely sent a letter to Nixon in Kansas City. Yet her calendar bears the entry "10/16 to meet R. Nixon in Kansas City, MO." (Re: letter: Safire, op. cit., p. 90, and detail at Forslund, op. cit., p. 29–.)

24. In her 1980 book Chennault said she responded by telling Mitchell she thought it unwise to "try to influence the Vietnamese." This seems at odds with her interviews with the author, cited earlier, in which she said she was told to promise the South Vietnamese they would get a better deal with Nixon in the White House. (not "try to influence": Chennault, op. cit., p. 190.)

25. A report from Rostow to President Johnson, ten days after the event, said that the "phone call to the Lady was at 1:41 P.M. EST. . . ." Agnew had arrived in Albuquerque at 1:15 P.M. EST. Another Rostow report, drawing on FBI surveillance, states that Chennault left her Washington apartment at 1:45 P.M. EST. In his reconstruction of the sequence of events for the president, Rostow referred to having received "new times" on Agnew's movements. The initial FBI report contained contradictory times. It also offered an earlier time—1:30 P.M.—for Chennault's departure from home. (Rostow ten days after: Rostow to president, Nov. 12, 1968; re: Rostow and Chennault 1:45 P.M.: Rostow to president, Nov. 2, 1968, both in "X" Envelope; initial FBI report: Cartha DeLoach to Clyde Tolson, Nov. 19, 1968, FBI 65-62098-266.)

26. Chennault told both this author and another researcher that she did not remember having received a call from New Mexico. She speculated that if she had been overheard referring to New Mexico, she was probably meaning to refer to New *Hampshire*, home state of Robert Hill, one of those she had nominated to Nixon as go-betweens. The documentary record,

however, seems to be more reliable on this matter than Chennault's memory. (Other researcher: conv. Catherine Forslund.)

27. It was Nixon who called Johnson, not vice versa, as is often reported. Having spoken with the president, the Senate minority leader Everett Dirksen had passed word that "something had to be done in a hurry to cool him off." According to William Safire, Dirksen thought Johnson was "ready to blow his stack—and blow the whistle on the Nixon campaign's attempt to defeat his peace efforts by getting President Thieu to hold back. Anna Chennault's name was mentioned." The message was so troubling that Nixon was roused from his bed and agreed to phone Johnson. (RN made call: Forslund, op. cit., citing LBJ sources, including Defense Communications Operations Unit; Safire, op. cit., p. 93, and *MEM*, p. 320, contradicting, for example, Witcover, op. cit., p. 442; "something had to be done": Safire, op. cit., p. 93.)

28. Anna Chennault insisted to the author in a 2000 interview that she had not spoken with Agnew while he was in Albuquerque. Clearly, however, Agnew was involved with the Vietnam issue and in touch with Nixon on the subject of a possible breakthrough in the peace talks. Nixon refers in his memoirs to a conversation with his running mate—in early October—in which Agnew briefed him on information he had learned on the subject from Johnson's secretary of state, Dean Rusk. On October 24, at a rally in St. Louis, Agnew said a development in the Paris peace talks was "fully expected." (Chennault insisted: int., March 2000; Agnew briefed Nixon: *MEM*, p. 324; Agnew/St. Louis; Jules Witcover, *White Knight: The Rise of Spiro Agnew*, New York: Random House, 1972, p. 270.)

29. Chennault said she was pressured not to talk by Herb Klein, Nixon law firm colleague Tom Evans, Senators Everett Dirksen and John Tower, and Robert Hill. (Chennault, op. cit., p. 193–; int. Herb Klein.)

30. Chennault did not reveal what she knew for a long time, but it is not surprising that Nixon's people were nervous. Interviewed before the 1969 inauguration by Tom Ottenad, a reporter on the trail of the story, she said: "You're going to get me in a lot of trouble. . . . I can't say anything . . . come back and ask me that after the inauguration. We're at a very sensitive time. . . . I know so much and can say so little." In September 1969 she asserted: "Whatever I did during the campaign the Republicans, including Mr. Nixon, knew about." In 1974 she further amplified that statement: "From the first conversation [with the South Vietnamese] I made it clear I was speaking for Mr. Nixon. . . . " By 1979, with Nixon long disgraced, she was starting to offer more detail. The blanket denials of the Nixon side had upset her, but, she said resignedly, "It was a very vicious campaign. Politics is a very cruel game." Tom Corcoran said in 1981: "People have used Chennault scandalously, Nixon in particular, I know exactly what Nixon said to her, and then he repudiated her." (Jan. 1969 int.: *Boston Globe*, Jan. 6, 1969; Sept. 1969 int.: *Washingtonian*, Sept. 1969; 1974 int.: Howe and Trott, op. cit., p. 48; 1979 int.: *Washington Star*, Aug. 20, 1979; Corcoran: *WP*, Feb. 18, 1981, cited at Forslund, op. cit., p. 52, fn.)

31. Two of Nixon's more forthright aides have expressed dismay. "It was not one of American politics' finest hours," wrote William Safire. Herb Klein, talking with the author of his reported postelection role—calling Chennault to warn her to keep quiet,—said it was "not something I was proud of." He justified it to himself, he said, because the Nixon side believed Johnson's peace initiative to be politically motivated. (Safire, op. cit., p. 91; Chennault, op. cit., p. 193; int. Herb Klein.)

32. Within two weeks of the 1968 election, Drew Pearson wrote of "unconfirmed reports that South Vietnamese leaders had even slipped campaign cash to Nixon's representatives," a notion not inconceivable perhaps in light of the evidence that Nixon took money from the Greek dictatorship that year. (See chapter 22.) A consultant to the House Judiciary Committee Impeachment Inquiry, Renata Adler, has written at length suggesting that this was the case four years later, in the 1972 campaign, and that it constituted the great secret of the Nixon presidency. The House Banking Committee, she noted, discovered "kickbacks by Vietnamese importers to American exporters" involving Swiss bank accounts. She also asked why as the Watergate crisis deepened, Nixon aides scurried to return a small contribution from a Philippine national, $30,000—via Anna Chennault. Adler's thesis seems based more on deduction than on evidence. Chennault, for her part, has denied all knowledge of election contributions by the Saigon government. (Pearson: *WP*, Nov. 17, 1968; Adler: *Atlantic*, Dec. 1976, *New York Review of Books*, Dec. 2(?), 1977; ints. Renata Adler; $30,000: E, 1, p. 721; 23, p. 11155; Stans, *Terrors*, op. cit., p. 371.)

Chapter 24

1. Tom Wicker followed Nixon's career as a senior correspondent and columnist for the *New York Times*. His book *One of Us: Richard Nixon and the American Dream*, was published in 1991. (New York: Random House).

2. Haldeman's family was in fact of Swiss origin. (Michael Medved, *The Shadow Presidents*, New York: Times Books, 1979, p. 306.)

3. The wireman, John Ragan, was hired by Robert Hitt, the Republican official who, along with his wife Patricia, made an appearance in the Anna Chennault Vietnam peace talks sabotage episode, reported in the previous chapter. (Wise, *American Police State*, op. cit., p. 12.)

4. This is the detective's report referred to at p. 303–. Robert Kennedy was reportedly provided with information on the Nixon visits to Hutschnecker, passed on by the singer Frank Sinatra, in those days a Kennedy supporter. Perhaps fearful of counterrevelations about his brother John, not least concerning the long-secret fact that he had Addison's disease, the younger Kennedy did not use the report. A copy survived, however, and was supplied to Drew Pearson in 1968. (Kelley, op. cit., pp. 279, 530, citing *WP*.)

5. The patient was William Block, a commercial photographer and one of several Hutschnecker patients Pearson interviewed. The doctor denied having made such comments and, without naming Block, suggested in his book *The Drive for Power* that Pearson's source was a "very sick former patient of mine." To rebut Robert Winter-Berger, who said Hutschnecker had talked about Nixon at a dinner party (see p. 94), he also insinuated that Winter-Berger was ill. Taking everything into consideration, the author is skeptical of the doctor's denial of such quotes. (*WP*, Nov. 20, 1968; Hutschnecker, *Drive for Power*, op. cit., pp. 8, 25.)

Chapter 25

1. The author sent interview requests to both Nixon daughters. Julie Nixon Eisenhower did not reply to repeated letters, while Tricia Nixon Cox wrote courteously declining. (Julie: Robbyn Summers to Julie Nixon Eisenhower, Aug. 25, 1998, May 13, June 28, July 23, 1999; Tricia: corr., May 13, June 10, 1999.)

2. Nixon later relented, and black tie became acceptable at many dinners. (Thomas, *Dateline*, op. cit., p. 125.)

3. It was illegal under the 1966 Foreign Gifts Act for U.S. government officials to keep gifts from foreign officials worth more than a hundred dollars, and there were rancorous claims and counterclaims when it turned out the Nixons' record keeping on such largess was at best poor. "If she lies to me," Pat's press secretary burst out in frustration at one point, "I have to lie to you." None of the Nixons' foreign gifts was turned over to the Protocol Office during the presidency, and the president's attorneys reportedly argued that he might be exempt from the Gifts Act. Legal wrangling over them continued for years afterward. A General Services Administration probe concluded that virtually all gifts to the Nixons had been returned or accounted for by 1978. Tricia was allowed to keep two wedding gifts, a silver vase given by Ethiopia's Haile Selassie and a rare temple carving from South Vietnam's President Thieu. (Cheshire with Greenya, op, cit., pp. 87–140; *WP*, Sept. 22, 1974; Knight News Service, Apr. 4, 1979.)

4. The massacre had occurred on March 16, 1968. The young veteran who sparked the first serious inquiry was former helicopter gunner Ronald Ridenhour, who wrote to the House Armed Services Committee. The story made its way into the press thanks to the investigative efforts of Seymour Hersh, then a freelance journalist. (Ridenhour: Mollenhoff, op. cit., p. 543; *NYT*, May 11, 1998; Hersh break: Obst, op. cit., p. 159.)

5. White House ombudsman Clark Mollenhoff had written to Nixon in January 1970, urging presidential supervision of the My Lai investigations. Haldeman later told him there was "no need to give such a project . . . priority." Mollenhoff recalled that Haldeman was "unconcerned . . . unless it threatened to embarrass the President or the administration." (Mollenhoff, op. cit., p. 77.)

6. The official in charge of the program in Vietnam in 1969, future CIA Director William Colby, was to deny the assassination activity. A number of veterans of Phoenix have contradicted him. One of the officials behind the program, John Paul Vann, had conferred with Nixon in the Oval Office that year. Vann reportedly encouraged Colby to pursue the Phoenix program. (Colby: William Colby and Peter Forbath, *Honorable Men,* New York: Simon & Schuster, 1978, p. 311–; veteran contradicted: Prados, *Secret Wars,* op. cit., p. 309; Vann: Sheehan, op. cit., p. 732.)

7. The detailed allegation of plotting against Sihanouk was made by a former U.S. Navy yeoman, Samuel Thornton, who served at naval headquarters in Saigon in early 1969. Henry Kissinger has said Washington was not involved in Sihanouk's overthrow, "at least not at the top level." (Thornton: Hersh, *Price of Power,* cit., p. 179–; Kissinger: Shawcross, op. cit., p. 222.)

8. The Senate Intelligence Committee received conflicting testimony on whether Track II ever ended. It could find no trace of a new Nixon order that, Kissinger claimed, terminated it. CIA Deputy Director Thomas Karamessines testified that Track II "was never really ended . . . what we were told to do was to continue our efforts." (U.S. Senate, *Assassination Plots,* op. cit., p. 253–.)

9. The box had been a gift from lobbyist Robert Keith Gray, on January 25, 1969. (*HD*, p. 21.)

Chapter 26

1. See supra., p. 314.
2. See supra., p. 227–. In an interview with the Senate Watergate Committee, Davies admitted being acquainted with Caulfield and Ragan but said he knew nothing about wiretaps. (Int.: John Davies, by Michael Herschman and Wayne Bishop, July 18, 1973, Box B 343, E, NA.)
3. ITT was deeply involved with the CIA throughout Latin America, especially in Chile, where it owned the telephone network. (Hersh, *Price of Power,* op. cit., pp. 260, 264.)
4. Criticizing the *Times* for revealing the Cambodia bombing, Nixon would claim it was "directly responsible for the deaths of thousands of Americans because it required the discontinuance of a policy that saved American lives." In fact, the bombing continued for a full year after the offending story ran. (*Newsweek,* March 22, 1976.)
5. There were prosecutions of both guardsmen and students, but no one went to prison. In 1973, civil litigation resulted in payment to students and their families, and twenty-eight guardsmen signed a statement "deeply regretting" the shootings. (*Newsday,* May 4, 1995.)
6. While Butterfield recalled briefing the president in the evening, an early White House tape suggests this occurred early in the morning. (Butterfield: *Journal of American History,* vol. 75, March 1989, p. 1252; WH tape: recording of 8:00 A.M., Feb. 16, 1971, reported by AP, Oct. 5, 1999.)
7. Rose Woods, Charles Colson, and Haldeman apparently expressed suspicion of Butterfield. It remains just that: their suspicion. (Haldeman and DiMona, op. cit., p. 203–, and int. Colson, in *Argosy,* March 1976, p. 32.)
8. Although Kissinger claimed he was informed of the tapes only in the spring of 1973, a Haldeman diary entry states that Nixon told him in November 1972 to "let Henry know that obviously the EOB and the Oval Office and the Lincoln Room have all been recorded for protection. . . ." Haldeman may not have passed on the message. (Spring 1973: Kissinger, *Upheaval,* op. cit., p. 110; Haldeman entry: *HD,* p. 538, entry for Nov. 19, 1972, and see *Washington Times,* Oct. 18, 1996; message not passed?: *Prologue,* vol. 20, Summer 1988, p. 87.)
9. Nixon was to authorize massive financial concessions for the dairy industry, apparently as a reward for two million dollars in campaign contributions, an abuse that became yet another element in the wider Watergate scandal. A House Judiciary Committee summary concluded that the president ordered the concessions "on the basis of his own political welfare." Nixon refused to cooperate with the committee. (R, Summary of Information, July 19, 1974, p. 149–.)
10. Nixon Library archivist Susan Naulty challenged the reported content of this September 8, 1971, White House tape. Naulty said the charge of anti-Semitism was "very questionable," citing statements defending Nixon by Jewish groups and the airlift of arms to Israel during the 1973 Middle East War. A check of the tape by the author's researcher in 2000, however, established that the president did indeed refer gratuitously to "the Jews . . . stealing . . ." In a conversation recorded five days later, moreover, he again made abusive remarks about Jews. (Naulty: *Washington Times,* Jan. 28, 1997; check for author: report of Robert Lamb, June 27, 2000; five days later: WHT, Sept. 13, 1971, transcribed for author—Jews described by Nixon as "cocksuckers.")
11. Former Congresswoman Shirley Chisholm, who did campaign in the presidential primaries in 1972, was "aghast" when told of this tape evidence in 1996. Jesse Jackson said his people had no truck with such schemes. (*Independent* [London], Nov. 29, 1996.)
12. As reported later in this chapter, it was steelworkers who formed the vanguard of the construction workers' assault on student protesters in New York in May 1970. There was an inquiry into the episode, which may explain why a year later Nixon and Haldeman deemed it wiser to turn to the Teamsters Union when recruiting thugs. (Steelworkers in NYC: *NYT,* May 9, 1970.)
13. Hoffman suffered his injury and was arrested on the afternoon of May 3. He was taken to the Kennedy Stadium, where thousands of others were being held, and then fled to New York, where he was rearrested hours after the Nixon-Haldeman conversation. While parts of the tape of the conversation are of poor quality, the use of the word "got" in the portion about Hoffman may indicate that Haldeman already knew of the injury inflicted on May 3. (Sequence of events reflected in AP picture captions, May 6, *NYT,* May 7, 1971; Hoffman int. in *San Francisco Examiner,* Sept. 30, 1981; see also Benjamin Spock, *Spock on Spock,* New York: Pantheon, 1989, p. 192, for his recollection and the extent of Hoffman's injuries.)
14. A *Newsday* investigation listed Lanza as "Family soldier . . . arrests for bookmaking and policy (twice); convicted of bookmaking and policy (twice); never jailed." The Glaziers Union official convicted of extortion, just a month earlier, was Sidney Glasser. Charley Johnson, of the Brotherhood of Carpenters, was said by witnesses to the Senate Committee on Improper Activities in the Labor or Management Field (the "Rackets Committee") in 1959 to have drawn four concurrent salaries from his union. Thomas Gleason, of the International Longshore-

men's Association, had attended an ILA meeting along with Tough Tony Anastasia and Frank ("Machine Gun Sonny") Campbell. (Lanza: *Newsday,* March 1, 1969; companions: *Scanlan's,* Sept. 1970.)

Chapter 27

1. That Rebozo and Nixon were together en route by air to Camp David, and on the day mentioned by Watts, is confirmed by the April 24, 1970, entry in Haldeman's diary. Three aides—William Watts, Roger Morris, and Anthony Lake (later President Clinton's national security adviser)—opposed the Cambodia operation and resigned when it went ahead. (Camp David trip: *HD,* p. 154; staff resignations: Kissinger, *White House Years,* op. cit., p. 493–; ints. William Watts.)
2. After a visit in July 1969 to Vietnam, where he was impressed by the troops, Nixon told Haldeman "never to let the hippie college-types in to see him again." (*HD,* p. 77.)
3. The makeup had presumably been applied for the press conference the previous evening.
4. The report that Hutschnecker attended Nixon in Florida came from former lobbyist Robert Winter-Berger, who had known the doctor for several years. Hutschnecker later denied having made the visit, just as he also claimed he had treated Nixon only in his capacity as an internist. Today not much weight need be given to the doctor's denial, which came during a congressional appearance in 1973, in which he described his contacts with Gerald Ford, then vice presidential nominee to replace Spiro Agnew. Nixon was still president at the time, though beleaguered by Watergate, and Hutschnecker probably deemed it judicious to protect their relationship. As reported in this chapter, Hutschnecker has since acknowledged that Nixon did secretly summon him to the White House just *before* his strange behavior during the Cambodia crisis. There is no special reason to doubt that he also consulted him in Florida the following week. Finally, it is clear from this author's interviews with the doctor that his sessions with Nixon went beyond the normal treatments of an internist. (Winter-Berger on Florida: Winter-Berger, op. cit., p. 257; Hutschnecker denied: Hutschnecker testimony, Hearings, Committee on Rules and Administration, U.S. Senate, 93 Congress, 1st Session, on Nomination of Gerald Ford to be Vice President, Nov. 7, 1973, p. 194; secret summons: JA, p. 404, citing int. Hutschnecker, 1991.)
5. For the false story about an oil discovery, see p. 2.
6. Kissinger erroneously dates the hijacking as having occurred on a Saturday. In fact, it took place on Friday, August 29, the day of the Nixon party. (*NYT* Aug. 30, 1969.)
7. In his book *White House Years* Henry Kissinger described the episode as a major crisis. His analysis did not, however, have the cataclysmic overtones of the Nixon characterization. The "biggest problem" with Nixon's posture, he wrote, "was to keep the courage from turning into recklessness and the firmness into bravado." (Kissinger, *White House Years,* op. cit., p. 600.)
8. The late George Carver served as special assistant to three CIA directors and on Kissinger's Washington Special Actions Group (WSAG), the National Security Council's subcommittee for crisis management. His comments on the Nixon drinking episode are attributed to him by former intelligence official Barry Toll, who grew close to Carver during congressional probes of Vietnam POW and MIA issues. (Carver: Kissinger, *White House Years,* op. cit., p. 1182, and see p. 183 re: WSAG [*NYT,* June 30, 1994]; Toll: Statement of Barry Toll, June 14, 1992, Senate Select Committee on P.O.W. and M.I.A. Affairs, C.I.S. No. H.381-89.4, p. 94–; affidavit of Barry Toll, Aug. 2, 1994, provided to author.)

Chapter 28

1. Julie Nixon was soon to take up a teaching post at a school in Atlantic Beach, Florida, and staff members had complained she was receiving preferential treatment. The school to which she had been assigned was only four blocks from where she would be living, whereas other teachers had to drive miles to work. (*NYT,* May 28, 1971.)
2. This was Anthony Ulasewicz, veteran New York policeman and, like Caulfield, a former member of the New York City Police Department's intelligence unit, the Bureau of Special Service and Investigation. Ehrlichman had hired him in April 1969 at a clandestine meeting at La Guardia Airport. Ulasewicz's pay was handled by Herb Kalmbach, Nixon's personal attorney. (Ulasewicz, op. cit., pp. 4–, 176–; *NM,* p. 14–.)
3. The former White House aide who described Nixon as "overjoyed" was Jeb Magruder. Magruder cannot have witnessed Nixon's immediate response to the news, for he did not join the White House until three months after the accident. Neither the Haldeman diary, though, nor an account by William Safire, who spoke with Nixon soon after the news broke, reflects the sympathy Nixon claimed to have felt. The president's immediate response was fascination and a resolve to "push hard" to take advantage of the tragedy. ("overjoyed": Jeb Magruder, *From Power to Peace,* Waco, Texas: Word Books, 1978, p. 32; joined staff: R, Report, p. 14; Haldeman, Safire: *HD,* p. 72–; Safire, op. cit., p. 149–.)

4. Future Watergate burglar Howard Hunt, hired by Ehrlichman at Colson's suggestion in July 1971, was given Chappaquiddick as his first assignment. In 1974, in a pitch to a prospective publisher, Hunt claimed that "Mary Jo Kopechne was pantyless and braless when found" and that "Kennedy did not go down in the creek with Mary Jo in the car—she was passed out on back seat; Ted K. was in front seat with another girl . . . he was attempting to lay; they didn't even know Mary Jo was in back seat of the Pontiac." A modified version of this theory appeared in Hunt's published book *Undercover*. Kopechne's body was found with no panties under her slacks, but she was wearing a bra. There was speculation that a second woman had been in the car because a handbag belonging to another of the night's partygoers, Rosemary Keough, had been recovered from the vehicle. Keough said she had left the handbag in the car after a shopping trip earlier in the day. (Hunt assignment: Hunt, *Undercover*, op. cit., p. 148–; underwear, second passenger?: ibid., p. 205, but especially Alfred Ulmer letter to William Colby, March 28, 1974, enclosing G. P. Putnam's internal memo, Feb. 8, 1974, re: *Privilege* [New York: Dell, 1988], pp. 12, 283, 411 [re: underwear]; Keough, bag: ibid., pp. 8, 28, but see pp. 371, 384, and Nelson Thompson, *The Dark Side of Camelot*, Chicago: Playboy Press, 176, p. 132.)
5. Haldeman recalled Nixon's ordering "24-hour surveillance," and instructions to that effect went out on June 23, 1971. The surveillance was modified in the fall of the year, after Caulfield advised that coverage of that extent could not be kept secret. (Haldeman on order: Haldeman with DiMona, op. cit., p. 60; instructions: Gordon Strachan testimony, July 12, 1973, R, Statement of Information, Bk. VII, Pt. 2, p. 658–; John Caulfield testimony, March 16, 1974, ibid., p. 656–; modified: ibid., and John Dean testimony, June 25, 1973, ibid., p. 661.)
6. The current rumor was that Kennedy was involved with Amanda Burden, daughter of CBS chairman William Paley and former wife of a New York Democratic councilman. Nixon referred on the White House tapes to her recent weekend with Kennedy and another couple aboard a Kennedy boat. Several press articles linked Kennedy romantically with Burden at a time he was married to his first wife, Joan. (RN, rumor: *WHT*, Sept. 7, 11, 1972; *AOP*, pp. 133, 138; Burden: Dunleavy and Brennan, op. cit., p. 165–; Peter Collier and David Horowitz, *The Kennedys*, London: Pan, 1984, p. 554.)
7. The private detective was Michael McMinoway, code-named by the Nixon people Sedan Chair II. The bumper sticker mischief was just one of the dirty tricks pulled by Donald Segretti, who had been hired by Chapin, Nixon's close aide. (McMinoway: E, Final Report, p. 192–; E, Bk. 11, pp. 4480–, 4489–, 4493–; Segretti: E, Final Report, p. 160.)
8. The right-wing *Manchester* (New Hampshire) *Union Leader* published a letter from Florida from a "Paul Morrison" concerning a derisive comment Muskie had allegedly made about "Canucks," a disparaging reference to French Canadians living in the United States. Morrison was never traced, and this was probably a dirty trick involving future Watergate burglars Howard Hunt and Gordon Liddy. A later letter to the *Union Leader* told of two men in Florida having paid a man a thousand dollars to write the letter. The name Morrison was picked out of the phone book. The "Canucks" letter was dated February 17, 1972, and Hunt and Liddy had been in Florida the previous week. Separately, Ehrlichman quoted Hunt as confiding that he knew about the letter. Months later White House Deputy Communications Director Kenneth Clawson would be quoted by a *Washington Post* reporter as saying *he* had written the letter. There seems little doubt Nixon's people were indeed behind the smear. ("Morrison" letter: facsimile Arthur Egan file, Box B343, NA; later letter: *Bangor Daily News*, Sept. 27, 1972, at E, Bk. 11, p. 4812–; Hunt, Liddy in Florida: E, Report, p. 165–; "generator": John Ehrlichman testimony, July 27, 1973, R, Bk. IV, Pt. 1, p. 516; Clawson: Ben Bradlee, *A Good Life*, New York: Simon & Schuster, 1995, p. 335; *NM*, p. 163.)
9. With John Mitchell's approval, ten thousand dollars were committed to a plan to persuade a sufficient number of registered voters away from Wallace to make him ineligible to qualify for the 1972 ballot. The scheme did not work. It later emerged that half the money wound up with the Southern California Nazi party. (*NM*, p. 149; Magruder, *American Life*, op. cit., p. 188–.)
10. For discussion of probable deception on the tapes, see chapter 26, p. 349; *AOP*, p. xx; *WHT*, May 11, 1973; *AOP*, p. 466; and Ehrlichman, op. cit., p. 371. For examples of document destruction, see Ehrlichman—on tampering by Plumber David Young—at Ehrlichman, op. cit., p. 370. Also, Gordon Liddy, on his own destruction of documents, at Liddy, op. cit., p. 340. And perhaps most important, on the shredding of papers after the Watergate break-in by Haldeman aide Gordon Strachan, at Haldeman's request, see E, Bk. 6, pp. 2442, 2473–, 2490, Haldeman with DiMona, op. cit., p. 15.
11. Ellsberg had never been Kissinger's student. There is no evidence that he shot at peasants in Vietnam or that he and his wife had sex in front of their children. He had years earlier taken part in experiments with LSD conducted at UCLA and, according to a friend, "got stoned" on occasion after returning from Vietnam. About the same time, by his own account, he had re-

sponded to a newspaper ad inviting people to attend "an orgy." He had been married twice, first to the daughter of a marine colonel and—in 1970—to Patricia Marx, daughter of toy manufacturer Louis Marx. (Never student: Rudenstine, op. cit., p. 122; LSD: Investigations of Unauthorized Disclosures of Classified Information, Aug. 9, 1971, p. 12, in J. Edgar Hoover to Haldeman, Aug. 10, 1971, NA; "got stoned," "orgy": *Harper's,* October 1973.)

12. Kissinger has argued he knew when not to follow Nixon's commands, see p. 369–. Haldeman, Ehrlichman, and other aides have claimed much the same. "I have an uneasy feeling," Nixon himself said in a memo to Haldeman in 1969, "that many of the items that I sent out for action are disregarded when any staff member reaches the conclusion that it is unreasonable or unattainable. . . . I respect this kind of judgement." (Haldeman: Haldeman with DiMona, op. cit., pp. xxi, 58; Ehrlichman: Ehrlichman in Miller Center, eds., op. cit., p. 128; Ehrlichman cited in Wicker, op. cit., p. 530 and fn. same page; other aides: Safire, op. cit., p. 112–; Hillings, op. cit., p. 121; ints. John Sears, William Rhatigan; "many of the items": RN to Haldeman memo, June 16, 1969, cited at *JA,* p. 414.)

13. The operative who testified about being given the fire-bombing suggestion was John Caulfield. Colson, for his part, said he did not recall making it, that it may have been only a joke. Caulfield's colleague Ulaswicz remembered reconnoitering Brookings in the fall. The operatives who worked up a variant on the scheme were future Watergate burglars Gordon Liddy and Howard Hunt. (Caulfield: E, Bk. 22, p. 10359; Colson: Colson testimony in *U.S. v. John Mitchell,* Dec. 5, 1974, NA; Ulasewicz: Ulasewicz, op. cit., pp. 233, 249; Liddy, Hunt: Liddy, op. cit., p. 236–; Lane, op. cit., p. 202, but see Hunt denial, E, Bk. 9, p. 37891.)

14. See p. 141 and Note 10 for Chapter 13.

15. Writing of another episode, Hunt's role in the scandal over the allegation that ITT traded a contribution to the Republican cause for an antitrust settlement, Nixon stated: "I later learned the man's name: E. Howard Hunt." The ITT episode occurred in March 1972, some seven months *after,* as the tapes show, he discussed Hunt in detail with Colson. (*MEM,* p. 582.)

16. John Dean would later recall Krogh's telling him "he had received his orders right out of the Oval Office." In interviews with the author, Krogh said he thought Dean had misinterpreted this. What he meant to say was that Nixon authorized his work but not specifically a break-in. (Dean: John Dean testimony, E, Bk. 3, p. 1007.)

17. Ehrlichman was obviously referring to the attempt to obtain Ellsberg's psychiatrist's files, abandoned after the failed break-in. By shielding the president from the details once the operation had gone wrong, he may have been using the "deniability" ploy. A similar example would be the policy CIA officials followed when discussing Castro's removal with Eisenhower and Kennedy. They reportedly avoided discussing assassination plots, once the principle was established, so that the presidents could legitimately deny involvement. This Ehrlichman exchange does not mean that Nixon might not earlier have approved the assignment. As discussed later, Ehrlichman surmised that he did do so—through Colson.

18. After being released from prison in 1974, Krogh visited Ellsberg's psychiatrist, Dr. Lewis Fielding, and apologized in person for the break-in of his office. Then he drove to San Clemente to see Nixon, who had resigned less than a week earlier. In the course of their conversation Nixon asked: "Did I know about that [the office break-in] in advance?" Krogh replied that he had no information that Nixon had been aware of it. "If you had come to me," Nixon responded, "I would have approved it." (Ints. Egil Krogh.)

19. Ehrilichman said the two aides were Frank Gannon and Diane Sawyer, former White House staffers who stayed on after the resignation to help with Nixon's memoirs.

20. The original "skeletal operations plan" to get "derogatory information" on Ellsberg came to Colson in the form of a memo from Howard Hunt. One scheme specifically mentioned was to "Obtain Ellsberg's files from his psychiatric analyst." It was Colson whom Ehrlichman asked for a "game plan" on how, if the operation was successful, the resulting information could best be used. During Watergate, on the White House tapes, Nixon said flatly: "I never talked to Colson about Ellsberg." This was not true, as several 1971 taped exchanges show. ("Plan": Howard Hunt to Charles Colson, July 28, 1971, E, Bk. 9, p. 3886; "game plan": John Ehrlichman to Charles Colson, Aug. 27, 1971, E, Bk. 6, p. 2651; "I never talked": WHT, March 27, 1973; *AOP,* p. 265; 1971 exchanges: WHT, RN-Colson conversations, June 29, July 2, Sept. 18, and see Aug. 12, 1971, *AOP,* pp. 6, 15, 34, 27.)

21. The other Nixon attorney was Len Garment.

22. The author of the study was Robert Fink, who had worked with Bob Woodward of the *Washington Post.* Senator Abourezk inserted the results in the *Congressional Record* (vol. 120, No. 153, Oct. 9, 1974, "The Unsolved Break-ins").

Chapter 29

1. Nixon's personal attorney, Herbert Kalmbach, held money remaining from the 1968 campaign, plus other sums, until passing them to the reelection campaign treasurer in early 1972.

He testified that it amounted at that time to $915,000. (Kalmbach testimony: E, Bk. 17, p. 7580.)

2. Khashoggi; see p. 282–.

3. Nixon later called it a "hypocritical myth" that his administration "sold" ambassadorships. It is true that he was not the first president to give the London embassy to a rich supporter—*vide* Roosevelt's appointment of Joseph Kennedy—but the White House tape passage cited demolishes his claim. ("myth": Nixon, *Arena*, op. cit., p. 32–, and see *Fortune*, June 1970.)

4. Nixon seriously considered dropping Vice President Agnew for the second term, hoping to replace him with John Connally, whom the president saw as his "logical successor." (*AMII*, p. 457, July 20, 1971, entry; *HD*, CD.)

5. This was the controversial donation that would eventually lead to CREEP fund-raiser Stans and John Mitchell being indicted for perjury and conspiracy to obstruct justice. They were acquitted in 1974, while the indictment against Vesco for the same matter remains outstanding today. (Schoenebaum, op. cit., p. 445.)

6. Curtis Counts double-dated with Nixon and Pat when they were courting. See p. 31.

7. The author interviewed one of the agents, the late John Daley, while researching two previous books, and his widow kindly made his papers available for this project.

8. Leads included information brought to the Watergate Special Prosecution Force that Teamsters official Salvatore Briguglio raised five hundred thousand dollars as a bribe to obtain a pardon for Hoffa, which was allegedly delivered in a Las Vegas restaurant. Mob associate and convicted racketeer Allen Dorfman had a receipt, purportedly signed by John Mitchell, for one hundred thousand dollars. A "financial diary," handed over to authorities in 1979 by reputed mob hit man Gerald Denomo, contained an entry that appeared to reflect a bribe to Nixon involving Dorfman and Fitzsimmons. It read: "Fitz OK. Al Dorfman Chi OK. Tony Pro [mobster and Teamsters official Provenzano] OK. ($500.-to C.C. (equals) Nix OK.)" "$500" has been taken to indicate five hundred thousand dollars. The *Arizona Republic* reported that law enforcement officials thought the diary implicated Nixon and key aides, including Colson, in the Hoffa deal. A Nixon spokesman denied it, and Colson dismissed it as a "discredited story." Another mob hit man, Charles Allen, claimed that he and another man delivered a briefcase containing forty thousand dollars to John Mitchell on Hoffa's behalf. (Briguglio: William Lynch to Charles Ruff, Aug. 9, 1976, WSPF, NA; Moldea, op. cit., p. 397; Dorfman: Friedman and Schwarz, op. cit., p. 131; Scheim, op. cit., p. 301; Denomo: AP, *San Francisco Examiner*, Nov. 16, [?]1979; Provenzano: Scheim, op. cit., p. 30; Allen: *WP*, Feb. 13, 1980.)

9. A front-page story in the *Manchester* (New Hampshire) *Union Leader*, published at the height of Watergate, alleged that funding for the burglars' operations came in part from "gambling interests in Las Vegas" and the Teamsters. Liddy, the article claimed, had visited Nevada twice and had picked up $250,000. Hunt reportedly later flew to Vegas to collect an additional $150,000. The *Leader* article was retracted after Murray Chotiner sued over references in it to him. Liddy apparently made two visits to Las Vegas in early 1972. Hunt knew Liddy had been to the city but denied having been there himself. Both Hunt and Liddy and their accomplice James McCord said the interest there was the safe of Las Vegas newspaper publisher Hank Greenspun, supposedly because he had information on Senator Muskie. (*Union Leader: Manchester* (New Hampshire) *Union Leader*, Apr. 27, 1973; Hunt: int. Howard Hunt; Hunt testimony, E, Bk. 9, p. 3686, E, Bk. 20, p. 9345; Hunt, *Undercover*, op. cit., p. 193–; McCord: James McCord testimony, E, Bk. 1, p. 204; *WHT*, Apr. 13, 1973; *AOP*, p. 312.)

10. Congresswomen Shirley Chisholm was one of the black politicians Nixon and his aides had discussed secretly financing, as a device to take votes away from the Democrats in 1972. See p. 355.

11. Dean claimed he told Haldeman that the Liddy plan was "unnecessary and unwise" and that the White House should have nothing to do with it. He did not say flat out that the plan itself should be dropped. Haldeman at first accepted that Dean had spoken along such lines, but later said he could not recall the episode. It was claimed recently that Dean could not have met Haldeman as he asserted, on the ground that Haldeman was out of Washington on the day of the alleged meeting, February 4, 1972. Persuasive evidence, however, suggests that he *was* in town. Interested readers should compare the passage at pages 119 and 258 of *Silent Coup*, op. cit., with p. 94 of Fred Emery's *Watergate*, op. cit., (Dean on seeing Haldeman: E, Bk. 3, p. 930.)

12. Mitchell would deny in testimony that he gave the go-ahead. His aide Fred LaRue, also present, claimed that Mitchell said the decision need not be taken at that meeting. Haldeman aide Gordon Strachan, however, recalled that Magruder called from Florida to tell him Mitchell had decided the project could proceed. Liddy said he got the "go" from Magruder's assistant Robert Reisner. Either Mitchell or Magruder evidently lied about this, or the meeting in Florida produced one of the most fateful misunderstandings in U.S. history. The wider controversy has been thrashed out most controversially in the book *Silent Coup*, by Len Colodny

and Robert Gettlin, op. cit., which blames John Dean for massive deceptions. The most balanced account is Fred Emery's *Watergate: The Corruption and Fall of Richard Nixon* (New York Times Books, 1994; see also E, Report, p. 25.)

13. Haldeman's aide Gordon Strachan testified that directly after the March 30 meeting with Haldeman in Florida, Magruder phoned to say a "sophisticated political intelligence-gathering system had been approved with a budget of $300,000." Strachan then prepared a Political Action Memorandum for Haldeman, advising him of the development, and Haldeman checked the relevant paragraph to indicate he had read it. Strachan outlined the matter again in the Talking Paper prepared for Haldeman's meeting with Mitchell on April 4. He testified that both documents were among those he shredded within days of the Watergate arrests, in line with Haldeman's order to "make sure our files are clean." A copy surfaced at the National Archives, however, during research for the television documentary series made for the BBC and the Discovery Channel in 1994. A second copy was found later by an archivist and drawn to John Dean's attention. The copy retrieved by the documentary makers bears a circled letter that is either an incomplete *P* or an odd *F*. The copy provided to Dean bears a scribbled "OK/LH," suggesting it was originally copied to Haldeman's assistant Larry Higby. White House logs show that Nixon met with Mitchell and Haldeman for thirty-seven minutes on April 4, after Mitchell and Haldeman had talked separately for about an hour. (Strachan on Magruder call, documents: Gordon Strachan testimony, E, Bk. 6, pp. 2452, 2454, 2459, 2490; *P/F?* copy: *Watergate: The Break-in,* Program 1, Brian Lapping Associates Production for Discovery Channel and BBC, Discovery Communications, 1994, [home video] interviews of Dean and Haldeman reflected in program; "OK/LH" copy: provided to author by John Dean; RN met Mitchell: George to Jim memo, Aug. 3, 1973, and WSPF Summary "Prior Knowledge of the DNC Break-in," Folder 53A-Z, Nixon memoranda, witness files, WSPF, NA, Apr. 4, 1972, entry, *HD,* CD.

14. Suspect intrusions in early 1972 include four targetings of John Meier, a former aide to Howard Hughes then campaigning for the U.S. Senate; an apparent break-in at the office of Las Vegas newspaper publisher Hank Greenspun; the theft of a safe from the law office of Ralph Denton, who represented Greenspun; and the theft of interview tapes from the office of Benjamin Schemmer, who was writing a book on Howard Hughes. Nixon White House concern about Hughes at this time is reported later in this chapter. CBS newscaster Dan Rather interrupted a burglary at his home in April 1972. Valuables and cash had been left untouched, but Rather's files had been disturbed. Rather, who had angered Nixon on occasion, asked the police to look into the burglary again after Watergate. One of the Watergate burglars, Frank Sturgis, later said he had taken part in two break-ins at the office of Sol Linowitz, former diplomat and senior adviser to Senator Muskie. Linowitz's firm represented the Chilean government of Salvador Allende at the time, and there were also break-ins at the Chilean Embassy and the homes of Chilean diplomats. Sturgis said that he and some of the Watergate Cubans took part in the embassy break-ins. The Linowitz and embassy entries allegedly involved the installation or removal of bugs. As Haldeman noted in his diary, the Hunt men reportedly admitted later that they had "dropped bugs all over town." In May 1973, a recently released tape shows, Nixon said the Chilean Embassy break-in was "part of the burglar's plan, as a cover." (Meier: *Playboy* [Sept. 1976]; Greenspun: Emery, op. cit., pp. 93, 97; Denton: int. Sally Denton; Schemmer: "Anatomy of a Break-in," unpublished article in Jim Hougan collection; ints. Benjamin Schemmer; Rather: Wise, *Police State,* op. cit., p. 166–; *WP,* June 5, 1973; Linowitz: int. Andrew St. George; Robert Fink, "The Unsolved Break-ins," *Congressional Record,* Oct. 9, 1974, p. S18595; Chilean Embassy: ibid., and Wise, *Police State,* op. cit., p. 178; *WP,* March 8, 1973; "bugs all over town": Jan. 13, 1973, entry *HD,* p. 568, and see *NYT,* Jan. 14, 1973; RN "part of plan": WHT, May 16, 1973, cited in *WP,* Feb. 26, 1999.)

15. The first psychiatrist to see Bremer under arrest said he believed he "might be a mental case." The following day Bremer spit on a doctor and threatened to kill him. He had an obsession about germs. Of ten psychiatrists who eventually examined him, six found he had been sane on the day of the shooting, three thought not, and one was undecided. (C. W. Bates to Mr. Shroder, May 15, 1972, FBI 44-52576-15, Acting Director to Acting A.G., May 17, 1972, FBI 44-52576-3, Milwaukee to Acting Director, May 18, 1972, FBI 44-52576-68, SAC Baltimore to Director, Sept. 7, 1973, FBI 44-52576-772.)

16. Colson referred to the events of May 15–16 in two memos, dated May 16 and June 20, 1972. This author shares the suspicion that the "May 16" document was created during the flap after the Watergate arrests—and composed to cover the real facts. The June 20 memo, meanwhile, glosses over his exchange with Hunt in the aftermath of the Wallace shooting. (May 16: memo to file, Oudes, op. cit., p. 445; June 20: memo for the file, re: Howard Hunt, E, Bk. 3, p. 1170–.)

17. In a summary of his concerns passed to FBI Director Clarence Kelley in 1975, Wallace said he thought Bremer "would not have had the money to buy an automobile and two guns . . . and

rent a limousine and stay at the Waldorf Astoria. . . . How was he able to . . . tail me all over the country?" Wallace also questioned the authenticity of Bremer's diary, saying: "I believe somebody else wrote it and he copied it." Others shared such doubts. (Wallace doubts: letter from [name censored] to FBI Director Clarence Kelley, Jan. 7, 1975, FBI 44-52576; others' doubts: William Turner article in Blumenthal and Yazijian, eds., op. cit., p. 56, and Gore Vidal article in Scott, Hoch, and Stetler, eds., op. cit., p. 386.)

18. The offices burglarized two floors above the DNC, on May 6, were those of the Bank Operations Division of the Federal Reserve Board. The office broken into elsewhere in the complex, on May 15, was that of a law firm, Fried, Frank, Harris, Shriver and Kampelman. Patricia Harris was acting chairperson of the Democratic Credentials Committee, and Sargent Shriver—a Kennedy brother-in-law—was occasionally mentioned as a possible vice presidential candidate. Max Kampelman was an intimate of Hubert Humphrey's, and another partner, Richard Berryman, was cocounsel for the Humphrey campaign. Harris and Shriver were on the "enemies list." The FBI would sweep the offices for bugs following the June 17 arrests elsewhere in the Watergate and, according to Shriver, found a bug in Harris's phone. (Federal Reserve: "The Unsolved Break-ins," *Congressional Record,* vol. 120, No. 153, Oct. 9, 1974; Fried, Frank break-in: ibid.; bug found?: *Miami Herald,* Aug. 20, 1972.)

19. See pp. 66 and 504 n. 15 for references to Russell's role with Nixon on the Hiss case and later on the Onassis operation. The Washington investigator and lobbyist for whom he worked in the late sixties and early seventies was James Juliana, whose links with Caulfield, Colson, Chotiner, and Mitchell are acknowledged in Juliana's interview with staff of the Senate Watergate Committee. Juliana had been in charge of ballot security and thus in touch with Chotiner and Mitchell. He said he knew Nixon "quite well," and the president appointed him to his Committee on Retardation. Juliana had helped in a White House effort to get information on the medical condition of ailing AFL-CIO leader George Meany. The information on Russell's request to see Nixon, and his meeting with Rose Woods, comes from Anatoli Granovsky, who arranged the visit, and from Woods's testimony. The Washington stockbroker whom Russell met not long after the White House visit was William Birely. Birely told the author in 1998 that he had known Nixon since 1947, and Rose Woods about as long. Russell's role in the White House probe of Chappaquiddick was mentioned by his daughter, Jean, his doctor, George Weems, and Clifton DeMotte, a Howard Hunt contact Russell had visited. Russell's daughter, Jean Hooper and his friend Ruth Thorne, have been useful sources. (Juliana: Paul Summit to Terry Lenzner, re: conversation with James Juliana, Nov. 5, 1973, Hughes-Rebozo file 804, WSPF, NA, and deposition of James McCord, Dec. 17, 1981, summary, in files of Henry Rothblatt, courtesy of Rothblatt family, *Washington Evening Star & Daily News,* Oct. 12, 1972; Meany: *WP,* June 28, 1974; report on Russell: director, FBI to attorney general, Apr. 14, 1971, FBI 67-37816; Woods, Russell: D. E. Moore to C. D. Brennan, subject Anatoli Granovsky, Aug. 17, 1970, FBI 100-356092, and Woods testimony, E, Bk. 22, p. 10250, and see Rose Woods to Lou Russell, Jan. 9, 1971, Lou Russell papers supplied to author by Jean Hooper; Birely: ints. William Birely, *Washington Evening Star & Daily News,* Oct. 12, 1972; Chappaquiddick: note of DeMotte int. by Jim Hougan, cited in Hougan to Philip Manuel, transcript of int. Dr. George Weems, and Hougan notes of int. Jean Russell Hooper, all in Hougan Collection and *Washington Evening Star & Daily News,* Oct. 12, 1972; Russell daughter. int. Jean Hooper.)

20. In his book *Secret Agenda,* which challenged the conventional account of Watergate, Jim Hougan raised multiple questions about the bugging evidence. He pointed out that, on checking after the Watergate arrests, neither FBI agents nor Watergate technicians found any bugging devices in any DNC phone.

A bug did turn up in Spencer Oliver's office phone months later, in September, following a report of a malfunction by an Oliver secretary. The bug was defective, however, and a reading of FBI technical reports suggests it could never have made the transmissions logged by Baldwin. The consensus, Hougan wrote, was that it was a "throwaway," a device planted in the phone with the intention that it be found. Some, including Nixon and Robert Finch, suspected this bug was "one they [the Democrats] planted themselves" to keep the story alive.

The burglar responsible for planting the bugs, James McCord, claimed to the contrary that the bug removed in September was one of the two he claimed to have installed. The second, McCord claimed in his book and in grand jury testimony, remained in place—"on an extension off a telephone call director carrying Larry O'Brien's lines"— until early April 1973. An FBI report, however, says an April 9, 1973, check of all DNC phones found no second device.

How to explain the muddle? Acting U.S. Attorney Earl Silbert thought the FBI "goofed" in its initial check of the DNC phones and missed finding the bugs. Internal FBI correspondence denied any such lapse but declared the anomalies "insoluble." So must this author. He agrees with author Hougan that the discrepancies are serious and were never sufficiently aired or investigated. (Hougan, *Agenda,* op. cit., pp. 218–, 243; O. T. Jacobson to Director, July 5, 1974, FBI 139-4089-2790; R. E. Gebhardt to Mr. Felt, Apr. 6, 1973; re: DNC search following McCord grand jury testimony: FBI 139-4089-1975, W. W. Bradley to Mr. Conrad, Apr. 9, 1973; re: negative result of DNC search: FBI 139-4089-1988, and McCord, op. cit., p. 24–. Nixon's discussion of a DNC "plant" is in WHT, Sept. 15, 16, 1972; *AOP,* pp. 147, 152.)

21. Mitchell testified that he did not see Liddy between early February and June 15 and that his records showed Magruder had never shown him the logs. Magruder's assistant Robert Reisner, however, recalled his boss handing him GEMSTONE material at the relevant time in preparation for a meeting with Mitchell. Liddy, for his part, has denied Magruder's claim that Mitchell called him into such a meeting and chastised him over the useless product from the bugging. By one account, Liddy suggested Magruder confused Mitchell with Strachan, who, Liddy acknowledged, summoned him to the White House to tell him that the take from the phone intercepts was useless. Anthony Lukas, author of *Nightmare,* reported that most contemporary investigators seemed to believe Magruder's version rather than Mitchell's denial. (Mitchell testimony: E, Bk. 4, p. 1620; Reisner: E, Bk. 2, p. 494; Liddy denied: Liddy, op. cit., p. 497; Magruder confused: Hougan, *Agenda,* op. cit., p. 166; contemporary investigators: *NM,* p. 203.)

22. See p. 229–.

Chapter 30

1. It was also suggested, Hunt said, that funds were reaching the Democrats from North Vietnam. (Int. Howard Hunt in Wise, *Police State,* op. cit., p. 159.)

2. Sturgis may have been referring to the burglary of May 15 at the offices in the Watergate complex of Fried, Frank, Harris, Shriver and Kampelman, which housed several leading Democrats. See Chapter 29, Note 18.

3. The author knew the late Frank Sturgis and spoke extensively with Andrew St. George, who conducted the Sturgis interview cited here. Although Sturgis was a swashbuckling, controversial character, there is no reason to doubt the essential points of his account.

4. See p. 176–.

5. See p. 191.

6. The Castro plots, discussed in chapters 16 and 17, continued during the Kennedy administration.

7. See pp. 157 and 279–.

8. See p. 198.

9. Charles Colson, who was also at the Hofstra conference, dismissed this Magruder account of the motive for the break-in as "a convenient answer to a question he's never been able to answer before." (Colson Oral History Interview, June 15, 1988, NP, NA.)

10. The transmissions from the functioning DNC bug were supposedly first noted by Baldwin in longhand, then typed up for transmission to Liddy. Liddy then edited them before showing them to colleagues, and apparently shredded them following the Watergate arrests. Magruder burned the copies in his possession. The tape and transcript of an interview Baldwin did with the *Los Angeles Times* were sealed by the Court of Appeals for the District of Columbia in early 1973. Although most of the transcript was unsealed in 1980, passages relating to the contents of the intercepted conversations remain censored. Baldwin declined to tell the Senate Watergate Committee about the content of the conversations he overheard, citing a federal statue prohibiting the divulging of intercepted communications. According to Baldwin and McCord, none of the intercepted conversations was recorded even though there were two tape recorders in Baldwin's room at the Howard Johnson's. McCord said he had been unable to hook them up to the receiving units, a claim that defies belief. If tapes were in fact made, what became of them? (Baldwin note process: Alfred Baldwin testimony, E, Bk. 1, pp. 401–, 410; McCord, op. cit., p. 26; Liddy edited: Liddy, op. cit., p. 323; destroyed: ibid., pp. 340, 347–; Magruder burned: Magruder, *American Life,* op. cit., p. 226; *LAT* tape, transcript sealed: Charles Morgan, Jr., *One Man, One Voice,* New York: Holt, Reinhart, & Winston, 1979, p. 217–; *LAT* transcript unsealed: transcript of int. Alfred Baldwin by Jack Nelson and Ronald Ostrow, released with redactions, Oct. 3, 1980, *U.S. v. G. Gordon Liddy, et al.,* Case 1827-72, U.S. Dist. Ct. for D.C.; Baldwin declined: Alfred Baldwin testimony, E, Bk. 1, p. 400; not recorded: *LAT* transcript, *supra.,* p. 62–; summary of Baldwin's Watergate trial testimony, Jan. 17, 1973, FBI 139-4089-2144; Liddy, op. cit., p. 322; Emery, op. cit., p. 123–; Hougan, *Agenda,* op. cit., p. 162.)

11. The author obtained the tape of an April 1973 conversation in the White House between John Ehrlichman and Jeb Magruder, in which Magruder said the Baldwin logs he saw included the conversations of a "young Democrat politician" who "was calling girls in Mississippi saying, 'Honey, I'll be down there for the weekend,' and discussing the bipartisan group Young American Political Leaders. Stuff like that." Mitchell's assistant Fred LaRue, with whom Magruder

also talked, recalled Magruder's saying that "one of the conversations involved Spencer Oliver talking to someone down in Mississippi about a date." (Transcript of Ehrlichman meeting with Magruder and attorneys, Apr. 14, 1973, Ref. SR 7304141, NP, NA, and see John Ehrlichman testimony, E, Bk. 7, p. 2764; LaRue: int. Fred LaRue, and see Emery, op. cit., p. 124.)

12. The key was seized by arresting officers from one of the burglars, Rolando Martinez, on the night of June 16–17, 1972. When Martinez reached for his pocket, having been told to raise his hands above his head, Officer Carl Shoffler thought he might be going for a gun. Instead Shoffler found a notebook, with a key taped to it, in Martinez's pocket. The FBI discovered that the key, a Vanguard model HL-311, fitted the desk of Maxie Wells, and according to a veteran locksmith, the chances it would have fitted any other DNC desk were "slim to zero." Wells has said that both she and her colleague Barbara Kennedy, who had been given a copy during Wells's recent vacation, still had their keys after the break-in. She had no idea why her desk should have been of special interest to the burglars, and said that the only reason she kept it locked was to prevent colleagues from taking her office supplies. Burglar Martinez claimed total ignorance of the key when interviewed in 1981 but in 1990 vaguely recalled having been given the key by either Liddy or Hunt before the break-in. The latter have both denied it. Martinez said he was also given a chart of the DNC office, marked with crosses to denote burglary targets. Targets so marked included Spencer Oliver's desk and others nearby. If Martinez had the key to Wells's desk, how to explain the fact that the only two known keys were still in the possession of the two secretaries at the time of the break-in? Since Kennedy was not given her key until early June, one could speculate that it was in the desk at the time of the May 28 break-in, and the burglars took an impression of it then. But why was there any special interest in Maxie Wells's desk? It is an important issue, one that was apparently never properly investigated. (Key seized: police lists of seized items, Exhibits in *Ida Maxwell Wells v. G. Gordon Liddy*, Case JFM-97-946, U.S. Dist. Ct. for Dist. of MD, N. Div., provided to author; ints. former officers Paul Leeper, Carl Shoffler, and John Barrett; Barrett testimony in *U.S. v. G. Gordon Liddy, et al.*, Case 1827-72, U.S. Dist. Ct. for D.C., p. 670; key fitted: FBI agent Michael King report, June 26, 1972, FBI WFO 139-166-356; Wells, Kennedy: reports of ints. Maxie Wells by FBI agent Michael King, June 27, 1972, and Barbara Kennedy, also June 27, both FBI WFO 139-166-359; Wells no idea: Wells int. by Jim Hougan, 1983, Hougan Collection; Martinez ignorance: int. Martinez by Jim Hougan, 1981, Hougan Collection; Martinez vaguely recalled: Benton Becker to files, March 13, 1990, on meeting with Martinez, supplied to author; Liddy denied: ibid.; Hunt denied: John Garrick to Joan Hoff, March 3, 1998, www.watergate.com.)

13. Spencer Oliver's secretary Maxie Wells has repeatedly denied having had any knowledge of or involvement in a phone's having been used for such a purpose. Alfred Baldwin, who monitored the bugged calls that apparently emanated from the Oliver phone, has said that he "can categorically state, from the conversations that were obtained, that no such [call girl ring] operation was being conducted, at least from the conversations I was monitoring." More recently he testified that had ordinary members of the public heard the conversations, many might have thought they were prostitution-related. Fred LaRue, who heard Magruder describe the logs, said he mentioned nothing that touched on prostitution. Former DNC treasurer Robert Strauss testified recently that "among many wild rumors" he had heard was one that "some of the state chairmen would . . . use the phone to make dates for that night." Maxie Wells's former colleague Barbara Kennedy testified that there was "a rumor at the time" that a "call girl operation" was being run from the DNC. Kennedy said, "No one paid any attention to it." Former staffer Margaret Shannon reportedly spoke privately even before Watergate of women at the DNC being "assigned" for sex. She no longer maintained that when interviewed by the author in 1998. (Wells denied: Maxie Wells int. by Jim Hougan, 1981, Hougan Collection, and Ida Maxwell Wells deposition, Sept. 19, 1997, *Wells v. Liddy*, Case CR 67231.0, p. 369; Baldwin "no such operation": Baldwin int. transcript, "Watergate: The Secret Story," CBS News, June 17, 1992, p. 5; more recently: Baldwin deposition, July 28, 1997, *Ida Maxwell Wells v. G. Gordon Liddy*, Case JFM-97-946, p. 155; LaRue: int. Fred LaRue; Strauss: Robert Strauss deposition, June 24, 1996, *Maureen and John Dean v. St. Martin's Press et al.*, Case 92-1807 (HHG), at www.watergate.com/strauss/.htm; Kennedy: Barbara Kennedy Rhoden deposition, July 17, 1996, *Deans v. St. Martin's Press et al.*, supra., pp. 23–68; Shannon: conv. Michael Ewing, former congressional investigator and staffer for Senator Harold Hughes and ints. Margaret Shannon.)

14. Dean told the author he saw Rothblatt's move as no more than "an effort by defense counsel to harass a plaintiff and make pursuing their lawsuit as unpleasant as possible." (John Dean to author, Nov. 12, 1997.)

15. In a 1996 deposition Dean said his comments to Ziegler about the Hollander affair were just "teasing" and that his office had concluded "there wasn't going to be any embarrassment"

from the Hollander case. He seemed to suggest that the passage on the subject in his book *Blind Ambition* was overwritten by his ghostwriter, Taylor Branch. Dean has recently appeared to disavow parts of that book, but Pulitzer Prize winner Taylor Branch and his publisher, Alice Mayhew, have stood by Branch's reporting. ("teasing" etc.: John Dean deposition, Jan. 22, 1996, *Maureen and John Dean v. St. Martin's Press et al.*, above, pp. 133, 139–; Branch role: *Tampa Tribune,* Apr. 22, 1993; *Washington Times,* Feb. 12, Sept. 15, 1996; *New York Post,* Feb. 15, 1996.)

16. Erika Rikan, known as Heidi from her schooldays, has been at the center of allegations of a prostitution link between the Columbia Plaza apartments and the DNC. After intensive research, including interviews with people who lived with Rikan or knew her well, the author found no evidence that she was a prostitute or call girl. The only reference to her located in police files was for a minor driving infraction. Publicity about Rikan, notably in the 1991 book *Silent Coup,* has relied on the notion that she was one and the same as Cathy Dieter, named by Phillip Bailley as having run a call girl operation in apartment 204 at the Columbia Plaza. Two witnesses interviewed for this book said Rikan had an apartment in the Columbia Plaza, but then so did well over a thousand other people, including at one time Julie Nixon Eisenhower. The arrest record of the madam known to have operated from the Plaza, Barbara Ralabate, shows that *she* was the madam at apartment 204 in 1971–72, so Dieter hardly could have been. Bailley, who has spun various fantasies around his core story, may have built his Dieter story onto what he knew of the operation actually being run out of apartment 204. Ralabate did recall a woman of foreign origin called Erika having worked for her at a different Plaza apartment at another time. Police records show that a woman named Erika, with a different last name, was charged with prostitution in 1970. Shown a photograph of Erika Rikan, Ralabate was sure it was not of the Erika who had worked with her. The name Dieter meanwhile meant nothing to her. The author has seen no reliable evidence, let alone legal proof, that Rikan and Dieter were the same person. Yet Cathy Dieter did exist. Former Assistant U.S. Attorney John Rudy recently testified that a woman using that name was associated with a Columbia Plaza call girl operation and cooperated with his investigation. (Suggestions re: Rikan: see refs. Colodny and Gettlin, op. cit.; Dieter and apt. 204: int. Phillip Bailley by Jim Hougan, Hougan Collection; author's interviews re: Rikan: Edith Meck, Carolyn Rainear, John Dean, Pete Kinsey, Josefina Alvarez, Adrienne Grady Clark, Sam Kay, Rebecca Sutton Nesline, Fortunato Mendes, Alvin Kotz, Langhorne Rorer, former police officer Carl Shoffler, and convs. journalists Jim Hougan and Phil Stanford and author Len Colodny; driving offense: charge slip for Erika L. Rikan, ticket no. 8879779, Sept. 10, 1972, D.C. Superior Ct.; Rikan apt. Plaza: ints. Adrienne Grady Clark, Sam Kay; Julie Nixon: *Miami Herald,* July 15, 1974; Ralabate: charge sheets of Lillian Lori and int. Barbara Ralabate; other "Erika": 1970 charge sheet for Erika K[name withheld], D.C. Ct. of General Sessions; no convincing evidence Dieter identical with Rikan: Author's view takes into account the research reported in G. Gordon Liddy's Consolidated Reply re: Motion for Summary Judgment in *Ida Maxwell Wells v. G. Gordon Liddy,* Civil Action JFM 97-946, at [Introduction] pp. 60, 63; letter from Collier, Shannon, and Scott to Stephen Contopoulos, June 11, 1992, supplied to author, and "Heidi Rikan was also known as Cathy Dieter," Defendant Len Colodny's Motion for Partial Summary Judgment, Dec. 1996, re: *Maureen and John Dean v. St. Martin's Press et al.,* Case 92-1807 (HHG), U.S. District Ct. for D.C., Core 1, p. 13–; Rudy on Dieter: John Rudy deposition, June 19, 1996, *Maureen and John Dean v. St. Martin's Press* et al., Case 91-1807 (HHG) (AK), pp. 508, 690–.)

17. Flanigan has denied that he called the U.S. attorney's office, as reported in the *Washington Star.* (Colodny and Gettlin, op. cit., p. 144.)

18. The woman's name is withheld here for legal and privacy reasons.

19. There is good reason to think the White House remained very sensitive to what O'Brien might have on the Nixon relationship with the Greek dictatorship, and not only because of the illegal funding for Nixon's 1968 campaign. (See p. 284–.) The go-between in that affair, millionaire Thomas Pappas, remained extremely close to the administration and hosted Nixon's brother on an Athens visit from which, as a vice president of Marriott Corporation, he came away with a contract to provide inflight catering for Olympic Airways. Pappas was cochairman of the Nixon fund-raising effort for 1972. The behavior of Nixon aides, meanwhile, demonstrates that the White House believed a real threat was posed by the exiled Greek journalist Elias Demetracopoulos, who had originally taken the information on the colonels' 1968 funding to O'Brien. (See p. 286.) In 1971, after allusions to Pappas's role in testimony to a House Foreign Affairs subcommittee, Nixon's confidant Murray Chotiner told Demetracopoulos to his face to "lay off" Pappas or risk deportation. Undeterred, Demetracopoulos submitted a memorandum to the House subcommittee that, he told the author, included sensitive information on the 1968 malfeasance. On January 24, 1972, at a political luncheon,

John Mitchell raged about Demetracopoulos, threatening to deport him—this three days before presiding over the first of the GEMSTONE meetings with Gordon Liddy.

Spencer Oliver, whose DNC phone was apparently bugged by Liddy's people, has suggested another potential motive for the surveillance. The Nixon side would have had an intense interest in the Democratic party's debate on whether McGovern's candidacy should go forward. This was being hotly debated in June 1972, and as head of the party's state chairmen's group Oliver was deeply involved. Hence, perhaps, CREEP's concern with his telephone conversations. (Pappas: *Detroit Sunday News*, Nov. 11, 1973; Roger Witten to File 306, Dec. 20, 1973, Jan. 11, 1974, and Witten to Stans interview file, Dec. 3, 1974, WSPF; *WP*, March 22, 1972; Pappas, Donald Nixon: *NYT*, June 4, 1970; *WP*, Feb. 16, 1972; Donald Nixon testimony, E, Bk. 22, p. 10675; Bob Muse to Terry Lenzner, undated, re: int. John Meier, Hughes-Rebozo investigation, WSPF, and see Dean, *Ambition*, op. cit., p. 165; Demetracopoulos testimony: Demetracopoulos testimony, July 12, 1971, Hearings, Committee on Foreign Affairs, Subcommittee on Europe, 92d Congress, 1st Session, p. 64–; Chotiner: ints. Elias Demetracopoulos, *Nation* [May 31, 1986]; memo to subcommittee: Demetracopoulos memo, Sept. 17, 1971, subcommittee on Europe, above, p. 450–; Mitchell raged: Louise Gore to Elias Demetracopoulos, Jan. 24, 1972, Demetracopoulos Papers; Oliver suggested motive: conv. Seymour Hersh, citing Spencer Oliver in *Houston Post*, June 15, 1972.)

Chapter 31

1. Russell apparently came to the attention of the FBI because McCord's phone records showed he had made a recent call to a phone at Russell's rooming house. Under questioning, Russell admitted that he had been at the Howard Johnson's restaurant, across from the Watergate, between 8:30 P.M. and 10:30 P.M. on the night of the arrests. He claimed he was there "for sentimental reasons" because it was where he had originally met a woman friend. Russell's accounts of his movements that evening were inconsistent, however. The best reconstruction, by investigative writer Jim Hougan, shows that in fact he returned to Washington from the suburbs after midnight, after telling his daughter he had to "do some work for McCord." McCord has refused to discuss Russell. Russell's friend Ruth Thorne, traced by the author in 2000, recalled his telling her that he was "outside watching" on the night of the arrests. (FBI ints.: ints. Louis J. Russell, June 27, 1972, July 5, 1975, by agents Rodney Kicklighter and James Hopper, FBI 139-166, and int. Russell by Donald Sanders and Harold Lipset, Apr. 12, 1973, with Russell letter to E, chief counsel, in Lou Russell file, Box C103, E. NA; Hougan reconstruction: Hougan, *Agenda*, op. cit., p. 181; McCord refused: ibid., p. 185; "outside": int. Ruth Thorne.)

2. In his 1978 memoirs, Haldeman recalled Nixon having first discussed the arrests with him (in Key Biscayne) during a phone call from the Bahamas on the morning of Sunday, June 18. Nixon told him, "Track down Magruder and see what he knows." Haldeman called Magruder, Ehrlichman, and Colson, then phoned Nixon back. Haldeman's diary, released on CD-ROM in 1994, offers a different account. It has Haldeman talking with Ehrlichman, Magruder, and Colson on his own initiative that Sunday morning. "The P," according to the diary entry, was at that time still "not aware of all this, unless he read something in the paper, but he didn't mention it to me." White House logs, meanwhile, reflect a four-minute call by Nixon to Haldeman at 10:58 A.M. on Saturday, June 17 and also an eighteen minute call from Nixon to Haldeman on Sunday, June 18. The following day, Monday, June 19, Nixon phoned Colson and Haldeman twice and met with Haldeman before flying back to Washington. This is not necessarily a complete record. (Memoirs: Haldeman with DiMona, op. cit. pp. 7, 12; diary: *HD*, CD, entries of June 17, 18, 19, 1972; logs: President's Daily Diary, June 17, 18, 1972, NP, NA; "First Conversations Concerning the Break-In," Witness Files: Nixon, Folder 53A.2, Investigative files, WSPF, NA.)

3. See pp. 403 and 526 n. 13.

4. In his memoirs Nixon would question the competence of the technical experts consulted by the prosecutors, and cite criticism of the findings by other organizations. The House Judiciary Committee, however, pointed out that neither Dektor Counterintelligence & Security nor Home Service, Inc.—the two principal organizations in question—examined the controversial June 20 tape or the recorder Woods used, or reviewed the experiments with the expert panel. Nixon also failed to mention that his own attorney had Dr. Michael Hecker of the Stanford Research Institute review the experiments and confer with the panel. Dr. Hecker agreed with the panel's approach and its expertise, and declared himself "in substantial agreement" with its final report. (RN questioned: *MEM*, p. 951; criticisms of findings: see technical article by George O'Toole, *New Republic*, March 9, 1974, citing Allan Bell of Dektor, and Summary of Information, R. Hearings, p. 114 nl; Hecker; ibid., p. 114.)

5. Nixon said in his memoirs that he knew he had not deliberately erased the tape segment and that he believed Woods's similar denial. In a later book he enlarged on his claim that the court-

appointed experts' report had been flawed (see Note 4, supra.) and dismissed the suggestion that he or any staff member had erased incriminating conversation as "the most preposterous myth." He said the prosecutors overlooked the fact that Haldeman's "Complete notes" of the meeting contained "nothing out of the ordinary." Haldeman, however, emphasized in his own memoirs—and in the context of the eighteen-and-one-half-minute gap—that his notes were often incomplete. The issue should be viewed in the context of other evidence of deception and destruction of evidence (RN denial: *MEM*, pp. 919, 948–; "myth": Nixon, *Arena.* op. cit., p. 32; Haldeman on notes: Haldeman with DiMona, op. cit., p. 42.)

6. "Everybody bugs everybody else," Nixon said, quoting Barry Goldwater, on June 23, 1972. There is in fact no good evidence that the Democrats bugged the Republicans in 1972, in spite of allegations to that effect. The author has, however, made some investigation of a fascinating angle to the case: that the Democrats had advance warning of the Watergate break-in. Good evidence, in the form of testimony and correspondence gathered by the Senate Watergate Committee, establishes that O'Brien was warned nearly three months before the fateful break-in of "very disturbing stories about GOP sophisticated intelligence techniques." A Democratic official then met with the source of this information, a private investigator with an intelligence background named Arthur Woolston-Smith. He obscured *his* source but revealed to the author in 1996 that it had in fact been none other than the veteran wireman who had long worked for Nixon himself, John Ragan. (See above, pp. 314 and 341.) Ragan, now dead, had been security officer for the Republican National Committee until the fall of 1971 and was thus the predecessor of CREEP's James McCord, who went on to become the electronics man for the Watergate break-ins.

The Democrats almost certainly did anticipate the break-in even if they did not know when to expect it. Veteran Democratic aide Frank Mankiewicz, who was with O'Brien when he learned of the arrests, thought the DNC chairman seemed "not very excited, by any means." Former *Washington Post* editor Ben Bradlee has recalled that his paper was notified within hours of the arrests by the Democrats' attorney, Joe Califano. Califano filed a suit against CREEP on the second possible business day after the arrests, an action so speedy that, Haldeman said, "As the mystery of Watergate deepened, we would wonder about his swiftness. Seemingly the Democrats had this lawsuit, with its complex legal briefs, all cranked up and ready to go." Woolston-Smith, the source of the Democrats' information, told the committee he thought O'Brien had "formulated a plan" and recalled that the DNC official he had been in touch with seemed "elated" after the arrests. He told the author that the notion that the Democrats "entrapped" the burglars is "pretty close." O'Brien dismissed such ideas in his memoirs as "preposterous." Whatever the truth, there is wonderful irony in the fact that the warning about Republican dirty tricks apparently originated with, of all people, the wireman Nixon himself had long used. ("Everybody bugs": WHT, Sept. 15, 1972, *AOP,* p. 147; allegations: *MEM*, p. 67; Lasky, op. cit., p. 326; DNC had advance warning?: summarized in Fred Thompson, *At This Point in Time,* New York: Quadrangle, 1975, p. 225–, and see John Stewart deposition, Feb. 28, 1973, *DNC v. McCord et al.,* Civil Action 1233-72; William Haddad testimony, Oct. 4, 1973, Box B79, E, NA; Arthur Woolston-Smith testimony, Oct. 10, 1973, Apr. 29, 1974, Box C129, E, NA; Woolston-Smith revealed: ints. Arthur Woolston-Smith; Ragan, RNC: John Caulfield testimony, E, Bk. 1, p. 235; O'Brien "not excited": *George,* June 1997; *WP* tipped: Bradlee, *Good Life,* op. cit., p. 324–; "As the mystery": Haldeman with DiMona, op. cit., p. 14; "preposterous": O'Brien, op. cit., p. 342.)

7. As reproduced by the House Judiciary Committee, Nixon's June 20 Dictabelt note mentioned that he had tried to cheer up Mitchell and that Mitchell had responded by regretting that he had not controlled his people better. Special Prosecutor Jaworski, however, later referred in his memoir to a Dictabelt note in which Mitchell "gave Nixon his first hard information on the details of the Watergate burglary. . . . When we subpoenaed that belt, the only words on it were: 'John Mitchell called me at two o'clock, and John said. . . .' The rest was erased." Either Jaworski was mistaken about the contents of the known June 20 Nixon call to Mitchell, or this passage must refer to a different—hitherto unknown—call. (Jaworski, *Confession,* op. cit., p. 237.)

8. See p. 177–.

9. The tape in question is of a conversation between Nixon and Haldeman on June 23, 1972. (Conversation Number 343-036, monitored for author by researchers Julie Ziegler and Robert Lamb.)

10. CIA Director Helms's posture troubled Watergate prosecutors and has never been satisfactorily resolved. Walters did intervene at the FBI, and the bureau did suspend its Mexico interviews, although the CIA admitted it had no legitimate objection to the interviews' going forward. Only some two weeks later, after the CIA had turned down an FBI request to put its concern in writing, did the Mexico probe resume. "I had no way of knowing I was being asked

to lie," Helms would later testify, claiming he and Walters had "held the line" against the White House appeal for help. He disputed having instructed Walters to ask the FBI not to let the investigation go beyond the five arrested burglars. Helms has yet to explain, however, a memo he wrote to Walters on June 28, 1972, stating: "We still adhere to the request that they confine themselves to the personalities already arrested or directly under suspicion and that they desist from expanding this investigation into other areas which may well eventually run afoul of our operations." In a letter to the author in 2000, Helms said: "I have wracked my memory, but I find nothing which is clarifying." His replies are not credible, for the episode is central to the CIA's part in the Watergate scandal. (Helms's posture: discussed best at Ben-Veniste and Frampton, op. cit., p. 72–; Wise, *Police State,* op. cit., p. 242–; memo: Richard Helms to Deputy Director, June 28, 1972, R, Bk. II, p. 459; "I have wracked": Helms to author, Apr. 2, 2000.)

11. Nixon acknowledged in his memoirs that he had talked with Colson "in sheer exasperation" of how "it would help if someone broke into our headquarters and did a lot of damage." He also admitted that he had discussed with Haldeman the idea of responding to Democratic bugging accusations by charging "that we were bugged and maybe even plant a bug and find it ourselves." The former president wrote as though he hoped readers would believe this was merely idle chat, but the extensive taped exchange with Colson on fabricating a break-in does not read that way. The journalist Ron Rosenbaum guessed, as early as 1982, that these passages in the memoirs were "preemptive pre-tape release" efforts by Nixon to explain away the compromising conversations. Sure enough, the phony break-in proposal did turn up in the tape release of November 1996. (Memoirs: *MEM,* pp. 637, 645; Rosenbaum: *New Republic,* June 23, 1982; 1996: WHT, July 1, 1972, *AOP.* p. 90; *WP,* Feb. 15, 1997.)

12. RN wrote in his memoirs that Colson was "ecstatic" over the Lungren break-in and wanted to use it as propaganda, that Ehrlichman was leery of appearing to have "set it up," and that he himself gave orders that it be investigated. (*MEM,* p. 713.)

13. Strauss had been the target of CREEP eavesdropping as early as January 1972, when James McCord bugged a conversation about fund-raising on the Democrat's car phone (Liddy, op. cit., p. 264.)

14. The identity of Deep Throat remains a secret. Some have doubted that he even existed, including David Obst, the literary agent who acted for Woodward and Bernstein on their Watergate books. Obst told the author Deep Throat did not appear at all as a character in the first draft manuscript of *All the President's Men,* and speculated that he was invented to make the book more viable as a movie. The author Don Wolfe, who worked on the film, said he heard Woodward telling director Alan Pakula that there was no one source behind the nickname. Both Woodward and Bernstein, however, have insisted in numerous interviews that Throat did exist and was one man with "a career in government." Available clues, if accurate, suggest he was a smoker, a Scotch drinker, and a gossip. According to former *Washington Post* editor Ben Bradlee, he was given his famous name by the paper's managing editor, Howard Simons— "deep" for deep background, the terms on which he offered information, and "Deep Throat" after the pornographic film of that title, which had opened in June 1972. Woodward and Bernstein apparently shared the true identity of their source with Bradlee, but with no one else. The two reporters have said they will be free to reveal the man's name only after his death—and Bernstein indicated that he was still alive as recently as 1999. (Obst int.: David Obst; David Obst, *Too Good to Be Forgotten,* New York: John Wiley, 1998, p. 240–; Wolfe ints.: Don Wolfe; Woodward and Bernstein on Throat: int. Carl Bernstein, *Time.* May 3, 1976; "Watergate: The Secret Story," CBS News Special Program, June 17, 1992, transcript, p. 13; *Today,* June 17, 1997, transcript, p. 5; *WP,* Oct. 1, 1997; Bradlee: Ben Bradlee, *A Good Life,* op. cit., pp. 333, 365; *Meet the Press,* June 15, 1997, transcript, p. 25–; alive 1999?: *Hartford Courant,* July 28, 1999.

15. In contrast with the 1973 settlement, which permitted North Vietnamese troops to remain in the South, the cease-fire accord signed at Geneva provided for the Vietminh (Ho Chi Minh's original movement) to withdraw from the South, and the French from the North, pending a nationwide election. (1973 agreement: ibid., pp. 663, 665; Kissinger, *White House Years,* op. cit., pp. 1347, 1391, 1469–; Nixon, *Real Peace,* op. cit., p. 284; Geneva: Karnow, op. cit., p. 220.)

16. Beecher had filed a report in mid-December reporting that renewed bombing was being considered, but the story was shelved because Kissinger had told a somewhat different version of events to James Reston. (Hersh, *Price of Power,* op. cit., p. 622–.)

17. See p. 295– for initial coverage of the Madman Theory. Former U.S. Army operations intelligence specialist Barry Toll, whose firsthand recollections are reported in chapter 33, said he learned from colleagues that—allegedly after drinking or using sedatives—Nixon issued orders for a nuclear strike during the Christmas 1972 offensive. Military chiefs ignored him, accord-

ing to Toll. It is Toll who has quoted the CIA's top Vietnam specialist, George Carver, as having made a similar allegation about Nixon's conduct when North Korea shot down a U.S. plane in 1969 (See p. 372.)

18. Connally, a leading Democrat, had served Nixon as treasury secretary in the second half of the first term. He founded Democrats for Nixon in 1972 and later became adviser to the president on domestic and foreign affairs.

Chapter 32

1. McCord did this in a letter to Judge Sirica, read aloud in court on March 23, 1973. It caused a sensation and was a huge fillip to the Senate probe. That McCord posed a serious danger to the White House had become most evident on December 28, 1972, when he wrote to John Caulfield that "if the Watergate operation is laid at CIA's feet, where it does not belong, every tree in the forest will fall . . . if they want it to blow, they are on exactly the right course." (Letter to Sirica: Emery, op. cit., p. 269–; "every tree": R, Bk. III, p. 40.)

2. On March 21, 1973, White House counsel Dean had the now-celebrated meeting with Nixon at which he told him that Watergate had become a "cancer on the presidency," that money had been paid to the burglary defendants and much more would yet be needed. Nixon later said he found this "distressing" information. The tape of the conversation, however, shows no sign that it came as a surprise or that he found it alarming. (WHT, March 21, 1973, prepared by R, Rec. Grp. 460, WSPF, NA, and see Ben-Veniste and Frampton, op. cit., p. 200–; "distressing": RN speech, Aug. 15, 1973, Drossman and Knappman, eds. op. cit., vol. 2, p. 42, and see Ben-Veniste and Frampton, op. cit., p. 201.)

3. See p. 284–.

4. Re: the Hoover allegation, see p. 314. In a 1996 interview former FBI Assistant Director Cartha DeLoach said Nixon's plane was not bugged in 1968. "Johnson did not order any such thing," he maintained, "and from the standpoint of electronics it was not possible to get anything from a bug on a plane." The surveillance Johnson did demand, DeLoach said, had been limited to coverage of the South Vietnamese Embassy and of Anna Chennault and to followup checks on calls made by the Agnew entourage at Albuquerque. Why, then, would Hoover have told Nixon his plane was bugged by Johnson? DeLoach claimed in his 1995 memoir that the director had merely "embellished" the facts and he added that he later learned that Nixon himself knew the charge was false. In fact, the tapes reveal that Haldeman, informed that the only surveillance the FBI had undertaken against the Republican campaign was to check phone records, informed Nixon of that fact. The next step, he suggested, was to "distort" the issue, and Nixon agreed with him. Until the end of his life Nixon, however, spoke as though he believed his plane had been bugged. (DeLoach: ints. of DeLoach 1996, shared with the author by Gus Russo, DeLoach, op. cit., p. 407; Haldeman discovered: WHT, March 22, 1973, conv. no. 422-020, WSPF, NA; RN to end of life: Crowley, *Off the Record*, op. cit., p. 17.)

5. See p. 297–. In old age, according to a former National Archives specialist, Nixon went out of his way to block the release of records on the subject. Key phrases from the Haldeman diary entry on the Johnson matter were the only passages censored under the national security rubric when *The Haldeman Diaries* were published in 1994. The full text was released only in 1999, while this book was being written. (Archives specialist: "Watergate's Final Victim: A Journey Through Archival Purgatory & Hell," by Maarja Krusten, updated version of draft supplied to NA and attorneys in civil case 92-662-NHJ, supplied to the author by Ms. Krusten; censored: Jan. 12, 1973, entry, HD, p. 567, and see Stephen Ambrose, Introduction, HD, p. 11.)

6. There has been an effort to discredit Dean in recent years, notably in the 1991 book *Silent Coup*, by Len Colodny and Robert Gettlin. The authors' theory was that Dean was personally responsible not only for ordering the DNC break-ins but also for the cover-up, including the attempt to use the CIA to prevent further FBI investigation. The authors asserted, too, that Dean had a special interest in "salacious political material" and ascribed to him a personal motive for promoting the break-in that led to the Watergate arrests. Dean and his wife, Maureen, sued the authors and publisher of *Silent Coup* for libel in a case that has been settled. A separate case brought by the Deans against Gordon Liddy was dismissed. The Senate Watergate Committee chief counsel Sam Dash, and Richard Ben-Veniste, assistant special prosecutor to the Watergate Task Force, both said in interviews for this book that they believed Dean's original testimony remains as credible today on all principal points as it was in 1973. Dean's memory was stunningly corroborated by the Nixon tapes. (1991 book: Len Colodny and Robert Gettlin, *Silent Coup*, New York; St. Martin's Press, 1991; Dean suits: *Tampa Tribune*, Feb. 25, 1998, Sept. 28, 1999; int. Kerrie Hook; Dean testimony credible: ints. Sam Dash and Richard Ben-Veniste.)

7. The claim that Nixon made disparaging remarks about returning American POWs comes from the book *Inside the White House* by former longtime *Washington Post* reporter Ronald Kessler, citing an unnamed former Secret Service agent. Secret Service agents more often than

not request anonymity, and the author's conversations with Kessler led him to believe the information was authentic. (Ronald Kessler, *Inside the White House*, New York: Pocket, 1995, p. 64; int. and corr. Ronald Kessler.)

8. When Ehrlichman referred to possible impeachment, the tape of April 25, 1973 indicates, Nixon merely said repeatedly: "That's right." Ehrlichman wrote in his memoirs: "The tapes show that after I left the room, Nixon dramatically recoiled from my remark. I guess that was the first time anyone used the word 'impeachment' in Nixon's presence." The author was unable to find a reference in the taped dialogue at which the president might have "recoiled." ("The tapes show": Ehrlichman, op. cit., p. 353; "That's right": WHT, Apr. 25, 1973, conv. 430-004, WSPF, NA, p. 27.)

9. Andrew Johnson was impeached in 1868 for violating the Tenure of Office Act. He was acquitted by the Senate.

10. A former member of the Executive Protection Service, the uniformed branch of the Secret Service, told the author that the president's tapes were in fact insecure, that duplicate copies existed. The Secret Service had its own microphone, in multiple White House locations, as part of the protection system, and these made Nixon's privacy additionally vulnerable. Former FBI Assistant Director William Sullivan, moreover, said in 1977 that senior FBI officials had long been aware Nixon was taping his conversations. Some Secret Service agents involved with the taping were also former FBI agents, and Hoover aides were able to gain access to the tapes. Some, Sullivan said, even borrowed them on occasion to play Nixon's conversational faux pas at parties. If these assertions are correct, the recording system was never the top secret installation most sources have always assumed—with potential ramifications for the Watergate story. (Int. former EPS officer, who has requested anonymity: re: Sullivan, see Summers, *Official & Confidential*, op. cit., p. 407–.)

11. The author was unable to question Dr. Hutschnecker on this point. While he had been astonishingly articulate when first interviewed, at age ninety-seven, he lost the power of speech after a subsequent accident.

12. Russell had initially been hospitalized on May 18, 1973, shortly after writing to the Senate Watergate Committee to deny having any information that would help the investigation and three hours before James McCord began testifying. Russell was released from the hospital in June, but died on July 2 of what the death certificate described as "acute coronary occlusion." There was no autopsy. Russell's claim that he had been poisoned was made to his daughter shortly before his death. More intriguing than the manner of his death, for this author, is the fact that in the months between the Watergate arrests and his death Russell had far more money than usual. He made two bank deposits during that period, one for $4,750 and a second for $20,895. William Birely, Nixon's stockbroker friend (see pp. 409 and 527 n. 19) had lent him a pleasant apartment and a car after Watergate and helped him invest his recent financial windfalls. Birely and McCord, who had continued to employ Russell, both attended his funeral. (Illness, death: Hougan, *Agenda*, op. cit., p. 306–; death certificate: in Jim Hougan Collection; Russell money: Best study is memo "Lou Russell Funds," John Williams memo to Gordon Liddy, Oct. 22, 1996, seen by author; Birely, funeral: int. of William Birely by Jim Hougan, Hougan Collection; McCord, funeral: Hougan, *Agenda*, op. cit., p. 239.)

13. Cox had been solicitor general during the Kennedy administration, but he was reportedly nonpartisan "to the point of prickliness" during the Watergate affair. His biographer points out that the Watergate scandal involved both pro- and anti-Nixon people with links to former Democratic administrations (Ken Gormley, *Archibald Cox, Conscience of a Nation*, Reading, Mass.: Perseus Books, 1997, pp. 246, 266–.)

14. See p. 250–.

15. All, including Admiral Moorer, agreed that Nixon was not present at the meeting that night. Moorer and CIA Director Colby have maintained that messages from the president were relayed to the meeting by Kissinger. Helmut Sonnenfeldt, on the National Security Council staff, has said: "Nixon didn't participate in most of these discussions and approved the recommendations early in the morning of the following day. I have always felt that decisions were made on the issues at hand rather than in terms of the President's own personal considerations. That is perhaps a more dramatic example of the kind of problem that we had to deal with in the declining phase of the Nixon presidency." (Moorer, Colby: Strober, eds., op. cit., p. 156–; Sonnenfeldt: ibid., and Miller Center, eds., op. cit., p. 325.)

16. Speechwriter Raymond Price, who was present at the dinner, has denied Nixon was drunk. (eds. Strober, *Nixon*, op. cit., p. 494; Price, op. cit., p. 94–.)

17. Reports of heavy drinking by Pat Nixon, first published in Woodward and Bernstein's *Final Days*, aroused controversy. Her press aide, Helen McCain Smith, insisted that "liquor was never a problem." In an article she wrote in response to *Final Days*, Julie Nixon emphasized how busy her mother was, "hardly the schedule of a reclusive heavy drinker...." Helen Thomas, the veteran White House correspondent, who quoted the First Lady as claiming she

did not drink or smoke, believed she simply avoided doing so in public. As cited earlier, one former Secret Service agent said she was at stages "almost an alcoholic," so much so that friends arranged counseling. Former Secret Service agent Marty Venker, who was on the Nixon detail after the resignation, thought "she was more of a drinker than him at that stage." The columnist Nick Thimmesch, who had once been a Nixon aide, wrote in 1979: "The face she showed to the world was never quite the whole picture. . . . In private she enjoys her martinis or margaritas. She smokes, swears . . . rarely attends church services. . . ." (*Final Days*: Woodward and Bernstein, op. cit., p. 172–; "never": UPI, June 13, 1976; Julie comments: *Newsweek,* May 24, 1976; Thomas: *Dateline,* op. cit., p. 160; "almost alcoholic": Kessler, op. cit., p. 41; int., Ron Kessler; "she was more": int. Marty Venker; Thimmesch: *McCall's,* Apr. 1979.)

Chapter 33

1. Hillary Rodham, then just out of law school, had been recommended to Judiciary Committee Special Counsel John Doar by her former professor at Yale, Burke Marshall. Marshall had also recommended her husband-to-be, future President Bill Clinton, but he turned the committee job down. He was already planning to run for public office in Arkansas, where Nixon had a major following, and reportedly feared being identified with the impeachment. (Zeifman, op. cit., p. 11–; David Maraniss, *First in His Class,* New York: Simon & Schuster, 1995, p. 297.)

2. As a legal technique, naming Nixon as an unindicted coconspirator meant that his conversations could be used in evidence against his former aides. Psychologically, in this case, it had far greater significance.

3. Speechwriter Ray Price, at a dinner in California with Nixon on July 21, observed Kissinger's deputy General Brent Scowcroft shuttling between Nixon, at the table, and a telephone. He thought Nixon "for that brief moment . . . again in his element." Kissinger, however, gives an impression of a president paying less than sufficient attention. (Price, op. cit., p. 312.)

4. See p. 432.

5. The author has used Kissinger's dating of this discussion between the secretary and Haig. In his memoirs Haig said their first such conversation took place not at San Clemente but later, on July 31, in Washington. While Kissinger also recalled a discussion that day, he indicated it was the second time the subject was seriously broached. (Haig, op. cit., p. 477; Kissinger, *Upheaval,* op. cit., pp. 1196–, 1198.)

6. In her biography of her mother, Julie said Cox was opposed to resignation at the family meeting on August 2. In his memoirs Nixon said his son-in-law remained opposed after that date. Woodward and Bernstein's account, in *Final Days,* which the author has used here, is irreconcilable with the Nixon family accounts. Although it is also unattributed—the book has no source notes—the author here relies on a contact with former Senator Griffin, who confirmed the calls from Cox took place, and on conversations with both Woodward and with Bernstein. (*MEM,* pp. 1060, 1062, 1072; *PAT,* p. 420; Woodward and Bernstein, *Final Days,* op. cit., p. viii; Griffin in 2000: research of Rebecca John, for BBC/History Channel.)

7. Schlesinger told the author he thought the conversation with Laitin took place not on the phone but in his office. Both agreed it took place in the spring, between April and June, 1974.

8. See p. 463, for the December 1973 Nixon meeting with the Joint Chiefs.

9. See earlier references to General Cushman. The general served in the marines in World War II, was assigned to the CIA from 1949 to 1951, and to Nixon as vice president from early 1957. Nixon named him deputy director of the CIA in 1969. He remained at the Agency until his appointment as Marine Corps commandant in December 1971. Although witnesses differed on details, it was established that Cushman responded to Howard Hunt's request for CIA assistance in 1971. The agency provided Hunt and Liddy with false identity papers, disguises, and a miniature camera, all of which they used in the burglary operation against the office of Ellsberg's psychiatrist. (For a brief summary, see Schoenebaum, ed., op. cit., p. 158–; Wise, *Police State,* op. cit., p. 250–.)

10. Toll testified under oath to having seen such orders at a closed session of the Senate Select Committee on P.O.W./M.I.A. Affairs on June 26, 1992. Theodore White, a man with excellent access to sources, wrote that at the time of the resignation "by order of Defense Secretary Schlesinger, all military commands had been warned to accept no direct orders either from the White House or from any source without the counter-signature of the Defense Secretary himself." Advised of Toll's statement, Schlesinger told the author he could see how Toll might have seen an order along the lines described in the final days of the presidency—although it would more likely have barred taking orders from "the White House" without checking, rather than specifically from "the president." There would not, he thought, have been an order to disobey the president, who was, after all, the Commander in Chief. Dr. Schlesinger was surprised, however, by Toll's claim to have seen earlier, similar orders relating to times when Nixon was

allegedly drunk. "On that," he said, "you would have to ask not people in the military chain of command, but White House personnel." (Toll testified: Committee Classified Testimony of Barry Toll, U.S. Senate Select Committee on P.O.W./M.I.A. Affairs, June 26, 1992, provided to author; "by order": White, *Breach of Faith,* op. cit., p. 22–; Schlesinger on Toll: int. James Schlesinger.)

11. Schlesinger's actions on the eve of the resignation became public after he discussed them with Pentagon reporters over lunch two weeks later. His comments were "not for attribution" but were only thinly veiled when published. President Ford later wrote in his memoirs that "he had to admonish" Schlesinger for having speculated on such a matter to the press, which he deemed unfair to the armed forces. Alexander Haig said in a 1997 interview that Schlesinger's action had been "wrong . . . outrageous." Nixon, for his part, in 1984 dismissed as "incredible" the notion that he might have used U.S. troops to retain power. (Schlesinger comments: *WP,* and *Chicago Sun-Times,* Aug. 24, 1974; "had to admonish": Ford, op. cit., p. 332; "outrageous": int. Alexander Haig; "incredible": transcript, int. Richard Nixon, "The American Parade," CBS TV, Apr. 10, 1984.)

12. Haig stated within weeks of the resignation that he had never worried about possible military intervention. "The danger," he said, "was from outside forces, that from so much frustration somebody would take events into his own hands and use extraconstitutional means or some distortion of the 25th Amendment." He later called the end of the presidency "one of the most dangerous periods of American history" and said lawful change was "not a foregone conclusion at the time." (*Time,* Sept. 30, 1974; *Newsweek,* July 16, 1979 and see Woodward and Bernstein, *The Final Days,* op. cit., p. 425, re: Nixon refusal to be "forced out by some legislative coup.")

13. See references to Nixon and Theodore Roosevelt's "man in the arena" speech at pp. 20, 169.

A Note on Sources

- Where an interview "by the author" is indicated in the text, or as "int." in the Source Notes, this refers to interviews done either by the author himself, his wife and colleague Robbyn Swan, or one of the research team who worked on the book.
- Recordings of White House conversations (designated in the Source Notes as "WHT") are often of poor quality. Where the author was concerned that there might be confusion as to what was said, a researcher has monitored tape extracts to check the accuracy of available transcripts.
- The conversion of monetary sums to their equivalent at today's values has in all cases been made in consultation with Rob Grunewald of the Federal Reserve Bank in Minneapolis, which provides such a service.

Source Notes

See list of abbreviations on pages 609–610.

Prologue

Graham/Walker: Int. Ronald Walker.

death: *NYT, Newsday, WP,* Apr. 24, 1994.

RN "specified": *HD,* p. 151.

"instructed": *WP,* Apr. 28, 1994.

"planted": *NYT,* Apr. 27, 1994.

"Air Force One": BBN wire report, Apr. 26, 1994.

"42,000": *LAT,* Apr. 28, 1994.

Ford: *New Leader,* May 9–23, 1994.

funeral: *NYT, LAT, WP, Chicago Sun-Times,* Apr. 28, 1994.

Nixonian faithful: (Walker) *NYT,* Apr. 28, 1994; int. Ron Ziegler; int. Peter Flanigan; int. Len Garment; (Walters) *NYT,* Apr. 28, 1994.

poll: Durham (NC) *Herald-Sun,* May 4, 1994.

Hiss: *Newsday,* Apr. 24, 1994.

Maheu: int. Robert Maheu and Robert Maheu, *Next to Hughes,* New York: HarperCollins, 1992, pp. 42–, 79–.

RN denied: In *Supplementary Detailed Staff Reports on Forgein and Military Intelligence,* U.S. Sen. Select Cttee. to Study Gov. Operations with Respect to Intelligence Activities, 94th Cong., 2nd sess., FR, Vol. IV, p. 157–.

violence: Reported and sourced in later chapters.

Agnew: ("feared") Spiro Agnew, *Go Quietly . . . Or Else,* New York: William Morrow, 1980, p. 190; (never spoke) *NYT,* Apr. 28, 1994.

"menacing": *LAT,* Apr. 28, 1994.

"prisoner of war": int. Sam Dash.

Saluted: *New Republic,* May 23, 1994.

Hunt comment: int. Howard Hunt.

McCord believes: James McCord, Jr., *A Piece of Tape, The Watergate Story: Fact or Fiction,* Rockville, MD: Washington Media Services, 1974, p. 259.

Ehrlichman: ("duped") *Newsweek,* Aug. 26, 1974, p. 19; (never spoke) int. John Ehrlichman; (Haldeman/Ehrlichman respect) int. John Ehrlichman in eds. staff at the Miller Center, University of Virginia, *The Nixon Presidency: Twenty-two Intimate Perspectives of Richard M. Nixon,* Lanham, MD: University Press of America, 1987, p. 139; H. R. Haldeman with Joseph DiMona, *The Ends of Power,* New York: Times Books, 1978, p. 72.

"kick-em": *NM,* p. 11.

Dean: ("evil") *NM,* p. 334; (lawsuit) *Maureen K. Dean and John W. Dean v. St. Martin's Press, Inc.,* et al., California Superior Court, Jan. 29, 1992; (book) Len Colodny and Robert Gettlin, *Silent Coup, The Removal of a President,* New York: St. Martin's Press, 1992.

Kalmbach: (vast sums) *NM,* p. 109–; (ambassadorships) ibid., p. 134; (present) ibid., p. 160; (phony names) ibid., p. 251 and cf. Bobby Baker, *Wheeling and Dealing,* New York: Norton, 1978.

Alzheimer's: int. Robert King.

"intentionally": *Newsday,* Jan. 13, 1995 and memo, Jan. 10. 1974, Woods files, NA release Feb. 16, 1995.

Rebozo/hospital: int. Sloan McCrae.

obstructed: E, FR, pp. 931, 1071.

Liu: Anthony Summers, *Official & Confidential, The Secret Life of J. Edgar Hoover,* New York: Putnam, 1993, p. 371–; (sued) *LAT,* Sept. 18, 1976; (cemetery) int. Marianna Liu.

Khashoggi: int. Adnan Khashoggi; int. Pierre Salinger; Anthony Sampson, *The Arms Bazaar,* New York: Viking, 1977, p. 188, *WP,* June 27, 1976.

"peacemaker": *LAT,* Apr. 28, 1994.

inaugural: Alexander Haig, Jr., *Inner Circles, How America Changed the World,* New York: Warner, 1992, p. 181.

Vietnam: (dead) ed. Spencer Tucker, *Encyclopedia of the Vietnam War,* Chicago: Ivan Dee, 1995, p. 1093; ("peace with honor") *AMIII,* citing Public Papers of the Presidents, 1973, p. 55–.

suspicion 1968: William Bundy, *Tangled Web, The Making of Foreign Policy in the Nixon Presidency,* New York: Hill & Wang, 1998, p. 35–; (Chennault) ints. Anna Chennault.

"Pat": Frank Gannon int. of RN, "The Real Richard Nixon," Part 2 (videotape), CPM 1374.

Other memories: reported and sourced in later chapters.

broke down: Monica Crowley, *Nixon in Winter,* New York: Random House, 1998, p. 392.

Hutschnecker: ints. Dr. Arnold Hutschnecker.

Haldeman: Haldeman with DiMona, op. cit., p. 62.

small episodes/serious implications: reported and sourced in later chapters.

Hutschnecker: (urging) *FB,* p. 332; (concern) Drew Pearson; *WP,* Nov. 20, 1968.

Kissinger confided: letter, Fawn Brodie to Henry Kissinger, Jan. 6, 1977, comment can be dated to summer 1968 in int. of Bob Woodward by FB, FBP.

"Mitty": Henry Kissinger, *Years of Upheaval,* Boston: Little, Brown, 1982, p. 1182–.

Chapter 1

"He belongs": FB, p. 54.

RN Sept. 1919: int. Mary George Skidmore in Renée Schulte, ed., *The Young Nixon, An Oral Inquiry,* California State University, Fullerton Oral History Program, Richard M. Nixon Project, 1978, p. 78.

Sears: int. John Sears.

George: int. Mary George Skidmore in ed. Schulte, op. cit., pp. 78, 81, 84.

tears/quavering: Pat, p. 427, Stephen M. Bauer, *At Ease in the White House,* New York: Birch Lane Press, 1991, p. 156.

farewell: *Time,* Aug. 19, 1974, p. 15; *WP,* Aug. 10, 1974.

bar exam: Richard Gardner, Richard Nixon, *The Story of a Fighting Quaker,* unpub. ms., Whittier College Library, p. 86; *AM1,* p. 84.

oil: int. Dr. Paul Smith, president emeritus of Whittier College and professor of RN, in ed. Schulte, op. cit., p. 147; FB, p. 30–.

TB: (Harold) *AM1,* p. 50; (Arthur) *AM1,* p. 41 and see detail in this chapter.

Buzhardt: Bob Woodward and Carl Bernstein, *The Final Days,* New York: Avon, 1976, pp. 78, 92; FB, p. 520, n. 17 for chapter 2.

Hiss: *Psychology Today,* Oct. 1974, p. 116.

1968 speech: *NYT,* Aug. 9, 1968.

met Pat: (Athletes) *Public Papers of the President,* 1969–1974, Washington, D.C.: U.S. Government Printing Office, 1971–75, citing National Football Foundation speech, Dec. 9, 1969; (RN) Bela Kornitzer, *The Real Nixon,* Chicago: Rand McNally, 1960, p. 134; *MEM,* p. 23.

French: Tad Szulc, *The Illusion of Peace, Foreign Policy in the Nixon Years,* New York: Viking, 1978, p. 766; (History) MO, p. 123.

chopsticks: Bruce Oudes, ed., *From: The President, Richard Nixon's Secret Files,* New York: Harper & Row, 1989, p. 383.

Kissinger: Henry Kissinger, *White House Years,* Boston: Little, Brown, 1979, p. 505.

candor: Fred Emery, *Watergate, The Corruption and Fall of Richard Nixon,* New York: Times Books, 1994, p. 414, but see *MEM,* p. 948.

"blameless": *AOP,* p. 476.

Scott: *NYT,* Dec. 10, 1974; James D. Barber, *Political Science Quarterly,* II. 4, p. 597.

Goldwater: ("danger") *Watergate, The Secret Story,* CBS, June 17, 1992; (losing mind) Robert A. Goldberg, *Barry Goldwater,* New Haven, CT: Yale University Press, 1995, pp. 278–.

Tricia: *Ladies' Home Journal,* March 1974, p. 132.

Sears: int. John Sears; *LAT,* Apr. 24, 1994.

Garment: *Burden of Proof,* CNN, Feb. 28, 1997; Leonard Garment, *Crazy Rhythm,* New York: Times Books, 1997, p. 115; int. Leonard Garment.

"dissembling": *SF Chronicle,* Oct. 28, 1982, citing *Good Morning America,* ABC-TV.

Kissinger: Kissinger, *White House Years,* op. cit., p. 1094.

Ehrlichman: Paul Theroux, *Sunrise with Seamonsters,* New York: Penguin, 1985, p. 177.

Kornitzer: (secretary) int. Evlyn Dorn by FB, FBP.

mother: (oil) *Good Housekeeping,* June 1960, p. 54–; (photo) Kornitzer, op. cit., p. 90; ("campaign") *LAT,* Feb. 25, 1960.

pies: David Wise, *The Politics of Lying,* New York:Random House, 1973, p. 328.

aides struck: John Ehrlichman, *Witness to Power,* New York: Pocket Books, 1982, p. 147; Kissinger, *Upheaval,* op. cit., p. 1183.

"mother taught me": Crowley, *Winter,* op. cit., p. 362.

Hannah origins: *MO,* p. 24–.

clannish: ibid., p. 25.

meets Frank: ibid., p. 36.

Frank origin: ibid., p. 32.

"below her station": int. Dr. Paul Smith in ed. Schulte, op. cit., p. 151.

Frank and women: Edwin Hoyt, *The Nixons, An American Family,* New York: Random House, 1972, p. 183; Jessamyn West, *Hide and Seek,* New York: Harcourt Brace Jovanovich, 1973, p. 239–; *FB,* p. 39.

"bad girl": *MO,* p. 37; int. Dr. Smith, *supra.,* p. 151.

kings: *JA,* p. 11.

Nixon name: Kornitzer, op. cit., p. 26.

circumstances: ("hunger") int. John Lindsay by FB, FBP; ("poor") Hoyt, op. cit., p. 182; (cornmeal) Joseph Dmohowski, "From a Common Ground, The Quaker Heritage of Jessamyn West and Richard Nixon," *California History,* Fall 1994, p. 222; (Alsop) Stewart Alsop, *Nixon and Rockefeller,* New York: Doubleday, 1960, p. 185; (advance) *JA,* p. 10; (lemons) *MO,* p. 65–; (pony) Theodore White, *The Making of the President 1960,* New York: Atheneum, 1960, p. 302; int. Hugh Sidey in eds. Miller Center, op. cit., p. 306; (RN on train) ibid., Wise, *Politics,* op. cit., p. 329; (mother and train) Kornitzer, op. cit., p. 49; (tractor/car) *MO,* p. 55; (Hannah did return) ibid., pp. 57, 67; (well-to-do) ibid., p. 55; ($5,000) ibid., p. 67.

Whittier house: ibid., p. 71.

piano: ibid., p. 61; (at three) *Legacy, Journal of the Nixon Library and Birthplace Foundation,* Spring 1997, p. 4.

"psychohistory": see David Abrahamsen, M.D., FB; Eli S. Chesen, M.D., Bruce Mazlish, Vamik Volkan, et al., and Arthur Woodstone cited in full in bibliography.

fighter: *MEM,* pp. 12, 6.

punishments: (Frank beaten) *MO,* p. 33; (dodged) ibid., pp. 65, 194; ("mother never") Barber, op. cit., p. 408; (screams/playmates) *MO,* p. 64–; ("animal") Abrahamsen, op. cit., p. 91; (canal) int. Jessamyn West by FBP, *FB,* p. 40.

"cruel": int. Jessamyn West, *supra.*

"brusque": *MEM,* p. 7.

Hutschnecker: int. Dr. Arnold Hutschnecker by *FB,* FBP.

mother: ("gentlest") Alsop, op. cit., p. 185; ("kind") int. Blanche McClure in ed. Schulte, op. cit., p. 8; ("throttle") *JA,* p. 14; ("holy, holy") int. Helene Drown by *FB,* FBP; ("cranky") *FB,* p. 54; ("steel") Richard Arena cited at *MO,* p. 98, but see Abrahamsen, op. cit., p. 89; (paddling) *Good Housekeeping,* June 1960; (neighbor) int. Mrs. Cecil Pickering in ed. Schulte, op. cit., p. 21; (switch) *MO,* p. 62, *FB,* p. 59–; (Sears) int. John Sears, *Richard M. Nixon, A Self-Portrait,* 1968 film script, FBP.

Arthur: (cigarettes) ibid., p. 5, Kornitzer, op. cit., p. 64; (hoping for daughter) ibid., p. 62–; (kiss) ibid., p. 65; *JA,* p. 25.

mother: (Bergholz) Gerald and Deborah Strober, *Nixon, An Oral History of His Presidency,* New York: HarperCollins, 1994, p. 38; (kissing) *JA,* p. 15; ("never heard") Richard Nixon, *In the Arena,* New York: Pocket Books, 1990, p. 94; ("projected") *JA,* p. 15.

Hutschnecker: int. Dr. Arnold Hutschnecker, Nov. 7, 1976 by *FB,* FBP.

Arthur death: (rock) Gardner, op. cit., p. 23; *FB,* p. 89; Edward Nixon to author, May 8, 1996; int. Donald Nixon, Jr., and other relatives; *MO,* p. 881 n.84; (certificate) *FB,* p. 89; (root cause) *MEM,* p. 10; Nixon, *Arena,* op. cit., p. 192; (nightmare) *MO,* p. 43–; ("staring") *FB,* p. 90; (cried) *MEM,* p. 10.

Harold: Abrahamsen, op. cit., p. 87; *MO,* p. 87–; (TB) ibid., p. 94–; (raw milk) *JA,* p. 23; (Richard/Don sick) ibid., pp. 23, 27; ("catastrophic") RN to Pat Buchanan, Feb. 10, 1971, NP, NA; (sold land) int. Harry Schuyler in ed. Schulte, op. cit., p. 251.

tough period: *MO,* p. 98–, *Richard M. Nixon, A Self-Portrait,* 1968 film script, FBP, p. 6; (shirts/breath) *Good Housekeeping,* June 1960; (meat) int. Merle West and see *Good House-keeping,* June 1960; (Arizona) *MO,* p. 94–; (afraid) ibid., p. 96; (carnival) *FB,* p. 97; (conspired) *AM1,* p. 44; (wiretap) *MO,* p. 97.

Harold death: ("guilt") Henry Lawton, "Milhous Rising," *Journal of Psychohistory,* Spring 1979, p. 533; ("Why?") Jessamyn West, *Double Discovery,* New York: Harcourt Brace Jovanovich, 1980, p. 138; (punishment) *MO,* p. 44, *JA,* p. 48; ("God's decision") Kornitzer, op. cit., p. 60.

religion: (two churches) unpub. essay by John Rothmann, JFRP; int. Jane Milhous Beeson in ed. Schulte, op. cit., p. 62–; (Quaker background) *Encyclopedia Brittanica,* Charles Henderson, *The Nixon Theology,* New York: Harper & Row, 1972; *MO,* pp. 23–, 27; int. Edward Nixon; ("four times") Nixon, *Arena,* op. cit., p. 95; (quiet) *MO,* p. 86; (closet) ibid., p. 31; *JA,* p. 338; (her life) int. Jane Beeson in ed. Schulte, op. cit., p. 63; ("firebrand") Jessamyn West, "Four Years, For What?," *Whittier College Bulletin,* May 1954; (cheeks) West, *Hide and Seek,* op. cit., p. 239–; ("reawakening") *AM1,* p. 41; (devotees) *NYT,* Jan. 26, 1969; (RN rethought) *JA,* p. 54–; (Trohan) int. Walter Trohan; (Peale) Rothmann unpub. essay, *supra.;* ("backslider") Marshall Frady, *Billy Graham,* Boston: Little, Brown, 1979, p. 446; (Catholicism) int. John Ehrlichman, int. John Ehrlichman in eds. Miller Center, op. cit., p. 135, Colson cited in *WP,* Apr. 24, 1994, p. C1 and Douglas Hallet article in *NYT* Magazine, Oct. 20, 1974; (anathema) *MO,* p. 23; (stopped holding) Marianne Means, Boston *Herald-American,* Sept. 26, 1973, John Osborne in *New York,* Apr. 21, 1975; ("guidance") Michael Medved, *The Shadow Presidents,* New York: Times Books, 1979, p. 326; (Colson) Charles Colson, *Born Again,* New York: Bantam, 1977, p. 203; (Lincoln table) *SF Chronicle,* May 26, 1977; (Korff) int. Baruch Korff and Baruch Korff, *The President and I,* Providence, RI: Korff Foundation, 1995, p. 74; ("peace") ibid., p. 167; ("Life of Christ") UPI, Mar. 19, 1975; *MEM,* p. 78; (Bible) int. WSPF attorney; (old age) Crowley, *Winter,* op. cit., p. 339–; ("I believe") *This Week* magazine, Sept. 18, 1960; (repudiate) int. Dr. Paul Smith in ed. Schulte, op. cit., p. 177; Henderson, op. cit., p. 32–; *FB,* p. 62; int. Rev. Eugene Coffin, East Whittier Friends Church by *FB,* FBP; (RN's "great trouble") int. Walter Trohan; ("victim") int. Dr. Arnold Hutschnecker.

Chapter 2

"One man may . . .": Richard Nixon, *Six Crises,* New York: Doubleday, 1962, p. xvi.

Whittier presidency: *MO,* p. 151–.

jail: Charles Elliott, *Whittier College,* Redondo Beach, CA: Legends Press, 1986, p. 157–.

privy: Ralph de Toledano, *One Man Alone, Richard Nixon,* New York: Funk & Wagnall, 1969, p. 26; *JA,* p. 37–.

schooling: (teacher) int. Mary George Skidmore in ed. Schulte, op. cit., p. 78; ("My mother") Nixon, *Arena,* op. cit., p. 103; (light) *FB,* p. 54; ("Richard always"); *MO,* p. 61; (good grades) Nixon, *Arena,* op. cit., p. 102, *MO,* p. 60, int. Mary George Skidmore in ed. Schulte, op. cit., p. 78; (fifth grade) *JA,* p. 23; (Carnegie/music) ibid., p. 24; *AMI,* p. 39–, int. Jane Milhous Beeson in ed. Schulte, op. cit., p. 57; (woodwork) Kornitzer, op. cit., p. 54; (klutz) *AMI,* p. 43, int. John Ehrlichman; (steady A) *JA,* p. 23; *MO,* p. 90; Nixon, *Arena,* op. cit., p. 104; (award) *JA,* p. 29, *MO,* p. 110; (offered scholarship) int. Dr. Paul Smith in ed. Schulte, op. cit., p. 149–; (Richard was needed) *MO,* p. 110, *JA,* p. 31; (scholarship) unpub. Whittier College study by John Rothmann, JFRP; Hoyt, op. cit., p. 195.

society: (Franklins) *MO* p. 117–; (Orthogonians) *FB,* p. 114, *AMI,* p. 60; ("two left feet") Kansas City *Star,* Nov. 3, 1955; (motto) *FB,* p. 114; (song) Elliott, op. cit., p. 150; (raw flesh) *FB,* p. 115; *JA,* p. 35; (injured) *MO,* p. 120; ("have-nots") "The Mystery of Richard Nixon" *Saturday Evening Post,* July 12, 1958.

family fortunes: (open-necked shirts) *JA,* p. 33; (West) *MO.* p. 137–; (Welch) ints. Ola Florence Welch Jobe; (Smith) int. Dr. Paul Smith in ed. Schulte, op. cit., p. 151.

place in society: (Bassett) int. James Bassett by *FB,* FBP; ("My dad") Carl Solberg, *Hubert Humphrey,* NY: Norton, 1984, p. 313; ("not children") Garment, op. cit., p. 69; ("working class") Herbert Parmet, *Richard Nixon and His America,* Boston: Little, Brown, 1990, p. 23; (destroy establishment) Douglas Hallett article, *New York,* Oct. 20, 1974; (Bork) *Bar Report,* Dec./Jan. 1998, p. 8; ("start sucking") WHT, Sept. 15, 1972, conv. no. 779–002, p. 30; ("screw the universities") Elmo Zumwalt, Jr., *On Watch,* Arlington, VA: Adm. Zumwalt & Assoc. Inc.,1976, p. 419; ("All money stops") eds. Strober, *Nixon,* op. cit., p. 83, int. John Ehrlichman in eds. Miller Center, op. cit., p. 129, and see *Time,* Apr. 25, 1988, p. 56; (Bok) int. Alexander Butterfield in eds. Strober, *Nixon,* op. cit., p. 50; (Clawson) *WP,* Aug. 9, 1979, (clubs) *Good Housekeeping,* July 1968; (Watts) int. William Watts.

RN at college: (liberal) Earl Mazo, *Richard Nixon, A Political and Personal Portrait,* New York: Harper, 1959, p. 26; *MO,* p. 150; (black man) Mazo, op. cit., p. 23; (dynamo) Alsop, op. cit., p. 220; ("Dick lived") ibid., p. 219; ("not . . . popular") ibid., p. 218; ("stuck-up"/"cock-sure-ness") ibid., p. 135, Kornitzer, op. cit., p. 100; ("I classified") Philip Blew to FB, 1974, FBP;

("incredible combination") Alsop, op. cit., p. 218; (Tolstoy) *MEM*, p. 15; ("didn't do bad things") Kornitzer, op. cit., p. 108; (acting) Abrahamsen, op. cit., p. 98; ("I taught him") Mazo, op. cit., p. 23; Alsop, op. cit., p. 132–; Henry Spalding, *The Nixon Nobody Knows,* Middle Village, New York: Jonathan David, 1972, p. 121.

debating: (team) *AMl,* p. 68; MO, p. 30; *Good Housekeeping,* June 1960; (Vincent) Theodore White, *Breach of Faith,* London: Jonathan Cape, 1975, p. 58; William Costello, *The Facts About Nixon,* New York: Viking, 1960, p. 23; (Johns) *FB,* p. 81; (Elliott) Abrahamsen, op. cit., p. 111; (others remember) int. Eugene Pumpian-Mindlin by FB, FBP.

Longfellow: *MEM,* p. 13; *Life,* Nov. 6, 1970.

second in class: unpub. Whittier College study by John Rothmann, JFRP.

lawyer ambition: int. Jane Beeson in ed. Schulte, op. cit., p. 55–; Mazo, op. cit., pp. 13, 14.

minister: Kornitzer, op. cit., p. 238; Nixon, *Six Crises,* op. cit., p. 295.

politics: (1920) int. Merle West; Abrahamsen, op. cit., p. 67; ("crooked politicians") Mazo, op. cit., p. 14; (McKinley) *This Week* magazine in *LAT,* Sept. 18, 1960; (Lincoln) Kornitzer, op. cit., p. 40; unpub. Whittier study *supra.;* (LaFollette) ibid., p. 21–; (Wilson) Nixon, *Arena,* op. cit., p. 88; (desk) William Safire, *Before the Fall,* New York: Belmont Tower, 1975, p. 105; Kissinger, *Upheaval,* op. cit., p. 1183.; int. Dr. Paul Smith in ed. Schulte, op. cit., p. 161; (Roosevelt) unpub. Whittier study, *supra.,* Nixon, *Arena.* op. cit., p. xi, *MEM,* p. 109; (teacher prophesied) Kansas City *Star,* Oct. 30, 1955; (father's forecast) int. Harry Schuyler in ed. Schulte, op. cit., p. 257; ("he wanted to go") Alsop, op. cit., p. 222; ("I would like") *JA,* p. 27.

Duke University: ("the proudest day") Laurie Nadel, *The Great Stream of History,* New York: Atheneum, 1991, p. 16; ("I don't believe") Spalding, op. cit., p. 99; (prodigiously) Alsop, op. cit., p. 234; MO, p. 165; (took jobs) ibid., p. 163; int. William King, Duke archivist, Richard M. Nixon Collection, Duke University Archive; (accommodation) Kansas City *Star,* Nov. 4, 1955; Alsop, op. cit., p. 232; (solitary figure) *JA,* p. 69; Alsop, op. cit., p. 237; (cripple) San Antonio *Light,* Nov. 20, 1968; *JA,* p. 69; (racial bias) Alsop, op. cit., pp. 230, 235–; (before dawn) ibid., p. 231; ("shot full") *Life,* Nov. 6, 1970; (special occasions) Alsop, op. cit., pp. 235, 237–; (Morrah) Abrahamsen, op. cit., p. 121; (Fuller) *Life,* Nov. 6, 1970; (Farley) *FB,* p. 127; (graduation) *MEM,* p. 22; MO, p. 181; (Bar Assn.) *Life,* Nov. 6, 1970, Abrahamsen, op. cit., p. 120.

Break-in: Kornitzer, op. cit., p. 120; Hoyt, op. cit., p. 214; *FB,* p. 131; MO, p. 171–; *JA,* p. 71; Abrahamsen, op. cit., p. 118; (newspaper) Charlotte (NC) *Observer,* July 22, 1973; Jack Anderson syndicated column, May 16, 1973; (more sinister?) Duke *Chronicle,* Nov. 18, 1976, Dorothy Marshall to Drew Pearson, citing Prof. Dumont of University of Michigan, DPP; ("finesse") Hoyt, op. cit., p. 214; Kornitzer, op. cit., p. 120; ("There are ways . . .") WHT, Sept. 15, 1972, conv. no. 779-002, p. 3.

Duke disowns: (honorary doctorate) *Newsweek,* Apr. 19, 1954; *SF Chronicle,* Sep. 4, 1981; Durham (NC) *Herald-Sun,* Apr. 24, 1994; *NYT,* Apr. 6, 1954; (Library) *SF Examiner,* Sept. 4–5; AP, Aug. 31, 1981; (petition) Durham (NC) *Herald,* Durham *Sun,* Oct. 31, 1973; (portrait) *SF Examiner,* Sep. 4, 1981.

FBI: RN application form, Apr. 23, 1937, FBI 69-102459-1.

NY lawfirms: Mazo, op. cit., p. 25–; *JA,* p. 76.

Horack: *JA,* p. 76.

Bewley job: MO, p. 182–.

prophesies: (teenager) *JA,* p. 61; (astrologer) Ehrlichman, op. cit., p. 331; int. John Ehrlichman.

Chapter 3

"Sometimes I think . . .": *Life,* Nov. 6, 1970.

RN and girls: (washing-up) Mazo, op. cit., p. 13; Barber, op. cit., p. 402; *Time,* Aug. 25, 1952, p. 13; Abrahamsen, op. cit., p. 59; (garlic) *JA,* p. 23; (". . . hated girls."/roller-coaster)Kornitzer, op. cit., p. 54; ("stuffy") MO, p. 141; ("aloof") Spalding, op. cit., p. 54; ("he didn't know . . .") *Life,* Nov. 6, 1970, p. 60; (". . . wasn't sexy.") MO, p. 142, *FB,* p. 124; (male friends) int. Charles Kendle in Schulte, op. cit., p. 193; Alsop, op. cit., p. 223; (slowest driver) Abrahamsen, op. cit., p. 111.

Ola Welch: (main sources) ints. Ola Florence Welch Jobe; "Whittier '34 Most Likely to Succeed," article by Lael Morgan (friend of Welch), *LAT West* magazine, May 10, 1970; *JA,* p. 58–; MO, pp. 109–, 141–, 159–, et al., *FB,* pp. 108–, 122–; (catcalls) *MEM,* p. 14; ("Would you think . . . ?) *AM1,* p. 38; (A-grade student) MO, p. 141; *JA,* p. 59; *LAT West,* May 10, 1970, p. 34; ("smartest") MO, p. 109; Bruce Mazlish, *In Search of Nixon,* New York: Basic Books, 1972, p. 63; (car) *AM1,* p. 46; (mother professed) *Good Housekeeping,* June 1960; ("stripteaser"/"very normal") MO, pp. 145, 142; ("no hanky-panky") *FB,* p. 123; ("never comfortable") int. Ola Florence Jobe by William Cran, notes supplied to author; (parents disliked) main sources, *supra.,* but see *JA,* p. 60; ("He had never . . .") *FB,* p. 124; MO, p. 159; ("nothing to it") *Good Housekeeping,* June 1960; ("nasty temper") Mazlish, op. cit., p. 63; ("on the string") Mazlish, op. cit., p. 64; (ceased seeing women) Alsop, op. cit., p. 236; *FB,* p. 128; MO,

p. 175; ("You'll never hear") Mazlish, op. cit., p. 64, and cf. *LAT West* magazine, May 10, 1970; (RN silent re. Ola) *FB*, p. 128, see Gardner, Kornitzer, Mazo, de Toledano, ops. cit.; (WH reception) int. John Lindsay by FB, FBP, int Ola Florence Welch Jobe; (memoirs) *MEM*, pp. 14, 18–19; ("broke his heart") int. Hubert Perry; (Harlow) int. Bryce Harlow, Jr.; Wicker, op. cit., p. 652 and int. Bryce Harlow in White Burkett Miller Center, University of Virginia, eds., *The Nixon Presidency*, New York: University Press of America, 1987, p. 9–; (Feb. 2, 1936 letter) *JA*, p. 64; (mother never uttered) Nixon, *Arena*, op. cit., p. 94; ("play-acting") *FB*, p. 123, Abrahamsen, op. cit., p. 107.

audition: (date) *JA*, p. 86; (previous role) *MEM*, p. 23; (colleague) *MO*, p. 204; (roles) ibid., *Saturday Evening Post*, Sept. 6, 1952.

Pat Ryan: ("That night . . .") *MEM*, p. 23; (Cloes) int. Elizabeth Cloes in ed. Schulte, op. cit., p. 236; ("nuts") Mazo, op. cit., p. 31; (birth) birth certificate, filed Apr. 7, 1912, County of White Pine, Nevada; (Rose Bowl) *FB*, p. 147, citing RN speech to National Football Foundation dinner, Dec. 9, 1969, and see Ch. 1 *supra.*; ("silly") *NYT*, Nov. 4, 1952; ("must not permit") *FB*, p. 26; ("near midnight") *PAT*, p. 17; WH bios., June 12, 1969 and Dec. 21, 1971, NA, contrary to physician's information on birth certificate; ("Thelma" in childhood) Artesia (CA) *News*, July 18, 1952; (father/"Pat") Pat cited in *Miami Herald*, Jan. 19, 1969; ("took Pat") *JA*, p. 87; *MEM*, p. 23; *PAT*, p. 34; (Haldeman) *Parade*, Feb. 5, 1995.

Pat background: *PAT*, unless otherwise indicated; (hold-up) Lester David, *The Lonely Lady of San Clemente*, New York: Thomas Crowell, 1978, p. 31; (timing of move to "Pat") *PAT*, p. 34; (married before?) Cheshire, op. cit., p. 110–; *Time*, May 13, 1974.

loan lawsuit: *FB*, pp. 134–, 527; Abrahamsen, op. cit., p. 122–; *MO*, p. 189.

orange juice: *MO*, p. 195–; *JA*, p. 83; int. Evlyn Dorn by FB, FBP.

divorce cases: (open air sex) ibid.; (good-looking girl) Alsop, op. cit., p. 195.

virgin: *JA*, p. 104, citing Lt. Jim Stewart.

dinner invitations: *PAT*, p. 56.

courtship: except where indicated source is *PAT*, which includes the couple's letters; ("insisted") *MO*, p. 218; David, op. cit., p. 51; (brick fireplace) *NYT*, Aug. 10, 1971; (adjoining plots) Traphes Bryant with Frances Spatz Leighton, *Dog Days at the White House*, New York: Macmillan, 1976, p. 247; (no Whittier weekends) *MO*, p. 218; (LA dates) *PAT*, p. 59; David, op. cit., p. 52; (poor dancer) int. Hortense Behrens in ed. Schulte, op. cit., p. 226; (skating) int. Evlyn Dorn by FB, FBP; *Life*, Nov. 6, 1970, p. 64; *JA*, p. 91; (RN Beast) Mazo, op. cit., p. 34; (LA club) *JA*, p. 91; *PAT*, p. 61.

RN and drink: (alcohol ban) *MO*, p. 200, *Saturday Evening Post*, undated, summer 1971, Jean Lippiatt article; (SF bar) *MEM*, p. 18; ("Those parties . . .") Nixon, *Arena*, op. cit., p. 147; (Blew) Blew letter to FB, Dec. 16, 1974, FBP; *MO*, p. 199; (objections to Nixon film) Charles Colson and William Safire in *NYT*, Nov. 27, Dec. 28, 1995; Herb Klein in San Diego *Union-Tribune*, Dec. 19, 1995.

wedding: Pat, p. 69–; *MO*, p. 233.

cruise: C. L. Sulzberger, *The World and Richard Nixon*, New York: Prentice Hall, 1987, p. 26; *PAT*, p. 72; *JA*, p. 94.

Cuba: (gambling) Dennis Eisenberg, Uri Dan, Eli Landau, *Meyer Lansky*, New York: Paddington Press, 1979, p. 227; (Havana as attorney) Mazo, op. cit., p. 35; *MO*, p. 233; Hoyt, op. cit., p. 330; int. Evlyn Dorn by FB, FBP; int. Earl Mazo.

RN in War: (OPA) *MO*, p. 242; (against family wishes) *MEM*, p. 27; *MO*, p. 243–; *Life*, Nov. 6, 1970, p. 64; (pose in uniform) *FB*, p. 165; ("in the foxholes") *MO*, p. 281; ("when the bombs . . .") Alsop, op. cit., p. 143; Spalding, op. cit., p. 137; (could curse) ibid., p. 140.

poker: (since Duke) RN application to FBI, including poker as "recreation," Apr. 23, 1937, FBI 67-102459-1; Alsop, op. cit., p. 144; *JA*, p. 108; *Life*, Nov. 6, 1970, p. 66; Kornitzer, op. cit., p. 147–; Mazo, op. cit., p. 37–; de Toledano, op. cit., p. 40; (1960) Chicago *Sunday Tribune*, Nov. 6, 1960; (in WH) int. Paul Ziffren by FB, FBP; (as VP) Tip O'Neill with William Novak, *Man of the House*, New York: Random House, 1987, p. 157–.

"Pollyanna . . .": *Time*, Oct. 9, 1972.

Chapter 4

"They tried . . .": Margaret Truman, *First Ladies*, New York: Random House, 1995, p. 199–.

RN marriage: (license) *JA*, p. 92; ("Pat never told") ibid., p. 88; ("hundreds of times . . .") *PAT*, p. 83; (hugs in future) Helen Thomas, *Dateline: White House*, New York: Macmillan, 1975, p. 169; int. John Lindsay by FB, FBP; (Dorn) int. Evlyn Dorn by FB, FBP; (Dixon) *FB*, p. 144; (Quakers kiss) int. Mary George Skidmore in ed. Schulte, op. cit., p. 86; ("both were shy") *PAT*, p. 63; (avoided scenes) ibid., p. 57; (Priest) Fr. John Cronin, cited in *Esquire*, July 1994; (clothes scattered) int. Gloria Steinem; ("I . . . don't tell all") *Time*, Aug. 19, 1974; (Mazo) David, op. cit., p. 73–; int. Earl Mazo; (Winchester) Kandy Stroud article, *Ladies' Home Journal*, Mar. 1975; (Dr. Smith) *FB*, p. 141; ("baggage") *FB*, p. 145; (Steinem) int. and corr. Gloria

Steinem; (Stroud) int. Kandy Stroud; (Ehrlichman) int. John Ehrlichman; (Dean) int. John Dean and John Dean, *Lost Honor*, LA: Stratford Press, 1982, p. 22–; (Watts) int. William Watts; (Bork) int. Robert Bork by FB, FBP; (Sidey) int. Hugh Sidey in eds. Miller Center, op. cit., p. 313; ("The moneyed class") *PAT*, p. 47; (Steinem) int. Gloria Steinem, corr. with author, 1998; Steinem in *New York*, Oct. 28, 1968; ("didn't respect him") corr. Gloria Steinem, July 7, 2000.

Pat personality after marriage: (Pierpoint) Robert Pierpoint, *At the White House*, New York: Putnam, 1981, p. 185; ("Coppelia") London *Spectator* article, reprinted in *The New Republic*, Dec. 22, 1958; (Pat claimed) Thomas, op. cit., p. 116 and unid. clip during Soviet visit, 1972, author's collection; (smoked) *PAT*, p. 89; Bauer, op. cit., p. 116; int. Tom Korologos; (lung cancer) *NYT*, June 23, 1993; ("incessantly") J. F. terHorst and Col. Ralph Albertazzie, *The Flying White House*, New York: Coward McCann & Geoghegan, 1979, p. 35; ("I once saw . . .") Thomas, op. cit., p. 160; ("drinking heavily") Woodward and Bernstein, *Final Days*, op. cit., p. 173; denied in *Star*, Apr. 27, 1976; Betty Beale in *SF Sunday Examiner and Chronicle*, May 2, 1976, by Julie Eisenhower in *Newsweek*, May 24, 1976, by Helen M. Smith, *Good Housekeeping*, July 1976, and int. Lucy Winchester; ("PN had a problem") Ronald Kessler, *Inside the White House*, New York: Pocket, 1993, p. 41, and int. Ronald Kessler.

RN and women: (Portnoy's) *HD*, p. 127; (Fleming) Timothy Crouse, *The Boys on the Bus*, New York: Ballantine, 1972, p. 8; ("B-girls") int. Lou Cannon in eds. Miller Center, op. cit., p. 189; Wise, *Politics*, op. cit., p. 330–; Ed Reid, *Mickey Cohen, Mobster*, New York: Pinnacle, 1973, p. 140; (Sears) int. John Sears; ("If you ever . . .") William Safire, *Before the Fall*, New York: Belmont Tower, 1975, p. 19–; ("have him give . . .") *HD*, p. 423; ("trouble finding Henry") Jimmy Breslin, *How the Good Guys Finally Won*, New York: Viking, 1975, p. 66; O'Neill, op. cit., p. 253–; ("built for you, Henry.") *Atlantic Monthly*, May 1982, p. 45; ("Can you imagine . . . ?") int. Hugh Sidey in eds. Miller Center, op. cit., p. 301; (Hutschnecker) ints. Dr. Arnold Hutschnecker and int. Dr. Hutschnecker by FB, Nov. 7, 1976, FBP.

Hannah to DC: int. Jessamyn West, citing her mother, Hannah's sister, by FB, FBP.

Chapter 5

parade for Ike: *Life*, Dec. 13, 1953; Eric Sevareid, *Candidates, 1960*, New York: Basic Books, 1959, p. 130.

letter: *MO*, p. 270–.

no political plans: ("never occurred . . .") Kornitzer, op. cit., p. 151; (never discussed) Mazo, op. cit., p. 34; Earl Mazo,"Is It Worth It?," *Good Housekeeping*, 1959; (speeches) *MO*, pp. 201–, 233; ("We shall realize . . .") *PAT*, p. 68; (President someday) ibid., p. 58; (male friends) *MO*, p. 200.

Voorhis campaign: (Perry) *MO*, p. 270, Kornitzer, op. cit., p. 153–; (peers/press) Jerry Voorhis, *The Strange Case of Richard Milhous Nixon*, New York: Popular Library, 1972, p. 12; (studying Voorhis) int. Evlyn Dorn by FB, FBP; (pads) *MO*, pp. 285, 288, 290; int. Bryce Harlow in eds. Miller Center, op. cit., p. 8; ($580) *MO*, p. 292; ("Hit 'em") int. John Rothmann; (Hoover) *SF Chronicle*, Oct. 14, 1946; ("infiltration") Athan Theoharis, *Beyond the Hiss Case*, Philadelphia: Temple University Press, 1982, p. 80–; (Republican Women) *MO*, p. 326; (Tricia/Pat) *PAT*, pp. 87–, 89; Kornitzer, op. cit., p. 155; (Dixon) int. Tom Dixon and int. FB, FBP, *FB*, p. 178; (RN satisfaction) LA *Examiner*, Nov. 7, 1946; (Chandlers) *Esquire*, Nov. 1977, p. 202–; conv. Pat Bradshaw, citing Buff Chandler; (Hannah . . . never saw) *Good Housekeeping*, June 1960; (stolen pamphlets) *PAT*, p. 90, *Saturday Evening Post*, Sept. 6, 1952; (irons/toasters) Paul Bullock, *Jerry Voorhis: The Idealist as Politician*, New York: Vantage, 1978, p. 277; (false stories) Jerry Voorhis, *Confessions of a Congressman*, New York: Doubleday, 1947, p. 342; *MO*, p. 302; (Voorhis realized) Bullock, op. cit., p. 271fn.; (booed) *MO*, p. 322; (Businessmen/bank admonished) Voorhis, *Confessions*, op. cit., p. 342, NY *Post*, Oct. 19, 1955; (leaflet) *MO*, p. 330; (PAC ploy) Bullock, op. cit., p. 246–; *AMI*, p. 129–; (anonymous calls) Bullock, op. cit., p. 275–, denied at 276; *AMI*, p. 138, but see Gellman, op. cit., p. 84–; ("I suppose . . .") Alsop, op. cit., p. 188; ("The important thing . . .") Bullock, op. cit., p. 280; Greg Mitchell, *Tricky Dick and the Pink Lady*, New York: Random House, 1998, p. 43.

'46 financing: ("We drew . . .") *Saturday Evening Post*, Sept. 6, 1952; (N. claimed) *MEM*, p. 34; ("so broke . . .") *Saturday Evening Post, supra.*; (job back) *MO*, p. 285 but see *New England Journal of History*, Winter '99/Spring '00, Vol. 56, p. 19; (savings intact) Mazo, op. cit., p. 38; Spalding, op. cit., p. 176; *AMI*, p. 136; (Adams) *MO*, pp. 279, 331; (pre-primary financing) *MO*, p. 304; (total spend) *MO*, p. 337, but see *JA*, p. 43; ("typical") *MEM*, p. 42; (Voorhis claimed) Voorhis, *Confessions*, op. cit., p. 331, but see Gellman, op. cit., p. 59–; (Wray) int. Merton Wray in ed. Schulte, op. cit., p. 207; (oil/liquor) *MO*, pp. 257, 261; (Perry) *AMI*, p. 118; (Somebody else) Kornitzer, op. cit., p. 153; (unnamed friend) Hoyt, op. cit., pp. 238, 242; (unpub. draft) *MO*, p. 336; (oil money) *MO*, pp. 278, 308, 332; (Marshall) *MO*, pp. 242,

338; (Marsh) *MO*, p. 308, but see *AMI*, p. 127; (Ackerman) Ackerman/FB corr. 1979; int. Mrs. William Ackerman.

Call/Chandler: *MO*, p. 309–; Robert Gottleib and Irene Wolt, *Thinking Big: The Story of the Los Angeles Times*, New York: Putnam, 1977, p. 277.

Palmer: (tout) *MO*, p. 299; (meets) *MO*, p. 298; Kornitzer, op. cit., p. 160; (Hartmann) Gottleib and Walt, op. cit., p. 271–; ("old head . . .") Mitchell, op. cit., p. 88; ("He looks . . .") Kornitzer, op. cit., p. 161; (Sinclair) *MO*, pp. 268, 299; (no Douglas photo) *Nation*, Mar. 9, 1998; (Palmer wrote) ibid.; (ad. space) *MO*, p. 301; (RN pines) ints. Pat Brown and Paul Ziffren by FB, FBP.

Chandlers: (orders IRS) *American Journalism Review*, Apr. 1997, *NYT*, Mar. 24, 1997; ("I would never . . .") Letter RN to N. Chandler, Dec. 29, 1960, VP, NA.

Copley: *San Diego Reader*, July 28, 1994.

Klein: ibid.; Herbert G. Klein, *Making It Perfectly Clear*, New York: Doubleday, 1980, p. 77; *MO*, p. 297.

W. E. Smith: Smith to Drew Pearson, Oct. 27, 1952, DPP.

Chapter 6

Salerno: Sid Blumenthal and Harvey Yazijian, *Government by Gunplay*, New York: Signet, 1976, p. 130.

Chotiner: (background) int. Nancy Chotiner; *MO*, pp. 292, 270, FBI 161-1495; (described) *MO*, pp. 292, 703, 780; (no name) *NYT*, Oct. 12, 1970; ("Macchiavelli") Garment, op. cit., p. 57; ("not beyond . . .") int. Nancy Chotiner; (first set eyes) Kornitzer, p. 153–; (1950) *MO*, p. 528; (Pink Sheet) Mitchell, op. cit., p. 141; *MO*, p. 581; ('52) *MO*, p. 741; ('54) *AMI*, p. 354; ("campaign school") *NYT*, May 13, 1956; ("textbook") Costello, op. cit., p. 44; (Garment) eds. Strober, *Nixon*, op. cit., p. 30; (uniform scam/check) *NYT*, Apr. 25, 1956 and Bellino Papers, held by family; (accountant) *NYT*, Apr. 25, 1956; (delaying tactics) Washington *Evening Star*, Apr. 26, 1956; (testifies) St. Louis *Globe-Democrat*, May 5, *NYT*, May 4, 1956; (McCarthy) *Washington Post Times Herald*, June 4, *NYT*, May 4, 1956.

Reginelli: (background) *NYT*, May 4, Newark *Evening News*, May 25, 1956; (221 cases) "List of Criminal Actions Defended by Chotiner & Chotiner in the Superior Ct. of the State of CA, & the County of LA, 1949–June 1, 1952," Murray Chotiner file, 1956, Box 178C, File 4, McClellan Collection, Ouachita Baptist University, AK, article by William L. Roper, *Nation*, July 2, 1955; unid. clip, "Chotiner's Dual Role in California Politics Told," by Mary Ellen Leary, DPP; Drew Pearson letter to radio stations, Apr. 1956, DPP; (RN claimed) Nichols to Tolson, May 1, 1956, FBI 63-2766.

RN/Chotiner relations: ("no contact . . .") Drew Pearson column, Nashville *Tennessean*, May 1, 1956; ("on behalf of the VP . . .") ibid., (Seelye) int. Howard Seelye; (letters to RN) *Washington Post Times Herald*, Apr. 29, 1956; (dropped) Washington *Daily News*, May 8, *NYT*, May 22, June 3, 4, 1956; ("tragedy") Alsop, op. cit., p. 193; (rift) int. Jerry Pacht by FB, FBP; ("without guts . . .") Bellino Papers; (1960) Cleveland *Press*, Oct. 26, 1960; (1962) int. John Rothmann, *AMI*, p. 656–; int. Chapin in eds. Strober, *Nixon*, op. cit., p. 340; ('62 forecast) *SF Chronicle*, Nov. 24, 1964; (1968) Richard Whalen, *Catch the Falling Flag*, New York: Houghton Mifflin, 1972, p. 53; Garment, op. cit., p. 156; undated story by Vera Glaser, DPP; (RNC chairmanship?) Rowland Evans and Robert Novak, *Nixon in the White House*, London: Davis-Poynter, 1972 p. 71; (FBI check) FBI HQ 161-6284; (pay) *WP*, Apr. 11, 1969.

Chotiner misdeeds: ("brilliant") *MEM*, pp. 39, 87; (Hughes) memo, DeOreo to Lenzner, Dec. 7, 1973 and int. John Meier, Oct. 23, 1973, WSPF(H-R); (extortion) Sam Ervin, Jr., *The Whole Truth, The Watergate Conspiracy*, New York: Random House, 1980, p. 264; *NYT*, May 3, 1974 and—dating back—*Nation*, July 2, 1955; (Greek exile) ints. Elias Demetracopoulos, Stanley Kutler, *The Wars of Watergate*, New York: Knopff, 1990, p. 207; (Townhouse) memo, Ruff to McBride, Aug. 3, 1973, Box 23, Folder 4, Archibald Cox Papers, Harvard Law School Library and Victor Lasky, *It Didn't Start with Watergate*, New York: Dell, 1977, p. 349; (IRS) Joan Hoff, *Nixon Reconsidered*, New York: Basic Books, 1994, p. 278; (Goldberg) *WP*, Aug. 21, 24, 1973, Jan. 23, Feb. 4, 1998, and see Aug. 13, 1972 entry *AOP*, p. 129; (Vesco) *Boston Globe*, Apr. 3, 1974, citing Vesco; Dan Moldea, *Interference*, New York: William Morrow, 1989, p. 458; (mafiosi) int. John Dean in U.S., June 14, 1977; *Scanlan's Monthly*, Sept. 1970; *NYT*, May 26, 1970; int. Michael Ewing; John Dean, *Blind Ambition*, New York: Simon & Schuster, 1976, p. 36; (scam) Oakland *Tribune*, May 4, 1973; Blumenthal and Yazijian, op. cit., p. 135; (Hoffa) *WP*, May 3, 1973; int. Harry Hall; Clark Mollenhoff, *Game Plan for Disaster*, New York: Norton, 1976, p. 45; *Newsweek*, Nov. 26, 1973 and Chotiner int, May 24, 1973, FBI WFO 58-1344; (Marcello) Walter Sheridan, *The Rise and Fall of Jimmy Hoffa*, New York: Saturday Review Press, 1972, pp. 492, 504; (Pajamas) *WP*, May 3, 1973; (offices) *NM*, p. 6; (telephone) Winzola McClendon, *Martha, The Life of Martha Mitchell*, New York: Random House, 1979, p. 167; (woman on payroll) Washington *Star-News,* Aug. 19, 1973; (Chapin) int. Chapin in eds. Strober, *Nixon,* op. cit., p. 340.

Pat disapproval: *PAT,* p. 92; (letterhead) *AMI,* p. 124.

Cohen: (principal story) SAC Sacramento to director, Apr. 22, 1969, FBI 161-6284-21, (hereafter "Sacramento FBI"); SAC LA to director, Oct. 10, 1962, FBI 92-3156-338; ed. John Peer Nugent, Mickey Cohen, *In His Own Words,* Englewood Cliffs, NJ: Prentice-Hall, 1975, p. 231; Reid, op. cit.; (Siegel) George Carpozi, Jr., *Bugsy,* New York: SPI, 1992; Fox, op. cit., p. 283–; Rappeleye and Becker, op. cit., p. 100 et al.; ("a power") Nugent, op. cit., p. 78; (Goodfellow's/pols.) Nugent, op. cit., p. 96, (Goodfellow's/meeting) Sacramento FBI, *supra.;* (Irvine) *NYT,* Oct. 17, 1959; *History of the Irvine Ranch,* pamphlet,1965, Troop 36, Irvine Ranch, history, 1953; www. ocbsa.org., Charlie S. Thomas file, corr. files; Series 320, Box 753, VP, NA; (footnote on Chotiner cases) *Nation,* July 2, 1955; *Behind the Scenes* magazine, Mar. 1956 [issued January 1956] FBI HQ 161-6284, Apr. 18, 1969, p. 74; (letter) Carey McWilliams to Drew Pearson, June 23, 1955, Box G230, DPP; (Sicas et al.) FBI 161-6284-21 and name entries, Sifakis, op. cit.; (Samish) Stephen Fox, *Blood & Power,* New York: Morrow, 1989, p. 126; (Pearson background) Oliver Pilat, *Drew Pearson,* New York: Pocket, 1973, esp. p. 3; *NYT,* Sept. 2, 1969; (1956) Chotiner letter to radio station WTSP, St. Petersburg, FL, May 23, 1956, Pearson letters to radio stations, May 23, 31, June 5, 13, 1956, Box G230, DPP; (1959) Chotiner letter to Pearson and subsequent corr., Box G281, DPP; (1962) Sacramento FBI, *supra.,* Nugent, op. cit., p. 231; (1968) ibid., and *WP,* undated, prob. Oct. 31, 1968; (first lead) P. Thafker telegrams to Pearson, May 8, 23, 1956, Box G230, DPP; (" I don't know . . .") LA *Examiner,* May 14, 1956 (refused), FBI 161-6284-21 and undated Pearson memo, May 1956, Box G198, DPP; ("ratting") SAC LA to director, Oct. 10, 1962, FBI 92-3156-338; (Chotiner demand) Pearson blind memo, June 16, 1959, Box G281, DPP.

Syndicate control?: ("the proper persons . . .") Nugent, op. cit., p. 80; (Costello/Lansky) ints. Hank Messick, Lansky biographer and Richard Hammer, Luciano biographer, for author's book *Official & Confidential,* op. cit., p. 240; (Sheridan) Miami *Herald,* Jan. 22, 1983; int. Pete Hamill by Julie Ziegler.

RN backing: ("I want you . . .") *MO,* p. 314; (Schuyler) int. Schuyler in ed. Schulte, op. cit., pp. 247, 248–, 264; (Stout) *MO,* p. 284.

Chapter 7

Safire: Christopher Andrew, *For the President's Eyes Only,* New York: HarperCollins, 1995, p. 351.

DC debut: (*Washington Times-Herald*) Jan. 21, 1947; (Reedy) int. George Reedy by FB, FBP; (suits/shoes) Kissinger, *White House Years,* op. cit., p. 662; *FB,* p. 59; Crowley, *Nixon in Winter,* op. cit., p. 4; int. Hugh Sidey in eds. Miller Center, op. cit., p. 305; Safire, op. cit., p. 606; (Trohan) int. Walter Trohan and Walter Trohan, *Political Animals,* New York: Doubleday, 1975, p. 367; (arrival DC) *PAT,* Ch. 10; (thing of the past) *PAT,* p. 97; (attic) *MO,* p. 356; int. George Reedy by FB, FBP; ("suppose . . . elated") Christopher Mathews, *Kennedy & Nixon,* New York: Simon & Schuster, 1996, p. 45; ("lost feeling") *MO,* p. 356; ("smash . . . bosses") Costello, op. cit., p. 179; (champions bill) *MO,* p. 344.

"pacing": *Time,* Aug. 25, 1952.

Eisler: *MO,* p. 344; Allen Weinstein, *Perjury,* New York: Random House, 1997 (hereafter *PERJ*), p. 77–.

Hiss main sources: *PERJ;* Sam Tanenhaus, *Whittaker Chambers,* New York: Random House, 1997; John Chabot Smith, *Alger Hiss, The True Story,* New York: Penguin, 1977; Morton and Michael Levitt, *A Tissue of Lies,* New York: McGraw-Hill, 1979; William Reuben, *The Honorable Mr. Nixon and the Alger Hiss Case,* New York: Action Books, 1957; Nixon, *Six Crises,* op. cit.

Hiss detail: (Great Fear) David Caute, *The Great Fear,* New York: Simon & Schuster, 1978; ("A Lesson") *MO,* p. 500; (RN told aides) *PERJ,* p. 554; ("How he loved") Haldeman and DiMona, op. cit., p. 49; (Dean) int. John Dean and WHT, Feb. 28, 1973, WSPF, NA.

job seeking: (NY law firms) *MEM,* p. 21; *MO,* p. 179–; Toledano, *One Man Alone,* op. cit., p. 31; Mazo, op. cit., p. 26; (Donovan) Thomas Troy, *Donovan and the CIA,* Frederick, MD: Aletheia Books, 1981, p. 23; G.J.A. O'Toole, *Honorable Treachery,* New York: Atlantic Monthly Press, 1991, p. 417; ("highest hope") Mazo, op. cit, p. 26 and cf. *SF Chronicle,* Nov. 4, 1968; (Dulles) Peter Grose, *Gentleman Spy,* Amherst, MA: University of Massachusetts Press, 1994; Leonard Mosley, *Dulles,* New York: Dial Press/James Wade, 1978; ("very particular") Grose, op. cit., p. 92; (Wise) David Wise, *The American Police State,* New York: Random House, 1976, p. 130fn; (Loftus) John Loftus and Mark Aarons, *The Secret War Against the Jews,* New York: St. Martin's Press, 1994, pp. 220–, 557; int. John Loftus; (Dulles fall 1945) Grose, op. cit., p. 256; (Phleger) William Ackerman to FB, Jan. 2, 1979, FBP; Lurie, *The Running of Richard Nixon,* op. cit., p. 163; *Who's Who in America,* 1982, p. 2653; (toured Europe) Grose, op. cit., p. 280; Parmet, op. cit., p. 326; Mosley, op. cit., p. 243; (dinners) *JA,* p. 246; (brief RN) Mosley, op. cit., pp. 394, 466; William Corson, *The Armies of Ignorance,* New York: Dial Press/James Wade, 1977, p. 36; (RN met brothers) *MEM,* p. 57.

Hiss OSS counsel?: Troy, op. cit., p. 80.

warnings about Hiss: (Donovan) *Spectator* [London], Nov. 23, 1996; (Dulles) ibid.; (run-in) Grose, op. cit., p. 297fn; (close touch) ibid, p. 272; (advisors) ibid, p. 288; Mosley, op. cit., p. 218.

FBI: (application) Apr. 23, 1937, FBI 67-102459, in Hoover Official & Confidential file 8, NA; (Dean) Horack to Hoover, May 11, 1937, Richard M. Nixon Collection, Duke University Archive; ("Not Qualified") investigation brief, Aug. 10, 1937, O & C 8, FBI 67-102459; (explanations) Hoover introduction of RN at FBI National Academy, June 11, 1954, FBI 298948-80; John Mohr testimony, Inquiry into the Destruction of Former FBI Director J. Edgar Hoover's Files, FBI Recordkeeping, Hearings, House Government Information and Individual Rights Subcommittee on Government Operations, 1975, p. 70; *MEM,* p. 21; (Assistant Directors) William Sullivan and Bill Brown, *The Bureau,* New York: Norton, 1979, p. 196; Norman Ollestad, *Inside the FBI,* New York: Lyle Stuart, 1967, p. 57; (another account) notes of Carmine Bellino, citing Agent Roy Morgan, Bellino Papers, held by family—FBI documents show Vincent was SAC; (Richfield) application form, *supra.*; Hoover to SAC Los Angeles, July 23, 1937; inspector's interview, Aug. 2, 1937, FBI 67-102459-15; (incoming congressman) Summers, *Official & Confidential,* op. cit., p. 194; ("good man") Ovid Demaris, *The Director,* New York: Harper's Magazine Press, 1975, p. 121–; the attorney was Bradshaw Mintener; (meets Hoover) *MEM,* p. 595; *Newsweek,* June 9, 1947; (RN/Hoover relations) Summers, *Official & Confidential,* op. cit., pp. 180, 262, 293, 368; (RN feared) ibid., p. 371 [citing Pete Pitchess] and Demaris, op. cit., p. 96 [citing William Sullivan]; ("Constitution . . . in such danger") Merle Miller, *Plain Speaking,* New York: Berkley, 1973, p. 416.

Hiss suspicions: (alleged Communists) *PERJ,* p. 311–; (mail) *Nation,* Fred Cook article, Oct. 11, 1980, p. 342; (Agents interviewed) *PERJ,* p. 302; (code clerk) ibid., p. 311; (Bentley) ibid., p. 316; (top leaders) ibid., p. 307; (tailing) *Nation,* Oct. 11, 1980, p. 342; (Chambers reinterviewed/leaks) *PERJ,* p. 327.

RN claimed: Nixon, *Six Crises,* op. cit., p. 4 and cf. Notes of RN int. by Herbert Parmet, Parmet papers.

Cronin: *MO,* pp. 351, 396 et al.; Garry Wills, *Nixon Agonistes,* Boston: Houghton Mifflin, 1969, p. 26–; (within month) Kornitzer, op. cit., p. 172–; Frank Donner, *Age of Surveillance,* New York: Vintage, 1981, p. 174fn, Cronin int. in "The Trials of Alger Hiss," History on Film, [documentary script], 1979, supplied to author by Producer/Director John Lowenthal, p. 40–; de Toledano, *One Man Alone,* op. cit., p. 76; Mazo, op. cit., p. 51; ("stacked deck") *Esquire,* Nov. 1975, p. 76, citing Cronin int. 1974; ("hard-core") Lowenthal script, *supra.,* p. 41; (Hummer) *Esquire,* Nov. 1975, p. 76, but see *JA,* p. 155, Gellman, op. cit., p. 234 and RN int. by Parmet, *supra.;* (Nichols/former agents) Nichols to Tolson, Dec. 2, 1948; Ladd to director, Dec. 9, 1948; FBI Hiss file in FBI Reading Room.

Russell: (triggered?) Seattle *Post-Intelligencer,* Feb. 17, 1954; Jerris Leonard memo, July 19, 1974, Jim Hougan Collection; (traveled with RN) int. William Birely; (phone with RN) int. Jean (Russell) Hooper; (reported to Hoover) Hottel to Hoover, Sept. 2, 1948; Nichols to Tolson, Dec. 2, 1948; Ladd to Hoover, Dec. 9, 1948; Hiss file, *supra.;* Nichols to Tolson, Jan. 14, 1949, FBI [hard to decipher] ?37816-260; (Democrat) int. William Birely; ("liberal") Robert Carr, *The House Committee on Un-American Activities, 1945–1950,* Ithaca, New York: Cornell University Press, 1952, p. 268; see also int. Gordon Hess by Jim Hougan, Hougan Collection, and cf. refs. in *MO* and Smith, *Alger Hiss,* op. cit.

Chapter 8

"They're trying . . . ": Crowley, *Nixon in Winter,* op. cit., p. 305.

RN and Hiss: (Harvard/Whittier) Stripling int. in "The Trials of Alger Hiss," History on Film, [documentary script], 1979, supplied to author by Producer/Director John Lowenthal, p. 38–; ("opportunistic") ibid., p. 163; ("hat set") *Esquire,* Nov. 1975, p. 78; ("sonofabitch") Lowenthal script, *supra.,* p. 39; (visits) Nixon, *Six Crises,* op. cit., p. 22–; (trick answer) *MO,* p. 420; (accommodation/car) *PERJ,* p. 133; (farm) ibid., pp. 47–, 134; *MO,* p. 348.

homosexuality: (RN/"queers") *Esquire,* Nov. 1975, p. 152; (Chambers admission) *PERJ,* p. 103–; (tried to force) *PERJ,* p. 343; (secret) *PERJ,* p. 104; (threesome) *PERJ,* p. 91–; (stepson) *PERJ,* p. 359; Bert and Peter Andrews, *A Tragedy of History,* Washington, D.C.: Luce, 1962, p. 751; (Chambers denied) *PERJ,* p. 358; ("closest") Nixon, *Six Crises,* op. cit., p. 43; (numerous items) Meyer Zeligs, *Friendship and Fratricide,* New York: Viking, 1967, p. 233; ("He never"/"His attitude") *PERJ,* p. 526; Levitt, op. cit., p. 299fn; (unrequited) *PERJ,* p. 521.

espionage not involved: *MO,* p. 452.

RN behavior: Tannenhaus, op. cit., p. 291–; *MO*, p. 459; *Esquire*, Nov. 1975, p. 147; ("proof") *MO*, p. 473; (promised Pat) Nixon, *Six Crises*, op. cit., p. 46; *PAT*, p. 101; ("exhausted") Kornitzer, op. cit., p. 177; (RN phoned) *MO*, p. 463; (after Christmas) Robert Stripling, ed. Bob Considine, *The Red Plot Against America*, New York: Arno Press, 1977, p. 145; (Miller) William Miller as told to Frances Spatz Leighton, *Fishbait, The Memoirs of the Congressional Doorkeeper*, Englewood Cliffs, NJ: Prentice-Hall, 1977, p. 41–; (logs) Smith, *Alger Hiss*, op. cit., p. 257; ("Attempt") *MO*, p. 467.

typewriter: (in court) Smith, *Alger Hiss*, op. cit., p. 355; *PERJ*, p. 426; Harold Rosenwald int. in Lowenthal script, *supra.*, p. 148; ("murder weapon") int. Alger Hiss; ibid., p. 151; (RN "major factor") *PERJ*, p. 493; (same machine) *MO*, p. 474; *PERJ*, p. 515; (junk dealer) *PERJ*, p. 351; (Woodstock matched) *PERJ*, p. 354 and cf. 351; Hoover to Sen. Karl Mundt, May 3, 1957, Mundt Archives, Grp. 1, Box 162, File 7, Dakota State College; (convinced jury) *PERJ*, p. 515, FB, p. 231; (documents sufficient?) int. Agent Jack Danahee; *PERJ*, p. 519; (RN "key witness") Nixon, *Six Crises*, op. cit., p. 59; ("contention") Levitt, op. cit., pp. 162, 191; (doubt) ibid., p. 162fn; *Nation*, June 26, 1986, p. 780; (Hiss possession?) *Nation*, May 12, 1962, p. 416–, but cf. *PERJ*, p. 352; (manufactured too late?) ibid., p. 776–; Levitt, op. cit., p. 188–, but cf. *PERJ*, pp. 262fn, 364, 523–.

Typewriter forgery?: (Hiss "forgery") Levitt, op. cit., p. 163; (RN "fingerprint") *PERJ*, p. 493, Nixon, *Six Crises*, op. cit., p. 60; (replica) *PERJ*, p. 517; (supporters) ibid., p. 518; Levitt, op. cit., p. 197–; (successful forgery) Montgomery Hyde, *Room 3603*, New York: Farrar, Strauss, 1963, pp. 135, 145; William Stevenson, *A Man Called Intrepid*, New York: Ballantine, 1976, pp. 204, 294, 296, and photo of "30 Ottobre 1941" letter.

Finding typewriter: (*World Telegram*) Dec. 13, 1948; (HUAC Report) Levitt, op. cit., p. 206; (McDowell) *Nation*, May 12, 1962, p. 420; (Sullivan) Peter Irons article, *Real Paper*, Mar. 12, 1975; Summers, *Official & Confidential*, op. cit., New York: Putnam, 1993, p. 167; ("On Dec. 13") Nixon, *Six Crises*, op. cit., p. 60; (sequel) *Nation*, May 12, 1962, p. 421; (RN/Oval Office) WHT, Mar. 10, 1972, transcribed for author; ("we built") Dean, *Blind Ambition*, op. cit., p. 57; (Colson/RN reactions) *PERJ*, p. 493; (Dean's notes) int. John Dean by FB, FBP; (Canada site) Stevenson, op. cit., pp. 222, 204.

Schmahl: Jim Hougan, *Spooks*, New York: William Morrow, 1978, p. 289; *PERJ*, cites, esp. p. 584–; Levitt, op. cit., p. 202–; *Nation*, Oct. 7, 1978, p. 336.

Hoover/framing: *Nation*, Nov. 10, 1984, p. 468; ("Had Nixon asked") Sullivan, op. cit., p. 95.

Diem: *NYT* News Service, Apr. 29, 1973; H. R. Haldeman and Joseph DiMona, *Ends of Power*, New York: Times Books, 1978, p. 161; WHT, Sept. 18, 1971; *AOP* p. 35, and for Apr. 28 and May 8, 1973 at pp. 371, 416; *HD*, p. 672; Howard Hunt, *Undercover*, New York: Berkley, 1974, p. 179; FB, p. 498, citing Ehrlichman; *NM*, p. 84; *New Yorker*, Seymour Hersh article, Dec. 14, 1992, p. 761; (Wallace) WHT, May 15, 1972; *AOP*, p. 38; Gordon Liddy, *Will*, New York: St. Martin's Press, 1980, p. 309; Hunt, *Undercover*, op. cit., p. 217–; Emery, op. cit., p. 116.

Volkogonov: John Lowenthal monograph, Oct. 4, 1996, supplied to author, citing *Bulletin*, Oct. 14, 1992, Cold War International History Project, Washington, D.C.: Woodrow Wilson Foundation, Issue 2, Fall 1991, p. 33; Dmitri Simes int. by Kai Bird and John Taylor int. Apr. 14, 1994 and *NYT*, Oct. 29, 1992 and see "Venona and Alger Hiss," in *Intelligence & National Security* [UK: Frank Kass, forthcoming Autumn 2000], the author has sought a comment from John Taylor, director of the Nixon Library and Birthplace, but he did not respond to letters on this, Dec. 20, 1998, Jan. 20, May 7, 1999, and follow-up call Apr. 3, 1999; (RN exploded) Crowley, *Nixon in Winter*, op. cit., p. 304–.

Field: (Hiss link) *PERJ*, p. 174; Allen Weinstein and Alexander Vassiliev, *The Haunted Wood*, New York: Random House, 1999, pp. 4–, 44; (interrogations) *New Republic*, Nov. 8, 1993; Maria Schmidt article; *Nation*, Nov. 8, 1993, Ethan Klingsberg article; (starved/beaten) ibid., p. 530–; (Massing/FBI) *PERJ*, p. 176; (consistent with messages in Soviet files) *PERJ*, p. 182–; Weinstein and Vassiliev, op. cit., p. 4–.

Weinstein/NKVD files: ibid., acknowledgments, p. xv–; *PERJ*, pp. 182–, 204, 325; (ten messages) Weinstein and Vassiliev, *supra.*, pp. 5, 7, 8, 10, 79, 80, 267–; (clear text) ibid., pp. 5, 79–.

Gordievsky: Christopher Andrew and Oleg Gordievsky, *KGB, The Inside Story*, New York: HarperCollins, 1990, pp. 2, 285.

Sudoplatov: Pavel Sudoplatov and Anatoli Sudoplatov with Jerrold and Leona Schecter, *Special Tasks*, London: Little, Brown, 1994, p. 277–.

Pavlov: Vitaly Pavlov, *Operation Snow*, Moscow: Goya, 1996, p. 50 of translation supplied to author.

"ALES": eds. Robert Benson and Michael Warner, *Venona, Soviet Espionage and the American Response, 1939–1957*, Washington, D.C.: National Security Agency/CIA, 1996, p. 423; John Haynes and Harvey Klehr, *Venona*, New Haven, CT: Yale University Press, 1999, pp. 126–,

170–, 352; Nigel West, *Venona, The Greatest Secret of the Cold War*, London, HarperCollins, 1999, p. 234–; *PERJ*, p. 325–; Weinstein and Vassiliev, op. cit., p. 267–; *NYT*, Oct. 23, 1978.

Weinstein/"NKVD reports": (never saw?) *Nation*, May 24, 1999; (deal) Weinstein and Vassiliev, op. cit., pp. xv, xi; (no response) Swan to Weinstein, Jan, 28, Mar. 15, Apr. 13, 1999.

Lowenthal: ints. John Lowenthal; *Times* [London] *Literary Supplement*, Feb. 7, 1999.

HUAC files sealed: *PERJ*, p. xxiiifn.

VENONA: (new release) Mar. 20, 1945 message, Washington to Moscow, obtained under Freedom of Information Act and kindly provided to author by John Lowenthal; (1946) eds. Benson and Warner, op. cit., p. xxi and Daniel Patrick Moynihan, *Secrecy*, New Haven, CT: Yale University Press, 1998, p. 61; (re. Truman) ibid., p. 71; (FBI) ibid., and cf. Robert Lamphere and Tom Shachtman, *The FBI-KGB War*, New York: Random House, 1996; (Donovan provided) ibid., p. 84 & cf.; eds. Benson and Warner, op. cit., p. xviii.

RN paradigm: ("bullshit!") *Esquire*, Nov. 1975, p. 152; *PERJ*, p. 492; (Trohan) int. Walter Trohan; ("He developed") Trohan to Lou Nichols, Jan. 10, 1974, Nichols collection; (RN/judge) *PERJ*, p. 418; (RN/foreman) Levitt, op. cit., p. 116; ("They couldn't") *JA*, p. 176; (Kennedy) *AOP*, pp. 24–, 28, 234–; (Stevenson) *MO*, pp. 752, 859–; (Vazzana) *Esquire*, Nov. 1975, p. 151; ("I was spending") Nixon, *Six Crises*, op. cit., p. 40–; (pills) ibid.; ("He wouldn't") *Good Housekeeping*, June 1960; Kornitzer, op. cit., p. 177; (Pat reluctant) *PAT*, p. 101; ("absorption") *JA*, p. 164; (visits) *MO*, p. 512; RN note to staff, Oct. 6, 1959, VP NA; ("loving care") Whittaker Chambers, *Cold Friday*, New York: Random House, 1964, p. 57; ("Nixie") Whittaker Chambers, *Witness*, New York: Random House, 1952, p. 793; (less than loyal) Chambers to Ralph de Toledano, May 12, 1959, in ed. Ralph de Toledano, *Notes from the Underground*, Washington, D.C.: Regnery, 1997, p. 317–; ("pity") Henry Grunwald, *One Man's America*, New York: Doubleday, 1997, p. 280; ("difficult time") *Saturday Evening Post*, Sept. 6, 1952; (discontent) *PAT* p. 97.

Chapter 9

"Whenever a man": *The Oxford Dictionary of Quotations*, London, Oxford University Press, 1974, p. 268.

McCarthy: (speech) David Oshinsky, *A Conspiracy So Immense*, New York: Free Press, 1983, p. 108, William Manchester, *The Glory and the Dream*, Boston: Little, Brown, 1973, p. 520–; ("Listen, you bastards") Thomas Reeves, *The Life and Times of Joe McCarthy*, New York: Stein & Day, 1982, p. 233; (RN on McCarthy) *MEM*, p. 149; ("hard core buddies") int. Bobby Baker; (RN in 1952) Reeves, op. cit., p. 451; Costello, op. cit., p. 274; (Alsop) Alsop, op. cit., p. 151; (Sevareid) Sevareid, op. cit., p. 87; (Cronkite) Walter Cronkite, *A Reporter's Life*, New York: Knopf, 1996, p. 228; (Dewey) Leonard Lurie, *The Running of Richard Nixon*, New York: Coward, McCann, & Geoghegan, 1972, p. 172; (wedding) ed. Toledano, *Notes from the Underground*, op. cit., p. 145; ("McCarthy's a friend") int. Dr. Arnold Hutschnecker; (at Eisenhower's behest) *MEM*, p. 144; (RN "hatchetman") Abrahamsen, op. cit., p. 165; int. Roy Cohn by FB, FBP; (Khrushchev) Pierre Salinger, *P.S., A Memoir*, New York: St. Martin's Press, 1995, p. 148; ("but anything!") unpub. journal of James Bassett, supplied by Cynthia Bassett; (RN/censure motion) Manchester, op. cit., p. 718; Oshinsky, op. cit., p. 490 and see *MEM*, p. 148–; (funeral) ibid., p. 506.

Rayburn: ("next thing to McCarthy") D. B. Hardeman and Donald Bacon, *Rayburn*, Austin, TX: Texas Monthly Press, 1987, p. 381–; ("ugly fellow") Alsop, op. cit., p. 30.

Douglas campaign: ("went for broke") int. Willard Espy by FB, FBP; (soundings) *MO*, p. 524; (Palmer) int. Paul Ziffren by FB, FBP; (nine backed RN) Parmet, op. cit., p. 190; (no photographs) Mitchell, op. cit., p. 251; (Hearst) *MO*, p. 589; ("letters") ibid., p. 603; (brand as leftist) ibid., p. 565 and see Gellman, op. cit., p. 298; (Douglas background) ibid., p. 528–; (Chotiner/P.R.) ibid., p. 602; (blimp) notation, Oct. 2, 1952, Box G201 73, DPP; ("prizes galore!!!") ibid., *Avant-Garde*, Jan. 1968; *The Reporter*, Apr. 19, 1956; ("nothing but pictures") *MO*, p. 602; (hard sold) ads. preserved in DPP.

smears/dirty tricks: ("Pink Lady") Mitchell, op. cit., p. 4; (pink paper) *MO*, p. 581, but see Gellman, op. cit., p. 12; ("purely fortuitous?") int. John Rothmann and cf. Mitchell, op. cit., p. 141, "Fundamentals of Campaign Organization," address by Murray Chotiner, Box 6 230, DPP; (flyers dumped) Mitchell, op. cit., p. 230; *MO*, p. 602; (phoney propaganda) Oshinsky, op. cit., p. 177; (pickets) *MO*, pp. 568, 602, 609, 618; (drenching Douglas) ibid., p. 562; Douglas, op. cit., p. 312; (forced off road) Mitchell, op. cit., p. 212; (Douglas pelted) *MO*, p. 603; Douglas, op. cit., p. 334.

Democrats' abuse: (Tuck) "An Evening with Dick Tuck," broadcast sound tape, available at some libraries; (Pat complained) *Saturday Evening Post*, Sept. 6, 1952; (overturned car) *MO*, p. 600; (Douglas lash back) Ingrid Scobie, *Center Stage*, New York: Oxford University Press, 1972, p. 280; (evoking fascism) *MO*, p. 600.

"**Did you know?**": *MO*, p. 610, Douglas, op. cit., p. 332, but see *New England Journal of History*, Winter 1999/Spring 2000, Vol. 56, p. 24.

RN in '50 campaign: ("we covered California") *Saturday Evening Post*, Sept. 6, 1952; (station wagon) *MO*, pp. 564, 573; Mitchell, op. cit., p. 51.

RN backers: (oil-banking) *MO*, p. 572; (Haldeman) ibid., pp. 573, 636; (Murchison/Richardson) int. Allan Witwer, San Diego *Union*, Aug. 11, 1955; (Dana Smith) *MO*, pp. 528, 546, 632; (Brewster) ibid., p. 576, letter, Owen Brewster to Nathan Buckman, Apr. 15, 1952, Box G128 and memo of int. Henry Grunewald, Oct. 27, 1955, Box G 281, DPP; (total cost?) Gellman, op. cit., p. 334; *New England Journal of History*, Winter 1999/Spring 2000, Vol. 56, p. 26; *MO*, p. 615–; (giving away cash) ibid., p. 575; (so broke) ibid., p. 577–; Mitchell, op. cit., p. 179; (RN/election day) *Saturday Evening Post*, Sept. 6, 1952.

RN on campaign: ("Tricky Dick") *MEM*, p. 77; (no mention) *MEM*, p. 71–; (plaintively) *MEM*, p. 73; (anyone who checked) *MEM*, p. 78.

RN responsibility: ("A perfectionist") *MO*, p. 566, Mitchell, op. cit., p. 108; ("Nixon knew") ints. Tom Dixon, Georgia Sherwood, and Tom Dixon by FB, FBP; (Arnold) William Arnold, *Back When It All Began*, New York: Vantage, 1975, p. 12–; ("pink to underpants") Gottlieb and Wolt, op. cit., p. 278; *MO*, p. 598; Dan Rather and Gary Paul Gates, *The Palace Guard*, New York: Harper & Row, 1974, p. 114; *FB*, p. 292; Douglas, op. cit., p. 327; (nod & wink) *MO*, p. 598; David Halberstam, *The Powers That Be*, New York: Knopf, 1979, p. 263; ("Hesselberg"/slur) *MO*, p. 599; Mitchell, op. cit., pp. 230, 234, 261; Lurie, op. cit., p. 93; (team propositioned) New York *Post*, Oct. 30, 1952; (phone calls) Douglas, op. cit., p. 326.

RN regrets?: (general) Willard Espy to FB, FBP; (Kempton) Mitchell, op. cit., p. 126; *New Yorker*, Mar. 1, 1993, p. 50; *WP*, Apr. 23, 1994; (Astor) *New Republic*, May 5, 1958, but cf. *JA*, p. 191.

Chapter 10

"**masculine self-image**": unpub. ms. shown to author by Dr. Hutschnecker.

Strain: ("mean") Nixon, *Six Crises*, op. cit., p. 40–; (nine secretaries) *JA*, p. 196; (not home for dinner) *PAT*, p. 111; ("Many times") *FB*, p. 337, citing Earl Chapman int. in California State Archives; (pain) *PAT*, p. 111; (book/Downey) *Collier's*, July 9, 1954; int. Dr. Arnold Hutschnecker; ("in the grips") *Contemporary Authors*, Vol. 81–84, Detroit, MI: Gale Research, 1979, p. 256; ("the interaction") Arnold Hutschnecker, *The Will to Live*, New York: Simon & Schuster, 1983 [orig. ed. 1951], Introduction.

Dr. Arnold Hutschnecker: (general sources) testimony, Dr. Arnold Hutschnecker, Hearings, Nom. of Gerald R. Ford of MI to be Vice Pres. of US, Cttee. on Rules and Admin., U.S. Senate, 93rd Cong., 1st Sess., Nov. 7, 1973 and, except where indicated otherwise, direct quotes of Dr. Hutschnecker in this chapter are from interviews with the doctor, conducted by Robbyn Swan, 1995, 1996; ("a sort of Pavlovian") Mazlish, op. cit., p. 7; (famous clients) Robert Winter-Berger, *Washington Pay-off*, Secaucus, NJ: Lyle Stuart, 1972, p. 256, and letter, Henry Altschuler to Drew Pearson, Nov. 27, 1960(?), Box G281 1/3, DPP; ("psychoanalytically oriented") UPI, Nov. 14, 1968, reporting Drew Pearson address to National Press Club citing Hutschnecker, reprinted at Arnold Hutschnecker, *The Drive for Power*, New York: Evans & Co., 1974, p. 311 and *WP*, Nov. 14, 1968; ("Dr. Strangelove") *WP*, Nov. 20, 1973; (Graham/Peale) see Ch. 1; (Dixon) Ehrlichman, op. cit., p. 331; int. John Ehrlichman; (Woods call) int. Hutschnecker; (first four years) UPI, citing Hutschnecker, *supra.*; (five consultations) Arthur Woodstone, *Nixon's Head*, New York: St. Martin's Press, 197, p. 4; (escort) Hutschnecker, *Drive for Power*, op. cit., p. 3; (military doctor) int. Arnold Hutschnecker by FB, FBP; Hutschnecker, *Drive for Power*, op. cit., p. 312; (privately NYC) *JA*, p. 197; (Hutschnecker lunched) int. Hutschnecker and Hutschnecker, *Drive for Power*, op. cit., p. 84; (McCarthy/Dulles disturbed?) ibid.; (RN/Woods note) RN to JDH & RMW, Oct. 6, 1959, Corr. Files, Series 320, Box 147, VP; (1960 summons) *WP*, Nov. 23, 1968; (early '61 visit/disastrous bid) int. Hutschnecker; ("to see the shrink") Harriet Van Horne column, NY *Post*, Nov. 15, 1968; (Hutschnecker at WH) int. Hutschnecker; Hutschnecker, *Drive for Power*, op. cit., p. 156–; Woodstone, op. cit., p. 1–; ("Pavlovian technique") Roger Rapoport, *The Super-Doctors*, Chicago: Playboy Press, 1975, p. 156–, apparently citing Robert Winter-Berger; ("Our old intimacy") *JA*, p. 404; int. Hutschnecker; (he avoided) int. Hutschnecker and Hutschnecker, *Drive for Power*, op. cit., p. 29; (looselipped) Winter-Berger, op. cit., p. 255–; (elephants) FB, p. 335; ("Nixon wondered") Woodstone, op. cit., p. 5; (RN on "direct relation") *Time*, Apr. 2, 1990.

depression: (part of RN problem) int. Herb Klein; ("more depressed") *PAT*, p. 157; ("is Nick still seeing?") Harrison Salisbury, *Disturber of the Peace*, London: Unwin, 1989, p. 304; (Garment) int. Len Garment.

Hutschnecker insights: (general) Wicker, op. cit., p. 30–; ("deep-seated inhibitions") unpub. ms. shown to author by Dr. Arnold Hutschnecker; ("brutal & cruel") int. Hutschnecker; ("brutalized") int. Arnold Hutschnecker by FB, FBP; ("I was convinced . . .") Hutschnecker unpub. ms., *supra.*; (Bassett on "impotence") FB notes and author's transcript of int. Bassett friends Paul and Mickey Ziffren by FB, FBP, FB, p. 331; ("ambivalence") Hutschnecker, *Will to Live*, op. cit., p. 179–; ("Nixon is happiest") Winter-Berger, op. cit., p. 258; ("It is safer") *Columbia Journalism Review*, Mar./Apr. 1974, p. 9.

RN anti-psychiatry: ("I've never done") Jules Witcover, *The Resurrection of Richard Nixon*, New York: Putnam, 1970, p. 212; (Ailes) Joe McGinniss, *The Selling of the President*, New York: Penguin, 1969, p. 100–; ("except see a shrink") Garment, op. cit., pp. 299, 85–; int. Leonard Garment.

Comments on RN's personality: ("He would be depressed") int. George Christopher; ("paranoid") taped int. Pat Brown by FB, FBP; ("Black spells") Sevareid, op. cit., p. 90; (O'Donnell) eds. Strober,*Nixon*, op. cit., p. 302; ("Dick's expression") San Diego *Weekly Reader*, July 28, 1984; ("he seemed unbalanced") Cronkite, op. cit., p. 227; ("Hamlet-type") int. Robert Greene by FB, FBP; ("walking box") int. John Lindsay by FB, FBP; ("acting so strangely") int. John Herbers; ("off his rocker") Jerome Zeifman, *Without Honor*, New York: Thunder's Mouth, 1995, p. 79; (Secret Service) Kessler, op. cit., p. 39, and int. Ronald Kessler re. SS source; (Deep Throat) Carl Bernstein and Bob Woodward, *All the President's Men*, New York: Simon & Schuster, 1974, p. 319; (White) *Readers' Digest*, May 1975; ("Here was the leader") Richard Kleindienst, *Justice*, Ottawa, IL: Jameson Books, 1985, p. 168–; ("losing control") Agnew, op. cit., p. 79; (Saxbe) "The American Experience," transcript, WGBH (Boston) TV program, Oct. 15, 1990; (Butterfield) *New York*, Apr. 21, 1975, eds. Strober, *Nixon*, op. cit., p. 40; *Journal of American History*, Mar. 1989, p. 1251; (Haldeman) ibid.; ("From close observation") *New York*, May 10, 1976; ("flat dark side") White, *Breach of Faith*, op. cit., p. 163; (Kissinger) Kissinger, *Years of Upheaval*, op. cit., pp. 431, 1181–; ("Did you hear?") Walter Isaacson, *Kissinger*, New York: Simon & Schuster, 1992, p. 145 and cf. Woodward and Bernstein, *The Final Days*, op. cit., p. 214; ("four years 'on the couch'") letters, FB to Kissinger, Feb. 6, 1977, Feb. 10, 1978; transcript int. Bob Woodward by FB, FBP; (Kissinger declines) letter, Kissinger to FB, Mar. 6, 1978 and int. Bruce Brodie.

Analyst other than Hutschnecker?: (issue raised) FB, p. 466fn; Witcover, op. cit., p. 34; (Bassett) int. James Bassett by FB, FBP; (Herbert Katcher) int. Herbert's brother, NY *Post* journalist Leo Katcher by FB, int. Daniel Ellsberg by FB, who tipped Brodie off to Leo Katcher as a source, FBP; (Hutschnecker on woman doctor) int. Dr. Hutschnecker; (Finch) taped int. of Robert Finch by FB, FBP; (Sherwood) ints. Foster and Georgia Sherwood and *FB*, p. 467fn; (died in sixties?) int. Daniel Ellsberg by FB, FBP; ("deeply troubled") int. Leo Katcher by FB, FBP; (also interviewed on area) ints. Mrs. Herbert (Ina) Katcher, Edward Katcher, Mrs. Ralph (Hildi) Greenson, Joe Wyatt.

Hutschnecker on RN state of mind: (concern) WP, Nov. 14, 20, 23, 1968; ("I detected no sign") *Look*, July 15, 1969; (old theme) Hutschnecker, *The Drive for Power*, op. cit., p. 318.

Kubie: "Nixon on the Couch," draft ms. by Irving Wallace for Chicago *Sun-Times*, June 1972, and corr. Irving Wallace to FB, FBP.

new book: Hutschnecker, *The Drive for Power*, op. cit.

"I am in no position": ibid., p. 85.

files withheld: researcher report to author on Hutschnecker file review VP, NA, Jan. 23, 1997.

stress on candidates: ("The awful burden") int. Paul Smith in ed. Schulte, op. cit., p. 177; (Ehrlichman) Ehrlichman, op. cit., p. vii– and int. John Ehrlichman; ("They've nearly all") int. Len Garment; ("Deep down") *Time*, Mar. 15, 1999; ("You could well say") int. Elliot Richardson in eds. Miller Center, op. cit., p. 63.

Chapter 11

"man of great character": MEM, p. 964.

Rebozo friendship: (prescription) *JA*, p. 198; (Finch) int. Robert Finch by FB, FBP; (Reedy) int. George Reedy by FB, FBP; (Danner) *Sundance* magazine, Nov./Dec. 1972, article by Pulitzer winner Jeff Gerth—this article and subsequent versions of it by Gerth included pioneering research on Nixon's apparent links to crime [see also ed. Steve Weissman, *Big Brother and the Holding Company*, Palo Alto, CA: Ramparts Press, 1974, p. 251 and *Penthouse*, July 1974]; (Smathers's tips) ints. George Smathers, Sloan McCrae; ("Gorgeous") Anthony Summers, *Goddess, The Secret Lives of Marilyn Monroe*, New York: Macmillan, 1985, p. 225; (did not go well) ints. George Smathers, Sloan McCrae, Jake Jernigan; (uncle/alone) int. Donald Berg, int. Perry O'Neal by FB, FBP; Safire, op. cit., p. 613; *PAT*, pp. 148–, 319; *Life*, July 31, 1970.

span of RN/Rebozo friendship: (1952) RN to Rebozo, Nov. 28, 1952, from VP files, FBP; ("lick wounds") Miami *News*, Nov. 9, 1958; (1960) *Life*, July 31, 1970; int. Jake Jernigan; (1962) RN to Rebozo, Mar. 23, 1962, in VP files, FBP; int. Mary Spotswood in Miami *Herald*, Oct. 16, 1994; ed. Marvin Miller, *The Breaking of a President*, City of Industry, CA: Therapy Productions, 1974, Vol. IV, p. 509; (midsixties) ibid., p. 510; (1968 decision) MEM, p. 292; (relaxed) John Curton to John Vermilye, Miami Police Intelligence, Nov. 13, 1968, Miami Records Center; *NYT,* Nov. 20, 1968; (inaugural address/1 day in 10) *Newsday,* Oct. 13, 1971; (run of WH) int. Robert Finch by FB, FBP; (own phone) McClendon, op. cit., p. 167; (jacket) *U.S. News* & *World Report,* Oct. 11, 1971; (cruised) Kissinger, *White House Years,* op. cit., p. 498; (movies) *PAT,* p. 320; (slip into WH) int. Robert Finch by FB, FBP and *FB,* p. 549n 29; (false name) int. Dan Rather by FB, FBP, *FB,* p. 476, Thomas, op. cit., p. 144; (first to tell) Miami *News,* June 18, 1974; (exile) AP, Aug. 12, 1974; (deathbed) int. Sloan McCrae; ("I say to myself") Miami *News,* June 18, 1974.

Rebozo background: (cover name) *FB,* p. 483 and see *WP,* Feb. 11, 1978; ("Be-be") *Life,* July 31, 1970, ed. Miller, *Breaking of President,* Vol. IV, op. cit., p. 506; ("best-looking") ibid., int. Sloan McCrae; (laundries/real estate) *Life,* July 31, 1970; *National Observer,* Feb. 2, 1974; (profits) *Boston Globe* magazine, Oct. 4, 1970; *Life, supra.;* (exorbitant rate) *Newsday,* Oct. 6, 1971—the *Newsday* series of this month directed by Robert Greene remains the most penetrating study of Rebozo's connections; (hostess) *Ladies' Home Journal,* Nov. 1973; ("Blue suits") *Life,* July 31, 1970.

marriages: (Gunn) *Boston Globe* magazine, Oct. 4, 1970, by Clay Blair, *Ladies' Home Journal,* Nov. 1973, *National Observer,* Feb. 2, 1974; ints. Eric Larson [Gunn's last husband], Mrs. William Gunn [sister-in-law], Rebozo/Gunn divorce Final Decree, Dec. 5, 1934, Brevard County [FL] Records Office; (Lucke) *Boston Globe, Ladies' Home Journal, supra.;* ("antiseptic") *FB,* p. 474.

RN/Rebozo relationship: ("screwball!") int. George Smathers; ("He's meditating") *Newsday,* Oct. 13, 1971; int. Sloan McCrae; int. Bob Greene by FB, FBP; (Maroon) ibid.; ("sensuality") int. Dan Rather by FB, FBP; (steward) int. Thomas Kiernan by FB, FBP; ("definitely") Florence Fuller, cited in int. and corr. with John Hunt, 1995; int. Pamela Fuller Dychess; ("limp wrist") Roger Morris, *Haig, The General's Progress,* Chicago: Playboy Press, 1982, p. 127; Woodward and Bernstein, *Final Days,* op. cit., p. 211; (woman to Rebozo) int. Norman Casper; (Giancana) Antoinette Giancana and Thomas Renner, *Mafia Princess,* New York: William Morrow, 1984, p. 161; (Hitchcock) int. Thomas Kiernan by FB, FBP; (lover of JFK) Stephen Dunleavy and Peter Brennan, *Those Wild, Wild Kennedy Boys,* New York: Pinnacle, 1976, p. 76–; ("ladies' man) *Life,* July 31, 1970; (man-about-town) *Boston Globe* magazine, Oct. 4, 1970; (statuesque) *Newsday,* Oct. 6, 1971; ("orgies") int. George Reedy and Robert Greene by FB, FBP; (nurses) *New Yorker,* Dec. 14, 1992, conv. Seymour Hersh; ("fornicating") George Rush, *Confessions of an Ex-Secret Service Agent, The Marty Venker Story,* New York: Donald Fine, 1988, p. 195; David Frost, *"I Gave Them a Sword,"* New York: William Morrow, 1978, p. 171; (inflatable legs) Rebozo-Cronkite interview, Dec. 19, 1973 in *Historic Documents,* 1973, Washington, D.C.: Congressional Quarterly, 1974, p. 980; (full-sized?) int. Mary DeOreo (Ervin Cttee. investigator) by FB, FBP; (girl on beach) int. Marty Venker; Rush, op. cit. p. 195; ("adolescents") int. John Lindsay by FB, FBP; ("like lovers") int. Bobby Baker; (Baker/Rebozo) *AOP,* p. 124; Baker with Larry King, op. cit. p. 248; ("boyhood bond") int. Herb Klein; ("held hands" 1962) Bryant, op. cit., p. 241; (clasping hands) int. Jerome Zeifman; ("unilateral") int. John Ehrlichman in eds. Miller Center, op. cit., p. 139; (Paar) Jack Paar, *P.S. Jack Paar,* New York: Doubleday, 1983, p. 131; (Fineman) Miami *Herald,* Apr. 23, 1994; (Lucke) int. Sloan McCrae; ("N was his God") int. Jake Jernigan; (Safire) Safire, op. cit., p. 614; (Pat/"sponge") *Good Housekeeping,* July 1976 and see Ehrlichman, op. cit., p. 50; ("do you talk to") Charles Colson int. by Dick Russell, in *Argosy,* Mar. 1976; ("golfing partner") West, *Double Discovery,* op. cit., p. 139; int. Jessamyn West by FB, FBP.

Rebozo political role: ("truly social") Miami *Herald,* Nov. 1, 1973; (culivated senators) *Life,* July 31, 1970; (Rebozo/Kennedy) Miami *Herald,* Jan. 12, 1974; *JA,* p. 198fn; (dirt on JFK) FB research note, FBP, the divorcée was Durie Malcolm; Dunleavy and Brennan, op. cit., p. 21–; ("so careless") Crowley, *Nixon Off the Record,* op. cit. p. 33; (1968 meeting) Whalen, op. cit., p. 182; (previous Christmas) *MEM,* p. 292; (Danner) Danner deposition, Sept. 4, 1973, *Plaintiff v. Hughes Tool Co.,* and Danner to Rebozo, Mar. 17, 1970, E files, Box B-56, NA; ("political influence") int. John Ehrlichman; Ehrlichman, op. cit., p. 51–; ("Nixon once sent") Haldeman with DiMona, op. cit., p. 89; ("quarter million") *AOP,* p. 4—the candidate was Raymond Guest; (Muskie) ibid., p. 124; (Wallace) *HD,* p. 408; (Vietnam policy) William Shawcross, *Sideshow,* New York: Simon & Schuster, 1979, pp. 140, 142; Woodward and Bernstein, *Final Days,* op. cit., p. 204; (hated Castro) Kissinger, *White House Years,* p. 641; ("did not usually") ibid., p. 1155; ("edgy") Haldeman with DiMona, op. cit., p. 341.

RN/Rebozo money: ("never had the urge") Nixon, *Arena,* op. cit., p. 122–; ("means nothing") Miami *Herald,* Nov. 1, 1973; (Bassett) int. James Bassett by FB, FBP; (investment advice) Klein, op. cit., p. 149; (dining/beer) *Newsday,* Oct. 13, 1971; (invested Cuba?) *Rolling Stone,* May 20, 1976; (FBI informant) Moore to Belmont, Jan. 9, 1959, FBI 480–1542; (motel) *Newsday,* Oct. 7, 13, 1971; int. Bob Greene by FB, citing Maroon, FBP; (dig derogatory information) Hunt, *Undercover,* op. cit., p. 183; ("selfless")Tampa *Tribune,* June 26, 1958; ("They'll never get . . .") Miami *Herald,* June 15, 1958; ("Nixon never . . .") int. George Smathers; (Nixon worth 1960–) Stephen Hess and David Broder, *The Republican Establishment,* New York: Harper & Row, 1967, p. 162.

Key Biscayne Bank: (described) *Nation,* Nov. 12, 1973, Paar, op. cit., p. 131; (shovel) *Newsday,* Oct. 9, 1971; (bust) *Nation,* Nov. 12, 1973; (bank's function) ibid.; (Rebozo at bank) *NM,* p. 363, Miami *Herald,* Dec. 6, 1974; (Continental) *Life,* July 31, 1970; (sticker) *Sundance,* Nov./Dec. 1972, p. 35.

RN/Rebozo property: ("loved property") int. George Smathers; (Fisher's) *Newsday,* Oct. 13, 1971; ("After the 1968 election . . .") *MEM,* p. 952; (Rebozo proposed) *Newsday,* Oct. 13, 1971; ("two houses") *MEM,* p. 952; (Rebozo/Key Biscayne/San Clemente properties) *NM,* p. 346–; (house for Julie) Miami *Herald,* Feb. 26, 1974, Boston *Globe,* May 29, 1974; (Rebozo concern) Ehrlichman, op. cit., p. 51; ("If there's something") *NM,* p. 368; ("help Bebe") Ehrlichman, op. cit., pp. 47, 51.

Rebozo in Watergate: (IRS investigation) Miami *Herald,* Oct. 11, 1973; *NYT,* Feb. 27, Apr. 23, 1974; (targeted) closing memo, Oct.16, 1975, WSPF(H-R), p. 5–; *NM,* p. 364; ints. Sam Dash, Terry Lenzner; (hush money) ibid., p. 145–; (Rebozo obstructed) E, Report, pp. 931, 1071; (left country) ibid., p. 1071–; (RN IRS) *AOP,* p. 31; (Baruffi) int. Andrew Baruffi; (Senior IRS source) int. retired IRS official who requested anonymity; (hearings aborted) ints. Sam Dash, Scott Armstrong and Sam Dash, *Chief Counsel,* New York: Random House, 1976, p. 245; ("evidence would not support") WSPF Report, p. 84; ("Star Chamber") *MEM,* p. 967.

Rebozo dubious business activity: (federal loan) *Newsday,* Oct. 6, 1971, *National Observer,* Feb. 2, 1974, Miami *Herald,* Aug. 20, 1972; (shopping center) *Newsday,* Oct. 7, 1971; (Buttari) Miami *Herald,* Feb. 8, 1969, Miami *News,* Feb. 9, 1969, eds. Peter Dale Scott, Paul Hoch, Russell Stetler, and Sylvia Meagher, *The Assassinations: Dallas and Beyond,* New York: Vintage, 1976, p. 404; ("kid gloves") *Newsday,* Oct. 7, 1971, Miami *Herald,* Oct. 7, 8, 1971; (bank application) *NYT,* Oct. 17, 1973; Providence *Journal,* Nov. 6, 1973; (Rebozo held funds?) *NM,* p. 366; (RN net worth) *Newsday,* Dec. 9, 1973; *Congressional Quarterly Almanac,* 1973, p. 1046–; (Rebozo net worth) ed. Miller, *Breaking of the President,* op. cit., Vol. IV, p. 518, Miami *Herald,* Nov. 5, 1973; (Stans) int. Maurice Stans; (earrings) *WP,* July 11, 1974, *NM,* p. 367; Safire, op. cit., p. 615; (RN rebuttal) *MEM,* p. 952; (Anderson) Miami *Herald,* Mar. 20, 1974; ("totally false") *MEM,* p. 953; (Rebozo dismissed) *NYT,* Mar. 21,1974.

Rebozo/organized crime: (Danner) *Sundance,* Nov./Dec. 1972, Hank Messick, *Lansky,* New York: Putnam, 1971, p. 189; (Miami hotels) Special Committee to Investigate Organized Crime in Interstate Commerce, U.S. Sen., 81st Cong., Washington, D.C., U.S. Govt. Printing Office, Interim Report, p. 7–; (Smathers arranged) int. George Smathers; (Lansky associates) ed. Weissman, op. cit., p. 263; (RN/Mackles friendly) *Washington Star,* Dec. 25, 1968, *Ladies' Home Journal,* June 1971; ("fronting") *Sundance,* Nov./Dec. 1972; (Frederich) *Newsday,* Oct. 13, 1971; (Fincher) *Newsday,* Oct. 13, 1971; (Fincher links) Moldea, *Interference,* op. cit., p. 292–; (Orowitz) *Penthouse,* July 1974, p. 106; (Polizzi picked/1943 conviction/Cleveland boss/petitions) *Newsday,* Oct. 7, 1971; (Grand Council) Los Angeles FBI report, Dec. 23, 1957, FBI 92-3229-5; (smuggling booze) *Village Voice,* Aug. 30, 1973; (Kefauver) ibid., *Newsday,* Oct. 7, 1971; Estes Kefauver, *Crime in America,* Garden City, NY: Doubleday, 1951, p. 64; ("one of the most") David Scheim, *Contract on America,* New York: Shapolsky, 1988, p. 298, re. 1964 Senate narcotics hearings; (FBI bug) Cleveland FBI report, June 21, 1965, FBI 92-3229-59, and see Louis Mastriana testimony, Sept. 18, 19, 1973; Sen. Permanent Subcttee. on Investigations, Cttee on Govt. Ops., U.S. Senate, 93rd Cong., 1st Sess. , Pt. II, p. 181–; (Berg) *Newsday,* Oct. 13, 1971, int. Donald Berg, *Village Voice,* Aug. 30, 1973, *Nation,* Nov. 12, 1973; (associate of Lansky/Hoffa) Allen Friedman and Ted Schwartz, *Power and Greed, Inside the Teamsters,* New York: Franklin Watts, 1989, p. 155; ed. Weissman, op. cit., pp. 264, 267—the associate was Arthur Desser; (Secret Service) *Newsday, supra.;* (Berg/RN 1994) int. Donald Berg.

Stolen stocks case: *Newsday,* Oct. 9, 1971; *LAT,* Sept. 12, 1970; ints. Ron Kessler, Jake Jernigan; *WP,* Oct. 25, 1973—major report by Ron Kessler but see Rosen to Sullivan, Sep. 12, 1970, FBI 87-102621-18, SA [name redacted] Miami to SAC Miami, Sep. 11, 1970 and other corr. in FBI 87-102621 and 62-112-974; (Salerno/Beckley) ibid., Messick, *Lansky,* op. cit., p. 193; Sifakis, op. cit., p. 314; (King) *WP,* Oct. 25, 1973; *Penthouse,* July 19, 1974; ed. Weissman, op. cit., p. 263–; (Kotz) int. and corr. Alvin Kotz; (Teresa) closing memo, Oct. 16, 1975, WSPF (H-R); Vincent Teresa with Thomas Renner, *My Life in the Mafia: The True Confessions of a Mob Leader,* London: Grafton, 1974, p. 288–; (Mastriana) testimony, Sept. 18, 19, 1973, Hearings of Perm. Subcttee. on Investigations, Cttee. on Govt. Ops., U.S. Sen., 93rd Cong., 1st. Sess.; (Alo/Lansky) Teresa, op. cit., p. 220–; Lacey, op. cit., p. 290– and see SAC Dallas to director, Aug. 20, 1971, FBI 92-128-23-5; (long-held suspicions) Eisenberg, Dan, and Landau, op. cit., p. 258; Messick, *Lansky,* op. cit., p. 187–; (Gallinaro) ints. William Gallinaro.

"non-member associate": ints. and corr. Michael Ewing, former congressional investigator of organized crime and Watergate; Ewing was given the designation by former FBI Agent Charles Stanley.

RN promise re: crime: *LAT,* Oct. 21, 1968.

Newsday series: Oct. 6, 7, 9, 11, 12, 13, 1971; (reaction/reprisals) McDermott to Jenkins, June 25, 1974, FBI 74575-150; Henry Ruth to Clarence Kelley, Feb. 27, 1974, FBI 62-112974; Wise, *American Police State,* op. cit., p. 129 and Wise, *The Politics of Lying,* op. cit., p. 324–, Joseph Spear, *Presidents and the Press,* Cambridge, MA: MIT Press, 1984, p. 130; Donner, op. cit., p. 351, Hunt, *Undercover,* op. cit., p. 183; Caulfield testimony, E, Bk. 22, p. 10368–; (agents' surveillance) *WP,* June 28, 1974; ("worse than foolish") Safire, op. cit., p. 615.

RN "resented": Pierpoint, op. cit., p. 82.

Smathers: int. George Smathers.

Finch: int. Robert Finch by FB, FBP.

"nails pulled out": ed. Miller, *Breaking of a President,* op. cit., Vol. IV, p. 511.

"never going to blab": Safire, op. cit., p. 615.

Chapter 12

"All you have got to do": *U.S. News & World Report,* Oct. 3, 1952.

"end is power": Hess and Broder, op. cit., p. 143.

hero/preacher: Mazo, op. cit., p. 85.

"A few friends": *MO,* p. 629.

Eisenhower meetings: (1949) *MO,* p. 507; (1950/51) ibid., pp. 577, 644–.

"prat boy": RN in Frank Gannon int. transcript, CBS *60 Minutes,* Apr. 8, 1984; Wicker, op. cit., p. 160.

Dewey: ("a possibility") Mazo, op. cit., p. 90; ("you can be President") *MEM,* p. 84; Nixon, *Six Crises,* op. cit., p. 299; (tempted Nixon?) *Frontier,* Apr. 1962; *MO,* p. 684–.

Warren: (questionnaire) *FB,* p. 253; Vernon O'Reilly unid. article, Sept. 26, 1952, Box G 281, DPP; (at convention) ed. Sevareid, op. cit., p. 76; Costello, op. cit., p. 86; James to Wilma Bassett, July 9, 1952, Bassett Papers, courtesy of Cynthia Bassett; Leo Katcher, Earl Warren, *A Political Biography,* New York: McGraw Hill, 1967, p. 290–; Earl Warren, *The Memoirs of Earl Warren,* New York: Doubleday, 1977, p. 252–; *MO,* pp. 691, 719–; Arnold, op. cit., p. 29–; (The most distasteful") int. John Rothmann and see Louis Kohlmeier, Jr., *God Save This Honorable Court,* New York: Charles Scribner's, 1972, p. 93; (" 'Tricky' . . . despicable") William Buckley column, Mar. 20, 1975, *National Review* and see Jack Harrison Pollack, *Earl Warren,* Englewood Cliffs, NJ: Prentice-Hall, 1979, p. 142.

1952 convention: (Ike's list) Sherman Adams, *Firsthand Report,* New York: Harper, 1961, p. 34; Eisenhower press conference, May 31, 1955, James Hagerty Papers, DDEL; (smoke-filled rooms) Manchester, *The Glory and the Dream,* op. cit., p. 619; (RN picked) *MO,* p. 732; Richard Norton Smith, *Thomas Dewey and His Times,* New York: Simon & Schuster, 1982, p. 596; ("Surprised") ibid., p. 597; (argued with Pat) *PAT,* p. 114–; *MEM,* p. 85–; (Pat surprised) *Saturday Evening Post,* Sept. 6, 1952; (platform) Smith, *Thomas Dewey,* op. cit., p. 597; (photographers) *Time,* Feb. 29, 1960; *PAT,* p. 117; (Ike irritated) Lurie, op. cit., p. 116–; (*Time*) *Time,* Aug. 25, 1952.

scandals: (Truman plagued) *MO,* p. 642–; ("When we are through") Nathan Miller, *Stealing from America,* New York: Marlowe, 1996, p. 331.

Fund Crisis: (*Post*) New York *Post,* Sept. 18, 1952; (tip etc.) Washington *Sunday Star,* Sept. 21, 1952; Robert Humphreys to Sherman Adams, Feb. 7, 1959, DDEL; *MO,* p. 757–; ed. Sevareid, op. cit., p. 88, but see Katcher, op. cit., p. 294; (use of money) New York *Post,* Sept. 18, 1952; *U.S. News & World Report,* Oct. 3, 1952; ("all wrong") Mazo, op. cit., p. 107; ("just . . . fund") *MO,* p. 759; Nixon, *Six Crises,* op. cit., p. 73–; ("nothing to worry") ibid., p. 78; (Edson story) Chicago *Daily News,* Sept. 18, 1952; (Ike response) *MO,* p. 770; ("hounds tooth") *NYT,* Sept. 21, 1952; ("Hiss crowd") *MO,* pp. 772, 774–; (call to withdraw) *MO,* p. 780–; (Dewey/resign) *MO,* p. 803; (Ike called Nixon) *MO,* p. 807.

Checkers speech: (no rehearsal?) Nixon, *Six Crisis,* op. cit., p. 112; *MEM,* p. 103; *Look,* Feb. 24, 1953; (witness) James Kearns in St. Louis *Post-Dispatch,* Sept. 28, 1952; (delayed?) *Variety,* Sept. 21, 1954 and draft article, both in Box G 281, DPP; (60 million) Barry Goldwater, *With No Apologies,* New York: William Morrow, 1979, p. 67; *MO,* p. 827; (text of speech) *U.S. News & World Report,* Oct. 3, 1952; (Pat sat close) *Westporter Herald,* Sept. 25, 1952; (Lincoln quote) Nixon, *Six Crises,* op. cit., p. 103; Wills, op. cit., p. 104; (hands reaching) *MEM,* p. 104; (hurled notes) *Look,* Feb. 24, 1973; Mazo, op. cit., p. 131; *PAT,* p. 124; ("I was a failure") *JA,* p. 218; (euphoric) *MO,* p. 844; (fur coats) Washington *Times-Herald,* Sept. 30; *Wall Street Journal,* Oct. 10, 1952; (RN "stripped") Wicker, op. cit., p. 107.

Ike response to Checkers: (watched) Robert Humphreys to Sherman Adams, Feb. 17, 1959, Humphreys papers, DDEL; (Mamie wept) *MEM,* p. 105; (telegram lost) *PAT,* p. 124; *MO,*

p. 839; (Chotiner intercepted) Pat Hillings with Howard Seelye, *Irrepressible Irishman,* privately published: Harold Dean, 1993, p. 61; *MO,* p. 840–; ("You're my boy") *MEM,* p. 106; (RN endorsed) *MEM,* p. 107; (RN weeps) ibid.; (drama coach) Kornitzer, op. cit., p. 106 and John Rothmann, unpub. ms., p. 36—coach was Albert Upton; ("amazing") int. Bryce Harlow in eds. Miller Center, op. cit., p. 7.

Dog: (collars, etc.) Nixon, *Six Crises,* op. cit., p. 125; (lived on) Madeleine Edmondson and Alden Duer Cohen, *The Women of Watergate,* New York: Pocket, 1975, p. 102; *NYT,* July 3, 1968; (exhume?) CNN Website, citing AP and *U.S. News & World Report,* Apr. 28, 1997; (Order of . . . Tooth) Nixon, *Six Crises,* op. cit., p. 125; Arnold, op. cit., p. 23; *Colliers,* July 9, 1954, James Bassett unpub. ms., Apr. 9, 1954; Bassett Papers.

RN reminded: *PAT,* p. 126, Crowley, *Winter,* op. cit., p. 19.

"truth on my side": Monica Crowley, *Nixon Off the Record,* New York: Random House, 1996, p. 63.

press on fund: *New Republic,* Oct. 6, 1952.

problems with RN's answers: (needed home) New York *Post,* Sept. 18, 1952; (no maid) ibid., *MO,* p. 757; ($20,000) *U.S. News & World Report,* Oct. 3, 1952; *MO,* p. 653; (decorator) ibid.; *PAT,* p. 111; (RN admitted) Costello, op. cit., p. 110; (acquired maid) *New Republic,* Sept. 29, 1952; (increased prosperity) New York *Post,* Oct. 31, 1952; (could not have been charged) *MO,* p. 856; (RN told newsman) Costello, op. cit., p. 95; (speech fees) *Look,* Feb. 24, 1953; (sheet on desk) *MO,* p. 762, citing int. Leo Katcher; (two accounts?) memo to DP, Oct. 20, 1952, citing Jiggs Donohoe, and AP, Oct. 18, 1952, memo citing Judge Thurman Clark, Box G 281, DPP; (three funds) Washington *Daily News,* Feb. 26, 1953.

fund contributors: ("We've been paying") *MO,* p. 762; (Chotiner) Lurie, op. cit., p. 127; ("Who's Who") *MO,* p. 636; (millionaires) DP column "Why?," fall 1952, not run in local papers, Box G 272, DPP; ("We realized") article by Richard Donovan, one of three journalists who developed fund story, *The Reporter,* Oct. 14, 1952; (within a week) *MO,* p. 632; (Woodward/Anderson) Pilat, op. cit., p. 302; DP broadcast, Nov. 2, 1952, Box G 281, DPP; *MO,* p. 650; (Ghormley) ibid. and see Kornitzer, op. cit., p. 190–; (Crail) Costello, op. cit., p. 216–; (Adams/Rowan bros.) *New Republic,* Sept. 29, 1952—Adams does not appear in *U.S. News & World Report,* Oct. 3, 1952 version of contributors list; ("Never . . . a phone call") *U.S. News & World Report,* Oct. 3, 1952; (Hammond call) DP column, "Did Nixon's Angels benefit?" Box G 281, DPP.

Dana Smith: (friend/host) int. Jean Smith Goodrich, Smith's daughter; (IRS problem) *NYT,* Sept. 24, 1952; AP wire copy, Sept. 23, 1952, Box G 281, DPP; St. Louis *Post-Dispatch,* Oct. 30, 1952.

Smith/Nixon? and Cuba: (RN to Embassy) AP wire copy, Oct. 29, *NYT,* Oct. 30, 1952, DP column, Oct. 29, 1962, with detail from embassy files, and see *MO,* p. 941n., p. 649; ("routine") *NYT,* Oct. 30, 1952; (office insisted) *Look,* Feb. 24, 1953; (RN reported in Cuba) St. Louis *Post-Dispatch,* Oct. 30, 1952; (demands retraction) RN to Ted Bates agency, Nov. 3, 1952, cited in full in Harrington telegram to DP, Box G 281, DPP; (claims Hawaii) *Look,* Feb. 24, 1953; *MEM,* p. 108; (Link background) *NYT,* Feb. 15, 1974; int. Theodore Link, Jr.; (Freeman/5 witnesses) memo to DP, Box G 281, DPP; ("Nixon agreed") Messick, *Lansky,* op. cit., p. 190; (Culbertson) ed. Tyler Abell, *Drew Pearson Diaries, 1949–1959,* New York: Holt, Rhinehart & Winston, 1974, p. 335, entry for Oct. 27, 1954; (other Rothman ints.) FBI summaries, "Norman Rothman, Internal Security—Cuba," June 26/27, director to Asst. AG Byron White, July 25, 1961, and SAC Miami to director, FBI 97-4030-20 in FBI Cosa Nostra files supplied to House Select Cttee. on assassinations, released 1998, JFK Collection, NA; (Rothman covered up?) ibid. and ed. Abell, op. cit., p. 335.

mob in Cuba: (controlled) Eisenberg, Dan, and Landau, op. cit., p. 253–; Sifakis, op. cit., p. 29–; (Sans Souci described) briefing in Box G 281, DPP; (Lansky control) Legat, Havana to director, Jan. 14, 1948, FBI 62-75147-210-102; Gus Russo, *Live by the Sword,* Baltimore, MD: Bancroft Press, 1998, p. 50; memo to DP, Sept. 26, 1952, Box 281, DPP, and Eisenberg, et al., op. cit., Ch. 30.

Lansky and Smith, RN: Eisenberg, et al., op. cit., p. 258; (Danner) Jeff Gerth article, *Penthouse,* July 1974.

Horner: int. Norman Casper.

Clarke: int. Jack Clarke.

"Italian money": Moore to Belmont, Jan. 9, 1959, FBI 109-480-1542.

Alo: (background) Sifakis, op. cit., p. 7; Ed Reid, *The Grim Reapers,* New York: Bantam, 1970, p. 92; Lacey, op. cit.; (responses on RN) int. Vincent Alo.

Lansky: ("impressed") Messick, *Lansky,* op. cit., p. 190; Messick contacts with author, 1991; (Stacher) Eisenberg, et al., op. cit., p. 232.

Giancana: Sam and Chuck Giancana, *Double Cross,* New York: Warner, 1992, p. 193.

Arvey: Peter Dale Scott, *Deep Politics and the Death of JFK,* Berkeley, CA: University of California Press, 1993, pp. 77, 158–, 179, 200.

Cohen refused: FBI report, originating Los Angeles, Dec. 29, 1958, FBI 92-3156-122.

RN innocent victim of smears?: e.g., *AMI,* p. 295–.

Chapter 13

"The top officials": RN in call for resignation of RNC Chairman Guy Gabrielson, Oct. 8, 1951, DP column, Box G 281, DPP.

Malaxa: (Pearson/TV) transcript broadcast, Nov. 2, 1952, Box G 281, DPP; (GSA) Compliance Division report, Dec. 29, 1949, Box G 172, DPP; (U.S. concern) DP memo to editors re. CIA/State, June 5, 1962, Box G 192, DPP; *WP,* Nov. 16, 1979; Seymour Hersh, *The Dark Side of Camelot,* Boston: Little, Brown, 1997, p. 158–; (20 drawers) *Saga,* Nov. 1962; (Goering bros.) ibid.; Howard Blum, *Wanted: The Search for Nazis in America,* New York: Quadrangle, 1977, p. 117; Charles Higham, *American Swastika,* New York: Doubleday, 1985, p. 211; (captured cable) German minister, Bucharest to Berlin, Jan. 8, 1941 cited at DP to editors, June 5, 1962, and in letter, Rep. Frank Kowalski to AG Robert F. Kennedy, Apr. 9, 1962, Box G 192, DPP; (1941 coups) I. Glickman, sec. of United Romanian Jews of America to Rep. Jacob Javits, May 14, 1953, Box G 192, DPP; *Saga, supra.,* Higham, op. cit., p. 211 and Elizabeth W. Hazard, *Cold War Crucible,* New York: Columbia University Press, 1996, p. 223–; (simply refusing) Kowalski to AG Kennedy, *supra.*

Malaxa/Nixon: (lawyers call) *Saga, supra.; MO,* p. 647 and deposition of Thomas Bewley in *Malaxa v. Pearson,* Washington, D.C. District Court, Civil Action, No. 5549-55, Box G 192, DPP; (Bewley backed RN) *MO,* pp. 369, 379, 528; (pure chance) ibid. and Walter Land memo, Oct. 9, 1952, Box G 192, DPP; (RN/Western Tube offices) Bewley deposition, *supra.;* Pearson draft entitled "Nicolae Malaxa," Box G 192, DPP, G. T. Vincent to DP, Oct. 26, 1952, Box G 281, photo of office directory, Box G 192, DPP; (never produced) *NYT,* Oct. 7, 1962; ("paper shuffling") DP memo to editors, June 5, 1962, *supra.,* and blind memo citing Bewley deposition, p. 48, Box G 192, DPP; (Shelley) *NYT,* Oct. 7, 1962; (private bill) Blum, op. cit., p. 119; ("important, strategically") RN and William Knowland to Manley Fleischman, Sept. 14, 1951, Box G 192, DPP; (massive advantages) Loftus and Aarons, op. cit., pp. 224, 558 and blind memo, *supra.;* (RN telephone) ibid., p. 558; Blum, op. cit., p. 120; (RN/Hillings) Kowalski to AG Kennedy, *supra.;* (Rogers) blind memo, *supra.,* Blum, op. cit., p. 121.

alleged bribe: (DP notes) handwritten notes/witness list, Box G 192, DPP; (Wisner/Romania) Evan Thomas, *The Very Best Men,* New York: Simon & Schuster, 1995, p. 20–; (Pearson/CIA report) "Friendly Questions for DP," document prepared for lawsuit, Box G 192, DPP; (Cadillacs/jewelry) *Saga,* Nov. 1962; (Wisner/recruitment) Thomas, op. cit., p. 35; (recruited Malaxa?) Loftus and Aarons, op. cit., p. 559n.33.

Gordon Mason: int. Gordon Mason and Hazard, op. cit., p. 223–; Hersh, op. cit., p. 158.

Visoianu widow: int. Mrs. Constantine Visoianu.

Malaxa in US: (5th Ave.) *Saga,* Nov. 1962; (death) Blum, op. cit., p. 122.

Election 1952: (vanished) Klein, op. cit., p. 49; (*Time*), Ralph de Toledano, *Nixon,* New York: Duell Sloan & Pearce, 1960, p. 149; (vacation) *NYT,* Miami *Herald,* Nov. 11, 21, 1952, Nixon to Rebozo, Nov. 28, 1952, Rebozo file, Series 320, Box 622, VP, NA; (fish) Rebozo to RN, Dec. 5, 1952, Michael Ewing Collection; int. P.R. man John Tassos.

RN enemies: (Harriman/Douglas campaign) Douglas, op. cit., p. 324; (Harriman/dinner) *FB,* p. 244; Rudy Abramson, *Spanning the Century,* New York: William Morrow, 1992, p. 412; (topic) ibid., p. 686; (Eleanor Roosevelt) *FB,* p. 244–; (J. F. Kennedy) Douglas, op. cit., p. 325; (Kent/Stevenson) Mazo, op. cit. p. 8; (Celler) ibid. and see Toledano, *Nixon,* op. cit., p. 151; (Lippmann) *Radical History Review,* Fall 1994, p. 138; (Ball) George Ball, *The Past Has Another Pattern,* New York: Norton, 1982, p. 128; (Pepper) Claude Pepper with Hayes Gorey, *Pepper: Eyewitness to a Century,* New York: Harcourt Brace Jovanovich, 1987, p. 240; (Redlich) cited in Boston *Phoenix,* Aug. 13, 1974.

Truman: (re: "traitors") Kornitzer, op. cit., p. 213; *MEM,* p. 112; Miller, *Plain Speaking,* op. cit., 178; ("crooks") *The Reporter,* Apr. 19, 1956; ("Goddamn liar") Miller, *Plain Speaking,* op. cit., p. 178–: ("doesn't understand") ibid., p. 335.

Rich: *NYT,* Apr. 24, 1994.

RN response to 1952 attacks: ("My instinct") *MEM,* p. 109; (Stripling) *Esquire,* Nov. 1975.

RN temper: ("The hotter") *Saturday Evening Post,* Sept. 6, 1952; ("blowing . . . stack") ed. Sevareid, op. cit., p. 80; Alsop, op. cit., p. 153; (Klein/Hillings) Klein, op. cit., p. 133–; *JA,* p. 223; ("obligation") ed. Sidney Kraus, *The Great Debates,* Bloomington, IN: Indiana University Press, 1962, p. 397; (slap) notes of int. Zita Remley by FB, FBP, *FB,* p. 236—name is Zita, not Vita, as rendered by FB (Remley to DP, Oct. 7, 1952, Box G 281, DPP).

1952 violence: (Oregon) Mazo, op. cit., p. 117–; (Long Beach) ed. Abell, op. cit., p. 229; (Rogan) Los Angeles *Sun News,* Nov. 2, 1952; ("When we're elected") Costello, op. cit., p. 6; (Heavey)

Weekly News Letter, CA State Federation of Labor, Nov. 3, 1954; Robert Allen to DP, Nov. 13, 1953, Box G 281, DPP; Chotiner to Agent Paul Paterni, Feb. 2 and to William Rogers, Feb. 10, and complaint for damages, 443705, Superior Court of California, (San Francisco) Nov. 26, 1954, summary of incident, Bogen/Pearman (police) Heckler Report, Oct. 29, 1954; Nelson to RN, Dec. 7, 1954, William Rogers Papers, DDEL; *NYT*, Oct. 30, Nov. 27, 1954.

RN depression/weeping: ("He almost needed") MO, p. 763; ("the full weight") Nixon, *Six Crises*, op. cit., p. 87; ("irritable") MO, p. 793; ("sponge") ibid., p. 799; (Drown) PAT, p. 120; ("blow up") MO, p. 793; (Mother message/Hillings) Hillings with Seelye, op. cit., p. 60; *Good House-keeping*, June 1960, but see Kornitzer, op. cit., p. 192–; (tears after Checkers) Matthews, op. cit., p. 84; Mazo, op. cit., p. 131; (tears on plane) ibid., p. 134; (tears/Knowland) MO, p. 849; ("Dick's state of mind") Kornitzer, op. cit., p. 193; (tried frantically) int. Dr. Arnold Hutschnecker.

Pat in '52 campaign: (doubts) see Ch. 12, *supra.*; MEM, p. 86; (prattled) *American Weekly*, Aug. 24, 1952; (Pat on campaigning) Los Angeles *Herald & Express*, July 25, 1952; (she urged) MEM, p. 98; PAT, p. 120; ("Of course you can") MEM, p. 103; ("great") PAT, p. 124; (total silence) MEM, p. 108; ("Why . . . keep taking?") Mazo, op. cit., p. 119; ("kitten") PAT, p. 119; ("So much pain") ibid., p. 126; ("would hate politics") MEM, p. 108.

Hannah in fund: (babysitting) Kornitzer, op. cit., p. 191; (Frank wept) MEM, p. 109; (Hannah on phone) MEM, p. 99; (Hannah/Ike telegram) Kornitzer, op. cit., pp. 192, 205–; MEM, p. 107; (inauguration note) MEM, p. 117.

RN promised to retire: *NYT* magazine, Sept. 13, 1970; Mazo, op. cit., p. 139.

1952 inauguration: Lurie, op. cit., p. 159.

RN on peace: e.g., 1969 inaugural address in full in *Whittier Rock*, Spring 1969.

"exaltation": PAT, p. 132.

portents: (Haldeman) MO, pp. 825, 826; (father) MO, pp. 573, 636; *U.S. News & World Report*, Oct. 3, 1952; (Goldberg in '52) *U.S. News & World Report*, Feb. 23, 1998; (Goldberg in Watergate) Washington *Star-News*, Aug. 19, 1973; WP, Aug. 20, 1973, Feb. 4, 1998; (Goldberg re. Lewinsky) ibid. and *LAT Book Review*, Mar. 14, 1999; (meets Hunt) int. Howard Hunt; Hunt, *Undercover*, op. cit., p. 127: (Hunt card) Hunt Corr file, VP, NA; (Ervin sworn in) Paul Clancy, *Just a Country Lawyer*, Bloomington, IN: Indiana University Press, 1974, p. 155.

Chapter 14

poem: David, op. cit., p. 13–.

Duke Zeibert's: James Bassett unpub. ms., pp. 52, 234.

Bassett: (background) Klein, op. cit., p. 137–; Bassett letters to Wilma Bassett, 1952, 1954, 1960, Bassett Collection, Bassett ms., *supra.*, p. lxv–; Nixon, *Six Crises*, op. cit., p. 329–; int. Cynthia Bassett, Gottlieb & Wolt, op. cit., p. 279; ("intense") Bassett ms., p. 52; ("affable") int. James Bassett by FRB, FBP; ("son") ibid.; ("oldest") JB to Wilma, June 3, 1954, Bassett Collection; (P-55) Bassett ms., pp. 46, 60; ("judgement") JB to Wilma, June 3, 1954, *supra.*; ("chlorophyll") Bassett ms., p. 27; ("ice") ibid., p. 13; ("subliminal") James Bassett int. by FB, FBP; ("I remember") Bassett ms., p. lxx; ("balls") James Bassett int. by FB, FBP; ("retreat") Bassett ms. p. 52; ("lonesome") JB to Wilma, June 3, 1954, *supra.*; ("grimness") Bassett ms., p. lxix.

RN and drink: (RN writing) Nixon, *Arena*, op. cit., Ch. 11; (protestations) e.g., int. Robert Cushman by FB, FBP; ("we ordered") Bassett ms. p. 11; ("fabulous Cad") ibid., p. 27–; ("Scotches") ibid., p. 164; ("We'd arrived") ibid., p. 244; ("Rarely") *Time*, Aug. 25, 1952; ("At 5 P.M.") Bellino autobiographical notes, Bellino Papers; ("wonderful catalysts") Bobst to RN, Apr. 20, 1956, corr. files, Series 320, Box 90, VP, NA; (gin) Elmer Bobst, *Bobst*, New York: David McKay, 1973, p. 273; ("won't drink") *Colliers*, July 9, 1954; (hair way down) JB to Wilma, June 10, 1960, Bassett Collection; ("after Martinis") James Bassett int. by FB, FBP and see Haldeman and DiMona, op. cit., p. 45; ("not a shit!") JA, p. 343.

RN and Eisenhower: ("errand boy") *Life*, Dec. 14, 1953; ("Asst. President") ibid.; (Johnson) Jeff Shesol, *Mutual Contempt*, New York: Norton, 1997, p. 79; (Reston) Blanche Wiesen Cook, "Dwight David Eisenhower: Antimilitarist in the White House," *Forums in History*, St. Charles, MO: Foreign Press, 1974, p. 3; (immature) Wicker, op. cit., p. 196 and *AMI*, p. 379; (liability) int. Robert Finch in eds. Miller Center, op. cit., p. 260; ("tea-drinkers") Bassett unpub. ms., *supra.*, p. 27–; ("dumb") JB to Wilma, Mar. 6, 1954, Bassett Collection; (RN . . . smiled) MEM, p. 145; ("slip . . . a gadget") Bassett unpub. ms., *supra.*, p. 48—entry for Mar. 12, 1954; ("You know boys") AMI, p. 334fn; (Ike "remembered") WP, Mar. 15, 1997; (Ike castigating) AP, Oct. 21, 1979; AMI, p. 349; ("snake's belly") Bassett ms., p. 207; ("six times") *Newsday*, Apr. 25, 1994, citing H. R. Haldeman notes, Apr. 1969; (Ike golf) Lurie, op. cit., p. 160; ("furious dedication") ibid.; (RN cheated?) London *Daily Express*, Aug. 9, 1996; ("Nixon fired") Bassett ms., p. 17–; ("RN complained"/bridge) int. Walter Trohan; (not in private quarters) int. John Rothmann, citing Bryce Harlow; ("never asked") White,

1960, op. cit., p. 66; ("Hutschnecker") Winter-Berger, op. cit., p. 257; (de Toledano) Lurie, op. cit., p. 161, citing PBS program, Oct. 14, 1971.

Rejections: (Duke) *COQ* magazine, Jan. 1974; (Whittier) Mazo, op. cit., p. 139 and JB to Wilma, June 10, 1954, Bassett Collection; ("pained") *Good Housekeeping*, June 1960; (few friends) int. Walter Trohan; ("uncomfortable") Nancy Dickerson, *Among Those Present*, New York: Random House, 1976, p. 1976; ("wooden") int. Patricia Alsop by FB, FBP, *FB*, p. 336; (aversion) Alsop, op. cit., p. 28–.

"bone tired": Mazo, op. cit., p. 152.

"through with politics": *MEM*, p. 163.

agreed with Pat: *JA*, p. 234.

Bassett bet: Alsop, op. cit., p. 155.

Ike illness: (heart attack) Adams, op. cit., p. 180; Manchester, op. cit., p. 752; (RN reaction) Press Secretary Jim Hagerty acct., Hagerty papers, DDEL; *MEM*, p. 164; *American Weekly*, Mar. 4, 1956; Nixon, *Six Crises*, op. cit., p. 132; ("voice hoarse") James D. Barber, professor of political science, Duke University, *Political Science Quarterly*, Winter 1977–78, p. 588; (RN presided) Adams, op. cit., p. 186; ("leaned backward") ibid., p. 185; (Dulles's biographer) Hoopes, op. cit., p. 304–; (Randall/"pray") cabinet notes, July 4–Aug. 1, 1956, Clarence Randall Papers, Box 3, DDEL–the note was reported by economist Gabriel Hauge; ("I would be next") *MEM*, p. 167; (Hall) Henry Brandon, *Special Relationships*, New York: Atheneum, 1988, p. 140.

Ike handling of vice presidency, 1956: (shortlist) entries for Dec. 13, 14, 1955, James Hagerty papers, DDEL; ("I've watched Dick") Emmet Hughes, *The Ordeal of Power*, New York: Atheneum, 1963, p. 173; (cabinet post suggested) *AMI*, p. 387; (Some would insist) Bob Considine column, Oct. 10, 1974, citing Milton Eisenhower, *The President Is Calling*, New York: Doubleday, 1974; Adams, op. cit., p. 230; ("be very gentle") diary note, Eisenhower secretary Ann Whitman, Feb. 9, 1956, DDEL; (cat-and-mouse) *AMI*, p. 384; ("agonizing") Nixon, *Six Crises*, op. cit., p. 161; ("anguish") Bryce Harlow cited at *FB*, p. 350; ("hurt") Mazo, op. cit., p. 164—perhaps citing Chotiner, see Leonard Lurie, *Party Politics*, New York: Stein & Day, 1980, p. 245; ("fury") int. Walter Trohan; ("depressed") *PAT*, p. 157.

Chotiner: ("April meeting") Ann Whitman diary, Apr. 26, 1956, DDEL; *AMI*, p. 398 and see NY *World-Telegram & Sun*, Apr. 27, 1956; (revelations emerge) Federal Trade Commission Order 6236, Dec. 22, 1955, Box 230, DPP; (FBI) Nichols to Jones, Jan. 25, 1956, FBI 63-2766-2; (furor) *Behind the Scenes* magazine, Mar. 1956—issued Jan.; *LAT*, Jan. 12, 1956; (untrue claim) *WP*, Jan. 4, 1956; (probe) NY *World-Telegram & Sun*, Washington *Daily News*, Apr. 27, 1956; (RN to tell the press) Ann Whitman diary, Apr. 26, 1956, DDEL; *AMI*, p. 398.

RN in '56 campaign: (campaign plane) *Time*, Nov. 5, 1956; (Pat/mike) *U.S. News & World Report*, Oct. 5, 1956; (Haldeman) H. R. "Bob" Haldeman deposition, May 22, 1973; *DNC vs. McCord*, Civil Action 1233-72, U.S. District Court, Washington, D.C., p. 10; H. R. "Bob" Haldeman to RN, May 22, 1956, Series 320, Box 311, VP, NA.

Hughes: (background) Donald Barlett and James Steele, *Empire*, New York: Norton, 1979; Charles Higham, *Howard Hughes, The Secret Life*, London: Pan, 1994; (bribery) Barlett and Steele, op. cit., p. 147–; Higham, Hughes, op. cit., p. 151; (Truman) Noah Dietrich and Bob Thomas, *Howard, The Amazing Mr. Hughes*, Greenwich, CT: Fawcett, 1972, p. 241–; (Dewey) ibid.; (Hughes's politics) Barlett and Steele, op. cit., p. 178; ("I can buy") Higham, Hughes, op. cit., frontispiece; ("He figured") Dietrich and Thomas, op. cit., p. 241–.

RN and Hughes: ("Never met") int. of RN by Prof. Herbert Parmet, supplied to author and see Parmet, op. cit., p. 403–; (Haldeman) *HD*, p. 397; Parmet, op. cit., p. 409; *JA*, p. 259; (St. Johns) *MO*, p. 592 citing Richard St. Johns and conv. Roger Morris; ("old buddy") int. Donald A. Nixon; ("encountered") int. Herbert Klein; ("happy . . . over seeing you") JDH to RN, memo, Jan. 23, 1959, Howard Hughes file, VP, NA, *AMI*, p. 599; (Don Hughes) int. Gen. Don Hughes; (from the very start) Michael Drosnin, *Citizen Hughes*, New York: Bantam, 1986, pp. 311, 519; (RN praise) Peter Brown and Pat Broeske, *Howard Hughes, The Untold Story*, New York: Signet, 1997, p. 341; (Giancana) Sam and Chuck Giancana, op. cit., p. 211; int. Sam Giancana (nephew).

Stassen: (1956 bid) Fullest accounts, see *U.S. News & World report*, Aug. 3, 1956; Mazo, op. cit., p. 158–; ("aloof") Nixon, *Six Crises*, op. cit., p. 167; ("scared") Mazo, op. cit., p. 179.

Maheu: (background) Maheu and Hack, op. cit.; Hougan, op. cit., p. 278–; (early work for Hughes) Maheu and Hack, op. cit., p. 55–.

Anti-Stassen operation: Maheu and Hack, op. cit., p. 79–; int. Robert Maheu; (basket) Hougan, *Spooks*, op. cit., p. 280; ("cannot . . . be told") Alsop, op. cit., p. 72; (polls announced) Maheu and Hack, op. cit., p. 82, Mazo, op. cit., p. 182; ("no gratitude") int. Robert Maheu, and Maheu and Hack, op. cit., p. 82; ("malleable") ibid., pp. 79.

Hughes loan: (Waters's call) Noah Dietrich, int. transcript, p. 126; Charles Higham Collection, Mary Norton Clapp Library, Occidental College, and Dietrich, op. cit., p. 281; (Donald Nixon business) Donald Nixon personal statement, 1960, File 804, Box 104, WSPF; ("smell") Dietrich, op. cit., p. 281; (lease worth less than half) ibid., p. 282; *The Reporter,* Aug. 16, 1962 and detail in Nicholas North-Broome, *The Hughes-Nixon Loan,* New York: American Public Affairs Inst., 1972; (Dietrich warning) Dietrch, op. cit., p. 283; ("family comes ahead") Dietrich int. transcript, *supra.;* (loan secrecy) Drew Pearson column draft, Oct. 25, 1960 and see Donald Nixon personal statement, *supra.;* (to bury further) *The Reporter,* Aug. 16, 1962; (supposedly used) Dietrich, op. cit., p. 281; ("Pull 'em off") Dietrich int., *supra.;* Dietrich, op. cit., p. 284; (leaked) *The Reporter,* Aug. 16, 1962; ("I had nothing") RN int. with Larry Collins; Long Beach *Independent,* undated, 1962, Box G 281, DPP; (lot transfer) Dietrich, op. cit., p. 285; (owner until '62) North-Broome, op. cit., p. 93 and see Frank Waters to William Gay, Jan. 4, 1963, Box 92, WSPF; (waived rights) letter agreement between F. Waters and H. Nixon, Dec. 12, 1954, ibid.; (Ridgeley) North-Broome, op. cit., p. 86; Parmet, op. cit., p. 405; ("call Dick," etc.) int. Philip Reiner; New York *Post,* Nov. 1, 1960; (RN to Cal.) ibid.; (ensure no tax) DP column, Oct. 27, 1960, Box G 281, DPP; (RN on list) ibid. and DP column draft, Oct. 25, 1960; (suggested Carnation) int. Dietrich, *supra.,* p. 126; (Carnation post) North-Broome, op. cit., pp. 94, 99 and see *MO,* pp. 637, 650; (no impropriety) RN to Ben Bradlee, *Meet the Press,* TV program transcript, VI.37, Oct. 7, 1962, p. 10; ("won't answer") int. Frank Waters; ("really for Richard") int. C. Arnholt Smith; (new house) *NYT,* UPI, June 4, 1957; ed. Sevareid, op. cit., pp. 106, 138; (mortgage) *MEM,* p. 243; (before selling) ed. Abell, op. cit., p. 384; (foes speculated) Kline to Champion; (Gov. Pat Brown Staff), Feb. 11, 1961, Nitze-Nixon folder, RFK papers, AG's general corr., Box 42, JFKL; (Medical Institute & IRS) Barlett and Steele, op. cit., p. 198; (airplane purchases/TWA) ibid., p. 217–; (concessions to TWA) ed. Miller, *Breaking of a President,* op. cit., Vol. 3, p. 113; Jack Anderson with James Boyd, *Confessions of a Muckraker,* New York: Random House, 1979, p. 329; (TWA president) North-Broome, op. cit., p. 14, *MO,* pp. 573, 746—the president was Charles Thomas; ("curious"/"bargain?") Dietrich, op. cit., p. 285; ("draw your conclusions") *WP,* Feb. 6, 1972; ("not philanthropist") Benjamin Schemmer unpub. ms. provided to author, p. 214; ("In back of mind") *WP,* Dec. 16, 1973; ("damaging") Nixon, *Six Crises,* op. cit., p. 243.

RN/Pat marriage: (Pat titles) Gil Troy, *Affairs of State,* New York: Free Press, 1997, p. 175; (supportive) *PAT,* p. 157; (silly things) *NYT,* Aug. 21, 1956; (clothing) Paul Boller, *Presidential Wives,* New York: Oxford University Press, 1988, p. 404; ("actress") *PAT,* p. 143; ("gadding") *PAT,* p. 162; ("I can think . . .") *NYT,* Aug. 21, 1956; ("serious problem") Ann Whitman diary, Mar. 13, 1956, DDEL; ("terror") Pierpoint, op. cit., p. 186; ("blowing stack") Bryant, op. cit., p. 249; ("temper") Alsop, op. cit., p. 59; ("chewed hell") Wills, op. cit., p. 30; ("one of her moods") JB to Wilma, Sept. 4, 1960, Bassett Collection; ("wasn't speaking") int. Jessamyn West by FB, FBP; ("Dick sent me") Garry Wills in *Esquire,* July 1994; ("They would always") int. James Bassett by FB, FBP; (adopt?) *PAT,* p. 161; (restaurant incident) int. James Bassett by FB, FBP, the date of the incident was probably Nov. 1957; ("Deadass!") ibid.

Frank Nixon death: ("Dear Dad") int. Evlyn Dorn by FB, FBP; (rupture) *PAT,* p. 159; ("I shall always") Nixon, *Arena,* op. cit., p. 91, but see *MEM,* p. 176 for another version; (carpet) int. Nathaniel George by FB, FBP; (pie) ed. Sevareid, op. cit., p. 105; ("I could hear") int. James Bassett by FB, FBP; ("strictly personal") ed. Sevareid, op. cit., p. 106; (Buffalo) *NYT,* Oct. 16, 17, 1956; ("I remember my father") Woodstone, op. cit., p. 42.

Strange RN behavior 1956: ("Get me away") int. James Bassett by FB, FBP, *FB,* p. 425; ed. Sevareid, op. cit., pp. 80, 98; (vomited) int. Herb Klein for BBC/History Channel; (punched in face) Woodstone, op. cit., p. 39; (disoriented) Woodstone, op. cit., p. 39–; (nonexistent crowd) ed. Sevareid, op. cit., p. 97; (Reston) Woodstone, op. cit., p. 40; ("Before gray-colored draperies") Haldeman and DiMona, op. cit., p. 45; (rambling typical) ibid. and int. John Ehrlichman; ("What scares the hell") int. James Bassett by FB, FBP.

Hutschnecker: ints. Dr. Arnold Hutschnecker.

"I have a feeling": RN to Rebozo, Sept. 8, 1956, Series 320, Box 622, Rebozo file, VP, NA.

Biscayne trip: *AMI,* p. 422.

Chapter 15

"Does a man enjoy?": Nixon, *Six Crises,* op. cit., p. xv.

foreign gifts: *NYT,* UPI, June 4, 1957.

50 plus countries: ed. Sevareid, op. cit., p. 126.

Far East trip: ("What . . . doing?") *AMI,* p. 318; (briefings/meetings) ed. Sevareid, op. cit., p. 123–; *MEM,* p. 120; *AMI,* p. 319; *JA,* p. 228; (RN would recall) *MEM,* p. 134; (Indonesia) ibid., p. 120; (Kuwait gift) int. Joseph Dmhowski; ("vanity") *MEM,* p. 121; (uniforms) Dickerson, op. cit., p. 164; (Nehru/Gandhi) *MEM,* p. 131; *AMI,* p. 325; (cad) Costello, op. cit., p. 250; *AMI,* p. 325; (Khan) *MEM,* pp. 133, 256; ("not printable") Kissinger, *White House Years,* op. cit., pp. 848, 878; (despised) Michael Genovese, *The Nixon Presidency,* New York: Greenwood Press, 1990, p. 157 and see Dickerson, op. cit., p. 164; (1971 "tilt" to Pakistan) research paper for author by Greg Murphy; (RN considered nuclear weapons) *Time,* July 29, 1985 and see Kissinger, *White House Years,* op. cit., p. 909; (Formosa visit) *MEM,* p. 126; (no recognition) Costello, op. cit., p. 250; ("Someday") James Humes, *Confessions of a White House Ghost-writer,* Washington, D.C.: Regnery, 1997, p. 137; (Shah personal friend) AP, July 5, 1979; (Op. Ajax) Andrew, op. cit., p. 203–; (no consultation) Washington *Spectator,* Oct. 15, 1976; secret House Intelligence Committee report, published in *Village Voice,* Feb. 16, 1976; Wicker, op. cit., p. 663, but see Henry Kissinger, *Years of Renewal,* op. cit., p. 583; (alcoholic) Ball, op. cit., p. 454–; (gifts "missing") WP, Aug. 22, 1977; (Marcos contributions) Kutler, op. cit., p. 207; Nathan Miller, *Spying for America,* New York: Paragon House, 1989, p. 385fn, NY *Observer;* (Joe Conason column), Oct. 21, 1996; Russell Howe and Sarah Trott, *The Power Peddlers,* Garden City, NY: Doubleday, 1977, p. 481–, but see Stans, op. cit., p. 371–; ("buying influence") "Insights with Robert Novak," America's Voice—Net cable, May 19, 1998.

RN on dictators: Nick Thimmesh int. in *LAT,* undated, 1978.

"go on . . . offensive": *MO,* p. 629.

Vietnam: (Bao Dai) *MEM,* p. 122; ("outpost of freedom") ibid., p. 124; ("husks") ibid., p. 125; (80 percent costs) Neil Sheehan, *A Bright Shining Lie,* London: Jonathan Cape, 1989, p. 172; (advisers) Manchester, op. cit., p. 918; *MEM,* p. 150; ("The boys") WP, June 15, 1997, citing Eisenhower Oval Office recording, Feb. 24, 1955; (RN "if . . . take the risk") Manchester, op. cit., p. 685; Cook, op. cit., p. 7.

European papers: Lurie, op. cit., p. 186; (RN's real view) Apr. 16, 1954 journal entry, James Hagerty Papers, DDEL; *MEM,* p. 152; Nixon Oral History, Feb. 21, 1966, John Foster Dulles Oral History Collection, Princeton University; *AMI,* p. 345; (Bassett) JB to Wilma Bassett, Apr. 16–17, 1954, Bassett Collection; ("own baby") Bassett unpub. ms., p. 89; (Op. Vulture) Dulles to Eisenhower, Apr. 23, 1954, DDEL, Parmet, Eisenhower, op. cit., p. 364; Hoopes, op. cit., p. 210–; ed. Cttee of Concerned Asian Scholars, *The Indochina Story,* New York: Pantheon, 1970, p. 19, Bernard Brodie, *War and Politics,* New York: Macmillan, 1973, p. 144–; (LeMay) *FB,* p. 322; ("Stone Age") Stanley Karnow, *Vietnam,* London: Random House, 1994, p. 48; (Ike "must be crazy") Brendon, op. cit., p. 290; (RN nuclear attitude) Cook, op. cit., p. 7; John Prados to author, Jan. 24, 1997, and see *AMI,* p. 344, *FB,* p. 322; (not necessary to mention) *MEM,* p. 154; ("guts") Bassett unpub. ms., p. 96, entry for Apr. 21, 1954; ("sun . . . shining") ibid., p. 117, on cong. leadership meeting, May 3, 1954; (Zeibert's) ibid., p. 119–, entry for May 5, 1954; (Ike notified France) Ranelagh, op. cit., p. 431; (RN/promote invasion) Cook, op. cit., p. 7; ("folly") ibid.; (JFK sends advisers) Karnow, op. cit., p. 270; (RN long supports war) *AMII,* pp. 43–, 142–; Shawcross, op. cit., p. 85.

Latin American visit: (main sources) Marvin Zahniser and Michael Weis, *Diplomatic History,* Vol. 13, Spring 1989, p. 163–; Mazo, op. cit., p. 206–; (Mazo covered the trip as a reporter), *MEM,* p. 185–; Nixon, *Six Crises,* op. cit., p. 183–; Vernon Walters, *Silent Missions,* Garden City, NY: Doubleday, 1978, p. 313; ("weird . . . character") ibid., p. 204; ("unable to wear") RN to Eisenhower, May 12, 1958, Ann Whitman Administrative file 28, DDEL; ("hailed") *MEM,* p. 188; (relations suffered) Zahniser and Weis, op. cit., p. 178; ("splotches") *MEM,* p. 189; ("French Revolution") Manchester, op. cit., p. 831; (RN on Caracas ambush) Nixon, *Six Crises,* op. cit., p. 217–; (looked like Eisler) Mazo, op. cit., p. 233; (damage/wounds) ibid.; Nixon, *Six Crises,* op. cit., p. 219; Nixon, *Arena,* op. cit., p. 206; Walters, op. cit., p. 330; ("heard attacker") Nixon, *Six Crises,* op. cit., p. 219; (On advice) ibid., p. 220; Walters, op. cit., p. 332; (Pat calm) ibid., p. 333; (Woods) int. Robert Cushman by FB, FBP; *JA,* p. 252; (relaxing) Walters, op. cit., p. 234, Mazo, op. cit., p. 237; (Molotov cocktails) ibid., p. 235; U. E. Baughman, *Secret Service Chief,* New York: Harper, 1962, p. 248–; ("I don't think") ibid., p. 246–; (Esterline) int. Jacob Esterline; (Op. Poor Richard) Manchester, op. cit., p. 833; Zahniser and Weis, op. cit., p. 182; (placards) ibid., p. 184; ("Rock and Roll) *LAT,* May 26, 1958 and club papers, corr. files, Series 320, Box 649, VP, NA; (showed courage) int. former Assistant Secretary of State Roy Rubottom, Jr.; Walters, op. cit., p. 337; (RN on Peru) Nixon, *Six Crises,* op. cit., p. 198; ("terrible test") ibid., p. 204; (analytical) *FB,* p. 369; ("When someone") ibid.; ("Those who hate you") *MEM,* p. 1089; ("felt . . . urge") Nixon, *Six Crises,* op. cit., pp. 204, 207; ("both barrels") ibid., p. 216; (Hughes) *JA,* p. 253; (RN made no move) *AMI,* p. 473; (defying S.S. rule) Baughman, op. cit., p. 247; ("can't be helped") ibid., p. 248; ("command decision) Alsop, op. cit., p. 75; ("worn out") Nixon, *Six Crises,* op. cit., p. 205; ("wrung-out") Mazo, op. cit., p. 238; ("My reaction") Alsop, op. cit., p. 198; ("avoidable") Baughman, op. cit., p. 249; (Esterline) ints. Jacob Esterline; ("damn nose") James Blight and Peter Kornbluh, *Politics of Illusion,* Boulder, CO: Lynne Rienner, 1998, p. 23; ("political decision") Grose, op. cit., p. 455; ("not qualify") Alsop, op. cit., p. 76; ("self-bamboozlement") *AMI,* p. 482; ("melee") Baughman, op. cit., p. 249–; (San Jose) *MEM,* p. 492–; ed. Strober, *Nixon,* op. cit., p. 25; ("like Caracas") ibid.

Moscow 1959: (arrival) Nixon, *Six Crises,* op. cit., p. 246–; ("hope") ibid., p. 243; (Hungary) *MEM,* p. 181; ("Butcher") ibid., p. 179; ("ready") Nixon, *Six Crises,* op. cit., p. 245; (preparations) ibid., pp. 235–, 240; (no sleep) ibid., p. 248; ("shit") *MEM*, p. 207, but see Salisbury, op. cit., p. 302; ("Go fuck") Louis and Yazijian, op. cit., p. 93; (Safire) Safire, op. cit., p. 3; (RN/Khrushchev/exhibit) Nixon, *Six Crises*, op. cit., p. 256–; (gesturing) Safire, op. cit., p. 4–; ("remarkably able") Salisbury, op. cit., p. 302–; (RN disgraced self) Michael Beschloss, *Mayday*, New York: Harper & Row, 1986, p. 183, citing ints. Milton Eisenhower and Vladimir Toumanoff and see Safire, op. cit., p. 5; ("businessman") Salisbury, op. cit., p. 174; ("S.O.B.") *FB*, p. 391; (help JFK?) Pilat, op. cit., p. 260; ("stick fist") Bobst, op. cit., p. 274.

Hughes: ("Mr. Thomas") int. Don Hughes; (suggestion) Parmet, op. cit., p. 409; *HD*, p. 397; (record) Nixon, *Six Crises*, op. cit., p. 246; New Orleans *Times-Picayune*, Aug. 8, 1959; (publicity) ibid., Aug. 8, 9, 17, 19, 20, 1959; (Thomas) ibid., Aug. 17, 1959.

PepsiCo: (Pepsi Moscow) int. Donald Kendall; Louis and Yazijian, op. cit., p. 92; Parmet, op. cit., p. 396–; London *Guardian*, undated ?Jan. 1969.

RN foreign policy: ("Tell . . . them") *AMI*, p. 520; ("To me . . . the concept") RN's radio television address from Moscow, Aug. 1, 1959, reprinted in Speeches and Statements of the Vice President of the United States, Richard Nixon in Connection with His Visit to the Soviet Union and Poland, 1959, JFRP; (for home consumption) Nixon, *Six Crises*, op. cit., p. 319.

Guatemala: ("swore to secrecy") Hunt, op. cit., p. 96; (CIA coup) David Wise and Thomas Ross, *The Invisible Government*, New York: Random House, 1964, p. 165; Thomas, op. cit., p. 111; Andrew, *For the President's Eyes Only*, op. cit., p. 206; (Phillips) David Phillips, *The Night Watch*, New York: Atheneum, 1977, p. 50.

Cuba: ("Cuba, Cuba . . .") David Phillips, *The Night Watch*, New York: Atheneum, 1977, p. 86; (1898) ed. Peter Kornbluh, *Bay of Pigs Declassified*, New York: New Press, 1998, p. 267; ("strongest . . . advocate") *Reader's Digest*, Nov. 1964, p. 288.

Chapter 16

"neuralgic": Kissinger, *White House Years*, op. cit., pp. 633, 641.

"Obsession": int. James Schlesinger.

RN and "Bay of Pigs" documents: (HRH) Haldeman and DiMona, op. cit., p. 53; ("distressed") Sept. 18, 1971, WHT, transcribed for author by Dennis Effle, 1997; (four times) June 24, July 1, 2, 27, 1971 cited in *AOP*; ("get started") WHT, Sept. 18, 1971, *supra.*; (Ehrlichman Sept. 18 note) John Ehrlichman handwritten notes, R, Statement of Information, App. III, p. 197; (end of week) *HD*, p. 356; (vast archive) ed. Peter Kornbluh, *Bay of Pigs Declassified*, New York: New Press, 1998, p. 1; (Colonel's report) Thomas Powers, *The Man Who Kept the Secrets*, New York: Pocket, 1979, p. 327—colonel was Jack Hawkins; ("incomplete") *MEM*, p. 515 and see Haldeman and DiMona, op. cit., p. 53.

RN/anti-Kennedy motive: ("chance to indict") Whalen, op. cit., p. 97; (1971 motive) June 24, July 1, 27, Sept. 18, 1971; *AOP*, pp. 4, 7, 34—see esp. RN: "We're going to expose them . . . first things I want [are] the Cuban missile crisis and . . . the Bay of Pigs"; (June 24) *MEM*, p. 513; Ehrlichman, op. cit., p. 325; (1973) WHT, May 14, 1973; *AOP*, p. 494; (Buzhardt) int. Elias Demetracopoulos.

cause of RN concern: ("need") *MEM*, p. 650; ("concern") ed. Strober,*Nixon*, op. cit., p. 50; ("cease/desist") Haldeman and DiMona, op. cit., p. 53; ("to protect") WHT, Sept. 18, 1971, *supra.*; ("what to duck") John Ehrlichman note, Oct. 8, 1971, R, Statement of Info., App. III, p. 202; (JE puzzled) int. John Ehrlichman; π John Ehrlichman note, Sept. 18, 1971, R, *supra.*, p. 198; ("N knew more") Haldeman and DiMona, op. cit., p. 54.

Rebozo letter: Jan. 15, 1955, Rebozo file, VP, NA.

Batista: (books argue) see Mario Lazo, *Dagger in the Heart*, New York: Twin Circle, 1968, pp. 92, 96–; Rufo Lopez Fresquet, *My 14 Months with Castro*, Cleveland, OH: World Publishing, 1966, p. 9–; (murders) Georgie Ann Geyer, *Guerrilla Prince*, Kansas City, MO: Andrews & McMeel, 1993, p. 121; Lacey, op. cit., p. 248; John Dorschner and Roberto Fabricio, *The Winds of December*, New York: Coward, McCann, & Geoghegan, 1980, p. 90; Manchester, op. cit., p. 860—JFK, in his second debate with RN, Oct. 7, 1960, said twenty thousand Cubans were killed under Batista's final seven-year rule, Box 40, FBP; (Lansky deal) Dorschner and Fabricio, op. cit., p. 65–; Sifakis, op. cit., p. 179.

RN Cuba trip: (briefing) notes, Jan. 31, 1955, Series 36, Box 1, VP, NA; (attach) int. Lionel Krisel; (exiles' letter) Feb. 1, 1955, sixty-three signatories, Series 36, Box 1, VP, NA; (visit) *NYT, WP*, Feb. 8, 9, 1955; Havana *Post*, Feb. 7, 10, 1955; Philip Bonsal, *Cuba, Castro, & the United States*, Pittsburgh, PA: University of Pittsburgh Press, 1971, p. 13; (cabinet) Mar. 11, 1955 notes, James Hagerty Papers, DDEL, Arthur Minnick Papers, DDEL; (opening line/reading) Dorschner and Fabricio, op. cit., pp. 67, 159.

1959 Revolution: (fled) ibid., p. 493; ("suitcases") Phillips, op. cit., p. 77; ($17 million) Eisenberg, Dan and Landau, op. cit., p. 256.

"short of war": *Alleged Assassination Plots Involving Foreign Leaders,* Select Cttee. to Study Govt. Ops. with Respect to Intelligence Activities, U.S. Senate, Interim Report, Nov. 20, 1975, p. 1.

casinos: (Castro view) Enrique Meneses, *Fidel Castro,* London: Faber & Faber, 1966, p. 58, citing 1958 int.; (reopen) Lopez-Fresquet, op. cit., p. 88; (jailings) Lacey, op. cit., p. 253; Summers, *Not in Your Lifetime,* New York: Marlowe, 1998, p. 338; U.S. Senate, *Assass. Plots,* op. cit., p. 74n2.

Lansky: (bounty) Geyer, op. cit., p. 297; (tight lipped) Eisenberg, Dan, and Landau, op. cit., p. 259; (Stacher) ibid., p. 258; (CIA benign) Scott, op. cit., p. 338n26; Amb. Earl Smith testimony to Sen. Cttee on Judiciary, 1965, cited in Peter Dale Scott, unpub. ms., Jonathan Marshall Papers; Dorschner and Fabricio, op. cit., pp. 70, 144–; unpub. ms. outline by Ladislas Farago, Box 25, Folder 10, Mugar Library, Boston University, citing arms dealer Sam Cummings; Tony Ulasewicz, *The President's Private Eye,* Westport, CT: Macsam Pub., 1990, p. 74; (Castro concern) int. Andrew St. George, also with Castro in mountains; (FBI) Lacey, op. cit., p. 254.

Pawley: (background) *NYT,* Jan. 8, 1977, Select Cttee. on Assassinations, U.S. House of Reps., X, pp. 83, 138; Gaeton Fonzi, *The Last Investigation,* New York: Thunder's Mouth, 1993; Summers, *Not in Your Lifetime,* op. cit., p. 326; "The Ghosts of November," *Vanity Fair,* Dec. 1994, p. 192; Miami *Herald,* Oct. 3, 1972, Jan. 8, 1977; (dress) Dorschner and Fabricio, op. cit., p. 159; (Trujillo) Warren Hinckle and William Turner, *Deadly Secrets,* New York: Thunder's Mouth, 1981, p. 192; (time to go) Dorschner and Fabricio, op. cit., pp. 29, 152–; (junta plan?) ibid., p. 158; (Pawley/Guatemala) Miami *Herald,* Aug. 22, 1971; ("aggressive action") Report on the Covert Activities of the CIA, (known as Doolittle Report), Sept. 1954, NA and see Hinckle and Turner, op. cit., p. 44; ("Find me man") Miami *Herald,* Jan. 8, 1977; (niece) int. Anita Pawley.

Castro U.S. visit: (astonishes) *Newsweek,* May 4, 1959; (dilemma) Geyer, op. cit., p. 227, Maurice Zeitlin and Robert Scheer, *Cuba, Tragedy in Our Hemisphere,* New York: Grove Press, 1963, p. 81; (C. grumbled) James Blight, Bruce Allyn, and David Welch, *Cuba on the Brink,* New York: Pantheon, 1993, p. 178; (C. refused) Lopez-Fresquet, op. cit., p. 106; (RN claimed) *Reader's Digest,* Nov. 1964; (chandelier) Geyer, op. cit., p. 234; (nervous) RN memo on meeting, Apr. 25, 1959 (full version), as sent to Sen. Mansfield, *Diplomatic History,* Vol. 4, No. 4, Fall 1980, p. 426; ("looked like") *Reader's Digest,* Nov. 1964; ("teenager") Wyden, op. cit., p. 26; (uncle) int. Bob Stephenson, former State Dept. official; (report) RN memo, Apr. 29, 1955, *supra.;* ("S.O.B.") Geyer, op. cit., p. 235; (RN didn't look) int. Constantine Kangles; ("arms around") int. Bob Stephenson; ("going to work") Dean Rusk, *As I Saw It,* New York: Viking, 1991, p. 208; ("Outright Communist") int. Herb Klein, Matthews, op. cit., p. 125; int. Don Hughes; ("dedicated") int. Jack Drown; ("characterized Fidel") *New Republic,* Apr. 23, 1977; int. Ken Bode.

Droller: Lopez-Fresquet, op. cit., p. 110; Bonsal, op. cit., p. 64.

Castro and communism: see esp. Dorschner and Fabricio, op. cit., pp. 506; Geyer, op. cit., pp. 187, 284–; Lopez-Fresquet, op. cit., p. 202; (at odds?) ibid., p. 111; Nestor Carbonell, *And the Russians Stayed,* New York: William Morrow, 1989, p. 62; Geyer, op. cit., p. 236–; (U.S. tool?/diplomat) eds. Blight and Kornbluh, op. cit., p. 36–; citing former Soviet Cuba specialist Oleg Daroussenkov; (anti-American) Carbonell, op. cit., p. 62, Geyer, op. cit., pp. 44, 181, 191; ("We will check") Grose, op. cit., p. 467.

Castro seizes U.S. business: Dorschner and Fabricio, op. cit., p. 150.

"find dramatic things": memo of NSC meeting 429, Dec. 16, 1959, cited at Newman, op. cit., p. 118–.

Nixon role: Robert Keith Gray, *Eighteen Acres Under Glass,* Garden City, NY: Doubleday, 1961, p. 278; ("deputy"/& NSC) RN int.; *U.S. News & World Report,* May 16, 1960; (briefing) Peter Wyden notes of int. Robert Cushman, supplied to author; ("apt pupil"/"friend") Corson, op. cit., p. 36 and see Mosley, op. cit., p. 394; ("didn't see fit") int. Marion Boggs.

Dulles Dec. 16: Newman, op. cit., p. 120.

listening to Pawley: Nixon, *Six Crises,* op. cit., p. 652—RN dined with Pawley Dec. 15; CIA memo, Cuban political matters, Dec. 16, 1959, CIA release 1993, NA.

King "recommended actions": U.S. Senate, *Assassination Plots,* op. cit., p. 92.

euphemisms: ibid., pp. 64, 93.

Cuba covert war: (March decision) ed. John Glennon, *Foreign Relations of the United* States, Vol. VI, Cuba, Washington, D.C.: U.S. Gov. Printing Office, 1991, Mar. 16, 17, p. 850–; (Pluto) John Prados, *The Presidents' Secret Wars,* New York: William Morrow, 1986, p. 178–; (AM/THUG) Thomas, *The Very Best Men,* op. cit., p. 206; ("pressure") int. Thomas McCoy and see schedule Newman, op. cit., p. 125; (Ike admonition) ed. John Glennon, op. cit., p. 861; (confided in four) San Diego *Union,* Mar. 25, 1962; ("trump card") Wyden, op. cit., p. 68; (Klein 1997) ints. Herb Klein.

RN prime mover?: (myth) *AMI*, p. 550; Thomas, *The Very Best Men*, op. cit., p. 208n; ("by no stretch") ibid.; (Pfeiffer noted) Pfeiffer to FB, Mar. 1, 1978, FBP; ("father") Bonsal, op. cit., pp. 174, 196; (Smith) Joseph B. Smith, *Portrait of a Cold Warrior*, New York: Putnam, 1976, p. 325; (CIA/Costa Rica) Howard Hunt, *Give Us This Day*, New Rochelle, NY: Arlington House, 1973, pp. 23, 29–; (Figueres) *New Republic*, Apr. 23, 1977; (Halpern) int. Sam Halpern by Gus Russo supplied to author; (Haig) int. Alexander Haig by Gus Russo supplied to author; ("monitor") Jacob Esterline, int. for CIA history by Jack Pfeiffer, Nov. 1975, transcript obtained by author and ints. Esterline; (luncheon) Howard Hunt, *Give Us This Day*, op. cit., p. 39; ("chief architect") Hunt testimony, Inquiry into the Alleged Involvement of the CIA in the Watergate and Ellsberg Matters, Special Subcttee. on Intelligence, House Cttee. on Armed Services, 94th Cong., 1st Sess., p. 500, and Hunt, *Undercover*, op. cit., p. 131; ("How the hell") Wyden notes of int. Robert Cushman supplied to author; (Ike's caution) ed. Glennon, op. cit., p. 1060; ("What's hurry?") Grose, op. cit., p. 514; (Cushman/pressure) int. Robert Cushman by FB, FBP; (CIA frustration) int. Jack Pfeiffer by FB, FBP; Thomas, *The Very Best Men*, op. cit., p. 384n13; Hunt, *Give Us this Day*, op. cit., pp. 28, 40, 43; (Ike/Pawley) ed. Glennon, op. cit., pp. 789, 1128, 1130–.

Kohly: (background) petition for writ of certiorari, U.S. Court of Appeals, by William Grosh and Mario Garcia Kohly, Oct. 16, 1964, No. 1061, p. 4, Kohly bio. notes in files of Assassination Archive and Research Center, Washington, D.C.; Marshall Diggs to RN, Dec. 9, 1966, Robert Morrow Papers, supplied by John Williams, University of Wisconsin-Stout; (Flemming) Thomas, *The Very Best Men*, op. cit., p. 207; ("Sucker") ed. Glennon, op. cit., p. 950–; (Rebozo/Kohly) int. Gerry Hemming; Kohly's son confirmed in 1996 that Hemming worked with the Kohlys; ("hated") Kissinger, *White House Years*, op. cit., p. 641; (in touch within months) int. Dr. Mario Garcia Kohly, Jr.; (Brewster investigated) Mitchell, op. cit., p. 53; (Diggs) RN/Diggs corr. 1953, 1960, VP, NA; (RN/Kohly met) Kohly Writ, *supra.*, pp. 353, 358, 398–, 675 and Diggs/RN corr, July 29, Sept. 3, 1960, VP, NA; int. Barrett Prettyman—former U.S. assistant attorney general; (counterfeiting) int. attorney James Cardiello, Kohly writ, *supra.*; Hinkle and Turner, op. cit., p. 197–; Arthur Schlesinger, *Robert Kennedy and His Times*, New York: Houghton Mifflin, 1978, p. 487n.; (discuss with Pawley) Peter Wyden notes of Robert Cushman int. supplied to author; (CIA/RN disagreement) FB notes of int. CIA historian Jack Pfeiffer, FBP; (RN ensured) int. Robert Thornton, former junior associate at Nixon, Mudge, Rose, Guthrie and Alexander; (wrote to judge) RN to U.S. District Judge Edward Weinfeld, Mar. 9, 1965, reprinted in full in *First Hand Knowledge*, by Robert Morrow, op. cit., p. 357; ints. Mario Garcia Kohly, Jr.; James Cardiello and Schlesinger, op. cit., p. 487n.; ("medal") int. Robert Thornton; (RN suggested jumping bail) transcript Edward Von Rothkirch; int. conducted for Rep. Thomas Downing, in Morrow, *First Hand Knowledge*, op. cit., p. 281; (RN sanction of killings?) Mario Garcia Kohly affidavit, July 15, 1975, Robert Morrow Papers, *supra.*, and see reproduced in Morrow, *First Hand Knowledge*, op. cit., p. 364, and see Schlesinger, op. cit., p. 487n.; ints. Mario Kohly, Jr.

Chapter 17

"The determination to kill": Harry Rositzke, *The CIA's Secret Operations*, New York: Reader's Digest Press, 1977, p. 200.

CIA assassinations: ("nail Jell-O") Wise, *American Police State*, op. cit., p. 214; (Lumumba/Trujillo/Castro summary) U.S. Sen. *Assass. Plots*, op. cit., p. 4–; ("Eisenhower's view") int. Marion Boggs; ("never without approval") Allen Dulles in *The Craft of Intelligence* cited at FB, p. 393; (other CIA officials) see Wise, *American Police State*, op. cit., p. 225, and ed. Weber, op. cit., p. 299, citing Richard Helms and Rositzke, op. cit., pp. 190, 238; (Sen. Cttee concluded) U.S. Sen., *Assass. Plots*, op. cit., p. 109; (Bissell/authorization) ibid., p. 110, transcript of int. Richard Bissell by CIA historian Jack Pfeiffer, p. 16–; ("Didn't inquire") int. Richard Bissell by Jan Weininger, supplied to author, and see *World Intelligence Review*, Nov./Dec. 1996, p. 3; Thomas, *The Very Best Men*, op. cit., pp. 27, 208n, 234–; (nod/wink) U.S. Sen., *Assass. Plots*, op. cit., pp. 111, 117, 148; ("I think we all") ibid., p. 148; ("almost everybody") *Newsweek*, Oct. 2, 1978, p. 62.

RN/assassination role?: (RN/Sen. Cttee. negotiations) UPI, July; *NYT*, Nov. 26, 1975; *This World*, Mar. 21, 1976; ("compromise") int. Joe Dennin; (Hart) int. Gary Hart; ("pernicious") *This World*, Mar. 21, 1976; (RN responses on assass.) in *Supplementary Detailed Staff Reports on Foreign and Military Intelligence*, U.S. Sen. Select Cttee. to Study Gov. Ops. With Respect to Intelligence Activities, 94th Cong., 2nd sess. FR, Vol. IV, pp. 143, 157–; ("I was amazed") *Newsweek*, May 19, 1986; (Brodie re: Jan. '60) FB handwritten notes of Pfeiffer briefing, Feb. 27, 1978, FBP; (RN briefing/goon squads) Thomas, *The Very Best Men*, op. cit., p. 208n, re: Mar. 2, 1960 CIA briefing of RN by Bissell; (Pawley/"somebody") Jacob Esterline int. by CIA historian Pfeiffer, transcript p. 22 and see memo re. Esterline/Pawley contact, Mar. 30, 1960, CIA 1994 release, NA.

bizarre plots: (Flemming) Thomas, *The Very Best Men*, op. cit., p. 207; (fatuous schemes) ibid., p. 208n; CIA inspector general, *Report on Plots to Assassinate Fidel Castro*, 1967; (Montecristo) int. Constantine Kangles; (in-house history) Thomas, *The Very Best Men*, op. cit., p. 208n; (Medical Services Dr.) CIA I.G., *Report on Plots, supra.*, p. 12; U.S. Sen., *Assass. Plots*, op. cit., p. 73.

Hunt in April: ("Assassinate Castro") Hunt, *Give Us This Day*, op. cit., 38; (denied) ibid. and letter to Robbyn Swan Summers, Jan. 22, 1996; (Colson) *Argosy*, Mar. 1976; (Putnam memo) CIA counsel John Warner to WSPF Chief Counsel Jaworski, Apr. 9, 1974 enclosing Mar. 29 letter and attachment from Alfred Ulmer to CIA Director William Colby, released to NA by CIA 1994.

CIA file Pawley: (contact's offer) July 13, 1960 message to director, released 1993, NA; ("I'm in touch") Pawley to RN, July 18, 1960, VP, NA, cited at Michael Beschloss, *The Crisis Years*, New York: Edward Burlingame, 1991, p. 136 and see Howard Hunt testimony to House Select Cttee. on Assassinations, Nov. 3, 1978, transcript, part 2, p. 39—Hunt was in touch with Pawley.

accident plot: (CIA manual) "A Study of Assassination from CIA Manual Distributed at Time of 1954 Guatemala Coup," released 1977 and reprinted in *Harper's* magazine, Aug. 1977, p. 22; ("accident" cables) U.S. Sen, *Assass. Plots*, Interim Report, op. cit. p. 73; (King/Barnes) ibid. and Thomas, *The Very Best Men*, op. cit., p. 209–; (Esterline knew) ibid.

Marita Lorenz: (Rorke) NY *Daily News*, Apr. 20, 1975, June 13, 1976, partial transcript of int. Lorenz by Senate Intelligence Cttee. investigator Gaeton Fonzi, Feb. 3, 1976, unnumbered release, p. 9–; NA, Marita Lorenz with Ted Schwarz, *Marita*, New York: Thunder's Mouth, 1993; (Rorke/Pawley) Fonzi. op. cit., p. 88 and Newman, op. cit., p. 109 and see *Vanity Fair*, Nov. 1993—except where indicated the above are main cites for Lorenz episode; ("right with God") Lorenz and Schwarz, op. cit., p. 46; (Sturgis background) authoritatively in Fonzi, op. cit.; (CIA backed?) "NY *Daily News*, June 13, 1976; (Sturgis on plot) ibid. and Fonzi, op. cit., p. 89; (Hoover warned) Hoover to DCI, Oct. 18, 1960, cited at U.S. Sen., *Assass. Plots*, Interim Report, op. cit., p. 79; (Cobb) Newman, op. cit., pp. 106, 545–; (surveillance re. Lorenz/Rorke) ibid., p. 108—CIA memo for record, Feb. 21, 1975, CIA release 1994, Folder 30, NA, confirms Cobb worked for Castro and was "of operational interest" to CIA and surveilled from June 1960. Her Office of Security No. was 216 264; (RN office routing) Newman, op. cit., p. 108, citing June 6, 1960 document in Cobb 201 file, featuring name of Nixon military aide Robert Cushman; (Cobb aide to Orta) ibid., p. 547n63, conv. John Newman.

CIA-Mafia plots: (Dulles knowledge/authorization) U.S. Sen., *Asass. Plots*, Interim Report, op. cit., p. 91–; testimony of Richard Helms, Select Cttee. On Assass., Box 2, #14719, NA, but see "Castro, Plans to Assassinate" refs. in Grose, op. cit.; (CIA-Mafia efforts) U.S. Sen., *Assass. Plots*, Interim Report, op. cit., p. 74–; I.G. report on plots, *supra*, (Gambling Syndicate), p. 14– and see Hinkle and Turner, op. cit., p. 76–.

Varona: (and Hunt) Hunt, *Give Us This Day*, op. cit., e.g. p. 44–; (Varona/key officer/Pawley) Pawley to Assistant Secretary of State Thomas Mann, Mar. 3, 1961; Sheffield Edwards to DCI, Dec. 22, 1959, CIA releases 1993–94, NA; (Varona/Lansky) Select Cttee. on Assass., Staff Report, U.S. House of Reps.,Vol. X, p. 171—former Cong. investigator Michael Ewing indentified "Cuban exile leader" referred to on this page as Varona (corr. with author).

Rothman/CIA: ibid., p. 183; NY *Daily News*, Apr. 23, 1975; list of State Department material on Rothman, HSCA release, 1994, NA and CIA memo for the record on Rothman, Apr. 25, 1973, released 1993, NA.

semicoded exchanges: Beschloss, op. cit., p. 136.

Diggs/Pulley: ("in close contact") Diggs to RN, July 29, 1960, Diggs corr. file, VP, NA; (RN reply) RN to Diggs, Sept. 3, 1960, Diggs corr. file, VP, NA; (Diggs's secretary) Sallie Mullin to Gen. Cushman, Aug. 1, 1960, Diggs corr. file, VP, NA; (empty envelopes) Brewster Papers, Bowdoin College, Brunswick, ME; (Pulley Trafficante liaison?) ints. late Robert Morrow; Morrow, *First Hand Knowledge*, op. cit., p. 41; Robert Morrow, *The Senator Must Die*, Santa Monica, CA: Roundtable, 1988, pp. 49, 178—as reported in this chapter, Morrow was arrested for counterfeiting with Mario Garcia Kohly; (date Mafia plots start) U.S. Sen., Assass. Plots, Interim Report, op. cit., p. 74.

Maheu: (W. C. Fields) Schorr, op. cit., p. 159; (Maheu role) ints. Robert Maheu; Maheu and Hack, op. cit., p. 108–; I.G. *Report on Plots, supra*, pp. 15–, 35, 57–; (told Hughes) U.S. Sen., *Assass. Plots*, Interim Report, op. cit., p. 72, Drosnin, op. cit., p. 271; (Hughes/other operations) Peter Dale Scott, "Watergate, Cuba, & the China-Vietnam Lobby," unpub. ms., p. 19, citing Miami *Herald* and SF *Chronicle* on Hughes's use of Caribbean islet Cay Sal and Higham, op. cit., p. 247; ("good idea") Drosnin, op. cit., p. 250.

King: (since war) int. Robert King; Kornitzer, op. cit., p. 150; (counterintelligence) docs. in King corr. files, Series 320, Box 411, File 1, VP, NA; (lobbied) King to RN, Dec. 4, 1952, ibid.; ("protection") FB, p. 338 citing *NYT*; (aide '56) FBI Grapevine, Nov. 1956; ("alter ego") Beschloss, op. cit., p. 136, citing VP; (King/Rebozo) e.g., King/Rebozo corr., Mar. 25, 27, 1957, VP, NA; (left RN office) UPI, Oct. 9, 1959, showing move from Winter Olympics post and Maheu/King partnership announcement, VP, NA; (King/'60) Maheu and Hack, op. cit., p. 84.

Onassis: (Eisenhower) memo on NSC meeting, July 2, 1954, DDEL; (anti-Onassis op.) Maheu and Hack, op. cit., p. 41–; Hougan, op. cit., p. 281–; Hougan article in *Playboy*, Sept. 1978, CIA I.G., *Report on Plots, supra.*, p. 72; ints. Robert Maheu, Kevin Gerrity, Jean Connor, conv. Michael Ewing; (RN on killing Onassis) int. Robert Maheu, Maheu and Hack, op. cit., p. 45, also Maheu int. in "Aristotle Onassis: The Golden Greek," Reputations, BBC-TV 1994; ("sounded tough") int. Robert Maheu.

"draw a blank": int. Robert King, conv. Michael Ewing re. his King int.

"no reason": ints. Robert Maheu.

"one of the last": Maheu and Hack, op. cit., p. 131.

Salinger: int. Pierre Salinger; (knew Maheu) Drosnin, op. cit., p. 271.

1971 sequence re. "Bay of Pigs: (Lenzner/Lackritz role) int. Terry Lenzner, Lenzner/Lackritz memo to Sen. Ervin, date obscured, Feb. 1974, subject "Relevance to S. Res. 60 of John Roselli's testimony about his CIA activities," Box 441-3, JFK Collection, HSCA, Record Grp. 233, NA; (Anderson) syndicated articles, Jan. 18, 19, 1971 reproduced at Exhibits 2, 3, E, Bk. 21, p. 9911–; (Mitchell/Maheu call) chronology attached to Lenzner/Lackritz/Sen. Ervin memo, *supra.*, and Maheu and Hack, op. cit., p. 126; (Maheu/Vegas prosecution) ibid.; (Mitchell "shaking") conv. Michael Ewing, citing Maheu; (Maheu/Justice Dept. officials) Lenzner/Lackritz memo, *supra.*, Maheu and Hack, op. cit., p. 126; (Wilson) int. Terry Lenzner; (Caulfield background) *NM*, p. 13–; (Caulfield memos) Caulfield to John Dean, Jan. 22, 25, Feb. 1, 1971, E, Bk 21, p. 9748–; (Caulfield conceded) ibid. p. 9723; (Lenzner/Lackritz asked CIA) int. Lenzner, CIA memo for record, Mar. 14, 1974, and [name censored] to director of security, Aug. 20, 1975, CIA release May 1989; (Ervin blocked) int. Terry Lenzner and subpoena request in Lenzner/Lackritz/Ervin memo, *supra.*; ("duck"/"protect") see p. 177.

"Bay of Pigs" = Kennedy Assassination?: (Haldeman) Haldeman and DiMona, op. cit., p. 68.

"fixation"/"Not rational": Salisbury, op. cit., p. 306.

Chapter 18

"I felt crushed": ed. William Buckley, *Odyssey of a Friend: Whittaker Chambers' Letters to William Buckley, 1952–1961*, Washington, D.C.: Regnery, 1987, p. 287.

RN and JFK: (meeting) Matthews, op. cit., p. 44—a key source for the relationship; ("bookends") *MEM*, p. 42; (Pennsylvania) ibid., Matthews, op. cit., p. 51; (reminisced) *JA*, p. 136; ("genuine") Matthews, op. cit., p. 17; (began meeting) *JA*, p. 135; (books) ibid., p. 136; (shy) ibid., p. 135 and *MEM*, p. 43; (Paris women) *JA*, p. 136; ('50 donation) *MEM*, p. 75; Arnold, op. cit., p. 14, but see suggestion donation much larger at O'Neill, op. cit., p. 81; (denial) Detroit *Free Press*, July 13, 1960; ("mistake") Douglas, op. cit., p. 325, citing *Look's* John Cowles and Judge Charles Wyzanski; (fast friends) Arnold, op. cit., p. 6; ("good luck") *MEM*, p. 91; (RN sponsoring) Matthews, op. cit., p. 91; (wedding) ibid., p. 93; (offices) Ralph Martin, *A Hero for Our Time*, New York: Macmillan, 1983, p. 221.

JFK on RN: ("enormous ability") Peter Lisagor int. April 1966, JFK Oral History Program, JFKL; (Smathers) int. George Smathers, JFK Oral History Program, July 1964, JFKL; ("split personality") Martin, op. cit., p. 221–.

RN re. JFK: (Reardon) Matthews, op. cit., p. 65; (snake charmer) *TW60*, p. 298; ("Poor Jack") Agent Rex Scouten, citing RN; *JA*, p. 137; (fruit) Mathews, op. cit., p. 102; (suite) *JA*, p. 137; ("admired") Matthews, op. cit., p. 100; ("liked") int. Jack Drown; ("loved him") int. Edward Nixon.

RN to run?: ("powers that be") ed. Abell, op. cit., p. 403; (Chandler meeting) int. Paul Ziffren by FB, FBP—citing Buff Chandler; (Pat miles) *NYT*, July 27, 1960; (Cronin) UPI, undated, 1974, Robert Hartmann Papers, Gerald R. Ford Library.

Convention: (mother's ints.) Kornitzer, op. cit., p. 88, int. Evlyn Dorn by FB, FBP; (sat like bird) Ehrlichman, op. cit., p. 147; (no sleep) *JA*, p. 271; (Overture) Len Hall, cited in FB int. John Lindsay, FBP; (acceptance speech) *TW60*, p. 206–; (JFK acceptance) ibid., p. 177; (O'Neill) cited in Matthews, op. cit., p. 127; (Hillings) ibid., p. 126; ("worried") *PAT*, p. 188; (opium) NY Daily *News*, July 29, 1960.

campaign: (small towns) *TW60*, p. 277–; *Saturday Evening Post*, Nov. 5, 1960; (Reston) Thimmesch, op. cit., p. 80; (RN weight) John Tower, *Consequences*, Boston: Little, Brown, 1991, p. 16; (Pat press-ganged) *PAT*, p. 189; (Pat thin/tired) *Saturday Evening Post*, Nov. 5, 1960, Jim Bassett letter to wife, Wilma, Sept. 25, 1960, Bassett Papers, *TW60*, pp. 302, 307; (Jackie) Herbert Parmet, *Jack: The Struggles of John F. Kennedy*, New York: Dial Press, 1980, p. 438; Martin, op. cit., p. 207–; ("No ease") Salisbury, op. cit., p. 304; (RN/hecklers) Klein, op. cit., p. 97, int. Herb Klein; (JFK never lost) *TW60*, p. 301; ("blew stack") ed. Sevareid, op. cit., p. 81; ("firey") Chicago *Sunday Tribune*, Nov. 6, 1960; (Sherwood) Troy, op. cit., p. 177;

(kick seat) Haldeman and DiMona, op. cit., p. 75; int. Don Hughes; (RN in plane) *Readers' Digest,* May 1975, p. 238-, Robert Finch Oral History, Columbia University; (pride/old age) Crowley, *Nixon Off the Record,* op. cit., p. 11; (wasteful?) e.g., Robert Finch Oral History, *supra.;* ("clerks") *TW60,* p. 314; (Plans Board) ibid., p. 264 and see Garment, op. cit., p. 116; (horse and jockey) int. James Bassett by FB, FBP; (Alaska) *TW60,* pp. 262, 267; Klein, op. cit., p. 25; *PAT,* p. 191; ("Dick has painted") James Bassett to wife, Wilma, Oct. 3, 1960, Bassett Papers; (Bassett/tempers) int. Cynthia Bassett; ("scarey isn't it?") James Bassett to Wilma, Nov. 2, 1960, Bassett Papers.

prelude to first debate: (law change) Nixon, *Six Crises,* op. cit., p. 323; Klein, op. cit., p. 102; (JFK accepted) int. Pierre Salinger; Salinger, op. cit., p. 83; int. Leonard Reinsch, JFK Oral History Program, JFKL, p. 13; ("one way") Richard Goodwin, *Remembering America,* Boston: Little, Brown, p. 112; (why resist) Martin, op. cit., p. 222; Nixon, *Six Crises,* op. cit., p. 323, Gray, op. cit., p. 316-; ("no debates!") int. Len Hall by FB, FBP; Klein, op. cit., p. 102-; (RN announced) ibid., p. 103, James Bassett to Wilma, Oct. 24, 1960, Bassett Papers; (Hall asked) int. Len Hall by FB, FBP; ("I can take") Reinsch Oral History, *supra.,* p. 10; ("I'll murder") Goodwin, op. cit., p. 112; ("might clobber") James Bassett to Wilma, Oct. 24, 1960, Bassett Papers; (make "conditions") int. James Bassett by FB, FBP; ("Make sure") Reinsch Oral History, *supra.,* p. 15; (haggling) ibid., p. 14-; Klein, op. cit., p. 103; *TW60,* p. 282; (Secret Service) Baughman, op. cit., p. 249-, citing agent's report; (injury) ibid. and RN on *Tonight* show, NBC-TV, Aug. 26, 1960, transcript in final report of U.S. Sen. Cttee. on Commerce, Subcttee on Communications, Dec. 11, 1961, Part 3, p. 10; (hospital) Nixon, *Six Crises,* op. cit., p. 326.

Ike remark: ("If you give") Aug. 24, 1960 press conf. transcript, *Public Papers of the Presidents,* Washington, D.C.: U.S. Govt. Printing Office, 1961, p. 268-; (apologize) Wicker, op. cit., p. 225; *PAT,* p. 192; ("lack of warmth") Ann Whitman Diary, Aug. 30, 1960, DDEL; (did endorse) Eisenhower statement, Oct. 17, 1960, JFRP; ("tough S.O.B.") Crowley, *Nixon Off the Record,* op. cit., p. 15; ("godammit") *Newsweek,* Oct. 9, 1961 and see Wicker, op. cit., p. 242, citing William Ewald and Leonard Hall.

RN after hospital: (marathon) *PAT,* p. 190-; Nixon, *Six Crises,* op. cit., p. 330; (fever) ibid., p. 331; ("pills/liquor") Ehrlichman, op. cit., p. 21, but see *PAT,* p. 192; (coma) *JA,* p. 288; (blood pressure?) ed. Sevareid, op. cit., p. 75; (denial) *Congressional Quarterly,* Aug. 12, 1960, p. 1395.

first debate: (70 million) *TW60,* op. cit., pp. 283–87; (JFK preparations) ibid., p. 283-; (prostitute) C. David Heymann, *A Woman Called Jackie,* New York: Birch Lane Press, 1994, p. 242 citing longtime aide Langdon Marvin, who says JFK had him arrange for the prostitute; (RN studied?) Nixon, *Six Crises,* op. cit., p. 337; ("totally refused") Robert Finch cited in Matthews, op. cit., p. 147; ("didn't look") int. James Bassett by FB, FBP, Klein, op. cit., p. 105; (Rogers) Matthews, op. cit., p. 147; (reject make up) Klein, op. cit., p. 105; Nixon, *Six Crises,* p. 338; *TW60,* p. 285; (banged knee) Chicago *Sun-Times,* April 24, 1994, Matthews, op. cit., p. 148, citing Klein int.; (Hewitt) ibid.; (clothes hanging) David Halberstam, *The Fifties,* New York: Villard Books, 1993, p. 731; Klein, op. cit., p. 105; (lost 10 lbs.) Nixon, *Six Crises,* op. cit., p. 341; (face/suit) ibid.; int. Leonard Reinsch, JFK Oral History Program, JFKL, p. 60; (make up offer) Matthews, op. cit., p. 149; (JFK powder) Goodwin, op. cit., p. 115 and see Halberstam, *The Fifties,* op. cit., p. 731; (Lazy Shave) Klein, op. cit., p. 105; Nixon, *Six Crises,* op. cit., p. 338; ("You look great") David Halberstam, *The Unfinished Odyssey of Robert Kennedy,* London: Barrie & Jenkins, 1968, p. 181-; Martin, op. cit., p. 222; ("nearly blinded") int./corr. Leonard Miall, former BBC head of television talks; ("macho") Klein, op. cit., p. 105, Matthews, op. cit., p. 149; (JFK fazed) ibid., p. 148-; ("spraddled") int. Edward Morgan, JFK Oral History Program, JFKL, p. 15; ("drooping") *TW60,* p. 289; ("A man severed") Goodwin, op. cit., p. 115; (Daley) cited by Rep. Roman Puchinski in eds. Strober, *Kennedy,* op. cit., p. 31; (Copley) San Diego *Reader,* July 28, 1994; (Woods/Hannah) *PAT,* p. 341; Nixon, *Six Crises,* op. cit., p. 340; (Pat) *Newsweek,* Oct. 17, 1960 and see *PAT,* p. 191; (RN seemed to think) Klein, op. cit., p. 106 and int. Len Hall by FB, FBP; (aides/"all right") Goodwin, op. cit., p. 115; ("I know I can") Matthews, op. cit., p. 155; (radio v. TV) *TW60,* p. 290, Edward Morgan Oral History, *supra.,* p. 16; PAT, p. 192; (Gallup) *TW60,* p. 294; (Baker) Halberstam, *The Fifties,* op. cit., p. 732; (JFK crowds) *TW60,* p. 291, Goodwin, op. cit., p. 116; (good make up) *TW60,* p. 289; (milk shakes) Nixon, *Six Crises,* op. cit., p. 341; (Lodge) int. Murray Frampson (CBS) by FB, FBP.

dirty tricks: (Tuck) An Evening with Dick Tuck, broadcast tape, available at Library of Congress, Halberstam, *Odyssey,* op. cit., p. 71; Orrin Klapp, *Symbolic Leaders,* Chicago: Aldine, 1964, p. 207; ("no sleaze") int. Pierre Salinger; (2nd debate) Salinger, op. cit., p. 84, Leonard Reinsch Oral History, *supra.,* p. 18; (New Nixon?) *Democratic Digest,* Nov./Dec. 1960; (not "alley fighter") *TW60,* p. 303; (Ehrlichman) Ehrlichman, op. cit., pp. 6, 30; ("most ruthless") *MEM,* p. 225.

religious issue: ("dirtiest trick") Lasky, op. cit., p. 37; (Catholic issue) *TW60*, p. 237–; (RN proud) Nixon, *Six Crises*, op. cit., pp. 307, 364, 367–; *JA*, p. 280; (Kennedys "repeatedly") *MEM*, p. 226; (hate mail) Lasky, op. cit., pp. 35, 45; *MEM*, p. 775; (anon. calls) J. W. Sorrells to Gov. Brown (CA), Nov. 3, 1960, Box 434, DPP; (Peale) Nixon, *Six Crises*, op. cit., p. 327–; Billy Graham, *Just As I Am*, San Francisco: Harper, 1973, p. 391–; (Graham) ibid., pp. 390–, 442–; Salinger, op. cit., p. 75; Frady, op. cit., p. 438–; *Esquire*, Apr. 10, 1979; ("I wonder") Graham, op. cit., p. 442.

bedroom dirt: (Rebozo parties) int. Lloyd Cutler, eds. Strober, *Kennedy*, op. cit., p. 30; ("I knew . . .") Crowley, *Nixon Off the Record*, op. cit., p. 33; (request to Hoover) Jack Anderson int. in *Star*, Mar. 23, 1976—referring to aide Luther Huston; int. Ann Noble Huston; (Hoover complied) ibid., Sullivan, op. cit., p. 48; (political research) Summers, *Official & Confidential*, op. cit., p. 262; (secret marriage) ibid., p. 292; Hersh, op. cit., Durie Malcolm refs.; (busy sex life) Summers, *Official & Confidential*, op. cit., p. 264–; (Raab) Hersh, op. cit., p. 120n; (Hall/other marriage) notes on "first marriage," Ladislas Farago Papers, Mugar Library, Boston University; ("counter-productive") San Francisco *Examiner*, (review of TV show *Richard Nixon Reflects*), May 4, 1990; (Hoover/Goldwater) Ladislas Farago Papers, *supra*; (women vote) Laurence Leamer, *The Kennedy Women*, London: Transworld: 1994, p. 509.

burglaries: (doctors' offices) Beschloss, op. cit., p. 187; Lasky, op. cit., p. 37; (RN office raid) Humes, op. cit., p. 133.

Democratic bugging: (Bush) statement by Hon. George Bush, Box 120, Korff Papers, Brown University; (detectives) reports on and affidavits of John Frank, Oliver Angelone, Edward M. Jones, John Leon, Joseph Shimon, June/July 1973, Box 120, Korff Papers, Brown University; int. Oliver Angelone; Lasky, op. cit., p. 46–; Jim Hougan, *Secret Agenda*, New York: Random House, 1984, p. 310; (subcommittee) ibid., p. 311n10; (RN "convinced") Kissinger, *Years of Upheaval*, op. cit., p. 1182; ("victimized") Crowley, *Winter*, op. cit., p. 314; (RFK "worst") Crowley, *Nixon Off the Record*, op. cit., p. 32.

JFK/RN and Mafia: (Kennedy/Mafia) Summers, *Official & Confidential*, op. cit., pp. 261, 268–; NY *Daily News*, Oct. 6, 7, 8, 1991 (series by author); Hersh, op. cit., Ch. 10; (RN/Cuba informant) int. Jack Clarke; (JFK compromised) Thelma Lansky (widow) int. *60 Minutes*, June 25, 1989, CBS transcript; (Trafficante) Frank Ragano and Selwyn Raab, *Mob Lawyer*, New York: Charles Scribner's, 1994, p. 84; int. Frank Ragano; ("we'll contribute") Sam & Chuck Giancana, op. cit., p. 286–; (Marcello bribe) int./corr. Michael Ewing, Dan Moldea, *The Hoffa Wars*, New York: Paddington Press, 1978, pp. 108, 260; (Hunter) Mollenhoff memo for files, Jan. 22, 1970, Box 74, Folder 10, Mollenhoff papers, Gerald R. Ford Library, Sheridan, op. cit., pp. 140, 156, 165–; *WP*, Jan. 5, 1961; (Hoffa on JFK) ibid., pp. 143, 146, 151, 157–; ("be assured") Cushman to Mrs. Ernest Wild, Oct. 24, 1960, Hoffa folder, VP, NA; (indictment stopped) Sheridan, op. cit., pp. 5, 158; (reactivated) ibid., p. 159; ("remained unpaid") ibid., p. 5.

Hughes loan in '60: (main sources) *The Reporter*, Aug. 16, 1962; James Phelan article, Schemmer, unpub. ms., op. cit., p. 216–; Maheu, op. cit., p. 83–; int. Robert Maheu; (RN panicked) int. Noah Dietrich, Higham Collection, Mary Norton Clapp Library, Occidental College; (RN decision) Klein, op. cit., p. 415; int. Herb Klein; ("sucker") *The Reporter*, Aug. 16, 1962; NY *Post*, Nov. 1, 1960, Gladwin Hill, *Dancing Bear*, New York: World Publishing, 1968, p. 175; (Pearson provoked) articles Oct. 25, 27, 1960, Box G281, DPP; (Don N.) Oct. 30, 1960 statement, File 804, Box 104, WSPF, NA; (accountant re. decisions) NY *Post*, Nov. 1, 1960; (RN on effect) Haldeman and DiMona, op. cit., p. 45, Drosnin, op. cit., p. 519–, citing Rebozo Watergate testimony (RFK too) *NYT*, Nov. 13, 1960 and see Maheu, op. cit., p. 85.

"filthy lying": Goodwin, op. cit., p. 105.

election day: (surge/ebb) Arthur Schlesinger, *A Thousand Days*, Boston: Houghton\Mifflin, 1965, p. 74; (Gallup/Cone) *Time*, Oct. 31, 1960; (Election Day) *Time*, undated on election; *JA*, p. 288–; *Good Housekeeping*, Mar. 1962; Nixon, *Six Crises*, op. cit., p. 377–; (Chotiner/Rebozo) ibid., p. 393; *Life*, July 31, 1970; Klein, op. cit., p. 36; (never conceded) Leonard Reinsch Oral History, *supra*, p. 29; Nixon, *Six Crises*, op. cit., p. 390; *TW60*, p. 24; (Pat grief) ibid., *NYT*, Sept. 13, 1970; (bony arm) FB to Paul Ziffren, recounting Wilma Bassett int., in Ziffren int, FBP and *FB*, p. 432–; (RN prowled) ibid, citing James Bassett; (election result) *TW60*, pp. 350, 386.

Vote fraud?: (Illinois) Earl Mazo and Stephen Hess, *President Nixon*, London: MacDonald, 1968, p. 242–; *Look*, Feb. 14, 1961; ("With . . . help") Benjamin Bradlee, *Conversations with Kennedy*, New York: Pocket, 1976, p. 33; ("mafiosi" role documented) Richard Mahoney, *Sons & Brothers*, New York: Arcade, 1999, p. 80–; (Blakey) ibid., p. 83; ("If it wasn't") Judith Exner with Ovid Demaris, *My Story*, New York: Grove Press, 1977, p. 194; (Chuck) Sam and Chuck Giancana, op. cit., p. 290; ("I know") Cohen with Nugent, op. cit., p. 236; (Republicans cheated?) Parmet, *Nixon*, op. cit., p. 355; Bradlee, op. cit., p. 33; Wicker, op. cit., p. 252; ("The point") ibid.; (Dems. worried) Brandon, op. cit., p. 155; Matthews, op. cit., p. 184;

("could not subject") *MEM*, p. 224 and see Nixon, *Six Crises*, op. cit., p. 413; ("finest hour") e.g., Miller, *Stealing from America*, op. cit., p. 341; ("RN was bitter") int. Ralph de Toledano by FB, FBP, *FB*, p. 433 and see de Toledano, *One Man Alone*, op. cit., p. 309–; ("not really") Crowley, *Off the Record*, op. cit., pp. 114, 147.

RN reaction: ("He started") int. Leonard Hall by FB, FBP; ("depressed") Mathews, op. cit., p. 183; ("difficult to speak") Klein, op. cit., p. 373.

RN/JFK after election: (meeting) ibid.; Nixon, *Six Crises*, op. cit., p. 404, RN cited by AP, Apr. 12, 1984; (JFK denied) Matthews, op. cit., p. 186; ("just as well") Kenneth P. O'Donnell, David F. Powers with Joe McCarthy, *Johnny, We Hardly Knew Ye*, Boston: Little, Brown, 1970, p. 227–; ("I've saved") Matthews, op. cit., p. 188; ("I had the wisdom") *MEM*, p. 226; ("Dick blew"/"never cut out") *TW60*, p. 317.

Halsey: *The New Republic*, undated 1958, sent to Harry Truman by Paul Butler, Apr. 9, 1958, Richard M. Nixon, general corr. file, Box 109, postpresidential papers, Truman Library.

RN unbalanced: ("How did you ever?") eds. Strober, *Nixon*, op. cit., p. 302, citing Colson; ("sick"/"unsound") Bradlee, op. cit., pp. 32n, 116; ("not know who was") J. K. Galbraith citing JFK, *Esquire*, LXXXI, 1974.

Hutschnecker: int. Hutschnecker citing female patient who knew Joseph Kennedy; Kitty Kelley, *His Way*, New York: Bantam, 1986, p. 530; "Nixon on the Couch," article ms. by Irving Wallace, FBP.

pressure: ("when he broke") *TW60*, p. 315 and see ed. Sevareid, op. cit., p. 108, re. "black spells"; ("I have faith") int. Hannah Nixon, *This Week*, Sept. 18, 1960.

JFK inauguration: ("trying") Bobst, op. cit., p. 276; (night drive), Nixon, *Six Crises*, op. cit., p. 417, *MEM*, p. 227, *Good Housekeeping*, Mar. 1962.

"terrible blow": int. Fletcher Knebel, citing JFK, JFK Oral History Program, JFKL.

"cannot imagine": letter, Mar. 16, 1960, ed. Buckley, op. cit., p. 287.

Chapter 19

"He can't help it . . .": *Ladies' Home Journal*, Nov. 1962.

Pat after 1960: ("banshee") Cheshire with Greenya, op. cit., p. 111, citing Kelly; ("I've given up") David, op. cit., p. 73; ("mother took") *McCall's*, Oct. 1973 and see ibid, May 1971; ("We won") *Ladies' Home Journal*, Mar. 1975 and see Bobst, op. cit., p. 275; ("turning point") *PAT*, p. 204; ("one of her 'moods'") James Bassett to wife, Wilma, Sep. 4, 1960, Bassett Papers.

Nixon after '60: (Bahamas '61) Nassau *Daily Tribune*, Jan. 20, 1961; Nassau *Guardian*, Jan. 23, 24, 25, 31, 1961; Bobst, op. cit., p. 276; (cut short/"shallow talk") Nixon, *Six Crises*, op. cit., p. 423; ("limbo") *PAT*, p. 203; ("bachelor apt.") *MEM*, p. 231; (grand address) Hoyt, op. cit., p. 289–; Nixon lived first at the Statler, then the Gaylord.

new L.A. house: (move) *PAT*, p. 204, *Good Housekeeping*, Mar. 1962; (described) *Newsweek*, June 26, 1961; *Esquire*, Feb. 1962; (price/ownership) *WP*, Dec. 16, 1973.

Murchison: (owner) ibid., Jane Wolfe, *The Murchisons*, New York: St. Martin's Press, 1989, p. 316; (contributor) ibid.; James Conaway, *The Texans*, New York: Knopf, 1976, p. 81; (gifts) e.g., "12 quarts of chili"—Rose Mary Woods to Bessie, Feb. 26, 1957, cited at Bruce Adamson, *Oswald's Closest Friend*, Aptos, CA: self-published, 1993, vol. 5, p. 89; (hosted) Wolfe, op. cit., p. 316; (Teamsters' financing) *LAT*, May 17, 1962, *Esquire*, Feb. 1962; Nancy Manella memo to Joe Wershba, (*60 Minutes*) June 4, 1973, FBP.

RN income: ("After 8 years") *Atlantic Monthly*, Aug. 1983; (Adams) Hoyt, op. cit., p. 286– and MO refs; full name of firm was Adams, Duque, & Hazeltine; (writing contracts) *Good Housekeeping*, Mar. 1962; *Esquire*, Feb. 1962; (butler) ibid.; (car) *Good Housekeeping*, Mar. 1962; (more in a year) *PAT*, p. 204; *Esquire*, Feb. 1962; ("Hallelujah") David, op. cit., p. 74.

Pat happy?: *PAT*, p. 204.

"If you ever": notes of int. Adela St. Johns by FB, FBP.

McGuire/Hopkins: (Bahamas) Nixon, *Six Crises*, op. cit., p. 418; (Southern Air) *NYT*, Sept. 1, 1973; (Hopkins) Louis and Yazijian, op. cit., p. 170.

Bay of Pigs: (Dulles) *MEM*, p. 233; ("JFK called") ibid., p. 234; (RN/JFK meeting) ibid., p. 234–; ("shit") *JA*, p. 295; (JFK/assurances) Schlesinger, *1,000 Days*, op. cit., pp. 250, 295; *MEM*, p. 234 and see James Binder, *Lemnitzer: A Soldier for His Time*, Washington, D.C.: Brassey's, 1997, p. 270; ("worst experience") ed. Kornbluh, *Bay of Pigs*, op. cit., p. 3; (RN calls) Wills, op. cit., p. 31; ("should not start") *MEM*, p. 236; ("Jack handled") *Newsweek*, Oct. 9, 1961; ("doomed") *MEM*, p. 233; ("Do you think?") Crowley, *Nixon in Winter*, op. cit., p. 302; (Ike/"down drain") Roger Morris, *Uncertain Greatness*, New York: Harper & Row, 1977, p. 174; ("I was hard-line") Witcover int. in *Saturday Evening Post*, Feb. 25, 1967; (U.S. force 60,000?) ed. Kornbluh, *Bay of Pigs*, op. cit., p. 322, re. contingency plan; (option excluded) ibid., pp. 111, 274; ("find legal cover") *MEM*, p. 234; (CIA damned?) e.g., Hunt, *Give Us This Day*, op. cit., Chap. 16; Summers, *Not in Your Lifetime*, op. cit., p. 177.

Esterline on RN/Bay of Pigs: ("It is very wrong", et seq.) int. Jacob Esterline, 1975 conducted by CIA historian Jack Pfeiffer for CIA in-house history, leaked transcript, pp. 12–, 39–, and ints. by Gus Russo, 1996, 1998, provided to author; (RN re. JFK "never . . . accountable") Crowley, *Nixon in Winter,* op. cit., p. 302; ("Bay of Pigs Thing") WHT, June 23, 1972.

RN activity '61: ("I found") MEM, p. 232; (weekly report) int. Stephen Hess in eds. Miller Center, op. cit., p. 364; (speeches) *Good Housekeeping,* Mar. 1962.

Six Crises: ("7th crisis") Nixon, *Six Crises,* op. cit. [Garden City, NY: Doubleday, 1962], p. xii; ("barricaded") Neil Morgan article, *Esquire,* Feb. 1962; (1990 Introduction) Richard Nixon, *Six Crises,* New York: Simon & Schuster, 1990, p. xii; ("I was hired") int. Alvin Moscow; (Adela St. Johns) cited by (former Whittier College president) Paul Smith in ed. Schulte, op. cit., p. 169; ("written for him") conv. Seymour Hersh, citing RN spokesman Jack Brennan, corroborated in. int. John Sears; ($345,000) estimate with *Life* serial included, *Esquire,* Feb. 1962; ("wisdom") circular letter by Doubleday chairman Douglas Black, Feb. 1, 1962, Box G281, DPP; (sent to writers) int. Jack Langguth.

advice on '62 run: (Bobst) Bobst, op. cit., pp. 277, 324; (Chambers) Chambers to RN, Feb. 2, 1961 and Rose Woods memo, Aug. 1, 1961, found in Box 36, FBP; (Dewey) Dewey to RN, Nov. 13, 1961, Thomas Dewey Papers, Series 8, Box 26A, University of Rochester; (colleagues) MEM, p. 237–; PAT, p. 205; (Klein) San Diego *Reader,* July 28, 1994, citing Klein to RN, June 28, July 10, 1961; (Bassett) int. James Bassett by FB, FBP.

Pat and '62 decision: (council) Pat article *Ladies' Home Journal,* Nov. 1962; MEM, p. 239; PAT, p. 206 and see Klein, op. cit., p. 47; (brother Tom) PAT, p. 205; ("trapped") ibid., p. 207; (restaurant) FB, p. 454, and see LAT, Feb. 11, 1968.

RN/Brown race: ("I welcome") SF Examiner, Sep. 28, 1962; (RN/Communism) RN remarks, Manhattan Beach, June 1, 1962, JFRP; Hess and Broder, op. cit., p. 164; (no mess) AMI, p. 651; ("yokels") John Osborne, *The Third Year of the Nixon Watch,* New York: Liveright, 1972, p. 167; ("sweat off balls") eds. Strober, *Nixon,* op. cit., p. 12.

covenant: Box G281, DPP and see AMI, p. 661; Klein, op. cit., p. 25; Ehrlichman, op. cit., p. 15, RN corr. with Herman Edelsberg (Anti-Defamation League) Sep./Oct. 1956—sources differ as to whether the covenant furor applied to a Nixon home in Washington or California; perhaps homes in both places were involved.

Hughes Loan '62: (justice officials) NYT, Jan. 24, 1972; (Chinatown) Herbert Baus and William Ross, *Politics Battleplan,* New York: Macmillan, 1968, p. 293; Matthews, op. cit., p. 215; Mankiewicz, op. cit., p. 27; conv. John Rothmann—sources conflict as to the location either L.A. or San Francisco; (Braden raised) MEM, p. 242–; transcript of Nixon/Brown discussion, Fairmont Hotel, San Francisco, Oct. 1, 1962, JFRP; (*Meet the Press*) program transcript, Oct. 7, 1962, p. 10; (Braden audits) int. Tom Braden by FB, FBP; (RN thought handicap) MEM, p. 243; (Brown/advantage) James Phelan obit., NYT, Sept. 12, 1997; (Brown denied) Fairmont Hotel transcript, *supra.,* p. 10.

John Davies: ints. Alvin Moscow and see Whitcover, op. cit., p. 36.

RN on Dem. bugging: ("We were bugged") WHT, Sep. 15, 1972, WSPF, NA; ("victimized") Crowley, *Winter,* op. cit., p. 314.

Watergate names '62: (Haldeman/Ehrlichman/Ziegler/Kalmbach/Woods) Nixon for Governor staff directory, VP, NA, (Stans) Stans, op. cit., p. 100; NYT, Apr. 15, 1998; (Kalmbach jail) SF Examiner, Mar. 26, 1985; NM, pp. 111n, 135n; (Chotiner) Frontier, Oct. 1962, WP, Feb. 23, 1969; (constituent) Mrs. Clarence Bentson to Brown, July 11, 1961, Brown Papers, Bancroft Library, University of California at Berkeley.

Knight: NYT. Sep. 29, 30, Oct. 5, 1961; Barry Lerner to DP, Nov. 20, 1961, undated clippings, Oceanside (CA) *Blade Tribune* and Longbeach *Telegram.*

phoney propaganda: statement to editors from Democratic official Don Kimball, Oct. 27, 1962, attaching false photos and rebuttal; WP, Feb. 23, 1969; NYT, Oct. 19, 1962; SF Examiner, Oct. 23, 1962; (mailing) Mankiewicz, op. cit., p. 63– and p. 219; reprinting Supreme Court Judgment, Case 526150, Oct. 30, 1964, "Poll Selection" facsimile, JFRP; *Nation,* May 28, 1973; (RN/"asshole") RN to Ehrlichman, Oct. 16, 1972; AOP, p. 165; (Colson/RN '72) Oct. 7, 1972 entry; AOP, p. 156.

Missile Crisis: ("hedgehog") London *Evening Standard,* Oct. 30, 1997; (effect on election) MEM, p. 244; Witcover, op. cit., p. 31.

'62 Election Day: (in suite) ibid., p. 13; ("dreary drama") MEM, p. 244; ("haggard") Klein, op. cit., p. 55; int. Herb Klein; ("Screw them") Witcover, op. cit., p. 14; ("The hell with") Hillings with Seelye, op. cit., p. 94; ("no shape") Klein, op. cit., p. 56; ("hurtling") Hillings with Seelye, op. cit., p. 94; (Haldeman) Rather and Gates, op. cit., p. 129; (RN speech) reprinted in full; Hill, op. cit., p. 274–.

RN and press '62: (angry in '60) TW60, p. 336; Fletcher Knebel in Minneapolis *Tribune,* undated, Jan. 1961; *U.S. News & World Report,* Nov. 26, 1962; (*LA Times* 1962) int. Paul Ziffren by

FB, FBP, *American Journalism Review,* Apr. 1997; (not unfair) Klein, op. cit., p. 58; ("ridiculous") int. Maurice Stans; ("What unnerved") Hill, op. cit., p. 177.

RN after speech: ("in the ass") David, op. cit., p. 124–; Witcover, op. cit., p. 22, citing *Time,* uses "behind" rather than "ass"; (leaves for home) ibid.; (drive by self) Klein, op. cit., p. 372.

RN alcohol election night: (8th Ave.) int. Jack Langguth; (concluded drink) e.g., James Wrightson, editor Sacramento *Bee,* in eds. Strober, *Nixon,* op. cit., p. 14; int. Richard Bergholz by FB, FBP; (description omitted) Ehrlichman, op. cit., p. 18; ("perversely stimulating") Hill, op. cit., p. 164; ("one or two") Hillings with Seelye, op. cit., p. 93; Parmet, *Nixon,* op. cit., p. 429; Witcover, op. cit., p. 13; (Ehrlichman) Ehrlichman, op. cit., pp. 21, 17; int. John Ehlrichman in eds. Miller Center, op. cit., p. 121; int. John Ehrlichman.

insomnia: (long-term) int. Leonard Hall by FB, FBP; ("more tired") *MEM,* p. 237.

RN/Pat relations '62: (watching Pat) *McCall's,* Oct. 1972, citing aide Nick Ruwe; *Cronkite,* op. cit., p. 221; (cruise) int. John Ehrlichman; Ehrlichman, op. cit., p. 12; ("tension") int. Ronald Ziegler; ("never forget") int. Howard Seelye; ("bubbling") SF *News Call-Bulletin,* Sep. 28, 1961; ("weapon") *Newsweek,* Oct. 29, 1962; ("just stick") int. Richard Bergholz by FB, FBP; ("Keep mouth shut") int. Judge Jerry Pacht by FB, FBP.

Pat after election: (aides preventing) Ehrlichman, op. cit., p. 17; (Pat sobbing) Witcover, op. cit., p. 13; (Pat "berserk") Cheshire, op. cit., p. 112; (return home) Witcover, op. cit., p. 22; ("Oh, Dick" etc.) *PAT,* p. 213.

RN rages: ("irrational") int. Robert Finch by FB, FBP; ("deep dark") Safire, op. cit., p. 364.

Pat temper: e.g., Alsop, op. cit., p. 59.

"martinis' great": 1968 presidential aide who requested anonymity.

RN physical abuse: (Woodward) ints. Bob Woodward and also Carl Bernstein, David Obst; (Hersh) convs. Seymour Hersh, transcripts Hersh int. on NBC *Today* and CNBC *Hardball,* June 23, 1998; (Brown) transcript of int. Pat Brown by FB, FBP; (Cullen) int. Frank Cullen; (van Petten) int./corr. Jon Ewing and re. Van Petten career, corr. Tom Wolfe; (Ehrlichman on RN drink) Ehrlichman, op. cit., p. 21–; ints. John Ehrlichman and int. John Ehrlichman in eds. Miller Center, op. cit., p. 121–; (Sears) ints. John Sears; (background) Garment, op. cit., pp. 107, 113; Wise, *Police State,* op. cit., p. 56–; Susan Trento, *The Power House,* New York: St. Martin's Press, 1992, p. 72; Safire, op. cit., p. 167; (Taylor background, not re. beating) int. Waller Taylor III; (Taylor father—Reese) see Reese and Waller Taylor files, Series 320, VP, NA and Dennis Effle report to author, July 18, 1996; (service station) Winter-Berger, op. cit., p. 247; (Bohemian Grove) RN to Reese Taylor, July 31, 1961, corr. files, Series 320, VP, NA; (Segretti) Waller Taylor to RN, May 26; Finch to Waller Taylor, May 29, 1959, corr. files, Series 320, VP, NA; ('60 Convention) Waller Taylor to RN, July 11; RN to Taylor, July 22, 1960, corr. files, Series 320, VP, NA; ("He knows Pat") int. Lou Cannon by FB, FBP; (psychologist/abuse) int. and corr. Gaye Humphries, counseling psychologist, formerly with Irish Defense Forces.

RN/trousers: int. Sarah McClendon and see *Parade,* Oct. 31, 1971.

"more reserved": *NYT* magazine, May 13, 1962.

"mother lay": *PAT,* p. 214.

"sadness for years": ibid., p. 216.

divorce?: int. Arnholt Smith and int. John Sears.

depression/impotence?: (Bassett) notes and transcript of int. Bassett friends, Paul and Mickey Ziffren by FB, FBP, *FB,* p. 331; (RN observed) Harriet Van Horne column, New York *Post,* Nov. 15, 1968 and see Woodstone, op. cit., p. 8; (Hutschnecker) ints. Arnold Hutschnecker.

Woods/dinner: int. James Bassett by FB, FBP; (just "kind of thing") int. Nancy Chotiner.

RN finished?: (Eisenhower) int. Leonard Hall by FB, FBP; (*Time*) Witcover, op. cit., p. 25; ("unelected") *NYT,* Nov. 9, 1962; ("shot down") int. Bryce Harlow in eds. Miller Center, op. cit., p. 7; (JFK gloated) Parmet, *Nixon,* op. cit., p. 437; (JFK/Brown) SF *Examiner,* Dec. 6, 1998 citing JFK/Brown taped call, JFKL, released 1998; (JFK: "nobody . . .") Bradlee, op. cit., p. 32n; (RN/Graham) Graham, op. cit., p. 443; (Chotiner) SF *Examiner,* Nov. 24, 1962.

Pat griping: Witcover, op. cit., p. 41.

$4 billion: *PAT,* p. 61.

Chapter 20

"I was accused": Nixon, *Arena,* op. cit., pp. 36–, 122.

Paradise Island: (background) Lisa Gubernick, *Squandered Fortune,* New York: Putnam, 1991, p. 124–; Paul Albury, *Paradise Island Story,* London: Macmillan, 1984, p. 94–; Gigi Mahon, *The Company That Bought the Boardwalk,* New York: Random House, 1980, p. 27; Alan Block, *Masters of Paradise,* New Brunswick, NJ: Transaction, 1991, p. 61–; ("Meyer's Island") Nassau *Guardian,* Feb. 16, 1978 citing Vincent Teresa deposition; (RN arrival '62) Nassau Weekend *Guardian,* Nov. 17/18, 1962, Witcover, op. cit., p. 36–; (Davies) ibid.; ints. Huntington Hartford and (former wife) Diane Hartford; (not charged) Denny Walsh article, *NYT,* Jan.

21, 1974; (RN family arrive) *MEM,* p. 247, Nassau *Daily Tribune,* Nov. 28, 1962; (Paar) Paar, op. cit., p. 132; ("morose") int. Seymour Alter; *NYT,* Jan. 21, 1974; (cigarette box) ibid.; ('67 visits) London *Daily Mail,* Jan. 8, 1968; *Look,* Apr. 2, 1968; DP column, undated (Oct.?),1968; Gubernick, op. cit., p. 176.

Island take-over: (Crosby/Davis) Nassau *Tribune,* Dec. 14, 1968; (Lansky meeting) Gubernick, op. cit., p. 170–; Block, op. cit., p. 43; (bribe/exemption) "Masters of Paradise Island: Organized Crime, Neo-Colonialism & the Bahamas" by Alan Block and Patricia Klausner in *Dialectical Anthroplogy,* Vol. 12, Dordrecht, The Netherlands: Martinus Nijhoff, 1987, p. 92, citing "Report to Control Commission with Reference to the Casino License Application of Resorts International Hotel, Inc., Vol 3, (1978), p. 15, and Report of Commission of Inquiry into the Operation of the Business of Casinos in Freeport & Nassau, Nassau, 1967, pp. 20, 102; Henry Petersen to Fred Vinson, Mar. 24, 1967, citing Louis Chesler, admission to Peloquin, Messick Papers, Alan Block Collection; (informant on cheating) IFB report, Nov. 9, 1964, Phelps No. 92-2831, File 92–102, Justice Dept. Org. Crime & Racketeering Section, Block Collection; (Peters trailed) *Saturday Evening Post,* Feb. 25, 1967; (been cartons) Miami *Herald,* Apr. 12, 1967; (Hartford furious) Gubernick, op. cit., p. 156 and see 153–; Block, op. cit., p. 62–; Mahon, op. cit., p. 65; (license in 1966) *Dialetical Anthropology, supra.,* p. 94; Mahon, op. cit., p. 68–; (Groves) Block, op. cit., pp. 27–, 34–; Mahon, op. cit., p. 60–; *Saturday Evening Post,* Feb. 25, 1967.

Crosby: (background) *Manhattan, Inc.,* Feb. 1987; (Groves/*Life*) *NYT,* Jan. 17, 1979; (real estate project) Mahon, op. cit., p. 208–; ("The funds amassed") Block, op. cit., p. 81; (Fiduciary Trust) ibid., p. 82–; (Enforcement Div. opposed) *Barrons,* Sept. 26, 1977, *Manhattan, Inc.,* Feb. 1987; *Hollywood Reporter,* Dec. 5, 1978; *Wall St. Journal,* May 22, 1970, p. 15.

"ripe for skim": Block, op. cit., p. 70.

Cellini: (Director) company bio., Resorts International stockholder's report, 1967, Block Collection; (banned/removed) *NYT,* Jan. 17, 1979, [Brunswick, NJ] *Home News,* Jan. 24, 1979; (claimed innocent) *Dialectical Anthroplogy, supra.,* p. 96; *Bergen County Record,* Oct. 14, 1976; Las Vegas *Sun,* Mar. 21, 1971, Mahon, op. cit., p. 86; (Eddie Cellini/Cuba/Kentucky) CIA Inspector General's Report on Plots to Assassinate Fidel Castro, op. cit., p. 30; Messick, *Lansky,* op. cit., p. 217; *Dialectical Anthropology, supra.,* p. 96; Jerry Shields, *The Invisible Millionaire,* Boston: Houghton Mifflin, 1986, p. 226; Hank Messick, *Secret File,* New York: Putnam, 1969, p. 323–; [Brunswick, NJ] *Home News,* Jan. 24, 1979.

Lansky/Dino Cellini indictment: Jeff Gerth article, *Penthouse,* July 1974.

Teresa: (testified) Perm. Subcttee. on Investigations, Cttee on Gov. Ops., 92nd Cong., 1st Sess., U.S. Sen., Hearings on Organized Crime (Stolen Securities), July 27, 1971, p. 814; Nassau *Guardian,* citing Jan. 31, 1978 testimony in *Resorts International Inc., v. Straight Arrow Publishers Inc.,* U.S. Dist. Court, S. Dist. of Florida, No. 76144551-CIV-WMH, and see Teresa and Renner, op. cit., p. 222; (inspector) Ray Clark, cited in undated memo, 1973, Warren Adams to John Sablich of Fidelifacts; (corporate investigators for plaintiff Huntington Hartford in suit v. James Crosby, Resorts International, et al), supplied to author, p. 536; (FBI agent) Frank Smith, cited in memo Dec. 10, 1973, John Sablich to Mr. Moerdler, ibid., p. 583.

Skyjector: Mahon, op. cit., p. 55.

Chesler: Jeff Gerth article, *Sundance,* Nov./Dec., 1972; Blumenthal & Yazijian, op. cit., p. 139.

Alter: ("old Lansky man") Smith cited in memo, Dec. 10, 1973, John Sablich to Mr. Moerdler, Fidelifacts report, *supra.,* p. 584; (Block) Block, op. cit., p. 61; (Alter/Lansky) ibid., pp. 62, 78n16; Miami *Herald,* Mar. 20, 1976; (officials oppose) *NYT,* Sept. 2, 1979; (violations/bribery) NY State Liquor Authority docs., transcript of Alter grand jury testimony, 1962, all in Block Collection; *NYT,* Dec. 13, 1978, Feb. 18, Sept. 2, 1979 and Block, op. cit., p. 61; Gubernick, op. cit., p. 172; Mahon, op. cit., p. 231–; (RN/Rebozo relations) *NYT,* Jan. 21, 1974; int. Seymour Alter; ("Treat well") Judith Denny memo to files on DeBoer int., Aug. 15, 1975, Box 98, WSPF, NA.

RN and Paradise Island: ("in on negotiations") Frank Smith cited in memo, Dec. 10, 1973, John Sablich to Mr. Moerdler, Fidelifacts report, *supra.,* p. 586; (RN/Crosby $100,000) int. Seymour Alter, *NYT,* Jan. 21, 1974; (RN/benefactor dine) Nassau *Tribune,* June 11, 1968; (Cosa Grande) Nevada State *Journal,* Oct. 31, 1968; undated memo, Warren Adams to John Sablich, Fidelifacts report, *supra.,* p. 545; (Crosby Wh. House) *HD,* p. 25; *Barrons,* Sept. 26, 1977; (Golden background) memos Jim Rowe to Scott Armstrong, Oct. 17, 1973; Armstrong to Terry Lenzner, Oct. 22, 1973; Sen. Int. memo folder 807, Box 101, WSPF; Nassau *Tribune,* Aug. 8, 1969, Resorts International stockholder's report, (1969?), Block Collection; (close to RN) Frank Smith cited in memo, Dec. 10, 1973, John Sablich to Mr. Moerdler, Fidelifacts report, *supra.,* p. 588; ("Nixon's man") *Rolling Stone,* May 20, 1976; (Ehrlichman) int. John Ehrlichman; Ehrlichman, op. cit., p. 52; (S.S. advice) *Barrons,* Sept. 26, 1977; ("significant investment") London *Daily Mail,* Jan. 8, 1968.

"giving the shaft": Moldea, *Interference,* op. cit., p. 174.

Paradise Island Bridge: (suit) Nassau *Tribune,* Oct. 9, 1973; Gubernick, op. cit., p. 210; (Bridge facts) Nassau *Tribune,* Jan. 27, 1966, Oct. 9, 1973, Aug. 31, 1984; (percentages) IRS informant Sally Woodruff, wife of Ed Woodruff, text, *supra;* report on Sy Alter, P.I. Bridge Co., Ltd., p. 4, Block Collection; ("reason to believe") Nassau *Tribune,* Oct. 9, 1973; (RN Swiss deposits?) Moldea, *Interference,* op. cit., p. 458n6 and convs./corr. Dan Moldea; (Crosby denied) Mahon, op. cit., p. 50; (Smith) cited in memo, Dec. 10, 1973; John Sablich to Mr. Moerdler, Fidelifacts report, *supra.,* pp. 578, 586–; (Butler background) Block, op. cit., pp. 141–, 157n24 and 37, Hutchison, op. cit., refs.; (Butler/bridge) ibid., p. 281–; Hougan, *Spooks,* op. cit., p. 180; (Mitchell) int./corr. Jim Hougan, investigative journalist who conducted interview.
"20 a day": int. Carl Feldbaum.
"A sound basis": Carl Feldbaum to Henry Ruth, May 15, 1974, Investigative Corr. Box 14, WSPF (H-R), NA.
Pictures '69: ("Rebozo feared") Spear, op. cit., p. 69; (Silk) ints. George Silk.
Silberman: (call to FBI) June 8, 1973 FBI memo, "Re: James Walter McCord, et al. Burglary of Dem. Party HQ, June 17, 1972" and associated corr., probably all in file containing FBI 139-4089-2624; (Buckley) Feldbaum to Ruth memo, May 15, 1974, *supra.,* and accompanying docs.; (male associates) former FBI informant, now security consultant, and former entertainment industry executive, both of whom requested anonymity; (background) ints. David Silberman, Elsie Silberman (wife), Kathy Silberman (daughter), Dee Anne Hill (secretary), Jack Cassinetto (former colleague), Gene Henry and Alvin Lotzcar (coin dealers); (murder conviction) Oakland *Tribune,* Oct. 21, 1979, Oct. 23, Nov. 25, Dec. 18, 1980; (signed photo) int. Dee Anne Hill; (*Life* pic. in bar) ints. Kent Woods, John Cassinetto; (S. Service agents) ints. Art Godfrey, Earl Moore by Phil Stanford, Robbyn Swan, and author; (Feb. Group) association directory, Dec. '94/Jan. '95, *NYT, WP,* Apr. 26, 1977; *Newsweek,* undated, 1978; *SF Chronicle,* Dec. 8, 1978; (Youngblood) *WP,* Oct. 19, 1971; (Edward Kennedy) June 13, Sept. 7, 1972 entries; *AOP,* pp. 40, 132; *WP,* Feb. 8, 1997; (McGovern) Nick Akerman to files, Nov. 19, 1973, citing int. John Dean, WSPF, NA; Marc Lackritz, undated memo, "Campaign Practices," GEMSTONE file, E, NA; (Don Nixon) *Wall St. Journal,* Dec. 4, 1973; ("perversion") *NYT,* Feb. 18, 1974; (Morgan) notes of int. Pacific News Service, Nov. 2, 1982, Stanley Kutler Papers; (Ehrlichman) int. John Ehrlichman; (FBI doc.) C. A. Nuzum to Mr. Long, May 23, 1974, FBI 139-4089-2761.
Laxalt: (crime links?) Sacramento *Bee,* Nov. 1, 1983; Scheim, op. cit., p. 308–; Dan Moldea, *Dark Victory,* New York: Viking, 1986 p. 347; *Crime Control Digest,* May 28, 1984; (Hughes Donation) Maheu, op. cit., p. 167; (re: Hoffa) Moldea, *Dark Victory,* op. cit., p. 259; (Laxalt denial) Tom Loranger to author, Nov. 8, 1999.
gold window: Safire, op. cit., p. 509–; Wicker, op. cit., pp. 543–, 545–; Theodore White, *The Making of the President 1972,* New York: Atheneum, 1972 (henceforth *TW72*), p. 64–; James Reston, Jr., *The Lone Star: The Life of John Connally,* New York: Harper & Row, 1989, p. 403–; Genovese, op. cit., p. 68–; *MEM,* p. 518–; ints. Don Adams, asst. dir. of international finance, Federal Reserve, George Shultz, Peter Flanigan, Darwin Beck; (Volcker) Safire, op. cit., p. 515.
Selix: ints. Janice Selix, Rose Wilkins.
study as described: int. Ronald Ziegler.
woman invited: ints. Patti Clarke.
3 witnesses: Dee Anne Hill (Silberman's secretary), Robin Sargeant (cousin), and Carol Adams.
Newell background: ints. Elizabeth Newell, Bill Gill, Michael Hershman.
DeBoer: (ad./"honest") Stephen Haberfield to Hughes-Rebozo file, re: int. of DeBoer, Jan. 10, 1974, Folder 809, WSPF, NA; Mahon, op. cit., p. 34; (wife/Rebozo) ibid. and DeBoer executive session testimony, Aug. 8, 1973, p. 2–, E, NA—DeBoer said once that he met Rebozo a year before getting the job, once that he met him only two weeks earlier; (knew Crosby/partner [I.G. Davis]) ibid., p. 51, Fidelifacts report, *supra.,* p. 486–; (Crosby/Davis accounts) *NYT,* Jan. 21, 1974; WPLG-TV News, July 20, 1973, in Fidelifacts report, *supra.,* p. 1537; *Village Voice,* Dec. 20, 1973; (SEC bar/Exchange expulsion) *WP,* Oct. 25, 31, 1973; *NYT,* Jan. 5, 1971, Nov. 9, 1973; (jail) Miami *Herald,* June 19,(?) 1977; (Newell revelations) ints. Elizabeth Newell, Kent Blacklidge [nephew], Newell original contemporary notes and calendar, supplied to author; ("losing" money) int. Elizabeth Newell, contemp. Newell notes of DeBoer convs.; (Alter) ibid.; (Woodruff) Nassau *Guardian,* July 29, 1971; Warren Adams to John Sablich, undated memo, Fidelifacts report, *supra.,* p. 544; (Stearns) Linda Noonan to Paul Michel, Nov. 15, 1974; summary ints. re: Alter, O'Sullivan, DeBoer, Box 113, WSPF, NA; (giftshop) Linda Noonan to Paul Michel, Nov. 15, 1974, re: Alter on matters testified to by Stearns, summary IRS int., Box 112, WSPF, NA; *NYT,* Jan. 21, 1974; (Rebozo instructions) Alter note in papers of Carmine Bellino, Ervin Cttee. chief investigator, supplied to author; Miami *Herald,* Nov. 29, 1973; ("lots of things") Judith Denny to files, Aug. 15, 1974, DeBoer folder, Box 98, WSPF, NA; ("bagman") *NYT,* Jan. 21, 1974; (tapes made) ints. Newell, Michael Hershman, Bill Gill, Carl Feldbaum, Newell transcript, Paul Michel to Henry Ruth, Oct. 16, 1975, p. 244, "re.

Closing Memo on Hughes-Rebozo Unreported Campaign Funds," File 309-804, Final Report, WSPF, NA, and Jack Anderson in *WP,* Dec. 11, 1973, *NYT,* Jan. 27, 1974; (fabrication?) ibid. and see memo of DeBoer int. by IRS, Nov. 8, 1974, File 804, WSPF, NA—DeBoer acknowledged knowing Newell.

"no foreign accounts": Frost, op. cit., p. 192.

"Operation Tradewinds": Block, op. cit., p. 6–; ints. Richard Jaffe, Norman Casper; (RFK/Reno commended) copies supplied to author by Jaffe.

Castle Bank: (access obtained) ints. Norman Casper, Richard Jaffe, Casper and Jaffe testimony, Nov. 4, 1975, Hearings Subcttee. of Cttee. on Gov. Ops., Oversight Hearings into the Operation of the IRS, U.S. House of Reps., 94th Cong., 1st Sess., p. 137–; (suspect) ibid., p. 140; (print-out found) ibid., pp. 141, 157–, 179–, 182, 207, 211–; (list obtained) ibid., 142–, 178–; Castle Bank Account List, 1972, Jaffe handwritten notes, Block Collection re: list obtained Jan. 15, 1973, & (re: briefcase) *U.S. Petitioner v. Jack Payner,* US-65LEd21468, 100, S. Ct., U.S. Supreme Court Reports, p. 473; (2nd copy) Miami *Herald,* July 1, 1980; (names) ibid., Castle List, *supra.; Wall St. Journal,* Apr. 18, 1980; Hank Messick article, *Rolling Stone,* May 20, 1976 [inc. Hall] and see TW-24 memo, "Subject Tom Ferguson," Apr. 25, 1974, Casper Papers; (files purged?) IRS Oversight Hearings, *supra.,* p. 207–; Richard Jaffe to Levoy Venable, May 15, 1974, at p. 187; Sartiano ref. at Steadman Stahl Summary, Nov. 3, 1981, Jaffe Papers, TW-24 to file, June 11, 1973, May 10, 1974, Casper Papers; (denial) Nassau *Tribune,* Oct. 29, 1976; ("absolutely positive") int. Samuel Pierson; (Bahamians prohibited) Nicki Kelly to author, Sept. 27, 1987, Burton Kanter to Anthony Marro, June 29, 1975, Casper Papers; (computer) Nassau *Tribune,* Nov. 4, 1972; ("not prepared") int. Alan Bickerton, IRS Oversight Hearings, *supra.,* p. 187; (IRS upheaval) Wise, *American Police State,* op. cit., p. 348; Lernoux, op. cit., p. 90–; Miami *Herald,* Apr. 7, 1976 and undated Jan. 1977, July 1, 1980, Nassau *Tribune,* Sept. 27, 1975; *WP,* Nov. 5, 1977; *Rolling Stone,* May 20, 1976; *LAT/WP* Service, Dec. 6, 1975.

Casper reaction to discovery: ("disturbed me") Oversight Hearings, *supra.,* p. 212; (respected) ints. Charles Wey [former adviser to IRS asst. commissioner], Richard Jaffe, Dallas *Morning Star,* Nov. 23, 1975; (knew RN/Rebozo) ints. Norman Casper; (Republican) ints. Norman Casper; (Rebozo/Casper mtg.) Jaffe diary note, Feb. 12, 1976, Block collection, Casper to Jaffe, Feb. 17, 1976, Casper Papers, int. Norman Casper; (Casper wondered?) Oversight Hearings, *supra.,* p. 179.

Cosmos: (briefcase contents) Jaffe statement to be read to Inspection Service, Sept. 5, 1975, Jaffe Papers, Oversight Hearings, *supra.,* p. 143; (photographs) ibid., pp. 142, 178; (use of initials) Paul Michel to Henry Ruth, closing memo, *supra.,* WSPF, NA; (Clesner) int. Virginia Clesner—who still as relevant documents from her husband's files; (Hartford) int. and orig. notes of Dan Moldea—to whom the author is grateful; Moldea, *Hoffa Wars,* op. cit., p. 458n6; ("Do you want?") int. Huntington Hartford; (Crosby stock) Fidelifacts report, *supra.,* p. 907; (20 percent P.I. Bridge) *Barrons,* Sept. 26, 1977, file of Sy Alter, compiled by IRS informant Sally Woodruff, p. 5, Block collection; Stockholder's List, P.I. Bridge Co., Cosmos Bank, Box B78, E, NA; (bank details) unid. economics journal, Sept. 14, 1974, Casper Papers, *Euromoney,* Oct. 1974, *Bankers Directory,* New York: Rand McNally, 1973, p. F466, Fidelifacts report, *supra.,* p. 902–.

Morgenthau: (Sixties) Leslie Waller, *The Swiss Bank Connection,* New York: Signet, 1972, p. 90–; Messick, Lansky, op. cit, pp. 249, 257, 268–; (Suspicion re: RN) ints. Robert Morgenthau; (Paris attorney) James Traub notes of Morgenthau int., supplied to author; int. James Traub and see Traub article, *The New Yorker,* July 28, 1997; (Morgenthau/Committee/removal) Waller, op. cit., p. 90–; Messick, *Lansky,* op. cit., p. 270.

anon. communication: letter and enclosure, Morgenthau to author, June 5, 1998.

Cantrade: *Bankers' Almanac,* 1969/70, p. 885, Vol I, Jan. 1998, p. 1441, Vol. II, p. 3623, and Website information from Cantrade Investment Managment Ltd., June/July 1998.

"Rebozo/nice guy": int. Maurice Stans.

de Gendre: int. Raoul de Gendre.

Chapter 21

"He has been vaporized": int. Bryce Harlow in eds. Miller Center, op. cit., p. 7.

RN after '62 defeat: (hurting for money?) Witcover, op. cit., p. 41; (promise) ibid., *NYT Magazine,* Sept. 13, 1970; (intimates/"cake") Witcover, op. cit., p. 40–; (wanted job) ibid., p. 42.

Nixon, Mudge, Rose: (Rebozo/Ball) ed. Weisman, op. cit., p. 262, citing *Women's Wear Daily,* 1969; (RN/Bobst) MEM, p. 247; Bobst, op. cit., p. 326–; (big business) *Saturday Evening Post,* Feb. 25, 1967; ("faces commanding") Hugh Sidey in *Life,* undated, 1967 and see White, *Breach,* op. cit., p. 73.

Nixons in NY: (apartment) PAT, p. 56; Witcover, op. cit., p. 52, Washington *Evening Star,* July 31, 1970; (no party) int. Maurice Stans; ("vacation") Troy, op. cit., p. 178; (mink) *NYT,* July 3,

1968; (Chapin) *PAT,* p. 219; (Deb.'s) *New York,* June 9, 1980, *NYT,* July 3, 1968; ("didn't want") Witcover, op. cit., p. 42 and see Kissinger, *White House Years,* op. cit., p. 20; (often alone) int. Walter Trohan; (NY bar) AP, undated 1964 with text of RN essay, and *SF Chronicle,* (?) July 1973; (office) *Saturday Evening Post,* Feb. 25, 1967.

law firm business: (Kendall) int. Don Kendall, Mazo and Hess, op. cit., p. 285; (Abplanalp) AP, May 26, 1973; (Rose) Louis and Yazijian, op. cit., p. 174; (Niarchos) Hougan, *Spooks,* op. cit., p. 281; (Smith) int. attorney Richard Hodge, recalling case involving Susquehanna Corp.; (Vietnam client) 275 Federal Supplement p. 860, re: *Hellenic Lines Ltd., plaintiff, v. The Embassy and Republic of S. Vietnam, Defendants,* no. 67 Civ 860, U.S. Dist. Court, S.D. NY, Dec. 1, 1967, Box G 281, DPP; (Trujillo hunt) *Mayday,* undated, 1968, Box G 119, DPP; Murray Kempton in NY *Post,* undated; Washington *Observer,* cited in Hinckle and Turner, op. cit., p. 202; William Turner, *Power on the Right,* Berkeley: Ramparts Press, 1971, p. 156 and see William Taub, *Forces of Power,* New York: Grossett & Dunlap, 1979, p. 216.

RN/Kennedy: ("cheap bastard") Bradlee, op. cit., p. 76; ("Bastards") Lasky, op. cit., p. 65; (audits) *MEM,* p. 247; *WP,* Jan. 3, 1997; Crowley, *Winter,* op. cit., p. 296; (Papal audiences) int. Walter Trohan, RN Library archivist Susan Naulty to author, Apr. 16, 1998; (JFK "hello") *MEM,* p. 250.

JFK assassination: (Baker Hotel) William Manchester, *The Death of a President,* New York: Popular Library, 1968, p. 101; Witcover, op. cit., p. 59; ("get Kennedys out") *NYT,* Nov. 22, 1963; (outbursts) *WP,* Apr. 21; *U.S. News & World Report,* Oct. 14, 1963; *MEM,* p. 253; (JFK irritated) Jim Bishop, *The Day Kennedy Was Shot,* New York: Bantam, 1975, p. 23; ("courteous reception") Witcover, op. cit., p. 59; (RN flight) Manchester, *Death,* op. cit., p. 132; (NY arrival) Bishop, op. cit., p. 197; (cab ride/doorman) *MEM,* p. 252; (daughters/TV) *PAT,* p. 219; (Hess) int. Stephen Hess in eds. Miller Center, op. cit., p. 370; (Jacqueline letter) *MEM,* p. 253–; ("keen intelligence") *Reader's Digest,* Nov. 1964, p. 298; ("mythology") Parmet, *Nixon,* op. cit., p. 25; ("neither respected") int. H. R. Haldeman in eds. Miller Center, op. cit., p. 82; ("it sometimes seemed") Rush, op. cit., p. 186, citing former agent Marty Venker; ("History intervened") Garment, op. cit., p. 71; ("already assessing") int. Stephen Hess in eds. Miller Center, op. cit., p. 371.

return to politics: ("never had") *SF Examiner,* Jan. 11, 1964, reporting RN to Jackie Gleason on *Arthur Godfrey Show;* ("If all I had") *MEM,* p. 265; (World's Fair) *PAT,* p. 219; Stans, *Terrors,* op. cit., p. 129; (Europe) ibid., p. 221; ('64 campaign) *TW64,* pp. 140–, 150, 153, 215; Witcover, op. cit., Chaps. 3, 4; ("Because I know") Wicker, op. cit., p. 272; (Garment joined) int. Leonard Garment, Garment, op. cit., pp. 62, 65, 68; (night in '65) int. Leonard Garment; Garment, op. cit., p. 85.

de Gaulle: ("Great Man") Michael Beschloss in *WP,* May 1, 1994; (revered) *JA,* p. 336; Richard Nixon, *Leaders,* New York: Simon & Schuster, 1990, p. 40; C. L. Sulzberger, *The World and Richard Nixon,* New York: Prentice-Hall, 1987, p. 150–; (Paris base) Witcover, op. cit., p. 43; (paying court '63) *MEM,* p. 248; Nixon, *Leaders,* op. cit., p. 61–; *JA,* p. 318; (first met) Nixon, *Leaders,* op. cit., p. 42; (Elysee '63) *JA,* p. 318– and see Sulzberger, op. cit., p. 160; (JFK funeral) Nixon, *Leaders,* op. cit., p. 52; (every trip) ibid., p. 62; (emissary) *NYT,* Sept. 21, 1968– RN emissary was Gov. William Scranton; (respect mutual) Kissinger, *White House Years,* op. cit., p. 387; ("equal") eds. Strober, *Nixon,* op. cit., p. 84; ("awe") int. H. R. "Bob" Haldeman, 1989; (RN writing on de G.) esp. Nixon, *Leaders,* op. cit., p. 40–; (RN Library) *JA,* p. 377; ("as if royalty") Dickerson, op. cit., p. 36; (Finch) ibid., p. 157 and see int. Robert Finch by FB, FBP and Safire, op. cit., p. 691; (Haldeman) *HD,* pp. 59, 230; ("giant") Kissinger, *White House Years,* op. cit., p. 107; George W. Johnson, ed. *The Nixon Presidential Press Conferences,* New York: Earl Coleman Enterprises, 1978, p. 31; (RN "not a giant") int. James Schlesinger.

RN travel: ('63 "vacation") *JA,* p. 318–; *MEM,* p. 248; ("As we were talking") AP story, July 24, 1963; (Wheeler) London *Sunday Telegraph,* Feb. 18, 1996; (Moscow '65) *WP,* May 25, 1972; Safire, op. cit., p. 6; *AP* stories, Apr. 11, 12, 17, 18, 1965; ("stupid") Witcover, op. cit., p. 112; (225,000 miles) Thimmesch, op. cit., p. 92; (Japan) *JA,* p. 329; (phlebitis) *PAT,* p. 223; ("shoestring") RN brief for press responses, undated, Gil Troy papers; (Rebozo companion) e.g., Witcover, op. cit., p. 101; Hong Kong *Standard,* Aug. 11, 1966; (*Reader's Digest*/Pepsi) Thimmesch, op. cit., p. 92, Louis and Yazijian, op. cit., p. 114; ("paid off in end") int. Hugh Sidey in eds. Miller Center, op. cit., p. 303; (photographs) *Saturday Evening Post,* Feb. 25, 1967; Whalen, op. cit., p. 25.

'66 campaign: (48-hour period) Hess and Broder, op. cit., p. 142; (victory) Witcover, op. cit., p. 169; Klein, op. cit., p. 148.

'68 campaign: (tight-lipped) *Saturday Evening Post,* Feb. 25, 1967, Witcover, op. cit., p. 177.

mother's death: (stroke) *JA,* p. 338–; *MEM,* p. 287; int. Evlyn Dorn by FB, FBP; (last conv.) *MEM,* p. 288–; Nixon, *Arena,* op. cit., p. 94; (father's death) see Chap. 14, p. 159–, *supra.*

decision to run: (Christmas '67) *MEM,* p. 294; *PAT,* p. 234; ("depressed") *PAT,* p. 233; ("Mother needed") ibid., p. 227; ("Miss Ryan"/"failure"?) ibid; ("flatly") *PAT,* p. 230; ("never been anybody") int. Ed Nixon.

Scarney: Ehrlichman, op. cit., p. 21; int.John Ehrlichman.

"I was looking for wife": int. Arnholt Smith, San Diego *Reader,* Mar. 26, 1992.

Marianna Liu: ("affair" reported) *NYT,* June 22, 1976; (*Enquirer*) *National Enquirer,* Aug. 10, 24, 1976; ("One of my contacts") int. Dan Grove and see Summers, *Official & Confidential,* op. cit., p. 371–; (surveillance) *SF Examiner,* Feb. 8, 1981; (RN visits) *NYT,* June 22, 1976; Hong Kong *Standard,* Feb. 8, Mar. 21, Apr. 6, 8, 1964, Sept. 2, 3, 1965, Aug. 9, 11, 12, 1966, Apr. 8, 1967; (Liu sued) *SF Examiner* and *SF Chronicle,* Feb. 8, 1981; *LAT,* Sept. 18, 1976 and int. Marianna Liu; (Liu 1996) int. for author by Kari Huus, then with *Far Eastern Economic Review,* and Huus report to author; (RN/Chinese women) *Ladies' Home Journal,* June 1970; ("had too much to drink") int. Mickey Ziffren by FB, FBP.

Christmas debate: ("resigned") *MEM,* p. 292; ("volunteer") *LAT,* Feb. 11, *Newsweek,* Dec. 2, 1968 and see *SF Chronicle,* Aug. 15, 1968; (applauding self) Joe McGinniss, *The Selling of the President,* New York: Penguin, 1969, p. 157; (not introduced) *PAT,* p. 241; ("Mr. Nixon publicly") John Osborne, *The Last Nixon Watch,* Washington, D.C.: New Republic Book Co., 1975, p. 3; ("I love it") Wills, op. cit., p. 22; ("what their readers want") *LAT,* July 1, 1968; (Steinem) *New York,* Oct. 28, 1968; *Writers Digest,* Feb. 1974, int. Gloria Steinem.

Chapter 22

"I am inclined to believe": Walt Rostow, special asst. for national security to President Johnson, memo for record, May 14, 1973, in "X Envelope," Chennault, Anna–South Vietnam and U.S. Policy folder, LBJL.

'68 campaign: ("DC") Whalen, op. cit., p. 34; Strober,*Nixon,* op. cit., p. 16–; Stans, *Terrors,* op. cit., p. 134; (preparations/HQ) Garment, op. cit., p. 121–; Raymond Price, *With Nixon,* New York: Viking, 1977, p. 10–; Whalen, op. cit., p. 10–; (men in suits) Garment, op. cit., p. 122 and photo section; (Haldeman/Ehrlichman) ibid., James Reichley, *Conservatives in an Age of Change,* Washington, D.C.: Brookings, 1981, p. 60, Ehrlichman, op. cit., p. 22; (Chotiner) int. E. C. Mueller, stepson; *NYT,* Jan. 14, 1970; Whalen, op. cit., p. 53; Vera Glaser column, undated, end '68, Box G281, DPP.

Mitchell: (background) *NM,* p. 4–; article by Martha Mitchell and Winzola McClendon, *Ladies' Home Journal,* Dec. 1974; *MEM,* p. 279; (DeBoer contacts) WPLG News special report, Aug. 2, 1973, transcript cited in memo, John Sablich to Moerdler, Fidelifacts (corporate investigators) p. 1537, author's collection, Linda Noonan to Paul Michel re: Richard Stearns, Nov. 15, 1974, Analysis Hughes-Rebozo, Box 113, WSPF, NA, Michael Hershman blind memo, Aug. 7, 1973, Box B 343, E, NA; ("understated") Kleindienst, op. cit., p. 46; (blank) *Mayday,* Jan. 3, 1969; ("leader against crime") *NM,* p. 5; (jail) ed. Eleanora Schoenberg, *Profiles of an Era,* New York: Harcourt, Brace, Jovanovich, 1979, p. 445.

Primaries: *TW68,* Chap. 5, Witcover, op. cit., p. 233–; int. Sandy Vanocur, ("very troubled") Ehrlichman, op. cit., p. 24–; int. John Ehrlichman in eds. Miller Center, op. cit., p. 121–; int. John Ehrlichman; ("New" RN) e.g., Witcover, op. cit., p. 244–; *TW68,* p. 170; ("runs as President") ibid., p. 149.

RFK death: ("We can beat") Whalen, op. cit., p. 96; ("We've just seen") Ehrlichman, op. cit., p. 24; ("Why does Bobby?") Whalen, op. cit. p. 136; (welcomed) ibid., p. 97; *Oregonian,* undated, RFK Papers, '68 Pres. Campaign, National HQ files, Pres. Div., Box 11, JFKL; ("wanted to beat") Whalen, op. cit., p. 143; (RN/King funeral) ibid., p. 148–; ("tragic") int. Ed Nixon; (funeral/Bahamas) *MEM,* p. 306; *NYT,* Jan. 21, 1974.

Convention: (arrival) *The New Yorker,* Nov. 16, 1968; (nomination) *TW68,* p. 287.

VP choice: (Bush) George Bush with Victor Gold, *Looking Forward,* New York: Doubleday, 1987, p. 5; (Ford) James Cannon, *Time and Chance,* New York: HarperCollins, 1993, p. 95; (RN focused) ibid.; *MEM,* p. 312; Witcover, op. cit., p. 353; ("gasps"/"centrist"/"mediocre") ibid., pp. 353, 355; Whalen, op. cit., p. 202; *JA,* p. 356; (Dem. commercials) Melvin Small, *The Presidency of Richard Nixon,* Lawrence, KS: University of Kansas Press, 1999, p. 24; (RN knew corrupt) *JA,* p. 356.

acceptance: ed. Bill Adler, *The Wit and Humor of Richard Nixon,* New York: Popular Library, 1969, p. 109.

campaign PR: (RN/TV) McGinniss, op. cit., p. 33; ("3-bump") Woodstone, op. cit., p. 106, and see Gloria Steinem in *New York,* Oct. 28, 1968; ("controlled") McGinnis, op. cit., p. 39; (elephant) Whalen, op. cit., p. 192–; (Humphrey) int. Lawrence O'Brien, 1987, LBJL, McGinniss, op. cit., p. xiii; Joseph Califano, Jr., *A Presidential Nation,* New York: Norton, 1995, p. 105; (Price) ibid.; ("image not man") Whalen, op. cit., pp. 210, 212; (quits) ibid., p. 212; Garment, op. cit., p. 126.

RN campaign style: (Sidey) *Life,* Oct. 4, 1968; (Cronkite) Cronkite, op. cit., p. 227; ("None of us") Whalen, op. cit., p. 176; ("It hasn't changed") ibid., p. 154.

RN and hecklers: ("may have something") *Time,* May 18, 1970; (told staffers) Safire, op. cit., p. 80; ("We would go in") int. Ron Walker; (Ehrlichman) Ehrlichman, op. cit., p. 33; int. Ehrlichman, *NYT,* Sept. 24, 1981; (paid cash) Ehrlichman, op. cit., p. 33; (busloads) Howard Smith, *Events Leading Up to My Death,* New York: St. Martin's Press, 1996, p. 343.

spy on plane: *WP,* Sept. 4, 1973; Ehrlichman, op. cit., p. 32; (Dewey) *MEM,* p. 102, Manchester, *Glory and the Dream,* op. cit., p. 633; (RN registered) *TW68,* p. 5.

RN on lying: (Sears) *LAT,* Apr. 24, 1974; ("Your never going") Garment, op. cit., p. 115, transcript of int. Garment, CNN "Burden of Proof," Feb. 28, 1997.

contributions '68: (money matters) Whalen, op. cit., p. 156; (RN/Humphrey spending) Stans, *Terrors,* op. cit., p. 142; ("refused always") ibid., p. 134; *LAT,* Oct. 27, 1973; (president admitted) *LAT,* Feb. 19, 1976—Phillips president was W. W. Keeler; (Crosby $100,000) *NYT,* Jan. 20, 1974; int. Seymour Alter; Mahon, op. cit., p. 117, and see *supra.,* Chapter 20, p. 243; ("ecstatic") Stans, *Terrors,* op. cit., p. 135, int. Maurice Stans; (Smith) *San Diego* magazine, Nov. 1976, int. Arnholt Smith, *Ramparts,* Oct. 1973; int. former IRS agent, San Diego Dep. DA David Stutz; (Pat on Smith) *Life,* Mar. 24, 1972; (Alessio) *Time,* Nov. 25, 1972; Penthouse, July, 1974; (Alessio prison) *Life,* Mar. 1972; (Smith prison) San Diego *Union-Tribune,* June 10, 1976; (WH efforts) int. David Stutz, and see Summers, *Official & Confidential,* op. cit., p. 411; (Crosby/Rebozo) int. Seymour Alter; (Davis bros.) Paul Michel to Henry Ruth, closing memo, Hughes-Rebozo, Oct. 16, 1975, WSPF, NA, Miami *Herald,* May 17, 18, 1974.

Getty: PAT, p. 228; ed. Miller, *Breaking,* op. cit., Vol. IV, p. 517; *WP,* May 13, 1973; closing memo, Hughes-Rebozo, *supra.,* pp. 8, 71, 84, 214–; *Rolling Stone,* May 20, 1976; Haldeman and DiMona, op. cit., p. 21; Rebozo/Getty corr., Aug. 22, 1966, Jan. 27, Mar. 8, 16, 1972, Lancing Hayes to Paul Michel, Apr. 17, 1975, and Exhibits, J. Paul Getty Contributions, 1968–1972, Box 19, WSPF, NA, Robert Lenzner, *Getty,* London: Grafton, 1987, p. 300.

cash from Hughes: ("You must remember") Barlett and Steele, op. cit., p. 451, citing Maheu testimony in *Maheu v. Hughes Tool Co.;* ("I am determined") Drosnin, op. cit., pp. 47, 309; ("If we select") ibid., pp. 47, 311; (million for LBJ) Maheu, op. cit., p. 202–; Barlett and Steele, op. cit., p. 346; ($50,000 for Humphrey) Elaine Davenport and Paul Eddy, *The Hughes Papers,* London: Andre Deutsch, 1987, p. 119–; (Humphrey denied) ibid., p. 24, but see *NYT,* Mar. 2, 1974; ("I want you to go see") E, Report, p. 933n7; (Two demands) Davenport and Eddy, op. cit., p. 129; (helicopter losses) ibid., Barlett and Steele, op. cit., p. 359–; ("in his debt") Maheu, op. cit., p. 206; int. Maheu; (Danner diary) For 1968, 1970, 1973, Box 15, WSPF, NA; (RN /Rebozo asked) E, Report, pp. 934, 1053, 1055, E, Vol. 20, p. 9503; (Hughes laughed) Maheu, op. cit., p. 211; (intermediary/Democrat) ibid.—ref. to Edward Morgan; (RN "no time") ibid. p. 212, E, Report, p. 938; (signed receipt?) ibid, p. 953; (2 $50,000 deliveries) int. Robert Maheu, Maheu, op. cit., pp. 213, 225; E, Report, p. 944–; ("laid the bundles") Barlett and Steele, op. cit., p. 452; (participants' accounts) E, Report, p. 944–, summary at Barlett and Steele, op. cit., p. 452fn.; Davenport and Eddy, op. cit., p. 157–; (Air West) ibid., p. 160–; E Report, p. 965–; (Mitchell/anti-trust) E, Report, p. 983–; Davenport and Eddy, op. cit., p. 159–; ("obligations") E Report, p. 988; ("house project") ibid., p. 939; (fate of money) E Report, p. 1030–; (RN's attorney recalled) ibid., p. 1063—the attorney was Herbert Kalmbach; (brothers'/Rebozo's denial) ibid., p. 1052, 1066; (Woods denied) E, Vol. 22, p. 10279; (total much higher?) int. Terry Lenzner; Stephen Haberfield of WSPF to Leon Jaworski, Mar. 5, 1974, cited at Higham, *Howard Hughes,* op. cit., p. 304; ("go to Key Biscayne") Maheu, op. cit., p. 222–; (Meier) Gerald Bellett, *Age of Secrets,* Maitland, Ontario, Can.: Voyageur North America, 1995, p. 46–; (Maheu/courier denied) ints. Robert Maheu, Ken Wright; (Meier background) Ehrlichman, op. cit., p. 162; *NM,* p. 66; *LAT,* Aug. 30, 1978; ("There is evidence") E, Report, p. 946; ("Mr. Rebozo persisted") ibid., p. 1071, and see p. 932; ("And unfortunately") ibid.

Khashoggi: ("arms dealer") Sampson, op. cit., p. 188; *Vanity Fair,* Sept. 1989; ("connector") *Fortune,* June 1977; (RN relationship) int. Adnan Khashoggi; (Khashoggi and prosecutors) Paul Michel to Files, Aug. 13, 1975, re: int. Khashoggi, Box 95, Michel to Henry Ruth, closing memo, Hughes-Rebozo, Oct. 16, 1975, pp. 9, 79, 92, 218–, WSPF, NA; (plane '67) int. Adnan Khashoggi, Sampson, op. cit., p. 188; (account) WSPF refs. *supra.,* and see *WP,* June 27, 1976; ("looks suspicious"/burglary/"If RN asked me") ibid.; ("he'd given $1 million") int. Pierre Salinger; (houseboat) int. Adnan Khashoggi; (inaugurals) Michel to Files, Aug. 13, 1975, *supra.;* *NYT,* Jan. 21, 1969; (" jewelry") *WP,* Nov. 22, 1979; (K. confirmed) int. Adnan Khashoggi—author also questioned Soraya Khashoggi.

foreign contributions: Kenneth Geller to Philip Lacovara, opinion on 18USC.613, Jan. 14, 1974, file 306, Box 23 (Pappas), WSPF, NA.

Pappas: (at Convention) NY *Daily News,* Aug. 9, 1968; (background) *NYT,* May 4, 1969, Jan. 18, 1988; Detroit *Sunday News,* Nov. 11, 1973; Boston *Globe,* Oct. 31, 1968; Pappas file, FBI 190-HQ-1262376; Roger Witten to File 306, Feb. 7, 1974, Pappas, Box 23, WSPF, NA; (knew

RN) int. former counsel of House Select Cttee. on U.S. Intelligence Agencies & Activities, 1975—unidentified at his request; (photographs) *NYT,* May 4, 1969; (wedding) Detroit *Sunday News,* Nov. 11, 1973; (WH dinners) guest lists, *WP,* Mar. 22, 1972; Winter-Berger, op. cit., p. 32; (Box) ibid., Detroit *Sunday News,* Nov. 11, 1973; ("good old") RN to Rose Woods, WHT, May 23, 1973; *AOP,* p. 549; ("Greek bearing") John Dean/RN conv., Mar. 21, 1973; *AOP,* p. 256.

Agnew choice: ("Nixon's decision") *WP,* Sept. 25, 1968, cited at Paul Hoffman, *Spiro!,* New York: Tower, 1971, p. 87; (Agnew origins) ibid., p. 35; *NYT,* Aug. 10, 1968; Detroit *Sunday News,* Nov. 11, 1973; ("good word") *NYT,* Aug. 10, 1968; (RN admitted) London *Sunday Times,* Sept. 29; *New York,* Oct. 28, 1968.

junta rule: *Encarta Encyclopaedia,* 1993–98, Microsoft Corp.; Seymour Hersh, *The Price of Power,* New York: Summit, 1983, p. 136–; Stephen Rousseas, *The Death of a Democracy,* New York: Grove Press, 1967, p. 103.

Demetracopoulos: (background) ints. Elias Demetracopoulos, Hearings, House Cttee. on Foreign Affairs, Subcttee. on Europe, 92nd Cong., 1st Sess., statement of Elias Demetracopoulos, July 12, 1971; Howe and Trott, op. cit., p. 414–; (political/journalists' respect) ibid. pp. 427, 433–.

junta cash for RN campaign: (Gore) Winter-Berger, op. cit., p. 282–; Howe and Trott, op. cit., pp. 423, 425; Baltimore *News-American,* July 17, 1975; (Agnew initial position) ibid.; ints. Elias Demetracopoulos; (from here on "ED"), transcript int. of ED by Stanley Kutler, 1987, Kutler Papers; (turnabout) text of remarks of Gov. Spiro Agnew, National Press Club, Sept. 27, 1968; text of ED press conf., Sept. 28, 1968, Cong. Record, Oct. 9, 1968; ("What happened?") Gore to ED, Sept. 27, 1968, handwritten on Fairfax notepaper, copy supplied by ED; (regime's $549,000) ints. ED and *WP,* Nov. 1, 1968, June 15, 1997; Kutler, op. cit., p. 205–; (Tsimas) int. of Tsimas by Stanley Kutler, E. Gordon Fox Professor of American Institutions at University of Wisconsin, reported in his book *Wars of Watergate,* pp. 205, 651, Kutler letters to ED, Jan. 5, 1987, Kutler Papers; (Tasca) author int. with counsel for House Select Cttee. on Intelligence, *supra.*; author's conv. Seymour Hersh and see Hersh, *Price of Power,* op. cit., p. 138; (details withheld) int. ED, and see Hearings, House Cttee. on Foreign Affairs, Subcttee. on Europe, 92nd Cong., 1st Sess., p. 463, last par.; (Demetracopoulos/O'Brien contacts) ints. ED, transcript Stanley Kutler int. of ED, 1985; (O'Brien cite of report) Democratic National Cttee. News Release, Oct. 31, 1968, in ED papers; (LBJ motive) e.g., Robert Dallek, *Flawed Giant,* New York: Oxford University Press, 1998, p. 580.

Chapter 23

"How many American soldiers?": Karnow, op. cit., p. 17.

Kimmons story: (wives) ints. Charlotte Higgins—first wife, Gabrielle Kimmons, second wife, also Mrs. Hollis Kimmons—mother, Joyce Hagan—employer, and Harry Oldaker—friend; (RN inscription) ints. Gabrielle Kimmons, Mark Vardakis, Gerard Stodolski; article by Ralph Blumenthal, *NYT,* Feb. 17, 1985; int. Ralph Blumenthal; int. Forbes archivist Robin Tromer; *Pen & Quill*—magazine of Universal Autograph Collectors Club, Jan/Feb. 1985—original inscription, with associated documents in Forbes Archive, Forbes Gallery, NYC; (RN '64 visit) *NYT,* Apr. 2; *LAT,* Mar. 24, Apr. 2, 3, 4, 5; Pacific *Stars & Stripes,* Apr. 5, 1964; *MEM,* p. 257–; ("trip political") Herbert Parmet to author, June 7, 1999 sending transcript of RN answer and Parmet, *Nixon,* op. cit., p. 452; ("unfortunate episode") Appendix, Michael Forrestal to McGeorge Bundy, Subject South Vietnam, May 26, 1964, Southeast Asia Folder, 1961–1964, Vietnam General, FRUS 1964-1968, Vol. 1, Doc. 178, NA; (footnote) ed. John Glennon, *Foreign Relations of the United States, Vietnam 1964,* Vol. 1, Washington, D.C.: U.S. Gov. Printing Office, 1992, p. 389fn.4; ("good deal more") oral history int. John Michael Dunn, LBJL, pp. I, 24; (Schreck) pp. in draft of unpub. ms supplied to author by (son) Terry Schreck; ints. Terry and (widow) Sandie Schreck, and (former wife) Rose Mary Kelly; (Hughes) int. John Hughes; (Green Berets/SOG) John Plaster, *SOG, The Secret Wars of America's Commandos in Vietnam,* New York: Simon & Schuster, 1997, p. 19; John Prados, *The Hidden History of the Vietnam War,* Chicago: Ivan Dee, 1995, p. 76–; Sheehan, op. cit., p. 376–; NYT, Apr. 14, 1995; (camps/Cambodia border) Richard Stewart, Dept. of the Army Special Ops. Command to author, undated, 1996, with camp locations at Trang Sup and Loc Ninh; (Fr. Hoa) *Saturday Evening Post,* May 20, 1961; *Life,* Mar. 16, 1962; obit. *Central Daily News* (Taipei), Jan. 20, 1993; Douglas Valentine, *The Phoenix Program,* New York: Morrow, 1990, p. 37–; int. the late Bernard Yoh; (Lansdale) Valentine, op. cit., p. 25; Cecil Currey, *Edward Lansdale, The Unquiet American,* Boston: Houghton Mifflin, 1988, p. 218; Sheehan, op. cit., refs.; (Lansdale/RN) e.g., Lansdale to RN, Nov. 20, 1960; Allen Dulles corr. file, Box 228, VP, NA, RN to "Ed," Sept. 13, Oct. 29, 1965, Lansdale Collection, Box 54, Hoover Institution; David Halberstam, *The Best and the Brightest,* New York: Random House, 1969, p. 207; (order to Special Forces) S3 Daily Journal of 5th Special Forces, 0700 Apr. 1–5, 1964, Military Section, NA, (Suitland); ('64 no prisoner exchange) Dept. of Defense Prisoner of War/Missing in Action

Office, Ref. Doc., *U.S. Personnel Missing in Southeast Asia,* March 1998; int. John Horn, Dept. of Defense.

RN/Vietnam '64–'68: (casualties '64) Defense Dept. statistics supplied by Center for Military History, Washington D.C.; ('67/'68 casualties) ed. Tucker, op. cit., p. 1093; (Truman-Johnson line) Karnow, op. cit., p. 30; (JFK right) Crowley, *Off the Record.* op. cit., p. 35/36; (advisers/backup) Karnow, op. cit., p. 270–; (RN urged/RFK "win") ibid., p. 272; ("nothing less") *NYT,* Apr. 4, 1964; (lacked "will") *Reader's Digest,* Aug. 1964; ("win for America") Parmet, *Nixon,* op. cit., p. 454; (RN "victory") transcript, *Meet the Press,* NBC-TV, Sept. 12, 1965; ("no substitute") *Reader's Digest,* Dec. 1965; (McNamara '66) Robert McNamara with Brian VanDeMark, *In Retrospect: The Tragedy and Lessons of Vietnam,* New York: Times Books, 1995, p. 236–; (de Gaulle urged) *NYT,* Sep. 2, 1966; (de G./RN then) Sulzberger, op. cit., p. 157–; (De G./RN later) *MEM,* p. 374 and see Kissinger, *White House Years,* op. cit., p. 110; ("Uncle Elmer") Bobst, op. cit., p. 270; ("disaster") Garment, op. cit., p. 86; ("We must stop") Bobst, op. cit. p. 329; ("idealism") Garment, op. cit., p. 85; ("more than enough"/swing) Witcover, op. cit., p. 155–; ("World War III") ibid. p. 137, speech to Nat. Assn. of Manufacturers, Dec. 3, 1965, and commencement address, University of Rochester, June 5, 1966, both in Series 8, Box 26A, Dewey Papers, University of Rochester; ('67 casualties) ed. Tucker, op. cit., p. 1093; ("escalation threatened") McNamara with VanDeMark, op. cit., p. 269; (Helms) ibid., p. 293, citing Sept. 12, 1967 report; ("other war") ibid., p. 266, citing May 19, 1967 memo; ("Oh, sure, honest") Halberstam, *The Best and Brightest,* op. cit., p. 207—the U.S. official was Edward Lansdale; ("how soon?") Terry Dietz, *Republicans and Vietnam,* New York: Greenwood Press, 1986, p. 117, citing *NYT;* ("massive pressures") Deborah Shapley, *Promise and Power,* Boston: Little, Brown, 1993, p. 428; ("most Americans") McNamara with VanDeMark, op. cit. p. 266; (20,000 march) ibid. p. 303; (limits to protest) RN statement re. Prof. Eugene Genovese of Rutgers University, Oct. 24, 1965, enc. in RN to Tom Dewey, and University of Rochester commencement address, June 5, 1966, both in Series 8, Box 26A, Dewey Papers, University of Rochester; (hawkish doubts) Whalen, op. cit., p. 17; ("flexibility") ibid., p. 18.

RN/Vietnam '68: ("What the hell?") ibid., p. 26; ("peace with honor") address by Pres. Nixon, Jan. 23, 1973, *Historical Documents,* Congressional Quarterly, 1973, p. 117–; *AMII,* pp. 190, 195, 224; *AMIII,* pp. 34, 40, 42; *MEM,* p. 757; Safire, op. cit., pp. 7, 48, 178; (nuclear weapons) Whalen, op. cit., p. 27; ("upsweep") ibid., p. 29; ("mistake"/no RN reply) ibid., p. 76–; (tougher tactics call) *NYT,* Feb. 6, 1968, cited in Lyndon Johnson, *The Vantage Point,* New York: Holt, Rinehart & Winston, 1971, p. 399; ("national interest") *SF Chronicle,* Jan. 1, 1968; ("last ditch") Whalen, op. cit., p. 80; (World War III) *SF Chronicle, supra.;* ("If in November") *LAT,* Mar. 6, 1968; Witcover, op. cit., p. 258; Karnow, op. cit., p. 597; *MEM,* p. 298; ("Nothing lay") Whalen, op. cit., p. 91; (Halberstam) Halberstam, *The Best and the Brightest,* op. cit., p. 661; (Sheehan) *NYT,* Apr. 28, 1994; ("substantively"/"stupid war") Whalen, op. cit., Ch. VIII; (speech drafted) full planned text at ibid., p. 283; (LBJ astonishing) Robert Dallek, *Flawed Giant,* New York: Oxford University Press, 1998, p. 529; (RN would refrain) *AMII,* p. 149–; ("pragmatic splitting") Whalen, op. cit., p. 135; ("political stroke") ibid., p. 144; ("no way to win") ibid., p. 137.

"Madman Theory": ("I call it . . .") Haldeman and DiMona, op. cit., pp. 83–; eds. Miller Center, op. cit., p. 82; (RN claimed "not remember") Hoff, op. cit., p. 177; (Colson) *U.S. News & World Report,* May 2, 1994; ("convey to Dobrynin") Kissinger, *White House Years,* op. cit., p. 305; ("impression . . . 'crazy' ") Garment, op. cit., pp. 174, 176–.

RN/Hatfield: ("He gave assurances") Mark Hatfield to Robert Klass, July 16, 1968, JFRP; (Hatfield announced) AP, June 27,(?) 1968; (end war 1st year) Haldeman and DiMona, op. cit, p. 121; (end war 6 months) int. John Rothmann, citing RN in meeting at NY apartment, 1967; ("stop it with victory") int. by Flora Rheta Schreiber, *Good Housekeeping,* July 1968; ("in the Democratic process") Hatfield, cited at Whalen, op. cit., p. 220.

Vietnam Peace Talks: (LBJ effort) described inter alia in Bundy, op. cit., p. 20; Clark Clifford with Richard Holbrooke, *Counsel to the President,* New York: Random House, 1991, p. 567–; ed. David Barrett, *Lyndon B. Johnson's Vietnam Papers,* College Station, TX: Texas A & M University Press, 1997. The author also read extensively in the holdings of the Lyndon B. Johnson Library, notably the daily diary, Ted Johnson's notes of meetings, Boxes 3 & 4, Clark Clifford Papers, Box 6, NSF, Country file Vietnam, "Memos to the President/Bombing Halt Decision," Vols. 1–14, Boxes 137, 138, NSF, files of Walt Rostow, "Nixon, Richard—Vietnam," Box 5, "Vietnam: July–Dec. 1968," Box 115, diary backup, Oct. 31, 1968, Box 114, Nov. 11, 1968, Box 115, office files of Harry McPherson, Box 67, and numerous oral histories all in LBJL. See also "The 1968 Presidential Election & Peace in Vietnam," article by Kent G. Seig, U.S. State Dept. Historian, in *Presidential Studies Quarterly,* XXVI. 4, Fall 1996, p. 1062; (Thieu announced) *AMII,* p. 212; ("not in cards") Nguyen Tien Hung and Jerald Schecter, *The Palace File,* New York: Harper & Row, 1986, p. 21; (Humphrey promise re: bombing) Clifford with

Holbrooke, op. cit., p. 572fn; (reductions) *AMII*, p. 197; ("a chance") Hung and Schecter, op. cit., p. 21—Hung was the close aide.

RN and peace initiative: ("country above party") transcript, RN on CBS Radio, Oct. 28, 1968, available in CO-4664, Dirksen Congressional Center, Pekin, IL; ("neither he nore I") *NYT*, Nov. 1, 1968; (In private) *AMII*, p. 207 and see p. 216; ("probably decisive") Clifford with Holbrooke, op. cit., p. 582; ("no truth at all") note from Jim Jones, Nov. 3, 1968; Ref. File, "Chennault, Anna," from folder "South Vietnam & U.S. Policies," labeled "The 'X' Envelope," LBJL, hereafter referred to as X.

Anna Chennault/RN: (background) biographical note, Appendix II, *World Journal*, Taiwan, Apr. 21–26, 1994, ints. Anna Chennault; Catherine Forslund, *Woman of Two Worlds: Anna Chennault and Informal Diplomacy in US.–Asian Relations, 1950–1990*, Ph.D. dissertation, spring 1997, Washington University at St. Louis; Anna Chennault, *The Education of Anna*, New York: Times Books, 1980; (Chennault '68) *WP*, Nov. 1, 1968, Jan. 12, 1969; Boston *Globe*, Jan. 6, 1969; *Washingtonian*, Sept. 1969; Washington *Star*, Aug. 20, 1979; (joined Republicans) Chennault, op. cit., p. 163; int. Chennault; (Chennault/RN first contacts) Chennault, op. cit., p. 163–; ints. Chennault—first in 1954, according to *World Journal*, Taiwan, Apr. 21–26, 1994; (Vietnam contacts) ints. Anna Chennault; Forslund, op. cit., p. 188–; (tough views) Chennault to RN, Mar. 25, Apr. 4, June 24, 1968, Folder 20, Box 124, Robert C. Hill Papers, Hoover Institution; (phone calls '67) *World Journal, supra.*; (NY meeting '67) ibid; Chennault, op. cit., p. 170–; ("RN would like to see") Dick Allen to DC, July 3, 1968, cited in Safire, op. cit., p. 89; ("victory") Chennault, op. cit., p. 170; ("if elected") ibid., p. 175; (met Thieu) Hung and Schecter, op. cit., p. 19;("only contact") ibid. and see Bui Diem with David Channoff, *In the Jaws of History*, Boston: Houghton Mifflin, 1987, p. 237; ints. Chennault, Bui Diem; (Chennault/Thieu) Chennault, op. cit., p. 187; ints. Chennault; ("better deal") ints. Chennault; (Thieu messages) int. Chennault; (other messengers) ibid. and Hung and Schecter, op. cit., p. 23; (Mitchell silent) int. Bui Diem; (changed number) Chennault, op. cit., pp. 174; (Hill, Woods, Hitt) Chennault to RN, June 24, 1968, *supra.* and re: Hitt background, int. Patricia R. Hitt, Patricia Hitt Oral History, Bancroft Library, University of California; (RN publicly mouthed) e.g., *LAT* and AP, Oct. 18, 1968—urging support for LBJ so as not "to play politics with peace"; (resentment) *MEM*, p. 326; (LBJ devoted to peace/too hesitant) e.g., minutes of foreign policy advisers group meeting, Oct. 14, 1968, citing LBJ not wanting it said "one man died who could have been saved by this plan . . . we'll be scared, but we'll try it," Tom Johnson meeting notes, Box 4, LBJL and Clifford with Holbrooke, op. cit., p. 80, citing LBJ as labeling aides "a bunch of duds"; (Agnew briefed) Kent Crane to Agnew, Oct. 15, 16, 1968, Folder 31, Box 125, Robert C. Hill Papers, Hoover Institution; (two days later) Chennault calendar entry re: meeting Bui Diem, 10 A.M. Oct. 18, shared with author by Catherine Forslund; (A few days after) ibid., for 11 A.M. Oct. 25; ("Call from payphone") Hung and Schecter, op. cit, p. 24; (Bui Diem on messages) Bui Diem, op. cit., p. 244, citing messages Oct. 23 and 27; int./corr. Bui Diem; (Read version) Bundy, op. cit., p. 42, int./corr. Bundy; (NSA Intercepts) ibid. and Powers, op. cit., p. 252; (CIA/Diem) ibid; (device/Thieu) ibid., pp. 235, 252; Hung and Schecter, op. cit., p. 80; (Thieu overheard) Walt Rostow to president, "Literally Eyes Only," Nov. 2, 1968, citing intelligence item of Oct. 26, Item 51, NSF files, Box 137, Vol. 4, LBJL; (Oct. 29 meeting) foreign policy group meeting, Oct. 29, 1968; (2:30 A.M.–) Tom Johnson meeting notes, Box 4, LBJL, and see Clifford with Holbrooke, op. cit., p. 586; (LBJ re: RN "conniving") Oct. 28, 1968 meeting notes, *supra.*, pp. 20, 21; ed. Barrett, op. cit., p. 817– and 3 memos, Walt Rostow to LBJ and 2 memos Eugene Rostow to Walt Rostow, Oct. 29, 1968, and Walt Rostow, memo for the record, May 14, 1973, all in X, LBJL; ("all adds up") Tom Johnson meeting notes, *supra.*; (wiretaps/surveillance ordered) memos in "June" folder, FBI HQ 65-62098, released to author, Dec. 1999; (LBJ heavy hint) Forslund, op. cit., p. 221, and see *MEM*, p. 322—although the latter does not mention LBJ's hint, a reference to subversive activity by "old China hands"; (panic in RN camp) Lewis Chester, Godfrey Hodgson, Bruce Page, *An American Melodrama*, London: Andre Deutsch, 1969, p. 727; Godfrey Hodgson to author, Dec. 6, 1996; (Chennault not get through) Chester, et al., op. cit., p. 733; (Chennault/Mitchell call) Chennault, op. cit., p. 190–; (Thieu announced) *WP*, Nov. 2, 1968—reporting announcement same day Saigon time; (RN underhand way) Witcover, op. cit., p. 438; Bundy, op. cit., p. 34; (Rostow/no hard evidence) Walt Rostow to LBJ, Oct. 29, 1968 (8:50 A.M.) in Vietnam, July–Dec., 1968, Box 6, NSF Rostow Papers, LBJL; (FBI/Sheraton Park call) teletype, director FBI to W. Hse. situation rm., Nov. 1, 1968, X, LBJL—partly conf. by Chennault calendar entry, Oct. 31, 1968, Chennault, op. cit., p. 190–; (Nov. 2 Chennault/Diem call) SAC Washington field office, 3, to director FBI, WFO 105-9894, sent as enciphered teletype to W. Hse. situation rm., FBI 65-62298-204, Nov. 2, 1968, both released to author, 1999.

Agnew/Albuquerque: Seymour Hersh article, *NYT*, June 27, 1973; (LBJ ordered checks) Cartha DeLoach to Clyde Tolson, Nov. 19, 1968, re: Nov. 12 order, FBI 65-62098; (Hoover warned Chennault) int. Anna Chennault; (Hoover/DeLoach conspired) Cartha DeLoach, *Hoover's*

FBI, Washington, D.C.: Regnery, 1995, p. 396–; (call to Hitt) Cartha DeLoach to Clyde Tolson, *supra.*; (Robert Hitt) "Special Inquiry," Murray Chotiner, Apr. 21, 1969, FBI HQ 161-6284, and re: cash–E, II, pp. 541, 573, 588–; (paymaster) Wise, *Police State*, op. cit., pp. 3–, 12; (Pat Hitt) *Who's Who in American Politics*, 1995/96, unid. clipping in Theodore White Papers, 1968, Box 32, JFKL, *SF Chronicle*, Feb. 1, 1975—and see main text *supra*. re: being named by Chennault; (Rostow to LBJ re: Albuquerque) Rostow to LBJ, "Eyes Only memo," Nov. 12, 1968, X, LBJL; (Rostow surmised) Nov. 2, 1968, X, LBJL.

Chennault/S.Vietnam Embassy contacts: (overheard Nov. 7) Special Agent in Charge, WFO to director FBI, 3 messages, Nov. 7, 1968, FBI 65-62098, Serials 226, 228, 256, released to author 1999; (Thieu congratulations) Special Agent in Charge, WFO to director, FBI, Nov. 7, 1968, FBI 65-62098-227; (RN in FL) *MEM*, p. 335; *PAT*, p. 248.

LBJ/RN/Humphrey: (LBJ furious) *MEM*, p. 329; Harry McPherson and James Rowe, Jr., ints., Oral History Collection, LBJL; (late Friday night) Safire, op. cit., p. 93; (on her own) Witcover, op. cit., p. 442; George Christian, *The President Steps Down*, New York: Macmillan, 1970, p. 93; ("laughter") Chester, et al., op. cit., p. 734; Godfrey Hodgson to author, Dec. 6, 1996; ("Johnson certain") Joseph Califano, Jr., *The Triumph & Tragedy of Lyndon Johnson*, New York: Simon & Schuster, 1991, p. 328; int. Joseph Califano, Jr.; ("horrendous"), ibid.; (Humphrey told/reaction) int. James Rowe, Jr., *supra.*; Grant, op. cit., p. 311; McClendon, op. cit., p. 61; Austin *American*, July 9, 11, 1969; Hung and Schecter, op. cit., p. 485, Solberg, op. cit., p. 397–; ("What kind of guy?") Lawrence O'Brien int., Oral History Collection, LBJL; (might "want to consider") int. Max Kampelman in "Wheeler on America," Prog. 1, BBC-TV, Feb. 18, 1996; Bundy, op. cit., p. 551n92; ("very well blow") Cartha DeLoach to Clyde Tolson, Nov. 4, 1968, FBI 65-62098-170, released to author, 1999; (advisers decided) "Eyes Only memo," Walt Rostow to president, Nov. 4, 1968, NSF Files (item 27A), Vol. 4, Box 137, and int. Harry McPherson, Oral History Collection, LBJL; ("blow whistle" query) "Literally Eyes Only" memo, Walt Rostow to president, Nov. 8, 1968, X, LBJL.

RN reverses position: (LBJ "actively sought") Rostow memo for record, May 14, 1973, X, LBJL, and see Hung and Schecter, op. cit., p. 486n32; (LBJ/Humphrey forecast) Tom Johnson meeting notes, Oct. 29, 1968, Box 4, LBJL—citing LBJ as saying "Nixon will double-cross after Nov. 5," and ibid., Nov. 20, 1968—citing Humphrey as saying "Nixon will move and fast. He'll sell them down the river"; (strong word) Dallek, op. cit., p. 597; ("flabbergasted") int. Anna Chennault; Chennault, op. cit., p.193; (Chennault harried) ibid.; int. Herb Klein; (fended enquiries) Chennault, op. cit., p. 195–; St. Louis *Post-Dispatch*, Jan 8, 1979; *NYT*, July 23, 1969; (feared for safety) int. Anna Chennault; ("I've certainly paid") Chennault, op. cit., p. 197–.

SE Asia conflict in presidency: (casualties final 5 weeks): supplied by U.S. Dept. of Defense Electronic Records; (Holbrooke) int. Richard Holbrooke for BBC/History Channel; ("a man so consumed") Califano, *Triumph & Tragedy*, op. cit., p. 328.

Thieu reaction: (champagne) *Newsweek*, Nov. 18, 1968, but see U.S. Embassy Saigon to Sec. of State, Nov. 15, 1968, Box 6, Clark Clifford Papers, LBJL; ("We did it") Chicago *Daily News*, Nov. 15, 1968; (Thieu felt) Hung and Schecter, op. cit., pp. 483n1, 31, 34; (Thieu would defy) *MEM*, pp. 584, 690–, 702, 707, and see Clifford with Holbrooke, op. cit., p. 593fn; (at first meeting) Hung and Schecter, op. cit., p. 30; (RN reassured) ibid., p. 34.

RN in WH: (Cambodia deaths) Cambodian Genocide Project, Yale University, New Haven, CT; (RN bombing N. Vietnam) George Herring, *America's Longest War*, New York: Knopf, 1986, p. 250–; *Radical History Review*, Fall 1994, p. 185, and see Karnow, op. cit., p. 658–; Shawcross, op. cit., pp. 217–, 260; (RN argued) Richard Nixon, *No More Vietnams*, New York: Touchstone, 1990, p. 277; (contrary case) *SF Chronicle*, Mar. 4, 1984; Arthur Pearl, *Landslide*, Secaucus, NJ: Citadel Press, 1973, p. 97; George McGovern in *Rolling Stone*, June 16, 1994; (RN/peace "won") Nixon, *No More Vietnams*, op. cit., pp. 206, 277; ("I agree war mistake") int. Sen. George McGovern in eds. Strober, *Nixon*, op. cit., p. 171, and McGovern article, *Rolling Stone*, June 16, 1994—Sen. McGovern was Kissinger's visitor in early 1969.

Chapter 24

"This really is": *NYT*, June 23, 1993.

Election '68: (Harris poll) *TW68*, p. 446; (aboard plane) ibid., p. 452–; (Op. Eagle Eye) Garment, op. cit., p. 141 and see Whalen, op. cit., p. 14; (Op. Integrity) *Life*, Sep. 5, 1969, ed. Miller, *Breaking of the President*, op. cit., vol. 3, p. 68; int. J. Edgar Nichols; (nervy) *MEM*, p. 332; (RN election night) *TW68*, p. 455–; *MEM*, p. 331; (RN urged Humphrey) ibid., p. 320; Wicker, op. cit., p. 361; ("tell Hubert to quit") *MEM*, p. 333; Wicker, op. cit., p. 383; (women isolated) *PAT*, p. 246; (Pat vomited) ibid.; (voting figures) *TW68*, p. 462–; (Graham) Graham, op. cit., p. 449–; *PAT*, p. 247; (Woods weeping) *NYT* News Service, Nov. 11, 1968; ("bring together") full text at Adler, op. cit., p. 124; ("verge of victory") Graham, op. cit., p. 450; ("Victory at Sea") *MEM*, p. 335; *PAT*, p. 248; (pirouette) ibid.; (Air Force One) Safire, op. cit.,

p. 107; ("Mr. President") ibid., p. 248; (S. Service) ibid., p. 249; (Searchlight) John Curtin to John Vermilye, (Miami Police Intelligence), Nov. 13, 1968, supplied to author by Gordon Winslow; (Starlight) Walker, op. cit., front matter; ("very strange") Matthews, op. cit., p. 270.

Transition: ("Baloney!) int. John Ehrlichman in eds. Miller Center, op. cit., pp. 122, 135; (Pierre) Carl Brauer, *Presidential Transitions*, New York: Oxford University Press, 1986, p. 131; Stans, *Terrors*, op. cit., p. 140; (*Who's Who*) int. John Ehrlichman in eds. Miller Center, op. cit., p. 135; Whalen, op. cit., p. 224–; (Ehrlichman/AG?) int. John Ehrlichman in eds. Miller Center, op. cit., p.123; ("no politician") Smith, *Dewey*, op. cit., p. 631; ("RN's right arm") ed. Schoenebaum, op. cit., p. 444; ("take care") int. Dwight Chapin in eds. Strober,*Nixon*, op. cit., p. 295; (RN/Martha) Bryant with Leighton, op. cit., p. 256, Haldeman with DiMona, op. cit., p. 9; (alcohol problems) int. Chapin *supra.*; McClendon, op. cit., p. 63.

Haldeman: (Ike: "S.O.B.") Haldeman with DiMona, op. cit., p. 54; ("pluperfect") ibid.; (quiet) White, *Breach*, op. cit., p. 92; ("fine guy") notes of Haldeman int., Nov. 22, 1968, Theodore White Papers, Box 40, JFKL; (accounts) William Shannon, *They Could Not Trust the King*, New York: Macmillan, 1974, p. 149; Medved, op. cit., p. 307; ("dream") int. Larry Higby; ("swam too far") White, *Breach*, op. cit., p. 92; (Germans/"Nazi") Haldeman with DiMona, op. cit., p. 55; Lewis Chester, Cal McCrystal, Stephen Aris, and William Shawcross, *Watergate*, New York: Ballantine, 1973, p. 13; Bernstein and Woodward, *Men*, op. cit., p. 304; eds. Strober, *Nixon*, op. cit., p. 55; (dined once) Haldeman with DiMona, op. cit., p. 65; ("didn't see as person") ibid., p. 74; ("never asked") ibid., p. 72; ("machine") ibid., p. 74; ("Executioner") ibid., p. 111.

friends dumped: (Klein) int. Herb Klein; Brauer, op. cit., p. 135; (Klein decent) e.g., Dickerson, op. cit., p. 153; ("Zig-zag") *NM*, p. 391; (Woods moved) *NM*, p. 461; int. Patricia Hitt, and see Safire, op. cit., p. 113–; ("Go fuck!) Wicker, op. cit., p. 400.

W.H. young men: (Magruder/Chapin/Huston/Strachan/Colson) *NM*, pp. 7, 11, 30, 151–, 187–; Magruder, *American Life*, op. cit., p. 3; ("Judas") *AOP*, p. 606; ("viciously") *NM*, p. 11; ("please boss") ibid., p. 280; ("If Nixon told") int. Tom Huston, 1973, in *Harpers*, Oct. 1974; (obedience) e.g., int. John Ehrlichman; eds. Miller Center, op. cit., p. 129, int. John Ehrlichman; Haldeman with DiMona, op. cit., pp. 59, 319; and Medved, op. cit., p. 319; Haldeman, op. cit., p. 59–; Safire, op. cit., p. 285, William Doyle, *Inside the Oval Office: The White House Tapes from FDR to Clinton*, New York: Kodansha Int., 1999, pp. 171–, 177.

Cabinet announcement: Klein, op. cit., p. 298, Brauer, op. cit., p. 144; (domestic bore/Moynihan) Wicker, op. cit., p. 421; ("I've always thought") *TW68*, p. 171; (RN intended) *MEM*, p. 340.

Kissinger appointment: (Humphrey/"clown") Shawcross, op. cit., p. 79; ("hopeless") Kissinger to Averell Harriman, Aug. 16, 1968, cited at Kent Seig, "The 1968 Presidential Election and Peace in Vietnam, *Presidential Studies Quarterly*, Vol. XXVI, No. 4, Fall 1996 p. 1078n83; ("most dangerous") *WP*, Aug. 23, 1972 ; ("not fit") Marvin Kalb and Bernard Kalb, *Kissinger*, Boston: Little, Brown, 1974, p. 16; *NYT Magazine*, Nov. 14, 1971; ("disaster") Iassacson, op. cit., p. 127; (gentler) Marvin Kalb and Bernard Kalb, op. cit., p.15; (and Brzezinski) Iassacson, op. cit., p. 133; ("shit" files) ibid. and Hersh, *Price of Power*, op. cit., p. 14; (Kissinger leaked) Iassacson, op. cit., p. 129; *MEM*, p. 340—but see Kissinger, *White House Years*, op. cit., p. 10; (Steinem) Iassacson, op. cit., p. 134; ("Guten Morgen") Haldeman with DiMona, op. cit., p. 14.

Hoover at Pierre: (warning) Summers, *Official & Confidential*, op. cit., p. 370 and sources; (embellished) DeLoach, op. cit., p. 407; (RN raises on WHT) *AOP*, pp. 75, 92, 147, 168, 175–, 196–, 198, 204, and see *Historical Documents*, 1973, pub. by *Congressional Quarterly*, pp. 663, 666, and blind memo, re: Potential Matters for Discussion with Sen. Baker, June 12, 1973, John Dean folder, Wh. Hse. Staff files, NA; ("Little men") Haldeman with DiMona, op. cit., p. 80, amended in int. H. R. "Bob" Haldeman, 1989.

Nixon worry re: bugs: (wireman) Wise, *Police State*, op. cit., pp. 4, 10; ("Let's get off") Louis and Yazijian, op. cit., p. 219; ("shh!") Hillings with Seelye, op. cit., p. 187; (LBJ "obsessed") Crowley, *Off the Record*, op. cit., pp. 17, 136; (former presidents' taping) best reported in Doyle, *Inside the Oval Office*, op. cit, and re: Ike, see July 16, 1954 cabinet notes, James Hagerty Papers, DDEL; (JFK bedroom phone) Beschloss, *Crisis Years*, op. cit., p. 346; (LBJ "extensive") Bill Gulley with Mary Ellen Reese, *Breaking Cover*, New York: Warner, 1980, pp. 19, 95; ("As any tenant") Haldeman with DiMona, op. cit., p. 80–; *Prologue*, XX, Summer 1988, p. 80 and int. Robert Finch in eds. Miller Center, op. cit., p. 266.

RN state of mind '68: ("as 1968 came to end") *MEM*, p. 361–; ("nervousness") Kissinger, *White House Years*, op. cit., p. 11; ("I would call") Haldeman with DiMona, op. cit., p. 66; ("between midnight & 3 A.M.") int. Len Garment, Garment, op. cit., p. 143–.

RN alcohol/drugs: ("like a Spartan") *Saturday Evening Post*, Feb. 25, 1967; ("couldn't take a drink") notes of int. Jan. 22, 1969, Nixon folder, Theodore White Papers, Box 40, JFKL; ("pills to ease mind") int. George Christopher; ("some medication") int. Edward Nixon for BBC/History Channel.

Dilantin: (Dreyfus background) *Life*, Sept. 29, 1967; Jack Dreyfus, *A Remarkable Medicine Has Been Overlooked*, New York: Continuum; 1997, Barry Smith and Jack Dreyfus, *The Broad Range of Clinical Use of Phenytoin*, New York: Dreyfus Medical Foundation, 1992; int. Jack Dreyfus; int. Jack Dreyfus for BBC/History Channel; (Tkach) *LAT*, Dec. 29, 1973; Nixon, *Six Crises*, op. cit., p. 326; (compliant doctor?) int. John Ehrlichman; (FDA status of Dilantin) int. Dr. Lawrence McDonald; *Physician's Desk Reference*, 1998, p. 2242; (Price) Wicker, op. cit., p. 393; (Korff) int. the late Rabbi Baruch Korff; (Graham) int. Billy Graham in *Esquire*, Apr. 10, 1979.

Pearson/Hutschnecker '68: (contacts) NY *Post*(?), Nov. 14, 1968; *WP*, Nov. 14, 20, 23, 1968; UPI, Nov. 14, 1968, reporting Pearson address to National Press Club; Pearson handwritten notes, Box G 281, DPP, reprinted at Hutschnecker, *Drive for Power*, op. cit., p. 7–, 311; Woodstone, op. cit., p. 4; ("felt we had to be ready") Klein, op. cit., p. 413, int. Herb Klein; (Klein call) ibid. and Hutschnecker, *Drive for Power*, op. cit., p. 314; (Ford) Winter-Berger, op. cit., p. 258–; (Klein/Chotiner visits) Klein, op. cit., p. 412–, int. Klein; (Pearson re: "pyschiatric"/"pressure") *WP*, Nov. 14, 20, 23, 1968; ("untrue") *WP*, Nov. 20, 1968; (RN "depressed") int. Herb Klein; (Steinem) int. Steinem and see Hutschnecker, *Drive for Power*, op. cit., p. 8–.

"attract scandal": Kleindienst, op. cit., p. 209.

O'Brien: (Humphrey campaign) Davenport and Eddy, op. cit., p. 132; (Hughes hires) Maheu, op. cit., p. 206–; Drosnin, op. cit., p. 273–; Lawrence O'Brien, *No Final Victories*, Garden City, NY: Doubleday, 1974, p. 255–; (Castro plots hint) Drew Pearson in *SF Chronicle*, Mar. 3, 1967—column not run in some papers; (O'Brien knew re: Pappas) see p. 286, "*supra.*; (O'Brien knew re: Chennault) Lawrence O'Brien oral history int., p. XXVI.13, LBJL; (O'Brien/Edward Kennedy) *TW68*, p. 449–; O'Brien, op. cit., p. 262.

Inauguration: (ceremony) *MEM*, p. 365–; *PAT*, p. 251; Leon Panetta and Peter Gall, *Bring Us Together*, New York: J. B. Lippincott, 1971, p. 59; ("Oops!") *WP*, Jan. 21, 1969; (Pat outfit) Lady Bird Johnson, *A White House Diary*, London: Weidenfeld and Nicolson, 1970, p. 776; (Warren loathed) int. John Rothmann; William Buckley, Jr., in *SF Chronicle* (?), Mar. 25, 1975; Kohlmeier, op. cit., p. 93; (RN's voice) Johnson, op. cit., p. 779; (Isaiah) *MEM*, p. 366; (from RN's pen) Price, op. cit., p. 48; (protesters) *MEM*, p. 366; *PAT*, p. 252; *NYT*, Jan. 21, 1969; (balls) ibid., *WP*, Jan. 21, 1969; *LAT*, Jan. 20, 1969; St. Petersburg [FL] *Times*, Jan. 21, 1969; (Rebozo) *NYT*, Jan. 20, 1969; (Khashoggi) *NYT*, Jan. 21, 1969; int. Adnan Khashoggi; (Hitt) *LAT*, Jan. 21, 1969; (Lombardo) *NYT*, Jan. 21, 1969; (turning on lights) *PAT*, 253–; (exultant) Kissinger, *White House Years*, op. cit., p. 3; (Harlow) Cannon, op. cit., p. 98; ("This is your house") *WP*, Jan 22, 1969.

Chapter 25

"The office neither elevates": George Reedy, *The Twilight of the Presidency*, New York: New American Library, 1970, p. 18.

"He was obsessed": int. Robert Finch, in eds. Strober, *Nixon*, op. cit., p. 80.

Excess in RN presidency: (no need?) *U.S. News & World Report*, Nov. 8, 1968; (silk) Kessler, op. cit., p. 55, citing Bill Gulley, and see *HD*, pp. 29, 30; (bed) Kessler, op. cit., p. 55; Cheshire with Greenya, op. cit., p. 176; (LBJ/RN airplanes) Manchester, *Glory and Dream*, op. cit., p. 1162; (Air Force One refurbished) Helen Thomas, *Front Row at the White House*, New York: Scribner, 1999, p. 171; (further $750,000) ibid., p. 173 and see higher figure in Kessler, op. cit., p. 57; (in-laws/aides used) Manchester, *Glory and Dream*, op. cit., p. 1162; Gulley with Reese, op. cit., p. 189; (Biscayne/San Clemente/$10.5 million) *NYT*, Dec. 19, 1973; Manchester, *Glory and Dream*, op. cit., p. 1161; (special features cost) Gulley with Reese, op. cit., p. 189; (C. David pool) ibid., p. 179; (nine offices) David, op. cit., p. 71, citing *Fortune*, John Herbers, *No Thank You, Mr. President*, New York: Norton, 1976, p. 64; (household expenses) Manchester, *Glory and Dream*, op. cit., p. 1162.

absences: *Newsweek*, Aug. 24, 1970; Herbers, op. cit., p. 64; (RN word on his work habits) *New York*, May 10, 1976; Small, op. cit., p. 230; (Butterfield) *People*, May 19, 1975 and see Kissinger, *Renewal*, op. cit., p. 70.

coats: *NYT*, Dec. 21, 1968.

Julie bent custom: Edmondson and Cohen, op. cit., p. 157.

nicknames: *Parade* magazine, *WP*, undated, 1967.

Tricia: (in room/figurines) Edmondson and Cohen, op. cit., pp. 106–, 114; Ehrlichman, op. cit., p. 42; ("Louis XV") Edmondson and Cohen, op. cit., p. 111; ("tough-and-troubled") Ehrlichman, op. cit., p. 42; (embassy party) ibid., p. 43; (steward staring) Kessler, op. cit., p. 43; (hassock) Bryant with Leighton, op. cit., p. 323; ("Goody-Two-Shoes") int. Lou Campbell, former agent with executive protection service; (agents urinating) Rush, op. cit., p. 192, citing former agent Marty Venker; (Tricia/Charles) UPI, Aug. 16, 1979, citing Prince Charles, Cheshire with Greenya, op. cit., p. 117, Bryant with Leighton, op. cit., p. 291; (Cox background) *WP*, Apr. 19, 1970, *NYT*, Mar. 17, 1971; (*60 Minutes* viewers/Rather) Troy, op. cit., p. 193.

uniforms: (Brussels) Dan Rather with Mickey Herskowitz, *The Camera Never Blinks*, New York: William Morrow, 1977, p. 221; (India) Dickerson, op. cit., p. 164; (Ruritanian) E. J. Applewhite, *Washington Itself*, Lanham, MD: Madison Books, 1993, p. 88; ("cross between") Bryant with Leighton, op. cit., p. 283; (RN & caps) *Newsweek*, Dec. 19, 1977; (dieting) Dickerson, op. cit., p. 164; (Iowa bands) *SF Chronicle*, May 16, June 18, UPI, Nov. 10, 1980; (Alice Cooper) *SF Chronicle*, June 18, 1980; ("something more formal") Magruder, *American Life*, op. cit., p. 60; ("stupid") int. Peter Flanigan.

RN style: (memo four days after) ed. Oudes, op. cit., p. 11; ("He saves everything") E, 22, p. 10267–; ("Things got regal") Bryant with Leighton, op. cit., p. 239; ("Problems with signals") *HD*, p. 29; (white tie) *U.S. News & World Report*, Feb. 24, Aug. 11, 1969; ("above salt") ibid.; (higher chair) Joseph Califano, Jr., *Governing America*, New York: Simon & Schuster, 1981, p. 429; (Sidey) *Life*, Mar. 10, 1972.

RN and Royalty: (Windsors) int. Robert K. Gray; *HD*, p. 146; (Pat "statistics") int. Jessamyn West by FB, FBP; (jewels) Cheshire with Greenya, op. cit., pp. 87–, 116–, 128–, 174; *WP*, May 14, 15, 16, Sep. 22, 23, 24, 1974; Paul Michel to Henry Ruth, Hughes-Rebozo closing memo, Oct. 16, 1975, WSPF, NA; Howe and Trott, op. cit., p. 500; Knight News Service, Apr. 4, 1979; ints. Fred Graboske, Donald Nixon, Jr.; (royal lineage) UPI, Apr. 10, 1975; ("I often felt") Klein, op. cit., p. 323; (RN denied) *MEM*, p. 771; ("aloof & imperial") O'Neill and Novak, op. cit., p. 240–; (Burns) int. Arthur Burns in eds. Miller Center, op. cit., p. 160; ("He just doesn't listen") Smith, *Dewey*, op. cit., p. 633; ("like Naploeon") int. Arnholt Smith, and see San Diego *Reader*, Mar. 19, 1992; ("regal") int. Leonard Hall by FB, FBP.

RN and cabinet: (initial intent) agenda for cabinet mtg., Jan. 22, 1969, Box 40, Theodore White Papers, JFKL; (RN "never intended") eds. Strober, *Nixon* , op. cit., p. 88, and see *HD*, p. 100; (Schlesinger) ibid., p. 89; ("We began to get") int. John Ehrlichman in eds. Miller Center, op. cit., p. 130–; (RN "never trusted") int. Richard Helms by Stanley Kutler, Kutler Collection kindly provided to author; ("Screw the Cabinet") WHT, April 1971 revealed in court case *Justice Dept. v. Nixon Estate*, reported in *WP*, Dec. 27, 1998.

RN and Congress: ("He simply didn't want") int. John Ehrlichman in eds. Miller Center, op. cit., p. 133 and see Robert Dole in *WP*, July 29, 1973; (Timmons) cited in Reichley, op. cit., p. 87; (blocking bills, etc.) Smith, *Events Leading Up to My Death*, op. cit., p. 352; Paul Clancy, *Just a Country Lawyer*, Bloomington, IN: Indiana University Press, 1974, p. 252–; Dick Dabney, *A Good Man: The Life of Sam Ervin*, Boston: Houghton, Mifflin, 1976, p. 250: Thomas Cronin cited in *NYT*, Apr. 24, 1994; (Phillips) Arthur Pearl, *Landslide*, Secaucus, NJ: Citadel, 1973, p. 226; ("Divine Right") *NYT*, Apr. 3, 1973.

RN presidency and press: ("that fucking bunch") Theodore White notes of conv. with RN, Nov. 23, 1968, Box 40, Theodore White papers, LBJL; ("Why don't we all get") Wise, *Politics of Lying*, op. cit., p. 316—the aide was Roy Goodearle; (cutoff *NYT*, *WP*, etc.) *HD*, p. 60; Safire, op. cit., p. 345; (moon rocks) Wise, *Politics of Lying*, op. cit., p. 315–; (grander quarters) ibid., p. 342, Thomas, *Dateline*, op. cit., p. 126; (press conferences) Wise, *Politics of Lying*, op. cit., p. 359; (RN claimed/Agnew) ibid., pp. 336, 339; *MEM*, p. 411; (Sidey on "non-news") Wise, *Politics of Lying*, op. cit., p. 360.

Vietnam and first presidency: ("Without the V. War") Haldeman with DiMona, op. cit., p. 79; (safe) *MEM*, pp. 336, 369; ("Who knows") T. White notes of conv. RN, Dec. 2, 1968, *supra.*; ("Peace cannot") Nixon address, May 14, 1969, as reprinted by U.S.I.S.; (RN/Thieu meeting) Hung and Schecter, op. cit., pp. 32–, 40; (RN withheld) ibid., p. 41; (tigers) ibid., p. 109; (Vietnamization) ibid., p. 34; *MEM*, pp. 395; (Critics claimed) e.g., eds. The Committee of Concerned Asian Scholars, *The Indochina Story*, New York: Pantheon, 1970, pp. 132, 136.

Cambodia: (bombing) Kissinger, *White House Years*, op. cit., p. 242–; Shawcross, op. cit., p.26–; Hersh, *Price of Power*, op. cit., p. 54–; "Secret Bombing of Cambodia," Congressional Quarterly, *Historical Documents 1973* Washington, D.C., 1974, p. 729–; (impeachment issue) Hersh, *Price of Power*, op. cit., p. 62fn.; Kissinger, *White House Years*, op. cit., p. 249; Bundy, op. cit., p. 471; (RN public lies) transcript RN speeches, *NYT*, May 15, 1969, May 1, 1970, int. John Rothmann.

Spy plane: (incident) Kissinger, *White House Years*, op. cit., pp. 247, 313–; Hersh, *Price of Power*, op. cit., p. 69–; *MEM*, p. 384; ("strong action") *HD*, p. 50; ("sweet-ass") Bryant with Leighton, op. cit., p. 253; ("I'll turn Right") *WP*, Dec. 27, 1998, citing RN/Kissinger call, April 1971.

Calley: (My Lai event) *TW72*, p. 58, Chicago *Sun-Times*, Nov. 13, 1969, [Seymour Hersh piece] *NYT*, May 11, 1998, obit. Ronald Ridenhour, June 5, 1998, obit. Col. Oran Henderson; Mollenhoff, op. cit., p. 74–; David Obst, *Too Good to Be Forgotten*, New York: John Wiley, 1998, p. 161; Sheehan, op. cit., p. 689; ("abhorent") RN press statement, Nov. 26, 1969, cited in Daniels letter, *WP*, Apr. 7, 1971, and see RN press conference in ed. Helen Thomas, *The Nixon Presidential Press Conferences*, New York: Earl Coleman, 1978, re: RN comments Dec. 8, 1969, p. 70; (spy order) Hersh, *Price of Power*, op. cit., p. 135; ("rotten Jews") ibid., citing

Alexander Butterfield; (confinement conditions) Sheehan, op. cit., p. 689; Obst, op. cit., p. 172; (life story/Hymm) ibid.; (Daniel Letter) *WP*, Apr. 7, 1971; int. Aubrey Daniel.

Phoenix program: (budget meeting) Hersh, *Price of Power*, op. cit., p. 135; (Phoenix) ibid., p. 80; Prados, *President's Secret Wars*, op. cit., p. 309; Sheehan, op. cit., p. 732.

Sihanouk assassination plan: Hersh, *Price of Power*, op. cit., p. 178–.

"Highest level": e.g., Summers, *The File on the Tsar*, New York: Harper & Row, 1976, p. 92, citing U.S. Ambassador Nelson Page reference to Italian royal family.

Nixon efforts against Allende: (Kendall) Hersh, *Price of Power*, op. cit., pp. 260, 273, the Kendall associate was Augustin Edwards, Chilean newspaper owner and focal point of opposition to Allende; (Kendall/Council) Louis and Yazijian, op. cit., p. 172; (Helms to act) U.S. Senate, *Assassination Plots*, op. cit., p. 227–; ("talking into a gale") int. Richard Helms in ed. Weber, op. cit., p. 275; ("furious") William Colby and Peter Forbath, *Honorable Men*, New York: Simon & Schuster, 1978, p. 303; ("aberrational") Cord Meyer, *Facing Reality*, Washington, D.C.: University Press of America, 1980, p. 184; (What did RN order?) see analysis at Hersh, *Price of Power*, op. cit., p. 274; (Colby "blackmailing") Scowcroft Memcon of Kissinger/Ford conversation, Mar. 5, 1975, NSC doc. 1781000410307, released in 1997 under JFK Assass. Records Collection Act; (RN "wanted something done") U.S. Senate, *Assass. Plots*, op. cit., p. 227–; (RN distanced himself) Sen. Cttee. to Study Gov. Ops., Final Report, Supplementary Detailed Staff Reports on Foreign and Military Intelligence, Bk. IV, p. 162; ("blurred account") *MEM*, p. 489.

Allende death: (coup) *NYT, WP*, Sept. 12, 13, 15, 1973; (advance warning) *NYT*, Sept.13, 1973; ('99 release on U.S. reaction) *USA Today*, June 30, July 1, 1999 and see Asst. Sec. of State Jack Kubisch to Kissinger Nov. 16, 1973, in 1998 release to National Security Archive; ("severe repression") *USA Today*, June 30, 1999; (RN on death) *MEM*, p. 490; (suicide?) *NYT*, Sep. 13, 20, *WP*, Sep. 22, 1973; (Sra. Allende re: "murdered") *NYT*, Sep. 20, 1973 but see study in Nathaniel Davis, *The Last Years of Salvador Allende*, Ithaca, NY: Cornell University Press, 1985, Chap. 11; (U.S. involvement in coup) ibid., p. 350, and Prados, *Secret Wars*, op. cit., p. 320; (Ryan) Davis, op. cit., p. 352; (Ryan report) Ryan to Dept. of Defense, U.S. Milgroup, Situation Report 2, Oct. 1, 1973, released to National Archives, 1998.

Morales: (background) Fonzi (former staff investigator, Hse. Cttee. on Assass.), op. cit., refs.; Noel Twyman, *Bloody Treason*, Rancho Santa Fe, CA: Laurel, 1997, refs; ("hit man") Fonzi, op. cit., p. 380; (Morales confided) ints. Robert Dorff and Dorff letter to author, Oct. 27, 1997—Dorff had interviewed Morales's lifelong friend Ruben Carbajal.

Phillips: (and Morales) Fonzi, p. 382; (and anti-Allende project) Phillips, op. cit., pp. 219–, 246–; (Head Western Hemisphere) ibid., p. 234–; (testimony doubted) Summers, *Not in Your Lifetime*, op. cit., p. 280; Fonzi, op. cit., pp. 336, 410; int. Gaeton Fonzi; (disinformation) Summers, *Not in Your Lifetime*, op. cit., pp. 371, 374, 381, 385; (Track II closed down) Phillips, op. cit., p. 223; (letter to Sra. Allende) excerpts from transcripts of 1981 int. sent to author by Mike Ewing, 1997; (RN "never cause to consider") page 190.

"Won't be the first P to lose": *HD*, p. 90.

Vietnam effort: (frustrated) *MEM*, p. 393, Kissinger, *White House Years*, op. cit., p. 277; (deliberate leak) *MEM*, p. 400; ("bad guys") *HD*, pp. 105, 110.

RN and protest: (Oct./Nov.'69 demonstrations) *MEM*, p. 398; *HD*, p. 98; ("Don't get rattled") *MEM*, p. 403; ("aloof") ibid., p. 401; (major address) ibid., p. 404–; ("The line we took") int. William Watts; ("talk softly") *MEM*, p. 410; (speech) ibid., p. 409; (switchboard swamped) *MEM*, p. 410, *HD*, p. 104; (telegrams) *MEM*, p. 410; Kissinger, *White House Years*, op. cit., p. 307; (Butterfield) int. Alexander Butterfield; *WP*, Jan. 23, 1999 reporting Butterfield testimony in Nixon estate dispute; (Phillip) *HD*, p. 105; ("you heard a lot") Ehrlichman TV int. cited in ed. Howard K. Smith, *Every Four Years*, Kent, OH: PTV Publications, 1980, p. 59; ("liberal bastards") Magruder, op. cit., p. 53; (new demonstration—Nov. 13, '69) *HD*, p. 107–; (soldiers concealed) Gulley, op. cit., p. 198; Hersh, *Price of Power*, op. cit., p. 130fn; (Mitchell) Breslin, op. cit., p. 6–; ("like St. Petersburg") int. William Watts; (RN ordered analysis) Andrew, op. cit., p. 354; (RN & candles) *HD*, p. 107–; ("Of all choices") Kissinger, *White House Years*, op. cit., p. 227; (V'nam casualties) Tucker, op. cit., p. 1193.

Music box: Medved, op. cit., p. 317 and see *HD*, p. 21.

Chapter 26

"You talk . . . police state": Wise, *Police State*, op. cit., p. 31.

Kraft: (Kraft bugging) Wise, *Police State*, op. cit., p. 3—most complete account; (Allende) ibid., p. 23 John Caulfield testimony, E, Bk. 21, p. 9699–; (investigated member Dem. Cttee.) Wise, *Police State*, op. cit., p. 13; int. A. J. Woolston-Smith; (advance knowledge of burglars' activity) int. A. J. Woolston-Smith; (bogus card) John Caulfield testimony, E, Bk. 21, p. 9692–, but see notes of int. John Davies, Aug. 3, 1973, Box B342, E, NA.

Caulfield: (background) *NM*, p. 13; (at RN's request) *WP*, May 19, 1973, citing bio. Caulfield used as job application; (hired) *NM*, p. 13; Caulfield testimony, E, Bk.21, p. 9687–; ("top man") Wise, *Police State*, op. cit., p. 14.

"no climate of fear": Theodore White notes of RN int., Jan. 23, 1969, Box 40, Theodore White Papers, JFKL, *TW68*, p. 504.

Tapping of journalists: (episode chronicled) Wise, *Police State*, op. cit., p. 31–; Szulc, op. cit., p. 181–; R, Report, p. 146, "Nixon on National Security Wiretaps," Historic Documents of 1976, *Congressional Quarterly*, 1977, p. 159; ("We were in Key Biscayne") Haldeman with DiMona, op. cit., p. 101; ("enraged") *Newsweek*, May 28, 1973; (RN on Kraft) *MEM*, p. 389; ("never helped us") RN to Dean, Feb. 28, 1973, WHT and see re: "helped" Wise, *Police State*, op. cit., p. 73; (RN & Kissinger try to dodge) Szulc, op. cit., p. 182; Hersh, *Price of Power*, op. cit., p. 96; ("Henry ordered") RN to Ronald Ziegler, May 14, 1973, on WHT, *AOP*, p. 491; ("approved by President") int. Alexander Haig by David Wise, transcript provided to author, and author's int. Alexander Haig; ("highest authority") int. William Sullivan by Robert Fink, provided to author; ("only to President") memo May 12, 1973, FBI 67-205182; ("cloak-and-dagger") Haldeman with DiMona, op. cit., p. 103; (RN "100%") ibid., p. 101; ("I was para-noiac") transcript of RN int. on *60 Minutes*, Vol. XVI, 30, Apr. 8, 1984, p. 6—the int. was conducted by Frank Gannon, a Nixon staffer after the presidency; (warning) Summers, *Official & Confidential*, op. cit., p. 398–; *NYT*, July 21, 1973; John Dean testimony, E, Bk. 3, p. 920–; Robert Mardian testimony, E, Bk. 6, p. 2393; ("Will he rat") WHT, RN to Ehrlichman, Oct. 25, 1971, WHT; (Ehrlichman/Sullivan job) Edward Epstein, *Agency of Fear*, London: Verso, 1990, p. 219; (impeachment) R, Report, p. 3; (agents lurked/photos) *WP*, Sep. 30, 1974; Miller, *Fishbait*, op. cit., pp. 3, 290; (Finch suspected) int. Robert Finch by FB, FBP; (Albertazzie) ter Horst and Albertazzie, op. cit., p. 270.

events of summer 1970: (general) summarized at Manchester, *Glory & Dream*, op. cit., p. 1211; ("bums") *NYT*, May 2, 1970; *AMII*, p. 350–; ("When dissent . . .") Barber, op. cit., p. 437; (knockdown story) J. Edgar Hoover to Clyde Tolson et al., July 24, 1970, Tolson staff file, Vol. 8, FBI 67-9524; (promote re. sniper) *Newsday*, May 4, 1995; ("What are we going to do?") Shawcross, op. cit., p. 154.

Plan to combat threat: (summary and detail) U.S. Sen. Cttee to Study Gov. Ops with Respect to Intelligence Activities, Final Report, Bk. III, p. 934—the RN aide was Tom Huston; ("Gestapo") *WP*, June 1, 1973; ("With presidential authority") Sen. Cttee. on Gov. Ops., *supra.*, p. 955; (RN/Frost exchange) Frost, op. cit., p. 183–; (Mitchell) John Mitchell int. by Stanley Kutler, transcript supplied to author.

taping system: (Butterfield) int. Alexander Butterfield, *Journal of American History*, Vol. 75, Mar. 1989, p. 1252; ("How does it work") WHT, Feb. 16, 1971, reported by AP, Oct. 5, 1999; ('62 request) int. specialist cited *supra.*, p. 227; (removal of LBJ equipment) int. Donald Kendall, int. Robert Finch in eds. Miller Center, op. cit., p. 266; *Newsweek*, May 2, 1994; (preoccupied with record) *Prologue*, Vol. 20, summer, 1988, p. 80–; (Blake on Disraeli) ints. Elliot Richardson, in eds. Miller Center, p. 68, and with Stanley Kutler, transcript provided to author; ("You assume") Alexander Butterfield testimony, July 2, 1974, R, Hearings, Bk. I, p. 31–, and int. Butterfield cited in *New York*, Apr. 21, 1975; ("He seemed to me") citing Butterfield E testimony; (note takers) *Prologue*, Vol. 20, Summer, 1988, p. 81–; (Walters) ibid., p. 82; Walters, op. cit., p. 575; (LBJ changes mind) AP, July 2, 1975, *JA*, p. 496; (Kissinger steal thunder) Ehrlichman, op. cit., p. 283; int. John Ehrlichman in eds. Strober, *Nixon*, op. cit., p. 124 and in eds. Miller Center, op. cit., p. 141; ("Great consternation") *HD*, p. 57; (location of devices) "A History of the White House Tapes," prepared by NP, Mar. 1995, NA, William Doyle, op. cit., p. 168, and see plan in illustrations; ("tell nobody") int. H. R. "Bob" Haldeman in eds. Strober, *Nixon*, op. cit., p. 381, *Prologue*, Vol. 20, Summer, 1988, p. 86; (not Rose Woods) Haldeman with DiMona, op. cit., p. 196; (Pat & girls not told) *PAT*, p. 307; ("appalled") UPI, Feb. 20, 1975; ("love letters") Edmondson and Cohen, op. cit., p. 295; (WH board tapped) *HD*, p. 76; (Secret Service handled) processing manual, Appendix A(7), WHT, NP, NA; Alfred Wong testimony in *O'Brien et al v. McCord et al.*, CA no. 1233-72, p. 861–; (Haldeman on Butterfield) Haldeman with DiMona, op. cit., p. 203–; (4 in know) *Prologue*, Vol. 20, Summer, 1988, p. 86; (Ehrlichman not told) ibid., int. John Ehrlichman in eds. Miller Center, op. cit., p. 141; (Ehrlichman taped) E, Bk. 5, p. 2173, Bk. 7, p. 2828–, Bk. 12, p. 4942; Rather with Herskowitz, op. cit., p. 223; (Kissinger excluded) Kissinger, *Years of Upheaval*, op. cit., p.110; (K. staff made notes) int. William Watts; ("We're going to look fools") John Ehrlichman citing Kissinger in *Parade*, Feb. 5, 1995.

Suspicions of tapes: (Douglas-Home) *JA*, p. 496; (Haldeman/Kissinger memo) Kissinger, *Years of Upheaval*, op. cit., p. 112; (O'Neill) O'Neill, op. cit., p. 243–; (RN oblivious) RN int. and Alexander Butterfield testimony, cited in *New York*, Apr. 21, 1975, p. 40, *Prologue*, Vol. 20, Summer, 1988, p. 86; ("could see occasions") Kissinger, *Upheaval*, op. cit., p. 113; (Baker) Bob Woodward, *Shadow*, New York: Simon & Schuster, 1999, p. 122, citing ints. Howard Baker;

(dog keeper guessed) Bryant with Leighton, op. cit., p. 258; ("moments when I should") Colson, op. cit., p. 114; (Dean) Dean, op. cit., pp. 260–, 263, 300–; (Dean/Colson hoped) ibid., p. 332, int. Sam Dash, Colson, op. cit., p. 114; ("You never heard") May 29, 1974 entry, diary of Rep. Jerome Waldie, supplied to author; (RN claimed "not comfortable") *MEM*, p. 501; ("room not tapped") WHT, Mar. 23, 1971, Conv. 051-001, WSPF, NA.

war over tapes: (trucks prevented) Cannon, op. cit., pp. 356, 365, Gulley, op. cit. p. 274–; (tape releases) int. Pat Anderson, archivist, NP, NA; *AOP*, p. xiv.

content of tapes: ("Daddy has cautioned") *MEM*, p. 976; ("Imagine your own feeling") Haldeman with DiMona, op. cit., p. 208–; (Naulty) Washington *Times,* Jan. 28, 1997; ("Here's this voice") Waldie diary entry, cited in *SF Examiner,* Aug. 9, 1984.

RN swearing: (computer check) Hoff, op. cit., p. 315–; (changing goddams) *AOP*, p. xv; ("Little shits") Richard Reeves in *New York,* May 10, 1976; ("fucking") WHT entries, June 11, June 19, 1973; *AOP*, pp. 598, 611; (Rebozo) AP, Nov. 4, 1974; (Finch) int. Robert Finch in eds. Miller Center, op. cit., p. 267–; (Kissinger) *Time,* Mar. 15, 1999; (Cushman) int. Robert Cushman by FB, FBP; (Price) eds. Strober, *Nixon,* op. cit., p. 384; (Hess) int. Stephen Hess in eds. Miller Center, op. cit., p. 372; (mother) *Good Housekeeping,* June 1960; (Mazo) Lurie, *Running,* op. cit., p. 40; (diplomatic dinner) int. Walter Coombs [former head of World Affairs Council] by FB, FBP; ("Fuck Volpe") *Harper's,* Aug. 1994; ("fucking Trudeau") William Watts cited in Hersh, *Price of Power,* op. cit., p. 106; ("motherfucking cocksucker") tapes diary entry of James Doyle, chief spokesman Watergate special prosecutor, Oct. 30, 1973, provided to author; (three obscenities) Ed Rollins with Tom DeFrank, *Bare Knuckles and Back Rooms,* New York: Broadway Books, 1996, p. 71; (RN in old age) Crowley, *Nixon in Winter,* op. cit., p. 289; (Lincoln) *New Republic,* June 23, 1982; (RN on Truman) Kansas City *Times,* Oct. 13, 1960, letter in *SF Examiner*(?), June 17, 1974; ed. Sidney Kraus, *The Great Debates,* Bloomington, IN: Indiana University Press, 1962, p. 197; (Paar) Paar, op. cit., p. 132; ("son-of-a-bitching Watergate") WHT, Apr. 30, 1973, *AOP*, p. 381, also monitored for author and re: slurring; WP, Nov. 29, 1996.

RN worry re: tapes: Spiro Agnew in letter to Prof. Stanley Kutler, Feb. 1, 1989, Kutler Collection; (Hearst) ed. Miller, *Breaking of the President,* op. cit., Vol. IV, p. 221; ("real love") Frady, op. cit., p. 478; ("spider") Kissinger, *Years of Upheaval,* op. cit., p. 113; ("definite image") RN notes, Sep. 7, 1969, Nov. 28, Dec. 6, 1970, Nixon Presidential Files, Box 186, NP, NA.

RN and ethnic slurs: (women) WP, Dec. 27, 1998; (Mexicans) ibid., AP, Mar. 9, 1999; (Italians) WP, Dec. 27, 1998; Breslin, op. cit., p. 151; O'Neill, op. cit., p. 256–; (RN/Immigration Act) RN Record as Favoring Anti-Italian Quota Barriers, Box 240, DPP; *NYT,* Oct. 10, 13, 1952, *Congressional Record,* 1952, p. 8267; ("shit-asses") James Doyle taped journal entry, early Sept. 1974, citing Leon Jaworski, supplied to author; (Zumwalt) Zumwalt, op. cit., p. 479, int. late Adm. Elmo Zumwalt.

RN anti-Semite?: ("Show me") Garment, op. cit., p. 199; int. Leonard Garment; ("not an ounce") Korff, op. cit, p.165; ("You can't believe") Henry Kissinger cited by Alan Dershowitz, *SF Examiner,* June 18, 1991; (RN on "Jewish traitors") Ehrlichman cited in Isaacson, op. cit., p. 148; ("Jews . . . liberalizing") May 26, 1971; *HD,* p. 292; ("find one") WHT, July 2, 1971; *AOP*, p. 20; ("cabal") SF *Examiner,* Sept. 11, 1988, cited Frederick Malek memo; ("youth, black, Jew") July 18, 1970; *HD, CD*; (objected to having rabbi again) March 7, 1971, ibid.; ("the Jews . . . stealing") WHT, Sep. 8, 1971; *AOP*, p. 29; ("please get me the names") WHT, Sep. 13, 1971; *AOP*, p. 31; (IRS "full of Jews") WHT, Sep. 14, 1971; *AOP*, p. 32; ("a kike") WHT, Oct. 7, 1971, cited in *American Journalism Review,* Apr. 1997; AP, Mar. 9, 1999; ("avoiding the Jews") WHT, Mar. 29, 1973; *AOP*, p. 288; (Jews disloyal, etc.) WHT, summer 1971, cited in *WP,* Oct. 6, 1999.

RN not anti-Semite: (some continued) Nixon Library archivist Susan Naulty article, Washington *Times,* Jan. 28, 1997; Safire, op. cit., p. 569; (Jewish group defended) Korff. op. cit., p. 164–, Washington *Times, supra.* 6, the reference is to an episode in 1950; (Soviet Jews) Korff, op. cit., pp. 4, 128.

RN and blacks: ("incompetent") WHT, Mar. 8, 1971, in *WP,* Dec. 27, 1998; (great grandfather) Mazo, op. cit., p. 280; (mother welcomed) Nixon, *Arena,* op. cit., p. 93; (college & black youth) Mazo, op. cit., p. 23; (at Duke) Alsop, op. cit., p. 235; *MO,* p. 177; (black Senate attendant) int. Robert Parker; (black on TV crew) Rather and Herskowitz, op. cit., p. 227; (drink in basement) int. Lou Campbell; ("most dangerous") Taylor Branch, *Parting the Waters,* New York: Simon & Schuster, 1988, p. 219, citing King letter, 1958; ("racist reflexes") John Osborne, *The Nixon Watch,* New York: Liveright, 1970, p. 165; (Bork) int. Robert Bork by FB, FBP; ("niggers"/"jigs") Hersh, *Price of Power,* op. cit., p. 110; ("never . . . an adequate black nation") *HD,* p. 53; (Biafra) Howe and Trott, op. cit., p. 184; Hoff, op. cit., p. 247; Wicker, op. cit., p. 673; Morris, *Uncertain Greatness,* op. cit., p.131; (white S. Africa) Small, op. cit., p. 142–; ("Let's leave the niggers") Hersh, *Price of Power,* op. cit., p. 111; ("presented different sides") int. Ehrlichman in eds. Strober, *Nixon,* op. cit., p. 384; ("just down from trees")

Seymour Hersh article, *The New Yorker*, Dec. 14, 1992; ("would do his best") int. John Ehrlichman and see Ehrlichman, op. cit., p. 196; (black admiral, etc.) Patrick Buchanan, *The New Majority*, Girard Bank, 1973, p. 36; (excoriated re: busing) e.g., Panetta, op. cit., p. 6; Reichley, op. cit., p. 174; ("nothing beyond the law") Aug. 4, 1970 entry; *HD*, CD, Genovese, op. cit., p. 85; ("No gain") Aug. 4, 1970, *HD*, CD; ("make sure") Morris, *Uncertain Greatness*, op. cit., p. 131; ("We do not make votes") *Newsday*, Apr. 25, 1994; (Michigan busing) Ehrlichman, op. cit., p. 207, the aide sent was Mike Bolzano, on Charles Colson's orders; (Chisholm/Bond/Jackson ploy) *AOP*, p. 33; London *Independent*, Nov. 20, 29, 1996.

"Thugs" conversation: (RN/ Haldeman meeting) WHT, May 5, 1971, transcribed for author and see Conv. No. 491-014, WSPF, Record Grp. 460, NA; (Fitzsimmons mtg.) James Neff, *Mobbed Up*, New York: Atlantic Monthly Press, 1989, p. 163–; (demonstrations) Charles DeBenedetti with Charles Chatfield, *An American Ordeal*, Syracuse, NY: Syracuse University Press, 1990, p. 291; Szulc, *Illusion*, op. cit., p. 389–; ed. Clifton Daniel, *Chronicle of the Twentieth Century*, Mt. Kisco, NY: Chronicle Pub., 1987, p. 1032; *HD*, p. 284; (Chicago Seven) DeBenedetti, op. cit., pp. 246, 452n101.

Hoffman/injury: AP pictures (showing bandaged nose) and captions, May 6, 7, 1971, *SF Examiner*, Sep. 30, 1981 and unid. alternative press clip, 1981, citing Hoffman; int. Anita Hoffman.

Haldeman and "thugs" conversation: (declined comment) *NYT*, Sep. 24, 1981, May 5, 1971 entry, *HD*, CD.

NY construction workers: (attack on protestors) *NYT*, May 9, 1970; (construction workers demo.) *NYT*, May 16, 20, 1970; Wise, *Politics of Lying*, op. cit., p. 287; (RN received) *NYT*, May 27, 1970; (Brennan described) Colson, op. cit., p. 38; Scheim, op. cit., p. 297; ed. Schoenebaum, p. 68; ("Thank God for hard hats") Safire, op. cit., p. 678 and see *Time*, June 8, 1970.

Triggered by RN high command?: int. Richard Howard and *NYT*, Sep. 24, 1981 citing John Ehrlichman.

San Jose incidents: Washington *Evening Star*, Oct. 30, 1970; Safire, op. cit., p. 327–; *MEM*, p. 492; ("We wanted confrontation") *HD*, p. 205.

Monroe Cornish: John Dean statement, E, Vol. 3, p. 917–; *NM*, p. 10; *WP*, June 27, 1973; (Quaker HQ ransacked) Robert Fink article in *Rolling Stone*, Oct. 10, 1974.

"Billy Graham Day": memo Ron Walker to Haldeman, Oct. 14, 1971, Haldeman testimony, E, Bk. 8, pp. 3150–, 3322–, and see Frady, op. cit., p. 455–; Rush, op. cit., p. 55–; int. Ron Walker; int. John Dean in *Playboy*, undated 1975, Box 168, Baruch Kroff papers, Brown University; (without incident) Sen. Sam Ervin, at E, Bk. 8, p. 3153; (Weicker) ibid., p. 3152; (McGrory) *NY Post*, June 26, 1973.

Chapter 27

"Sick of mind"?: as cited in *New York*, Apr. 21, 1975 and see Osborne, *Last Nixon Watch*, op. cit., p. 189.

RN personality in presidency: ("What do with him?") Safire, op. cit., p. 112; ("so drained") Kissinger, *White House Years*, op. cit., p. 319; ("frustration") notes of int. Arthur Burns, John Osborne Papers, Library of Congress; ("embarrassing rattle") Magruder, *American Life*, op. cit., p. 57; (need for control) Nixon, *Six Crises*, op. cit., pp. xv, 219 and see John Osborne, *The Second Year of the Nixon Watch*, New York: Liveright, 1971, p. 58; ("flew into rage") Kissinger, *White House Years*, op. cit., p. 495; (Patton) Shawcross, op. cit., p. 134; ("walking add") ibid., p. 144.

Cambodia decision: ("flipped out") Morris, *Haig*, op. cit., p. 141; ("your ass") int. William Watts; ("bold stroke") Ehrlichman calendar entry, Apr. 25, 1970 sited in *LAT*, July 1, 1984; ("show who's tough") int. William Watts; (decision in pool) Kissinger, *Upheaval*, op. cit., p. 3; ("tensions of planning"/Patton again) Kissinger, *White House Years*, op. cit., p. 498–; (Patton 5 times) Morris, *Haig*, op. cit., p. 141; (signed twice) facsimile, Kissinger, *White House Years*, op. cit., p. 499; (up all night/slurred) Shawcross, op. cit., p.146–; (made much of role) Schlesinger, *Imperial Presidency*, op. cit., p. 187–; (public reaction) *NYT*, May 1, 1970; (manufactured) *NYT*, May 8, 1970; (questionable results) e.g., *AMII*, p. 360; (RN's "unbridled ebullience") Westmoreland, op. cit., p. 388; (macho) *AMII*, p. 348; ("Everyone misunderstands") *JA*, p. 404.

Hutschnecker visit: (worried re: trigger) DP column, *WP*, Nov. 23, 1968, and see page 97–; (summoned) *JA*, p. 404; (RN/H during presidency) int. Dr. Arnold Hutschnecker, Hutschnecker, *Drive for Power*, op. cit., p. 154– and see Dec. 1, 1969 entry, *HD, The Complete Multimedia Edition*, Santa Monica, CA: Sony, 1994 [henceforth *HD* CD]; ("intimacy" absent) *JA*, p. 404–, citing int. Hutschnecker.

Lincoln Memorial episode: (machine guns) White, *Breach of Faith*, op. cit., p. 131; ("nervous breakdown") ibid; (Dickerson) Dickerson, op. cit., p. 171–; (46 calls) log at Safire, op. cit., p. 204; (accounts of episode) RN to Haldeman, May 13, 1970; ed. Oudes, op. cit., p. 127–,

MEM, p. 459–; Safire, op. cit., Ch. 8; (RN declines to visit Wall) Crowley, *Off the Record,* op. cit., p. 186; (Pelletier, et al.) Price, op. cit., p. 168; Toledo, OH, *Blade,* May 10, 1970; ("dislocation") Dickerson, op. cit., p. 175; (RN at Capitol) int. Egil Krogh; ("Very weird") May 9, 1970 entry, *HD,* p. 163; ("weirdest") ibid; (FL decision) ibid; ("could be rough") May 14, 1970 entry, *HD,* p. 166; ("only tip") Kissinger, *White House Years,* op. cit., p. 514; ("unwinding not succeeding") May 15, 1970 entry, *HD,* p. 166; ("More same") May 16 entry, ibid.; ("emergency housecall") Winter-Berger, op. cit., p. 257; int. Robert Winter-Berger; (Blue Heart) May 18, 1970 entry, *HD,* p. 167 and *MEM,* p. 466; (RN to CA) May 28– May 31, 1970 diary entry, *HD,* CD; (trouble sleeping) May 29, 1970 entry, *HD* CD; ("recovering . . .") Kissinger, *Upheaval,* op. cit., p. 1184–; ("back to schedule") June 8, 1970 entry, *HD,* p. 173; (AP on times spent away) May 31, 1970 entry, *HD,* CD; ("in a daze") Thomas, *Dateline,* op. cit., p. 136; ("erratic") Dickerson, op. cit., p. 175.

Doubts re: RN condition: ("never happened before") Osborne, *Watch2,* op. cit., p. 61; (frequent slips) ibid., p. 129; (The staff habit) ibid., p. 73; ("created impression") Brandon, op. cit., p. 260–; ("might go bats") Osborne, *Last Watch,* op. cit., p. 5; ("letting himself slip") May 14, 1970 entry, *HD,* p. 166; (Tormented) Bryant with Leighton, op. cit., p. 314.

Romania: Price, op. cit., p. 302–; Aug. 2, 1969 entry, *HD,* p. 77–; Dennis McCarthy with Philip Smith, *Protecting the President,* New York: William Morrow, 1985, p. 192–.

Alcohol in presidency: ("occasional sip") Spalding, op. cit., p. 116fn; (researchers) *The New Yorker,* Dec. 14, 1992; ("I got a call") int. Hugh Sidey in eds. Miller Center, op. cit., p. 305; ("given to exploding") int. William H. Sullivan in eds. Strober, *Nixon,* op. cit., p. 99; ("Two glasses") Kissinger, *Renewal,* op. cit., p. 54; ("occurred rarely") ibid., p. 55; ("drunken friend") Morris, *Haig,* op. cit., p. 108; ("We caught glimpses") Hersh, *Price of Power,* op. cit., p. 108; ("Oh, screw 'em") Woodward and Bernstein, *Final Days,* op. cit., p. 204; ("He just got pissed") int. Marty Venker; ("People who knew") Morris, *Uncertain Greatness,* op. cit., p. 147; (weekend Aug. '69) Aug. 28–31, '69 entries, *HD,* CD; ("bomb" the airport) Kissinger, *Renewal,* op. cit., p. 57; int. and corr. Melvin Laird; int. Len Garment; ("ghastly game") *MEM,* p. 483; ("K woke me") Sept. 17, 1970 entry, *HD,* p. 195; ("tough guy" orders") Kissinger, *Renewal,* op. cit., p. 57; ("wouldn't have been good day") Osborne, *Watch2,* op. cit., p. 74; ("Stuff that will look belligerent") Kissinger, *White House Years,* op. cit., p. 695–.

RN nuclear talk: ("nuclear war each week!) Isaacson, op. cit., p. 145; ("ranting & raving") Hersh, *Price of Power,* op. cit., p. 88; (Vietnam/1954) see page 165–; ("blow that would end") Reichley, op. cit., p. 117; ("got to nuke 'em") Hersh, *Price of Power,* op. cit., p. 396—Young cited by Ehrlichman aide Egil Krogh; (Colson on *Sequoia*) Colson, op. cit., p. 40–; May 18, 1971 entry, *HD,* CD.

Chapter 28

"He hated . . . ": eds. Strober, *Nixon,* op. cit., p. 45.

"Enemies" lists: (Buckley) Buckley cited in intro. by Eugene McCarthy, *White House Enemies,* New York: New American Library, 1973, opening p. of intro.; (Kilpatrick) Providence [RI] *Journal,* Jan. 5, 1974; (Mollenhoff) Mollenhoff, op. cit., pp. 29, 107–, and Mollenhoff affidavit, June 4, 1974, R, Stmt. of Inf., Bk. VIII, p. 38; (Chotiner office) *NYT,* Jan. 14, 1970; (RN "did not like") *NYT,* July 17, 1974, cited in Congressional Record, Aug. 1, 1974, p. 26439; ("ruthless sonofabitch") *WHT,* May 13, 1971, cited in *WP,* Jan. 3, 1997; (priority list for "activity") memo, [Colson aide] George Bell to John Dean, et al., June 24, 1971, E, Bk. 4, p. 1693–; (Haldeman and Colson would claim) E, Final Report, p. 132; (Dean: "screw our enemies") memo, Aug. 16, 1971, E, Bk. 4, p. 1689–; ("We have the power") *WHT,* Sept. 8, 1971; *AOP,* p. 29 and monitored for author; (Walters) ints. Johnnie Walters, George Shultz; *WP,* Jan. 3, 1997; ("kick Walter's ass") *WHT,* Sept. 15, 1972, conv. no. 779-002, WSPF, NA, p. 5; ("blue eyes") ibid., p. 2; ("candy ass") *WP,* Jan. 3, 1997, citing Dean testimony; (list of 200+) E, Bk. 4, p. 1692, intro. McCarthy, op. cit.; ("keep a good list") E, Bk. 3, p. 958; (Van Horne and RN/Hutschnecker) page 90; (2 lower ranking officials) *NM,* pp. 24, 106–, 148, memo re: int. Roger Barth, July 31, 1975; Howard Clesner Collection supplied to author, *WHT,* Aug. 19, Sept. 7, 1972, *AOP,* p. 107– [referring to Roger Barth and Vernon Acree]; (journalists audited) *WP,* June 28, 1973; (Greene) E, Final Report, p. 135; *NM,* p. 24; ("The guy that's running") *WHT,* Sep. 14, 1971; *AOP,* p. 32; ("The IRS is battering") *WHT,* Sep. 13, 1971; *AOP,* p. 31.

milestone meeting: ("attack" on Julie) May 28, 1971 entry, *HD,* p. 292 and see Ehrlichman, op. cit., p. 300; ("more wiretapping") *WHT,* May 28, 1971, transcribed for author.

RN and Edward Kennedy: ("ill at ease") Kissinger, *White House Years,* op. cit., p. 100; (Asst. Majority Leader) Theodore Sorensen, *The Kennedy Legacy,* New York: New American Library, 1969, p. 229.

Chappaquidick: (RN "called me over") *HD,* p. 72: (probe at RN's behest) ibid. and Haldeman notes, *Newsday,* Apr. 25, 1994; *MEM,* p. 543; (undercover man) Ulasewicz, op. cit., pp. 4–, 178, 181, 187–; Wise, *Police State,* op. cit., p.107; (RN/astronauts) *HD,* p. 72–; Rather and

Herskowitz, op. cit., p. 221; (RN reached Ehrlichman) Wise, *Police State*, op. cit., p. 115; (phone to radio) entry, July 6, 1969, *HD*, p. 75; (RN "sorry"/took aside) *MEM*, p. 542–; *HD*, p. 79; and see Safire, op. cit., p. 154–; (phone records) John Davies, *The Kennedys*, New York: S.P.I. Books, 1992, p. 716; (inquest transcript) memo, Mary DeOreo to Terry Lenzner, Dec. 10, 1973; Hughes-Rebozo investigation, Teamsters File, WSPF, NA; (Kopechne house phone) Wise, *Police State*, op. cit., p. 155–; (reports to Chotiner/Rebozo) *WP*, Aug. 1, 1973; (cost $100,000) Rather and Herskowitz, op. cit., p. 226.

RN pursuit of Edward Kennedy: (Al Capp) Seymour Hersh in *The New Yorker*, Dec. 14, 1992; *NYT Magazine*, Oct. 20, 1974; Boston *Globe*, June 25, 1970; Brit Hume, *Inside Story*, Garden City, NJ: Doubleday, 1974, p. 60–; ("catch him in sack") Haldeman with DiMona, op. cit., p. 60; (Colson and "catch Kennedy") *The New Yorker*, Dec. 14, 1992; (photo/princess) *HD*, p. 293, Magruder, *American Life*, op. cit., p. 66; Matthews, op. cit., p. 289; Hunt, *Undercover*, op. cit., p. 206; (polls spring '71) *NYT Magazine*, July 22, 1973; ("Nothing for Teddy?") WHT, Apr. 9, 1971, transcribed for author; (one not enough) WHT, July 6, 1971; *AOP*, p. 25; (Colson man) Hunt, *Undercover*, op. cit., pp. 160, 178, 205; (NY apartment) Wise, *Police State*, op. cit., p. 120; Hunt, *Undercover*, op. cit., p. 208; (Vegas girls) ibid., p. 182; ("No evidence) blind memo, re: EMK Visit to Honolulu, Aug. 1–19, 1971, Exhibit 34-4, E, Bk. 3, p. 1117; (RN disappointed) WHT, Sep. 8, 1971; *AOP*, p. 29; (False "drunk" story) Cheshire, op. cit., p. 190–; (Gallup) *WP*, Dec. 9, 1971; ("Do you think") Seymour Hersh article, *The New Yorker*, Dec. 14, 1992; (RN still insisting) int. Tim Wyngaard, by Stanley Kutler, supplied to author; ("Plant one, plant two guys") WHT, Sep. 7, 1972; *AOP*, p. 132 and see *WP*, Feb. 8, 1997; (Butterfield) ibid.; eds. Strober, *Nixon*, op. cit., p. 263; *Journal of American History*, Mar. 1989, p. 1253; ("might get lucky") WHT, Sep. 7, 1972, transcribed for author; ("Did we") WHT, Mar. 13, 1973, R, Stmt. of Inf., Bk. III, Pt. 2, p. 874.

RN White House and Humphrey: (impropriety?) Ulasewicz, op. cit., p. 183–, citing Woods memo and see WHT entries, Sep. 8, 1971; *AOP*, p. 28; (detective etc.) Magruder, *American* Life, op. cit., p. 202, E, Final Report, p. 192; *NM*, p. 165; ("lay off") WHT, Aug. 3, 1972; *AOP*, p. 115.

RN White House and Muskie: ("all out attack") Sep. 26, 1970 entry, *HD*, CD; ("lib" mailings) *HD* p. 213, and see WHT, Jan. 12, 1972, cited in *WP*, Oct. 30, 1997; (trawled Maine) Wise, *Police State*, op. cit., p. 132, citing Ulasewicz int., John Caulfield testimony, E, Bk. 19, p. 9276; ("monkish") WHT, Sep. 8, 1971; *AOP*, p. 29; (docs. photographed) E, Final Report, p. 187–; (RN was told) WHT, Mar. 21, 1973, Record Grp. 460, Box 171, NA; (Chapin orchestrated) E, Final Report, p. 163–; *NM*, p. 158; ("massive mailing") WHT, Jan. 12, 1972, cited in *WP*, Oct. 30, 1997; (Humphrey/Jackson smears) *NM*, p. 157–, E, Final Report, p. 169–; (Chapin pleased) ibid., p. 170; (home address) ibid., p. 165; (set at throats) ibid., p. 158–; *NM*, p. 158; ("Let's prove") E, Report, p. 164; (RN approved?/write-in for Kennedy) ibid., p. 202, Jeb Magruder citing Charles Colson to this effect; (article re: Mrs. Muskie) *NM*, p. 162–, and see Mark Lane, *Plausible Denial*, New York: Thunder's Mouth, 1991, p. 202–, citing Gordon Liddy's testimony, Sep. 25, 1973, R, Bk. VII, Pt. 2, p. 3769; (Muskie tears) *NM*, p. 163; ("tear to pieces") WHT, Aug. 7, 1972; *AOP*, p. 124; ("chicken shit") WHT, May 11, 1973; *AOP*, p. 454.

RN and Wallace: ("most seriously") *MEM*, p. 542; (Sherry Netherland handover) "Safe Deposit Boxes" file, Carmine Bellino Papers, courtesy of Bellino family, E, Bk. 5, p. 2142–, E, Bk. 4, p. 1536–; (RN behind payments) WHT, Mar. 21, 1973, *HD*, p. 168; (IRS probe) Mollenhoff, op. cit., pp. 109, 114, and see Dan Carter, *The Politics of Rage*, New York: Simon & Schuster, p. 389–.

Vietnam '71: ("Can you believe?") Wise, *Politics of Lying*, op. cit., p. 19–; (N. Viet. troops) "Kissinger and the Betrayal of S. Viet." by Stephen Young, 1995, orig. draft for *Wall Street Journal*, provoided to author and transcript; Seymour Hersh int. of John Negroponte, provided to author; ("thugs") see Chap. 26, *supra*.

Tricia wedding: ("Family proud of") Troy, op. cit., p. 193; (chefs/cakes) Bryant with Leighton, op. cit., p. 311; Troy, op. cit., p. 193; (jokes) *NYT Magazine*, Oct. 20, 1974; (wedding described) *NYT*, June 13, 1971; (RN/Pat dance) Troy, op. cit., p. 193, Klein, op. cit., p. 3; int. Herb Klein.

Pentagon Papers: ("another headline") *MEM*, p. 508; (publication saga) David Rudenstine, *The Day the Presses Stopped*, Berkeley, CA: University of California Press, 1976, and Sanford Ungar, *The Papers and "The Papers,"* New York: Dutton, 1972; (98%) *MEM*, p. 509, and see eds. Strober, *Nixon*, op. cit., pp. 206, 209.

5 perjurers: ed. Hedda Garza, *The Watergate Investigation Index*, Wilmington, DE: Scholarly Resources, 1985, p.vii, the fifth man was Herbert Porter.

RN/Kiss. reaction: ("Get story out") Rudenstine, op. cit., p. 74; ("clear disloyalty") *HD*, CD, June 14, 1971; ("no contact") ibid., June 15, 1971; ("fired/"wants to be sure") ibid., June 17, 1971; ("pleasure") ibid., June 16, 1971; (Kissinger) Rudenstine, op. cit., p. 72; ("Too unsteady") Kissinger, *White House Years*, op. cit., p. 730; ("destroying us") Colson, op. cit., p. 59; ("irrational") Pete Kinsey, memo to files, re: Colson int. Jan. 13, 1975, Box 16, Farago Papers, Mugar Library, Boston University; (cables) Colson, op. cit., p. 60; int. Charles Colson for "Watergate: The Break-in," Part 1, Brian Lapping Associates Production for Discovery Channel and BBC, Discovery Communications, 1994, home video.

Ellsberg: (background) Rudenstine, op. cit., p. 33–; Sheehan, op. cit., p. 12–; ("bloody") Shapley, op. cit., p. 487; ("murder") eds. Strober, *Nixon*, op. cit., p. 200; ("shut me up") ibid., p. 201; ("brightest") Rudenstine, op. cit., p. 121–; ("weird sexual habits . . .") Haldeman with DiMona, op. cit., p.110; (sex/children) Hersh, *Price of Power*, op. cit., p. 385; (Hiss) *HD* CD, June 17, 20, 24, 29, July 1, 1971; (RN "weakling") Haldeman with DiMona, op. cit., p. 110.

"Bombing halt"/Brookings: (RN ordered/"blackmail"), *MEM*, p. 512; *WHT*, June 17, 1971, transcribed for author; *WP*, Jan. 24, 1997; ('68 ploy) e.g., *MEM*, p. 327; ("I wanted it back") *MEM*, p. 512; ("Implemented") *WHT*, June 17, 1971, *supra.*; ("You're to break into") *WHT*, June 30, 1971, transcribed for author and see *AOP*, p. 6; *WP*, Nov. 22, 1996, Jan. 24, 1997, also *SF Examiner*, Nov. 21, 1996; ("Now you do it") *WHT*, July 1, 1971, transcribed for author, and see *AOP*, p. 7, *SF Examiner*, Nov. 24, 1976; *WP*, Nov. 22 & 23, 1996, Jan. 24, 1997; *NYT*, Oct. 31, 1997; ("Who's going to?") *WHT*, July 1, 1971, Conv. 534-5, Segmt. 1, transcribed for author; *AOP*, pp. 10, 13; ("I really meant it") *WHT*, July 2, 1971; AP, Oct. 5, 1999; *AOP*, p. 17.

Brooking break-in attempts: (Caulfield) E, Bk. 22, p. 10359–; (Dean) eds. Strober, *Nixon*, op. cit., p. 225; Dean, *Blind Ambition*, op. cit., p. 47, and Dean article in *Rolling Stone*, Sep. 8, 1974; ("cased the joint") handwritten notes of John Dean int., Watergate Task Force, Box 125, 1 of 3, E, NA; (veteran guard) *WP*, Nov. 23, 1996, re: Roderick Warrick; (2nd reconnaissance) Ulasewicz with McKeever, op. cit. p. 232; (other operatives) Liddy, op. cit., p. 236; Liddy testimony, Mark Lane, *Plausible Denial*, New York: Thunder's Mouth, 1991, p. 202, operatives were Gordon Liddy and Howard Hunt, see this Ch., note 13; (Colson disclaimer) Charles Colson testimony Dec. 5, 1974, *U.S. v. John Mitchell*, NA; (Ehrlichman called off/RN knew) Ehrlichman, op. cit., p. 368; ("Don't discuss") *WHT*, June 30, 1971, transcribed for author.

Howard Hunt: ("talk to Hunt") *WHT*, June 30, 1971, transcribed for author; ("Colson never told me") *WHT*, Apr. 28, 1973; *AOP*, p. 372; (RN mentioned Hunt's name) *WHT*, June 30, 1971, transcribed for author; ("kind of a tiger") *WHT*, July 1, 1971; *AOP*, p. 13; (Colson knew) Colson, op. cit., p. 62; (Haldeman/Hunt) *WHT*, July 1, 2, 1971; *AOP*, pp. 14, 19; ("first-rate analyst") *WHT*, Aug. 12, 1971; *AOP*, p. 27; (Colson/Hunt/6 men) Colson, op. cit., p. 62; ("dirty guy") *HD*, CD, July 2, 1971; ("I want to alert") transcript of call, July 7, 1971, R, St. of Info., Bk. II, p.467.

Plumbers: (RN/San Clemente) Wicker, op. cit., p. 644–; Pete Kinsey, memo to files, re: int. Charles Colson, Jan. 20, 1975, Box, Farago Papers, Mugar Library, Boston University; ("Mr. Young") *MEM*, p. 514; *NM*, p. 80–; (Krogh inexperienced) White, *Breach*, op. cit., p. 149.

Liddy: (and Nazi Germany) Liddy, op. cit., p. 22–; Hougan, *Secret Agenda*, op. cit., p. 37–; (guns/killing) Summers, *Official & Confidential*, op. cit., pp. 406, 413; *NM*, p. 86; Magruder, *American Life*, op. cit., p. 174; ("cowboy") *NM*, p. 87; ("LIDDY" Page) advertisements on the "Official G. Gordon Liddy Web Page, Real Time Internet Services, Inc. 1996–2000, posted March 2000; ("best memo") Liddy, op. cit., p. 250.

RN/Hoover/Ellsberg: (RN wanted Hoover gone) Summers, *Official & Confidential*, op. cit., p. 412; ("Hoover assigned") Ehrlichman, op. cit., p. 143 and see *MEM*, p. 513; ("2 people") Ehrlichman testimony, E, Bk. 6, p. 2626; (disappointed/E'man approval) Bud Krogh and David Young to John Ehrlichman, Aug. 11, 1971, E, Bk. 6, p. 2644; (actual break-in) *NM*, p. 97–; ("vital importance") E, Report, p. 120, citing Nixon speech, May 22, 1973 and see R, Trans. of Recorded Pres. Conv., Mar. 21, 1973, p. 112; ("had to be discredited") *MEM*, p. 513; ("painted evil") Haldeman with DiMona, op. cit., p.116; Douglas Hallett, Colson aide in *NYT Magazine*, Oct. 20, 1974; ("neutralized") E, Report, p. 121; (Krogh told author) ints. Egil Krogh; ("direct action") Ehrlichman, op. cit., p. 365 and int. John Ehrlichman; ("I briefed Ehrlichman") RN/Colson conversation, *WHT*, Aug. 12, 1971; *AOP*, p. 27–; ("one little operation") RN/Ehrlichman, Sept. 8, 1971, transcribed for author; ("There wasn't anything") Ehrlichman testimony, E, Bk. 7, p. 2804; ("Goddamn to hell") RN/Ronald Ziegler, May 14, 1973; *AOP*, p. 492; ("I am stuck with") RN/Alexander Haig, Fred Buzhardt, May 16, 1973; *AOP*, p. 512; ("I believe somehow") ibid., p. 510; ("I did not authorize") E, Report, p. 120, citing Nixon speech, May 22, 1973; ("Did I know about it?") ints. Egil Krogh; ("I was so damn mad") Haldeman with DiMona, op. cit., p. 114, Ehrlichman, op. cit., p. 367 and int. John Ehrlichman; ("I do not believe") *MEM*, p. 514; (Ehrlichman surmised) Ehrlichman, op. cit., p. 368; (Colson denied) Charles Colson testimony, R, Bk. III, pp. 271, 455 and Colson, op. cit., pp. 225, 251; (Colson privy) Howard Hunt to Charles Colson, July 28, 1971, E, Bk. 9, p. 3886, Ehrlichman to Colson, Aug. 27, 1971, E, Bk. 6, p. 2651; ("It would be hard") int. Alexander Haig in eds. Strober, *Nixon*, op. cit., p. 224.

Other break-ins: ("horse's-ass crap") *WHT*, May 16, 1973, to Haig and Buzhardt; *AOP*, p. 516; (National Archives) *WHT*, Sep. 10, 18, 1971, transcribed for author; ("additional burglaries")

Nixon/Buzhardt, June 7, 1973, WHT; *AOP*, p. 494; ("break-ins sanctioned") Kissinger, *Years of Upheaval*, op. cit., p. 75; (100 break-ins) Sen. James Abourezk, presenting article by Robert Fink, "The Unsolved Break-ins, 1970–1974," Congressional Record, Oct. 9, 1974, Vol. 120, No. 153; (Ellsberg wife's burglary) Wise, *American Police State*, op. cit., p. 157fn–; (NAACP) Congressional Record, *supra.*; *NYT*, May 31, 1973; Dorris Hendricks, NAACP to researcher Robert Fink, June 3, 1974; (Potomac Associates) John Caulfield to John Dean, July 6, Aug. 9, 1973, E, Bk. 21, p. 9765–; Jack Caulfield testimony, E, Bk., 21, p. 9727, E, Report, pp. 143, 234; Roger Witten, Justice Dept. to Phil Heyman, July 2, 1973, enclosing July 9 letter to Heyman from Mitchell Rogovin, Congressional Record, Oct. 9, 1974, *supra.* re: June 27, 1973 break-in attempt; int. William Watts; (Lou Harris) ibid.; (Caplin) ibid. and re: Caplin support of Dem. protest, E, Bk. 7, p. 2978, and re: Enemies List, E, Bk.4, p. 1707 and, re: Dec. 31, 1973 break-in, research note by Robert Fink; (Weicker) individual views of senators of the Select Cttee., E, Final Report, pp. 1193, 1217.

"Let me be sure": *MEM*, p. 541.

69,000 troops: ibid., p. 584.

Christmas '71: (CBS) Troy, op. cit., p. 194; ("did his bit") *HD*, p. 383; (avoid schmaltz) *HD*, CD, Nov. 22, 1971; (boat parade) Dec. 28, 1971, ibid.; (Hunt) int. Howard Hunt; Hunt, *Undercover*, op. cit., p. 187.

Hoover: (in limousine) int. Kenneth Whittaker; (Tully) int. Andrew Tully; Las Vegas *Sun*, July 22, 1973.

Chapter 29

"We are lucky": int. Bryce Harlow in eds. Miller Center, op. cit., p. 16.

Funds: ("Jesus God!") WHT, July 2, 1971, transcribed for author; (Rose Mary's Baby) *Newsweek*, July 23, 1973; *The New Yorker*, Mar. 11, 1974, E, Bk. 22, pp. 10209, 10232; ($60 million) *NYT*, Sep. 29, 1973; (by suitcase) int. Larry Dubois, coauthor of *Playboy* series, Sep. 1976 and Apr. 1977.

Foreign donations: (Shah) int. Joseph Spear; Howe and Trott, op. cit., p. 492; ("we Arabs") Sampson, op. cit., p. 189; (Marcos) Kutler, op. cit., p. 207; (illegal) E, Report, p. 573.

Fundraising in U.S.: (business leaders' mtg) Washington *Spectator*, Oct. 15, 1976; (Phillips, Ashland, Gulf, Goodyear) *NYT*, Nov. 14, 1973; (Braniff) ibid., *NYT, LAT*, Mar. 24, 1976; (American) *Aviation Week and Space Technology*, July 16, 1973; *NYT*, Nov. 14, 1973; (Occidental) Louis and Yazijian, op. cit., p. 216; ($5 million) *WP*, Jan. 2, 1974; (cabinet officials) Providence [RI] *Journal*, Nov. 15, 1973; (Grumman) *NYT*, Sep. 14, 1976; *LAT*, Mar. 20, 1980; (McDonald's) William Dubrovir, Joseph Gebhardt, Samuel Buffone, Andra Oakes, *The Offenses of Richard Nixon*, New York: Quadrangle, 1974, p. 80–; (NY architect) *NYT*, Dec. 10, 1973; (Steinbrenner) Breslin, op. cit., p. 196, E, Report, p. 451; ("Anybody that wants") WHT, June 23, 1971, transcribed for author; (13 ambassadors) *NM*, p. 134–; (Annenberg) Emery, op. cit., p. 502; Howe and Trott, op. cit., p. 483; (Rebozo in bar) Darius Davis testimony, E, Bk. 22, p. 10564; (Manzi) UPI, Feb. 15, 1979, citing witness Anthony Mansueto.

Vesco: ("largest security fraud") *Time*, Mar. 12, 1973; (pending indictment) *WP*, June 21, 1995; ("Vesco is crook") WHT, July 11, 1973; *AOP*, p. 625; (VIP dinner) Arthur Herzog, *Vesco*, New York: Doubleday, 1987, p. 21–; ('68 contribution) F. Donald Nixon testimony, Apr. 5, 1973, E, Bk. 22, p. 10711–; (Rose Bowl) int. A. L. "Ike" Eisenhauer; A. L. Eisenhauer and Robin Moore, *The Flying Carpetbagger*, New York: Pinnacle, 1976, p. 91–, and see *NYT*, Jan. 2, 1969; (Mitchell "pressure") Hutchison, op. cit., p. 205–; Jospeh Persico, *Casey*, New York: Viking, 1990, p. 148; McClendon, op. cit., p. 197; *NYT*, Mar. 6, 1974; (aide suggested) *Time, Newsweek*, Mar. 12, 1973, the aide was CREEP vice president and former WH aide Daniel Hofgren; (Vesco aide to US) *Time*, Mar. 12, 1973, the aide was Laurence Richardson, Jr.; ("surrogate") Magruder, *American Life*, op. cit., p. 183; (Edward helped arrange) *NYT*, Apr. 6, 1974; int. Edward Nixon; (Donald Sr. '68) F. Donald Nixon testimony, E, Bk. 22, p. 10711; (son/Vesco) int. Donald A. Nixon, refs.; Eisenhauer and Moore, op. cit.; ("Ah . . . let's go on") transcript of Cronkite–Vesco int., Apr. 2, 1974; ed. Miller, *Breaking of the President*, Vol. 4, op. cit., p. 69; Boston *Globe*, Apr. 3, 1974.

RN and Teamsters: ("The P apparently met") Dec. 9, 1971 entry, *HD*, p. 382; ("The President wants you") Haldeman to Colson, Sept. 8, 1970; ed. Oudes, op. cit., p. 157–; (Mollenhoff opposed) Mollenhoff memo to files, Sep. 12, and to John Ehrlichman, Sep. 17, 1969, Mollenhoff Papers, Gerald R. Ford Library; (Chotiner "handling") Mollenhoff, op. cit., p. 45, citing call from former Justice Dept. official Walter Sheridan; ("substantial sums") Quarles to McBride, Aug. 30, 1973 enclosing Tab B, Colson memo to Krogh, June 6, 1970, Campaign Contributions Task Force, Box 803, WSPF, NA; (Hoffa barred) ed. Shoenebaum, op. cit., p. 303; (Teamsters endorsement) Colson to RN, July 17, 1972, WH Special Files, staff members and Office, NP, NA; (*Time* probe) *Time*, Aug. 31, 1981; (Hall) ibid., Cleveland *Plain Dealer*, Aug. 23, 24, 1981, NYT, July 20, 1975; ints. Harry Hall, the late John Daley, and former IRS Supervisor

Marty Philpott, and refs., Neff, op. cit., refs.; (Colson/Vegas) *Time,* Aug. 8, 1977, citing FBI sources; (Colson attorney for Teamsters) ed. Schoenebaum, op. cit., p. 139.

"Intelligence" plans: ("For God's sake") Hunt, *Undercover,* op. cit., p. 185; ("800–300") attachment to Oct. 27, 1971 memo, Gordon Strachan to H. R. "Bob" Haldeman, R, Stmt. of Inf., App. IV, p. 45; ("intelligence capability") memo, Gordon Strachan to H.R. "Bob" Haldeman, Dec. 2, 1971, p. 59; ("When going to do something") Haldeman with DiMona, op. cit., p. 10–; (Liddy/Mitchell mtg.) E, Report, p. 21, and see useful summary at Emery, op. cit., p. 89–; (frieze) White, *Breach,* op. cit., p. 156; ("Smart, isn't he") WHT, Oct. 25, 1971, conv. no. 601-033, WSPF, NA; (GEMSTONE) Liddy, op. cit., p. 270; ("beyond pale") Mitchell testimony, E, Bk. 4, p. 610; (too expensive) Liddy, op. cit., p. 276–; Dean, *Blind Ambition,* op. cit., p. 85; Magruder, *American Life,* op. cit., p. 179.

"overall political plan": *HD,* p. 403.

Digest dinner/Wallaces: *WP* magazine, July 27, 1997; ($ in Bahamas?) John Sablich to Mr. Moerdler, Dec. 10, 1973, JSFF, pp. 490, 555; (*Digest* editor brokered) Paul Michel to files, Feb. 7, 1975, Campaign Contributions Task Force, File 804, Box 99, Paul Michel to files, May 27, 1975, Campaign Contrib. Task Force, File 804, Box 111, WSPF, NA; (Oobie-doobie girl) *WP* magazine, July 27, 1997; Bryant with Leighton, op. cit., p. 257–6, the singer was Carole Feraci; (RN angry memo) RN to Colson and Haldeman, Jan. 28, 1972, WH Special Files, H. R. Haldeman, Pres. Memos, 1971–1973, Box 230, NP, NA.

2nd Meeting: E, Report, p. 22, Emery, op. cit., p. 92–.

Liddy went to Colson: summarized and sourced at E, Report, p. 23–; Emery, op. cit., p. 99; ("the President wanted") int. Jeb Magruder for "Watergate: The Break-in," Part 1, Brian Lapping Associates Production for the Discovery Channel and BBC, Discovery Communications, Inc., 1994, transcript p. 52, provided to author by Brian Lapping Associates.

Political position early '72: (polls) Manchester, *Glory & Dream,* op. cit., p. 1273—Harris poll in January showed RN and Muskie neck and neck at 42 percent, and Wallace at 11 percent, *MEM,* p. 541–; ("coronation") int. Charles Colson for "Watergate: The Break-in," *supra.,* transcript p. 39.

Mitchell go-ahead?: summarized at E, Report, p. 24–; Emery, op. cit., p. 101; Magruder, *American Life,* op. cit., p. 193; (shift to McGovern) E, Report, p. 27.

RN/Mitchell meeting and "P"/"F" document: Apr. 4, 1972 entry, *HD* CD, Nixon to Rodino, June 9, 1974, Box 8, Edward Hutchinson Papers, Gerald R. Ford Library and see WHT, Apr. 25, 1973, conv. 430-004, WSPF, NA, and report of Peter Vea to author.

Others on RN/Mitchell meetings: (Butterfield) eds. Strober, *Nixon,* op. cit., p. 249; (Korff/Mitchell/RN) Korff, op. cit., p. 120, and ints. the late Baruch Korff, Zamira Korff (daughter).

Early talk of DNC break-in: E, Report, p. 22, John Dean testimony, E, Bk. 3, p. 929, *NM,* p. 173, referring to Dean and Magruder and James McCord testimony, E, Bk. 1, pp. 145–, 183–, re: discussions of DNC as early as Jan. or Feb.

"entries" at Convention/nominee HQ: E, Report, p. 25.

Hoover death: Summers, *Official & Confidential,* op. cit., pp. 10, 422–.

Bizarre orders: (RN raging over offensive) *HD,* p. 435, and see esp. p. 448; ("The bastards") WHT, Apr. 4, 1972, in *LAT* June 29, 1974; (RN kicked desk) Hersh, *Price of Power,* op. cit., p. 508; (demand for flag) Liddy, op. cit., p. 303–; Magruder, op. cit., p. 205–; Hunt, *Undercover,* op. cit., p. 211; ints. Bernard Barker, Howard Hunt; (melee) *Saturday Review,* Sep. 11, 1973; *Time,* Oct. 23, 1972; int. Liddy in *George,* June 1997; FBI ints. Pablo Fernandez, FBI Miami 139-328, Angel Ferrer, 302 int., unnumbered and handwritten notes of WSPF int., in Michael Ewing Collection, int. Ellsberg, *Rolling Stone,* Nov. 8, 1973, and *NM,* p. 196.

Wallace shooting: (actual event) *WP,* May 15, 16, 1972; (RN on surface) ibid.; *MEM,* p. 608; ("agitated") Bernstein and Woodward, *Men,* op. cit., p. 329, citing int. Charles Colson; (Bremer "leftist") ibid., p. 326, citing White House aide Kenneth Clawson, ("Don't worry") May 16, 1972 entry, *HD,* CD; ("times that it's best") WHT, May 16, 1972, transcribed for author; (Nixon/Colson dine) May 15, 1973 entry, *HD,* CD, Henry Hecht to William Merrill, Aug. 14, 1973; int. Colson in Bremer released docs. folder, WSPF, NA; ("Nixon having") Emery, op. cit., p. 116, citing NA oral history; (Nixon/Colson phone call) WHT, May 15, 1972; *AOP,* p. 38; *WP,* June 17, 1997; (Colson admitted) C. L. McGowan to Mr. Gebhardt, Aug. 13, 23, 1974, FBI 44-52576, serials 808 and 809, Hunt referred to call in "late afternoon," Colson to call at 10 P.M.; (Hunt said too late) Hunt, *Undercover,* op. cit., p. 216, and see Liddy, op. cit., p. 309; NY *Daily News,* Dec. 8, 1992; (RN strategy depended) NY *Review of Books,* Dec. 13, 1973, the colleague was Robert Finch; ("With the needle sticking") *TW72,* p. 238; (Simons) Bernstein and Woodward, *Men,* op. cit., p. 326; (Wallace suspicions) e.g., C. L. McGowan to Mr. Gebhardt, Jan. 15, 1975, FBI 44-52576-814; *McCall's,* Sept. 1974; int. former Wallace aide Elvin Stanton.

Gilday: SAC (Washington Field Office) to director, May 23, 1974, FBI 139-4089, notes of interviews by Jim Hougan, Jim Lesar (author's attorney), and Julie Ziegler (author's researcher); ("I did things") WHT, Jan. 2, 1973, transcribed for author.

anti-Anderson plans: (Hughes payments) *WP*, Aug. 6,1971; (on ITT) Emery, op. cit., p. 101; (Indo-Pakistan conflict) Hersh, *Price of Power*, op. cit., pp. 444–, 659; Jack Anderson with George Clifford, *The Anderson Papers*, New York: Ballantine, 1974, p. 260–, and research paper prepared for author by Greg Murphy, *West* magazine [San Jose *Mercury News*], Nov. 20, 1983; *WP*, Feb. 16, 1972; *MEM*, pp. 531–, 574, 580–; and see Jack Caulfield to H. R, Haldeman, re: Anderson Leaks, Feb. 11, 1971; ed. Oudes, op. cit., p. 215; ("foes") Ehrlichman, op. cit., p. 25; (information to WSPF) John Lydick to Jack Anderson file, Oct. 21, 1975, and Michael Lehr to files, Oct. 28, 1975, WSPF, NA; *WP*, Sep. 30, *Time*, Oct. 6, 1975; ("They charged us") int. Gordon Liddy, *High Times*, June 1981; Liddy court testimony in Lane, op. cit., p. 204; (Liddy meeting with CIA doctor) Liddy, op. cit., p. 286–; (Hunt affidavit) Mar. 21, 1978 in *Jack Anderson v. Richard Nixon et al.*, Civ. Act. no. 76-1794; ("spiking his drink") AP, Aug. 17, 1973, cited in eds. Scott, Hoch and Stetler, op. cit., p. 387, citing former covert actions specialist Miles Copeland.

"political intelligence" operation continued: (phoney support) *NM*, p. 166; int. Robert Odle; (Cuban's demonstration) Liddy, op. cit., p. 307–; ("our next job") Hunt, *Undercover*, op. cit., p. 213; (McCord reconnaissance) E, Report, p. 27; McCord, op. cit., p. 22; (O'Brien office & apt.) ibid., p. 19.

Baldwin: Angelo Lano and Daniel Mahon report of int. Alfred Baldwin, July 11, 1972, FBI WFO 139-166, Baldwin testimony, E, Bk. 1, p. 395–.

Russell: see this chapter, author's note 19; (probing Anderson) Rodney Kicklighter and James Hopper report of int. Louis Russell, June 28, 1972, FBI 139-166; (security service) Don Sanders to file, Oct. 8, 1973, citing Russell file at General Security Services, Howard Leibengood file, E, NA and int. Ken Prestia, Jim Hougan Collection.

RN in Moscow: (sleep eludes) Szulc, *Illusion*, op. cit., p. 56; *MEM*, p. 610; (meetings/"never loosened") John Osborne, *The Fourth Year of the Nixon Watch*, New York: Liveright, 1973, p. 92.

Cubans/first break-in: (hotels) *NM*, p. 197; ("We're going to") transcript, *LAT* int. of Alfred Baldwin, in *U.S. v. G. Gordon Liddy et al.*, Case 1827-72, U.S. Dist. Court DC, p. 43; (photographed papers) Hunt, *Undercover*, op. cit., pp. 228; Washington *Evening Star and Daily News*, Sep. 1, 1972; Hougan, *Agenda*, op. cit., p.156; (bugs according to McCord) McCord, op. cit., p. 25; E, Report, p. 157.

RN no diary/Moscow bugs: *MEM*, p. 618–.

First fruits of bugs: (Baldwin) int. Alfred Baldwin by FBI agents Angelo Lano and Daniel Mahon, July 10, 1972, FBI WFO 139-166, p. 10; (O'Brien bug failed) McCord, op. cit., p. 26; Liddy, op. cit., p. 321–; (content of calls intercepted) FBI int. of Baldwin, July 10, 1972, *supra*. pp. 9, 11, WFO to director, July 10, 1972, FBI 139-4089-504, *NM*, p. 201, Magruder, *American Life*, op. cit., p. 209, and see author's note 22 for this chapter.

CREEP/WH reaction to logs: (stationery) E, Report, p. 30; Liddy, op. cit., p. 323; Nick Akerman to files, Oct. 26, 1973; int. of Sally Harmony, p. 3–, Box 63, WSPF, NA; (Magruder shows Mitchell?) Jeb Magruder testimony, E, Bk. 2, p. 797; Magruder, *American Life*, op. cit., p. 210; (backed by assistant) Robert Reisner testimony, E, Bk. 2, p. 494; (Strachan saw) Jeb Magruder testimony, E, Bk. 2 pp. 797, 827; ("Strachan called me") Liddy, op. cit., p. 326; (Haldeman denied knowledge) H. R. Haldeman testimony, E, Bk. 7, p. 2880, opening statement on behalf of H. R. Haldeman, Nov. 26, 1974, *U.S. v. Mitchell, et al.*, Case 74-110, U.S. Dist. Court D.C., p. 7590–; ("best of knowledge") H. R. Haldeman testimony, E, Bk. 7, p. 2880; (declines to answer) DNC deposition of H. R. Haldeman, May 22, 1973, summary deposition folder, Box 115, *DNC v. McCord*, WSPF, NA; ("whether any result") Richard Ben-Veniste and George Frampton, *Stonewall*, New York: Touchstone, 1977, p. 371.

Nixon after foreign trip: (polls) *U.S. News & World Report*, May 2, 1994; ("We need savage") June 9, 1972 entry, *HD*, CD, p. 470; (RN urged Colson) WHT, June 13, 1972; *AOP*, p. 40; (S.S. agent passed info.) Rush, op. cit., p. 61; ("hit McGovern") Liddy, op. cit., p. 324; (Magruder wanted) ibid.; (Mitchell denied) John Mitchell testimony, E, Bk. 4, p. 1620; ("Tell me what room") Ben-Veniste and Frampton, op. cit., p. 375; Charles Colson testimony, Dec. 4?, 1974, *U.S. v. Mitchell et al.*, Rec. Grp. 21, NA, p. 9378, and see Emery, op. cit., pp. 127, 504n38; (Liddy/Mitchell June 15) Liddy, op. cit., p. 328; (200 calls) *NM*, p. 201.

Chapter 30

"My God!": WHT, June 20, 1972; *AOP*, p. 49.

Motive for Watergate: ("basic issue") opening statement of Henry Rothblatt on behalf of Bernard Barker et al., in *U.S. v. McCord*, Rothblatt Papers, and see Bernstein and Woodward, *Men*, op. cit., p. 230; ("To this day") *NYT*, Nov. 30, 1987, and see int. H. R. Haldeman in eds. Miller Center, op. cit., p. 95.

Cuba motive?: (hoped find foreign funding") int. Howard Hunt and see Wise, *Police State,* op. cit., p. 159; (accomplices) e.g., Virgilio Gonzalez, New Haven *Register,* June 16, 1997 and int. Bernard Barker; (McGovern pressing) *WP,* undated, summer 1972; (phoney) e.g., int. Prof. Sam Dash (Chief Counsel, Sen. W'gate Cttee.); (Sturgis) Andrew St. George int. of Frank Sturgis, *True,* Aug. 1974; ints. Andrew St. George; (Rosselli attorney) Rappelye and Becker, op. cit., p. 307, attorney was Leslie Scherr; (RN: "Hunt . . . open that scab") WHT, June 23, 1972, conv. no. 741-002, WSPF, NA; ("very bad to have this fellow Hunt") WHT, June 23, 1972, transcribed for author; ("The obsession of the administration") Terry Lenzner and Mark Lackritz to Sen. Ervin, date obscured, Feb. 1974, Subject: Relevance to S. Res. 60 of John Rosselli's testimony about his CIA activities, Box 441-3, JFK Collection, HSCA, Rec. Grp. 233, NA.

O'Brien/Hughes motive: ("Colson can talk") Haldeman with DiMona, op. cit., p. 18; ("Operation O'Brien") ed. Oudes, op. cit., p. xxix, citing Haldeman memo to Lyn Nofziger, Mar. 9, 1970; (Chotiner reported) ibid., citing memo to Haldeman, Mar. 12, 1970; (RN memo on Air Force One) The President to H. R. Haldeman, Jan. 14, 1971, Box 140, H. R. Haldeman Papers, "Extra Copies," W. Hse. central files, NA; ("shake . . . skeletons") Jack Caulfield to John Dean, Feb. 1, 1971, E, Bk. 21, p. 9755; (Anderson/Hughes contributions) *WP,* Aug. 6, 1971; (RN: "I said: 'Get word out' ") Nixon/Frank Gannon int., "American Parade," CBS-TV, Apr. 10, 1984, transcript, p. 2, and see *Larry King Weekend,* CNN, June 21, 1997 (rerun), transcript p. 5; (O'Brien "attacked") Lawrence O'Brien Oral History, Dec. 10, 1987, XXXI, p. 40–, JFKL; (no irregularities) E, Report, p. 1027; ("possible wrongdoing") ibid., p. 1025; ("A.G. called today") Jan. 31, 1972 entry, *HD,* p. 405, the Hughes aide was Noah Dietrich—see also entries for Jan. 16, 17 and this book page 279–; (Irving) Drosnin, op. cit., p. 440–; Dean *Blind Ambition,* op. cit., p. 390–; (Schemmer) ints. Benjamin Schemmer, Enc. to Schemmer to Robert Herrema, May 24, 1973, File 804, Campaign Contributions Task Force, E, Anatomy of a Break-in, unpub. article in Jim Hougan collection; ("Nixon-Hughes Loan" book) Gordon Liddy to John Mitchell, May 15, 1972, attached to Gordon Strachan to John Ehrlichman, May 18, 1972, Donald Nixon file, John Ehrlichman papers, W. Hse. special files, NP, NA and Higham, op. cit., p. 348; ("planned burglary") *NYT,* Nov. 30, 1987; ("Plan hatched") Haldeman note, Mar. 28, 1973, *HD,* CD; ("to find out what O'Brien had") Liddy, op. cit., p. 325; ("mainly Hughes") WHT, July 8, 1973, WSPF, NP, NA.

Sex information motive: ("background checks") Anthony Ulasewicz testimony, E, Bk. 7, p. 2774–; ("all telephone calls") U.S. Attorney, DC Earl Silbert response to Charles Morgan, Jr., Report, FBI 139-4089-2708, p. 20, int. Charles Morgan; (attention to "sexual") Alfred Baldwin deposition, July 25, 1996, Exhibit 13, p. 86; *Maureen and John Dean v. St. Martin's Press et al.,* Case 92-1807 HHG AK, U.S. Dist. Court DC; (record sealed) Emery, op. cit., p. 238; ("personal matters") Alfred Baldwin int., reprinted from *LAT,* Oct. 6, 1972, in FBI 139-4089-1355; ("extremely personal") Earl Silbert response, *supra.,* ("calls of sexual nature") Washington *Times,* Sep. 29, 1996; (Ehrlichman handwritten notes) E, Bk. 7, p. 2940; ("What they were getting") WHT, Apr. 14, 1973, conv. no. 428-028, WSPF, NP, NA; (Oliver prime mover) "Nomination of Earl Silbert to be Untied States Attorney for the District of Columbia, U.S. Senate Committee on the Judiciary, Statement of Spencer Oliver," Apr. 30, 1974, p. 200.

Maxie Wells: (background) Ida Maxwell Wells deposition, Sep. 19, 1997; *Wells v. Liddy,* Case JFK-97-946, U.S. Dist. Court Dist. of MD, N. Div., pp. 97–; ("I've developed crisis") M. Wells letter to J. Roberts, Exhibit 21, in *Wells v. Liddy, supra.;* ("pretty wild") Wells deposition, *supra.,* p. 99; ("kind of appalled") ibid., p. 111–; ("Marty & I") ibid., pp. 85, 88, 101; ("talk to sweeties") ibid., p. 245.

Bailley: (allegation) Hougan, *Agenda,* op. cit., p. 129; *WP,* June 10, 1972; (convicted) *WP,* Oct. 26, 1972.

Plans to use prostitutes: ("call girl bit") John Mitchell testimony, E, Bk. 4, p. 1610; (houseboat) Liddy, op. cit., p. 274; Howard Hunt testimony, E, Bk. 9, p. 3741; (Baltimore madam) Dean, *Blind Ambition,* op. cit., p. 83; int. John Dean, in "Watergate: The Break-in," Lapping series, *supra.;* (Prostitute use in DC) Jeb Magruder testimony, E, Bk. 2, p. 788; Magruder *American Life,* op. cit., p. 178; Liddy, op. cit., p. 286; (Hunt re: "accusations") G. Goldman to file, re: int. Bernard Barker, Sep. 13, 1973, Barker memo folder, Box 99, E, NA; (straitlaced?) int. Lawrence Higby; eds. Strober, *Nixon,* op. cit., p. 62; ("perverted") notes of int. Edward Morgan, for Pacific News Service, in Stanley Kutler collection.

Columbia Plaza prostitution/Ralabate record: (arrest records) records of Superior Court, D.C. and Metropolitan PD criminal history record for Lillian Lee Lori listing offenses 1963–1972, including notations of addresses at Apts. 204 and 901 at 2440 Virginia Ave., NW (Columbia Plaza Apt.) re: "disorderly house" charge, Apr. 4, 1972. Research for author by Alex Kramer Research, ints. Eugene Zoglio, deposition of Carl Shoffler, Mar. 13, 1995, *Maureen and John Dean v. St. Martin's Press et al.,* Case 92-1807(HHG), U.S. Dist. Court DC, p. 55, deposition of John Rudy (former asst. U.S. attorney), June 19, 1996, *Maureen and John Dean v. St. Martin's Press et al., supra.,* p. 202–, int. Barbara Ralabate (aka Lil Lori); (Democrats involved)

Rudy deposition, *supra.,* p. 245–; ("arranged for liaisons") ibid., p. 321–; (filmed/recorded) ibid., p. 246–.

Russell: (and Washington whores) int. William Birely; int. Gordon Hess (former police officer) in Jim Hougan Collection; Hougan, *Agenda,* op. cit., p. 116; int. Wm. Birely; ("I had 3 or 4") int. Robert Smith, and see Hougan, *Agenda,* op. cit., p. 118 (re: similar information of Kennard Smith and Bernard Fensterwald), int. Gordon Hess, *supra.;* (Russell named prostitute) ibid.

Sex angle in Oval Office: (Dean briefs RN) WHT, Sep. 15, 1972, conv. 779-002, WSPF, NP, NA, p. 39, the lawyer was Henry Rothblatt; (Dean/Haldeman memo) John Dean to H. R. Haldeman, Sep. 12, 1972, E, Bk. 3, p. 1177–, and see E, Bk. 4, p. 1470, the copy of the original memo, supplied to the author by John Dean, bears a checked capital "P," probably indicating that Nixon saw or discussed the memo; (Maroulis) int. Peter Maroulis, Donna Rothblatt was also interviewed.

Xaviera Hollander case: (Colson tip) Charles Colson to John Dean, attaching note from *Life's* Bill Lambert, Oct. 27, 1971, and John Caulfield's report Nov. 22, 1971 report to John Dean, supplied to author; (Mosbacher) ibid., and Terry Lenzner to Mark Lackritz, Sep. 22, 1973, re: T. Ulasewicz Investigations, in Defendant Len Colodny's Motion for Partial Summary Judgment, *John and Maureen Dean v. St. Martin's Press et al., supra.,* Exhibit 226; ("blackmail" headline) *NYT,* Nov. 20, 1971; (Hollander book) Xaviera Hollander with Robin Moore and Yvonne Dunleavy, *The Happy Hooker,* New York: Dell, 1972; ("one of the hierarchy") Xaviera Hollander, *Xaviera,* New York: Warner, 1973, p. 419; (deported) *NYT,* Nov. 19, 1971, Apr. 18, 29, 1972; (wiretapper fled) *NYT,* Sep. 15, 17, 1972, ints. Robin Moore, Theodore Ratinoff; ("Thank you, Tricky") Hollander, *Xaviera,* op. cit., p. 13; ("W. Hse. . . . kicked out") ints. Robin Moore; (report revealed) House Select Cttee. on Intelligence report ("Pike Report"), disclosed at length in *Village Voice,* Feb. 16, 1976; (King Hussein) Wise, *Police State,* op. cit., pp. 184, 411; ("whatever his taste") int. Carl Feldbaum; (Ziegler denial) int. Ronald Ziegler; ("white as a sheet") Dean, *Blind Ambition,* op. cit., p. 41.

Mosbacher: (job) Safire, op. cit., p. 129; Mar. 1, 1970 entry, *HD,* p. 133; (resignation) WHT, June 23, 1972, conv. no. 741-002, p. 8, WSPF, NA; (dead) Aug. 13, 1997, at Mosbacher entry, britannica.com.

Ruwe: (i/c social events) Apr. 14, 1969 entry, *HD,* p. 49; (veteran) Witcover, op. cit., pp. 10, 124, 134, 170, 233; Ehrlichman, op. cit., pp. 14, 24, 30; *TW68,* p. 6; int. Robert Odle; ("We have 10 Arabs") int. Bill Bagley.

Rikan: (background) see author's note for this chapter, number 17; (knew Dean & [later wife] Maureen) Maureen Dean with Hayes Gorey, *Mo,* New York: Simon & Schuster, 1975, pp. 13, 15, 40, 48, 63, 79, 264, 272; ("Heidi is identified in index as Heidi Rikan) Dean, *Blind Ambition,* op. cit., pp. 328–; "Erika AKA Heidi L. Rikan Certification of Death," State of PA, Jan. 27, 1990, Reading [PA] *Eagle,* Jan. 28, 1990; (maid) Mary Banks deposition, Sep. 28, 1993, *Maureen and John Dean v. St. Martin's Press et al., supra.,* pp. 10–, 25, 33, 35; Washington *Star*/Dean follow-up: (story) *Evening Star,* June 9, 1972; ("big folderol") int. Pete Kinsey; (Rudy/Dean mtg.) John Dean deposition, Sep. 12, 1995; *Maureen and John Dean v. St. Martin's Press et al., supra.,* pp. 118, 122, 123; John Dean deposition, Sep. 15, 1995, *supra.,* p. 64–; John Rudy deposition, Apr. 11, 1996, *supra.,* p. 185–; transcript of Len Colodny int. of John Rudy, Apr. 4, 1989, defendant Len Colodny's motion for partial summary judgment; *John and Maureen Dean v. St. Martin's Press et al., supra.,* refs. in Exhibits, and int. John Dean by Jim Hougan, Jim Hougan Collection.

Ruwe after resignation: *Good Housekeeping,* July 1976, *SF Chronicle,* June 12, 1981; "Newsmakers" column, *Newsweek,* Aug. 24, 1981; February Group Directory, Summer 1979.

"The directions that I received": deposition of John Rudy, June 19, 1996; *Maureen and John Dean v. St. Martins' Press et al., supra.,* pp. 203, 205.

"balance of terror": Liddy, op. cit., p. 251.

Magruder: John Ehrlichman mtg. with Jeb Magruder and attorneys, Ref. no. 7304141, NP, NA.

Sturgis: int. Frank Sturgis by Andrew St. George, *True,* Aug. 1974; int. Andrew St. George.

O'Brien as target: ("Op. O'Brien") ed. Oudes, op. cit., p. xxix; (home burglaries/phones) Lawrence O'Brien oral history, Dec. 10, 1987, transcript, XXXI, p. 16–, JFKL; Lawrence O'Brien, *No Final Victories,* Garden City, NY: Doubleday, 1974, p. 346– and see [re: intent to burgle/bug apartments] McCord, op. cit., p. 19 and James McCord testimony, E, Bk. p. 174; (Hunt "alternate plan") Schorr, op. cit., p. 14; (get "information that CREEP") Lawrence O'Brien oral history, Dec. 11, 1987, transcript, XXXI, p. 38, JFKL; ("simple as that") O'Brien, op. cit., p. 345; (Liddy on what Democrats had) Liddy, op. cit., p. 325; ("shit file") int. Frank Sturgis by Andrew St. George, *True,* Aug. 1974; ("believe in Santa Clus") int. Len Garment in eds. Strober, *Nixon,* op. cit., pp. 319, 322; (Liddy/"war") Ulasewicz, op. cit., p. 237.

Chapter 31

"**Watergate has done**": int. Robert Finch in ed. Miller, *Breaking of the President*, op. cit., Vol. 1, p. 130.

Vann ceremonies: Sheehan, op. cit., pp. 3–, 753–.

RN to Bahamas: *MEM*, p. 625, June 16, 1972 entry, *HD*, CD.

Burglary June 16/17: (movements/evening) *NM*, p. 203–; Hougan, *Agenda*, op. cit., p. 178–; Hunt, *Undercover*, op cit., p. 239–; Liddy, op. cit., p. 331–; (Baldwin) *LAT*, Oct. 5, 1972; (*Puppet People*) Hougan, *Agenda*, op. cit., p. 195; (burglars' tasks) *NM*, p. 206; McCord, op. cit., p. 30; ("I personally checked") int. Bernard Barker in eds. Strober, *Nixon*, op. cit., p. 305; (police picked up) ints. Paul Leeper, John Barrett, Carl Shoffler, Thomas Herlihy, Metropolitan Police Dept. Intelligence Division, to John Hughes, June 16, 1972, Hougan Collection; (Russell) int. Ruth Thorne, citing Russell; int. Jean Hooper (daughter) and see Hougan, *Agenda*, op. cit., p. 192–; (Herlihy report) see Herhlihy to Hughes, *supra*.

RN/news of arrests: (told nation June 17) address to the nation about the Watergate investigations, Apr. 30, 1973, Public Papers of the Presidents of the United States, Richard Nixon, 1973, Washington, D.C.: U.S. Gov. Printing Off., 1974, p. 328; (memoirs/Sunday) *MEM*, p. 625; (Abplanalp) *JA*, p. 468; (did not accompany) Emery, op. cit., p. 149fn; (Rebozo/Saturday) int. *Miami Herald*, Mar. 22, 1990; ("They did WHAAT?") *JA*, p. 468; (Haldeman) Haldeman with DiMona, op. cit., pp. 5, 8–; ("ashtray") Charles Colson testimony, R, Bk. III, p. 259; Haldeman with DiMona, op. cit., p. 37; and transcript of int. Charles Colson by Mike Wallace, "Watergate: The Secret Story," CBS News, June 17, 1992; Emery, op. cit., p. 154; int. Charles Colson for BBC/History Channel; ("Why did he telephone?") Haldeman with DiMona, op. cit., p. 37.

First response: ("Track down Magruder") ibid., p. 31–; (first statement) Magruder, *American Life*, op. cit., p. 220; ("Idea—get it confused") Haldeman note of Magruder call, June 18, 1972, NP, NA, and see Emery, op. cit., p. 155–.

destruction of evidence: (Liddy) Liddy, op. cit., pp. 34–, 347, 359; (McCord deputy) Hougan, *Agenda*, op. cit., p. 224–; *NM*, p. 226; (Hunt safe) John Dean testimony, E, Bk. 3, pp. 935, 937; Dean, *Blind Ambition*, op. cit., p. 114; int. Pete Kinsey; (Gray) Patrick Gray testimony, E, Bk. 9, 0. 3468; ("Maybe . . . little fire") Magruder, *American Life*, op. cit., p. 225–; (Mitchell destroyed) McClendon, op. cit., p. 274–.

Tuesday morning meeting: R, Statement of Inf., Bk. II, p. 23; Emery, op. cit., p. 170; ("make sure files clean") Gordon Strachan testimony, E, Bk. 6, p. 2458; Haldeman with DiMona, op. cit., p. 39–.

RN Tuesday: (alone) RN daily diary, June 20, 1972, R, Bk. II, p. 243; (sees Ehrlichman) ibid.; (Watergate discussed) Emery, op. cit., p. 173; Ehrlichman, op. cit., p. 318, but see R, Summary of Inf., p. 37–; (Haldeman meeting) ibid., p. 38.

18½ minute gap: (Haldeman's notes) R, Statement of Inf., Bk. II, p. 246; ("serious thing") transcript of proceedings, Nov. 21, 1973, Subpoena Duces Tecum Issued to Pres. Richard M. Nixon for Production of Tapes, Misc. No. 47-73; Rose Mary Woods Legal Corr., Box 20, WH Central files, NP, NA; (ludicrous scene) Ben-Veniste and Frampton, op. cit., p. 177–; Doyle, op. cit., p. 257–; (experts concluded) "Report on Technical Investigation—The EOB Tape of June 20, 1972," by Advisory Panel on White House Tapes, Box C11 and E, NA, Technology Review, Feb. 1976, *Newsweek*, Jan. 28, 1974; (Woods insisted only 5 min.) Ben-Veniste and Frampton, op. cit., p. 177; ("Don't worry") Ben-Veniste and Frampton, op. cit., p. 177; ("framed") int. James Bassett by FB, FBP; int. Cynthia Bassett; (RN reviewed tapes) *MEM*, pp. 902, 918, 975; R, Bk. IX, Pt. 2, p. 528–; Leon Jaworski with Mickey Herskowitz, *Confession & Avoidance*, Garden City, NY: Anchor Press, 1979, p. 237; ("pushed buttons") R, Bk. IX, Pt. 2, p. 530; (RN around Woods) "Fact Sheet," *supra.*; ("Most likely the President") Jill Wine Banks, formerly Volner, *The Washington Lawyer*, July/Aug. 1999; ("Only the President") Jaworski with Herskowitz, op. cit., p. 236; (Haldeman reconstruction) Haldeman with DiMona, op. cit., p. 17.

Other events Tuesday, June 20: (RN refused release tapes) R, Summary of Inf., p. 38fn; ("A lot of people think") WHT, June 20, 1972, conv. no. 342-027, WSPF, NA; (further meeting with Haldeman) WHT, June 20, 1972, transcribed for author and *AOP*, p. 47–; ("nice touch") Emery, op. cit., p. 178, citing WHT, June 20, 1972 [Haldeman/RN 4:35 P.M.–5:25 P.M.]; (evening call Mitchell) R, Summ. of Inf., p. 38, R, Stmt. of Inf., BK. II, p. 310; (Dictabelt "tapered with") "First Conversations Concerning the Break-in," p. 7, folder 53A.2, Nixon Memoranda, WSPF, NA; (no tapes of 4 calls) ibid., p. 2; Emery, op. cit., p. 508n32, R, Stmt. of Inf., BK II, p. 244; ("A lot of people think . . . anti-Castro Cubans") Haldeman with DiMona, op. cit., p. 24.

Rebozo and Watergate: (name came up) WHT, June 21 [3 times], June 22 [twice]; *AOP*, pp. 52, 57, 61, 63, 65; ("Is Rebozo safe?") ibid., p. 65 and monitored for author; (lines to Barker/Martinez) Hinckle and Turner, op. cit., pp. 338, 352; ed. Weissman, op. cit., p. 258; eds. Scott, Hoch, and Stetler, op. cit., p. 395; (Ameritas as cover) Watergate Hotel booking records May 26–28, 1972 and refs. to bookings, June 10–19, 1972, police report, June 20, 1972, James Hougan Collection and testimony of Miguel Suarez, *U.S. v. Liddy et al.*, re: Manger Hamilton Hotel booking record, Michael Ewing Collection, *NM*, p. 197–.

"no involvement . . . this particular incident": Emery, op. cit., p. 186.

Cover-up: (get FBI "turned off") WHT, June 21, 1972; *AOP*, p. 50; ("You can't cover this") WHT, June 30, 1972; *AOP*, p. 89; ("The worst thing") WHT, July 19, 1972; *AOP*, p. 93; ("cover-up . . . hurts you") WHT, Sep. 11, 1972; *AOP*, p. 138; ("A cover-up . . . main ingredient") WHT, Feb. 14, 1973, conv. no. 855-010.

June 23, 1972 tape: (FBI one step away) R, Summ. of Inf., p. 39, and Emery, op. cit., p. 186–; (Haldeman offers solution) WHT, June 23, 1972 [2 convs.]; *AOP*, p. 67–; ("All right, fine") ibid., p. 68; ("You call them in") ibid., p. 69; ("no problem") ibid., p. 70; ("time bomb") WHT, June 29, 1972; *AOP*, p. 76.

RN/tape peril: ("complicates things") WHT, June 20, 1972; *AOP*, p. 48.

RN needing rest: ("trying to get rest") RN address to nation, Apr. 30, 1973, *Historical Documents,* 1973, Washington, D.C.: Congressional Quarterly, 1974; (time at Key Biscayne, Camp David, San Clemente) June 2–5, June 7–9, June 28–29, July 1–18, 1973; *HD,* CD; (aides blame fatigue) Osborne, *Watch 4,* op. cit., p. 106; ("According to associates") ibid.; (vist to Capitol) McCarthy with Smith, op. cit., p. 21–; (Campbell) int. Lou Campbell.

RN in control of campaign: McClendon, op. cit., p. 275; int. Elliot Richardson in eds. Miller Center, op. cit., p. 56; Barry Goldwater with Jack Casserly, *Goldwater,* Garden City, NY: Doubleday, 1988, p. 261; ed. Miller, *Breaking of the President,* Vol.5, p. 573, citing Robert Mardian.

little public consciousness: (Gallup) Manchester, *Glory & Dream,* op. cit., p. 1287; (Woodward/Bernstein) Barry Sussman, *The Great Cover-Up,* Arlington, VA: Seven Locks Press, 1992, p. 59–; *NM,* p. 274; (Nelson) *LAT,* Oct. 5, 1972, with Ron Ostrow, he obtained an early exclusive in interviewing Alfred Baldwin.

RN on popular reaction to Watergate: ("I think the country") WHT, June 21, 1972; *AOP*, p. 54; ("don't give a shit about repression") ibid., p. 59; ("average guy") WHT, Sep. 8, 1972; *AOP*, p. 136; ("chicken shit") WHT, May 1, 1973; *AOP*, p. 392.

crimes/plotting continue: ("There should be rifling") WHT, July 1, 1972; *AOP*, p. 90; *WP*, Feb. 15, 1997; (Lungren break-in) Dr. John Lungren affidavit, Nov. 2, 1973, E, Bk. 12, p. 5065–; (Haldeman aide called) Felt, op. cit., p. 223, and Acting FBI Director Patrick Gray testimony, May 31, 1973, Inquiry into the Alleged Involvement of the CIA in the Watergate and Ellsberg Matters, Special Subcttee. on Intelligence, Cttee. on Armed Services, U.S. Hse. of Reps., 94th Cong., 1st Sess., p. 239.

getting at Democrats/O'Brien persisted: ("still talking in those terms") int. Jeb Magruder; eds. Strober, *Nixon,* op. cit., p. 355; Magruder, op. cit., p. 37–; (Fontaineblue bugging?) transcript, *NBC Nightly News,* Oct. 4, 1973, press files, Box 16, WSPF, NA; (groundwork) Schorr, op. cit., p. 14fn; (Gerstein office break-in) *Miami News,* Aug. 28, 1972; (Strauss break-in) AP, June 3, 1973; Robert Strauss deposition, May 29, 1973, *DNC v. McCord et al.,* Civic Action 1233-72, U.S. District Court, DC; ("Go gung-ho") *Atlantic Monthly,* June 1989; ("What, if anything?") WHT, Aug. 3, 1972; *AOP*, p. 113; ("Get everything") WHT, Sep. 8, 1972; *AOP*, p. 136; (tried hard) Roger Barth testimony, June 6, 1974, E, Bk. 23, p. 11223, Aug. 27, 28, 1972 entries, *HD* CD, R, Bk. VIII, pp. 334, 337, 345; Johnnie Walters affidavit, June 10, 1974, R, Summary Inf., pp. 142, 222; Reston, op. cit., p. 448; (unlawfully) R, Bk. VIII, p. 28; ("send him to jail") John Ehrlichman testimony, Feb. 8, 1974, R, Bk. VIII, p. 225; ("cleanest campaign") Pat Buchanan memo, Nov. 15, 1972, President's Office File, Box 90, NP, NA.

Democratic convention: (disaster) *TW72,* p. 158; Boller, op. cit., p. 334–.

Eagleton: (crisis) *TW72,* p. 193; Schoenbaum, op. cit., p. 178–; ed. Bruce Westley, *Journalism Monographs,* 35, Aug. 1974, p. 1–; (RN letter) *MEM,* p. 663–; ("Supposing") *TW72,* p. 201; (Deep Throat/Eagleton) Bernstein and Woodward, *Men,* op. cit., pp. 133, 316, Bradlee, *Good Life,* op. cit., p. 333; (CREEP plant) *NM,* pp. 162–, 168; (overheard discussion) St. Louis *Post-Dispatch,* June 24, 1973; (Ehrlichman had possession) Bernstein and Woodward, *Men,* op. cit., p. 316– and see WHT, May 17, 1973; *AOP*, p. 521; ("Haldeman once intimated") int. Alexander Butterfield; in eds. Strober, *Nixon,* op. cit., p. 266; (RN/Haldeman on exploiting) WHT, July 26, 1972; *AOP*, p. 106–; (McGovern on Eagleton drink/sedatives) eds. Strober, *Nixon,* op. cit., p. 265.

Republican Convention: (background) *TW72,* p. 239; ("Everything was scheduled") Cannon, op. cit., p. 126; (Ehrlichman praised) Dickerson, op. cit., p. 201; (Movies) ibid., p. 200, *TW72,* p. 244; ibid., p. 200, *TW72,* p. 244; (podium) Spear, op. cit., p. 181; ("join our majority") *TW72,* p. 243; (Gallup) *WP,* Aug. 30, 1972.

'72 election: (results) *TW72,* p. 341–; ("preoccupied") *WP,* Apr. 23, 1994; (tooth snapped) *MEM,* p. 715; (RN/music) ibid.; *PAT,* p. 352; (with Colson) Colson, op. cit., p. 7–; ("good feeling shattered") Kissinger, *White House Years,* op. cit., p. 1406; (resignations) ibid.; Richard Nathan, *The Plot That Failed: Nixon & the Administrative Presidency,* New York: Wiley, 1975, p. 63; Hillings, op. cit., p. 163; ("maniacal") Kissinger, *White House Years,* op. cit., p. 1407; ("1984") Colson, op. cit., p. 79.

Christmas bombing: (background) *Historical Documents,* 1973, Washington, D.C.: Congressional Quarterly, 1974, p. 115, and see Karnow, op. cit., p. 65, 651–; ("peace at hand") Kissinger, *White House Years,* op. cit., p. 1399; (Nixon wanted resolution) Karnow, op. cit., p. 666; ("any terms") Kissinger, *White House Years,* op. cit., p. 1446–; ("The P said . . . rather bomb Monday") Dec. 15, 1972 entry, *HD,* p. 556; (offensive described) Hersh, *Price of Power,* op. cit., p. 621; Karnow, op. cit., p. 667–, *U.S. News & World Report,* Feb. 5, 1973; ("win war") *MEM,* p. 734; ("Brutality nothing") Kissinger, *White House Years,* op. cit., p. 1469; ("peace with honor") address to the nation, Jan. 23, 1973, *Historical Documents,* 1973, Washington, D.C.: Congressional Quarterly, 1974, p. 117; ("have it break with a year") *MEM,* citing RN diary, p. 734; (N. Viet. troops remained) Nixon, *Real Peace,* op. cit., p. 284; ("biggest flaw") Crowley, *Winter,* op. cit., p. 256; (RN would insist) Nixon, *Real Peace,* op. cit., p. 278; Crowley, *Winter,* op. cit., pp. 256, 261–; ("stupid") ibid., p. 256; ("won war") ibid. and Nixon, *Real Peace,* op. cit., p. 278.

RN state of mind during bombing: (Churchill on mind) *MEM,* p. 736; ("most difficult/heartrending") *MEM,* pp. 734, 735; ("This is Dec. 24") ibid., p. 739; ("terrible personal ordeal") transcript of RN Apr. 30, 1973 address, in ed. Edward Knappman, *Watergate & the White House,* New York: Facts on File, 1973, Apr.–May, 1973, p. 37; (ordeal in private) *PAT,* p. 354, Dec. 20, 1972–Jan. 1, 1973 entries, *HD, CD;* Hersh, *Price of Power,* op. cit., p. 629; ("into hiding") Thomas, *Dateline,* op. cit., p. 145; ("withdrawn/hostility") Kissinger, *White House Years,* op. cit., p. 1149; (press views) *MEM,* p. 738; (Saxbe) ed. Schoenebaum, op. cit., p. 569; ("throwing stuff") Hersh, *Price of Power,* op. cit., p. 622; ("did not care") Richard Wilson note, cited in Thomas Hughes article, *Atlantic Monthly,* Oct. 1974.

"awesome power": Oct. 16, 1972 entry, *HD, CD.*

"I want the most comprehensive": WHT, Sep. 15, 1972, conv. 779-002, WSPF, NA.

extend presidency?: (getting brother, etc. to run) Dec. 10, 1972 entry, *HD,* p. 552; (Dean/Zeifman) Zeifman, op. cit., p. 49; ("to mountaintop") *Life,* Dec. 1979; ("intended to control") Magruder, *Power to Peace,* op. cit., p. 31; (choice as successor) Goldwater, *Apologies,* op. cit., p. 248; Lee Edwards, *Goldwater,* Washington, D.C.: Regnery, 1995, p. 389; Cannon, op. cit., pp. 124–, 136–, 182–, 210–; ints. Charles Young and John Galbraith by FB, FBP.

RN state of mind late '72: ("troubled man") int. James Keogh in eds. Miller Center, op. cit., p. 207; ("strange shudder") Ehrlichman, op. cit., p. 331; ("strange dream") WHT, July 20, 1972; *AOP,* p. 101.

Chapter 32

"We kept one step . . .": WHT, Apr. 26, 1973, transcribed for author.

'73 inaugural: (events) *MEM,* p. 751; *LAT, WP,* Jan. 20, 1973; *NYT, LAT, WP,* Jan. 21, 1973; *Radical History Review,* fall 1994, p. 138; Dickerson, op. cit., p. 199; (Bork) int. Robert Bork by FB, FBP; ("some jerk") *Rolling Stone,* Sep. 8, 1994 and see *MEM,* p. 753; (jurors watch) *NYT,* Jan. 21, 1973.

hush money: (payments method) R, Summary of Information, p. 52, E, Final Report, p. 51; Ben-Veniste and Frampton, op. cit., p. 53–; (RN re: "myth") *Time,* Apr. 2, 1990; (RN stated flatly) RN statement, May 22, 1973, R, Hearings, Bk. I, p. 39 and see RN statement, Aug. 15, 1973; Evan Drossman and Edward Knappman, eds., *Watergate & the White House,* Vol. 2, New York: Facts on File, 1974, p. 40– and RN address, transcript, Apr. 29, 1974; eds. Drossman and Knappman, *supra.,* Vol. 3, p. 101; ("It's worth it") WHT, Aug. 1, 1972, transcribed for author; ("Goddamn hush money") WHT, Jan. 8, 1973, in Bob Woodward and Scott Armstrong article, *WP,* May 1, 1977; ("We could get that") WHT, Mar. 21, 1973, prepared by R, Rec. Grp. 460, WSPF, NA, pp. 62–, 93; (Pappas/tapes) WHT, Mar. 2, 7, 21, 1973 May 23, June 6, 1973; *AOP,* pp. 217–, 225–, 544–, 580–, Apr. 26, 1973, Conv. No. 905–008 & 905–009, WSPF, NA.

RN tried to use Johnson '68 bugging: WHT, June 17, July 1, 1972, transcribed for author, Sep. 15, Oct. 17, Nov. 3, 1973 and Jan. 8, 11, Feb. 6, 1973; *AOP,* also WHT, Mar. 1, 1973, Conv. No. 866-003, WSPF, NA, p. 8, Nov. 2, 3, 4, 1972, Jan. 8, 11, 12, 1973, *HD, CD,* and Haldeman testimony, Aug. 1, 1973, E, Bk. 8, p. 3204–, and John Dean testimony, June 25, 1973; (Haldeman note) H. R. "Bob" Haldeman note, Jan. 12, 1973, Haldeman Papers, NP, NA; (diary entry) Jan. 12, 1973 entry, *HD, CD;* (returned to idea) WHT, Feb. 6, 1973 (two convs.), *AOP,* p. 207–.

Patman: (probe) int. Jake Lewis, *Washington Monthly,* Apr. 1973; *WP,* June 13, 1982; ("very smart fellow"/"get off asses") WHT, Sep. 15, 1972, Conv. No. 779-002, WSPF, NA, pp. 30, 38–.

Post: ("damnable problems") WHT, Sept. 15, 1972, *supra.*, p. 35; (TV licenses) Miami *Herald,* Jan. 6, 1970; ints. Sloan McCrae, Cromwell Anderson, WHT, Aug. 9, 1972; *AOP,* p. 126; Katharine Graham, *Personal History,* New York: Alfred Knopf, 1997, pp. 387, 479–, 497; int. Ben Bradlee in "Watergate: The Secret Story," June 17, 1992, transcript p. 17; Spear, op. cit., p. 133; ("tit in wringer") Bernstein and Woodward, *Men,* op. cit., p. 105; (wringer/breast on neck) Bradlee, *Life,* op. cit., p. 330fn.

Kennedy "holding action": Bernstein and Woodward, op. cit., p. 247; ("thugs") ibid. , p. 260.

Decision on Sen. Probe: Sam Ervin, *Preserving the Constitution,* Charlottesville, VA: Michie, 1984, p. 318; Dabney, op. cit., p. 261.

RN and Ervin Committee: ("I don't see") WHT, Feb. 6, 1973; *AOP,* p. 207; ("old fart") WHT, May 29, 1973, *AOP,* p. 559; ("old shit"/"unpatriotic") WHT, June 2, 1973; *AOP,* p. 565; ("asshole"/"ass") WHT, July 12, 1973; *AOP,* pp. 629, 635; (Baker "off reservation") WHT, Mar. 16, 1973; *AOP,* p. 231; ("destroy . . . chances") ibid., p. 232; ("flaw") ibid., p. 232; ("simpering") WHT, July 12, 1973; *AOP,* p. 631; ("never W. Hse. Again") WHT, ibid.; *AOP,* p. 633–; ("hotshots") WHT, Mar. 16, 1973; *AOP,* p. 231; (Weicker & higher-ups) Mar. 25, 26, 27, 1973 entries, *HD,* CD; ("We've got to play") WHT, Mar. 30, 1973; *AOP,* p. 290; (RN raging) Apr. 1, 2, 4, 17, 18, 19, 1973, *HD,* CD; (break-in) "The Unsolved Break-Ins," by Robert Fink, *Congressional Record,* Oct. 9, 1974; ("only friend") WHT, July 12, 1973, *AOP,* p. 631; (Gurney supporters) Miami *Herald,* July 2, 1973, *WP,* July 3, 1973; Colson friend was Charles Morin; (Gurney posture) "Nixon's Man on the Watergate Panel: Sen. Edward Gurney of Florida," *Today's Speech,* Fall, 1975, p. 7–; ("If the many allegations") E, Bk. 1, p. 1–.

Crack-up in spring: well chronicled in Emery, op. cit., p. 249–.

Dean defection: ("skillful"/"finger in dikes") WHT, Sep. 15, 1972; *AOP,* p. 148; ("innocent accomplice") WHT, Mar. 27, 1973; *AOP,* p. 265; (Dean testimony) E, Bk. 3, p. 911–, Bk. 4, p. 1348–; (effect) summary at Emery, op. cit., p. 363–; (Goddamn him") WHT, May 8, 1973; *AOP,* p. 407; ("Judas") WHT, June 13, 1973; *AOP,* p. 606.

Mitchell: ("protect him") WHT, Feb. 3, 1973; *AOP,* p. 206; (Ehrlichman—"jig up") WHT, Apr. 14, 1973, Conv. No. 428-019, WSPF, NA, p. 26–; (told Haldeman) Emery, op. cit., p. 346, citing Haldeman note, Apr. 17, 1973; (Martha/"espionage operation") McClendon, op. cit., pp. 11–, 222–.

Apr. 17 statement: Edward Knappman, *Watergate & the White House,* Vol. 1, New York: Facts on File, 1973, p. 29; (hands shaking) Bernstein and Woodward, *Men,* op. cit., p. 291.

Haldeman/Ehrlichman resignations: (Justice Dept. advice) Emery, op. cit., p. 341; ("no running room") Garment, op. cit., p. 259–; (day of resignations) Haldeman with DiMona, op. cit., p. 289–; Ehrlichman, op. cit., p. 356–; *MEM,* p. 847–; (RN crying) Ehrlichman, op. cit., p. 367; int. John Ehrlichman in "Nixon," *American Experience,* WGBH–TV, Oct. 15, 1990, transcript p. 37; ("really guilty one") *HD,* p. 672; (RN shook hand) ibid.; (RN call/misspelling) int. John Ehrlichman.

Post **firings speech/aftermath:** (text) transcript, Apr. 30, 1973, in ed. Knappman, op. cit., Vol. 1, p. 37; (wan) *Newsweek,* May 14, 1973; (retreat to Lincoln Sitting Room) *PAT,* p. 369; (calls later) WHT, Apr. 30, 1973, with Haldeman, Rogers, Billy Graham, Elliott Richardson, Hobart Lewis, Charles Colson, *AOP,* p. 381 and monitored for author re: sound of voice/drunk.

Liquor/pills Apr. 1973: int. John Dean, Dean, *Blind Ambition,* op. cit., p. 258; John Dean at "An American Forum," American University School of Communications, Jan. 31, 1996, forum re: Oliver Stone film *Nixon;* (Dilantin) Dreyfus, op. cit., p. 218; int. Jack Dreyfus.

Concern for months: ("eyes seemed") Thomas, *Dateline,* op. cit., p. 192; ("tremor") John Osborne, *The Fifth Year of the Nixon Watch,* New York, Liveright, 1974, p. 45; (man in distress) McCarthy and Smith, op. cit., p. 19–; ("agitated") Kissinger, *Upheaval,* op. cit., p. 75; ("Good God") WHT, Apr. 27, 1973, transcribed for author; ("Ron, it's over") int. Ronald Ziegler; (shoved FBI man) Klein, op. cit., p. 354; Kleindienst, op. cit., p. 169; ("No sooner") ibid.; (RN/Key Biscayne) Woodward and Bernstein, *Final Days,* op. cit., p. 16; (P.O.W. dinner) *MEM,* p. 865–; Troy, op. cit., p. 200; *Radical History Review,* Fall 1994, p. 186.

RN lying: (CIA psychologists) *New Times,* June 25, 1976, citing former CIA technical service division psychologist Jim Keehner; (Scott) UPI, Dec. 9, 1974; Stanley Kutler, *Wars of Watergate,* New York: Knopf, 1990, p. 270; ("just be damned sure") WHT, Mar. 21, 1973; transcript for R, Box 171, Rec. Grp., 480, NA, p. 102; ("I don't lie") WHT, Apr. 25, 1973, *AOP,* p. 339; ("lie like hell") WHT, Apr. 26, 1973, Conv. No. 905–008, WSPF, NA, transcript, p. 47; ("anemone") Ehrlichman, op. cit., p. 308; ("I began to feel") int. John Ehrlichman in eds. Miller Center, op. cit., p. 138.

Resignation talk 1973: ("we'll even consider") WHT, Apr. 17–18, 1973; *AOP,* p. 321; ("put in next draft") Price, op. cit., p. 100–; Cannon, op. cit., p.157; (resignation/family) *PAT,* p. 372; *SF Examiner,* Sep. 4, 1974; ("cat in Kool-aid") Ehrlichman, op. cit., p. 353; int. John Ehrlichman.

Defiance: ("totally blameless") WHT, May 11, 1973; *AOP,* p. 474; ("I wouldn't give a damn") WHT, May 16, 1973; *AOP,* p. 503; ("I came away feeling") *Newsweek,* May 28, 1973.

RN inattention/distraction: Kissinger, *Upheaval,* op. cit., pp. 78, 322–; ("disintegration"/"Like a figure") ibid., p. 105; ("to concede . . . impaired") ibid., p. 289; ("deprived") ibid., p. 263; (RN snapped) Osborne, *Watch5,* op. cit., p. 118; ("By the end") Kissinger, *Upheaval,* op. cit., p. 300.

Cox appointment: WSPF Report, Oct. 1975.

Impeachment foreseen: (impeachment defined) R, "Impeachment, Selected Materials," p. 705; ("The time is going") Breslin, op. cit., p. 12; O'Neill, op. cit., p. 242; (Rodino present) O'Neill, op. cit., p. 242; Breslin, op. cit., p. 13; ("just in case") Zeifman, op. cit., pp. 32, 40.

Ervin/RN call: Sam Ervin, Jr., *The Whole Truth,* New York: Random House, 1980, p. 209; Sam Dash, *Chief Counsel,* New York: Random House, 1976, p. 168–; ints. Sam Dash, Rufus Edmisten.

Tapes discovered: ("Frankly, I don't want) WHT, Apr. 9, 1973; *AOP,* p. 292; (ordering change) WHT, Apr. 9, 1973; *AOP,* p. 297–; *WP,* Oct. 30, 1997; (A week later) *WP,* Oct. 30, 1997; ("I don't think it should ever get out") WHT, Apr. 26, 1973, Conv. No. 905-008, WSPF, NA, transcript, p. 31; *NYT,* May 1, 1977, citing Apr. 27, 1973 conv; (Butterfield reveals) *Journal of American History,* Mar. 1989, p. 1222–; int. Alexander Butterfield, June 30, 1974; *People,* May 19, 1975; int. Scott Armstrong; (Dean's tape suspicions) John Dean testimony, June 25, 1973, E, Bk. 3, p. 1016–; (RN appalled) *MEM,* p. 900; ("You dirty bastard") *NM,* p. 461; (Democrats hastened) *MEM,* p. 900; (Kennedy Library) Richard Burke with William and Marilyn Hoffer, *The Senator,* New York: St. Martin's Press, 1992, p. 36–; (discuss what to do) *MEM,* p. 900; ("Should have destroyed") *MEM,* p. 901; ("I know what I did") *JA,* p. 500, citing Alexander Haig; (tape releases) int. Pat Andersen, archivist; ("absolute power") Schlesinger, *Imperial Presidency,* op. cit., p. 271–; ("Unlike monarch") ibid., p. 272.

RN mental condition summer '73: ("Do you think . . . mentally ill?") June 27, 1973 entry, taped diary of James Doyle provided to author; (Elfin) *Newsweek,* June 18, 1973; int. Mel Elfin by FB, FBP; ("relaxed & confident") New Orleans *Times–Picayune,* Aug. 21, 1973; (shoving incident) *NYT Week in Review,* Aug. 26, 1973; Rather with Herskowitz, op. cit., p. 243–; int. Ronald Ziegler; (drunk?) Osborne, *Watch5,* op. cit., p. 135; ("uppers") Herbers, op. cit., p. 92; ("Sullivan on speed") *Newsweek,* Sep. 3, 1973; (not on medication) *NYT Week in Review,* Aug. 26, 1973; Herbers, op. cit., p.92; (seeing psychiatrist?) ibid., p. 90; int. John Herbers; (Hutschnecker letter) Dr. Arnold Hutschnecker to RN, July 3, 1973, "Material Removed from President's Desk," Pres. Personal File, Box 188, NP, NA; (reporters armed with photos) Herbers, op. cit., p. 93; (Hutshnecker in *NYT) NYT,* July 4, 1973; ("Millions of us") *WP,* Aug. 24, 1973; (*Star-News*/presidents' illness) Washington *Star-News,* Aug. 31, 1973; ("that thing"/"main fear") Dabney, op. cit., p. 261–.

RN/Kissinger relationship late '73: ("Haig is keeping") int. Mel Elfin by FB, FBP; (RN not attend) Edward Rowny, *It Takes One to Tango,* McLean, VA: Brassey's, 1992, p. 59.

Middle East War start: (RN not one mtg.) Elmo Zumwalt, *On Watch,* Arlington, VA: Adm. Zumwalt & Associates, 1976, p. 434; (RN clear on essentials/"preoccupied") Kissinger, *Upheaval,* op. cit., p. 495; ("anti-Semitic bastard") Max Lerner, "Eros and Power," *Playboy,* Nov. 1978.

Agnew resignation: (charges) Washington *Star-News,* Oct. 11, 1973; Richard Cohen and Jules Witcover, *A Heartbeat Away,* New York: Viking, 1974, Chapter 4–; (RN letter) ibid. , p. 356; ("mortal enemy") Agnew, op. cit., p. 189; (feared being killed) ibid. and int. by Helen Dudar, *WP,* Apr. 20, 1980.

Murders feared: ("Everyone's life") Bernstein and Woodward, *Men,* op. cit., p. 317; int. Carl Bernstein; (threat to Dean) Dash, op. cit., p. 161; Providence [RI] *Journal,* May 16, 1974; Zeifman, op. cit., p. 50; Dean, *Blind Ambition,* op. cit., p. 271; ints. John Dean, Sam Dash; (Ervin) int. Sam Dash; (Cox) Ken Gormley, *Archibald Cox,* Reading, MA: Perseus, 1997, p. 279; (danger to burglars) int. Andrew St. George (re: fear for Al Baldwin), int. Charles Colson by Jim Hougan (discussion of Frank Sturgis's fear), in Hougan Collection, and see Liddy, op. cit., pp. 419–, 455 (re: thoughts of killing Hunt, Dean); (McCord bomb threat) McCord, op. cit., p. 36; ("if the administration") James McCord testimony, E, Bk. 1, p. 141, summary of McCord deposition, Dec. 17, 1981 (431–435) in Rothblatt Papers; (Russell death) Hougan, *Agenda,* op. cit., p. 306.

RN and congressional leadership: (acting . . . strange") O'Neill, op. cit., p. 253; Breslin, op. cit., p. 66–.

Ford ceremony: Dickerson, op. cit., p. 208; Kissinger, *Upheaval,* op. cit., p. 511; *WP,* editorial, Oct. 14, 1973; ("most repellent") *NYT,* Oct. 15, 1973; ("wallowing") Robert Hartmann, *Palace Politics,* New York: McGraw-Hill, 1980, p. 26; ("Can you imagine?") Kutler, *Wars,* op. cit., p. 419; ("disintegrating") Kissinger, *Upheaval,* op. cit., p. 511.

Cox firing: (planning removal) *MEM*, p. 928–; Kissinger, *Upheaval*, op. cit., p. 535; (Cox/Harvard/Kennedys) ibid., p. 910; ("We can get rid of") int. Elliot Richardson by James Doyle, Doyle Collection, provided to author; ("The FBI just entered") Zeifman, op. cit., p. 59; (Bork/dismissal letter) Doyle, op. cit., p. 192–; (staff hurried) ibid., p. 195–; (tapes smuggled out) ibid. fn. and p. 165–; ints. James Doyle, Carl Feldbaum—Feldbaum's wife got the tapes out; (Rebozo admitted) Memo re: "Rebozo's Credibility," Box B 135, E, NA; ("Constitutional crisis" etc.) *MEM*, p. 935; *AMIII*, p. 249–; (Gallup) ibid., p. 250; ("miscalculation") *MEM*, p. 935–.

Kissinger to Moscow: (RN "driven") Kissinger, *Upheaval*, op. cit., p. 543; ("get off my back") ibid., p. 552.

Oct. 24 alert crisis: (Kissinger account) Kissinger, *Upheaval*, op. cit., p. 581–; (principal concern) ibid.; (RN "upstairs drunk') Morris, *Haig*, op. cit., p. 257; ("tired") Alexander Haig with Charles McCarry, *Inner Circles*, New York: Warner, 1992, p. 416; int. Alexander Haig; ("I will say it straight") Kissinger, *Upheaval*, op. cit., p. 583; ("should I wake up") ibid., p. 585; (another discussion with Haig) ibid., p. 586; (DefCon decision) ibid., p. 587–; Zumwalt, op. cit., p. 443; "On the Brink: Doomsday" TV documentary for The Learning Channel, Towers Productions, transcript, p. 37–; *Newsweek* Nov. 5, 1973; (stern reply) Kissinger, *Upheaval*, op. cit., p. 591; (RN "clear-headed & crisp") ibid., p. 593; (RN lecture/Dr. Morgan) O'Neill, op. cit., p. 254, and see Kissinger, *Upheaval*, op. cit., p. 593; (physician) Uniontown [PA] *Herald-Standard*, Jan. 26, 1976; *NYT*, Aug. 2, 1995; (tell press "indispensable") ibid., p. 598; ("the most serious thing") Haig, op. cit., p. 415; (Zumwalt recalled) Zumwalt, op. cit., p. 444–; (RN not mentioned) ibid., p. 448; ("The reason we had to") int. Elmo Zumwalt; (Haig put up") ints. James Schlesinger, 1997 and 2000 (the latter for the BBC/History Channel); (advisers wondered) Kissinger, *Upheaval*, op. cit., p. 589.

Disney World: (points covered) Boston *Herald-American*, Dec. 4, 1973; *Newsweek*, Nov. 26, 1973; ("not a crook") excerpts of exchange with press, Drossman and Knappman, eds., op. cit., Vol. 2, p. 117; ("couple of belts") terHorst and Albertazzie, op. cit., p. 261–.

RN condition: (Bork) int. Robert Bork by FB, FBP; (Kelley) Kutler, *Wars of Watergate*, op. cit., p. 437; (Simon) Woodward and Bernstein, *The Final Days*, op. cit., p. 101.

Goldwater on dinner: Goldwater with Casserly, op. cit., p. 266–; Goldberg, op. cit., p. 278.

RN and Joint Chiefs: int. Elmo Zumwalt, Zumwalt, op. cit., p. 459–; *Atlantic Monthly*, Aug. 1983—Zumwalt acknowledged to author he was the "four-star officer" referred to in the latter; President Nixon's daily diary, Dec. 13, 22, 1973, Boxes FC-41 and RC-13, NP, NA.

RN family Christmas: (low spirits) *PAT*, p. 395; (Yankee Stadium) Edmondsen and Cohen, op. cit., p. 110–; (Julie appearance) *McCall's*, Feb. 1974; (Will) Dallas *Morning News*, Apr. 26, 1994; (San Clemente flight) *PAT*, p. 396; (4 weekends) Elizabeth Drew, *Washington Journal*, New York: Random House, 1974, p. 138; (diplomat) David, op. cit., p. 168; (agents to Pat's aide) ints. Lou Campbell; (Pat drinking) int. Mark Barnett citing the late John Ehrlichman; (resignation discussed/notepad) *MEM*, p. 970, *PAT*, 397–.

Chapter 33

"I suppose inevitable": journal entry for July 29, 1974, kindly provided to author by Jerome Waldie.

"mirrors/smoke": Breslin, op. cit., p. 33.

"I convinced myself": *MEM*, p. 976.

State of Union: ibid., p. 978–, eds. Knappman and Drossman, op. cit., Vol. 3, p. 21.

Investigations' momentum: (Jaworski) *NM*, p. 446–; Ben-Veniste and Frampton, op. cit., p. 187–; Emery, op. cit., p. 421; (Jaworski stunned) ibid., p. 420; ("psychopaths around him") Jan. 10, 1974 entry, James Doyle taped diary, provided to author; ("something missing") ibid., Feb. 20, 1974 entry; ("RN culpably involved") Emery, op. cit., p. 420, citing Jaworski oral history; ("get finest . . . lawyers") ibid., p. 422.

Impeachment: (Judiciary Cttee process) R, Report, p. 6; (Rodham) Zeifman, op. cit., p. 11–.

Longworth party: Dickerson, op. cit., p. 213, eds. Knappman and Drossman, op. cit., Vol. 3, p. 23.

Colleagues depart: (Haldeman/Ehrlichman charges) WSPF Report, pp. 155, 157; (Klein) Schoenebaum, op. cit., p. 359; (Laird) Schoenebaum, op. cit., p. 371; (Harlow) int. Bryce Harlow in eds. Miller Center, op. cit., p. 21; *WP*, Feb. 18, 1987; (Chotiner death) *WP*, Jan. 27, 1974; *NYT*, Jan. 31, 1974; Hillings with Seelye, op. cit., p. 124, int. Nancy Chotiner; ("ally . . . friend") *WP*, Jan. 31, 1974; ("almost incommunicado") int. Bryce Harlow in eds. Miller Center, op. cit., p. 21; (Ziegler) Zumwalt, op. cit., p. 479.

Colleagues face trial: (Krogh) WSPF Report, p. 157; (Kalmbach) ibid., p. 161; (Colson) ibid., p. 157; (Magruder) ibid., p. 156; (Mitchell) ibid.; (Chapin) ibid., p. 162; (Dean) ibid., p. 155; (Haldeman/Ehrlichman) ibid., p. 155; (14 associates) ibid., p. 155–.

Grand jury/"unindicted co-conspirator": (letter to RN) Kutler, *Wars of Watergate,* op. cit., p. 445; (juror ints.) *SF Chronicle,* June 19, 1982, citing *20/20* program, and int. Vladimir Pregelj, jury foreman; (21-page memo) Carl Feldbaum, George Frampton, Gerald Goldman, Peter Rient to Leon Jaworski, "Recommendations for Action by the Watergate Grand Jury," Feb. 12, 1974, WSPF, NA; int. Carl Feldbaum; (details of jury episode) Ben-Veniste and Frampton, op. cit., p. 211–; Doyle, op. cit., pp. 270–, 308–; *NM,* pp. 476, 480, 495; ("stopped beating wife") *NM,* p. 476.

Pat and daughters early 1974: ("hasn't done wrong") Boston *Herald Examiner,* citing *McCall's,* Jan. 22, 1974; ("She seemed emaciated") Rabbi Baruch Korff diary note, Apr. 11, 1974, provided to author by Zamira Korff; ("We do believe") *Ladies' Home Journal,* Apr. 1974; ("Nixon came out") int. Norman Casper; (Pat pain) John Osborne, *The Last Nixon Watch,* Washington, D.C.: New Republic Book Co., 1975, p. 81; (Grand Opry) Helen McCain Smith article, *Good Housekeeping,* July 1976, and see *PAT,* p. 404; ("He never ate") int. Robert Keith Gray.

April transcript release: ("Any more") *MEM,* p. 994; (transcript process/TV appearance) *NM,* p. 483–; (troubling discrepancies) WHT, Mar. 22, 1973, in eds. *The New York Times, The White House Transcripts,* New York: Bantam, 1974, p. 208, and R, Transcripts of Eight Recorded Presidential Conversations, p. 164; (at RN's behest) *NM,* p. 483–; (Ford previously) Hartmann, op. cit., p. 103; ("The time has come") ibid., p. 120, citing Eastern Illinois University address; ("deplorable") *NM,* p. 491; ("The thing that hurt") int. Sen. Barry Goldwater, *Newsweek,* May 27, 1974; (Judiciary Cttee. Reaction) *NM* p. 493–.

Rumors: (Phoenix hospital) May 9, 1974 entry, taped journal of James Doyle, provided to author, and see *MEM,* p. 996; (resignation rumors) ibid.; *NM,* p. 507; (walk on water) Bauer with Leighton, op. cit., p. 154.

Phlebitis: (difficult to walk) Szulc, *Illusion,* op. cit., p. 773—re: limp on departure; (Haig Salzburg) Haig with McGarry, op. cit., p. 458; *MEM,* p. 1010; (flouting advice) Haig with McGarry, op. cit., p. 459; ("I thought I would die") ints. Arnold Hutschnecker; (physician worried agent commented) Korff, op. cit., p. 51, Woodward and Bernstein, *Final Days,* op. cit., p. 233–; (plunged crowds/open cars) ibid.; Rush, op. cit., p. 186; ("impeachment diplomacy") *NM,* p. 505; ("beyond hoping") Kissinger, *Upheaval,* op. cit., p. 1124; ("sadness all about") Osborne, *Last Watch,* op. cit., p. 150; ("We sensed") Kissinger, *Upheaval,* op. cit., p. 1142.

Rebozo: ("Christopher") Thomas, *Dateline* op. cit., p. 144; ("You betta") Miami *Herald,* June 18, 1974.

Soviet trip: Kissinger, *Upheaval,* op. cit., p. 1151–; *MEM,* p. 1023–; ("since little girl") ibid., p. 1033; ("in a daze") Thomas, *Dateline* op. cit., p. 212; ("No mention Watergate") int. Viktor Sukhodrev in eds. Strober, *Nixon,* op. cit., p. 168; ("the biggest obstacle") Kissinger, *Upheaval,* op. cit., p. 1163–.

RN lost form: (stumbled statistics) *AMIII,* p. 373; (meet in car) *MEM,* p. 1027; (careless) Oleg Gordievsky, cited in Andrew, op. cit., p. 394.

Foreign affairs slippage: (Portugal coup/India test/Colby) Andrew, op. cit., p.393–; 603n181; (Cyprus crisis) Kissinger, *Upheaval,* op. cit., p. 1190–; (only 6 days) White, *Breach,* op. cit., p. 306; (Dean/Watergate traffic) Szulc, *Illusion,* op. cit., p. 796; ("in no position") Kissinger, *Upheaval,* op. cit., p. 1191.

"Ever since . . . something lost": *MEM,* p. 1049.

Committee releases: (Sen. Cttee) WP, July 14, 1974—the Final Report eventually made available is 1,250 pages long; ("tragic happenings") E, Final Report, p. xxiii; (Judiciary Cttee) eds. Staff of the *NYT, The End of a Presidency,* New York: Bantam, 1974, p. 267; Woodward and Bernstein, *The Final Days,* op. cit., p. 269.

RN arithmetic: Kissinger, *Upheaval,* op. cit., p. 1181, *MEM,* p. 1041–; (call to Wallace) ibid., p. 1049–; Haig, op. cit., p. 471.

Supreme Ct.: (crucial unknown) *MEM,* p. 1043; (decision) *NM* p. 515–; (RN & news) Haig, op. cit., p. 472; ("exploded") *NM,* p. 518.

June 23 tape: ("There is one tape") Haig, op. cit., p. 472–; ("This . . . smoking gun") ibid.; (clear evidence) R, Report, p. 2, WSPF Report, p. 128; Ben-Veniste and Frampton, op. cit., p. 292; ("No one is to listen") Haig, op. cit., p. 455– and see *MEM,* p. 1000; (hidden from own people) Haig, op. cit., p. 490–.

State of Nixon after Ct. decision: ("His coloring pallid") Kissinger, *Upheaval,* op. cit., p. 1195–; ("gone too far") ibid., p. 1196; (not left compound) *NM,* p. 537; (Napoleon) ibid.; (after swim) *MEM,* p. 1053.

Impeachment articles: R, Report, pp. 1–, 10–.

Kissinger/Haig agreed: Kissinger, *Upheaval,* op. cit., p. 1196.

Nixon resignation/indecision: ("Dick, make deal") Cannon, op. cit., p. 285–, citing int. John Mitchell by Hal Bruno; (spins tape Tuesday) White, *Breach,* op. cit., p. 10; (4:00 A.M.) *MEM,*

p. 1056; ("Once this tape gets out") Haig, op. cit., p. 476; ("like stroke victim") Bob Woodward, *Shadow,* New York: Simon & Schuster, 1999, p. 3, citing int. Alexander Haig; ("tell Ford") Haig, op. cit., p. 480; (two Ford meetings) ibid., p. 480–; Hartmann, op. cit., p. 124–; (back to tapes) *MEM,* p. 1058; ("You can't do it") ibid.; (Julie first) *PAT,* p. 417–; (canceled plans) ibid., p. 418; Clem Conger, White Hse. curator, in *Ladies' Home Journal,* Mar. 1975; (family/transcripts) *MEM,* p. 1060; *PAT,* p. 419–; ("fighting to finish") *MEM,,* p. 1061–; ("Quite late") Haig, op. cit., p. 487; (weekend Aug. 3–4) *MEM,* p. 1061; Haig, op. cit., p. 488–; Price, op. cit., p. 329–; (Options A/B) AP, Dec. 15, 1997, citing Raymond Price; (Monday transcript release) Haig, op. cit., p. 491–; Price, op. cit., p. 336; White, *Breach,* op. cit., p. 20–; (cruise) *MEM,* p. 1063; *PAT,* p. 420–; (cabinet meeting) *MEM,* p. 1065, Kissinger, *Upheaval,* op. cit., p. 1202; Haig, op. cit., p. 492–; Hartmann, op. cit., p. 148–; ("Nixon had never") Kissinger, *Upheaval,* op. cit., p. 1205; ("tilting") ibid.

Edward Cox phone call: Woodward and Bernstein, *Final Days,* op. cit., p. 437– and Griffin conversation with BBC/History Channel producer Rebecca John in 2000.

Suicide?: (never crossed mind) Crowley, *Off the Record,* op. cit., p. 193; ("leave a man") Haig, op. cit., p. 496; ("I told White House doctors") *WP,* Dec. 25, 1995 and see Woodward and Bernstein, *Final Days,* op. cit., p. 447; (David worries) Woodward & Bernstein, *Final Days,* op. cit., p. 377; ("given to sudden rages") *NM,* p. 562.

Concern re: stability: ("A new element") Ben-Veniste and Frampton, op. cit., p. 145; ("He gave us strange arguments") int. Harold Evans on ABC-TV's *20/20,* June 1982, cited in research paper by Michael Ewing supplied to author and see Woodward and Bernstein, *Final Days,* op. cit., pp. 115, 270; (legislators/Brown) Kessler, op. cit., p. 40; (Cranston) int. notes of FB, FBP; ("He made sure") int. Margaret Shannon; (Buchen/Whitehead) Woodward and Bernstein, *Final Days,* op. cit., p. 230–.

Schlesinger precautions: (Laitin) int. Joseph Laitin by author and transcript of int. for BBC/History Channel, and see Seymour Hersh article, *Atlantic Monthly,* Aug. 1983; (Zumwalt/Schlesinger) ibid., int. Elmo Zumwalt; ("paranoid") Zumwalt, op. cit., pp. 459, 495; ints. Elmo Zumwalt, James Schlesinger; (Schlesinger kept informed) ibid.; Chicago *Sun-Times,* Aug. 24, 1974; (Schlesinger/Brown) ints. James Schlesinger by author and transcript of int. for BBC/History Channel; (Brown confirmed) int. George Brown by Bernard Shaw, transcript, *CBS Evening News with Walter Cronkite,* Oct. 10, 1974; (meeting/Holloway) int. James Holloway and notes of Michael Ewing int. with Joseph Laitin—re: dinner conversation with Holloway—by Michael Ewing, supplied to author; ("hands shaking") int. Joseph Laitin for BBC/History Channel; (Security Act) Chicago *Sun-Times,* Aug. 28, 1974; ("I did assure myself") *WP, SF Chronicle,* Aug. 24, 1974; ("be sure no idiot") Gerald Ford, *A Time to Heal,* Norwalk, CT: Easton Press, 1987, p. 322; (Air Force) Chicago *Sun-Times,* Aug. 24, 1974; (Cushman) Brig. General Robert Cushman to Chief AFSWP, re: "Advanced Orientation Course," Apr. 18, 1959, VP, NA; (82nd during demos) Gulley, op. cit., p. 198; (Ford spokesman/no measures) *WP,* Aug. 27, 1974; ("The last week or so") ints. Barry Toll; (Toll background) army record, including decorations—Vietnam Cross of Gallantry, Bronze and Palms, Bronze Star for Heroism, Presidential Unit citation, evidence Battle Staff Team, CINCLANT Airborne Command Post, Aug. 2, 1974, and honorable discharge certificate, Aug. 15, 1975; ("Haig was in touch") Kissinger, *Upheaval,* op. cit., p. 1199; ("The end of RN presidency") int. James Schlesinger for BBC/History Channel and for author; ("Secretary had responsibility") int. Geroge Brown, CBS-TV, *supra.*

Haig Aug. 7: Haig, op. cit., p. 496–; int. Alexander Haig; Goldwater with Casserly, op. cit., p. 277; Goldwater, *No Apologies,* op. cit., p. 266–.

Republican leaders/RN meeting: ("We sat there") int. Barry Goldwater, transcript "Watergate: The Secret Story," CBS News, June 17, 1992; ("how things stood") Goldwater, *No Apologies,* op. cit., p. 267; (stared at seal) *MEM,* p. 1073; ("irrevocably") ibid.

Evening Aug. 7: (Ed/Griffin) Woodward and Bernstein, *Final Days,* op. cit., p. 466; (dinner/Kissinger meeting) drawn from *MEM,* p. 1074–; *PAT* p. 423–; Kissinger, *Upheaval,* op. cit., p. 1207–; ("drunk") Woodward and Bernstein, *Final Days,* op. cit., p. 472; (Price) int. Raymond Price in eds. Strober, *Nixon* op. cit., p. 472.

Thursday Aug. 8: (morning/Haig) Haig, op. cit., p. 499–; *MEM,* p. 1078; ("I know good job") ibid.; (Lenion/Gandhi) Haig, op. cit., p. 502; (*"you don't quit"*) ibid., ("no tears") *MEM,* p. 1073; (cried with Kissinger?) Woodward and Bernstein, *Final Days,* op. cit., p. 470–; ("I just hope") *MEM,* p. 1082; (TV telling nation) Haig, op. cit., p. 503; ("May God's grace") *MEM,* p. 1084; ("slow . . . huddle") ibid.; (Pat/window) ibid., p. 1085; (curtains) Dickerson, op. cit., p. 220; ("I let you down") Garment, op. cit., p. 296 and transcript, "Watergate: The Secret Story," CBS-TV, June 17, 1992; (Haig found Nixon) Haig, op. cit., p. 503–; ("Dear Mr. Secretary") *NM,* p. 568; ("Oh, Dick") *PAT,* p. 426; (speech) eds. Knappman and Drossman, op. cit.,

Vol. 3, p. 224–; ("Have a nice trip") *MEM*, p. 1089; ("so sad") *MEM*, p. 1090; (transition moment) terHorst and Albertazzie, op. cit., p. 48; ("nightmare") Hartmann, op. cit., p. 172; (martini) terHorst and Albertazzie, op. cit., p. 49–; (call-sign change) ibid., p. 51; (mere colonel) int. James Schlesinger; ("black box") AP, BBC, Apr. 26, 1999, int. Barry Toll; (Haig confided) ints. John Barker and see int. Richard Ben-Veniste; (No box on board) terHorst and Albertazzie, op. cit., p. 43–; ("God Bless America") int. Howard Seelye; terHorst and Albertazzie, op. cit., p. 58–; *PAT*, p. 429.

Aftermath: (Nixon plays "God Bless America") unidentified clipping, [*SF Chronicle*?], July 14, 1986; ("He's Back") *Newsweek*, May 19, 1986; (Carter/other presidents consulted) *JA*, p. 552–; Crowley, *Winter*, op. cit., p. 130–; ("running for ex-presidency") *SF Chronicle*, Dec. 2, 1978; (pardon) *AMIII*, p. 461; (foreman) int. Vladimir Pregelj; ("That's justice?") *SF Chronicle*, June 19, 1982; (Krogh) *JA*, p. 530; int. Egil Krogh; (contrition) *AMIII*, p. 461; int. Benton Becker; ("won't grovel") *JA*, p. 538; ("I did wrong") *Newsweek*, Oct. 20, 1975, citing Rev. Eugene Coffin; ("only a footnote") Colson, op. cit., p. 270; (Churchill quote) *SF Chronicle*, Mar. 8, 1985; ("obeyed Mark Twain") Knight News Service, Jan. 8, 1981; ("Nixon and his apologists") Magruder, *Power to Peace*, op. cit., p. 177; ("If there was dominant sentiment") Shannon, op. cit., p. 11.

List of Abbreviations

AMI	Stephen Ambrose, *Nixon: The Education of a Politician,* Vol. 1, New York: Simon & Schuster, 1987.
AMII	Stephen Ambrose, *Nixon, The Triumph of a Politician,* Vol. 2, New York: Simon & Schuster, 1989.
AMIII	Stephen Ambrose, *Nixon, Ruin and Recovery,* Vol. 3, New York: Simon & Schuster, 1991.
AOP	Stanley Kutler, *Abuse of Power: The New Nixon Tapes,* New York: The Free Press, 1997.
DDEL	Dwight D. Eisenhower presidential Library.
DPP	Drew Pearson Papers, Lyndon B. Johnson Presidential Library.
E	Senate Select Committee on Presidential Campaign Activities, chaired by Senator Ervin.
FB	Fawn Brodie, *Richard Nixon: The Shaping of His Character,* New York: W. W. Norton, 1981.
FBP	Fawn M. Brodie Papers, Marriott Library, Special Collections, University of Utah.
FR	Final Report (applies to government documents).
HD	H. R. Haldeman, *The Haldeman Diaries,* New York: Putnam, 1994.
HD, CD	H. R. Haldeman, *The Haldeman Diaries,* The Complete Multimedia Edition, Santa Monica, CA: Sony, 1994.
JA	Jonathan Aitken, *Nixon: A Life ,* Washington, D.C.: Regnery, 1993.
JFKL	John F. Kennedy presidential Library.
JFRP	John F. Rothmann Papers.
LAT	*Los Angeles Times.*
LBJL	Lyndon B. Johnson presidential Library.
MEM	Richard Nixon, *The Memoirs of Richard Nixon,* New York: Simon & Schuster, 1990.
MO	Roger Morris, *Richard Milhous Nixon: The Rise of an American Politician,* New York: Henry Holt, 1990.
NA	National Archives.
NM	J. Anthony Lukas, *Nightmare,* New York: Penguin, 1988.
NP, NA	Nixon Presidential Materials Project, National Archives housed at College Park, MD.
NSF	National security file.
NYT	*New York Times.*
PAT	Julie Nixon Eisenhower, *Pat Nixon: The Untold Story,* New York: Simon & Schuster, 1986.
PERJ	Allen Weinstein, *Perjury,* New York: Random House, 1997.
R	U.S. House of Representatives, Committee on the Judiciary, 93rd Congress, 2nd Session, "Impeachment Inquiry" [pursuant to House Resolution 803], chaired by Rep. Peter Rodino.
RN	Richard M. Nixon.

TW60	Theodore H. White, *The Making of the President, 1960,* New York: Atheneum, 1962.
TW64	Theodore H. White, *The Making of the President, 1964,* New York: Atheneum, 1965.
TW68	Theodore H. White, *The Making of the President, 1968,* New York: Atheneum, 1969.
TW72	Theodore H. White, *The Making of the President, 1972,* New York: Atheneum, 1973.
VP, NA	Richard M. Nixon Pre-Presidential Papers, National Archives, housed at Laguna Niguel, CA.
WHT	White House tapes. The tapes themselves are housed at the National Archives, College Park, MD. Where so indicated, tapes have been transcribed by the author's researcher, Robert D. Lamb.
WP	*Washington Post.*
WSPF	Watergate Special Prosecution Force.
WSPF (H-R)	Hughes-Rebozo Investigation, Watergate Special Prosecution Force.

Acknowledgments

More than a thousand people were interviewed for this book. We thank them all, but draw the reader's special attention to the following. Of Richard Nixon's surviving family, his brother Edward and his nephew Donald talked with us. Tricia Nixon courteously declined an interview request while Julie did not respond. From amongst Nixon's friends, Jack Drown and Donald Kendall were interviewed. We could not see the late Bebe Rebozo, who had suffered a stroke, and Robert Abplanalp did not reply to letters. The late C. Arnholt Smith was interviewed, as were former Senator George Smathers and Adnan Khashoggi. Dr. Arnold Hutschnecker, the psychotherapist with whom Nixon had a long relationship as patient and friend, gave three extensive interviews.

Of Nixon's staff, the following granted interviews: Alexander Butterfield, Dwight Chapin, John Dean, the late John Ehrlichman, Peter Flanigan, Leonard Garment, Alexander Haig, Herb Klein, Egil Krogh, John Sears, Ron Walker, and Ronald Ziegler. So, too, did former Defense Secretaries Melvin Laird and James Schlesinger (who also served as chairman of the Atomic Energy Commission and director of the Central Intelligence Agency). Brent Scowcroft, former military assistant to the president and deputy assistant for national security affairs, was helpful. The late Maurice Stans, who served Nixon as commerce secretary and on several occasions chaired his campaign finance committees, gave a long interview at his home in California. The late Admiral Elmo Zumwalt, former chief of naval operations, displayed a fine memory and perceptive insights. George Shultz, who served as labor secretary, director of the office of management and budget, and treasury secretary, also talked with us. Cynthia Bassett, daughter of Nixon's early press spokesman, provided her father's intimate correspondence and diaries.

Of those involved directly in the break-ins at the Watergate and the office of Daniel Ellsberg's psychiatrist, we spoke with Howard Hunt, Bernard Barker, and Rolando Martinez.

We are grateful to Lou Campbell, who served at the Nixon White House as an executive protection officer, and to Barry Toll, a former head of one of the battle staff units that stand ready to brief the president and top commanders on procedures in a nuclear crisis, for their patient assistance.

Former Representative Jerome Waldie, who served on the House Judiciary Committee during the Watergate investigation, gave us access to his "impeachment diary." Both he and Lowell Weicker, former senator and member of the Senate Watergate Committee and later governor of Connecticut, impressed us with their evident devotion to the core principles of American democracy. John Doar and Jerome Zeifman, special counsel and general counsel, respectively, to the House Judiciary Committee, were both interviewed. Professor Sam Dash, former chief counsel of the Senate Watergate Committee, gave a long interview at his Georgetown University office. Richard Ben-Veniste, former assistant special prosecutor on the Watergate Special Prosecution Force, was as impressive in interview as he was in court. James Doyle and John Barker, who worked closely with special prosecutors Archibald Cox and Leon Jaworski as public affairs assistants, were both interviewed; Doyle kindly gave us access to his taped Watergate journal. Robert Morgenthau, the veteran district attorney of New York County, was helpful as in the past. Former IRS supervisor Marty Philpott explained the probe into Teamsters' contributions to the Nixon White House. The family of the late, brilliant IRS agent John Daley allowed us to rummage in the treasure trove of his filing system. Norman Casper, the IRS informant whose field craft led to exposure of Caribbean banking scams, was endlessly cooperative.

President Johnson's assistant secretary of state, William Bundy, special assistant Joseph Califano, Jr., and national security adviser Walt Rostow threw light on Republican interference with the Vietnam peace initiative in 1968. Anna Chennault and former South Vietnamese ambassador Bui Diem gave detailed accounts of that episode. Although recovering from an operation, Howard Hughes's longtime troubleshooter Robert Maheu talked with the author at length. Huntington Hartford and Seymour Alter, who were also unwell, offered memories of Nixon's Paradise Island connection. The brave Elizabeth Newell told, for the first time, what she had learned from a Rebozo bank official of Nixon's alleged offshore investments. In prison in California, David Silberman offered his account of an alleged Nixonian financial scam. Alvin Kotz, also in jail when interviewed, was informative on stolen securities and much else. The relatives of both men put up with a barrage of questions over many months, as did Silberman's former secretary, Dee Anne Hill.

The indefatigable Greek journalist Elias Dematrocopoulos sat for many interviews and provided a cornucopia of documentation, especially on the allegation that Nixon accepted an illegal contribution from the Greek dictatorship in 1968.

An investigative book on this scale owes much to the labors of those who have gone before. Special thanks are due to John Rothmann, a sometime Republican activist in California who maintains a unique and extraordinary private archive, and to Michael Ewing, a former congressional investigator with an encyclopedic knowledge of organized crime.

Of the many authors and journalists who have written about Nixon, Roger Morris's published work on the early years—and the help he gave the author—was invaluable. Charles Elliott, Jr., guided the author through Nixon's hometown of Whittier. Gil Troy, who has written about Pat Nixon, allowed us to copy his files. John Lowenthal, lawyer and longtime believer in the innocence of Alger Hiss, offered the most evenhanded advice he could muster. Charles Higham and Benjamin Schemmer, respectively published and unpublished biographers of Howard Hughes, readily supplied documentation. Peter Wyden, John Prados, and Evan Thomas, authors knowledgeable on intelligence matters and the Bay of Pigs, were all helpful. So, too, were Jerry Hunt and former reporters who investigated Nixon's relationship with Marianna Liu. Catherine Forslund, now assistant professor of history at Rockford College, Illinois, made available her dissertation and expertise on the Anna Chennault episode. Alan Block, professor of the administration of justice at Penn State University, opened up his files on organized crime in the Bahamas, as did Jerry Shields. Lisa Gubernick provided unique archival material on Paradise Island. Jeff Gerth's work on how Nixon's world intersected with that of organized crime was an important resource, as was that of former *Newsday* editor Robert Greene and Jonathan Marshall. Professor Joan Hoff gave us access to a mass of material arising from a recent Watergate lawsuit. The author Ron Kessler submitted to a grilling about his sources, and Peter Dale Scott, Berkeley professor and devoted student of the world of intelligence and organized crime, helped once again.

Anthony Lukas, author of a Watergate account no researcher of the subject can be without, died tragically while this book was being written. He had given us thoughtful guidance early in the project. The authors of three other indispensable works on Watergate, Fred Emery, Jim Hougan, and Stanley Kutler—professor of American institutions at the University of Wisconsin—offered every encouragement. Emery dipped into old files, and both Hougan and Kutler opened their archives to us. David Wise lived up to his name and supplied out-of-print congressional volumes. Seymour Hersh allowed us to carry away files by the boxload, and helped with contacts. Former Senate intelligence committee investigator Scott Armstrong dug deep in memory in a lengthy interview. Carl Bernstein and Bob Woodward were helpful and supportive. Where our path crossed their old Watergate tracks, we concluded that "Woodstein" deserved their accolades.

Of the several skilled journalist-researchers who worked on the project, Robert D. Lamb performed long and sterling service. We thank him especially. Sondra Feldstein, who holds an advanced degree in American history and who worked for us on a previous book, read and annotated judiciously the many books we could not read thoroughly ourselves. The skills of Kari Huus, Greg Murphy, Gus Russo, Phil Stanford, and Julie Ziegler were valuable as we identified tough investigative areas. Cinda Elser especially, and Alex Kramer, traced elusive people and records. Researchers Blair Campbell, Brian Connolly, Mark Herman, James Rosen, and Monisha Saldanha, starting out on their careers, gave us willing help in the early days. In Nassau, Nicki Kelly shared her expertise on the Bahamas. Brenda Brodie and Gordon Winslow gave us the benefit of their knowledge of anti-Castro activities. Bill Pugsley labored to get unreleased material freed up at the Johnson Library, and Warren Rabe trawled the Truman Library on a purely volunteer basis.

Librarians and archivists for the National Archives—Pat Andersen, David Paynter, and Karl Weissenbach of the Nixon Presidential Materials Project at College Park, Maryland, and Paul Wormser of the Nixon Pre-Presidential Papers holdings at Laguna Niguel, California—were most cooperative. So, too, were Lyndon B. Johnson Library director Harry Middleton, David DeLorenzo at Harvard, Tom Harkins at Duke University, Mike Sutherland of the Mary Norton Clapp Library at Occidental College, and Stan Larsen and Nancy Young at the manuscript division of the University of Utah. All were generous with time and facilities, and so, too, once again, was Waterford County Librarian Donal Brady in Ireland.

The Richard Nixon Library and Birthplace, in our experience of it, proved less helpful than other presidential or private libraries. Its director, John Taylor, who has often spoken on the record, turned down our interview request. Archivist Susan Naulty did respond helpfully to some specific questions. The overall impression, however, was that the Nixon Library is more committed to promoting the virtues of the late president than to providing a wholly open service to researchers and scholars. We found it disquieting, too, that numerous interviewees told us they felt they needed to "check with the Library" before being interviewed. In the end, we did not visit the Library.

James Lesar, an attorney and Freedom of Information Act wizard, once again did battle with recalcitrant agencies. Terry Murphy worked magic on old photographs, as did John Lombard on computers. Patrick Farren of Alex International made vast quantities of books and paper travel backward and forward across the Atlantic. Simi Kerman and Stephen Aaron and Nancy Pulley stored our research in the basements of their homes. Larry and Lesley McDonald offered hospitality in Delaware, and Michael and PJ Dempsey gave us refuge after we were robbed at gunpoint.

Against all the odds, Jeanette Mundy is still prepared to work as our assistant after more than ten years, and Zvenka Kleinfeld ran the office during research stints in the United States. Jennifer O'Leary struggled with the earliest chapters in Cork. Pauline Lombard was mistress of the file and tape system and myriad related books at our Irish base. Jenny and Sally Brittain, Jenny Barlow, Breeda O'Connell, Ann Dalton, and Anne-Marie Ronayne photocopied hundreds of thousands of pages of documents over the years. James Ronayne drove thousands of miles to and from airports and courier offices. A trusty friend, Tiddy Rowan, flew in to the rescue when more hands were needed.

Sincere thanks to my editor at Viking, the talented Rick Kot, his assistant, Brett Kelly, and to Tory Klose, the managing editor who made a crazed schedule work. That extraordinary New York publishing potentate Phyllis Grann ensured that the book and its author survived its grueling five-year birth process. Wayne Lawson got it right, once again, at *Vanity Fair.* My effective agents, Sterling Lord in New York and Jonathan Lloyd at Curtis Brown in London, supplied business sense and friendship in equal measure. Former BBC colleague Bill Cran, at the helm of his own distinguished freelance documentary film company, Invision Productions, fashioned two fine films for the BBC and the History Channel from the clay of our draft manuscript.

The true sustaining strength behind us, however, has been that of our family. The love and understanding of Bob and Terry Swan, Robbyn's parents, have been central to keeping our spirits up. Our five fine children, from the eldest to the youngest, have good reason to resent the five-year presence of the Nixon project in their lives. In many different senses, though, the effort has been for them.

A.S. and R.S.
Ireland, 2000

Photo Credits

1. Whittier College
2. The Richard Nixon Library and Birthplace
3. The Richard Nixon Library and Birthplace
4. Whittier College
5. Whittier College
6. Whittier College
7. AP/Wide World Photos
8. Whittier Daily News
9. *The Washington Post*
10. Bettmann/CORBIS
11. Private Collection
12. AP/Wide World Photos
13. AP/Wide World Photos
14. AP/Wide World Photos
15. Courtesy of Carmine Schiavone Studios
16. James Shepley/TimePix
17. Bettmann/CORBIS
18. AP/Wide World Photos
19. AP/Wide World Photos
20. AP/Wide World Photos
21. AP/Wide World Photos
22. Bettmann/CORBIS
23. Sygma/CORBIS
24. AP/Wide World Photos
25. Hank Walker/TimePix
26. AP/Wide World Photos
27. Ralph Crane/TimePix
28. Bettmann/CORBIS
29. *Hong Kong Standard*
30. Houston Metropolitan Research Center, Houston Public Library
31. Bettmann/CORBIS
32. Stanley Toogood/Courtesy of Michael A. Toogood Photography
33. Private Collection
34. Courtesy of Adnan Khashoggi
35. George Silk/TimePix
36. Black Star
37. Lyndon Baines Johnson Library
38. Bettmann/CORBIS
39. Courtesy of Herb Klein
40. TimePix
41. Fred J. Maroon
42. Bettmann/CORBIS
43. National Archives
44. AP/Wide World Photos
45. Arthur Schatz/TimePix
46. Bettmann/CORBIS
47. National Archives
48. National Archives
49. Fred J. Maroon
50. *The New York Times*
51. Fred J. Maroon
52. National Archives
53. National Archives
54. Bettmann/CORBIS
55. Bettmann/CORBIS
56. Bettmann/CORBIS
57. AP/Wide World Photos
58. CORBIS
59. Courtesy of Anna Chennault
60. Courtesy of Elias Demetracopoulos
61. Courtesy of Cora Cummins
62. Courtesy of Sam Kay
63. FBI Archives
64. Bettmann/CORBIS
65. National Archives
66. CBS News Photos
67. Bettmann/CORBIS
68. Sygma/CORBIS
69. Bettmann/CORBIS
70. National Archives
71. AP/Wide World Photos
72. Dirck Halstead/TimePix
73. AP/Wide World Photos
74. Bill Pierce/TimePix
75. Courtesy of Lester Sloan
76. Sygma/CORBIS
77. Sygma/CORBIS
78. AP/Wide World Photos
79. TimePix
80. AP/Wide World Photos

Selected Bibliography

Books About Richard Nixon

Abrahamsen, David, M.D. *Nixon vs. Nixon*. New York: Farrar, Straus & Giroux, 1977.

Aitken, Jonathan. *Nixon: A Life*. Washington, D.C.: Regnery, 1993.

Allen, Gary. *Richard Nixon*. Boston: Western Islands, 1971.

Ambrose, Stephen E. *Nixon: The Education of a Politician, 1913–1961*. New York: Simon & Schuster, 1987.

———. *Nixon: The Triumph of a Politician, 1962–1972*. New York: Simon & Schuster, 1989.

———. *Nixon: Ruin and Recovery, 1973–1990*. New York: Simon & Schuster, 1991.

Andrew, Christopher. *For the President's Eyes Only*. New York: HarperCollins, 1995.

Andrews, Philip. *This Man Nixon*. Philadelphia: John Winston, 1952.

Anson, Robert Sam. *Exile*. New York: Simon & Schuster, 1984.

Brodie, Fawn M. *Richard Nixon*. New York: W. W. Norton, 1981.

Cavan, Sherri. *20th Century Gothic: America's Nixon*. San Francisco: Wigan Pier Press, 1979.

Chesen, Eli S., M.D. *President Nixon's Psychiatric Profile*. New York: Peter Wyden, 1973.

Costello, William. *The Facts About Nixon*. New York: Viking, 1960.

Crowley, Monica. *Nixon Off the Record*. New York: Random House, 1997.

———. *Nixon in Winter*. New York: Random House, 1998.

Elliott, Charles, Jr. *Whittaker College: The First Century on the Poet Campus*. Redondo Beach, CA: Legends Press, 1986.

Evans, Rowland and Robert D. Novak. *Nixon in the White House*. London: Davis-Poynter, 1971.

Gardner, Richard. *Fighting Quaker*. Unpub. ms. held at Whittier College, Whittier, CA.

Gellman, Irwin, F. *The Contender: Richard Nixon, The Congress Years 1946–1952*. New York: The Free Press, 1999.

Hamburg, Eric, ed. *Nixon: An Oliver Stone Film*. New York: Hyperion, 1995.

Higgins, George V. *The Friends of Richard Nixon*. New York: Ballantine, 1974.

Hoff, Joan. *Nixon Reconsidered*. New York: Basic Books, 1994.

Hoyt, Edwin P. *The Nixons: An American Family*. New York: Random House, 1972.

Korff, Baruch. *The President and I*. Providence, RI: Baruch Korff Foundation, 1995.

Kornitzer, Bela. *The Real Nixon*. New York: Rand McNally, 1960.

Lurie, Leonard. *The Running of Richard Nixon*. New York: Coward, McCann & Geoghegan, 1972.

Mankiewicz, Frank. *Perfectly Clear*. New York: Quadrangle, 1973.

Mazlish, Bruce. *In Search of Nixon*. New York: Basic Books, 1972.

Mazo, Earl. *Richard Nixon*. New York: Avon, 1960.

——— and Stephen Hess. *President Nixon: A Political Portrait*. London: McDonald, 1968.

Morris, Roger. *Richard Milhous Nixon*. New York: Henry Holt, 1990.

Oudes, Bruce. *From: The President*. London: André Deutsch, 1989.

Parmet, Herbert S. *Richard Nixon and His America*. Boston: Little, Brown, 1990.

Price, Raymond. *With Nixon*. New York: Viking, 1977.

Rather, Dan and Gary Paul Gates. *The Palace Guard*. New York: Harper & Row, 1974.

Safire, William. *Before the Fall.* New York: Belmont Tower Books, 1975.

Schell, Jonathan. *The Time of Illusion.* New York: Alfred Knopf, 1975.

Schlesinger, Arthur M., Jr. *The Imperial Presidency.* Boston: Houghton Mifflin, 1973.

Schulte, Renée K. *The Young Nixon: An Oral Inquiry.* Fullerton, CA: California State University, 1978.

Spalding, Henry D. *The Nixon Nobody Knows.* New York: Jonathan David, 1972.

Strober, Gerald S. and Deborah Hart Strober. *Nixon: An Oral History of His Presidency.* New York: HarperCollins, 1994.

Sulzberger, C.L. *The World and Richard Nixon.* New York: Prentice-Hall, 1987.

Toledano, Ralph de. *Nixon.* New York: Duell, Sloan and Pearse, 1960.

———. *One Man Alone: Richard Nixon.* New York: Funk & Wagnalls, 1969.

Turner, William. *Nixon's Vendetta and the Old Boy Network, Part VII.* Unpub. ms. 1986.

Volkan, Vamik, Norman Itzkowitz, and Andrew Dod. *Richard Nixon: A Psychobiography.* New York: Columbia University Press, 1997.

Voorhis, Jerry. *The Strange Case of Richard Milhous Nixon.* New York: Popular Library, 1973.

Wicker, Tom. *One of Us.* New York: Random House, 1991.

Wills, Garry. *Nixon Agonistes.* Boston: Houghton Mifflin, 1970.

Witcover, Jules. *The Resurrection of Richard Nixon.* New York: G. P. Putnam's Sons, 1970.

Woodstone, Arthur. *Nixon's Head.* New York: St. Martin's Press, 1972.

On Richard Nixon's Campaigns

Alsop, Stewart. *Nixon and Rockefeller.* New York: Doubleday, 1960.

Chester, Lewis, Godfrey Hodgson, and Bruce Page. *An American Melodrama: The Presidential Campaign of 1968.* New York: Viking, 1969.

Crouse, Timothy. *The Boys on the Bus.* New York: Ballantine, 1973.

Harris, Mark. *Mark the Glove Boy.* New York: Macmillan, 1964.

Pearl, Arthur. *Landslide: The Hows and Whys of Nixon's Victory.* Seacaucus, NJ: Citadel, 1973.

McGinniss, Joe. *The Selling of the President.* New York: Penguin, 1988.

Sevareid, Eric, ed. *Candidates 1960.* New York: Basic Books, 1959.

Schynkel, Sharon Lee. *A Thesis on Speeches by R.N. from 1960 & 1969 Presidential Campaigns.* Whittier, CA: Whittier College, June 1969.

White, Theodore H. *America in Search of Itself: The Making of the President 1956–1980.* Norwalk, CT: Easton Press, 1986.

———. *The Making of the President 1960.* New York: Atheneum, 1962.

———. *The Making of the President 1964.* New York: Atheneum, 1965.

———. *The Making of the President 1968.* New York: Atheneum, 1969.

———. *The Making of the President 1972.* New York: Atheneum, 1973.

Witcover, Jules. *1968: The Year the Dream Died.* New York: Warner Books, 1997.

Books by Richard Nixon

In the Arena. New York: Touchstone, 1990.

Leaders. New York: Touchstone, 1990.

The Memoirs of Richard Nixon. New York: Simon & Schuster, 1990.

1999: Victory Without War. New York: Simon & Schuster, 1988.

Real Peace/No More Vietnams. New York: Touchstone, 1990.

The Real War. New York: Touchstone, 1990.

Seize the Moment. New York: Simon & Schuster, 1992.

Six Crises. Garden City, NY: Doubleday, 1962.

On Pat Nixon

David, Lester. *The Lonely Lady of San Clemente.* New York: Thomas Crowell, 1978.

Eisenhower, Julie Nixon. *Pat Nixon: The Untold Story.* New York: Simon & Schuster, 1986.

Troy, Gil. *Affairs of State.* New York: The Free Press, 1997.

On the Hiss Case

Andrews, Bert and Peter. *A Tragedy of History: A Journalist's Confidential Role in the Hiss-Chambers Case.* Washington, D.C.: Robert B. Luce, 1962.

Haynes, John Earl and Harvey Klehr. *Venona: Decoding Soviet Espionage in America.* New Haven, CT: Yale University Press, 1999.

Levitt, Morton and Michael. *A Tissue of Lies: Nixon vs. Hiss.* New York: McGraw Hill, 1979.

Reuben, William A. *The Honorable Mr. Nixon.* New York: Action Books, 1956.

Smith, John Chabot. *Alger Hiss: The True Story.* New York: Penguin, 1977.

Tanenhaus, Sam. *Whittaker Chambers.* New York: Random House, 1997.

Weinstein, Allen. *Perjury: The Hiss-Chambers Case*. New York: Random House, 1997.
———— and Alexander Vassiliev. *The Haunted Wood: Soviet Espionage in America, The Stalin Era*. New York: Random House, 1999.
West, Nigel. *Venona: The Greatest Secret of the Cold War*. London: HarperCollins, 1999.
Zeligs, Meyer A. *Friendship or Fratricide*. New York: Viking, 1967.

On the McCarthy Years

Caute, David. *The Great Fear*. New York: Simon & Schuster, 1978.
Oshinsky, David M. *A Conspiracy So Immense: The World of Joe McCarthy*. New York: Free Press, 1983.

On Helen Gahagan Douglas

Mitchell, Greg. *Tricky Dick and the Pink Lady*. New York: Random House, 1998.

On Nixon's Vice Presidential Years

Keogh, James. *This Is Nixon*. New York: G. P. Putnam's Sons, 1956.
The Speeches of Vice President Richard M. Nixon Presidential Campaign of 1960. Washington, D.C.: U.S. Government Printing Office, 1961.

On Nixon and John F. Kennedy

Beschloss, Michael. *The Crisis Years: Kennedy and Khrushchev 1960–1963*. New York: Harper-Collins, 1991.
Collier, Peter and David Horowitz. *The Kennedys: An American Drama*. London: Pan Books, 1984.
Halberstam, David. *The Best and the Brightest*. New York: Random House, 1969.
Hersh, Seymour. *The Dark Side of Camelot*. New York: Little, Brown, 1997.
Matthews, Christopher. *Kennedy and Nixon*. New York: Simon & Schuster, 1986.

On the Nixon Presidency

Atkins, Ollie. *The White House Years*. Chicago: Playboy Press, 1977.
Buchanan, Patrick J. *The New Majority*. Philadelphia: Girard Bank, 1973.
Doyle, William. *Inside the Oval Office*. New York: Kodansha International, 1999.
Johnson, George W., ed. *The Nixon Presidential Press Conferences*. New York: Earl M. Coleman 1978.
Kessler, Ronald. *Inside the White House*. New York: Pocket Books, 1993.
Kutler, Stanley. *Abuse of Power*. New York: The Free Press, 1997.
Mollenhoff, Clark R. *Game Plan for Disaster*. New York: W. W. Norton, 1976.
Nathan, Richard. *The Plot That Failed: Nixon and the Administrative Presidency*. New York: John Wiley, 1975.
Osborne, John. *The Nixon Watch*. New York: Liveright, 1970.
————. *The Second Year of the Nixon Watch*. New York: Liveright, 1971.
————. *The Third Year of the Nixon Watch*. New York: Liveright, 1972.
————. *The Fourth Year of the Nixon Watch*. New York: Liveright, 1973.
————. *The Fifth Year of the Nixon Watch*. New York: Liveright, 1974.
————. *The Last Nixon Watch*. Washington D.C.: New Republic Book Company, 1975.
Osgood, Robert, et al. *Retreat from Empire: The First Nixon Administration*. Baltimore, MD: Johns Hopkins University Press, 1973.
Reichley, A. James. *Conservatives in an Age of Change*. Washington D.C.: The Brookings Institute, 1981.
Schell, Jonathan. *Observing the Nixon Years*. New York: Pantheon, 1989.
Schoenebaum, Eleanora, Ph.D. *Profiles of an Era: The Nixon/Ford Years*. New York: Harcourt Brace Jovanovich, 1979.
Small, Melvin. *The Presidency of Richard Nixon*. Lawrence, KS: University Press of Kansas, 1999.
Smith, Howard. *Every Four Years: A Study of the Presidency*. Philadelphia, PA: WHYY, 1980.
Spear, Joseph. *Presidents and the Press*. Cambridge, MA: MIT Press, 1984.
Staff of the Miller Center, eds., University of Virginia. *The Nixon Presidency: 22 Intimate Perspectives of Richard M. Nixon*. Lanham, MD: University Press of America, 1987.
Whalen, Richard. J. *Catch the Falling Flag*. Boston: Houghton Mifflin, 1972.

On Nixon's Policies

Brandon, Henry. *The Retreat of American Power*. New York: Doubleday, 1973.
Bundy, William. *A Tangled Web: The Making of Foreign Policy in the Nixon White House*. New York: Hill and Wang, 1998.
Dent, Harry S. *The Prodigal South Returns to Power*. New York: John Wiley, 1978.

Keogh, James. *President Nixon and the Press*. New York: Funk & Wagnalls, 1972.
O'Reilly, Kenneth. *Nixon's Piano*. New York: Free Press, 1995.
Ravenal, Earl C. *Large Scale Foreign Policy Change: The Nixon Doctrine as History and Portent*. Berkeley, CA: University of California, 1989.
Schurmann, Franz. *The Foreign Politics of Richard Nixon*. Berkeley, CA: University of California, 1987.
Sulzberger, C.L. *The World and Richard Nixon*. New York: Prentice-Hall, 1987.
Szulc, Tad. *The Illusion of Peace*. New York: Viking, 1978.
Thornton, Richard C. *The Nixon-Kissinger Years*. New York: Paragon House, 1989.

On Spiro Agnew

Agnew, Spiro T. *Go Quietly or Else*. New York: William Morrow, 1980.
Cohen, Richard, and Jules Witcover. *A Heartbeat Away*. New York: Viking, 1974.
Hoffman, Paul. *Spiro*. New York: Tower Publications, 1971.
Witcover Jules. *White Knight: The Rise of Spiro Agnew*. New York: Random House, 1972.

On Henry Kissinger

Blumenfeld, Ralph and the Staff and Editors of the *New York Post*. *Henry Kissinger*. New York: New American Library, 1974.
Hersh, Seymour. *The Price of Power*. New York: Summit, 1983.
Isaacson, Walter. *Kissinger*. New York: Simon & Schuster, 1992.
Kalb, Martin and Bernard. *Kissinger*. Boston: Little, Brown, 1974.
Kissinger, Henry. *White House Years*. Boston: Little, Brown, 1979.
———. *Years of Upheaval*. Boston: Little, Brown, 1982.
———. *Years of Renewal*. New York: Simon & Schuster, 1999.
Morris, Roger. *Uncertain Greatness*. New York: Harper & Row, 1977.
Valeriani, Richard. *Travels with Henry*. Boston: Houghton Mifflin, 1979.

On Vietnam

Bui Diem and David Chanoff. *In the Jaws of History*. Boston: Houghton Mifflin, 1987.
Chennault, Anna. *The Education of Anna*. New York: Times Books, 1980.
Currey, Cecil, B. *Edward Lansdale: The Unquiet American*. Boston: Houghton Mifflin, 1988.
DeBenedetti, Charles, assisted by Charles Chatfield. *An American Ordeal: The Antiwar Movement of the Vietnam Era*. Syracuse, NY: Syracuse University Press, 1990.
Dietz, Terry. *Republicans and Vietnam*. New York: Greenwood Press, 1986.
Karnow, Stanley. *Vietnam: A History*. London: Pimlico, 1991.
McNamara, Robert S. with Brian VanDeMark. *In Retrospect*. New York: Random House, 1995.
Nguyen Tien, Hung and Jerrold Schecter. *The Palace File*. New York: Harper & Row, 1986.
Plaster, John L. *SOG: The Secret Wars of America's Commandos in Vietnam*. New York: Simon & Schuster, 1997.
Podhoretz, Norman. *Why We Were in Vietnam*. New York: Simon & Schuster, 1982.
Prados, John. *The Sky Would Fall: Operation Vulture, The U.S. Bombing Mission in Indochina, 1954*. New York: Dial Press, 1983.
Pratt, John Clark. *Vietnam Voices: Perspectives on the War Years 1941–1982*. New York: Viking, 1984.
Rudenstine, David. *The Day the Presses Stopped*. Berkeley, CA: University of California, 1996.
Scott, Peter Dale. *The War Conspiracy*. New York: Bobbs-Merrill Company, 1972.
Shawcross, William. *Sideshow*. New York: Pocket Books, 1970.
Sheehan, Neil. *A Bright Shining Lie*. London: Jonathan Cape, 1989.
Ungar, Sanford J. *The Papers and the Papers*. New York: Dutton, 1972.

Books by Individuals Associated with the Watergate Scandal

Colson, Charles W. *Born Again*. New York: Bantam, 1976.
———. *Life Sentence*. Lincoln, VA: Chosen Books, 1979.
——— with Ellen Santilli Vaughan. *Kingdoms in Conflict*. New York: William Morrow, 1987.
Connally, John with Mickey Herskowitz. *In History's Shadow*. New York: Hyperion, 1993.
Dean, John. *Blind Ambition*. New York: Simon & Schuster, 1976.
———. *Lost Honor*. Los Angeles: Stratford Press, 1982.
Ehrlichman, John. *Witness to Power*. New York: Pocket Books, 1982.
Garment, Leonard. *Crazy Rhythm*. New York: Random House, 1997.
Haldeman, H.R. with Joseph DiMona. *The Ends of Power*. New York: Times Books, 1978.
Haldeman, H.R. *The Haldeman Diaries*. New York: Putnam, 1994.
Hunt, E. Howard. *Give Us This Day*. New York: Arlington House, 1973.
———. *Undercover*. New York: Berkeley, 1974.

Kleindienst, Richard. *Justice.* Ottawa: Jameson Books, 1985.

Liddy, Gordon. *Will.* New York: St. Martin's, 1980.

McCord, James W. *A Piece of Tape: The Watergate Story, Fact and Fiction.* Rockville, MD: Washington Media Services, 1974.

Magruder, Jeb Stuart. *An American Life.* New York: Atheneum, 1974.

———. *From Power to Peace.* Waco, TX: Work Books, 1978.

Malek, Frederick V. *Washington's Hidden Tragedy.* New York: The Free Press, 1978.

O'Brien, Lawrence. *No Final Victories.* New York: Doubleday, 1974.

Stans, Maurice H. *The Terrors of Justice.* New York: Everest House, 1978.

———. *One of the Presidents' Men: Twenty Years with Eisenhower and Nixon.* Washington, D.C.: Brassey's, 1995.

Ulasewicz, Tony with Stuart A. McKeever. *The President's Private Eye: The Journey of Detective Tony U. from N.Y.P.D. to the Nixon White House.* Westport, CT: MACSAM, 1990.

Books by or About Watergate Probers

Annis, J. Lee, Jr. *Howard Baker.* New York: Madison Books, 1995.

Ben-Veniste, Richard and George Frampton, Jr. *Stonewall.* New York: Simon & Schuster, 1977.

Cox, Archibald. *The Court and the Constitution.* Boston: Houghton Mifflin, 1987.

Dash, Samuel. *Chief Counsel.* New York: Random House, 1976.

Doyle, James. *Not Above the Law.* New York: William Morrow, 1977.

Ervin, Sam J., Jr. *The Whole Truth.* New York: Random House, 1980.

Gormley, Ken. *Archibald Cox: Conscience of a Nation.* Reading, MA: Perseus Books, 1997.

Jaworski, Leon. *The Right and the Power.* New York: Reader's Digest Press, 1976.

——— with Mickey Herskowitz. *Confession and Avoidance.* New York: Anchor Press, 1979.

——— with Dick Schneider. *Crossroads.* Elgin, IL: David Cook, 1981.

Sirica, John J. *To Set the Record Straight.* New York: W. W. Norton, 1979.

Thompson, Fred D. *At That Point in Time.* New York: Quadrangle, Times Books, 1975.

Zeifman, Jerry. *Without Honor.* New York: Thunder's Mouth Press, 1995.

Books on Watergate

Berger, Raoul. *Impeachment.* New York: Bantam/Harvard University Press, 1974.

Bernstein, Carl and Bob Woodward. *All the President's Men.* New York: Simon & Schuster, 1974.

Black, Charles L., Jr. *Impeachment: A Handbook.* New Haven, CT: Yale University Press, 1974.

Breslin, Jimmy. *How the Good Guys Finally Won.* New York: Viking, 1975.

Buschel, Lee, Al Robbins, and Bill Vitka. *The Watergate File.* New York: Flash Books, 1973.

Chester, Lewis with Cal McCrystal, Stephen Aris, and William Shawcross. *Watergate.* New York: Ballantine Books, 1973.

Colodny, Len and Robert Gettlin. *Silent Coup.* New York: St. Martin's, 1991.

Dent, Harry S. *Coverup.* San Bernardino, CA: Here's Life Publishers, 1986.

Dobrovir, William with Joseph Gebhardt, Samuel Buffone, and Andra Oakes. *The Offenses of Richard M. Nixon: A Guide for the People of the U.S.* New York: Quadrangle, 1974.

Dorman, Michael. *Dirty Politics.* New York: Delacorte Press, 1979.

Drew, Elizabeth. *Washington Journal.* New York: Random House, 1975.

Edmondson, Madeleine and Alden Duer Cohen. *The Women of Watergate.* New York: Pocket, 1975.

Emery, Fred. *Watergate: The Corruption of American Politics and the Fall of Richard Nixon.* New York: Times Books, 1994.

Fields, Howard. *High Crimes and Misdemeanors.* New York: W. W. Norton, 1978.

Friedman, Leon. *United States v. Nixon.* New York: Chelsea House, 1974.

Frost, David. *I Gave Them a Sword.* New York: William Morrow, 1978.

Havill, Adrian. *Deep Truth.* New York: Birch Lane Press, 1993.

Hougan, Jim. *Secret Agenda.* New York: Random House, 1984.

Knappman, Edward W. *Watergate and the White House, June 1972–September 1974, Vols. 1, 2, 3, 4.* New York: Facts on File, 1973–1974.

Kurland, Philip. *Watergate and the Constitution.* Chicago: University of Chicago Press, 1978.

Kutler, Stanley. *The Wars of Watergate.* New York: Alfred A. Knopf, 1990.

Lasky, Victor. *It Didn't Start with Watergate.* New York: Dell, 1977.

Lukas, Anthony. *Nightmare.* New York: Penguin, 1988.

Lurie, Leonard. *The Impeachment of Richard Nixon.* New York: Berkley, 1973.

McCarthy, Mary. *The Mask of State: Watergate Portraits.* New York: Harcourt Brace Jovanovich, 1974.

McMenamin, Michael and Walter McNamara. *Milking the Public.* Chicago, IL: Nelson-Hall, 1980.

Mankiewicz, Frank. *Nixon's Road to Watergate.* London: Hutchinson, 1973.

————. *U.S. vs. Richard M. Nixon*. New York: Quadrangle, 1975.
Miller, Marvin. *The Breaking of a President, Vols 1, 2, 3, 4*. City of Industry, CA: Collectors Publications, 1974, 1975.
Oglesby, Carl. *The Yankee and Cowboy Wars*. Mission, KS: Sheed, Andrews and McMeel, 1976.
Rangall, Leo. *The Mind of Watergate*. New York: W. W. Norton, 1980.
Schudson, Michael. *Watergate in American History*. New York: Basic Books, 1992.
Shannon, William. *They Could Not Trust the King*. New York: Collier Books, 1974.
Smith, Franklin B. *The Assassination of President Nixon*. Rutland, VT: Academy Books, 1976.
Smith, Myron J. *Watergate: An Annotated Bibliography of Sources in English, 1972–1982*. Metuchen, NJ: Scarecrow Press, 1983.
Sussman, Barry. *The Great Coverup*. Arlington, VA: Seven Locks Press, 1992.
Szulc, Tad. *Compulsive Spy*. New York: Viking, 1974.
The Staff of the *New York Times*, eds. *The End of Presidency*. New York: Bantam, 1974.
————. *The White House Transcripts*. New York: Bantam, 1974.
The Staff of the *Washington Post*, eds. *The Presidential Transcripts*. New York: Dell, 1974.
————. *The Fall of a President*. New York: Dell, 1974.
Weissman, Steve. *Big Brother and the Holding Company*. Palo Alto, CA: Ramparts Press, 1974.
White, Theodore, H. *Breach of Faith*. London: Jonathan Cape, 1975.
Woodward, Bob and Carl Bernstein. *The Final Days*. New York: Avon, 1976.
Woodward, Bob. *Shadow: Five Presidents and the Legacy of Watergate*. New York: Simon & Schuster, 1999.
Woodward, C. Vann. *Responses of the Presidents to Charges of Misconduct*. New York: Dell, 1974.

On Alexander Haig

Haig, Alexander, Jr., with Charles McGarry. *Inner Circles*. New York: Warner Books, 1992.
Morris, Roger. *Haig: The General's Progress*. Chicago: Playboy Press, 1982.

On Gerald Ford

Cannon, James. *Time and Chance*. New York: HarperCollins, 1993.
Ford, Gerald R. *A Time to Heal*. Norwalk, CT: Easton Press, 1987.
Hartmann, Robert T. *Palace Politics*. New York: McGraw-Hill, 1980.
Mollenhoff, Clark R. *The Man Who Pardoned Nixon*. New York: Giniger, in association with St. Martin's Press, 1976.

On Financial Irregularity

Bahama Islands, Report of the Commission of Inquiry into the Operation of the Business of Casinos in Freeport and in Nassau. London: H.M.S.O., 1967.
Examination of President Nixon's Tax Returns for 1969 through 1972. Washington D.C.: U.S. Government Printing Office, 1974.
Howe, Russell U. W. and Sarah Hays Trott. *The Power Peddlers: How Lobbyists Mold America's Foreign Policy*. Garden City, NY: Doubleday, 1977.

On Howard Hughes

Barlett, Donald L. and James B. Steele. *Empire*. New York: W. W. Norton, 1979.
Bellett, Gerald. *Age of Secrets*. Ogdensberg, NY: Voyageur North America, 1995.
Brown, Peter Harry and Pat H. Broeske. *Howard Hughes: The Untold Story*. New York: Signet, 1997.
Davenport, Elaine with Paul Eddy and Mary Hurwitz. *The Hughes Papers*. London: André Deutsch, 1977.
Dietrich, Noah with Bob Thomas. *Howard: The Amazing Mr. Hughes*. Greenwich, CT: Fawcett, 1972.
Drosnin, Michael. *Citizen Hughes*. New York: Bantam, 1985.
Higham, Charles. *Howard Hughes: The Secret Life*. New York: Putnam, 1993.
Maheu, Robert and Richard Hack. *Next to Hughes*. New York: HarperCollins, 1992.
North-Broome, Nicholas. *The Hughes-Nixon Loan*. New York: American Public Affairs Institute, 1972.
Schemmer, Benjamin F. *The Howard Hughes Affair*. Unpub. ms., supplied to author by Schemmer.

On Robert Vesco

Eisenhauer, A.L. with Robin Moore and Robert J. Flood. *The Flying Carpetbagger*. New York: Pinnacle Books, 1976.
Herzog, Arthur. *Vesco*. New York: Doubleday, 1987.
Hutchison, Robert. *Vesco*. New York: Praeger, 1974.

On Jimmy Hoffa

Moldea, Dan E. *The Hoffa Wars*. New York: Paddington Press, 1978.
Mollenhoff, Clark. *Tentacles of Power: The Story of Jimmy Hoffa*. New York: World, 1965.
Sheridan, Walter. *The Fall and Rise of Jimmy Hoffa*. New York: Saturday Review Press, 1972.

On Organized Crime

Block, Alan. *Masters of Paradise: Organized Crime and the Internal Revenue Service in the Bahamas*. New Brunswick, NJ: Transaction Publishers, 1991.
Cohen, Mickey as told to John Peer Nugent. *Mickey Cohen*. Englewood Cliffs, NJ: Prentice-Hall, 1975.
Eisenberg, Dennis with Uri Dan and Eli Landau. *Meyer Lansky: Mogul of the Mob*. New York: Paddington Press, 1979.
Lacey, Robert. *Little Man*. Boston: Little, Brown, 1991.
Messick, Hank. *Lansky*. New York: Berkley, 1973.
Mollenhoff, Clark. *Strike Force: Organized Crime and the Government*. Englewood Cliffs, NJ: Prentice-Hall, 1972.
Ragano, Frank and Selwyn Raab. *Mob Lawyer*. New York: Scribner's, 1994.
Rappleye, Charles and Ed Becker. *All American Mafioso: The Johnny Roselli Story*. Garden City, NY: Doubleday, 1991.
Scheim, David. *Contract on America: The Mafia Murder of President John F. Kennedy*. New York: Shapolsky, 1988.
Sifakis, Carl. *The Mafia File: The A–Z of Organized Crime in America*. Wellingborough, U.K.: Equation/Thorsons, 1987.

On Intelligence-Related Subjects

Donner, Frank. *The Age of Surveillance: The Aims and Methods of America's Political Intelligence System*. New York: Vintage, 1980.
Grose, Peter. *Gentleman Spy: The Life of Allen Dulles*. Amherst, MA: University of Massachusetts Press, 1994.
Hinckle, Warren and William Turner. *Deadly Secrets*. New York: Thunder's Mouth, 1981.
Hougan, Jim. *Spooks*. New York: William Morrow, 1978.
Loftus, John and Mark Aarons. *The Secret War Against the Jews: How Western Espionage Betrayed the Jewish People*. New York: St. Martin's Press, 1994.
Powers, Thomas. *The Man Who Kept the Secrets*. New York: Pocket Books, 1979.
Prados, John. *The President's Secret Wars*. New York: William Morrow, 1986.
Ranelagh, John. *The Agency: The Rise and Decline of the CIA*. New York: Simon & Schuster, 1986.
Rositzke, Harry. *The CIA's Secret Operations*. New York: Reader's Digest Press, 1977.
Smith, Joseph B. *Portrait of a Cold Warrior*. New York: G. P. Putnam's Sons, 1976.
Sudaplatov, Pavel. *Special Tasks*. Boston: Little, Brown, 1994.
Thomas, Evan. *The Very Best Men*. New York: Simon & Schuster, 1995.
Wise, David. *The Politics of Lying*. New York: Random House, 1973.
———. *The American Police State*. New York: Random House, 1976.
——— and Thomas Ross. *The Espionage Establishment*. New York: Bantam, 1967.

Biographies and Autobiographies

Anderson, Jack with George Clifford. *The Anderson Papers*. New York: Ballantine, 1974.
Ashman, Charles and Sheldon Engelmayer. *Martha: The Mouth That Roared*. New York: Berkley Medallion, 1973.
Bauer, Stephen. *At Ease in the White House*. New York: Birch Lane Press, 1991.
Bradlee, Ben. *A Good Life*. New York: Simon & Schuster, 1995.
Bryant, Traphes with Frances Spatz Leighton. *Dog Days at the White House*. New York: Macmillan, 1975.
Buchanan, Patrick J. *Right from the Beginning*. Washington D.C.: Regnery Gateway, 1990.
Carter, Dan. *The Politics of Rage: George Wallace: The Origins of the New Conservatism and the Transformation of American Politics*. New York: Simon & Schuster, 1995.
Cheshire, Maxine with John Greenya. *Maxine Cheshire, Reporter*. Boston: Houghton Mifflin, 1978.
Clifford, Clark with Richard Holbrooke. *Counsel to the President*. New York: Random House, 1991.
Dallek, Robert. *Hail to the Chief*. New York: Hyperion, 1996.
Davis, Deborah. *Katharine the Great*. New York: Sheridan Square, 1991.

Dean, Maureen with Hays Gorey. *Mo: A Woman's View of Watergate.* New York: Simon & Schuster, 1975.

Goldwater, Barry. *With No Apologies.* New York: William Morrow, 1979.

Graham, Katharine. *Personal History.* New York: Knopf, 1997.

Gubernick, Lisa Rebecca. *The Life and Times of Huntington Hartford.* New York: Putnam, 1991.

Gulley, Bill with Mary Ellen Reese. *Breaking Cover.* New York: Simon & Schuster, 1980.

Harding, Luke with David Leigh and David Pallister. *The Liar: The Fall of Jonathan Aitken.* London: Penguin, 1997.

Hillings, Patrick with Howard Seelye. *The Irrepressible Irishman: A Republican Insider,* privately published, 1993.

Hollander, Xaviera with Robin Moore and Yvonne Dunleavy. *The Happy Hooker.* New York: Dell, 1972.

Hollander, Xaviera. *Xaviera: Her Continuing Adventures.* New York: Warner, 1973.

Hutschnecker, Arnold. *The Drive for Power.* New York: Evans, 1974.

———. *The Will to Live.* New York: Simon & Schuster, 1983.

Klein, Herbert G. *Making It Perfectly Clear.* New York: Doubleday, 1980.

McLendon, Winzola. *Martha.* New York: Random House, 1979.

Miller, William Fishbait. *Fishbait: The Memoirs of the Congressional Doorkeeper.* Englewood Cliffs, NJ: Prentice-Hall, 1977.

Nofziger, Lyn. *Nofziger.* Washington D.C.: Regnery Gateway, 1992.

Obst, David. *Too Good to Be Forgotten.* New York: Wiley, 1998.

O'Neill, Tip with William Novak. *Man of the House: The Life and Political Memoirs of Tip O'Neill.* New York: Random House, 1987.

Pierpoint, Robert. *At the White House: Assignment to Six Presidents.* New York: G. P. Putnam's Sons, 1981.

Pilat, Oliver. *Drew Pearson: An Unauthorized Biography.* New York: Pocket Books, 1973.

Reston, James, Jr. *Lone Star: The Life of John Connally.* New York: Harper & Row, 1989.

Rush, George. *Confessions of an Ex-Secret Service Agent.* New York: Donald I. Fine, 1988.

Ruskin, Jonah. *For the Hell of It: The Life and Times of Abbie Hoffman.* Berkeley: University of California Press, 1995.

Schlesinger, Arthur M., Jr. *A Thousand Days: John F. Kennedy in the White House.* Boston: Houghton Mifflin, 1965.

———. *Robert Kennedy and His Times.* Boston: Houghton Mifflin, 1978.

Schorr, Daniel. *Clearing the Air.* New York: Berkley, 1978.

terHorst, J.F. and Col. Ralph Albertazzie. *The Flying White House: The Story of Air Force One.* New York: Coward, McCann and Geoghegan, 1979.

Thomas, Evan. *The Man to See.* New York: Simon & Schuster, 1991.

Trento, Susan B. *The Power House: Robert Keith Gray and the Selling of Access and Influence in Washington.* New York: St. Martin's, 1992.

Walters, Vernon A. *Silent Missions.* New York: Doubleday, 1978.

Wills, Garry. *Reagan's America: Innocents at Home.* Garden City, NY: Doubleday, 1987.

Zumwalt, Elmo R., Jr. *On Watch.* Arlington, VA: Admiral Zumwalt & Consultants, 1976.

Index

Abourezk, James, 392
Abplanalp, Robert, 108, 252, 257, 261, 325, 370, 426, 496*n*, 511*n*, 512*n*
Abrahamsen, David, 487*n*, 488*n*
Abrams, Creighton, 297, 463
Acheson, Dean, 136
Ackerman, William, 47, 48, 123
Adams, Earl, 46, 221
Adams, Morgan, 124
Adams, Sherman, 148, 496*n*
Adenauer, Konrad, 265
Adonis, Joe, 111
Agnew, Spiro, 96, 515*n*, 518*n*, 519*n*, 525*n*
  as Nixon's running mate, 275, 284–86
  Nixon-Thieu agreement and, 296, 298, 300, 302–4
  resignation of, xii, 275, 457–58, 459
  as vice president, 330, 331, 351, 451
Ailes, Roger, 94, 506*n*
Air Force One, x, 38, 39, 101, 105, 262, 310, 324–25, 326, 333, 368, 394, 462, 484–85
Aitken, Jonathan, 487*n*, 490*n*, 513*n*, 515*n*
Ajax, Operation, 163
Albert, Carl, 453
Albertazzie, Ralph, 38, 344, 462
Albrink, Freddie, 21
ALES code name, 77–78
Alessio, John, 278, 279
Alexander, Donald, 255
Allen, George, 115
Allenberg, Abe, 111
Allende, Salvador, 335–37, 526*n*
Alo, Vincent ("Jimmy Blue Eyes"), 114, 128, 488*n*
Alsop, Patricia, 147
Alsop, Stewart, 6, 82, 170, 488*n*

Alter, Sy, 240, 243, 252
Ambrose, Stephen, 298
AM/THUG, 184
Anagnostopoulos, Theodoros, 284
Anderson, Jack, 56, 111, 197, 198, 319, 407, 408, 409, 413, 415
Anderson, Robert, 257–58, 513*n*
Anderson, William, 124
Angelone, Oliver, 212
Annenberg, Walter, 397
Arbenz, Jacobo, 500*n*
Armstrong, Scott, 509*n*
Army Security Agency, 76, 78
Arnold, William, 86, 201
Arvey, Jake, 129
Associated Press, 219, 367, 462
Astor, David, 87
Ayub Khan, Mohammed, 163

Baerwald & DeBoer, 258–59
Bagley, William, 421
Bailley, Phillip, 418, 423, 530*n*
Baker, Bobby, 82, 104
Baker, Howard, 349, 446–47
Baker, Russell, 208
Baldwin, Alfred, 408, 409, 410, 416–17, 426, 528*n*–29*n*
Ball, Ed, 260
Ball, George, 136, 164
Banco de Londres y Mexico, 396
B & C Investments, 257
Bank Cantrade, 258–59
Bank of America, 42, 47, 131, 133
Bao Dai, 164
Bardot, Brigitte, 242
Barker, Bernard, 107, 431
Barnes, Tracy, 186, 192
Baruffi, Andy, 109
Bassett, James, 17, 82–83, 93,

97, 107, 143–50, 159, 160, 165, 166, 202, 205, 206, 221, 225, 237, 429
Bassett, Wilma, 143, 216
Batista, Fulgencio, 126–27, 128, 178–79, 181, 182, 194
Baughman, U. E., 168, 169–70, 171
Bay of Pigs invasion, 175, 176–78, 185, 187, 191, 197–99, 222–24, 274, 414, 432
Beckley, Gil ("The Brain"), 113, 496*n*
Beecher, William, 440, 533*n*
Beeson, Jane, 487*n*
Behn, Gerald, 511*n*
Bellino, Carmine, 51, 52, 144–45, 212, 507*n*
Benguet Consolidated, 244–45
Bentley, Elizabeth, 65
Ben-Veniste, Richard, 477, 534*n*
Berg, Donald, 113
Bergholz, Richard, 9, 233
Berlanti, Louis, 513*n*
Berle, Adolf, 490*n*
Bernstein, Carl, 38–39, 95–96, 234, 369, 434, 436, 446, 458, 533*n*, 535*n*, 536*n*
Beschloss, Michael, 264
Bewley, Knoop and Nixon, 131, 133
Bewley, Tom, 29, 131–32, 156
Bible, 13, 322, 365
Bickerton, Alan, 254
Binder, David, 515*n*
Birely, William, 409, 527*n*, 535*n*
Bissell, Richard, 186, 189, 503*n*
Blake, Robert, 346
Blekey, Robert, 217
Blew, Philip, 32
Blind Ambition (Dean), 72–73
Block, Alan, 242, 243, 510*n*
Block, William, 520*n*

Blum, Harold, 132
Bobst, Elmer, 145, 173, 225, 260, 264, 293, 483
Boggs, Marion, 184, 188–89
Bohemian Grove, 117, 235
Bok, Derek, 17
Bolívar, Simón, 168, 170
Bond, Julian, 355
Bonsal, Philip, 185
Bork, Robert, 17, 354, 443, 459, 462
Braden, Tom, 226–27
Bradlee, Benjamin, 218, 532n, 533n
Bradley, Omar, 78
Brandon, Henry, 368
Bremer, Arthur, 405–6, 526n–27n
Brennan, Peter, 17, 358
Breslin, Jimmy, 465
Bretnall, Harold, 73
Brewster, Owen, 85, 186, 194
Brezhnev, Leonid, 296, 393, 452, 460, 461, 471
Bright Shining Lie, A (Sheehan), 425
Briguglio, Salvatore, 525n
Brinegar, Claude, 12
Brodie, Fawn, 96–97, 190, 488n, 494n
Brookings Institution, 385–88, 390–92
Brown, Bertram, 477
Brown, Edmund ("Pat"), 56, 225, 226–27, 233, 234, 237–38, 260, 268, 286
Brown, George, 479, 481
Brown, Jerry, 503n
Bryant, Traphes, 327, 349
Brzezinski, Zbigniew, 313
Buchanan, Ruth, 203
Buchen, Philip, 478
Buchwald, Art, 39
Buckley, Jim, 388
Buckley, Michael, 245
Buckley, William, 374
Bui Diem, 299–301, 302, 304–5
Bull, Stephen, 348
Burden, Amanda, 523n
Burger, Warren, 473
Burke, Richard, 454
Burning Tree Club, 146–47, 187, 201
Burns, Arthur, 329, 353, 361
Bush, George, x, 212, 275, 476, 485
Butler, Allan, 245
Buttari, Edgardo, 110
Butterfield, Alexander, 17, 96, 325, 338, 345, 346, 348, 351, 374, 380, 403, 436, 454
Buzhardt, Fred, 2, 177, 392, 473, 482–83

Caine Mutiny, The (Wouk), 477
Califano, Joseph, Jr., 305, 307, 532n

California Democratic Council (CDC), 229–30
Call, Asa, 48
Calley, William, 334
Cambodia, 307
  bombing campaigns against, 3, 332–33, 342–43, 474
  U.S. invasion of, 90, 344–45, 362–63, 367, 370, 393
Campbell, Judith, 213, 511n
Campbell, Lou, 433
Camp David, 101, 325, 327, 347, 349, 363, 369, 411, 429, 438, 441, 448–49, 454, 461
Candor, Operation, 3
Cannon, James, 436
Cannon, Lou, 235
Caplin, Mortimer, 393
Capp, Al, 379
Capri, George, 55
Carter, Jimmy, x, 4, 485
Carver, George, 372, 522n, 534n
Casey, William, 211–12
Casper, Norman, 104, 127, 253–57, 512n
Cassinetto, Jack, 246
Castle Bank and Trust Company, 253–57
Castro, Fidel, 106, 127, 230, 336, 500n, 501n, 502n, 503n, 508n–9n, 524n
  CIA assassination plots against, 175, 180–81, 184–99, 222, 223, 320–21, 335, 337, 388, 412–14, 415, 424, 432
  as Communist, 180, 181, 183
  dictatorship of, 179, 182, 239, 241
  mob contract on, 178–81, 193–99
  Nixon's meeting with, 181–83
  Nixon's opposition to, 176–99
  Nixon's views on, 175, 182–83
Castro, Raúl, 179, 183, 187, 189, 192
Catholic Church, 12, 13, 209–10, 212, 216
Catlett, Raymond, 491n
Caulfield, John, 198, 342, 376, 387, 514n, 524n, 534n
Ceaucescu, Nikolai, 368
Celler, Emanuel, 136
Cellini, Dino, 241
Cellini, Eddie, 242, 243
Central Intelligence Agency (CIA), 286, 339, 421
  in Allende overthrow, 335–37
  in Bay of Pigs invasion, 176–78, 197–99, 222–24
  Castro assassination plots of, 175, 180–81, 184–99, 222, 223, 320–21, 334–335,

337, 388, 412–14, 415, 424, 432
  congressional investigation of, 188–90, 191, 193, 335, 336, 337, 345
  Cuban covert operations of, 174–75, 188–89, 192
  Hiss investigated by, 63, 73–74, 77–78
  in Malaxa affair, 131, 132–34
  mob connections attributed to, 193–99
  Nixon-Thieu agreement investigated by, 298, 300–301
  in Watergate scandal, 432–33, 473, 474
Chambers, Whittaker, 60–61, 63, 65–66, 68–69, 70, 71, 72, 75, 79, 80, 200, 219, 225, 489n, 490n, 499n
Chandler, Dorothy ("Buff"), 202, 203
Chandler, Norman, 43, 48, 202
Chandler, Otis, 48–49
Chapin, Dwight, 53, 54, 312, 359, 380–81, 384, 467
Chapman, Earl, 88
Chappaquiddick affair, 378–79, 380, 409
Charles, Prince of Wales, 326
Checkers (Nixon's dog), 120, 121–22, 261, 326
Chennault, Anna, xiv, 298–306, 322, 518n–19n, 534n
Chennault, Claire, 298, 518n
Cheshire, Maxine, 29, 488n
Chesler, Lou, 243, 510n, 513n
Chiang Kai-shek, 163, 298
Chicago Seven, 357
Chile, 335–37, 342
China, People's Republic of:
  Nixon's trip to (1972), 3, 115, 163, 314, 371, 393, 433, 437, 482, 484
  Nixon's views on, 163, 166, 295, 371–72
  as UN member, 229
  U.S. relations with, 264
Chisholm, Shirley, 355, 400, 521n, 525n
Chotiner, Jack, 52, 55
Chotiner, Murray, 525n, 530n
  background of, 50
  death of, 467
  FBI investigation of, 53
  mob connections attributed to, 50–59, 149
  in Nixon's congressional campaign (1946), 42–43, 46, 51, 54–58
  in Nixon's gubernatorial campaign (1962), 52–53, 228, 229
  in Nixon's presidential campaign (1968), 53, 273, 277, 319

in Nixon's presidential campaign (1972), 54
Nixon's relationship with, xi, 50–58, 216, 238, 353, 398
in Nixon's Senate campaign (1950), 51, 54–57, 83–84, 85, 86
in Nixon's vice-presidential campaign (1952), 51, 117, 118, 121, 123, 137, 139
in Nixon's vice-presidential campaign (1956), 148, 149, 150
reputation of, 51–52, 149
as special counsel, 53, 375
in Watergate scandal, 53, 54
Chotiner, Nancy, 50, 237
Christian, George, 445
Christopher, George, 95, 317
Churchill, Winston S., 65, 328, 439, 486
Civil Aeronautics Board, 157–58, 281
civil rights movement, 204, 355
Clarke, Jack, 128, 498n
Clawson, Ken, 17, 523n
Clements, William, 461, 462
Clesner, Herschel, 257
Clifford, Clark, 298, 306
Clinton, Bill, x, 53, 105, 122, 141, 158, 401, 485
Clinton, Hillary Rodham, 466, 536n
Cloes, Elizabeth, 27
Cobb, June, 193
Cohen, Mickey, 54–57, 85, 129, 217, 226, 489n
Cohn, Roy, 82
Colby, William, 335, 472, 520n
cold war, 322
Colodny, Len, 534n
Colson, Charles, 485, 524n, 525n, 526n, 528n, 533n
  Brookings Institution raid and, 387, 388
  "enemies list" prepared by, 375
  as Nixon's aide, 12–13, 61, 72–73, 105, 191, 218, 221, 295, 312, 372–73, 379, 380, 384–85, 398, 399, 405–8, 411, 436, 437
  at Nixon's funeral, xii
  in Nixon's presidential campaign (1972), 74–75
  Plumbers' Unit and, 394, 402, 405–8, 427–28
  in Watergate scandal, xii, 230, 390, 391, 394, 402, 405–8, 414, 415, 420, 427–32, 434, 444, 448, 467
  White House tapes and, 349
Committee for the Preservation of the Democratic Party in California, 229–30
Committee to Re-Elect the President (CREEP), 54, 245,

395–98, 400–403, 405, 408, 409, 412, 416, 419, 424, 430, 432, 436
Communists:
  Hoover's measures against, 43, 65, 74
  McCarthy's crusade against, 45, 61, 81–83, 145, 146
  Nixon's opposition to, 22, 43, 44–45, 67, 81–85, 119, 120, 164, 165, 166–74, 182, 183, 187, 203, 226, 229–30, 264, 295–97
  in State Department, 45, 60–61, 65, 66, 69, 76, 77, 81–82
  Vietnam War insurgency of, 164–66, 292, 293, 294, 295–97, 332, 404, 439
  see also Hiss, Alger
Connally, John, 330, 441, 525n, 534n
Conniff, Ray, 401
Constitution, U.S., 65, 136, 140, 149, 189, 261, 310, 343, 393, 441, 451, 453, 456, 459, 463, 474, 480, 481
Copley, James, 49, 95, 208
Coppola, Michael ("Trigger Mike"), 112, 241
Corbin, Paul, 507n
Corcoran, Tom, 519n
Cornish, Monroe, 359
Cosmos Bank, 256–59
Costello, Frank, 57, 489n
Counts, Curtis, 31, 398
Courtney, Max, 127–28, 241, 513n
Cox, Archibald, 95, 452, 455, 458–59, 466, 477, 535n
Cox, Ed, 326, 328, 383, 441, 463, 475, 476, 482, 536n
Cox, Tricia Nixon, 520n
  birth of, 43
  diary of, 350, 472
  gifts for, 283, 284, 328
  marriage of, 326, 328, 383
  in New York City, 261, 262, 271
  at Nixon's funeral, xi
  Nixon's political career and, 3, 216, 222, 225, 268, 309, 310
  Nixon's resignation and, 451, 475, 476, 483
  Pat Nixon and, 233–34, 236
  Watergate scandal and, 451, 463, 468, 472
  in White House, 326
Crail, Joseph, 124
Cranston, Alan, 477
Cretzianu, Alexandre, 132, 134
Crocker, William, 47
Cronin, John, 66, 159, 203, 490n
Cronkite, Betsy, 232, 398
Cronkite, Walter, 82, 95, 115, 276

Crosby, James, 241–44, 251, 252, 257, 278, 279, 510n
Crosby, Peter, 510n, 513n
Crozier, Ross, 501n
Cuba:
  CIA operations in, 174–75, 188–89, 192
  currency of, 186, 191, 192
  economy of, 178, 182, 186, 191, 192
  Eisenhower's policy on, 181, 182, 183, 184–86, 188–89, 197, 223
  Mafia gambling operations in, 178–81, 193, 239, 241
  Nixon's interest in, 32–33, 107, 124–29, 135, 176–99, 412–14
  Nixon's visits to, 33–34, 41, 124–29, 135, 178, 180–81, 194, 213, 412–14
Cuban Missile Crisis, 230, 461
Culbertson, Horace, 126
Cullen, Frank, 234
Cummings, Homer, 157
Curtis, Tony, 254
Cushman, Robert, 174, 184, 185–86, 190, 191, 193, 194, 196, 388, 480, 536n
Cutler, Lloyd, 211

Daley, John, 525n
Daley, Richard, 208, 217, 309
Dalitz, Moe, 253
Dan, Uri, 127
Daniel, Aubrey, 334
Danner, Richard, 100–101, 106, 111, 126, 127, 280–81, 282, 495n
Dash, Sam, 453, 534n
Davidson, Irving, 507n
Davies, John, 228, 240, 521n
Dean, Dizzy, 472
Dean, John, 525n, 526n, 529n–30n, 534n
  "enemies list" as viewed by, 375–76
  memoir of, 72–73
  as presidential legal counsel, 312, 343, 387, 394, 421–23, 441, 443–44
  resignation of, 449
  in Watergate scandal, xiii, 21–22, 61, 312, 400, 428, 447, 454, 458, 467
  White House tapes and, 349, 380
DeBoer, Franklin, 251–53, 259, 274, 459, 512n
Declaration of Independence, 326
"Deep Throat," 95–96, 436, 458, 533n
de Gaulle, Charles, 264–65, 293, 326–27, 379
de Gendre, Raoul, 259
DeLoach, Cartha ("Deke"), 303, 314, 445, 534n

Demetracopoulos, Elias,
285–87, 321, 500*n*, 515*n*,
530*n*–31*n*
Democratic National Committee
(DNC), 129, 321, 342
Watergate burglary of, 21–22,
44, 284, 403–4, 408, 416,
423–33, 444–45, 447
Watergate wiretapping of,
408–11, 416–23, 430
Democratic National Conventions:
of 1960, 203, 235
of 1968, 357*n*
of 1972, 380, 400–403, 418,
435–36
Democratic party, *see specific
elections and individuals*
Dennin, Joe, 190
Dennis, Eugene, 168
Denomo, Gerald, 525*n*
de Toledano, Ralph, 147,
217–18
Dewey, Thomas E., 63, 65, 82,
117, 118, 119, 128–29,
151, 225, 278, 311, 329,
498*n*
Dickerson, Nancy, 147, 265,
364, 365, 367, 467
Dick Nixon Special, 150
Dien Bien Phu, battle of, 165–66
Dieter, Cathy, 530*n*
Dietrich, Noah, 151, 153, 155,
157, 158
Dietrich, W. Q., 490*n*
Diggs, Marshall, 186, 194
Dilantin, 317–18, 449, 455
DiMona, Joseph, 505*n*
Dirksen, Everett, 519*n*
Disraeli, Benjamin, 346
Dixon, Gloria, 43
Dixon, Jeane, 89
Dixon, Tom, 36, 43, 86
DNC, *see* Democratic National
Committee
Dobrynin, Anatoly, 295, 452,
459, 460
Dole, Bob, x
Donovan, Leisure, Newton, and
Lombard, 62, 73–74
Donovan, William ("Wild Bill"),
62, 63, 73–74, 78
Dorfman, Allen, 525*n*
Dorn, Evelyn, 29–30, 36
Douglas, Helen Gahagan, 489*n*
Communist accusations
against, 51, 84, 85, 86
Senate campaign of (1950),
51, 83–87, 88, 100, 135,
201
Douglas, Melvyn, 86
Douglas-Home, Alec, 348
Downey, Sheridan, 88
Doyle, James, 455
Dragna, Jack, 55
Dreyfus, Jack, Jr., 317, 318,
449
Drinan, Robert, 332

Drive for Power, The (Hutsch-
necker), 98
Droller, Gerry, 183
Drown, Helene, 8, 139, 158
Drown, Jack, 138, 183, 202
Duke, Francis Vincent, 488*n*
Duke University Law School,
20–22, 25–26, 31–32, 64,
147, 354
Dulles, Allen, 62–63, 65, 77, 78,
133, 134, 170, 181–86,
189–93, 222, 489*n*, 490*n*,
492*n*, 502*n*
Dulles, John Foster, 62–63, 90,
148, 489*n*
Dump Nixon movement, 153,
154
Dunn, Mike, 290, 516*n*

Eagleburger, Lawrence, 372,
460, 482
Eagle Eye, Operation, 309
Eagleton, Thomas, 436
Edge of the Sword, The (de
Gaulle), 265
Edlund, Elayne, 467–68
Edson, Peter, 119, 215–16, 497*n*
Edwards, Willard, 204
Edward III, King of England,
328
Ehrlichman, John, 523*n*, 524*n*,
528*n*–29*n*, 535*n*
Brookings Institution raid
and, 385–88
Nixon as viewed by, 3, 12,
37, 74, 96, 99, 199,
234–35, 244, 247, 268–69,
311, 317, 338, 353, 354,
355, 368, 413, 451
in Nixon's gubernatorial campaign (1962), 228, 232
in Nixon's presidential campaign (1960), 206, 209
in Nixon's presidential campaign (1968), 273, 274,
277, 316, 320
Pat Nixon as viewed by, 37,
464
Rebozo and, 105, 106, 109
resignation of, 348, 448–52
tax audits and, 375–76
in Watergate scandal, xii,
313, 384, 389, 390, 391,
392, 416, 417, 429, 432,
446–52, 467, 468
as White House counsel, 176,
178, 311, 312, 325, 329,
330, 342, 363, 378, 394,
436
White House tapes and, 347,
348, 386–87
wiretapping activities and,
343, 348
Eisenhower, David, 108–9, 326,
368, 441, 475, 476, 477
Eisenhower, Dwight D., 62, 115,
205, 315, 499*n*, 501*n*,
506*n*, 508*n*

Cuban policy of, 181, 182,
183, 184–86, 188–89, 197,
223
death of, x
foreign policy of, 145–46,
164, 174–75, 195–96
golf played by, 146–47, 148
Hannah Nixon's telegram to,
139–40
heart condition of, 148–49,
206
Nixon as running mate of,
116–22, 135–40, 153, 154,
195, 201
Nixon presidential campaign
and (1960), 206, 217–18
Nixon's relationship with, x,
82, 83, 116–22, 133–34,
138, 139, 140, 145–50,
158, 162, 167, 183–84,
206, 217–18, 237, 261,
267, 311
Nixon's views on, 41, 116,
120, 121, 482
presidential campaign of
(1952), 116–22, 129, 134,
135–40
presidential campaign of
(1956), 51–52
tape recording system of, 146,
315
Vietnam policy of, 164–66
Eisenhower, Julie Nixon, 522*n*,
535*n*
birth of, 60
diary of, 268
finances of, 108–9
gifts for, 283, 284, 328
media coverage of, 377
in New York City, 261, 262,
271
Nixon as viewed by, 34, 36
at Nixon's funeral, xi
Nixon's political career and,
268, 309, 310
Nixon's resignation and, 451,
475, 476, 482, 483
Pat Nixon as viewed by,
28–29, 30, 79–80, 139,
220–21, 233–34, 236, 268
poem written by, 143
Watergate scandal and, 451,
463, 468
in White House, 326, 368,
393–94
Eisenhower, Mamie, 121, 145,
271
Eisenhower, Milton, 171, 172
Eisler, Gerhart, 60, 168, 489*n*
elections:
of 1920, 20
of 1944, 151
of 1946, 41–49, 51, 54–58,
60, 62, 64, 83, 84, 153,
210
of 1950, 51, 83–87, 88, 100,
135, 201, 210, 213
of 1952, 36, 51, 64–65, 79,

82, 90, 101, 116–22, 129, 134, 135–40
of 1954, 51, 148
of 1956, 51–52, 92, 134, 140, 148, 149–50, 153, 154, 158, 159–61, 195
of 1958, 101
of 1960, 21, 29, 36, 52, 65, 90, 92, 95, 101, 105, 107, 156, 171, 173, 174, 184–85, 186, 200–224, 231, 232, 235, 242–43, 267, 276, 309, 310, 321
of 1962, 48, 52–53, 56, 90, 97, 101, 104–5, 225–33, 236, 237–38, 240, 260, 314, 345, 368, 377, 464
of 1964, 225, 263, 267, 268–69
of 1966, 267, 268
of 1968, xiv, 2, 3, 37, 39, 53, 56, 94, 101, 105–6, 108, 110, 113, 177, 196, 243, 265, 267, 271–87, 309–10, 313, 316, 318–20, 355, 378, 397, 399
of 1970, 379
of 1972, 54, 74–75, 106, 164, 197, 230, 278, 283, 355–56, 377, 378, 379, 380–82, 395–99, 401, 402, 405, 408, 411, 424, 434–38, 440, 441, 446
Elfin, Mel, 455
Elizabeth II, Queen of England, 328
Elliott, Lois, 19, 487n
Ellsberg, Daniel, 385–92, 401, 403, 404, 407, 408, 425, 428, 435, 467, 494n, 523n–24n
Emancipation Proclamation, 13
Ervin, Sam, 141, 198, 330, 345, 446, 447, 456–57, 458, 486
Esterline, Jacob ("Jake"), 168, 170, 185, 192, 223–24, 500n, 502n
Evans, Harold, 477
Ewing, Michael, 214
executive privilege, 189, 453, 455
Exner, Judith Campbell, 213, 511n

Fahd, Prince, 328
Faisal, King of Saudi Arabia, 328
Farley, Ethel, 21
February Group, 247
Federal Bureau of Investigation (FBI), 53, 115, 422
  Hiss investigated by, 64–66, 68, 70, 72–75, 76, 78, 79
  Kennedy investigated by, 211, 213
  Nixon investigated by, 64, 269, 298, 301–5, 314

Rebozo investigated by, 113–14, 128
Wallace shooting investigated by, 405–6
Watergate investigation of, 429–35, 459, 473
wiretapping by, 129, 342–44
Feldbaum, Carl, 245, 421
Felt, Mark, 434
Field, Noel, 75–76, 492n
Fielding, Lewis, 524n
Fifth Amendment, 189, 451
Figueres, José, 183, 185
Final Days, The (Bernstein and Woodward), 234
Finch, Carol, 225
Finch, Robert, 97, 100, 115, 207, 211, 234, 265, 324, 329, 344
Fincher, Richard, 112
Fink, Robert, 524n
Finletter, Thomas, 124
Fitzsimmons, Frank, 356, 398–99, 525n
Flanigan, Peter, xi, 326–27, 422
Fleeson, Doris, 208
Fleming, Ian, 186, 191
Fleming, Karl, 39
Fonda, Henry, 33
Ford, Betty, 29, 324, 484
Ford, Gerald R., 4, 99, 275, 319, 324, 335, 446, 502n, 537n
  Nixon pardoned by, x, 485
  as president, 478, 480, 482, 484
  as vice president, 458, 460, 475, 476
  White House tapes and, 350, 470
Fourth Amendment, 393
Franco, Francisco, 265
Frank, John, 507n
Frederich, Walter, 112
Freeman, Warren, 126
Freidin, Seymour, 277–78
Frost, David, 104, 253, 345
Fuller, Lon, 21

Galindez, Jesús de, 491n
Gallinaro, William, 114
Gallup, George, 216
Gandhi, Indira, 39, 163
Gandhi, Mohandas K., 482, 483
Gardner, Ava, 154
Garment, Len, xi, 3–4, 50, 51, 92, 94, 99, 263, 264, 278, 293, 296, 316, 353, 424, 448, 483
Gelb, Leslie, 384
Gellman, Irwin, 488n, 494n
GEMSTONE project, 400–403, 410, 418, 428
General Service Administration (GSA), 131, 327
George, Mary, 1, 15
Gerrity, John, 196
Gerstein, Richard, 435

Gerth, Jeff, 495n
Gettlin, Robert, 534n
Getty, J. Paul, 279, 283
Ghormley, Alfond, 124, 157
Giancana, Antoinette, 104
Giancana, Chuck, 129, 153, 213, 217
Giancana, Sam, 129, 193, 213, 217, 504n, 507n, 511n
Gilday, William, 406
Gladding, McBean, 47–48, 63
Glasser, Sidney, 521n
Gleason, Thomas, 521n–22n
Godfrey, Art, 247
Goldbaum, Hy, 55
Goldberg, Lucianne, 53, 141, 506n–7n
Golden, James, 244
gold price, 245–50
Goldwater, Barry, 3, 211, 228, 263, 462–63, 470, 481–82, 483, 532n
Goodwin, Richard, 208, 216
Gorbachev, Mikhail, 485
Gordievsky, Oleg, 76, 472
Gore, Louise, 285
Göring, Hermann, 131
Graham, Billy, ix, 12, 13, 89, 106, 210, 310, 318, 322, 352, 359, 367, 377, 451
Graham, Katharine, 446
Grant, Ulysses S., 20
Gray, Pat, 405, 428
Gray, Robert Keith, 183, 469
Great Depression, 16, 43
Greece, 53, 284–87, 320, 321, 424, 430, 445, 472
Green Berets, 291, 292
Greene, Robert, 95, 376–77
Greenspun, Hank, 526n
Griffin, Robert, 476, 482
Grose, Peter, 489n
Grove, Dan, 269
Groves, Wallace, 241
GRU, 76–78
Guatemala, 174–75, 181
Guccione, Bob, 254
Guevara, Che, 179, 187
Gunn, Donald, 102
Gurney, Edward, 447

Hagerty, James, 149
Haig, Alexander, 39, 103, 185, 343, 391, 451, 454, 457–62, 466, 467, 470, 472–77, 481–84, 501n, 536n, 537n
Halberstam, David, 294
Haldeman, Henry, 85, 141
Haldeman, H. R. ("Bob"), 500n, 505n, 517n, 523n, 526n, 531n, 532n, 534n
  background of, 311–12
  Brookings Institution raid and, 385–88
  diary of, 327, 333, 348, 353–54, 355, 357, 359, 366, 367, 368, 370, 371,

Haldeman, H. R. ("Bob")
  (cont.)
  diary of, 377, 378, 382, 388,
    394, 398, 401, 403, 405,
    438, 441, 445, 448
  Kissinger and, 314, 342
  memoirs of, 414
  Nixon as viewed by, xv, 12,
    96, 161, 205, 263, 265,
    295, 296, 312, 326, 327,
    339, 342, 361, 384, 394,
    449, 451
  in Nixon's gubernatorial cam-
    paign (1962), 227, 228,
    229–30, 231, 232
  in Nixon's presidential cam-
    paign (1960), 205
  in Nixon's presidential cam-
    paign (1968), 273, 275,
    309, 310, 316, 320
  resignation of, 448–52
  Talking Paper prepared for,
    399–400, 402–3
  tax audits requested by,
    374–75
  in Watergate scandal, xii,
    21–22, 61, 197, 198, 199,
    230, 313, 331, 384, 391,
    399–404, 410, 412,
    414–15, 416, 420, 427–33,
    442, 444–52, 467, 468,
    473
  as White House chief of staff,
    61, 140–41, 146, 150,
    176–78, 311, 330, 337,
    338, 355–56, 363, 394,
    411, 414, 434–37, 438, 440
  White House tapes and, 315,
    346–48, 350, 356–58, 386,
    453–54, 473
  wiretapping activities and,
    343, 377
Hall, Harry, 399
Hall, Leonard, 149, 203, 205–6,
    211, 218, 254, 329
Halpern, Sam, 185
Halsey, Margaret, 218
Hamlet (Shakespeare), xv
Happy Hooker, The (Hollan-
    der), 421
Harding, Warren G., 19–20
Harlow, Bryce, 26, 121, 237,
    260, 320, 322, 395, 467
Harriman, Averell, 135, 344
Harris, Lou, 208, 393
Harris, Patricia, *527n*
Hart, Gary, 190, 230
Hartford, Huntington, 239–41,
    244, 257
Hartmann, Robert, 48, 458
Hatfield, Mark, 296
Haykal, Mohammed, 396
Hearst, William Randolph, 83,
    239
Hearst, William Randolph, Jr.,
    352
Heavey, James, 138
Hecker, Michael, *531n*

Hefner, Hugh, 254
Helms, Richard, 177, 189, 286,
    293, 330, 335, 337, 339,
    432, *500n*, *532n–33n*
Hempstone, Smith, 456
Herbers, John, 95
Herlihy, Thomas, 427
Hermann, Albert, 212
Hersh, Seymour, 211, 224–25,
    234, 434, *507n*
Herter, Christian, 153
Hess, Stephen, 116, 230,
    262–63
Hewitt, Don, 207
Higby, Larry, 338, 347, 348,
    526n
Hill, Dee Anne, 246
Hill, Gladwin, 231, 232
Hill, Robert, 299–300, *518n*
Hillings, Patrick, 84, 132, 137,
    145, 153, 203, 231, 235,
    314
Hiss, Alger, 60–80, *489n, 490n,*
    492n
  Chambers's accusations
    against, 60–61, 63, 65–66,
    68–69, 70, 71, 72, 75
  CIA investigation of, 63,
    73–74, 77–78
  conviction of, 61, 70–71
  FBI investigation of, 64–66,
    68, 70, 72–75, 76, 78, 79
  guilt of, 61, 67, 75–79
  media coverage of, 69–70, 72,
    75, 77
  Nixon's investigation of, xi,
    2, 60–80, 81, 88, 117, 119,
    137, 224, 385, 388
  Soviet intelligence files on, 67,
    73, 75–79
  typewriter evidence against,
    70–75
Hiss, Donald, *491n, 492n*
Hiss, Priscilla, *490n, 492n*
Hiss, Timothy, 68, 77
Hitchcock, Joan, 104
Hitler, Adolf, 33
Hitt, Patricia, 300, 304, 322
Hitt, Robert, 303–4
Ho Chi Minh, 164, 295
Hoff, Joan, *517n*
Hoffa, Jimmy, 54, 113, 213–15,
    221, 249, 398–99, *525n*
Hoffman, Abbie, 357, *521n*
Holbrooke, Richard, 306
Hollander, Xaviera, 421–23,
    529n–30n
Holloway, James, 479
Holt, Joe, 84
Hoover, Herbert, 50
Hoover, J. Edgar, *490n, 514n,*
    534n
  Castro assassination plots
    and, 193
  Communist threat as viewed
    by, 43, 65, 74
  death of, 404
  Kennedy investigated by, 211

Nixon's relationship with,
    64–65, 73, 74, 77, 78, 211,
    262–63, 303, 314, 315,
    389, 394, 400, 404, 445
  White House tapes and, 348
  wiretapping approved by,
    342–43
Hopkins, Harry, 115
Hopkins, Lindsay, 222
Horack, Dean, 22
Horner, Arch, 127
Horton, Herman, 134
Hougan, Jim, *527n–28n, 531n*
House of Representatives, U.S.:
  Assassinations Committee of,
    213, 336
  Banking and Currency Com-
    mittee of, 258, 446
  Education and Labor Com-
    mittee of, 60
  Intelligence Committee of, 421
  Judiciary Committee of, 332,
    343, 466, 468, 469–70,
    473, 474
  Labor Committee of, 200
  Un-American Activities Com-
    mittee of (HUAC), 2, 45,
    60–80, 353
Howard, Mike, *55*
Howard, Richard, 358
*How to Win Friends and Influ-
    ence People* (Carnegie), 15
Hubbard, Henry, 95
Hughes, Don, 151–53, 169,
    183, 205
Hughes, Emmet, 149
Hughes, Harold, 478
Hughes, Howard, *490n, 497n,*
    504n, 514n–15n, 526n
  as anti-Communist, 151, 153
  Nixon loan of, 154–58,
    215–16, 226–27, 235, 320
  in Nixon's presidential cam-
    paign (1968), 279–82
  Nixon's relationship with,
    xiii, 53, 134, 150–58, 195,
    196, 197, 198, 249, 251,
    279–82, 321, 407, 414–16,
    424, 430, 459
  political influence of, 53, 106,
    109n, 134, 150–58, 196
  wealth of, 150–58
Hughes, John, 289, 290–92,
    516n
Hughes Medical Institute, 157,
    158
Humes, James, 212
Hummer, Ed, 66
Humphrey, Hubert H., 17, 207,
    286, 297, 320, *517n, 527n*
  Nixon-Thieu agreement and,
    300, 301, 305–6, 321
  presidential campaign of
    (1968), 276, 277–78, 280,
    310, 313, 319, 378
  presidential campaign of
    (1972), 377, 378, 380–81
Hunt, E. Howard, *499n, 500n,*

502n–3n, 523n, 524n, 525n, 536n
Brookings Institution raid and, 388
as CIA agent, 174, 175, 185, 191, 192, 194, 388, 414
memoirs of, 191
as Nixon's aide, 74, 107, 141
in Plumbers' Unit, 388–90, 392, 394, 399–404, 406, 407–8, 409, 418, 424, 426–27, 431, 444
in Watergate scandal, xii, 192, 412, 428, 480
Hunter, Oakley, 214
Hussein, King of Jordan, 371, 421
Huston, Tom, 312
Hutschnecker, Arnold, 494n, 495n, 520n, 522n, 535n
Nixon as viewed by, 7–8, 9, 13, 40, 88–89, 237, 455–56, 470
Nixon's consultations with, xiv–xv, 7, 8n, 40, 82, 88–99, 100, 139, 147, 161, 219, 237, 318–20, 363, 366, 376

IBM, 113–14
Immigration and Naturalization Act, 352–53
Immigration and Naturalization Service (INS), 131, 132
India, 163, 326, 407, 472
Integrity, Operation, 309
Internal Revenue Service (IRS), 48, 53, 104, 109, 126, 157, 158, 227, 242, 253–59, 282, 353, 374–77, 382, 399, 415, 435, 447
International Telephone and Telegraph (ITT), 72, 342, 407
Iran, 163–64, 396
Irvine, Myford, 55
Irving, Clifford, 415
Isaiah, Book of, 322
Israel, 354, 370, 371

Jackson, Donald, 514n
Jackson, Henry M. ("Scoop"), 381, 382
Jackson, Jesse, 355–56
Jackson State University shootings, 344
Jaffe, Richard, 253, 254, 255
Jameson, Bob, 247
Javits, Jacob, 243, 477
Jaworski, Leon, 429, 466, 468, 477, 532n
Jefferson, Thomas, 81, 96–97, 316
Jernigan, Jake, 105
Jews, 86, 128, 131
Jobe, Gail, 487n
John F. Kennedy, 370–71
Johns, Mildred, 19

Johnson, Andrew, 452, 535n
Johnson, Charley, 521n
Johnson, Justin, 497n
Johnson, Lyndon B., 177, 324, 329, 331, 351, 517n–18n, 519n, 534n
death of, x, 445–46
Nixon's relationship with, 145–46, 310, 311, 445, 482
presidential campaign of (1968), 280, 282, 286, 287, 295
tape recording system of, 314, 315, 345–46, 347
vice-presidential campaign of (1960), 203
Vietnam policy of, 280, 287, 291, 292–308, 331, 383, 385
Johnson, Robert, 501n–2n
Johnson Library, 132, 298
Joint Chiefs of Staff (JCS), 78, 164, 372, 438, 461, 463, 479–80, 481
Jones, Ed, 212
Jorgensen, Frank, 49
Juliana, James, 527n
Justice Department, U.S., 109, 112, 214, 226, 241, 242, 405, 448
J. Walter Thompson, 275, 311, 312

Kalmbach, Herb, xiii, 228–29, 246, 281, 444, 467, 524n–25n
Kampelman, Max, 527n
Kangles, Constantin, 182
Kapenstein, Ira, 515n
Katcher, Herbert, 97
Katcher, Leo, 97, 118–19, 494n–95n
Kaufman, Samuel, 79
Kearns, Henry, 85
Keeler, W. W., 278
Kefauver Committee, 112, 126
Kelley, Clarence, 462
Kellogg, Francis, 509n
Kelly, Tom, 220
Kemper, Ronnie, 365
Kempton, Murray, 86
Kendall, Donald, 173, 261, 335, 504n
Kennedy, Barbara, 529n
Kennedy, Edward M., 79, 197, 215, 247, 321, 377, 378–80, 387, 406–7, 409, 428, 446, 467, 523n
Kennedy, Jacqueline Bouvier, 201, 204, 211, 263, 513n
Kennedy, John F., 115, 351, 502n, 505n, 506n, 507n, 508n, 516n–17n, 520n
assassination of, x, 197, 198–99, 213, 247, 262–63, 310, 315, 483
Bay of Pigs invasion approved

by, 175, 177, 187, 197–99, 222–24
campaign style of, 209–18
Castro assassination plots and, 197–99
as Catholic, 209–10, 212
as congressman, 200–201, 202
expected presidential campaign of (1964), 225, 263
funeral of, 263, 265
health problems of, 202, 204, 211–12
mob connections attributed to, 213, 217
Nixon as viewed by, 201, 216, 218–19, 237–38, 262
Nixon's debates with, 205–9, 212, 276
Nixon's gubernatorial campaign and (1962), 226, 237–38
Nixon's relationship with, 33, 56, 57, 60, 74, 95, 135, 200–202, 262–63, 328, 329, 331, 375, 377, 378
Nixon's views on, 199, 200, 201, 202, 203, 218, 262–63
presidential campaign of (1960), 52, 101, 105, 129, 156, 173, 202–24, 276, 309, 310
previous marriage attributed to, 211
RFK's relationship with, 115, 187, 197
as senator, 201
sexual liaisons of, 201, 207, 211, 213
tape recording system of, 314, 315, 454
Vietnam policy of, 74, 166, 292, 384
Kennedy, Joseph P., Sr., 201, 213, 218, 219, 525n
Kennedy, Robert F., 51, 56, 212, 292, 491n, 502n, 509n, 520n
assassination of, 274, 275, 277, 320–21
as attorney general, 213, 214, 253, 277–78, 377, 398
in Kennedy's presidential campaign (1960), 207, 210, 216
Kennedy's relationship with, 115, 187, 197
presidential campaign of (1968), 177, 196, 274
Kennedy Library, 454
Kent, Roger, 135–36, 230
Kent State University shootings, 344, 358
Keogh, James, 441
Keough, Rosemary, 523n
Kersten, Charles, 489n
Kessler, Ronald, 488n, 534n,

Kessler, Ronald *(cont.)*
    535*n*
Key Biscayne Bank, 107–11,
    112, 250–53, 255, 259,
    274, 283
KGB, 75, 76, 77
Khashoggi, Adnan, xiii, 282–84,
    322, 396, 515*n*
Khashoggi, Soraya, 283
Khrushchev, Nikita, 82, 203,
    229, 230
    Nixon's meetings with,
        171–74, 206, 266
Kilpatrick, James, 374, 515*n*
Kimmons, Gaby, 288
Kimmons, Hollis, 288–92, 516*n*
King, Bob, 195, 196
King, Coretta Scott, 354
King, James, 114
King, J. C., 181, 184, 190, 192
King, Martin Luther, Jr.,
    274–75, 354
King Lear (Shakespeare), x
King Timahoe (Nixon's dog),
    346, 433
Kinsey, Pete, 422 –23
Kirkpatrick, Lyman, 498*n*
Kissinger, Henry A., 487*n*,
    511*n*, 515*n*, 517*n*, 521*n*,
    522*n*, 524*n*, 533*n*, 536*n*
    background of, 313
    diary of, 369
    memoirs of, 96, 295
    as national security adviser,
        96, 295–96, 313–14, 330,
        335, 337, 342, 353,
        370–72, 384–85
    Nixon as viewed by, xv, 3, 4,
        40, 96–97, 99, 163, 176,
        265, 308, 315, 322, 333,
        338, 339, 361, 362, 363,
        364, 366–67, 369, 437,
        450, 451–52, 471, 472,
        476
    at Nixon's funeral, x–xi
    Nixon's relationship with,
        223, 347, 348–49, 353,
        370–72, 440
    Nixon's resignation and, 476,
        481, 482, 483
    Pentagon Papers as viewed by,
        384–85
    Rebozo and, 101, 106, 186,
        362, 367
    as secretary of state, 96, 457,
        458, 459–62, 471, 472,
        476, 481, 483
    sexual liaisons of, 39–40, 458
    in Vietnam peace negotia-
        tions, 332, 372, 439
    Watergate scandal and, 392,
        450, 451–52, 457, 458,
        459–62, 471, 472, 475
    White House tapes and, 348,
        349, 352
    wiretapping activities and,
        342–43
Klein, Herbert, 49, 104, 137,

151, 183, 185, 204–9, 215,
    218, 225, 231–33, 267,
    312, 319, 320, 328, 467,
    494*n*, 508*n*, 519*n*
Kleindienst, Richard, 96, 351,
    399, 405, 449, 450
Klingsberg, Ethan, 492*n*
Knight, Goodwin, 229
Knowland, William, 138
Knudsen, Thomas, 497*n*
Kohly, Mario García, 186–87,
    194, 261–62, 501*n*
Kohly, Mario García, Jr., 186,
    187
Kohn, Howard, 489*n*–90*n*,
    510*n*
Kopechne, Mary Jo, 379, 523*n*
Korean War, 85
Korff, Baruch, 13, 318, 353,
    403, 468
Kornitzer, Bela, 5
Kotz, Alvin, 114
Kraft, Joseph, 341, 342
Krogh, Egil, 365–66, 389, 391,
    403, 467, 485, 524*n*
Kubie, Lawrence, 98
Kutler, Stanley, 164
KYP, 286

labor unions, 204, 214, 398–99
Lackritz, Mark, 197, 198
Lacovara, Philip, 459
Laird, Melvin, 296, 370–71,
    384, 467, 517*n*
Laitin, Joseph, 478, 479, 480,
    536*n*
Lamphere, Robert, 492*n*
Lansdale, Edward, 291
Lansing, Robert, 490*n*
Lansky, Jake, 111, 127, 180,
    241
Lansky, Meyer, 55, 57, 111,
    112, 113, 114, 127–29,
    178–81, 194–95, 213, 239,
    240–43, 246, 258, 448*n*,
    489*n*, 498*n*, 510*n*
Lanza, Biagio, 358, 521*n*
Laos, 3
Larson, Willard, 47
LaRue, Fred, 525*n*, 528*n*–29*n*
Lasky, Victor, 53, 209, 506*n*–7*n*
Laxalt, Paul, 248–50, 280, 514*n*
Lee, Harold, 270
LeMay, Curtis, 166
Lenin, V. I., 482
Lenzer, Terry, 197, 198, 414
Leon, John, 212
Lerner, Max, 457
"Lesson for the American Peo-
    ple, A" (Nixon), 61
Levy, David, 266
Lewinsky, Monica, 141, 158
Lewis, Anthony, 440, 458
Liddy, G. Gordon, 523*n*,
    525*n*–26*n*, 528*n*, 534*n*,
    536*n*
    at Nixon's funeral, xii
    in Plumber's Unit, 389–90,

392, 399–404, 407, 408,
    410, 411, 416, 418, 423,
    424, 426–27
    in Watergate scandal, xii,
        389, 418, 428
Life, 74, 84, 145, 242, 245–48,
    420
Lincoln, Abraham, x, 13, 19,
    20, 120, 121, 351
Lindsay, John, 104
Link, Theodore, 125–26
Linowitz, Sol, 526*n*
Lippmann, Walter, 136
Liv, Marianna, xiii, 269–70,
    514*n*
Lodge, Henry Cabot, 208, 290,
    516*n*
Loftus, John, 62–63, 489*n*
Lombardo, Guy, 322
Lombardozzi, John, 510*n*
Longfellow, Henry Wadsworth,
    19
Longworth, Alice Roosevelt,
    466–67
Look, 97–98
Lorenz, Marita, 192–93, 503*n*
Los Angeles Times, 48–49, 83,
    122, 202, 231
Lowenthal, John, 77
Luciano, Charles ("Lucky"),
    128–29
Lucke, Jane, 105, 366, 495*n*
Lukas, Anthony, 477, 528*n*
Lumumba, Patrice, 188,
    501*n*–2*n*
Lungren, John, 434–35, 533*n*
Lynn, Laurence, 334

McCarran, Pat, 82
McCarthy, Dennis, 433, 450
McCarthy, Joseph R.:
    anti-Communist crusade of,
        45, 61, 81–83, 145, 146
    Nixon's relationship with,
        51–52, 81–83, 90, 145,
        146
McClendon, Winzola, 448
McCord, James, in Watergate
    scandal, xii, 400, 408, 409,
    426, 427, 428, 444, 458,
    525*n*, 527*n*, 528*n*, 531*n*,
    532*n*, 534*n*, 535*n*
McCoy, Thomas, 184–85
McCrae, Sloan, 103, 257, 495*n*
McDonald, Lawrence, 318
McDonald's, 396
McDowell, John, 72
McGinnis, Joe, 275–76
McGovern, George, 53, 230,
    247, 378, 380, 402, 405,
    408, 411, 412, 430, 431,
    435, 436, 437, 531*n*
McGrory, Mary, 237, 359–60
McGuire, Perkins, 222
Machiavelli, Niccolò, 50
McInerney, James, 215
McKinley, William, 20
Mackle family, 111–12

McMinoway, Michael, 523*n*
McNamara, Robert, 292–93, 516*n*
McPherson, Harry, 306
Madala, John, 495*n*
"Madman Theory," 295–97, 440
Mafia:
  Castro contract of, 178–81, 193–99
  Chotiner's connections to, 50–59, 149
  Cuban gambling operations of, 178–81, 193, 239, 241
  FBI wiretapping of, 129
  Kennedy's connections to, 213, 217
  Nixon's connections to, 50–59, 85, 111–15, 124–29, 149, 180–81, 194–99, 213–15, 221, 226, 240–45, 249–50
  Rebozo's connections to, 111–15, 127, 128, 180, 181, 243, 244–45
Magruder, Jeb, 312, 362, 402, 404, 411, 416, 417, 423, 428, 435, 441, 451, 467, 486, 522*n*, 525*n*–26*n*, 528*n*–29*n*, 531*n*
Maheu, Robert A., xi–xii, 153–54, 195–99, 215, 279, 280–82, 321, 413–14, 491*n*, 505*n*, 507*n*
Mahon, George, 461
Mahoney, Richard, 217
Malaxa, Nicolae, 130–35, 498*n*
Malcolm, Durie, 507*n*
Manckiewicz, Frank, 436, 532*n*
Mansfield, Mike, 446, 456
Manzi, Albert ("Toots"), 397
Mao Zedong, 3, 371–72, 393
Marbury, William, 491*n*
Marcello, Carlos, 54, 112, 213–14
March, Harry, 47
Marcos, Ferdinand, 164, 298, 396
Marcos, Imelda, 39, 164
Maroon, Hoke, 103, 107, 108, 324
Maroulis, Peter, 420
Marshall, J. Paull, 47
Martinez, Rolando, 431, 529*n*
Mason, Gordon, 133–34
Massing, Hede, 76, 489*n*
Massing, Paul, 489*n*
Mastriana, Louis, 114, 510*n*
Mazo, Earl, 36, 116, 351
Meany, George, 527*n*
Meet the Press, 210, 227
Meier, John, 282, 526*n*
Meir, Golda, 39
Mental Health of Our Leaders, The (Hutschnecker), 97–98
"Menu" bombing campaign, 332–33
Messick, Hank, 128, 129

Milhous, Jane, 11, 15, 19
Milhous, Olive, 6
Milhous Scholarship, 15, 16
Miller, Merle, 498*n*
Miller, William ("Fishbait"), 70, 344, 506*n*
Mitchell, John, 245, 345, 509*n*, 523*n*, 525*n*–26*n*, 528*n*, 531*n*, 532*n*
  as attorney general, 49, 197, 198, 274, 281, 311, 339, 342, 394, 397, 409, 410, 413, 416
  in Nixon's presidential campaign (1968), 273–74
  Nixon-Thieu agreement and, 298–302, 306
  in Watergate scandal, xii, 274, 349, 384, 399–402, 410, 411, 418, 428, 430, 446, 447–48, 451, 467, 475
Mitchell, Martha, 311, 408, 448
Mohammad Reza Shah Pahlavi, 37, 162, 163–64, 396
Moldonado, Jorge, 500*n*
Mollenhoff, Clark, 374–75, 398, 520*n*
Mondale, Walter F., 188
Moore, Earl, 247
Moore, Robin, 421
Morales, David, 336
Morgan, Edward, 247
Morgan, Thomas, 461
Morgenthau, Robert, 258–59, 513*n*
Morrah, Bradley, 21
Morris, Roger, 369, 370, 460, 487*n*, 489*n*, 494*n*
Morrow, Robert, 501*n*
Morton, Robert Geddes, 504*n*
Mosbacher, Emil, 420, 421, 423
Moscow, Alvin, 224, 227–28
Moynihan, Daniel Patrick, 313
Murchison, Clint, 85, 221
Muskie, Edmund, 106, 377, 378, 381–82, 402, 407–8
Muskie, Jane, 381
My Lai massacre, 333–34

NAACP Legal Defense Fund, 392
National Archives, U.S., 98–99, 355, 369, 380, 392, 429
National Citizens' PAC (NC-PAC), 45
National Enquirer, 269–70, 379
national security, 190, 196, 307, 353–54, 384, 390, 474
National Security Act, 479–80
National Security Agency (NSA), 76, 300
National Security Council (NSC), 148, 174, 183–84, 186, 195–96, 290, 457
Naulty, Susan, 350, 514*n*, 521*n*
Navasky, Victor, 491*n*
Nazis, 62–63, 131, 190

Nelson, Jack, 434
Nesline, Joe, 114
New Deal, 43, 83
Newell, Elizabeth, 250–53
New Frontier, 203, 209
Newsweek, 39, 91, 103, 271, 485
New York Post, 118, 122
New York Times, x, 75, 77, 100, 123, 160–61, 237, 247, 269, 290, 330, 342, 383, 384, 385, 406, 420, 440, 455, 456
Ngo Dinh Diem, 74, 516*n*–17*n*
Nguyen Khanh, 291
Nguyen Van Thieu, *see* Thieu, Nguyen Van
Niarchos, Stavros, 261
Nichols, Louis, 66, 489*n*
Nick's Snack Shack, 33
Nixon, 32, 505*n*
Nixon, Arthur, 2, 6, 8–10, 11, 13, 20, 23
Nixon, Donald, 6, 7, 9, 10, 113, 122, 134, 151, 154–58, 215–16, 281, 282, 398, 399, 504*n*, 510*n*
Nixon, Donald, Jr., 151, 398
Nixon, Edward, xi, 6, 8, 9, 15, 202, 268, 275, 281, 317, 397–98, 441
Nixon, Frank:
  background of, 5–6
  death of, 159–60, 268
  as grocer, 6–7, 11, 16, 17, 64
  lemon grove owned by, 1, 2, 5
  as Methodist, 5, 11
  Nixon's relationship with, 7–8, 11, 13, 19, 20, 60, 92, 93, 137, 139, 159–60, 268, 275
  Nixon's views on, 1–2, 7, 120, 275, 483
  personality of, 7–8, 137, 139
  as Quaker, 5, 11
Nixon, Hannah Milhous:
  background of, 5, 15, 16
  death of, 268
  Hughes loan and, 156, 215, 235
  marriage of, 6, 7–8, 92
  Nixon as viewed by, 4–5, 20, 24, 139–40, 160, 351
  Nixon's relationship with, 1, 2, 5, 8, 9, 11, 13, 15, 19, 26–27, 40, 43–44, 60, 79, 92–93, 138, 147, 203, 208, 219, 264, 268, 275, 293
  Nixon's views on, 1–2, 5, 7, 8, 26, 120, 275, 483
  Pat Nixon and, 30, 159
  personality of, 5, 8
  pies baked by, 5, 7, 160
  as Quaker, 5, 6, 10, 11, 12, 13, 19, 33, 92–93, 264, 275, 293, 310
  race relations as viewed by, 354

Nixon, Harold, 2, 6, 7, 10–11, 15
Nixon, Henry Richard, 512*n*
Nixon, King Richard, 512*n*
Nixon, Mudge, Rose, Guthrie and Alexander, 260–63
Nixon, Richard Milhous:
 in amateur theatricals, 18, 24, 27, 121
 ambition of, 42, 45, 78, 115, 116, 148, 158, 170, 172–73, 184–85, 186, 307
 anger of, 18–19, 67, 79, 137–38, 167, 169, 204–5, 231–32, 234, 274, 330, 361, 370–72, 376, 404, 428, 440–41
 anticommunism of, 22, 43, 44–45, 67, 81–85, 119, 120, 164, 165, 166–74, 182, 183, 187, 203, 226, 229–30, 264, 295–97
 anti-Semitism ascribed to, 353–54, 457
 arrest of, 14, 64
 as assistant city attorney, 32
 autograph of, 289
 Bahamas visits of, 221, 222, 238, 239–45, 253–59, 275, 325, 426
 Bel Air home of, 221, 226, 227, 230, 232
 Berlin visit of (1969), 378
 big business support for, 46–48, 85, 123–24, 260–61, 396
 biographies of, 4, 5, 62
 birth of, 1, 6
 business failure of, 29, 31
 cabinet of, 313, 327, 329–30, 438, 450, 476
 campaign financing of, xiii, 45–48, 54–58, 62, 64–65, 85, 86, 101, 106, 109, 111, 114, 118–24, 132, 133, 164, 201, 213, 221, 226, 243, 251–52, 276, 278–87, 320, 321, 395–99, 401, 407
 campaign style of, 43–49, 83–87, 150, 209–18, 226–32, 273–78
 Checkers speech of, 27, 118–24, 136–41, 226
 childhood of, 1–11, 20, 42
 China trip of (1972), 3, 115, 163, 314, 371, 393, 433, 437, 482, 484
 as Commander in Chief, 463, 477–81, 484
 congressional campaign of (1946), 41–49, 51, 54–58, 60, 62, 64, 83, 84, 153, 210
 congressional relations of, 330, 362–63, 437, 441
 as congressman, 59–80, 88, 116, 123, 200–201, 202

 correspondence of, 25–26, 30–31, 32, 34, 35–36, 159
 corruption charges against, 27, 51, 54–58, 85, 90, 92, 101, 118–24, 125, 129, 130–41, 149, 151–58, 164, 226
 dating and courtship by, 22, 23–32
 as debater, 18–19, 44, 45, 92, 95, 205–9, 212, 276, 449
 depressions of, 92–93, 95–96, 138–39, 144, 149, 216–17, 237, 240, 268, 315–20
 diary of, 430, 439–40, 465
 domestic policies of, 313, 372–73
 drinking by, 3–4, 31–32, 43–44, 82–83, 106, 144–45, 159, 161, 166, 172, 232–35, 240, 268–70, 274, 316, 351, 368–73, 391, 437, 449–50, 460–62, 476, 481, 482
 in Duke break-in, 21–22, 64
 Eastern Establishment distrusted by, 17–18, 63, 67, 79, 202, 261, 459, 463
 education of, 1, 2, 3, 14–22, 24–25
 emotional reticence of, 9, 13, 18, 21, 26–27, 36, 39, 59, 92–94, 147, 202
 "enemies list" of, 274–77, 378, 393, 408
 enemies of, 21–22, 48–49, 105, 117, 135–38, 353, 372–94, 408
 ethnic prejudices of, 352–53
 European fact-finding mission of (1947), 63
 final illness and death of, ix–xv, 101, 270
 finances of, 2, 29, 33, 37, 41, 45–46, 47, 106–11, 118–24, 151–58, 221–22, 238, 239–61, 281, 282, 304, 325, 459, 462
 football played by, 16, 135
 foreign assets of, 253–59
 foreign policy expertise of, 140, 142, 163, 173–74, 225, 226, 260, 263–67, 292, 472
 foreign policy of, xi, 313, 330, 355, 362–63, 368–72, 384, 393, 409, 441
 friendships of, 25, 104–5
 funeral of, ix–xv, 270
 gambling by, 33–34, 41, 124–29, 135, 178, 180–81, 194, 213, 412–14
 golf played by, 101, 105, 106, 146–47, 189
 gravesite of, 122, 270
 as grocery store clerk, 10–11, 15

 gubernatorial campaign of (1962), 48, 52–53, 56, 90, 97, 101, 104–5, 225–33, 236, 237–38, 240, 260, 314, 345, 368, 377, 464
 health of, 101, 182, 189, 206–7, 208, 221, 266, 453–54, 470
 history's kindness to, 485–86
 Hong Kong visits of, 269–70
 hospitalization of, 453–54
 humor attempted by, 31, 36–37, 39, 104
 "imperial presidency" of, 324–31
 inaugurations of, 101, 322–23, 342, 443–44
 insecurity of, 10, 20–21, 29, 59–60, 121, 135–40, 144, 359–60
 insomnia of, 39, 79, 88, 91, 169, 206, 232, 264, 316, 318, 366, 368–69, 409, 475, 476
 interviews of, 151, 190, 253, 267, 275, 345, 449
 Kennedy's assassination and, 262–63
 Key Biscayne home of (Florida White House), 100–101, 103, 107, 108, 113, 243, 255, 281, 325, 370, 427–28, 439, 450
 "kick around" speech of, 231–32, 233, 237–38, 330
 Latin America trip of (1958), 166–71, 185, 261, 359
 as lawyer, 2, 17, 19, 22, 27, 29–30, 31, 32, 46, 47, 62, 64, 107, 131, 221–22, 224, 225, 235, 237, 260–63, 267, 273, 314
 leadership of, x, 98, 263, 294, 362, 439–40, 465–66
 legal studies of, 2, 20–22, 25–26, 31–32, 62, 64
 leisurely work habits of, 325
 lies of, 2–4, 18–19, 64, 217–18, 278, 332–33, 450–51, 468, 473–74, 486
 at Lincoln Memorial protest, 364–66, 371
 loyalty to, 312–13
 media coverage of (non-Watergate), 43, 48–49, 56–59, 69–75, 83, 86, 94, 118–19, 121–26, 137, 138, 144, 146, 156, 159–61, 204–9, 220, 226–27, 230–33, 237, 262, 263, 266, 269–76, 311, 330–31, 338, 364, 376
 medications used by, 316–18, 449–50, 455, 476–77
 memoirs of, 4, 15, 26, 45, 53, 86, 100, 108, 110, 111, 135, 163, 164, 177, 201, 222, 223, 240, 275, 283,

289, 298, 334–37, 346,
349, 366, 378, 383–91,
405, 410, 427, 436,
465–66, 485
middle-class background of,
6–7, 16–17
Milhous relations of, 5, 6, 15,
16
military service of, 30, 33, 41,
42, 47, 62
Moscow visits of, 151,
171–74, 204, 266, 404–5,
409–11, 433, 437, 471–72
name of, 1
in New Orleans, 455, 456
"new" vs. "old," 93, 209,
273, 274
in New York City, 260–63,
271, 273, 278, 314
nocturnal phone calls of, 364,
368–71, 380, 449, 482,
483
non-autobiographical writ-
ings of, 11–12, 61, 72, 78,
82, 224–25, 262, 263, 362
note-taking by, 103, 205,
464, 475
offices of, 144, 325, 347
as outsider, 16, 60, 146–47
papers of, 194
pardon of, x, 485
Paris visits of, 264–65
patient records of, 434–35
phlebitis of, 266, 470
piano played by, 7, 15, 103,
469
poker played by, 33–34, 41,
203, 329
political appointments of,
311–14
political career of, 101,
105–6, 115, 154–55,
158–59, 170, 202–3, 216,
220–21, 222, 225, 232–38,
260, 263, 264, 267, 268,
271–72, 279, 280–82, 283,
309, 310
as politician, 3–4, 14, 18,
19–20, 22, 24, 40, 41–49,
57–58, 135–40, 144, 148,
267, 294, 306, 307, 308
"poor boy complex" of, 17
portfolio of, 251–52, 256–59,
274, 459
as president, xiv, 98, 99,
189–90, 218, 219, 237,
244, 274, 307, 311–15,
324–31, 339–40, 359–60,
438, 441–42, 451–52,
455–64, 470, 475, 485–86
presidential campaign of
(1960), 21, 29, 36, 52, 65,
90, 92, 95, 101, 105, 107,
156, 171, 173, 174,
184–85, 186, 200–224,
231, 232, 235, 242–43,
267, 276, 309, 310, 321
presidential campaign of

(1968), xiv, 2, 3, 37, 39,
53, 56, 94, 101, 105–6,
108, 110, 113, 243, 265,
267, 271–87, 309–10, 313,
316, 318–20, 355, 378,
397, 399
presidential campaign of
(1972), 54, 74–75, 106,
164, 197, 230, 278, 283,
355–56, 377, 379, 380–82,
395–99, 401, 402, 405,
408, 411, 424, 434–38,
440, 441, 446
as Quaker, 11–13, 31, 33, 36,
93, 127, 140, 209–10, 264,
267, 322, 359
racist remarks attributed to,
354–56
reading by, 15, 18, 19, 265
real estate owned by, 107,
108, 112, 113, 238,
239–45, 325
recklessness of, 169–71, 359
as "red-baiter," 22, 43,
44–45, 84–85
rehabilitation of, ix–xv, 101,
189–90, 485–86
religious convictions of,
11–13, 310, 448
reputation of, ix–xv, 135–40,
147, 154–55, 214, 346–47,
352, 485–86
San Clemente home of (Western White House), 32, 91,
108, 189–90, 249, 250,
325, 366–67, 370, 433,
463–64, 472, 474, 484–85
Senate campaign of (1950),
51, 83–87, 88, 100, 135,
201, 210, 213
as senator, 87, 88, 116, 123,
124–25, 201
sexual experiences of, xiii, 30,
39–40, 93, 103–4, 237,
268–70
speeches of, ix, 1–2, 17, 27,
42, 43, 48, 55, 61, 101,
116–24, 136–41, 146, 150,
159, 160, 165, 172, 174,
203, 205, 224, 226,
231–32, 233, 237–38, 263,
275, 283, 294–95, 322,
330–33, 337–39, 363, 449,
455, 466, 467, 483–84
staff of, 3, 39, 52, 125, 184,
185, 294, 310, 311, 326,
343, 367, 369, 437–38,
467
State of the Union address of
(1974), 466, 467
swearing of, 350–51
Swiss bank account of,
256–59
tax audits requested by,
21–22, 48–49, 353,
374–77, 393, 447
tax returns of, 109, 228, 262,
375, 377, 462, 474

transition team of (1968),
311, 320
as "Tricky Dick," 86, 494n
trust fund of, 111, 259, 462
unstable personality of,
xiv–xv, 9, 18, 26–27,
59–60, 79, 92–99, 143–44,
147, 160–61, 182, 199,
201–5, 218–19, 231, 236,
237–38, 315–20, 328–29,
359–60, 361–73, 433–42,
449–52, 453, 455–64,
470–71, 476–81, 482
Upper East Side apartment of,
261, 262, 278, 299
vetoes of, 330
as vice president, 22, 33, 39,
89, 107, 140, 143–99, 202,
219, 261, 298, 319, 354,
388, 433
vice-presidential campaign of
(1952), 36, 51, 64–65, 79,
82, 90, 101, 116–22, 129,
134, 135–40
vice-presidential campaign of
(1956), 51–52, 92, 134,
140, 148, 149–50, 153,
154, 158, 159–61, 195
Watergate scandal of, see Watergate scandal
White House press corps and,
330–31
White House remodeled by,
324–25
White House tapes of (non-
Watergate), 48, 72, 74,
104, 106, 111, 146, 176,
177, 315, 330, 345–60,
369, 375–76, 382, 384,
386–87, 397, 405–6, 436
in Whittier, Calif., 6–20, 42
women as viewed by, 23,
39–40, 159, 276, 352
world tours of, 140, 145,
162–74, 265–67, 326,
470–71
Nixon, Thelma Catherine
("Pat"), 488n, 520n,
535n–36n
anger of, 220–21, 222,
233–34
background of, 27, 28–29,
30, 35
biographies of, 28–29, 30,
79–80, 139, 220–21
birth of, 28, 130
death of, xiv
divorce considered by,
236–37
drinking and smoking by,
38–39, 464
Eastern Establishment as
viewed by, 37
education of, 29
as First Lady, 216, 322, 326,
327, 328, 383, 394, 443
funeral of, 91
gifts for, 101, 111, 162, 328

Nixon, Thelma Catherine
  ("Pat") *(cont.)*
  grave of, x, xiv, 122
  interviews of, 271–72
  Julie Eisenhower's views on,
    28–29, 30, 79–80, 139,
    220–21, 233–34, 236, 268
  in Key Biscayne, 255
  Latin America trip of (1958),
    166, 167, 168, 169–70
  media coverage of, 158, 159,
    220, 233, 271–72
  in Moscow (1959), 171
  name of, 28, 35
  in New York City, 261, 271,
    273
  in Nixon's congressional cam-
    paign (1946), 43, 44,
    45–46
  Nixon's courtship of, 27–32,
    35
  Nixon's first meeting with, 3,
    27–28
  in Nixon's gubernatorial cam-
    paign (1962), 225, 232–33
  Nixon's marriage to, xiv, 32,
    34, 35–39, 43, 60, 69–70,
    79–80, 92, 93, 120, 139,
    140, 148, 158–59, 202–3,
    220–21, 232–37, 269, 270,
    271–72, 383, 464, 468–69,
    471
  and Nixon's political career,
    158–59, 202–3, 220–21,
    222, 225, 232–37, 238,
    260, 263, 268, 271–72
  Nixon's possible physical
    abuse of, 232–36, 464
  in Nixon's presidential cam-
    paign (1960), 202–3, 204,
    208, 216, 218, 220–21
  in Nixon's presidential cam-
    paign (1968), 268, 271–72,
    278, 309, 310
  Nixon's resignation and, 451,
    475, 482, 483, 484
  in Nixon's Senate campaign
    (1950), 84, 85
  in Nixon's vice-presidential
    campaign (1952), 118,
    120, 121, 135, 139
  in Nixon's vice-presidential
    campaign (1956), 149,
    150, 158
  personality of, 28, 36, 37–39,
    54, 105, 118, 158–59,
    233–34, 236, 464
  previous marriage attributed
    to, 210
  Watergate scandal and, 44,
    450, 451, 463–64, 466,
    468–69
  wedding of, 32
  White House tapes and, 347
  world tours of, 162–74
Nixon Archives, 151
Nixon for President committee,
  267, 273

"Nixon Girls," 204
Nixon Library, x, 7, 22, 85, 99,
  122, 283, 350
"Nixonophobia," 147
Nixon's Inc., 154–58
NKVD, 76, 77
Norodom Sihanouk, Prince,
  334–35, 520n
North Atlantic Treaty Organization (NATO), 117
North Korea, 333, 372
North Vietnam, 294–97, 307,
  333, 337, 383, 438–41,
  450
Novak, Robert, 285
nuclear war, 293, 294, 295–97,
  371–72
nuclear weapons, 165–66, 280,
  282, 371, 393, 461

O'Brien, Lawrence, 197, 198,
  286, 287, 320–21, 408,
  409, 411, 414–16, 419–20,
  424, 426, 430, 435, 527n,
  530n, 532n
O'Brien, Operation, 414–16,
  424
Obst, David, 533n
O'Donnell, Kenneth, 95, 218
Office of Strategic Services
  (OSS), 62, 63, 73–74, 77,
  78, 132, 133
oil industry, 46–48, 83, 85, 124,
  195, 261, 396
Oliver, Spencer, 409, 410, 417,
  418, 527n, 529n, 531n
Onassis, Aristotle, 153–54,
  195–96, 261, 408, 491n,
  504n
O'Neill, Thomas P. ("Tip"),
  33–34, 95, 203, 329,
  348–49, 352, 453, 458,
  461
Operation Ajax, 163
Operation Candor, 3
Operation Eagle Eye, 309
Operation Integrity, 309
Operation O'Brien, 414–16, 424
Operation Pluto, 184–86, 192,
  501n
Operation Poor Richard, 168
Operation Townhouse, 53
Operation Tradewinds, 253–59
Operation Vulture, 165–66
Order of the Hound's Tooth,
  122, 168
Orowitz, Max, 112, 513n
Orta, Juan, 193–94
Ortman, Fred, 47–48
Osborne, John, 271, 361, 367,
  371, 449–50, 471
Oswald, Lee Harvey, 262–63,
  513n
Oswald, Marina, 513n
Ottenad, Tom, 519n

Paar, Jack, 105, 206, 240, 351
Pakistan, 163, 407

Pakula, Alan, 533n
Palestinian terrorists, 370–71
Palmer, Harriet, 23
Palmer, Kyle, 48, 83
Paonessa, Alfred, 29
Pappas, Thomas, 284–87, 321,
  445, 504n, 515n,
  530n–31n
Paradise Island, 238, 239–45,
  251, 252, 257, 258, 275,
  278
Parmet, Herbert, 290, 499n,
  517n–18n
Partin, Edward, 213–14, 507n
Patman, Wright, 446
Patton, 362, 363
Patton, George S., 362
Pauker, Ana, 133
Paul VI, Pope, 262
Pavlov, Vitaly, 76
Pawley, William, 181, 183, 184,
  186, 190, 191–92, 193,
  194
Peale, Norman Vincent, 12, 89,
  210, 469
Pearson, Drew, 56–57, 130–35,
  197, 202, 215, 216,
  318–20, 407, 497n, 498n,
  499n, 519n
Pelletier, Joan, 365
Pentagon Papers, 383–92, 425
Pepper, Claude, 136
PepsiCo, 173, 252, 262, 266,
  289, 314
Perdue, Bill, 21
*Perjury: The Hiss-Chambers
  Case* (Weinstein), 76
Perot, Ross, 338
Perry, Herman, 42, 46–47, 116,
  131
Perry, Hubert, 26
Peru, 166–67, 168
Peters, Dan ("Dusty"), 241
Peters, Jean, 154
Petersen, Henry, 451
Pfeiffer, Jack, 185, 190
Phillips, David, 175, 336
Phillips, Kevin, 330
Phleger, Herman, 63
Phoenix program, 334
Pierpoint, Robert, 38, 158
Pierson, Samuel, 254
Pinochet, Augusto, 335–36
Pistell, Richard, 511n
Pluto, Operation, 184–86, 192,
  501n
Political Action Committee
  (PAC), 44–45
Polizzi, Alfred ("Big Al"),
  112–13
Poor Richard, Operation, 168
Porter, Charles, 137
Portnoy's Complaint (Roth), 39
Potter, Philip, 204
Power of Positive Thinking, The
  (Peale), 12
president-worship, 486
Price, Ray, 276, 294, 318,

368–69, 451, 482, 536n
Price of Power, The (Hersh),
234
Primakov, Yevgeny, 76
Pulley, C. H. ("Jim"), 194–95,
503n
Pumpkin Papers, 61, 69–75, 79

Quarter Deck Yacht Club, 126,
135

Raab, Maxwell, 211
Radford, Arthur, 165
Ragan, John, 341–42, 520n,
532n
Ragano, Frank, 213
Ralabate, Barbara, 418–20,
530n
Randall, Clarence, 148
R & M Properties, 257
Rather, Dan, 39, 103, 326, 526n
Rayburn, Sam, 83
Read, Benjamin, 300
Reader's Digest, 251–52, 263,
266, 401
Reagan, Ronald, 267, 274, 485
Reardon, Ted, 202
Rebozo, Charles Gregory
("Bebe"), 495n, 496n–97n,
510n, 512n, 514n, 522n
background of, 101–5
banking interests of, 107–11,
112, 250–53, 255, 259,
274, 283
Ehrlichman and, 105, 106,
109
FBI investigation of, 113–14,
128
finances of, 102, 106–11,
255–59, 325
Kissinger and, 101, 106, 186,
362, 367
media coverage of, 103, 107,
376–77
mob connections attributed
to, 111–15, 127, 128, 180,
181, 243, 244–45
Nixon's first meeting with,
100–101
at Nixon's funeral, xiii
Nixon's political career and,
101, 105–6, 115, 267, 279,
280–82, 283, 309, 310
Nixon's relationship with,
100–115, 135, 161, 178,
195, 211, 216, 238–60,
266, 270, 275, 280, 282,
322, 351, 354, 367, 369,
370, 382, 394, 397, 459,
462, 471
Nixon's resignation and, 101,
464, 475
real estate deals of, 102, 107,
108, 112, 113, 240–41,
243, 244–45, 257
sexual liaisons of, 102–4
Watergate scandal and, xiii,
101, 105, 106, 109, 114,

281, 282, 283, 415, 416,
427, 428, 431, 446, 450,
459, 462, 464, 471
Rebozo, Claire Gunn, 102–3
Redlich, Norman, 136
Reedy, George, 59, 100, 104,
324
Reeves (Nixon's butler), 222
Reginelli, Marco ("The Little
Guy"), 52
Reiner, Philip, 507n–8n
Reinsch, Leonard, 206
Reisner, Robert, 528n
Remley, Zita, 488n, 499n
Reno, Janet, 253
Republican National Commit-
tee, 53, 81, 120, 121, 211,
342
Republican National Conven-
tions:
of 1952, 117–18
of 1956, 153, 154, 159
of 1960, 203, 214
of 1964, 263, 268–69
of 1968, 2, 275
of 1972, 436–37
Republican party, 41–49, 72
*see also specific elections and
individuals*
Reston, James, 146, 160–61,
170, 204, 440, 533n
Resurrection (Tolstoy), 18
Rich, Frank, 136–37
Richard I, "the Lionheart," King
of England, 6
Richardson, Elliot, 96, 99, 346,
459
Richardson, John, 517n
Richardson, Sid, 85
Richfield Oil, 47, 64
Rickenbacker, Eddie, 260
Ridgeley, William, 156
Rikan, Heidi, 422, 530n
Ritter, Frank, 241
Rock and Roll Club, 168
Rockefeller, David, 18
Rockefeller, Nelson, 209, 261,
267, 458
Rodgers, Richard, 310
Rodino, Peter, 352, 453, 469
Rogan, Richard, 56, 138
Rogers, Ted, 160, 207
Rogers, William, 51, 132, 135,
207, 211, 214, 362, 369,
396
Rollins, Ed, 351
Romania, 130–35, 368
Romney, George, 267, 329
Roosevelt, Eleanor, 83, 135, 237
Roosevelt, Elliott, 151
Roosevelt, Franklin D., 24, 65,
115, 151, 315, 492n, 525n
Roosevelt, Theodore, 2, 20,
137, 484, 499n
Rorke, Alexander, 192, 193
Rose, Milton, 261
"Rose Mary's Baby" list, 395
Rosenbaum, Ron, 533n

Rosenstiel, Lewis, 489n
Rositzke, Harry, 188
Rosselli, Johnny, 413, 504n
Rostow, Walt, 273, 302, 304,
306, 518n
Roth, Philip, 39
Roth, Samuel, 490n
Rothblatt, Henry, 420, 529n
Rothman, Norman, 125, 127,
194
Rothmann, John, ix, 117
Roufogalis, Mikalis, 286
Ruckelshaus, William, 459
Rudy, John, 418, 419, 423,
530n
Rummel, Sam, 56
Rusk, Dean, 183, 519n
Russell, Lou, 66, 68, 408–9,
419, 426, 458, 491n, 504n,
527n, 531n, 535n
Ruwe, Nick, 421–22
Ryan, Kate, 28, 35
Ryan, Patrick, 336
Ryan, Will, 28, 30, 35

Sachs, Alexander, 301
Safer, Morley, 288
Safire, William, 59, 105, 115,
234, 519n, 522n
St. George, Andrew, 501n
St. Johns, Adela Rogers, 151,
222, 224
St. Louis Post-Dispatch,
125–26, 215, 330
Saldana, Luis, 57
Salerno, Ralph, 50
Salerno, Tony ("Fats"), 113
Salinger, Pierre, 196–97, 209,
283
Salisbury, Harrison, 92, 172,
199, 204
Samish, Art, 56
Sampson, Marty, 418
Sanchez, Fina, 261, 513n
Sanchez, Manolo, 261, 364–66,
513n
Sanders, Donald, 454
Sands, Stafford, 510n
San Jose, Calif., antiwar protest
in, 358–59
San Marcos University, 166–67
Sans Souci casino, 124–29, 194
Saralegui, Francisco, 496n
Saratoga, 370–71
Saudi Arabia, 195–97, 283, 328,
329
Saxbe, William, 96, 440, 476
Scarney, Shelley, 514n
Schatzkin, Lynn, 365
Schee, Marie, 488n
Schemmer, Benjamin, 415–16
Scherr, Leslie, 413
Schlesinger, James, 176, 265,
329, 461, 462, 478–81,
484, 536n–37n
Schmahl, Horace, 73–74, 491n,
504n, 507n
Schmidt, Maria, 491n–92n

Schreck, Paul, 289, 290, 291–92, 516n
Schuyler, Harry, 57–58
Schweitzer, Albert, 267
Scott, George C., 362
Scott, Hugh, 3, 450–51, 470
Scowcroft, Brent, 536n
Sears, John, 3, 8, 39, 235, 236, 237, 278, 509n
Secret Service, U.S., 38, 39, 89, 101, 104, 113, 115, 138, 140, 166–71, 202, 206, 219, 244–48, 263, 277, 299, 310, 315, 316, 326, 346, 348, 364–70, 411, 433–34, 443, 455, 464, 470, 478
Securities and Exchange Commission (SEC), 251, 397
Seelye, Howard, 52, 232–33
Segretti, Donald, 235
Selix, Alfred, 248, 250, 511n
Selling of the President, The (McGinnis), 275–76
Senate, U.S.:
  Intelligence Committee of, 188–91, 193, 335, 336, 337, 345
  Investigations Subcommittee of, 51, 114
  Judiciary Committee of, 452
  Watergate Committee of, xiii, 96, 141, 197, 198, 212, 312, 359–60, 410, 452, 453, 458
Sequoia, 363, 372–73, 470, 475–76, 477
Sevareid, Eric, 82, 95
Shah of Iran, 37, 162, 163–64, 396
Shakespeare, William, ix, x, xv
Shannon, Margaret, 478, 529n
Sheehan, Neil, 294, 425
Shelley, John, 131–32
Shepley, Jim, 207
Sheridan, Walter, 57, 214
Sherwood, Foster, 97
Sherwood, Jack, 204
Shimon, Joseph, 507n
Shoffler, Carl, 529n
Shriver, Sargent, 527n
Shultz, George P., 17, 376, 478
Sica, Fred, 55
Sica, Joe, 55
Sidey, Hugh, 37, 261, 266–67, 276, 327–28, 331, 369, 441
Siegel, Benjamin ("Bugsy"), 54
Signal Corps, U.S., 344, 368
Sihanouk, Prince Norodom, 334–35, 520n
Silberman, David, 245–50, 511n
Silberman, Elsie, 246, 247
Silberman, Kathy, 247
Silbert, Earl, 417, 527n
"Silent Majority," 337–39
Silk, George, 245
Simes, Dimitri K., 75

Simon, William, 462
Simons, Howard, 406, 533n
Sinatra, Frank, 219, 520n
Sinclair, Upton, 48
Sindona, Michael, 512n
Sirica, John, 412, 429, 534n
Six Crises (Nixon), 61, 72, 78, 82, 224–25, 262, 362
Six-Day War, 283
Smathers, George, 100–101, 103, 107, 108, 111, 115, 181, 201, 298, 501n, 511n
Smith, Arnholt, 157, 236, 261, 269, 278–79, 329, 489n, 514n
Smith, Dana, 85, 118, 119, 123, 124–29, 180–81, 497n
Smith, Frank, 243, 244–45
Smith, Gerald, 86
Smith, Helen McCain, 469, 535n–36n
Smith, Paul, 16, 36, 99
Smith, Walter Bedell, 133–34
Smith, W. F., 49
Sonnenfeldt, Helmut, 535n
Sons and Brothers (Mahoney), 217
Southern California, University of, 29, 84
South Vietnam, 164–66, 261, 288–308, 383
Soviet Union:
  collapse of, 203
  Nixon's visits to, 151, 171–74, 204, 266, 404–5, 409–11, 433, 437, 471–72
  U.S. relations with, 171–74, 264, 295, 371
Spock, Benjamin, 357
Stacher, Joseph, 127, 128–29, 180
Stalin, Joseph, 65
Standard Oil, 46, 47
Stanley, Charles, 114
Stans, Maurice, 111, 228, 231, 259, 278, 311, 396, 525n
Stassen, Harold, 153, 154
State Department, U.S., 124–25, 164, 330
  Communists in, 45, 60–61, 65, 66, 69, 76, 77, 81–82
  Malaxa affair and, 131
  Nixon-Thieu agreement and, 300–301
Stearns, Richard, 252
Stein, Herb, 353
Steinbrenner, George, 397
Steinem, Gloria, 37–38, 271–72, 313, 320
Stephenson, Bob, 182–83
Steuer, Otto, 488n
Stevenson, Adlai, 79, 120, 129, 136, 138
Stewart, Jim, 488n
Stone, Oliver, 32, 505n
Stout, Osmyn, 58
Strachan, Gordon, xii–xiii, 312, 381, 410, 428, 525n, 526n,

528n
Strauss, Robert, 435, 529n
Stripling, Robert, 67, 69, 70, 78, 79, 137
Stroessner, Alfredo, 166
Stroud, Kandy, 37
Sturgis, Frank, 192, 193, 413, 424, 526n
Stutz, David, 514n
Sudoplatov, Pavel, 76, 492n
Sukarno, 163
Sukhodrev, Viktor, 471
Sullivan, William, 64, 72, 74, 343, 369, 535n
Supreme Court, U.S., 267, 350, 362–63, 433, 455, 473, 474, 475

Taiwan, 163, 166, 298
Taiwan Strait, 371–72
Tasca, Henry, 286, 515n
Taylor, John, 75
Taylor, Reese, 235
Taylor, Waller, 235–36, 237
Teamsters Union, xii, 53–54, 213–15, 221, 226, 233, 356–58, 398–99
Teapot Dome scandal, 19, 20
television, 48, 119–21, 146, 160, 172, 183, 205–9, 275–76, 309, 363, 483
Teresa, Vincent, 114, 242, 511n
Theroux, Paul, 4
Thieu, Nguyen Van, xiv, 287, 296–308, 318–21, 322, 332, 385, 424, 438–39, 445, 517n, 519n
Thimmesch, Nick, 536n
Thomas, Charles, 173
Thomas, Helen, 38, 367, 440, 449, 471, 535n–36n
Thorne, Ruth, 531n
Thrower, Randolph, 375
Time, 29, 34, 37, 118, 135, 144, 215, 216, 237, 337, 399
Timmons, Bill, 330
Tkach, Walter, 317–18, 365, 470
Tobin, Jack, 233, 509n
Toll, Barry, 480–81, 533n–34n, 536n–37n
Tolson, Clyde, 64
Tolstoy, Leo, 18
Toumanoff, Vladimir, 172
Tourine, Charles ("Charlie the Blade"), 241
Tourison, Sedgwick, 291
Townhouse, Operation, 53
Toynbee, Arnold, 441
Tradewinds, Operation, 253–59
Trafficante, Santo, 112, 127, 193, 194–95, 213, 504n
Trans World Airlines (TWA), 150, 157–58, 173
Tricia, 276
Trifa, Viorel, 498n
Trohan, Walter, 12, 13, 59–60, 78–79, 147

Trudeau, Pierre, 351
Trujillo, Rafael, 181, 188, 261–62, 491n, 496n
Truman, Harry S., 4, 65, 73, 78, 86, 99, 115, 118, 120, 126, 134, 136, 151, 315, 329, 331, 351, 498n, 499n
Truman, Margaret, 35
Tsimas, Kostas, 286
Tuchman, Barbara, 486
Tuck, Dick, 84, 208–9, 226, 494n
Tully, Andrew, 394
Twenty-fifth Amendment, 456
Twenty-second Amendment, 441

Udall, James, 33
Ulasewicz, Tony, 444, 522n, 524n
Union Bank of Switzerland, 258–59
United Fruit Company, 32, 174–75
United Nations, 65, 229
United States:
  Chinese relations of, 264
  Soviet relations of, 171–74, 264, 295, 371
Upton, Albert, 18

Van Horne, Harriet, 90, 376
Van Le, 288
Vann, Jesse, 425–26
Vann, John Paul, 425–26, 520n
Van Petten, Bill, 234–35
Vardakis, Mark, 290, 516n
Varona, Antonio de, 194, 498n, 503n
Vassiliev, Alexander, 77
Vaughan, Harry, 115
Vazzana, Nicholas, 79
Venezuela, 167–70, 185
Venker, Marty, 536n
VENONA intercepts, 76–78, 492n, 493n
Vesco, Robert, 53, 245, 397–98
Viet Cong, 288–92, 297, 334
Vietnam War, 288–308
  bombing campaigns in, 292, 293, 295, 297, 298, 300, 301, 307, 310, 332–33, 385, 404, 408, 438–41
  Communist insurgency in, 164–66, 292, 293, 294, 295–97, 332, 404, 439
  domestic opposition to, 337–39, 344–45, 356–60, 363–65, 372–73, 383, 401, 404
  Eisenhower's policy on, 164–66
  French phase of, 164–66, 332
  Johnson's policy on, 280, 287, 291, 292–308, 331, 383, 385
  Kennedy's policy on, 74, 166, 292, 384

Nixon's policy on, xiii–xiv, 3, 90, 106, 165–66, 171, 244–45, 248–49, 292–96, 310, 322, 331–34, 337–39, 342–43, 356–60, 363–65, 372–73, 382–91, 393, 401, 404, 408, 425–26, 438–41, 450, 480
Nixon's POW mission in (1964), 288–92
Nixon's "secret plan" for, 3, 294–97
Nixon-Thieu agreement in, xiv, 287, 296–308, 318–19, 320, 321, 322, 332, 385, 424, 445
peace negotiations on, xiv, 287, 292–308, 313, 314, 318–19, 320, 321, 322, 332, 372, 383, 385, 438–39, 445
Tet offensive in, 294
U.S. advisers in, 165–66, 266, 292
U.S. casualties in, xiv, 207, 293, 306, 331, 339, 369, 383, 438
Vietnamization of, 332, 385
Vincent, John, 64
Vincent, Mrs. Clifford, 19
Visoianu, Constantin, 132, 134
Volcker, Paul, 250
Volkogonov, Dmitri, 75, 76
Volpe, John, 351, 397
Voltaire, 16
von Hoffman, Nicholas, 456
Voorhis, Jerry, 42–49, 51, 57, 60, 62, 63, 64, 83, 84, 200, 489n
Vulture, Operation, 165–66

"Wa, Father," see Nguyen Lao Hoa
Waldie, Jerome, 349, 350, 465
Walker, Ron, ix, xi, 277, 422
Wallace, DeWitt, 401
Wallace, George, 74–75, 106, 310, 382, 402, 404–6, 408, 437, 473, 526n–27n
Walt Disney Productions, 311–12
Walters, Barbara, 485
Walters, Johnnie, 376
Walters, Vernon, xi, 265, 346, 432, 532n, 533n
Warren, Earl, 50, 117, 118, 123, 237, 322, 497n
Warren Commission, 199
Wary, Merton, 46
Washington, George, 99, 372
Washington Post, 149, 284, 330, 338, 351, 422, 436, 440, 446, 496n
Watergate scandal, 388–485
  arrests in, 426–27, 434, 442, 444, 452, 458, 473
  CIA involvement in, 432–33, 473, 474

congressional investigation of, xiii, 96, 141, 197, 198, 212, 312, 359–60, 410, 445–49, 452–53, 458, 466, 467–70, 473–74
cover-up of, 21, 350, 428–35, 444–55, 458–59, 465–70, 473–74
Cuban group in, 404, 408, 409, 426–27, 431, 444–45
DNC burglary in, 21–22, 44, 284, 403–4, 408, 416, 423–33, 444–45, 447
DNC wiretapping in, 408–11, 416–23, 430
evidence destroyed in, 428–29
executive privilege in, 453, 455
FBI investigation in, 429–35, 459, 473
foreign policy affected by, 452, 457, 458, 459–62, 470–72
grand jury indictments in, 467–68
"hush money" in, 431, 444–45
impeachment proceedings in, 22, 332, 343, 451, 452–53, 466, 468, 474, 475, 478, 479, 482
independent prosecutor in, 13, 95, 114, 245, 350, 452, 455, 458–59, 466, 477
legacy of, 485–86
media coverage of, 427, 428, 434, 446, 449–50, 455, 459, 461, 462, 468
military role as concern in, 463, 477–81
motives of participants in, 411, 412–24
Nixon's credibility in, 3, 449–50
Nixon's farewell speech in, 1–2, 483–84
Nixon's finances investigated in, 109, 251, 252–53, 254, 281, 282, 304, 459, 462
Nixon's mental state in, 451–52, 453, 455–64, 470–71, 476–81, 482
Nixon's public statements on, 430, 431, 449–50, 466
Nixon's resignation and, x, 1–2, 3, 91, 96, 101, 178n, 234, 253, 350, 391, 451, 464, 470, 474–76, 478, 481–86
Nixon's response to, 95–96, 427–35, 444–86
Nixon's role in, xi, 21–22, 98, 210, 211, 212, 245, 273, 310, 314, 388–94, 403, 426–86
nuclear threat in, 456–57, 459–62, 477, 484

Watergate scandal *(cont.)*
  obstruction of justice in, 427–35, 444–45, 451, 467–68, 473–74
  Plumber's Unit in, 388–92, 394, 399–429, 431, 444–45
  political impact of, 427, 433, 439, 451–52, 457–59, 471
  prostitution ring in, 416–23
  "Saturday Night Massacre" in, 458–59
  sensitive information revealed in, 53, 134, 177–78, 196–99, 407, 412–24, 430
  White House tapes in, xiii, 4, 141, 178n, 228, 230, 276, 284, 349, 390–92, 403, 411, 413–14, 429–34, 442, 444, 451, 453–54, 458–59, 466, 468–70, 473–74, 475
Watergate Special Prosecution Force, 13, 114, 245, 350, 452
Waters, Frank, 155–57
Watts, William, 18, 37, 338, 362–63, 392–93
Weicker, Lowell, 359–60, 393, 447
Weinberger, Caspar, 449
Weiner, Myron ("Mickey"), 503n–4n
Weinstein, Allen, 76, 77, 490n, 491n, 492n
Welch, Dorothy, 22, 25
Welch, Guy, 64
Welch, Ola Florence, 16, 22, 23–27, 30, 64, 487n
Wells, Maxie, 417–18, 529n
West, Jessamyn, 7, 11, 16, 20, 105, 159, 328
West, Merle, 19–20, 24
West, Nigel, 492n
Western Tube Corporation,

131–32
Westmoreland, William, 290, 291, 363, 516n
Whalen, Richard, 274, 276–77, 294, 295
"What Can I Believe?" (Nixon), 11–12
Wheeler, Charles, 266
White, Harry Dexter, 492n
White, Theodore, 96, 202, 204, 208, 218, 219, 274, 311, 316, 321, 330, 331, 342, 406, 437, 536n
Whitehead, Clay, 478
White House Communications Agency, 315, 348
White House police, 326–27
White House Preservation Committee, 17
Whittaker, Kenneth, 394
Whittier College, 14, 15–20, 58, 64, 67, 120, 147, 367
Wicker, Tom, 217, 236, 310
Will, George, 463
Wills, Garry, 271
Will to Live, The (Hutschnecker), 88–89, 93
Wilson, Henry, 20
Wilson, Pete, x
Wilson, Richard, 440–41
Wilson, Will, 197
Wilson, Woodrow, 20
Winchell, Walter, 89, 219
Winchester, Lucy, 36
Wine-Banks, Jill, 429
Wingert and Bewley, 29
Winter-Berger, Robert, 94, 494n, 520n, 522n
wiretapping, 11, 129, 212, 227–28, 240, 300–305, 314, 341–44, 377, 393, 408–11, 416–23, 430
Wise, David, 62
Wisner, Frank, 132, 133, 134

Witcover, Jules, 266
Witwer, Allan, 85
Wolfe, Don, 533n
Wolstonecraft, Michael, 512n
Woodruff, Ed, 252
Woods, Rose Mary, 527n, 531n
  as Nixon's secretary, 89, 90, 144, 168, 208, 229, 237, 281, 310, 312, 327, 339, 342, 347, 359, 380
  Watergate scandal and, xiii, 347, 409, 429, 454, 467, 469, 482
Woodward, Bob, 38–39, 95–96, 234, 369, 434, 436, 533n, 535n, 536n
Woodward, Tyler, 124
Woolston-Smith, Arthur, 532n
World War I, 20
World War II, 30, 33, 71, 73, 78, 116, 151, 190, 206, 322
Wouk, Herman, 477
Wrightson, James, 171

"X" Envelope, 298

Yalta Conference, 65, 77
Yeltsin, Boris, 75
Yom Kippur War, 39, 452, 457, 458, 459–62
Yorba Linda, Calif., x, 1, 6–7, 20, 367
Young, David, 372, 389
Youngblood, Rufus, 247

Zeifman, Jerome, 441, 453, 459
Ziegler, Ron, xi, 229, 232, 312, 390, 394, 404, 421, 450, 455, 456, 467, 484
Ziffren, Mickey, 270
Zumwalt, Elmo, 17, 353, 461–62, 463, 479